C...
& Turkey

> "Lighthearted and sophisticated, informative and fun to read. *[Let's Go]* helps the novice traveler navigate like a knowledgeable old hand."
> —*Atlanta Journal-Constitution*

> "The guides are aimed not only at young budget travelers but at the independent traveler, a sort of streetwise cookbook for traveling alone."
> —*The New York Times*

▣ Let's Go writers travel on your budget.

> "Retains the spirit of the student-written publication it is: candid, opinionated, resourceful, amusing info for the traveler of limited means but broad curiosity."
> —*Mademoiselle*

> "The writers seem to have experienced every rooster-packed bus and lunar-surfaced mattress about which they write."
> —*The New York Times*

> "All the dirt, dirt cheap."
> —*People*

▣ Great for independent travelers.

> "A world-wise traveling companion—always ready with friendly advice and helpful hints, all sprinkled with a bit of wit."
> —*The Philadelphia Inquirer*

> "Lots of valuable information for any independent traveler."
> —*The Chicago Tribune*

▣ Let's Go is completely revised each year.

> "Unbeatable: good sight-seeing advice; up-to-date info on restaurants, hotels, and inns; a commitment to money-saving travel; and a wry style that brightens nearly every page."
> —*The Washington Post*

> "Its yearly revision by a new crop of Harvard students makes it as valuable as ever."
> —*The New York Times*

▣ All the important information you need.

> "Enough information to satisfy even the most demanding of budget travelers...*Let's Go* follows the creed that you don't have to toss your life's savings to the wind to travel—unless you want to."
> —*The Salt Lake Tribune*

> "Value-packed, unbeatable, accurate, and comprehensive."
> —*The Los Angeles Times*

Let's Go Publications

Let's Go: Alaska & the Pacific Northwest 1998
Let's Go: Australia 1998 **New title!**
Let's Go: Austria & Switzerland 1998
Let's Go: Britain & Ireland 1998
Let's Go: California 1998
Let's Go: Central America 1998
Let's Go: Eastern Europe 1998
Let's Go: Ecuador & the Galápagos Islands 1998
Let's Go: Europe 1998
Let's Go: France 1998
Let's Go: Germany 1998
Let's Go: Greece & Turkey 1998
Let's Go: India & Nepal 1998
Let's Go: Ireland 1998
Let's Go: Israel & Egypt 1998
Let's Go: Italy 1998
Let's Go: London 1998
Let's Go: Mexico 1998
Let's Go: New York City 1998
Let's Go: New Zealand 1998 **New title!**
Let's Go: Paris 1998
Let's Go: Rome 1998
Let's Go: Southeast Asia 1998
Let's Go: Spain & Portugal 1998
Let's Go: USA 1998
Let's Go: Washington, D.C. 1998

Let's Go Map Guides

Berlin	New Orleans
Boston	New York City
Chicago	Paris
London	Rome
Los Angeles	San Francisco
Madrid	Washington, D.C.

Coming Soon: Amsterdam, Florence

**Let's Go
Publications**

LET'S GO
Greece
& Turkey
1998

Patrick K. Lyons
Editor

Ziad W. Munson
Editor

James J. Castanino
Assistant Editor

St. Martin's Press ≈ New York

HELPING LET'S GO

If you want to share your discoveries, suggestions, or corrections, please drop us a line. We read every piece of correspondence, whether a postcard, a 10-page email, or a coconut. Please note that mail received after May 1998 may be too late for the 1999 book, but will be kept for future editions. **Address mail to:**

Let's Go: Greece & Turkey
67 Mount Auburn Street
Cambridge, MA 02138
USA

Visit Let's Go at **http://www.letsgo.com,** or send email to:

fanmail@letsgo.com
Subject: "Let's Go: Greece & Turkey"

In addition to the invaluable travel advice our readers share with us, many are kind enough to offer their services as researchers or editors. Unfortunately, our charter enables us to employ only currently enrolled Harvard-Radcliffe students.

About Let's Go

THIRTY-EIGHT YEARS OF WISDOM

Back in 1960, a few students at Harvard University banded together to produce a 20-page pamphlet offering a collection of tips on budget travel in Europe. This modest, mimeographed packet, offered as an extra to passengers on student charter flights to Europe, met with instant popularity. The following year, students traveling to Europe researched the first, full-fledged edition of *Let's Go: Europe,* a pocket-sized book featuring honest, irreverent writing and a decidedly youthful outlook on the world. Throughout the 60s, our guides reflected the times; the 1969 guide to America led off by inviting travelers to "dig the scene" at San Francisco's Haight-Ashbury. During the 70s and 80s, we gradually added regional guides and expanded coverage into the Middle East and Central America. With the addition of our in-depth city guides, handy map guides, and extensive coverage of Asia and Australia, the 90s are also proving to be a time of explosive growth for Let's Go, and there's certainly no end in sight. The first editions of *Let's Go: Australia* and *Let's Go: New Zealand* hit the shelves this year, expanding our coverage to six continents, and research for next year's series has already begun.

We've seen a lot in 38 years. *Let's Go: Europe* is now the world's bestselling international guide, translated into seven languages. And our new guides bring Let's Go's total number of titles, with their spirit of adventure and their reputation for honesty, accuracy, and editorial integrity, to 40. But some things never change: our guides are still researched, written, and produced entirely by students who know first-hand how to see the world on the cheap.

HOW WE DO IT

Each guide is completely revised and thoroughly updated every year by a well-traveled set of over 200 students. Every winter, we recruit over 140 researchers and 60 editors to write the books anew. After several months of training, Researcher-Writers hit the road for seven weeks of exploration, from Anchorage to Adelaide, Estonia to El Salvador, Iceland to Indonesia. Hired for their rare combination of budget travel sense, writing ability, stamina, and courage, these adventurous travelers know that train strikes, stolen luggage, food poisoning, and marriage proposals are all part of a day's work. Back at our offices, editors work from spring to fall, massaging copy written on Himalayan bus rides into witty yet informative prose. A student staff of typesetters, cartographers, publicists, and managers keeps our lively team together. In September, the collected efforts of the summer are delivered to our printer, who turns them into books in record time, so that you have the most up-to-date information available for your vacation. And even as you read this, work on next year's editions is well underway.

WHY WE DO IT

We don't think of budget travel as the last recourse of the destitute; we believe that it's the only way to travel. Living cheaply and simply brings you closer to the people and places you've been saving up to visit. Our books will ease your anxieties and answer your questions about the basics—so you can get off the beaten track and explore. Once you learn the ropes, we encourage you to put *Let's Go* down now and then to strike out on your own. As any seasoned traveler will tell you, the best discoveries are often those you make yourself. When you find something worth sharing, drop us a line. We're Let's Go Publications, 67 Mount Auburn Street, Cambridge, MA 02138, USA (email fanmail@letsgo.com).

HAPPY TRAVELS!

Contents

About Let's Go v
Maps ix
Researcher-Writers xi
Acknowledgments xii
Let's Go Picks xiii
How to Use This Book xx

ESSENTIALS 1

Planning Your Trip 1
Getting There 29
Once There 37

GREECE 47

Essentials 47
Life and Times 55

Athens   66

Near Athens 86
The Petalion Gulf Coast 89
Evia (Euboea) 98

Central and Northern Greece   104

Thessaly 104   Macedonia 118
Evritania 111   Halkidiki 131
Epirus 112   Thrace 133

Peloponnese   138

Corinthia and Argolis 138   Messenia 166
Elias and Achaïa 153   Laconia 171
Arcadia 163   Mani 175

Greek Islands

Crete   182

Central Crete 184
Western Crete 193
Eastern Crete 203

Cyclades   216

Mykonos 216   Tinos 248
Delos 221   Syros 252
Ios 222   Andros 255
Santorini (Thira) 226   Milos 258
Paros 233   Sifnos 261
Naxos 240   Serifos 264
Amorgos 245

Dodecanese   266

Rhodes (Rodos) 266   Astypalea 292
Kos 277   Karpathos 293
Kalymnos 284   Symi 298
Patmos 288   Nisyros 300

Saronic Gulf Islands   **303**
Aegina 303   Hydra (Idra) 309
Poros 306   Spetses 311
Sporades   **314**
Skiathos 314   Alonissos 320
Skopelos 317   Skyros 322
Northeast Aegean Islands   **326**
Chios 326   Thassos 340
Lesvos (Lesbos) 329   Samothraki (Samothrace) 342
Samos 335   Limnos 343
Ikaria 338
Ionian Islands   **346**
Corfu (Kerkyra) 346   Ithaka (Ithaki) 358
Zakinthos 352   Cephalonia 360
Lefkada (Lefkas) 355

TURKEY 364

Essentials 364
Life And Times 370
Istanbul   **382**
Northwestern Turkey   **406**
Aegean Coast   **422**

Western Turkey

Northern Coast 422   Bodrum Peninsula 448
Ephesus and Environs 434   Marmaris Coast 454
Pamukkale and Environs 443

Anatolia

Black Sea Coast   **460**
West to Trabzon 460
East of Trabzon 474
Mediterranean Coast   **481**
Fethiye Coast 481   Antalya Gulf Coast 495
Kaş Coast 487   Eastern Mediterranean Coast ..502
Central Anatolia   **512**
Ankara 512   Cappadocia 532
Konya and Environs 526   Eastern Anatolia 546

CYPRUS 551

Essentials 551
Life and Times 554
Northern Cyprus   **579**

APPENDIX 595

Holidays and Festivals 595
Climate 596
Telephone 596
Time Zones 598
Weights and Measures 598
Glossary 599
Greek Language Index 605

INDEX 609

Maps

Greece .... xiv-xv
Turkey: Regions .... xvi-xvii
Major Pre-Classical, Hellenic, and Byzantine Sights .... xviii-xix
Eastern Mediterranean Sea 31
Greece 48-49
Athens City Overview 67
  Athens Central City 68-69
  Acropolis 81
  Delphi 93
Northern Greece 105
  Thessaloniki 120-121
  Mount Olympus 129
  Mount Athos 133
Peloponnese 139
  Patras 155
  Ancient Olympia 161
Crete 183
  Iraklion 185
Greek Islands 214-215
  Mykonos 217
  Santorini (Thira) 227
  Paros and Antiparos 235
  Naxos 241
  Tinos 249
  Syros 253
  Andros 257
  Sifnos 261
  Rhodes 267
  Kos 279
  Karpathos and Kassos 295
  Aegina 305
  Skiathos and Skopelos 315
  Alonissos and Skyros 321
  Chios 327
  Lesvos 331
  Corfu 347
Turkey 366-367
Istanbul 384-385
  Central Istanbul 386-387
  Topkapı Palace 399
Bursa 415
Aegean Coast 423
  Izmir Central City 429
  Ephesus 438
Western Black Sea 461
  Trabzon 471
Eastern Black Sea 475
Mediterranean Coast 483

Antalya City Overview 497
Central Anatolia 513
    Old Ankara 515
    Downtown Ankara 517
Cyprus 553
    South Nicosia 559
    Larnaka 561
    Limassol 569
    Lefkoşa 581

Researcher-Writers

Elif Batuman *Central Anatolia, Mediterranean Coast, Northern Cyprus*
After dodging several international intelligence agencies, Elif's fabulous work (and especially marginalia!) had us rolling on the floor. Because of her vibrant descriptions of central Turkey and northern Cyprus, those of us back in Cambridge spent hours on the phone with travel agencies asking about fares to Ankara and Girne. Elif was also the only one of our researchers to experience the thrill of deportation.

Mark Coumounduros *Aegean Coast, Northwestern Turkey*
Mark, the draft horse of the book team, plowed through fields of new cities on the Aegean Coast. With his tireless writing and attention to historical detail, visitors to this area now have a terrific guide to use. For his clear vision and solid understanding of Turkey, he gets an award for a much improved section of the book. It is obvious to us that he worked long hours. We just hope he had time for a little *ouzo*. We were particularly proud of Mark's special relationship with MCI.

Alexandra DeLaite *Mainland Greece, Sporades, Northeast Aegean Islands, Corfu, Istanbul*
Alex rules. What more can we say? Sure, we cried when she got stuck for 8 weeks or something on Skiathos; but, hey, we knew she'd catch up. When she finally did get off the island, we came to the office early and left late, hoping she'd call so we could live the Greek life vicariously through her. And if we ever needed to figure out which town to cut, Alex was right there with a suggestion or two. Thanks, Alex, for helping us when we really needed you.

Aykan Erdemir *Istanbul, Northwestern Turkey, Black Sea Coast*
Without Aykan's strong language skills and intimate knowledge of Turkey, we never would have been able to plan itineraries of places we covered last year, much less add an entire new region of Turkey to the book. We truly admired his ability to sniff out telnet connections even in the most remote corners of Turkey.

Demetra Koutsoukos *Athens, Cyclades, Dodecanese*
Demetra's strong Canadian sensibility is what kept us from printing the lyrics to "God Bless America" instead of the listing for the Acropolis. But seriously folks, Demetra's coverage of Athens and the islands strengthened what is probably the most read section of the book. Without her tireless work and great advice, we could never have done this book. Have a great time in England, Demetra, and check the baseball standings—the Brewers are 10 games ahead of the Jays!

Christian Lorentzen *Cyprus, Crete, Mt. Athos, Lefkoşa, Black Sea Coast*
Christian had the longest itinerary in G&T history. He is the only one of us (as well as the only one we know) to actually visit all four countries in the book and then read a *few* histories on each locale he visited. We can't believe how much work he did and can only surmise that he has developed some *Star Trek*-esque way of replacing his need for sleep with photovoltaic cells implanted into his arm. Thanks, Christian, for bailing us out when we had our little problem.

Emily Wong *Peloponnese, Ionian Islands, Saronic Gulf Islands*
Emily is one of the most conscientious people we know. Trudging around the Peloponnese, she checked facts for us that were, shall we say, suspiciously out-of-date. We think she even counted the number of pebbles in each campground. She also overcame the inevitable problems of the road with courage and tenacity that made us office potatoes proud. We couldn't have asked for more from Emily. Just keep those balcony doors locked!

Acknowledgments

When we were first hired, we couldn't believe the job we had in front of us. But our thoughts of fleeing to Bonaire were soon replaced with a growing sense of hope, thanks mostly to those who helped us. Sara, our managing editor, guided us through the spring and summer and taught us the ropes of editing and format. Katherine, our intern, did a fabulous job creating our Greek language index. That section of the book is thanks to you, Katherine. Melissa, who we must have driven crazy with our questions, never grew impatient with us, although we wouldn't have blamed her if she had. Special thanks to Melanie and Dave who worked with us through crashes, disappearing files, viruses, network problems, printer "issues," and all the Framemaker quirks. Thanks also to: Andrew Nieland (the typing was way above and beyond), Jessica Wolf, Jennifer Burns, Rob Shanshiry, Katherine Ingman, Sam Brooks, Chuck O'Toole, and the Hotel Sezgin (for keeping our fax machine warm). Patrick and James would like to pay homage to the Game of Baseball, the Milwaukee Brewers, and the Boston Red Sox. Without baseball, we would both be lost.

Ziad and James, we made it through sixteen editions of morale charts! Enough said. I owe you both a Guinness or four. Thanks to my best friend Jennifer for her love, help, and volts. Thanks to Christopher for the walking tour of Oxford (sorry about the gimp). Thanks to Kev for the All-Star Game, the highlight of my baseball life (I forgot all about baseball games in the 1980s). Rose, thanks for your advice. I only wish you could have come out to Cambridge again this summer. **-PKL**

James and Pat—thanks for so graciously enduring my bad jokes and compulsive need to organize everything. A million thanks to Amy for putting up with the long hours and the countless stories about *Let's Go* office foibles and trials. **-ZWM**

Pat and Ziad—a great summer and a great book. Thank you to my wonderful family for all of your support. You guys are the best. Thanks to John H. for being a great friend. And Zrenda, Dewey, Vincent, and Ohnnie. Have a day! **-JJC**

Editor	Patrick K. Lyons
Editor	Ziad W. Munson
Assistant Editor	James J. Castanino
Editorial Intern	Katherine Boas
Managing Editor	Sara K. Smith
Publishing Director	John R. Brooks
Production Manager	Melanie Quintana Kansil
Associate Production Manager	David Collins
Cartography Manager	Sara K. Smith
Editorial Manager	Melissa M. Reyen
Editorial Manager	Emily J. Stebbins
Financial Manager	Krzysztof Owerkowicz
Personnel Manager	Andrew E. Nieland
Publicity Manager	Nicholas Corman
Publicity Manager	Kate Galbraith
New Media Manager	Daniel O. Williams
Associate Cartographer	Joseph E. Reagan
Associate Cartographer	Luke Z. Fenchel
Office Coordinators	Emily Bowen, Chuck Kapelke
	Laurie Santos
Director of Advertising Sales	Todd L. Glaskin
Senior Sales Executives	Matthew R. Hillery, Joseph W. Lind
	Peter J. Zakowich, Jr.
President	Amit Tiwari
General Manager	Richard Olken
Assistant General Manager	Anne E. Chisholm

Let's Go Picks

Let's Go: Greece and Turkey can make one claim that no other book in the *Let's Go* series can make—we cover, in our unique pages, four out of the seven wonders of the ancient world: the Colossus of Rhodes (Rhodes Island, Greece), the Temple of Zeus (Olympia, Greece), the mausoleum at Halicarnassus (Bodrum, Turkey), and the Temple of Artemis (Ephesus, Turkey). In case you were wondering, the other three are: the Hanging Gardens of Babylon, the Lighthouse at Alexandria, and the Great Pyramids at Giza. But these are far from the only wondrous sights to be seen in Greece, Turkey, and Cyprus. Here is a sampling of some of the places we feel are above and beyond the ordinary travel experience. Admittedly, this is a subjective list. Perhaps we should include a Reader's Picks '99? Send us a postcard of your favorite haunts.

Best place for a kiss

In **Greece:** pucker up and head to a quiet corner of the Acropolis (p. 80). But be respectful—Athena was a virgin. In **Turkey:** keep your clothes on long enough to make it to the legendary Blue Lagoon of Ölüdeniz, where crystal waters and gentle sands will have you seeing stars (p. 485). Or, stand on the Galata Bridge in Istanbul and watch the sun set over two continents (p. 382). In **Cyprus:** cuddle up as you gaze over the stunning Kaledonia Falls in the Troodos (p. 572).

Where to rock around the clock

In **Greece:** the truly hardcore partiers make a beeline to Ios in the Cyclades (p. 222), where late-night revelers can hold their liquor but can't hold onto their clothes. In **Turkey:** forget your worldly cares in Bodrum (p. 448), where the rockin' harborside never sleeps. In **Cyprus:** Agia Napia (p. 565), Cyprus's overnight clubbing wondertown, won't disappoint those in search of the perfect nightlife.

Best aesthetic experience

In **Greece:** grab your camera, stock up on postcards, and prepare yourself to experience Delphi's Oracle (p. 92), the top of the acropolis of Lindos (p. 276), or southern Corfu (p. 351). In **Turkey:** where do we begin? Lace up your hiking boots and climb to the Sümela Monastery on the Black Sea (p. 473), or enjoy the more relaxing atmosphere of Antakya (p. 508) or the fishing village of Ayvalık (p. 422). In **Cyprus:** the Karpaz Peninsula (p. 593) is second to none.

Required visiting

In **Greece:** how could you miss the Greek Popular Musical Instruments Museum (p. 85)? In **Turkey:** without a doubt, fans of Atatürk, the father of modern Turkey must check out the Anıt Kabir in Ankara (p. 522), where even clouds show respect. No visit to Turkey is complete without a visit to the Hair Museum (p. 537). In **Cyprus:** act out your colonial fantasies over a steak and kidney pie at Planter's Bar and Bistro (p. 586).

Where to watch the sunset over a drink

In **Greece:** grab your shades and a few thousand *drachmae,* and pay for the view at the old harbor in Santorini (p. 232). In **Turkey:** watch the sun dip into the Black Sea as you stroll the Kordon in Ordu (p. 469). In **Cyprus:** enjoy the twinkling twilights while dining on the harbor of Girne (p. 584).

Places to crash

In **Greece:** try the Art Gallery Hotel in Athens (p. 77) or make a pilgrimage (men only!) to Mount Athos (p. 132). In **Turkey:** sleep in a cave cum pension in Cappadocia (p. 533), or do your best Tarzan imitation by sleeping in one of Olympos's tree houses (p. 494). In **Cyprus:** stay at the best-named hotel in the Mediterranean basin, Xenis Rooms (p. 566).

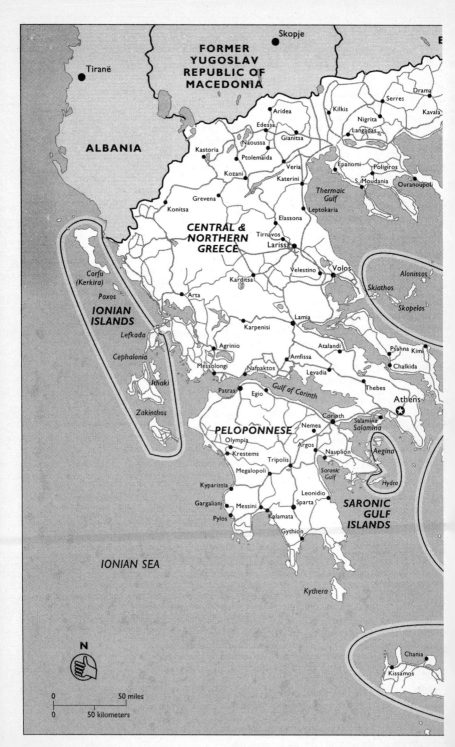

FORMER
YUGOSLAV
REPUBLIC OF
MACEDONIA

Skopje

Tiranë

ALBANIA

Aridea

Edessa

Kilkis

Serres

Drama

Kavala

Nigrita

Langadas

Náoussa

Gianitsa

Kastoria

Ptolemaida

Veria

Epanomi

Poligiros

Kozani

Katerini

S. Moudania

Ouranoupoli

Grevena

Thermaic
Gulf

Konitsa

Elassona

Leptokaria

CENTRAL &
NORTHERN
GREECE

Tirnavos

Larissa

Corfu
(Kerkira)

Karditsa

Velestino

Volos

Alonissos

Skiathos

Paxos

Arta

Skopelos

IONIAN
ISLANDS

Karpenisi

Lamia

Lefkada

Atalandi

Psahna Kimi

Cephalonia

Agrinio

Amfissa

Chalkida

Messolongi

Nafpaktos

Levadia

Ithaki

Patras

Egio

Gulf of Corinth

Thebes

Zakinthos

Athens

Corinth

Salamina
Salamina

PELOPONNESE

Nemea

Olympia

Argos

Nafplion

Aegina

Krestems

Tripolis

Megalopoli

Saronic
Gulf

Hydra

Kyparissia

Leonidio

SARONIC
GULF
ISLANDS

Gargaliani

Messini

Sparta

Pylos

Kalamata

Gythion

IONIAN SEA

Kythera

N

Chania

Kissamos

0   50 miles
0   50 kilometers

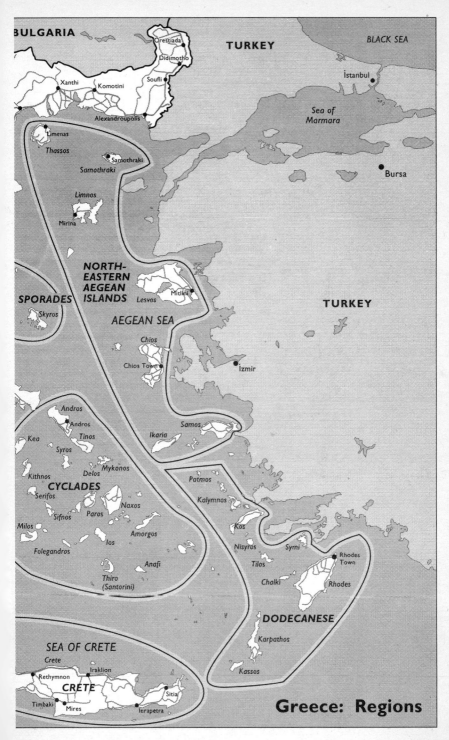

Greece: Regions

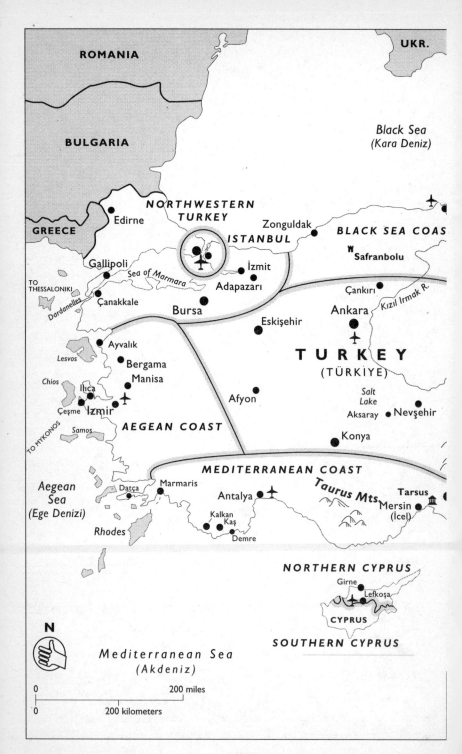

ROMANIA

UKR.

BULGARIA

Black Sea
(Kara Deniz)

GREECE

NORTHWESTERN TURKEY

Edirne

Zonguldak

BLACK SEA COAS

ISTANBUL

Safranbolu

Gallipoli

Sea of Marmara

İzmit

TO
THESSALONIKI

Adapazarı

Çankırı

Kızıl Irmak R.

Dardanelles

Çanakkale

Bursa

Ankara

Eskişehir

T U R K E Y
(TÜRKİYE)

Lesvos

Ayvalık

Bergama

Manisa

Chios

Ilıca

Çeşme

İzmir

Afyon

Salt
Lake

Aksaray

Nevşehir

AEGEAN COAST

Samos

TO MYKONOS

Konya

Aegean
Sea
(Ege Denizi)

MEDITERRANEAN COAST

Datça

Marmaris

Antalya

Taurus Mts.

Tarsus

Mersin
(İcel)

Kalkan
Kaş

Rhodes

Demre

NORTHERN CYPRUS

Girne

Lefkoşa

CYPRUS

SOUTHERN CYPRUS

N

Mediterranean Sea
(Akdeniz)

0   200 miles

0   200 kilometers

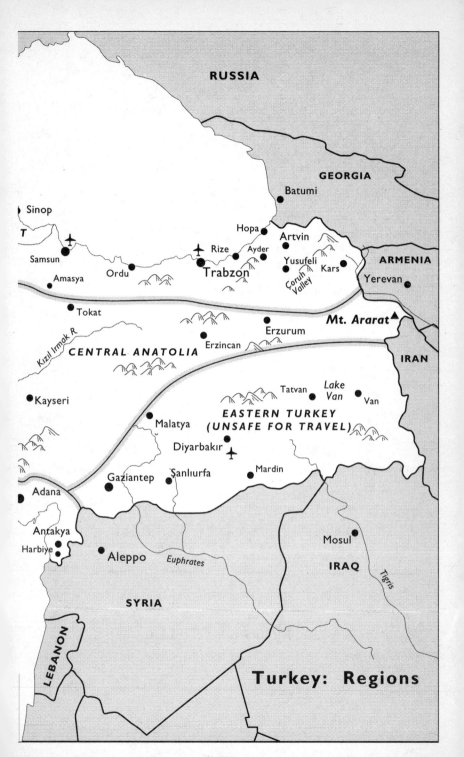

Turkey: Regions

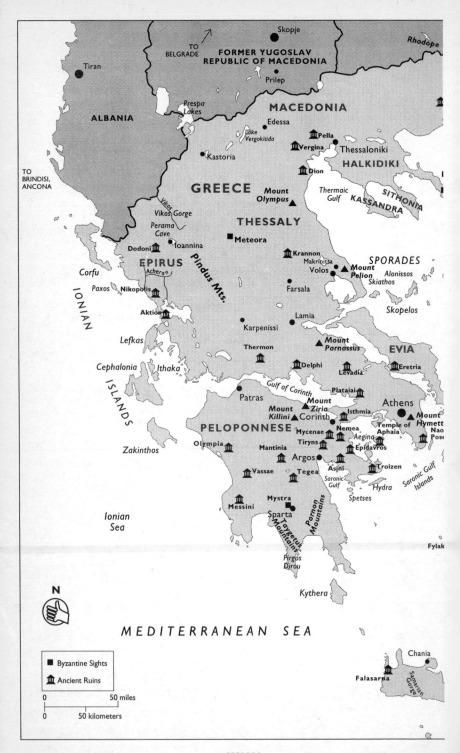

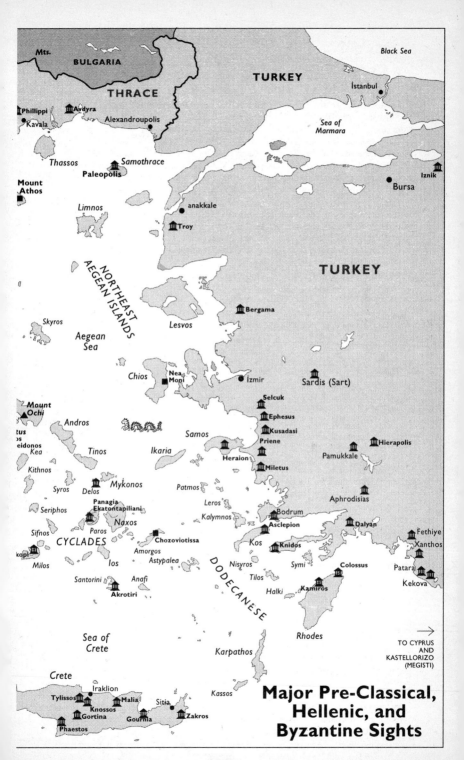

Major Pre-Classical,
Hellenic, and
Byzantine Sights

How to Use This Book

Traveling through the lands of the northeastern Mediterranean, you are walking in the footsteps of philosophers, conquerors, sufis, kings, apostles, writers, generals, sultans, and saints. Perhaps no where else in the world does the majesty and tragedy of human history confront visitors with such force as in Greece, Turkey, and Cyprus.

Of course, our job here at *Let's Go* is to help you enjoy the majesty while avoiding any tragedies of your own. To that end, we have comprehensive practical information on each town that you may visit. From hospitals to hotels, cops to cafes, we give you the addresses and phone numbers you need to make your visit smooth.

This year's edition sees some major changes from past editions. We have added new coverage along the Black Sea Coast in Turkey, improved our coverage by adding almost 50 new pages to the book, added 30 new maps (including of popular sights like the Acropolis and Topkapi Palace), created a Greek-language index of place names, and reorganized the book to make it easier for you to take day trips.

Planning a trip to Greece, Turkey, and Cyprus is a good way to learn the difference between theory and reality. In theory, ferries leave on time; buses arrive as scheduled; pensions are open; and cafes serve food until midnight. In reality, the ferry from Skiathos got cancelled because not enough passengers bought tickets; the bus from Antalya to Istanbul took an extra 15 hours; the pension owner is on vacation in May; and the restaurant ran out of everything but octopus. This doesn't mean that your trip won't be the most stimulating, exciting, beautiful, and entertaining one you've ever taken; it just means you need to be flexible and work with a rough itinerary rather than a firm one.

This book is organized in three major sections: Greece, Turkey, and Cyprus. Within each portion of the book, introductions offer general information to help you decide where to visit and enhance your trip once there. Be sure to check out the **Essentials** section at the beginning of the book, as well as the **Appendix** for quick reference. Also, if you don't know any Greek, the aforementioned **Greek Language Index** in the Appendix is designed to help you make sense out of street signs and schedules by giving you the name of cities in both Greek and English, as well as the page number where the city can be found in the book.

Within each city, we offer: information on orienting yourself; practical information like the hours and location of the post office and tourist police; several lodging recommendations; our favorite restaurants, bakeries, bars, and clubs; and the most interesting sights in the area. Virtually every listing in our book has a telephone number, so if you get lost in, say, Ankara, you could call the Museum of Anatolian Civilization to ask how to get there from the Parliament Building. Please note that listings of hotels and restaurants are ranked in order of the researchers' preference.

We hope you love Greece, Turkey, and Cyprus as much as the people who have worked on this book do. So, Πάμε! *Hadi gidelim!* Let's Go!

A NOTE TO OUR READERS

The information for this book is gathered by *Let's Go*'s researchers from late May through August. Each listing is derived from the assigned researcher's opinion based upon his or her visit at a particular time. The opinions are expressed in a candid and forthright manner. Other travelers might disagree. Those traveling at a different time may have different experiences since prices, dates, hours, and conditions are always subject to change. You are urged to check beforehand to avoid inconvenience and surprises. Travel always involves a certain degree of risk, especially in low-cost areas. When traveling, especially on a budget, always take particular care to ensure your safety.

ESSENTIALS

The three countries that make up the northeast corner of the Mediterranean cast a wide shadow over the entire region's life. Greece, Turkey, and Cyprus have set world standards in art, architecture, military power, and natural beauty. These and other factors come together to give visitors an experience that is both visceral and unique. Tourism is a major industry in these countries. You may feel overwhelmed in the colorful sea of American, German, Japanese, and other tourists at the larger destinations. But if you can avoid getting lost in the crowds, secluded beaches, remote mountain trails, and quiet ruins beckon.

Plan ahead to get the most out of your vacation, but be flexible with your itinerary: schedules change without notice, national holidays pop up unannounced, and everything takes longer than you'll anticipate. An astounding amount of travel information is available to best facilitate your trip; stop by your local travel agency or library, or see **Useful Information.**

PLANNING YOUR TRIP

▓ When To Go

Summer is high tourist season in Greece, Turkey, and Cyprus. If you visit between late July and early September, expect to run into tour groups. If you feel annoyed by crowds or taxed by the frantic pace of summer travel, consider visiting during off season (Sept.-May), when inexpensive airfares are easier to obtain and lodging is cheaper. A few facilities and sights may close down, but residents are often more receptive and the weather is far more pleasant. Even during the winter months, some areas continue to be mild. These countries also have winter sports, with ski areas at Parnassos, Mt. Pelion, Metsovo, Bursa, and Troodos. Ferry schedules become more capricious in winter, but mainland travel is less affected by season. Refer to the climate chart in the appendix for average temperatures and rainfall.

▓ Useful Information

The following organizations and agencies offer a wealth of information. If you don't know where to begin, write a few polite letters. Calling offices directly (or faxing, if you have the means) is always an option and may be necessary if you're in a rush.

GOVERNMENT INFORMATION OFFICES

Greek National Tourist Organization (GNTO): In **Australia,** 3rd Fl., 51 Pitt St., Sydney, NSW 2000 (tel. (2) 241 1663; fax 235 2174). In **Canada,** Head Office, 1300 Bay St., Toronto, Ontario M5R 3K8 (tel. (416) 968 2220; fax 968-6533); 1233 rue de la Montagne, Suite 101, Montréal, Québec, H3G 1Z2 (tel. (514) 871-1535; fax 871-1498; email gnto@ael.com). In **U.K.,** 4 Conduit St., London W1R DOJ (tel. (171) 734 5997; fax 287 1369). In **U.S.,** Head Office, Olympic Tower, 645 Fifth Ave., 5th Floor, New York, NY 10022 (tel. (212) 421-5777; fax 826-6940); 168 N. Michigan Ave., 6th floor, Chicago, IL 60601 (tel. (312) 782-1084; fax 782-1091); 611 W. Sixth St. #2198, Los Angeles, CA 90017 (tel. (213) 626-6696; fax 489-9744). Provides pamphlets on different regions and tourist literature, including the booklet *General Information About Greece* and Travel Agent's Manual.
Turkish Cultural and Information Office: In **Australia,** Suite 101, 280 George St., Sydney, NSW 2000 (tel. (2) 9223 3055; fax 9223 3204). In **Canada,** Constitution Square, 360 Albert St., Suite 801, Ottawa, Ontario K1R 7X7 (tel. (613) 230-8654;

fax 230-3683). In **U.K.,** 170-173 Piccadilly, 1st Fl., London W1V 9DD (tel. (0171) 629 7771; fax 491 0773; email eb25@cityscape.co.uk). In **U.S.,** Turkish Centre, 821 United Nations Plaza, New York, NY 10017 (tel. (212) 687-2194; fax 599-7568; email tourny@soho.ios.com); 1717 Massachusetts Ave. NW, Suite 306, Washington, D.C. 20036 (tel. (202) 429-9844; fax 429-5649).

Cyprus Tourism Organization (CTO): In **Cyprus,** P.O. Box 4535, CY1390, Nicosia, Cyprus (tel. (2) 33 77 15; fax 33 16 44; email cto@cyta.com.cy). In **U.K.,** 213 Regent St., London W1R 8DA (tel. (171) 734 9822; fax 287 6534). In **U.S.,** 13 E. 40th St., New York, NY 10016 (tel. (212) 683-5280; fax 683-5282; email gocyprus@aol.com; http://www.cyprustourism.org). Ask for the *Cyprus Travelers Handbook.*

TRAVEL ORGANIZATIONS

Council on International Educational Exchange (CIEE), 205 East 42nd St., New York, NY 10017-5706 (tel. (888)-COUNCIL (268-6245); fax (212) 822-2699; http://www.ciee.org). A private, not-for-profit organization, Council administers work, volunteer, academic, internship, and professional programs around the world. They also offer identity cards (including the ISIC and the GO25), and a range of publications, among them *Student Travels.* Call or write for further info.

Federation of International Youth Travel Organizations (FIYTO), Bredgade 25H, DK-1260 Copenhagen K, Denmark (tel. (45) 33 33 96 00; fax 33 93 96 76; email mailbox@fiyto.org; http://www.fiyto.org). An international organization promoting educational, cultural and social travel for young people. Member organizations include language schools, educational travel companies, national tourist boards, accommodation centers, and other suppliers of travel services to youth and students. FIYTO sponsors the GO25 Card (http://www.go25.org).

International Student Travel Confederation, Herengracht 479, 1017 BS Amsterdam, The Netherlands (tel. (31) 20 421 2800; fax 20 421 2810; email istcinfo@istc.org; http://www.istc.org). A nonprofit confederation of student travel organizations whose focus is to develop and promote travel among young people and students. Member organizations include International Student Surface Travel Association, Student Air Travel Association, IASIS Travel Insurance, and the International Association for Educational and Work Exchange Programs.

USEFUL PUBLICATIONS

Hippocrene Books, Inc., 171 Madison Ave., New York, NY 10016 (tel. (212) 685-4371; orders (718) 454-2366; fax 454-1391; email hippocre@ix.netcom.com; http://www.netcom.com/~hippocre). Free catalogue. Publishes travel reference books, travel guides, foreign language dictionaries, and language learning guides which cover over 100 languages.

Specialty Travel Index, 305 San Anselmo Ave. #313, San Anselmo, CA 94960 (tel. (415) 459-4900; fax 459-4974; email spectrav@ix.netcom.com; http://www.spectrav.com). Published twice yearly, this is an extensive listing of "off the beaten track" and specialty travel opportunities. One copy US$6, one-year subscription (2 copies) US$10.

INTERNET RESOURCES

Along with everything else in the 90s, budget travel is moving rapidly into the information age, with the **Internet** as a leading travel resource. On today's net, people can make their own airline, hotel, hostel, or car rental reservations. You can connect personally with others abroad and become your own budget travel planner. **NetTravel: How Travelers Use the Internet,** by Michael Shapiro, is a very thorough and informative guide to this process (US$25). The form of the Internet most useful to net-surfing budget travelers is the World Wide Web. **Search engines** are often a good place to start; **Lycos** (http://www.lycos.com) and **Infoseek** (http://guide.infoseek.com) are two of the more popular. **Yahoo!** is a slightly more organized search engine; check out its travel links at http://www.yahoo.com/Recreation/Travel. You might also take a peek at:

The CIA World Factbook (http://www.odci.gov/cia/publications/nsolo/wfb-all.htm). Tons of vital statistics on any country you might want to visit.

Cybercafe Guide (http://www.cyberiacafe.net/cyberia/guide/ccafe.htm) can help you find cybercafes, as well as net access, worldwide.

Foreign Language for Travelers (http://www.travlang.com) is an excellent resource for learning Turkish and Greek words and phrases.

Rent-A-Wreck's Travel Links (http://www.rent-a-wreck.com/raw/travlist.htm). Contrary to what its name implies, very good and very complete.

Shoestring Travel (http://www.stratpub.com). A travel magazine, with feature articles, links, user exchange, and accommodations information.

TravelHUB (http://www.travelhub.com) is a great site for cheap travel deals.

▓ Documents and Formalities

File all applications weeks or months in advance. The agency might deem your applications inadequate and return them, so leave enough time to resubmit them. Apply off-season (August to December) for speedier service. When you travel, always carry on your person two or more forms of identification, including at least one photo ID. Never carry all your forms of ID together, however; you risk being left entirely without ID or funds in case of theft or loss.

EMBASSIES AND CONSULATES

Greek Embassy: In **Australia,** 9 Turrana St., Yarralumla, Canberra, ACT 2600 (tel. (6162) 773-158; fax 732-620). In **Canada,** 7680 MacLaren St., Ottawa, Ontario K2P 0K6 (tel. (613) 238-6271; fax 238-5676). In **Ireland,** 1 Upper Pembroke St., Dublin 2 (tel. (1) 676-7254; fax 661-8892). In **South Africa,** 995 Pretorius St., Arcadia 0083, Pretoria (tel. (12) 437-351, -2, -3; fax 434-313). In **U.K.,** 1A Holland Park, London W11 3TP (tel. (0171) 229 3850; fax 229 7221). In **U.S.,** 2221 Mass. Ave. NW, Washington, D.C. 20008 (tel. (202) 939-5800; fax 939-5824; email greece@greekembassy.org).

Greek Consulates: In **Australia:** 366 King William St., 1st Fl., **Adelaide,** SA 5000 (tel. (618) 211-8066; fax 211-8820); Stanhill House, 34 Queens Road, **Melbourne** Vic. 3004 (tel. (613) 866-4524, -5; fax 866-4933); 15 Castlereagh St., Level 20, **Sydney,** NSW 2000 (tel. (612) 221-2388; fax 221-1423); 16 St. George's Terrace, **Perth,** WA 6000 (tel. (619) 325-6608; fax 325-2940). In **Canada:** 1170 Place du Frère André, 3ème Etage, **Montréal,** Québec H3B 3C6 (tel. (514) 875-2119; fax 875-8781; email congrem@citenet.net); 365 Blue St. E, Suite 1800, **Toronto,** Ontario M4W 3L4 (tel. (416) 515-0133, -4; fax 515-0209); 500-688 West Hastings, **Vancouver,** B.C. V6B 1P1 (tel. (604) 681-1381, -1366; fax 681-6656). In **New Zealand,** 57 Willeston St., 10th Fl., Box 24066, Wellington (tel. (644) 473 7775, -6; fax 473 7441). In **U.S.:** 2211 Massachusetts Ave. NW, Washington DC 20008 (tel. (202) 939-5818; fax 234-2803); 69 East 79th St., **New York,** NY 10021 (tel. (212) 988-5500; fax 734-8492); 650 North St. Clair St., **Chicago,** IL 60611 (tel. (312) 335-3915, -6, -7; fax 335-3958); 2441 Gough St., **San Francisco,** CA 94123 (tel. (415) 775-2102, -3; fax 776-6815); 12424 Wilshire Blvd., Suite 800, **Los Angeles,** CA 90025 (tel. (310) 826-5555; fax 826-8670); 86 Beacon St., **Boston,** MA 02108 (tel. (617) 523-0100; fax 523-0511; open Mon.-Fri. 9am-1pm, Wed. 2pm-5pm); Tower Place, Suite 1670, 3340 Peachtree Rd. NE, **Atlanta,** GA 30326 (tel. (404) 261-3313, -91; fax 262-2798); 1360 Post Oak Blvd., Suite 2480, **Houston,** TX 77056 (tel. (713) 840-7522; fax 840-0614); World Trade Center, 2 Canal St., Suite 1946, **New Orleans,** LA 70130 (tel. (504) 523-1167; fax 524-5610).

Turkish Embassy: In **Australia,** 60 Muggaway, Red Hill, ACT 2603 (tel. (6) 295 0227; fax 239 6592). In **Canada,** 197 Wurtemburg St., Ottawa, Ontario K1N 8L9 (tel. (171) 393 0202; fax 393-0066). In **Ireland,** 11 Clyde Rd. Ballsbridge, Dublin 4 (tel. (01) 668 5240; fax 284 7738). In **New Zealand,** 15-17 Murphy St., Level 8, Wellington (tel. (4) 472 1290, -2; fax 472 1277). In **South Africa,** 1067 Church St., Hatfield 0181 Pretoria (tel. (12) 342 6053; fax 342 6052). In **U.K.,** 43 Belgrave Sq., London SW1 X8PA (tel. (0171) 393 0202; fax 393 0066). In **U.S.,** 1714 Mass. Ave. NW, Washington, D.C. 20036 (tel. (202) 659-0742).

Turkish Consulates: In U.S.: 360 N. Michigan Ave. Suite 1405, **Chicago,** IL 60601 (tel. (312) 263-1295; fax (312) 263-1449); 4801 Wilshire Blvd. Suite 310, **Los Angeles,** CA 90010 (tel. (213) 937-0110; fax (213) 932-0061); 1990 Post Oak Blvd. Suite 1300, **Houston,** TX 77056 (tel. (713) 622-5849; fax 623-6639; email turcon@ix.netcom.com); 821 United Nations Plaza, 5th Fl., **NY,** NY 10017 (tel. (212) 949-0160).

Cypriot Embassy: In Australia, 30 Beale Crescent, Deakin-Canberra ACT 2600 (tel. (6) 281-0832, -4; fax 281-0860). In **U.K.,** 93 Park St., London W1Y 4ET (tel. (0171) 499 8272; fax 491 0691). In **U.S.,** 2211 R St. NW, Washington, D.C. 20008 (tel. (202) 462-5772; fax 483-6710).

Cypriot Consulates: In Canada: Toronto, 365 Bloor St. E., Suite 1010, Box #43, **Toronto,** Ontario M4W 3L4 (tel. (416) 944-0998; fax 944-9149); 2930 Rue Edouard Mont Petit, Suite PH2, **Montréal,** Quebec H3T 1J7 (tel. (514) 735-7233).

Northern Cyprus Representative Offices: In Canada, 328 Highway East, Suite 308, Richmond Hill, Ontario L4B 3P7. In **U.K.,** 29 Bedford Square, London WC 1 B3EG (tel. (0171) 631 1920, -30; fax 631 1948. In **U.S.:** 821 United Nations Plaza, 6th Fl., **New York,** NY 10017 (tel. (212) 687-2350; fax 949-6872; email trncny@aol.com); 1667 K St. NW, Suite 690, **Washington,** D.C. 20006 (tel. (202) 887-6198; fax 467-0685; email kktc@aol.com).

PASSPORTS

Citizens of the United States, Canada, the United Kingdom, Ireland, Australia, New Zealand, and South Africa all need valid passports to enter Greece, Turkey, and Cyprus, and to re-enter their own country. If you plan a long stay, you may want to register your passport with the nearest embassy or consulate; notify them or the police immediately if your passport is lost or stolen. Your consulate can issue you a new passport or temporary traveling papers. If you lose your passport in Istanbul, first go to your consulate to get a citizen certificate and then to the tourist police.

Before you leave, **photocopy** the page of your passport that contains your photograph and identifying information. (Especially important is your **passport number.**) Also copy all the pages in your passport that are stamped with visas, and leave a duplicate with a friend. Consulates recommend that you carry an expired passport or an official copy of your birth certificate in a separate part of your luggage from other documents. U.S. citizens can request a duplicate birth certificate from the Bureau of Vital Records and Statistics in their region of birth.

Losing your passport can be a nightmare. A replacement may take weeks, and may be valid only for a limited time. Immediately notify the local police and the nearest embassy or consulate of your home government. Provide all the information that you had previously recorded and photocopied, and show identification and proof of citizenship. Some consulates issue new passports within two days. In an emergency, ask for immediate temporary traveling papers that will permit you to return to your home country. Remember, your passport is a public document that belongs to your nation's government. You may have to surrender your passport to a foreign government official; if you don't get it back in a reasonable time, inform the nearest mission, consulate, or embassy of your home country.

Australia: Citizens must apply for a passport in person at a post office, a passport office, or an Australian diplomatic mission overseas. An appointment may be necessary. Passport offices are located in Adelaide, Brisbane, Canberra City, Darwin, Hobart, Melbourne, Newcastle, Perth, and Sydney. A parent may file an application for a child who is under 18 and unmarried. Adult passports cost AUS$120 (for a 32-page passport) or AUS$180 (64-page), and a child's is AUS$60 (32-page) or AUS$90 (64-page). For more info, call toll-free (in Australia) 13 12 32.

Canada: Application forms in English and French are available at all passport offices, Canadian missions, many travel agencies, and Northern Stores in northern communities. Citizens may apply in person at any 1 of 28 regional Passport Offices across Canada. Travel agents can direct applicants to the nearest location. Canadian citizens residing abroad should contact the nearest Canadian embassy or consulate. Children under 16 may be included on a parent's passport. Passports cost CDN$60, are valid for 5 years, and are not renewable. Processing takes approximately 5 business days for applications in-person; 10 days if by mail. For additional info, contact the Canadian Passport Office, Department of Foreign Affairs and International Trade, Ottawa, Ontario K1A 0G3 (tel. (613) 994-3500; http://www.dfait-maeci.gc.ca/passport). Travelers may also call (800) 567-6868 (24hr.); in Toronto (416) 973-3251; in Vancouver (604) 775-6250; in Montréal (514) 283-2152. Refer to the booklet *Bon Voyage, But...*, free at any passport office or by calling InfoCentre at (800) 267-8376, for further help and a list of Canadian embassies and consulates abroad. You may also find entry and background information for various countries by contacting the Consular Affairs Bureau in Ottawa (tel. (800) 267-6788 (24hr.) or (613) 944-6788).

Ireland: Citizens can apply for a passport by mail to either the Department of Foreign Affairs, Passport Office, Setanta Centre, Molesworth St., Dublin 2 (tel. (01) 671 1633), or the Passport Office, 1A South Mall, Cork (tel. (021) 627 2525). Obtain an application at a local Garda station or request one from a passport office. The new Passport Express Service, available through post offices, allows citizens to get a passport in 2 weeks for an extra IR£3. Passports cost IR£45 and are valid for 10 years. Citizens under 18 or over 65 can request a 3-year passport that costs IR£10.

New Zealand: Application forms for passports are available in New Zealand from travel agents and Department of Internal Affairs Link Centres in the main cities and towns. Overseas, forms and passport services are provided by New Zealand embassies, high commissions, and consulates. Applications may also be forwarded to the Passport Office, P.O. Box 10526, Wellington. Standard processing time in New Zealand is 10 working days. The fees are adult NZ$80, and child NZ$40. An urgent service is also available for an extra NZ$80. Different fees apply at overseas posts: nine posts including London, Sydney, and Los Angeles offer both standard and urgent services (adult NZ$130, child NZ$65, plus NZ$130 if urgent). The fee at other posts is adult NZ$260, child NZ$195, and a passport will be issued within three working days. Children's names can no longer be endorsed on a parent's passport—they must apply for their own, which are valid for up to 5 years. An adult's passport is valid for up to 10 years.

South Africa: Citizens can apply for a passport at any Home Affairs Office. Passports are valid for 10 years and cost SAR80. For further information, contact the nearest Department of Home Affairs Office.

United Kingdom: British citizens, British Dependent Territories citizens, British Nationals (overseas), and British Overseas citizens may apply for a **full passport,** valid for 10 years (5 years if under 16). Application forms are available at passport offices, main post offices, many travel agents, and branches of Lloyds Bank and Artac World Choice. Apply in person or by mail to one of the passport offices, located in London, Liverpool, Newport, Peterborough, Glasgow, or Belfast. The fee is UK£18. The London office offers same-day, walk-in service; arrive early. The formerly available **British Visitor's Passport** (valid in some western European countries and Bermuda only) has been abolished; every traveler over 16 needs a 10-year standard passport. The U.K. Passport Agency can be reached by phone at (0990) 21 04 10, and info is on the Internet at http://www.open.gov.uk/ukpass.

United States: Citizens may apply for a passport at any federal or state **courthouse** or **post office** authorized to accept passport applications, or at a **U.S. Passport Agency,** located in Boston, Chicago, Honolulu, Houston, Los Angeles, Miami, New Orleans, New York, Philadelphia, San Francisco, Seattle, Stamford, or Washington, D.C. Refer to the "U.S. Government, State Department" section of the telephone directory or the local post office for addresses. Parents must apply in person for children under age 13. You must apply in person if this is your first passport, if you're under age 18, or if your current passport is more than 12 years old or was issued before your 18th birthday. Passports are valid for 10 years (5 years if under 18) and cost US$65 (under 18 US$40). Passports may be **renewed** by mail or in person for US$55. Processing takes 3-4 weeks. **Rush service** is available for a surcharge of US$30 with proof of departure within 10 working days (e.g., an airplane ticket or itinerary), or for travelers leaving in 2-3 weeks who

require visas. Given proof of citizenship, a U.S. embassy or consulate abroad can usually issue a new passport. Report a passport lost or stolen in the U.S. in writing to Passport Services, 1425 K St. NW, U.S. Department of State, Washington, D.C. 20524 or to the nearest passport agency. For more information, contact the U.S. Passport Information's **24-hour recorded message** (tel. (202) 647-0518). U.S. citizens may receive consular information sheets, travel warnings, and public announcements at any passport agency, U.S. embassy, or consulate, or by sending a self-addressed stamped envelope to: Overseas Citizens Services, Room 4811, Department of State, Washington, D.C. 20520-4818 (tel. (202) 647-5225; fax 647-3000). Additional information about documents, formalities and travel abroad is available through the Bureau of Consular Affairs homepage at http://travel.state.gov, or through the State Department site at http://www.state.gov.

ENTRANCE REQUIREMENTS AND VISAS

Citizens of the U.S., Canada, E.U. members, Australia, and New Zealand do not need to get a visa ahead of time to visit **Greece.** Non-E.U. members will be automatically granted leave for a three-month stay (not valid for employment), but South Africans do need a visa. Apply to stay longer at least 20 days prior to the three-month expiration date at the **Aliens Bureau,** 175 Alexandras Ave., Athens 11522 (tel. 642 3094), or check with a Greek embassy or consulate. Bona fide tourists with valid passports from Australia, Canada, Great Britain, Ireland, New Zealand, and the U.S. do not need a visa to enter either Cyprus or Northern Cyprus for stays of up to 90 days; South Africans and Turks do need visas (fee: C£5). It is suggested that tourists wishing to stay longer leave and then re-enter. Citizens of Australia, Canada, and New Zealand do not need a visa for visits to **Turkey** of up to three months. South African nationals need a visa, and they may stay up to one month. Three-month sticker visas, not valid for employment, are available for cash at ports of entry for citizens of the U.S. ($20), U.K. (£5), and Ireland.

CUSTOMS: ENTERING

Greece: Upon entering Greece, you must declare cameras, typewriters, portable radios, and musical instruments. One of each may be brought in duty-free as long as they will be taken with you upon departure. You must also register all currency above US$1000, or you may not take it with you when you leave. Duty-free limits include: 10kg of foodstuffs and beverages; 200 cigarettes, 50 cigars, or 250g tobacco; 5 boxes of matches; 2 packs of playing cards; and 1L of alcoholic beverage or 2L of wine. Children under 15 may bring in 5000dr worth of gift articles, everyone else up to 9000dr worth. Bicycles must be declared when entering; they may be used freely throughout, but they must be taken with you when exiting the country. Weapons and explosives are strictly prohibited. Prescription medications for personal use are the only admissible drugs, and even these may need to be accompanied by the prescription.

Turkey and Northern Cyprus: Travelers entering Turkey or Northern Cyprus may bring along: 1 camera and 5 rolls of film; 1 video camera with 5 blank cassettes; 1 personal stereo and 5 cassettes or compact discs; 1 video player or slide projector; no more than 3 musical instruments; 200 cigarettes (or 50 cigars); 200g tobacco or 50g chewing tobacco; 1.5 kg coffee; 1.5kg instant coffee; 500g tea; 1kg chocolate; 1kg sweets; and 5 100cc or 7 70cc bottles of wine and/or spirits. In addition to these allowances, it is possible to purchase 400 cigarettes, 100 cigars, and 500g pipe tobacco from Turkish duty-free shops on entering the country. No sharp instruments or firearms of any sort may be brought in, and under no circumstances should you bring any illegal drugs into Turkey or Northern Cyprus. To avoid problems when you transport prescription drugs, ensure that the bottles are clearly marked, and carry a copy of the prescription to show the customs officer.

Republic of Cyprus: Cyprus allows travelers to bring in duty-free not more than 250g tobacco, 1L spirits, 0.75L wine, and 0.3L perfume. Other personal effects are permitted, up to a total value of C£50. Travelerd entering Cyprus after a stay abroad of less than 72 hours are allowed to import free of duty only 250g of tobacco. Travelers importing more than $1000 worth of foreign currency should declare it on form D (NR), especially if they want to take it out of the country later. Firearms, live animals, ammunition, plants, agricultural products, and uncooked meat are prohibited. Illegal drugs, of course, are not to be imported.

CUSTOMS: GOING HOME

Upon returning home, you must declare all articles acquired abroad and pay a **duty** on the value of the goods that exceed the allowance established by your country's customs service. Goods and gifts purchased at **duty-free** shops abroad are not exempt from duty or sales tax upon return; you must declare these items as well. "Duty-free" merely means that you need not pay a tax in the country of purchase.

Australia: Citizens may import AUS$400 (under 18 AUS$200) of goods duty-free, in addition to 1.125L alcohol and 250 cigarettes or 250g tobacco. You must be over 18 to import alcohol or tobacco. There is no limit to the amount of Australian and/or foreign cash that may be brought into or taken out of the country, but amounts of AUS$10,000 or more, or the equivalent in foreign currency, must be reported. All foodstuffs and animal products must be declared on arrival. For information, contact the Regional Director, Australian Customs Service, GPO Box 8, Sydney NSW 2001 (tel. (02) 9213 2000; fax 9213 4000).

Canada: Citizens who remain abroad for at least 1 week may bring back up to CDN$500 worth of goods duty-free any time. Citizens or residents who travel for a period between 48 hours and 6 days can bring back up to CDN$200. Both of these exemptions may include tobacco and alcohol. You are permitted to ship goods except tobacco and alcohol home under the CDN$500 exemption as long as you declare them when you arrive. Goods under the CDN$200 exemption, as well as all alcohol and tobacco, must be in your hand or checked luggage. Citizens of legal age (which varies by province) may import in-person up to 200 cigarettes, 50 cigars or cigarillos, 400g loose tobacco, 400 tobacco sticks, 1.14L wine or alcohol, and 24 355mL cans/bottles of beer; the value of these products is included in the CDN$200 or CDN$500. For more information, write to Canadian Customs, 2265 St. Laurent Blvd., Ottawa, Ontario K1G 4K3 (tel. (613) 993-0534), phone the 24hr. Automated Customs Information Service at (800) 461-9999, or visit Revenue Canada at http://www.revcan.ca.

Ireland: Citizens must declare everything in excess of IR£142 (£73 per traveler under 15 years of age) obtained outside the EU or duty and tax-free in the EU above the following allowances: 200 cigarettes, 100 cigarillos, 50 cigars, or 250g tobacco; 1L liquor or 2L wine; 2L still wine; 50g perfume; and 250mL toilet water. Goods obtained duty and tax paid in another EU country up to a value of £460 (£115 per traveler under 15) will not be subject to additional customs duties. Travelers under 17 may not import tobacco or alcohol. For more information, contact The Revenue Commissioners, Dublin Castle (tel. (01) 679 27 77; fax 671 20 21; email taxes@iol.ie; http://www.revenue.ie) or The Collector of Customs and Excise, The Custom House, Dublin 1.

New Zealand: Citizens may import up to NZ$700 worth of goods duty-free if they are intended for personal use or are unsolicited gifts. The concession is 200 cigarettes (1 carton), 250g tobacco, 50 cigars, or a combination of all 3 not to exceed 250g. You may also bring in 4.5L of beer or wine and 1.125L of liquor. Only travelers over 17 may import tobacco or alcohol. For more information, contact New Zealand Customs, 50 Anzac Ave., Box 29, Auckland (tel. (09) 377 35 20; fax 309 29 78).

South Africa: Citizens may import duty-free: 400 cigarettes, 50 cigars, 250g tobacco, 2L wine, 1L of spirits, 250mL toilet water, and 50mL perfume, and other items up to a value of SAR500. Amounts exceeding this limit but not SAR10,000 are dutiable at 20%. Certain items such as golf clubs and firearms require a duty higher than the standard 20%. Goods acquired abroad and sent to the Republic as unaccompanied baggage do not qualify for any allowances. You may not export or import South African bank notes in excess of SAR500. For more information, contact the Commissioner for Customs and Excise, Private Bag X47, Pretoria 0001 for the pamphlet *South African Customs Information.* Citizens residing in the U.S. should contact the Embassy of South Africa, 3051 Massachusetts Ave. NW, Washington, D.C. 20008 (tel. (202) 232-4400; fax 244-9417) or the South African Home Annex, 3201 New Mexico Ave. NW #380, Washington, D.C. 20016 (tel. (202) 966-1650).

United Kingdom: Citizens or visitors arriving in the U.K. from outside the EU must declare goods in excess of the following allowances: 200 cigarettes, 100 cigarillos, 50 cigars, or 250g tobacco; 2L still table wine; 1L strong liquors over 22% volume or fortified or sparkling wine; 2L other liqueurs; 60cc perfume; 250cc toilet water; and UK£136 worth of all other goods including gifts and souvenirs. You must be over 17 to import liquor or tobacco. These allowances also apply to duty-free purchases within the EU, except for the last category, other goods, which has an allowance of UK£71. Goods obtained duty and tax paid for personal use (regulated according to set guide levels) within the EU do not require any further customs duty. For more information, contact Her Majesty's Customs and Excise, Custom House, Nettleton Road, Heathrow Airport, Hounslow, Middlesex TW6 2LA (tel. (0181) 910-3744; fax 910-3765).

United States: Citizens may import US$400 worth of accompanying goods duty-free and must pay a 10% tax on the next $1000. You must declare all purchases, so have sales slips ready. The $400 personal exemption covers goods purchased for personal or household use (this includes gifts) and cannot include more than 100 cigars, 200 cigarettes (1 carton), and 1L of wine or liquor. You must be over 21 to bring liquor into the U.S. If you mail home personal goods of U.S. origin, you can avoid duty charges by marking the package "American goods returned." For more information, consult the brochure *Know Before You Go,* available from the U.S. Customs Service, Box 7407, Washington, D.C. 20044 (tel. (202) 927-6724).

YOUTH, STUDENT, & TEACHER IDENTIFICATION

The **International Student Identity Card (ISIC)** is the most widely accepted form of student identification. Flashing this card can procure discounts for sights, theaters, museums, accommodations, meals, train, ferry, bus, airplane transportation, and other services. Present the card wherever you go, and ask about discounts even when none are advertised. It also provides insurance benefits, including US$100 per day of in-hospital sickness for a maximum of 60 days, and US$3000 accident-related medical reimbursement for each accident (see **Insurance,** p.20). In addition, cardholders have access to a toll-free 24hr. ISIC helpline whose multilingual staff provides assistance in medical, legal, and financial emergencies overseas.

Many student travel agencies around the world issue ISICs, including STA Travel in Australia and New Zealand; Travel CUTS in Canada; USIT in Ireland and Northern Ireland; SASTS in South Africa; Campus Travel and STA Travel in the U.K.; Council Travel, Let's Go Travel, and STA Travel in the U.S.; and any of the other organizations under the auspices of the International Student Travel Confederation (ISTC); see **Budget Travel Agencies** (p.29) for more information. When you apply for the card, request a copy of the *International Student Identity Card Handbook,* which lists by country some of the available discounts. You can also write to Council for a copy. The card is valid from September to December of the following year and costs US$19 or CDN$15. Applicants must be at least 12 years old and degree-seeking students of a secondary or post-secondary school. Because of the proliferation of phony ISICs, many airlines and some other services require other proof of student identity, such as a signed letter from the registrar attesting to your student status and stamped with the school seal or your school ID card. The US$20 **International Teacher Identity Card (ITIC)** offers the same insurance coverage, and similar but limited discounts. For more information on these cards, consult the organization's web site (http:\\www.istc.org; email isicinfo@istc.org).

The Federation of International Youth Travel Organizations (FIYTO) issues a discount card to travelers who are under 26 but not students. Known as the **GO25 Card,** this one-year card offers many of the same benefits as the ISIC, and most organizations that sell the ISIC also sell the GO25 Card. A brochure that lists discounts is free when you purchase the card. To apply, you will need a passport, valid driver's license, or copy of a birth certificate, and a passport-sized photo with your name printed on the back. The fee is US$19, CDN$15, or UK£5. Information is available on the web at http://www.fiyto.org or http://www.go25.org, or by contacting Travel CUTS in Canada, STA Travel in the U.K., Council Travel in the U.S., or FIYTO headquarters in Denmark.

DRIVING PERMITS AND CAR INSURANCE

If you plan to drive a car while abroad, you must have an **International Driving Permit (IDP),** though certain countries allow travelers to drive with a valid American or Canadian license for a limited number of months. Most car rental agencies don't require the permit. Call an automobile association to find out if your destination country requires the IDP. It may be a good idea to get one anyway, in case you're in a position (such as an accident or stranded in a smaller town) where the police may not read or speak English.

Your IDP, valid for one year, must be issued in your own country before you depart. A valid driver's license from your home country must always accompany the IDP. An application for an IDP usually needs to be accompanied by one or two photos, a current local license, an additional form of identification, and a fee. Australians can obtain an IDP by contacting their local **Royal Automobile Club (RAC),** or the **National Royal Motorist Association (NRMA)** if in NSW or the ACT, where a permit can be obtained for AUS$12. Canadian license holders can obtain an IDP (CDN$10) through any **Canadian Automobile Association (CAA)** branch office in Canada, or by writing to CAA Central Ontario, 60 Commerce Valley Drive East, Thornhill, Ontario L3T 7P9 (tel. (416) 221-4300). Citizens of Ireland should drop into their nearest **Automobile Association (AA)** office where an IDP can be picked up for IR£4, or phone (01) 283 3555 for a postal application form. In New Zealand, contact your local **Automobile Association (AA),** or their main office at 99 Albert Street, PO Box 5, Auckland (tel. (09) 377 4660; fax 309 4564), IDPs cost NZ$8 plus NZ$2 for return postage. In South Africa visit your local **Automobile Association of South Africa** office, where IDPs can be picked up for SAR25, or for more information phone (011) 466 6641, or write to P.O. Box 596, 2000 Johannesburg. In the U.K., IDPs are UK£4 and you can either visit your local **AA Shop,** or call (01256) 49 39 32 and order a postal application form (allow 2-3 weeks). U.S. license holders can obtain an IDP (US$10) at any **American Automobile Association (AAA)** office or by writing to AAA Florida, Travel Agency Services Department, 1000 AAA Drive (mail stop 28), Heathrow, FL 32746-5080 (tel. (407) 444-4245; fax 444-4247).

■ Money Matters

CURRENCY AND EXCHANGE

Before leaving home, exchange US$50 or so for the currency of Greece, Turkey, or Cyprus. You'll pay a higher exchange rate (and you may have to call your bank in advance to find Greek *drachmae,* Turkish *lira,* or Cypriot pounds), but this will save time and exasperation, especially if you arrive when the banks are closed. When exchanging currency, you'll usually lose money due to commissions and high exchange rates; ordinarily exchange in fairly large sums in order to minimize the loss.

Greek *drachmae* are issued in both paper notes (100, 200, 500, 1000, 5000, and 10,000dr) and coins (10, 20, 50, and 100dr). If you're carrying more than US$1000 in cash when you enter Greece, you must declare it upon entry in order to export it legally (this does not apply to traveler's checks). You can bring up to US$445 worth of *drachmae* into Greece. In addition, no more than 20,000 *drachmae* can be taken

A note on prices: throughout the guide, we quote prices effective in the summer of 1997. Since inflation and exchange rates fluctuate considerably, be advised that listed prices could rise by an additional 10-30% by 1998. Because inflation in Turkey generally keeps pace with the devaluation of the *lira,* prices are quoted in U.S. dollars and should be slightly more stable than those in Greece.

out of the country when you leave. It is not difficult to exchange money in Greece. Commission-free ATMs are located in most major cities.

The official currency in Turkey and Northern Cyprus is the Turkish *lira* (TL). Coins are divided into 50, 1000, 2500, 5000, 10,000, and 25,000 lira pieces, and paper currency comes in denominations of 5000, 10,000, 20,000, 50,000, 100,000, 250,000, 500,000, and 1,000,000 *lira* notes. It is difficult to get change for bills of 250,000TL or more at museum entrances and cheap restaurants. Once in Turkey, currency can be exchanged almost anywhere, but banks and exchange bureaus offer the best rates. Turkey has 24-hour currency exchanges at border crossings, major airports, and train stations; major tourist areas have places to change money on weekends. Even better, commission-free 24-hour ATMs are centrally located in the larger cities. Hold on to exchange slips, since you may have to present them when you're re-converting your cash. If you take gifts out of Turkey, you may have to prove that they were bought with legally exchanged foreign currency. There is no limit to the amount of foreign currency that can be brought into Turkey, but no more than US$5000 in *lira* may be brought into or taken out of the country. If you are coming from Greece, exchange your money before arriving. The banks that accept *drachmae* exchange them at an absurdly high rate.

The main unit of currency in the Republic of Cyprus is the pound (£), which is divided into 100 cents. Coins come in 1, 2, 5, 10, 20, and 50 cent sizes; bank notes in denominations of £1, 5, 10, and 20. Cyprus imposes no limit on the amount of foreign currency that may be imported upon entering the country, but amounts in excess of US$1000 should be declared on Customs form D (NR). No more than £50 in Cypriot currency may be brought into or taken out of the country.

TRAVELER'S CHECKS

Traveler's checks are one of the safer and least troublesome means of carrying funds. Several agencies and many banks sell them, usually for face value plus a 1% commission. (Members of the American Automobile Association can get American Express checks commission-free through AAA.) American Express and Visa are the most widely recognized, though other major checks are sold, exchanged, cashed, and refunded with almost equal ease. Keep in mind that in small towns, traveler's checks are less readily accepted than in cities with large tourist industries. Nonetheless, there will probably be at least one place in every town where you can exchange them for local currency. Each agency provides refunds if your checks are lost or stolen, and many provide additional services. (Note that you may need a police report verifying the loss or theft.) You should expect a fair amount of red tape and delay in the event of theft or loss of traveler's checks. To expedite the refund process, you should: keep your check receipts separate from your checks and store them in a safe place or with a traveling companion; record check numbers when you cash them and leave a list of check numbers with someone at home; and ask for a list of refund centers when you buy your checks. Keep a separate supply of cash or traveler's checks for emergencies. Be sure never to countersign your checks until you're prepared to cash them and always be sure to bring your passport with you when you plan to use the checks.

American Express: Call (800) 25 19 02 in Australia; in New Zealand (0800) 44 10 68; in the U.K. (0800) 52 13 13; in the U.S. and Canada (800) 221-7282. Elsewhere, call U.S. collect (801) 964-6665. American Express traveler's checks are now available in 10 currencies. They are the most widely recognized worldwide and the easiest to replace if lost or stolen. Checks can be purchased for a small fee (1-4%) at American Express Travel Service Offices, banks, and American Automobile Association offices (AAA members can buy the checks commission-free). Cardmembers can also purchase checks at American Express Dispensers at Travel Service Offices at airports and by ordering them via phone (tel. (800) ORDER-TC (673-3782)). American Express offices cash their checks commission-free, although they often offer slightly worse rates than banks. Request the American Express booklet "Traveler's Companion," which lists travel office addresses and stolen check hotlines for each European country. Visit their online travel offices (http://www.aexp.com).

Citicorp: Call (800) 645-6556 in the U.S. and Canada; in Europe, the Middle East, or Africa (44) 171 508 7007; from elsewhere call U.S. collect (813) 623-1709. Sells both Citicorp and Citicorp Visa traveler's checks in U.S., Australian, and Canadian dollars, British pounds, German marks, Spanish pesetas, and Japanese yen. Commission is 1-2% on check purchases. Checkholders are automatically enrolled for 45 days in the Travel Assist Program (hotline (800) 250-4377 or collect (202) 296-8728) which provides travelers with English-speaking doctor, lawyer, and interpreter referrals as well as check refund assistance and general travel information. Citicorp's World Courier Service guarantees hand-delivery of traveler's checks when a refund location is not convenient. Call 24hr. per day, 7 days per week.

Thomas Cook MasterCard: For 24hr. cashing or refund assistance, call (800) 223-9920 in the U.S. and Canada; elsewhere call U.S. collect (609) 987-7300; from the U.K. call (0800) 622 101 free, (1733) 502 995 collect, or (1733) 318 950 collect. Offers checks in U.S., Canadian, and Australian dollars, British and Cypriot pounds, French and Swiss francs, German marks, Japanese yen, Dutch guilders, Spanish pesetas, South African rand, and ECUs. Commission 1-2% for purchases. Thomas Cook offices may sell checks for lower commissions and will cash checks commission-free. Thomas Cook MasterCard Traveler's Checks are also available from **Capital Foreign Exchange** (see **Currency and Exchange**) in U.S. or Canadian dollars, French and Swiss francs, British pounds, and German marks.

Visa: In the U.S., call (800) 227-6811; in the U.K. (0800) 895 492; from anywhere else in the world call collect (01733) 318 949. Any of the above numbers can tell you the location of their nearest office. Any type of Visa traveler's checks can be reported lost at the Visa number.

CREDIT CARDS

Depending on where you are in Greece, Turkey, or Cyprus, credit cards are either accepted in all but the smallest businesses or, in some places, only recognized in fancy hotels and restaurants. However, some benefits of credit cards can be reaped just about everywhere. Major credit cards—**MasterCard** and **Visa** are the most welcomed—can be used to extract cash advances from associated banks and teller machines throughout a great deal of the region, and in local currency. Credit card companies get the wholesale exchange rate, which is generally 5% better than the retail rate used by banks and even better than that used by other currency exchange establishments. However, you will be charged ruinous interest rates if you don't pay off the bill quickly, so be careful when using this service. **American Express** cards also work in some ATMs, as well as at AmEx offices and major airports. All such machines require a **Personal Identification Number (PIN),** so be sure to ask your credit card company to assign you a PIN before you leave; without it, you will be unable to withdraw cash with your credit card outside the U.S. Keep in mind that MasterCard and Visa have different names elsewhere ("EuroCard" or "Access" for MasterCard and "Carte Bleue" or "Barclaycard" for Visa).

American Express (tel. (800) 843-2273) has a hefty annual fee (US$55) but offers a number of services. AmEx cardholders can cash personal checks at AmEx offices outside the U.S., and U.S. Assist, a 24hr. hotline offering medical and legal assistance in emergencies, is also available (tel. (800) 554-2639 in U.S. and Canada; from abroad call U.S. collect (301) 214-8228). Cardholders can take advantage of the American Express Travel Service; benefits include assistance in changing airline, hotel, and car rental reservations, baggage loss and flight insurance, sending mail-grams and international cables, and holding your mail at one of the more than 1700 AmEx offices around the world.

MasterCard (tel. (800) 999-0454) and **Visa** (tel. (800) 336-8472) are issued in cooperation with individual banks and some other organizations; ask the issuer about services that go along with the cards.

CASH CARDS

Cash cards—popularly called **ATM** (Automated Teller Machine) cards—are wide-spread in Europe and elsewhere. Depending on the system that your bank at home uses, you will probably be able to access your own personal bank account whenever you're in need of funds. (Be careful, however, and keep all receipts–even if an ATM won't give you your cash, it may register a withdrawal on your next statement). Happily, ATMs get the same wholesale exchange rate as credit cards. Despite these perks, do some research before relying too heavily on automation. There is often a limit on the amount of money you can withdraw per day (usually about US$500, depending on the type of card and account), and computer network failures are not uncommon. Be sure to memorize your PIN code in numeral form since many machines often don't have letters on the keys. Also, if your PIN is longer than four digits, ask your bank whether the first four digits will work, or whether you need a new number. Many ATMs are outdoors; be cautious and aware of your surroundings.

The two major international money networks are **Cirrus** (U.S. tel. (800) 4-CIRRUS (424-7787)) and **PLUS** (U.S. tel. (800) 843-7587). Cirrus now has international cash machines in 80 countries and territories. It charges US$3-5 to withdraw non-domestically depending on your bank. If possible, carry two cards, one linked to each network.

GETTING MONEY FROM HOME

One of the easiest ways to get money from home is to bring an **American Express** card. AmEx allows cardholders to draw cash from their checking accounts at any of its major offices and many of its representatives' offices, up to US$1000 every 21 days (no service charge, no interest). AmEx also offers Express Cash, with over 100,000 ATMs located in airports, hotels, banks, office complexes, and shopping areas around the world. Express Cash withdrawals are automatically debited from the Cardmember's checking account or line of credit. Cardholders may withdraw up to US$1000 in a seven-day period. There is a 2% transaction fee for each cash withdrawal, with a US$2.50 minimum/$20 maximum. To enroll in Express Cash, Cardmembers may call (800) CASH NOW (227-4669). Outside the U.S. call collect (904) 565-7875. Unless using the AmEx service, avoid cashing checks in foreign currencies; they usually take weeks and a US$30 fee to clear.

Money can also be wired abroad through international money transfer services operated by **Western Union** tel. (800 325-6000). In the U.S., call Western Union any time at (800) CALL-CASH (225-5227) to cable money with your Visa, Discover, or MasterCard within the domestic United States and the U.K. The rates for sending cash are generally US$10 cheaper than with a credit card, and the money is usually available in the country you're sending it to within an hour, although this may vary.

Another way to send money abroad is in cash via **Federal Express.** On the plus side, it's reasonably reliable, avoids transmission fees and taxes, and is quite easy. On the minus side, it is **illegal** and involves an element of risk. It also requires that you remain at a legitimate address for a day or two to wait for the money's arrival.

In emergencies, U.S. citizens can have money sent via the State Department's **Overseas Citizens Service, American Citizens Services,** Consular Affairs, Room 4811, U.S. Department of State, Washington, D.C. 20520 (tel. (202) 647-5225; nights, Sundays, and holidays (202) 647-4000; fax (on demand only) (202) 647-3000; http://travel.state.gov). For a fee of US$15, the State Department will forward money within hours to the nearest consular office, which will then disburse it according to instructions. The office serves only Americans in the direst of straits abroad; non-American travelers should contact their embassies for information on wiring cash. The quickest way to have the money sent is to cable the State Department through Western Union.

■ Safety and Security

PERSONAL SAFETY

> Road travel in Turkey is dangerous by European standards. *Let's Go* lists emergency, police, and consulate numbers in every large city. For more information, see **Turkish Buses,** p.368.

Tourists are particularly vulnerable to crime for two reasons: they often carry large amounts of cash and they are not as street savvy as locals. To avoid unwanted attention, try to **blend in** as much as possible. Respecting local customs (in many cases, dressing more conservatively) may placate would-be hecklers. The gawking cameratoter is a more obvious target than the low-profile traveler. Walking directly into a cafe or shop to check a map beats checking it on a street corner. Better yet, look over your map before setting out. Muggings are more often impromptu than planned; nervous, over-the-shoulder glances can be a tip that you have something valuable to protect. An obviously bewildered bodybuilder is more likely to be harassed than a stern and confident 98-pound weakling.

When exploring a new city, extra vigilance is wise, but no city should force you to turn precautions into panic. Find out about unsafe areas from tourist information, from the manager of your hotel or hostel, or from a local whom you trust. Especially if you travel alone, be sure that someone at home knows your itinerary. Never say that you're traveling alone. You may want to carry a small **whistle** to scare off attackers or attract attention; memorize the emergency number of the city or area.

Let's Go does not recommend **hitchhiking,** particularly for women—see **Getting There** (p. 29) for more information on its hazards and general undesirability.

There is no sure-fire set of precautions that will protect you from all of the situations you might encounter when you travel. A good self-defense course will give you more concrete ways to react to different types of aggression, but it often carries a steep price tag. **Impact, Prepare,** and **Model Mugging** can refer you to local self-defense courses in the United States (tel. (800) 345-KICK). Course prices vary from $50-400. Women's and men's courses are offered. Community colleges frequently offer inexpensive self-defense courses.

For official **United States Department of State** travel advisories, call their 24-hour hotline at (202) 647-5225 or check their website (http://travel.state.gov), which provides travel information and publications. Alternatively, order publications, including a free pamphlet entitled *A Safe Trip Abroad,* by writing to Superintendent of Documents, U.S. Government Printing Office, Washington, D.C. 20402, or by calling them at (202) 512-1800. Official warnings from the **United Kingdom Foreign and Commonwealth Office** are online at http://www.fco.gov.uk; you can also call the office at (0171) 238 4503. The **Canadian Department of Foreign Affairs and International Trade** (DFAIT) offers advisories and travel warnings over the phone ((613) 944-6788 in Ottawa, (800) 267-6788 elsewhere in Canada) and on the web (http://www.dfait-maeci.gc.ca). Their free publication, *Bon Voyage, But...,* offers travel tips to Canadian citizens; you can receive a copy by calling (613) 944-6788 from Ottawa or abroad, or (800) 267-6788 from elsewhere in Canada.

FINANCIAL SECURITY

Among the more colorful aspects of large cities are **con artists.** Con artists and hustlers often work in groups, and children are among the most effective. Hucksters possess an innumerable range of ruses. Be aware of certain classics: sob stories that require money, rolls of bills "found" on the street, mustard spilled (or saliva spit) onto your shoulder distracting you for enough time to snatch your bag. Be especially alert in these situations. Do not respond or make eye contact, walk quickly away, and keep a solid grip on your belongings. Contact the police if a hustler is particularly insistent or aggressive.

Don't put a wallet with money in your back pocket. Never count your money in public and carry as little as possible. If you carry a purse, buy a sturdy one with a secure clasp, and carry it crosswise on the side, away from the street with the clasp against you. Secure packs with small combination padlocks which slip through the two zippers. (Even these precautions do not always suffice: moped riders who snatch purses and backpacks sometimes tote knives to cut the straps). A **money belt** is the best way to carry cash; you can buy one at most camping supply stores. A nylon, zippered pouch with belt that sits inside the waist of your pants or skirt combines convenience and security. A **neck pouch** is equally safe, although far less accessible. Refrain from pulling out your neck pouch in public; if you must, be very discreet. Avoid keeping anything precious in a fanny-pack (even if it's worn on your stomach): your valuables will be highly visible and easy to steal.

In city crowds and especially on public transportation, pick-pockets are amazingly deft at their craft. Rush hour is no excuse for strangers to press up against you on the bus. If someone stands uncomfortably close, move away and hold your bags tightly. Also, be alert in public telephone booths. If you must say your calling-card number, do so very quietly; if you punch it in, make sure no one can look over your shoulder. **Photocopies** of important documents allow you to recover them in case they are lost or filched. Carry one copy separate from the documents and leave another copy at home. Keep some money separate from the rest to use in an emergency or in case of theft. Label every piece of luggage both inside and out.

Be particularly careful on **buses** (for example, carry your backpack in front of you where you can see it), don't check baggage on trains, and don't trust anyone to "watch your bag for a second." Thieves thrive on **trains;** professionals wait for tourists to fall asleep and then carry off everything they can. When traveling in pairs, sleep in alternating shifts; when alone, use good judgement in selecting a train compartment: never stay in an empty one, and use a lock to secure your pack to the luggage rack. Keep important documents and other valuables on your person and try to sleep on top bunks with your luggage stored above you (if not in bed with you).

Let's Go lists locker availability in hostels and train stations, but you'll need your own padlock. Lockers are useful if you plan on sleeping outdoors or don't want to lug everything with you, but don't store valuables in them. Never leave your belongings unattended; crime occurs in even the most demure-looking hostel or hotel. If you feel unsafe, look for places with a curfew or a night attendant. When possible, keep valuables or anything you couldn't bear to lose at home.

If you travel by **car**, try not to leave valuable possessions—such as radios or luggage—in it while you're off rambling. Radios are especially tempting. If your tape deck or radio is removable, hide it in the trunk or take it with you. If it isn't, at least conceal it under a lot of junk. Similarly, hide baggage in the trunk (although savvy thieves can tell if a car is heavily loaded by the way it sits on its tires).

Travel Assistance International by Worldwide Assistance Services, Inc. provides its members with a 24-hour hotline for assistance. Their year-long frequent traveler package ($235-295) includes medical and travel insurance, financial assistance, and help in replacing lost documents. Call (800) 821-2828 or (202) 828-5894, fax (202) 828-5896, or write them at 1133 15th St. NW, Suite 400, Washington, D.C. 20005-2710. The **American Society of Travel Agents** provides extensive informational resources, both at their website (http://www.astanet.com) and in their free brochure, *Travel Safety*. You can obtain a copy by sending a request and self-addressed, stamped envelope to them at 1101 King St., Alexandria, VA 22313.

ESSENTIALS

DRUGS AND ALCOHOL

Laws vary from country to country, but, needless to say, **illegal drugs** are best avoided altogether; the average sentence for possession outside the U.S. is about seven years. Some countries do not differentiate between "hard" drugs and more mainstream ones such as marijuana. Buying or selling *any* type of drug may lead to anything from a prison sentence to the death penalty. A meek "I didn't know it was illegal" will not suffice. Remember that you are subject to the laws of the country in which you travel, not to those of your home country, and it is your responsibility to familiarize yourself with these laws before leaving. If you carry **prescription drugs** while you travel, it is vital to have a copy of the prescriptions themselves readily accessible at country borders. Avoid **public drunkenness;** it is against the law in many countries. It can also jeopardize your safety and earn the disdain of locals.

■ Health

Common sense is the simplest prescription for good health while you travel: eat well, drink and sleep enough, and don't overexert yourself. Travelers complain most often about their feet and their gut, so take precautionary measures. Drinking lots of fluids can often prevent dehydration and constipation, and wearing sturdy shoes and clean socks, and using talcum powder can help keep your feet dry. To minimize the effects of jet lag, "reset" your body's clock by adopting the time of your destination immediately upon arrival. Most travelers feel acclimatized to a new time zone after two or three days.

> For **medical emergencies** in Greece, dial 166. In Turkey and Northern Cyprus, dial 112 or call your consulate. In the Republic of Cyprus, dial 190.

Greece, Turkey, and Cyprus require few medical preparations. If you heat-sterilize your **contact lenses,** you should consider switching temporarily to a chemical system, as your heater will not work properly without a converter, and the availability of equivalent devices in Greece or Turkey is slim. When traveling in Greece and Turkey, don't underestimate the dangers of sun and heat, and educate yourself about **heatstroke.** Heatstroke, sunburn, food poisoning, bladder infections, diarrhea, exotic flus—all these could strike you in Greece, Turkey, and Cyprus.

Pharmacies *(farmakeia)* in Greece and Cyprus have sophisticated staffs with more prescribing power than you may be accustomed to in the United States or Western Europe. In emergencies you will be given free treatment in state hospitals. The Turkish pharmacy *(eczane)* will have remedies for minor troubles; more serious medical problems should be taken to the *klinik* (private ones tend to be much better than state-run, and are not much more expensive for foreigners, who must pay for care in any case). Pharmacies in Greek, Turkish, and Cypriot towns stay open all night on a rotating basis; each should have a sign in the window telling which is on duty that night (the open one is known as *efimerevon* in Greece, *nöbetçi* in Turkey). They sell small rectangles of mosquito repellent to be burned slowly on little heat pads which plug into the wall and light up (*bayvap* in Greece and Cyprus, *esem mat* in Turkey and Northern Cyprus).

BEFORE YOU GO

Though no amount of planning can guarantee an accident-free trip, preparation can help minimize the likelihood of contracting a disease and maximize the chances of receiving effective health-care in the event of an emergency.

For minor health problems, bring a compact first-aid kit, including bandages, aspirin or other pain killer, antibiotic cream, a thermometer, a Swiss Army knife with tweezers, moleskin, a decongestant for colds, motion sickness remedy, medicine for diarrhea or stomach problems, sunscreen, insect repellent, and burn ointment.

   In your passport, write the names of any people you wish to be contacted in case of a medical emergency, and also list any allergies or medical conditions you would want doctors to be aware of. If you wear glasses or contact lenses, carry an extra prescription and pair of glasses or arrange to have your doctor or a family member send a replacement pair in an emergency. Allergy sufferers should find out if their conditions are likely to be aggravated, and obtain a full supply of any necessary medication before the trip, since matching a prescription to a foreign equivalent is not always easy, safe, or possible. Carry up-to-date, legible prescriptions or a statement from your doctor, especially if you use insulin, a syringe, or a narcotic. While traveling, be sure to keep all medication with you in carry-ons.

   Take a look at your **immunization** records before you go; some countries require visitors to carry vaccination certificates. Travelers over two years old should be sure that the following vaccines are up to date: Measles, Mumps, and Rubella (MMR); Diptheria, Tetanus, and Pertussis (DTP or DTap); Polio (OPV); Haemophilus Influenza B (HbCV); and Hepatitis B (HBV). A booster of Tetanus-diptheria (Td) is recommended once every 10 years, and adults traveling to developing countries in Africa, Asia, Latin America, the Middle East, the Indian subcontinent, and most of the New Independent States of the former Soviet Union should consider an additional dose of Polio vaccine if they have not already had one during their adult years. Hepatitis A vaccine and/or Immune Globulin (IG) is recommended for travelers to all areas except Japan, Australia, New Zealand, Northern and Western Europe, and the United States and Canada. If you will be spending more than four weeks in a developing country, you should consider the typhoid vaccine as well. Check with a doctor for guidance through this maze of injections, and try to remember that no matter how bad the needles are, they're better than the diseases they prevent.

   For up-to-date information about which vaccinations are recommended for your destination, and region-specific health data, try these resources: The **United States Centers for Disease Control and Prevention** (based in Atlanta, Georgia), an excellent source of information for travelers around the world, maintains an international travelers' hotline (tel. (404) 332-4559; fax 332-4565; http://www.cdc.gov). Or write directly to the Centers for Disease Control and Prevention, Travelers' Health, 1600 Clifton Rd. NE, Atlanta, GA 30333. The CDC publishes the booklet "Health Information for International Travelers" (US$14), an annual global rundown of disease, immunization, and general health advice, including risks in particular countries.

   Those with medical conditions (e.g. diabetes, allergies to antibiotics, epilepsy, heart conditions) may want to obtain a stainless steel **Medic Alert** identification tag (US$35 the first year, and $15 annually thereafter), which identifies the disease and gives a 24-hour collect-call information number. Contact Medic Alert at (800) 825-3785, or write to Medic Alert Foundation, 2323 Colorado Ave., Turlock, CA 95382. Diabetics can contact the **American Diabetes Association**, 1660 Duke St., Alexandria, VA 22314 (tel. (800) 232-3472) to receive copies of the article "Travel and Diabetes" and a diabetic ID card, which carries messages in 18 languages explaining the carrier's diabetic status.

   If you are concerned about being able to access medical support while traveling, two services are particularly valuable: **Global Emergency Medical Services (GEMS)** has products called *MedPass* that provide 24-hour international medical assistance and support coordinated through registered nurses who have online access to your medical information, your primary physician, and a worldwide network of screened, credentialed English-speaking doctors and hospitals. Subscribers also receive a personal medical record that contains vital information in case of emergencies. For more information call (800) 860-1111, fax (770) 475-0058, or write: 2001 Westside Drive #120, Alpharetta, GA 30201. The **International Association for Medical Assistance to Travelers (IAMAT)** offers a membership ID card, a directory of English-speaking doctors around the world who treat members for a set fee schedule, and detailed charts on immunization requirements, various tropical diseases, climate, and sanitation. Membership is free, though donations are appreciated and used for further research. Contact chapters in the **U.S.,** 417 Center St.,

Lewiston, NY 14092 (tel. (716) 754-4883; fax (519) 836-3412; email iamat@sen-tex.net; http://www.sentex.net/~iamat); **Canada,** 40 Regal Road, Guelph, Ontario, N1K 1B5 (tel. (519) 836-0102) or 1287 St. Clair Avenue West, Toronto, Ontario M6E 1B8 (tel. (416) 652-0137; fax (519) 836-3412); or **New Zealand,** P.O. Box 5049, Christchurch 5.

PREVENTING DISEASE

You can minimize the chances of contracting a disease while traveling by taking a few precautionary measures. Always avoid animals with open wounds, and beware of touching any animal at all in developing countries. Often dogs are not given shots, so that sweet-faced pooch at your feet might very well be disease-ridden. If you are bitten, be concerned about **rabies**. Clean your wound thoroughly and seek medical attention immediately to find out whether you need treatment. The danger of rabies is greatest in rural areas.

Many diseases are transmitted by insects—mainly mosquitoes, fleas, ticks, and lice. Be aware of insects in wet or forested areas, while hiking, and especially while camping. **Mosquitoes** are most active from dusk to dawn. Wear long pants and long sleeves (fabric need not be thick or warm; tropic-weight cottons can keep you comfortable in the heat) and buy a bed net for camping. Wear shoes and socks, and tuck long pants into socks. Use insect repellents; DEET can be bought in spray or liquid form, but use it sparingly, especially on children. Soak or spray your gear with permethrin, which is licensed in the U.S. for use on clothing. Natural repellents can also help: taking vitamin B-12 pills regularly can eventually make you smelly to insects, as can garlic pills. Still, be sure to supplement your vitamins with repellent. Calamine lotion or topical cortisones (like Cortaid) may stop insect bites from itching, as can a bath with a half-cup of baking soda or oatmeal. **Ticks**—responsible for Lyme and other diseases—can be particularly dangerous in rural and forested regions. Brush off ticks periodically when walking, using a fine-toothed comb on your neck and scalp. Do not try to remove ticks by burning them or coating them with nail polish remover or petroleum jelly. Topical cortisones may help quell the itching.

FOOD AND WATER-BORNE DISEASES

To ensure that your food is safe, make sure that everything is cooked properly (deep-fried is good, for once), and be sure the water you drink is clean. Don't order meat "rare," and eggs should be thoroughly cooked, not served sunny-side up.

In Turkey, you should never drink unbottled water which you have not treated yourself—the risk of contracting traveler's diarrhea or other diseases is high. To purify your own water, bring it to a rolling boil (simmering isn't enough), or treat it with iodine drops or tablets. Don't brush your teeth with tap water, and don't even rinse your toothbrush under the faucet. Keep your mouth closed in the shower. Don't be fooled by the clever disguise of impure water—the ice cube. Stay away from salads: uncooked vegetables (including lettuce and coleslaw) are full of untreated water. Other culprits are raw shellfish, unpasteurized milk, and sauces containing raw eggs. Peel all fruits and vegetables yourself, and beware of watermelon, which is often injected with impure water. Watch out for food from markets or street vendors that may have been washed in dirty water or fried in rancid cooking oil. Beware juices and peeled fruits, and always wash your hands before eating. Your bowels will thank you.

Parasites (tapeworms, etc.) also hide in unsafe water and food. *Giardia,* for example, is acquired by drinking untreated water from streams or lakes all over the world. It can stay with you for years. Symptoms of parasitic infections in general include swollen glands or lymph nodes, fever, rashes or itchiness, digestive problems, eye problems, and anemia. Boil your water, wear shoes, avoid bugs, and eat cooked food.

Traveler's diarrhea is the dastardly consequence of ignoring the warnings against drinking untreated water. The illness can last from three to seven days, and symptoms include diarrhea, nausea, bloating, urgency, and malaise. If the nasties hit you, have quick-energy, non-sugary foods with protein and carbohydrates to keep your strength up. Over-the-counter remedies (such as Pepto-Bismol© or Immodium©) may counteract the problems, but they can complicate serious infections. Avoid anti-diarrheals if you suspect you have been exposed to contaminated food or water, which puts you at risk for other diseases. The most dangerous side effect of diarrhea is dehydration; the simplest and most effective anti-dehydration formula is 8 oz. of (clean) water with a ½ tsp. of sugar or honey and a pinch of salt. Also good are soft drinks without caffeine, and salted crackers. Down several of these remedies a day, rest, and wait for the unpleasantness to run its course. If you develop a fever or your symptoms don't go away after four or five days, consult a doctor. Also consult a doctor if children develop traveler's diarrhea, since treatment is different.

Common sense goes a long way toward preventing **heat exhaustion:** relax in hot weather, drink lots of non-alcoholic fluids, and lie down inside if you feel awful. Continuous heat stress can eventually lead to **heatstroke,** characterized by rising body temperature, severe headache, and cessation of sweating. Wear a hat, sunglasses, and a lightweight long-sleeve shirt to avoid heatstroke. Victims must be cooled off with wet towels and taken to a doctor as soon as possible.

Always drink enough liquids to keep your urine clear. Alcoholic beverages are dehydrating, as are coffee, tea, and caffeinated sodas. If you'll be sweating a lot, be sure to eat enough salty food to prevent electrolyte depletion, which causes severe headaches. Less debilitating, but still dangerous, is **sunburn.** If you're prone to sunburn, bring sunscreen with you (it's often more expensive and hard to find when traveling), and apply it liberally and often to avoid burns and risk of skin cancer. If you get sunburned, drink more fluids than usual.

Visitors to higher climes in Greece and Anatolia should remember that extreme cold is just as dangerous as heat. Overexposure to cold brings the risk of **hypothermia.** Warning signs are easy to detect: body temperature drops rapidly, resulting in the failure to produce body heat. You may shiver, have poor coordination, feel exhausted, have slurred speech, feel sleepy, hallucinate, or suffer amnesia. *Do not let hypothermia victims fall asleep* if they are in the advanced stages—their body temperature will drop more and if they lose consciousness they may die. Seek medical help as soon as possible. To avoid hypothermia, keep dry and stay out of the wind. In wet weather, wool and most synthetics, such as pile, will keep you warm but most other fabric, especially cotton, will make you colder. Dress in layers, and watch for **frostbite** when the temperature is below freezing. Look for skin that has turned white, waxy, and cold, and if you find frostbite do not rub the skin. Drink warm beverages, get dry, and slowly warm the area with dry fabric or steady body contact. Take serious cases to a doctor as soon as possible.

Travelers to **high altitudes** must allow their bodies a couple of days to adjust to lower oxygen levels in the air before exerting themselves. Also be careful about alcohol, especially if you're used to U.S. standards for beer—many foreign brews and liquors pack more punch, and at high altitudes where the air has less oxygen, any alcohol will do you in quickly.

WOMEN'S HEALTH

Women traveling in unsanitary conditions are vulnerable to urinary tract and bladder infections, common and severely uncomfortable bacterial diseases which cause a burning sensation and painful and sometimes frequent urination. Drink tons of vitamin C-rich juice, plenty of clean water, and urinate frequently, especially right after intercourse. Untreated, these infections can lead to kidney infections, sterility, and even death. If symptoms persist, see a doctor. If you often develop vaginal yeast infections, take along enough over-the-counter medicine, as treatments may not be readily available in Greece, Turkey, or Cyprus. Women may also be more susceptible to vaginal thrush and cystitis, two treatable but uncomfortable illnesses that are likely to flare up in hot and humid climates. Wearing loosely fitting trousers or a skirt and cotton underwear may help. Tampons and pads are sometimes hard to find when traveling; certainly your preferred brands may not be available, so it may be advisable to take supplies along. Refer to the *Handbook for Women Travelers* by Maggie and Gemma Moss (published by Piatkus Books) or to the women's health guide *Our Bodies, Our Selves* (published by the Boston Women's Health Collective) for more extensive information specific to women's health on the road.

BIRTH CONTROL

Reliable contraceptive devices may be difficult to find while traveling. Women on the pill should bring enough to allow for possible loss or extended stays. Bring a prescription, since forms of the pill vary a good deal. The sponge is probably too bulky to be worthwhile on the road. Women who use a diaphragm should have enough contraceptive jelly on hand. Though condoms are increasingly available, you might want to buy your favorite brand before you go; availability and quality vary.

Women overseas who want an **abortion** should contact the **National Abortion Federation Hotline** (tel. (800) 772-9100; Mon.-Fri. 9:30am-12:30pm, 1:30-5:30pm), 1775 Massachusetts Ave. NW, Washington, D.C. 20036. The hotline can direct you to organizations which provide information on the availability of and techniques for abortion in other countries. For information on contraception, condoms, and abortion worldwide, contact the **International Planned Parenthood Federation,** European Regional Office, Regent's College Inner Circle, Regent's Park, London NW1 4NS (tel. (0171) 487 7900; fax (0171) 487 7950).

AIDS, HIV, STDS

Acquired Immune Deficiency Syndrome (AIDS) is a growing problem around the world. The World Health Organization estimates that there are around 13 million people infected with the HIV virus. Well over 90% of adults newly infected with HIV acquired their infection through heterosexual sex; women now represent 50% of all new HIV infections. For more information on AIDS, call the **U.S. Center for Disease Control's** 24-hour hotline at (800) 342-2437; in Europe, write to the **World Health Organization,** Attn: Global Program on AIDS, 20 Avenue Appia, 1211 Geneva 27, Switzerland (tel. (22) 791-2111). Or write to the **Bureau of Consular Affairs,** #6831, Department of State, Washington, D.C. 20520. Council's brochure, *Travel Safe: AIDS and International Travel,* is available at all Council Travel offices.

Sexually transmitted diseases (STDs) such as gonorrhea, chlamydia, genital warts, syphilis, and herpes are a lot easier to catch than HIV, and can be just as deadly. It's a wise idea to actually *look* at your partner's genitals before you have sex. Warning signs for STDs include: swelling, sores, bumps, or blisters on sex organs, rectum, or mouth; burning and pain during urination and bowel movements; itching around sex organs; swelling or redness in the throat, flu-like symptoms with fever, chills, and aches. If these symptoms develop, see a doctor immediately. When having sex, condoms may protect you from certain STDs, but oral or even tactile contact can lead to transmission.

■ Insurance

Beware of buying unnecessary travel coverage—your regular insurance policies may well extend to many travel-related accidents. **Medical insurance** (especially university policies) often cover costs incurred abroad, check with your provider. **Medicare's** "foreign travel" coverage is valid only in Canada and Mexico. Canadians are protected by their home province's health insurance plan for up to 90 days after leaving the country; check with the provincial Ministry of Health or Health Plan Headquarters for details. Australia has Reciprocal Health Care Agreements (RHCAs) with several countries; when traveling in these nations Australians are entitled to many of the services that they would receive at home. The Commonwealth Department of Human Services and Health can provide more information. Your **home-**

owners' insurance (or your family's coverage) often covers theft during travel. Homeowners are generally covered against loss of travel documents (passport, plane ticket, railpass, etc.) up to US$500.

ISIC and **ITIC** provide basic insurance benefits, including US$100 per day of in-hospital sickness for a maximum of 60 days, and US$3000 of accident-related medical reimbursement (see **Youth, Student, and Teacher Identification,** p. 9). Card-holders have access to a toll-free 24-hour helpline whose multilingual staff can provide assistance in medical, legal, and financial emergencies overseas. **Council** and **STA** offer a range of plans that can supplement your basic insurance coverage, with options covering medical treatment and hospitalization, accidents, baggage loss, and even charter flights missed due to illness. Most **American Express** card-holders receive automatic car rental (collision and theft, but not liability) insurance and travel accident coverage (US$100,000 in life insurance) on flight purchases made with the card. Customer Service proffers up pearls of insurance-related wisdom at (800) 528-4800.

Remember that insurance companies usually require a copy of the police report for thefts, or evidence of having paid medical expenses (doctor's statements, receipts) before they will honor a claim and may have time limits on filing for reimbursement. Always carry policy numbers and proof of insurance. Check with each insurance carrier for specific restrictions and policies. Most of the carriers listed below have 24-hour hotlines.

Access America, 6600 West Broad St., P.O. Box 11188, Richmond, VA 23230 (tel. (800) 284-8300; fax (804) 673-1491). Covers trip cancellation/interruption, on-the-spot hospital admittance costs, emergency medical evacuation, sickness, and baggage loss. 24hr. hotline (if abroad, call the hotline collect at (804) 673-1159 or (800) 654-1908).

The Berkely Group/Carefree Travel Insurance, 100 Garden City Plaza, P.O. Box 9366, Garden City, NY 11530-9366 (tel. (800) 323-3149 or (516) 294-0220; fax 294-1096). Offers 2 comprehensive packages including coverage for trip cancellation/interruption/delay, accident and sickness, medical, baggage loss, bag delay, accidental death and dismemberment, and travel supplier insolvency. Trip cancellation/interruption may be purchased separately at a rate of US$5.50 per US$100 of coverage. 24hr. hotline.

Travel Assistance International, by Worldwide Assistance Services, Inc., 1133 15th St. NW, #400, Washington, D.C. 20005-2710 (tel. (800) 821-2828 or (202) 828-5894; fax (202) 828-5896; email wassist@aol.com). TAI provides its members with a 24hr. free hotline for travel emergencies and referrals. Their Per-Trip (starting at US$52) and Frequent Traveler (starting at US$226) plans include medical, travel, and financial insurance, translation, and lost document assistance.

Travel Insured International, Inc., 52-S Oakland Ave., P.O. Box 280568, East Hartford, CT 06128-0568 (tel. (800) 243-3174; fax (203) 528-8005; email travelins@aol.com). Insurance against accident, baggage loss, sickness, trip cancellation and interruption, travel delay, and default. Covers emergency medical evacuation and automatic flight insurance.

■ Alternatives to Tourism

Because most visitors see Greece, Turkey, and Cyprus only through the eyes of a tourist, those who go in order to study or work can expect a particularly unique and rewarding experience. There are several general resource organizations for those interested in alternatives to tourism.

STUDY

Foreign study programs vary tremendously in expense, academic quality, living conditions, degree of contact with local students, and exposure to local culture and languages. There is a plethora of exchange programs for high school students. Most American undergraduates enroll in programs sponsored by U.S. universities, and many colleges have offices that give advice and information on study abroad. Ask for the names of recent participants in these programs, and get in touch with them in order to judge which program is best for you.

The Athens Centre, Archimidous 48, Athens, Greece 11636 (tel. (01) 701 2268; fax 701 8603; email athenscr@compulink.gr), offers a modern Greek language program. Semester and quarter programs on Greek civilization in affiliation with U.S. universities. Offers 4-6 week summer Classics programs, a yearly summer theater program and a Modern Greek Language program in July on Spetses island.

Beaver College Center for Education Abroad, 450 S. Easton Rd., Glenside, PA 19038-3295 (tel. (888) BEAVER 9 (232-8379); fax (215) 572-2174; email cea@beaver.edu; http://www.beaver.edu/cea/). Operates study abroad programs in Australia, Austria, **Greece,** Ireland, Mexico, and the U.K. as well as offering a Peace Studies program. Summer and graduate study programs also available. Applicants must have completed three full semesters at a university. Call for info.

College Year in Athens (tel. (01) 726 0749) runs a 2-semester program for undergraduates (usually juniors), which includes travel as well as classroom instruction (in English). The program has two tracks, one in Ancient Greek civilization and one in Mediterranean area studies. Scholarship available. College Year in Athens also runs 3- to 6-week summer programs. From the U.S. call (617) 494-1008 or write to College Year in Athens, P.O. Box 390890, Cambridge, MA 02139.

Council on International Education Exchange, 205 E. 42nd St., New York, NY 10017 (tel. (888) COUNCIL (268-6245); fax (212) 822-2699; email info@ciee.org; http://www.ciee.org) sponsors over 40 study abroad programs throughout the world. Contact them for more information.

Your best bet for information on study in Turkey is the education office at the nearest tourist office. You may also enroll in one of several small colleges in Cyprus; contact the Department of Education in Nicosia. **Council** sponsors over 40 study abroad programs throughout the world. Contact them for more information or see **Travel Organizations** on p.2.

WORK

There's no better way to immerse yourself in a foreign culture than to become part of its economy. It's easy to find a **temporary job,** but it will rarely be glamorous and may not even pay for your plane fare, let alone your accommodations. Officially, you can hold a job in most countries only with a **work permit.** Your employer must obtain this document, usually by demonstrating that you have skills that locals lack—not the easiest of tasks. There are, however, ways to make it easier. Friends in your destination country can help expedite work permits or arrange work-for-accommodations swaps. Be an au pair; advertise to teach English. Many permit-less agricultural workers go untroubled by local authorities. European Union citizens can work in any EU country, and if your parents were born in an EU country, you may be able to claim dual citizenship or at least the right to a work permit. (Beware of countries where citizenship obligates you to do military service.) Students can check with their universities' foreign language departments, which may have connections to job openings abroad. Call the Consulate or Embassy of the country in which you wish to work to get more information about work permits. Volunteer jobs are readily available in Greece, Turkey, and Cyprus. You may receive room and board in exchange for your labor. Opportunities include archaeological digs and community projects. The organizations that arrange placement sometimes charge high application fees in addition to the workcamps' charges for room and board. You can sometimes avoid this extra fee by contacting the individual workcamps directly; check with the organization.

The Archaeological Institute of America, 656 Beacon St., Boston, MA 02215-2010 (tel. (617) 353-9361; fax 353-6550; email aia@bu.edu; http://csaws.bryn-mawr.edu:HH31aia.html), puts out the *Archaeological Fieldwork Opportunities Bulletin* (US$11 non-members) which lists over 300 field sites throughout the world. This can be purchased from Kendall/Hunt Publishing, 4050 Westmark Dr., Dubuque, Iowa 52002 (tel. (800) 228-0810).

Gençtur Turizm ve Seyahat Ac. Ltd. (Tourism and Travel Agency), Head Office: Professor K. İsmail Gürkan Cad., No. 14 Flat 4, Sultanahmet, Istanbul (tel. (212) 520 5274; fax 519 0864). Taksim Branch: İstiklal Cad., Zambak Sok., 15/5 Taksim, Istanbul (tel. (212) 249 2515; fax 249 2554). Organizes teenage, group, or international voluntary work camps and study tours in Turkey.

Office of Overseas Schools, A/OS Room 245, SA-29, Dept. of State, Washington, D.C. 20522-2902 (tel. (703) 875-7800; http://www.state.gov/www/about_state/schools/). Keeps a list of schools abroad and agencies that arrange placement for Americans to teach abroad.

Finding work in Greece, Turkey, and Cyprus is difficult. Job opportunities are scarce and the governments try to restrict employment to citizens and visitors from the EU. Be persistent; the informality of local life will work to your advantage.

For long-term employment in Greece, you must first get a work permit from your employer; permits are available at the **Ministry of Labor,** 40 Pireos St., Athens 10437 (tel. (01) 523 3110). Make all arrangements and negotiations before you leave home.

For **hotel jobs** (bartending, cleaning, etc.) arrive in the spring and early summer to search for work. Most night spots have meager pay. Check the bulletin boards of hostels in Athens and the classified ads in the *Athens News.* Another possibility is to work as a farm laborer. In Greece, the **American Farm School** runs a summer work and recreation program for high school students. Write 1133 Broadway, New York, NY 10010 (tel. (212) 463-8434; fax 463-8208; email NYO@amerfarm.com; www http://afs.edu.gr); or in Greece, P.O. Box 23, GR-55102, Thessaloniki (tel. 30 (31) 471 803, -825; fax 472 345).

The brightest prospect for working in Turkey is probably **teaching English.** Students with university credentials might fare quite well, but having your credentials verified can take some time. Various organizations in the U.S. will place you in a (low-paying) teaching job, but securing a position will require patience, because teaching English abroad has become enormously popular in the past few years.

The process for obtaining a job in Cyprus is similar. Before you arrive, you must find an employer who can assert that you are particularly suited for your position due to academic interest or experience, and that there are no suitably qualified local employees available in your field.

■ Specific Concerns

WOMEN TRAVELERS

Women traveling in the Mediterranean, whether alone or in groups, are likely to experience verbal harassment which can be just as intimidating as physical abuse. Be adventurous, but avoid unnecessary risks. Trust your instincts: if you'd feel better somewhere else, move on. Always carry extra money for a phone call, bus, or taxi. You might consider staying in hostels which offer rooms that lock from the inside or in religious organizations that offer rooms for women only. Communal showers in some hostels are safer than others; check them before settling in. Stick to centrally-located accommodations and avoid solitary late-night treks or metro rides. **Hitching** is never safe for lone women, or even for women traveling together. Choose train compartments occupied by other women or couples; ask the conductor to put together a women-only compartment if he or she doesn't offer to do so first.

When in a foreign country, the less you look like a tourist, the better off you'll be. Look as if you know where you're going (even when you don't) and consider approaching women or couples for directions if you're lost or feel uncomfortable. In general, dress conservatively, especially in rural areas. Shorts and t-shirts, though unrevealing, may identify you as a foreigner and should be avoided. Trying to fit in can be effective, but wearing much more makeup than usual to match the natives or dressing to the style of an obviously different culture may cause you to be ill at ease and a conspicuous target.

If you spend time in cities, you may be harassed no matter how you're dressed. Your best answer to verbal harassment is no answer at all (a reaction is what the harasser wants). In crowds, you may be pinched or squeezed by oversexed slime-balls. Wearing a conspicuous **wedding band** may help prevent such incidents. The look on the face is the key to avoiding unwanted attention. Feigned deafness, sitting motionless and staring at the ground will do a world of good that reactions usually don't achieve. You might also turn to an older woman for help; her stern rebukes will usually be enough to embarrass the most determined jerks. If, at any time, unwanted attention becomes physical, you should yell, scream, and make getting away your first priority. In Greek, screech "vo-EE-thee-ah" (help) or "as-te-no-MEE-ah" (police). In Turkish, holler "eem-DAHT" (help) or "PO-lees" (police).

Don't hesitate to seek out a police officer or a passerby if you are being harassed. *Let's Go* lists emergency numbers (including rape crisis lines) in the **Practical Information** listings of most cities. Memorize the emergency numbers in the countries you visit. Carry a **whistle** or an airhorn on your keychain (available at many airports and travel stores), and don't hesitate to use it in an emergency. A **Model Mugging** course will not only prepare you for a potential mugging, but will also raise your level of awareness of your surroundings as well as your confidence (see **Safety and Security,** p. 14). Women also face additional health concerns when traveling (see **Health,** p. 16). Other resources which might be helpful include:

Handbook For Women Travelers by Maggie and Gemma Moss (UK£9). Encyclopedic and well-written. Available from Piatkus Books, 5 Windmill St., London W1P 1HF (tel. (0171) 631 07 10).

Women Travel: Adventures, Advice & Experience by Miranda Davies and Natania Jansz (Penguin, US$13). Info on several foreign countries plus a decent bibliography and resource index. The sequel, *More Women Travel,* costs US$15. Both from Rough Guides, 375 Hudson St. 3rd Fl., New York, NY 10014.

Women Going Places is a women's travel and resource guide geared toward lesbians which emphasizes women-owned enterprises. Advice appropriate for all women. US$15 from Inland Book Company, 1436 W. Randolph St. Chicago, IL 60607 (tel. (800) 243-0138; fax (800) 334-3892) or a local bookstore.

OLDER TRAVELERS

Senior citizens are eligible for a wide range of discounts on transportation, museums, movies, theaters, concerts, restaurants, and accommodations. If you don't see a senior citizen price listed, ask, and you may be delightfully surprised. Agencies for senior group travel (like **Eldertreks,** 597 Markham St., Toronto, Ontario M6G 2L7; tel. (416) 588-5000; fax 588-9839; email passages@inforamp.net) are growing in enrollment and popularity.

BISEXUAL, GAY, AND LESBIAN TRAVELERS

Greeks and Cypriots have a relatively tolerant attitude towards homosexuality. Homosexual sex is legal, although homosexuality as a declared lifestyle is frowned upon. In Turkey and Northern Cyprus, social conservatism and religious dictates keep most activity discreet. If problems arise, plan on authorities being almost uniformly unsympathetic.

In Greece, Athens in particular offers a variety of gay bars, clubs, and hotels. For further information, consult the multilingual **Greek Gay Guide,** TΘ 4228, Athens 10210 (tel. (01) 381 5249; English speaker Mon.-Fri. 7-9pm). The islands of Hydra, Lesbos, Paros, Rhodes, and Mykonos also offer gay and lesbian resorts, hotels, bars, and clubs. Turkey's urban centers do not lack bars or informal cruising areas (men only), although they may be less obvious. Contact Turkey's gay and lesbian organization **Lamartin,** c/o İbrahim Eren, Lamartin Cad. 23/6, Tuslim, Istanbul for more details.

Ferrari Guides, P.O. Box 37887, Phoenix, AZ 85069 (tel. (602) 863-2408; fax 439-3952; email ferrari@q-net.com; http://www.q-net.com). Gay and lesbian travel guides: *Ferrari Guides' Gay Travel A to Z* (US$16), *Ferrari Guides' Men's Travel in Your Pocket* (US$16), *Ferrari Guides' Women's Travel in Your Pocket* (US$14), *Ferrari Guides' Inn Places* (US$16), *Ferrari Guides' Gay Paris* (Spring 1997). Available in bookstores or by mail order (postage/handling US$4.50 for the first item, US$1 for each additional item mailed within the U.S. Overseas, call or write for shipping cost).

Giovanni's Room, 345 S. 12th St., Philadelphia, PA 19107 (tel. (215) 923-2960; fax 923-0813; email giolphilp@netaxs.com). An international feminist, lesbian, and gay bookstore with mail-order service which carries many of the publications listed here.

International Gay and Lesbian Travel Association, P.O. Box 4974, Key West, FL 33041 (tel. (800) 448-8550; fax (305) 296-6633; email IGTA@aol.com; http://www.rainbow-mall.com/igta). An organization of over 1300 companies serving gay and lesbian travelers worldwide. Call for lists of travel agents, accommodations, and events.

Spartacus International Gay Guides, published by Bruno Gmunder, Postfach 61 01 04, D-10921 Berlin, Germany (US $33; tel. (30) 615 00 34; fax (30) 615 91 34). Lists bars, restaurants, hotels, and bookstores around the world catering to gays. Also lists hotlines for gays in various countries and homosexuality laws for each country. Available in bookstores and in the U.S. by mail from Lambda Rising, 1625 Connecticut Ave. NW, Washington, D.C. 20009-1013 (tel. (202) 462-6969).

DISABLED TRAVELERS

Greece, Turkey, and Cyprus are only slowly beginning to respond to the needs of travelers with disabilities. Many cruise ships that sail the Greek islands are equipped to accommodate those with disabilities. Special air transportation is available aboard Olympic Airways to many of the larger islands. Some hotels, train stations, and airports have recently installed facilities for the disabled; many of the archaeological sites throughout the region, however, are still not wheelchair-accessible. There are also a number of more general books helpful to travelers with disabilities. The following organizations provide info or publications that might be of assistance:

Facts on File, 11 Penn Plaza, 15th Fl., New York, NY 10001 (tel. (212) 967-8800). Publishers of *Disability Resource,* a reference guide for travelers with disabilities (US$45 plus shipping). Available at bookstores or by mail order.

Moss Rehab Hospital Travel Information Service (tel. (215) 456-9600, TDD (215) 456-9602). A telephone information resource center on international travel accessibility and other travel-related concerns for those with disabilities.

Society for the Advancement of Travel for the Handicapped (SATH), 347 Fifth Ave., #610, New York, NY 10016 (tel. (212) 447-1928; fax 725-8253; email sath-travel@aol.com; http://www.sath.org). Publishes a quarterly color travel magazine *OPEN WORLD* (free for members or on subscription US$13 for nonmembers). Also publishes a wide range of information sheets on disability travel facilitation and accessible destinations. Annual membership US$45, students and seniors US$30.

The following organizations arrange tours or trips for disabled travelers:

Directions Unlimited, 720 N. Bedford Rd., Bedford Hills, NY 10507 (tel. (800) 533-5343; in NY (914) 241-1700; fax 241-0243). Specializes in arranging individual and group vacations, tours, and cruises for the physically disabled. Group tours for blind travelers.

Flying Wheels Travel Service, 143 W. Bridge St., Owatonne, MN 55060 (tel. (800) 535-6790; fax 451-1685). Arranges trips in the U.S. and abroad for groups and individuals in wheelchairs or with other sorts of limited mobility.

The Guided Tour Inc., Elkins Park House, 114B, 7900 Old York Rd., Elkins Park, PA 19027-2339 (tel. (800) 783-5841 or (215) 782-1370; fax 635-2637). Organizes travel programs for persons with developmental and physical challenges and those requiring renal dialysis. Call, fax, or write for a free brochure.

DIETARY CONCERNS

Vegetarians should have no problem finding suitable cuisine. Most restaurants have vegetarian selections on their menus, and some cater specifically to vegetarians. *Let's Go* often notes restaurants with good vegetarian selections in city listings. Vegetarian dishes in Greece, Turkey, and Cyprus include succulent fruits, colorful salads, tasty breads, *fasolia* (beans, *fasülye* in Turkish), *spanakopita* (spinach-filled pastry), and *tyropitakia* (cheese-filled pastry, *börek* in Turkish). In Turkey and Cyprus, *meze* appetizers are plentiful. In summer fresh produce abounds in the outdoor markets; vegetarians find plenty of fresh vegetables, fruits, and interesting cheeses. Travelers who keep **kosher** will be hard pressed to find a synagogue or kosher restaurant in the land of mosques and Greek Orthodox churches. Your own synagogue or college Hillel may have a list of Jewish institutions in the region. If you are strict in your observance, consider preparing your own food on the road.

The International Vegetarian Travel Guide was last published in 1991 (UK£2). Order back copies from the Vegetarian Society of the UK (VSUK), Parkdale, Dunham Rd., Altringham, Cheshire WA14 4QG (tel. (0161) 928 0793). VSUK also publishes other titles, including *The European Vegetarian Guide to Hotels and Restaurants.* Call or send a self-addressed, stamped envelope for a listing.

The Jewish Travel Guide lists synagogues, kosher restaurants, and Jewish institutions in over 80 countries. Available from Ballantine-Mitchell Publishers, Newbury House 890-900, Eastern Ave., Newbury Park, Ilford, Essex, U.K. IG2 7HH (tel. (0181) 599 8866; fax 599 0984). It is available in the U.S. from Sepher-Hermon Press, 1265 46th St., Brooklyn, NY 11219 (tel. (718) 972-9010; US$15 plus US$2.50 shipping).

TRAVELERS WITH CHILDREN

Greeks, Turks, and Cypriots alike adore children. Expect a stream of compliments, advice, candy, and substantial discounts on transportation throughout Greece, Turkey, and Cyprus. Children under two generally fly for 10% of the adult airfare on international flights (this does not necessarily include a seat). International fares are usually discounted 25% for children from two to 11. Family vacations will be most enjoyable if you slow your pace and plan ahead. Be sure that your child carries some sort of ID in case of an emergency or he or she gets lost, and arrange a reunion spot in case of separation when sight-seeing (e.g., the Parthenon). Consider using a papoose-style device to carry your baby on walking trips.

Backpacking with Babies and Small Children, published by Wilderness Press, 2440 Bancroft Way, Berkeley, CA 94704 (US$10; tel. (800) 443-7227 or (510) 843-8080; fax 548-1355; email wpress@ix.netcom.com).

Travel with Children, by Maureen Wheeler (US$12, postage US$1.50). Published by Lonely Planet Publications, Embarcadero West, 155 Filbert St., #251, Oakland, CA 94607 (tel. (800) 275-8555 or (510) 893-8555, fax 893-8563; email info@lonelyplanet.com; http://www.lonelyplanet.com). Also at P.O. Box 617, Hawthorn, Vic. 3122, Australia.

TRAVELING ALONE

There are many benefits to traveling alone, among them greater independence and challenge. Without distraction, you can write a great travel log, in the grand tradition of Mark Twain, John Steinbeck, and Charles Kuralt. As a lone traveler, you have greater opportunity to meet and interact with natives. On the other hand, you may also be a more visible target for robbery and harassment. Lone travelers need to be well-organized and look confident at all times. No wandering around back alleys looking confused. Try not to stand out as a tourist. If questioned, never admit that you are traveling alone. Maintain regular contact with someone at home who knows your itinerary. Still, a number of organizations can find travel companions for solo travelers who so desire.

American International Homestays, P.O. Box 1754, Nederland, CO 80466 (tel. (303) 642-3088 or (800) 876-2048). Lodgings with English-speaking host families all over the world.

Connecting: News for Solo Travelers, P.O. Box 29088, 1996 W. Broadway, Vancouver, BC V6J 5C2, Canada (tel. (604) 737-7791 or (800) 557-1757). Bimonthly newsletter with features and listings of singles looking for travel companions. Annual directory lists tours and lodgings, subscription US$25.

Traveling On Your Own, by Eleanor Berman (US$13). Lists information resources for "singles" (old and young) and single parents. Write to Crown Publishers, Inc., 201 East 50th St., New York, NY 10022.

■ Packing

Plan your packing according to the type of travel you'll be doing (multi-city backpacking tour, week-long stay in one place, etc.) and the area's high and low temperatures. If you don't pack lightly, your back and wallet will suffer. The more things you have, the more you have to lose. The larger your pack, the more cumbersome it is to store safely. Before you leave, pack your bag, strap it on, and imagine yourself walking uphill on hot asphalt for the next three hours. A good rule is to lay out only what you absolutely need, then take half the clothes and twice the money.

LUGGAGE

Backpack: If you plan to cover most of your itinerary by foot, a sturdy backpack is unbeatable. Many packs are designed specifically for travelers, while others are for hikers; consider how you will use the pack before purchasing one or the other. In any case, get a pack with a strong, padded hip belt to transfer weight from your shoulders to your hips. Be wary of excessively low-end prices, and don't sacrifice quality. Good packs cost anywhere from US$150 to US$420.

Suitcase or trunk: Fine if you plan to live in 1 or 2 cities and explore from there, but a bad idea if you're going to be moving around a lot. Make sure it has wheels and consider how much it weighs even when empty. Hard-sided luggage is more durable and doesn't wrinkle your clothes, but it is also heavier. Soft-sided luggage should have a PVC frame, a strong lining to resist bad weather and rough handling, and its seams should be triple-stitched for durability.

Duffel bag: If you are not backpacking, an empty, lightweight duffel bag packed inside your luggage will be useful: once abroad you can fill your luggage with purchases and keep your dirty clothes in the duffel.

Daypack, rucksack, or courier bag: Bringing a smaller bag in addition to your pack or suitcase allows you to leave your big bag behind while you go sightseeing. It can be used as an airplane carry-on to keep essentials with you.

Moneybelt or neck pouch: Guard your money, passport, railpass, and other important articles in either one of these, available at any good camping store, and keep it with you *at all times*. The moneybelt should tuck inside the waist of your pants or skirt; you want to hide your valuables, not announce them with a colorful fanny-pack. See **Safety and Security** for more information on protecting you and your valuables.

CLOTHING AND FOOTWEAR

Clothing: When choosing your travel wardrobe, aim for versatility and comfort, and avoid fabrics that wrinkle easily (to test a fabric, hold it tightly in your fist for 20 seconds). Stricter dress codes (especially for women) in Greece, Turkey, and Cyprus call for something besides the basic shorts, t-shirts, and jeans. Women should pack at least one long skirt. Always bring a jacket or wool sweater.

Walking shoes: Well-cushioned **sneakers** are good for walking, though you may want to consider a good water-proofed pair of **hiking boots.** A double pair of socks—light silk or polypropylene inside and thick wool outside—will cushion feet, keep them dry, and help prevent blisters. Bring a pair of flip-flops for protection in the shower. Talcum powder in your shoes and on your feet can prevent sores, and moleskin is great for blisters. Break in your shoes before you leave.

Rain gear: A waterproof jacket and a backpack cover will take care of you and your stuff at a moment's notice. Gore-Tex is a miracle fabric that's both waterproof and breathable; it's all but mandatory if you plan on hiking. Avoid cotton as outer-wear, especially if you will be outdoors a lot.

MISCELLANEOUS

Sleepsacks: If you plan to stay in **youth hostels,** don't pay the linen charge; make the requisite sleepsack yourself. Fold a full size sheet in half the long way, then sew it closed along the open long side and one of the short sides. Less industrious folk can buy a sleepsack at any HI outlet store.

Washing clothes: *Let's Go* attempts to provide information on laundromats in the **Practical Information** listings for each city, but sometimes it may be easiest to use a sink. Bring a small bar or tube of detergent soap, a rubber squash ball to stop up the sink, and a travel clothes line.

Electric current: The standard electrical outlet in Greece produces 220 volts AC using the two-pronged plug used in Europe. Although Turkey uses the same plug, be careful and ask the exact voltage, since both 110 volts and 220 volts are used. In Cyprus, 220 volt outlets require either the two or three-pronged outlets used in Africa and Asia. North American appliances are designed for 110 volts AC and the prong won't fit. If you're bringing a beloved electrical appliance, you'll need a converter and a three-pronged adapter, both available in department and hardware stores. Visit a hardware store for an adapter (which changes the shape of the plug) and a converter (which changes the voltage). Don't make the mistake of using only an adapter (unless appliance instructions explicitly state otherwise, as with some portable computers), or you'll melt your radio.

Other useful items: First-aid kit; eyedrops; sealable plastic bags (for damp clothes, soap, food, shampoo, and other spillables); alarm clock; waterproof flip-flop sandals for showers; waterproof matches; sun hat; moleskin (for blisters); needle and thread; safety pins; sunglasses; a personal stereo (Walkman) with headphones; pocket knife; plastic water bottle; collapsible porcupine; compass; string (makeshift clothesline and lashing material); towel; padlock; whistle; rubber bands; toilet paper; flashlight; cold-water soap; small shatterproof mirror; earplugs; inflatable neck rest; insect repellant; electrical tape (for patching tears); clothespins and short clothesline; maps and phrasebooks; tweezers; garbage bags; sunscreen; vitamins. Some items not always readily available or affordable on the road: deodorant; razors; condoms; tampons.

DRESS FOR SUCCESS

If you know you will encounter situations which require more than the jeans and t-shirt uniform, remember that simple is elegant, not boring. Black is ideal because it is always in fashion and you can't tell if it's been worn five times. Women should bring a simple, solid color, cotton (or other versatile fabric) dress or a nice pants outfit. Men should bring a pair of khakis, which can be both dressy and casual, and the essential white button-up shirt. Both are useful everyday and dressy when paired together. If you have the inclination and the room, you might decide to bring an extra pair of shoes so you don't ruin that dressy outfit, although some say that hiking boots go with everything.

GETTING THERE

■ Budget Travel Agencies

Students and people under 26 ("youth") with proper ID qualify for enticing reduced airfares. These are rarely available from airlines or travel agents, but instead from student travel agencies which negotiate special reduced-rate bulk purchase with the airlines, then resell them to the youth market. Return-date change fees also tend to be low (around US$35 per segment through Council or Let's Go Travel). Most flights are on major airlines, though in peak season some agencies may sell seats on less reliable chartered aircraft. Student travel agencies can also help non-students and people over 26, but probably won't be able to get the same low fares.

Let's Go Travel, Harvard Student Agencies, 17 Holyoke St., Cambridge, MA 02138 (tel. (617) 495-9649; fax 495-7956; email travel@hsa.net; http://hsa.net/travel). Railpasses, HI-AYH memberships, ISICs, ITICs, FIYTO cards, guidebooks (including every *Let's Go*), maps, bargain flights, and a complete line of budget travel gear. All items available by mail; call or write for a catalogue (or see the catalogue in center of this publication).

Council Travel (http://www.ciee.org/travel/index.htm), the travel division of Council, is a full-service travel agency specializing in youth and budget travel. They offer discount airfares on scheduled airlines, railpasses, hosteling cards, low-cost accommodations, guidebooks, budget tours, travel gear, and international student (ISIC), youth (GO25), and teacher (ITIC) identity cards. U.S. offices include: Emory Village, 1561 N. Decatur Rd., **Atlanta,** GA 30307 (tel. (404) 377-9997); 2000 Guadalupe, **Austin,** TX 78705 (tel. (512) 472-4931); 273 Newbury St., **Boston,** MA 02116 (tel. (617) 266-1926); 1138 13th St., **Boulder,** CO 80302 (tel. (303) 447-8101); 1153 N. Dearborn, **Chicago,** IL 60610 (tel. (312) 951-0585); 10904 Lindbrook Dr., **Los Angeles,** CA 90024 (tel. (310) 208-3551); 1501 University Ave. SE #300, **Minneapolis,** MN 55414 (tel. (612) 379-2323); 205 E. 42nd St., **New York,** NY 10017 (tel. (212) 822-2700); 953 Garnet Ave., **San Diego,** CA 92109 (tel. (619) 270-6401); 530 Bush St., **San Francisco,** CA 94108 (tel. (415) 421-3473); 1314 NE 43rd St. #210, **Seattle,** WA 98105 (tel. (206) 632-2448); 3300 M St. NW, **Washington, D.C.** 20007 (tel. (202) 337-6464). **For U.S. cities not**

listed, call 800-2-COUNCIL (226-8624). Also 28A Poland St. (Oxford Circus), **London,** W1V 3DB (tel. (0171) 287 3337); **Paris** (tel. (146) 55 55 65); and **Munich** (tel. (089) 39 50 22).

STA Travel, 6560 Scottsdale Rd. #F100, Scottsdale, AZ 85253 (tel. (800) 777-0112 nationwide; fax (602) 922-0793; http://sta-travel.com). A student and youth travel organization with over 150 offices worldwide offering discount airfares for young travelers, railpasses, accommodations, tours, insurance, and ISICs. Sixteen offices in the U.S. including: 297 Newbury Street, **Boston,** MA 02115 (tel. (617) 266-6014); 429 S. Dearborn St., **Chicago,** IL 60605 (tel. (312) 786-9050); 7202 Melrose Ave., **Los Angeles,** CA 90046 (tel. (213) 934-8722); 10 Downing St., Ste. G, **New York,** NY 10003 (tel. (212) 627-3111); 4341 University Way NE, **Seattle,** WA 98105 (tel. (206) 633-5000); 2401 Pennsylvania Ave., **Washington, D.C.** 20037 (tel. (202) 887-0912); 51 Grant Ave., **San Francisco,** CA 94108 (tel. (415) 391-8407); **Miami,** FL 33133 (tel. (305) 461-3444). In the U.K., 6 Wrights Ln., **London** W8 6TA (tel. (0171) 938 47 11 for North American travel). In New Zealand, 10 High St., **Auckland** (tel. (09) 309 97 23). In Australia, 222 Faraday St., **Melbourne** Vic. 3050 (tel. (03) 349 69 11).

■ By Plane

The **airline industry** attempts to squeeze every dollar from customers; finding a cheap airfare will be easier if you understand the airlines' systems. Call every toll-free number and don't be afraid to ask about discounts; if you don't ask, it's unlikely they'll be volunteered. Have knowledgeable **travel agents** guide you; better yet, have an agent who specializes in the region(s) you will be traveling to guide you. An agent whose clients fly mostly to Nassau or Miami will not be the best person to hunt down a bargain flight to Athens or Istanbul. Travel agents may not want to spend time finding the cheapest fares (for which they receive the lowest commissions), but if you travel often, you should definitely find an agent who will cater to you and your needs, and track down deals in exchange for your frequent business.

There is also a steadily increasing amount of travel information to be found on the Internet. The *Official Airline Guide* now also has a website (http://www.oag.com) which allows access to flight schedules (one-time hook-up fee US$25 and a user's fee of 17¢-47¢ per minute). The site also provides information on hotels, cruises, and rail and ferry schedules. **TravelHUB** (http://www.travelhub.com) will help you search for travel agencies on the web. The **Air Traveler's Handbook** (http://www.cis.ohio-state.edu/hypertext/faq/usenet/travel/air/handbook/top.html) is an excellent source of general information on air travel. Marc-David Seidel's **Airlines of the Web** (http://www.itn.net/airlines) provides links to pages and 800 numbers for most of the world's airlines. The newsgroup **rec.travel.air** is a good source of tips on current bargains. And a few airlines have begun holding auctions on their websites, including **Icelandair** (http://www.centrum.is/icelandair) and **Finnair** (http://www.us.finnair.com).

COMMERCIAL AIRLINES

The commercial airlines' lowest regular offer is the **Advance Purchase Excursion Fare (APEX);** specials advertised in newspapers may be cheaper, but have more restrictions and fewer available seats. APEX fares provide you with confirmed reservations and allow "open-jaw" tickets (landing in and returning from different cities). Generally, reservations must be made seven to 21 days in advance, with seven- to 14-day minimum and up to 90-day maximum stay limits, and hefty cancellation and change penalties (fees rise in summer). Book APEX fares early during peak season; by May you will have a hard time getting the departure date you want. Also look into flights to less popular destinations or on smaller carriers. Even if you pay an airline's lowest published fare, you may waste hundreds of dollars. For the adventurous or the bargain-hungry, there are other, perhaps more inconvenient or time-consuming options, but before shopping around it is a good idea to find out the average commercial price in order to measure just how great a "bargain" you are being offered.

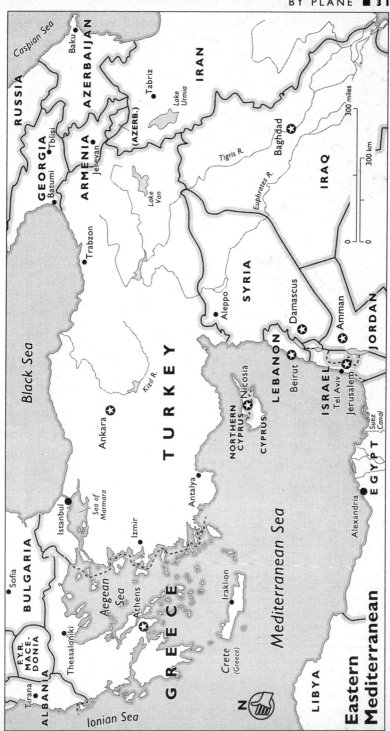

Eastern Mediterranean

Upgrades: Timing is Everything

While round-trip tickets may be cheaper during the week than on weekends, they also mean crowded flights, which in turn means competition for that Holy Grail of the budget traveler, the frequent-flier upgrade. Scheduling weekend flights is more expensive, but less crowded, and proves the best bet for using frequent-flier upgrades. Most business travelers travel on Thursdays, which makes stiff competition for upgrade hunters. Saturdays and Sundays present the best opportunities for frequent fliers.

TICKET CONSOLIDATORS

Ticket consolidators resell unsold tickets on commercial and charter airlines at unpublished fares. The consolidator market is by and large international; domestic flights, if they do exist, are typically for cross-country flights. Consolidator flights are the best deals if you are traveling: on short notice, (you bypass advance purchase requirements, since you aren't tangled in airline bureaucracy); on a high-priced trip; to an offbeat destination; or in the peak season, when published fares are jacked way up. Fares sold by consolidators are generally much cheaper; a 30-40% price reduction is not uncommon. There are rarely age constraints or stay limitations, but unlike tickets bought through an airline, you won't be able to use your tickets on another flight if you miss yours, and you will have to go back to the consolidator to get a refund, rather than the airline. Keep in mind that these tickets are often for coach seats on connecting flights on foreign airlines, and that frequent-flyer miles may not be credited. Decide what you can and can't live with before shopping.

Not all consolidators deal with the general public; many only sell tickets through travel agents. **Bucket shops** are retail agencies that specialize in getting cheap tickets. Although ticket prices are marked up slightly, bucket shops generally have access to a larger market than would be available to the public and can also get tickets from wholesale consolidators. Look for bucket shops' tiny ads in the travel section of weekend papers; in the U.S., the *Sunday New York Times* is a good source. In London, a call to the **Air Travel Advisory Bureau** (tel. (0171) 636 50 00) can provide names of reliable consolidators and discount flight specialists. Kelly Monaghan's *Consolidators: Air Travel's Bargain Basement* (US$7 plus US$2 shipping) from the Intrepid Traveler, P.O. Box 438, New York, NY 10034 (email intreptrav@aol.com), is an invaluable source for more information and lists of consolidators by location and destination.

Be smart and check out the competition. Among the many reputable and trustworthy companies are, unfortunately, some shady wheeler-dealers. Contact the local Better Business Bureau to find out how long the company has been in business and its track record. Although not necessary, it is preferable to deal with consolidators close to home so you can visit in person, if necessary. Ask to receive your tickets as quickly as possible so you have time to fix any problems. Get the company's policy in writing: insist on a **receipt** that gives full details about the tickets, refunds, and restrictions, and record who you talked to and when. It may be worth paying with a credit card (despite the 2-5% fee) so you can stop payment if you never receive your tickets. Beware the "bait and switch" gag: firms will advertise a super-low fare and then tell a caller that it has been sold. Although this is a viable excuse, if they can't offer you a price near the advertised fare on *any* date, it is a scam to lure in customers—report them to the Better Business Bureau. Also ask about accommodations and car rental discounts; some consolidators have fingers in many pies.

CHARTER FLIGHTS

Charters are flights a tour operator contracts with an airline (usually one specializing in charters) to fly extra loads of passengers to peak-season destinations. Charters are often cheaper than flights on scheduled airlines, especially during peak seasons, although fare wars, consolidator tickets, and small airlines can beat charter prices.

ESSENTIALS

Better Safe than Sorry

Everyone who flies should be concerned with airline safety. The type and age of the aircraft used often indicate the airline's safety level—aircraft not produced by Boeing, Airbus, McDonnell Douglas, or Fokker sometimes fall below acceptable standards, and aircraft over 20 years old require increased levels of maintenance. Travel agencies can tell you the type and age of aircraft on a particular route, as can the *Official Airline Guide* (http://www.oag.com); this can be especially useful in Eastern Europe where less reliable equipment is often used for inter-city travel. If you're flying a foreign airline, especially to Third World countries, consult one of the following organizations: The **International Airline Passengers Association** (tel. (972) 404-9980) publishes a survey of accident rates on foreign airlines and provides safety information on carriers worldwide. The **Federal Aviation Administration** (http://www.faa.gov) reviews the airline authorities for countries whose airlines enter the U.S. and divides the countries into three categories: stick with carriers in category 1. Call the **U.S. State Department** (tel. (202) 647-5225; http://travel.state.gov/travel_warnings.html) to check for posted travel advisories which sometimes involve foreign carriers.

Some charters operate nonstop, and restrictions on minimum advance-purchase and minimum stay are more lenient. However, charter flights fly less frequently than major airlines, make refunds particularly difficult, and are almost always fully booked. Schedules and itineraries may also change or be cancelled at the last moment (as late as 48 hours before the trip, and without a full refund), and check-in, boarding, and baggage claim are often much slower. As always, pay with a credit card if you can, and consider traveler's insurance against trip interruption.

Try **Interworld** (tel. (305) 443-4929, fax 443-0351); **Travac** (tel. (800) 872-8800; fax (212) 714-9063; email mail@travac.com; http://www.travac.com) or **Rebel**, Valencia, CA (tel. (800) 227-3235; fax (805)-294-0981; http://rebeltours.com; email travel@rebeltours.com) or Orlando, FL (tel. (800) 732-3588). Don't be afraid to call every number and hunt for the best deal.

Eleventh-hour **discount clubs** and **fare brokers** offer members savings on European travel, including charter flights and tour packages. Research your options carefully. **Last Minute Travel Club,** 100 Sylvan Rd., Woburn, MA 01801 (tel. (800) 527-8646 or (617) 267-9800), and **Discount Travel International** New York, NY (tel. (212) 362-3636; fax 362-3236) are among the few travel clubs that don't charge a membership fee. Others include **Moment's Notice,** New York, NY (tel. (718) 234-6295; fax 234 6450; http://www.moments-notice.com), air tickets, tours, and hotels; US$25 annual fee and **Travelers Advantage,** Stamford, CT (tel. (800) 548-1116; http://www.travelersadvantage.com; US$49 annual fee); and **Travel Avenue** (tel. (800) 333-3335). Study these organizations' contracts closely; you don't want to end up with an unwanted overnight layover.

■ By Train

Greece is served by a number of international train routes that connect Athens, Thessaloniki, and Larissa to most European cities. Count on at least a three-day journey from Trieste or Vienna to Athens. Istanbul, **Turkey** is accessible by rail from points in Europe. Trains are among the cheaper transportation options, but not the more convenient—Eurail is not valid in Turkey. The Turkish rail system is rivaled only by the Greek system as Europe's most antiquated and least efficient. There is no rail system in Cyprus.

■ By Ferry

Ferry travel is a popular way to get to and travel between Greece, Turkey, and Cyprus. Reservations are recommended for many ferries, especially in high season.

Be warned that **ferries run on irregular schedules.** Check in at *least* two hours in advance; late boarders may find their seats gone. If you sleep on deck, bring warm clothes and a sleeping bag. Bicycles travel free, and motorcycles are transported for an additional charge (check each agency). Don't forget motion sickness medication, toilet paper, and a hand towel. Bring your own food to avoid high prices on board.

The major ports of departure from Italy to Greece are Ancona and Brindisi, on the southeast coast of Italy. Bari, Otranto, and Venice also have a few connections. If coming from the north of Italy, be aware that gassing and theft are not unheard of on the overnight trains from Rome to Brindisi. Some ferry lines offer free deck passage on a space-available basis (you could get bumped by a paying passenger), but all passengers still need to pay the port tax (L10,000, or $6.25, in Brindisi) and, in high season, a supplementary fee of L19,000 ($12). Boats travel primarily to Corfu (10hr.), Igoumenitsa (12hr.), and Patras (20hr.). Prices range L50,000-105,000 ($31-66); in low season L22,000-45,000 ($13-29). For schedules from Greece to Italy, see Patras, Cephalonia, Corfu, or Igoumenitsa.

From Çeşme, Turkey, an **Ertürk** ferry offers service to Chios (May-June 3-4 per week, July-April 1 per week). Prices are one way $25, same-day return $30, open round-trip $35. Rhodes is connected by ferry to Marmaris (one way 10,000dr, round-trip 12,000dr), as well as to Limassol, Cyprus (2 per week, 17hr., 18,500-22,000dr), and Haifa, Israel (2 per week, 36hr., 28,500-33,000dr). These Limassol and Haifa services provide student and youth discounts of 20% year-round.

From **Northern Cyprus,** the easiest crossing is Taşucu, Turkey to Girne (Kyrenia) on the northern coast of the island (7hr.). Boats run twice per day in the summer, less frequently in winter. Ertürk and **Fergün** tourism companies sell discounted tickets. You can also cross from Mersin (10hr.).

Hydrofoils (Flying Dolphins) are a tempting mode of traveling. They run more frequently and reliably than ferries at twice their speed, but cost twice as much.

■ By Bus

Road travel in Turkey is dangerous by European and U.S. standards (see p. 368).

Though European trains and railpasses are extremely popular, the long-distance bus networks of Greece and Turkey are more extensive, efficient, and often more comfortable than train services.

Eurolines, 4 Cardiff Rd., Luton LU1 1PP (tel. (01582) 40 45 11; fax (01582) 40 06 94; in London, 52 Grosvenor Gardens, Victoria; tel.(0171) 730 82 35), is Europe's largest operator of Europe-wide coach services, including Eastern Europe and Russia. A Eurolines Pass offers unlimited 30-day (under 26 and over 60 UK£159; 26-60 UK £199) or 60-day (under 26 and over 60 UK£199, 26-60 UK£249) travel between 20 major tourist destinations. Eurolines also offers **Euro Explorers,** eight complete travel loops throughout Europe with set fares and itineraries. **Eurobus,** P.O. Box 3016 Workingham Berkshire RG40 2YP (tel.(0118) 936 23 21; fax (0118) 936 23 22; http://www.eurobus.uk.com), offers cheap bus trips in 25 major cities in 10 major European countries for those between ages 16 and 38. The buses, with English speaking guides and drivers, stop door-to-door at one hostel or budget hotel per city, and let you hop on and off. Tickets are sold by zone; for any one zone US$225, for any two zones US$400, for all three zones US$525. Travelers under 26 are eligible for discounts on all tickets. For purchase in the United States contact Council Travel or STA; in Canada contact Travel CUTS (see **Budget Travel Agencies,** p. 29).

ONCE THERE

■ Getting Around

The Greek government frowns on tourists taking advantage of cheaper fares to Greece for easy access to Turkey, and the information you receive on how to travel between the two countries may be confusing. Contrary to what tourist authorities may lead you to believe, there's no law that prevents crossing the borders. Many travelers make one-day excursions, but you should check into regulations on longer trips. If you fly to Greece on a European charter flight, you can't travel to Turkey.

Athens and Istanbul are connected by **Euroways Eurolines** bus and by train. If you have a railpass and are traveling from Greece to Turkey, take the train as far as Alexandroupolis, and ride the bus from there. Beware: the 38-hour ride from Athens will wear out even the most seasoned traveler. The quickest but most expensive option is an Olympic Airways **flight** to Istanbul or other points in Turkey.

Those who **hitch** between Turkey and Greece usually try to make it to Istanbul in one ride from Alexandroupolis or Thessaloniki; there isn't much traffic, and people are not permitted to walk across the border. Those who have decided to hitch say they made sure their driver's license plate number did not get stamped in their passports (but rather on some other, disposable piece of paper), or they would have needed to produce the car to leave the country. Again, *Let's Go* does not recommend hitchhiking.

BY TRAIN

European trains retain the charm and romance of a bygone era, but charm and romance don't satisfy those earthly needs. Bring food and a water bottle because the on-board cafe can be pricey, and train water undrinkable. Lock your compartment door and keep your valuables on your person. Many train stations have different counters for domestic and international tickets, seat reservations, and info—check before lining up. Even with a railpass, reservations are often required on major lines, and are advisable during the busier holiday seasons; make them at least a few hours in advance at the train station (US$3-10). For overnight travel, a tight, open bunk called a **couchette** is an affordable luxury (about US$20; reserve at the station at least several days in advance).

BY BOAT

Travel by boat is a bewitching alternative favored by Europeans but overlooked by most foreigners. Most European ferries are comfortable and well-equipped; the cheapest fare class sometimes includes a reclining chair or couchette where you can sleep. You should check in at least two hours early for a prime spot and allow plenty of time for late trains and getting to the port. Avoid the astronomically priced cafeteria cuisine by bringing your own food. Fares jump sharply in July and August. Ask for discounts; ISIC holders can often get student fares, and Eurail passholders get many reductions and free trips (check the brochure that comes with your railpass). You'll occasionally have to pay a small port tax (under US$10). Advance planning and reserved ticket purchases through a travel agency can spare you days of waiting in dreary ports for the next sailing. Reservations are recommended, especially in July and August. Bring toilet paper. Ferries run on erratic schedules, with similar routes and varying prices. Shop around, and beware of dinky, unreliable companies which don't take reservations.

BY MOPED AND MOTORCYCLE

Motorized bikes have long spiced up southern European roads with their flashy colors and perpetual buzz. They offer an enjoyable, relatively inexpensive way to tour coastal areas and countryside, particularly where there are few cars. They don't use much gas, can be put on trains and ferries, and are a good compromise between the high cost of car travel and the limited range of bicycles. However, they're uncomfortable for long distances, dangerous in the rain, and unpredictable on rough roads and gravel. Always wear a helmet, and never ride with a backpack. If you've never been on a moped before, a twisting Alpine road is not the place to start. Expect to pay about US$20-35 per day; try auto repair shops, and remember to bargain. Motorcycles normally require a license. Before renting, ask if the quoted price includes tax and insurance, or you may be hit with an unexpected additional fee. Avoid handing your passport over as a deposit; if you have an accident or mechanical failure you may not get it back until you cover all repairs. Pay ahead of time instead.

BY THUMB

Let's Go strongly urges you to consider seriously the risks before you choose to hitch. We do not recommend hitching as a safe means of transportation, and none of the information presented here is intended to do so.

No one should hitch without careful consideration of the risks involved. Not everyone can be an airplane pilot, but any bozo can drive a car. Hitching means entrusting your life to a random person who happens to stop beside you on the road and risking theft, assault, sexual harassment, and unsafe driving. In spite of this, there are gains to hitching. Favorable hitching experiences allow you to meet local people and get where you're going, where public transportation is sketchy. The choice, however, remains yours.

Depending on the circumstances and the norms of the country, men and women traveling in groups and men traveling alone might consider hitching (called "autostop" in much of Europe) beyond the range of bus or train routes. If you're a woman traveling alone, don't hitch. It's just too dangerous. A man and a woman are a safer combination, two men will have a harder time, and three will go nowhere.

If you do decide to hitch, consider where you are. Where one stands is vital. Experienced hitchers pick a spot outside of built-up areas, where drivers can stop, return to the road without causing an accident, and have time to look over potential passengers as they approach. Hitching (or even standing) on super-highways is usually illegal: one may only thumb at rest stops or at the entrance ramps to highways. In the **Practical Information** section of many cities, we list the tram or bus lines that take travelers to strategic points for hitching out.

Finally, success will depend on what one looks like. Successful hitchers travel light and stack their belongings in a compact but visible cluster. Most Europeans signal with an open hand, rather than a thumb; many write their destination on a sign in large, bold letters and draw a smiley-face under it. Drivers prefer hitchers who are neat and wholesome. No one stops for anyone wearing sunglasses.

Safety issues are always imperative, even for those who are not hitching alone. Safety-minded hitchers avoid getting in the back of a two-door car, and never let go of their backpacks. They will not get into a car that they can't get out of again in a hurry. If they ever feel threatened, they insist on being let off, regardless of where they are. Acting as if they are going to open the car door or vomit on the upholstery will usually get a driver to stop. Hitchhiking at night can be particularly dangerous; experienced hitchers stand in well-lit places, and expect drivers to be leery of nocturnal thumbers (or open-handers).

■ Accommodations

HOSTELS

A Hosteler's Bill of Rights
There are certain standard features that we do not include in our hostel listings. Unless we state otherwise, you can expect that every hostel has: no lockout, no curfew, a kitchen, free hot showers, secure luggage storage, and no key deposit.

For tight budgets and those lonesome traveling blues, hostels can't be beat. Hostels are generally dorm-style accommodations, often in single-sex large rooms with bunk beds, although some hostels do offer private rooms for families and couples. They sometimes have kitchens and utensils for your use, bike or moped rentals, storage areas, and laundry facilities. There can be drawbacks: some hostels close during certain daytime "lock-out" hours, have a curfew, impose a maximum stay, or, less frequently, require that you do chores. Fees range from US$5 to $25 per night and hostels associated with one of the large hostel associations often have lower rates for members. If you have Internet access, check out the **Internet Guide to Hostelling** (http://hostels.com), which includes hostels from around the world in addition to oodles of information about hostelling and backpacking worldwide. **Eurotrip** (http://www.eurotrip.com/accommodation/accommodation.html also has information on budget hostels and several international hostel associations. Reservations for over 300 **Hostelling International (HI)** hostels (see listing below) may be made via the International Booking Network (IBN), a computerized system which allows you make hostels reservations months in advance for a nominal fee (tel. (202) 783-6161). If you plan to stay in hostels, consider joining one of these associations:

An Óige (Irish Youth Hostel Association), 61 Mountjoy St., Dublin 7 (tel. (01) 830 4555; fax 830-5808; anoige@iol.ie One-year membership is IR£7.50, under 18 IR£4, family IR£7.50 for each adult with children under 16 free. Prices from IR£4.50-9.50 a night. 37 locations.

Hostelling International-American Youth Hostels (HI-AYH), 733 15th St. NW, Suite 840, Washington, D.C. 20005 (tel. (202) 783-6161; fax 783-6171; email hiayhserv@hiayh.org; http://www.hiayh.org). Maintains 35 offices and over 150 hostels in the U.S. Memberships can be purchased at many travel agencies (see p. 29) or the national office in Washington, D.C. One year membership US$25, under 18 US$10, over 54 US$15, family cards US$35; includes *Hostelling North America: The Official Guide to Hostels in Canada and the United States*. Reserve by letter,

phone, fax, or through the International Booking Network (IBN), a computerized reservation system which lets you book from other HI hostels worldwide up to 6 months in advance. Basic rules (with much local variation): check-in 5-8pm, check-out 9:30am (although most urban hostels have 24hr. access), max. stay 3 nights, no pets or alcohol allowed on the premises. Fees US$5-22 per night.

Hostelling International-Canada (HI-C), 400-205 Catherine St., Ottawa, Ontario K2P 1C3 (tel. (613) 237-7884; fax 237-7868). Maintains 73 hostels throughout Canada. IBN booking centers in Edmonton, Montreal, Ottawa, and Vancouver; expect CDN$9-22.50/night. Membership packages: 1-yr., under 18 CDN$12; 1-yr., over 18 CDN$25; 2-yr., over 18 CDN$35; lifetime CDN$175.

Scottish Youth Hostels Association (SYHA), 7 Glebe Crescent, Stirling FK8 2JA (tel. (01786) 891400; fax 891333; email syha@syha.org.uk; http://www.syha.org.uk). Membership UK£6, under 18 UK£2.50.

Youth Hostels Association of England and Wales (YHA), Trevelyan House, 8 St. Stephen's Hill, St. Albans, Hertfordshire AL1 2DY (tel. (01727) 855215; fax 844126). Enrollment fees are: UK£9.50; under 18 UK£3.50; UK£19 for both parents with children under 18 enrolled free; UK£9.50 for one parent with children under 18 enrolled free; UK£130 for lifetime membership. Overnight prices for under 18 UK£4.25-17.20, for adults UK£6.25-20.50.

Youth Hostels Association of Northern Ireland (YHANI), 22 Donegall Rd., Belfast BT12 5JN (tel. (01232) 324733, 315435; fax 439699). Prices range from UK£8-12. Annual memberships UK£7, under 18 UK£3, family UK£14 for up to 6 children.

Youth Hostels Association of New Zealand (YHANZ), P.O. Box 436, 173 Gloucester St., Christchurch 1 (tel. (643) 379 9970; fax 365 4476; email info@yha.org.nz; http://www.yha.org.nz). Annual membership fee NZ$24.

Hostel Association of South Africa, P.O. Box 4402, Cape Town 8000 (tel. (021) 24 2511; fax 24 4119; email hisa@gem.co.za; http://www.gen.com/hisa). Membership SAR45, group SAR120, family SAR90, lifetime SAR250.

■ Camping & the Outdoors

CAMPING AND HIKING EQUIPMENT

Purchase equipment before you leave. This way you'll know exactly what you have and how much it weighs. Spend some time examining catalogues and talking to knowledgeable salespeople. Whether buying or renting, finding sturdy, light, and inexpensive equipment is a must.

Sleeping bags: Most good sleeping bags are rated by "season," or the lowest outdoor temperature at which they will keep you warm ("summer" means 30-40°F, "three-season" means 20°F, and "four-season" or "winter" means below 0°F). Sleeping bags are made either of down (warmer and lighter, but more expensive, and miserable when wet) or of synthetic material (heavier, more durable, and warmer when wet). Prices vary, but might range from US$65-100 for a summer synthetic to US$250-550 for a good down winter bag. Sleeping bag **pads,** including foam pads (US$15 and up) and air mattresses (US$25-50) cushion your back and neck and insulate you from the ground. Another good alternative is the **Therm-A-Rest,** which is part foam and part air-mattress and inflates to full padding when you unroll it.

Tents: The best tents are free-standing, with their own frames and suspension systems; they set up quickly and require no staking (except in high winds). Low profile dome tents are the best all-around. When pitched their internal space is almost entirely usable, which means little unnecessary bulk. Tent sizes can be somewhat misleading: two people *can* fit in a two-person tent, but will find life more pleasant in a four-person. If you're traveling by car, go for the bigger tent; if you're hiking, stick with a smaller tent that weighs no more than 3-4 lbs. Good two-person tents start at US$150, four-person tents at US$400, but you can some-

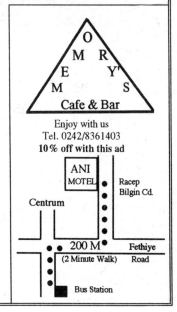

times find last year's model for half the price. Be sure to seal the seams of your tent with waterproofer, and make sure it has a rain fly.

Backpacks: If you intend to do a lot of hiking, you should have a **frame backpack. Internal-frame packs** mold better to your back, keep a lower center of gravity, and can flex adequately to allow you to hike difficult trails that require a lot of bending and maneuvering. **External-frame packs** are more comfortable for long hikes over even terrain since they keep the weight higher and distribute it more evenly. Whichever you choose, make sure your pack has a strong, padded hip belt, which transfers the weight from the shoulders to the legs. Any serious backpacking requires a pack of at least 4000 cubic inches. Allow an additional 500 cubic inches for your sleeping bag in internal-frame packs. Sturdy backpacks cost anywhere from US$125-500. This is one area where it doesn't pay to economize—cheaper packs may be less comfortable, and the straps are more likely to fray or rip. Before you buy any pack, try it on and imagine carrying it, full, a few miles up a rocky incline.

Boots: Be sure to wear hiking boots with good **ankle support** which are appropriate for the terrain you are hiking. Your boots should fit snugly and comfortably over one or two wool socks and a thin liner sock. Be sure that the boots are broken in—a bad blister can ruin your day (or a couple of them).

Other necessities: Rain gear should come in two pieces, a top and pants, rather than a poncho. **Synthetics,** like polypropylene tops, socks, and long underwear, along with a pile jacket, will keep you warm even when wet. When camping in autumn, winter, or spring, bring along a **"space blanket,"** which helps you retain body heat and doubles as a groundcloth (US$5-15). Plastic **canteens** or water bottles keep water cooler than metal ones do, and are virtually shatter- and leak-proof. Large, collapsible **water sacks** will significantly improve your lot in primitive campgrounds and weigh practically nothing when empty, though they can get bulky. Bring **water-purification tablets** for when you can't boil water. Though most campgrounds provide campfire sites, you may want to bring a small **metal grate** or **grill** of your own. For those places that forbid fires or the gathering of firewood (this includes virtually every organized campground in Europe), you'll need a **camp stove.** The classic Coleman starts at about US$30. In Europe, consider the "GAZ" butane/propane stove. Its little blue cylinders can be purchased anywhere on the continent—just don't try to take them onto a plane. Campers heading to Europe should also look into buying an **International Camping Carnet.** Similar to a hostel membership card, it's required at a few campgrounds and provides discounts at others (available in North America from the **Family Campers and RVers Association,** and in the U.K. from **The Caravan Club**). A **first aid kit, swiss army knife, insect repellent, calamine lotion,** and **waterproof matches** or a **lighter** are essential camping items. Other items include: a **battery-operated lantern,** a **plastic groundcloth,** a **nylon tarp,** a **waterproof backpack cover** (although you can also store your belongings in plastic bags inside your backpack), and a **"stuff sack"** or plastic bag to keep your sleeping bag dry.

WILDERNESS AND SAFETY CONCERNS

Stay warm, stay dry, and **stay hydrated.** The vast majority of life-threatening wilderness problems stem from a failure to follow this advice. On any hike, however brief, you should pack enough equipment to keep you alive should disaster befall. This includes **rain gear, hat** and **mittens, a first-aid kit, high energy food,** and **water.** Dress in warm layers of **synthetic materials** designed for the outdoors, or **wool.** Pile fleece jackets and Gore-Tex raingear are excellent choices (see **Camping and Hiking Equipment**). Never rely on **cotton** for warmth. This "death cloth" will be absolutely useless should it get wet. When camping, be sure to bring a proper tent with rain-fly and warm sleeping bags. Check **weather forecasts** and pay attention to the skies when hiking. Weather patterns can change instantly. If on a day hike when the weather turns nasty, turn back. If on an overnight, start looking immediately for shelter. Whenever possible, let someone know when and where you are going hiking, either a friend, your hostel, a park ranger, or a local hiking organization. Do not attempt a hike beyond your ability—you may be endangering your life.

See **Health** (p. 16) for information about outdoor ailments such as giardia, rabies, and insects, as well as basic medical concerns and first-aid. A good guide to outdoor survival is *How to Stay Alive in the Woods,* by Bradford Angier (Macmillan, US$8).

■ Keeping in Touch

MAIL

Mail can be sent internationally through **Poste Restante** (the international phrase for General Delivery) to any city or town; it's well worth using, generally without any surcharges, and much more reliable than you might think. Mark the envelope, for example, "Jennifer <u>GANDHI</u>, *Poste Restante,* Athens, GREECE." The last name should be capitalized and underlined. As a rule, it is best to use the largest post office in the area; sometimes, mail will be sent there regardless of what you write on the envelope. When possible, it is usually better to send mail express or registered.

It helps (though is not imperative) to use the appropriate translation of *Poste Restante* (*Postrestant* in Turkey and Northern Cyprus, *Poste Restante* in Greece and Southern Cyprus). Cyprus has official postal codes for the North, but your best bet may be to send letters via Turkey using the postal code **Mersin 10, Turkey**. When picking up mail, bring your passport or other ID. If the clerks insist that there is nothing for you, have them check under your first name as well. In a few countries you may have to pay a minimal fee per item received. *Let's Go: Greece & Turkey* lists post offices in the **Practical Information** section for each city and most towns.

Aerogrammes, printed sheets that fold into envelopes and travel via airmail, are available at post offices. It helps to mark them with "airmail" or *par avion.* Most post offices will charge exorbitant fees or refuse to send Aerogrammes with enclosures. Airmail from Europe and the U.S. averages one to two weeks. Much depends on the national post office which handles the mail before it leaves the country.

If regular airmail is too slow, there are a few faster, more expensive, options. **Federal Express** (U.S. tel. (800) 463-3339) can get a letter from New York to Paris in two days for a whopping US$29.07; rates among non-U.S. locations are prohibitively expensive (Paris to New York, for example, costs upwards of US$60). By U.S. Express Mail, the same letter would arrive in two to three days and would cost US$21, although rates vary according to country. For more information on U.S. mail options, check out their web site at http://www.usps.gov.

Surface mail is by far the cheapest and slowest way to send mail. It takes one to three months to cross the Atlantic and two to four for the Pacific—appropriate for sending large quantities of items you won't need to see for a while. It is vital, therefore, to distinguish your airmail from surface mail by explicitly labeling "airmail" in the appropriate language. When ordering books and materials from abroad, always include one or two **International Reply Coupons (IRCs)**—a way of providing the postage to cover delivery. IRCs should be available from your local post office as well as abroad (US$1.05).

American Express travel offices throughout the world will act as a mail service for cardholders if you contact them in advance. Under this free **"Client Letter Service,"** they will hold mail for 30 days, forward upon request, and accept telegrams. Check the **Practical Information** section of the countries you plan to visit; *Let's Go* lists AmEx office locations for most large cities.

TELEPHONES

You can place **international calls** from most telephones. To call direct, dial the universal international access code followed by the country code, the city code (see the city's **Essentials** listings), and the local number. Country codes and city codes may sometimes be listed with a zero in front (e.g., 033), but after dialing the interna-

Calling There, Calling Home

The country codes for the countries covered in this book are as follows:

Cyprus: 357
Greece: 30
Northern Cyprus: 90 392
Turkey: 90

Need to check up on your yacht or mansion back home? Call the caretaker!

AT&T
Greece	00 800 1311
Turkey and Northern Cyprus	00 800 12277
Cyprus	080 90010

MCI
Greece	00 800 1211
Turkey and Northern Cyprus	00 800 11177
Cyprus	080 90000

Sprint
Greece	00 800 1411
Turkey and Northern Cyprus	00 800 14477
Cyprus	080 90001

tional access code, drop successive zeros (with an access code of 011, e.g., 011 33). In some countries, especially in small villages, you may have to go through the operator. In others, you must wait for a tone after the international access code. Note: Wherever possible, use a calling card (see **calling cards** below) for international phone calls, as the long distance rates for national phone services are often unpredictable and exorbitant.

You can usually make direct international calls from **pay phones,** but you may need to drop your coins as quickly as your words. In Greece, Turkey, and Cyprus, pay phones are card-operated; some even accept major credit cards. Be wary of more expensive, private pay phones; look for pay phones in public areas, especially train stations. If private pay phones are to be feared, one should all but flee from the in-room hotel phone call. Although incredibly convenient, these calls invariably include an arbitrary and sky-high surcharge (as much as US$10 in some establishments). If you really don't want to leave your hotel, find a pay phone in the lobby.

English-speaking operators are often available for both local and international assistance. Operators in most countries will place **collect calls** for you. It's cheaper to find a pay phone and deposit just enough money to be able to say "Call me" and give your number (though some pay phones can't receive calls).

Some companies, seizing upon this "call-me-back" concept, have created callback services. Under these plans, you call a specified number, ring once, and hang up. The company's computer calls back and gives you a dial tone. You can then make as many calls as you want, at rates about 20-60% lower than you'd pay using credit cards or pay phones. This option is most economical for loquacious travelers, as services may include a US$10-25 minimum billing per month. For information, call **America Tele-Fone** (tel. (800) 321-5817), **Globaltel** (tel. (770) 449-1295), **International Telephone** (tel. (800) 638-5558), and **Telegroup** (tel. (800) 338-0225).

A **calling card** is probably your best and cheapest bet; your local long-distance service provider will have a number for you to dial while traveling (either toll-free or charged as a local call) to connect instantly to an operator in your home country. The calls (plus a small surcharge) are then billed either collect or to the calling card. For more information, call **AT&T** about its **USADirect** and **World Connect** services (tel. (888) 288-4685; from abroad call (810) 262-6644 collect), **Sprint** (tel. (800) 877-4646; from abroad, call (913) 624-5335 collect), or **MCI WorldPhone** and **World Reach** (tel. (800) 444-4141; from abroad dial the country's MCI access number). In Canada, contact Bell Canada **Canada Direct** (tel. (800) 565 4708); in the

U.K., British Telecom **BT Direct** (tel. (800) 34 51 44); in Ireland, Telecom Éireann **Ireland Direct** (tel. (800) 250 250); in Australia, Telstra **Australia Direct** (tel. 13 22 00); in New Zealand, **Telecom New Zealand** (tel. 123); and in South Africa, **Telkom South Africa** (tel. 09 03).

MCI's WorldPhone also provides access to MCI's **Traveler's Assist,** which gives legal and medical advice, exchange rate information, and translation services. Many other long distance carriers and phone companies provide such travel information; contact your phone service provider.

In many countries, you can also buy **pre-paid phone cards,** which carry a certain amount of phone time depending on the card's denomination. The time is measured in minutes or talk units (e.g. one unit/one minute), and the card usually has a toll-free access telephone number and a personal identification number (PIN). To make a phone call, you dial the access number, enter your PIN, and at the voice prompt, enter the phone number of the party you're trying to reach. A computer tells you how much time or how many units you have left on your card.

Also, remember **time differences** when you call. Greece, Turkey, and Cyprus are two hours ahead of GMT (which is five hours ahead of Eastern Standard Time).

OTHER COMMUNICATION

Between May 2 and Octoberfest, **EurAide,** P.O. Box 2375, Naperville, IL 60567 (tel. (630) 420-2343; fax (630) 420-2369; http://www.cube.net/kmu/euraide.html), offers **Overseas Access,** a service useful to travelers without a set itinerary. The cost is US$15 per week or US$40 per month plus a US$15 registration fee. To reach you, people call, fax, or use the internet to leave a message; you receive it by calling Munich whenever you wish, which is cheaper than calling overseas. You may also leave messages for callers to pick up by phone.

If you're spending a year abroad and want to keep in touch with friends or colleagues in a college or research institution, **electronic mail (email)** is an attractive option. With minimal computer knowledge and a little planning, you can beam messages anywhere for no per-message charges. One option is to befriend college students as you go and ask if you can use their email accounts. Or, look for bureaus that offer access to email for sending individual messages. Search through http://www.cyberiacafe.net/cyberia/guide/ccafe.htm to find a list of **cybercafes** around the world from which you can drink a cup of joe and email him too. See **Internet Resources,** p. 2, for more information on global travel's newest twist.

GREECE ΕΛΛΑΔΑ

Even before Odysseus made his epic voyage across the Mediterranean, Greece was a land for wanderers. The country exhibits an extraordinary range of landscapes and attractions. Its historical ruins are among the most spectacular in the world, and its surprisingly varied topography among the most exquisite. The uniformity of classical aesthetics has given way to a mix of popular and ethnic influences and, today, the struggles of the past remain visible in the beauty of present-day Greece.

For visitors, Greece is a country in which utterly hedonistic vacation pleasures and weighty cultural offerings co-exist in successful harmony. By and large, Greece lacks the Club Med feel of other built-up tourist areas. Visitors should expect to simply soak up Greece's offerings, natural and man-made, without high expectations for amenities or chic service. In other words, don't allow your hotel's lack of room service or the unreliable ferry schedules ruin the blissful relaxation you could find while hiking, swimming late at night, eating olives, or visiting a medieval city. All these things can be better done in Greece than anywhere else.

ESSENTIALS

▓ Money

US$1 = 290 Greek Drachmae (dr)	100dr = US$0.35
CDN$1 = 208dr	100dr = CDN$0.48
UK£1 = 462dr	100dr = UK£0.22
IR£1 = 418dr	100dr = IR£0.24
AUS$1 = 215dr	100dr = AUS$0.46
NZ$1 = 186dr	100dr = NZ$0.54
SAR1 = 61dr	100dr = SAR1.63
1000TL = 1.75dr	100dr = 57,069TL
C£1 = 532dr	100dr = C£0.19

▓ Once There

TOURIST OFFICES

Two national organizations oversee tourism in Greece: the **Greek National Tourist Organization (GNTO)** and the **tourist police** *(touristiki astinomia)*. The GNTO can supply general information about sights and accommodations throughout the country. Offices in the U.S. and other countries are listed under tourist offices on p. 1; the main office is at 2 Amerikis St., Athens (tel. (01) 322 4128). Note that the GNTO is known as **EOT** in Greece. The tourist police deal with more local and immediate problems: where to find a room, what the bus schedule is, or what to do when you've lost your passport. They are open long hours and are willing to help, although their English is limited. Tourist info for Greece is available in English 24 hours a day by calling 171. **Nikis** and **Filellinon Streets** in Athens are lined with agencies and organizations geared towards budget and student travelers. We also list similar establishments in different cities in the **Orientation and Practical Information** section for most cities.

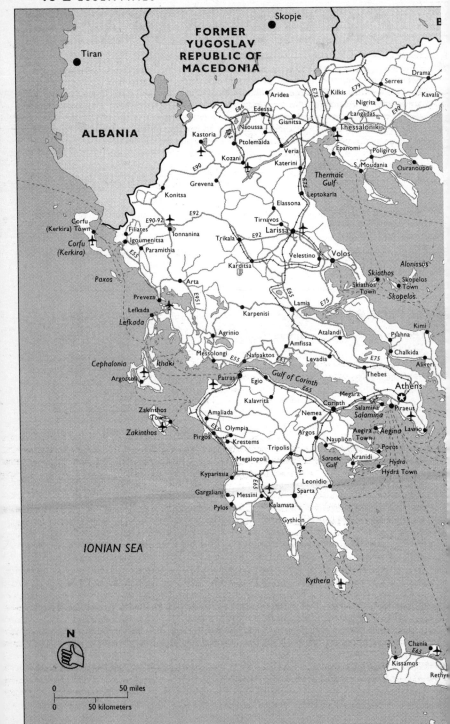

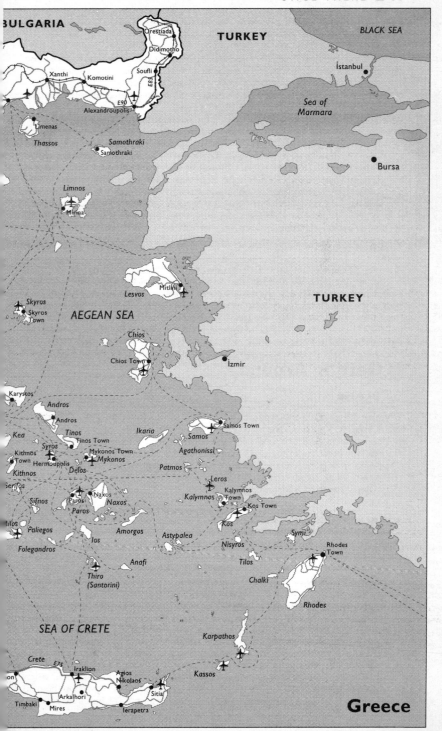

Greece

BUSINESS HOURS

Most **shops** close on Sundays; only restaurants, cafes, and bakeries remain open. During the week business hours vary, but most places open early (around 7am), close after 2pm for a siesta, and re-open at roughly 6pm. Most **banks** are open Monday-Friday 8am-1:30pm, and in some larger cities, open again 3:30-6pm. Banks offer the best **currency exchange** rates. **Post offices** are generally open Monday through Saturday 7:30am to 2pm. The **OTE**, the Greek phone company, is often open until 7:30pm or later in larger cities. Shops and **pharmacies** are open Monday, Wednesday, and Saturday 8am-2:30pm and Tuesday, Thursday, and Friday 8am-1pm and 5-8:30pm. There's usually a pharmacy open 24 hours on a rotating basis; its address should be posted on the doors of all other pharmacies or in the local daily newspapers. **Grocery stores** have longer hours. Government-run **museums** and **archaeological sites** close on Mondays, and have slightly shorter hours from mid-October to mid-May. On holidays, sights often have Sunday opening hours and, in many cases, do not charge admission on these days. All banks and shops close on major holidays (see **Holidays and Festivals,** p. 595). In general, travelers from punctuality-obsessed countries should be aware that many establishments in Greece have flexible and variable hours.

EMERGENCIES

In each regional section, under **Orientation and Practical Information,** we list police telephone numbers. We also list the telephone numbers for ambulances, medical emergency centers, local hospitals, clinics, and pharmacies. Emergency phone numbers, applicable throughout most of Greece and operating 24 hours, include **police** (tel. 100), **first aid** (tel. 166), **fire** (tel. 199), **hospitals** on duty (tel. 106), and **tourist police** (171 in Athens, 922 7777 for the rest of Greece). For **U.S. citizen's emergency aid** call (01) 722 3652 or 729 4301.

■ Getting Around

BY PLANE

Olympic Airways, 96-100 Syngrou Ave., 11741 Athens (tel. (01) 929 2111), serves many large cities and islands within Greece. While flying is quickest, it may not be the most convenient or flexible option for travel; coverage in some areas is spotty. In the U.S., call the **New York** office, 645 Fifth Avenue, NY 10022 (tel. (800) 223-1226; fax 735-0215). In England, call the **London** office, 11 Conduit St., London W1R OLP (tel. (0171) 409 2400; fax 493 0563). For further flight information within Greece, check the regional **Practical Information** listings of airports, flight destinations, and prices, or pick up an Olympic Airways booklet at any Olympic office.

BY BUS

Spending time in Greece invariably means traveling by bus. Service is extensive in most areas, and fares are cheap. On major highways, buses tend to be more modern and efficient than in the mountainous areas of the Peloponnese or Northern Greece. The **OSE** (see **By Train,** p. 51) offers limited bus service from a few cities. Unless you're sticking close to train routes, **KTEL** bus service should be sufficient.

Always ask an official about scheduled departures (posted schedules are often outdated, and all services are curtailed significantly on Sat. and Sun.), and try to arrive at least 10 minutes ahead of time (Greek buses have a habit of leaving early). In major cities, KTEL bus lines have several different stations for different destinations. In villages, a cafe often serves as the bus station, and you must ask the proprietor for a schedule. Ask the conductor before entering the bus whether it's going to your destination (the signs on the front are often misleading or wrong), and make clear where you want to get off. If the bus passes your stop, stand up and yell *Stasi!* On the road, stand near a *Stasi* (ΣΤΑΣΗ) sign to pick up an intercity bus. KTEL buses are generally green or occasionally orange, while intercity buses are usually blue. For long-distance rides, you should buy your ticket beforehand in the office. (If you don't, you may have to stand throughout the journey.) For shorter trips, pay the conductor after you have boarded. Some lines offer round-trip fares with a 20% discount. In towns and cities, local buses and trolleys charge roughly 80dr for a ride.

BY TRAIN

In general, Greek trains are not quite as comfortable as the sleek, modern lines in northern Europe and have more limited service. Service to some areas is painfully slow, and lines do not go to the west coast. Trains are not very useful for traveling to remote areas or many archaeological sites, either.

New air-conditioned intercity trains have been put into service on many lines and although they are slightly more expensive and rare, they are worth the price. **Eurail** passes are valid on Greek trains. **Hellenic Railways Organization (OSE)** connects Athens to major Greek cities. For schedules and prices in Greece, dial 145 or 147.

BY CAR

Driving might be the ideal way to tour Greece. There are highways on the mainland, and ferries take you island hopping if you pay a transport fee for the car. Drivers should be comfortable with a standard transmission , winding mountain roads, reckless drivers (especially in Athens), and the Greek alphabet. Signs in Greek appear roughly 100m before the transliterated versions, which are placed at the turn-offs.

Agencies quote low daily rates, but these prices exclude the 20% tax and Collision Damage Waiver (CDW) insurance. Without CDW, the driver is responsible for the first 15,000dr worth of damage if theft or accident is not the driver's fault, and the full amount otherwise. CDW insurance (2000dr per day) is strongly recommended. Read the fine print. Some places quote lower rates but hit you with hidden charges, such as exorbitant refueling bills if you come back with less than a full tank, 1½-2½dr per km drop-off or special charge, or 100km per day minimum mileage. Most companies won't permit driving the car outside Greece. Hertz and InterRent rent to 21-year-old drivers, but most other companies rent only to those 23 and older.

The cheaper and larger rental agencies are Just, InterRent, and Retca, with offices in Athens and other mainland cities, as well as on Crete and several islands. **Avis, Hertz, Europcar,** and **Budget** operate throughout Greece; their rates are steeper, but service is reliable. It is often cheaper to make arrangements with these companies while still in your home country.

Foreign drivers are required to have an **International Driver's License** and an **International Insurance Certificate** to drive in Greece; see **Driving Permits and Car Insurance,** p.10). The Automobile and Touring Club of Greece (ELPA), 2 Messogion St., Athens 11527 (tel. 779 7401), provides assistance and offers reciprocal membership to foreign auto club members. They also have 24-hour **emergency road assistance** (tel. 104) and an **information line** (tel. 174; open Mon.-Fri. 7am-3pm).

BY MOPED

Motorbiking is a popular way of touring Greece, especially the islands. Bikes are cheaper than cars and offer more freedom than buses, particularly for visiting remote areas. Plenty of places offer scooters or mopeds for rent, but the quality of bikes, speed of service in case of breakdown, and prices for longer periods vary drastically. Nearly all agencies are open to bargaining. Expect to pay at least 2700dr per day for a 50cc scooter, the cheapest bike still able to tackle steep mountain roads. More powerful cost 20-30% more, and usually require a Greek motorcycle license. Many agencies request your passport as a deposit, but it's wiser just to settle up in advance. If they have your passport and you have an accident or mechanical failure, they may refuse to return it until you pay for repairs. Before renting, ask if the quoted price includes the 20% tax and insurance, or you'll be hit for several hundred unexpected *drachmae*. A word of caution about travel by moped: the majority of tourist-related accidents each year occur on mopeds. Regardless of your experience driving a moped, winding, often poorly maintained mountain roads and reckless drivers make driving a moped hazardous.

BY FERRY AND HYDROFOIL

Ferries are the cheapest way to cross the Mediterranean, but be prepared for delays and hassle (see **By Ferry,** p. 35). Hydrofoils are twice as swift and twice as expensive. Ferry travel is notoriously unreliable. Always confirm your departure times with the tourist or boat office. Don't bother planning an itinerary far in advance. Although boat connections between major islands are frequent during summer, departure times fluctuate from year to year. To get to smaller islands, you often have to change boats several times, and some islands are accessible only a few times per week. Direct connections are less expensive than longer routes (the more stops, the higher the price), but also tend to be less frequent. The English-language weekly newspaper *Athens News* prints summer ferry and Athens bus schedules.

BY FOOT

Let's Go describes hikes and trails in town and city listings; local residents and fellow travelers can suggest even more. Always make sure you have comfortable shoes and a map. Remember that hiking under the hot sun at a high altitude may be more strenuous than you expect. Good sunscreen, a hat, and water are essential.

BY THUMB

Consider fully the risks involved before you decide to hitchhike. *Let's Go* does not recommend hitching as a means of travel. That said, it's hard to generalize about hitching in Greece. Greeks are not eager to pick up foreigners, and foreign cars are often full of other travelers. Sparsely populated areas have little or no traffic. Those who do hitchhike write their destination on a sign in both Greek and English letters, and try to hitch from turn-offs rather than long stretches of straight road.

■ Accommodations

Relative to the U.S. and elsewhere in Europe, Greece's accommodations remain a bargain. Off-season prices average 20-40% cheaper than during high season. Prices quoted in the guide are from summer 1997; expect them to rise by 10-20% in 1998.

HOSTELS

Greek youth hostels are an excellent, reasonable alternative to hotels. At the time of publication, **Hostelling International (HI)** had yet to reach an agreement with Greek hostels, and it endorses only one hostel in the entire country. Nevertheless, hostels that are not currently endorsed by HI are in most cases still safe and reputable. To obtain an HI membership, please refer to **Hostels** on p. 39.

Greek youth hostels generally have fewer restrictions than those farther north in Europe. Most are open year-round and have midnight or 1am curfews (which are strictly enforced, and may leave you in the streets if you come back too late). In summer, they usually stay open from 6-10am and 1pm-midnight (shorter hours in winter). The larger hostels offer breakfast. Some hostels have a maximum stay of five days. It's advisable to book in advance in the summer at some of the more popular hostels in Athens, Santorini, or Nauplion.

If you arrive in Greece without an HI card, you can buy an International Guest Card (2600dr), either from the Greek Youth Hostel Association, 4 Dragatsaniou St., Fl.7, Athens (tel. (01) 323 4107; fax 323 7590) or the Athens International Hostel (HI), 16 Victor Hugo St., Athens (tel. 523 1095).

HOTELS

The government oversees the construction and the seemingly random classification of most hotels. Proprietors are permitted to charge 10% extra for stays of less than three nights, and 20% extra overall in high season (July-Sept. 15). In order to get more *drachmae* out of you, they may only offer their most expensive rooms, compel you to buy breakfast, squeeze three people into a hostel-like triple and charge each for a single, or quote a price for a room that includes breakfast and private shower and then charge extra for both.

If proprietors offer a room that seems unreasonably expensive, stress that you don't want luxuries and they may tell you of a cheaper option. Late at night, in the off season, or in a large town, it's a buyer's market. You may consider bargaining. As a security deposit, hotels may ask for your passport and return it when you leave. You can often leave your luggage in the reception area during the afternoon, though check-out is at 11am or noon. Be skeptical about offers to be driven to a pension or hotel. Let the driver show you the destination on a map; it may be miles out of town.

The tourist police are on your side. If a hotel flagrantly violates the prices shown by law at the front desk or on a chart behind each room's front door, or if you think you've been exploited, threaten to report the hotel to the tourist police. The threat alone often resolves "misunderstandings."

One note on Greek toilets: if a trash container is within reach of the toilet, this is where used toilet paper goes. Flushing toilet paper will probably jam the toilet. Many Greek toilets are flushed by pulling a handle that hangs from the ceiling. Also, some hotels may only have pit toilets; check before accepting a room. Most D- and E-class hotels start at 3500dr for singles and 5000dr for doubles. A hotel with no singles may still put you in a room by yourself. More information is available from the **Hellenic Chamber of Hotels,** 24 Stadiou St., Athens (tel. 323 7193; fax 322 5449).

ROOMS TO LET

Wherever there are tourists, you'll see private homes with signs offering *domatia* (rooms to let). As you arrive at more popular destinations, proprietors hustling their rooms to let will greet your boat or bus. Peddling rooms at bus stops or ports is illegal according to the tourist police. Generally, you should have a set destination in mind and head there. On occasion the rooms offered to you at the port or bus stop may be cheap. Nonetheless, it is imperative that you make owners pinpoint the exact location of their houses. "Ten minutes away, near the beach," can mean a 45-minute hike from the main town. Most rooms are cheap and perfectly dependable. There may not be locks, towels, or telephones, but there may be warm offers of coffee at night and friendly conversation. Then again, in the more touristed areas, there may be more locks than conversation. Prices here are especially variable, so be sure that you're paying no more than you would at a hotel. If in doubt, ask the tourist police: they'll usually set you up with a room and conduct all the negotiations themselves. Most private rooms operate only in high season, and they're a good option for those arriving without reservations. Sleeping on hotel roofs used to be a cheap option. Now it's illegal.

TRADITIONAL SETTLEMENTS

Greece has several traditional villages and buildings which have been preserved and restored by the government in an effort to maintain the country's architectural heritage. The restoration of some Greek villages promises to offer a taste of small town Greek life to visitors and to improve the regional economy. Thus far, more than ten settlements have been converted into guest houses: Makrinitsa and Vizitsa on Mt. Pelion, Mesta on Chios, Psara Island, Fiscardo on Cephalonia, Kapetanakos in Areopolis, and Papingo-Zagohoria in Epirus. There are 12 reconstructed towers in Vathia (Mani) and an expensive hotel in the Kastro in Monemvassia. Doubles range from 5000 to 10,000dr; tourist offices can make reservations and provide information.

With the EU's new open-door policy, European businesses have been buying and tearing down traditional buildings in order to build modern hotels cheaply. In an effort to preserve traditional architecture, conservation groups have been buying traditional settlements.

CAMPING

Camping is an easy way to escape the monotony of barren hotel rooms, hostel regulations, and the other limitations of conventional lodgings. More importantly, it's one of the cheapest ways to spend the night.

In Greece, the GNTO is primarily responsible for campgrounds. Most of the official GNTO campgrounds have good facilities, including drinking water, lavatories, and electricity. The Hellenic Touring Club also runs a number of campgrounds. In addition, Greece has many campgrounds run by private organizations which may include pools, discos, and minimarkets.

The prices charged at campgrounds depend on the facilities; you'll usually pay roughly 1200dr per person, plus 1000dr per tent. GNTO campgrounds tend to be ritzier and more expensive (up to 1700dr in some places).

On many islands, campers just take to the beaches. Free-lance camping outside campgrounds is illegal, but during July and August, when hotels and pensions are booked solid, illegal camping becomes commonplace. Penalties run the gamut from a stern chastisement to a 50,000dr or higher fine. At peak season when camps are crowded, the police may sometimes ignore sleeping-bagged bodies sprawled in the sand. Those who decide to free-lance camp should make sure to clean up after themselves. Many beaches offer beach huts as well as designated camping sections. We urge you to consider the safety risks inherent in free-lance camping and sleeping on beaches. *Let's Go* does not recommend illegal free-lance camping.

▓ Keeping in Touch

Most Greek **post offices** are open Monday-Friday from 7:30am-2pm, although services (such as mailing parcels) may close early. Some larger offices keep longer hours. To register a letter, ask for *systemeno;* for express, *katepeegon;* for air mail, *aeroporikos,* and write "air mail" on the envelope. A letter or postcard to the U.S. costs 120dr to mail and takes as little as four days or as long as two weeks, sometimes longer from smaller villages.

Even if you have no fixed address while in Greece, you can receive mail through the Greek post office's **Poste Restante** (General Delivery) service. Mark the envelope "HOLD," and address it: "Jennifer GANDHI, c/o Poste Restante, Main Post Office, the address of the appropriate office, the postal code, GREECE (in capital letters)." Write "Air Mail" on the side of the envelope and use a first class stamp. If you are expecting Poste Restante to arrive for you after you leave a town, arrange at the post office to have it forwarded to another Poste Restante address. American Express offices hold mail for up to 30 days, but often charge a small fee if you aren't a cardholder or don't use their traveler's checks.

Long-distance and collect **phone calls** and telegrams should be placed at the **OTE** (the Greek Telephone Organization) offices. In small villages, offices are usually open Monday-Friday 7:30am-3pm, in towns 7:30am-10pm (shorter hours or closed on weekends), and in larger cities 24 hours. If you visit one of the latter in the middle of the night, the door may be locked, but ring and they'll let you in. There's often a long line; try, if at all possible, to call early in the morning. You can also purchase a phone card from OTE offices or kiosks to make calls from any of the numerous card phones.

To make **direct calls** to the **U.S.** or **Canada,** dial 001 and then the area code and number. If you plan on talking for a while, ask the other party to call right back, since rates from the U.S. are cheaper. To make **direct calls** from the **U.S.** to **Greece,** dial 011-3, then the city code, then the number. If you call the U.S. collect, you'll be charged the U.S. person-to-person rate; in most cases, you'll still save money over expensive hotel surcharges. To call the U.S. **collect,** dial 008 00 13 11 (AT&T) or 008 00 12 11 (MCI). This method only works on the card phones. To use a **calling card,** see the access numbers on p. 45. Also, complete phone codes are listed in the **appendix,** p. 596. An even better option is buying a *telekarta* for 1000dr (and up) at a kiosk or OTE; you can use it at the ubiquitous *kartotilephona* and buy a new one when it runs out. Slide the card into the phone and press "i" on the phones for English language instructions. Remember the time difference.

LIFE AND TIMES

■ History

ANCIENT GREECE

Archaeological evidence dates the first settlements of Greece to as far back as 6500 BC. Prehistoric agricultural sites existed on the mainland near Thessaloniki, on Crete, and in the Cyclades. Far from the simple-minded farmers one may envision, these pioneers of Greek culture produced pottery, designed crafts, and eventually established regional and international trade routes. On the mainland and Crete, they produced terra cotta votive figurines which they placed on the tops of mountains. Such peak sanctuaries served as religious centers for the deities they worshiped. In the Cyclades, they carved intricate marble statuettes and deposited them in graves.

Eventually, competition for trade routes, increased migration, and cultural diffusion led to more complex lifestyles. By the 3rd millennium BC, the development of weapons, government, social hierarchy, and a written script led to the construction of intricate palaces. During this time, the balance of power shifted to **Minoan Crete,** where the major palaces at Knossos, Gournia, Malia, Phaistos, and Zakro served both as distribution centers and venues for religious activities such as bull leaping and libation pouring. An earthquake and series of tidal waves following the eruption of the Thera volcano allowed the palace at **Knossos** to gain supremacy over an Aegean marine empire and to remain dominant until a third trauma, probably a Mycenaean invasion, shook its walls. In the **Mycenaean Era,** war iconography was common both at Mycenae and Tyrins. Homer's *Iliad* and *Odyssey* most famously chronicle this era.

The **Dark Age** stretched from the 9th to the 11th century BC. Despite the negative connotation of the period's name, the Dark Age was an influential precursor to the **Archaic Period.** Shortly thereafter, the *polis,* or city-state, became the predominant form of political organization. While individual city states were relatively autonomous, Hellenic peoples shared a strong sense of unity. They carefully distinguished themselves from foreigners by referring to non-Hellenes as *Barbaroi,* a term that connoted foreign speech (to them, anything but Greek sounded like *bar bar bar*). The period also saw the birth of the **Olympic Games** as a source of political and athletic pride. Seafaring states like Corinth, Megara, and Miletus established colonies as far away as Spain and the Black Sea, while Sparta and Athens ultimately emerged as the most powerful of the *poli.* Sparta, relatively defenseless on its agriculturally rich plain, developed an extremely militaristic culture. Children were separated from their parents at the age of seven to begin a military life while unhealthy babies were left to die. In addition to its military supremacy, Sparta was an economic and cultural center of Ancient Greece. Athens also reached its pinnacle during this period; philosophy and the first successful attempts at democracy, however limited by contemporary standards, immortalized Athenian life. Despite an intense rivalry which later culminated in war, Sparta and Athens united against the Persian King Darius in the early 5th century BC, defeating the Persians at Salamis and Platea and defending Greece from foreign domination.

The Classical Age often refers to the apex of Athenian civilization, from 480 to 323 BC. In the words of classicist Edith Hamilton, "What was then produced in art and thought has never been surpassed and very rarely equalled, and the stamp of it is on all the art and all the thought of the Western world." The spectacular Acropolis of Athens, including the Parthenon, dates from this period. Athenian playwrights like Sophocles and Aristophanes also wrote during this era. These cultural achievements were made possible by the wealth Athens accrued from trade and its command of the **Delian League**, which had been formed as an alliance against Persia.

The rivalry between Sparta and Athens came to a head in the **Peloponnesian Wars,** which lasted 27 years and ended in a nominal defeat for Athens after a hopeless attack on Syracuse. Athens retained its cultural supremacy, however, even in defeat. Some of Athens's more notable artists (Scopas, Praxiteles), philosophers (Socrates, Plato, Aristotle), and scientists (Hippocrates) found inspiration in the conflict and flourished during this period.

Socrates: A Scholar and a Gentleman?

In some respects, following in the steps of greats like Socrates may have a meaning altogether different from what people have traditionally envisioned. There is no doubt that Socrates was one of the greatest philosophers of all time. His legendary technique of using questions to sway his students and listeners has been immortalized as the "Socratic Method." Socrates did not write down any of his teachings, so all that is known of his work comes from the writings of his students, Plato and Xenophon. In *Oeconomicus*, Xenophon portrays Socrates not only as a great logician but also as a man with a keen knowledge of agriculture. Similarly, Plato immortalized the power of his mentor's intellect in works like *Dialogues*. Evidence suggests, however, another side to Socrates not as well-known as his philosophical brilliance. In *Symposium*, Plato describes some of Socrates's scholarly gatherings as raucous drinking parties full of lewd comments and jokes. Socrates is alleged to have been responsible for light-hearted comments like "Is that a Doric column in your toga, or are you just happy to see me?" While some may argue about the propriety of such remarks, Socrates appears to have had a quick wit and a real sense of humor.

In the midst of the Peloponnesian War a new political force was gaining strength in **Macedonia.** Between 360 and 320 BC, the Macedonians, under King Philip II, conquered many Greek cities. After establishing a powerful confederacy known as the Hellenic League of Corinth in 338 BC, **Alexander the Great,** King Philip's illustrious son, embarked on an historic expedition in 336 BC to crush the extensive Persian Empire. In only 13 years, Alexander amassed one of the largest empires the world has ever seen, spreading Hellenic rule deep into Africa and as far east as India.

Following Alexander's death, violent conflicts ravaged his empire. Nevertheless, Hellenic culture continued to spread throughout the region. In 146 BC, after 50 years of skirmishes and political intrigue, Rome filled the power vacuum left after the fall of Greece. While Roman legions took hold of Greek lands, Hellenic culture took hold of Roman society. The Romans adopted what they believed to be the best aspects of the Greek cultural legacy and added their own improvements and innovations to create a new culture which would be enormously influential around the world. By the middle of the first century AD, the culture of Alexandria and Antioch had begun to surpass Hellenism in reputation if not in scope. Two hundred years later, after the conversion of the Roman Empire to Christianity and the establishment of the **Byzantine Empire,** the focal point of Hellenic culture finally shifted from the Peloponnese to Byzantium.

Although Greek culture remained strong following the Frankish conquest of Byzantium in 1204, Greece suffered a more devastating conquest in 1453. Byzantium, renamed Constantinople after emperor **Constantine,** fell to the Ottomans, ushering in four centuries of Ottoman rule. During this time, Greek culture retreated to the private sphere, centering around village life and the Greek Orthodox church.

GREEK INDEPENDENCE

After 400 years of Ottoman rule and numerous false starts, Peloponnesian and Aegean rebels began battling Ottoman armies in early 1821, eventually declaring independence on March 25. From the start, foreigners took an interest in the Greek nationalist cause. First to intervene on behalf of the nationalists was the leader of Egypt, Muhammad Ali. In 1827, at the **Battle of Navarino,** European intervention in the form of the British, French, and Russian navies defeated the Ottoman fleet, ending Ottoman control of Greece.

After their intervention, the three European powers took the lead role in determining Greece's future. They drew up borders for the infant state incorporating all the territories with an ethnic Greek majority, but not all of the modern Greek state. Consequently, Greek politics for the next hundred years were driven by the vision of the **Megali Idhea** (Great Idea) which called for the unification of the scattered Greek population around the Mediterranean into a unified state. Although major lands were indeed added to the Greek state (e.g., Crete), the ultimate goal of controlling Istanbul remained elusive.

MODERN HISTORY

The assassination of Greece's first elected president thwarted the country's first attempts at modern democracy. After the assassination, European powers tried to create a constitutional monarchy in Greece by installing the German Prince Otho as King. In 1843, the military forced the reticent Otho to finally agree to a constitution, which he proceeded to ignore. Twenty years later Otho was unseated and replaced by King George I (of Denmark). George I made some half-hearted attempts at land reform and tried to develop Greece's infrastructure, but the country remained predominantly agricultural throughout the 19th century, with most capital concentrated in the hands of a few large families.

In 1910, the election of Eleftherios Venizelos as premier inaugurated a period of economic development and geographic expansionism. The **Balkan Wars** of 1912-13 resulted in Greece conquering Crete and parts of Thessaly and Macedonia. Due to the new king's ties with Germany, Greece remained neutral during much of WWI. Venizelos, however, saw the war as a chance to expand Greece's borders and finally realize the *Megali Idhea*. He set up his own revolutionary government, which entered the war in 1917. At Versailles, Venizelos pressed Greek claims to Smyrna (Izmir), but Allied distaste for expansion, Venizelos's defeat in the 1920 elections, and the failed Anatolian campaign against Turkey dashed Greek aspirations. Far from gaining additional territory, Greece agreed to a population exchange with Turkey, resulting in the forced resettlement of millions of Greeks and Turks who had been living in the other country.

> On October 28, 1940, his famous "Οχι!" (No) to Mussolini's demand to occupy Greece brought the country into WWII.

The next decade saw a chaotic succession of monarchies, military rule, and brief intervals of democracy. **General Metaxas,** appointed prime minister in 1936, was an autocrat and ardent Greek nationalist. On October 28, 1940, his famous "Οχι!" (No) to Mussolini's demand to occupy Greece brought the country into WWII. In 1941, Greece fell to German invaders. For the next four years, the Axis powers occupied Greece, resulting in the destruction of ancient sites, widespread starvation, large-scale executions, and the Nazi extermination of Greece's Jewish community, which had been among the largest in the Balkans. The communist-led EAM/ELAS organized resistance which received broad popular support. But Churchill's reluctance to allow a communist movement to ascend to power made for a difficult transition to a post-liberation government, and civil war broke out in 1947. Ultimately, Greece became one of the first arenas of American Cold War military intervention. The U.S. provided vast quantities of aid and numerous military advisers to the Greek government as part of the **Truman Doctrine** and **Marshall Plan** in an attempt to contain the spread of communism. Consequently, the last ELAS guerillas were defeated in 1949. During the next 15 years the U.S. continued its involvement in Greek politics.

On April 21, 1967, the army, apparently feeling threatened by increasing liberalism and political disarray, staged a coup that resulted in rule by a junta for seven years. The regime made extensive use of torture, censorship, and arbitrary arrest to maintain power, but it also encouraged foreign investment and therefore continued to enjoy U.S. support. Martial law suppressed student demonstrations in Athens in 1973, and a year later, General Ionnidis's attempt to overthrow Cyprus's president provoked a Turkish invasion of Cyprus that ultimately led to the junta's downfall. Former president Karamanlis returned from his self-imposed exile to take power. As the new prime minister, Karamanlis orchestrated parliamentary elections and organized a referendum to determine the fate of the government. After the monarchy was defeated by a two-thirds vote, a constitution was drawn up in 1975 which established a parliamentary government with a ceremonial president appointed by the legislature.

Under Prime Minister **Andreas Papandreou,** the leftist Panhellenic Socialist Movement (PASOK) won landslide electoral victories in 1981 and 1985. Papandreou promised a radical break with the past and initially oversaw the passage of women's rights legislation and advances in civil liberties. But he also pursued economic nationalization and economic austerity policies in exchange for a European Community (EC) loan. At the same time, Papandreou's heated anti-NATO rhetoric and his friendship with Qadhafi and Arafat sparked international alarm. In September, 1988, Papandreou underwent major heart surgery. He attempted to run the country while hospitalized, refusing to appoint an interim leader. After returning to work, Papandreou discovered an embezzlement scandal involving George Koskotas, the chair of the Bank of Crete, which threatened to implicate a number of government officials in corruption and bribery. After Koskotas made allegations against Papandreou himself, the beleaguered prime minister managed to keep only 125 seats in the 300-seat parliament.

> After the monarchy's defeat, a constitution was drawn up which established a parliamentary government

In the wake of the scandals **Tzannis Tzannetakis,** who was accepted by both conservatives and leftists, became Prime Minister-designate through a compromise decision of the communist-right coalition. As part of the compromise, the opposing conservative New Democracy Party (*Nea Demokratia;* ND) and the Communist Party of Greece (*Kommunistiko Komma Ellados;* KKE) forged a short-term alliance to oppose the incumbent socialist leadership. In 1990, after three general elections within the space of 10 months, **Constantine Mitsotakis** of the ND became Prime Minister. Although the ND was only able to obtain 47% of the total vote, the vagaries of Greek electoral law left the party with a slim majority in parliament.

Mitsotakis attempted to lead Greece into the mainstream of European politics and to solve some of the country's festering economic and diplomatic problems. In an attempt to bring Greece's huge debt under control, he imposed an austerity program that limited wage increases and authorized the sale of state enterprises. The state agencies, however, provided jobs for large numbers of Greeks who valued the security of work in the public sector. As a result, he lost a 1993 emergency election, and Andreas Papandreou returned to power. In January 1996, Papandreou finally stepped down due to persisting health problems. His Socialist Party named **Constantinos Simitis** as its new Prime Minister. Elections in September 1996 maintained the Socialists in power with Simitis still as prime minister.

■ Religion

Worship of the **pantheon** of pre-Classical and Classical gods and goddesses ended after the death of the Roman Emperor Julian. In the post-classical period, Greece saw the rise of cults associated with mysteries like the Eleusinian and Orphic, in which members enacted rituals associated with the afterlife. Participants swore to keep the rituals secret, so almost all that's known of the mysteries comes from disapproving Christian authors.

Power and influence of the **Orthodox Church** rapidly grew following the conversion of Constantine. The Christian faith had been officially permitted by the Edict of Milan, issued by Emperor Licinius in 313. Constantine, for his part, summoned the first of seven Ecumenical Councils, held in Nicaea, in order to codify the tenets of the faith. During that time Christianity flourished in ascetic monastic communities such as those on Mt. Athos and at Meteora. The schism between East and West occurred, according to some scholars, in 1054 when three legates of the Pope came to the Church of the Holy Wisdom (Hagia Sophia) in Constantinople and placed a Bull of Excommunication at the altar. During the middle of the 9th century, Orthodox missionaries spread Christianity to Slavic peoples in Russia, Serbia, Romania, and Bulgaria. The Patriarch of Constantinople was recognized as the head of an Orthodox Christian "nation." The Ottomans tolerated Christians, but required them (as with all non-Muslims) to pay a special tax. Today, Greek Orthodoxy is the **national religion,** although the constitution guarantees freedom of religion. The Church includes the archbishop of Athens, 85 bishops in 77 dioceses, and 7500 parishes.

Like the Catholic Church, Greek Orthodoxy insists upon the hierarchical structure of the church, Apostolic succession, the episcopate, and the priesthood. Rome upholds the universal jurisdiction and infallibility of the Pope, but Greek Orthodoxy stresses the infallibility of the church as a whole and does not have cardinals or a pope. The Greek Orthodox believe the Spirit proceeds through the Father, while Catholics believe that the Spirit proceeds from the Father and the Son. Timothy Ware's *The Orthodox Church* provides a thorough description of both the history of the church and the exegesis behind Greek Orthodox beliefs. Greek Orthodox priests, who are easily recognizable by their long black robes, beards, and cylindrical hats, are closely associated with their parishes. Celebrations in churches include weddings, baptisms, and celebrations on the feast day of the patron saint.

■ Language

The language barrier that tourists find upon entering Greece may not crumble as easily as one may expect. Pronunciation, dialects, and vocabulary vary from region to region, from Greece to Cyprus. Although most Greek youths under the age of 25 speak at least marginal English, bus destinations, many all-night pharmacies, advertisements, and street signs are in Greek. It may be helpful to brush up on the **Greek alphabet** before you go. Learning how to read ferry schedules may be more important than being able to ask for directions to the Acropolis if you can't understand the reply. If you're at a loss for words, most tourist agencies and the trusty tourist police speak English and are willing to help.

Be conscious of Greek body language. To indicate a negative, Greeks lift their heads back abruptly (as if they're actually nodding "yes"), while raising their eyebrows. To indicate the affirmative, they emphatically nod once. Greeks wave a hand up and down in a gesture that seems to say "stay there" when they mean "come." Be careful when waving goodbye; keep your fingers loose because gesturing with an open palm and extended fingers may be interpreted as an insult. Also, eye contact is a key way for a Greek man to communicate with a woman. Be aware that returning the intense glare is another way of saying, "yup, I'm interested—approach me."

A note on transliteration: There is no fully satisfactory system of transliterating one alphabet to the other. Greek letters do not have an exact correspondence with English letters. Like those of the Greek government, *Let's Go*'s transliterations are different for each word; the process follows no rigid rules, but is based on historical connotation, local usage, and chance. Bear in mind that when we write "ch," we're trying to represent the guttural "h" sound; for a more detailed explanation, see **Greek pronunciations,** p. 599.

■ Art and Architecture

DECORATIVE ARTS

Ancient Greek art can be divided into periods roughly corresponding to historical eras. During the **Bronze Age** (3000-1100 BC), the Minoans and Mycenaeans produced exquisite pottery, detailed wall paintings, intricate jewelry, bronze implements, religious icons, and earthquake-proof architecture. Bull's heads, horns of consecration, marine life, and human figures were popular Bronze Age subjects.

In the **Geometric Period** (900-700), artists developed new techniques and more expressive styles of sculpture and painting. Pottery decoration became more elaborate; jars were completely covered with bands of meanders, zig-zags, and identically posed animals and people. Architects of the time created simple structures and designed one-room temples with columned porches and raised altars. Examples of Geometric architecture are concentrated at Olympia.

The **Archaic Period** (700-480) marked the transition from the Geometric Period to the more elaborate and realistic forms of the Classical Period. The cylindrical Doric column and the fluted Ionic column were developed in this period. At the end of the 7th century, large-scale standing figural sculptures appeared in sanctuaries. These *kouroi* (feminine, *kori*) evolved into more graceful, simplified figures. The depiction of life and movement became prime concerns in sculpture. Vase painting similarly became more concerned with a realistic portrayal of life. The rigid friezes of marching animals and people of the Geometric Period were replaced with narrative scenes from mythology and later, with genre scenes. The black figure technique, in which figures were glazed black and details incised into them, gave artists greater precision. At the end of the 6th century, vase painters adopted the Attic red-figure technique in which the figures were emblazoned against a black background and the details painted in with a fine brush.

The arts flourished during the **Classical Period** (480-323), as Athens reached the pinnacle of its cultural, military, and economic power under Pericles and his successors. Sculptors such as Praxiteles and Scopas developed the heroic nude form, which idealizes the human body's severe and somber beauty. The Olympia Museum houses Praxiteles' statue of Hermes holding the baby Dionysus. Architecture of the Classical period, like Athens' Parthenon, features greater spaciousness, fluidity, and grace than the massive temples of the Archaic Period.

ARCHITECTURE

The famous Corinthian column, a fluted column with a multi-leafed top, was first designed during the **Hellenistic Period** (323-first century BC). The Monument of Lysicrates in Athens typifies this architectural design. Several amphitheaters were built at this time, most notably those at Argos and Epidavros, where the acoustics are so precise that more than 2000 years after their construction, a coin dropped on the stage can be heard in the theater's last row. The Romans adopted the Hellenistic style and introduced it to the rest of Europe.

In 395 AD, the Roman Empire split into the Western Empire and the Eastern (or Byzantine) Empire. As Constantine Christianized the Byzantine Empire, Greek artists began to incorporate Christian symbols into their work. During the **Byzantine Period** (500-1200), many churches were built and Christian iconography developed an elaborate repertoire of symbols. Figures of veneration generally appeared in symbolic postures, the most unusual of which is the *anapezousa*, or sleeping Christ, in which the Christ figure is depicted lying down with his eyes open, expressing God's vigilance at all times. The most notable examples of Byzantine art include the monasteries built at Osios Loukas, Daphni, Mt. Athos, and Meteora, as well as the churches at Mystra. The churches were built in a cruciform style, with a narthex (small chamber) added at one end and an apse (half-dome) at the other. The transept, or crossing, of the two lengths of the church was capped by a domed ceiling. Byzantine artists created beautiful, ornate icons and mosaics to decorate their churches. A mosaic of Christ *Pantocrator* (Creator of All Things) usually adorns the dome or apse.

MODERN ART IN GREECE

Nationalist sentiment after the Greeks attained independence from the Ottomans led the government to subsidize Greek art. The Polytechniou, Greece's first modern art school, was founded in 1838. Many artists since have gone abroad to study and **Modern Greek Art** has followed the European artistic trends of the 19th and 20th centuries. Theophilos, Alexis Kontoglou, George Bouzanis, Yiannis Spiropoulos, Sotiris Sorongas, and Michael Tombros are among the familiar modern Greek artists.

Greek **folk art** continues to fascinate both the most casual onlooker and the discerning shopper. Handicrafts include hand-painted, polychromatic terra cotta bowls and ceramics; thick, wooly woven blankets and mats; polished metalwork; intricately carved wooden furniture and gadgets; finely embroidered linens and shirts; and handmade lace. Old women try to sell these goods on the street, and many visitors are lured by their colorful offerings, sun-worn crinkles, and big brown eyes.

▓ Literature

CLASSICAL AND BYZANTINE WRITING

The earliest appearances of the Greek language are Minoan palace record tablets inscribed in duo-syllabic scripts called **Linear A and B.** These treasury records, somewhat uninspiring in content and probably dating from the end of the Bronze Age (roughly 1100 BC), were often preserved, ironically, by baking in the fires that destroyed the palaces themselves. From the 11th to the 8th centuries BC, the Greeks were generally illiterate, and it was not until the **Homeric** *Iliad* and *Odyssey* that written material first appears. Scholars still question whether Homer actually composed these works. While the stories show evidence of origin in an oral tradition, it is possible that either Homer or a group of poets worked on the actual hard copy. **Hesiod,** roughly Homer's contemporary, composed *Works and Days,* a farmer's-eye view of life, as well as the *Theogony,* the first systematic account in Greek of the creation of the world and the exploits of the gods. During the 7th century BC, **Archilochus** of Paros began to write anti-heroic, anti-Homeric elegies, including the often-imitated fragment in which he expresses no shame at abandoning his shield in battle to save his own life. On the island of Lesvos, during the 5th century, the gifted lyric poet **Sappho** and her contemporary **Alcaeus** sang of love and the beauty of nature. Pindar (518-438), acclaimed by the ancients as the greatest of lyric poets, wrote Olympic odes commissioned by nobles to commemorate athletic victories.

> **Scholars still question whether Homer actually composed the "Iliad" and "Odyssey."**

Literature flourished in the **Classical Period. Aeschylus, Sophocles,** and **Euripides** developed ritualistic dramas and staged innovative tragedies while **Aristophanes** produced raucous comedies. Orators like Gorgias practiced rhetoric, and the sophists taught methods of philosophical dialogue. Herodotus, the so-called "Father of History," captured the monumental battles and personalities of the Greco-Persian conflict in the *Persian Wars* while **Thucydides** immortalized the Athenian conflict with Sparta in his *Peloponnesian Wars.* Callimachus (c. 305-240) wrote Alexandrian elegies, of which only fragments remain. His influence, was felt during the Alexandrian revival in Rome, when poets like **Catullus** took his warning *mega biblion, mega kakon* (long book, big bore) to heart.

During the **Byzantine Era,** religious poetry flourished, though not necessarily to the exclusion of secular works. Photios (c. 820-893 AD), who was twice appointed Patriarch of Constantinople, admired the "pagan" works of Homer and encouraged their study. Photios himself wrote several important works, including the massive *Biblioteca.* Later, under the Franks (1204-1460), Greeks developed the pseudo-historical romance, including *Life of Alexander,* and personal love poems, such as *Eroto-paegnia* (Love Games). **Bandits** composed stirring folk ballads in the 16th century when they weren't raiding Ottoman installations.

1821 AND BEYOND

The **Ionian School** (beginning with the revolution in 1821) saw the rise of **Andreas Kalvos** (1796-1869) and **Dionysios Solomos** (1798-1857). Kalvos' lyrical poetry, known for powerful tributes to freedom, earned him high esteem among modern poets. Solomos is often called the "national poet of Greece," and his *Hymn to Liberty* became the Greek national anthem. During the second half of the 19th century, revolutionary hero John Makriyiannis (1797-1864) wrote his vivid *Memoirs,* considered a masterpiece of Greek literature. The 20th century has seen the emergence of many poets, including Angelos Sikelianos, Constantine P. Cavafy, and Kostas Varnales. Cavafy, who won the Nobel Prize in 1963, has had a wide-ranging influence, attracting the attention of writers such as E.M. Forster and W.H. Auden. Also among modern greats are Kostas Karyotakes and the lyricist Nikos Karvounes, who was the first to translate Walt Whitman's works into Greek.

Greek writers produced a wide variety of poetry in the 20th century. While **George Seferis's** poems evoke the legacy of the past, the mystical, erotic works of 1979 Nobel laureate **Odysseus Elytis** celebrate nature. Yiannis Ritsos blends revolutionary and mythological symbolism. Stratis Haviaris' *When The Tree Sings* depicts WWII through the eyes of a young boy. Perhaps the best known modern Greek author is **Nikos Kazantzakis.** His many works include *Odyssey,* a modern sequel to the Homeric epic, *Report to Greco, Zorba the Greek* (1946), and *The Last Temptation of Christ* (1951), of which the latter two were adapted for the cinema.

The landscape of Greece has also inspired some of the more inventive travel writing by English-speaking authors, such as Edward Lear's lively journals of his years in Greece, Henry Miller's classic *The Colossus of Maroussi,* and the varied works of Lawrence and Gerald Durrell, who lived in a house still visible on Corfu (see p.351).

■ Classical Mythology

Greek mythology is second only to the Bible in its influence on the Western imagination. Greek myths were passed from generation to generation, region to region, and gradually embellished to reflect local concerns. The anthropomorphic gods and goddesses lived as immortal beings with divine power. Often tired of the tedium of divinity, they descended to earth to intervene romantically, mischievously, or combatively in human affairs. Traditionally, there are **14 major deities:** Zeus, king of gods; his wife Hera, who watches over child-bearing and marriage; Poseidon, god of the sea; Hephaestus, god of smiths and fire; Aphrodite, goddess of love and beauty; Ares, god of war; Athena, goddess of wisdom; Apollo, god of light and music; Artemis, goddess of the hunt; Hermes, the messenger god and patron of thieves and tricksters; Hades, lord of the underworld and wealth; Demeter, goddess of the harvest; Dionysus, god of wine; and Hestia, goddess of the hearth.

In addition to the gods, many humans and minor deities figured prominently in Greek mythology. The three Fates—Atropos, Clotho, and Lachesis—spun, measured, and snipped the threads of humans' lives. The Furies, also optimistically called *Eumenides,* or "kindly ones," punished evildoers. The nine Muses brought inspiration to poets, artists, and musicians. Dryads and naiads inhabited trees and streams; nymphs cavorted in the fields; satyrs, or goat-men with long beards and tails, frolicked with maenads in the holy groves. Humans had their place in mythology as well, though not always willingly: the talented weaver Arachne, because she dared compete with Athena, was turned into a spider, lending her name to taxonomy; Tantalus was condemned to stand in a pool in Tartarus, forever tormented by hunger and thirst and surrounded by food and water just beyond his grasp; and Europa was ravished by Zeus disguised as a bull.

The extramarital exploits of **Zeus** are even more infamous than those of less powerful but equally randy minor deities. Zeus was a sexual gymnast, ready and willing to bed down with just about anyone, as long as his baleful wife Hera wasn't looking. Zeus' mortal lovers, however, were not always willing or easily accessible: Danae, imprisoned in a tower by her father, was impregnated by Zeus in the form of a golden shower; Ganymede, a Trojan shepherd, was snatched up from earth to be the cupbearer of the gods. Worse still for mortals, Hera, powerless to injure her husband directly, would lavish her vengeance on the object of his lust. Io was turned into a cow and chased by an enormous gadfly; Leto, pregnant with Artemis and Apollo, was forbidden to rest on solid ground until the itinerant island of Delos lent its shore for her to give birth; Callisto, who got off relatively easy, was changed into a bear. Semele, one of Zeus' voluntary cohorts, dissolved into ash. The overarching lesson of stories involving Zeus and sex seems to be that **mortals never win.**

An accompanying book of mythology might inspire your Greek travels. Both Edith Hamilton's and Bullfinch's *Mythology* are eminently readable. Another excellent choice is Ovid's *Metamorphoses,* a principal source for our knowledge of mythology. Keep in mind that the 1st-century AD Roman poet uses the gods' Latin names (Jupiter for Zeus, Venus for Aphrodite, etc.).

■ Music and Dance

Musical instruments date from the Bronze Age on Crete, reinforcing scholars' belief that early poetry was often sung or chanted. As drama evolved, **choruses** played a major role in Greek plays. Before the 5th century BC, the Greeks had no system of musical notation, yet they managed to develop a **theory of harmonics.**

Throughout the Byzantine era, **folk music and dances** assumed regional traits: the south emphasized tragic and mourning dances, the north produced war and rural harvest dances, and religious and burial dances were performed on Crete. These regional influences are still evident. For example, pontic-influenced dances like *kotsari* are danced only in the north, while the islands have their own dances called *nisiotiko.* Nonetheless, dances have become somewhat more standardized. *Tsamiko* and *kalamatiano,* for example, are now danced throughout the country.

Today it's common to see a wide circle of locals and tourists, hands joined, dancing to the tunes of clarinets and lyre (originating in Crete). The leader of the dance per-

---

Cries from the Underground

Much of Greek lyric song is romantic and poetic, but at the end of the 19th century a new style of music began to develop on Turkey's western coast that would unsettle these classical notions. *Rembetika* was popularized in Greek cities by convicts who embraced the lustful strains of the music and lamented about smoking hashish and life on the run. During the exchange of populations with Turkey in the 1920s, the music was invigorated by the scores of refugees who lived in shantytowns on the outskirts of major Greek cities. This music that had been the voice of the underground emerged, in its mature state, as the cry of the underclass. *Rembetika,* the music of Smyrna cafés and Greek jails, is still played on the *bouzouki* and *baglama* and features lyrics such as these from the *Little Old Monk* (1929). For more information, consult Holst's *Road to Rembetika.*

> I'll become a little old monk and wear a monkish habit
> And I'll carry a string of beads, sweetheart, just to please you.
> Your lips tell me one thing…and your friends tell me another.
> I'd rather be stabbed twice…than hear the words you're saying.
> I fixed myself up as a monk, stayed in a monastery.
> Then I fell into your hands, nagging bitch,
> And got myself defrocked.

forms the fancy footwork, winding around a white handkerchief and twirling around in circles, sometimes throwing in a few backward somersaults. Don't hesitate to join in; the dance steps for the followers are repetitive, so you'll learn quickly. Just stamp your feet, yell *Opa*, and have fun.

To see authentic Greek dancing, check out the **Dora Stratou Folk Dance Theatre,** (tel. 324 4395, 921 4650; fax 324 6921, email gzdance@hol.gz), which performs at the open-air theater at Philopappus Theatre and on 8 Scholion St., both in Athens, at 10pm from May through September. From June through October, in the old city of Rhodes, the **Nelly Dimoglou Troupe** features dances from northern and central Greece and the Dodecanese. Greek dancing is particularly enjoyable at one of the many village or church festivals held throughout the summer in various parts of Greece. Generally, the festival takes place when the church celebrates its patron saint. Check the **Entertainment** listings in major cities for additional information and ask tourist officials about local festivals.

Rembetika, a grittier, more urban variety of music that developed in the 1930s, uses traditional Greek instruments to sing about drugs, prison, and general alienation. *Rembetika* became popular again in the 1970s but is played only in a few clubs today. Greek popular music continues to evolve, incorporating influences from *rembetika* as well as gypsy and traditional folk music.

■ Food and Drink

Greek food is simple and healthful. Recent medical studies have highlighted the Greek diet as a good model for healthy eating; its reliance upon unsaturated olive oil and vegetables has prevented heart attacks in a fairly sedentary population.

A Greek restaurant is known as a *taverna* or *estiatorio* while a grill is a *psistaria.* Before ordering, see what others are eating. If you don't know the word for what you want, point. Most places have a few fixed-price dishes available anytime; make sure they have your dish before you sit down. Waiters will ask you if you want salad, appetizers, or the works, so be careful not to wind up with mountains of food (Greek portions tend to be large). Don't be surprised if there is an extra charge for the tablecloth and bread, often listed on the menu as the *couvert.* Service is always included in the check, but it is customary to leave a few *drachmae* as an extra tip.

Breakfast can be bread, *tiropita* (cheese pie), or a pastry with *marmelada* (jam) or *meli* (honey). A particular breakfast favorite among Greeks is *patsa* (a soup made of calf or lamb tripe), served only in the early morning and particularly soothing to a travel-weary stomach. **Lunch** is eaten between noon and 3pm. The **evening meal** is a leisurely affair served late by American standards, usu-

> A breakfast favorite among Greeks is "patsa," a soup made of calf or lamb tripe, particularly soothing to a travel-weary stomach.

ally after 8 or 9pm, and as late as 11pm to 1am during the summer in the larger cities. Greek restaurants divide food into two categories—*magiremeno,* meaning cooked, or *tis oras* (of the hour), indicating grilled meat. The former is generally cheaper. *Tis oras* includes grilled *moschari* (veal), *arni* (lamb), or *koto-poulo* (chicken), served with *patates* (french fries), *rizi* (rice), or *fasolia* (beans). Popular *magiremeno* dishes include *moussaka* (chopped meat and eggplant covered with a rich cream *béchamel*), *pastitsio* (a lasagna-like dish of thick noodles with *béchamel*), *yemista* (tomatoes and peppers stuffed with rice or meat), *dolmadhes* (grape leaves stuffed with rice and minced meat), and *youvarelakia* (meatballs covered with egg and lemon sauce). Fried zucchini, stuffed eggplant, *tzatziki* (spicy cucumber and yogurt salad), and/or *horta* (greens, either beet or leeks, served with oil and lemon) accompany meals at most *taverna.* Feel free to order these vegetables as the main dish. **Vegetarians** might also try *spanakopita* (spinach-filled pastry) or *tiropita* (cheese pie in a similar flaky crust). *Briam,* potatoes and other vegetables cooked in oil, is another delicious possibility. **Seafood** is as readily available as you'd expect in a such an ocean-begotten nation, but it's more expensive than you'd think. Don't leave without trying fresh *chtopodi* (octopus) marinated in olive oil and oregano, and don't miss the *taramosalata* (dip made with caviar) or the *Merenda* (Greece's version of Nutella).

You can hardly avoid *souvlaki,* a large skewer of steak, generally pork or lamb. A *souvlaki pita,* appropriately known as "the budget food of the masses," consists of a pita crammed full of skewered meat and fillings (only about 300dr). Gyros also abound in street vendor fast-food stands. *Bifteki* are a more tender, spicy version of hamburgers; you are usually served two as well as fries. For a healthy staple at a *taverna,* try a *choriatiki,* a "Greek" salad containing olives, tomatoes, onions, cucumbers, and hefty chunks of feta cheese. (Ask for it *horees ladhi* if you don't want it swimming in olive oil.) Usually accompanied by a basket of bread and a glass of water, these salads make inexpensive and satisfying meals.

■ Media

Several years ago, much of Greek media was state-owned and thus prone to expositions of government policy. More recently, private companies have bought several outlets. Many Greek language **newspapers** are still sensationalistic— akin to New York *Newsday* or London's *Sun.* A few reputable papers are *Eleftherotipia, Kathimerini* (daily) and *Bima* (published every Sun.). Unlike most of their newsprint counterparts, glossy Greek **magazines** are worthwhile. *Diabazo* and *Anti* are more scholarly journals, *Clique* caters to the teeny-bopper crowd, and *Taxydromos* is a more sophisticated glamor magazine. American and British magazines like *Vogue* and *Cosmopolitan* also circulate (in Greek). The most noticeable change in Greek media has been in the **television** industry. Whereas ERT1 and 2 were the original stations, both state-owned and private channels like Mega Channel and ANT-1 have brought hi-tech production and, of course, more **wacky American sitcoms** to the Greek viewing public. Greek radio plays a wide range of music in large cities, but in the remote locales you'll only be able to tune in that loud Greek-pop that bus drivers insist on playing at full blast during long trips.

■ Sports

Sports fanatics may be quick to associate Greek sports lore with the country's ancient "sound mind, sound body" principle. Although everything from handball to water polo is popular, soccer and basketball are the country's games of choice. Of the several Greek A-League **soccer** teams, three stand out in the hearts and apparel of Greek sports fans: *Olympiakos* (red), *Panathinaikos* (green), and *AEK* (yellow). Even the least devout of sports fans wear their favorite team's colors that, for some, are revered on a level beyond religion. Although British hoodlums don't frequent soccer matches in Greece, the experience is significantly more rowdy than an afternoon at an American baseball game. **Basketball** is the country's newfound passion. The primary teams are the same as in soccer, but unlike the soccer league, Greek basketball is one of the premier European leagues. It has featured such foreign NBA stars as Roy Tarpley, Dino Radja and Dominique Wilkens. *Olympiakos* is another basketball powerhouse. For golfers, there are 18-hole courses in Athens, Rhodes, Corfu, and Porto Carras on Halkidiki. **Tennis** has also gained great popularity among Greeks, especially with the success of native son Pete Sampras. There are public tennis clubs throughout the country. **Watersports** are what most sports enthusiasts who visit Greece dream about. Windsurfing, water skiing, sailing, and other sea sports can be found at most popular beaches. **Scuba diving** is generally forbidden in Greek waters; it is allowed only under supervised conditions in Chalkidiki, Mykonos, Corfu, Cephalonia, and Zakynthos. Surprisingly, **skiing** has become popular among Greeks, and ski resorts can be found throughout the country.

Athens ΑΘΗΝΑ

The city of Athens sits astride a remarkable past and a beckoning future. Still overshadowed by the glory of its ancient inhabitants, modern Athens grew up around the foot of the breathtaking Acropolis. Although war, occupation, liberation and expansion have perhaps led the city's development and progress astray, recent efforts have made modernization a priority. Visitors harboring mental images of togas and philosophers may be disappointed to find a 20th-century city in every sense of the word—Athens is crowded, noisy and polluted. The neoclassical mansions that graced the city's streets only 30 years ago have largely been replaced by white monolith towers to accommodate a growing population of 4.5 million residents. The Plaka neighborhood, which borders the Acropolis, is one of the few remnants of Athens' ancient grandeur; column-bound temples stand as proud reminders of the faith of the ancient Athenians. Modernity, however, cannot rest on teetering ruins—the city needs a comprehensive subway system, a manageable communications system, and space for its citizens to live. Nevertheless, the city center is a mosaic of Byzantine churches, ancient ruins, neoclassical cafes, traditional outdoor *tavernas* and modern shopping centers. Plagued by the incessant roar and exhaust from buses, cars, and motorcycles, certain areas can be deafening and suffocating.

■ History

A competition between **Poseidon** and **Athena** determined how Athens (*Athena* in Greek) would be named. The gods of Olympus decreed that whoever gave the city the most useful gift would become its patron deity. Poseidon struck the rock of the Acropolis with his trident and salt water came gushing forth. The populace was awestruck, but Athena's wiser gift, an olive tree, won her the right to rule.

Athens was an important town as early as the 16th century BC. Around the 8th century, the city became the artistic center of Greece, known especially for its geometric-style pottery. This initial fame merely foreshadowed the future. After dramatic victories over the Persians at Marathon and Salamis in the 5th century BC, Athens enjoyed a 70-year Golden Age, reaching its apogee under the patronage of Pericles. It was during this time that Iktinos and Kallikrates designed the Parthenon; Aeschylus, Sophocles, and Euripides wrote tragic masterpieces, and Aristophanes penned ribald comedies. Early historians, Herodotus in particular, challenged the assumption that gods, not human beings, govern history. Hippocrates, with a similar interest in human autonomy (and anatomy), developed the study of medicine.

The bloody and drawn-out campaigns of the **Peloponnesian War** (431-404 BC) between Athens and Sparta heralded the demise of Periclean Athens. Political power in Greece then shifted north to the court of Philip of Macedon and his son **Alexander the Great.** Through the 5th and 4th centuries BC, however, Athens remained important as a cultural center, producing three of the most influential western philosophers, Socrates, Plato, and Aristotle, as well as the great orator Demosthenes. By the 2nd century, the ravenous Roman Empire had feasted on Athens and drained the city. By the time the **Byzantine Empire** split off from the foundering remains of the Roman Empire (285 AD), Athens was no more than an overtaxed backwater specializing in Neoplatonism. The city remained the center of Greek education with elaborate institutes of learning, but its status (and buildings) lapsed into ruin when Justinian banned the teaching of philosophy in 529.

Around 1000, **Basil II,** the Holy Roman Emperor of Byzantium, visited Athens. After praying to the Virgin Mary in the Parthenon, Basil ordered craftsmen to restore Athens to its former glory. Under successive conquerors—the Franks in 1205, the Catalans in 1311, and the Accajioli merchant family in 1387—Athens underwent a renaissance. **Ottoman rule** in 1456 and Greek independence in 1821 brought further waves of renovation and restoration. Modern Athens, with its *plateias* (squares),

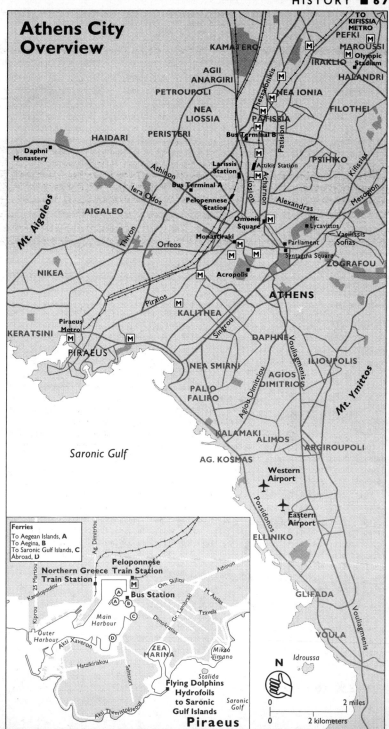

Athens City Overview

KAMATERO

AGII ANARGIRI

PETROUPOLI

NEA LIOSSIA

HAIDARI

PERISTERI

Daphni Monastery

Athinon

Iera Odos

 Thivon

AIGALEO

Mt. Aigaleos

NIKEA

Pirxios

Singrou

KERATSINI

Piraeus Metro

PIRAEUS

Bus Terminal B

Larissis Station

Bus Terminal A

Peloponnese Station

Omonia Square

Monastiraki

Orfeos

Acropolis

KALITHEA

Attikis Station

Liosion

Acharnon

Patision

Thessalonikis

TO KIFISSIA METRO

PEFKI

MAROUSSI

Olympic Stadium

IRAKLIO

HALANDRI

NEA IONIA

FILOTHEI

PATISSIA

PSIHIKO

Kifissias

Mesogion

Alexandras

Mt. Lycavittos

Parliament

Syntagma Square

Vasilissis Sofias

ZOGRAFOU

ATHENS

ZOGRAFOU

DAPHNE

NEA SMIRNI

PALIO FALIRO

Agios Dimitriou

Vouliagmenis

ILIOUPOLIS

AGIOS DIMITRIOS

Saronic Gulf

KALAMAKI

ALIMOS

ARGIROUPOLI

AG. KOSMAS

Mt. Ymittos

Western Airport

Poseidonos

Eastern Airport

ELLINIKO

GLIFADA

Vouliagmenis

VOULA

N

Idroussa

0   2 miles

0   2 kilometers

Piraeus

Ferries
To Aegean Islands, **A**
To Aegina, **B**
To Saronic Gulf Islands, **C**
Abroad, **D**

25 Martiou

Kanelopoulou

Kiprou

Ag. Dimitriou

Northern Greece Train Station

Train Station

Om. Skilitsi

Athinon

Peloponnese Train Station

Bus Station

A

A

B

C

D

Main Harbour

Outer Harbour

Akti Xaveron

Hatzikiriakou

Saltoun

Akti Themistokleous

M. Assias

G. Lambraki

Dimokratias

Tzavela

ZEA MARINA

Mikro Limano

Stalida

Flying Dolphins Hydrofoils to Saronic Gulf Islands

Saronic Golf

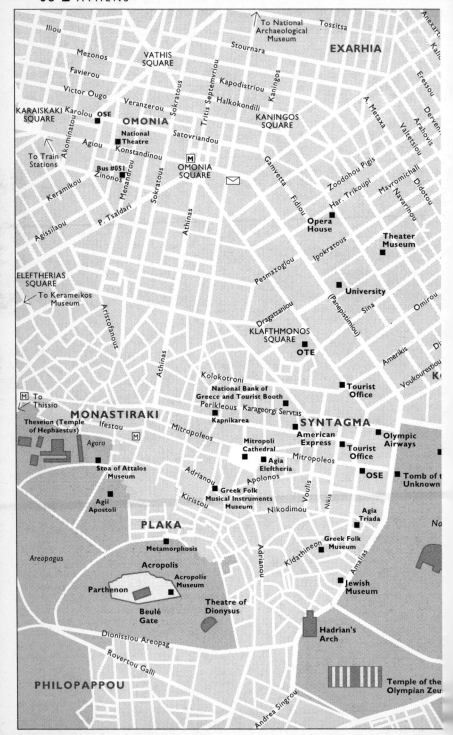

Athens Central City

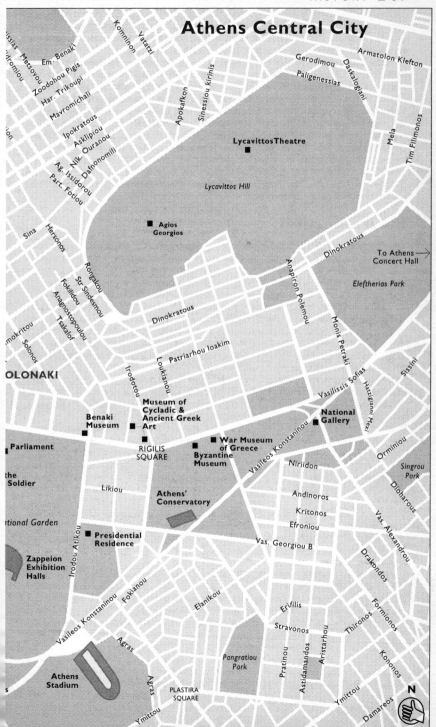

Armatolon Klefton
Gerodimou
Paligenessias
Daskalogiani
Komninon
Vatatzi
Em. Benaki
Zoodohou Pigis
Har. Trikoupi
Mavromichali
Ipokratous
Asklipiou
Nik. Ouranou
Dafnonomili
Ag. Issidorou
Part. Fotiou
Apokarkon
Sinessiou Kirinis
Mela
Tim Filimonos

Lycavittos Theatre

Lycavittos Hill

Sina
Hersonos
Rongakou
Str Sindesmou
Fokilidou
Anagnostopoulou
Tsakalof
mokritou
Solonos

■ **Agios Georgios**

Anapiron Polemou
Dinokratous
To Athens Concert Hall →
Eleftherias Park

Dinokratous
Patriarhou Ioakim
Irodotou
Loukianou
Monis Petraki
Vasilissis Sofias
Hatzigianni Mexi
Sissini

OLONAKI

Benaki Museum ■
Museum of Cyclidic & Ancient Greek Art ■
RIGILIS SQUARE

■ **National Gallery**

■ **Parliament**
the Soldier
tional Garden

War Museum of Greece ■
Byzantine Museum

Vasileos Konstaninou
Niriidon
Orminiou
Singrou Park

Likiou
Athens' Conservatory

Andinoros
Kritonos
Efroniou
Dioharous
Vas. Alexandrou

■ **Presidential Residence**
Irodou Atikou

Zappeion Exhibition Halls

Vas. Georgiou B
Drakondos
Formionos
Thironos

Vasileos Konstaninou
Fokianou
Elanikou
Erifilis
Stravonos
Pratinou
Astidamandos
Aristarhou
Ymittou
Kononos

Agras

Athens Stadium

Agras
Ymittou
PLASTIRA SQUARE
Pangratiou Park
Damareos

N

wide boulevards, and tranquil National Garden, embodies plans drawn up by German architects under the direction of the Bavarian **King Otto,** who was awarded the newly created kingdom of Greece in the late 19th century.

In the 20th century, Athens has grown exponentially in population and industry. In 1923, Greece agreed to a population exchange with Turkey, producing a great burden on the burgeoning city. As with all industrial cities, Athens has also attracted workers from destitute regions of the country. The past century has seen the population of the city explode from 169 families to almost half the population of Greece—4.5 million people. In an attempt to counteract noise and pollution, the transit authority now bans cars from a number of streets in the historic Plaka district and limits driver access downtown on alternate days. The **subway,** only partially completed, has eliminated much of the traffic and noise in the immediate city center, but continual construction adds to the dust. Zeus' thunderbolt now shakes down acid rain, and longtime residents rue the infamous *nephos* (smog cloud) that settles in a most sinister fashion over Athens in summer.

■ Orientation

Coming from either airport, the bus stops at **Syntagma (Constitution) Square.** The center of modern Athens, this bustling plaza is packed with overpriced outdoor cafes, luxury hotels, and flashy banks. A pale yellow Neoclassical building, formerly the royal palace and now home to the Greek Parliament, gazes over the toe-nipping traffic of Syntagma. The **Greek National Tourist Office (EOT), post office, American Express office, transportation terminals,** and a number of **travel agencies** and **banks** surround the square. **Filellinon Street** and **Nikis Street,** parallel thoroughfares which head out from Syntagma towards Plaka, contain many of the city's budget travel offices, cheap hotels, and dance clubs. Unfortunately, Syntagma is currently being torn up for subway construction; cranes and dirt will detract from the square's charm for several more years.

If you come by ferry, you can reach Syntagma Sq. from Peiraias (where the ferries dock) by walking left (facing inland) along the waterfront to Roosevelt St., then taking the subway to Montastiraki. Turn right up Ermou St., and Syntagma Sq. will be a 5-minute walk away.

Northwest of Syntagma, **Omonia Square** is the site of the city's operational central subway station from which trains run to Kifissia (40min.), Monastiraki (3min.), and Peiraias (20min.), among other destinations. Inexpensive shops for food, clothing, and jewelry abound, but with the influx of refugees in recent years, this cosmopolitan area has become increasingly unsafe. There are, however, many cheap lodgings here. Mind your own business and try to be inconspicuous. *Above all, don't travel alone at night.* Two parallel avenues connect Syntagma Sq. to Omonia Sq. (Panepistimiou and Stadiou). The **university** and **library** are on Panepistimiou St., between Syntagma and Omonia. North on Patission St., which intersects the two avenues just before Omonia, is the **National Archaeological Museum.** Both train stations, **Larissis** and **Peloponnese,** are on Konstantinoupoleos St. northeast of **Karaiskaki Square** and can be reached along Deligiani St.

Make use of the free **maps** available at the tourist office. The city map includes bus and trolley routes, while a more detailed street plan graces the pages of *Greece-Athens-Attica* magazine. Athenian geography mystifies newcomers and natives alike; if you lose your bearings, ask for directions back to the well-lit Syntagma or look for a cab. The **Acropolis** provides a useful reference point. Be alert when crossing the street, as drivers rarely pause for pedestrians. Be aware that Athenian streets often have multiple spellings or names. Lysikrateus is also known as Lisicratous or Lissi Kratous; Aiolou as Eolou and Eolu; Victoriou Ougo as Victor Hugo. Panepistimiou St. is commonly called Eleftheriou Venizelou; Peiraias is Tsaldari. Many streets also change names along the way—Amerikis, for example, becomes Lykavittou.

Several publications list general information about Athens. Pick up a free copy of the tourist office's *This Week in Athens*, which gives addresses, hours, and phone numbers for in English for a variety of attractions. News, movie, restaurant, and exhibit listings appear daily in Athens' English-language newspaper, the *Athens News* (300dr). The *Weekly Greek News* (300dr) and *Greece's Weekly* focus on Greek politics and some international news. The monthly *Athenian* magazine features stories about Greek culture.

In summer, businesses are generally open Monday and Wednesday from 8:30am to 3pm; Tuesday, Thursday, and Friday from 8am to 2pm and from 5:30 to 8:30pm, and Saturday from 8am to 3pm. High season officially runs from mid-June to mid-September; however, be aware that each Greek may have his or her own version of "high season" (i.e., May-August, July-August, when you're there).

■ Practical Information

Tourist Office: Information window at the **National Bank of Greece,** 2 Karageorgi Servias, Syntagma Sq. (tel. 322 2545). Bus, train, and ferry schedules and prices; lists of museums, embassies, and banks; colorful brochures on travel throughout Greece. Ask for the detailed Athens map. Open Mon.-Fri. 9am-6:30pm, Sat. 9am-2pm. There is also an office open the same hours in the **East Terminal** of the airport (tel. 969 4500). The **central office,** 2 Amerikis St. (tel. 322 4128), off Stadiou St., is not as helpful as the others. Open summer Mon.-Fri. 11am-2pm; winter Mon.-Fri. 11:30am-2:30pm.

Tourist Police: 77 Dimitrakopoulou St. (tel. 171). English spoken. Open 24hr.

Tourist Agencies: For **ISIC/FIYTO** purchases, see **Identification** (p. 9). In Athens, you can buy the ISIC for 2500dr at either **USIT Youth Student Travel,** 3 Filellinon St. (tel. 324 1884; fax 322 5974; open Mon.-Fri. 9am-5pm, Sat. 10am-2pm), or **I.S.Y.T.S.L.T.D.,** 11 Nikis St., 2nd floor (tel. 322 1267; fax 322 1531; open Mon.-Fri. 9am-5pm, Sat. 9am-1pm). The latter sells FIYTO cards as well. Travel agencies along Nikis and Filellinon St. off Syntagma Sq. offer student discounts on international plane and train travel. **Magic Travel Agency** (formerly **Magic Bus**), 20 Filellinon St. (tel. 323 7471, -4; fax 322 0219), stands out. Extremely competent, English-speaking staff. Open Mon.-Fri. 9am-7pm, Sat. 9am-2:30pm. You might also visit **Consolas Travel,** 100 Aiolou St. (tel. 325 4931; fax 321 0907), next to the post office. They have a second office on 18 Filellinon St (tel. 323 2812). Generally, it is best to shop around and look for specials at the agencies.

Greek Youth Hostel Association, 4 Dragatsaniou St., 7th floor (tel. 323 4107; fax 323 7590), elevators on right as you enter the arcade. Lists hostels in Greece. Open Mon.-Fri. 9am-3pm.

The Hellenic Chamber of Hotels: (tel. 323 7193; fax 322 5449). In the National Bank of Greece next to the tourist office. Provides information and reservations for A, B, C, D, and E-class hotels throughout Greece and some less expensive ones in Athens. All reservations require a cash deposit in trusty *drachmae.* Open Mon.-Fri. 8:30am-2pm, Sat. 9am-12:30pm.

Embassies: Comprehensive listing of embassies available at the tourist office. **Albania,** 1 Karahristrov St. (tel. 723 4412). Open Mon.-Fri. 8:30am-noon. **Australia,** 37 D. Soutsou St. (tel. 644 7303). Open Mon.-Fri. 8:30am-12:30pm. **Bulgaria,** 33 A Stratigov Kalari St. (tel. 721 3039). Open Mon.-Fri. 8:30am-noon. **Canada,** 4 Ioannou Genadiou St. (tel. 725 4011). Open Mon.-Fri. 8:30am-12:30pm. **Czech Republic,** 6 Seferi St. (tel. 671 3755, 671 9701). Open Mon.-Fri. 9am-noon. **European Community,** 2 Vasilissis Sofias (tel. 725 1000). Open Mon.-Fri. 8:30am-1pm. **Germany,** 3 Karaoli Dimitriou St. (tel. 728 5111). Open 9am-noon. **Hungary,** 6 Kalrou St. (tel. 672 5337, 672 3753). Open Mon.-Fri. 8:30am-12:30pm. **Ireland,** 7 Vas Konstantinov Ave. (tel. 723 2771). Open Mon.-Fri. 9am-3pm. **Romania,** 7 Em Benaki St. (tel. 671 8020). Open Mon.-Fri. 8am-1pm. **South Africa,** 60 Kifissias St. (tel. 680 6645). Open Mon.-Fri. 8am-1pm. **Turkey,** 8 Vas Georgiov B. St. (tel. 724 5915). Open Mon.-Fri. 8:30am-12:30pm. **United Kingdom,** 1 Ploutarchou St. (tel. 723 6211), at Ypsilantou St. Open for visas Mon.-Fri. 8:30am-1pm. **United States,** 91 Vasilissis Sofias (tel. 721 2951; fax 645 6282). Open Mon.-Fri. 8:30am-5pm. Call in advance to inquire about hours of specific department you need. Open for visas 8-

11am. **Yugoslavia,** 106 Vasilassis Sofias (tel. 777 4344, 777 4355). Open Mon.-Fri. 8:30am-1pm.

Banks: National Bank of Greece, 2 Karageorgi Servias St., Syntagma Sq. (tel. 322 2738, -7). Open Mon.-Thurs. 8am-2pm and 3:30-6:30pm, Fri. 8am-1:30pm and 3-6:30pm, Sat. 9am-3pm, Sun. 9am-1pm only for currency exchange. American Express, the post office, some hotels, and other banks (list available at tourist office) **exchange currency.** Expect commissions of around 5%. Most banks close at 2pm on weekdays and are closed on weekends. Currency exchange at the airport is available 24hr., but the fee is high.

American Express: 2 Ermou St., P.O. Box 3325 (tel. 324 4975, -9), above McDonald's in Syntagma Sq. Air-conditioned and filled with Americans, the office cashes traveler's checks with no commission, runs a travel agency, holds mail for one month, and provides other special services for cardholders. Open Mon.-Fri. 8:30am-4pm, Sat. 8:30am-1:30pm (only travel and mail services on Sat.).

Flights: From Athens, take the express bus #090 and 091 from either Syntagma Sq. or Stadiou St. near Omonia Sq. Buses run every 30min. from 6am-9pm, every 40min. from 9pm-11:30pm, and then every hour on the ½hr. from 11:30pm-5:30am. **East Terminal,** foreign airlines and some charters; **West Terminal,** Olympic Airways domestic and international service; **New Charter Terminal,** most charters. From the airport to Athens, look to your left after exiting customs for the blue and yellow express buses (160-200dr). A taxi costs 1500-2000dr, with an extra 55dr charge for each piece of luggage. Watch drivers very carefully; some rig the meters. Drivers may be unwilling to pick up travelers laden with luggage and might also make you share a cab. Express buses and cabs are the most reliable travel option.

Trains: Call 145, 146, or 147 for timetables. **Larissis Train Station** (tel. 524 0601) serves northern Greece (Thessaloniki 3720dr) and several European destinations (primarily Eastern Europe). Take trolley bus #1 from El. Venizelou (also called Panepistimiou St.) in Syntagma (every 10min. 5am-midnight, 75dr). **Peloponnese Railroad Station** (tel. 513 1601) is in a Victorian building with a silver roof. From Larissis, exit to your right and go over the foot-bridge, or take blue bus #057 from Eleftheriou Venizelou (every 15min. 5:30am-11:30pm, 75dr). Serves Patras (1580dr) and major towns in the Peloponnese. Also has OSE buses to Bulgaria, Albania, and Turkey. For more info, call **Hellenic Railways (OSE)** (tel. 323 6273).

Buses: Unlike just about anything else in Greece, the KTEL (KTEΛ) buses are punctual, so be there and be square. For Athens and its suburbs, buses are blue and designated by 3-digit numbers. Fare is 100dr. Good for travel across the city, they are also ideal for daytrips to places like Daphni and Kesariani. For longer trips, take the orange or green buses. There are two main blue bus terminals, **Terminal A,** 100 Kifissou St. (tel. 512 4910), and **Terminal B,** 260 Liossion St. (tel. 831 7181). Terminal A serves most of Greece and can be reached by blue bus #051, caught at the corner of Zinonos and Menandrou near Omonia Sq. (every 10min. 5am-11:30pm, 75dr). The "information" booth at Terminal A is a privately-run agency; don't get duped into buying useless "vouchers." Terminal B (Mavromateon stop, at one corner of Areos park), serving some destinations in central Greece, can be reached by blue bus #024, caught at El. Venizelou Panepistimiou St. (every 25min. 5am-midnight, 75dr). Buy a ticket at a kiosk from a station vendor and stamp it yourself at the orange machine on board. Kiosks only sell tickets for Athens and its suburbs; it is a good idea to buy several tickets at once if you intend to use the buses and trolleys frequently during your stay in Athens. If you don't stamp your bus, trolley, or subway ticket (even when it seems nobody is there to make you pay) and hold onto it, you may get caught by police in a spot-check and fined 1500dr for not paying for the 75dr ticket.

Subway: The subway system in Athens is under construction. The 1-line system running from Peiraias Harbor to Kifissia in north Athens with 20 stops in between, including Omonia, is the *elektriko.* A train departs from either end of the line every 10min. 5am-midnight. Tickets are 75dr for local travel and 100dr for greater distances. Buy tickets in the station, at booths, or automatic machines (which do not provide change). As with the bus system, hold on to your ticket.

Trolleys: Yellow, crowded, and sporting 1- or 2-digit numbers. Fare 75dr. Trolleys no longer accept money. Buy a ticket (same as bus ticket) ahead of time at a kiosk. Frequent service; convenient for short hops within the city.

Ferries: Most dock at **Peiraias** and go to all Greek island groups except the Sporades (which leave from Ag. Konstantinos or Volos) and the Ionian Islands (which leave from Patras in the Peloponnese). To: Thera (Santorini) (9hr., 5350dr); Mykonos (6hr., 4380dr); Ios (8hr., 4725dr); Aegina (1¼hr., 1270dr); Paros (5hr., 4260); Rhodes (15hr., 7890dr); Haifa; Alexandria; and Limassol. For more info, contact the **Port Authority of Peiraias** (tel. 422 6000). From Athens to Peiraias, take the subway to the last stop, or take green bus #40 from Filellinon and Mitropoleos St. (every 10min.). Boats also leave from **Rafina,** a port suburb east of Athens, to Andros, Tinos, and Mykonos. To Kea or Kithnos, take a ferry (1650-2300dr) from **Lavrio.** The orange bus to Lavrio leaves from Mavromateon St. near Areos Park (take bus or taxi from Syntagma) for 700dr. Always check schedules prior to departure at the tourist office, in the *Athens News,* with the Port Authority of Peiraias, or any travel agency. Ferry information is in any Greek newspaper or dial 143 for a Greek-recorded timetable.

Flying Dolphins: Hydrofoils serve the mainland and the Argosaronic, Sporades, and Cyclades islands. **Ceres' Flying Dolphins** (tel. 428 0001) and **Ilios Lines' Dolphins** (tel. 322 5139) are the two main companies (both open Mon.-Sat. 8am-6:30pm, Sun. and holidays 8am-1pm). The hydrofoils, roughly twice as expensive and twice as fast as ferries, leave from **Zea Port** near Peiraias, Agios Konstantinos, and Volos.

Taxis: Meters start at 200dr, with an additional 60dr per km within city limits, 120dr per km in the suburbs (and rates double between midnight and 5am). If the taxi is caught in traffic, you will be charged 33dr per stationary minute. There is a 300dr surcharge for trips from the airport and a 160dr charge from ports, bus, and railway terminals in addition to the 55dr for each piece of luggage. Hail your taxi by shouting your destination—not the street address, but the area (i.e., "Kolonaki"). The driver may or may not pick you up, depending on whether he is inclined to head in that direction. Get in the cab and *then* tell the driver the exact address or site. Most drivers don't speak English so have your destination written down (in Greek if possible) and include the area of the city (keep in mind some streets in different parts of the city have the same name). Empty taxis are rare. It is common to ride with other passengers going in the same direction. For an extra 400dr, call a radio taxi (Ikaros, tel. 513 2316; Hermes, tel. 411 5200; Kosmos, tel. 420 0042). A full list of radio taxis appears in the *Athens News.* Pay what the meter shows, rounded up to the next 50dr, but be wary of drivers who tinker with their meters.

Car Rental: Places abound on **Singrou Ave.,** all charging 8000-13,500dr for a small car with 100km free mileage (prices include tax and insurance). Credit cards accepted and international drivers license is not necessary. Most require drivers to be 23 or older and to have driven for at least a year.

Luggage Storage: At the airport, 100m outside on your right as you exit baggage claim and customs; look for the yellow "lockers" sign. Keep your ticket stub to reclaim; pay when you collect. 700dr per piece per day. After midnight you pay for an extra day. Open 24hr. There are also several offices on Nikis and Filellinon St., including **Pacific Ltd.,** 26 Nikis St. (tel. 324 1007; fax 323 3685). Per piece: 300dr per day, 600dr per week, 1800dr per month. Open Mon.-Sat. 7am-8pm, Sun. 7am-2pm. Many hotels have free or inexpensive luggage storage.

International Bookstores: Eleftheroudakis Book Store, 4 Nikis St. (tel. 322 9388). A pleasure to browse through, with Greek, English, French, and German books, classical and recent literature, and many travel guides, including *Let's Go.* Open Mon.-Fri. 9am-8:30pm, Sat. 9am-3pm. **Pantelides Books,** 11 Amerikis St. (tel. 362 3673), overflows with a huge variety of books; self-proclaimed best philosophy/critical theory selection in town. Open Mon. and Wed. 8am-4pm, Tues. and Thurs.-Fri. 9am-2:30pm and 5-8:30pm, Sat. 9am-3pm. **Compendium Bookshop,** 28 Nikis St. (tel. 322 1248). Popular, large used book selection. Open Mon. and Wed. 8:30am-3:30pm, Tues. and Thurs.-Fri. 8:30am-8:30pm, Sat. 9am-3pm. Also houses a new children's book room—part bookshop, part library. Open Mon. and Wed. 9am-5pm, Tues. and Thurs.-Fri. 9am-8pm, Sat. 9am-3pm.

GREECE

Libraries: In the **Hellenic American Union,** 22 Massalias St. (tel. 362 9886; fax 363 3174), behind the university, there is an **American Library** (tel. 363 7740) on the 4th floor. Open Mon. and Thurs. 3-7pm, Tues.-Wed. and Fri. 11am-3pm. The Union also houses a **Greek Library,** with English books on Greece, nestled on the 7th floor. Open Mon.-Thurs. 9am-8pm, Fri. 9am-5pm; closed in August. The **British Council Library,** Kolonaki Sq. (tel. 363 3215), also has English reading material. Open Tues.-Fri. 9:30am-1:30pm. All also sponsor **cultural events.**

Laundromats: The Greek word for laundry is *plinitirio,* but most places have signs reading "Laundry." Try **10 Angelou Geronta St.** in Plaka, **9 Psaron St.** (tel. 522 2856), and **41 Kolokinthous and Leonidou St.** (tel. 522 6233), near the train stations. Expect to pay roughly 2000dr per load for wash, dry, and detergent.

Pharmacies: Identifiable by a red or green cross hanging over the street. The daily *Athens News* (300dr) lists each day's emergency pharmacies and their hours in its Useful Information section. One is always open 24hr. (refered to as *efimerevon* in Greek). They alternate. To find out which pharmacies are open after hours, dial 107 or 102.

Hospitals: Geniko Kratiko Nosokomio (Public State Hospital), 154 Mesogion (tel. 777 8901; fax 770 5980). **Hegia,** 4 Erithrou Stavrou (tel. 682 7904; fax 684 5089), is a top-notch private hospital in Marousi. Closer to the center of Athens, try the **Aeginitio** state hospital at 72 Vas. Sofias (tel. 722 0811, -2), and at 80 Vas. Sofias (tel. 777 0501; fax 777 6321). Near Kolonaki is a **public hospital** at 45-47 Evangelismou (tel. 722 0101; fax 729 1808). In Greek, "hospital" is *nosokomio.*

Emergencies: For **doctors** (2pm-7am), call 105; for an **ambulance,** 166; for **poison control,** 779 3777. For the **AIDS Help Line,** 722 2222. The daily emergency hospitals are listed in the *Athens News.* Tourists can receive free emergency health care.

Police: (tel. 100). Speak broken English.

Main Post Office: 100 Aiolou St. (tel. 321 6023), Omonia Sq. **Postal Code:** 10200. **Syntagma Sq.** (tel. 322 6253), on the corner of Mitropolis. **Postal Code:** 10300. **60 Mitropoleos** (tel. 321 8143), a few blocks from Syntagma Sq. All open Mon.-Fri. 7:30am-8pm, Sat. 7:30am-2pm, Sun. 9am-1:30pm. **Parcel post** for sending packages abroad at **29 Koumoundourou** (tel. 524 9359; open Mon.-Fri. 7:30am-8pm), and **4 Stadiou** (tel. 322 8940). Open Mon.-Fri. 7:30am-2pm.

OTE: 15 Stadiou St. (tel. 33 02 121). Offers overseas collect calls, recent phonebooks for most European and Anglophone countries, and currency exchange (until 3pm). Open 24hr. For information on **overseas calls,** dial 161; for **directory assistance** in Athens, 131; outside Athens, 132. Most **phone booths** in the city operate by **telephone cards** that cost 1500, 6500, or 12,000dr at OTE offices, kiosks, and tourist shops. Push the "i" button on the phones for English instructions. For **telephone information** call 134; for **complaints,** 135; for a **domestic operator** speaking English, 151 or 152. **Telephone Code:** 01.

■ Accommodations

Concentrated within the city center, budget hotels often provide unwelcome background noise—ask for a room that faces away from the street. Although the noise is bearable, light sleepers might consider earplugs. Stays less than three nights may incur a 10% surcharge, but very few hotel owners take advantage of this option. In the past, stranded travelers could sleep on the roof of a hotel when no rooms were available. Get your bird's eye room of Athens from the Acropolis instead; sleeping on rooftops is now illegal.

Many hotel hawkers meet trains at the station. Some will distribute maps to decent places near the station; others will lure you to dumps way out of town. There have been cases where unsuspecting travelers have been harmed by deceitful hawkers in the past. Call ahead to reserve a room or search one out on your own. Following a hawker is safest when traveling in large groups. Insist that he point the hotel suggestion out on a large city map and set a firm price in writing before leaving the station. Men arriving by bus from the airport should be aware of "friendly barkeepers" who may direct you to brothels rather than budget hotels. Do not sleep in the city parks; camping anywhere in Athens is illegal and dangerous.

Several hotels offer breakfast for about 1000dr. For significantly less, you can buy milk or juice and fresh rolls or baked goods at any bakery.

Note that the prices quoted below are from mid-1997 and are expected to increase in the next year. In 1998, expect a 10-20% rise from the prices in these listings. Prices are 20-40% less in the off season (September through May).

PLAKA-SYNTAGMA AREA

Most of the city's cheap hotels cluster in this central and busy part of town. If you're looking for convenience, relative safety, quiet, and a good venue for people watching, this is the place to stay. During the summer months, make a reservation if possible—these qualities draw a crowd.

Student's and Traveler's Inn, 16 Kidathineon (tel. 324 4808; fax 321 0065), in the heart of Plaka. With its convenient locale, friendly owner and staff, outdoor courtyard, and hardwood floors, this hotel is more than worthwhile. 24hr. hot showers. Singles 6500dr; doubles 8000dr; triples 10,000dr; quads 11,500dr. Breakfast served 6am-noon (800-1000dr). 10% discount with student ID or Youth Card.

Dioskouros House, 6 Pitakou (tel. 324 8165), across the street from Hadrian's Arch. The hotel is sheltered from, yet remarkably close to, the city center. Popular with weary travelers, the outdoor bar and courtyard serves beer and non-alcoholic beverages until 11pm. 10am checkout. No singles available—hook up with fellow visitors and share. Doubles 8000dr; quads 18,000dr.

Thisseos Inn, 10 Thisseos St. (tel. 324 5960). From Syntagma Sq., take Karageorgi Servias (which becomes Perikleous); Thisseos St. is on the right. This home-turned-hostel is popular with students who want to stay near Syntagma's sights but far from its noise. Very quiet at night. TV in reception area, full kitchen facilities, common showers (24hr., with hot water). The extra-friendly reception staff more than makes up for the 2am curfew—ask and they may bend the rules. Dorm beds 2500dr; doubles 5500dr.

Hotel Phaedra, 16 Herefondos St. (tel. 322 7795). From Hadrian's Arch on Amalias, walk 1 block up Lysikrateous St. to the intersection with Herefondos. Owned and run by two brothers since 1963, Phaedra has a friendly family atmosphere. In addition to the scenic park that flanks it, the hotel boasts a view of the Acropolis from almost every room. Noon checkout. Singles 7000dr; doubles 8500dr; triples 10,000dr; quads 12,000dr. Breakfast 1500dr. Bargaining may prove rewarding. Prices slashed in winter.

Hotel Festos, 18 Filellinon St. (tel. 323 2455). Come as a guest and stay as an employee! Hotel Festos hires travelers to work in the lounge and behind the desk. Although the shared bathroom facilities are a bit run down, the student travelers who frequent this hotel claim to come for the friendly atmosphere. Wide range of food served includes a vegetarian menu. Cable TV. Luggage storage 200dr per day. Hot showers morning and evening only. Checkout 9am. Dorm beds 3000dr; doubles 7000dr; triples 10,500dr; quads 14,000dr.

Economy Hotel, 5 Klisthenous St. (tel. 522 0520; fax 522 0640). From Omonia Sq., go up Athinas and turn right after the town hall onto Kratinou St., which leads to the hotel's front door. Central location with clean rooms. Singles with bath 7000dr; doubles with bath 9000dr. Breakfast 1000dr, served 6:30-9am.

MONASTIRAKI-THISSION AREA

Near the central food and flea markets, this neighborhood has an ever-increasing, never-ceasing noise problem. But it's also near the Acropolis and the subway, practically on top of the Agora site, and home to some souvenir bargains.

Hotel Tempi, 29 Aiolou St. (tel. 321 3175; fax 325 4179). From Syntagma Sq., follow Ermou St. and take a right on Aiolou (also spelled Eolu and Eolou); hotel is in Monastiraki. 24hr. hot water. Public phone in the reception area. Free short and long-term luggage storage. Singles 4500dr, with bath 6500dr; doubles 7500dr, with bath 8500dr; triples 9000dr. Laundry service 1000dr.

GREECE

Pella Inn, 104 Ermou St. (tel. 325 0598, 321 2229; fax 325 0598), a 10-min. walk down Ermou from Syntagma Sq., 2 blocks from the Monastiraki subway station (entrance on Karaiskaki St.). Dine in the lounge where the bright yellow and orange furniture is sure to wake you up. Better yet, take your food to the exceptional terrace and enjoy the breathtaking view of the Acropolis. Free luggage storage. Singles 5000-7000dr, with bath 9000dr; doubles 7000-9000dr, with bath 9000dr. Breakfast 1000dr.

RAILWAY STATION AREA

This overcrowded business and residential center is too far away from Syntagma for week-long stays, but ideal for a stopover because of its proximity to trains, buses, and (via the Victoria or Omonia subway stop) Peiraias. Be wary of pickpockets around the Omonia Sq. area.

Athens International Hostel (HI), 16 Victor Hugo St. (tel. 523 4170; fax 523 4015). From Omonia Sq., walk down Third September St. and take a left on Veranzerou; it will become Victor Hugo after crossing Marni St. The only HI-affiliated youth hostel in Greece. HI membership required. Six 250dr per night stamps on a membership card obtained at this hostel fulfill all HI membership requirements. All beds 1500dr per night, including sheets. Make reservations in the summer.

Hostel Aphrodite, 12 Einardou St. (tel. 881 0589 or 883 9249; fax 881 6574). From the subway stop at Victoria Sq., follow Heiden for 2 blocks, then Paioniou for 2 more. Take a right on Michail Voda and a left 2 blocks later onto Einardou. From the train station, follow Filadelfias until Michail Voda. Easy access to both the train station and Victoria Sq. Friendly basement bar, travel services (ask about the 20-day island pass for 9000dr). Dorm beds 2000dr; doubles 6500dr; triples 8000dr; quads 9000dr. Breakfast 900-1200dr. 10% discount with student ID.

Hostel Argo, 25 Victor Hugo St. (tel. 522 5939; fax 864 1693). Noon checkout. No curfew. Breakfast 600dr. Laundry 1500dr. Free luggage storage. Singles 4000dr; doubles 6000dr, with bath 6600dr; triples 7000dr with bath; quads 8000dr. *Let's Go* users get a 10% discount.

Hotel Appia, 21 Menandrou St. (tel. 524 5155, -4561; fax 524 3552). From Omonia Sq., follow Tsaldari St. to Menandrou St. Popular with international travelers, the reception staff is fluent in English, Spanish and French. Telephones, ceiling fans, and radios in all rooms. Breakfast 900dr more. 24hr. hot water. Check-out noon. Singles 3500dr, with bath 5500dr; doubles 6000dr, 7500dr; triples 7000dr; quads 9000dr. Reserve for July-Sept.

Hotel Arta, 12 Nikitara St. (tel. 382 7753, 382 2881). From Syntagma or Omonia, take Stadiou to Benaki, turn left, and take the 3rd left on Nikitara. Convenient hotel in a quiet part of the city center. Endearing non-English speaking reception. Immaculate rooms with desks and phones. Free luggage storage. Reception always open. Breakfast 1500dr. Room for bargaining. Singles 6000dr, with bath 7500dr; doubles 7500dr, with bath 10,000dr; triples 9000dr, with bath 13,000dr.

SOUTH OF THE ACROPOLIS

These rooms are in relatively quiet residential areas. To the west, Koukaki and Veikou require 15 to 20-minute uphill hikes to the Acropolis or Syntagma Sq. To the east, Pangrati, a one-hour walk from Syntagma, can be easily reached by trolley.

Youth Hostel #5 Pangrati, 75 Damareos St., Pangrati (tel. 751 9530; fax 751 0616). Take trolley #2 or 11 from Syntagma Sq. to Filolaou, or walk through the National Garden, down Eratosthenous St. to Plastira Sq., 3 blocks on Efthidiou to Frinis, and down Frinis St. until Damareos on the right (40min. walk). There is no sign for the hostel on the street, just the number "75" and a dark gray door. Curfew midnight. Only the bare necessities, and at a cost. Hot shower 50dr. Sheets 100dr. Pillowcases 100dr. Blankets 50dr. Laundry 700dr. Key deposit 300dr. Dorm beds 1500dr; singles 3500dr; doubles 5000dr.

Marble House Pension, 35 Zini, Koukaki (tel. 923 4058 or 922 6461). From the southern side of Acropolis, follow Erechthiou St. until it ends and turn right onto

When in 172-1011, do as the 172-1011's do.

All you need for the clearest connections home.

Every country has its own AT&T Access Number which makes calling from overseas really easy. Just dial the AT&T Access Number for the country you're calling from and we'll take it from there. And be sure to charge your calls on your AT&T Calling Card. It'll help you avoid outrageous phone charges on your hotel bill and save you up to 60%.* For a free wallet card listing AT&T Access Numbers, call 1 800 446-8399.

It's all within your reach.

AT&T

http://www.att.com/traveler

Clearest connections from countries with voice prompts, compared to major U.S. carriers on calls to the U.S. Clearest based on customer preference testing. *Compared to certain hotel telephone charges based on calls to the U.S. in November 1996. Actual savings may be higher or lower depending upon your billing method, time of day, length of call, fees charged by hotel and the country from which you are calling. ©1997 AT&T

Greetings from Let's Go Publications

The book in your hand is the work of hundreds of student researcher-writers, editors, cartographers, and designers. Each summer we brave monsoons, revolutions, and marriage proposals to bring you a fully updated, completely revised travel guide series, as we've done every year for the past 38 years.

This is a collection of our best finds, our cheapest deals, our most evocative description, and, as always, our wit, humor, and irreverence. Let's Go is filled with all the information on anything you could possibly need to know to have a successful trip, and we try to make it as much a companion as a guide.

We believe that budget travel is not the last recourse of the destitute, but rather the only way to travel; living simply and cheaply brings you closer to the people and places you've been saving up to visit. We also believe that the best adventures and discoveries are the ones you find yourself. So put us down every once in while and head out on your own. And when you find something to share, drop us a line. We're **Let's Go Publications,** 67 Mount Auburn St., Cambridge, MA 02138, USA (email: fanmail@letsgo.com; http://www.letsgo.com). And let us know if you want a free subscription to **The Yellowjacket,** the new Let's Go Newsletter.

Veikou, which will intersect Zini. There are several buildings with this same address. Make sure to head to the one at the end of the small dead-end side street. Noon check-out. Singles 5000dr, with bath 6000dr; doubles 7000dr, with bath 8000dr; triples 8000dr. Breakfast 750dr.

Art Gallery Hotel, 5 Erechthiou St., Veikou (tel. 923 8376 or 923 1933; fax 923 3025). From the southern side of the Acropolis, Erechthiou stretches directly towards this pension. This welcoming family business is a 5min. walk from the Acropolis (downhill) and a 20min. walk from Syntagma Sq. The popularity of this establishment is indicative of its exceptional service. Spotless rooms and, even more importantly, staff that extends itself beyond the call of duty. English, French and Italian spoken. Singles 10,800dr; doubles 13,000dr; triples 15,000dr; quads 16,900dr. No credit cards. Reserve room a month in advance during high season.

Hotel Greca, 48 Singrou St., Veikou (tel. 921 5262 or 923 3229; fax 360 1438). Rooms resemble those of a typical hospital room—bland yet functional. 24hr. reception does not always have English-speaking staff on hand. Check-out before noon. Singles 7000dr, with bath 8000dr; doubles 8000dr, with bath 10,000dr; triples 12,000dr, with bath 18,000dr. Cash only.

■ Food

Athens offers a melange of stands, open-air cafes, outdoor side street *tavernas,* and intriguing dim restaurants frequented by grizzled Greek men. Athens' culinary claim to fame is cheap and plentiful *souvlaki* (250-400dr), either on a *kalamaki* (skewer) or wrapped in *pita.* Served quickly and eaten on the go if necessary, *souvlaki* is the Greek version of fast food. A *tost,* a grilled sandwich of variable ingredients (normally ham and cheese) for 250-500dr is another option. Beer (usually Amstel and Heineken, the latter also known as "Green Beer," for its green bottle) runs roughly 200dr per bottle. *Tiropita* (hot cheese pie) and *spanakopita* (hot spinach pie) go for around 300dr. Ice cream is sold at almost every kiosk. A *koulouri,* a donut-shaped, sesame-coated roll, makes a good breakfast for 50-100dr.

The most popular place for tourists to eat is Plaka. You'll find many interesting places up and down Adrianou and Kidatheneon St. Once seated at the joint of your choice, relax: Greek restaurants are not known for their speedy service. Women should know that Plaka is a popular spot for *kamakia* (literally "octopus spears," or pick-up men) who enjoy making catcalls at women as they walk by. Sometimes they may even follow you, but keep walking and ignore them; in most cases, harassment is only verbal. Places in Plaka serve early or all day, but outside these touristed quarters few restaurants open before 8pm. Restaurants tend to be deserted at 6pm, near-empty before 10pm, and crowded from 11pm to 1am.

PLAKA-SYNTAGMA

For do-it-yourself meals, various **minimarkets** on Nikis St. and in Plaka sell basic groceries. The Thisseos Inn in particular offers noteworthy kitchen facilities.

To Gerani, 14 Tripodon St. (tel. 324 7605). From Kidatheneon, one of Plaka's busiest strips, Tripodon is a side street. In a quiet niche with a wonderful balcony, To Gerani is cheaper than most. Claims to be "the most traditional restaurant" are substantiated by entrees named after the owner's grandmother. The rotating menu limits your choices, but any 2 dishes make a good meal (900-1100dr each).

Hermion Cafe and Restaurant, 15 Pandrossou (tel. 324 6725, 324 7148). Just down the street from the Metropolis (the central Greek Orthodox Cathedral), Hermion has a beautiful outdoor terrace that is generally full. Popular for its extensive and traditional Greek menu, specialties include roast lamb with potatoes (2300dr) and eggplant with ground beef (1900dr). Visa accepted.

Eden Vegetarian Restaurant, 12 Lissiou (tel. 324 8858), on the corner of Minissikleous on the west side of Plaka. Signs will direct you to this otherwise secluded restaurant. Popular with both herbivores and omnivores. Soy-meat in traditional dishes like *moussaka* (1500dr). The Spanish special, a combination of rice, cheese, carrots and cream, is a filling favorite (1700dr).

Zorbas, 15 Lissiou (tel. 322 6188), down and across the street from Eden. Entrees 1500-3000dr. Try the lamb Zorbas (1900dr), chicken Artmenis (1800dr) or beef Stamnas (1900dr), all of which combine two Greek favorites, the grill and cheese. Pumpkin balls (700dr) are a good way to tease your appetite. Gum available upon request—absolutely necessary.

Orpheas, 6 Arsakiou (tel. 322 7103). Enter the air-conditioned neoclassical arcade with the glass roof after Pezmezoglou St., coming down Stadiou St. Serves a wide array of light meals and desserts, each with a special twist. Have a creamy frappe for 730dr or a rich baguette sandwich for 1100dr. Open Mon.-Sat.

Souvlaki ee Lievadia, 7 Gladstonos St. (tel. 383 2413). Walk along Patissan St. and take the first left away from Omonia Sq. Inexpensive and delicious, they've been making *souvlaki* (230dr) for 32 years. Also enjoy their all-you-can-eat free bread.

Nikis Cafe, 3 Nikis St (tel. 323 4971). A self-described pasta bar, Nikis serves the basic starch and sauce for 1500dr, but also has a variety of sandwiches and quiche. Thirsty? Skip the meal and choose one of the frozen margaritas in delicious cherry, mango or strawberry flavors.

T. Stamatopoulos, 26 Lissiou St. (tel. 322 8722). The fenced-off, outdoor terrace keeps outsiders from peeking in, especially in the summer when live music catches their attention. A family-owned restaurant, this *taverna* works on Greek time—it doesn't open for dinner until 8pm, but serves until at least 2am. The popular veal special (1950dr) is a safe choice.

Golden Flower, 30 Nikis St. (tel. 323 0113). Tired of Greek food? A nice Chinese place. Vegetable dishes 1400-1650dr, chow mein 2050dr. Closed 4-7pm.

Cafe Plaka, 1 Tripodon (tel. 322 0388). A dessert lover's haven, Cafe Plaka serves authentic French crepes smothered in innumerable choices. Choose ham, mushrooms, chicken or cheese for a meal, or sin a little and opt for the chocolate-banana option. Take-out crepes are identical to those served inside but half the price (500dr compared to 1000dr).

For a less touristy atmosphere, and less expensive food, wander outside Plaka:

Restaurant of Konstantinos Athanasias Velly, Varnava Sq., Plastira. Take trolley #2, 4, 11, or 12 to Plastira Sq., walk 3 blocks up Proklou St. to Varnava Sq. The restaurant is at the square's far right corner, in a small white house with flowers in front. No English spoken, but your stomach can growl and you can point. Tomato salad 500dr, *keftedes* (Greek meatballs) with potatoes 900dr, and *fasolia* (bean soup) 400dr. Kosta and Nitsa have been cooking here for over 30 years. Their *keftedes* would bring a Greek Betty Crockeropoulous to tears of joy.

To Meltemi, 26 Zinni St. (tel. 924 7606), Koukaki, near the Marble House Pension. Menu changes daily at this authentic *taverna.* Medium-sized variety plate 1500dr. Pork in the oven 1300dr and *gemista* (stuffed peppers and tomatoes) 900dr.

For an after-dinner treat, there are tons of **sweet shops** in Plaka, many virtually indistinguishable from their neighbors. *Baklava* tends to go for 250-400dr, ice cream 150-300dr per scoop. **Lalaggis,** 13 Speusippou St. in Kolonaki, is an excellent sweet shop in the heart of the city (*baklava* 250dr). Check out their branch in Pagrati, at 29 Empedokleous St. **Artos & Zoe,** 73 Ermou St., has lots of yummy cookies and breads (*tiropita* 200dr). **Floca** is a chain, but also tends to be quite good.

■ Entertainment

Visitors to Athens often restrict themselves to the familiar Plaka and Monastiraki neighborhoods. Don't be fooled into thinking that nights here consist only of dancing the Zorba and breaking dishes. On the contrary, Athenian nightlife is diverse enough to please highbrow, chic sophisticates as well as down and dirty backpackers. Nightlife is very different in the off season when many outdoor spots close, but there is still plenty to do throughout the year.

CLUBS AND NIGHTLIFE

During the summer months, young and hip Athenians head to the seaside clubs on Poseidonos Ave. in Glyfada (past the airport). The most popular clubs are right on the beach, with calming ocean views to help cool off the frenzied interiors. Dance clubs play American or British tunes from 11pm or midnight until 2 or 3am, when either Greek music is played or a Greek singer takes the stage. Put on your best Euro-suave outfit because many of these clubs will not admit anyone in shorts. Covers range 2000-3000dr, and drinks are often ridiculously priced (cheap beers run 1000-2000dr, cocktails 1500-3000dr).

The best bars are all conveniently lined up nearby, off the water on Vouliagmenis St. Some excellent clubs include **La Mamounia at La Playa** and **Amphitheatro** for dance beat, **Wild Rose** for rock, and **Prinz** for people-watching. **Privilege** and **Empire** are the current hotspots—you will wait in line on Friday and Saturday night. Cover charge for these places is roughly 3000dr. You'll need to take a cab back to Plaka (1500-2500dr). Just get in and tell them what club you're going to and "Glyfada" they'll know where to go. As always, be careful of cabbies trying to rip you off.

To quiet hungry stomachs, ask your taxi driver to take you to the **meat market** (no, this is not another club) on Athinas St. between Syntagma and Omonias, where popular early-morning restaurants replace the meat market (3-7am). Simply go into the kitchens and point away; *patsa* soup may calm a hangover, but don't order it sober—it's made with sheep entrails.

If you're determined to stay around Plaka, there are several forgettable bars and clubs near Nikis and Filellinon. Be prepared to rub shoulders with other tourists or Athenians trying to pick up foreigners. The posh **Kolonaki** district, on the way to Lycabettos, sports Gucci shoes in chic shop windows which cost more than your whole vacation; however, a coffee or beer at any of the outdoor *tavernas* will not break the bank. While in the area, dig **Jazz Club 1920**, 10 Ploutarchou St. (tel. 721 0533), just up from the British Embassy (open nightly 10:15pm-1:15am for jazz, blues, latin, and rock). In Kifissia, a hip residential area north of Athens, you can find a number of slick *tavernas* and discos. Here you'll find the **Divina**, 2 Argiropoulou (tel. 801 5884), where you can dance in air-conditioned comfort. For **gay clubs** (primarily male), try **Lembessi St.** off Singrou.

OTHER DIVERSIONS

The **Athens Festival** runs annually from June until September, featuring classical theater groups performing in the **Odeon of Herodes Atticus**. Performances are also staged in **Lycabettos Theater** at the top of Lycabettos Hill, and in Epidavros (see p.152). The Greek Orchestra performs during this festival, as do visiting groups, which have ranged from the Bolshoi to B.B. King, from the Alvin Ailey Dance Company to Classical Greek dramas, and from Pavarotti to the Talking Heads. The **Festival Office** (tel. 322 1459, -3111; ext. 240) is in the arcade at 4 Stadiou St. Student tickets are generally affordable and available (3000-5000dr; open Mon.-Fri. 8:30am-2pm and 5-7pm, Sat. 8:30am-1pm, Sun. 10am-1pm). The **Athens Box Office of the National Theater** (tel. 522 3242), at the corner of Agiou Konstandinou and Menandrou St. sells tickets for the four classical productions put on annually (2500-3500dr, students 2000dr; closed in summer).

If you've had enough to drink, the hokey **Sound and Light Show** (which depicts the Parthenon over the centuries) on Pnyx Hill (opposite the Acropolis) can be quite entertaining, though you'll leave unsure whether the title refers to the program or the click and flash of cameras (tel. 322 1459, after 2pm tel. 922 6210; April-Oct. shows daily in English 9pm; in French Wed.-Thurs. and Sat.-Mon. 10:10pm; in German Thurs.-Fri. 10pm; admission 1200dr, students 600dr). Nearby in Dora Stratou Theatre on Philopappou Hill, **Greek dancers** kick and holler to live music on an open-air stage, celebrating traditions from all regions of the country. For information, call 324 4395 from 9am-3pm; after 7:30pm call 921 4650 (shows May-Sept. nightly 10:15pm, and also Wed. and Sun. at 8:15pm; tickets 2500-3000dr).

Athens' two principal markets attract everyone from bargain-hunters to inveterate browsers. The **Athens Flea Market,** adjacent to Monastiraki Sq., has a festive, bazaar-like atmosphere and offers a potpourri of second-hand junk, costly antiques, and everything in between. Although parts of it have become overtouristy, there is still the occasional treasure to be found and lots of neo-hippies to watch (open Mon., Wed., and Sat.-Sun. 8am-3pm, and Tues., Thurs.-Fri. 8am-8pm). On Sunday, the flea market overflows the square and Fillis Athinas St., and a huge indoor-outdoor **food market** lines the sides of Athinas St. between Evripidou and Sofokleous St. The **meat market** is huge, but not for vegetarians or the faint of heart (open Mon.-Sat. 8am-2pm). Even the smell can be overwhelming. Livers, kidneys, and skinned rabbits complete with cottontails hang throughout. There are also less visually challenging foods, such as fruits, vegetables, breads, and cheeses. It's open the same hours as regular food stores, but Athenian restaurateurs go early and purchase the choice meat and fish. Restaurants in the meat market are open at night.

■ Sights

ACROLIS

The **Acropolis,** particularly the **Parthenon,** is Athens' highlight. Its name means "high city" and it has, with its strategic position overlooking the Aegean Sea and Attic Plains, served through the ages as both a military fortress and religious center. The heights afford an expansive view of Athens and the Aegean. Today, the hilltop's remarkable ruins grace otherwise rubble-strewn grounds. Ongoing renovations require that steel scaffolding cling to the ancient marble columns.

In the 13th century BC, wealthy landowners overthrew the monarchy in Athens who had ruled the city safely from their fortress in the Acropolis. The new rulers, the *Aristoi* (excellent ones), shifted the center of their government away from the Acropolis, ruling the *polis* (city-state) from the lower foothills of the city. The Acropolis, far from being abandoned, was then used as a shrine devoted to two aspects of the goddess **Athena:** Athena Polias, goddess of crops and fertility, and Athena Pallas, military guardian of the city. The original shrine was made of wood. Following the Greek custom of putting money under the protection of a deity, the Acropolis also housed the city treasury.

In 507 BC, the tyrannical *Aristoi* were overthrown and Athens began its successful experiment with **democracy.** In 490 BC, Athenians began constructing a temple on the Acropolis; this time out of marble. When the Persians sacked the temple 10 years later, the Greeks threw the violated religious objects off the side of the Acropolis and buried the litter (now displayed in the Acropolis Museum).

In response to the Persian threat, Aegean rulers formed the Delian League. **Pericles** appropriated part of the taxes paid by the league to beautify Athens. Among his projects were the temples of the Acropolis, the Temple of Hephaestus in the *agora,* and the Temple of Poseidon at Sounion. These developments slowed during the **Peloponnesian War** (431-404 BC), but by then the Athenians were committed to Pericles' plans, and construction sputtered along throughout the war and after his death in 429 BC. Four of the buildings erected at that time still stand today: the Parthenon, the Propylaea, the Temple of Athena Nike, and the Erechtheum. They were designed and sculpted by Iktinos, Kallikrates, and a slew of eager-beaver apprentices all trying to outdo each others' artistry. Their construction has had an unrivaled influence on Western architecture.

Through the Hellenistic and Roman periods, the function of the Acropolis altered as often as it changed hands. The **Byzantines** converted it into a church worship. In a good example of Christianity appropriating older "pagan" symbols, the Parthenon became the Church of St. Sophia ("Sophia," like "Athena," means wisdom). In 1205, when Athens was liberated from the Byzantines by **Frankish crusaders,** the Acropolis once again became a fortress, serving as palace and headquarters for the Dukes de la Roche. When the political situation later settled down, the Parthenon was trans-

GREECE

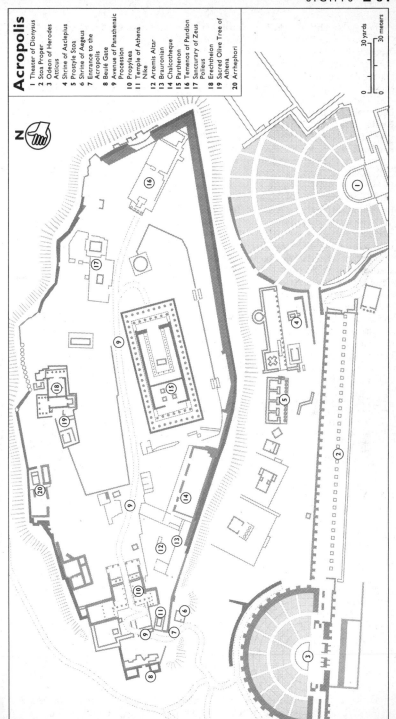

Acropolis

1 Theater of Dionysus
2 Stoa Proper
3 Odeon of Herodes
   Atticus
4 Shrine of Asclepius
5 Prostyle Stoa
6 Shrine of Aegeus
7 Entrance to the
   Acropolis
8 Beulé Gate
9 Avenue of Panathenaic
   Procession
10 Propylaea
11 Temple of Athena
   Nike
12 Artemis Altar
13 Brauronian
14 Chalcotheque
15 Parthenon
16 Temenos of Pandion
17 Sancturary of Zeus
   Polieus
18 Erechtheion
19 Sacred Olive Tree of
   Athena
20 Arrhephori

N

0 ——————— 30 yards
0 ——————— 30 meters

formed into a Catholic church (Notre Dame d'Athènes). In the 15th century, **Otto-mans** turned the Parthenon into a mosque and the Erechtheum into the Ottoman commander's harem.

Tragedy befell the Acropolis during the **Venetian siege** in 1687, when an Ottoman supply of gunpowder stored in the Parthenon was hit by a shell and came tumbling down, destroying many sculptures. The reconstructed temple is what you see before you. The ramp that led to the Acropolis in classical times no longer exists. Today's visitors make the five-minute climb to the ticket window, enter through the crumbling **Beulé Gate** (added by the Romans and named after the French archaeologist who unearthed it), and continue through the **Propylaea,** the ancient entrance. Unfortunately, the site is not wheelchair-accessible.

The Propylaea became famous for its ambitious multi-level design, although the entrance itself, begun by Mnesicles between 437 and 432 BC, was never completed. In Roman times, the structure extended as far as 80m below the Beulé Gate. At the cliff's edge, the tiny **Temple of Athena Nike** was built during a respite from the Peloponnesian War, the so-called Peace of Nikias (421-415 BC). Known as the "jewel of Greek architecture," this temple with eight miniature Ionic columns once housed a winged statue of the goddess Nike (not yet a brand-name label). One day, in a paranoid frenzy, the Athenians feared that their deity (and peace) would flee the city, so they clipped Athena's wings. Below the temple are the remains of the 5m-thick **Cyclopean wall** (so named for its one-eyed architects), which once surrounded the whole of the Acropolis.

The **Erechtheum,** to the left of the Parthenon as you face it, was completed in 406 BC, just prior to Athens' defeat by Sparta. Lighter than the Parthenon, the Erechtheum is a unique two-level structure that housed a number of cults, including those of Athena, Poseidon, and the snake-bodied hero Erechtheus. The east porch, with its six Ionic columns, was dedicated to Athena Polias and sheltered an olive wood statue of her. On the south side of the Erechtheum, facing the Parthenon, are the **Caryatids,** six columns sculpted in the shape of women. Their artful tunics are plaster replicas—the originals were moved to the Acropolis Museum to protect them from acid rain.

THE PARTHENON

Looming over the hillside, the **Parthenon,** or "Virgin's Apartment," keeps vigil over Athens and its world. Designed by the architects Iktinos and Kallikrates, the Parthenon was the first building completed under Pericles' plan to revive the city. It once housed the legendary gold and ivory statue of Athena Parthena (Virgin Athena) sculpted by Phidias. The temple intentionally features many almost imperceptible irregularities; the Doric columns bulge in the middle and the stylobate (pedestal) of the building bows slightly upward in order to compensate for the optical illusion in which straight lines, viewed from a distance, appear to bend. Originally made entirely of marble except for a long-gone wooden roof, the building's stone ruins attest to both the durability of the structure and the elegance of the Classical Age.

Metopes around the sides of the Parthenon portray victories of the forces of order over disorder. On the far right of the south side, the only side which has not been defaced, the Lapiths battle the Centaurs; on the east the Olympian gods triumph over the giants; the north depicts a faintly visible victory of the Greeks over the Trojans; and on the west, the triumph of the Greeks over the Amazons. A better-preserved frieze in bas-relief around the interior walls shows the Panathenaic procession in Athena's honor. The **East Pediment,** the formerly triangular area that the columns propped up, once depicted the birth of Athena, who according to legend, sprang from the head of Zeus. The **West Pediment,** on the opposite facade, formerly documented the contest between Athena and Poseidon for Athens' eternal devotion. Various fragments of the originals are now housed in the Acropolis and British Museums.

To avoid massive crowds and the broiling midday sun, visit early in the morning. Warm water is available from sink-like fountains at the top of the Acropolis; bring bottled water to avoid the overpriced refreshment stand at the entrance (soda 600dr). You can reach the entrance, which is on the west side of the Acropolis (tel. 321

0219), from Areopagitou St. south of the Acropolis, or by walking uphill from Plaka. Follow the spray-painted signs at intervals in the narrow passageway. Open in summer Mon.-Fri. 8am-6:30pm, Sat.-Sun. and holidays 8:30am-2:30pm; in winter 8:30am-4:30pm. Admission 2000dr, students 1000dr.

The **Acropolis Museum** (tel. 323 6665), footsteps away from the Parthenon, contains a superb collection of sculptures, including five of the Caryatids of the Erechtheum (the sixth now resides in the British Museum). Most of the treasures housed here date from the transition period from Archaic to Classical Greek art (550-400 BC). You can trace this development in the faces of the statues, from the stylized, entranced faces and static poses of Archaic sculpture—seen in the famous *Moschophoros* (calf-bearer)—to the more familiar, naturalistic (though idealized) figures of Classical Art. Only a few pieces from the Parthenon are here—Lord Elgin helped himself to the rest, which are now in the British Museum—but the collection is nonetheless impressive. Cameras without flash are allowed, but no posing next to the objects, heathen tourist (open Mon.-Sat. 8am-6:30pm, Sun. 8:00am-2:30pm; admission included in Acropolis ticket). From the southwest corner of the Acropolis, you can look down on the reconstructed **Odeon of Herodes Atticus,** a still-functioning theater dating from the Roman Period (160 AD). Nearby are the ruins of the classical Greek **Theater of Dionysus** (tel. 322 4625; entrance on Dionissiou Areopagitou St.), the **Asclepion,** and the **Stoa of Eumenes II.** The Theater of Dionysus dates from the 4th century BC (open daily 8:30am-2:30pm; admission to all three 500dr, students free with ID).

NEAR THE ACROPOLIS

The **Athenian Agora,** at the foot of the Acropolis, was the administrative center and marketplace of Athens from the 6th century BC through the late Roman Period (5th-6th centuries AD). However, prehistoric habitation and cemeteries have been unearthed here as well. The decline of the Agora paralleled the decline of Athens, as barbarian attacks buffeted both the city and the square from 267 BC to 580 AD. It was in the Agora and on the **Pnyx** (the low hill and meeting place of the assembly, 1km to the south) that Athenian democracy was born and flourished. Socrates frequented the Agora, as did Aristotle, Demosthenes, Xenophon, and St. Paul. According to Plato, Socrates' preliminary hearing was held at the **Stoa Basileios** (Royal Promenade), which has been recently excavated and lies to the left as you cross the subway tracks upon leaving the Agora.

The sprawling archaeological site features three remarkable constructions. The **Temple of Hephaestus,** on a hill in the northwest corner, is the best-preserved classical temple in Greece. Built around 440 BC, it is especially notable for its friezes which depict the labors of Hercules and the adventures of Thisseos. The ruins of the **Odeon of Agrippa** (concert hall), built for the son-in-law of the Emperor Augustus, stand in the center of the Agora. In 150 AD the roof collapsed, and the Odeon was rebuilt as a lecture hall half its former size. The actors' dressing room was made into a porch supported by colossal statues (the ruins of three of these statues remain to guard the site). To the south, the elongated **Stoa of Attalos,** a multi-purpose building for shops, shelter, and informal gatherings, was rebuilt between 1953 and 1956 and now houses the **Agora Museum** (tel. 321 0185). The original structure, built in the 2nd century BC, was given to Athens by Attalos II, King of Pergamon, in gratitude for the education he had received in the city. The museum contains a number of relics from the site and offers a cool sanctuary from the sweltering summer sun (agora and museum open Tues.-Sun. 8:30am-3pm; admission to both 1200dr, students with ID 600dr, seniors 900dr). There are several entrances to the Agora, including one at the edge of Monastiraki, one on Thission Sq., and one on Adrianou St. You can reach the Acropolis from here by exiting the south side of the Agora (follow the path uphill) and then turning right. The most commonly used gate is the one near the Acropolis entrance (turn right as you leave the Acropolis).

Northwest of the Agora, on the other side of the tracks at Thission Station, 148 Ermou St., is **Kerameikos.** This is the site of the 40m-wide boulevard that ran from the Agora, through the Diplyon gate, and 1.5km to the sanctuary of Akademos, where Plato founded his academy in the 4th century BC. Public tombs for state leaders, famous authors, and battle victims were constructed along this road. Worshipers began the annual Panathenaean procession to the Acropolis at the Diplyon Gate, one of the two gates excavated at this site. The sacred road to Eleusis, traversed during the annual Eleusian processions, ran through the Sacred Gate, the second gate on the site. Family tombs adorn either side of the Sacred Road outside the gate. A **museum** on the site (tel. 346 3552) exhibits finds from recent digs as well as an excellent pottery collection (site and museum open Tues.-Sun. 8:30am-3pm; admission to both 400dr, students 200dr).

The **Temple of Olympian Zeus,** Vas. Olgas and Amalias Ave. (tel. 922 6330), also deserves a visit. Fifteen majestic columns are all that remain of the largest temple ever built in Greece. Started in the 6th century BC, the temple was completed 600 years later by the Roman emperor Hadrian. The Corinthian columns stand in the middle of downtown Athens, below the National Garden. The remains of a Roman bath, tiles and all, are also here (open Tues.-Sun. 8:30am-3pm; admission 500dr, students 300dr). Next to the Temple is **Hadrian's Arch,** which was built in the 2nd century BC to mark the boundary between the ancient city of Thisseos and the new city built by Hadrian.

MUSEUMS

The **National Archaeological Museum,** 44 Patission St., 28 Oktovriou next to Metsovion Polytechnion (tel. 821 7717), is well worth delaying your jaunt to the islands. It's a 20-minute walk from Syntagma down Stadiou until Aiolou and then onto 28 Oktovriou. Take trolley #2, 4, 5, 9, 11, 15, or 18 from the uphill side of Syntagma or trolley #3 or 13 from the north side of Vasilissis Sofias. Pieces that would be the prizes of lesser collections seem almost unremarkable amid the general magnificence. Invest a couple of hours to explore.

After checking your bags at the cloakroom (mandatory; no charge), go straight ahead into the **Mycenae exhibit** of Heinrich Schliemann's digs at Mycenae, including the golden "Mask of Agamemnon" (which is really the death mask of a king who lived at least three centuries earlier than the legendary Agamemnon). Also displayed are samples of Bronze Age jewelry and pottery from Mycenae, other sites in the Peloponnese, and various prehistoric sites in Greece. This primary exhibit is skirted by findings from other tombs found in different parts of Greece and displayed in side rooms. In the red room is the bronze statue, **Artemisian Jockey** (140 BC).

Don't leave without viewing the **kouroi,** or standing males, in the left wing of the museum. They are displayed chronologically and in the buff, allowing you to see the evolution of this "form." The **wall paintings from Akrotiri,** Santorini, (1 flight up) are intriguing. These painted architectural and artistic treasures were buried during a volcanic eruption believed to have occurred around 1500 BC and present a unique glimpse into Bronze Age life. The bronze statue of **Poseidon,** also in the left wing, is eerily life-like. With its hollowed-out eye sockets, it is impressive, as are many of the other bronze sculptures. The **mask of a slave from Diplyon** (2nd century BC), with a wide, toothless grin and crazy eyes, seems amused by the starkly stoic statues which surround it. The right wing of the museum hosts a beautifully preserved **Aphrodite-Panas-Eros** from the Hellenistic Era. Look for the statue of the **Sleeping Maenad.** Wander towards the back to view the temporary exhibitions that change several times a year. Also worth viewing is the extensive **vase collection** (on the same floor as the wall paintings)—Red and Black Ware, Narrative, and Geometric styles. Museum open Mon. 12:30-7pm, Tues.-Fri. 8am-7pm, Sat.-Sun. and holidays 8:30am-3pm. Admission 2000dr, students 1000dr, seniors 1500dr, free Sun. and holidays. No flash photography.

Opened in 1986, the **Goulandris Museum of Cycladic and Ancient Greek Art,** 4 Neophytou Douka St. (tel. 722 8321) near Kolonaki, is accessible by trolley #3 and 13 (75dr). It has a stunning collection in a modern building with air conditioning. Cycladic art is famous for its sleek, marble, Picasso-esque figurines. Some even exhibit painted details, possibly representing tattoos. Many figurines were either looted from archaeological sites at the turn of the century or found buried with the dead in graves on the Cycladic Islands. Their precise use in antiquity is still an enigma; however, plenty of theories have arisen and range from representations of goddesses to *psycho-pompoi* (tour guides to the Underworld) to kept women. The bronze jewelry from Skyros, as well as to the collection of Greek vases and statues from 2nd century BC to the 4th century AD, are also impressive. The new wing of the museum, on the corner of Vas. Sofias and Herodotou, is an extension of the Cycladic collection (open Mon. and Wed.-Fri. 10am-4pm, Sat. 10am-3pm; admission 400dr, students 200dr).

Inside an elegant Florentine building with serene courtyards, the **Byzantine Museum,** 22 Vasilissis Sofias (tel. 723 1570), has an excellent and extensive collection of Christian art from the 4th through the 19th centuries. The collection includes early Byzantine sculptures, an icon collection containing works from the entire Byzantine period, and a reconstructed early Christian basilica. One wing of the building features an array of well-preserved frescoes and mosaics. The exhibits are poorly labeled, however; consider buying a book (2500dr) before you visit (open Tues.-Sun. 8:30am-3pm; admission 500dr). Next door to the Byzantine Museum is the **War Museum** (tel. 729 0543). It traces the history of Greek armaments from neolithic eras, through the 5th century BC Persian invasion and expeditions of Alexander the Great, to the submachine guns of the modern era. The primary emphasis is on the modern Greek arsenal (open Tues.-Sun. 9am-2pm; free).

The **National Gallery** (Alexander Soutzos Museum) is set back from Vasilissis Sofias at 50 Vasileos Konstandinou (tel. 721 7643). The museum exhibits Greek artists' works supplemented by periodic international displays. The permanent collection includes some outstanding works by El Greco. The drawings, photographs, and sculpture gardens are also impressive. Consult *This Week in Athens* or call the museum for information on current exhibits (open Mon. and Wed.-Sat. 9am-3pm, Sun. 10am-2pm; free). The **Theater Museum,** 50 Akadimis St. (tel. 362 9430), displays costumes, models, photographic paraphernalia, and dressing rooms (open Mon.-Fri. 9am-2:30pm; admission 300dr). In Plaka, the **Greek Folk Art Museum,** 17 Kidatheneon St. (tel. 322 9031), exhibits *laiki techni* (popular art) from all over Greece, including embroidered textiles, costumes, and puppets. Ornamental ecclesiastical silverwork and household pottery are also on exhibit. Don't miss the wall paintings by folk artist Theophilos Hadzimichail (open Tues.-Sun. 10am-2pm; admission 500dr, students and seniors 300dr; no flash photography). The **Greek Popular Musical Instruments Museum,** 1-2 Diogenous St., Plaka (tel. 325 0198), has an interactive display of an array of musical instruments used in the 18th, 19th and 20th centuries (open Tues. and Thurs.-Sun. 10am-2pm, Wed. noon-6pm; free).

On the south side of the Acropolis, just off Dionysiou Areopagiotou St., you can satiate your lust for gold at the **Ilias Lalounis Jewelry Museum** (tel. 922 1044). This private museum houses over 3000 designs created by Lalounis, as well as collections displaying the history of jewelry in Greece from ancient to modern times, including a workshop where visitors can observe different jewelry-making techniques. Open Mon. and Wed. 9am-9pm, Thurs.-Sat. 9am-3pm. Admission 800dr, students and seniors 500dr, free after 3pm on Wednesdays.

The **Jewish Museum,** 36 Leoforos Amalias, third floor (tel. 323 1577), is in the 19th-century building with a United Nations flag. An impressive collection of textiles, religious artifacts, and documents traces the roots of the Greek Jewish communities dating from the Hellenistic period. The museum also contains the reconstructed Synagogue of Patras (open Sun.-Fri. 9am-1pm; free). The **Children's Museum,** 14 Kidathineon St. (tel. 331 2995, -6), is a colorful, friendly, hands-on experience in the heart of Plaka. The museum's philosophy is "I hear and I forget; I see and I remember; I do and I understand." Go to the attic to play dress-up in a quaint bedroom from times past (open Mon., Fri. 9:30am-1:30pm, Wed. 10am-7pm, Sat.-Sun. 10am-2pm; hours can be erratic so call in advance; free).

CHURCHES

Byzantine sanctuaries, like their Classical counterparts, have been incorporated into the urban landscape. Traffic on Ermou St. must go around **Kapnikaria Church,** which is stranded in the middle of the street, one block beyond Aiolou St. Walking down Mitropoleos from Syntagma, you may also notice a tiny church on the corner of Pentelis St., around which a modern building has been built. Other Byzantine churches in Athens include the **Agia Apostoli,** at the east edge of the Agora; **Metamorphosis,** in Plaka near Pritaniou St.; **Agia Triada,** on Filellinon St., a few blocks from Syntagma; and **Agios Eleftherios,** next to the **Mitropoli Cathedral,** on Mitropoleos St. Viewing hours are at the discretion of each church's priest since he locks the door after the early evening service. Mornings are the best bet. Dress appropriately: skirts for women, long pants for men, and sleeved shirts for everyone.

The **Chapel of St. George,** on top of rocky **Lycabettos Hill,** offers a beautiful view of the city. Burn off dinner by walking up, or take the funicular (1000dr round-trip, children 500dr) to the top—the station is a healthy hike at the end of Ploutarchou St. The funicular leaves every 10-15 minutes for its dark but somewhat exciting two-minute uphill journey (chapel open Mon.-Wed., Fri.-Sun. 8:45am-12:15am, Thurs. 10:30am-12:15am). The cool, pleasant **National Garden,** adjacent to Syntagma Square, is an escape from the noise, heat, and frantic pace of Athens. Walk along its tranquil paths and visit the duck pond and sad little zoo. Women should avoid strolling here alone (open sunrise to sunset).

When you're passing through Syntagma Sq., don't miss the changing of the guard in front of the **Parliament** building. Every hour on the hour, two sets of enormously tall *evzones* (guards) slowly wind up like toy soldiers, kick their heels about, and fall backwards into symmetrical little guardhouses on either side of the **Tomb of the Unknown Warrior.** Unlike their British equivalents, *evzones* occasionally wink and even smile at tourists. Their jovial manner is as delightful as their attire—pom-pom-laden clogs, short pleated skirts *(foustanela),* and tasseled hats. Every Sunday at 10:45am the ceremony occurs with the full troop of guards and a band.

NEAR ATHENS

■ Kesariani and Daphni ΔΑΦΝΗ

If you're worn down by Athens' insane congestion, visit the **Monastery of Kesariani** (tel. 723 6619) for serenity and salvation. Located near the top of scenic **Mt. Hymettus** and providing a bird's eye view of Athens, the site was originally a temple to Dimitra, goddess of agriculture and nature. In the Roman period (200-300 AD), another temple was erected in its place. The structure's stones were used in the 14th century to build the existing monastery. The 17th-century frescoes (painted by Ioannis Ypatios) and the sacred atmosphere are splendid. Come alone or with a spiritual friend; tour buses are likely to whirl you through too quickly.

To reach Kesariani take blue bus #224 from the KTEL (ΚΗΠΟΣ) stop two blocks up Vas. Sofias from Syntagma Sq. (every 15min., 20min., 75dr). Get off at the last stop, follow the left-hand road uphill and, when you reach the overpass, bear right under it, staying to the right through two forks. A bit farther up the road splits, the right going up the mountain, the left coming down from it. Once again, stick to the right. Roughly a five-minute jaunt farther uphill, just as the road bends left, two branches spring from the right side. Ignore the barred one on the right, and take the stone path left up to the monastery. The entire walk takes 40-50 minutes, so be sure to bring lots of water. Avoid the temptation to accept a ride from one of the speeding motorists that fly by next to the all-too-narrow pedestrian path. If you drain your water bottles, a 15-minute walk up the main road leads to a small store and a drinkable fountain. For a fabulous view overlooking Athens all the way to the sea, keep walking for 15 more minutes past the store. Many hiking trails meander away from the road throughout the area. The Monastery makes a wonderful spot for a picnic (open Tues.-Sun. 8:30am-3pm; admission 800dr, seniors 600dr, students with ID 400dr, EU students free).

To reach Daphni (daph-NI) from Athens, take bus #A16 from **Pl. Eleftherias** (from Omonoia Sq., go up Peiraias St./Tsaldari St.; about 10min. on foot). A bus leaves every 30 minutes and the trip should take 20 minutes. From Peiraias Port, take #804 or #845 (every 15min., 6am-11:30pm, 35min.). From the final stop, go to the highway and cross it to get to the monastery. Built on the site of the ancient Temple of Daphnios Apollo and surrounded by a high fortified wall is the **Monastery of Daphni** (tel. 581 1558), a peaceful retreat 10km west of Athens, along the Ancient Sacred Way. Cool breezes sweep the area, and the 11th-century structure is pock-marked with birds' nests and populated by a dozen cats. The monastery has served as both an army camp and an insane asylum, which may help explain the pronounced scowl on Christ's face as he stares down from the masterful mosaic dome (open daily 8:30am-3pm; admission 800dr, students 400dr, seniors 600dr, EU students free; no flash photography).

■ Peiraias ΠΕΙΡΑΙΑΣ

The natural harbor of Peiraias has been Athens' port since the early 5th century BC, when Themistokles began fortifying Peiraias, then an island, as a base for the growing Athenian fleet. In approximately 450 BC, Pericles added the Long Walls from Athens to Peiraias, bridging the land masses. Though the opening scenes of both Kazantzakis' *Zorba the Greek* and Plato's *Republic* depict Peiraias as a charming port town, these days Peiraias has lost that loving feeling—its pollution rivals Athen. A mere block away from the tourist-laden port, neighborhoods are run-down and dirty. The waterfront is lined with stores selling cheap tourist trinkets and "aged" pastries glistening with grease. Use Peiraias only as the point of departure to the Greek isles. To get there, take the subway to the last stop in the Peiraias direction, or take blue bus #049 on Athinas St. just off Omonoia Sq. From Syntagma Sq., take green bus #040 on Filellinon St. and get off at the Public Theater (Demotikon Theatron) and head down the hill toward the port. The subway takes roughly 20 minutes, while the bus is a 40 minute ride. Long-distance trains for Patras and the Peloponnese leave daily from the station on Akti Kalimassioti. Long-distance trains for northern Greece (Larissis) leave daily from the station on Ag. Dimitriou across the harbor.

ORIENTATION AND PRACTICAL INFORMATION

Ferries ply the waters from Peiraias to nearly all Greek islands except the Sporades and Ionians. There is a small but invaluable map of Peiraias on the back of the Athens map (available at the tourist office in Syntagma Sq.). Most of the boats and ticket agencies are on two streets, **Akti Poseidonos** and **Akti Miaouli**. The subway deposits you at the top of Akti Poseidonos; facing the water, head left. It merges with Akti Miaouli at **Themistokleous Square,** where you arrive if you walk down **Vas. Georgiou** (from the bus stop at **Korai Square**). Themistokleos Sq. is also the departure point for boats to the Saronic Gulf Islands and **hydrofoils** to Aegina (every 2hr. 8am-8pm, 40min., 25,500dr, students 21,700dr). The larger ferries dock at Akti Miaouli; international ferries are at the end toward the Customs House. Small ferries depart from Akti Poseidonos. **Kentriko** (tel. 412 1181 or 412 1172; fax 413 3193), in the subway station with a large blue-lettered sign, offers luggage storage (300dr) and extremely helpful advice on where to find your boat in the glut of vessels in the port (open daily 5:30am-10pm). Inquire about their special 20-day unlimited island-hopping packages, available after June 15 (9500dr). It is harder to avoid **banks** than to find them in this town—most are located on the waterfront. The **National Bank of Greece,** 3 Antistasseos St. (tel. 417 4101), is one block up from Themistokleous Sq. Open Mon.-Thurs. 8am-2pm, Fri. 8am-1:30pm. There is a **Citibank** with **ATMs** at 47-49 Akti

Miaouli (tel. 417 2153). All banks change currency, as does the **Thomas Cook,** one block down Akti Poseidonos from the subway. **OTE** is at 14-16 Akti Poseidonos (open daily 7:15am-1pm). This office is for general inquiries only. For 24hr telephone service, head to Karaoli-Dimitriou, a block away from the National Bank. After midnight, ring the doorbell for the security guard. **Telstar Booksellers,** 57 Akti Miaouli (tel. 429 3618), offers an impressive array of magazines in English, French, and Arabic (open Mon.-Fri. 7am-8pm, Sat. 8am-4pm). **Port Police:** tel. 422 6000. **Post Office:** Tsamadou St. (tel. 412 4202), on the right off Antistasseos St., one block inland from Themistokleous Sq. The subway station offers travelers a smaller post office, to the right of the Akti Poseidonos doors (open Mon.-Fri. 7:30am-8pm, Sat. 8am-2pm, Sun. 9am-1:30pm). **Postal code:** 18503. **Telephone Code:** 01.

On the opposite side of the peninsula is the port of **Zea.** Hydrofoils depart from here to the other Saronic Gulf islands and to Kea and Kithnos. Along the water and under the sidewalk (to the right if you are coming from inland) at Zea are a **port police** office (tel. 459 3145, 459 3144), a **post office** (open Mon.-Fri. 7:30am-2pm), and a **tourist office** upstairs (tel. 413 5716; open Mon.-Fri. 8am-2:30pm); look for the EOT sign. Private boats dock in the harbor on the left (facing the water); hydrofoils await on the right. To get to Zea, walk away from the water on any of the roads off Akti Miaouli; it takes 10 minutes to get there.

ACCOMMODATIONS, FOOD, AND SIGHTS

Head away from the water, where the hotels will at least be safe. **Hotel Phidias,** 189 Koundouriotou St. (tel. 429 6480; fax 429 6251), is close to Zea on a side street off Boumboulinas, which itself springs from Akti Miaouli (singles 11,000dr; doubles 14,500dr; triples 17,400dr, all with bath). **Hotel Glaros,** 4 Char. Trikoupi St. (tel. 451 5421 or 453 7887; fax 453 7889), on a street which runs away from the lower part of Akti Miaouli, offers cheaper rates (singles 4800dr, with bath 6500dr; doubles 7000dr, with bath 8500dr; triples with bath 12,000dr). Don't sleep in the dirty and dangerous park at Themistokleos Sq.

Inexpensive fast food restaurants line the dock, offering mediocre fare at uniform prices. To find a good, cheap meal, the best approach is to do it yourself at the **Peiraikon Supermarket** (tel. 417 6495). Go one block up Antistasseos St., and turn left at the National Bank of Greece; the supermarket is at the end of that block (open Mon.-Thurs. 8am-8pm, Fri. 8am-9pm, Sat. 8am-3pm). The bakery **Europa,** 166-168 Koundouriotou (tel. 412 2577), near Hotel Phidias, offers cheap, mouth-watering treats (*baklava* 300dr). For inexpensive and delicious pita roll-ups, visit **Drosopigi,** 24 Akti Moustopoulou (tel. 452 0585, 428 0645). Although the menu is extensive, the 17 sandwich varieties, including vegetarian options, are the most popular choices. Sit outside and eat along the Zea boardwalk.

The prize possession of the **Archaeological Museum,** 31 Char. Trikoupi St. (tel. 452 1598), is the ancient "Peiraias Kouros," a large hollow bronze statue with outstretched arms (open Tues.-Sun. 8:30am-3pm; admission 500dr, students 400dr, EU students free, seniors 400dr; no charge for video, no flash allowed). Near the museum is the 2nd-century BC **Hellenistic theater.** Farther south at Zea, facing the harbor and underneath the sidewalk on Akti Themistokleous, is the **Maritime Museum** (tel. 451 6822), which traces the history of the Greek navy using detailed ship models. The courtyard is home port to torpedo tubes, naval weapons, and anchors (open Tues.-Fri. 8:30am-2pm, Sat.-Sun. 9am-1pm; admission 500dr).

THE PETALION GULF COAST

■ Cape Sounion

Local legend has it that the remains of fabled **Atlantis,** the continent which sank into the sea millennia ago, lie off the coast of Cape Sounion. A strikingly similar local legend exists in Akrotiri, Thera (Santorini). Take your pick. At Sounion, tourist-oriented schedules, including bus routes and temple viewing, are fixed according to the sunset. It is popular belief that the sunset at Sounion is the most breathtaking in all of Greece. The **Temple of Poseidon** (tel. 39 363) still stands on a promontory high above the coast. The original temple was constructed around 600 BC, destroyed by the Persians in 480 BC, and rebuilt by Pericles in 440 BC. The 16 remaining Doric columns still suggest the graceful symmetry of the original temple. Scattered remains of the **Temple of Athena Sounias,** the patron goddess of Athens, litter the lower hill. Sunrise is the ideal time to view the temples. If you sleep in, try to visit before early afternoon (when the tour buses funnel in) or around sunset (after they've drained out). Pack a lunch and bypass the pricey cafeteria (temples open daily 9am-sunset; admission 800dr, students 400dr, EU students free). Last bus to Athens departs according to the hour of the sunset (usually 8:30-9pm in summer). Check the schedule at the bus station upon arrival.

To reach the ocean, follow one of the many paths from the inland side of the temple. The agile and adventurous can negotiate the cliff on the ocean side. Swarmed with vacationing families, the **beaches** along the 70km **Apollo Coast** between Peiraias and Cape Sounion have a crowded carnival atmosphere, especially on summer weekends. Some are owned by hotels, which charge a 150dr admission fee, but towns usually have free public beaches as well and some seaside stretches along the bus route remain almost empty. The driver will let you off almost anywhere.

Two orange-striped KTEL buses travel the 65km road to Cape Sounion. One goes along the coast and stops at all points on the Apollo Coast, leaving every hour on the half hour (6:30am-6:30pm, 2hr., 1200dr) from the 14 Mavromateon St. stop in the square just below Areos Park in Athens. It provides a beautiful, pleasant ride with crystal blue water in sight the whole time (catch a seat on the right side of the bus to enjoy the scenery). The other bus leaves from Areos Park every hour on hour (6am-6pm, 2¼hr., 1200dr), and follows a slightly less scenic inland route. Every hour on the half hour, buses head from Cape Sounion to the port of **Lavrio** (20min., 200dr). Buses depart from Athens to Lavrio to catch the ferries (every 30min. 5:50am-7pm, 8:15pm, 9:30pm, 1½hr., 900dr). **Ferries** go from Lavrio to Kea (1¼hr., 1750dr) and Kithnos (2½hr., 2300dr). For tickets call 26 177.

If you want to spend the night to see the temples, or if you miss the last bus to the ferry at Lavrio, you can find pricey accommodations at **Aegaeon Hotel** (tel. 39 200; fax 39 234), located five minutes from the bus stop toward the temples (if you plan to stay, get off the bus at the main stop rather than up at the temples). Look for the large yellow building down by the beach on the right (singles 12,000dr; doubles 16,000dr, all with bath). The **Belle Epoque Hotel,** 33 Klioni St at Lavrio (tel. 27 130 or 26 059), has reasonably priced rooms (singles 5000dr; doubles 9000dr; triples 15,000dr; full breakfast 1500dr). To find it, walk a very short distance from the bus stop away from the port and the center of town. **Telephone Code:** 0292.

■ Near Peirais: Rafina

Rafina might as well be named "Little Peiraias." Situated across from its larger twin on the Attic Peninsula, Rafina is more pleasant on the eyes, ears, and lungs than its bigger, badder counterpart. Uphill from the port, life centers on the white-paved town square.

The ramp up from the waterfront leads to Plastira Sq. The **Commercial Bank** (tel. 25 182) is located on the far left corner of the square (open Mon.-Thurs. 8am-2pm, Fri. 8am-1:30pm) and the **Ionian Bank** (tel. 24 152), which is equipped with an **ATM** as well, is two blocks farther inland (open Mon.-Thurs. 7:45am-2pm, Fri. 7:45am-1:30pm). Both banks offer **currency exchange.** English-speaking offices along the waterfront offer information and ferry tickets. **Strintzis Lines, Gatsos Lines, Agoudimos Lines,** and **Ventouris Ferries** operate various ferries, while **Ilios Lines** and **Hermes Lines** operate hydrofoils. **Taxis** line up right in front of the square. There is a **pharmacy** one block down Kyprion St. off the left side of the square. Look for the green cross (open Mon. and Wed. 8:30am-2pm, Tues. and Thurs. 8:30am-2pm and 5:30-9pm). With the water at your back, the **post office** (tel. 23 777) stands two streets to the right on Eleftheriou Venizelou (open Mon.-Fri. 8am-3pm). **Postal Code: 19009.** The **OTE** (tel. 25 182) is across the street from the post office on the far side of the square (open Mon.-Fri. 7:30am-2:30pm). **Telephone Code:** 0294.

Rafina is accessible by frequent **buses** from 29 Mavromateon St., two blocks up along Areos Park in Athens (every 30min. 5:45am-10:30pm, 1hr., 440dr). **Ferries** sail to: Karystos in Evia (2-3 per day, 1¾hr., 1950dr); Marmari in Evia (4-6 per day, 1¼hr., 1340dr); Andros (2-3 per day, 2hr., 2340dr); Tinos (2-3 per day, 4hr., 3370dr); Mykonos (2 per day, 5hr., 3825dr); Paros (1 per week, 8hr., 3770dr); and Naxos (6hr., 3800dr). **Hydrofoils** sail to: Andros (2 per day, 1hr., 4530dr), Tinos (2 per day, 2hr., 6925dr), and Mykonos (2 per day, 2½hr., 7830dr). There is also a daily **super-Catamaran** to the Cyclades in summer. Mr. Rigos at **Auromar tourist office** (tel. 28 666) on the port can help. The **port authority** (tel. 22 300) has more info.

Be prepared to pay heartily for the dubious pleasure of spending a night in Rafina. **Hotel Korali** (tel. 22 477), in Plastira Sq., offers cramped but clean rooms with shared baths (singles 5500dr; doubles 8000dr; triples 12,000dr). **Hotel Avra's** (tel. 22 780, -3; fax 23 320) similar rooms are immeasurably enhanced by ocean views. Visible from the port, this enormous brown concrete building can be reached by heading left at the top of the ramp leading away from the boats (singles 15,000dr; doubles 19,000dr). Those who wish to **camp** can head to the beach of **Kokkino Limanaki** (tel. 31 604 or 78 780; fax 31 603), 1½km from the port; there is a blue and white sign at the top of the ramp (1250dr per person; 1100dr per small tent; 1250dr per large tent; shower included with 24hr. hot water).

For those catching early ferries, the **Arktopeio** is the place for a quick and inexpensive bakery. Head to the left side of the square, with your back to the water, for fresh bread (160dr), filled croissants (from 160dr), yogurt, milk and juice (open daily 5am-11pm). The pier is lined with innumerable *psarotavernas* (fish restaurants), all of which display their catch in storefront, ice-filled counters. If you can't stand the smell of octopus, there is a small grill next to the bakery that can fill you with *souvlaki* and pita bread.

■ Marathon

In 490 BC, when the Athenians defeated the Persians at the bloody battle of Marathon, the messenger Pheidippides ran 42km to Athens to announce the victory and then collapsed dead from exhaustion. Today, international marathons (*sans* fatal collapse) replicate this act. Runners trace Pheidippides' route twice annually, beginning at the commemorative plaque. Beautiful **Lake Marathon,** with its huge marble dam, rests 8km past the otherwise uninspiring town. Until WWII, the lake was Athens' sole water source. At **Ramnous,** 15km to the northeast, lie the ruins of the Temples of Nemesis, goddess of retribution, and Themtis, goddess of law, and justice.

On the coast near Marathon, **Schinias** to the north and **Timvos Marathonas** to the south are popular beaches. Many people camp at Schinias since the trees offer protection, but the mosquitoes are thirsty and mean, and freelance camping is illegal.

The **bus** for Marathon leaves from 29 Mavromateon St. by Areos Park in Athens (every hr. 5:30am-10:30pm, 1hr., 750dr). To get to the **Archaeological Museum of Marathonas** (tel. 55 155), ask the driver to let you off at the sign for the museum

("Mouseion and Marathonas"). Follow the signs and don't despair; the museum is 2km farther at the end of the paved road (open Tues.-Sun. 8:30am-3pm; admission 500dr, students 300dr, seniors 400dr). To reach the Marathon Tomb or the nearby beach, walk 1.5km back toward Athens. Lake Marathon, Amphiareion, and Ramnous are accessible by automobile only.

■ Delphi ΔΕΛΦΟΙ

As any Delphinian will proudly attest, this small city of 2500 marks the *omphalos* (navel) of the earth. Local legend claims that, to satisfy his curiosity, Zeus simultaneously released two eagles, one from the East and one from the West. The birds impaled each other with their beaks over Delphi and fell to the ground where the sacred stone still marks the spot of the ill-fated rendezvous. The Oracle of Apollo was later built around this landmark, welcoming troubled citizens who sought Pythia's guidance. Pythia, ancient Greece's fortune teller, inhaled the vapors emitted from a chasm in the temple floor, entered a state of ecstasy, and uttered incoherent words then interpreted by a priest and announced in cryptic verse.

ORIENTATION AND PRACTICAL INFORMATION

The municipal **tourist office** (tel. 82 900), housed in the town hall with entrances on both Pavlou and Apollonos St., is run by friendly and tetra-lingual Mrs. Efi. Come here to get tips on just about anything under the Delphic sun, including bus schedules, hotels, and camping rates (open Mon.-Fri. 7:30am-2:30pm). If the office is closed, head to the bus station/Cafe Castri, 14 Frangou St., where English-speaking staff can help decipher complicated bus schedules and provide directions (open daily 8am-10pm). The **tourist police** (tel. 82 220) and the general **police station** (tel. 82 222) are located at 3 Angelos Syngrov St., directly behind the church at the peak of Apollonos St. (open daily 9am-2pm, but staffed 24hr.). The **National Bank** (tel. 82 622; open Mon.-Thurs. 8am-2pm, Fri. 8am-1:30pm) is at 30 Pavlou St. and has an **ATM** which accepts MasterCard. At the foot of Pavlou St. across from Hotel Pythia are free **public toilets** and the **taxi stand** (tel. 82 000). The **post office** (tel. 82 376; open Mon.-Fri. 7:30am-2pm) is at 25 Pavlou St. **Postal Code:** 33054. The **OTE** is at 10 Pavlou St. (open Mon.-Sat. 7:30am-3:10pm, Sun. 9am-2pm). **Telephone Code:** 0265.

Buses leave Athens from the station at 260 Liossion St. for Delphi (tel. (01) 831 7096; 5 per day, 3½hr., 2700dr). To get to the station, take blue bus #024 from Amalias Ave. at the entrance to the National Garden or El. Venizelou (Panepistimiou) by Syntagma Sq. Buy your ticket at the booth labeled Δελφοι (Delphi). Arrive early to avoid long lines. With a railpass, take a train to Levadia; from there, buses head to Delphi (700dr). From Delphi buses leave for: Thessaloniki via Volos, Larissa, and Katerini (7 per week, 5½hr., 6200dr); Patras (1-2 per day, 3hr., 2200dr); Lamia (3 per day, 2hr., 1600dr); Nafpaktos (4 per day, 2½hr., 1900dr); Amphissa (7 per day, 30min., 340dr); Itea (7 per day, 30min., 320dr); and Galaxidi (4 per day with a switch in Itea, 50min., 650dr).

ACCOMMODATIONS

Delphi is chalk full of hotels. Closest to the bus station is the **Hotel Athina,** 55 Pavlou St. (tel. 82 239), with balconied rooms and marvelous views of the gulf of Corinth. Check-out is 11am (singles 5000dr; doubles 6000dr, with bath 7000dr; triples 8000dr, with bath 9000dr). Right next door, **Hotel Pan** offers similar breathtaking views but includes a filling breakfast and private bath to enjoy along with the view in the price of your room. Also accepts credit cards and offers free luggage storage (tel. 82 294; singles 5000dr; doubles 6000-10,000dr). If you don't mind sharing a bathroom, head over to **Pension Odysseus** on Filellinon (tel. 82 235), parallel to and below Pavlou, where Mrs. Toula will show you to one of her clean and breezy rooms (singles 4900dr; doubles 6300dr). **The Sun View Rooms,** 84 Apollonos St. (tel. 82 349), are new and in pristine condition. Look for the last house on Apollonos before the European center and ring the bell at the brown door under the "rooms to let" sign (doubles 7500dr; triples 9500dr, but you'd be wise to bargain). The nearest campsite is **Apollo Camping** (tel. 82 762, -50; fax 82 639), 1.5km down from the bus station (1200dr per person; 750dr per tent; 700dr per car). **Delphi Camping** (tel. 82 363; 1200dr per person; 800dr per tent; 700dr per car) is 4km down the road and **Chrissa Camping** (tel. 82 050) is 10km out of town (1300dr per person; 900dr per tent). The bus can drop you at any of these campsites.

FOOD AND ENTERTAINMENT

Delphi's *tavernas* have terraces that overlook the mountains and the Gulf of Corinth. **Taverna-Restaurant Sunflower,** 33 Pavlou St. (tel. 82 442, -686), offers a filling assortment of *mezedes* (hors d'oeuvres) that allow you to taste several Greek specialties at once. Entrees, including their specialty, *yiouvetsi* (meat and kritharaki cooked in a ceramic pot), range from 1000-3000dr. If your stomach grumbles later in the evening, head over to **Thimios,** 51 Pavlou St. (tel. 83 130), for a deliciously cheap *souvlaki* (250dr; open daily 7:30pm-midnight). **Markets** can be found along Apollonos and Pavlou St. For great fresh breads and pastries, take a left at the whitewashed church on the peak of the hillside Apollonos St. and follow the clearly marked signs to the **Artotechniki Bakery** (tel. 82 042). Your small effort will be rewarded with *voutimata* (dipping cookies for coffee/milk) and the regional specialty, *kourabiethes* (almond cookies covered in icing; open daily 5am-10pm).

The only places to shake a leg after dark are **Club No Name,** 33 Pavlou St. (tel. 82 600), and **Katoi** (tel. 82 053), across the street from the bus station, where you can mingle with Delphi's youth for a 500dr cover, sipping 500dr beers or 1000dr cocktails. Both open at 10pm and stay open until sunrise if customers are enjoying themselves. If your timing is lucky, there is also a **Festival of Ancient Greek Drama** put on in July and August by the **European Cultural Center of Delphi** (tel. 82 731, -92; fax 82 733). The Center, open daily 9am-2pm, also has temporary international art exhibitions. To find it, walk down the Amphissa/Itea road and follow the signs back uphill. Delphi is home to several other summer festivals, so ask around and keep a sharp eye out for posters when you arrive. Also, from April to October **Villa Symposio** offers nightly food, drink, and Greek folk dances. Call **Delphi Consultants** (tel. 82 086) for information on prices and transportation.

SIGHTS

The ancient Greek gods expressed their wishes to humans through oracles. Politically, **Delphi's oracle** was supreme—leaders throughout the Mediterranean sought its infallible advice. Whenever a Greek city won a battle, its leader would erect a dedicatory offering to the oracle. As a result, the entrance to the sanctuary was cluttered with tributes from all over Greece.

Legend has it that Apollo slew the monster Python, which had presided over Delphi. The snake, an earth-spirit, continued to speak to postulants through an intermediary, an elderly woman known as the **Pythia,** who could be seen only by specially elected priests. Sitting directly over the *omphalos,* the Pythia inhaled the vapors wafting up from the chasm below, became entranced, and then chanted deliriously. Her incoherent mutterings were "versified" by the priests, who would announce her prophecies to the waiting public.

The main body of structures, known as the **Sanctuary of Apollo,** lies 300m east of town on the road to Athens (follow the highway and take the paved path on your left to the ruins and museum, a 5min. downhill walk out of town). **Maps** of the first century BC reconstruction of the site are available in the shops in town or at the kiosk across from the bus station for 300dr. The *Delphi* brochure, free at the tourist information office, has a smaller map. The **guidebooks** available at the museum (1500-2500dr) are most useful in the museum, where Greek and French dominate.

Now as then, the **Temple of Apollo** is the prime attraction in the area. The building burned in 548 BC and the 373 BC reconstruction was shattered by an earthquake.

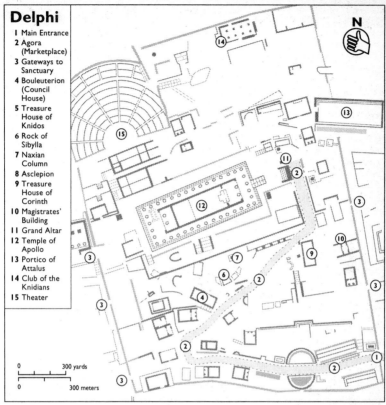

Delphi

1 Main Entrance
2 Agora (Marketplace)
3 Gateways to Sanctuary
4 Bouleuterion (Council House)
5 Treasure House of Knidos
6 Rock of Sibylla
7 Naxian Column
8 Asclepion
9 Treasure House of Corinth
10 Magistrates' Building
11 Grand Altar
12 Temple of Apollo
13 Portico of Attalus
14 Club of the Knidians
15 Theater

0 ———— 300 yards
0 ———— 300 meters

What stands today are the remains of a second reconstruction. Oracular priests announced the Pythia's verdicts. The huge walls were once inscribed with famous maxims of Greek philosophers. Scamper up the hills past tour groups to the stadium, sit and relax, then meander down the mountain at your leisure, pitying the tour groups huffing and puffing their way up (site open in summer Mon.-Fri. 7:30am-7:15pm, Sat.-Sun. 8:30am-2:45pm; off-season Mon.-Fri. 7:30am-5:15pm, Sat.-Sun. 8:30am-2:45pm; admission 1200dr, students and seniors 600dr, EU students free). Delphi's **Archaeological Museum** (tel. 82 312), located just before the Pythian Sanctuary along the path from town, contains the frieze of the Siphnian Treasury and the Charioteer of Delphi. Open Mon.-6:30pm, Tues.-Fri. 7:30am-7:15pm, Sat.-Sun. 8:30am-2:45pm. Admission 1200dr, students 600dr.

The unfenced ruins of the **Temple of Pronaia Athena** are roughly 200m past the main set of ruins heading away from town (the entrance is just past the exit sign). On your way, you'll pass the **Castelian Spring,** where pilgrims cleansed themselves both physically and spiritually before calling upon the oracle. Drinking from the spring is said to confer the gift of eloquence. To your right is the millennia-old **Gymnasium.** The three remaining Doric columns of the circular 4th-century **Tholos** at Athena's sanctuary are the most photographed of Delphi's ruins. Although scholars have inferred from ancient texts that the Tholos was an important part of the Delphic complex, no one now knows exactly what function it served. Next to the *Tholos* lies the **Treasury of Marseilles,** a gift from the citizens of ancient France attesting to the extent of the oracle's prestige (ruins open 24hr.; free).

■ Near Delphi

LEVADIA ΛΕΒΑΔΙΑ

For oracle enthusiasts who want a second opinion, the **Oracle of Trophonios** is on a cliff overlooking Levadia (ancient Lebadea). The site once attracted pilgrims on their way to Delphi. In the 14th century, Frankish crusaders built a **castle** over the site of the oracle. It is the best-preserved castle in the area, and only a 15-minute walk from town. From the bus station, turn right, walk uphill to the square, and go right again onto Venizelou St. Turn right at the end of the street, then left at the church. The oracle once stood at the stream; the castle ruins are 200m farther.

To ponder the oracle's inspiration, make your way to **Xenia,** a trendy bar and restaurant built directly over the waterfall. Sip refreshing fruit granitas (950dr) or a variety of iced coffees (500dr) to the peaceful sound of rushing water (open daily 9am-3am). For an inexpensive yet filling meal, follow the *pezedromos* (pedestrian path) that branches off the south side of the main square. **Geros** (tel. 28 492), a bakery that also serves cheese pie and fresh sandwiches (200-400dr), is on the left (open daily 7am-10pm). Otherwise, try one of the snack bars that line Papaspyrou St. next to Hotel Levadia (chicken or pork *souvlaki* and pita 400dr).

Buses to Athens (2hr.) via Thebes (45min.) leave every hour from 6am to 8pm (2050dr). Athens is also accessible by train from Levadia, but the station is 5km from town. If the scarcity of bus connections compels you to spend the night in Levadia, **Hotel Levadia,** 4 Papaspyrou (tel. (02061) 23 611; fax 28 266), is near the top of the town square. All rooms have bathrooms (singles 10,000dr; doubles 14,000dr). The popular ski slopes of Mt. Parnassos, only 65km away, make winter the high season here.

OSIOS LOUKAS

Although it is toilsome to reach, the **Osios Loukas** monastery is worth the trouble for those who seek the combination of spiritual and natural divinity. This pastoral and inspiring spot may give you pangs of longing for the monkhood. More than 1700m above sea-level, the stone monastery complex contains magnificent mosaics and affords tremendous views. Dress modestly (no shorts or bare shoulders, no pants for women); makeshift coverings are available at the gate.

To allow for transportation difficulties, give Osios Loukas a full afternoon preceded by a morning jaunt in Levadia. There is only one daily **bus** which climbs the mountain to Osios Loukas, leaving Levadia at 1:40pm (45min., 480dr); make sure you tell the driver you are headed for the monastery or he might just skip the mountain route altogether and go directly to Distomo. In the summer months, the monastery closes between 2 and 4pm, just in time to welcome those arriving on the 1:40pm bus from Levadia with barred doors. From Athens, take blue bus #024 from Amalias St. or El. Venizelou to the Liossion St. bus station (every 20min., 30min., 75dr) and buy a ticket to Levadia (every hr. 5:50am-8:30pm, 2hr., 2150dr). Six buses per day leave from Delphi (700dr). If you miss the sole direct bus to Osios Loukas, head over to Distomo. Take the Distomo bus from Levadia (30min., 440dr), or, if you get one of the Delphi-Athens buses, get off at the cross road for Distomo (tell the driver well in advance so that he doesn't miss the turn-off; 400dr) and walk 3km to Distomo, then take a taxi to the monastery (9km, 1000-2000dr).

Getting out of Osios Loukas may also be problematic. Travelers used to mooch lifts from commercial tour **buses,** but drivers are increasingly wary of police and thus reluctant to let people bum rides. The bus station in Distomo is a joke—buses, when they come, only go to Levadia. One bus leaves Distomo for Arachova at 4pm (45min., 280dr). The best bet to anywhere else is to share yet another taxi (4000dr). You can **change money** at the **post office,** down the hill near the bus stop (open Mon.-Fri. 7:30am-2pm). The **OTE** is a few buildings down the road (open Mon.-Fri. 7:30am-3pm). For **medical emergencies** dial (0267) 22 791.

There are two hotels up the hill to the right of the main intersection in Distomo. The first you'll come to is **Hotel America** (tel. (0267) 22 079, -80; singles 4500dr; doubles 7000dr). **Koutiaris Hotel** (tel. (0267) 22 268), near Hotel America, offers slightly larger rooms with bath, phone, and TV (singles 6480dr; doubles 7980dr). To make your own meal, choose one of several mini-supermarkets on 10th Ioniov 1944 St. for cheese or sweet hazelnut-chocolate spreads, then head to **Matina Bakery,** across from the bus station, for fresh bread (60-130dr). Right next door, **Cafeteria In & Out** (tel. 22 420, open daily 9am-2:30pm and 5pm-2am) will make you a sandwich for 500dr. If you seek a full meal, **Odysseus** (tel. 22 616) is only a five-minute walk away from the bus stop on 10th Ioniov St. Although the road appears deserted, persist until the gas station—the restaurant is right next door. Your effort will be rewarded with grilled meats and traditional (albeit greasy) Greek cuisine.

Kill some time at the **archaeological museum,** up the road to Osios Loukas (open Mon.-Fri. 8am-6pm, Sat.-Sun. 9:30am-3pm; admission 400dr). Ask to be let into the locked half in order to see a few cool mosaics. The main building in the Osios Loukas complex, the arresting **Church of St. Luke,** is dedicated to a local hermit known for his powers of healing and prophecy. According to locals, when Luke died in his cell in 953 AD, a myrrh tree sprouted from the cold floor. The entrance to the 10th-century church is adorned with Byzantine **mosaics,** most notably a faceless doubting Thomas inserting his finger in Christ's wound. The more beautiful mosaics, the Nativity, Presentation at the Temple, and Baptism, are tucked into the squinches that support the dome. Although not as famous as the ones in the upper church, the 11th-century **frescoes** that cover most of the **crypt's** interior are every bit as gorgeous; use a flashlight for best viewing. Don't miss the frescoes removed from their original homes and now displayed in a building at the very back of the complex, off the courtyard behind the churches. Despite Osios Loukas' indoor attractions, the flowers, birds, and encompassing mountains outside the monastery are most enthralling (tel. (0267) 22 797; open daily 7:30am-2pm and 4:30-7pm; admission 800dr, students 400dr, seniors 600dr).

ARACHOVA ΑΡΑΧΩΒΑ

Stacked onto the slopes below Mt. Parnassos 10km east of Delphi, the village of Arachova revels in its own relaxed atmosphere in summer and caters to skiers in winter. This is a perfect place to collapse after you've spent the day fighting the crowds at Delphi. It's a charming mountain town with narrow streets and little shops. Even though Arachova lives the intensity of a ski resort in winter, a breezy summer afternoon spent wandering and enjoying the mountainous view can be a delight. The area's culinary distinctions are its amber honey and tasty *saganaki* (fried cheese). The main street oozes with *souvlaki* and souvenirs. The sweaters, woven rugs, and coonskin-type hats that you'll find befit the town's popularity in winter.

The **Cooperative Office Kiparissos** (tel. 31 519) serves as a **tourist office** with information on the town and accommodations. To find it, continue on the main road in the direction of Athens. You'll soon see the school, a stone building with a red painted entrance. The cooperative office is right next door (look for the red and yellow sign). In the first of the town's three squares you'll find the **post office** (open Mon.-Fri. 7:30am-2pm), which **exchanges money.** Stay on the main road and head farther into town to find the **National Bank** on your left (open Mon.-Thurs. 8:30am-2pm, Fri. 8:30am-1pm). If it's closed, don't pout—it has an **ATM.** The **police** are across from the bus station, on the second floor (tel. (0267) 31 133). Farther east, past the third square, is a **pharmacy** (tel. (0267) 31 186). The **OTE** is across from the post office (open Mon.-Fri. 7:30am-3:10pm). **Postal Code:** 32004.

Roughly five **buses** per day run between Athens and Delphi, stopping in Arachova, while an additional eight make the run from Arachova to Delphi (20min., 160dr). All buses to Delphi go to Itea (1hr., 500dr) and two make connections from Itea to Galaxidi (15min., 150dr). A brown and yellow "Celena" sign identifies the **bus station** (tel. (0267) 31 790), which doubles as a cafe and restaurant. The owner can usually be found sipping coffee in the square directly across the street.

Near the first square (coming from Delphi) are several hotels, pensions, and rooms to let. The **Apollon Inn,** on the first left off the main road coming from Delphi (appropriately called Delphi St.), has single and double rooms with bath for 5000dr and 7000dr respectively. **Pension Nostas** (tel. 31 385; email nostosstravelling.gr), farther up the main road and on the last right before the central square, has beautiful rooms and an incredibly friendly manager/owner. Doubles with bath, TV, and refrigerator range between 8000-13,000dr. The closest **campground** is west of Delphi (see p. 91). Moderately priced *tavernas* include **Liakoura** (tel. 31 783) next to the OTE (*saganaki* 800dr, *souvlaki* 1250dr), and **Lakka** below the police station (salad 700-1000dr, *saganaki* 500dr). The more daring, non-vegetarians can head over to **Dasargiri** (tel. 31 291) for *kokoretsi* (1500dr) and *kontosouvli* (1800dr)—both delightfully cooked animal viscera.

Apollo and the Muses now share their abode with ski buffs on **Mt. Parnassos** (2700m). If you're interested in hiking up in summer, take a taxi to the **Mt. Parnassos Ski Center,** 27km northwest of Arachova. From the ski center, it's a steep 2km climb up to the summit, where vultures glower overhead. The ski season on Mt. Parnassos runs from November to May. There are 14 lifts and tickets average 6000dr per day; rentals are 4000dr per day. Renting in Arachova can save you about 2000dr if you have a means of transporting equipment to the slopes.

Founded in 1996, the **Hellenic Center of Mountain Sports in Arachova** (tel. (0267) 31 846) organizes mountain biking, skiing, trekking, and snowboarding excursions to Mt. Parnassos. There's a small information booth next to Cafe Neo on the main road. To stay in the area, try Delphi or Arachova, but you'll have to pay 7000-8000dr for the round-trip cab, since the taxi lobby won't allow public buses to run to the ski center (taxi tel. (0267) 31 566). Alternately, make a daytrip from Athens (bus leaves 6am, 3hr., 2500dr round-trip). For information on skiing, find Mr. Kostas Koutras at his **ski shop** (tel. 31 841, -767) on the first left coming from Delphi. In addition to information, Mr. Koutras rents skis for 2500dr and snowboards for 5000dr per day. He also sells new equipment at decent prices. In the summer, when his shop is closed, Mr. Koutras is a good source of tourist information—find him in the main square drinking coffee with the bus manager.

ITEA ITEA

A quiet escape from Delphi, this semi-industrial town offers only a rocky beach and the long waterfront boardwalk lined with cafes and *tavernas.* Enjoy the view in the afternoon when the construction has silenced and the sun glints on the water. The beach east of town is equipped with outdoor showers. A cleaner and more solitary beach is **Kira Beach,** 2km from town. The **post office** is along the beach near the bus stop (open Mon.-Fri. 7:30am-8pm, Sat. 7:30am-2pm). A **bank** is across the street (open Mon.-Thurs. 8am-2pm, Fri. 8am-1:30pm). Itea also has the only **motorbike rental** shop in the Delphi area; inquire at the **tourist shop** Tsonos (tel. (0267) 33 317), past the post office 100m to the left of the bus station (small motorbikes 3000-5000dr per day). Frequent **buses** run from Delphi to Itea (11 per day, 6:30am-8:20pm, 1hr., 320dr). The last bus back to Delphi from Itea is at 5:45pm; a **taxi** (tel. (0267) 32 200) is a good option for late returns (1200-2500dr according to the number of passengers). It's a five- to six-hour walk uphill to Delphi. If you want to stay here, try the **Hotel Galini** (tel. (0267) 32 278; fax 32 323) on the waterfront street Akti Poseidonos (singles 7000dr; doubles 9500dr; all rooms have bath). Or, continue to walk with the water on your right, down the street to **Hotel Akti** (tel. 32 015, -257), which is cheaper but not quite as clean (singles 4000dr; doubles 6000dr, with bath 7500; triples 7000dr). Moderate cuisine for moderate prices can be found along the waterfront. The **Dolphin II Restaurant,** on the water as you walk away from town, has superb seafood, as do most of the *tavernas* on the beach.

GALAXIDI ΓΑΛΑΞΙΔΙ

Asking the origin of Galaxidi's name can pit neighbor against neighbor. Men are likely to claim that the mermaid Galaxa rose from the sea to establish a seaside town—hence the name in her honor. Women will tell a different story. A combination of *gala* (milk) and *xithi* (vinegar), the town's name reflects the bittersweet existence of a seaman's wife. Stemming from Galaxidi's history as a prominent naval base, this story is now out of date. Navy wives no longer sit impatiently for news of a safe voyage—instead, they await a speedy return from the local *taverna.*

The bus drops off at one end of **Nik. Mama,** the main street in the town center that leads down to the waterfront and harbor. Though Galaxidi is pretty sleepy most of the year, things get hectic here just before Easter. Food fights break out over Mardi Gras, and pies are the weapon of choice. The town's children dancing in traditional garb offer more sedate entertainment. The **OTE** is down the first right from the bus stop off Nik. Mama (tel. (0265) 41 42 199; open Mon.-Fri. 7:30am-3:10pm). For indigestion and other post-party traumas, head to the **pharmacy** (tel. (0265) 41 122), one block to the right of the bus station on Nik. Mama. Galaxidi's **post office** is at the end of Nik. Mama (open Mon.-Fri. 7:30am-2pm). **Postal Code:** 33052.

From the bus stop, turn right and head down Nik. Mama St. to find **Hotel Poseidon** (tel. 41 246, -271), a breezy old home turned hotel blessed with a friendly manager, Costas, who is likely to break open a bottle of ouzo the evening of your arrival (singles 4000dr; doubles 8000dr). **Pension Votsalo** (tel. (0265) 41 788, -542) is pricier but near the waterfront. Cross the square from the bus stop and go down Novorhou Ageli St. at the right side of the square until you see the pension on your left. Don't be put off by the twists and turns of the street; you'll see the place soon enough (doubles 10,000dr; longer stays get better deals). On a summer weekend, expect the prices to be 20% higher. There are also a few **rooms to let**; ask at the bus station/*taverna* or other restaurants, or keep your eyes peeled for signs.

To dine by the water, head for **Omilos,** a restaurant with tables that extend onto a pier (tel. 42 111, -0). In keeping with the surroundings, fresh fish is the entree of choice, but stretch your imagination and sample grilled sardines and the secret recipe mussels (2500dr). Prices may require a bit of a splurge, but view and quality make it well worth the strain on your daily budget.

If local clientele is a sign of authenticity, **Cafe Mezethoglentopoleion** (meat, drink, and merriment) is *the* place for ouzo and *garthouba* (1500dr). A block away from the bus station, it welcomes visitors to a relaxed atmosphere. Just follow the laughter and shouts. But perhaps the best deal is a trip to either of the supermarkets on Nik. Mama, followed by a swing through **To Konaki** (tel. 42 258), an excellent **sweet shop** next to the supermarket closest to the bus stop (ice cream 200dr, special soupy almond concoction 1900dr per kg).

For wonderful swimming, head to the forest side of the harbor (over the "bridge" as you walk down Nik. Mama past Restaurant Steki, all the way around). Small islands sit offshore and flooded caves overhang scant beaches. The **Church of St. Nicholas,** near the museum, houses many fine mosaics. The 13th-century **Monastery of Transfiguration,** with sublime century-old wood carvings and a great view of town, is 500m from Galaxidi on the uphill road outside of town. Coming from Itea, make a right before the gas station.

Many travelers continue from Galaxidi to **Nafpaktos,** close to the mouth of the Gulf and to the ferry crossing for the Peloponnese at **Antirion.** The **bus** to Nafpaktos runs out of Delphi and stops in Galaxidi (2½hr. from Delphi, 2hr. from Galaxidi). If you stay, try the **Aegli** (tel. (0634) 27 271; singles 4000dr; doubles 7000dr).

■ Thebes (Thiva) ΘHBA

Thebes once ranked among the most powerful cities in ancient Greece. Its location gave it control over the strategic routes connecting the Peloponnese and Attica with northern Greece, and its fertile soil ensured the town's prosperity. Thebes is most famous as the birthplace of Hercules and as the setting for the story of Oedipus. The sphinx that guarded the gates of Thebes was a blight to the town's trade and prosperity until Oedipus came along and did away with the dreadful monster by solving its riddle: "What animal walks on four legs in the morning, two in the afternoon, and three in the evening?" (Answer: Man.) Modern Thebes can't compete with its racy past. Razed by Alexander the Great in the 4th century BC, it never fully recovered.

The **National Bank of Greece,** 94 Pindarou (tel. (0262) 27 782), one street over from Eparminon, also has an **ATM** (open Mon.-Thurs. 8am-2pm, Fri. 8am-1:30pm). Thebes' new **bus station** is on Kiprou St., which meets Epaminon near the top of the hill. Street signs are rare but people are more than willing to give directions. Bus service is frequent to the Liossion St. terminal in Athens (every hr., 1½hr., 1500dr). To travel to Chalkis, take the frequent Athens bus to the Skimatari stop (30min., 500dr). Across the street, the Athens-Chalkis bus runs every 30 minutes (10min., 300dr). For a **taxi,** call 27 077. The town's **hospital,** 2 Tseva (tel. (0262) 28 101), is located directly across the street from the museum while the **post office,** 17 Drakou St. (tel. (0262) 27 810), is near the top of Epaminon St. (open Mon.-Fri. 7:30am-2pm). **Postal Code:** 32200. The **OTE** at 2 Vousouba (tel. (0262) 27 799) is in the center of town (open Mon.-Fri. 7:30am-3pm).

If you are obliged to spend the night here, the **Hotel Niovi,** 63 Epaminon St. (tel. (0262) 29 888), may be your best bet (doubles 7560dr, with bath 9180dr). In the evening, the many *tavernas* that line Epaminon and Pindari streets provide lively R&R for the neighboring military base.

Follow Epaminon St. downhill, take a right past the ruins, and on your left will be the **Archaeological Museum** (tel. 27 913). Be sure to see the **Mycenaean larnakes,** clay coffins adorned with paintings of funerary rites, mosaics, and reliefs. The guidebook is particularly informative (open Tues.-Sun. 8:30am-3pm; admission 500dr, students 300dr, senior citizens 400dr). The scanty remains of the **House of Kadmos,** a Mycenaean palace dating from the 14th century BC, are visible from Pindarou St. An extensive **Mycenaean palace and acropolis** lie beneath the modern town of Thebes. Historians and archaeologists begrudge Thebes' every new building, fearing construction may endanger what little remains of the Mycenaean civilization.

EVIA (EUBOEA) ΕΥΒΟΙΑ

Wrenched from the mainland by an ancient earthquake (or perhaps by Poseidon's trident), Evia grazes the coastline north of Athens. The second largest island in Greece (after Crete), Evia was, in ancient times, a major trading center and maritime power. It boasts a central mountain range choked with chestnuts and pines—paradise for hikers. And though several beaches are sprinkled around the coast of Evia, it has yet to be infested with too many resorts.

■ Chalkida (Chalkis) ΞΑΛΚΙΖ

Bus travelers through Evia will almost inevitably encounter the suffocating port town of Chalkida. But spending time here may be not be as uneventful as you think. Aristotle was desperate because of his inability to comprehend what still may be the most interesting thing about Chalkida—the bizarre tidal flow through the straits between Evia and the mainland. Aristotle threw himself in the nearby Evia strait in a fit of anguish (*Let's Go* does not recommend following in his footsplashes). Scientists still can't explain why the water changes direction at the narrowest point between the land masses—up to six times daily around full moons, one to four times per day during the rest of the month.

The English-speaking **tourist police,** 32 El. Venizelou (tel. 22 100), are located two flights above the police station and can help with bus schedules (open Mon.-Fri. 7am-2:30pm; someone's there 24hr.). You can **change money** closer to the water at the **National Bank** (open Mon.-Thurs. 8am-2pm, Fri. 8am-1:30pm). The

bus station is at 28 Favrierou St. in the center of town. A **bus** from Liossion Station in Athens goes to Chalkida (every 30min., on Sun. every 45min., 1½hr., 1450dr). The **train** runs nearly as frequently from the Larissa station (18 per day, 2hr., 880dr). Arrival by train leaves you on the mainland; just cross the bridge to the island and the busier section of Chalkida. E. Venizelou St. runs uphill about five blocks to the left of the bridge. If you get off at the bus depot, look for Papanastasiou and turn right; walk down one block to El. Venizelou St. **Flying dolphins** leave from the dock to the right of the bridge as you face the mainland. Purchase tickets to Limni, Aedipsos, and the Sporades at the shack on the waterfront just in line with the dock (tel. 21 521, -621). For **taxis,** dial 24 411. To get to a **pharmacy** (tel. 24 646), head down El. Venizelou and make a left on A. Gobiou St. just before the waterfront. The **post office** is on Karamourzouni St., the second left off El. Venizelou as you walk uphill from the water (open Mon.-Fri. 7:30am-8pm). **Postal Code:** 34100. The **OTE** is located on Papiadaiou St.; walk up El. Venizelou four blocks from the water (2 blocks after the park with the fountain), then make a left on Papiadaiou, continuing for one block (tel. (0221) 22 599, open Mon.-Fri. 7am-10pm). The **telephone code** is 0221.

If you must spend the night, try **Hotel Kentriko** (tel. 22 375, 27 260), the pink building at 5 Ageli Gobiou St., the last left off El. Venizelou just before the waterfront (singles 7000dr; doubles 8000dr, with bath 9500-10,500dr). Prices vary depending on season; ask for a discount with a student ID. A couple doors down on Aggeli Gobiou St., **John's Hotel** (tel. (0221) 24 996, -7, -8) is a little bit more expensive, but offers TV, CNN, A/C, and baths in all its rooms (singles 9500; doubles 13,000).

Baltas Bakery, 49 Eleftheriov Venizelou (tel. 22 228), will overwhelm you with baked goods appropriate for breakfast on a bus. *Tsoureki,* a Greek specialty sweet bread baked in braid form, will leave you craving a second loaf (220dr; open daily 6am-4pm and 5:30-9pm). The waterfront is lined with trendy cafes, outdoor tables and colorful umbrellas that shade die-hard people-watchers. Order a frappe (600dr) and join in the fun, but eat elsewhere—the prices will give you heartburn. Instead, make a right onto Ermou St. at the far right end of the pier (facing the water), and join the local Chaldikians for traditional Greek foods at **O Thanasis.** Salted codfish with garlic paste and sauteed *okra* and green beans in tomato sauce display the sign of a good home-cooked meal—you'll need a thick piece of bread to wipe your plate (tel. (0221) 24 241; open daily 7:30am-10pm). Several vegetarian options are available, but little for the calorie-conscious.

The **Archaeological Museum** (tel. 76 131), on El. Venizelou across from the police station, is a roomful of findings from the Classical and Roman eras (open Tues.-Sun. 8:30am-3pm; admission 500dr, students 300dr, senior citizens 400dr). Facing the big pink building, head down the street and turn right on the little downhill road. Look for the **Folklore Museum** on your left at 4 Skalkola St. (tel. 21 817; open Wed. 10am-1pm and 6-8pm, Thurs.-Sun. 10am-1pm; free).

■ Eretria

First inhabited between the 15th and 17th centuries BC, permanent occupation of Eretria began in the 8th or 9th century BC. The town rivaled ancient Chalkis as the most important city on the island, its importance stemming from its convenient location for trade between Greece (and later Italy) and the Near East. In the 3rd century BC, Menedimos, the town's most famous son and a disciple of Plato, founded a school of philosophy here. The Roman era saw a decline in Eretria's fortunes and the town was only sporadically occupied from the first century AD onwards. More recently, the town's easy access from Chalkida (30min. by bus) and from Oropos on the mainland (30min. by ferry) has led to a resurgence in this now modest town.

ORIENTATION AND PRACTICAL INFORMATION

The first, and more convenient, of the two bus stops is at the lower end of the main commercial street, **Menedimos.** A little farther along, the same road leads to the **National Bank,** which **changes money** and has an **ATM** (open Mon.-Thurs. 9:15am-1:30pm, Fri. 9:15am-1pm). The bright lights and whizzing bumper cars of an amusement park overlook the fenced ruins to the right of the main intersection. Continuing straight ahead you'll find one wing of the town's waterfront lined with *tavernas* and, eventually, the town's few hotels. A right down the other waterfront road yields more *tavernas* and the ferry dock for boats to Oropos. Eretria is accessible by **bus** from Chalkida because everything heading south to Karystos, Kimi, or Amarinthos swings through here (about every 30min., 400dr). There is also a **ferry** from Oropos on the mainland (every 30min. 5am-9pm and every hr. until 11:45pm, 30min., 350dr). **Taxis** wait by the water, or call 62 500. A map of the town sits at the intersection of Menedimos and **Archaiou Theatrou,** two blocks up from the bank. A left turn brings you to the **post office** (open Mon.-Fri. 7:30am-8pm, Sat. 8:30am-2pm), which also changes money. The **Archaeological Museum,** an extensive area of low-lying ruins, and the scant remains of the ancient theater lie at the end of the street. **Postal Code:** 34008. A right at the main intersection leads to the **OTE** (open Mon.-Fri. 7:30am-3:10pm), a few blocks down on the right. **Telephone Code:** 0229.

ACCOMMODATIONS

Pension Diamanto (tel. 62 214), along the waterfront stretch of Archaiou Theatrou St., has rooms with bath, fridge, and A/C above the Babylon Cafe (doubles 9000dr; triples 11,000dr). A full breakfast including freshly squeezed orange juice is available for 1000dr. Farther down the street, turn left at the sign and walk 200m inland for the modern apartments (all with kitchen, fridge, A/C, and bath) of the **Eretria Sun Rise Hotel** (tel. 60 004; fax 60 648). Sadly enough for the budget traveler, this hotel is one of the better deals in town (doubles 12,000dr; triples 14,000dr; quads 16,000dr). Ask at *tavernas* for rooms.

FOOD, ENTERTAINMENT, AND SIGHTS

If all the fresh air whets your appetite, look for **La Cubana** (tel. 61 665) on Archaiou Theatrou near the waterfront and try the *dolmadakia* (900dr) or a plate of *moussaka* (1100dr). On the other waterfront stretch across the dock is **Dionisos** (tel. 61 728), which prides in its *kolokythakia* (fried zucchini 700dr) and fresh fried squid (1400dr). For dessert, **Stamatoukos** (tel. 60 909), the large sweet shop on Archaiou Theatrou, serves homemade ice cream in 24 delicious flavors (200-250dr per scoop). Nightlife hotspots serve beer for 500dr and cocktails for 1000dr.

The **Archaeological Museum** (tel. 62 206) is at the inland end of Archaiou Theatrou St. It's not the biggest collection around, but there are some quality pieces, such as a gorgeous terra cotta Gorgon's head from the 4th century BC, and the mysteriously six-fingered Centaur of Lefkandi, which dates from 750-900 BC (open Tues.-Sun. 8:30am-3pm; admission 500dr, students and senior citizens 300dr, EU students free). Exhibits are in Greek and French, but you can get the red guidebook in English (2000dr). Beyond the museum is a large excavated area of the old city. You also might explore the creatively named **House with the Mosaics.** You must find someone at the museum to bring you to the site (300m away) and unlock it, but it's definitely worth the effort. The four works in two separate rooms are among the best preserved and oldest (4th century BC) of all Greek mosaics. Because of their age and importance, they are enclosed in a room which visitors can't enter without special permission, but the glass walls afford a good view. The Swiss School of Archaeology in Greece has put out a brochure (in Greek, English, French, and German) explaining the house's history (available from the museum for 1000dr).

■ Karystos ΚΑΡΥΣΤΟΣ

Surrounded by mountains and flanked by two long sandy beaches, Karystos, which takes its name from the son of the centaur Chiron, is easygoing despite being the largest town in South Evia. Pointed round straw umbrellas, like the mushrooms in *Fantasia,* dot the sands that extend in either direction from the port.

ORIENTATION AND PRACTICAL INFORMATION

The bus stops one block above the main square, next to the **National Bank** (open Mon.-Thurs. 8am-2pm, Fri. 8am-1:30pm); look for the KTEL sign above a restaurant roasting chickens in the window. The **OTE** is on Amerikis, the next cross-street beyond the square, across from the Church of St. Nicholas (tel. 22 399; open daily 7:30am-3pm). **Buses** from Karystos travel twice daily to: Chalkis (2 per day, 4hr., 2100dr); Stira (2 per day, 1¼hr., 600dr); Marmari (3 per day, 30min., 300dr). Three to four **ferries** per day head to Rafina (2hr., 1950dr) and Marmari (1½hr., 1340dr). In Karystos, ferry tickets are sold across from where the boat docks. **South Evia Tours** (tel. (0224) 25 700; fax 22 461; open 8am-10pm), on the left of the square as you face the water, sells tickets for **flying dolphins** which go three times weekly to: Andros (2870dr); Tinos (5350dr); and Mykonos (6510dr). **Taxis** (tel. 22 200) queue in the square. To find the **police station** (tel. (0224) 22 252), turn into the small alley past the bank and climb the stairs. To reach the **post office** from the OTE, turn left on Amerikis and then take the first right past the playgrounds; you'll see the round yellow sign (open Mon.-Fri. 7:30am-2pm). **Postal Code: 34001.**

ACCOMMODATIONS

The tourist kiosk, at the center of the waterfront, is stocked with colorful pamphlets and tour suggestions. English-speaking staff are helpful with cryptic bus schedules. **George and Bill Kolobaris,** 42 Sachtouri St. (tel. (0224) 22 071), offer cozy rooms and boundless hospitality. George may pick you up on his motorbike and sing to you on the way to his pension. Rooms include hot water and use of fully-equipped kitchen (doubles 8000dr; triples 8000dr). Carry on along the waterfront (200m) to the more luxurious rooms of **Hotel Karystion** (tel. (0224) 22 391; fax 22 727). The proprietor, the amiable Charis Mitros, is the president of the local Tourist Association and a good source of information about the area; he also speaks fluent English. Rooms all have bath, TV, A/C, and free breakfast (singles 7000-8000dr; doubles 10,1000-11,000dr; triples 12,900-14,940dr).

FOOD, ENTERTAINMENT, AND SIGHTS

The yummy octopi *(oktopodia)* lined up and drying in the sun give fair warning of the town's favorite food. Find incomparable food and prices at **Kabontoros,** one block inland on Parodos Sachtouri St., in the alleyway a half block right of the main square (sauteed green beans in olive oil with a pureed garlic sauce, 800dr), or walk to the very end of the strip (on the far right facing the water) until you come to the all-Greek crowd at **Kalamia** (tel. 22 223; stuffed tomatoes 650dr). If you're not stuffed after your meal, skip down the alleyway off Parodos Sachtouri St. to the water and find **Tsimis' sweet shop.** The regional specialty, almond cookies covered in icing, are about 200dr each.

Various seaside pubs and cafes are popular day and night. **Archipelagos,** on the beach at the right edge of town, offers beer for 500dr. The view and heady sea air here may tempt you to linger. For serious dancing, head to the **Barbados Disco** (tel. 24 119), 3km from town towards the mountains. The 1300dr cover includes your first drink. A cab will run 500dr, probably more after midnight.

Peek into one of the holes at the back of the **Fort of Bourtzi,** the impossible-to-miss structure on the waterfront. In the 11th century, your peep-hole was used to pour boiling oil on attackers. Today, the fort opens only to host summer student theatrical productions. The new **Archaeological Museum,** provides a better glimpse into the area's history of military prestige. Located on the waterfront past the fort, it shares a building with the local library (tel. 22 472; open 9am-3pm; admission 500dr, students 300dr).

■ Near Karystos

If you have a free morning, you may wish to explore the villages north of Karystos. Follow Aiolou St., one block east of the square, out of town; continue straight at the crossroads toward **Palio Chora,** a village nestled among lemon and olive groves. For a more strenuous walk, turn right at the crossroads outside Karystos and head toward the village of **Mili.** The road ascends sharply, following a stream to the village, where water flows from the mouths of three lions in a small roadside fountain. From Mili, a 20-minute hike up the hill on the left and across the stone bridge leads to **Kokkino Kastro** (the Red Castle). This 13th-century Venetian castle is named for the blood spilled there during the war between the Greeks and the Ottomans. The village of **Agia Triada** is also worth a trek; take a left when you come to a crossroads and walk to this shady valley, where two small, rustic churches sit under gnarled trees.

For more extensive hiking, climb Evia's second-highest mountain, **Mt. Ochi** (1398m), where Zeus and Hera fell in love. The refuge hut on the mountain is a three to four-hour hike from Karystos. Some claim that the refuge, made of unmortared stone blocks during the Pelasgian Period, was a temple to Hera; others believe it was a signal tower. The ruin, now known as the "dragon's house," is allegedly haunted.

■ Limni

According to legend, Zeus married Hera in Limni. An infelicitous earthquake destroyed the wedding temple long ago, but today Limni still has much to offer. Activity centers on the long waterfront stretch overlooking rickety, bobbing rowboats and neon windsurfers. Adjacent to a rocky beach and connected by bus and hydrofoil to surrounding towns, Limni makes a pleasant base for exploring northern Evia. As tourists are few and transient, there are only a few hotels, so call for reservations, especially on weekends.

Buses run from Chalkis to Limni (4 per day, 2hr., 1400dr). Bus service also runs to Aedipsos (30min., 500dr) with connections to Istea (30min., 350dr) and Pefki (15min., 200dr). Buses drop off at the center of the waterfront next to the **bank** (tel. (0227) 31 223; open Mon.-Thurs. 8am-2pm, Fri. 8am-1:30pm). The **post office** is in the little square just off the waterfront, up the street from the bank (open Mon.-Fri. 7:30am-2pm). **Postal Code:** 34005. To find the **OTE,** walk down to the far left of the waterfront, uphill two blocks, and then look for the blue sign (open Mon.-Fri. 7:30am-3:10pm). **Telephone Code:** 0227.

Hotel Plaza's (tel. 31 235) lovable rooms are filled with antiques (doubles 5800dr, with bath 7000dr). **Hotel Limni's** (tel. 31 316) clean, spacious rooms have private baths. Its open March-Nov. and for special occasions in the off-season (singles 4500dr; doubles 7500dr; breakfast 100dr). Both are on the waterfront, but Limni's is a 10-minute walk from the centrally located bus stop. Facing the water, turn left and get moving.

Anyone with a sweet tooth can't help salivating at **Giannaro's Zacharoplasteio** (tel. 31 263; open daily 9am-1am). The ice cream is homemade. Taste it in a cone (300dr) or enhanced with toppings in an enormous sundae (1000dr). Also high in calcium and perhaps a little more traditional, *galactobounko* (milk custard layered between flaky phyllo dough) is the regional favorite (350dr). To reach this divine dessert house, turn left at the waterfront and walk less than half a block.

■ Aedipsos

The village of Aedipsos, 30km northwest of Limni, was praised by Herodotus, Aristotle, and Aristophanes for its healing sulphurous waters. Aedipsos is worth a daytrip for anyone who wishes to enjoy the hot springs' relaxing vibes. Locals advise that you swim no longer than 30 minutes, as hours of bathing will leave you in a therapeutic stupor. The bus drops off in a small square at Ermou St., where you will be able to see the waterfront. The **hot springs** are in a large complex on a road heading inland from the left end of the waterfront (facing the water) 200m past the post office. For more information call the **tourist information office** (tel. 23 500). They are open all year but extend their hours in summer (open May-Oct. 7:30am-1pm and 5-7pm). A variety of specialized pools and equipment is available. To hang with a younger crowd, experience the relaxing effect of the hot springs at the beach on the far left end of Poseidonos St. (the waterfront strip). Here, the hot springs water mixes with the sea water as it cascades down a small waterfall, cooling the temperature slightly while retaining the hot-tub quality (adults 300dr, children 150dr).

The **tourist police** are located on the first floor of 3 Oceanidon St. (tel. 22 456). Facing the water from the town square, take a right onto Ermou St., then your first left. **Buses** run between Athens and Aedipsos (3 pcr day, 3¼hr., 2450dr) and between Aedipsos and Limni (30min., 500dr). **Flying dolphins** connect Aedipsos with Limni, Chalkida, and the Sporades. The hydrofoil agent can be found in the center of the waterfront (tel. 23 760). To find the **post office,** 25th Martiou (tel. 22 252), make a left turn (facing the water) away from the water at the left end of the waterfront (open 6:30am-12:30pm and 5-6:30pm). **Postal Code:** 34300. The **OTE** is hidden behind a black gate and a garden in the square (tel. (0226) 60 399; open Mon.-Fri. 7:30am-3pm). **Telephone code:** 0226.

Aedipsos is brimming with hotels to accommodate the influx of relief-seeking bathers. **Hotel Artemi,** 11 Omirov St. (tel. (0226) 22 473, 24 009), is located on the second side street off the waterfront. Equipped with A/C, bath, TV, telephone, and refrigerator, rooms are priced at very reasonable rates (singles 6000-7000dr; doubles 8000-10,400dr; triples 10,000-13,000dr). A little more expensive, the **Minos Hotel** offers rooms with private bath, TV, and refrigerator (singles 7000-8000dr; doubles 9000-10,500dr). Turn left at the last side street off the waterfront—the hotel is no more than 20 paces away at 5 Byzantinon Autokratoron (tel. (0226) 22 294, 22 720).

GREECE

Central and Northern Greece

ΚΕΝΤΡΙΚΗ ΚΑΙ ΒΟΡΕΙΑ ΕΛΛΑΔΑ

Central and northern Greece may seldom find their way onto postcards, but it's not for a lack of beauty. Robust and free of pretension, the region waits to be discovered by adventurous travelers seeking refuge from swarming hotel owners and their over-priced establishments. Greece's forgotten regions are graced with mountain goat paths that lead to some of the country's more precious Byzantine treasures, springs, and breathtaking mountain top vistas. Green trees, lush vegetation, and intricate patchworks of cultivated farmland characterize this gorgeous region.

THESSALY ΘΕΣΣΑΛΙΑ

Outside its charmless industrialized urban centers, Thessaly's villages conceal some of the better nature trails in Greece. To the west of the cultivated Thessalian plain, the monasteries of Meteora cling to towering gray pinnacles. The rocky crags of Mt. Olympus, throne of the pantheon of Greek gods, watch over Aegean beaches with stark majesty. To the southeast, traditional mountain hamlets on Mt. Pelion lie scattered among forests, apple orchards, and grapevines that reach out to the sea.

■ Volos ΒΟΛΟΣ

Volos has remained a transportation center since Jason and the Argonauts set sail from this port on their quest for the Golden Fleece. With hydrofoils and ferries for the island-hoppers and a few large thoroughfares crossing the city, Volos is not a small town anymore.

ORIENTATION AND PRACTICAL INFORMATION

The **bus station** lies at the end of **Leof. Lambraki Street,** an easy 15-minute walk away from town and the waterfront. The **main road,** leading from the bus station to town, runs past the train station and the tourist office and splits to become the parallel **Dimitriados Street, Iasonos Street,** and **Argonafton Street.** The intersecting roads lead to various hotels and other services including banks, pharmacies, and the post office.

> **Tourist Office:** (tel. 23 500, 36 233) On the waterfront next to the town hall in Riga Fereou Sq. Ask here for information about Volos and the Pelion Peninsula. A map of Volos is available at the town hall (open Mon.-Fri. 7am-3pm). Open July-Aug. daily 7am-2:30pm and 5-7pm, Sept.-June daily Mon.-Fri. 7am-2:30pm.
>
> **Tourist Police:** #179 28th Octovriou St. (tel. 72 421). The street was recently renamed; locals still call it "Alexandras St." Help in English provided when the tourist office is closed. Open daily 7am-2:30pm, but available anytime.
>
> **Hospital:** (tel. 27 531) Next to the museum. Open 24hr.
>
> **Trains:** The station (tel. 28 555, 24 056) is 1 block west of the tourist office. From town, turn right at the kiosk past the tourist office and walk 2-3min. down the parking lot parallel to the tracks in the train yard. You must change in Larissa (16 per day, 1hr., 560dr) for Athens or Thessaloniki, unless you catch the daily train to Athens (2 per day, 5hr., 5410dr). Otherwise, to: Athens (7 per day, 6-7hr., 3330dr); Thessaloniki (1 per day, 4hr., 1780dr); and Kalambaka (4 per day, 3½hr., 1140dr). Only the express train has A/C.

Buses: (tel. 33 254) At the end of Leof. Lambraki St. In summer Mon.-Fri., buses travel to: Athens (10 per day, 5hr., 4950dr); Thessaloniki (5 per day, 3¼hr., 3330dr); Larissa (14 per day, 1¼hr., 1000dr); and Kalambaka (4 per day, 3½hr., 2800dr). Inquire at the bus station or tourist office about bus service to the Pelion villages, including: Portaria, Makrinitsa, Zagoria, Horefto, Afissos, Platania, Drakia, and Ag. Ioannis. Most villages have daily service and can be reached in less than 3hr. (service reduced on weekends and in winter).

Ferries: 3 boats travel daily to: Skiathos (3hr., 2700dr); Skopelos (4½hr., 3300dr); and Alonissos (6hr., 3600dr). Fewer on weekends and in the off season. Tickets are sold at the agencies on the waterfront (tel. 31 059), and on the pier itself.

Flying Dolphins: 3 hydrofoils run daily to: Skiathos (1¼hr., 5500dr); Skopelos (2¼hr., 6600dr); Alonissos (2¾hr., 7300dr); and Glossa (1¾ hr., 6200dr). Inquire at the agencies on the waterfront.

Car Rental: Avis, 41 Argonafton St. (tel. 22 880; fax 32 360). **European Car Rental,** 83 Iasonos St. (tel. 36 238, fax 24 192). High-season rentals start at 16,000dr per day.

English Bookstore: Bookstop, 163 Alexandras St. (tel. 22 924), behind Ag. Nikolaos church. Offers instructional language material. Open Wed.-Fri. and Sun. 8:30am-1:30pm and 5:30-9pm, Mon.-Tues. and Sat. 8:30am-2pm. **International Press** (tel. 27 054), just off the waterfront road, offers magazines and newspapers.

Police: (tel. 72 400) Open 24hr.

Post Office: On P. Mela St., off 28th Octovriou St. Open Mon.-Fri. 7:30am-8pm. **Postal Code:** 38001.

OTE: On the corner of Eleftheriou Venizelou and Sokratous St., across from the fruit market. Open 24hr. **Information:** 131. **Telephone Code:** 0421.

ACCOMMODATIONS

The amount of *drachmae* you may have to shell out for a room in Volos is enough for a down-payment on a mighty fine goat. Saying that you're a student and that you only want a simple room *(aplo domatio)* may procure a small discount. Prices vary with the season; expect to pay less in the winter.

Hotel Iasson, 1 P. Melo St. (tel. 26 075). Well-scrubbed rooms with private phones, bath, and TV. Singles 6000dr; doubles 9000dr; triples 10,000dr.

Hotel Admitos, 5 A. Diakou (tel. 21 117), on the corner of Dimitriados. Clean rooms with bath, TV, and phone. Singles 6000dr; doubles 9000dr.

Hotel Philippos, 9 Solones St. (tel. 37 607), on the corner of Dimitriados. Rooms with bath, TV, and phone. Singles 8800dr; doubles 12,800dr; triples 15,360dr.

FOOD, SIGHTS, AND ENTERTAINMENT

Cafes, *tavernas,* and *ouzeries* drench the waterfront like oil on a Greek salad. Well known for its *ouzeries,* Volos features *mezedhes* such as *spetzofai,* spicy sausages, and seafood. In late July and August, Volos hosts a **festival** in Riga Fereou Park featuring concerts, dances, and outdoor theater.

Volos' **Archaeological Museum,** 1 Athonassaki (tel. 25 285), displays finds from the latter part of the paleolithic era to the Roman period. The museum is set in a verdant floral garden in the east part of town and is well worth the 40-minute walk from the waterfront (open Tues.-Sun. 8:30am-3pm; admission 500dr, students 400dr). Inquire here or at the tourist office for information on the nearby archaeological sites at **Dimini** and **Sesklo.**

■ Mount Pelion Peninsula ΟΡΟΣ ΠΗΛΙΟ

In Greek mythology, the rugged Pelion Peninsula was home to centaurs—half-man, half-horse creatures—and to Chiron, their mentor. Chiron, a physician, chose Pelion as a stomping ground because it contained more than 1700 medicinal herbs. The diversity of plant life in the region stems from a cool, moist climate, appreciated today by sun-weary tourists. Pelion's rugged terrain once helped protect it from invasion and was a center of Greek nationalism while the rest of Greece was under Ottoman rule. These steep slopes now form a barrier to tourism, leaving many of the villages quiet and undisturbed.

MAKRINITSA ΜΑΚΡΥΝΙΤΣΑ

The winding road from Volos to tranquil Makrinitsa transcends noise and smog, but not souvenir stands. The wooden balconies and shuttered windows of this traditional settlement command views of the Aegean, earning its name as the Balcony of Pelion. Hiking trails weave past mountain springs in "goat-begotten" hills, each crowned by a church or monastery. From the bus stop, the road climbs upward past a small waterfall and the tourism-driven cafes and *domatia.* No traffic is allowed in the town's square or on the steep cobbled paths. The tiny one-room church of **Agios Yiannis the Beheaded** presides over the square. The 1000-year-old plane tree is older than all 11 of the nearby 18th-century churches and monasteries.

As you face Agios Yiannis, climb uphill to the clock tower to your right. Here, the austere **Xamiseos Theotokou,** the functioning church of Makrinitsa, houses the *krifto skolo.* A secret school taught the Greek language during the Ottoman era. Down the path past the map, signs reading MOYCEIO direct you to the **Museum of Folk Art and the History of Pelion.** The curator gives tours of the displays of authentic clothes, scabbards, and folk art (open Tues.-Sun. 10am-2pm and 6-9pm). The roof directly below the museum covers the **Metamorphosi,** another of Makrinitsa's churches. The churches remain open at the whim of whomever takes care of them, so early to mid-morning and evenings are your most likely opportunities to visit them. Most require modest dress (skirts for women and pants for men).

Makrinitsa has been designated a traditional settlement by the Greek National Tourist Organization, so staying here will cost an arm and a leg. Budgeteers either splurge on one of the town's posh pensions, or make the town a daytrip. For the cost of one night, you could buy bus tickets to several other villages on Pelion. Still, **Kentavros** (tel. (0428) 88 075), just before the square, offers beautiful rooms with private bath, TV, and lovely views of the sea (singles 8500dr; doubles 17,000dr). Next door, **Hotel Achilles** (tel. (0428) 99 177) is 14,000dr per room. Uphill from the Galini Restaurant, **Pension Archontiko Diomides** (tel. (0428) 99 430) features older rooms, with cozy communal living rooms and an outdoor terrace (singles 8000dr; doubles 10,000dr; triples 12,000dr; all prices higher in winter). The round-trip bus ticket to Makrinitsa from Volos costs 520dr and about 10 buses run per day. Inquire at the bus station and the tourist office in Volos for info about other villages on the Pelion Peninsula.

Tavernas, ouzeries, and cafes fill Makrinitsa's central square. Don't leave without looking at the Theophilos wall painting on the right wall of the cafe by the same name, **O Theophilos.** Makrinitsa offers paltry practical conveniences. Stamps can be bought with postcards, and there is a mailbox behind the fountain in the central square. The village of Portaria has a **post office** which also offers **currency exchange.**

▨ Meteora ΜΕΤΕΩΡΑ

The mysterious black rock formations of Meteora rise majestically above the surrounding Thessalian plain. One theory says that the rocks are large salt deposits from a primordial sea. Whatever their origin, the spectacle of the formations would be worth visiting even if they didn't hold 24 Byzantine monasteries with beautiful frescoes and astonishing views. Six of the 24 are still inhabited by religious orders and are open to the public. Although the site is one of the more popular in northern Greece, the monasteries themselves offer an experience both quieting and serene.

In the 9th century, hermits and ascetics began occupying the pinnacles and crevices of Meteora, where they built a church dedicated to the Virgin. As religious persecution at the hands of Serbian invaders increased in the 12th century, Christians flocked to take refuge on the summits of these impenetrable columns of rock. In 1356, the region's first monastic community was founded. In the late Byzantine period, when the Ottomans ruled most of Greece, Meteora became a bastion of Christian faith, eventually growing into a powerful community of 24 monasteries, each embellished by fine artists. The communities' wealth turned out to be their downfall. Quarrels over riches led to neglect and deterioration during the 16th century. All was not lost, however; some of the monasteries (**Grand Meteoron, Varlaam, Agia Triada,** and **Agios Nikolaos**) are still active, while others (**Agios Stephanos** and **Agia Barbara**) now serve as convents.

ORIENTATION AND PRACTICAL INFORMATION

Buses travel from the main square in Kalambaka to the **Grand Meteoron** (2 per day, 20min., 220dr). Flag down the bus at any of the blue *stasis* signs along its route or go to the central square with the large Meteora bus stop sign. The bus may stop at the different monasteries along the way to the Grand Meteoron, but it is best to begin your walking tour from the Grand Meteoron, the uppermost monastery, and then to visit the others on your way down.

Almost a full day is needed to see the monasteries properly. Grand Meteoron and **Varlaam** are the largest and cater to tourists; the others are more intimate but offer less spectacular displays. Modest dress (pants for men, skirts for women) is strictly enforced and visitors should cover their shoulders. Men with long hair may be asked to wrap it in a bun (as the monks do). Photography and filming inside the monasteries are forbidden; illicit attempts have been known to provoke the monks into fits of anger. The monasteries have staggered their closing days, but all are open Saturday, Sunday, and Wednesday from April until the end of September (9am-6pm; admission to each 400dr).

THE MONASTERIES

The Monastery of the Transfiguration, known as the **Grand Meteoron,** is the oldest and largest in the area. Built on the most massive of the occupied stone columns, the complex looms 500m above the Thessalian plain. Founded by Athanasios, a monk from Mt. Athos, the monastery rose in the hagio-hierarchy when John Uresis, grandson of the Serbian prince Stephen, retired here in 1388. The Grand Meteoron's central feature is the 16th-century **Church of the Transfiguration,** with brilliant frescoes of the Roman persecution of Christians in its narthex. Directly below lies a chamber filled with the remains of past monks (open daily 9am-1pm and 3:30-6pm).

GREECE

Highway to Heaven

The first ascetics scaled the sheer cliff faces by wedging timbers into the rock crevices, thereby constructing small platforms, traces of which can still be seen. After the monasteries were completed, visitors usually arrived by means of extremely long rope ladders, but when these were pulled up, the summit became virtually inaccessible. Visitors who were either too weak or too timid to climb with the ladders were hoisted up in free-swinging rope nets. The half-hour ascent, during which the rope could be heard slowly unwinding, no doubt fostered profound faith in God. Motorized winches have since replaced monk-powered, rope-spool cranes, and today only provisions, not pilgrims, are elevated. In 1922, steps were carved into the rocks and bridges built between the pillars, so even the vertigo-prone could feel secure.

Some 800m from the Grand Meteoron stands the **Varlaam Monastery,** the second largest monastery on Meteora. Built in 1518, the monastery's crowning glory is its chapel's 16th-century frescoes, including a disturbing depiction of the Apocalypse. Varlaam also has an extensive net and pulley system, now used for supplies, which shows how earlier visitors were hoisted up (open daily 9am-1pm and 3:30-6pm).

If you choose to visit more of the monasteries, follow the road down to **Agia Barbara** (also called Roussanoou). Visible from most of the valley, it is spectacularly situated and frequently photographed. Even with continued renovation, the interior cannot compare to the exterior (open in summer daily 9am-6pm, in winter Thurs.-Tues. only).

Walking back to Agia Barbara, a footpath across from the monastery leads to the road above. Follow the road to **Agios Stephanos.** Founded as a hermitage, it became a monastery in the 14th century and is now a convent. Stephanos is cleaner, lighter, and more spacious than Grand Meteoron and Varlaam. Of its two churches, the more modern **Agios Charalambos,** built in 1798, is open to the public. The museum displays artifacts of intricate detail (open Tues.-Sun. 9am-1pm and 3:30-6pm).

The Monastery of **Agia Triada** lies 3km back down the road towards the main intersection. Movie buffs will recognize it from the James Bond flick *For Your Eyes Only*. Looming above Kalambaka, the peak of Agia Triada gives a soul-searing view of the town and the distant, snow-capped **Pindos Mountains.** The monk Dometius built the monastery in 1476, but the wall paintings were added 200 years later. A 3km footpath to the right of the entrance leads to Kalambaka (closed for renovation).

Back down the road rests the Monastery of **Agios Nikolaos,** past the main intersection and only 2.5km before Kastraki. Built in 1388 and expanded in 1628, its highlight is the fresco work painted by the 16th-century Cretan master **Theophanes.** Visitors are admitted only in small groups, so wait in the entrance at the top of the steps for the door to open (open daily).

■ Near Meteora: Kalambaka ΚΑΛΑΜΠΑΚΑ

Once famous for its architecture, Kalambaka lost most buildings of importance to the occupying Nazis' brand of urban renewal. Today, the town caters to international tourists visiting Meteora, and many begin their visits in this convenient base.

ORIENTATION AND PRACTICAL INFORMATION

Kalambaka has two main squares. The first, two blocks from the **bus station,** is the town's central transit hub from which all major thoroughfares radiate. **Taxis** (tel. (0432) 22 310) congregate here at a small kiosk (open daily 6:30am-midnight). The second, a few blocks to the right facing Meteora, is full of shops and restaurants. The non-English-speaking but amiable **police,** 11 Hagipetrou St. (tel. (0432) 22 109), will not only enforce the law but also help travelers find rooms (open daily 9am-9pm, but officer on duty 24hr.). To get there from the bus station, walk one block uphill and take your first right. Facing the square is an **Ionian Bank,** with an **ATM** that accepts

Visa (open Mon.-Thurs. 8am-2pm and Fri. 8am-1:30pm). Down Ioanninon St. (look for signs for Ioannina and Grevena, at the top of the street) are the **OTE** and the **post office** diagonally across from each other. By way of Trikalon St. (the road to Trikala), you'll come to **Riga Fereou Square,** which, according to locals, is the town's "real" square because it boasts a pleasant, leafy park. Facing the park is a **National Bank.** Beyond the park, Trikalon St. becomes an all-out nightlife scene. There are **international bookstores** on both of the town's main squares, a **pharmacy** at the top of the square, and a **health center** (tel. (0432) 24 111) 1km from town (open 24hr.).

Trains depart from the station on the main "highway" behind the bus station and off to the left (tel. (0432) 22 451). They go to: Athens (7 per day, 7hr., 2700dr); Thessaloniki (6 per day, 6hr., 2220dr); Alexandroupolis (2 per day, 13hr., 5400dr); and Volos (4 per day, 4hr., 1140dr). Air-conditioned express trains cost 2200dr extra to Athens (2 per day) and 1110dr extra to Thessaloniki (3 per day). Be sure to change trains in Paleofrasis en route to Athens. From the bus station (tel. 22 432), buses go from Kalambaka to Meteora (2 per day, 20min., 190dr). The early bus ensures you time to hike around the monasteries, which are open 9am-1pm and 3:30-5pm. Most people walk back to Kalambaka (6km downhill), visiting monasteries along the way. Buses also go to: Volos (4 per day, 2800dr); Thessaloniki (3350dr); Athens (8 per day, 5000dr); Metsovo (2 per day, 1250dr); and Ioannina (2 per day, 2150dr).

ACCOMMODATIONS AND FOOD

Private rooms abound, but it's illegal for owners to solicit at the bus or railway stations. Those who do have been known to lure travelers with the promise of good prices and then add surcharges for supplementary services. Cozy, traditional, and utterly delightful, **Koka Roka** (tel. (0432) 24 554) warrants the 15-minute walk up from the bus station (singles 3000dr, with bath 4000dr; doubles 6000dr, with bath 7000dr; triples 7500dr). There are also **campgrounds** near Kalambaka.

Restaurant Panellinio, in the central square, has tasty and satisfying vegetarian entrees (900dr). The *taverna* at **Koka Roka** rewards wayfarers from the monasteries with delicious homemade specialties (entrees 1000dr). The largest of several **markets** is uphill past Hotel Astoria (open daily 7am-2:30pm and 5-9pm). In late July the town honors its patron saint with a **glendi** (celebration). Kalambaka holds a three-day **wine festival** with traditional dancing and **free wine** in late August.

SIGHTS

In the land of monasteries, it is no surprise that Kalambaka's foremost sight is the Byzantine **Church of the Dormition of the Virgin.** Follow the signs that are everywhere around the central square, and after several blocks you'll spy the graceful bell tower of the old church, haloed by a stork's nest. Built in the 11th century on the ruins of a 5th-century basilica, the main structure was remodeled in 1573. Unfortunately, the interior frescoes, painted by the Cretan monk **Neophytos,** have been badly blackened by centuries of candle flames and incense. George Dailianas is the church tour guide (when he's not planting trees) and is fond of practicing his English with visitors. Modest dress is preferred (open daily 9am-2pm; admission 400dr).

▓ Metsovo ΜΕΤΣΟΒΟ

As a consequence of Metsovo's official designation as a "traditional" settlement, junk shop owners promote a booming trade in postcards and handmade wooden trinkets. For better or for worse, this has profitably romanticized the subsistence agriculture and petty commerce economy it has replaced. But genuine charm prevails away from the central square, and Metsovo reveals its unique culture. Native Metsovans descend from the **Vlachi,** a people once thought to have emigrated from Romania, but now believed to have been Greeks. A snug mountain hamlet perched just below the 1690m Katara Pass, Metsovo retained its sovereignty and became wealthy after a rebel Ottoman king sought refuge here.

ORIENTATION AND PRACTICAL INFORMATION

On the wall of an outdoor cafe's patio in the square, a large English-language town map lists hotels, sights, monasteries, restaurants, discos, and the "sanitary station" for **medical emergencies** (tel. 41 111; 24hr.). There is a **National Bank** (tel. 41 203) in the square (open Mon.-Thurs. 8am-2pm, Fri. 8am-1:30pm) and a 24hr. **ATM** at the intersection of the main road entering the square. The municipal **police** (tel. 41 233) are on the right, downhill past the bus stop, with an English-speaking police chief (office open daily 8am-2pm and 4-6pm, but available 24hr.). **Buses** depart from the stop in the square to Ioannina (4 per day, 1¼hr., 1000dr) and Trikala via Kalambaka (2 per day, 2hr., 1700dr). Buses to Thessaloniki stop at the main highway above town (about 5 times per day). For **schedule information,** go to the cafe across from the bus stop. The **post office** (tel. 41 245) is uphill on the main road leaving the square (open Mon.-Fri. 7:30am-2pm; **postal code:** 44200). The **OTE** (tel. 42 199) is across the street from the police (open daily 7:30am-3:10pm; **telephone code,** 0656).

ACCOMMODATIONS

Inviting rooms characterize **Hotel Athens** (tel. 41 725), down the hill from the main square. Enjoy homemade specialties in their peaceful, parkside restaurant. Hikers and campers are welcome to store their gear here free of charge during visits to Pindos Mountain. The owners can also suggest good routes, and may in fact be your best source of information in Metsovo (singles 4000dr; doubles 6000dr; all rooms with private bath). If Hotel Athens is full, talk to the owners about staying in their slightly fancier **Hotel Filoxenia** (tel. 41 725), which boasts TVs, radios, phones, and beautiful mountain views (singles 6000dr; doubles 7000dr). The **Duros family** (tel. 42 415) offers appealing rooms on the path away from the square, downhill from the post office (singles 4000dr; doubles 6000dr). All prices are higher mid-July to early September.

FOOD, ENTERTAINMENT, AND SIGHTS

The **parkside restaurant** (tel. 41 725) in Hotel Athens serves delicious Greek specialties. The bean soup (700dr), a regional specialty, and stuffed vegetables (900dr) are of a price and quality generally superior to restaurants in the square. While in the square, locals favor the **Krifi Folia** (tel. 41 628) for its grilled meats. After dinner, head to one of the many cafes or bars that line the main road running uphill away from the center of town.

Off the main square, the **Museum of Modern Greek Art of the 19th and 20th Centuries** (tel. 41 210) alone merits a trip to Metsovo. The gallery houses the private collection of Metsovo's benefactor, politician and writer Averof-Tossizza. Although small, the gallery is still the second largest in Greece, rivaled only by the National Gallery in Athens (see p. 85). A refreshing treat, the fantastic display has information in English (Open Sept. 15-July 14 Wed.-Mon.10am-4:30pm, July 15-Sept. 14 10am-7pm. Admission 500dr, students 300dr.) A museum shop sells postcards and gallery publications, and in the summer months a terrace cafe reveals beautiful views of the Pindos Mountains. Inquire here about exhibits and events.

The **Tossizza Museum,** housed in a stone and timber mansion up the main road on the left (look for the sign opposite the Shell station), presents wonderful examples of earlier Metsovite life. *Vlachi* furniture and clothing show how Metsovite families spent long winters cooped up in their homes. The upper floor served as Vangeli Averof's apartment when he was a diplomat. Visitors wait at the door until the guide appears every 30 minutes. (open Fri.-Wed. 8:30am-1pm and 4-6pm; 500dr).

Signs near the square point to the **Agios Nikoloas Monastery,** which has a 14th-century chapel complete with period frescoes and icons. A family now lives in the monastery, so knock to be admitted. The family who owns Hotel Athens can direct you to other sights in the surrounding area.

EVRITANIA ΕΥΡΥΤΑΝΙΑ

At sunrise a rooster crows, calling you to the Timfristos mountainsides covered with the fragrant yellow blossoms of the wildflower Sparta. According to Greek legend, Evritania earned its name from the valiant archer Evritos who was slain by Apollo. It seems more likely that the fifth cleanest environment in the world is named for its pure mountain springs. Summer adventurers here enjoy some of the best hiking, climbing, and rafting in Greece. With the recent development of a ski center at Mt. Velouchi, winter tourists can now share in the lovely vistas and relax in the traditional villages surrounded by luxuriant pine forests. Tourism is new to Evritania, so enjoy the fresh air and your taste of Greek life.

■ Karpenisi ΚΑΡΠΕΝΗΣΙ

The goats that first fashioned the path to Karpenisi, capital of Evritania, never rode a teetering bus around its switchback turns. As a result, the tortuous route to this mountain city is not for the feeble of heart of weak of stomach. Yet the panoramic views and the relaxed town at the end of the journey are well worth the ride. The area has weathered a history of conquest by Ottomans, Albanians, and Germans, as well as by Mother Nature. The Germans burned Karpenisi in 1941, so there is little worth looking at in this town of whitewashed concrete. Karpenisi is, however, a comfortable base for visits to many of the nearby villages.

ORIENTATION AND PRACTICAL INFORMATION

Since Karpenisi is built on a slope, almost everything lies within a five-minute walk downhill from the **bus station.** The main road leading down from the bus station forks at the square. The **OTE** (open daily 7am-10pm) and the **police station** (tel. 25 100; open 24hr.) are in close succession along the road forking off to the right. Edging the square is a **National Bank** (open Mon.-Thurs. 8am-2pm, Fri. 8:30am-1:30pm) and the local **taxi stand** (tel. 22 666). The **bus station** is uphill from the square on the main road. **Buses** run to Athens (3 per day, 5hr., 4450dr); Lamia (4 per day, 1¾hr., 1300dr); Agrinio (1 or 2 per day, 3½hr., 1900dr); the villages of Proussou (2 per week, 45min., 600dr); and Mikro Horio and Megalo Horio (2 per day, 20min., 250dr). Ask at the bus station about bus service to smaller villages, which is available once or twice per week depending on the village. In the square facing the cafes is the **town hall,** which provides tourist information. Diagonally across the street from the Agricultural Bank, after Maxim's Cafe, is the Karpenisi chapter of the **Greek Mountaineering Club (EOS),** 2 Georgiou Tsitsara (tel. 23 051), which can field your questions concerning travel in the Timfristos Mountains. Also, **Trekking Hellas** (tel. 25 940) organizes hiking, climbing, and rafting trips to the mountains. For the **hospital,** call 22 315. **Postal Code:** 36100. **Telephone Code:** 0237.

ACCOMMODATIONS

From December to March, people flock to the hotels of Karpenisi to ski at the **Velouchi Ski Center** (12km away). Although none can compete with the view from the luxury **Hotel Montana** above Karpenisi, many balconies are available for reasonable rates in the summer, although prices rise on holidays and weekends. **Hotel Galini,** 3 R. Ferou (tel. 22 930, -14, fax 25 623) is on your first right after the Agricultural Bank. Its pleasant, clean rooms with private baths are a great bargain (singles 4000dr; doubles 8000dr; triples 12000dr). Just on the left past the square, the **Hotel Elvetia,** 7 Zinopoulou (tel. 22 465, -920), boasts TVs and private baths (singles 7000dr; doubles 10,000dr; triples 11,000dr). Farther down Zinopoulou, on your right, the newly remodelled **Hotel Anessis,** 50 Zinopoulou (tel 22 840, 23 021), features shower curtains and a fascinating shelf in each room that turns on the room's electricity when you set your keys on it (singles 800dr; doubles 12,000dr; triples 15,000dr). Through the tourist office, **Rooms To Let** can be arranged starting around 10,000dr in Karpenisi and 7000dr in the surrounding villages.

FOOD AND ENTERTAINMENT

Karpenisi's dining options begin with inexpensive meals from the many supermarkets or fruit stores. If you'd rather sit down to eat, grab one of the two and a half plaid booths, try a gyros (280dr), and *caht* with the Australian owner at **Yevsi Taste,** 10 Zinopoulou (tel. 23 777). On the left hand side at 33 A. Karpenisioti, the **Three Star Restaurant** (tel. 24 800, -222) serves all sorts of fast food, from an "American" breakfast of ham and eggs with a toasted hamburger bun, to a "Greek" breakfast of an Amstel and *patsas*. Although it will save you about 300dr, only the brave should try the local speciality, best described as floating fat. **Taverna Panorama** (tel. 25 976) offers a relatively varied menu and outdoor dining. Choices include several vegetarian options. Farther up the street and to the right, **Isi Oti Pis** (tel. 24 080), translated as "Whatever You Say," serves delicious lamb in a lovely stone dining room with small tables. Entrees at both *tavernas* start around 1400dr. If you have transportation or are willing to take a taxi, you can get fresh local trout and the more traditional sausages or *katiki*, a cheese spread, at the village *tavernas*. Regardless of where you eat dinner, relax in the square at any one of the cafes and sip a frappe (400dr), but look first to see that you are not entering a *kafeneo* where only older Greek men sit during the day. Just opposite the square, a pink and white sign advertises the sweet shop of **Georgos Kitsios and Co.,** 13 Zinopoulou (tel. 24 082), which sells *kourabies* and some of the best *baklava* you may ever taste.

SIGHTS

Throughout the summer, saints' days are celebrated in **local festivals** with religious services in the mornings and traditional cooking, music, and dance at night. Other possible activities while on the island include a trip to the **Monastery of Prousos** (33km from Karpenisi), which, as one of the most revered palaces of worship in Greece, is dedicated to the Virgin Mary and contains a miracle-working icon. Here you may also visit Karaiskakis' castles and the black cave. **Klafsion** (8km from Karpenisi) derived its name from the Greek verb "to cry," as a result of the terrible suffering of the village's people. The **St. Leonides Church** dates back to the 5th century and has a mosaic floor from the Byzantine era. For outdoor enthusiasts, hiking near **Krendi** and rafting on the **Agrafiotis River** provide days of adventure.

EPIRUS ΗΠΕΙΡΟΣ

Epirus is among the less touristy and more beautiful regions in Greece, featuring stark mountains, gorgeous wildflowers, and lush forests. In Epirus, traditional mountain villages inhabited by black-clad women and staff-holding shepherds can still be found. The region spent about 500 years under Ottoman rule and boasts ancient ruins, Roman artifacts, and Turkish mosques in proximity to one another. Epirus is also home to stellar mountain climbing, hunting, and hiking. The picturesque town and resplendent beaches of Parga see their share of visitors, but the mountains and timeless villages of Zagoria near the Vikos-Aoos National Park remain undisturbed.

■ Igoumenitsa ΗΓΟΥΜΕΝΙΤΣΑ

Igoumenitsa may be your first stop on the Greek mainland, since boats from Italy and Corfu stop here. If you begin exploring the country here, you can follow in Lord Byron's footsteps. Igoumenitsa is the consummate transportation hub, linking Central and Northern Greece, the Ionian Islands, and other destinations. There are no must-see sights or sprawling beaches, but you can stroll along a lovely waterfront.

ORIENTATION AND PRACTICAL INFORMATION

Buses depart from the station (tel. 22 309) to: Ioannina (10 per day, 2hr., 1700dr); Thessaloniki (1 per day, 8hr., 7250dr); Athens (3 per day, 8hr., 7750dr); Parga (4 per day, 1hr., 1050dr); and Preveza (2 per day, 2hr., 1950dr). To reach the bus station from the ports, walk up the street with the Ionian Bank on the corner. When you reach the town square, turn left and walk just over two blocks. The ticket office will be behind a cafe on your left. To reach the **OTE** (tel. 22 399), go left from the station, and turn left at the first corner (open daily 7am-10pm). The **post office** (tel. 22 209) is in the same building (open Mon.-Fri. 7:30am-2pm).

Igoumenitsa has three main ports, which you'll come to in rapid succession. The **old port** mostly sends boats to Italy and houses the multilingual **EOT tourist office** (tel. 22 227), which has timetables and brochures, a list of hotels and their prices, and a helpful **map** (open daily 7am-2pm and 5-10pm). Across the road from the old port is a string of banks, including the **National Bank** (tel. 22 415) with a 24hr. **ATM** and automatic **currency changer.** Near the National Bank is an **American Express** office (tel. 22 406, 24 333), which will **change money,** issue traveler's checks, and give you cash from your AmEx card (open Mon.-Sat. 7:30am-2pm and 4-11pm, Sun. 7:30-11am and 5:30-10pm). **Ferry tickets** to Corfu can be purchased at the **Corfu Port,** in the yellow kiosk in the parking lot, 100m farther to the left as you face the harbor. Across from the Corfu Port are the **police** (tel. 22 100), available 24hr., and the **tourist police** (tel. 22 222), who speak little English. Beyond the Corfu Port is the **New Port,** which sends boats to Italy and Corfu. The new port also houses a new **OTE** (open daily 7am-10pm), which **exchanges currency,** sells telephone cards, and provides fax and telephone services, and a second **EOT office** (tel. 27 757). **Ferries** go to Corfu (every hr., 4:30am-10pm, 2hr., 1500dr per person, 7200dr per car). For tickets to Italy or the former Yugoslav Republic of Macedonia, shop around at the waterfront agencies. "Budget" carriers vary from year to year, and some have student rates. Igoumenitsa's primary ferry agencies sell tickets for most shipping lines. Adriatica and HML accept Eurail and Inter-Rail passes. Destinations include Brindisi (15 day, 10hr., 8600dr); Ancona (2 per day, 22hr., 17,600dr); Venice (1 per day, 30hr., 18,800dr); and Bari (2 per day, 12hr., 8000dr). Prices do not include port dues (at least 1500dr in Greece, L4000 in Italy). The prices quoted for these ferries are estimates for the high season of July and August. Prices are lower in the off season. Most boats depart before noon; arrive early or plan to spend the night. In Igoumenitsa, there is a 24hr. **medical center** (tel. 24 420) that handles most health problems. If you need to go to a hospital, they will help you get to the one 15 minutes away. **Postal Code:** 46100. **Telephone Code:** 0665.

ACCOMMODATIONS AND FOOD

Most people try to arrange their transportation so that they pass through Igoumenitsa. If you are stuck, **Hotel Rex** (tel. 22 255) provides small but adequate rooms with shared baths (singles 2000dr; doubles 4000dr; triples 6000dr). From the port walk up the street with the Ionian Bank on the corner and turn left at the first corner. Look for their small sign on the white building with green shutters on your right in the middle of the block. **Hotel Egnatia** (tel. 23 648), whose sign is at the central square's far right corner, has rooms with bath, TV, and phone (singles 7000dr; doubles 10,000dr; off-season prices lower).

The Bakery Alexiou Spiridon (tel. 24 617) is just off the waterfront at 7 El. Venizelou St. Look for the Ionian Bank at the waterfront corner and try to catch the subtle white "Bakery" placard hanging a few storefronts inland. It offers a wonderful array of baked goods and sweets, including nutritious and hard-to-find whole-grain and special sugar-free breads. Early in the morning you might be lucky to get a piece of their delicious *spanakopita* (open daily 6am-6pm). While you wait for transportation, the **Meeting Cafe** across the street from the bus station has dim lights, air conditioning, cold drinks (cafe frappe or beer 400dr), and clean bathrooms.

■ Parga ΠΑΡΓΑ

Snug within an arc of green mountains, Parga is sheltered from the sea by a row of rocky islets and rests in coves of stunning, sand and turquoise beaches. It has not, however, been sheltered from tourism. Like much of the Sporades, Parga presents whitewashed buildings housing high-price jewelry shops and stone alleyways lined with t-shirt vendors. The beaches and waterfront *tavernas* draw a fun and sun-loving crowd, who partake in the effervescent nightlife. The narrow streets, neoclassical houses, and harbor views create a romantic mood that seems to have infected even the pink pastel supermarket.

ORIENTATION AND PRACTICAL INFORMATION

To reach the bus stop from the port, head to the corner of the waterfront (to the left, facing inland), and walk uphill and inland. You'll find the **National Bank** (tel. 31 719) one block inland (open Mon.-Thurs. 8am-2pm, Fri. 8am-1:30pm, and also in summer Mon.-Fri. 7-9pm). Continue uphill to pass the **OTE** (tel. 31 699) sporting a maroon facade (open in summer Mon.-Fri. 7am-3pm). Farther up, the **bus stop** sits at the intersection with the church on the corner, while the **post office** (tel. 31 295; open Mon.-Fri. 7:30am-2pm), **police station,** and **tourist police** (tel. 31 222; available 24hr.) are next door. The **port police** can be reached at 31 227, and a private **doctor** at 31 100. On the waterfront you'll find a **pharmacy** (tel. 31 635) open 8am-2pm Mon.-Sat. and some evenings. Next door, a **bookstore/newsstand** sells English books and papers.

    Tourist agencies pack the streets. They will help find rooms, rent mopeds, and arrange daytrips (all open Mon.-Sat. 9am-2pm and 5:30-10pm). They also sell **ferry tickets** to Paxos and Antipaxos (daily, 4500dr round-trip) and Corfu Town (2 per week, 7900dr), as well as provide information about **buses** connecting Parga with: Igoumenitsa (3-4 per day, 1½hr., 1050dr); Athens; and Thessaloniki. Of all the agencies, the charming staff of **Parga Tours** (tel. 31 580, fax 31 116) on the waterfront caters least to northern European package tours (open daily 8:30am-2:30pm and 5:30-10:30pm). **Postal Code:** 48060. **Telephone Code:** 0684.

ACCOMMODATIONS, FOOD, & ENTERTAINMENT

As the number of vacationers in Parga increases, the summer rooms more than keep up. But hotels in Parga are expensive. You can check out the rooms extolled by folks who greet incoming buses, or try off the beaten track, at the south end of the town and the top of the hill. Better yet, head to one of the helpful tourist agencies.

    As for food, remember that the waterfront can often be one long tourist trap. Above the town beach, under the blue tent, **Balthazar Restaurant** offers good value with 1000dr *moussaka* and 950dr stuffed vegetables. For a treat, head inland and one block downhill from the National Bank to catch sight of **To Kantoyni Taverna's** colorful tablecloths behind a small church. They play Greek music and serve delicious, traditional Greek foods (entrees 900-1100dr).

    Even the **bars** themselves recognize that there's not much to distinguish between them. Like the waterfront, they cater to tourists, with prices fixed around 500dr for beers, 1000dr for drinks, and 1300dr for cocktails.

SIGHTS

The **Venetian fortress,** the largest in the area, dominates the town. Constructed by the Normans, the Venetians controlled it from 1401 to 1797. Today the structure seems a mere shell beneath the shade of majestic pines. But in the afternoon heat it's a luscious spot for a picnic or snooze. Follow the steps from the harbor up the hill, only five minutes from the water (open daily 7am-10pm; free). A three-minute walk down and behind the castle lies **Valtos Beach,** a voluptuous crescent of fine pebbles and clear water. **Golfo Beach,** five minutes to the left of the town beach, is more secluded but has rocks the size of golfo balls. The town beach pales in comparison to

Valtos, but it's clean. A short swim or pedal boat ride will bring you to the islets 100m offshore, home to a small **church.** Boats sometimes travel to the smaller beaches.

The travel agencies book a variety of excursions, including the **River Styx,** the mythical pathway to the underworld, and the **Necromonteion,** the Oracle of the Dead. Just 3000dr for a Parga Tour-sponsored ticket to the underworld. You could also shop around for a larger, more expensive tour. But why would you want to?

■ Ioannina ΙΩΑΝΝΙΝΑ

With its Eastern flavor, staid castle walls, idyllic lake island, and racy, if troubled, past, Ioannina is much more than a mere transportation hub. It is Epirus's largest city, the capital of the region, and, curiously, the town with the most marked Turkish influence in all of Greece. Founded by Emperor Justinian in 527 AD, Ioannina was conquered by the Normans in 1082, Ottoman in 1430, and Greeks in 1913. Ioannina's most notorious foreign ruler was Ali Pasha, the Ottomans governor of Epirus just before the Greek Revolution. His ambition to secede from the Ottoman Empire and create a Greek-Albanian state was thwarted, and he eventually lost his head. But in the meantime, his exploits became infamous as he combed the region, amassing a harem of hundreds of young women and men to serve as concubines. Those who resisted were thrown into the lake.

ORIENTATION AND PRACTICAL INFORMATION

The names of the main thoroughfares in Ioannina change often, and many posted street signs are obsolete. The main bus station is between **Sina** and **Zossimadon Streets.** Zossimadon continues south, changing its name twice, to merge with **28 Octovriou Street** in front of the post office. The merged street crosses **Averof Street** at the town's largest intersection, and changes to **Vizeniou Street** as it continues behind the central park area to the town's second bus station. Averof St., running northeast, heads toward the Old Town, the castle, and the harbor before it narrows, then turns left, and becomes **Anexartissis Street,** which merges with Zassimadon going north from the main bus station. The city of Ioannina is built around **Lake Pamvotis,** which has an island in the middle. To reach the waterfront, walk straight down Averof St. and keep the castle walls on your right.

Tourist Office: EOT office (tel. 25 086), turn right onto Dodonis St. from Octovriou, with the central park on your left. Open daily in summer 7:30am-2:30pm and 5:30-8:30pm; in winter 7:30am-2:30pm.

Tourist Police: (tel. 25 673) from the main bus station, follow Zassimadon to post office and double back on 28 Octovriou until you reach the police station. Police and EOT have brochure including very helpful map (open daily 8am-10pm).

Hellenic Mountaineering Club: 2 Despotatou Ipirou (tel. 22 138), near the stadium. Information on mountain trips for the outlying region and excursions every Sun. or weekend Sept.-June (open Mon.-Sat. 7:30-9pm).

Banks: National Bank on Averof, on the right toward the waterfront from the central square. 24hr. **ATM** (open Mon.-Thurs. 8am-2pm, Fri. 8am-1:30pm).

Flights: To Athens (1-2 per day, 17,000dr) and Thessaloniki (1-2 per day, 10,700dr) The **Olympic Airways** office (tel. 26 218) sits across from the EOT office (open Mon.-Fri. 8am-3pm). An **airport branch** (tel. 26 218) is available for tickets and information (open 10am-5pm).

Buses: From **main terminal** (tel. 26 404) to: Athens (9 per day, 7hr., 6750dr); Igoumenitsa (10 per day, 2hr., 1700dr); Metsovo (4 per day, 1½hr., 1000dr); Thessaloniki (5 per day, 7hr., 5650dr); and Konitsa (1 per day, 1½hr., 1050dr). Check the schedule; changes are common, and buses may run more frequently at times. Buses leave from the **other station** (tel. 25 014) for Preveza (10 per day, 2hr., 1700dr) and Dodoni.

Laundromat: Express Wash, 86 Napoleon Zerva St. (tel. 66 493). Wash 900dr, dry 700dr, (open Mon.-Fri. 8:30am-3pm and 5-9pm, Sat. 8:30am-2:30pm).

Hospital: There are two hospitals, each about 5km from the center of town, that handle emergencies on alternating days of the week, one for even dates (tel. 80 111), another for odd days (tel. 99 111).

Police: (tel. 26 226) with the tourist police. Open 24hr.

Post Office: (tel. 25 498) at the intersection of 28 Octovriou St. and Zossimadon (open Mon.-Fri. 7:30am-8pm). **Postal Code:** 45221.

OTE: (tel. 22 350, 42 777) opposite the police behind the post office (open daily 7am-11pm). **Telephone Code:** 0651.

ACCOMMODATIONS AND FOOD

Hotel Tourist, 18 Koletti St. (tel. 26 443, 25 070), next to Hotel Metropolis. The virtually spotless rooms have TVs, and are available at reduced rates in the off season. Singles 5000dr, with bath 7000dr; doubles 8000dr, with bath 11000dr.

Hotel Metropolis (tel. 25 507, 26 207), on your left as you walk down Averof toward the waterfront. Singles 4000dr; doubles with shared bath 6500dr.

Hotel Paris (tel. 20 541), on a side street by the main bus terminal. Singles 5000dr, with bath 7000dr; doubles 8000dr, with bath 9000dr.

What may be the **best souvlaki** in Greece is found in the garden of an unnamed **souvlaki restaurant** (tel. 38 545). To find it walk down Averof toward the waterfront, turn left on the street just before the town hall, and walk one block. It is across the street from the library, where you'll probably see people waiting for tables (*souvlaki* 180dr, fries 450dr, salads 480dr, Greek salad 900dr). For something faster try the *bougatsa* (350dr) at the shop across from the National Bank of Averof. **Nikos Grill,** on Averof, toward the waterfront fixes hearty gyros (300dr).

SIGHTS

The massive stone walls of the **Castle of Ioannina** rise from the harbor. Today, they divide the old and new city. The streets of the old city also hold a **synagogue,** a testament to the city's once-large Jewish population.

The **Archaeological Site of the Inner Acropolis,** lies within the walls of the **Its Kale,** or inner fortress. It boasts fine views of the lake and city, a small cafe, and broad stone tunnels to explore (open Tues.-Sun. 7am-10pm). An excellent **Byzantine Museum** (tel. 25 989) is there and features icons and wood-carved iconostases. A **Silverworks Gallery,** housed in the former treasury building, displays beautiful, delicate examples of the region's silvercraft. The galleries have English information and are open Tues.-Sun. 8:30am-3pm (admission 500dr, students 300dr. Free on Sunday from Nov-March). During the summer on nights of the full moon, the museum holds free Byzantine music concerts within the walls of the Its Kale. The **Municipal Museum** (tel. 26 356) rather minimally relates the history of Ioannina's three communities: Jewish, Muslim, and Greek. It resides in the **Aslan Aga Mosque,** a splendid 18th-century reminder of the Ottomans' 500-year ascendancy in the province. (Open daily 8am-8pm in summer; 8am-3pm in winter. Admission 700dr, students 300dr.) The **Archaeological Museum's** (tel. 33 357) collection features minute stone tablets etched with political, romantic, and cosmological questions that Romans asked the oracle at Dodoni between the 6th and the 3rd century BC. The tablets are translated, and you are led to wonder how the oracle answered when asked, "Has Pistos stolen the wool from the mattress?" In a park off Averof Street, the museum is behind the clock tower. (Open Monday noon-6pm, Tues.-Fri. 8am-6pm, Sat. and Sun. 8:30am-3pm. Admission 500dr, students 300dr.)

If Ali Pasha's tomb in the Its Kale wasn't enough, you can get more on Ali Pasha at the diminutive **Ali Pasha Museum** on the site of Ag. Nikolaos monastery. Here, Ali Pasha sought refuge to no avail from the assailing Sultan's forces (open daily 9am-10pm; admission 100dr). **Boats** (tel. 25 885) leave for the unnamed **scenic island** (in summer every 30min., 8am-11pm, 10min., 200dr; in winter every hr. 7am-9pm). On the island, chickens wander among whitewashed **tavernas,** cheap **silver shops,** and curiously silent **monasteries.** A sign in the central square will direct you to any of the islands sights. On Averof St., just off of the waterfront, the **Athanasios Vrellis' Wax-Works Museum** (tel. 22 414) provides historical diversion, with greats like Socrates, Prometheus, and Alexander (open daily 9am-4pm, free). Unfortunately for wax figure buffs, the Vrellis brothers had something of a falling out, and Pavlos' larger museum (tel. 92 128) is 13km from Ioannina towards the village of **Bizani.**

Four kilometers northeast of Ioannina, the 17°C **Cave of Perama** (tel. 81 521) provides respite from Greece's summer heat. Discovered in 1941 by villagers seeking shelter from Italian bombings, the caverns are now accessed by a 163-step staircase. A 45-minute guided tour passes by spectacular stalagmite and stalactite formations, that are almost two million years old. (Open daily in summer 8am-8pm, and winter 8am-5pm. Admission 1000dr, students 500dr. Local bus #8, catch it behind the park across from 28 Octovriou travels there about every 20min., 300dr round-trip).

■ Vikos Gorge and Zagoria
ΒΙΚΟΣ ΚΑΙ ΖΑΓΟΡΙΑ

The spectacular combination of dramatic scenery and dozens of traditional villages inexplicably fails to attract more than a handful of adventurous travelers each year. For those who do make the trip, the Vikos and Aoos Rivers await, with hiking trails, kayaking routes, wildlife, and lovely views of the area's famous stone bridges. Avid hikers and climbers enjoy the ascent of Astraka and Gamila peaks, as well as the trek to Dragon Lake. For further information on the Zagorochoria, contact the **GNTO.** The city of Ioannina provides a good base from which to start your tour of the area. The local GNTO (tel. (0651) 22 138) provides information, including maps, as well as refuge locations and services for outdoor enthusiasts. Because of the region's proximity to Albania, do **not** hike in this area before contacting the EOS.

Kastoria and Florina, tucked against the Albanian and Macedonian borders, rarely receive tourists, particularly during periods of political upheaval in the neighboring countries. However, the Lake District offers stunning natural scenery, accessible to boaters, climbers, and skiers alike. The respite from tourism will give you an opportunity to test your Greek.

■ Dodoni ΔΩΔΩΝΗ

Ancient Dodoni rests at the foot of a mountain 22km south of Ioannina. Though the oracle at Delphi is better known, Homer (in both the *Iliad* and the *Odyssey*) and Herodotus refer to the oracle at Dodoni. It is here that Odysseus came for absolution after killing Penelope's suitors. A religious center for almost 4000 years, Dodoni began as an **oracle dedicated to Zeus.** According to legend, Zeus resided here as the roots of a giant oak while courting a nearby cypress tree. The Helloi interpreted the rustling of the huge oak's leaves as Zeus' advice, and the Argonauts had wood from the tree made into a ship keel, endowing the vessel with the ability to speak in times of need. A **temple** was built around 500 BC, then plundered (along with the oak tree) by the Romans in 167 BC. Christians later built a basilica on the site in an attempt to diminish pagan influences by incorporating them into Christianity.

The central attraction at Dodoni is a classical **amphitheater** last restored in the 3rd century BC. Originally designed to seat 18,000, Romans rebuilt it for **gladiator games,** and it still dominates the surrounding landscape. Bring your imagination, and you can walk in the footsteps of wily Odysseus or join the audience of a Sophoclian tragedy. In late July and August, the theater (tel. 82 287) hosts a festival of classical drama. Left of the theater are the remains of the oracle and foundations of several buildings, including the Christian basilica, and temples to Hercules and Aphrodite. Today there is little more than stones, weeds, and echoes (open daily 8am-7pm; admission 500dr, students 400dr).

For a site that has attracted gods, priests, gladiators, and rock stars, Dodoni is surprisingly difficult to visit. Groups can reach the oracle by hiring a car or **taxi** (at least

1000dr round-trip). In the summer, several buses run between Ioannina's second bus station and Meligi and Zotiko, villages near Dodoni (no buses on Tues. or Sun.; 320dr). Since all of the buses return to Ioannina immediately, you may want to go in the early morning and try to sweet-talk your way on a tour bus returning to Ioannina. Otherwise, go on Monday, Wednesday, or Friday when two buses run to nearby villages in the afternoon. Plan on hiking the 2km from the crossroads where the bus lets you off to the archaeological site.

MACEDONIA ΜΑΚΕΔΟΝΙΑ

Once the stomping ground of Alexander the Great, Macedonia, now the largest Greek province, retains its proud tradition. Thessaloniki, the focal point of Northern Greece, has emerged as a worthy competitor to Athens in fashion and nightlife. The countryside conceals the Lake District's natural splendor, and the excavations at Pella, Dion, and Vergina pay homage to the region's past. Macedonian pride is visible throughout this region of deep green foliage and red-roofed houses similar to those found in Eastern Europe. Men may find a trip to the monastic community of Mt. Athos the highlight of their trip—the peninsula is closed to women.

▓ Thessaloniki ΘΕΣΣΑΛΟΝΙΚΗ

Cosmopolitan Thessaloniki encircles its harbor and waterfront promenade with assurance. Wealthy and energetic, it proudly displays sophisticated shops, cafes, and a myriad of tree-lined avenues to passing visitors. The city is at its best in the markets that fringe popular squares, its thick-walled ruins, and Roman monuments. Its well-trafficked thoroughfares, lined with modern high rises, continue to accommodate splendid mansions. The old city's quiet, winding, castle-bound streets surprise the wayfarer with their residential charms and panoramic views. Few foreigners make it this far north, but those who do discover a pleasant anomaly—a Greek urban center that shows off its history without being overshadowed by it.

The capital of Macedonia and the second largest city in Greece, Thessaloniki teems with Byzantine churches and Roman ruins, and offers one of the best archaeological museums in Greece. On the crossroads of important trade routes, the city has flourished since its founding in 315 BC by Cassander, brother-in-law of Alexander the Great. Named for Cassander's wife, ancient Salonika prospered after the Roman conquest of Greece. Being the only port on the Via Egnatia (the ancient east-west highway) no doubt helped, and the city's cultural influence led the Apostle Paul, in the first century AD, to write two epistles to disciples of the churches he founded here (I and II Thessalonians). While Athens was in the throes of cultural decline, Thessaloniki usurped its position as the most important Greek city of the Byzantine Empire. After the 10th century, missionary followers of the brothers Methodius and Cyril (inventors of the Cyrillic alphabet) exerted their wide-ranging influence from headquarters here. In the early 20th century, the city's population, which included Slavs, Albanians, and a vast Jewish community, was more characteristically Balkan than Hellenic. More homogeneously Hellenic today, the city nonetheless continues to project cultural vigor. In recognition of this, Thessaloniki celebrated its year as the Cultural Capital of Europe in 1997.

ORIENTATION AND PRACTICAL INFORMATION

Running parallel to the water, the main streets are **Nikis, Mitropoleos, Tsimiski, Ermou,** and **Egnatia.** Intersecting all these streets and leading from the water into town are **Aristotelous** and **Agia Sophias.** The main shopping streets are Tsimiski, Mitropoleos, and Ag. Sophias. As it reaches the waterfront, Aristotelous forms Aristotelous Sq., which is lined by the tourist office, train office, airport bus terminal, and a string of overpriced cafes. The cheaper hotels are on Egnatia, banks and post office on Tsimiski, and waterfront bars and cafes on Nikis. The railway station is west of the square along Monastiriou St. The main park, fairgrounds, university, and Archeological Museum lie east of the downtown area, just inland from the **White Tower** (Lefkos Pirgos). Inland from Tsimiski, **Navarinou Square,** with its centerpiece of Roman ruins, is a captivating meeting ground for Thessaloniki's youth. Facing inland, head left on Mitropoleos, to reach the **Ladadika** district. This ex-red-light neighborhood has been restored into a charming pocket of turn-of-the-century cafes, bars, and authentic Greek *tavernas.* Roughly 15 blocks inland, north of Athinas St. and flanked by ancient castle walls, wind the streets of the **old town.** A marvelous place for morning or evening strolls, here you will find a welcome degree of tranquility, panoramic views, and cheap *tavernas.*

Tourist Offices: EOT (tel. 27 18 88, 22 29 35), off Aristotelous Sq. at #8, one block from the water. Take any bus on Egnatia to Aristotelous Sq. The office has free city maps, hotel listings, transportation schedules, and information about the **International Trade Fair, Song Festival,** the **Thessaloniki Festival of Film,** and the **Dimitria Cultural Festival,** all held between Sept. and Nov. Open Mon.-Fri. 8am-8pm, Sat. 8:30am-2pm. **United Travel System,** 28 Mitropoleos St. (tel. 28 67 56; fax 28 31 56), near Aristotelous Sq. There is no sign on the street, so ring the bell to be let in and go to the 7th floor. Ask for English-speaking Liza and make sure you're carrying *Let's Go.* Open Mon.-Fri. 9:30am-5pm. Other offices at the **port** (tel. 59 35 78) and the **airport** (tel. 42 50 11, ext. 215).

Tourist Police: 4 Dodekanissou St., 5th floor (tel. 55 48 70). Offers free maps and brochures. Some English spoken. Open daily 8am-11pm.

Banks: National Bank, 11 Tsimiski St. (tel. 53 86 21). Open for **currency exchange** Mon.-Fri. 8am-2pm and 6-8pm, Sat. 9am-1pm, Sun. 9:30am-12:15pm. Smaller banks charge slightly higher commissions. Many line Tsimiki, including **Citibank,** 21 Tsimiski St. (tel. 26 60 21), which handles sophisticated international banking needs and has 24hr. **ATMs.** Most banks open Mon.-Thurs. 8am-2pm, Fri. 8am-1:30pm.

American Express: Northern Greece representative at **Memphis Travel,** 23 Nikis St. (tel. 22 27 96), on the waterfront. Open Mon.-Fri. 10am-4pm, Sat. 9am-2pm.

Consulates: United Kingdom, 8 Venizelou St. (tel. 27 80 06). Open Mon.-Fri. 8am-3pm. **Bulgaria** (tel. 82 92 10). **Cyprus** (tel. 26 06 11). **Italy** (tel. 83 00 55). **Turkey** (tel. 24 84 59). Consulates generally open 9am-6pm. **U.S.,** 59 Nikis St. (tel. 24 29 00), on the waterfront west of the White Tower. Open Tues. and Thurs. 9am-noon.

Ministry of Northern Greece: (tel. 25 70 10) On the corner of Ag. Dimitiriou St. and Venizelou. After obtaining letters from their consulate, men wishing to visit Mt. Athos must obtain permits here in room 222 (see **Mt. Athos** p. 132). Open Mon.-Fri. 10am-2pm.

Flights: The airport (tel. 47 39 77) is 16km from town. Take bus #78 (110dr) or a taxi (1800dr). **Olympic Airways Office,** 3 Koundouriotou St. (tel. 23 02 40). Open Mon.-Sat. 8am-3:30pm. Call 28 18 80 for reservations Mon.-Sat. 7am-9pm. Flights to: Athens (9-10 per day, 21,700dr); Limnos (1 per day, 5:45am, 14,900dr); Lesvos (1 per day, 5:45am, 17,500dr); Crete (3 per week, 29,600dr); Rhodes (2 per week, 31,600dr); Ioannina (2 per week, 11,800dr); and Duluth, Minn. (1 per day, 20hr., 533,250dr). Flights also connect Thessaloniki with European cities and Larnaka in Cyprus.

Trains: the **main terminal** (tel. 51 75 17) is on Monastiriou St., in the western part of the city. Take any bus down Egnatia St. (75dr). Trains to: Athens (50 per day, 8hr., 3800dr); Kalambaka (6 per day, 5hr., 2300dr); Volos (10 per day, 4½hr., 1800dr); Edessa (7 per day, 2½hr., 850dr); Florina (5 per day, 4hr., 1400dr); Alexandropolis (3 per day, 7hr., 3000dr); Istanbul (1 per day, 20hr., 11,900dr); and Sofia (1 per day, 7hr., 5110dr). A **ticketing office** at the corner of Aristotelous and Ermou is open Tues.-Fri. 8am-8pm, Sat. and Mon. 8am-3pm.

Buses: The privately run **KTEL** bus company operates out of dozens of stations scattered throughout the city, each servicing a district of Greece named for its largest city. Although printed timetables and price lists are almost nonexistent, departure times are posted above ticket counters. In addition, the **EOT** has virtually complete information, in Greek, regarding bus schedules, fares, trip duration, station locations, and telephone numbers. There are buses to: Athens (10 per day, 7hr.,

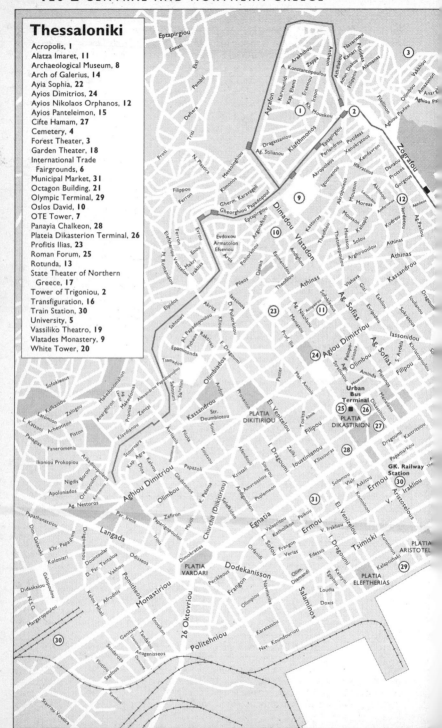

Thessaloniki

Acropolis, 1
Alatza Imaret, 11
Archaeological Museum, 8
Arch of Galerius, 14
Ayia Sophia, 22
Ayios Dimitrios, 24
Ayios Nikolaos Orphanos, 12
Ayios Panteleimon, 15
Cifte Hamam, 27
Cemetery, 4
Forest Theater, 3
Garden Theater, 18
International Trade
  Fairgrounds, 6
Municipal Market, 31
Octagon Building, 21
Olympic Terminal, 29
Oslos David, 10
OTE Tower, 7
Panayia Chalkeon, 28
Plateia Dikasterion Terminal, 26
Profitis Ilias, 23
Roman Forum, 25
Rotunda, 13
State Theater of Northern
  Greece, 17
Tower of Trigoniou, 2
Transfiguration, 16
Train Station, 30
University, 5
Vassiliko Theatro, 19
Vlatades Monastery, 9
White Tower, 20

Gulf of Thessaloniki

0		300 yards
0		300 meters

7700dr); Katerini (about every 30min., 6:30am-10pm, 1hr., 1150dr); Kozoni (about every hr., 6am-9pm, 2½hr., 2150dr); Veria (about every 45min., 6am-8pm, 1½hr., 1200dr); Volos (5 per day, 3½hr., 3300dr); Alexandropolis (6 per day, 6hr., 5200dr); and Kavala (every hr., 6am-10pm, 3hr., 2650dr). Call 142 for Greek language information on the telephone numbers and street addresses of all depots.

Public Transportation: An office across from the train station and the EOT provides limited scheduling information. #8, 10, 11, and 31 run up and down Egnatia St. Buy your ticket on the bus (75dr).

Ferries: Ticketing at **Karacharisis Travel and Shipping Agency,** 8 Kountourioti St. (tel. 52 45 44; fax 53 22 89). Open Mon.-Fri. 9am-9pm, Sat. 9am-3pm. Ferries travel to: Crete (24hr., 10,700dr); Paros (14hr., 8550dr); Naxos (14hr., 8050dr); Syros (12hr., 7900dr); Santorini (17hr., 9100dr); Tinos (13hr., 8350dr); and Mykonos (13hr., 8000dr). Ferries travel twice a week to: Limnos (7hr., 5100dr); Lesvos (9hr., 7700dr.); Chios (12hr. 7800dr); Rhodes (20hr., 13,200dr) and Kos (18hr., 11,500dr). Cabins without bath generally cost an additional 50% of quoted fare, and cabins with bath average twice the deck fare. In July and Aug., it is recommended that you reserve a seat 2-3 days in advance. Ferry service is reduced significantly in the winter.

Flying Dolphins: Hydrofoils travel daily (June-Sept. only) to Skiathos (3hr.), Skopelos (4hr.), and Alonissos (5hr.). Fares average 10,000dr. **Crete Air Travel,** 1 Dragoumi St. (tel. 54 74 07, 53 43 76), directly across from the main port, sells tickets. Open Mon.-Fri. 9am-9pm, Sat. 9am-3pm.

International Bookstore: Molcho Books, 10 Tsimiski St. (tel. 27 52 71), across from the National Bank. Excellent selection of English and other foreign language books. International daily newspapers. Open Mon., Wed., and Sat. 8:40am-2:50pm; Tues. and Thurs.-Fri. 8:40am-2:20pm and 5-8pm.

Laundromats: Bianca, 3 L. Antoniadou St. (tel. 20 96 02). Behind the church to your right as you face the Arch of Galerius. 1400dr per load includes wash, dry, and soap. You can leave your laundry and pick it up later in the day. Open Mon.-Fri. 8am-8:30pm, Sat. 8am-3pm.

Hospital: Ippokration Public Hospital, 50 A. Papanastasiou (tel. 83 79 20), some doctors speak English. **Red Cross First Aid Hospital,** 6 Kountourioti St. (tel. 53 05 30), located at the entrance to the main port. Free minor medical care.

Post Office: 45 Tsimiski St., midway between Agia Sophias St. and Aristotelous St. Open Mon.-Fri. 7:30am-8pm, Sat. 7:30am-2pm, Sun. 9am-1:30pm. **Postal Code:** 54101.

OTE: 27 Karolou Diehl St., at the corner of Ermou, 1 block east of Aristotelous. Open 24hr. **Telephone Code:** 031.

ACCOMMODATIONS

Many hotels sit along the western end of Egnatia St., between Vardari Sq. (500m east of the train station) and Dikastirion Sq. Be aware that Egnatia is loud at all hours. Prices may rise 25% between September and November during the international fair and festivals. Single women should avoid offers for cheap rooms touted by English-speaking tourist information impersonators at the train station.

Hotel Argo, 11 Egnatia St. (tel. 51 97 70). Old rooms, good bargains, and classical music. Singles 4000dr, with bath 5500dr; doubles 5000dr, with bath 7000dr. Just don't get stuck in room 21B, as it's essentially in the attic.

Hotel Amaila, 33 Ermou St. (tel. 26 83 21; fax 23 33 56). Clean, olive green rooms with bath, TV, and telephone. Singles 12,000dr; doubles 17,000dr.

Hotel Atlas, 40 Egnatia St. (tel. 53 70 46, 51 00 38; fax 54 35 07). Singles 5000dr; doubles 7000dr, with bath, TV, and A/C 10,000dr. Add 20% per extra bed.

Hotel Averof, at the intersection of Egnatia St. and L. Sofou St. 24 (tel. 53 88 40; fax 54 31 94). New furniture but old floors. Communal living room with TV. Singles 5500dr, with bath 7500dr; doubles 7500dr, with bath 9500dr.

Hotel Ilios, 27 Egnatia St. (tel. 51 26 20). Loudly patriotic red, white, and blue floors. Rooms with bath and A/C. Singles 9000dr; doubles 13,000dr.

Hotel Kastoria (tel. 53 62 80; fax 53 62 50), at the intersection of Egnatia St. 24 and L. Sofou St. 17. Tidy, dim rooms with baths. Singles 5000dr; doubles 6000dr.

Hotel Tourist, 21 Mitropoleos (tel. 27 63 35; fax 22 68 65), 1 block from Aristotelous Sq., on a pleasant, tree-lined street near the waterfront. Has 4.5m-high ceilings, cavernous hallways, and an old-fashioned salon and elevator. Singles 7500dr, with bath 9000dr; doubles with bath 10,000dr; triples with bath 17,000dr.

Youth Hostel, 44 Alex. Svolou St. (tel. 22 59 46; fax 26 22 08). Take tram #8, 10, 11, or 31 on Egnatia and get off at the Arch of Galerius. Walk toward the water and turn left 2 blocks later onto Svolou. Cheap accommodation (2000dr per person), but you'll want to wear your shoes everywhere. No curfew, but 11am-6:30pm lockout. Free showers available at all other times. 1-night max. stay without Hostel Membership, 3 nights with it.

FOOD

Don't go to Thessaloniki for the standard *moussaka* and Greek salad—this town is known and loved throughout Greece for its excellent *mezedes*. Prepared for locals, the food is almost sure to be cooked well and priced fairly. Thessaloniki's downtown is dotted with inexpensive self-service food outlets and shops. Lively and full of bargains, the marketplace *(agora)* is bounded on four sides by Irakliou, Egnatia, Aristotelous, and Venizelou St. To stock up on fruits, vegetables, bread, and groceries, visit the **open-air markets** of Vati Kioutou St. just off Aristotelous. The Aretsou Area, along the bay about 4km toward the airport, boasts excellent seafood. Explore the old town and Ladadika district for inexpensive, family-oriented *tavernas*.

The Brothers (tel. 26 64 32), in Navarino Sq., offers traditional Greek meals, at good prices (full meal 1500dr). They are popular, delicious, but very busy. Open daily noon-midnight.

Ta Spata, 28 Aristotelous (tel. 27 74 12), offers a wide selection of tasty, inexpensive, moderately sized entrees (1500dr). Lacks atmosphere. Open daily 11am-midnight.

To Chriso Pagoni, Alex. Svolou St., next to the hostel. Large portions, low prices.

To Palati, 3 Platcia Morichovou (tel. 55 08 88). Traditional Greek meals (1300-1600dr) in the restored Ladadika district.

New Ilyssia, 17 Leontos Sofou St. (tel. 53 69 96), a neighborhood restaurant and grill located off Egnatia St. Serves large helpings of traditional Greek food in an unpretentious setting. Entrees from 1250dr. Open daily 8:30am-2am.

ENTERTAINMENT

Cafes abound—try the **Journal** across from the Agia Sophia. The king of all cafe-hangouts for bohemian locals, however, is the **Milos** district, accessible by taxi. **Vilka** houses a similar scene in what used to be a brewery. On weekend evenings, mingle with Greeks along **Plaza Dhimitrio Gounari.** Fashion-conscious couples promenade from the waterfront to the Arch of Galerius. A more grunge crowd mellows out with a cup of coffee in the park and at **Navarinou Square,** one block west of D. Gounari. Lesbian and gay revelers head to **Taboo** on Kastritsiou St., one block from Egnatia. Turn toward the water on Mitropolitou Genadiou and take your first left. The Ladadika district has clubs and live Greek music. Prices are high with beers at 1000dr, drinks 1500dr, and cocktails 1800dr. All the big, noisy nightclubs that boom to the beat of techno and other music are near the airport. You can only get there by taxi (2000-2500dr). Thessaloniki's favorite is **Ab Fab** (as in Absolutely Fabulous), past the turn-off for the airport. Most clubs have a cover of about 2000dr that includes the first drink. **Natali Cinema,** 3 Vassilissis Olgas (tel. 82 94 57), on the waterfront, five minutes past the White Tower heading away from the city center, shows open-air movies in summer, as does the **Forest Theater** north of the center.

SIGHTS

If you have time for only one stop in the city, the superlative **Archaeological Museum** (tel. 83 05 38, -1037) is your destination. The museum spotlights a collection of Macedonian treasures, including gold *larnakes* (burial caskets) that once contained the cremated royal family of Vergina. When archaeologists first discovered this unpillaged tomb in 1979, the exquisite artifacts indicated that it belonged to a king. After putting together the skeleton from the bones in the tomb, they noticed two idiosyncracies: one leg was shorter than the other and the skull had a disfigured eye socket. Ancient historians had documented that King Philip the Great, father of Alexander, had been born with one leg shorter than the other and had suffered an eye injury caused by a spear thrown at him in an assassination attempt. Notice in the exhibit his special shin guards. To get there, take bus #3 from the railway station to Hanth Sq. Open Mon. 12:30-7pm, Tues.-Fri. 8am-7pm, Sat. and Sun. 8:30am-3pm; in winter Mon. 10:30am-5pm, Tues.-Fri. 8am-5pm, Sat.-Sun. 8:30am-3pm. Admission 1500dr, students and seniors 800dr, EU students and children under 18 free.

The **International Fairgrounds,** across from the museum, hold a variety of festivals in the fall, including the International Trade Fair in September (for info call 23 92 21). The fairgrounds also house the **Macedonian Museum of Contemporary Art** (tel. 24 00 02; fax 28 15 67). The new museum frequently hosts displays of internationally renowned modern artists. Open Tues.-Sat. 10am-2pm and 6-9pm, Sun. 11am-2pm. Admission 500dr, students 300dr, artists and groups free.

On the other side of the park looms the **Lefkos Pirgos** (tel. 26 78 32), all that remains of a 16th-century Venetian seawall. Formerly known as the Bloody Tower because an elite corps of soldiers was massacred within it, the structure was painted white to obliterate the gruesome memories. The tower now houses a museum of early Christian art, and a cafe in the turret (same hours as archaeological museum; admission 800dr, students 400dr, EU students and children under 18 free). The ruins of the **Eptapirgion Walls,** erected during the reign of Theodosius the Great, stretch along the north edge of the old city. Take bus #22 from Eleftherias Sq. on the waterfront. Eleftherias Sq. is also where buses #5, 33, and 39 leave for the **Ethnology and Popular Art (Folklore) Museum,** 68 Vas. Olgas St. (tel. 83 05 91). Under renovation in the summer of 1997, the costume exhibits were scheduled to reopen in September 1997 (open Fri.-Wed. 9:30am-2pm; admission 200dr).

The celebrated **Arch of Galerius** stands at the end of Egnatia St. at the corner of Gounari St., but remains under renovation and covered with scaffolding. Next to it and also closed for reconstruction, the **Rotunda** was designed as an emperor's mausoleum, but renamed **Agios Georgios** by Constantine the Great for use as a church. For further historical pursuits, head north of Dikastirion Sq. to the **Roman Market** between Filippou and Olibou St. The ruins, which include a somewhat hyper-restored theater, continue to be excavated. The centerpiece of the remains of the **Palace of Galerius,** near Navarino Sq., is the well-preserved octagonal hall.

Over the centuries, earthquakes and fire have severely damaged most churches in this region. Although the renovation has not beautified the lucky survivors, the churches of **Panagia Ahiropitos, Panagia Halkeon,** and **Agios Nikolaos Orfanos** still feature some brilliant mosaic work and frescoes from the late Byzantine era.

Another example of Byzantine art is the 9th-century mosaic of the Ascension in the dome of the **Agia Sophia,** modeled after the Hagia Sophia in Istanbul. For a glimpse of these churches' former glory, visit the **Crypt of Agios Dimitrios** (open Mon. 12:30-7pm, Tues.-Sat. 8am-8pm, and Sun. 10:30am-8pm; admission free). You can also visit the beautiful **Old Synagogue** at 35 Sigrou St. Although it is not in use, the caretaker at the **Jewish Community Center,** 24 Tsimiski St., will let you in.

■ Near Thessaloniki: Pella

Along the highway, the ruins of ancient Pella and Vergina make interesting day trips. Pella, where a farmer discovered the ruins in 1957, is located just 38km west of Thessaloniki. In ancient times, Pella served as a port when water from the Thermaiko Gulf covered the surrounding plain. Around 400 BC, King Archelaus opted to build his palace here, and Pella became the largest city in Macedonia. During Philip II's reign, Pella was the first capital of a united Greece; subsequently, his son Alexander the Great began his mission to unify the world under Macedonian rule in Pella. Across the highway, the small **Pella Museum** (tel. (0382) 31 278) contains the exquisite mosaics "Dionysus Riding a Panther" and "The Lion Hunt." These skillful works are the earliest-known mosaics that attempt three-dimensionality. (Open April 1-Oct. 20 Mon.-Fri. 8am-7pm, Sat.-Sun.8:30am-3pm, Oct.-March, open Tues.-Sun. 8:30am-3pm. Site and museum have separate tickets, but both are 500dr, 300dr for students and seniors.)

Buses to Pella depart from the 22 Anagenniseos depot near the train station in Thessaloniki (every 30-45min., 650dr). Walk down Octovriou St. past the courthouse and turn right onto Anagenniseos St. The KTEL is on the corner of Damonos St. Pella only takes an hour to see, but the museum alone makes the trip worthwhile. Buses to Thessaloniki (2-3 per hr.) pass the site, which is right on the main highway.

To travel between Pella and Vergina, take the bus (15min., 210dr) to Halkidona, 3km east of Pella. At the **Okostas Taverna** right off the central square, across from a gas station and next to a pharmacy, you can catch a bus to Veria (1½hr., 750dr). From the Veria bus station, the Alexandria bus stops at Vergina (30min., 260dr), but ask to be let off at the archeological site rather than at the village.

■ Vergina ΒΕΡΓΙΝΑ

The discovery of the ancient ruins of Vergina, 13km southeast of Veria, was an archaeological watershed. In 1977 Manolis Andronikos began excavating the remains of **royal tombs** and a large **palace** dating from 350 BC. The tombs display such superb artistry (and skeletal remains) that scholars believe that they could only have belonged only to the royal Macedonian family of **King Philip II**, father of Alexander the Great. These fabulous treasures are now on display in Thessaloniki's Archaeological Museum (see p. 122). The remains suggest that Vergina was the site of the ancient Macedonian capital of **Aigai.**

The bus stop is next to the complex housing the Royal Tombs. Here you can view four tombs in varying degrees of repair after time and pillaging. The spectacular painted facade and marble door protecting Philip II's tomb, found unpillaged, have yielded solid gold wreathes and burial caskets *(larnakes)* containing his cremated remains. Uphill, the open ruins of the 3rd-century BC **Palace of Palatitsa** can be reached by a 30-minute walk, and also leads past a theater and another tomb. A good selection of books on Vergina is available at the cafe/souvenir stand across the street from the tombs which will help you interpret the ruins. The site office up the hill at the entrance to the palace ruins also sells books, but has a smaller selection. (Tombs and palace open Tues.-Sun. June-Sept. 8am-7pm, Oct.-May 8:30am-3pm. Admission to the tombs is 1200dr, students 900dr. Admission to the palace is 500dr, students 300dr.) **Buses** run from Thessaloniki (every 30min., 2hr., 1150dr) and Edessa (6 per day, 800dr) to Veria, from which you can take the "Alexandria" bus and get off in Vergina (12 per day, 15min., 240dr).

■ Edessa ΕΔΕΣΣΑ

Greeks love Edessa because it contains the country's only waterfalls. Perched on top of a steep butte in the foothills of Mt. Vermion, the city was named Edessa, "the waters," by an occupying Bulgarian army. The town ends on the brink of a ravine, where numerous streams channelled through stone waterways and under Edessa's arched bridges cascade 32m to the valley floor. But it's not quite as magnificent as it sounds; concrete viewing balconies, overgrown weeds, litter, and danger signs along the water's edge detract from the experience. Even if Edessa's main attraction is not as spectacular as one might wish, the town's temperate climate, aromatic flowers, petite parks, and water-bound walkways give the town a relaxed atmosphere that is worth a visit.

ORIENTATION AND PRACTICAL INFORMATION

Hotels and the town center await at the top of **Pavlou Mela,** where the road intersects **Egnatia** and **Democratias Street** as they merge. Farther along, 18th Octovriou Street branches out from Democratias St. and terminates at the railroad tracks at the end of town. If you're in dire need of help, turn right at 20 Democratias (walking away from the bus station) and look for the **police station** (tel. 23 333) at the corner of Filippou and Iroon Polytechniou (open 24hr.). The **tourist information office** (tel. 20 300), located just to the right of the waterfalls, is open daily 9am-10pm from April to October and provides information about sights, hotels, and transportation. The **National Bank,** 1 Demicratias St., is surrounded by a fence on the corner of 2 Arch. Penteleiminos and has an **ATM** (open Mon.-Thurs. 8am-2pm and Fri. 8am-1:30pm).

The main **bus station** (tel. 23 511) is at the corner of Pavlou Mela and Filippou St. **Buses** run to: Athens (3 per day, 8hr., 8250dr); Thessaloniki (14 per day, 11 on Sun., 2hr., 1500dr); and Veria (6 per day, 1hr., 850dr). A **second depot,** marked by a bus sign, is located at a family-run sandwich shop and grill just up the block at Pavlou Mela and Egnatia (look for "KTEL" painted on the window). Buses go to: Kastoria (4 per day, 2½hr., 1800dr) and Florina (6 per day, 1½hr.). The **train station** (tel. 23 510) is at the end of 18th Octovriou St., a 10-minute walk from the post office. **Trains** run to: Florina (7 per day, 2hr., 720dr); Thessaloniki via Veria and Naoussa (8 per day, 2hr., 840dr); Kozani (7 per day, 2½hr., 820dr); and Athens (1 per day), either directly (7hr., 7500dr) or via Plati (9hr., 3940dr). **Taxis** (tel. 23 392, 22 904) congregate on 18th Octovriou St., near the bank. Edessa's **post office** (tel. 23 332), on Democratias St., one block from the *agora,* exchanges money for a commission (open Mon.-Fri. 7:30am-2pm). **Postal Code:** 58200. The **OTE** is a blue and white building facing the Byzantine clock tower on Ag. Dimitrios. **Telephone Code:** 0381.

ACCOMMODATIONS, FOOD, AND SIGHTS

The **Hotel Alfa** (tel. 22 221; fax 24 777), two blocks up from the bus depot and across the square, has clean rooms with TV and bath (singles 7500dr; doubles 11,000dr). You might also call **Hotel Elana** (tel. 23 218) or **Hotel Pella** (tel. 23 541).

Edessa has no shortage of the lethal twin-food demons known as cheese pies and rotisserie chicken. The fish *taverna* **Boulgouri,** near 18th Octovriou on the way to the train station, provides a pleasant atmosphere for a fish dinner (1200dr). A good way to appreciate the town is to walk west up Monasteriou St. (behind Egnatia and to the right of the **Byzantine Clock Tower**) to the **Byzantine Bridge,** under which flows the main rivulet that eventually splits off to form the many streams flowing through town. Many unpretentious cafes reside here. In the direction of the waterfalls, a few restaurants offer seats with a magnificent view of the mountains and the valley below, including the ruins of the ancient city, whose marble columns are visible in the distance. The **Public Waterfall Center Restaurant** (tel. 26 718), right at the top of the falls, has many seats and decent prices (goulash 1200-1600dr). Near the post office, a side street on the left of Democratias leads into a cluster of **bars,** which offer beers for 500dr, cocktails 1000dr.

Below the town to the east lie the 4th-century BC ruins of the ancient city which were unearthed in 1968. Until the discovery of the ruins at Vergina, Edessa was thought to be ancient **Aigai,** the capital of Macedonia. Except for a few churches, the only other attraction is a small **archaeological museum** in the mosque on Stratou St. at the edge of town. Inquire at the information office about the status of renovations to Varossi, the old town which remained a Christian enclave during the Ottoman occupation, and new industrial and folklore museums. Hopefully, the new sights will have more charm than the waterfalls themselves.

KATARRAKTON WATERFALL

To reach Edessa's largest waterfall, **Katarrakton,** keep to the stream farthest to your left (with your back to the bridge). As the stream forks, pursue the branch to your left. Alternately, walk down Democratios St. and watch for the large and clear waterfall signs. The roar of surging cascades and the vision of bustling souvenir stands will herald your arrival. Enthusiasts should continue down the path at the bottom of Katarrakton into the valley to see the three larger falls near the hydroelectric plant or stroll into the waterfall's none too impressive **cave** (50dr). Almost all the cliffside terraces spanning the east rim offer beautiful panoramic vistas of the agricultural plain below. You'll be able to spot a convent and the ruins of the ancient town.

▓ Kastoria and the Lake District
ΚΑΣΤΟΡΙΑ ΚΑΙ ΠΕΡΙΦΕΡΕΙΑ ΤΗΣ ΛΙΜΝΗΣ

Kastoria, Florina, and Pella, tucked against the borders of Albania and the former Yugoslav Republic of Macedonia, are rarely visited by tourists. The natural setting is stunning, the villages attractive and unassuming, the absence of sputtering buses refreshing, and English-speaking residents are scarce.

The city of **Kastoria** (named after Kastor, one of Zeus's sons) originally rested securely on an island in Lake Kastoria. Around the 10th century AD, the townspeople began dumping garbage into the lake in an attempt to build a causeway to the shore. Today, the bulk of the city is squeezed onto this narrow isthmus, and the island proper is nearly deserted. Savor the beauty of the lake from a distance, but don't even think about taking a dip. The town only recently stopped dumping raw sewage into the water, and the biological clean-up process is still years from completion.

ORIENTATION AND PRACTICAL INFORMATION

Tourist services (tel. 22 312) are available on the first floor of the town hall in room #3 (open Mon.-Fri. 7am-5pm and Sat. 10am-3pm). There are no tourist police, but the kindly **municipal police** (tel. 83 333), located behind the bus station on Gramou St., speak some English (open 24hr.). The **National Bank** (tel. 22 350) is on the mainland at 11 Noembriou St., off Gramou, bearing left as you head northeast uphill. They have a 24-hour **ATM** that accepts MasterCard or Cirrus (open Mon.-Thurs. 8am-2pm and Fri. 8am-1:30pm). The **post office** (tel. 22 991) is on the lakefront road, Megalou Alexandrou Ave., around the bend from the bus station. They also exchange currency (open daily 7:30am-2pm). The **OTE**, 33 Ag. Athanasiou St., is uphill midway between Davaki Sq. and Dexamenis Sq. (open daily 7am-10pm). The Olympic Airways office (tel. 22 275, 23 125) is on the waterfront (open Mon.-Fri. 8:30am-4pm). A taxi travels to the **airport** (12km away) in Argos for 1500dr. Flights go to Athens (Fri.-Wed., 17,900dr). Kastoria's main **bus terminal,** 3 Septemvriou (tel. 83 455), lies one block from the lake. Buses run to: Thessaloniki (6 per day, 3½hr., 3300dr); Edessa (4 per day, 2hr., 1850dr); Athens (2 per day, 9hr., 8600dr); Kozani (5 per day, 1¾hr., 1550dr); and Veria (2 per day, 2½hr., 2250dr). Multiple bus connections are required to reach Florina or Kalambaka. **Taxis** (tel. 82 100, -200) converge near the bus station (24hr.). To contact the **hospital,** call 28 341, -2, or -3. The **postal code** is 52100; **telephone code,** 0467.

ACCOMMODATIONS

Hotel Acropolis, 14 Gramou St. (tel. 83 587), one block behind the bus station. One of the better bargains in Kastoria. Opt for a higher floor for a view of the lake. Singles 4850dr, with bath 5500dr; doubles with bath 7300dr.

Hotel Anesis, 10 Gramou St. (tel. 83 908; fax 83 768), is near Acropolis, but fancier. Rooms with bath and TV. Singles 7800dr; doubles 10,500dr; triples 12,600dr.

Hotel Kastoria (tel. 85 508) is 1km to the right (facing the water) of the bus station on the waterfront road. Spacious, neat rooms. Singles and doubles 7000dr; triples 8000dr. Breakfast 1000dr.

Europa Hotel, 12 Ag. Athanasiou St. (tel. 23 826, -7; fax 25 154), on the main road out of Davaki Sq., running towards Dexamenis Sq. Professional, English-speaking staff. Spacious rooms with bath and TV. Singles 8400dr; doubles 10,400dr; triples 13,100dr. Breakfast 1100dr.

Camping (tel. 22 714) is available at Mavriotissa Church for about 1000dr per person. Get permission from the priest.

SIGHTS

In addition to its voluminous fur garment industry (some 5000 garments per day), Kastoria is renowned for its churches. There are 40 Byzantine and 36 post-Byzantine edifices scattered throughout the city, each with elaborate masonry and exquisite decoration. The tiny Byzantine **Panagia Koumblelidhiki,** in the center of town (open Tues.-Sun. 8am-6pm), and the **Mavriotissa Church,** 3km out of town, house particularly spectacular frescoes (open daily 9am-8pm). Unfortunately, these have been marred by modern graffiti. To visit Mavriotissa, stroll out of town past the hospital toward the island. The priest who lives in the church conducts tours (in Greek or German) and opens the churches between 9am and 10pm. If you want to be certain of gaining access to any of the town's churches, stop first at the **Byzantine Museum** (tel. 26 781), off Mitropoleos St. in Dexamenis Sq., and arrange for a guide to open the churches for you (open Tues.-Sun. 8am-6pm; free).

AROUND THE LAKE DISTRICT

One kilometer out of town stands **Mt. Psalida,** where Alexander the Average resolved to become Alexander the Great by conquering the world. Bounded by Yugoslavia, Albania, and Kastoria, the **Lake District** is an area of dense wilderness and swimming lakes. **Florina,** accessible from Edessa and Thessaloniki, makes a good base from which to explore the area. **Trains** run to the Florina **train station** (tel. (0385) 36 239) from Thessaloniki (7 per day, 4hr., 1340dr) and Edessa (7 per day, 2hr., 650dr). **Buses** run from Thessaloniki (6 per day, 3½hr., 2650dr) and to Edessa (6 per day, 2hr., 1350dr). For the Florina **bus station,** call (0385) 22 430. Florina has little to offer tourists apart from its location, a fragrant market area, and the **Hotel Ellenis** (tel. (0385) 22 671) in the town center (singles 7000dr; doubles 8500dr; triples 10,500dr). The **Alpine Club** runs a large refuge near the village of **Pissoderi** on Mt. Verna.

■ Mount Olympus ΟΛΥΜΠΟΣ

The charm of Olympus does not lie in its natural beauty; nor its physical
magnitude; the beauty of Olympus is spiritual, it is divine. . .
— Boissonade

Rising from the coastal plain 90km southwest of Thessaloniki, Mt. Olympus so impressed the seafaring ancient Greeks that they exalted it as a suitable home for the gods. First climbed in 1913, Olympus has been harnessed by a network of well maintained hiking trails that make the summit accessible to just about anyone with sturdy legs. The zenith rewards visitors with incomparable views and ethereal blue skies, particularly in June and September, when the air is clearest. Each winter, six or more feet of snow bury Mt. Olympus, so the climbing season lasts only from May to October, and you may meet snow even in late July. If you make the ascent between May and September, you'll need no special equipment besides sturdy shoes (hiking in sandals is a stupid idea), sunglasses, sunscreen, a hat, and at least two liters of water. If you plan on climbing the upper regions, you may need a waterproof windbreaker, an extra shirt, and gloves. Plan on a two or three-day trip to fully enjoy the wilderness, staying overnight in one of the refuges or camping on the mountain. In either case, bring warm clothes and leave your pack in Litohoro.

LITOHORO

The gateway to Olympus is the small village of **Litohoro.** Surprisingly, the friendly town is relatively free of souvenirs and other tourist accoutrements. On the main street, near the **bus station** before the main square, lies an information booth which acts as the town's **tourist office** (tel. (0352) 83 100), providing free maps of the area

Mount Olympus

GREECE

Legend:
- ▲ Peaks (elev.)
- ● Pits (elev.)
- ◖ Caves
- ◖ Waterholes
- ▬ Roads
- –·–· International trails
- –––– Trails and cart tracks

N

2 miles
2 kilometers
0

Litohoro

Moni. Ag. Dionysiou ■
Refuge D
Stavros ●

Mantrnies ▲

MAVROLOUNGO GORGE

E4

D

D

Petrostrougka, 2000 ▲
Strangos, 1910 ▲
Ag. Dionysiou

D

Mandres, 2154 ▲

D

D

Kardara, 916 ▲
Koromilies ▲
Maltas ▲

Pelekoudia, 1600 ▲
Livadaki, 2150 ▲
Rachi Achriani ▲

Prionia ▲

Simaioforos, 2366 ▲

Pagos, 2681 ▲

D

Kalogeros, 2701 ▲

Dragasia, 2253 ▲

Fragkou Aloni, 2684 ▲
2530 ●

E4

Refuge A

D

D

2320 ●

E4

Stavroities, 2676 ▲
Agios Antonios, 2815 ▲

Refuge C
2540 ●

Refuge SEO
Toumba, 2801 ▲
Stefani, 2903 ▲
Mytikas, 2917 ▲
Skala, 2866 ▲

Refuge B

E4

Ski Lift

Kakavrakas, 2618 ▲

Skolio, 2911 ▲

E4

2350 ●

Vrisopoules, 1800 ▲

(open mid-June to Sept. daily 9am-8pm). The **health center** (tel. (0352) 22 222) has **emergency facilities.** Litohoro's **National Bank** (tel. (0352) 81 025) is in the main square (open Mon.-Thurs. 8am-2pm and Fri. 8am-1:30pm) along with the **post office** (open Mon.-Fri. 7:30am-2pm). **Postal code:** 60200. The **OTE** sits on the main street.

   Trains (tel. (0352) 22 522) stop at Litohoro on the Thessaloniki-Larissa and Thessaloniki-Athens lines, but the station is 1km from the bus stop (by the BP station, left facing the water). The Katerini-Litohoro bus will take travelers the remaining 5km into town (every hour). **Buses** (tel. (0352) 81 271) from the KTEL station, opposite the church in the main square, travel from Litohoro to: Thessaloniki via Katerini (12 per day, 1½hr., 1500dr); Katerini (every hour 6am-9pm, 20min, 400dr); Larissa (10 per day, 2hr., 1200dr); and Athens (3 per day, 6½hr., 6750dr).

   From the main square, follow the signs to the offices of Greece's two alpine clubs—the **EOS Greek Mountaineering Club** (tel. (0352) 84 544), which offers a free map and brochure (open June-Aug. Mon.-Fri. 9am-12:30pm and 6:30-8:30pm, Sat.-Sun. 9am-noon), and the **SEO Mountaineering Club.**

   SEO's Main Refuge is the highest in the Balkans and offers a glorious view of the mountain, the valley, and Thessaloniki (2760m; open June-Sept.), but **EOS's Refuge A** (open May-Oct.) is closer to the end of the road and more accessible by car. Both refuges have running water and cost 2500dr per night, less for club members. The refuges fill up Friday and Saturday nights. Try to make reservations 3-4 days in advance through the club offices. EOS also owns three other refuges on Mt. Olympus. Both clubs provide maps and information about the mountain, maintain the trails, and organize emergency rescues.

   The pleasant **Hotel Aphroditi** (tel. (0352) 81 415; fax 22 123) is located on the uphill road from the main square. Many of the comfortable rooms offer stunning views of the mountain, and the friendly management can offer suggestions about other places to stay. They will hold baggage for 500dr (singles 8000dr; doubles 12000dr; triples 16000dr). A lovely *taverna* perches at the top of this road, serving Greek cuisine and views of the gorge. Four **campgrounds** squeeze between the railroad and the beach, 5km out of town across the highway. **Do not free-lance camp** on the north side of the road connecting the town and the highway, as it is a training ground for the Greek army.

THE PEAKS

Mt. Olympus has eight peaks: **Kalogeros** (2701m), **Toumba** (2785m), **Profitis Ilias** (2803m), and **Antonius** (2817m) are dwarfed by the thrones of **Skala** (2866m), **Skolio** (2911m), **Stefani** (also called the Throne of Zeus, 2909m), and **Mytikas** (or the Pantheon, 2917m). There are two approaches to the peaks from Litohoro. To reach the beginning of both trails, take the road that winds upward just before the square in Litohoro. There is no bus service between the trails and the village, so it's best to find a group to share a taxi (6000dr to Prionia). Those who hitch usually start early, since most climbers drive up in the morning; *Let's Go* does not recommend hitching. For the first approach, hiking alongside the Enipeas River from Litohoro to Prionia is an option; the 18km trail is wonderful but difficult. It begins past the town cemetery and Restaurant Mili in the upper part of Litohoro. At the fork in the trail, follow the yellow diamond marker uphill on the left side of the **Mavrolungo Gorge.** This path takes you up and down hills for four hours, but traverses astonishing scenery. You will also pass the charred shell of a monastery that gave refuge to Greek partisans during WWII until the Nazis burned it. If you decide not to hike through the gorge, walk to Prionia along the asphalt road (which eventually becomes an unpaved path).

   At **Diastavrosi,** just 14km from Litohoro, is the second approach to the peaks. This route offers views of the Aegean, the Macedonian plain, and the smog layer over Thessaloniki far below. You can find water in two places along this trail: at the turn-off between Barba and Spilia (1½hr. from the trail head), marked on the trail, and at the spring at Strangos. It's a long haul (5-6hr.) from the start of the trail to the **SEO refuge,** where you can seek shelter (2500dr). Ample blankets are provided and hot meals served throughout the day. At 2760m (only 157m from the summit of Olympus), this shelter is less frequented than its counterpart Refuge A below, and offers a magnificent view of the Stefani peak at sunrise. Just as exhilarating is the lunar landscape overlooking the **Plateau of the Muses,** named after the mythical Muses who inspire creativity. From here, the summit is a painless 90 minutes away.

Mytikas is the highest (2917m) and most climbed peak of Olympus. From Refuge A, take the path uphill and follow the red marks along mountain meadows strewn with indigo wildflowers. The last leg of the ascent to Mytikas is usually made by one of two routes. If you take the fork in the path at Refuge A, you'll see the peak **Skala** (2866m) to your left and the SEO Refuge to your right. From Skala, there is a sinuous descent a bit before the ascent to Mytikas. This trail to Mytikas, prone to rock slides and avalanches, is considered dangerous; it's not a good idea to lug a large pack along the route. Many trails are appropriate only for experienced hikers in excellent physical condition, particularly the rockslide-plagued **Locki.** If you return to Skala, it's a relatively easy walk to **Skolio,** the second highest peak (2911m) and the best point for viewing the sheer western face of Olympus. From Refuge A, you can go directly to Skolio, taking the path left or that to Skala.

HALKIDIKI ΧΑΛΚΙΔΙΚΗ

Three-pronged like Poseidon's trident, the Halkidiki Peninsula advances southward into the Aegean, yielding spectacular scenery and some of the finer sandy beaches in Greece. Tourists with money and tanning lotion swarm to the middle and western prongs, **Sithonia** and **Kassandra.** Although natural beauty tempers tourist gloss, they are devoid of monuments to any period of Greece's past. The eastern prong, **Mt. Athos** (or *Agion Oros*), is inaccessible to tourists and completely off limits to all women—a living link to the traditions of the Byzantine Empire. Visitation to Mt. Athos is strictly regulated, and reservations for serious male pilgrims should be made a month in advance (see p. 132). There are no bureaucratic hoops to jump through to reach Kassandra or Sithonia; just crack the codes of the Halkidiki public transportation system. Frequent **buses** run between the 68 Karakassi St. station in Thessaloniki (tel. (031) 924 444) and the three peninsulas, but bus service does not accommodate travelers wishing to hop from peninsula to peninsula. You may have to return to Thessaloniki in order to catch a bus to another peninsula. Moped rental is a viable and visually rewarding option on Halkidiki's quiet, beautiful roads. Accommodations on Halkidiki are among the most expensive in Greece. In the off season you may be able to find a double for 5000-6000dr, but in July and August expect to dish out no less than 9000dr. Camping at the many coastal campgrounds is the inexpensive option. Meals and lodging in the Mt. Athos monasteries are free.

■ Sithonia ΣΙΘΩΝΙΑ

Although it withstood the barrage longer than its western neighbor, Sithonia has recently been seduced by visitors sporting BMWs and fistfuls of *drachmae*. The area has since plunged into the sordid world of beachside villas and plastic souvenirs. On the more isolated beaches to the south, a measure of tranquility persists. Sithonia is popular as a beach and nature retreat from Thessaloniki and is quieter and generally more relaxed than Kassandra to the west.

NEOS MARMARAS

There are two back road routes through Sithonia—west via **Neos Marmaras** and east via **Vourvourou.** The Neos Marmaras **police** (tel. (0375) 71 111) are on a side street left of the main street, away from the church. The town **post office** (tel. (0375) 71 334; **Postal Code:** 61381) is in the second square, near the **Cafe Metro** (open Mon.-Fri. 7:30am-2pm). To reach the **OTE** from the bus stop, walk to the bottom left corner of the square, then hike up the street 2 minutes (open daily 7:30am-midnight).

The **National Bank** (tel. (0375) 72 793) is on the main street (open Mon.-Thurs. 8am-2pm, Fri. 8am-1:30pm, **currency exchange** only Sat. 9am-1pm).

Before arriving at Neos Marmaras (also called Marmaras), you'll pass the beach at **Agios Ioannis,** where some people stake tents. Numerous signs for official campgrounds line the roads. Neos Marmaras is a small, quiet, upscale vacation spot with jewelry stores and stylish bars. Rooms here are expensive (singles from 6000dr; doubles from 10,000dr). The English-speaking staff at **Doucas Tours** (tel. (0375) 71 959), near the bus stop, recommends rooms, sells **Flying Dolphin** tickets for Volos (1 per day, 2hr., 6200dr) and Skiathos (1 per day, 2½hr., 6300dr), **exchanges currency,** and books excursions (open daily 8am-3pm and 5-10pm). **Bus timetables** are posted outside of Dionysios's next door. They run to Thessaloniki (8 per day, 2hr., 2300dr) and smaller nearby towns. **Albatros Rooms To Let** (tel. (0375) 71 738), on Themistokli St., has spacious, modern, clean rooms with kitchenettes and large balconies. Inquire at Rigalo Jewelers, near the bus stop (doubles with bath and kitchen 6000-8000dr; triples 10,000dr). On the beach, **Camping Marmaras** (tel. (0375) 71 901) is 1km back and clearly marked by road signs (open June to early Oct.; 1400dr per person; 1300dr per tent).

Neos Marmaras enjoys its existence largely due to the **Porto Carras** (tel. (0375) 72 500) hotel complex situated just across the bay. The nearby amusement park contains restaurants, boutiques, beaches, a cinema, and a new casino, **Casino Porto Carras** (tel. (0375) 70 500). Although doubles start at 30,000dr, all rooms are fully booked in summer. Ferries shuttle between the second square and Propondis in Marmaras to Porto Carras (every 30min., 15min., 400dr). The 20-minute walk around the coast is free.

Dionysios Tavern (tel. (0375) 71 201) on the waterfront, serves good seafood (fried mussels 1200dr; open daily 8am-2am). Essentially one long bar divided in three: **Cool Bar, Sugar Bar,** and **Smile Bar** are all on the waterfront (open daily 9pm-2:30am). The **bus** around the peninsula to Sarti (4 per day, 1hr., 580dr) passes by the most deserted, desirable turf on Sithonia. After climbing the road 5km south of Porto Carras, you'll see a beach near **Agia Kiriaki,** with a small reef and an outlying island. It's a long, hard climb down, but well worth the effort.

■ Mount Athos ΑΘΩΣ–ΑΓΙΟΝ ΟΡΟΣ

The monasteries on Mt. Athos have been the standard bearers of asceticism for more than a millennium. Today, the easternmost peninsula of Halkidiki is an autonomous state comprised of 20 Eastern Orthodox monasteries and countless hamlets *(skites)*, with some 1400 monks. The absence of development has helped to preserve the peninsula's luxuriant foliage. Only the jagged marble peak of Mt. Athos itself, soaring 2033m above the encircling waves of the Aegean, is exposed. Against the background of this lush turf, the monks of Mt. Athos isolate themselves from the outside world in an attempt to transcend material pleasures and live a truly spiritual life. The community on Mt. Athos has existed since 883 AD, when Basil I issued an imperial charter to Athos preventing local military officials from interfering with the monks. A 1060 edict of Emperor Constantine, enforced to this day, forbids women and, believe it or not, female animals from setting foot on the peninsula.

Men who wish to see Mt. Athos first-hand should secure a permit (see below). Those without a permit can view the monasteries by boat. A **day cruise** from Thessaloniki costs 10,500dr. From Ouranoupolis, tours (roughly 3½hr.) cost 3000dr. Contact Doucas Travel, 8 Venizelou St., Thessaloniki (tel. (031) 26 99 84), or try Avdimiotis Theophilos in Ouranoupolis (tel. (0377) 51 207, -244).

PERMITS

A special entrance pass, issued **only to adult males,** is required in order to visit Mt. Athos. These passes are issued at **Ouranoupolis,** the main gateway to Athos, upon presentation of a special permit. To get this permit, call at least 15 days (in winter) or

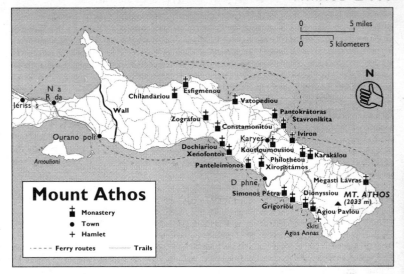

Mount Athos
† Monastery
● Town
+ Hamlet
- - - - Ferry routes   Trails

one month (in summer) in advance to make a reservation with the Ministry of Northern Greece in Thessaloniki (tel. (031) 26 4321). This office will offer you no special
favors and may even discourage you from visiting Mt. Athos. Because only 10 visitors
per day are admitted to Mt. Athos, visits are always booked well in advance. Arrive in
Thessaloniki at least two days before you plan to visit. Bring a letter of recommenda-
tion from your embassy or consulate (tell them you are a student interested in theol-
ogy, history, architecture, or Byzantine art); a letter from your university stating your
academic interest in Mt. Athos could also be helpful. Deliver this letter to the **Ministry
of Northern Greece,** room 222 Pl. Dikitirou, Thessaloniki (open daily 10am-2pm). In
Ouranoupolis, bring your permit and your passport to the **Athos office,** just uphill
from the bus stop by the gas station, by at least 9am of the day your visit begins.
Passes cost 5000dr for foreigners, 3000dr for students with ISIC. You must strictly
observe the **date of arrival** on your permit. If you arrive a day late, you will be turned
away. Without your **passport,** you will not be admitted. The **tourist office** in Thessaloniki has more information.

GETTING THERE

Permit in hand, arrive in Halkidiki the night before your entry date into Athos, or
catch the 6am bus leaving Thessaloniki for Ouranoupolis the day of your visit. **Hotel
Acrogiali** in Ouranoupolis (tel. (0377) 71 201) offers singles (4000dr) and doubles
(6000dr) with bathrooms for the Athos-bound. The standard approach to Athos is via
Ouranoupolis, by boat to Daphni, then by bus to the capital city of Karyes. **Buses** for
Ouranoupolis leave from Thessaloniki's Halkidiki station (tel. 92 44 44), located at 68
Karakassi St. (4 per day, 3hr., 2800dr). A bus for Thessaloniki will be waiting immedi-
ately after your arrival from the mountain.

THRACE ΘΡΑΚΗ

Thrace, separated into the Greek west and Turkish east by the Evros River, remains
the political and cultural frontier of both countries (see p. 406 for Turkish Thrace).
Ruled by the Ottomans until 1913, the region fell under Allied control during WWI. It
joined Greece in 1919. Continued Western influence resulted in the 1923 Laussane
Treaty which divided Thrace and ceded the eastern region to Turkey. The division,
however, left Greek communities in Turkey and Turkish communities in Greece.

GREECE

Most Greek Orthodox communities moved to Greece, but some Muslims have remained in Greek Thrace. The treatment of this minority group in Greece remains a significant question 75 years later. Unfortunately, if your travels include only modern Alexandroupolis, you will miss this tangle of cultures, mirrored in a chaotic landscape of rivers, swamps, and lonely rolling hills. But you will get up close and personal with the region's military forces centered at a base in Alexandroupolis.

■ Alexandroupolis ΑΛΕΞΑΝΔΡΟΥΠΟΛΗ

Traveling through Thrace inevitably means a stop at the modern city of Alexandroupolis, which lies on the main west-to-east highway and rail lines. Just a fisherman's village until the railway arrived in 1871, the city boasts no ancient ruins *(chora)* to explore. Russian occupiers created the gridlike street plan, which greatly simplifies transit, during the 1877 Russo-Turkish War. Today vacationers fill the streets in the summer, and accommodations become scarce and expensive, so to avoid an overnight stay here.

Alexandroupolis is also not the ideal departure point for Turkey, especially in the summer. Trains are hot, slow, and crowded. Most buses originate in Thessaloniki and overflow by the time they reach Alexandroupolis. People who hitch across the border make a trilingual sign asking for a ride, but *Let's Go* does not recommend hitchhiking. It is illegal to cross on foot. Expect at least an hour delay at the border.

ORIENTATION AND PRACTICAL INFORMATION

Walking inland from the **ferry** and **hydrofoil dock,** the active waterfront and Alexandrou Ave. stretch to your left, while the **train station** lies a few meters to your right in front of Eleftherias Square. The two main streets running parallel to Alexandrou lie about three blocks inland: L. Dimokratias Ave. and El. Venizelou. The **bus station** sits at the corner of El Venizelou and 14th Maiou, almost directly inland from the docks.

Tourist Police: 6 Karaiskaki (tel. 37 411), two blocks inland from the waterfront, just before the lighthouse. Provides city maps with transportation, accommodations, and sights marked. They speak some English. Open Mon.-Fri. 7am-2:30pm and 5-11pm, Sat.-Sun. 7am-2:30pm.

Banks: L. Dimokratias is one long string of banks, so if the **National Bank's** 24hr. **ATM** doesn't like your card, just try another. Banking hours are Mon.-Thurs. 8am-2pm and Fri. 8am-1:30pm.

Flights: Olympic Airways, 4 Ellis St. (tel. 26 361), offers flight to Athens (2 per day, 45min., 18,300dr). No buses run to the airport, but taxis only cost about 500dr. Office open Mon.-Fri. 9am-3pm.

Trains: (tel. 27 906) Station open 6:30am-11:30pm. Trains to Thessaloniki (5 per day, 6hr., 4500dr) and Istanbul (1 per day, 10hr., 6000dr).

Buses: (tel. 26 479) 6 buses per day head to Thessaloniki (5hr., 5200dr) via Xanthi (1½hr., 1950dr) and Kavala (2hr., 2700dr). The bus to Istanbul leaves from the train station and tickets can be bought there (1 per day, 7hr., 4000dr).

Ferries: Arsinoi and Saos (tel. 22 215), located at the corner of Kyprou St. and the waterfront, sends ferries to Samothrace (2-3 per day, 2hr., 2200dr) and Limnos (1 per week, 6hr., 3000dr). **Kikon Tours** (tel. 25 455) has one ferry per week to: Limnos (3hr., 3000dr); Lesvos (10hr., 4700dr); Chios (14hr., 6400dr); Samos (17hr., 7800dr); Ikaria (19hr., 7800dr); Kos (26hr., 10,000dr); and Rhodes (30hr., 10,700dr). Offices are open Mon.-Sat. 9am-2pm and 6-9pm, Sun. 9am-2pm. Services may be reduced in winter.

Flying Dolphins: In high season, **Arsinoi and Saos** send 1-3 Dolphins per day to Samothrace (1hr., 4300dr). Tickets may be bought on board.

Taxis: Run 24hr. (tel. 22 000, 27 700).

Hospital: 19 Dimitras St. (tel. 25 772). Open 24hr.

Police: (tel. 37 424) With the **tourist police,** open 24hr.

Post Office: Along the waterfront, past Karaiskaki St. Open Mon.-Fri. 7:30am-2pm. **Postal Code:** 68100.

OTE: Located on I. Kaviri in the block between L. Dimokratias and El. Venizelou. Open Mon.-Sat. 7am-10pm and Sun. 7am-6pm. **Telephone Code:** 0551.

ACCOMMODATIONS

Hotel Majestic (tel. 26 444), in Eleftherias Sq., visible from the train station. Rooms are old but clean. Singles 4500dr; doubles 7500dr.

Hotel Vergina (tel. 23 035), right across the street from the rumbling trains. Clean rooms with private shower and shared toilet. Singles 8000dr; doubles 10,000dr.

Hotel Mitropolis (tel. 26 443, 33 808), on the corner of Emporiou and Athan. From Platia Eleftherias, turn left onto Emporiou and walk down several blocks (to the left facing inland). Rooms are immaculate and include bath, radio, and phone. Singles 8500dr; doubles 12,000dr; triples 14,000dr.

Hotel Erika (tel. 34 115), near the Hotel Majestic on the waterfront. Rooms with TV, fridge, kitchen, and bath. Singles 10,000dr; doubles 12,500dr.

FOOD, SIGHTS, AND ENTERTAINMENT

As you walk left (facing inland) from the docks and train station, you arrive first at a cluster of fish *tavernas*. Slightly farther, at the intersection with Kyprou, the waterfront gives way to a cluster of *ouzeries*. The **Ouzerie Mynos,** opposite the post office on the waterfront, is unmistakable for its Dutch windmill and unforgettable for its sweet, permeating scent of olive oil and freshly baked bread. The rest of the waterfront merges into one endless cafe; only the chairs and music vary. For an inexpensive filling meal, grab a gyros (350dr) on any of the streets around Dimokratias.

Probably Alexandroupolis' most important site, the cathedral of Agios Nikolaos governs the **Ecclesiastic Art Museum.** An 18th-century icon of a limber Christ, their best piece, portrays Jesus with his legs forming a heart. The museum is worth a visit if an English-speaking priest can give you a tour, relating some Thracian history and distinctions between icon styles. The museum is two blocks inland from the National Bank (open Mon.-Sat. 8am-1pm; 200dr donation).

■ Kavala ΚΑΒΑΛΑ

The modern port city of Kavala, a tobacco town and a bastion of communism in the 1930s, reversed both its preferred commodity and political orientation after the end of WWII. Today, having born the brunt of Greco-Ottoman conflict and a Bulgarian occupation, Kavala remains a trading center. A bustling city with tree-lined avenues stretching from the seaside up the slopes of Mt. Simvolo, Kavala is well organized and relatively smog-free. Buried beneath the new city lies the 5000 year-old city of Neapolis, later Christoupolis, where the Apostle Paul once preached. Although modernized, Kavala retains a traditional appeal, as congested avenues give way to fruit vendors and flower markets, particularly around Kavala's old section, the Panagia District (District of the Virgin Mary).

ORIENTATION AND PRACTICAL INFORMATION

The city's main attraction, the **Panagia District,** sits east of the port on its own peninsula, hemmed in by ancient walls and under the shadow of the dominating **Byzantine fortress.** The entrance is near **Doxis Square.** Just outside the walls is **Eleftherias Square,** the main square from which Kavala's two major commercial streets, **Eleftheriou Venizelou** and **Erithrou Stavrou,** extend westward. **Vassileos Pavlou** runs along the waterfront near the Thassos ferry dock. Parallel to it, one block inland, is Erithrou Stavrou, two blocks inland Eleftheriou Venizelou.

Tourist Office: (tel. 22 24 25, 22 87 62 or 23 16 53) On its own little traffic island at the corner of El. Venizelou and Dragoumi, a block inland from the main port. Has city maps and a list of hotels. Open Mon.-Fri. 8am-2pm.

Tourist Police: (tel. 22 29 05) On the ground floor of the police station. Open daily 7:30am-2:30pm.

Bank: The **National Bank** (tel. 22 21 63), on the corner of Onomias and Paulo Mela St., 1 block north of the GNTO. Has a 24hr. **ATM and currency changer.** Open Mon.-Thurs. 8am-2pm, Fri. 8am-1:30pm.

Flights: Olympic Airways (tel. 22 36 22), across from Thassos ferry dock on the corner of Ethnikis Aristasis and Kavalas Hris. Open Mon.-Fri. 8am-2:30pm. Tickets to Athens (2 per day, 1hr., 18,000dr). Public buses to the airport run 2hr. before scheduled airplane departures (30min., 700dr), and from the airport to Kavala center immediately following flight arrivals.

Buses: (tel. 22 35 93) At the corner of Filkis Eterias and K. Mitropolitou St., a block from Vassileos Pavlou St. and the waterfront, around the corner from the OTE. Buses to: Thessaloniki (every hr., 3hr., 2650dr); Drama (every 30min., 1hr., 650dr); beaches to the west (take bus to Iraklitsa, every 20-30min., 20 min., 270dr); and Athens (3 per day, 10hr., 10,350dr). Contact the **KTEL Office** (tel. 22 22 94) near the post office (open daily 6am-8pm). For bus service to Alexandroupolis (6 per day, 3hr., 2600dr), go to the **Dore Cafe,** 35 Erithrou Stavrou St. (tel. 22 76 01), beyond the Oceanis Hotel, which sells tickets, posts departure times, and maintains the bus stop.

Ferries: Nikos Milades (tel. 22 64 17), on the corner of the main port, provides ferry information. Open daily 8:30am-1:30pm and 5:30-8:30pm. Ferries go to: Limnos (4 per week, 4½hr., 3500dr); Lesvos (3 per week, 11½hr., 6000dr); Chios (1 per week; 14hr., 6840dr); and Peiraias. Contact **Arsinoi Travel,** 16 K. Dimitriou (tel. 83 56 71), for info about the ferry to Samothrace (5 per week, 4hr., 2800dr) and Thassos (11 per day, 2hr., 750dr). Open daily 8am-9pm.

Flying Dolphins: Hydrofoils connect Kavala with nearby Thassos and Samothrace. For tickets and schedule information, head for the booths near the hydrofoil dock, opposite the OTE.

International Bookstore: Thodoros Theodoridis, 46 Omonoias, sells English publications. Open Mon. and Wed. 8am-2pm, Tues., Thurs., and Fri. 8am-3pm and 5:30-9:30pm.

Taxis: (tel. 23 20 01) Congregate in 28 Octovriou Sq. Available 24hr.

Hospital: 113 Amerikanikou Erithrou Stavrou (tel. 22 85 17). Open 24hr. Call 166 in case of **emergency.**

Police Station: 119 Omonias St., 4 blocks north of the port. Open 24hr. **Emergency** tel. 100. **Port police** (tel. 22 44 72) are in the OTE building. Open 24hr.

Post Office: Main branch at K. Mitropoliteou St., on the corner of Erithrou Stavrou one block north of the bus station. **Exchanges currency.** Open Mon.-Fri. 7:30am-8pm. **Postal Code:** 65110.

OTE: (tel. 22 26 99) West of the port at the corner of Eth. Andistassis and Averof St. Open in summer 8am-midnight, in winter 8am-10pm. **Telephone Code:** 051.

ACCOMMODATIONS

Many of Kavala's rooms overlook the port, but if you are a light sleeper, remember that the shipping industry does not shut down when you go to bed.

Hotel Akropolis, 29 El. Venizelou St. (tel. 22 35 43). Clean rooms with a view of the bay. The 75-year-old hotel has charm, and you can bargain with the owner for a much better price. Singles 7500dr; doubles 8000-10,000dr, with bath 14,000dr.

Hotel Panorama, 26 El. Venizelou (tel. 22 42 05; fax 22 46 85), entrance across the street from Hotel Akropolis. Adequate rooms. Singles 5000dr; doubles 7500dr, with bath 9000dr.

FOOD

Dining in Kavala may not be like savoring a crepe on the French Riviera (or in Athens for that matter), but it offers quality Greek food at reasonable prices. **Mihalakis,** 1 Kassanarou St., three blocks inland from the post office, sits on a quiet terrace away from waterfront pedestrian traffic (open daily for lunch and dinner). **Panos Zafeira,** 20 Dimitriou St., is situated on the waterfront and serves the perpetually expensive seafood (open daily 9am-midnight). Head up the hill toward the Byzantine castle to find a group of inexpensive fish *tavernas* dotting the cobbled street. Of them, **Antonia** seems to win locals' favor. In summer, **bars** in the center of Kavala empty out at 11pm, when locals head to beachside discos.

SIGHTS

The sprawling 13th-century **Byzantine Castle's** turreted walls dominate the city. Saunter atop them for a great view of the city; the guard often gives tours and would appreciate your tip (open 10am-7pm). A small **amphitheater** occasionally hosts musical and cultural performances here. For scheduled events, ask the guard or the people at the refreshment stand. During the **Eleftheria Festival** in late June, students celebrate Kavala's liberation from the Ottomans by performing dances at the castle. Visitors are welcome.

The 400-year-long Ottoman domination of Northern Greece left its mark on the city. The **Imaret** (Ottoman soup kitchen for the poor), the largest Muslim-built building in western Europe, is now a trendy cafe-bar. On the corner of Pavlidou and Mehmet Ali St. stands the **House of Muhammad Ali.** Born here in 1769, Ali was the self-appointed ruler of Egypt and an important force in Ottoman politics (tip 100dr).

Also be sure to check out the colossal 16th-century **Kamares Aqueduct** at the north edge of the old town near Nikotsara Sq. Süleyman the Magnificent had the graceful, double-tiered structure built to transport water from mountain springs above the city. On the other side of town, overlooking the water, the **archaeological museum** (tel. 22 23 35) on Erithrou Stavrou St. contains such treasures as polychrome busts of goddesses from Amphipolis and a Hellenistic dolphin mosaic from Abdera (open Tues.-Sun. 8:30am-6pm; admission 500dr, students 300dr, EU students free). Kavala has a small **municipal museum** (tel. 22 27 06), with folk art displays and a gallery of work by the famed Thassian artist Vagis (open Sun.-Fri. 8am-2pm and Sat. 9am-1pm; donation requested).

■ Near Kavala

Several sandy **beaches** west of Kavala are accessible by intercity bus. The closest is just outside the city of **Kalamitsa.** There's a **GNTO campground** (tel. 24 30 51) in **Batis,** 3km outside of Kavala, which you might just mistake for a parking lot (1200dr per person; 1500dr per large tent; 900dr per small tent; 750dr per child; 500dr to swim). They've got a supermarket and snack bar. Blue bus #8 treks to Batis from Kavala every 30 minutes.

Philippi, roughly 15km north of Kavala, lies in ruins. Philip of Macedon founded the city to protect Thassian gold miners from Thracian attacks. He modestly named the city after himself. Crucial battles of the Roman civil war dogged the city in 42 BC, when Marc Antony's soldiers defeated the army of Brutus and Cassius here. In 50 AD, missionaries Paul and Silas arrived from Anatolia to preach Christianity, and the first European Christian, **Lydia,** was baptized here. The **Cell of Paul** is the apostle's own budget accommodation. Shut the door and peek at the Roman **latrines;** most of the 42 marble seats are intact, but the lids have all been left up. Call 51 64 70 for more information (site open daily 8am-7pm; admission 800dr).

The entrance on the other side of the highway leads up to the **acropolis.** Classical drama is performed here on summer weekends. Ask at the theater or the Kavala GNTO for details (open daily sunrise-sunset; admission 200dr, students 100dr). There's an **archeological museum** nearby (tel. 51 62 51; open Tues.-Sun. 9am-3pm; admission 800dr, students 400dr). A **bus** to Philippi leaves every 20 minutes. Tell the driver you're going to the archaeological site, not the village. Otherwise, you'll end up in the boonies. The bus back to Kavala stops down the road from the site.

GREECE

Peloponnese
ΠΕΛΟΠΟΝΝΗΣΟΣ

Separated from the rest of the mainland by the Corinth Canal, the Peloponnese is a fertile hand-shaped plain that unites human achievement and natural beauty. The theater at Epidavros, the shell of a medieval city at Mystra, Agamemnon's palace at Mycenae, and Olympia, the site of the first Olympic games, are impressive architectural and artistic masterpieces. Beyond these massive ruins, however, the Peloponnese's rocky mountains hold undeveloped sandy beaches and wondrous mountain villages.

CORINTHIA AND ARGOLIS
ΚΟΡΙΝΘΙΑ ΚΑΙ ΑΡΓΟΛΙΔΑ

Argos, a grotesque beast covered with 100 unblinking eyes, once stalked vast stretches of the north Peloponnese, subduing unruly satyrs and burly bulls. Today's Argolis and Corinthia hold impressive monuments produced during the Peloponnese's 3,500-year history but, alas, no grotesque roving hundred-eyed stalker beasts. In summer, try to visit the sites at Mycenae, Corinth, Tiryns, and Epidavros early in the day, before tour groups arrive and the heat soars. Nauplion is a good base for visiting the nearby ruins.

■ New Corinth ΚΟΡΙΝΘΟΣ

New Corinth sits on the Gulf of Corinth just west of the canal that separates the Peloponnese from the rest of Greece. Like its ancient predecessor (7km southwest of the city), New Corinth has been a victim of several recent earthquakes. As a result, the city issues building permits for only the most shake-proof structures, and now Corinth sits low and secure. Tourists come here to see the surrounding ancient sites, so New Corinth itself caters primarily to its own citizens. Corinth's harbor makes the industrial city beautiful. The waterfront is surrounded by open-air restaurants, where Corinthians of all ages gather in the evenings to stroll and play.

ORIENTATION AND PRACTICAL INFORMATION

The easiest way to navigate New Corinth is to find the harbor, turn your back to the sea, and look inland at the perfect grid that is downtown Corinth. **Ethnikis Antistasis** is the main drag running perpendicular to the waterfront. Both **Ermou** (to the east) and **Kolokotroni** (to the west) are parallel to Ethnikis Antistasis. All three streets intersect **Damaskinou,** the street bordering the harbor. Two blocks inland, between Ethnikis Antistasis and Ermou, is the central park of the city. **Buses** drop off passengers here. The **train station** is a few blocks east of the center of town. To find the waterfront from the station, turn right out of the building onto **Demokratias** and then right again onto Damaskinou. While the city is relatively safe, the tourist police advise women not to walk alone in poorly lit areas after midnight.

> **Banks: Alpha Bank,** 7 Ethnikis Anastisis St. (tel. 24 149), on the first block in from the water. Offers **currency exchange.** Open Mon.-Thurs. 8am-2pm, Fri. 8am-1:30pm. The **ATM** outside offers instructions in English and accepts Visa and AmEx. Several more ATMs (connected to both PLUS and Cirrus networks) are located on the second block of Ethnikis Antistasis St.

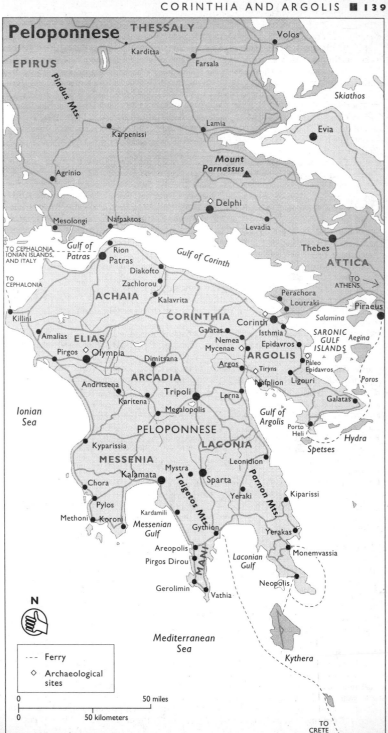

Peloponnese

Trains: Station (tel. 22 523) on Demokratias St. Trains run to Athens (15 per day, 2hr., 800dr) via Isthmia. Two major train lines serve the Peloponnese: one along the northern coast from Corinth to Pirgos and south to Kyparissia; the other south from Corinth to Tripoli and Kalamata. Trains go to Patras (8 per day, 8am-midnight, 2½hr., 1000dr); Pirgos (8 per day, 8am-midnight, 4½hr., 1440dr); Argos (6 per day, midnight-6pm, 1hr., 510dr); Tripoli (4 per day, noon-5pm, 2hr., 900dr); Kalamata (4 per day, 1-5pm, 5hr., 1640dr); Lefktro (1 per day, 6am, 3hr., 1120dr); Kyparissia (5 per day, 8am-midnight, 5hr., 2050dr); Kalavryta (5 per day, 8am-3pm, 1½hr., 1200dr); and Diakofto (13 per day, 8am-midnight, 1 hr., 600dr). Express trains can cost 400-1000dr extra. 25% off for round-trips. **Luggage storage** costs 270dr per piece per day.

Buses: Ermou and Koliatsou Station (tel. 24 481). Buses run until 10:10pm. Station on corner of Ermou and Koliatsou streets. Buses to Athens (32 per day, 5:30am-9:30pm, 1¼hr., 1450dr); Loutraki (every 30min., 6am-10pm, 20min., 260dr); Isthmia (5 per day, 10min., 210dr); and Nemea (7 per day, 1hr., 750dr). **Ethnikis Antistasis and Aratou Station** (tel. 24 403) is located at the corner of Ethnikis Antistasis and Aratou streets inside the cafe Zaxaroplasteio. Buses to Mycenae (40min., 650dr), Argos (1hr., 850dr), and Nauplion (1¼hr., 1050dr) leave at 7am and every hr. 8:30am-9:30pm. Note that the bus to Mycenae drops passengers at Fichtia, a 1½km walk from the site. To catch a bus to Sparta and other southern locations on the Peloponnese, take the Loutraki bus to the Corinth Canal and pick up buses coming from Athens to Sparta, Kalamata, Koroni, and Tripoli.

Taxis: (tel. 22 361 or 24 844), along the park side of Ethnikis Antistasis St.

Car Rental: Gregoris Lagos, 42 Ethnikis Antistasis St. (tel. 22 617). Prices start at 6500dr per day plus 2000dr for insurance and 18% tax. Minimum age 21. Open Mon.-Sat. 8am-1:30pm and 4-9pm.

Moped Rental: Liberopoulos, Ethnikis Antistasis St. (tel. 72 937), across the street from the car rental. Mopeds 5000dr per day. Open daily 8am-1:30pm and 5-8:30pm.

Public Toilets: Across from the park on Ethnikis Antistasis St. Avoid these like the plague. But if you gotta go, you gotta go. They're free and open 24hr.

Pharmacy: 23 Ethnikis Anastasis St. (tel. 22 515). Open Mon.-Fri. 8am-1:30pm. Many others on Koliatsou St.

Hospital: (tel. 25 711), on Athinaion St. Cross the train tracks and turn left. It's quite a walk, so use a cab or call for an ambulance in an emergency. Open 24hr.

Police: 51 Ermou St. (tel. 100), facing the park. Open 24hr., but travelers may be better off dealing with the English-speaking **tourist police** (tel. 23 282), upstairs, who can supply maps and brochures as well as assistance. Open Mon.-Sat. 8am-3pm and 5-8pm.

Post Office: (tel. 22 015), 35 Adimantou St., borders the park on the end farthest from the water. Open Mon.-Fri. 7:30am-2pm. **Postal Code:** 20100.

OTE: 32 Kolokotroni St. (tel. 22 111). Sells phone cards which are also available at kiosks near the harbor. Open daily 7am-10pm, collect calls Mon.-Fri. 7am-10pm.

Telephone Code: 0741.

ACCOMMODATIONS

Corinth's hotels are either on Ethnikis Antistasis St. or along the waterfront on Damaskinou St.

Hotel Acti, 3 Ethnikis Antistasis St. (tel. 23 337), near the waterfront. The best deal in town, this hotel is friendlier than it may seem at first. Rooms are tiny, but virtually spotless. A shared balcony at the end of the hall has a beautiful view of the water. Singles 3000dr.; doubles 6000dr.

Ephira Hotel, 52 Ethnikis Antistasis St. (tel. 24 021), two blocks inland from the park. Spacious rooms, A/C, TVs, private baths, and daily maid service. Singles 7500dr.; doubles 10,000dr.; triples 12,000dr. Continental breakfast 1000dr.

Campsites: Corinth's two beachfront campgrounds are pleasant and inexpensive alternatives to the city's hotels. To get to them, catch a bus (every ½hr., 210dr) on Kollatsou St. near Kolokotroni. Ask to be let out when you see the campground signs. **Camping Korinch Beach** (tel. 27 920; 1000dr per person, 500dr per tent) is just out of town and **Blue Dolphin** is 3km farther (tel. 25 766; campsites on the beach, 1300dr per person, 850dr per small tent, 1000dr per large tent, 700dr per car, electricity 800dr; tents rented for 2000dr). Catching a bus back in to New Corinth is tricky; you may end up walking.

FOOD

Restaurants and cafes dominate downtown Corinth, especially after 9pm. Most either aim for atmosphere or good food; few manage both. Speed also seems to be a culinary virtue in Corinth. Fast food joints abound, and waiters scurry even at the sit-down *tavernas*. **Kanita** (tel. 28 834) is one of the best of the harbor eateries. Its indoor *taverna* on Damaskinou is charming, and across the street is additional outdoor seating under a tent—be sure to sit under the right one, as all the restaurants claim waterfront space and the tables look the same. The tasty *tzatziki* (500dr) and fresh fish (1000dr) are both excellent (open 24hrs). **Neon** (tel. 84 950), also on the waterfront, is a good choice for vegetarians or anyone in a hurry. Fresh fruit and a salad bar (800dr) are a refreshing respite from the more greasy Greek fare. Sandwiches (500dr), hot dishes (1500dr), and delicious pastries (300-500dr) are all served cafeteria-style and displayed smartly in this airy, chrome and marble cafe (open 8am until the wee hours). **Fast Food** (tel. 85 335), on Ethnikis Antistasis St., features fries, gyros (1500dr), *souvlaki* (200dr), and fluorescent lights (open 24hrs).

ENTERTAINMENT AND SIGHTS

During the day Corinth is a serious, bustling town with little to offer the traveler except a bus to its neighboring ruins, but by 10pm Corinth lets down its hair. Motorcycle-mounted teenagers pop up from nowhere and head straight to **Kalami Beach.** West of the city, it can be reached by walking four blocks past the park along Ethnikis Anistasis St. Any right turn will take you there (about ten blocks). Instead of walking the 1.5km alone at night, women may prefer to get a taxi from the park (300dr). Just tell the driver "Thalisa" (the beach). There may not be any taxis waiting to take you back to the center of town, but you can ask any restaurant owner to call you one (about 500dr).

Kalami's strip has something for everyone. Behind the street and looking out at the dark water and sparkling lights of Loutraki are a line of happening cafes and clubs. Each tries to outdo the others with the volume of its bass beat and the span of its palm umbrellas. **La Plaza's** decor is based on green stained wood and **Montezuma's** on totem poles and cave paintings. Both offer beer (700dr), a spot to watch the motorcycles whiz by, and a DJ to mix your favorite 80s hits into techno dance songs.

On the beach side of the main drag humbler cafes like the **Kafeteria** draw family crowds. Children play as adults sip coffee (300dr) and beer (400dr) while they gaze at the ocean. **Pizza Ami** is also out of earshot of the raucous bars; families share pizza while couples share silence, a prelude to a stroll down to the pebbly beach.

If you'd rather stay downtown, an alternative to the beach is car-free Theotke St. Walking away from the harbor on Ethnikis Antistasis, turn right half way down the second block. Past the intersection with Koloktroni, the street becomes filled with outdoor tables from the numerous cafes, pubs, and small restaurants that line this lively block. The trendy **Aenaon Club** (tel. 21 773), where beer costs 700dr and you can sit and talk all night, is typical of these establishments. **Le Creperie** is unique on this street, serving cooked-to-order crepes with your choice of filling (open 9am-early morning; 500dr for chocolate filling, 600dr for meat).

■ Ancient Corinth ΑΡΧΑΙΑ ΚΟΡΙΝΘΟΣ

Strategically based on both the Corinthian and Saronic Gulfs, Corinth was a powerful commercial center and one of the most influential cities in ancient Greece. Corinth reached the apex of its power in the 5th century BC and allied with Sparta, its neighbor to the south, against the naval strength of Athens. This power struggle resulted in the Peloponnesian Wars. Ancient Corinth was greatly weakened in the fighting, but

Sparta became the leading city in Greece. Eventually Corinth was conquered by the Romans, who exterminated the city's population in 146 BC. Corinth remained deserted until Julius Caesar rebuilt it in 44 BC.

ORIENTATION AND PRACTICAL INFORMATION

Enveloping ruins that have seen eons pass, the village of Ancient Corinth offers the peace and serenity that its modern counterpart lacks. To get here from New Corinth, catch a green **bus** on Koliatsou near Kolokotroni. Tickets are sold on the bus, which leaves 10min. after every hour and returns every hour on the half-hour (6am-9pm, 20min., 210dr). The **post office,** along the road to New Corinth, offers **currency exchange** (open 8am-2pm). **Telephone Code:** 0741.

ACCOMMODATIONS AND FOOD

Spending the night in one of Ancient Corinth's pensions puts you in the difficult position of having to choose between two of Greece's most endearing proprietors. When you enter **Rooms Marinos** (tel. 31 209 or 31 180), Mama Elizabeth declares that you are no longer a tourist, but a member of her family. Like any mother, she'll talk your ear off but also treat you to free food and spotless rooms (singles 7500dr; doubles 11,000dr; triples 13,000dr). To get there, walk away from the ruins and turn right onto Sisyphos St. and continue uphill past the church, turning right again when you see the sign for Argos. Your other option is **Taverna Tassos** (tel. 31 225). It is a treat to meet the elderly proprietor, Dafini Tassos. With nods, smiles, and handshakes he will escort you to crisp, white rooms (singles 4000dr; doubles 5000dr) above his restaurant. Balconies provide views of Corinth Bay. To get to Mr. Tassos', walk down the road to Corinth away from the ruins. The *taverna* and pension will be on your left.

There are many touristy *tavernas* around the bus stop, but if you want a sit-down meal the best place is **Taverna Tassos** (tel. 31 225), a little walk down the road to Corinth away from the bus tours. Hot dishes such as *moussaka* and *pastisio* are 1000dr. A less expensive and more romantic alternative to a restaurant meal is a picnic among the ruins. A **bakery** (tel 31 291) at the bus stop sells bread for 100dr per loaf (open daily 8:30am-3pm and 6-10pm), and a small **supermarket** near the entrance to the site has yogurt (250dr), fruit (450dr), and cookies (170dr). If you decide to eat under the open sky, be sure to carry your trash off of the site.

SIGHTS

The remains of the ancient city stand at the base of the **Acrocorinth.** This is where the **Ministry of Culture Archaeological Museum** (tel. 31 207) and **archaeological site** are located (both open daily 8am-7pm; in winter 8am-5pm; admission to both 1200dr, students 600dr, free on Sun.). Columns, metopes, and pediments lie in fascinating chaos in the museum's courtyard. Facing the entrance of the museum, the Corinthian columns on your left are the facade of a Roman shrine. If you want a good guide, pick up Nikos Papahatzis' *Ancient Corinth* at the museum entrance (2200dr). The museum houses a wonderful collection of statues, well-preserved mosaics, tiny clay figurines, and pottery that traces Corinth's history through Greek, Roman, and Byzantine rule. The Roman frescoes and mosaics are from the same period as Pompeii, and the collection of pottery follows the evolution of Greek pottery from neolithic to Byzantine times. The museum's collections of sarcophagi (one with a skeleton under glass) and headless statues in the green, open-air courtyard are impressive and eerie. Especially weird is a collection of votive offerings from the sick to the god of medicine which includes misshapen phalluses, sore ears, and wart-afflicted hands.

As you exit the museum, down the stairs to your left is the archaeological site including the remains of the 6th century BC **Temple of Apollo.** Behind the museum is the **Fountain of Glauke,** named after Jason's second wife who drowned while trying to douse the flames that sprouted from an enchanted shirt given to her by Jason's first wife, Medea. If you stand at the Temple of Apollo and face the mountainous

Acrocorinth, the remains of the forum—the center of city-state life—lie in front of you. Walk down the middle of the row of central shops and you'll see the **Julian Basilica.** To the left a broad stone stairway descends into the **Peirene Fountain.** This is where the ancient Greeks believed winged Pegasus was drinking when he was captured by Bellerophon. Just past the fountain is the **Perivolos of Apollo,** an open-air court surrounded by columns. Near the Perivolos is the **public latrine.**

Getting to the **fortress** at the top of Acrocorinth is a tough 1½-hour walk. Alternatively, you can call a taxi (tel. 31 464) which will drive you to the site and wait for an hour (2500dr). The summit originally held a **Temple to Aphrodite,** which was served by "sacred courtesans" who initiated free-wheeling disciples into the "mysteries of love." The surprisingly intact remains are a medievalist's fantasy. Relatively empty, the fortress contains acres of towers, mosques, gates, and walls.

■ Near Corinth: Loutraki ΛΟΥΡΤΑΚΙ

The name may seem familiar. Much of the bottled water (½L, 80dr) you will be clutching during your travels gushes from Loutraki's sweet wells, but Loutraki hardly springs to mind as an ideal Mediterranean vacation spot. A clean little city, Loutraki rests across the crescent-shaped bay from Corinth (20min. bus ride, 240dr). If you're visiting Corinth, you might want to stop and tap the source of the town's allure. Stroll along the stone boardwalk that flanks the body-blanketed beach, shadowed by the **Yerania Mountains.** The main street is El. Venizelou, which runs parallel to the water, curves at the port, and becomes Georgiou Lekka St.

ORIENTATION AND PRACTICAL INFORMATION

To get to Loutraki from Isthmia, cross the canal bridge; the bus stop is next to a railroad station sign. Stay on the bus until the last stop, a triangular road island where **El. Venizelou Street** meets Periandou and Eth. Antistasis. English-speaking **tourist police** (tel. 65 678) respond to the needs of travelers (open daily 9am-9pm). Day boat excursions are available at the dock past the park. **Albona Cruises** goes to Lake Vouliagmeni, the "Blue Lake" (Tues.-Thurs., 2500dr). Cruises down the Corinth Canal leave Sundays at 10am and Thursdays at 5pm (3950dr). To get to the **National Bank,** 25 Martiou Square, bear left where the road forks (open Mon.-Thurs. 8:30am-2pm, Fri. 8:30am-1:30pm). At 10 El. Venizelou, you'll find the **OTE** (open Mon.-Fri. 7:30am-3:10pm). **Buses** (tel. 22 262) from Loutraki go to: Athens (8 per day, 6am-7:30pm, 1300dr, round-trip 2000dr); Corinth (every 30min. 5:30am-10:30pm, 20min., 240dr); Perachora (9 per day 6am-8pm, 20min., 190dr); and Vouliagmeni (July-Aug. only, departs 10am, returns 1pm, 45min., 700dr).

For **moped rentals,** make a right at the post office and turn at the second corner on the left to reach **Andreas** (tel. 23 812; Vespas 4000-5200dr, bikes 1000dr). Follow E. Venizelou St. (which changes to G. Lekka St.) toward the mountains. Periandrou St., the first side street on the right across from the bus station's road island, is home to **Laundry Self-Service** (tel. 63 854) which provides wash (1200dr), wash and dry (1600dr), and ironing (open Mon.-Tues. 8:30am-1:30pm, Wed.-Sat. 8:30am-1pm and 6-9pm). On the left, the densely congregated trees guard a **public fountain** that spouts Loutraki water; fill your bottle. For the **health center,** dial 63 444. The center itself is roughly 5km from the center of town. To reach it, walk 5 blocks up from El. Venizelou St., turn right, and continue along that road. There is a **pharmacy** at 21 El. Venizelou St. (tel. 21 787), and an outdoor movie theater opposite the tennis courts (summer only). From the bus station, walk down El. Venizelou Street with the water to your left, and you'll reach the **post office** at 28th Octovriou St. #4, one block down to the right (open Mon.-Fri. 7:30am-2pm). **Police** (tel. 63 000, 22 258) keep the peace across the street from the OTE. The **postal code** is 20300; **telephone code,** 0744.

ACCOMMODATIONS

There are only a few budget hotels in Loutraki. **Hotel Brettagne**, 28 G. Lekka St. (tel. 22 349), has a kindly, semi-English-speaking manager. Rooms and baths sparkle, and every floor has a refrigerator (singles 4300dr; doubles 6600dr; triples 8000dr). To find **Pension Marko** (tel. 63 542), go left from the bus station (facing the water) and take your second right onto L. Kalsoni St. Marko. All rooms have balcony and bath/shower (singles 6000dr; doubles 8000dr). **Camping** is at Lake Vouliagmeni, accessible by bus.

FOOD AND ENTERTAINMENT

The formula for the best food may simply be what is closest at hand. If applied to Loutraki, such culinary logic says fish. And that is what you will find strung along the 2km of white-tiled waterfront walkway. Vegetarians may have to work a little harder in the back streets and markets of Loutraki. **Horiatiki Taverna,** 70 El. Venizelos (tel. 22 228), has been serving fruits and stellar fish dishes for over 30 years. This *taverna's* staff (as its card suggests) are "specialists in fish." An elegant garden seating area and the freshest seafood draw large French and German crowds. **Kazino's** (tel. 22 332), on the waterfront, has an English menu and inexpensive fare including Greek salads (700dr) and stuffed tomatoes (1000dr; open 7am-2am). **Canadian Steak House** (tel. 23 993) is on the waterfront next to Kazino's—cute place, inaccurate name. From schnitzel (2000dr) to *souvlaki* (1900dr), carnivores of all stripes make the trek to the Steak House for atmosphere and copious protein (open 10am-4pm and 6pm-2 or 3am). For a little class you may want to swing over to the **Hotel Agelidis Palace,** 19 G. Lekka St. (tel. 28231). Though you may not want to sleep here (prices begin at 30,000dr), you may want to eat here.

Nightlife consists of a ritual alternation between eating and dancing. Waterfront restaurants swell in summer until midnight and beyond. Taxis lorry anxious feet to the discos on the fringe of the city. The flagship disco in Loutraki is undoubtedly **Baby-O.** Precariously placed between a vast and lonely looking bottling company and a shrub-covered wasteland, Baby-O caters to a weekend crowd of 1000 to 1500 people. Baby-O is the only disco open year-round in the Corinth-Loutraki area. Other discos include **Biblos** and **Club Bazaar,** both in town and near the waterfront (open in summer).

SIGHTS

The majority of Greek tourists go to Loutraki for the healing waters. Whirlpool baths and hydromassage are offered at the **Hydrotherapy Thermal Spa,** 26 G. Lekka St. (tel. 22 215). These will cure "rheumoatoarthritic, spondycarthritic" and "chronic gynecological diseases," or so the bilingual sign printed on the door promises (open Mon.-Sat. 8am-1pm). The waterfalls, on the edge of town away from Corinth, merit a visit. They are theme-park-like in construction but less impressive, although as pleasant to listen to as their cousins in nature. The water funnels to the top from a series of fountains at the base of the cliff. Hike around the waterfalls. You will see rows of tables along the side of the falls, as though the hill were terrace-farmed by the **cafe** that sits below (open daily 10am-3am).

■ Near Corinth: Isthmia

Ancient Greek jocks used to gather in Isthmia and Nemea to compete in the Pan-Hellenic Games, drink beer, and slap each other's backsides. Take the bus from Corinth heading toward Isthmia, and ask to be let out at the **museum,** a green building up and on the right of the road from the bus stop. The carefully diagrammed exhibits display finds from the Temple of Poseidon and the sites of the Isthmian games. Of particular interest are the glass *opus sectile* (mosaic panels), discovered at nearby Kenchreai, that managed to survive the earthquake of 375 AD. The entrance to the ruins lies to the right of the museum. All that remains of the **Temple of Poseidon** is its despoiled foundation. The **theater** is below and farther to the right of the temple. **Cult caves,** where many people enjoyed dinner and entertainment during the Archaic Period, lie above the theater. (Open Tues.-Sat. 8:45am-7pm; off season 8:45am-3pm, Sun. 9:30am-2:30pm; closed holidays.)

■ Near Corinth: Nemea

Pausanias wrote in the 2nd-century AD edition of *Let's Go: Nemea*, "Here is a temple of Nemean Zeus worth seeing although the roof has fallen in and the cult statue is missing." Were he to visit it today, he might be peeved that the temple has dwindled to three columns. The walkway takes you past a wall built around a glass-encased grave, complete with skeleton. Try not to miss the well-preserved **baths**. The **stadium** is 500m down the road to Corinth. The **museum** on the site (tel. (0746) 22 739) has excellent explanatory notes in English, some artifacts, and several reconstructions of the site (open Tues.-Sun. 8:30am-7pm; off season Tues.-Sat. 8:30am-3pm; admission 500dr, students 300dr). The ruins of Ancient Nemea are 4km from Modern Nemea, so if you are coming by bus from Corinth, ask to be let off at the ancient site (1hr., 700dr).

■ Mycenae MYKHNAI

Mycenae's hazy origins, its interactions with other Near Eastern civilizations, and its subsequent decline have long puzzled historians. The site was settled as early as 2700 BC by tribes from the Cyclades who were colonizing the mainland. Clay tablets written in Linear B, an early form of Greek, were found at Pylos and Knossos and serve as a record of the Mycenaeans' developed bureaucratic system of account-keeping. Mycenae flourished after the fall of Knossos around 1400 BC and Mycenaean culture spread as far as Cyprus, Syria, and Sicily. Mycenae was probably destroyed by Dorian tribes from the north led by disgruntled rivals of the House of Atreus.

The remarkable artifacts from the well preserved ruins of ancient Mycenae, which include an extensive fortress, Grave Circles A and B, and *tholos* (beehive) tombs, are now on display in the National Museum in Athens and are among the most celebrated archaeological discoveries in modern history. In summer, mobs stampede the famed Lion's Gate and Tomb of Agamemnon. Visit early in the morning or late in the afternoon to avoid the rush. Although most travelers make Mycenae a daytrip from Athens, Argos, or Nauplion, you can spend the night in the charming modern village, which is surprisingly peaceful since most bus tours drive straight through it.

The Curse of Atreus

Anyone who thinks that his or hers is a dysfunctional family should thank the gods that their problems are not of the epic proportions that bloodied the mythology of Mycenae. Atreus, Mycenae's first chosen ruler, brought the fabled curse upon himself and his progeny when he cooked his nieces and nephews for dinner and served them to his hated brother, Theytes. This culinary atrocity provoked the wrath of the gods, and out of sympathy for Theytes, who had just digested his own children, the Olympians put a curse on the House of Atreus. A leader of the Greek army in the Trojan War, Agamemnon decided to sacrifice his daughter Iphagenia to speed their journey across the Aegean. Years later when he returned to Mycenae a war hero, his wife Clytemnestra had not forgiven his murdering their daughter and killed him in his bath. Agamemnon's son Orestes later avenged the murder of his father by slaying his mother, and was haunted by the Furies, who torment those who kill their own family. Athena finally pardoned Orestes and lifted the curse from the House of Atreus.

ORIENTATION AND PRACTICAL INFORMATION

The only direct **buses** to Mycenae are from Nauplion (4 per day, 40min., 550dr) and Argos (4 per day, 30min., 260dr). A bus from Athens (15 per day, 2½hr., 1750dr) stops at Fihtia, 1.5km away. From Fihtia, the site is located on the Corinth-Argos road; simply follow the sign to Mycenae. Four buses make the return trip to Nauplion. They stop in the town of Mycenae (in front of the Hotel Belle Hellene) and at the site (a 20-minute walk from the town). **Trains** (5 per day) run from Athens via Corinth to Fihtia. Although the town has no banks, the **post office** has **currency exchange** (open April-Oct. Mon.-Fri. 9am-3:15pm). **Postal Code:** 21200. **Telephone Code:** 0751.

ACCOMMODATIONS

Mycenae has few cheap accommodations. If campgrounds aren't your thing, seek out private rooms. Look for the signs off the main road. You may want to browse, because prices vary considerably.

Belle Helene Hotel (tel. 76 225) serves as a bus stop on the main road. This quiet hotel opened its doors in 1862, and hosted Heinrich Schliemann and his excavating team for two years in the 1870s. If it is available ask for room #3, Schliemann's room with an iron bed and period furniture. Other rooms are modern, clean, and carpeted. In the lobby you can read framed photocopies of the Belle Helene's guest book which feature the signatures of Virginia Woolf, Claude Debussy, and Alan Ginsberg. Singles 5000dr; doubles 6000dr; triples 9000dr.

Hotel Klitemnistra (tel. 76 451), also on the main road, is closer to the ruins. It features enormous rooms, 24hr. hot water, and a restaurant. Breakfast included. Singles 4000dr; doubles 7000dr; triples 8500dr.

Camping Mykines (tel. 76 121; fax 76 247), in the middle of town. Popular because of the owner's reputation for hospitality, it is an ideal camping spot. Shaded by pine trees, the sights are close to an inexpensive outdoor restaurant where the owners prepare homemade food for campers (Greek salad 800dr). Washing machine available. Hot showers included. 1100dr per person; 800dr per tent.

FOOD

A few fun restaurants exist among the multitude built solely to feed the bus-borne masses. **Aristidis O Dikeos** (tel. 76 258), on the main street, is distinguishable by its flower-filled porch. Every once in a while, the friendly proprietor cranks up the music and leads guests in an enthusiastic folk dance (Greek salads 1000dr, *dolmadakia* 1200dr). **Restaurant/Taverna Micinaiko** (tel. 76 245), further down the hill, has nice folks and tasty food. Prices are marked in high season; otherwise, ask (Greek salad 800dr, chicken 1200dr, squid 1300dr).

SIGHTS

The excavated site of ancient Mycenae extends over a large tract of rough terrain tucked between Mt. Agios Elias to the north and Mt. Zara to the south. The site is enclosed by 13m-high, 10m-thick monstrous walls called "Cyclopean" by ancient Greeks. The ancients believed that Perseus and his descendant who founded the city could only have lifted the stones with the help of the Cyclops, one-eyed giants with superhuman strength. Modern historians have scarcely better explanations of how the stones were moved. The bulk of the ruins standing today date from 1280 BC, when the city was the center of the far-flung Mycenaean civilization.

German businessman, classics scholar, and amateur archaeologist **Heinrich Schliemann** uncovered Mycenae in 1874, having located the site by following clues in the writings of Homer and later Greek dramatists. Schliemann began digging just inside the citadel walls at the spot where several ancient authors indicated the royal graves should be located. Discovering 15 skeletons "literally covered with gold and jewels," Schliemann bedecked his new 16 year-old Greek wife with the baubles and had her pose for photographs. Schliemann believed he had unearthed the skeletons of Agamemnon and his followers. He sent a telegram to the Greek king that read: "Have gazed on face of Agamemnon." Moments after he removed its mask, the "face" underneath disintegrated. Modern archaeologists shudder at the thought of such high-spirited, incautious excavations, and with modern precision have dated the tombs to four centuries before the Trojan War.

Bring a flashlight when you visit the site, and a guidebook might prove useful. The book by S. E. Iakovidis, covering both Mycenae and Epidavros, includes a map and is well worth the 2500dr. For a more scholarly approach, try the book by George E. Mylonas, director of the excavation (1700dr). If you want information on other ruins, buy the larger guide, *The Peloponnese,* by E. Karpodini-Dimitriadi (3000dr). All are available at the entrance to the site in Greek, English, German, and French.

The bus will take you to the end of the asphalt road; the ruins are on your right. The gate and the **Cyclopean Walls** of the upper citadel date from the 13th century BC. The imposing **Lion's Gate,** with two lionesses carved in relief above the lintel, is the portal into ancient Mycenae. These lionesses were symbols of the house of Atreus and their heads (now missing) had eyes of precious gems. Schliemann found most of his artifacts (now on display in Athens) in **Grave Circle A.** These 16th-century BC shaft graves were originally located outside the city walls, but the city grew and now they rest to the right of the entrance. The **barracks** are up the stairs to your left immediately after the gate.

The ruins on the hillside are the remnants of various homes, businesses, and shrines. The **palace** and the **royal apartments** are at the highest part of the citadel on the right. The open spaces here include guard rooms, private areas, and more extensive public rooms. Look for the **megaron,** or royal chamber; it has a round hearth surrounded by the bases of four pillars. To the left of the citadel sit the remaining stones of a Hellenistic **Temple of Athena.** At the far end of the city, between the palace and the **postern gate,** is the underground cistern used as refuge in times of siege. Be careful as the steps are worn and slippery.

Follow the asphalt road 150m back toward the town of Mycenae to the **Treasury of Atreus** (tel. 76 585), the largest and most impressive *tholos* (beehive tomb). The tomb of Agamemnon can be reached through a 40m passage cut into the hillside. As you walk into the *tholos,* look up at the 120-ton lintel stones above you. The famous tomb was found empty, but is believed to have held valuables that were spirited away by thieves. To the right on the walk up to the main site are pathways to two often overlooked *tholoi,* the **tomb of Aegistheus** and the more interesting **tomb of Clytemnestra.** Bring a flashlight; the *tholoi* are dark inside. (Open April-Sept. 8am-7pm, Oct.-March 8am-5pm. Admission 1500dr, students 800dr, EU students free. Keep your ticket or you will pay twice.)

■ Argos ΑΡΓΟΣ

The inconvenience of having ancient ruins beneath your city doesn't seem to have discouraged construction in Argos. Archaeologists need to inspect each building site before a permit is issued, but the city has grown rapidly despite the red tape. Urban and dusty, Argos is too far from the shore to catch any sea breezes, but it is worth the trip just to see ancient ruins pop up in midst of a blandly modern city. Every Wednesday and Saturday the city hosts the largest **open-air market** in the Peloponnese in an empty square across from the museum. Evening festivals punctuate the summer months in the city's **theater,** drawing crowds from Athens and beyond (call 62 143 for program details).

ORIENTATION AND PRACTICAL INFORMATION

Most amenities, hotels, and restaurants can be found in or around Argos's main square. The large church of St. Peter marks the square, and behind the church, a small shady park extends towards the train station. Downtown Argos has few landmarks and navigation can be difficult beyond the square. Your best bet is to pick up one of the excellent laminated maps that the archaeological museum provides free.

Bank: National Bank (tel. 29 911), on a side street off the square behind the church. **Currency exchange, ATM.** Open Mon.-Thurs. 8am-2pm and Fri. 8am-1:30pm.

Trains: The **station** (tel. 67 212) is 1km from the main square. To get there from the main square, go to the OTE and follow the signs to Nauplion from the five-point intersection. At the next big intersection follow the sign to Athens and you'll see it at the end of the street. Five trains per day go to: Athens (3hr., 1040dr) and Corinth (1hr., 510dr). Trains also to: Tripoli (1hr., 590dr); Kalamata (4 per day, 4hr., 1280dr); Mycenae (10min., 105dr); and Nemea (20min., 210dr).

Buses: There are two stations. The **Argolida** station (tel. 66 300) is on Kapodistriou St. very near the square. From here buses go to: Athens (every hr., 2½hr., 2150dr); Nauplion (every 30min., 20min., 240dr); Nemea (2 per day, 1hr., 550dr); Mycenae (4 per day, 30min., 260dr); and Prosimni (2 per day, 30min., 280dr). There is also the **Arcadia-Laconia Station,** 24 Feidonos St. (tel. 67 157). Follow Vas. Olgas St. 2 streets past the museum, turn left, and walk past the Agricultural Bank. Buses leave from here for Tripoli (5 per day, 1hr., 1000dr). From Tripoli you can make connections to Sparta, Olympia, Andritsena, Gythion, and Monemvassia.

Hospital: (tel. 24 455) North of town on Corinth St., opposite St. Nicholas Church. Open 24hr.

Police: (tel. 67 222) On the corner of Inaxou and Papaoikonomou. Head out from Vas. Sofias. English spoken. Open 24hr.

Post Office: (tel. 68 066) Follow the signs from Hotel Telesilla. Open Mon.-Fri. 7:30am-2pm. **Postal Code:** 21200.

OTE: 8 Nikitara St. (tel. 67 599). Facing the park from the main square, take the street running on park's left side and look to your right. Open daily 7am-9pm.

Telephone Code: 0751.

ACCOMMODATIONS

Argos has few accommodations. Since the sights can be seen in half a day, it's possible to make Argos a daytrip from Nauplion or, if you want to camp, from Mycenae.

Hotel Apollon, 13 Papaflessa St. (tel. 68 065). Take Nikitara off the square, turn left at the red and yellow cafe, then turn right into the nearby alley. It's on the left; follow the signs. Sweet yellow and white rooms with TV, balcony, and tiny bath. Singles 4700dr; doubles 6800dr; triples 8500dr.

Hotel Telesilla, 2 Danan St. (tel. 68 317), just off Saint Peter's Sq. near the entrance to the park. A more luxurious hotel with air-conditioning, TVs, and private baths. Singles 8000dr; doubles 12,000dr.

Hotel Mycenae (tel. 68 754), in the main square across from the church. All rooms have a fan and private bath. Singles 6000dr; doubles 8000dr; triples 12,000dr.

FOOD AND ENTERTAINMENT

The food is discouragingly bad in Argos, so you might want to eat something quickly and get it over with. If, however, you're willing to shell out for overpriced cafe fare, you can sit in the air-conditioning indefinitely. Tough call. **Restaurant Egli** (tel. 67 266), in the corner of the square facing the church, has the most *taverna*-like menu of any establishment in the area (pizza 1500dr, spaghetti 1000dr, calamari 1000dr). **Retro Pub and Restaurant,** next to the Hotel Mycenae, is a sparkling chrome and plastic cafe. They serve spaghetti (1300dr), Greek salads (1000dr), and pizzas (1600dr). **Cafe Croissant** (tel. 63 013), past the archaeological museum, is the place to go for desert or an afternoon snack (ice cream 180dr, pastries 250dr). **Cafe Podon** sits in the square to the left of the church. Frequented by a young crowd, Polon has its own DJ at night and has lots of backgammon players (open until 2am).

SIGHTS

According to Homer, Argos was the kingdom of the hero Diomedes and claimed the allegiance of Mycenae's powerful king Agamemnon. Invading Dorians captured Argos in the 12th century BC, around the same time as the fall of Mycenae, and then used it as their base for controlling the Argolid Peninsula. Through the 7th century BC, Argos remained the most powerful state in the Peloponnese and even defeated its rival Sparta. In the famous 494 BC battle, Kleomenes and the Spartans nearly defeated Argos but failed to penetrate the city walls.

Argos' small but superb **archaeological museum** (tel. 68 819), west off the main square on Vas. Olgas St., has a collection of Mycenaean and pre-Mycenaean pottery and mosaics (open Tues.-Sun. 8:30am-7pm, 8:30am-3pm in off season; admission 500dr, students 300dr, EU students free).

Archaeologists hoped to uncover a large part of the ancient city of Argos, but most of it lies under the modern town. The principal **excavations** have occurred on the city's western fringe; digs are currently going on there and in different areas throughout the town. To get to the entrance to the site, walk past the post office, turn right, and walk to the end of Theatron St.

With a seating capacity of 20,000, the ancient **theater** was the largest in the Greek world when it was built in the 4th century BC. Though not as well-preserved as its famous counterpart in Epidavros, it is nonetheless striking. Next to the theater are the **Roman baths.** Segments of wall give a good impression of the original magnitude of these ancient social centers. The **Roman Odeon** is also here, as is the **agora,** with blue-and-white mosaics still in place. Past the Odeon are the remains of a smaller theater (all sites open Tues.-Sun. 8:30am-3pm; free).

In medieval times, Franks, Venetians, and Ottomans in turn captured and ruled Argos. They each had a hand in creating the **Fortress of Larissa,** a splendid architectural hodgepodge which includes classical and Byzantine elements. Getting to the fortress is a hike. You can walk along Vas. Konstantinou St. for roughly an hour, or climb the foot path from the ruins of the ancient theater. The ruins, which lie among overgrown weeds, are mainly of interest to scholars.

Hera was the patron deity of the Argives, and the temple of her cult, the **Argive Heraion,** is a short bus ride north of Argos (take the Prosimni bus, 220dr). The complex contains, among other things, a pair of temples, a *stoa,* and baths. At **Prosimni,** several kilometers northeast of Argos and past the Heraion, archaeology aficionados will delight in a series of prehistoric graves. A few kilometers east of Agias Trias lie the remains of the city of **Dendra,** where tombs yielded the completely preserved suit of bronze armor now on exhibit in the Nauplion museum.

■ **Nauplion** ΝΑΥΠΛΙΟ

The city of Old Nauplion is a soothing antidote to the hustle of Corinth and the crowds of sun-worshippers on the islands. Venetian architecture, shady squares, and hillside stairways that foil noisy mopeds make Old Nauplion a perfect base for daytrips into the Peloponnese and nearby ruins. In contrast, New Nauplion is unattractive and its design kindles thoughts of an ongoing construction site. Remnants of Nauplion's illustrious past include Palamidi, a Venetian fortress in which Ottomans imprisoned the Greek nationalist Kolokotronis before the Revolutionary War of 1821, and the Bourtzi, a Venetian stronghold that once housed retired executioners.

Nauplion's history has been both dramatic and unstable. Before the Venetians built it on swamp land in the 15th century, the city (named for Poseidon's son Nauplius) consisted entirely of the hilltop fortresses. It passed from the Venetians to the Ottomans and back again. In 1821, it served as headquarters for the Greek revolutionary government, and as the first capital of Greece (1829-1834). John Kapodistrias, the former president of Greece, was assassinated here in St. Spyridon Church. The bullet hole is still visible in the church walls; the assassins hid behind the fountain across the street. Recent years have brought fewer calamities to the city, and under the watchful eyes of its surrounding fortresses, Nauplion seems content to exist peacefully.

ORIENTATION AND PRACTICAL INFORMATION

The bus terminal, on **Singrou Street,** sits near the base of the Palamidi fortress. To reach **Bouboulinas Street,** the waterfront promenade, just walk right (facing the bus station) down Singrou to the harbor. The area behind Bouboulinas and Singrou is the old part of town, with many shops and *tavernas*. If you arrive by water, Bouboulinas St. will be directly in front of you, across the parking lot and parallel to the dock.

There are three other principal streets in the old town, all of which run off Singrou Street parallel to Bouboulinas. Moving inland, the first is **Amalias,** a shopping street. The second, **Vasileos Konstandinou,** ends in **Syntagma Square,** which has *tavernas,* a bookstore, bank, museum, and at night, scores of aspiring soccer stars. The third street is **Plapouta,** which becomes **Staikopoulou** in the vicinity of Syntagma Square. Here you will find good restaurants.

Across Singrou Street, Plapouta becomes **25th Martiou,** the largest avenue in town. This side of Singrou Street—everything behind the statue of Kapodistrias—is the new part of town. It radiates outward from the 5-way intersection split by the road to Argos and the road to Tolo. While ugly, the new town is where you'll find many of the city's inexpensive hotels.

Tourist Office: (tel. 24 444) On 25th Martiou, across the street from the OTE. English-speaking staff provides free pamphlets, maps, and changes money. Open 9am-1pm and 4:30pm-8:30pm.

Tourist Police: (tel. 28 131) With your back to the old town, walk along 25 Martiou, continuing 6 blocks past the turn-off for the road to Tolo. English-speaking police are helpful and cheerfully provide pamphlets and information. Open 7am-10pm.

Banks: National Bank (tel. 23 497), Syntagma Sq. Open Mon.-Thurs. 8am-2pm and Fri. 8am-1:30pm. Other banks in Syntagma Sq. and on Amalias St. charge 500-700dr commission for **currency exchange.**

Buses: Station on Singrou St. (tel. 28 555), off Kapodistrias Sq. Daily buses go to: Athens (15 per day, 3hr., 2350dr); Argos (every 30min., 30min., 240dr); Corinth (2hr. 1050dr); Mycenae (4 per day, 45min., 550dr); Epidavros (5 per day, 1hr., 550dr); Tolo (every hr., 20min., 240dr); Kranidi (3 per day, 2hr., 1400dr); Galatas (2 per day, 2hr., 1400dr); and Ligouri (7 per day, 30min., 500dr).

Flying Dolphins: Staikos Travel, 50 Bouboulinas St. (tel. 27 950) Open 9am-10:30pm. Purchase tickets 2 days before departure date. A Dolphin leaves Tues.-Sun. for Peiraias (4hr., 7615dr), stopping at: Spetses (1hr., 2840dr); Hydra (2hr., 3625dr); Poros (3hr., 5125dr); and Aegina (3hr., 6595dr).

Taxis: (tel. 27 393, 23 600) Congregate on Singrou St. across from the bus station. The trick is to get drivers who operate out of the destination you desire; they charge less if they're returning. Taxi to the top of the Palamidi fortress 700dr.

Bike/Moped Rental: Rent-A-Moto Europe (tel. 29 290). Walk past the post office toward the new town and turn left. Mopeds 3000dr per day. Open 9am-1pm and 5-8pm.

English Bookstore: Odyssey (tel. 23 430), Syntagma Sq. Books and magazines as well as translations of Classical Greek plays. Open daily 8am-11pm.

Hospital: Call the tourist police or visit **Nauplion Hospital** (tel. 27 309). Walk down 25th Martiou St. and turn left onto Kolokotroni St., which eventually becomes Asklipiou St. (a 15min. walk).

Police: (tel. 27 776) Praitelous St., a 15min. hike along 25th Martiou St. from the bus station. Follow the signs. Open 24hr.

Post Office: (tel. 24 230) The large yellow building on the corner of Sidiras Merarchias and Singrou St., one block from the bus station toward the harbor. Open Mon.-Fri. 7:30am-2pm. **Postal Code:** 21100.

OTE: 25th Martiou St. (tel. 22 139), on the left as you walk toward the new town. Open daily 7am-10pm. **Telephone Code:** 0752.

ACCOMMODATIONS

Prices have risen in the old part of town, but it's still the most pleasant district. Check the streets at the east end, below Dioscuri Hotel, for rooms.

Hotel Economou (tel. 23 955), on Argonafton off the road to Argos. A 15min. walk from the bus station, Hotel Economou offers swept rooms, pressed sheets, balconies, and pleasant company. 2000dr per person for dorm rooms.

Dimitris Bekas' Domatia (tel 24 594). Turn up the stairs onto Kokinou, following the sign for rooms off of Staikopoulou. Climb to the top, turn left and then climb another 50 steps. This place is worth the climb; it has a wonderful view of the city's rooftops, the sea, and the Palamidi. Sit on the rooftop terrace while enjoying the sunset. Doubles 4500dr.

Hotel Artemis (tel. 27 862), on the Argos road 1500m from the bus station. Located in the noisy new town, but it does have large clean rooms with balconies and private bath. Singles 6650dr; doubles 8000dr; triples 9000dr.

Hotel IRA, 9 Vas. Georgiou B St. (tel. 28 184), off Bouboulinas St. in the new part of town. Clean, airy rooms. Singles 4000dr; doubles 6000dr; triples 8000dr.

FOOD AND ENTERTAINMENT

The food in Nauplion is excellent, though not often cheap. At times the city may seem one *taverna*-packed back alley after another, lit by soft flood lights and strewn with plants, balconies, and people. The waterfront is lined with fish restaurants, which charge as much as 7000dr per entree. Better dining options occupy the street above Syntagma Sq., behind the National Bank, where proprietors will lure you with calls of "Good food, good food here."

Taverna O Vasiles (tel. 25 334), on Staikopoulou one street above the square, serves wonderful fresh fish, and a rabbit in onions (1400dr) that will delight even the most avid Beatrix Potter fan.

Zorba's Tavern (tel. 25 319), to the left of Basiles, caters to local tastes (*moussaka*, 1000dr) and offers some cheap starters (stuffed tomatoes, 900dr).

Ellas (tel. 27 278), in Syntagma Sq., is the cheapest restaurant around (chicken and fish entrees 950-1250dr), and boasts an international clientele including Marcello Mastroianni. It closes early though, and you may be asked to leave by 11pm.

The Old Mansion (tel. 22 449), between Syntagma Sq. and Ipsalidou St., is one of the treasures of Nauplion's back streets. Its specialty is veal in cream sauce (1800dr), and has an original menu featuring rooster with white wine sauce (1500dr).

Taverna Kauarapauns (pronounced Kakanapakis; tel. 25 371), on Vas. Olga St. one street closer to the water than the Old Mansion, serves only dinner. With greek salad (900dr) and stuffed vine leaves (1400dr), this *taverna* is a secluded relief from the crowds surrounding Syntagma and the waterfront.

Nauplion's discos have all relocated to **Tolo** (15min., 1400dr by taxi). For in-town action, stroll along the waterfront where the cafes and bars are crowded with twenty-somethings chatting and sipping frappes. At the far right end (facing the water) of the waterfront is **Luna Park,** a carnival where you can relive your childhood under the neon lights. Or take a **minicruise** of the harbor (which run until 7pm), and toodle around the Bourtzi. Small *caïques* leave from the end of the dock (500dr round-trip).

SIGHTS

A stroll through the streets of Nauplion is more edifying than that slide show in Architecture 101. Everywhere you look there is an impressive contrast of the building styles from various periods in history. An amazing example is the 18th-century **Palamidi fortress** (tel. 28 036). The 999 grueling steps that once provided the only access to the fort have been superseded by a 3km road. Taxis cost 700dr each way, or you can attack the road by foot. If you opt for the steps, bring water and climb in the morning. The views of the town, gulf, and much of the Argolid are spectacular. The steps begin on Arvanitias St., across the park from the bus station. A snack bar on the site opens at 9:30am and serves fresh juices, coffee, water, and snacks. The lion stelae that adorn some of the lower citadel's walls are Venetian. Years ago there were eight working cisterns at the site; today you can still tour the cool interiors of the two remaining underground reservoirs (open Mon.-Fri. 7:45am-7pm, Sat.-Sun. and off season 8:30am-3pm; admission 800dr, students 400dr, EU students free).

The walls of the **Acronauplion** were fortified by three successive generations of conquerors: Greeks, Franks, and Venetians. Approach the fortress by the tunnel that runs into the hill from Zigomala St., where you can take the Xenia Hotel elevator. The views of the Palimidi, the Gulf, and Old Nauplion are fantastic. Ludwig I, King of Bavaria, had the huge Bavarian Lion carved out of a monstrous rock as a memorial after seeing many of his men die in an epidemic in 1833-34. Today, a small park sits in front of it. To get there, make a left onto Mikh. Iatrou St. and walk 200m.

Nauplion's **Folk Art Museum,** winner of the 1981 European Museum of the Year Award, is closed for renovations until 1999. The **Military Museum,** toward the new town from Syntagma, has artifacts and high-quality black and white photographs from the burning of Smyrna (Izmir), the population exchanges of the 1920s, and WWII (open Tues.-Sun. 9am-2pm; free). The **archaeological museum** (tel. 27 502), in a Venetian mansion on Syntagma Sq., has a small but esteemed collection of pottery and idols, as well as a fantastic Mycenaean suit of bronze armor (open Tues.-Sun. 8:30am-3pm; admission 500dr, students 300dr).

Karathona Beach in Nauplion is accessible by foot; follow the road which curves around the left-hand side of Palamidi. There's also a footpath from the parking lot between the Palamidi and the end of Polizoidou St. It runs along the water from the left. The 45-minute walk will reveal three quiet, rocky coves. The beach is nothing special, but very convenient.

■ Near Nauplion

TIRYNS (TIRINTHA)

About 4km northwest of Nauplion on the road to Argos lie the Mycenaean ruins of **Tiryns** (or Tirintha), birthplace of Hercules. Perched atop a 25m-high hill, Tiryns (tel. 22 657), one of the finer prehistoric sites outside of Mycenae, was impregnable during ancient times—that is, until it was captured by the Argives and destroyed in the 5th century BC. Parts of the stronghold date as far back as 2600 BC, but most of what remains was built 1000 years later, in the Mycenaean era. Standing 8m in both height and width, the massive walls surrounding the site are evidence of the immensity of the original fortifications. They reach a width of 20m on the eastern and southern slopes of the ancient acropolis. Inside these structures lurk vaulted galleries. The palace's frescoes are in the National Archaeological Museum in Athens (see p. 84). One huge limestone block remains—the floor of the bathroom (open 8am-6:30pm. admission 400dr, students 200dr). The site is easily reached by the Argos bus from Nauplion (every 30min., 175dr).

TOLO (ΤΟΛΟ)

If you're staying in Nauplion and are desperate for a long, sandy beach, Tolo is the place to go. Buses leave Nauplion frequently, and on summer days, scads of pre-teens head for the water. You can rent jet skis (5000dr per 15min), umbrellas (2000dr per day), paddle boats (1500dr per hour) or wind surf (2000dr per hour) on the beach. It is advisable to make Tolo a daytrip, however, because the town has nothing to offer besides the beach, and the tourist industry here is unfriendly.

■ Epidavros ΕΠΙΔΑΥΡΟΣ

Henry Miller claimed that amid Epidavros's powerful serenity he heard the pounding "great heart of the world." It's easy to see why—the theater at Epidavros is acoustically impeccable and is conveniently situated atop the world's great heart. From the top of its graceful, perfectly preserved 55 tiers of seats, you can hear a *drachma* drop onstage. Even with the midday din of eager tourists and busloads of schoolchildren singing hymns and folk songs, Epidavros, surrounded by pine groves, is endowed with a sense of peacefulness that relaxes even the most frenzied of tourists.

Try to visit during the **Epidavros Festival** Friday and Saturday nights from late June to mid-August, when the **National Theater of Greece** and visiting companies perform plays from the classical Greek canon (Euripides, Sophocles, Aristophanes, etc.). Performances are at 9pm and tickets can be purchased at the site (open Mon.-Sat. 9am-5pm and Fri.-Sat. 5-9pm). You can also buy tickets in advance in Athens at the **Athens Festival Box Office** (tel. (01) 322 14 59; see p. 79). In Nauplion, buy tickets at **Bourtzi Tours,** 9 Thessaloniki St., near the Atlantic Supermarket (tel. 21 249). Tickets cost 3000-4500dr, 2000dr for students. Children under six are strictly prohibited. Performances are in Greek, so bring your favorite translation. **Telephone Code:** 0753.

Unless you're going to Epidavros for the theater, make the small town a daytrip from Nauplion, Athens, Corinth, or a Saronic Gulf Island. Buses travel to and from Nauplion (6 per day, 1hr., 550dr) and Galatas (2 per day). On performance nights, **KTEL** buses make the round-trip circuit, leaving Nauplion at 7:30pm (1500dr).

There is no town near the sight of Epidavros, so bring a picnic lunch and eat at the site, or shell out for a snack at the only place around, **Xenias.**

The theater is a grand structure, built in the early 4th century BC to accommodate 6000 people. In the 2nd century BC, the capacity was expanded to 14,000. Despite severe earthquakes in 522 and 551 AD, the theater was miraculously spared. Note the restored Corinthian columns supporting the entrances. Performances were staged here until the 4th century and began again in the 20th century.

While Mycenae, Nauplion, and Tiryns were all originally built as fortified cities, the small state of Epidavros was designed as an **Asclepion** or a sanctuary for healing. Its ruins, the remains of hospital rooms and sick wards, attest to the blurred boundaries between medicine, magic, and religion common in antiquity. From its founding in the 6th century BC, Epidavros was dedicated to gods of medicine—first Maleatas, then Apollo, and finally Apollo's son Asclepius.

The **museum** (tel. 22 009) is on the way from the theater to the ruins. The first room includes painted decorations from the ruins and huge stones containing inscriptions of hymns to Apollo and accounts of repairs to the temple. Hold onto your ticket stub for the museum. (Theater, site, and museum open Tues.-Sun. 8am-7pm and Mon. noon-7pm, closing at 5pm in the off season. Admission 1500dr, students 800dr, EU students free).

The ruins of the Sanctuary of Asclepius are extensive and can be confusing. Walking from the museum, you will first come across the **gymnasium** on your right, which contains the remains of an **odeon** built by the Romans. On your left are the remains of the **stadium.** In front and to the left are the ruins of the **Temple to Asclepius** and the famous **tholos,** thought to have been designed by Polykleitos, the architect of the theater. The *tholos* contains a maze, the purpose of which is unknown. Farther from the theater lie the ruins of the extensive baths built by the Romans before Sulla destroyed and looted the site in 89 BC.

ELIAS AND ACHAÏA ΗΛΕΙΑΣ ΚΑΙ ΑΧΑΙΑ

In the rural provinces of Elias and Achaïa, tomatoes ripen beneath the blazing sun as beachgoers redden to a similar hue. The area between Pyrgos and Patras, the capitals of Elias and Achaïa, is a vegetable farmer's dream. Corn fields, rimmed with golden-sand beaches, are studded with ancient, Frankish, and Venetian ruins. The locals call these regions of the Peloponnese "tame" as opposed to the "wild" landscape in other parts of Greece. The current tranquility of the Northwest Peloponnese hides centuries of diverse influence. The Achaïans from the Argolid were the first settlers of Achaïa, and in 280 BC the Achaïan Confederacy was created. In 146 BC the region fell to the Romans, in 1205 AD it was captured by the Franks, in 1460 it became Ottoman property, and from 1687 to 1715 it was a Venetian colony. Ruins from each of these periods stand to this day. In 1828 Achaïa became Greek again.

GREECE

■ Patras ΠΑΤΡΑΣ

Patras, Greece's third largest city, sprawls noisily along its harbor. Menacing semitrailers crowd the harbor roads of this transportation hub, threatening hapless pedestrians. Most tourists treat Patras as a stopover and leave the city having seen nothing but tour agencies, bars, and sleazy hotels. If you hope to enjoy Patras, buy your ferry ticket, store your luggage, and head for the hills. The upper city is peaceful and perfect for an afternoon stroll. Ruins from the city's long history dot the streets, and picturesque only begins to describe its beauty.

Patras provides a base to reach much of the Peloponnese, including **Olympia,** the northern coast, and a resort-free beach in Kalogria. It also has the second largest number of bars and pubs in Europe. From mid-January to Ash Wednesday, Patras hosts Carnival, featuring music, food, and an all-night fête. The city's port becomes one vast dance floor where Greeks and tourists alike are bumped and ground.

ORIENTATION AND PRACTICAL INFORMATION

If you're coming from Athens by car, choose between the **New National Road,** an expressway running inland along the Gulf of Corinth, and the slower, more scenic **Old National Road,** which hugs the coast. Those coming from the north can take a ferry from **Antirio** across to **Rio** on the Peloponnese (every 15min, 7am-11pm, 30min., 270dr per person, 1720dr per car) and hop on bus #6 from Rio to the station, four blocks uphill from the main station, at Kanakari and Aratou St. (30min., 200dr).

If you're arriving by boat from Brindisi or any of the Ionian Islands, turn right as you leave customs onto **Iroon Polytechniou Street** to get to the center of town. Just before the train station the road curves and its name changes to **Othonos Amalias Street.** Past the train station is the large **Trion Simahon Square,** with palm trees, cafes, and kiosks. **Agios Nikolaou** runs inland from the square and intersects the major east-west streets of the city. From the corner of Agios Nikolaou and Mezanos, three blocks from the water, turn right. You will see **Georgiou Square.** Between Georgiou Sq. and Olgas Sq. (3 blocks to the west) is the heart of new Patras. But skip the lower city's squares in favor of the upper's parks. Walk inland on Agios Nikolaou, climb the daunting steps, and you will be rewarded.

Tourist Office: (tel. 62 22 49), On the waterfront at the entrance to the customs complex. Multilingual staff gives free maps as well as bus and boat timetables and can help with accommodations. Open Mon.-Fri. 7am-9:30pm.

Tourist Police: (tel. 45 18 33 or 45 18 93), inside the customs complex. Offers same services as tourist office. Open 7:30am-11pm.

Consulates: British, 2 Votsi St. (tel. 27 73 29), on the corner of Othonos Amalias St. Variable hours, but most often Mon.-Fri. 9:30am until late morning.

Banks: National Bank (tel. 22 16 43), Trion Simahon Sq., on the waterfront, just past the train station. Open Mon.-Thurs. 8am-2pm, Fri. 8am-1:30pm. Another branch at customs complex (hours vary). **ATMs** on the first block of Agios Nickolaou.

Trains: (tel. 27 36 94), on Othonos Amalias St. To: Athens (8 per day, 2600dr) via Corinth (1000dr); Kalamata (2 per day, 4½hr., 1500dr); and Pyrgos (8 per day until 10pm, 2hr., 820dr); transfer here for Olympia. Expect delays and a shortage of seats, especially on the trains to Athens. Even if you have a railpass, reserve a seat at the ticket window before taking a train.

Buses: KTEL (tel. 62 38 86, -7), on Othonos Amalias between Aratou and Zaïmi. To: Athens (26 per day, 3hr., 3350dr); Kalamata (2 per day, 1hr., 1000dr); Pyrgos (11 per day, 1700dr); Tripoli (2 per day, 4hr., 2850dr); Ioannina (4 per day, 4050dr); Thessaloniki (3 per day, 7500dr); Kalavrita (4 per day, 1350dr); and Egion (15 per day, 650dr).

Ferries: From Patras, boats reach Cephalonia, Ithaka, and Corfu in Greece, and Brindisi, Bari, and Ancona in Italy. Most boats to Italy depart at night and have prices that vary according to the season. Ask about student discounts. If you have a railpass, got to **HML** (tel 45 25 21) on Iroon Polytechniou, past customs. Deck passages can be as low as 4500dr in off-season to 14,000dr in high season. Ask at each

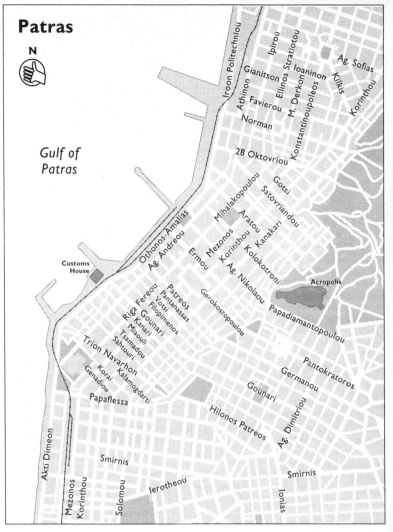

Patras

N

Gulf of Patras

Customs House

Acropolis

GREECE

agency about check-in and boarding. Ferries to Cephalonia and Ithaka leave daily and cost about 3000dr. For info about ferries to the Ionian islands go to **Strintzis Tours,** 14 Othonas Amalias St. (tel. 62 26 02). Open daily 9am-10pm.

Luggage Storage: In the pink building near the customs complex. Open daily 7am-9:30pm; 200dr per item per day. Also at train station (270dr per item).

International Bookstore: Biblia Clio, 27 Patreos. Scholarly collection, including Cambridge University Press.

Laundromat: On Zaïmi near Korinthou (tel. 62 01 19). Wash and dry 2000dr. Open Mon.-Sat. 9am-9pm.

Hospital: The **Red Cross Emergency Station** (tel. 27 386) is open 8am-8pm and dispenses first aid. It is on the corner of 28 Oktoviou and Agios Dionysiou. **Rio Hospital** of Patras University (tel. 99 91 11) is a large, modern hospital 5km away. Accessible by taxi or bus #6.

Post Office: (tel. 22 38 64) On Mezonos at the corner of Zaïmi. Open Mon.-Fri. 7:30am-8pm, Sat. 7:30am-2pm. **Postal Code:** 26001.

OTE: (tel. 42 19 98), at customs. Open daily 7:30am-10pm. For collect international calls, go to the OTE at Trion Simahon Sq. Open Mon.-Fri. 7am-2:30pm, Sat.-Sun. 7:20am-1pm. Also at the corner of Kanakari and Gounari St., up from the waterfront. **Telephone Code:** 061.

ACCOMMODATIONS

Cheap accommodations are threaded through the tangle of buildings on Agios Andreas St., one block up and parallel to the waterfront. If you pick a very cheap hotel that isn't listed here, be sure it's not a bordello (some are).

Youth Hostel, 68 Iroon Polytechniou St. (tel. 42 72 78). From the ferry, turn left (away from town) and walk 1½km. Currently housed in a dusty turn-of-the-century mansion, it sat empty for 40 years after being used as a German headquarters in WWII. This hostel is planning a move in the winter of 1997. Check at the tourist office for current information. It's a little cramped and there is at least one report of the men that hang out there getting a little too friendly, but it's your best bet in Patras (1700dr per night, sheets 150dr, breakfast 600dr).

Pension Nikos, 3 Patreos St. (tel. 22 16 43), off the waterfront. Go up to the third floor when you arrive. Clean rooms. Singles 3500dr; doubles 6000dr, with bath 8000dr.

Hotel Mediterranee, 18 Agios Nikolaou (tel. 27 96 02). Expensive for the budget traveler, but if you can't find anyplace else, treat yourself to a TV and a very hot shower. Singles 7500dr; doubles 13,500dr.

Camping: Rio Camping (tel. 99 15 85), 8km east of Patras. 1100dr per person; children 600dr; tent 1000dr; car 600dr; electricity 700dr. To get there, catch bus #6 at the corner of Aratou and Kamakari, get off at Rion, and follow the signs. **Rio Mare** (tel. 99 22 63), near Rio Camping, charges 1200dr per person; 800dr per small tent; 1100dr per large tent; 750dr per car. **Kavouri Camping** (tel. 42 21 45), 2km east of town, next to the Patras swimming pool. Crowded, but cheap. Take bus #1 from in front of Agios Dionysios Church; walk up Norman St. 1 block and turn left. 650dr per person; 300dr per small tent; 700dr per large tent; 480dr per car;

FOOD

Patras's waterfront restaurants are aimed at tourists, overpriced, and virtually indistinguishable from one another. If you ask locals for recommendations, they'll probably send you to one of the many **Goody's** that the city's young people love. These joints, where you can get a variety of pre-packaged burgers and chicken sandwiches (300-900dr) are clean and fast.

Taverna Nicolaras (tel. 22 52 53), three blocks inland on Agios Nikolarou, is a traditional *taverna*. It isn't as flashy, but the food is delicious, and the variety is wider than usual. The food is displayed in a case so you can choose between beans (800dr), *dolmades* (950dr), and salmon (1100dr). Great for **vegetarians.** You might also try the **Artopoisio Bakery** (tel. 27 41 39), on Agios Nikolarou at the foot of the stairs to the upper city. Inhale the delicious smell of baking bread. The delicious, yet inexpensive baked goods make a perfect snack after a jaunt around the castle. Large loaves of bread are 140dr, and ginger cookies are 28dr.

ENTERTAINMENT

It may not be the city of lights, but Patras may be the city of light beer. Although it is not immediately apparent, Patras's tiny side streets hide many small bars and cafes. Notable are **Caffé Luz,** off Olgas Square, on Aratoy St., and its neighbor **Napoli,** for beer, coffee, and backgammon. **Blue Monday,** along Radinou St., one street east of Olgas Sq., serves ordinary cafe fare, but plays more Elvis Presley than any other bar on the Peloponnese. It takes its name from an old rock song, and silver-screen idols provide labels for each chair (try Charlie Chaplin, Cary Grant, or Katherine Hepburn—all beside each other). Look for its red Coke-bottle cap sign.

Off of Mezonos between Agios Nikolarou and Kolokotronis there are two arcades lined with bars. These bars fill up at night. The wildest partygoers, however, head out of town at night. As with many large coastal cities, a beach town satellite is only min-utes away. **Rion** is a small city, roughly 8km to the northeast of Patras. This stretch of beach bars, clubs, restaurants, and discos is where Patras's nightlife transports itself in the summer months.

Decor is taken seriously at the beach bars. The most exciting bars resemble theme parks minus the rides. At **Mioiouia 105,** a bright yellow WWII plane hangs above the dance floor and plastic soldiers engage in desert combat under plexiglass at the bar. A beer will set you back 600dr, a frappe 500dr. **Soka Bay** goes for the jungle motif: green atmosphere lighting illuminates rope-wrapped trees and fake ruins. Play on the giant tree swing as you sip your beer (500dr). There are some more serious **restau-rants** that families frequent at Rion Beach. **La Piscina,** at the end of the strip, has a fountain, pizza (1600-2200dr), and a variety of fish (600-5500dr). **Gali Gali Deliplace** is new, bright, and spotless.

Buses run until 10pm to Rion. You may have to take a cab home (1000dr). Take bus #6 from the Kamakari and Araton St. (30min., 200dr). Once past the hospital, look for Hotel Apollo or the Castello Restaurant on Somerset St.; this is the nearest bus stop. Follow the signs to Camping Rion and they will take you to the strip.

SIGHTS

A 13th-century Venetian **castle** crowns the city. Built on the ruins of the ancient acropolis, it was once the site of the temple of the Panachaïan Athena. Playground equipment in the castle's park rewards kids who make the trek. From up here, you can see downtown Patras for the beehive that it is. This Eden-esque courtyard has chirping birds, olive trees, and bright flowers that will transport you to a remote countryside. The park is open daily until 7pm. In the summertime watch out for con-certs and theater at the park. Also in the upper city, west of the castle, is the **Ancient Odeum.** This ancient Roman theater was restored in brick in the 14th century. It is open during the day (8:30am-3pm). From June 15 until October 15, it hosts the **Patras Festival,** where Greek music groups perform every evening starting at 9pm (tickets average 1500dr). The **Archaeological Museum,** 42 Mezonos (tel. 22 08 29), next to Olgas Sq. at the corner of Mezonos St. and Aratou, shows vases, statues, and other artifacts (open Tues.-Sun. 8:30am-3pm; free).

The largest Orthodox cathedral in Greece, **Agios Andreas** is dedicated to St. Andrew, who lived and died in Patras. As he felt himself unworthy to die on the same kind of cross as Jesus, St. Andrew was martyred by crucifixion on an X-shaped ver-sion. A little more than 10 years ago, the Catholic Church presented the Bishop of Patras with the saint's head. To the right of the cathedral is the old church of St. Andrew, which houses a small **well** said to have been built by the saint himself. It can be reached by a doorway to the right of the church, and legend has it that whoever drinks from this well will return to Patras again. Photography and videotaping are prohibited and modest dress is appropriate (open daily 9am-dusk). To get here, fol-low the water to the west end of town, roughly 1.5km from the port (20min.).

Achaïa Clauss winery is 9km southeast of town. Its founder, Baron von Clauss, was consumed with lust for a woman named Daphne. Upon her death, he made a wine in her honor with his darkest grapes, called *Mavrodaphne,* "Black Daphne." to get there, take bus #7 (20min., 185dr) from the intersection of Kolokotroni and Kanakari St. (tours daily 9am-7:30pm; off season daily 9am-5pm; free).

The **carnival season** in Patras begins mid-January every year and lasts until Ash Wednesday. The locals describe *karnavali* as an undefinable energy that sweeps through town. The Carnival's last night is capped by a ritual burning of King Carnival, and an open, boozy party on the harbor that lasts all night. The last Sunday of Carnival is topped off with a 12-hour marathon parade that takes over the streets. In 1995, the Gypsy Kings performed here. With feasts every night, people of all ages dance in the streets. Patras's bash may be the best carnival in Greece. Call the Youth Hostel (tel. 42 72 78); they provide program details. In a nearly 100km radius, hotel rooms are booked for much of Carnival—advance reservations are a necessity.

■ Diakofto ΔΙΑΚΟΦΤΟ

Fruit trees and flowers overwhelm this town lying halfway between Patras and Corinth. Houses are hidden by orange and lemon trees, while magenta bougainvillea cover their facades. Diakofto is a quiet town with a beautiful rocky beach that lures tourists with its famous **rack-railway train** to Kalavrita.

ORIENTATION AND PRACTICAL INFORMATION

The train station cuts Diakofto's main road in half. If you walk inland toward the spectacular mountains that frame the town you will see the post office (open Mon.-Fri. 7:30am-2pm) and the **National Bank of Greece** (open Mon.-Fri. 8:45am-12:45pm), which offers **currency exchange.** If you walk down the main road toward the sea you will pass through a picturesque residential area and end up at the harbor and public beach. The train station (tel. 43 206) is the social center of Diakofto. Cafes and restaurants face it from both sides. Tiny rack-railway trains to Kalavrita make for an exhilarating ride (6 per day, 1¼hr, 630dr one-way, 1100dr round-trip).

ACCOMMODATIONS AND FOOD

Hotel Helmos (tel. 41 236) is on the main road on the inland side of the tracks. Convenient to everything in Diakofto, the rooms are small but spotless. Showers and toilets are shared, but heat and water pressure here are second to none. There are also private sinks in each room (singles 4000dr; doubles 6000dr; triples 8000dr). **Hotel Lemonides** (tel. 41 820) is halfway between the train station and the beach on the main road. It offers very clean, bright white, and spacious rooms with private baths. Downstairs is a pleasant *taverna*, and the surrounding neighborhood is lovely (singles 5000dr; doubles 7000dr; triples 8000dr). Cafes and bars line the train station and the main street inland from the station. The service is quick and the outdoor dining pleasant at **Festaria Taverna** (tel. 43 228), which offers delicious *souvlaki* (200dr), hot dinners (1200dr), and quick salads (800dr). Many eateries close between lunch and dinner, so you may have trouble finding an afternoon snack. An exception is **Revanche,** located to the left when you cross the railroad tracks.

SIGHTS

The famous monastery of **Mega Spilaeou** is 9km from Diakofto and getting there actually is half the fun. The train ride is breathtaking, the 3km climb will leave you panting, and your heart will jump at the surprise in the back of the monastery. It is best to start your trek early in the day, catching the first rack-train that leaves Diakofto at 8am (700dr round-trip). Be sure to bring a water bottle, long-sleeved shirt, and sturdy shoes. The 40 minute ride on the 19th-century railway has the same "will-we-make-it?" excitement as a rollercoaster's uphill climb. Sit in a window seat to enjoy the view of spectacular cliffs, stalactite-rich caves, and the rapids of the Vouraikos River. Anticipate your stop at Zahlorov, as the train stops briefly.

Zahlorov is a tiny mountain village reminiscent of *Heidi* even though it's in the wrong mountain range. The path that leads to the monastery is marked in English. Frequent water stops are a must and will give you a chance to admire the panoramic views with the occasional donkey or goat. You should reach a paved road after about 45 minutes of walking. Turn left and follow the road to the sign for Mega Spilaeou on your right. Stairs in front of the monastery lead to the main entrance. Modest (i.e., long sleeved) clothes are appreciated inside. A monk will lead you to the upstairs museum containing gold-encased relics and beautiful icons (some say one was painted by St. Luke). Photographs describe the destruction of the centuries-old monastery by an explosion of stored gunpowder in 1934. The new monastery is built up against the cliff wall, and one of the cliff's caves is accessible from the second floor of the building. Let the cool darkness of the cave envelop you as you peer into the darkness and look for the cave's surprise. On your way back down the mountain, be careful of loose rocks and the odd snake that might cross your path.

▓ Kalavrita ΚΑΛΑΒΡΥΤΑ

The clock of the town's church is set permanently to 2:34 to commemorate the Nazi massacre of all Kalavrita's men on December 13, 1943. A **memorial** to those slain in 1943 is located at the site of the massacre. To get there, follow the signs away from the central square on 13 Dekembriou. Kalivrita's **church** is in the shady central square. At the end of the rack-railway line, Kalavrita is a winter ski resort with little to offer a summer visitor. Budget accommodations are hard to find and you will do better down the line in Zahlorov or Diakofto.

ORIENTATION AND PRACTICAL INFORMATION

Two roads perpendicular to the train station lead to main square, **Konstantinov** (later called **Agios Alexiou**) to the left and **Syngrov** (later called **25 Martiou**) to the right. The **National Bank of Greece** is at #4 25 Martiou (tel 22 212; open Mon.-Thurs. 8am-2pm and Fri. 8am-1:30pm) and offers **currency exchange.** The **post office** is next to the park near the train station. The **police** (tel. 23 333) are three blocks beyond the OTE, off Agios Alexiou at 7 Fotina St. (open 24hr.). The **OTE** is at 10 Agios Alexiou (open daily 7:30am-3:10pm). The **telephone code** for Kalavrita is 0692.

ACCOMMODATIONS AND FOOD

Hotels in Kalavrita are pleasant but expensive (prices quoted here are higher during ski season). **Hotel Megas Alexandrous** (tel. 22 221) has spacious rooms with wood floors. The private bathrooms' showers are tiny. To find the hotel, turn right on Lex. B. Kapota from 25 Martiou (singles 5000dr; doubles 10,000dr; triples 12,000dr). The **Hotel Paradissos,** 18 Ethnikis Anistaseos (tel 22 303), offers white stucco walls, lace curtains, and private baths (no singles; doubles 9000dr; triples 12,000dr). Down the street and close to the main square, **Hotel Maria** (tel 22 296; fax 22 686) is luxurious with TVs, telephones, and lavender furniture (singles 6000dr; doubles 10,000dr; triples 14,000dr).

Agios Alexiou and 25 Martiou have many *tavernas* which are all more or less the same. **Taverna Stani** (tel. 23 000) has entrances on both streets and offers traditional fare (*tzaziki* 500dr, salads 500-100dr, seafood 1500dr), while the **Snack Bar** on 13 Dekembriou is less expensive with pizza (450dr), gyros (350dr), and beer (450dr).

▓ Killini ΚΥΛΛΗΝΗ

What is most amazing about Killini is its underdevelopment. Almost all of the myriad tourists who travel to Zakinthos have to travel through this port, yet Killini has no bus station and only one hotel.

The path to town from the dock leads to the **police** (tel. (0623) 92 202; no English spoken). The **port police** (tel. (0623) 92 211) are on the dock (open 24hr.). The **post office** is a few blocks farther down, on a side street leading inland (**postal code:** 27068; open daily 10am-noon). **Buses** travel to Pyrgos (4 per day until 4pm, ½hr., 400dr) and Patras (4 per day, 1hr., 1200dr). A daily bus to Athens leaves Killini at 9.30am. To get to Lehena, the nearest town on the main Patras to Pirgos highway, take a taxi (tel. 71 764, 2000dr) or one of the infrequent buses. **Ferries** sail from Killini to: Zakinthos (5 per day, 1hr., 1500dr); Cephalonia (5 per day, 1hr., 1500dr); Argostoli (daily at noon, 2½hr., 2700dr); and Poros (daily at 6:30pm, 1½hr., 2000dr). Buy tickets on the dock.

To find **accommodations,** turn right from the dock, cross the train tracks, and walk along the beach. **Hotel Ionion** (tel. 92 318) offers large rooms decorated in various shades of gray. Some have private baths (singles 7000dr; doubles 10,500dr; triples 12,150dr). On a side street just before the Ionion is **Voultses Domatia** (tel. 92 161) which offers a tiny room with a shared bath for 4000dr and a larger room with a private bath for 8000dr.

The Frankish **Chlemoutsi Castle** and the mineral springs of **Loutra Killinis,** a well-manicured resort with a long beach, are 20km from Killini. Getting to either is difficult unless you have your own transportation or are willing to pay for a taxi (1200dr to the castle, 3000dr to Loutra). Near Loutra is **Camping Killinis** (tel. (0623) 96 259). The campgrounds are close to the sea, and include a market and hot showers (1200dr per person; 650dr per small tent; 1200dr per large tent; 600dr per car). Three buses per day leave Loutra for the castle. Nearby is **Karitena,** the village pictured on the 5000dr bill. The birthplace of Kolokotronis, Karitena has ruins of a Frankish castle and a 13th-century church dedicated to St. Nicholas. Its beauty may entice you to stay. **Stamata Kondopoulos** (tel. (0623) 31 206) has rooms near the post office (singles 2500dr; doubles 4200dr).

■ Olympia ΟΛΥΜΠΙΑ

Were it not for the ruins of the site of the ancient Olympic games, modern Olympia would be a pleasant little town with absolutely no reason for tourists to set foot in it. As it stands, Olympia is as multicultural as the modern games that trace their heritage here. Walk the streets and hear English, Greek, French, German, Italian, and Japanese—and that's just from the restaurant patrons.

ORIENTATION AND PRACTICAL INFORMATION

Modern Olympia essentially consists of a 1km main street, **Kondili Avenue.** The bus will drop you off across from tourist information. Head out of town on the main road for a five-minute walk to the ruins and the archaeological museum. On the other side of town, towards Pirgos, sports enthusiasts will appreciate the **Museum of the Olympic Games** (tel. 22 544), with paraphernalia from each of the modern Olympic games. Located on Angerinou St., it's two blocks uphill from Kondili Ave. (open Mon.-Sat. 8am-3:30pm, Sun. 9am-4:30pm; admission 500dr). Since the town caters mainly to tourists, most restaurants open at 8am and close after 1am.

Tourist Office: (tel. 23 100), Kondili Ave., on the east side of town, towards the ruins. Open April-Sept. 9am-9pm; Oct.-Mar. 11am-5pm. Has a photocopy machine, stamps, and provides maps.

Bank: National Bank, on Kondili Ave., offers **currency exchange.** Open Mon.-Thurs. 8am-2pm, Fri. 8am-1:30pm. ATM accepts PLUS, Cirrus, MasterCard, and Visa.

OTE: Kondili Ave., past the post office. Open daily 7am-10pm.

Buses: The bus stop is directly across from the tourist information shack, which has an up-to-date schedule posted outside. To: Pirgos (15 per day, 6:30am-9:45pm, 40min., 360dr); Tripoli (3 per day, 3½hr., 2200dr); and Dimitsana (2 per week, 1300dr). Reduced service on weekends.

English Bookstore: Athanasia Bookshop, Kondili Ave., on the east end of town. Carries a large selection of English guidebooks, novels, and books on Greece. Open daily 8am-11pm.

Hospital: (tel. (0621) 22 222) in Pirgos, (tel. (0624) 22 222) in Olympia. Olympia uses Pirgos' hospital, but has a **health center** of its own. Walk from the ruins down Kondili St. Before the church (on your left), turn left. Continue straight, and after the road winds right, then left, take a left. Open Mon.-Fri. 8am-2pm.

Police: 1 Em. Kountsa Ave., 1 block up from Kondili (tel. 22 100). Open 9am-9pm, but someone's there 24hr. **Tourist police** may be around in the morning.

Post Office: (tel. 22 578), on a nameless, uphill side street just past the tourist information center. Open Mon.-Fri. 7:30am-2pm. **Postal Code:** 27065.

Telephone Code: 0624.

ACCOMMODATIONS

If all you want is a cheap place to crash, head for the youth hostel. Otherwise, choose from dozens of hotels, most of which offer private baths, balconies, and modern

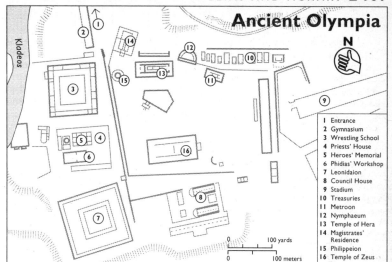

Ancient Olympia

N

1 Entrance
2 Gymnasium
3 Wrestling School
4 Priests' House
5 Heroes' Memorial
6 Phidias' Workshop
7 Leonidaion
8 Council House
9 Stadium
10 Treasuries
11 Metroon
12 Nymphaeum
13 Temple of Hera
14 Magistrates'
   Residence
15 Philippeion
16 Temple of Zeus

GREECE

rooms. Private rooms in Olympia are surprisingly large. Prices vary but hover around 5000dr per double. They are 20-40% less in the off season.

Youth Hostel, 18 Kondili Ave. (tel. 22 580). Convenient location. Membership not needed. No curfew. Check-out 10am. 1500dr per day. Breakfast 500dr.

Pension Possidon (tel. 22 567), turn uphill at the National Bank and go 2 blocks. Offers large clean rooms, some with private bath. Singles 4000dr; doubles 6000dr; triples 8000dr.

Hotel Hermes (tel. 22 577), Kondili Ave. At the end of town, just before the entrance for Camping Olympia. Clean, pink rooms, some with and some without bathrooms. Singles 4000dr; doubles 7000dr.

Rooms to let, ask at **O Fraka Restaurant** (tel. 22575), on Kondili closer to Pirgos than the site. Large rooms with bath and balcony. Singles 4000dr; doubles 6000dr. Or, inquire at the **Ambrosia Restaurant** (tel. 22 916), from which the Spiliopoulous rents rooms. Doubles 5000dr. Mention *Let's Go* for a 10% discount.

Camping Diana (tel. 22 314), uphill from the Sports Museum. Offers a clean pool, hot water, and breakfast (900dr). 1300dr per person; 800dr per car; 900dr per small tent; 1200dr per large tent. Electricity 800dr. 10-20% student discounts.

Camping Olympia (tel. 22 745), 1km west on the road to Pirgos, has a baby pool and larger pool. 1200dr per person; 700dr per car; 800dr per small tent; 900dr per large tent. Electricity 850dr.

FOOD

Most restaurants on Kondili Ave. are cramped and overpriced. A walk toward the railroad station and away from the busloads of tours reveals some charming *tavernas*. **O Kladeus,** behind Olympia's train station (its sign is obvious), is the *taverna* you've been waiting for. The menu features fish (1200dr) and Greek salad (700dr). The dirt floor, ramshackle canopy, ragged table settings, and the mysterious, potent "house wine" set the mood. Be sure to bring bug repellant. Just before O Kladeus, the management of **Ambrosia** (tel. 23 414) serves great food in a white building (entrees 1500-1700dr). For a shady afternoon drink or light meal, **Socrate 1908** on Kondili (next to the Youth Hostel) has an outdoor garden area (omelettes 800dr, *spaniko-pitou* 750dr). Along Kondili there are numerous markets where you can pick up the makings for a picnic lunch.

■ Ancient Olympia

This legendary site between the Kladeo and Alphios Rivers was never a city, but an event. Here, the leaders of rival city-states shed their armor and congregated in peace to enjoy the games and make offerings to the gods. Only game officials were permitted in the sacred town. The center of town was reserved for the **Altis,** a walled enclosure or sacred grove of Zeus. On the far-east side were the **stadium** and the **echo stoa,** which was said to have had a seven-fold echo. Facilities for both administrators and participants comprised the remaining three sides of the Altis. Over the centuries, council houses and treasuries were added to the site. In addition, victors often built monuments to the gods here.

The site's dimensions remain impressive, although the ruins are not especially well-preserved. The setting is also striking for its natural beauty and tranquility. Few sections are cordoned off and you can walk or climb on the colossal remains of the Temple of Zeus. A guide and map are vital, as the ruins are poorly marked. Two thorough guides are available at the site—the red *Olympia* by Spiros Photinos (2000dr) and the blue *Guide to the Museum and Sanctuary* by A. and N. Yalouris (2500dr).

TOURING OLYMPIA

As you enter the site, the thigh-high remains of the **Gymnasium,** dating from the 2nd century BC, lie to your right. To the left as you enter is the **Prytaneion,** with its sacred hearth. Past the Gymnasium stand the re-erected columns of the **Palaestra.** This building was the wrestling school, a place for athletes to practice and dress and philosophers to ruminate. The next group of buildings includes the **workshop of Phidias.** Phidias was a famous sculptor who came to Olympia, having been banished from Athens in a scandal connected to the statue of Athena he had created for the Parthenon. While in Olympia, he was commissioned to sculpt for the site. He produced a statue of Zeus so magnificent that it was named one of the **seven wonders of the ancient world.** Farther on is the huge **Leonidaion,** the lodgings of game officials.

To the left and raised by the Altis is the gigantic **Temple of Zeus,** which dominates the entire complex. Parts of the original mosaic floor can still be seen on the temple base. The nave of the temple once housed a statue by Phidias. Emperor Theodosius ordered that the gold and ivory statue be brought to Constantinople, where it was destroyed by fire in 475 AD.

On the north edge of the Altis lie the dignified remains of the **Temple of Hera.** Built in the 7th century BC, it is the oldest and most well-preserved building on the site, as well as the oldest Doric temple in Greece. Originally built for both Zeus and Hera, it was devoted solely to the goddess when Zeus moved to separate quarters in the south. The temple testifies to the ancient worship of female deities and mother earth. This temple was also featured in the **Heraia,** the first Olympic event for women—foot races for virgins. The **Olympic flame** is still lit here, then borne to the site of the modern games by the necessary vehicles, runners, school children, Hell's Angels, and anyone else wishing to join the Coca-Cola-sponsored panoply.

The archway on the east end of the Altis leads to the **stadium.** As originally constructed, the arena's artificial banks could accommodate 40,000 spectators. The **judges' stand** is still in place, as are the start and finish lines. Beyond the stadium flows the Alphios River, said to run underground all the way to Sicily. This was quite handy for Hercules when he had to clean the Augean stables (tel. 22 517; site open daily 8am-7pm; admission 1200dr, students 600dr, EU students free). **Free public bathrooms** and water fountains are inside the site.

The gleaming **New Museum** (tel. 22 742), across the street from the site, is set among marble pavilions and tree-lined avenues. It houses a large collection of well-displayed statues, including the Baby Dionysus attributed to the 4th-century BC sculptor Praxiteles, and a number of figurines, including the **Little Man with the Big Erection** pictured on postcards throughout the country. It also contains two impressive constructions made of surviving pieces of the pediments of the Temple of Zeus and miniature reconstructions of the site as it might have appeared in antiquity. (Open

Tues.-Fri. 8am-7pm, Sat.-Mon. 8:30am-3pm. Admission 1200dr, students 600dr; cameras with flash 500dr; video cameras 1000dr.)

ARCADIA ΑΡΚΑΔΙΑ

Poets since Theocritus have fancied Arcadia as the archetypal scene of pastoral pleasure. Gods, too, appreciated the area—Pan and Dionysus chose this lush, mountain-ringed land as the site of their gleeful dances. Rural serenity can still be found in the hidden bays, deep green vegetation, dramatic mountains, and vast fir forests. Elsewhere, as in the bustling metropolis of Tripoli, the modern era has brought a rumble of buses and cargo to the fields where satyrs once cavorted.

■ Tripoli ΤΡΙΠΟΛΗ

Tripoli is the transportation hub of Arcadia. Its crowded sidewalks and perilous streets, negotiated by motorists who demonstrate their driving prowess by narrowly missing pedestrians, can be initially dismaying. Buses to the wonderful mountain villages are infrequent, and travelers may have to spend the night. If you stay, don't despair; Tripoli has pleasant squares with cafes, churches, trees, and a tourist-free atmosphere. Nightlife may feel a bit adolescent, but Tripoli's integrity rests in its unspoiled, albeit modern, charm.

ORIENTATION AND PRACTICAL INFORMATION

Think of Tripoli as a cross. At the joint is **Agios Vasiliou,** a large square marked, unsurprisingly, by the Church of Agios Vasiliou. The square is the geographical center of the city. Four other squares form the ends of the cross along the four roads that radiate out from Agios Vasiliou. Most buses arrive at Arcadia station in **Kolokotronis Square,** the square to the east of the center. Georgiou St. will take you from here to Agios Vasiliou. Facing the Church of Agios Vasiliou, take the street on your left (Ethnikis Antistasis St.) to reach **Petrinou Square,** home to the police and recognizable by the large, neoclassical Maliaropouli theater. This is the north part of the cross and, along with Kolokotronis Sq., sees most of the city's activity. Continue along Ethnikis Antistasis (the main shopping street), looking to your right to find the **park** (occupying about eight city blocks) and a vast open square with a 5m-high statue of Kolokotronis. The blocks around the park house mostly boutiques, cafes, clubs, and hotels, and provide the best outpost for people-watching. The park's square is called **Palateia Areus.**

Tourist Office: (tel. 23 18 44) In the town hall past Petrinou Sq. on Ethnikis Antistasis St. Look for the flag and colored windows. Open Mon.-Fri. 8am-12:30pm.
Bank: National Bank (tel. 22 54 89 or 24 29 53), on Ethnikis Antistasis, is one block from Agios Vasiliou Sq. It offers **currency exchange** (open Mon.-Thurs. 8am-2pm, Fri. 8am-1:30pm). A 24hr. **ATM** is located 10m from the bank's entrance—look for the metal door on Ethnikis Antistasis.
Trains: The station (tel. 24 12 13) is 1km west of Kolokotronis Sq. Go through the bus station and turn right—the station is at the end of the street. 4 trains per day to: Athens (4hr., 1500dr); Corinth (2½hr., 900dr); and Argos (1½hr., 590dr); 3 per day to Kalamata (2½hr., 840dr).
Buses: Arcadias Station (tel. 22 25 60) in Kolokotronis Sq. has buses to: Athens (13 per day, 2hr., 2800dr); Dimitsana (1-2 per day, 1hr., 1500dr); Pirgos (1-2 per day, 3½hr., 2500dr); Andritsena (1 per day, 2hr., 1400dr); and Megalopolis (9 per day, 45min., 600dr). Buses go from the **KTEL Messinia and Laconia** bus depot (tel. 24 20 86), across from the train station, to: Kalamata (4 per day, 1½hr., 1450dr); Pylos (5 per day, 3hr., 2300dr); Sparta (8 per day, 1hr., 950dr); and Patras (2 per day, 3hr., 2850dr). **Blue buses** leave from the kiosk at Palateia Areus for Tegea and Mantinea (every hr., 15min., 190dr).

Hospital: (tel. 23 85 42) Located on Panargadon Rd. (on the far western ring of the city). Walk due west from Agios Vasiliou. The road becomes E. Stavrou, which intersects with Panargadon after 500m. At the intersection, turn left. After another 300m, look right.

Police: (tel. 22 24 11) On Eth. Antistasis St., next to the theater at the center of Petrinou Sq. Open 24hr.

Post Office: (tel. 22 2565) On Plapouta St. With your back to the church in Agios Vasiliou Sq., go straight on V. Pavlou St. (away from the church). Take the first right (Nikitara St.) and, after one block, the post office is across the street (open Mon.-Fri. 7:30am-2pm). **Postal Code:** 22100.

OTE: #29 Octovriou 28th St. (tel. 22 63 99). From Agios Vasiliou Sq., take Eth. Antistasis St. and bear left immediately on 28 Octovriou St.—you'll see its tower (open Mon.-Fri. 7am-10pm). **Telephone Code:** 071.

ACCOMMODATIONS

Tripoli is better suited for business conventions than for budget travelers, boasting numerous bloated and sub-par hotels with spotty lighting. Camping near Tripoli is non-existent, and impromptu camping illegal. But if you stay by the park, you do have some options.

Hotel Anactoricon (tel. 22 25 45), along Ethnikis Antistasis two blocks before the park. This is your best bet. With a magnificent main hall and high ceilings in the rooms, this place borders on elegant. TVs and private baths in rooms. Singles 3000dr, with bath 6000dr; doubles 6000dr, with bath 8000dr.

Hotel Alex, 26 Vas. Georgios St. (tel. 22 34 65), between Kolokotronis Sq. and Agios Vasiliou Sq., offers standard rooms in varying shades of puce. Ask for a room at the back, because the noise from the nearby bus station can make Tripoli seem like the city that never sleeps. Singles 4500dr, with bath 5500dr; doubles 7000dr, with bath 8000dr.

Hotel Artemis (tel. 22 52 21), right on the park, is a little pricey, but it offers large rooms with TVs and double beds. Singles 6000dr; doubles 10,000dr.

FOOD, ENTERTAINMENT, AND SIGHTS

The best food in Tripoli borders the park. **Kipos Sosoli Restaurant,** located in a garden-like backyard one block off Ethnikis Antistasis on Pavlou St., offers entrees under 1500dr. The menu is in Greek, but the staff will patiently translate for you. **Restaurant Lido** serves large portions of mostly Italian fare among roses on the far west side of the park's square (spaghetti 900dr, tuna salad 950dr). Also in the square, to the right of the bronze Kolokotronis, the **Park Chalet** restaurant offers ocean perch (1225dr), chicken with lemon (1375dr), and a "Greek country salad" (825dr). Overall, Tripoli lacks culinary inspiration, but if you subscribe to the quick-fix theory of dining out, a number of sandwich shops serve up tasty baguettes stuffed with meat and cheese (300-500dr). Just walk up and down Ethnikis Antistasis and Georgiou Sts.

At night you can rub shoulders with Tripoli's high school students at the bars along Ethnikis Antistasis after Petrinou Square. Especially popular is the **Cinema Classic Billiards Club** on the pedestrian street off of Ethnikis Antistasis. Air-conditioned and with a big screen TV, this place fills up every night (beer 400dr; 1hr. of pool 1600dr). In the summer, posters advertise dance groups, choirs, and plays which can be seen in the city's main squares and in nearby villages. The **Lera Panigyris** is a ten-day cultural festival that starts August 15. Traveling companies and local performance groups also stage Greek-language shows in the attractive **Maliaropoulio Theater,** which dominates Petrinou Sq. If you're interested, ask at the tourist office (tickets 1000-2000dr). During Easter, the town's bishop roasts a lamb in one of the squares, and all in attendance eat for free.

The new **Archaeological Museum** (tel. 24 21 48) is on Evangelistrias St., in a yellow flower-bedecked building. From Kolokotronis Sq. to Agios Vasiliou Sq., take the first left and turn left again. It's full of pottery from the Paleokastro tombs—look for the interesting spout designs (open Tues.-Sun. 8:30am-2:30pm; admission 500dr, students free). The large **Church of Agios Vasiliou** is in the square of the same name. Check out the shops under the church—they're great for religious art.

▓ Dimitsana & Stemnitsa
ΔΗΜΗΤΣΑΝΑ ΚΑΙ ΣΤΕΜΝΙΤΣΑ

West of Tripoli, the little villages of Dimitsana and Stemnitsa make good bases for hiking, walking, or just slowing down to enjoy the villages' natural beauty. This area is known as the "Switzerland of Greece" for its green mountains and chalet-like houses. The atmosphere, however, is far from Swiss. In Dimitsana and Stemnitsa, travelers can still discover the charms of traditional Greek village life. The Erimanthos, Menalo, and Oligirtos mountain ranges, upon which the villages are perilously perched, separate the old settlements of the West from the beach resorts of the East. The mountains are ancient and gnarled, and lush vegetation clings to all but the highest summits. When making treks into the mountains, don't be fooled by Greece's daytime heat—mountain towns get chilly after twilight, even in summer.

In **Dimitsana,** the bus deposits you on Labardopoulou St. across from a cafe which doubles as a **taxi stand.** You can see the **OTE** from here (tel. (0795) 31 955; open Mon.-Fri. 7am-2:30pm). Uphill from the cafe is **Pesonton Sq.** The **police** (tel. (0795) 31 205; open 24hr.; no English spoken) occupy a second-floor office in the square (the building with the Greek flag). Walking through the square and bearing left with the road you will come to the **National Bank** (tel. (0795) 31 503; open Mon.-Thurs. 8am-2pm, Fri. 8am-1:30pm). Just beyond the bank is the **post office** (tel. 22 007; open Mon.-Fri. 7am-2:30pm).

Dimitsana has been an educational center for more than 300 years and two institutions commemorate its scholarly achievements. The **museum within the library** (tel. 31 219) is at the peak of the mountain encircled by the main road. You can climb the steps either at the bus stop or at the main square. When you find yourself in a cobbled courtyard, enter through the library to see the 16th-century illuminated manuscripts and pistols of various war heroes (open Mon.-Fri. 9am-1:30pm, Sat. 8am-12pm). The **Icon Museum,** in the alley to the right of the main square, also merits a look (tel. (0795) 31 465; open Sat.-Tues. and Thurs. 9:30am-1:30pm). Transportation can be tricky in the mountains, and you'll find locals in the towns frustratingly indifferent to the passage of time. When planning connections, keep in mind that the two taxis in some towns might siesta all afternoon.

Buses run from Tripoli to Dimitsana (2 per day, 1½hr., 1100dr), and from Dimitsana to Tripoli (3 per day, 1hr., 1500dr). There are buses leaving for Tripoli, Pirgos, and Olympia from **Karkalou,** a 20-minute (1500dr) taxi ride away.

There's one hotel in town, the pretty but pricey **Hotel Dimitsana** (tel. (0795) 37 578), on the road to Stemnitsa (singles 8000dr; doubles 10,500dr; breakfast included). A better option is the **Enoikiazomena Domatia** off the main square. To find it, turn right on Grigoriou St. where the main road bears left. Their rooms are large, have kitchens and bathrooms, and afford spectacular views of the copper-roofed chapels and red-tiled roofs of Dimitsana (singles 5000dr; doubles 7000dr).

From Dimitsana, hike 11km along the road through perfumed wildflowers (or shell out 1000dr for a cab) to **Stemnitsa,** a perfect honeymoon location with beautiful homes, sun-dappled squares, and lovely restaurants. Completing the fantasy is a gorgeous hotel on the main road, **Hotel Triokolonion** (tel. (0795) 81 297; singles 6000dr; doubles 8000dr). The **post office** (tel. 81 280) is behind the church in the square (**postal code** 22024; open daily 7:30am-2pm). From among the squares' numerous cafes and tavernas, consider the tiny **Taverna Klinitsa** (tel. 81 438) for an inexpensive treat. Here Mama Roilos serves up original dishes, specializing in creative vegetarian fare (*fasolacia* 600dr, *briam* 500dr). If you're lucky, you may get to try Mama's special fried bread on the house. On the other side of the square, **Stemnitsa Bakery** (tel. 81 373) has great desserts (300dr), rumored to be aphrodisiacs.

Off the road from Dimitsana to Stemnitsa are several monasteries, some built right into the mountain face. One of these is the **Monastery of Agios Ioannis Prodromos,** 12km from Dimitsana. The road goes from asphalt to dirt, and finally becomes a foot-path on the mountain. Here you can see the icons painted on the bare stone walls and monastic cells almost defying gravity as they hang off the mountain. It is now inhabited by only twelve monks (open dawn-dusk to modestly dressed visitors; free, though a small donation is expected).

MESSENIA ΜΕΣΣΗΝΙΑ

An oasis in the arid Peloponnese, Messenia is a refreshing stop for travelers. Olives, figs, and grapes spring from the rich soil on the region's rocky coastline, which remains largely tourist-free. Most Messenians live at the head of the gulf, around sprawling Kalamata, a convenient town from which to tour Mani's west coast. More alluring is the port town of Pylos, strategically located for bus, moped, and car travel to Koroni, Methoni, and the beaches of the south.

■ Kalamata ΚΑΛΑΜΑΤΑ

Kalamata, the second largest city in the Peloponnese, flourishes as a port and beach resort. It was here that the Greek War of Independence began in 1821. On March 23, two days before the official start of the war, a group of Kalamatans, impatient to end Ottoman rule, massacred the enemy while they slept. The event is commemorated each year with a reenactment of the Greek victory, parades, and dancing. Today Kala-mata is pleasant, but there is little to merit a long stay.

ORIENTATION AND PRACTICAL INFORMATION

Kalamata sprawls inland from its long beachfront lined with hotels, restaurants, and tourist shops. Behind the beach, the city can be divided into three sections. Closest to the water is a residential section distinguished by the municipal park. Next is the cen-tral square, with the train station and most amenities. Finally, the old town, with its castle, market, and bus station, is 3km from the beach. Navigation from one end to the other can be very confusing, and you should get a map from the tourist police.

Navarinov Street runs along the water. Perpendicular to it, but never actually intersecting it, is **Aristomenous Street**, running along the park and then through **Georgiou Square,** the heart of downtown. Kalamata's efficient blue bus route can get you anyplace you need to go for 200dr. To get to the main stop from the intercity bus terminal, walk with the river bed on your left and cross at the second bridge you encounter. Continue straight for three blocks to 25 Martinou Sq.

Tourist Police: (tel. 95 555) Located in the port on Miaouli St., on the 2nd floor of a yellow building. They distribute an invaluable map. Open daily 7:30am-9:30pm. The regular police (tel. 22 622; open 24hr.) are located in Georgiou Sq. on Aris-tomenous St. The **port police** (tel. 22 218) are on the harbor near the tourist police in the blue building.

Bank: National Bank (tel. 28 047), on Aristomenous St., off the north end of Geor-giou Sq., and on Akrita St. at the waterfront. Both offer **currency exchange.** Open Mon.-Thurs. 8am-2pm, Fri. 8am-1:30pm. 24hr. **ATMs** at both locations.

Flights: To Athens daily at 9:25pm (30min., 12,700dr, under 24 10,800dr). **Olympic Airways,** 17 Sideromikou Stathmou St. (tel. 22 376), just before train station. Open daily 8am-3:30pm. Taxis to the airport (6km from town, near Messini) cost about 1500dr. From the KTEL station, catch a bus to Messini.

Trains: (tel. 95 056) Station at the end of Sideromikou Stathmou St. Turn right on Frantzi St. at the end of Georgiou Sq. and walk a few blocks. Cheap but slow. To: Athens (4 per day, 5:30am-3:40pm, 7hr., 2400dr) via Tripoli (2½hr., 840dr); Argos

(4hr., 1300dr); Corinth (5¼hr., 1700dr); Kyparissia (2hr., 600dr); Pirgos (3¼hr., 860dr); Patras (5½hr., 1500dr); and Olympia (3 hr., 900dr).

Buses: (tel. 28 581) Station provides info daily 7am-10pm. To: Athens (11 per day, 4hr., 3950dr) via Megalopolis (1hr., 950dr); Tripoli (2hr., 1450dr); the Corinth Isthmus (3hr., 2800dr); Patras (2 per day, 4hr., 3800dr) via Pirgos (2hr., 2800dr); Sparta (2 per day, 2hr., 1000dr) via Artemisia (30min., 400dr); Mavromati (2 per day, 1hr., 400dr); and Koroni (8 per day, 1½hr., 850dr). Some continue to Methoni (2 per day, 2hr., 1000dr) and Finikountas (2 per day, 2½hr., 1250dr). For Areopolis and Gythion, go via Itilo (4 per day, 2hr., 1250dr) and change buses for Areopolis (15min., 220dr) or Gythion (1½hr., 400dr).

City Bus: Depart from the bus depot near 25 Martiou Sq. Take the #1, which goes down Aristomenous Sq., then turns to run along the water, winding up at the waterfront or camping areas (200dr). Open daily 8am-10pm.

Moped Rental: Alpha Rental (tel. 93 423), Vironos St. Mopeds 3500dr per day. Near waterfront and open daily 8am-8pm. Also **Verga Rent-A-Car,** 202 Faron St. (tel. 95 190). Mopeds 3000dr per day. Open 10:30am-2pm and 6:30-10pm.

Taxi Service: (tel. 22 522) A ride to the campsites from the city costs 500dr.

Pharmacies: Places line Aristomenous St. Most open 8am-2pm and 5:30-9pm. For 24hr. pharmacy information, dial 100.

Hospital: Athinou St. (tel. 85 203).

Medical Emergency: Call 25 555.

Post Office: 4 Iatropolou St. (tel. 22 810), follow this street from the south end of Georgiou Sq. Another branch on the waterfront at the port next to the tourist police. Both are open Mon.-Fri. 7:30am-2pm. **Postal Code:** 24100.

OTE: Georgiou Sq., opposite the National Bank. Open daily 7am-9:30pm.

Telephone Code: 0721.

ACCOMMODATIONS

Most of Kalamata's hotels are on the waterfront. Accommodations abound, but rooms to let are uncommon here.

Hotel Nevada, 9 Santa Rosa (tel. 82 429), one block back from the water. Take bus #1 and get off as soon as it turns left along the water. Tons, and we mean *tons,* of potted plants inside and outside, on tables and posters. Singles 3000dr; doubles 4000dr; triples 6000dr.

Pension Avra, 10 Santa Rosa (tel. 82 759). Hard wood floors, shared bath, and kitchen. Singles 5000dr; doubles 7000dr; triples 10,000dr.

Hotel George (tel. 27 225), right near the train station. Clean, convenient, and cute. Singles 5000dr; doubles 6000dr.

Hotel Palace (tel. 93 924) is for anyone who craves a view of the sea. On Navarinou St., it has big rooms with shared bath. Singles 5000dr; doubles 8000dr.

Hotel Byzantian (tel. 86 824), on Sideromikou Stathmou just before the train station. Simple rooms, some with double beds, bath tubs, and balconies. Singles 5000dr; doubles 6000dr.

Camping Maria's Sea and Sun (tel. 41 060) is luxurious for a campsite. Take bus #1 east past the other campsites. Hot showers included. 1300dr per person; 800dr per car; 800dr per small tent; 1000dr per large tent; electricity 800dr.

FOOD AND ENTERTAINMENT

Before leaving town, sample the famous Kalamata olives and figs. The immense **New Market,** just across the bridge from the bus station, is a collection of meat, cheese, and fruit shops, as well as a daily farmer's market. It's a perfect place to assemble an inexpensive picnic. Great sit-down meals can be found along the waterfront. **Taverna Tzamaika** (tel. 24 940) is the best of the waterfront *tavernas,* but also the farthest (2km) away. It has its own outdoor oven, a large collection of farm implements that appear to have lingered since the Agricultural Revolution, and even a horse. Grilled lamb (1400dr) and stuffed tomatoes (900dr) get rave reviews. **Tampaki Restaurant** (tel. 23 225) is closer to town than Tzamaika, and serves good food at reasonable prices (*moussaka* 1100dr, stuffed vine leaves 1200dr; open for dinner around

7pm). **Exociko Kentro** (tel. 22 016), with a seating area over the beach, serves a mean lamb and potatoes (1400dr), veal (1500dr), and Greek salad (1000dr).

Nightlife in Kalamata revolves around the beach scene. Unfortunately the beach bar strip (1km east of the port) lacks some of the over-the-top fun that other cities boast. Expect lots of umbrellas and subdued techno music. Kalamata's newest disco, **Palladium**, costs a small fortune (cover 1200dr, including one drink), and is not to be confused with **The Million Dollars Club**, housed in the same building (it hosts strippers). Palladium attracts great crowds, but more moderately priced clubs surround it.

SIGHTS

Only a few sights remain in Kalamata. The **Castle of the Villehardouins**, which crowns a hill above the old city, has survived despite a violent history. Built by the Franks in 1208, it was blown up by the Ottomans in 1685 and restored by the Venetians a decade later. It was damaged in the 1986 earthquake and is still being repaired today. The castle houses an open-air theater which hosts "Cultural Summer of Kalamata" in July and August, with everything from jazz and rock to classical Greek drama (ticket prices average 2000dr). To get to the gates from 23 Martiou Sq., walk up Ipapandis St. past the church on the right side and take your first left. At the foot of the castle is the **Convent of St. Constantine and Helen**, where nuns sell their linen and lacework at bargain prices. At the far end of the site is the **Byzantine Church** where a doe-eyed Virgin Mary icon was found, giving the city its name, which means "good eyes" (open daily 8am-dusk; free). Also in the old city is the **Benaki Museum**, which displays local archaeological finds (open Tues.-Sun. 8am-2:30pm). There are also remains of a Byzantine church at the far edge of the site—scramble up for a sublime view (open daily 8am-dusk). At 221 Faron St., off the waterfront, Kalamata's **School of Fine Arts** exhibits work by Greek artists (open daily 9am-1pm and 6-10pm). Kalamata also supports two professional theaters and cinemas. Ask the **tourist police** for information on events in the **Pantazopoulion Cultural Center** on Aristomenon St.

Kalamata has had considerable success cleaning up its beaches. They are increasingly less crowded as you go eastward. With large shady trees, cafes, a performance area, and a duck pond, the **Train Park** (at the end of Aristomenous St., closer to the waterfront) extends several blocks toward Georgiou Sq. The main attraction are an old train station which has been converted into an ice cream parlor, and antique trains on the tracks.

■ Near Kalamata

For more antiquities, take the bus from Kalamata to **Mavromati** (2 per day, Mon.-Sat., 1hr., 400dr) to the well-preserved remains of **Ancient Messene** on Mt. Ithomi. The striking 4th-century BC wall is characteristic of the period's defensive architecture. An **agora, theater,** and **Temple to Artemis** also remain. Up the road is the fallen doorpost of the colossal **Arcadian Gate**, designed by Epaminondas, the architect of Megalopolis. Nearby is the 16th-century **Monastery of the Vourkano**, with some great frescoes. The only difficulty with this trip is the timing. If you want more than 15 minutes at the site, catch the morning bus and return on the post-Petralona leg of the evening bus, or take a taxi (4000dr). The road from Koroni to Kalamata hugs the east coast of the Messenian peninsula. Between Harokopi and the coastal town of **Petalidio** is a chain of beaches. **Koroni** is a pleasant fishing village with a long sand beach and a castle of its very own. Unfortunately, it is connected by bus only to Kalamata, making it difficult to reach. Pleasant **Koroni Camping** (tel. (0725) 22 119) is an option (1200dr per person; 600dr per car; 1000dr per tent).

■ Taygetus Mountains

South of Kalamata, the bus to Areopolis winds through the Taygetus Mountains, which soar to 2630m at their highest point. The alluring gray peaks of Mani loom behind olive-covered hillsides. The first major bus stop comes at the coastal village of

Kardamili. With its distinctive stone houses and long white pebble beaches, Kardamili is attracting more and more visitors. It doesn't feel like a tourist trap, and it's still possible to enjoy the charming town on a budget. The bus drops passengers off on the main road. At the Kalamata end there is a well-stocked **supermarket** and **bakery.** The road past the church leads to the main square. Beyond is the **post office** (open Mon.-Fri. 7:30am-2:30pm). Kardamili's **police station** (tel. 73 209) is on the main road further toward Itilo (open 24hr.). **Telephone Code:** 0721.

"Rooms to Let" signs are everywhere, but *domatia* can be expensive, especially those with a view. Follow signs across from the police station to **Olivia Koumanakou**'s tidy pension with a communal kitchen (tel. 73 623; singles 2500dr; doubles 5000dr). For good food with a beautiful waterfront view try the family-run **Taverna Kiki,** downhill from the main square (veal and potatoes 1150dr, rabbit 1200dr). To get to the beach, walk toward Kalamata from the main square and turn left at the signs for **Camping Melitsana,** 1.5km down the beach (tel. 73 461; 1150dr per person; 950dr per small tent; 1050dr per large tent; 650dr per car; 700dr for electricity). Buses go to Kalamata from Kardamili (5 per day, 1½hr., 650dr).

If you're bound for Areopolis, change buses in the village of **Itilo** immediately upon arrival—the bus leaves promptly. The frescoed **Monastery of Dekoulo** and the 17th-century Ottoman **fortress** are poised on a nearby hill. The entertainment consists of two cafes off the small square and a reasonably priced restaurant. The bus continues 3km down to the magnificent **Neo Itilo.** At the heart of an enormous natural bay encircled by monumental barren mountains, the white pebble beach is ideal for swimming. From Neo Itilo, the road winds uphill, affording a view of **Limani,** the old harbor of Areopolis. The tiny port is home to the Mavromichaeli **Castle of Potrombei.** From here, buses continue to Areopolis. Bad roads make this ride as much fun as putting your stomach through the spin cycle, but the views are rewarding.

▓ Pylos ΠΥΛΟΣ

Pylos does not boast any particular tourist attractions and perhaps for this reason is the perfect place to feel the undisturbed life of a Greek town. Steep stairways lead up from the waterfront square, and flower-laden buildings line the narrow streets. Pylos harbor has a unique silhouette marked by the perpendicular cliffs of Sfakteria Island. The town prides itself on the 1827 Battle of Navarino. As Ottoman forces battered the coast, English, French, and Russian fleets arrived and sunk the invaders' battalions.

ORIENTATION AND PRACTICAL INFORMATION

The **police** (tel. 22 316) are located on the second floor of a building on the left side of the waterfront (English spoken; open 24hr.). Continue around that turn to reach the **port police** (tel. 22 225). The **tourist police** (tel. 23 733) are in the same building (open daily 8am-2pm). The **post office** (tel. 22 247) is on Nileos St., uphill to the left (facing the water) from the bus station (open Mon.-Fri. 7:30am-2pm). A **National Bank** is on the main square (open Mon.-Thurs. 8am-2pm, Fri. 8am-1:30pm). To get to the **hospital** (tel. 22 315), take the road right of the square (open 24hr.). **Buses** (tel. 22 230) to Kalamata (9 per day, 1½hr., 850dr), Athens (2 per day, 6½hr., 4850dr); and Finikountas (4 per day, 1hr., 400dr) via Methoni (5 per day, 15min., 210dr). No buses travel directly to Koroni, but you can go to Finikountas and take a bus from there to Horokorio, the nearest stop to Koroni. Buses also leave for Kyparissia (5 per day, 1½hr., 1000dr), all stopping at Nestor's Palace (40min., 360dr) and Chora (45min., 360dr). **Auto Europe** (tel. 22 393) has a monopoly on **moped rentals** and as a result their prices are steep (5000dr per day; open 8am-1:30pm and 5:30-9pm). To get to the **OTE** (tel. 22 399), pass the post office and take your first left; then turn right (open Mon.-Fri. 7:30am-3:10pm). **Postal Code:** 24001. **Telephone Code:** 0723.

ACCOMMODATIONS AND FOOD

There are several "Rooms to Let" signs as the bus descends the hill. In general, expect to pay 3500-5000dr for singles, 4500-7000dr for doubles, and 5000-8000dr for triples. Try the large white rooms of **Terma Manakiov** (tel. 22 953), whose shared bathroom has spectacular views of the water. Another option is the **Pension** (tel. 22 748), just before the OTE, offering high-ceilinged rooms with private baths (singles 400dr; doubles 5000dr). **Navarino Beach Camping** (tel. 22 761) lies 6km north at Yialova Beach (1100dr per person; 800dr per small tent; 1000dr per large tent; electricity 600dr).

Many restaurants along the waterfront offer *taverna* staples and a beautiful view of the sunset over the turquoise water. **Ta Adelpha** (tel. 22 564), around the bend past the police station, is a little removed from the rest of the pack and offers an especially striking view and a traditional menu (*tzalziki* 550dr, *pasizzio* 950dr). Uphill from the main square, **La Plaza** is a haven for those seeking a non-*taverna* menu. Both pasta and pizza are delicious. Opens at 6:30pm for dinner (pasta 700-900dr; pizza 1300dr.)

SIGHTS

Fortresses guard both sides of Pylos' harbor. **Neokastro,** to the south, is easily accessible from the town; walk up the road to Methoni and turn right at the sign. The well-preserved walls enclose a church (originally a mosque), a citadel, and a collection of European Philhellene paintings. (Open Tues.-Sun. 8:30am-3pm. Admission 800dr, senior citizens 400dr, students free.) The **archaeological museum,** located just before the castle on the road to Methoni, houses finds from Hellenistic and Mycenaean tombs (Tel. 22 448 for both castle and museum. Open Tues.-Sun. 8:30am-3pm. Admission 500dr, students free.) The **Paleokastro,** north of Pylos, is harder to reach. The tourist police say making the dangerous trip is not worth the badly preserved remains. If you are undaunted, however, check with them for instructions (you must have transportation). To see **Sfakteria** up close, you can take a **boat tour** from the port. The hour jaunt around the island stops at various monuments to the allied sailors of the Battle of Navarino and shows off a sunken Ottoman ship. Boat captains try to organize groups for tours (roughly 10 people). Inquire at the small booth on the waterfront or at the neighboring coffee bar under the police station, where the captains often rest. The cost is 10,000dr for four people. The ride takes 90 minutes.

■ Near Pylos

In the Mycenaean world, Pylos was second only to Mycenae in economic prosperity and cultural breadth. The **palace** at Pylos, where Nestor met Telemachus in Homer's *Odyssey,* was built in the 13th century BC. The site is still being excavated and consists of three buildings. The main building, possibly the king's residence, originally had a second floor (and walls) with official and residential quarters and storerooms. To the southwest, archaeologists think that an older, smaller palace stood. To the northeast lie the ruins of a complex of isolated workshops and more storerooms. Important finds from Nestor's Palace are **Linear B tablets** explaining some of its administrative operations, jewelry, bronze objects, and ivory knick-knacks. Most are on display in the National Archaeological Museum in Athens (see p.84). Bring your own water. The site is covered and provides ample shade; but touring it does not fill all the time between buses. Bring a book, or read the University of Cincinnati's scholarly *Guide to Nestor's Palace* (500dr), available at the entrance. (Tel. (0763) 31 437, -358. Open Tues.-Sun. 8:30am-3pm. Admission 500dr, students free.)

■ Methoni ΜΕΘΩΝΗ

With its hibiscus-lined streets, Methoni is a refreshing reprieve for the weary traveler. Peer through the flowering trees at the spectacular 13th-century **fortress** along the beach. Forever "the Camelot of Greece," Methoni was once offered by Agamemnon to Achilles to cheer the sulking warrior. Cervantes was so taken with the place that he churned out romances even while imprisoned under Ottoman guard.

The town's two main streets form a "Y" where the Pylos-Finikountas buses stop. The beach is at the end of the lower street, and a little beachfront square is to the left. To get to the castle follow the upper street to the water. The **police** (tel. (0723) 31 203; open 24hr.) are near the bus station on the upper street, just past the bank. The **National Bank** is 40m down the right fork (open Mon.-Thurs. 8am-2pm, Fri. 8am-1:30pm). **Buses** go to Athens (7 per day, 5hr., 4900dr) via Pylos (15min., 210dr) and Kalamata (1hr., 1000dr). Another bus goes to Finikountas (4 per day, ½hr., 300dr). You can get bus information in the supermarket just across from the bus stop at the "Y," and catch connections to the rest of the Peloponnese in Pylos or Kalamata. The **post office** is open Mon.-Fri. 7:30am-2pm. **Postal Code:** 24006. The **OTE** (open Mon.-Fri. 7:30am-3:10pm) is difficult to find. It's a cream colored building with blue shutters. Go down the lower fork and turn left going toward the beachside square.

Hotel Giota (tel. (0723) 31 290, -1), offers clean, air-conditioned rooms on the beachside square (singles 5000dr; doubles 7000dr). There are dozens of "Rooms to Let" signs along both forks of the "Y." **Hotel Dionysus** (tel. 31 317), accessible from either fork, has rooms with private baths and beautiful white moldings (singles 4000dr; doubles 6000dr). **Camping Methoni** (tel. (0723) 31 228) is crowded but on the sea (950dr per person; 550dr per car; 650dr per small tent; 850dr per large tent).

No visitor to the southwest Peloponnese should miss Methoni's **Venetian fortress,** a 13th-century mini-city. Venture behind the fortified gate onto a windswept field of low shrubs that sticks out into the sea. Waves crash against the sand colored Ottoman buildings. At the tip a narrow bridge leads to an islet and its chapel. Views and wild-flowers are spectacular (open daily 8:30am-7pm, Sun. 9am-7pm).

■ Near Methoni: Finikountas ΦΟΙΝΙΚΟΥΝΤΑΣ

Halfway between Methoni and Koroni, Finikountas, a colorful fishing village, coaxes visitors to bask in sunshine and watch colorful *caïques* glide across the surface. For swimming, take the time to go to **Paradise Beach,** the cove beyond the rock jetty to the east. If you stay, change money in advance: Finikountas has neither a bank nor a post office. The **Supermarket Phoenix** sells stamps and houses an **OTE** (open daily 7am-1pm and 5-9pm). **Bus transportation** from Finikountas to anywhere but Kala-mata is tricky to figure out. The bus stops across from the Hotel Finikounta, but there is no station, so check out times. Buses go to Kalamata (3 per day, 2hr., 210dr). Some Kalamata buses go west via Methoni, but most go east stopping at Horokorio (30min.), the closest stop to Koroni. Check with drivers about routes. Look for **"Rooms to Let"** signs on the waterfront or on the road from Koroni as you enter town. Most restaurateurs either rent rooms or know who does. For a large room with a private bath, try asking at **Taverna Vasso** (tel. 0793 71 242), where singles are 5000dr and doubles 6000dr.

LACONIA ΛΑΚΩΝΙΑ

In the 10th century BC, a tribe of Doric warriors from the north invaded the south-west Peloponnese, drove out its Mycenaean inhabitants, and executed stragglers unlucky enough to get in their way. Famed for slaughtering their enemies, the region's new masters also distinguished themselves by their curt speech. While their northern counterparts argued in flowery rhetoric, Laconians often dispatched their opponents with a single, witty phrase. Thus, the reticent became "laconic." The ancient Laconian qualities are still manifest throughout the area, especially in the bar-ren peninsula. Although Laconia boasts three of the Peloponnese's most popular sites—Mani's Pirgos Dirou caves, Sparta's nearby Byzantine ruins of Mystra, and Mon-emvassia's "rock"—the region remains low-key. Laconia's friendly villages are a wel-come break from the urban atmosphere of other, more touristy areas.

▓ Sparta ΣΠΑΡΤΗ

The Spartans are often portrayed as the bad guys of the classical world—totalitarian war-mongers who insisted on pestering the civilized Athenian democrats. These stereotypes, however simplistic, hold true even today. Sparta's reputation for brutal, nononsense militarism is well deserved. Around 700 BC, after Sparta barely subdued a revolt of the Messenians, the leader Lycurgus instituted reforms that transformed Sparta into a war machine. For the next 350 years, it dominated the entire central Peloponnese with its invincible armies and austere discipline. Outside of war, Sparta contributed little to Greek history—no philosophy, art, or architecture is remembered from here. Weary of Athenian expansion, Sparta attacked, beginning the 28-year-long Peloponnesian War. After triumphing in 404 BC, Sparta emerged as *the* military power in the Hellenic world. The Spartans reveled in their power, not even bothering to build walls around the city. Only the combined effects of earthquakes, depopulation, and resistance of its neighbors broke Sparta's hegemony.

In their quiet city, today's Spartans prefer to make olive oil, not war. A few buildings and an abundance of orange trees challenge the Great Asphalt Conspiracy, but modern Sparta goes about its business, making little effort to win over the occasional tourist. Still, Sparta is the best and most convenient base from which to explore the Byzantine ruins of Mystra, only 6km away.

ORIENTATION AND PRACTICAL INFORMATION

Sparta is laid out in an appropriately spartan grid. Sparta's two main streets, **Paleologou** and **Lykourgou,** intersect in the center of town. To get to the center from the bus station, walk west on Lykourgou for about 10 blocks. The town square is one block to the right of the intersection on Lykourgou, and all of the necessary amenities are on these two streets. The ruins are on the north edge of town.

Tourist Office: (tel. 24 852) To the left of the town hall in the square. English spoken and very helpful. Bus schedules, hotels, and information. Map 400dr. Open daily 8am-2pm.

Banks: National Bank (tel. 26 200), on the corner of Dioskouron and Paleologou, 3 blocks down from the intersection, offers **currency exchange.** Open Mon.-Thurs. 8am-2pm, Fri. 8am-1:30pm. Other banks line Paleologou. An ATM (Cirrus and MC) is located on Dioskouron.

Buses: (tel. 26 441), walk down Lykourgou, museum-side away from the square. Continue past the fire station until the road peters out—it's on your right, 1500m from the center of town. Buses go to Athens (9 per day, 3hr., 3450dr), via Corinth (2hr., 2250dr) and Tripoli (1hr., 950dr). Buses also head to Neapolis (2-4 per day, 2½hr., 2350dr); Monemvassia (2-3 per day, 2hr., 1700dr); Pirgos Dirou and the caves (1 per day, 1½hr., 1350dr) via Areopolis (2 per day, 1½hr., 1150dr); Kalamata (2 per day, 2hr., 950dr); Gerolimenas (2 per day, 3hr., 1700dr); and Gythion (5 per day, 1hr., 750dr). For buses to Mystra, the station is at the corner of Leonidou and Kythonigou 2 blocks past the town hall (every 1½hr., 6:50am-8:20pm, 210dr). The schedule varies; call the tourist office to check.

Pharmacies: 117 Paleologou St. (tel. 27 212). Open daily 8am-2pm and 5:30-9pm. Three other pharmacies on Paleologou St. and many more throughout the city.

Hospital: (tel. 28 671, -5), Nosokomeio St. (Hospital St.), 1km to the north of Sparta. Open 24hr.

Police: 8 Hilonos St. (tel. 26 229). From the intersection, turn left on Lykourgou St. away from the square. The police are on a side street to the right, a block past the museum. Open 24hr. Helpful, earnest, English-speaking **tourist police** (tel. 20 492) are housed in the same building. Open daily 8am-3pm and 7-9pm.

Police Emergency: Dial 100.

Post Office: (tel. 26 565) On Arhidamou off Lykourgou, 5 blocks before the intersection. Open Mon.-Fri. 7:30am-2pm. **Postal Code:** 23100.

OTE: 11 Kleombrotou St., off Lykourgou (tel. 23 799). Open Mon.-Fri. 7am-9:40pm. **Telephone Code:** 0731.

ACCOMMODATIONS

Among Paleologous's numerous mid-range hotels, a bargain is hard to find, but TVs and a private bath are not. The cheapest place to stay is the **Hotel Panellinion** (tel. 28 031), just past the Lykourgou intersection, with minimalist but high-ceilinged rooms, balconies, and shared bathrooms (singles 4000dr; doubles 6000dr). Or try **Hotel Cecil** (tel. 24 980), five blocks north on the corner of Paleologou St. and Thermopilion St. Lemon yellow inside and out, you'll spot this small, adorable hotel from down the block (singles 5000dr; doubles 8000dr). The **Hotel Laconia** (tel. 28 952), also on Paleologou St., offers attractive dark wood furniture, TVs, and even shower curtains (singles 5000dr; doubles 7000dr)! Near Mystra is the new **Camping Castle View** (tel. 83 303), with pool, modern showers and toilets, and a mini-market (1200dr per person; 700dr per car; 700dr per small tent; 1000dr per large tent; electricity 700dr). To get to the campground, take the regular Mystra bus and ask the driver to let you off at the signs.

FOOD AND ENTERTAINMENT

Sparta's few restaurants serve expensive fast food. For a reasonably priced meal under the fluorescent lights of **Dhiethnes** (tel. 28 636), head to the far right of the main square. Also called **Restaurant in the Garden,** it offers good vegetarian food (700dr per plate). A grill called **O Finikas** (tel. 24 126) is across from the Hotel Cecil on Paleologou St. (*tzatziki* 400dr). At night, bop 2.5km down the road towards Gythion to the **Aithrio Disco.** The **Imago,** a hip, artsy bar, is in the alley behind the town hall and offers a gay-friendly atmosphere (open daily 10pm-3am).

SIGHTS

There is almost nothing left of ancient Sparta to clue us in to the people who lived there. At the north end of Paleologou St. stands an enormous **statue of Leonidas,** the famous warrior king of the Spartans. The Spartans built a large pseudo-tomb for their leader, who fell at the Battle of Thermopylae in 480 BC, in hopeful anticipation of his remains, which were never found. The tomb lies in the middle of a grove that is now a public park, to the left of the ancient ruins. The ruins themselves lie to the north of the modern city (facing the statue of Leonidas; bear left). The ruins (1km from the main square at the north edge of the modern city) consist of the outlines of one of the larger theaters of ancient Greece and some fragments of the acropolis.

Finding surrounding ruins may be a bit of a challenge. Before you set out, ask the tourist police for a hand-drawn map. Five kilometers away are three remaining platforms of the **shrine to Menelaus and Helen,** history's most sought-after beauty. The remains of the Spartans' **shrine to Apollo** are on the road to Gythion. A short walk

---

A Hard-Knock Life

A young Spartan's training for a life of war began early, even before conception. Lycurgus believed two fit parents produced stronger offspring, so he ordered all Spartan women to undergo the same rigorous training endured by men. Furthermore, newlyweds were permitted only an occasional tryst on the theory that the heightened desire of the parents would produce more robust children. If they weren't winnowed out as weak or deformed, boys began a severe regimen of training under an adult Spartan. The young were forced to walk barefoot to toughen their feet and wore only a simple piece of clothing in both summer and winter to expose them to drastic weather changes. The Spartan creed dictated that young men be guarded against temptations of any kind—strict laws forbidding everything from drinking to pederasty governed Spartans' actions. Moreover, young Spartans were given the plainest and simplest foods for fear that rich delicacies would stunt their growth. One visitor to Sparta, upon sampling the fare, allegedly quipped, "Now I know why they do not fear death."

east on the banks of the Eurotas River leads to the **sanctuary of Artemis Orthia.** Spartan youths had to prove their courage here by unflinchingly enduring public floggings. Headless statues beckon you to enter the **archaeological museum** (tel. 28 575), through its beautiful, well-kept park on Lykourgou St. (on the opposite side of Paleologou from the square). The collection includes spooky votive masks used in ritual dances at the sanctuary of Artemis Orthia, and a bronze boar which bristles in the room to the left of the entrance. Especially impressive are the "unpublished" mosaics from the Roman period (open Tues.-Sun. 8:30am-2:30pm; admission 500dr, students 300dr). For modern art, visit the **National Art Gallery,** 123 Paleologou St. (tel. 81 557; English not spoken). The permanent collection of 19th-century French and Dutch paintings is unusual for this part of the world. On the second floor are exhibits of watercolors by modern Greek artists (open Tues.-Sat. 9am-3pm, Sun. 10am-2pm; free).

For an evening excursion from Sparta, share a cab to the village of **Paroli,** 2km from Mystra. There you can sit in a *taverna* and watch the nearby waterfalls. Two kilometers farther is the village of **Tripi,** which has larger waterfalls, some of which run right under the excellent grill-restaurant **Exochiko Kentro** (tel. 98 314).

■ Near Sparta: Mystra ΜΥΣΤΡΑΣ

The extraordinary medieval ruins of Mystra (tel. (0731) 83 377) stand 6km west of Sparta. Overflowing with Byzantine churches and castle ruins, this site reveals the splendor of Byzantium's final flourish. In the late 14th century, Mystra, prospering from a lucrative silk industry, became an intellectual center. Many free thinkers, unhappy under the control of repressive feudal lords and clergy, surged into town and set up schools, tying Mystra to the Florentine humanist movement. Philosophers and students wandered the intricate network of paths that weaves the city together and today renders sightseeing a complex affair. Try tracing a path around several key sites on the three tiers that correspond to the sectors for the commoners, the nobility, and the royalty (in ascending order, naturally). Fortunately, Mystra is one of the better-labeled sites in Greece. Ask the bus driver to let you off at the **Kastro entrance.** This way you can make your way down the mountain instead of up. Aside from campsites, digs at Mystra are pricey—visit from Sparta.

The castle was Mystra's first building (the town developed downward), built by the crusader Guillaume de Villehardouin in 1249 AD. Don't miss the **Metropolis of St. Demetrios** in the lower tier, with its sanctuary and museum of architectural fragments. Wander on to the two churches of the monastery of **Vrontochion, St. Theodori,** and the **Aphentiko** (Hodegetria) with its magnificent two-story frescoes. On the same tier is the **Pantanassa,** a convent with a beautifully ornamented facade and a multitude of frescoes, not to mention a miracle-working Virgin Mary icon. Finally, at the extreme left of the lower tier, the **Church of Perivleptos** is perhaps Mystra's most stunning relic; every inch of the church is bathed in exquisitely detailed religious paintings, most of which were vandalized by invading Ottomans.

There are water taps inside the entrance through the main gate, at the Metropolis and at Pantanassa, but it's a good idea to bring your own water to combat Mystra's heat. Also, wear tough shoes—many of the paths are rocky. You'll enjoy Mystra more with a guidebook and a good map. Manolis Chatzidakis' *Mystras* is the best (2000dr). Even a cursory look at the site requires at least three hours, including the long climb to the top. Be warned: it's been years since bathrooms at the site were in working condition. In summer, try to be at the site by 8am, since the sun becomes unbearable as early as 10am. (Site open daily 8am-7pm in summer, 8:30am-3pm in winter. Admission 1200dr, students 600dr.) The site is 1.5km past the town.

MANI ΜΑΝΗ

Mani broke off from Sparta during the Roman Period and founded the League of Laconians. They ferociously resisted foreign rule, thereby gaining the name "Maniotes" (from the Greek *mania* or fury). Old Mani is best characterized as the Greek version of *The Godfather*'s Sicily—vendettas, organized crime, the works. Ultimately, the Maniotes' obstinacy paid off, as even today Maniotes boast that not a single Ottoman set foot on Mani soil. Today, Maniot culture has softened. Although they revel in their historical ferocity, the inhabitants make excellent hosts to visitors seeking beautiful beaches and views. The sparsely settled territory stoically circles the cinnamon-brown Taygetus Mountains, which border the sea. Towering buildings add muted greys and greens to the stark landscape.

▓ Gythion ΓΥΘΕΙΟ

The "Gateway to the Mani," Gythion, in the Northeast corner of the territory, has a more colorful and lively feel than the bleak but dramatic land to the south. Bright fishing boats bustle in and out of the port and dockside restaurants hang strings of octopuses out to dry. A causeway connects Gythion to the tiny island **Marathonisi,** where Paris and Helen consummated their ill-fated love. Beautiful sand and stone beaches are within easy walking distance, and this is the only city in the area where you can rent a motorbike to explore the hard-to-reach Mani on your own.

ORIENTATION AND PRACTICAL INFORMATION

The bus stop is on the north side of the waterfront. Small **Mavromichali Square** is in the middle of the waterfront near the quay. The harbor road continues to the right, where it eventually meets the causeway to Marathonisi. The **police** (tel. 22 100) are on the waterfront, halfway between the bus station and Mavromichali Sq. (English spoken; open 24hr). Before the causeway, past the square, you will find the **port police** (tel. 22 262). The post office and the OTE are both inland from the bus station. The **post office** (tel. 22 285) is on Ermou St. (open Mon.-Fri. 7:30am-2pm), and the **OTE** (tel. 22 799) is at the corner of Herakles and Kapsali St. (open Mon.-Fri. 7:30am-3:10pm). The **National Bank** (tel. 22 313), just beyond the bus stop toward the water, offers **currency exchange** (open Mon.-Thurs. 8am-2pm, Fri. 8am-1:30pm). Its 24hr. **ATM** is hooked up to Cirrus, MasterCard, and Visa.

The **bus station** (tel. 22 228), is on the north end of the waterfront. Buses head to: Athens (6 per day, 4hr., 4150dr), via Sparta (1hr., 750dr); Kalamata, via Itilo (2 per day, 1hr., 650dr); Gerolimenas (daily, 2hr., 1000dr), via Areopolis (4 per day, 1hr., 450dr); and Pirgos Dirou (daily, 1¼hr., 450dr). Buses also go to the campgrounds (including Meltemi, Gythion Beach, and Mani) south of town (6am, 10:15am, 1pm, and 7pm; 200dr). **Ferries** which depart from the quay between Mavromichali Sq. and the causeway go to Kythera (daily, 2hr., 1535dr) and Crete (2 per week, 7½hr., 4560dr). Theodore V. Rozakis (tel. 22 6500), the **travel agency** on the waterfront near the square, provides information and tickets (open daily 7am-11pm). For **taxis,** call 23 423 (open 24hr.). **Moto Mani** (tel. 22 853), on the waterfront near the causeway, rents mopeds. The **health clinic** (tel. 22 001, -2, -3) is on the water near the causeway. The **postal code** is 23200. The **telephone code** is 0733.

ACCOMMODATIONS

Many hotels and *domatia* that look out at the sea are prohibitively expensive, but there are some inexpensive and charming ones. Gythion's **campgrounds** are an alternative to city lodging. All are about 3km south of town, toward Areopolis. The bus is infrequent, and a taxi costs about 900dr.

Xenia Karlafti's (tel. 22 719) rooms are on the water just 20m from the causeway. Rooms are spacious and manager provides a breakfast area and washing machine for her guests. Singles 3000dr; doubles 5000dr; triples 6000dr.

Koutsouri Rooms (tel. 22 321) is a little hard to find. From Mavromichali Sq., go up Tzanaki Gregoraki, turn right at the clock tower, look for a sign past the bakery on your left. At the gate, go past the (chained-up) dogs, and you're there. Singles 4000dr; doubles 6000dr. Show your *Let's Go* book to get these prices.

Domatia Leoridas (tel. 22 389), a beautiful pink building in the heart of the water-front, has large rooms with TVs and balconies. May look too rich for the blood of budget travelers, but for groups of three it offers a great deal. Triples 9000dr.

Meltemi (tel. 22 833). 1180dr per person; 700dr per car; 1000dr per tent; electricity 800dr.

Gytheio Bay Campgrounds (tel. 22 522), charges: 1200dr per person; 700dr per car; tent 800dr; electricity 700dr.

Mani Beach (tel. 23 450) charges: 1050dr per person; 600dr per car; small tent 750dr; large tent 950dr; electricity 700dr.

FOOD AND ENTERTAINMENT

The fish *tavernas* along the water are not cheap, but they also are not a great deal more expensive than the typical *tavernas;* you may decide a view of Moratorisi at sunset is worth the price. **Saga** (tel. 23 220), on the water between the causeway and the square, has deliciously prepared food and tables pulled right up to the water. You can watch the fish swim by after it gets dark. Crispy grilled and seasoned bread replaces the usual staple, and vegetarian salads are cheap. (Boiled zucchini 500dr, eggplant salad 500dr, fresh kalamari 1800dr.) **Taverna To Nisi** is a charming outdoor *taverna* on Mavothonisi islet just across from the church. Besides a pleasant stroll, from here you get a great view of Gythion's unique architecture (*tzaziki* 400dr, grilled chicken 1000dr, minnows 1000dr). Mavromichali Sq. is the perfect place for lunch or a cheap dinner. The **grill** inland from the plastic chairs serves a delicious gyro for 300dr. Across the street is a **fruit store. Fournos Bakery** (tel. 23 193), on Ermou St. near the PTT, is the best bakery in town. The waterfront is the place to be at night, where people stroll and drink all night. For a drink, try **Statos,** where the hip crowd hangs in the middle of the main strip.

SIGHTS

The ancient **theater** of Gythion, tucked away in a corner, has endured the centuries remarkably well. Note the differences between the seats for dignitaries in front and the simpler seats farther back. To get there, walk down Herakles St. from the bus sta-tion, go to Ermou St., and then right onto Archaiou Theatrou St. to its end. If you arrive in the early evening, join the soldiers getting their nightly pep talk here. **Paliat-zoures Antique Shop,** #25 on the waterfront (tel. 22 944), is a treat for window shop-pers and is easy to spot, because the natives spill onto the sidewalk. Everything is expensive, but the collection of household items, artwork, and furniture spans all of Greek history. Only items made after 1453 AD are exportable by law, but if you are looking to buy, don't worry—most stuff is from the 19th century. This store is the last of its kind in the Peloponnese (open 10am-2pm and 5-10pm).

The Museum of the Mani (tel. 22 676) is in a Maniot tower and hidden by pines on Mavothonisi Island. Its main exhibit offers photographs, maps, and lengthy English captions, but is a little disappointing because few primary sources are displayed. An English traveler from the 1800s proves that the nuisances of travel are timeless when he complains of "squadrons of fleas and bugs that marched zealously to battle." The museum is open daily 9:30am-9pm.

There is a **public beach** just north of the bus station, but the best beaches are north and south of town. Three kilometers to the south is the long, sandy beach of **Mavro-vouni,** with a high surf and a number of surfer bars (mixed drinks 900-1000dr, beer 500dr). Three kilometers north is rocky **Selinitsa,** which has earned accolades from the European Union for its clean water. This beach is at its prettiest beneath the Lakonis bungalows. Neither beach is accessible by bus—ride a moped, take a taxi (700dr), or hike. Farther north than Selinitsa (500m past the bungalows) is a sandy beach which houses the remains of an abandoned drug-runner's ship.

When traveling from Gythion to Areopolis, look for the Frankish **Castle of Pasava** on the right (roughly 10km down the road; tours available). Farther along, the **Castle of Kelefa** looks out to sea.

■ Areopolis ΑΡΕΟΠΟΛΗ

The sun feels too close in the blinding, bright main square, but shade in the labyrinth of tower houses and tiny chapels is just a few steps away. Streets are cobbled and buildings constructed from the same sand-colored rock, giving monochromatic Areopolis a unique dignity that most towns lack. Though its restaurants are superb and its tower houses provide romantic and inexpensive accommodations, Areopolis remains under-touristed. Locals prefer to tell visitors stories over wine than sell them postcards and trinkets. Areopolis is a favorite spot for artists seeking inspiration from the stark landscape; you will understand why after an evening walk through rocky olive groves framed against the purple Taygetus Mountains.

ORIENTATION AND PRACTICAL INFORMATION

The bus stops in front of **Nicola's Corner** in the main square. The bus points toward the main street of the old town, **Kapetan Matapam Street**. All amenities can be found off this street or in the main square. The **police** (tel. 51 209) are in the square at the end of a little street that starts behind the statue (open 24hr.). The **post office** is just off the square on Kapetan Matapan St.(open Mon.-Fri. 7:30am-2pm). To get to the **National Bank,** walk down Kapetan Matapan St., turn right at the first small church, and continue up the street—it's before the Hotel Mani (open Mon.-Fri. 9am-noon; open Tues. and Thurs. only in the off season). The bus station and the post office will **exchange currency** and traveler's checks for a hefty fee. The **OTE** (tel. 51 399) is 50m down a street that starts in the main square; the statue's right hand (with the sword) points down the street. Opposite the OTE is a **health center** (tel. 51 242) that is open 24hr. Areopolis also has a hospital to which the health center may direct you.

The **bus stop** (tel. 51 229) is at Nicola's Corner. Four buses per day make the trip from Kalamata to Itilo (2hr., 1250dr), with connections to Areopolis. Buses from Areopolis go to: Kalamata (3 per day, 1600dr), via Itilo (30min., 450dr); Sparta (4 per day, 1½hr., 1150dr), via Gythion (30min., 450dr); and Athens (4 per day, 6hr., 4600dr). A bus goes from Areopolis to the Glyfatha Lake Caves (210 dr) three times per day and returns 1¾ hours later. A bus goes deep into the Mani from Areopolis three times per week, stopping in Gerolimenas (30min., 450dr) and Vatnia (1hr., 700dr). The **postal code** is 23062. The **telephone code** is 0733.

ACCOMMODATIONS

If you spend the night here, try to find a room in the old town, which best evokes Mani's intriguing, turbulent past. You may become a player in a feud if you decide to stay at either **Tsimovas Rooms** or the **Pension** just opposite. Both proprietors are balding men who stare menacingly at the other's door. Both are delightful, but choose at your own risk. To find them, turn left at the end of Kapetan Matapan St.

Tsimova (tel. 51 301) offers narrow doubles decorated with electric wall hangings. Kolokotronis supposedly slept here. Singles 5000dr; doubles 6000dr.

Pierros Bozagregos (tel. 51 354), just across the street, has spotless doubles with private baths. Rooms 6000-10,000dr.

O Barba Petros (tel. 51 205), off Kapetan Matapan St. above the restaurant, has the cheapest rooms in town. The small rooms all share two bathrooms and may feel bit tight. Singles 3000dr; doubles 4000dr; triples 6000dr; quads 8000dr.

GREECE

FOOD

Nicola's Corner (tel. 51 366), in the square, serves excellent traditional dishes. Greek salads (1000dr), a delicious vegetarian *ratatouille* (1000dr), and their trademark grill and seasoned bread (300dr).

Tsimova (tel. 51 219) serves veal with tomato sauce (1500dr) and the swordfish special (2000dr) with smiles. A good place to sip Greek coffee (150dr).

Pistaria O Alepis (tel. 51 436), on the main road. For something cheap and easy, try the *souvlaki* (200dr), chicken (2000dr per kilo), and other grill items.

■ Pirgos Dirou and Glyfatha Lake Cave
ΠΥΡΓΟΣ ΔΙΡΟΥ

With its subterranean river, the **Glyfatha Cave** (also known as Spilia Dirou or Pirgos Dirou) is one of Greece's most splendid natural attractions. The boat ride through the cave is 1200m and lasts about 30 minutes. Originally discovered at the end of the 19th century and opened to the public in 1971 (a new section was found in 1983), the cave is believed to be 70km long and may extend all the way to Sparta. Vermilion stalagmites slice through the water, 30m deep in places and squiggling with eels. Dripping water and dark depths contribute to a clammy coolness that is a little spooky but a welcome relief from summer heat. Don't miss **Poseidon's Foot,** a striking formation that looks like a giant foot hanging in the air. Since some guides speak only Greek, you may want to buy the small book *Caverns of Mani* from the store near the entrance (1500dr). After the boat trip, you can walk through more of the caves. The caves are 4km from town, accessible by bus from Areopolis (open June-Sept. 8am-4pm, Oct.-May 8am-2:30pm; admission 3500dr). There is a beautiful pebble beach and a cafeteria next to the caves, so it is worth allotting a couple of hours here. A small **museum** (tel. 52 222, -3) houses neolithic artifacts from the cave's early inhabitants, who were trapped when an earthquake sealed the entrance (open Tues.-Sun. 8:30am-3pm; admission 500dr, students 300dr).

■ Monemvassia ΜΟΝΕΜΒΑΣΙΑ

Travelers who have seen countless postcards of the Byzantine city of Monemvassia may be puzzled when the bus drops them off in the pleasant, albeit modern, town of **Gefyra.** Just beyond the breaking waves off Gefyra's shore lies an impressive island, dominated by spectacular vertical cliffs. From the mainland, "the rock" as it is known, looks uninhabited. Only after crossing the causeway and walking along the main road for 20 minutes will the gate of Monemvassia be revealed.

Today, one must pass through a covered gateway to enter Monemvassia's town (hence the name, which means "one way"). Entering old Monemvassia may give visitors an eerie feeling of having crossed into another time. The narrow streets are a delight to explore, full of stairways, child-sized doorways, flowered courtyards, and even the occasional cactus. No cars or bikes are allowed through the gate, so pack horses bearing groceries and cases of beer are led back and forth to restaurants. Visible immediately, a sinuous path lined with staircases serves as the main street and leads to shops and restaurants. Continue past the small strip of tourist traps to reach the **town square.** Facing the ocean, the **Christos Elkomenos** (Christ in Chains) church is on the left. The **Agia Sofia,** a Byzantine church modeled after the monastery at Daphni, presides on the edge of the ruins. Some of the original frescoes were restored 30 years ago.

ORIENTATION AND PRACTICAL INFORMATION

While spending as much time as possible wandering around the old city, budget travelers should take care of most of their needs on the mainland in the much cheaper Gefyra. An orange bus runs between the causeway and Monemevassia gate all day long (every 10min.). In Gefyra, **23rd Iouliou Street,** the principal thoroughfare, runs along the waterfront straight up to the causeway leading to the island. Across from the bus station is the **National Bank** (tel. 61 201; open Mon. and Wed. 9am-1:30pm and Fri. 9am-1pm), and next door, the **post office** (tel. 61 231; open Mon.-Fri. 7:30am-2pm). The **police station** (tel. 61 210) is on the same side of the street, toward the causeway (open 24hr.). The **tourist police** (tel. 61 941) are in the same building. Room listings are available. The **OTE** (tel. 61 399) is 200m uphill bearing left from the bus station. Look for it on the left in a second floor balcony (open Mon.-Fri. 7:30am-3pm). Helpful **Malvasia Travel** (tel. 61 752) houses the bus station and is opposite the post office (open daily 7am-2:30pm and 6-9:30pm). Ask the manager about **currency exchange** and **moped rental** (3500dr per day). **English language books** ranging from romances to *Zorba the Greek* are available at **Bibliopoleio Polilpono** (tel. 61 021; open daily 9:30am-1:30pm and 6-9pm).

The **bus station** (tel. 61 752) is on 23rd Iouliou St., in the Malvasia travel agency opposite the post office. Buses for all destinations either connect or stop in Molai. The only exception is the 4:10am direct express to Athens (daily, 6hr., 3500dr). Buses leave (2 per day) for: Sparta (2½hr., 1700dr); Tripoli (4hr., 2600dr); Corinth (5hr., 3850dr); and Athens (6hr., 5150dr), via Molai (20min., 400dr). Daily buses connect Molai to Gythion, leaving Monemvassia (1½hr., 1300dr). In the summer, **Flying Dolphins** go to Kythera (1¼hr., 4465dr) and Neapolis (1½hr., 3235dr) four times a week. One or two hydrofoils per day leave for Piraeus (3½hr., 7920dr) stopping at Spestes (2½hr., 3775dr) and Hydra (3hr., 4680dr). Check at the ticket office (tel. 61 219) for schedules (next to the Mobil station on the island of Monemevassia). The **postal code** is 23070. The **telephone code** is 0732.

ACCOMMODATIONS

There are many hotels in Gefyra, but they are rather expensive. Many *domatia* dot the waterfront.

Kritikos Domatia (tel. 61 439), about 200m away from the bus stop. A suite of rooms with a kitchen and bathroom costs 6000dr.

Hotel Aktaion, 23rd Iouliou St. (tel. 61 234), near the causeway, is more expensive but has clean, modern rooms with balconies, bug screens, and reading lamps. Singles 6000dr; doubles 8000dr; off-season 20-40% less.

Hotel Minoa (tel. 61 209), along the main road. Matching furniture, fridges, and A/C. Singles 6000dr; doubles 8000dr.

Malavasia Hotel (tel. 61 160) is a treat in the island's medieval village. It has some spectacular rooms, but they are also spectacularly expensive. Still, the stone floors, fireplaces, beamed ceilings, and woven decorations may be worth it. Singles 10,000dr; doubles 12,000dr.

Camping Paradise (tel. 61 123), 3.5km along the water on the mainland, is a more affordable choice. 1100dr per person; 750dr per car; 800 per small tent; 1100dr per large tent. Off-season prices lower. 20% discount for longer stays.

FOOD

Matoula (tel. 61 660) is somewhat expensive, but its old city location boasts fig trees and a pleasant stone terrace (*moussaka* 1300dr, stuffed tomatoes 1300dr). On the mainland, follow the water past the causeway to the harbor-side to: **To Limanaki** (tel. 61 619; stuffed eggplant 1150dr, kalamari 1250dr). The road to Camping Paradise has some of the best Greek food around. Try **Pipinellis Taverna** (tel. 61 004), located 2km from Monemvassia. The restaurant has featured home-grown produce for the past 25 years (stuffed tomatoes 1000dr, veal 1300dr).

▓ **Kythera** KYΘHPA

Myth holds that Zeus threw Chronus' severed genitalia into the ocean, and Kythera and Aphrodite later sprang from the surrounding waters. Kythera, just to the south of the Peloponnesian cities of Monemvassia, Neapolis, and Gythion, is a lovely isolated spot. The land's tranquil mountainous landscape harbors a collection of evergreens and flowering shrubs, secluded villages, and sandy beaches. Improved ferry schedules have recently made Kythera a more convenient destination for budget travelers. Travel by bus is still difficult, but mopeds are plentiful and cheap, and they allow travelers to expand their choices of inexpensive *domatia* and charming villages. It is easy to see Kythera's major sites in a day if you have transportation, but if you enjoy clean beaches and the relaxed pace of uncrowded islands, you will probably want to stay longer.

AGIA PELAGIA

Ferries dock in Kythera at the west port of **Agia Pelagia,** and Flying Dolphins dock at the newer port of **Diakofti.** The island's main road runs between Agia Pelagia and **Kapsali,** a lively port town with small villages connected by subsidiary roads. Besides the port towns, this road passes through **Potamos, Livadi,** and **Kythera** (Chora). Although Agia Pelagia is very small, it does have beaches to either side of the ferry quay, and almost everything a tourist could need is at hand. You may want to stay here instead of the south part of the island.

In a little cottage to the left (facing inland) of the quay is a very helpful **Volunteer Tourist Office** (tel. 33 815). The friendly staffers can provide information about accommodations and sights around the island (open daily July-Sept., 9am-1pm and 5-9pm. Across the road is **Conomos Travel** (tel. 33 490), an agency that sells tickets for ferries and flying dolphins (pen June-Sept. 9am-1pm and 4-8:30pm, reduced hours in winter). The **port police** (tel. 33 280) also provide schedules.

Ferries leave Agia Pelagia daily for the mainland, stopping at both **Neapolis** (50min., 1650dr) and **Gythios** (2½hr., 1550dr). Ferries also travel to Kastili on Crete (Mon. and Thurs., 5hr., 3750dr). A daily **bus** in July and August runs between Agia Pelagia and Kapsali; it leaves Agia Pelagia at 8am and returns from Kapsali at noon (300dr). You may even be able to hop on the school bus during other months. Ask at the tourist office for details.

If you decide to spend the night in Agia Pelagia, all of your needs can be taken care of in one building. Across from the quay, a little to the right, is **Taverna Faros** (tel. 33 343). This delicious *taverna* offers a great ocean view (breakfast 900dr, goat cheese and spaghetti 1300dr, Greek salad 1000dr). Simple rooms are above the restaurant (doubles 5000dr, August prices slightly higher). The tourist office has lists of other *domatia* owners and will put you in contact with them.

POTOMAS

The pleasant inland town of **Potomas** is 9km south of Agai Pelagia on the main road. Its square is home to many of the island's amenities. The **National Bank** (tel. 33 350) marks the main square (open Mon.-Thurs. 8am-2pm, Fri. 8am-1:30pm). The **post office** (tel. 33 225) is uphill from the square (open Mon.-Fri. 7:30 am). The **police station** (tel. 33 222) is behind the National Bank, tucked in a lemon-tree lined corner (no English spoken). The **hospital** (tel. 33 325) is on the road to Chora (many doctors speak English). The **postal code** is 80200. The **telephone code** is 0735.

The **Olympic Airlines** office (tel. 33 362) is in Potomas's square, but the airport is a taxi ride away on the eastern half of the island. Olympic runs three flights a day into Kythera (13,400dr to Athens, 11,400dr less for people under 24 or over 60; office open Mon.-Fri. 8am-4pm). **Taxis** park in Potomas's Square, or call 33 676.

For a treat, try **Chrisafiti Bakery** (tel. 33 244), in the main square. Their *focaccio* (350dr) is divine, and you can sit in the main square for a picnic.

CHORA (KYTHERA)

Chora, also called Kythera, is the capital of the island. Its whitewashed plaster houses will make you wonder if there is a city ordinance requiring everyone to paint their shutters blue. The effect is powerful under the bright sun, especially along the narrow main street that starts in the town's square and leads to the castle. You can see the azure sea and the small island called **Hydra,** which looks just like the Prudential rock, from many vantage points.

Chora's **post office** (tel. 31 274) is in the main square (open 7:30am-2pm), as is the **National Bank** (tel. 31 713; open Mon.-Thurs. 8am-2pm and Fri. 8am-1:30pm). To get to the **OTE** (tel. 31 299), go up the stairs next to Kithira Travel and turn left at the top (open 7:30am-2pm). Facing the water, Chora's main street starts from the square's lower left hand corner. About 500m down this street are the **police** (tel. 31 206), where the **tourist police** can be found in the morning.

In the square, **Kithira Travel** (tel. 31 390) has lots of information, including **Flying Dolphin** schedules (open 8:30am-1:30pm and 6:30-9:30pm). Flying Dolphins leave Diakofti (Mon., Wed., Sat., and Sun. at 5pm) and go to Piraeus (4hr., 9265dr), via Monemovassia (1hr., 4440dr), and Spestes (2hr., 6500dr). **Taxis** (tel. 31 320) from Chora to Diakofti cost about 3000dr.

Among Chora's sparkling white buildings are numerous "Rooms to Let" signs, but many are quite expensive. **Pension Pises** (tel. 31 070) has interestingly decorated rooms with great views and shared baths (doubles 6000dr). From the main road through town, turn left at the "pension" sign onto Ag. Elesis. Another place to try is **Domatia Nike** (tel. 31 488), which is on Kythera's highway past the turn-off for Chora on the way to Kapsali. Rooms have refrigerators, bathrooms, and sea views (singles 5000dr; doubles 6000dr).

At the end of Chora's main road are the remains of the town's **castle**. Wildflowers have sprouted around the old battlements, and the wind-swept plateau offers intoxicating views of Kapsali's double harbor. The **Archaeological Museum** is on Kythera's highway just before the turn-off for Chora. The small museum houses ancient pottery and 19th-century English gravestones (open Tues.-Sat. 8:45am-3pm and Sun. 9:30am-2:30pm; free).

KAPSALI

Downhill from Chora on the sea is **Kapsali,** a small beachfront town. You will find the island's most developed and least friendly tourist industry here.

The **port police** (tel. 31 222), are at the far left (facing the water) side of the harbor. Where the road from Chora ends, you will see **Nikos Moto-Rent** (tel. 31 190), which has motorbikes starting at 2000dr a day. On the main highway toward Chora is **Camping Kapsali** (tel. 31 580), sheltered in a shady evergreen forest. (850dr per person; 850dr per small tent; 950dr per large tent; 650dr per car; electricity 200dr; open mid-June to Sept.) Ask on the waterfront at the **Dawaris Supermarket** (tel. 31 847), for rooms in town. The large rooms are a few blocks uphill, and each has a refrigerator and small stove (doubles 6000dr). The charming blue and red tables of **Artena** (tel. 31 342) are located on the beach, and the food is reasonably priced (spaghetti 750dr, stuffed tomatoes 1000dr).

Although it does not compare to the **nightlife** on other Greek islands, Kapsali presents the best in the area. The waterfront is cluttered with outdoor cafes and clubs. The most popular is the new **Barbarosa Music Bar** (tel. 31 831). Drinks are a little expensive, but local music contributes to a pleasant environment. Also popular is the **Yachting Club** (tel. 31 909).

Crete ΚΡΗΤΗ

In middle of the sable sea there lies An isle call'd Crete, a ravisher of eyes,
Fruitful, and mann'd with many an infinite store; Where ninety cities crown
the famous shore, Mix'd with all-languag'd men.

—Homer, *Odyssey*

There is a Greek saying that a Cretan's first loyalty is to the island and second to the country. Indeed, some of Crete's rugged individualism, which treats even Greeks as foreigners, persists; simply look to the long-mustached men who sit by the harbor polishing their high black boots. Like the island, they are hospitable, but prefer to keep their distance, staid and stoic.

As far back as 6000 BC, the neolithic Cretans dwelled in open settlements and worshipped their deities by placing terra cotta statuettes on the tops of mountains, now referred to as peak sanctuaries. Crete's glory days, however, began when settlers arrived from Asia Minor around 3000 BC.

Since the third millennium BC, Crete has held a distinct cultural identity, expressed in the unique language, script, and architecture of the ancient Minoans through to the novels of Nikos Kazantzakis, several of which play out Crete's heroic struggle for freedom from foreign rule. In many ways Greek mythology had its beginnings on Crete's Mt. Ida, the mythical birthplace of Zeus. The myth of the man-eating Minotaur was enacted in the shadow of Mt. Ida, and the hybrid beast's slaying at the hands of Theseus, King of Athens, metaphorically transferred power from the Minoans of Crete to the Achaeans of mainland Greece.

Throughout the span of a few thousand years, these inhabitants created sophisticated palaces. Among the artifacts found from this time are gracefully-flared pottery shards, frescoes, jewelry, ceremonial horns, stone libation vessels, Linear A and B tablets, and figurines. This period lasted from 2800 to 1100 BC and was the height of the Minoan Civilization. The extensive ruins of this unique civilization, all unearthed during this century, offer visitors an impressive spectacle.

The Minoans not only survived three waves of destruction—an earthquake, a series of tidal waves following the eruption of the volcano on Santorini, and (probably) a Mycenaean invasion—but also rebuilt their civilization after each setback. These periods are now referred to as the Early, Middle and Late Minoan Periods, based on pottery styles. Iconography of enthroned females suggest that the Early Period may have been a matriarchy. This period is also famous because it was believed to have been the one and only time in human history when men and women lived together in pure peace, harmony, and equality. However, archaeological discoveries in recent years (weaponry and evidence of human sacrifice) suggest that the state of Minoan affairs may not have been so socially advanced after all. Crete's most glorious days were during the Middle Minoan Period, when the Palace at Knossos functioned as the center of an Aegean marine empire. Newly established trade routes fostered prosperity and sophistication, and Minoan artistry reached its climax.

In the 8th century BC, Dorians occupied the island; they introduced the Greek language, as jewelry-making, sculpture, and pottery thrived. The Roman conquest in 67 BC found the island increasingly unstable, with dominant aristocratic families and frequent intercity warfare. In the Medieval and Modern periods, Crete was ruled by a succession of empires, and in 1898, the island became an English protectorate. After the Balkan War of 1913, Crete finally joined the rest of Greece. This peace was interrupted by a WWII German occupation.

GETTING THERE

Olympic Airways has cheap, fast, domestic **flights** from Athens to Sitia on the east, Iraklion in the center, and Chania on the west. Air Greece also has flights to Crete, and their prices are often cheaper, but they service fewer destinations than Olympic

Crete

⊗ Capital city
● City or town
■ Point of interest
▲ Mountain peak
--- Ferry line

GREEK ISLANDS

RHODES
KARPATHOS
LIMASSOL (Cyprus)
HAIFA (Israel)
RHODES
HAIFA (Israel)

PIRAEUS

SANTORINI

PIRAEUS

PIRAEUS

Sea of Crete

Mediterranean Sea

Dia Island

Vai
Palaikastro
Moni Toplu
Mt. Prasino
Ano Zakros
Kato Zakros
Sitia
Koufonisi Island

Hametgatos
Agia Fotia
Thripte Mts.
Ierapetra
Mikronisio Island

Spinalonga
Agios Nikolaos
Neapolis
Gournia
Elounda
Lasithi Plateau
Kritsa
Dikti Mts.
Chrisi Island
Myrtos
Arvi

Heronissos
Malia
Tzermiado
Psychro

Ammissos
Knossos
Mirtia

Iraklion

Agia Pelagia
Tylissos
Skalavokambos
Agia Varvara
Gortina
Lendas

Panormos
Mt. Ida
Anogia
Kamares
Phaestos
Agia Triada
Kali
Limenes

Eleftherna
Gerakari
Mazala
Peximadia Island

Rethymnon
Spili
Mt. Kedros
Agia Galini

Plakias
Preveli

Georgioupolis
Frangokastello

Almirou Gulf
Souda Bay
Chora Sfakion

Airport
Akrotiri
Souda
Vamos
Lefka Ori
Samarian Gorge

Stavros
Laki
Xyloskalo
Agia Roumeli
Leutro

Chania

Tavronitis
Kastelli
Souga
Agia Triada
Paleochora

Falasarna
Platatios
Elafonisi

Gavdos Island

20 mile
20 kilometer

N

Airways. Most flights take less than an hour. Consult the **Orientation and Practical Information** listings in your destination city for more information.

Most travelers arrive in Crete by **ferry.** The island has frequent connections during summer, but boats often fall behind schedule. The larger the boat, the more frequently it runs, and the more dependable its schedule. All prices listed here are for deck-class accommodations. Boats run to Iraklion, Rethymnon, Chania, Agios Nikolaos, and Sitia. There are **international ferry** connections to Ancona in Italy, Çeşme in Turkey, Limassol on Cyprus, and Haifa in Israel. For Egypt, change boats in Cyprus. From April to October, the *Vergina* leaves Haifa on Sundays and travels to Cyprus, Rhodes, Iraklion, and Peiraias; deck-class costs roughly 20,000dr between any two ports. Those heading to Italy must go to Peiraias and change boats.

CENTRAL CRETE

▓ Iraklion (Heraklion) ΗΡΑΚΛΕΙΟ

Greece's fifth-largest city, Iraklion is both Crete's capital and its primary port. The city's chic native population supports a nightlife more diverse than those of nearby beach resorts, Malia and Herssonisos. With rich museums, Venetian monuments, ancient churches, and daytrip proximity to the Minoan palaces of Knossos, Phoistos, and Malia, Iraklion is an ideal base for a cultural tour of Crete.

ORIENTATION AND PRACTICAL INFORMATION

Though Iraklion spreads for miles, almost everything important lies within the circle formed by Dikeosinis Ave., Handakos St., Doukos Bofor Ave., and the waterfront. The city centers are **Venizelou Square,** known to tourists as **Lion Fountain Square** or **Four Lion Square,** where Handakos St. meets Dikeosinis and 25th Augustou Ave. in the center of town, and **Eleftherias Square,** at the intersection of Doukos Bofor and Dikeosinis Ave. on the east side of the old city.

Tourist Office: 1 Xanthoudidou St. (tel. 22 82 03, 24 46 62), opposite the Archaeological Museum in Eleftherias Sq. Free city maps, lists of hotels, message board for travelers, bus schedules, and some boat schedules. Staff is helpful but busy. Info on harvest jobs. Open Mon.-Fri. 8am-2:30pm and Sat. 10am-2:30pm.

Tourist Police: 10 Dikeosinis St. (tel. 28 31 90, 28 96 14), one block from intersection of 25th Augustou and Dikeosinis. Open daily 7am-11pm.

Tourist Agencies: Several agencies on 25th Augustou Ave. **Arabatzoglou Bros. Shipping Agents Travel Bureau,** #54 25th Augustou Ave. (tel. 28 86 08, fax. 22 21 84) has a friendly staff. Helpful with air and boat tickets. Open daily 8am-9pm. Many agencies **exchange currency** at bank rates.

Banks: The banks on 25th Augustou Ave. are open Mon.-Thurs. 8am-2pm and Fri. 8am-1:30pm. The **National Bank,** 25th Augustou Ave. is open Mon.-Thurs. 8am-2pm and Fri. 8am-1:30pm. Shops in Venizelou Sq. **exchange currency** after hours at lower rates.

Flights: Inquire at **Travel Hall Travel Agency,** 13 Hatzimihali Yiannari St. (tel. 34 18 62; fax 28 33 09), one block southwest of Eleftherias Sq. Sells tickets for Olympic Airways to: Athens (6 per day, 45min., 21,600dr); Mykonos (2 per week, 30min., 22,400dr); Rhodes (4 per week, 30min., 21,600dr); Thessaloniki (3 per week, 1hr., 29,600dr); and Santorini (3 per week, 30min., 15,100dr). Flights on **Air Greece,** which are less frequent but also less expensive, are also available. Open daily 8am-9pm. Bus #1 departs for the airport from Eleftherias Sq. every 10min. (200dr). Cabs to the airport cost 300-400dr.

Buses: There are several **KTEL** bus terminals, so match the station to your destination. **Terminal A** (tel. 24 50 17, -19), between the old city walls and the harbor near the waterfront, serves: Agios Nikolaos (24 per day, 1½hr., 1300dr); Lassithi (1-2 per day, 2hr., 1300dr); Hersonissos (every 30min., 45min., 550dr); Malia (every

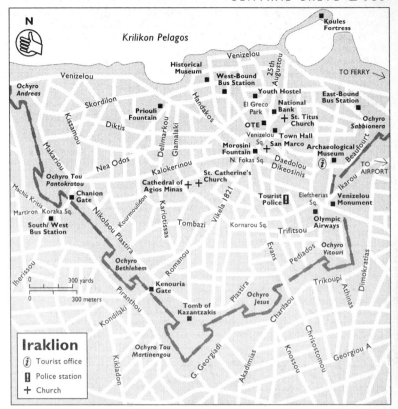

N

Krilikon Pelagos

Koules Fortress

Venizelou

TO FERRY →

Historical Museum

West-Bound Bus Station

Venizelou

Venizelou

Youth Hostel

El Greco Park

National Bank

East-Bound Bus Station

Ochyro Andreas

Skordilon

Handakos

Ochyro Sabbionera

Priouli Fountain

Diktis

St. Titus Church

OTE

Delimarkou

Giamalaki

Kissamou

Venizelou Sq.

Town Hall

San Marco

Archaeological Museum

Makariou

Morosini Fountain

N. Fokas Sq.

Daedolou Dikeosinis

ⓘ

TO AIRPORT →

Nea Odos

Kalokerinou

St. Catherine's Church

Ikarou

Beaufort

Ochyro Tou Pantokratou

Machis Kritis

Chanion Gate

Cathedral of Agios Minas

Viketa 1821

Tourist Police

Eleftherias Sq.

Venizelou Monument

Martiron

Koraka Sq.

Kariotissas

Koumoulidon

Olympic Airways

South/West Bus Station

Nikolaou Plastira

Tombazi

Kornarou Sq.

Trifitsou

Evans

Pediados

Ochyro Vitouri

Dimokratias

Ochyro Bethlehem

Romanou

Plastira

Ochyro Jesus

Charilaou

Trikoupi

Athinas

Iherissou

0   300 yards

0   300 meters

Piranthou

Kenouria Gate

Tomb of Kazantzakis

G. Georgiadi

Chrisostomou

Knossou

Georgiou A

Kondilaki

Kikladon

Ochyro Tou Martinengou

Akadimias

Iraklion

ⓘ Tourist office

🅟 Police station

✚ Church

30min., 1hr., 700dr); Sitia (5 per day, 3¼hr., 2650dr); Ierapetra (7 per day, 2½hr., 1950dr); Archanes (13 per day, 30min., 320dr); and Agios Pelagia (5 per day, 45min., 600dr). **Terminal B** (tel. 25 59 65), outside the Chania Gate of the old city walls, runs buses to: Phaistos (9 per day, 1½hr., 1150dr); Agios Galini (6 per day, 2¼hr., 1450dr); Matala (5 per day, 2hr., 1400dr); Lentas (1 per day, 3hr., 1500dr); Anogia (5 per day., 1hr., 700dr); and Fodele (2 per day, 1hr., 600dr). The **Chania/ Rethymnon Terminal** (tel. 22 17 65) is near the waterfront. Walk down 25th Augustou Ave. to the waterfront, turn right, and walk another 500m. The station will be on your right 200m before the ferry landing. It serves the same destinations as Terminal A, plus service to Chania (14 per day, 2500dr) and Rethymnon (17 per day, 1½hr., 1400dr).

Ferries: Boat offices on 25th Augustou Ave. Most open daily 9am-9pm. Boats leave for: Athens (2 per day, 12hr., 6500dr); Santorini (5 per week, 4hr., 2955dr); Paros (9 per week, 8½hr., 4800dr); Naxos (3 per week, 7hr., 4500dr); Mykonos (2 per week, 9hr., 5705dr); Rhodes (2 per week, 12hr., 6190dr); and Thessaloniki (6 per week, 11hr., 10900dr).

Taxis: Tariff Taxi of Iraklion (tel. 21 01 02). Open 24hr. When taking a taxi from the airport or port, beware of drivers drawing commission from a local hotel who may claim that the rival hotel you name is closed or full.

Car Rental: Rental car companies are scattered along 25th Augustou Ave. Shop around. Make the owners compete for your business by quoting prices from their neighbors. **Caravel** at #16 and #39 25th Augustou Ave. (tel. 24 53 45, -50; fax 22 03 62) will rent cars to anyone over 19. Prices average 9000dr per day. A copy of *Let's Go* will get you free insurance or a 40% discount on any car. Open 7am-10pm.

Moped Rental: Cheap rentals line Handakos St., El Greco Park, and 25th Augustou Ave. Check if the quoted price includes the 20% tax and insurance (50cc bikes

3500dr per day, tax and third-party liability insurance included). **Nikos Rent-a-Vespa,** 16 Doukos Bofor St. (tel. 22 64 25), across from Marin Hotel. Open daily 8am-8:30pm.

Laundromat: Washsalon, 18 Handakos St. (tel. 28 08 58; fax 28 44 42). 1000dr for wash and dry soap included. Also provides luggage storage (250dr, with locker 300dr). Open daily 8:30am-9pm.

Public Toilets: El Greco Park. Open daily 7am-9pm. 30dr per use. Also in public gardens near Eleftherias Sq.

Library: Vikelaia Municipal Library (tel. 24 65 50, -2), in Venizelou Sq. Limited number of books in English on the second floor. Open Mon.-Fri. 8am-3pm.

Bookstores: Newsstands in Eleftherias Sq. sell foreign newspapers like the *International Herald Tribune* as well as paperbacks. Open daily 8am-10pm. **Planet Bookstore** (tel. 28 15 58), a 5-floor megastore on the corner of Hortatson and Kidonias St. Open Mon.-Fri. 8:30am-2pm and 5:30-8:30pm, Sat. 8:30am-noon.

Pharmacy: (tel. 22 46 08) On Agiou Titou St. off 25th Augustou Ave. Open Mon.-Fri. 9am-10pm. One open 24hr. by rotation—its name and address is posted on the door of every pharmacy. All are marked by a red cross.

Hospital: (tel. 23 95 02, 26 93 73) On Venizelou St. Take bus #2 (20min.). Also **Panepistimiako Hospital** (tel. 26 91 11, -94 62).

Police: Same location as the tourist police. Open 24hr. One station services the east side of town (tel. 28 45 89, 24 34 66); another station in the same building takes care of the west (tel. 28 26 77, 28 22 43). **Port Police** (tel. 22 60 73).

Post Office: Main office (tel.24 38 96, 28 99 95), off Gianani St. Open Mon.-Fri. 7:30am-8pm. **Branch office** in El Greco Park. Open Mon.-Fri. 8:30am-3pm.

Postal Code: 71001.

OTE: 10 Minotavrou St. (tel. 28 23 99); follow signs on Minotavrou near El Greco Park. Open daily 7am-11pm. **Branch office** in Eleftherias Sq. Open March-Oct. Mon.-Fri. 8am-11pm, Nov.-Feb. Mon.-Fri. 1-9pm. **Telephone Code:** 081.

ACCOMMODATIONS

Iraklion has a bunch of cheap hotels and hostels, most near Handakos St. at the center of town. Others are on Evans and 1866 St. near the market.

Youth Hostel, 5 Vyronos St. (tel. 28 62 81, 22 29 47), off 25th Augustou Ave. Standard hostel rooms. Midnight curfew. Luggage storage 300dr. Check-out 10am. Larger rooms for families and couples. 1400dr per person; doubles 3800-4000dr. Breakfast 350dr, beer 350dr.

Rent a Room Hellas, 24 Handakos St., 2 blocks from El Greco Park (tel. 28 08 58). Formerly the HI Youth Hostel, offers sheets, verandas, and garden bar. Dorm beds 1500dr; singles 4000dr; doubles 5000; triples 6500.

Hotel Rea, Kalimeraki St. (tel. 22 36 38). Walking toward the harbor, turn right off Handakos St., 2 blocks above the waterfront. Clean, airy rooms. Hot showers included. Luggage storage free. Doubles 5500dr, with bath 6500dr; triples 7500dr, with bath 9000dr; dorm-like quads 8800dr. Breakfast 900dr.

Rent a Room Vergina, 32 Chortason St. (tel. 24 27 39). Walking toward the harbor, turn right off Handakos onto Kidonias, take your first left on Hortason, and walk down 2 blocks—it's on the right. Clean, homey rooms. High ceilings, new furniture. Free luggage storage. Check-out noon. Doubles 6000dr; triples 8000dr.

FOOD AND ENTERTAINMENT

Around the Morosini Fountain, near El Greco Park and in Eleftherias Sq., are ritzy cafes perfect for lounging. Take a left off 1866 St., one block from Venizelou Sq., to reach tiny Theodosaki St. Though not the most upscale place in town to dine, it's certainly colorful, with 10 *tavernas* jammed side by side serving Greek fare. The cheaper dishes go for roughly 650dr and the portions are impressive. If there's no menu, fix the price before you sit. For more elegant dining, try any of the *tavernas* on boutique-lined Daedolou St. *Souvlaki* joints abound on 25th Augustou Ave.

Thraka, 14 Platokallergon (4 Lions Square), is the most fun thanks to its 30-year tradition of only grilled ham meat gyros and *souvlaki*. No electricity here, only charcoal.

Try the *souvlaki* with bread crust (300dr). The manager of the **Minos Restaurant** on Daedalou St. will guide you in the kitchen to choose the dish that looks best. The same owner for 26 years has served a special of lamb with yogurt (lamb "Elvasan" yogurt 2500dr; open 11am-3pm and 6-10pm).

During the day, the best show in town is the **open-air market** on 1866 St., which starts near Venizelou Sq. Both sides of the boisterous, aromatic, narrow street are lined with stalls piled high with sweets, spices, fresh fruits, vegetables, cheeses, and meat in glass cases. The huge cauldrons of yogurt sold here far eclipse the filtered, pasteurized brands found elsewhere. For delicious yogurt try **Amalthia** (tel. 28 50 84). Named after the goat of Zeus, the store serves traditional sheep's milk yogurt (600dr per kg), as well as local cheeses like the special Cretan Gruyere (market open Mon-Sat. 8:30am-2:30pm, also Tues., Thurs., Fri. 5:30-9pm). The two **sweet shops** in Lion Fountain Sq. sell *bougatsa,* a cheese or cream-filled phyllo pastry (open daily 6am-11pm).

Antonios Nerantzoulis, 16 Agios Titoy St. (tel. 24 62 36), is behind the St. Titus Church. The bakery has been run by the same family since 1900. They're famous for *oktasporo* (8 grain leaves, 800dr) and *kaltsounia* (little cheese biscuits, 1800dr per kg; open Mon.-Sat. 7am-3pm and also Tues., Thurs.-Fri. 5-8pm).

Iraklion natives are the first to point out that the "in" places change rapidly, so ask around. Or try **Aktarika Cafe** (tel. 34 12 25), across from the Lion Fountain Square. All day and all night this huge atrium-like cafe teems with hip black-clad twenty and thirty-something Iraklionites and the people who watch them. (Frappes 600dr, cocktails 1500dr. Open daily 9am-2:30am. DJ on duty 11am-4pm and 7pm-2:30am.)

Iraklion's pulsing nightlife outdoes those of the resort towns, trading tourist kitsch for genuine urban energy. Cretans mingle with travelers and everybody gets it on. On the waterfront, **Factory** plays rave and disco Thursday to Saturday nights. For Greek music, head to **Cafe Aman. Disco Kazani** sports a young crowd.

Schedules for Iraklion's **movie theaters** are posted near the tourist police office. For an evening of free sociological entertainment, join Greeks and tourists at Venizelou Sq., where Iraklion's annual **summer festival** combines cultural events such as concerts, theater, ballet, and folk dancing. Shows begin at 9:30pm and cost up to 300dr. Students pay no more than 150dr. Pick up a schedule of events from the tourist police or tourist information office. Call 24 29 77 for more information.

SIGHTS

Iraklion's capital attraction is its superb **Archaeological Museum** (tel. 22 60 92), off Eleftherias Sq. While most museums in Cretan cities offer merely a hodgepodge of local finds strung across millennia, the Iraklion museum, which has appropriated major finds from all regions of the island, presents a comprehensive record of neolithic, Minoan, Hellenistic, and Roman stages of the island's history. Exhibits are organized chronologically from the neolithic period to Roman times. The museum's

---

It's El Greco to Me

Though he made his name at the Spanish court, Domenikos Theotocopoulos (1541-1614) clung to his Greek heritage throughout his artistic career. Born in Iraklion (then under Venetian rule), the Cretan artist incorporated his early Byzantine training with the teachings of the Venetian and Roman schools, where he trained with masters like Titian, Raphael, and Michelangelo. El Greco, as he came to be known, was a master of Mannerism, a style of painting that places internal emotions above nature and the ancients. His reputation was built on portraits and religious imagery that featured rigid figures filled with emotion. His best-known work, *The Burial of the Count Orgaz,* staged a historical event in the contemporary world, a strong tradition in Western art. Although El Greco moved to Toledo, Spain, in 1576, the Spanish subjects and contexts of his work never eclipsed his feeling that he was a stranger in that land. Throughout his career, El Greco would continue to sign his paintings in Greek.

most outstanding feature is the **Hall of the Minoan Frescoes.** An illustrated guide available at the museum's gift stand is well worth the 1500dr. The frescoes depict ancient Minoan life: ladies in blue offering libations, blue monkeys frolicking in palatial gardens, and Minoans in procession. (Open Mon. 12:30-7pm and Tues.-Sun. 8am-7pm. Admission 1500dr, students 800dr, under 18 free.)

Iraklion also has a **Historical Museum** (tel. 28 32 19) on the corner of Grevenon and Kalokerianou, two blocks from the Xenia Hotel. Unlike the crowded Archaeological Museum, the place is undervisited. Its collection includes Byzantine and medieval works, a folk collection, finely woven tapestries, photographs from the WWII Nazi invasion, and **View of Mt. Sinai and the Monastery of St. Catherine** (1578), the only work of **El Greco** on Crete. (Open Mon.-Fri. 9am-5pm and Sat. 9am-2pm. Admission 1000dr, students 750dr, children under 12 free.)

The austere **Tomb of Kazantzakis** has views of Iraklion, the sea, and Mt. Ida to the west, and offers a peaceful and green respite from the crowded city of Iraklion. To get there, either walk along the top of the Venetian walls to Martinengo Bastion at the south corner of the city, or go down Evans St. until you reach the walls and the bastion. Because of his heterodox beliefs, Kazantzakis, the author of *The Last Temptation of Christ,* was denied a place in a Christian cemetery and was buried here. True devotees can visit the **Kazantzakis Museum** (tel. 742451) in nearby Varvari. The carefully presented exhibit includes many of the author's original manuscripts, as well as photographs of his theatrical productions. A slide show (in English) provides historical background. A bus from Station A takes you to Mirtia (22km from Iraklion), only a short walk from the museum. For schedules, inquire at the station or call 24 50 17 or 24 50 19. (Open March 1-Oct. 31 Mon., Wed. and Sat.-Sun. 9am-1pm and 4-8pm, Tues. and Fri. 9am-1pm. Admission 500dr.)

Several interesting churches hide in the modern maze of Iraklion's city streets. Built in 1735 in Agia Ekaterinis Sq., the **Cathedral of Agios Minas** (tel. 28 24 02) piously graces the area (open daily 7am-8pm). **St. Catherine's Church of Sinai** (tel. 28 88 25), in the square, served as the first Greek university after the fall of Constantinople in 1453. The church features six icons by the Cretan master Damaskinos as well as other icons from monasteries and churches around Crete. (Open Mon., Wed., and Sat. 9am-1:30pm, Tues. and Thurs.-Fri. 5-8pm; admission 400dr). **St. Titus Church,** 25th Augustou Ave., is a mosque converted into a church. The **Armenian Church** (tel. 24 43 37) can be reached by heading away from the town center on Kalokerianou St. Take a right on the street just after the fruit market at 174 Kalokerianou St. and *oriste*—you're there. The priest gives tours of the grounds.

As you scamper around, take note of the various monuments built during the Venetian occupation of Iraklion: the 17th-century **Morosini Fountain** and the reconstructed **Venetian Loggia** in Lion Fountain Sq.; the **Venetian Arsenal,** off Kountouriotou Sq. near the waterfront; and the **Koules Fortress** (tel. 24 62 11), guarding the old harbor (open Mon.-Fri. 8am-6pm, Sat.-Sun. 10am-5pm; admission 500dr, students 300dr). For a dose of peace and beauty which will surprise you in Iraklion's urban context, climb up and walk along the southeast section of the **Venetian walls,** an olive tree-lined refuge.

◼ Near Iraklion

Iraklion is an ideal base for exploring Central Crete. Archaeological sites abound, including the Minoan palaces at **Knossos, Phaistos** (p. 190), and **Malia** (p. 205), as well as the lesser finds at Tylissos, Sklavokambos, and Gortina (p. 190).

KNOSSOS

Knossos is undoubtedly the most famous archaeological site in Crete, partially because of an ancient tale (see **Half-breeds, High Taxes, and Wax Wings,** p. 189). During the first millennium BC, Cretans were ridiculed for imagining that they sprang from such illustrious forebears as the **Minoans.** Time, however, has proven the Cretans right. **Sir Arthur Evans,** one of Heinrich "Troy" Schliemann's British cronies, pur-

Half-breeds, High Taxes, and Wax Wings

One of the most complex and resonant myths in all Greek mythology, that of **King Minos,** begins with a simple crime of ingratitude. When Minos withheld the sacrifice of a fine white bull, which Poseidon had granted him for that exclusive purpose, Aphrodite was dispatched to exact a twisted retribution—an unconquerable lust in Minos' queen **Pasiphaë** for the bull itself. To woo the bull she hired master engineer **Daedalus** to build a sexy cow costume that might rouse the bull's affections. After a lusty roll in the hay, Pasiphaë bore a **minotaur** to King Minos' disgust and dismay. With the head of a bull and a human body, the Minotaur fed on human flesh and was kept in the inescapable **labyrinth** designed by Daedalus. To feed his queen's child, Minos imposed an annual tax of seven maidens and seven youths upon mainland Greece. **Theseus,** an Athenian prince, volunteered for the sacrifice and, once within its labyrinth, slew the minotaur. With a ball of string given him by **Ariadne,** Minos' daughter (who had conspired with Daedalus to save her Athenian squeeze), Theseus retraced his way out of the labyrinth and escaped with Ariadne by ship. Although he had promised her marriage, he left Ariadne on the beach of Naxos to be swept off by Dionysus. Meanwhile, Minos imprisoned Daedalus and his son **Ikarus** as conspirators. Always resourceful, Daedalus constructed wings of wax for the two of them to make the ultimate jailbreak. With freedom in sight, Ikarus, in a fit of hubris, flew straight at the sun, melting his wings and sending him plummeting to his death.

chased the hill and spent the next 43 years and his fortune excavating it. His work showed that from 1700-1400 BC Knossos was indeed either a temple complex or distribution center that stood at the center of the first great European civilization.

Dr. Evans creatively, though in many instances inaccurately, restored large portions of the palace to what he believed were their original configurations based on evidence unearthed during the excavations. Walls, window casements, stairways, and columns were reconstructed in reinforced concrete, and copies of the magnificent frescoes were mounted in place of their original counterparts (which are now in Iraklion's Archaeological Museum). In some cases, restorations prevented the walls from falling down as the excavations continued, but Evans' reconstruction crossed the boundaries of preservation and reflected his own interpretation. While purists feel that the complex at Knossos is an outrage, it is nonetheless impressive.

The extended series of **magazines** (storage rooms with large clay jars) give the palace its labyrinthine architecture and are its claim to fame. The large open space in the middle of the site, imaginatively named the Central Court, was quite possibly an arena for bull-leaping (see **Bull Leaping, Minoan style,** p. 209). The **Throne Room,** to the left of the Central Court, enshrines the original throne. A replica sits in an adjacent room for your very own Kodak moment.

The throne faces an enigmatic structure known as a **lustral basin.** Iconography of the first palatial era, often depicting an enthroned queen or goddess surrounded by palm fronds, suggests that the Minoan civilization may have begun as a matriarchy. Note also the drainage system, occasional mason's marks on the shiny, cut-stone architecture, and the I-shaped cement bumps on the ground where doors ingeniously slid into the walls and let in, or kept out, the sunlight. The areas painted red around each window and door were actually constructed out of wood in antiquity; they cushioned the walls from frequent seismic shock. Don't miss the **Queen's Bathroom**—over 3000 years ago she could flush her own toilet. Finally, gaze upon the **Royal Road** in the complex's northwest corner. It served not only as an entryway, but also as a reception area for important guests.

For general reference, check out *Knossos and the Iraklion Museum,* by Costis Davaris (1500dr), *Knossos: The Minoan Civilization,* by Sosso Logadiou-Platonos (1200dr), and the new *Knossos: A Complete Guide to the Palace of Mines,* by Anna Michailidou (2000dr), all on sale at the site. Even more helpful and enlightening is an English-speaking tour guide (1000-2000dr for a 1hr. tour). Make sure that the guide is official and has the required papers. The ruins are open 8am-7pm (tel. 23 19 40; admission 1500dr, students 800dr, free on Sun.). Take bus #2 (every 20min., 210dr), which stops along 25th Augustou Ave., and look for signposts on the street.

PHAISTOS

Imperiously situated on a plateau with a magnificent view of the mountains, the palace at Phaistos (tel. (0892) 42 315) housed Minoan royalty. At the turn of the century, Halbherr began excavations here and unearthed two palaces. The first was destroyed by the earthquake that decimated Crete around 1700 BC; the second was leveled in a mysterious catastrophe in 1450 BC. Surprisingly enough, a final excavation in 1952 came upon traces of two even older palaces. Since the excavations, minor reconstruction work has been done on the walls, chambers, and cisterns. Built according to the standard Minoan blueprint, the complex included a great central court from which extended the private royal quarters, servants' quarters, storerooms, and chambers for state occasions. The grand staircase is intact. Phaistos may be disappointing to those not versed in Minoan archaeology because it's difficult to visualize what the palace looked like in its former glory days. Combined with a day at the Matala beach, Phaistos makes for an ideal day trip from Iraklion (open 8am-5pm; admission 1200dr, students 600dr). **Buses** from Phaistos go to: Iraklion (5-7 per day, 1½hr., 1100dr); Matala (3-5 per day, 20min., 200dr); and Agia Galini (3-5 per day, 25min., 200dr).

TYLISSOS, FODELE, AND GORTINIA

Although Knossos is secure in its status as the most popular site on Crete, it cannot lay claim to being the oldest. At **Tylissos,** 14km southwest of Iraklion, archaeologists have unearthed a Minoan city dating back to 2000 BC. Unlike Knossos, the ruins at Tylissos remain relatively unaltered. Halfway between Tylissos and Anogia are the remains of the Minoan villas at **Sklavokambos.**

Also accessible from Iraklion is **Fodele,** a village full of orange trees and famous as the home of **El Greco** (see **It's El Greco to Me,** p. 187). The first stop of historical interest on the road south, **Gortina** contains the ruins of the Greco-Roman city **Gortyn.** In 67 BC, when it fell to the Romans, Gortyn was made the island's capital. Most of the remaining ruins here are from the Roman occupation, including the **Roman Odeon** (music hall). One of the few remains from the Hellenic city, the **Law Code tablets** are the most important extant source of information regarding pre-Hellenistic Greek law. They are written in a Dorian dialect of Greek and date from 450 BC. The tablets were so well-cut the Romans used them as building materials for the odeon.

The site of ancient Gortyn, en route to Phaistos, is on your right as you come from Iraklion. The first thing you'll see is the 7th-century **Basilica of Saint Titus.** The odeon is behind the church. The site has a hall with 14 sculpted figures and a statue of a soldier. To get to Gortyn, take one of the **buses** that go to Matala or Phaistos.

■ Matala ΜΑΤΑΛΑ

LSD, psychedelic colors, and groovy music once filled the caves strewn along Matala's seaside cliffs. Anyone who visited Matala 20 years ago is likely to muster only intoxicated memories of a more hallucinogenic trip. Before you pack your rolling papers, be aware that hardly anything of these hedonistic fiestas remains, and Matala is now a resort town for families. Along the beach with the best waves in Crete, huge cliffs with tiers of caves have been inhabited since neolithic times.

ORIENTATION AND PRACTICAL INFORMATION

Matala has three main streets: one on the water, one behind it, and one that intersects both. On the first you'll find cafes, restaurants, souvenir stands, and a covered market; on the second, the bus station, motorbike rental agencies, and stores. At Matala's square, these two join the hotel and pension-lined road to Phaistos. Several motorbike rental places, all in the main square, handle **currency exchange. Monza Travel** (tel. 45 732) serves as an informal tourist office and provides information on hotels and beaches. Monza rents **mopeds** for 3000-9000dr per day, with reduced prices for longer rentals (open 9am-11pm). The **OTE,** in the beach parking lot, resembles a small prison (open Mon.-Sat. 8am-11pm, Sun. 9am-2pm and 5-10pm). The **laundromat,** across from the campground and up a small road in an unmarked white building, charges 2500dr per wash and dry (open Mon.-Sat. 9am-3pm). The **post office** is near the entrance to the beach parking lot (open Mon.-Fri. 8:30am-2pm). In summer, **buses** go to: Iraklion (3-6 per day, 1¾hr. 1400dr); Phaistos (5 per day, 20min., 500dr); and Agia Galini (3-5 per day, 45min., 600dr). The **police, hospital,** and **pharmacy** are in Mires, 17km northeast. In an **emergency,** call 22 222 for police or 22 225 for a doctor to drive to Matala (24hr.). **Public toilets** are located in the main square next to Monza Travel. **Postal Code:** 70200. **Telephone Code:** 0892.

ACCOMMODATIONS

Matala has more than a dozen hotels and pensions, but bargains are scarce. Singles cost as much as doubles and rarely drop below 3000dr in summer. Germans and Brits often pack the town in tour groups, but there are lots of **rooms to let** on the road forking off the main road 750m out of town. It may be a good idea to make Matala a daytrip. Cheaper accommodations are available in nearby villages. Don't try to sleep on the main beach or in the caves; it's illegal and police raid them. Your best bet in town is **Dimitri's Villa** (tel./fax (093) 32 07 37). From the town center, walk out of town 200m, turn right onto the winding road at the blue "Dimitri's Villa" sign, then follow the path around; call from the bus stop and one of the owners may come pick you up by motorbike. Dimitri has immaculate, shiny rooms with private bath, balconies, safes, and hot water. He also offers *Let's Go* users a myriad of advantages including: **currency exchange** without commission, 600dr breakfasts, a 25% discount on bike rentals, and a free ride from Mires to Matala to stay in his rooms (singles 2800dr; doubles 3500dr; triples 4300dr). Another fine option is **Pension Matala View** (tel. 45 114), on the pension-lined road running inland near the main square. They have tidy bedrooms with baths and balconies (singles 3500dr; doubles 5000dr; triples 6000dr). **Matala Camping** (tel. 45 720), on your right in the town center, has showers (950dr per person; 650dr per tent; 600dr per car; 1100dr per RV).

FOOD AND ENTERTAINMENT

As usual better food is farther from the mainstream hangouts. **Nassos** (tel. 45 250), near the waterfront, offers good *souvlaki* (250dr) and gyros (400dr; open daily 9am-1am). Tucked away near the end of the stream of bars that face the caves is **Skala** (tel. 45 489), a family-run restaurant known by its nickname, the "Fish Taverna." Try the Cretan salad, a sampler of all the *tzatziki*-related dishes Crete has to offer (2000dr; open 8am-midnight). **Antonio's Taverna** (tel. 45 552), near the turn-off for Dimitri's Rooms, has tasty charcoal-roasted chicken (1200dr; open in summer daily 10am-2am). The **bakery** (tel. 45 450) in front of the police station sells a large array of standard Greek pastries, biscuits, and loaves of fresh bread (open daily 7am-11pm). **Sirtaki** (tel. 45 001), one of the many restaurants on the beach, is the ideal setting for sunset dining. All meat and fish is cooked on the grill over hot coals. Mixed fish platter, including shrimp, and salad is 1500dr (open daily 8am-midnight).

Nightlife in Matala means drinking, dancing, and gazing at the ocean until dawn in bars built into the caves on the Easter ridge. At the **Seahorse Bar** (tel. 45 724), dig the reggae, hear the waves, sip the Metaxa, and gaze across to the caves from this porch-turned-bar with tropical plants and a water wall (open just about all day). **Kahlua** (tel. 45 253) is a more mellow nightspot. Sip coffee or brandy among patrons who are out to converse rather than carouse (open daily 5pm-late). **Yorgos** (tel. 45 722), the energetic bartender and owner of this lively bar, is bound to make you happy with his spunky dancing, chit-chat, and ice-cold beers (open daily 6pm-late).

SIGHTS

Matala's main attraction is its three tiers of **caves** next to the beach. Sit in their cool, dim interior and spy on the beach action while reflecting on the cave's possible previous occupants: singer-songwriter Joni Mitchell, Nazis searching for British submarines, and, long ago, Roman corpses (open 8am-5pm, free).

Matala has more than its share of great **beaches** too. Past the crashing waves rises the dim outline of Paximadia Island; check in with vacationing environmentalists who run a stand providing information about local **sea turtles,** endangered by the bright lights of big development. And if you're running low on clothes, pick up a turtle t-shirt (profits to benefit turtles, 3000dr). For an equally good shore and more secluded caves, bikini and Speedo-clad sun worshipers join nude bathers on **Red Beach,** 20 minutes down the path behind the church. Comparatively shut off, with a small community of free-lance summer residents and a lone *taverna,* **Kommos Beach** is a 5km walk from Matala. Archaeologists are currently excavating a Minoan site that overlooks the sea, arguably the bluest patch of water in Crete. The bus from Iraklion will let you off roughly 500m from the beach (bus schedule posted by the station in Matala). Bring water; the hike down is long and dusty.

■ Near Matala: Agia Galini ΑΓΙΑ ΓΑΛΗΝΗ

Agia Galini, once a tranquil fishing village west of Matala on the southwestern coast, has become a pleasant resort town with glitzy hotels, discos, and bars. Friendly locals make up for the busloads of people you could have met at home.

ORIENTATION AND PRACTICAL INFORMATION

Agia Galini is perched on a hill—no matter where you are in town, just head downhill to reach the sea. The **post office** is below the bus station on the left (open Mon.-Fri. 8am-2pm). **Cretan Holidays** provides essential services, such as **currency exchange,** tourist information, and **car rental** (open April-Oct. daily 8:30am-9pm; 13,000-16,000dr per day, insurance included). The **police** (tel. 91 210) and the **port police** (tel. 91 206) are near the water on the right side of the street with the bus stop (both open 24hr.). There are **public toilets** (100dr) next to the police. Several shops rent bikes, including **Biggis Bikes** (tel. 91 142), near the post office (open daily 8:30am-11:30pm; mopeds 4000dr). There is a **pharmacy** (tel. 91 168) farther down from the post office, toward the harbor on the left (open daily 9am-2pm and 5-9pm). A **doctor** (tel. 91 091) is a few doors down from the OPSIS office, toward the harbor (open Mon.-Fri. 10am-1:30pm and 7-8pm, Sat. noon-1pm and 7-8pm, Sun. 7-8pm). The **health center** (tel. 91 111) is in the police station. A doctor visits the health center two days per week; the exact schedule varies. When the doctor is out, it is essentially a first aid station. (Open in summer Mon.-Fri. 9am-2pm and 5:30-8:30pm; in winter 9:30am-1:30pm.) Facing the harbor, turn left at Biggis and then turn right onto **Vas. Ioannis Street,** Agia Galini's main drag. **Candia Tours** (tel. 91 278; fax 91 174; open in summer daily 9am-1pm and 5-9pm) and a **bookstore** called "Book Shop/Leather" (open daily 9am-11pm) are both on this street. The **postal code** is 74056. The **telephone code** reads a stunning 0832.

ACCOMMODATIONS

The pensions along the upper tier of Agia Galini are cheaper than the hotels in the center of town.

Hotel Manos (tel. 91 394), 25m from bus stop, has attractively furnished rooms with wide, comfortable beds and shared balconies. Doubles with bath 3000-5000dr.

Hotel Acteon (tel. 91 208) is about halfway up the main road or up the steps from the harbor. Turn right on the tier before the Hotel Daedalus. Decent, large rooms. Ask for the middle floor—it is high enough for a view of the water, but too low for the glorious panorama of the parking lot. Doubles 4000-5000dr; triples 6000dr. Prices negotiable in early high season. Reserve 2 weeks in advance.

Hotel Mirago (tel. 91 140, -494) is next door to the Hotel Acteon. Clean, bright rooms. Doubles 4000dr; triples 5000dr.

Camping Agia Galini (tel. 91 386) is on the road from Iraklion, at the turn-off 3km before town. From the harbor, follow the beachfront 500m and look for the sign. Walk across the tilted footbridge to the end of the beach, then walk another 150m. The grounds have gravel tent sites shaded by olive and carob trees. Beware of the dogs. 1000dr per person; 400dr per tent.

FOOD AND ENTERTAINMENT

Agia Galini has a multitude of restaurants, bars, and discos, all of which have similar prices. **Taverna Kosmas** (tel. 91 222), on the main street cluttered with nondescript *tavernas,* is exceptional. Traditional Cretan cuisine is served with a Cretan smile under the unusual upside-down tree-trunk lights made by Kosmas himself (the tree is called the "never die" tree by Greeks). Enjoy all the traditional specialties of Crete as well as homemade wine (500dr per 500mL) and organically grown vegetables. The tasty *dolmades* are stuffed vine leaves (750dr; open daily 11am-3pm and 6pm-late). **Charlie's Place** (tel. 91 065), still known by locals as Horiarti's, recently underwent a facelift but still serves good *taverna* fare at reasonable prices. Try the *tava* (oven roasted lamb ribs, 1000dr) or the rabbit (1400dr; open daily 6pm-1am). For a quick meal, head to **Mr. Karamouzos** (tel. 91 023) for a huge gyro (400dr; open daily Feb.-Nov. 10am-1am).

Nightlife in Agia Galini is dominated by roof garden bars and loud discos. **Paradiso** is a lively roof garden bar, and the **Juke Box Disco** fills with dancing tourists. Meet other dancing travelers at the nightly happy hour, when all cocktails are 700dr (daily 10pm-midnight). For a mellower scene and respite from the bar and disco crowds, **Incognito** (tel. 91 414) offers live guitar music and singing in a cozy, air-conditioned atmosphere. Couples and families come to enjoy coffees (*frappés* 350dr), cocktails (900-1200dr), and cider (700dr). They also serve tasty breakfasts (mushroom omelettes 750dr; open daily 8am-late).

WESTERN CRETE

While many of the resort towns of eastern Crete seem to have sprung from the brains of British booking agents, the vacation spots of western Crete have grown naturally around towns with rich histories and Cretan characters. The meld of Ottoman, Venetian, and Greek architecture in Rethymnon and Chania complement the blue waters of the southwest coast and the sheer cliffs of the Samaria Gorge.

■ Rethymnon ΡΕΘΥΜΝΟ

The Ottoman and Venetian influences pervading the cities of northern Crete are best appreciated in Rethymnon's harbor. Arabic inscriptions lace the walls of its narrow arched streets, minarets highlight the old city's skyline, and a Venetian fortress guards the harbor's west end. On any given day, even the most energetic travelers may inexplicably find themselves waking up just in time for the afternoon *siesta* and lounging until the wee hours of the next morning in a cafe by the sea.

ORIENTATION AND PRACTICAL INFORMATION

To get to **Arkadiou Street** and the waterfront from the bus station, follow Igoum Garrill St. from behind the station until it becomes **Kountouriotou Street,** and make a left onto **Varda Kallergi Street.** You'll find everything you need in the rough triangle formed by Arkadiou, **Antistassios,** and **Gerakari Street.**

Tourist Office: (tel. 29 148) Down by the waterfront, east of the old city. Staff provides free maps, bus and ferry schedules, museum hours, and a list of all-night pharmacies. They also suggest daytrips and local events. Open Mon.-Fri. 8am-5:30pm and Sat. 9am-2pm.

Tourist Police: 5 Venizelou St. (tel. 28 156; fax 53 450), 3 blocks from the fortress. Provides services similar to the tourist office. Open Mon.-Fri. 7am-10pm.

Banks: Bank of Crete, at the intersection of Kountouriotou and Varda Kallergi, has **currency exchange.** The **National Bank** is on Kountouriotou St. Both open Mon.-Thurs. 8am-2pm and Fri. 8am-1:30pm.

Flights: Olympic Airways, 5 Koumoundorou St. (tel. 24 333, 22 257), opposite the public gardens. Open Mon.-Fri. 8am-7:30pm and Sat. 8am-3:30pm.

Buses: Reythymnon-Chania station (tel. 22 212, -659), south of the fortress on the water at Igoum Gavril St. To: Iraklion (17 per day, 1½hr., 1400dr); Chania (18 per day, 1hr., 1350dr); Agia Galini (4 per day, 2hr., 1100dr); and Plakias (6 per day, 1hr., 850dr).

Taxis: (tel. 22 316, 24 316, 28 316). Available 24hr. in 4 Matrion Sq.

Moped Rental: Fahrrad Rent-a-Vespa, 15 Kountouriotou St. (tel. 29 331), across from the OTE. Mountain bikes 2000dr per day. Open daily 8am-2pm and 5-9pm.

International Bookstore: International Press, 15 Petichaki St. (tel. 24 111), near the water. Sells books and magazines. Open daily 9am-11pm. **Spontidaki Toula,** 43 Souliou St. (tel. 54307), buys and sells used books. Open 9am-11pm.

Laundromat: 45 Tombasi St. (tel. 56 196), next to the youth hostel. Wash and dry 2000dr. Open Mon., Wed., Sat. 8:30am-2pm and 4-8:30pm, and Tues., Thurs.-Fri. 8:30am-2pm and 4-7pm. Drop-off service available.

Hospital: Trantalidou St. (tel. 27 814), in the southwest corner of town. From Igoum Gavril St. at the bus station take Kriari St. to G. Trandalidor St. and bear left; it's on the left. Open 24hr.

Police: (tel. 25 247) Located in Iroon Square. Open 24hr.

Post Office: Main branch on Moatsou St., near the public gardens. **Caravan office,** on the beach. Both branches open Mon.-Fri. 7:30am-8pm and Sat. 7:30am-2pm.

Postal Code: 74100.

OTE: 28 Kountouriotou St. Open May-Oct. Mon.-Sat. 7am-midnight and Sun. 8am-11pm, Nov.-April daily 7am-10pm. **Telephone Code:** 0831.

ACCOMMODATIONS

Arkadiou St. and the harbor, near the fortress and the Venetian port, are lined with hotels and rooms to let. Most are spacious and expensive. The **Association of Rooms to Let,** 2 Petichaki St. (tel. 29 503), a block from the harbor, will tell you what is available. Off-season prices are 20-40% less.

Youth Hostel, 41-45 Tombazi St. (tel. 22 848), at the center of the old town. Rooms and outside bunk beds on the veranda or roof are available. Teeming in the summer with young people enjoying the pleasant garden areas and bar. Spontaneous parties and communal meals are known to form. Hot showers in summer 8-10am and 5-8pm. Reception open in summer daily 8am-noon and 5-10pm, in winter 8am-noon and 5-9:30pm. 1200dr per person. Breakfast 400dr.

Olga's Pension, 57 Souliou St. (tel. 29 851), on a restored street off Antistassios. Cheery decor in comfortable rooms, all with bath. Note the coin mosaic on your way up the front stairs. Coffee and meals can be brought up from Stella's. Warm, friendly owners. Singles 4500dr; doubles 5000dr; triples 7000dr; quads 9000dr.

Hotel Paradisos, 35 Igoum Gavril St. (tel. 22 419). From the bus station, walk down Igoum Gavril; the hotel is on the left, across from the public garden. Clean, quiet rooms. Singles 3000dr; doubles 4000dr; triples 5000dr. Hot showers 500dr.

Elizabeth Camping (tel. 28 694), 3km east of town at the beginning of the old road to Iraklion. Tent pitches on shaded grass. Free parking next to reception. The staff lends supplies, guitars, and books. Self-service *taverna* open 8:30am-1am. "Texas" BBQ every Thursday. **Buses** run here from the Rethymnon station (150dr). Open May-Oct. 3600dr for 2 people and a tent.

FOOD AND ENTERTAINMENT

Rethymnon has plenty of *souvlaki* (150dr) stands scattered throughout the city. There's also an **open-air market** on Thursdays next to the park, between Moatsou and Kountouriotou St. The market opens early (6 or 7am) and closes by midday (1 or 2pm). By 9 or 10am the selection is drastically diminished. For a thriving nighttime dining scene, tourists and locals head to Petichaki Sq. and fill the *tavernas*.

Dimitris, 35 Agios Varvaras St. (tel. 28 933). There is no menu in this *raki* bar, but the food is tasty. If you order alcohol made by the owner (150dr), you'll receive a plate of snacks, usually olives, cheese, and meat. Their specialty (besides *raki*) is oven-roasted potatoes (200dr). Open daily 8am-2pm and 5-11pm.

Taverna Kyria Maria, 20 Moskovitou St. (tel. 29 078). Rabbit (1300dr), lamb with potatoes (1300dr), and octopus (woo-hoo!) in wine sauce (1100dr). Free hot cheese pies drenched in honey after dinner. Pleasant atmosphere among chirping birds. Open mid-March to Oct. daily 10am-11pm.

Pontios, 34 Melissinou St. (tel. 57 024). Homemade Greek specialties: fresh, delicious stuffed *kalamari* (1300dr), Greek salad (500dr), and *souvlaki* with pita (300dr). The street closes every day at 3pm, making these outdoor tables beneath the Fortezza a pleasant place to dine. Open daily 8am-midnight.

Akri, 27 Kornarou St. (tel. 50 719), just off of Souliou St. in the old town. Enjoy Greek music and feast on house specialties (1500-2500dr; open 11am-4pm and 6pm-1am).

Stella's Kitchen, 55 Souliou St. (tel. 28 665). Family-run coffee shop below Olga's Pension serving homemade cakes (200-1000dr). Open 7am-midnight.

The bar scene at Rethymnon centers around Petichaki St. and Nearchou St. near the west end of the harbor. The happening **Rockafé Bar,** on Petichaki St., and the **Fortezza Disco Bar,** 14 Nearchou St. (tel. 21 493), book-end several Greek *bouzouki* places. Both have pricey beers (1000dr). Most wanderers end up at the **Lemon Tree.**

SIGHTS

Rethymnon has been occupied nearly continuously since the late Minoan period. At its apex in the 4th century BC it was overrun by Mycenaeans. During the Fourth Crusade, the Franks sold the island to the Venetians for 520 pounds of silver. The Venetians fortified Rethymnon, which was crucial to their chain of trading outposts. The Ottomans then took the city in 1646, enlarging it and incorporating Ottoman designs into the buildings.

Rethymnon's **Archaeological Museum** (tel. 54 668) is in a former Ottoman prison, adjacent to the fortress. Once inside, you'll feel like you've wandered into the storeroom of an absent-minded archaeologist—headless statues lean on walls behind rows of figurines, and Minoan sarcophagi lie next to Roman coins (open Tues.-Sun. 8:30am-3pm; admission 500dr, students 300dr). The **Historical and Folklore Museum,** 28-30 Vernardou St. (tel. 23 398), showcases traditional arts and farming tools (open Mon.-Sat. 9am-1pm and 6-8pm; admission 400dr, students 300dr).

New to Rethymnon is the **L. Kanakakis Center of Contemporary Art,** 2 Himaras St., at the corner of Salaminus St. Works by Rethymnon's Kanakakis are part of a larger collection of modern Greek paintings. The center also hosts temporary exhibitions (open Tues.-Sat. 10am-2pm and 6-9pm, Sun. 10am-3pm; admission 500dr).

At some point during your visit you should make a pilgrimage to the 1580 **Venetian Fortezza** (tel. 28 101). The walls of the citadel are in excellent condition, but most of the buildings inside the fortress were destroyed by Ottomans in the 17th century, and even more bit the dust three centuries later during WWII (open daily 8am-8pm; admission 500dr). The city's **Renaissance Festival,** featuring theater, concerts, and exhibitions, is held in the fortress in July and August.

Tattooed with graffiti and untamed by museum keepers, Rethymnos' Ottoman monuments blend uncelebrated into its scenery: the **Neratzes Minaret** on Antistassios St.; the **Nerdjes Mosque** a block farther, formerly a Franciscan church; the **Kara**

Pasha Mosque on Arkadiou St. near Iroon Sq.; and the **Valides Minaret,** which presides over **Porta Megali** gate at the beginning of Antistassios St. in 3 Martiou Sq. Cretans who sought refuge in the early Byzantine **Arkadi monastery** in 1866, 23km from Rethymnon, blew themselves up rather than surrender to the Ottomans. The monastery has a **museum** today (admission 200dr; 3 buses per day, 400dr).

Rethymnon's **Wine Festival** (in July or August) is a crowded all-you-can-drink fest. (First-night admission is 1000dr, descending 100dr per night. Required souvenir glasses 150dr.) A local dance troupe performs early in the evening. Rethymnon's own **craft shops** cluster around Arkadiou, Antistassios, and Gerakari St. The **Herb Shop,** 58 Souliou St. (tel. 29 664), stocks folk remedies and herbs exclusive to Crete. For 50 years this shop has sold dried Cretan herbs for cooking and healing. *Senes* is said to help heal stomach ailments (300dr for a small bag), and oregano tastes good on salad (500dr per bag; open Mon.-Sat. 10am-2pm and 6-11pm, Sun. 6-11pm).

■ Plakias ΠΛΑΚΙΑΣ

Sunny and secluded, Plakias has remained pleasantly underdeveloped and inexpensive compared to most other Cretan beach towns. The crystal-clear waters of the south coast, as well as mountain villages and remote monasteries within hiking distance, make Plakias an ideal budget escape from Crete's cosmopolitan north coast.

ORIENTATION AND PRACTICAL INFORMATION

Everything in Plakias lies either on the beach road or on the roads and foot paths that recede into the hills. **Buses** drop off and pick up visitors right on the beach. They run to: Rethymnon (7 per day, 850dr); Agia Galini (2 per day, 1200dr); Preveli (3 per day, 340dr); and Chora Sfakia (1 per day, 900dr). **Monza Travel** (tel. 31 882), on the beach road, has both British and Greek staff, rents cars (10,000dr) and mopeds (4000dr), arranges for scuba instruction and other watersports, and runs excursions to all parts of Crete (5000-10,000dr). A **doctor** and **pharmacy** (tel. 31 770), are behind Monza (open Mon.-Sat. 9:30am-1:30pm and 5-8:30pm, Sun. 5-8:30pm), but call the **hospital** in Rethymnon in an emergency (tel. (0831) 27 814). A **post office** trailer sets up on the beach for the summer (open Mon.-Fri. 8:30am-2pm), but a larger, year-round post office and the **police** (tel. 31 338), are 1km north in Mirthios. The **postal code** is 74060. The **telephone code** is 0832.

ACCOMMODATIONS

Follow several signs pointing inland to reach the **Plakias Youth Hostel** (tel. 32 118). The bungalows have dorm beds (1100dr) where a young, international set of backpackers spend quiet *siestas* between swims and hikes. The common refrigerator, bathroom, and lounge (with jukebox) are kept clean by a friendly staff. The roof provides a somewhat private getaway for couples. Reception is open 9am-noon and 5-9pm, but if you arrive during off-hours, grab an open bed and settle up in the morning. For private doubles (3500dr), ask at the Youth Hostel about **Fethra.**

FOOD, ENTERTAINMENT, AND SIGHTS

For a tasty switch from the usual *gyro* fare, try chicken in pita (450dr) or shrimp in pita (600dr) at **To Xechoristo,** on the beach road (tel. 31 214; open daily 2pm-5am). Over the tiny bridge to the west, **Lysseos** serves inexpensive traditional village meals (*moussaka* 1150dr). For those in search of **nightlife,** even far from the city lights, **Hexagon** and **Meltemi** dance clubs grind from midnight to 6am.

You may be too tired for such nocturnal activities after **hikes** through the surrounding hills. Follow posted signs or ask around town for a one-hour climb past the village of Mirthios to **Preveli Monastery** (open daylight hours; admission 500dr; modest dress required). Return the same way or climb down the cliff road to **Preveli Beach,** where you can hitch a ride back to Plakias on a passing ferry (1000dr).

■ Chania XANIA

Chania has survived an attack of WWII German paratroopers as well as Venetian, Egyptian, and Ottoman occupations. Although no longer Crete's official capital, Chania is still regarded by many islanders as the spiritual capital. Visitors meander through winding streets, absorb folk music from streetside cafes, or spend the day gazing at the old Venetian Harbor. No matter how tourist-oriented the waterfront cafes become, they don't mar the harbor's beauty, silhouetted at sunset by Ottoman-built domes.

ORIENTATION AND PRACTICAL INFORMATION

From the bus station, walk right on Kidonias St. for two blocks and turn left onto Platia 1866; going north, the road becomes Halidon St. and leads to the old **harbor,** the setting for much of Chania's nightlife. To lighten the load while looking for a room, **leave your bags** at the bus station (storage open 6am-8pm; 100dr per bag). Ferries dock in **Souda,** the nearby port. A bus from Souda drops you off at Chania's Municipal Market (10min., 250dr). Facing the market, turn left and walk two blocks on Gianari St., then right onto Halidon. Even with maps from the tourist office, finding your way around is challenging. Luckily, Chania is small, so you can't stay lost for long. Chania's business district is mostly contained within the area across from the market, around the intersection of **Gianari Street** and **Tzanakaki Street.**

Tourist Office: (tel./fax 92 624) First floor of Megaro Pantheon, Platia 1866, behind Greek Agricultural Bank. Information on flights, ferries, buses, hotels, and package tours; free maps. Open Mon.-Fri. 7:30am-2:30pm, Sat-Sun. 8am-3pm.

Tourist Police: 60 Karaiskaki St. (tel. 73 333), by the central bus station. In an **emergency,** call 100. Open daily 7:30am-8pm. **Port Police:** Tel. 98 888.

Banks: The **National Bank** is on the corner of Nikiforou and Foka St. Open Mon.-Thurs. 8am-2pm, Fri. 8am-1:30pm.

Flights: Olympic Airways, 88 Tzanakaki St. (tel. 57 701, -2, -3), near the public garden. Buses for the airport leave the main office on Tzanakaki 1½hr. before each flight. Tickets sold Mon.-Fri. 8am-3pm. Phone reservations Mon.-Fri. 7am-10pm, Sat. 8am-3pm. Flights to Athens (4 per week, 19,600dr).

Buses: Central bus station (tel. 93 052, -306), on the corner of Kidonias and Kelaidi St. Schedules change often so check before you go. To: Paleochora (5 per day, 1350dr); Chora Sfakion (3 per day, 1300dr); Kastelli (14 per day, 900dr); Samaria (4 per day, 1100dr, return 1200dr); Elafonissi (1 per day, 1350dr); Soagia (2 per day, 1300dr); Rethymnon (16 per day, 1350dr); and Iraklion (16 per day, 2650dr).

Ferries: ANEK Office (tel. 28 500), in Venizelou Sq., near National Bank. *Kriti* and *Aptera* go to Peiraias (8pm, 11hr., tourist-class 9550dr, deck-class 5750dr).

Moped Rental: Several on Halidon St. Mopeds rent for 4500-7000dr per day. **Olympic Rent-a-Car,** 74 Halidon St. (tel. 94 915; fax 88 025), rents **cars.** Fiat Panda 8000dr per day. 25% discount for *Let's Go* users. Open daily 8am-10pm.

Laundromat: (tel. 52 494), next to Hotel Fidias. Wash 800dr; dry 700dr. Soap free. Open daily 9am-9pm.

Hospital: (tel. 27 000) Corner of Dragoumi and Kapodistriou St., 5 blocks east of the harbor center. Outpatient clinic open Mon.-Sat. 12:30-2pm and 6-9pm, Sun. 8am-9pm. For **emergencies,** call 22 222. Available 24hr.

Post Office: 3 Tzanakaki St. Open Mon.-Fri. 7:30am-8pm. **Postal Code:** 73100.

OTE: 5 Tzanakaki St. Very efficient. Open in summer 6am-midnight; in the off season daily 7am-11pm. Telex and telegram Mon.-Fri. only. **Telephone Code:** 0821.

ACCOMMODATIONS

Most of the inexpensive pensions in the old town overlook the harbor, a convenient but noisy area. Small hotels sprout from the beaches on the west coast, but expect to lay out the cash for the brown sands of **Nea Kydonia** and **Agia Marina.** The **Association of Rooms to Let: Unikreta Travel Agency,** 20 Dor. Episkopou (tel. 43 601; fax

46 277), a block left of harbor center, can help find rooms (open Mon.-Fri. 9am-2pm). Be wary of the locals at the bus station who *illegally* try to entice visitors to stay in their private rooms. It is dangerous—they are dishonest about prices and intentions.

Meltemi Pension, 2 Agelou St. (tel. 92 802), at end of west side of harbor, next to the Naval Museum. Rooms have wooden floors, marble-topped desks, high ceilings, and some harbor views. The Meltemi Cafe downstairs serves *frappés* (500dr), breakfast, and drinks. Doubles 4000-7000dr; triples with private shower 8000dr.

Hotel Fidias, 6 Sarpaki St. (tel. 52 494), from Halidon St. turn right at the cathedral on Athinagora St., which becomes Sarpaki St. With poster-coated walls and linoleum floors, it looks like a clean college dorm. Hot common showers, TV, international calls. Reception open daily 7am-11pm. Dorm beds 1700dr per person; singles 3000-3500dr; doubles 3800-4000dr; triples 5000dr.

Ifigenia Rooms (tel. 99 184; mobile phone (094) 501 319). Head to Ifigenia III at 15 Theotokopolou St. at the Cafe Orio to find the manager. To get there, walk up Angelou St. from the Naval Museum and take a left on Theotokopolou St. Several buildings, all in the old town close to the harbor, with many rooms available. Most rooms have private bath, and some have kitchens. The cafe and pension are on the right. Prices for doubles range from 5000-9000dr, depending on season.

FOOD AND ENTERTAINMENT

The **public market,** at the south end of the old town at the intersection of Tzanakaki St. and Hatzi Michali Gianari St., is in a beautiful building built in about 1912. Produce, cheese, herb, and meat shops mix with leather shops and tiny seafood restaurants (open Mon-Sat. 8am-2pm, Tues. and Fri. 8am-2pm and 6-9pm). Small restaurants serve fresh fried seafood and delicious stews for good prices.

To Apovrado, 30 Isodion St. (tel. 58 151). Several shady tables along a narrow lane, a block off of Halidon St. Provides a cozy atmosphere for relaxed dining (salads 550dr, open daily 9am-1am).

Tamam, Zabeliou 49 (tel. 96 080). Intimate dinners of super veal with mushrooms (900dr), as well as vegetarian alternatives (open daily 7-11pm or 1am).

Dinos (tel. 41 865), famed all over Crete for outstanding seafood. To try a plateful of fresh local seafood, splurge on the mixed fish plate for two (6500dr). Garlic fans should request the special Greek sauce. Scenes from the film *Zorba the Greek* were filmed here (open daily noon-1 or 2am).

Chania's lively nightlife has a distinct dichotomy—the American music young Greeks groove to is on the west side of the harbor, and the Rembetika beats old men drink to is on the east side. Tiny **Fagotto Bar,** 16 Agelou (tel. 71 877), plays hot jazz and rhythm and blues from their huge collection (cocktails 1200dr; open daily 10pm-3am). For a hard-core Cretan experience head east to **Cafe Kriti**, 22 Kalergon St., which offers traditional music and dancing among the old men with the long mustaches and the big black boots. (Beer 500dr. Open 7pm-late. *Not for women traveling alone.*)

SIGHTS

Kastelli Hill, the area north of Kanevaro St., is studded with reminders of Chania's past. Remnants of Ancient Kydonia's Bronze Age prosperity are evident at the **Late Minoan House** (circa 1450 BC), on the corner of Kandanoleu and Kanevaro St. Unfortunately, the site is fenced off. In the Middle Ages, Venetian occupiers enriched the city's architecture, but WWII destroyed much of their artistry. The waterfront alleys, with a melange of Ottoman and Venetian architecture, reflect the city's past. Pass through several archways on Moshon St. to reach the **Venetian Chapel,** decorated with Latin and Turkish inscriptions. Young Greeks mellow out in the **Municipal Gardens,** *Dimotikos Kypos,* once the property of a *muezzin* (Islamic prayer caller). The garden also harbors a small zoo and an open-air movie theater that shows international films. UNICEF sets up an annual **International Fair** in the gardens—consult the tourist office for details. **Sfakianaki,** a 19th-century neighborhood with tree-lined streets, is beyond the gardens to the east, as is the **Historical Museum and Archives,** 20 Sfakianaki St. (tel. 52 606), which contains Cretan weaponry, photos of 19th-century generals, old clothing, and a tattered Cretan flag (open Mon.-Fri. 8am-1:30pm).

The **Venetian Inner Harbor** is a thriving social scene and an architectural relic that has retained its original breakwater and Venetian arsenal. Egyptians restored the Venetian **lighthouse** during their occupation of Crete in the late 1830s (enter at the east end of the harbor). On the opposite side of the main harbor, the **Naval Museum** (tel. 91 875), exhibits nautical pictures and pieces of boats (open in summer daily 10am-4pm; in winter 10am-2pm; admission 500dr, students 300dr). The **Archaeological Museum** (tel. 80 334), on Halidon St. opposite the cathedral, displays Cretan artifacts. Once a Venetian monastery, it also served as the mosque of Yusuf Pasha (open Mon. 12:30-7pm, Tues.-Fri. 8am-7pm, Sat.-Sun. 8:30am-3pm; admission 500dr, students 300dr). In the **Venetian Shiphouse** at the east end of the harbor, a temporary museum is set up with a new theme each summer, so stop by the shiphouse or consult the tourist office for current information.

■ Samaria Gorge

The most popular excursion from Chania, Rethymnon, or Iraklion is the five- to six-hour hike down Europe's longest gorge: the formidable 16km **Samaria Gorge.** Worn away by millions of years of river runoff, this pass through the White Mountains, **Lefka Ori,** retains its allure despite being mobbed by visitors and spotted with litter. Bird watchers can glimpse the rare bearded vulture, horticulturists can admire the wildflowers and shrubs which peek out from sheer rock walls, and goat lovers can spot the nimble *agrimi,* a wild Cretan species in one of its few remaining natural habitats. The towering beauty of the gorge is visible at all points, but only to those who stop long enough to take their eyes from their feet. Please observe Chania Forest Protection Service's rules concerning litter to preserve the trail's natural beauty.

The 44km, one-and-a-half-hour bus ride from Chania to **Xyloskalo,** at the start of the trail, offers spectacular scenery. Passing between cliff walls up to 300m high, the downhill path, only 3m wide at some points, winds down along a riverbed that runs nearly dry in the summer. Parts of the hike are shaded by clumps of pine trees, goats, and the towering walls of the gorge itself. The hike ends in Agia Roumeli on the south coast. From there a boat sails to Loutro and Chora Sfakion, where buses run back to Chania. Experienced hikers can hike from Agia Roumeli to Chora Sfakion (10hr.) along one of the more outstanding coastlines in the country. The downhill hike favored by most people (from Xyloskalo in the Omalos Plain to Agia Roumeli) takes four to six hours. A less traveled path ascends Mt. Gingilos to the west.

Whichever route you choose, bring plenty of water and trail snacks, and wear good walking shoes. The Gorge is dry and dusty in summer, and the stones on the path become slippery. Furthermore, the altitude often makes the top of the gorge cold and rainy. If you get tired on the hike, do not worry; you can always take the donkey taxis that patrol the trail. If all you want to see is the dramatic tail of the gorge, Agia Roumeli is a great place to start the journey. The path to the trail begins just behind Rooms Livikon. From the quay, walk straight to the rear of the village. Known as "Samaria the Lazy Way," the two-hour climb to the north takes you to the gorge's dramatic and narrow pass, the "Iron Gates." The gorge is open May 1 to October 15; during the winter and spring, the river goes back to work cutting its trail through the rock. Flash floods in the winter have claimed many lives. During the open months, passage is officially allowed through the gorge between 6am and 4pm (admission 1200dr). For gorge information, call the **Chania Forest Service** (tel. (0821) 92 287), or pick up information at the tourist offices in Chania, Rethymnon, or Iraklion.

Expensive accommodations for the night before the hike are available in Xyloskalo at the **Tourist Pavilion** (tel. (0821) 63 269). Reservations can be placed with the Chania tourist office. Some 5km north of Xyloskalo, **Omalos** has food at **Drakoulaki's**

Restaurant (tel. (0821) 67 269), with **rooms to let** (doubles 5000dr; triples 7000dr). On the plain of Omalos, take a left onto a dirt road for the 90-minute trek to the Spartan **Kallergis refuge huts.** Hikers can hike in the White Mountains from there.

Buses for Omalos and Xyloskalo leave Chania four times per day (1100dr). The 6:15, 7:30, and 8:30am buses will place you in Xyloskalo for a day's hike while the 4:30pm bus will put you in Omalos for a hike the next day. From Rethymnon, take the 6:15 or 7:00am buses through Chania to Omalos (2450dr). Intrepid early risers can take the 5:30am bus from Iraklion through Rethymnon and Chania (3750dr) to Omalos. Since Agia Roumeli is connected by ferries leaving at 90-minute intervals to Chora Sfakion, you can make the complete round-trip from Chania, Rethymnon, or Iraklion in one day, leaving on a morning bus. Taking the earliest bus will ensure cooler weather and less company for the hike. The last buses out of Chora Sfakion leave at 7:15pm for Chania (1300dr) and Iraklion (2650dr) via Rethymnon (1300dr). You can also plan a leisurely hike and spend the night in a coastal town.

A hot and dusty hike beyond the official exit of the gorge leads to **Agia Roumeli,** a seedy oasis for tired and thirsty hikers. Beyond Agia Roumeli proper is a town with little but its beach to offer. The black pebbles are unbearably hot, but the water is refreshing. The town itself exists mainly to sell food, souvenirs, and lodgings to tired and weak-willed hikers. If you do stay, you can sleep at **Hotel Livikon** (tel. 91 363), on the inland end of town (doubles 4500dr; triples 5500dr).

■ Paleochora ΠΑΛΕΟΧΩΡΑ

Once a refuge for the embattled rear guard of the 1960s counterculture, Paleochora is the stop for diehard devotees. Just 77km from Chania, Paleochora is a pleasant retreat with a sandy beach and a stunning backdrop of Cretan mountains. *Tavernas* and necessities line one main street and reasonably priced pensions dot the harbor.

ORIENTATION AND PRACTICAL INFORMATION

Paleochora is on a small peninsula. Running north-south through the town center is **Venizelou Street,** the main thoroughfare. It crosses **Kentekaki Street** which leads west to the beach and east to the harbor. **Buses** to Chania (5 per day, 2hr., 1250dr) stop at this intersection.

The **tourist office** (tel. 41 507) is on Venizelou St. (open Wed.-Mon. 10am-1pm and 6-9pm), as is a **bank** (open Mon.-Thurs. 8am-2pm, Fri. 8am-1:30pm) and the **OTE** (open Mon.-Sat. 7:30am-11pm, Sun. 9am-2pm and 6-11pm). The **police station** (tel. 41 111) is on Kentekaki, near the quay; **port police** can be reached at 41 214. **Econoline Travel** (tel. 41 529; fax 41 745) is helpful for ferry information, tickets, car rental (6000dr per day for a Fiat Panda), motorbike rental (2000-8000dr per day depending on type), and bicycle rental (1000dr per day), as well as basic information about the region. From Paleochora, one to two **ferries** per day leave for: Sougia (30min., 850dr); Agios Roumeli (1hr., 1900dr); Ch. Sfakion (3hr., 3200dr); and Loutro (2¾hr., 2600dr). One boat a day departs Paleochora at 10am and leaves from Elafonisi at 4pm (1hr., one way 1200dr). A post boat goes to **Gavdos** every Tuesday and Friday (4hr., 2800dr), and a regular ferry goes to Gavdos every Thursday, Saturday, and Sunday (2½hr., 2800dr). A bus departs for Samaria daily at 6am and returns to Paleochora by boat from Agia Roumeli at 4pm (3150dr round-trip). Entrance to Samaria costs 1200dr. A boat goes to Anidri Beach, Monday and Wednesday at 10:30am (1000dr). For a taxi, call **Paleochora Taxi Office** (tel. 41 128, -061). The **medical center** sits down the road from Interkreta Travel (from the office, make a right onto the cross street). Look for the sign with the blue cross (open Mon.-Fri. mornings until 2pm). The **pharmacy** (tel. 41 498) is on Venizelou St. (open Mon.-Sat. 9am-1:30pm and 6-10pm). The **post office** is on the beach next to the Galaxy Cafe (open Mon.-Fri. 7:30am-2pm). **Postal Code: 73001. Telephone Code: 0823.**

ACCOMMODATIONS

A walk along the road closest to the harbor will bring you to the small hotels. At the center of the harbor stands the tallest white building marked "Rooms for Rent" which is run by **Nikos Bubalis** (tel. 41 112). A kindly older couple has clean doubles and triples off a staircased area. All rooms have access to balconies which look out onto the picturesque harbor and the gorgeous mountains that descend to the sea (doubles 4000-6000dr; triples 7000dr). The **Cafe Alaloom,** adjacent to the OTE, books rooms at **Savas Rooms** (tel. 41 075) for reasonable prices (doubles 5000dr). Another good option, **Rooms Oriental Bay** (tel. 41 322), is right on Rocky Beach as you enter town (doubles 5000dr; triples 8000dr). **Christos Restaurant** (tel. 41 359), along the harbor, has clean rooms with private baths (doubles 5000dr; triples 6000dr). **Camping Paleochora** (tel. 41 120) rests 1500m east of town. To reach the campground, walk north on Venizelou (away from the harbor), turn right opposite the gas station, and take the second left on the last paved road before the beach which is 1km to the site. It's also convenient to Paleochora Club, the town's popular open disco that hosts some pretty wild parties (open March-Oct. 800dr per person; 600dr per tent; **moped rental** 200dr).

FOOD AND ENTERTAINMENT

Several markets stand in the center of the town and on Venizelou St. The waterfront sports a row of restaurants serving traditional Greek food from standard tourist menus at the usual mid-range prices (*tzatziki* 400-600dr, *moussaka* 850-1000dr, *baklava* 500-700dr). More *tavernas* line Venizelou St. and have similar menus. Vegetarians and carnivores alike should appreciate the fresh homemade Greek, Asian, and European vegetarian dishes prepared by the family at the **Third Eye Vegetarian Restaurant** (tel. 41 234). Everything is delicious, but you might hope to catch the vegetarian paella (700dr) or the vegetable curry (850dr). Nothing on the menu costs more than 850dr, unless, of course, you order something from the grill. Yes, they've kept a grill for meat lovers who just can't live without their *souvlaki* (open April-Oct. daily 8am-3pm and 5pm-midnight).

For inexpensive Greek baked goods, **George Vakakis's** bakery (tel. 41 069), close to the ferry dock (follow the signs), sells generously sized cheese, spinach, or sausage pies (200dr), chocolate croissants (150dr), and traditional biscuits (1000dr per kg). Cretan *kalitsinia* are fresh and tasty (1700dr per kg). They also bake fresh Cretan sweet bread served on special occasions like weddings and christenings. (600dr per kg. Open in summer daily 7:30am-3pm and 4-11pm; in winter 8am-2:30pm and 4:30-10pm.) **Paleochora Club,** near Camping Paleochora, is the town's open-air disco (beer 600-700dr; open daily noon-4am).

AROUND PALEOCHORA

Six kilometers above Paleochora lies the peaceful town of **Azogizes** which affords a lovely view of the promontory and the sea. Here you'll find the 13th-century caves of the 99 Holy Fathers and a museum featuring relics of the Turkish occupation dating from 1770. Farther inland, the frescoed churches of Kakodiki date back to the 14th century. To reach these mountain villages, take the bus toward Chania. Boats run five times per week (one takes 2½hr., the other 4hr.; 2800dr) to the nearly deserted island of **Gavdos,** the southernmost point of Europe.

The residents of nearby **Moni Chrisoskalitissis** can provide water and lodgings. **Buses** run daily from Kastelli to as far as Chrisoskalitissis (9:30am and 2:30pm, 900dr). From there, a 5km hike leads to a pinkish-white beach. You also can hook up with excursions leaving from Paleochora or Chania. Boats go from Paleochora to the beach across from Elaforisi daily (1200dr one way, 1hr.). The boat ride along the coast is astounding, and the cliffs diving into the deep sapphire blue sea at the extreme southwestern tip of Crete are inspiring. Even closer to Paleochora is beautiful **Anidri Beach.** Just a 30-minute walk west out of Paleochora brings you to one of the lovelier beaches in Crete (according to some locals). Alternately, the boat from Paleochora also goes to the beach (Mon. and Wed. at 10:30am, 1000dr).

■ Southwest Coast

CHORA SFAKION

The scenic town of Chora Sfakion lacks the intimacy of Plakias to the east or Loutro and Paleochora to the west, but serves as the transportation hub of the south coast. The town's pebbly cove and fishing fleet look tempting from afar, but up close you will see that the beach is littered. Since Chora Sfakion lacks the dusty heat that pervades Agia Roumeli, it is an adequate resting spot after a Samaria Gorge hike.

The **post office** is next to Sfakia Tours on the waterfront (open Mon.-Sat. 7:30am-2pm). The **OTE** is on the road leading away from town, near where buses leave (open Mon.-Fri. 7:30am-3:15pm). The **supermarket** is also on the street behind the harbor—a good place to stock up for a tour of remote beaches. The 24hr. **police station** (tel. (0825) 91 205) and **port police** (tel. (0825) 91 292) are on the corner of the waterfront near a travel office, **Sfakia Tours** (tel./fax (0825) 91 130), which sells bus tickets and rents mopeds (4500dr per day; open daily 8am-10pm).

Buses from Chora Sfakion go to Plakias (2 per day, 1¼hr., 1000dr) and then to Rethymnon (4 per day, 1½hr., 1300dr) to meet the ferry. At the same time, a bus leaves for Agia Galini (1 per day, 2hr., 2100dr) or Anapolis (4 per day, 30min., 300dr). Change buses at Rethymnon for Iraklion (2650dr). Four buses per day go to Chania (2hr., 1300dr), the last at 7:15pm. If your ferry is late, don't worry—the buses wait for the boats to arrive. **Boats** from Chora Sfakion travel to Agios Roumeli (5 per day, 1¼hr., 1200dr). Most routes stop in Loutro. These run from April to October; in winter, travelers go to Loutro by foot or fishing boat. It is a good idea to check schedules with the **ticket office** (tel. (0825) 91 221). Boats run from Chora Sfakion to Gavdos, an uninhabited island and the southernmost point in Europe, every Saturday and Sunday (departs 9am, returns 5pm). **Caïques** to Sweetwater Beach run twice daily.

There are plenty of cheap accommodations in Chora Sfakion. The cool, grotto-like **Hotel Xenia** (tel. (0825) 91 490; fax 91 491) has spacious, immaculate rooms (singles 6000dr; doubles 7500dr; triples 8500dr). **Lefka Ori** (tel. (0825) 91 209), on the waterfront, rents singles for 3500dr and doubles with small, dark bathrooms for 4500-5000dr. **Rooms Samaria** (tel. (0825) 91 261), on the east end of the back street, is large and cool, with wrought-iron balconies (open March-Nov.; doubles with terrace and bath 6000dr; triples 8000dr). The town's restaurants are basically limited to those downstairs from the hotels, where meals run from 1500-4000dr. The town's only disco, **Boomerang,** rocks nightly to, in the words of the owner, "whatever the people want" (10pm-morning free).

ELAFONISSI

The satisfying journey to miraculous **Elafonissi,** a small uninhabited island at the southwest corner of Crete, must be made on foot. Perhaps like nowhere else on earth, this place will leave you speechless and astounded. Boats can't make the crossing, but the sea is so shallow that you can wade out to the island. A recent influx of tourists has left this retreat strewn with litter, but the authorities are increasing their efforts to keep it clean. There are several small cantinas serving snacks and drinks, but you may want to pack a picnic to avoid high prices. A bus from Chania (7:30am, returning 4pm, 1350dr) makes a daily trek to the opposite beach.

EASTERN CRETE

The road east from Iraklion along the north coast passes first through overcrowded, overpriced beach resort towns. All traces of traditional culture have been wiped clean from these towns, but the road becomes gradually quieter and more scenic as it passes through smaller villages sustained not by tourism, but by thriving local agriculture. The endlessly winding main highway joining Malia and Hersonissos to Agios Nikolaos, Ierapetra, and Sitia is spectacular: it grips the side of the mountains, ascending and descending deep valleys. Seemingly psychotic bus drivers dart through these hills, passing mopeds and even other buses amid treacherous curves. Miraculously, perhaps due to the prayers of elderly village women in traditional dress who frantically make the Byzantine sign of the cross at every swerve, the buses actually arrive on time and charge reasonable prices. The locally favored destinations east of Agios Nikolaos are entirely worthwhile: white villages with small green gardens, olive plains, and an astonishingly blue sea.

▓ Hersonissos ΧΕΡΣΟΝΗΣΟΣ

This resort town, 26km east of Iraklion, is free of ancient sites, monasteries, and Cretan village culture. More than 40 bars, discos, and nightclubs cluster in a 500m radius, and the beach is never far away. If you're bored with Iraklion's nightlife, just hop on the bus; you probably don't have to know the Greek words for vodka and orange juice here because your bartender won't know them either—it's about as Greek as Las Vegas.

ORIENTATION AND PRACTICAL INFORMATION

There is one main road in Hersonissos, **Eleftheriou Venizelou,** with offices, markets, and discos. Perpendicular streets lead either to the beach or to the hills.

Tourist Police: 8 Minoas St. (tel. 21 000), toward the beach in the police station. Offers **currency exchange.** Open 7am-11pm.

Tourist Agencies: Mareland Travel has four branches, one conveniently located at 12 Minoas St. (tel. 24 424), across from the police station. Open daily 9am-midnight. **Zakros Tours,** 46 El. Venizelou (tel./fax 24 715). Open daily 8am-10pm. Both rent cars, sell boat tickets, exchange currency, and have maps.

Banks: Several on El. Venizelou that exchange currency. **National Bank** is on the east end of the road. Open Mon.-Thurs. 8:30am-2pm, Fri. 8am-1:30pm.

Buses: Several bus stops in Hersonissos, but there's no central bus station. Buses run every 30min. Service to Iraklion (45min., 550dr); Malia (20min., 200dr); Agios Nikolaos (45min., 850dr); Sitia (2½hr., 2150dr); and Ierapetra (2hr., 1500dr).

Taxi: Station (tel. 23 723, -722 -193) on the west end of El. Venizelou near the Hard Rock Cafe. Open 24hr.

Car and Motorbike Rental: Several agencies on El. Venizelou. **Odyssey,** 51 El. Venizelou (tel.24 649), rents bicycles (100-1500dr per day) and motorbikes (400-6000dr per day). Open daily 9am-10pm.

Laundromat: Wash Saloon Ilios, 3 Margaraki St. (tel.22 749), just up the street from Selena Pension and restaurant. Does laundry in 3hr. 1500dr per 6 kg, includes soap price. Open daily 9am-10pm.

Public Toilets: Across from Zakros tour office on El. Venizelou St. Free.

Pharmacies: Several on El. Venizelou. Get off the bus at the first stop in Hersonissos from Iraklion, cross the street, and after 2 or 3 blocks (or 30m), **Lambraki's Pharmacy** (tel. 22 473) will be on your left. Open Mon.-Fri. 9am-11pm. Consult the signs on the doors to find one open after hours and on Sundays.

Medical Services: Dr. Babis Kokodrulis (tel. 22 063; fax 21 987) has a medical office on El. Venizelou St., opposite the bus stop from Iraklion, before the pharmacy. Open daily 9am-10pm, but call ahead. For emergencies, call him at home (tel. 22

836) or on his mobile phone (tel. (094) 51 71 70). **Hersonissos Health Center,** 19 El. Venizelou (tel. 25 141), near the Hard Rock Cafe. Open 24hr.

Post Office: 122 El. Venizelou. Follow the signs. Open Mon.-Fri. 8am-2pm. **Postal Code:** 70014.

OTE: Behind the town hall on Eleftherias St., down El. Venizelou from PTT. Open Mon.-Sat. 7:30am-10pm, Sun. 9am-2pm and 5-10pm. **Telephone Code:** 0897.

ACCOMMODATIONS

Hersonissos's digs can be pricey and hard to come by. Tour companies book a majority of the rooms for the entire season. Before arriving, consult Iraklion's **"Rooms to Let Association"** (see **Iraklion,** p. 184).

Selena Pension (tel. 25 180) 13 Marogaki St., just off Main St. toward the waterfront. All immaculate rooms have private bath. Doubles 6000-7000dr.

Camping Hersonissos, (tel. 22 902) Anisara. Take a bus or walk 3km toward Iraklion—it's on the right. Restaurant, minimarket, bar, and hot water. 950dr per person. 640dr per tent.

Camping Caravan, (tel. 22 025) Limenas. Walk or take bus 2km east toward Agios Nikolaos until Nora Hotel, then another 300m. English spoken. Open March-Oct. 1200dr per person; 900dr per tent.

FOOD AND ENTERTAINMENT

The Hersonissos waterfront sports the usual assortment of restaurants serving "traditional Greek food" pre-packaged facsimiles, often inferior to the equally common western imitations. **Taverna Kavouri** (tel. 21 161) is a thoroughly enjoyable escape from the commercialized waterfront (walk toward Iraklion, turn right onto Irinis Kai Filias St. near the Hard Rock Cafe, and walk around the bend). Fifteen tables rest under grapevines and among hanging fishing equipment. Order from the menu or just go into the kitchen and point at whatever looks appealing. Full dinner combinations including fresh local vegetables and goat, chicken, beef, or lamb are priced at 1500dr or less. Delicious fried *tiganites* are served with ice cream (600dr; open noon-midnight). For less commotion, try **Selena Restaurant** (tel. 25 180), beneath Selena Pension. Selena serves house wine from their own vineyard and fresh rabbit (1500dr) from their farm (not on the menu—ask for it grilled or stewed in wine; open daily 8am-11:30pm; Greek salad 450dr, *tzatziki* 400dr).

Nightlife is the only reason to come to Hersonissos because the beach is mediocre relative to those south and east. The bars and dance clubs on El. Venizelou St. offer an essentially homogeneous facsimile of any variety of atmosphere. Their tourist patrons are rowdy and ready for hot action. Nightlife in Heronissos is "jammin'," as Greeks like to say. The bars and discos that line Main St. and the Paraliakos offer every kind of atmosphere, music, and drink imaginable. Try the **Black Cactus Bar,** 72 El. Venizulou (tel. 23 590), on Main St. (open daily 9am-6am). As the night progresses, hit the bars on Paraliakos and on the waterfront (beer 600dr). The dance floors of **Disco 99** (open daily 9pm-4:30am) or **La Luna** (tel. 22 014) are large and crowded by English tourists (La Luna open daily 10:30pm-5am). The hottest club in town is the **Camelot Dancing Club** (tel. 22 734), where both locals and tourists crowd in to dance to international rave and house (open daily 10pm-5:30am). The **Hard Rock Cafe** (tel. 25 255) offers live music from British rockers most nights (12:30pm-5am). The **Cine Creta Maris,** around the corner from the Hard Rock Cafe, is an outdoor summer cinema showing English-language (usually American) films nightly at 9:45pm (1500dr).

The open-air museum, **Lychnostatis** (tel. 23 660), located roughly 1km toward Agios Nikolaos, exhibits Cretan houses and offers windmill, ceramic, and weaving workshops as well as the opportunity to tread grapes or bake pumpkin pi. Open Tues.-Sun. 9:30am-2pm for visit 3 daily guided tours at 10:30, 11:30am, and 12:30pm for 2250dr. Admission 1000dr, 500dr for kids under 12.

■ Malia ΜΑΛΙΑ

Its Mediterranean climate and nearby Minoan palace aside, Malia, with its pubs and Guinness taps, comes closer to evoking the pages of Dickens or Joyce than those of Homer or Kazantzakis. Young British tourists, booked months in advance on pre-packaged holidays, descend on Malia's beach like salmon in the midst of a mating frenzy. The number of advertisements in languages other than Greek has no equal, matched only by the number of sandwich boards displaying kitschy photographs of food. Neverthe-less, the palatial Minoan site at Malia merits a visit. Malia is best as a daytrip or, if you must stay, the old village is cheaper than the glitzed-out, pre-sold waterfront. Bring lots of *drachmae,* a jersey from your favorite football (a.k.a. soccer) team, condoms, and a canonical knowledge of Irish drinking songs.

ORIENTATION AND PRACTICAL INFORMATION

The main road from Iraklion (Eleftheriou Venizelou) should satisfy most practical needs, while the path to the beach, with the discos and watering holes, panders to the primal. The old village between the main road and the inland hills has no discos, but just as many bars and cheaper rooms. **Stallion Travel and Tourism** (tel. 33 690; fax 32 031), next to the church on the main road, offers extensive, personalized ser-vices. Sarah, the British proprietor, secures 100% insurance on every **car** or **motor-bike rental.** This is the best source for **travel information** and **currency exchange.** . The **National Bank** is just off the main road. Bear left at the first street past the road to the beach (open Mon.-Thurs. 8am-2pm, Fri. 8am-1:30pm). **Buses** connect Malia with Iraklion (1hr., 700dr) via Hersonissos (every 30min. until 11pm, 20min., 200dr); Agios Nikolaos (25 per day, 30min., 650dr); and Lassithi (8:45am, returning at 2pm, 1½hr., 1100dr). **Taxis** (tel. 31 777) idle at the intersection of the main road and the beach path (open 24hr.). The **Wash Express Laundromat** (tel. 32 730) is on the beach road (open Mon.-Sat. 9am-9pm; wash and dry 2500dr). If you require medical assistance, Dr. Georgia (tel. 31 529) has a **medical office** on the main road, next to the bus stop, above the market. In case of **emergency,** call her at home (tel. 31 880), or on her mobile phone (tel. (094) 52 51 42). The **pharmacy** (tel. 31 332) is next to her office (open Mon.-Sat. 9am-10pm, Sun. on rotation). The **post office** is off the main street toward Iraklion (look for the sign), behind the church (open Mon.-Fri. 7:30am-2pm). **Postal Code:** 70002. The **OTE** is in the old village—follow signs from 25th Martiou at the Bimbo Cafe (open Mon.-Fri. 7:30am-3pm). **Telephone Code:** 0897.

ACCOMMODATIONS

Finding reasonably priced rooms in Malia is a challenge. If you can't find them, look for the cluster of pensions and rooms to let in the old village. You can wander off into 25th Martiou St. and look around for a place that suits your fancy. Walking east toward Agios Nikolaos and away from town, after the point where the bus drops you off on the main road, make a right onto 25th Martiou St. to reach **Pension Aspasia** (tel. 31 290), with large, balconied rooms and common baths (doubles 5000-6000dr; triples 7000-8000dr). Or, try **Pension Menios,** #2 25th Martiou St. (tel. 31 361), near the corner of the main road. It has new, immaculate rooms, wood furnishings, small balconies, and private baths (doubles 5000dr, 6000dr with bath; triples 6000dr). You can also consult **Stallion Travel** for rooms.

FOOD AND ENTERTAINMENT

The most popular dishes in Malia are the "English" breakfast (600dr), pizza (1500dr), and the "steak" dinner (1900dr). Ironically, or perhaps appropriately, the tastiest authentic Greek fare in Malia is prepared by the Dutch chef at **Petros** (tel. 31 887) in the old village. An excellent Greek salad (900dr) complements a plate of *stifado* (1900dr; open 5pm-1am). On the main road, **banana vendors** sell bunches for 400dr.

In order to experience Malia's thriving experience, there are two areas to visit. The waterfront road is home to many of Malia's (and Crete's) more popular dance clubs.

On Beach Rd., house, international, rave, and dance music also blare at **Zoo, Zig Zag,** and **Corkers,** while **Terma's** is the place for authentic Greek tunes. Clubs open around 9pm, get really packed by 1am, and stay that way until 3:30 or 4am during the week. Most of them rock all night (until 6am), Thursday through Saturday. For a quieter but still exciting night, head for the narrow, cobbled streets of the old town. Due to the presence of many Irish, English, and Scottish vacationers, there are many pubs at which you can imbibe. Ireland meets the Mediterranean at **The Temple Bar** (tel. 31 272), where huge tropical plants grow out of the bar tables, and Greeks and Celts lap up pints of Guinness on tap (1100dr per pint). Every hour is happy hour at this open-air pub, cocktails are always 700dr (next to St. Dimitrios Sq.; open daily 9am-3 or 4am). The **Stone House Pub** (tel. 32 268) serves good drinks in an open-air vine-covered bar area, as well as inside the cozy old stone house. Cool tunes waft through the mellow crowd on nights when there is no Greek dancing. There's a pool table and dart board inside. Most drinks are around 1000dr (open April-Oct. daily 7pm-morning). At the end of the beach road, current movies from Hollywood and old British comedies play all day and most of the night at **Charlie Chaplin's** and **Union Jack's**. Movies are free, and drinks and snacks are cheap (500dr or less; open 11am-1am).

SIGHTS

The **Minoan Palace** (tel. 31 597) at Malia, one of the three great cities of Minoan Crete, lacks the labyrinthine architecture and magnificent interior decoration of Knossos and Phaistos, but is still imposing. First built around 1900 BC, the palace was destroyed in 1650 BC, rebuilt on an even more impressive scale, but then destroyed again around 1450 BC. Notice the **Hall of Columns** on the north side of the large central courtyard, named for the six columns supporting the roof. The *loggia,* the raised chamber on the west side, was used for state ceremonies. West of the *loggia* are the palace's living quarters and archives. Northwest of the *loggia* and main site slumbers the **Hypostyle Crypt** that may have been a social center for Malia's intelligentsia. Follow the road to Agios Nikolaos 3km to the east and turn left toward the sea, or walk along the beach and then 1km through the fields (open Tues.-Sun. 8:30am-3pm; admission 800dr, Sun. free).

■ Agios Nikolaos ΑΓΙΟΣ ΝΙΚΟΛΑΟΣ

Agios Nikolaos has moved closer to the naughty mood of a nouveau chic resort town, but still retains some nice facets of a low-key fishing village. The town's visitors include beach-obsessed patrons, one-stop holiday-makers, and hikers on their way to more obscure destinations. There are few bargains in Agios Nikolaos or in its satellite beach towns, but the town's intense nightlife, its diverse selection of intriguingly glamourous tourists, and its remnants of indigenous Cretan culture make Agios Nikolaos a lively concoction—a place that's fun without the sense of having been used up and spit out by tourists.

ORIENTATION AND PRACTICAL INFORMATION

It's easy to get around Agios Nikolaos—the center of town is actually a small peninsula, with beaches on three sides and most services, hotels, restaurants, and discos in the center. If you've just gotten off the bus, walk to the end of the block (with the terminal on your right), and take the first right. Follow **Venizelou Street** to the monument, where it leads into **Roussou Koundourou,** which heads downhill to the harbor. The tourist office is to the left, across the bridge. Don't confuse the nepotistic street names: R. Koundourou, I. Koundourou, and S. Koundourou St.

Tourist Office: 21A S. Koundourou St. (tel. 22 357), at the bridge between the lake and the port. Assists with accommodations, **exchanges currency,** provides bus and boat schedules, and distributes a free brochure with a town map and practical information. Open Apr.-Oct. daily 8:30am-9:45pm.

Banks: National Bank (tel. 28 735), at the top of R. Koundourou St., near Venizelou Sq. Open for **currency exchange** Mon.-Thurs. 8am-2pm, Fri. 8am-1:30pm.

Flights: Olympic Airways (tel. 22 033), on Plastira St. overlooking the lake. Open Mon.-Fri. 8am-4pm. The closest airport is in Iraklion.

Buses: (tel. 22 234), Atlandithos Sq., in the opposite side of town from the harbor. To: Iraklion via Malia (24 per day, 1½hr., 1300dr); Lassithi (2 per day, 2½hr., 1050dr); Ierapetra (8 per day, 1hr., 700dr); Sitia (6 per day, 1½hr., 1350dr); and Kritsa (12 per day, 15min., 220dr). Buses to Elounda (15 per day, 20min., 220dr) and Plaka (6 per day, 40min., 320dr) leave opposite the tourist office.

Ferries: Globe Travel, 29 R. Koundourou St. (tel. 22 267). Air and ferry tickets for departures from Agios Nikolaos and other Cretan ports. Open daily 9am-11pm. For ferries to Peiraias, the Greek islands, Cyprus, and Israel, cross the street to **Nostos Tours,** 30 Koundourou St. (tel. 22 819). Open daily 8am-2pm and 5-9pm.

Car and Motorbike Rental: Economy Car Hire, 15 S. Koundourou St. (tel. 28 988); also an office at 5 K. Sfakianaki St. Fiat Panda 24,000dr for 3 days. 50cc mopeds for 3000dr, 100cc for 4000dr. Open daily 8am-10pm.

International Bookstores: Anna Karteri, 5 R. Koundourou St. (tel. 22 272). Books in English, German, and French. Open Mon.-Fri. 8am-10pm, Sat. 8am-2pm.

Pharmacies: Dr. Theodore Furakis (tel. 24 011), at the top of R. Koundourou St. Open Mon.-Tues., Thurs.-Fri. 8am-2pm and 5:30-9pm, Wed. 8am-2pm.

Hospital: (tel. 25 221), on Paleologou St., at the north end of town. From the lake, walk up Paleologou St., 1 block past the museum.

Police: (tel. 22 321) share the **Tourist Police** (tel. 26 900) building. Follow 28th Octovriou St. past Venizelou Sq. until it becomes G. Kontoghianni St. After a good 10 min. walk, it will be on the right.

Post Office: #9 28th Octovriou St. (tel. 22 062). Open Mon.-Fri. 7:30am-8pm, Sat. 7:30am-2pm. **Postal Code:** 72100.

OTE: (tel. 82 880), on the corner of 25th Martiou and K. Sfakianaki St. Open Mon.-Sat. 7am-midnight, Sun. 7am-10pm. **Telephone Code:** 0841.

ACCOMMODATIONS

As a result of Agios Nikolaos's popularity, many of the better hotels are booked months in advance by European tour groups. There are many pensions in town that offer clean, cheap rooms. They do fill up quickly, so it may be wise to call ahead and make a reservation. The tourist office has a bulletin board with many of Agios Nikolaos's pensions and their prices. Prices listed are 20-40% less in the off season.

Argiro Pension, 1 Solonos St. (tel. 28 707). From the tourist office, walk up 25th Martiou and turn left onto Manousogianaki. After 4 blocks, go right onto Solonos. Unsullied, cool rooms (with common or private baths) in a huge, stately old house with a serene, jasmine-scented garden. Quiet, yet close to town. Doubles 5000-5500dr; triples 6600-7000dr.

Christodoulakis Pension, 7 Stratigou Koraka St. (tel. 22 525), one block south of the lake. Spotless rooms, kitchen facilities, and friendly proprietors. Singles 4000-5000dr; doubles 5000-6000dr.

Pension Perla, 4 Salaminos St. (tel. 23 379). Big clean rooms, some with balconies and ocean views. Comfortable TV lounge. All but 2 rooms have private bath. Singles 4000dr; doubles 5000dr; triples 6000dr.

The Green House, 15 Modatsou St. (tel. 22 025). From the tourist office, turn left onto R. Koundourou, left again onto Iroon Polytechniou, and right onto Modatsou. Relax in the shady, tangled garden. If you're lucky, you'll get homemade Italian ice from the multilingual proprietors. Clean rooms and common baths. Laundry 1200dr per load. Singles 3500dr; doubles 5000dr.

FOOD AND ENTERTAINMENT

Agios Nikolaos is overrun by overpriced, touristy, mediocre restaurants claiming to serve "traditional Greek food." Many of these places are recognizable by their brightly colored menus with photographs of their food in front, along with pushy waiters who try to pull you in. Generally, the restaurants that are open all year (rather than just in the summer tourist season) cater to the native Greek clientele and serve more authentic food. **Itanos** (tel. 25 340), off the main square, serves large portions of fresh Greek salads (600dr), homemade barreled wine (1000dr per 1L), vegetarian entrees (plate of stuffed vegetables 900dr), and meat (entrees 600-1400dr; open daily 10am-11pm). If you don't mind relaxed service, go to **Stelio's,** at the bridge, for a dazzling harborside view and excellent *tzatziki* (500dr; open April-Oct. daily 8am-midnight). Next door, at the **Actaion** (tel. 22 289), fish dishes start at 1200dr (open April-Oct. daily 9am-midnight). The **New Kow Loon Chinese Restaurant,** 1 Pasifais St. (tel. 23 891), serves surprisingly decent Chinese cuisine. Egg rolls (850dr), mixed veggies (1150dr), and lemon chicken (1500dr) are an interesting surprise in Greece (open daily noon-3pm and 7pm-1am). **Xenakis Family Bakery,** 9 M. Sfakianaki St. (tel. 23 051), several blocks from the port on the street leading to Kitroplatia Beach, sells delicious loaves of freshly baked bread (150-300dr). Try their *tyropitas* (150dr) or their delicious raisin rolls (150dr; open Mon.-Sat. 7am-4pm).

For nocturnal pursuits, stroll around the harbor on I. Koundourou St., or walk up 25th Martiou St. **Rififi** (tel. 23 114) provides a meeting place for backpackers and young locals who sip coffee and alcohol on the harborside terrace. The **Sorrento Bar** on the waterfront is a good place to warm up before hitting the dance floors, especially on Thursday's 70s night (beer 600dr). **Sixties,** 40 R. Koundourou (tel. 82 451), serves a multigenerational crowd grooving to nostalgic tunes (the DJ takes requests) and smooth cocktails (1200dr). Alcohol-free drinks like the Temperance (lemon juice, egg yolk, and grenadine 900dr) are also served (open daily 9am-late). **Lipstick Night Club** (tel. 22 377), close to the Mediterraneo on the waterfront, attracts a touristy crowd looking for fun (specials on drinks like 2 cocktails for 1000dr; open 10pm-late). Each summer from mid-July to mid-September, the town celebrates with the **Lato Festival.** Visit the Tourist Office for details.

SIGHTS

According to legend, Artemis and Athena bathed at the "bottomless" lake, **Xepatomeni,** near the tourist office (it is actually 64m deep). In 1867, the regional governor dug a canal linking the lake with the sea, creating a perpetual flushing mechanism. Three beaches are within walking distance of the main harbor. With minimal effort, you can sunbathe on the concrete piers that jut out from S. Koundourou St. To reach a better spot, catch the bus, which departs every hour, headed to Ierapetra or Sitia and get off at **Almiros Beach,** 2km east of Agios Nikolaos. The sandy beach at **Kalo Chorio,** 10km farther along the same road, is less crowded. Get off the bus headed for either Sitia or Ierapetra at the Kavos Taverna (tell the driver to stop). Another beautiful beach on the road to Elounda is the **Harania Beach.** A winner of the European Blue Flag award for 1996, it is clean and secluded. Take the bus towards Elounda and get off at Harania.

For more cerebral pursuits, visit one of Agios Nikolaos's two museums, or see if anything is playing at the theater on M. Sfakianaki St. The **Archaeological Museum** (tel. 24 943), just outside the center of town, a few blocks down the road from Iraklion, houses a modest collection of Minoan artifacts (open Tues.-Sun. 8:30am-3pm; admission 500dr). The **Folk Art Museum,** in the tourist office's building, displays tapestries, embroidered clothes, furniture, icons, 16th-century manuscripts of contracts, and stamps for the holy bread at church (open Sun.-Fri. 9:30am-1:30pm and 6-930pm; admission 250dr, free on Sun.). To shop for inexpensive clothes, visit the weekly **market** on Ethnikis Antistassios St., next to the lake (open Wed. 7am-noon).

The archaeological site of **Gournia** is located 2km from Agios Nikolaos. Take the bus heading to Ierapetra or Sitia—ask the driver to stop (open Tues.-Sun. 9am-3pm; admission 800dr). One kilometer before Kritsa on the road from Agios Nikolaos, Crete's Byzantine treasure, the **Panagia Kera** (tel. 51 525), honors the Dormition of the Virgin. The interior is adorned with a patchwork of smoky 14th-century paintings in the central nave and 15th-century Byzantine frescoes in the wings (open Mon.-Sat. 9am-3pm, Sun. 9am-2pm; admission 800dr, free on Sun.).

Bull Leaping, Minoan-style

For those who might wonder what the Minoans did for kicks, the constantly recurring images of bulls and their horns in all of Crete's archeological museums conjure visions of a great bull kicking up dust and preparing to charge. Unlike modern bull-fighting in Spain, scholars now think that Minoan bulls' opponents had more in common with young Olympic gymnasts than a wily middle-aged moustached *toreador*. The bull games of the Minoans probably occupied the large central court of a palace and followed a boxing match. (Mike Tyson may have been living at the wrong time—ear-biting was probably legal.) For the main event, the court's ground level exits were blocked and fans crowded the upper windows and balconies. Well-trained and scantily clad (if not nude) boys and girls then engaged the bull in chases about the court. As things heated up, a youth might lure the bull to a platform, climb up, and then leap the bull as he clumsily attempted to follow. Other, more treacherous flips occurred at mid-court where the athlete grabbed the horns of the bull and used head rearing to launch a spectacular flip.

■ Ierapetra ΙΕΡΑΠΕΤΡΑ

Although German tourists have made inroads, Ierapetra hosts more Greeks than foreigners. The city sits in tourism's rare *purgatorio*—it teeters between the cosmopolitan and the rural. Ierapetra's star attraction is its remote island, **Chrisi,** eight nautical miles from the mainland. Several small ferries depart every day at 10:30am and return at 5 or 5:30pm. The trip to Chrisi takes one hour (ferries 2000-5000dr; 1500dr beach chair charge). Free from stores and crowds, Chrisi is completely flat, adorned by green pine, and surrounded by transparent green sea. Pack a lunch and bring water; you won't even find a small market, though there are two *tavernas* near the dock which are open all day.

ORIENTATION AND PRACTICAL INFORMATION

Most of Ierapetra's services are on the streets parallel to the waterfront. The **police station** also houses the **tourist police** (tel. 22 560) on the waterfront, a few blocks before Eleftherias Sq. (open 24hr.) The **port police,** 29 Kyvra St. (tel. 22 294), are near the excursion boat port. The **National Bank,** in Eleftherias Sq., is across the street from Ierapetra Express (open Mon.-Thurs. 8am-2pm, Fri. 8am-1:30pm). In Kanoupaki Sq., five blocks south of the bus station toward the port, is the **post office,** 3 Stilianou Hota St. (open Mon.-Fri. 7:30am-2pm). **Tourist agencies** on the street parallel to the water distribute free city maps. The **Ierapetra Express office,** 24 Eleftherias Sq. (tel. 28 673 or 22 411), is helpful (open daily 8am-1:30pm and 4-9pm). **Olympic Airways,** 26 Losthenous St. (tel. 22 444), has flight information and sells tickets (open Mon.-Tues., Thurs.-Fri. 9am-1:30pm and 6-8pm, Wed. and Sat. 9am-1:30pm). Across the street is the **bus station,** 41 Lasthenous St. (tel. 28 237). To get to the waterfront from there, head past the palm tree and you'll see signs for the beach. **Radio Taxi** (tel. 26 600) lines up cars in Kanoupaki Sq. **Free Rider** (tel. 22 571; fax 25 180), south of the bus station, rents bicycles (1000dr), motorbikes (4000dr), and cars (8000dr). The **hospital** (tel. 22 488) is north of the bus station, left off Losthenous Sq. at 6 Kalimerake St. (open daily 8:30am-1:30pm, open 24hr. for emergencies). The town has several **pharmacies,** including one (tel. 22 231) in Eleftherias Sq. (open Mon.-Fri. 8am-2pm and 5:30-9pm). **Postal Code:** 72200. The **OTE** is at 25 Koraka St., three blocks from the water (open Mon.-Fri. 7:30am-1pm). **Telephone Code:** 0842.

ACCOMMODATIONS

There's a sign at the bus station that leads visitors to the charming **Cretan Villa,** 16 Lakerda St. (tel. 28 522). The 200-year-old building hides a garden surrounded by beautiful, white stucco-walled, brick-floored, high-ceilinged rooms. The owner, a University of Missouri alum, speaks fluent English. All rooms have private bath. (Singles 5000dr; doubles 6000dr; triples 8000dr. Prices rise by 1000dr in high season.) The **Camiros Hotel** (tel. 89 930), 15 Michalis Kaothrais St., one block east of Venizelou Sq. offers clean rooms with private baths, breakfast (1000dr) and full reception services (singles 6000dr; doubles 8500dr). For your camping pleasure, **Ierapetra** (tel. 61 351) and, 7km from Ierapetra, the new **Koutsounari** (tel. 61 213), 9km away on the coastal road to Sitia, provide the ground, a restaurant, a bar, and a beach. Take the bus to Sitia via Makri Gialo (7 per day) and ask to be let off at the campgrounds. The bus costs 220dr and the 7km trip takes about 10min. (1200dr per person; 900dr per tent).

FOOD AND ENTERTAINMENT

Nearly all of Ierapetra's restaurants lie on the waterfront and feature identical prices (*moussaka* 800-1000dr). Among the touristy *tavernas,* **Notos,** with panoramic views of the harbor, near the Venetian Fortress offers traditional Greek fare (*moussaka* 800dr, *tzatziki* 500dr), as well as delicious grilled fresh seafood (delectable octopus 1250dr) and friendly service (open in summer daily 5am-3am; in winter 5am-midnight). At **Veterano** (tel. 23 175), in Eleftherias Venizelou Sq., you can peek in the gigantic kitchen where you may see old men alongside young boys shelling almonds, mixing frostings, and layering cakes. Sit in the shade with a large piece of fresh *baklava* (400dr) or Ierapetra's own *kalitsenia,* an individual-sized sweet cheese tart-like pie (200dr each; open daily 7:30am-midnight). The **public market,** two blocks up Konaki St. from Kanoupaki Sq. on the left, has fruit and vegetable stands as well as bakeries which sell cheap, fresh loaves of bread (250-300dr; market open Mon.-Tues. and Thurs.-Fri. 7:30am-2pm and 5-8 or 8:30pm, Wed. and Sat. 7:30am-2pm). On Saturdays there is also a **street fruit market** on the corner of Panagou and Kalimerake St. (open daily 7am-1:30 or 2pm).

Nightlife in Ierapetra is low key. The bars at the south end of the waterfront (closer to the Fortress) are frequented by locals and play mostly Greek music. **Bar Alexander** is packed with locals who come to groove to the DJ'd Greek tunes (cocktails 1200dr; open daily 9pm-3:30am). The bars on the other end of the harbor are busy with primarily German tourists. **Acropolis** (tel. 23 659) has a beautiful view from the center of the waterfront; inside, tourists enjoy oldies and jazz mixed by the DJ with rock, rave, and even Greek music (open 9am-8am; it gets crazy from midnight until 4am).

SIGHTS

There are loads of historical sights in Ierapetra; unfortunately, most are closed. Locals laud **Napoleon's House,** in the old town, where the French commander supposedly spent the night on June 26, 1798, en route to Egypt to battle the Mamluks. Also in the old town are a **mosque** and an **Ottoman fountain,** decaying and covered with Greek graffiti, built near the end of the 19th century. The restored **Venetian fortress** *(Kales),* at the extreme south end of the old harbor, was started in the early 13th century and is open daily for visiting. The **Kervea festival** each summer in July and August sometimes holds some of its music, dance, and theater performances at the fortress. Call the **town hall** (tel. 24 115) for information (open Mon.-Fri. 7:30am-2:30pm). Ierapetra's **Archaeological Museum,** at the beginning of Adrianou St. at Kanoupaki Sq. on the waterfront, has a small collection of Minoan and classical artifacts from the south coast (open Tues.-Sat. 9am-3pm; 500dr). The large, perfectly preserved Hellenistic sculpture of **Persephone,** Queen of Hades, proves Aphrodite wasn't the only beauty in the Greek pantheon.

■ Sitia ΣHTEIA

A scenic drive on coastal and mountain roads from Agios Nikolaos leads to Sitia, a sleepy fishing and port town. The wave of tourism that has engulfed the coast from Iraklion to Agios Nikolaos slows to a trickle before Sitia where pelicans walk the streets at dawn. Use Sitia as your base for exploring Crete's east coast.

ORIENTATION AND PRACTICAL INFORMATION

To get to the center of the waterfront from the bus station, head for the sign for Vai and Kato Zakros, then bear left. **Dimokritou** and **Venizelou Street** intersect with the waterfront at the square where you will find a small palm-treed traffic island, Sitia's restaurant strip, and several kiosks.

Tourist Police: 62 Therissou St. (tel. 24 200). From the square walk up Kapetan Sifi St. 2 blocks to Mysonos St. Take a left on Mysonos and continue until it turns into Therissou St.; it's several blocks up on the right. Open daily 7:30am-9pm.

Banks: National Bank (tel. 24 990), in Venizelou Sq., offers **currency exchange.** Open Mon.-Thurs. 8am-2pm, Fri. 8am-1:30pm.

Flights: To Karpathos (1½hr., 8400dr) and Kassos (1hr., 8400dr). There are also flights to Athens (3 per week, 22,800dr). No buses to airport. Taxis cost 300-400dr for the 1km uphill ride.

Buses: 4 Karamo St. (tel. 22 272), on the east end of the waterfront. To Agios Nikolaos (6 per day, 1½hr., 1300dr); Iraklion (5 per day, 3¼hr., 2650dr); Ierapetra (5 per day, 1½hr., 1150dr); Vai (3-4 per day, 1hr., 560dr); and Kato Zakros (2 per day, 1hr., 950dr).

Ferries: The *Kornaros* travels twice per week to Kassos (4hr., 600dr) and Karpathos (5hr., 3130dr) and thrice weekly to Peiraias (16-17hr., 7180dr) via Agios Nikolaos (1½hr., 1650dr) and Milos (7-8hr., 4530dr). The *Romilda* goes to Rhodes (580dr).

Porto-Belis Travel, 3 Karamanli St. (tel. 22 370), near the bus station, provides ferry information, rents rooms, sells airplane tickets, rents cars and mopeds, and **exchanges currency.** Open in summer daily 8:30am-9pm; in winter 8:30am-8pm.

Taxis: (tel. 23 810, 23 298, or 28 591) lounge in Venizelou Sq. Sometimes they run all night, sometimes they don't; usually cabs available 24hr. on weekends.

Moped Rental: Knossos (tel. 22 057) on Ithanou St. up the block from Sitia Rent-a-Car. Knossos rents cars and bikes and can help you find a room. Vespas 3000dr per day. Open daily 8am-8pm.

Pharmacies: Many on streets behind the waterfront. One is straight from the square up 1½ blocks, on the left. Open Mon. and Wed. 8am-1:30pm, Tues. and Thurs.-Fri. 8am-1:30pm and 5:30-8:30pm.

Hospital: (tel. 24 311), off Therissou St. just past the Youth Hostel, away from town. Follow the signs from the main square. Open 24hr.

Police: (tel. 22 266, -59), in the same building as the tourist police. Open 24hr.

Post Office: Main branch, 2 Ethnikis Antistasis St. (tel. 22 283). From the bus station, walk south and follow the road around to the right. Open Mon.-Fri. 7:30am-2pm.

Postal Code: 72300.

OTE: 22 Capitan Sifis St. (tel. 28 099), from the main square, turn inland at the National Bank, and walk uphill 2 blocks. Open Mon.-Sat. 7:30am-10pm.

Telephone Code: 0843.

ACCOMMODATIONS

It is difficult to find rooms in July and August, and during mid-August, when the Sultana Festival is held, it is nearly impossible. Off-season prices are 20-40% less. The youth hostel is friendly and informal, but for more privacy, head to the main road which leads up to the hostel, and to the back streets at the west end of the waterfront, especially Kornarou and Kondilaki St.

Youth Hostel, 4 Therissou St. (tel. 22 693). From the bus station, take a left on Ithanou (after road bends it becomes Papanastasiou), follow until the BP gas station, where road becomes Therissou, and uphill another 100m on the left. Reception open in summer daily 8:30am-10pm; but if no one is around, feel free to find a bed and register later. Call ahead and you may be picked up at the bus station for free. Common kitchen, book exchange. Hot water 24hr. 1300dr per person; private singles 2000dr; private doubles 3000dr; breakfast 600dr.

Porto-Belis, 34 Karamanli Ave. (tel. 22 370). Apartments, studios, and rooms above the Porto-Belis Travel Agency. The bright, sunny rooms in this new building are spacious and clean. All have large private baths, balconies, and refrigerators. Dou-

bles 4500-5300dr; triples 5500-6300dr; studio for 2-3 people with kitchenette 5200-5800dr; 2-room apartment with kitchenette for 3-4 people 7500-8500dr.
Venus Rooms to Let, 60 Kondilaki St. (tel. 24 307). Walk uphill from the OTE and take your first right. Green courtyard, sunny rooms with balconies, and kitchen facilities. Clean shared baths. Doubles upstairs have private bath, couch, and sea view balcony for 7500dr; doubles 6500dr; triples 9000dr.
Rooms to Let Apostolis, 27 Kazantzakis St. (tel. 22 993 or 28 172). Pleasant rooms with private baths. Wash basin and linens. Doubles 7000dr; triples 9000dr.

FOOD, ENTERTAINMENT, AND SIGHTS

Sitia's restaurants specialize in fresh fish and lobster. **Zorba's** (tel. 22 689), on the west side of the harbor, has a variety of good, moderately priced entrees (*moussaka* 950dr). Set menus of meat or fish, salad, wine, and dessert are sometimes a good, if touristy, bargain (1500-3000dr). For fresh fruits and veggies, you can visit one of the many produce markets on Fountalidou St. Try to catch the roaming Macedonian minstrel along the waterfront. He'll serenade you with the traditional *bazouki*, although he admits he'd rather be playing the Doors. Tucked away and removed from the touristy waterfront, **Taverna Michos,** 117 V. Kornarou (tel. 22 416), is, according to locals, Sitia's best restaurant. Swordfish-prawn *souvlaki* is served with rice and delicious Cretan vegetables (1400dr). For an appetizer try *damoudes,* grapes overstuffed with spicy goo (500dr; open daily noon-3pm and 6pm-1 or 2am).**Taverna Panorama** (tel. 25 160) in neighboring Agia Fotia on the road to Palaikastro and Vai, serves home-cooked traditional Cretan dishes. The menu varies daily, but specialties include yummy octopus cooked in red wine and tomato sauce, fresh fish, and grape leaves. It is usually only open for dinner, but call ahead, just in case. Bakeries are also a good place to find fresh, delicious nourishment. **Paradosiaka Glyka** (tel. 28 466), one block from the main square, specializes in traditional Cretan biscuits and pastries. *Kserotigano* are a special wedding pastry (they're round, sticky, and covered with sesame seeds, 2400dr per kg). *Kalitsenia* come in two varieties—an open tart-like pie and a small, soft roll-like biscuit and both are filled with cinnamon-spiced delicious Cretan cheese (950dr per kg; open daily 8:30am-2pm and 5-9 or 9:30pm).

During the middle of August, Sitia hosts the **Sultana Festival,** which features unlimited wine, dancing, and music for roughly 2000dr. Nightlife is not Sitia's strong point, but one exception is the **Planetarium Disco,** 2km west of the second pier on a sweeping balcony. The 1500dr cover includes first drink (open daily 1am-sunrise). **De Sitia Peris** is a "garden bar" in Sitia, past all of the *tavernas* on the harbor, near the end (no cover; beer 700dr, cocktails 1200-1500dr; open daily 10pm-4am).

The **fortress** at the hilltop provides a view of the town and the city's bay. The distant end of the town's **beach,** extending 3km east of Sitia toward Petra, is usually empty. Watch for signs for a performance of a classical Greek tragedy in the fortress. They are put on in Modern Greek, but if you learn the words for kill *(skotoso),* mother *(mitera),* and father *(pateras),* you'll be able to follow the action. The **Archaeological Museum** (tel. 23 917) houses a small collection from nearby sights, although most have been shipped off to Iraklion. Take a left on Ithanou; when you come to the sign for Iraklion, take another left on the road to Ierapetra. Be sure to note the Late Minoan **Palaikastro Kouros** statuette, one of the very first representations of Zeus (open Tues.-Sun. 8:30am-3pm; admission 800dr, students 300dr).

■ Near Sitia

Several kilometers of some of Crete's most scenic beaches stretch south to the **Minoan Palace** at **Roussolakos,** near Chiona Beach and the lazy village of **Palaikastro.** The village has all the necessities in its main square, including an OTE (tel. 61 222). You can find rooms and warm atmosphere in the home of Yiannis Perrakis (tel. 61 310). When you get off the bus, follow the road that forks to the right. Look for greenhouse-enclosed banana trees on your right; the pension is up the gravel path on the left. Lemon trees and magenta flowers invite you to bright rooms (singles 2500dr;

doubles 4000dr; triples 5000dr; prices lower in the off season). The **Hotel Hellas** (tel. 61 455) serves standard Greek food (Greek salad 590dr, stuffed eggplant 950dr).

Take a 6am bus from Sitia to Zakros Gorge (950dr). Walk the gorge, smaller and less crowded but equal in scenery to Samaria in the west, to the modest Minoan Palace of Kato Zakros on the coast. On the way, explore the **Caves of the Dead** which line the gorge and still conceal ancient bones.

VAI

Not long ago, tourists headed east to the sylvan palm beach at **Vai** for refuge from Sitia's crowds. Today, several buses roll into this outpost every day, depositing tourists eager to ponder Europe's only indigenous palm tree forest. According to local tradition, the forest is the legacy of the Arabs who conquered Crete in the 9th century (park open daily 8am-9pm; free). Most visit Vai via the crowded public bus from Sitia. Buses leave Sitia and stop at Palaikastro en route to Vai (4 per day, 1hr., Sitia-Vai 550dr, Palaikastro-Vai 220dr). Camping is forbidden in the park itself, but many unfurl sleeping bags in the cove to the south of the palm beach. If sandy pajamas and the possibility of arrest don't appeal to you, rent a room in quiet Palaikastro, a town 8km back toward Sitia. A **tourist office** and **currency exchange center** are located in the parking lot (open Apr.-Oct. daily 9am-10pm). When those places on which the sun don't usually shine start burning, slap on some more cocoa butter (and clothes) and check out the **watersports** on the far end of the beach, such as a **scuba diving center** (tel. (0843) 71 548; call ahead since it opens seasonally). At the Vai tourist shop, inquire about the nearby **Open Air Banana Plantations and Sub-Tropical Cultivations** (tel. (0843) 61 353). An old, retired sea captain gives tours in German, English, French, and Greek. A free banana awaits you at the tour's end. (open Apr.-Oct. daily 8am-8pm; admission 800dr, group rate 600dr). Beyond Vai sprawls the mellow and secluded **Itanos Beach** with beachside archeological sites.

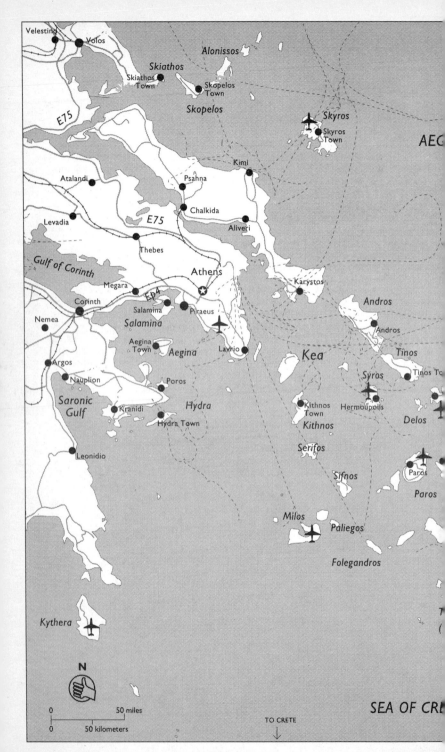

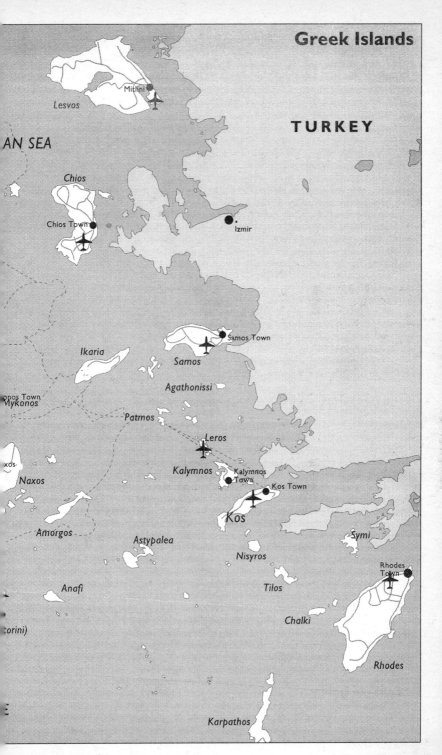

Greek Islands

Lesvos
Mitlini

TURKEY

AN SEA

Chios

Chios Town

Izmir

Samos Town

Ikaria

Samos

Agathonissi

onos Town
Mykonos

Patmos

Leros

xos

Naxos

Kalymnos

Kalymnos Town

Kos Town

Kos

Amorgos

Astypalea

Symi

Nisyros

Anafi

Tilos

Rhodes Town

orini)

Chalki

Rhodes

Karpathos

Cyclades ΚΥΚΛΑΔΕΣ

"Happy is the man, I thought, who, before dying, has the good fortune to sail the Aegean Sea."

—Nikos Kazantzakis

When people speak longingly of the Greek islands, they are probably talking about the Cyclades. Whatever your idea of the Aegean—peaceful cobblestone streets and whitewashed houses, *ouzo* sipped seaside during warm sunsets, inebriated revelry—you can find it here. In classical antiquity, the islands received their name from the shape of their layout. The ancient Greeks saw the Cyclades forming a circular, or "cyclical" pattern, spiraling around the sanctified Delos. Today, somewhat less romantically, the islands can be grouped into three broad categories. Although each has quiet villages and untouched spots, Santorini, Mykonos, and Ios are known to all as the party islands and are the most heavily touristed. Of these three, Santorini is the most chic, the most expensive, and offers an impressive history and some of the most spectacular views in all of Greece. Mykonos is a close second in sophistication (and price), but also provides some of Greece's most sizzling nightlife. Ios can be summed up in four words: American frat party run amok (all right, that was five words, but after a week on Ios you won't be able to count either). Paros, Naxos, and Amorgos are also popular but less frantic and more pristine. Syros, Tinos, Andros, Kea, Kithnos, Serifos, Sifnos, and Milos get few foreign visitors and are dependent primarily on Greeks. If you visit in the winter, you may be the only foreigner on some islands.

Note that tourist amenities on many of these islands, especially accommodations, are only open April through October.

MYKONOS ΜΥΚΟΝΟΣ

Mykonos has been the object of envy and desire since the 18th century, when pirates vied for the right to lounge on the island's long, blonde beaches. Today, the island is chic and sleek, playing host to sophisticated revelers who retain a strong sense of history and culture. The word Greeks use to describe this island is invariably *kosmopolitikos,* and it certainly is. The wealthy and well-dressed abound on Mykonos. After several years of decline, Mykonos's gay scene has begun to regain the acclaim that once made it the Mediterranean's hottest spot for gays. A word of caution: don't pester Petros the Pelican, the island's mascot. Although the current mascot is Petros II (Petros I was accidently run over by a taxi), he has a loyal fan club on the island—one that recently provided him with a new pink mate. The pair can be seen strolling the waterfront.

▨ Mykonos Town

If you stay in Mykonos long enough, you will most likely spend at least one drunken evening lost in Mykonos Town's maze of endless, winding alleys lined with indistinguishable whitewashed buildings. These labyrinthine streets, closed to motor traffic, were created to disconcert and disorient pirates. Perhaps they never bothered to straighten them out because they seem to work just as well for tourists. Despite the influx of visitors, the town has resisted large hotel complexes. Fishing boats in the harbor, basket-laden donkeys, drag queens, high-fashion models, and Petros the Pelican all help preserve the town's charm. Nevertheless, Mykonos is unmistakably a tourist town. Depending on your degree of homesickness, you will either exult in or grieve over the availability of cheeseburgers, milkshakes, fish and chips, Chinese food, and continental breakfasts. Don't come to Mykonos to experience unadulterated Greek culture; come instead to witness a world of Dionysian delight.

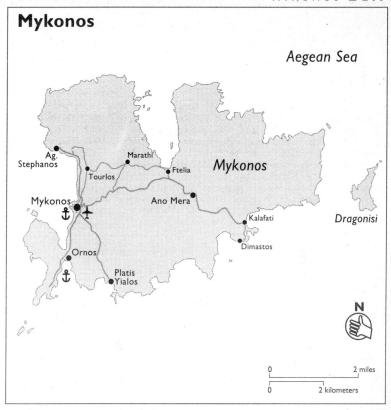

Mykonos

Aegean Sea

Ag. Stephanos

Marathi

Tourlos

Ftelia

Mykonos

Mykonos

Ano Mera

Kalafati

Dragonisi

Ornos

Dimastos

Platis Yialos

N

0   2 miles

0   2 kilometers

ORIENTATION AND PRACTICAL INFORMATION

Boats dock at a pier on the far left of the waterfront (facing inland). One road leads along the water past the town beach to **Taxi Square** and the center of town. Another road heads uphill to the **North Station** bus depot, then wraps around Mykonos Town to the **South Station.** Everything you need or want is near the waterfront—banks, travel agencies, shops, cafes, *tavernas,* bars, and discos—but much of the real shopping, fine dining, and partying goes on in the infamous narrow, winding back streets (especially Matogianni, Kalogera, Mitropoleas, and Enoplon Dinameon). On the right side of the waterfront is another pier for excursion boats headed primarily for nearby Delos. Past the pier is a series of churches, the lovely part of town called **Little Venice,** and a small hill with a line of windmills.

> **Tourist Police:** (tel. 22 482) In an office at the ferry landing. Very helpful English speakers. Open daily 8am-9pm.
> **Banks: National Bank of Greece** (tel. 22 234), in the center of the waterfront, offers **currency exchange** and **ATM.** Open June-Sept. Mon.-Thurs. 8am-2pm and 6-8pm (evening hours for currency exchange only), Fri. 8am-1:30pm, Sat.-Sun. 10am-1pm; Oct.-May, Mon.-Thurs. 8am-2pm, Fri. 8am-1:30pm.
> **American Express:** (tel. 22 422), left of the bank inside **Delia Travel Ltd.** Full travel services for cardholders. Open Mon.-Fri. 9am-9pm, Sat.-Sun. 9am-3pm and 6-9pm.
> **Flights: Olympic Airways** (tel. 22 490, -95 in town, 22 327 at airport). Flights to: Athens (6-7 per day, 40min., 17,300dr); Thessaloniki (3 per week, 25,100dr); Santorini (Wed.-Mon., 30min., 13,900dr); Iraklion (2 per week, 1hr., 20,400dr); and

Rhodes (3 per week, 1hr., 20,400dr). There are no buses to the airport; a taxi from Mykonos Town costs 1000dr.

Buses: North Station, uphill from the ferry dock, serves: Ag. Stefanos beach (every 30min., 210dr); Ano Mera and Kalafatis (every 2hr., 320dr); Elia Beach (6 per day, 290dr); and Kalo Livadi beach (2 per day, high season only, 290dr). **South Station,** uphill from the windmills at the opposite edge of town, serves: Plati Yalos beach (every 30min.); Paradise Beach (every 30min.); Ornos Beach (every 30min.); and Ag. Ioannis (every hr.). Schedules are posted at the stations (tel. for both 23 360).

Ferries: Boats sail to: Tinos (3-5 per day, 45min., 1340dr); Paros (2-3 per day, 2hr., 1800dr); Naxos (1-2 per day, 3hr., 1810dr); Syros (1-3 per day, 2½hr., 1610dr); Andros (1-3 per day, 3½hr., 2640dr); Santorini (1-3 per day, 6½hr., 3290dr); Ios (1-2 per day, 4hr., 3100dr); Peiraias (1-4 per day, 6hr., 4690dr); Iraklion (3 per week, 5550dr); Thessaloniki (3 per week, 8570dr); Samos (2 per week, 4700dr); Ikaria (2 per week, 3070dr); and Rafina (1-3 per day, 3890dr).

Flying Dolphins: Hydrofoils are faster but more expensive and have less reliable schedules. Daily to: Paros (3390dr); Santorini (6640dr); Naxos (3410dr); Ios (6260dr); Amorgos (2 per week, 6140dr); and Sikinos (1 per week, 6640dr). Also **SeaJet** service to: Tinos (2 per day, 2480dr); Syros (3020dr); Andros (2 per day, 5400dr); and Rafina (1-2 per day, 7900dr).

Taxi: (tel. 22 400, -700) Available at Taxi Sq., along the waterfront.

Moped Rentals: Agencies surround both bus stops. 2000-5000dr (depending on model) per day. Some rent jeeps as well (10,000-16,000dr per day).

International Bookstore: International Press (tel. 23 316), in small square opposite Pierro's, follow signs from the waterfront. Eclectic books, magazines, and newspapers in several languages, including English. Open 8am-midnight.

Laundry: Several facilities, especially near North Station. Go down the road (from the cluster of churches at Paraportiani) into Little Venice. Across from Montparnasse Bar, a store says "Laundry" (tel. 24 982). Laundry ready in 1½hr. Wash 2000dr, dry 1500dr. Open daily 9:00am-10:30pm.

Pharmacy: (tel. 23 250) On Matogianni St., right across from Pierro's. Open Mon.-Sat. 8:30am-1:30pm and 5-10pm.

Hospital: (tel. 23 994, -6) 1km east of Mykonos Town. Take the bus or taxi (600dr) to Ano Mera (8 per day, 190dr). For an emergency, call an **ambulance** at 166.

Police: (tel. 22 716, -215) In Laka past the South Station. Open 24hr.

Post Office: (tel. 22 238), around the corner from the police in Laka, behind South Station. **Exchanges currency.** Open Mon.-Fri. 7:30am-2pm. **Postal Code:** 84600.

OTE: (tel. 22 699) Left end of waterfront in big white building, uphill to the right of the dock. Open Mon.-Fri. 8am-3pm. **Telephone Code:** 0289.

ACCOMMODATIONS

Hotel proprietors take advantage of the island's wealthy clientele by charging exorbitant prices, particularly during the months of July and August. Even so, reasonable accommodations are available, especially if you are willing to stay outside the immediate town area. The information offices located on the dock are numbered according to accommodation type and are helpful—1 for hotels (tel. 24 540; open 9am-midnight), 2 for rooms to let (tel. 24 860; open daily 9am-11pm), and 3 for camping (tel. 23 567; open daily 9am-midnight). Follow one of the hawkers at your own risk. Many claim to have rooms "on the beach," but they are often miles from town. Remember free-lance camping is illegal. Prices are 20-40% less in the off season.

Hotel Terra Maria, 33 Kalogera St. (tel. 24 212; fax 27 112), in an alley off Kalogera. Don't confuse it with Chez Maria or the nearby Marios Hotel. A/C, private baths, and mini-bars. Despite central location, surrounding city park makes it very peaceful. Run by Petros, a former soccer star. Doubles 13,000-20,000dr; triples 16,000-24,000dr. Breakfast 1800dr.

Hotel Apollon (tel. 23 271, 22 223), on the waterfront. Oldest hotel in town—an old, antique-laden house with many rooms overlooking the harbor. Common baths. Singles 7000-10,000dr; doubles 9000-12,000dr; triples 12,000-15,000dr.

Hotel Karboni/Matogianni (tel. 22 217), on Matogianni St., inland from the waterfront. Pleasant and spotless. Ask about cheaper rear rooms. Doubles 15,000dr; triples 18,000dr. Breakfast 1000dr.

Hotel Phillippi, 25N. Kalogera St. (tel. 22 294, fax 24 680), next to Chez Maria. Friendly owners, gorgeous gardens, and clean rooms. Rooms with common bath cost as much as those with private bath. Singles 6,500-7,800dr; doubles 11,000-13,500dr; triples 15,500-19,000dr.

Chez Maria Pension, 27N. Kalogera St. (tel. 22 480). From the waterfront, turn inland next to Sea & Sky Travel Agency onto Matogianni St., turn right onto Kalogera at the yellow building across from the Credit Bank. There are signs to help. Above Chez Maria Restaurant—conveniently located meals, but perhaps a little noisy when others feast while you try to sleep. Doubles 12,000dr; triples 15,000dr.

Paradise Beach Camping (tel. 22 852, -129; fax 24 350), on beach 6km from the village. You can take a bus here (380dr round-trip). Situated directly on one of island's more popular beaches. Even though it's quite large, it often feels crowded. Because of its location, nude bathers on Paradise Beach are a common sight. Free shuttle service from port and airport. 1500dr per person; 800dr per small tent; 1000dr per large tent.

Mykonos Camping (tel. 25 915, -916; fax 24 578), near Paradise Beach. Smaller, quieter, and cleaner. 1500dr per person; 800dr per tent; 1500dr per tent rental.

FOOD

Klimataria (tel. 24 051), past Taxi Sq. on Florov Zouganeli St.—look for blue tables. Good prices and a 5-language menu, including English. Draws a tourist crowd, but serves authentic Greek cuisine. Try *Moussaka* (1100dr), rabbit stew (1700dr), or rooster in red sauce with pasta (1800dr). Open daily 9am-1am.

Alexi's (tel. 26 904), back of Taxi Sq. The oldest greasy spoon in Mykonos. Alexi puts on a show as he cooks up your *gyro*-pita (350dr), hamburger (450-650dr), or barbeque chicken with fries (1100dr). Open daily 22hr., closed 7am-9am.

Niko's Taverna (tel. 24 320), in a cluster of restaurants inland from excursion boat docks. A hoppin' place for traditional Greek cuisine. Taste the baked *kalamari* and cheese (2000dr), mussels with tomato and cheese (1500dr), lamb *kleftiko* (baked with cheese in aluminum foil, 2000dr). Open daily noon-2am.

La Mexicana (tel. 24 194), at the end of Kalogera St. Chicken enchiladas are 1900dr; chicken, beef, or shrimp fajitas 2500dr. A good choice for homesick Mexican food lovers. Happy hour daily 6:30-8:00pm—discount on sangria, frozen margaritas, and tequila shots.

The Donut Factory (tel. 22 672), at the intersection of Mitropoleos, Ipirou, and Enoplon Dinameon St., roughly 3 blocks down from South Station. Delightful donuts (300-450dr) and fresh fruit juices (500-600dr). Open daily 24hr.

Kyklamino/Klouras Bakery (tel. 23 229), around the bend off of Kalogera St., next to the electric company office. Head here for the island's sweet specialties—*amigthalota* (almond cookies) and *kalathakia* (pastry tarts filled with walnuts). Open daily 8:30am-10pm.

ENTERTAINMENT

Skandinavian Bar, near Niko's Taverna and the waterfront. This perennially packed party complex sprawls over 2 buildings and a patio. Evening mellowness becomes madness 'round midnight. *Everyone* passes through this place. Beer 700dr, cocktails 1500dr. Open Sun.-Fri. 10:30pm-3am, Sat. 10:30pm-4am.

Pierro's, on Matogianni St., reputedly the most happening place on Mykonos. Pierro's was the first gay bar in Greece. Best dancing around the island and loud music—the crowd spills out into the square. Beer 1000dr, cocktails 2000dr.

Nepheli-Blue Bar, upstairs from Pierro's. A popular gay hangout, but like most gay bars on the island, everyone is welcome. Beer 1000dr, cocktails 1400-1600dr. Next door, **Icaros** has a similar atmosphere.

Montparnasse (tel. 23 719), Agion Anargyron St., in the Little Venice district. Step into a Toulouse-Lautrec and have a cocktail by the bay window overlooking the water while being serenaded by cabaret tunes from a live piano. Groovy and sophisticated. Wine 800dr, cocktails 900-2000dr. Open daily 7pm-3am.

Caprice Bar, on the water in Little Venice. Popular and crowded, with a fruit motif befitting a waterfront bar. A popular place to watch breathtaking sunsets. So close to the water that windy days are not as pleasant. Open daily 4:30pm-4am.

Mykonos Bar, in Little Venice, next to the Caprice Bar. Watch Greek dancers perform the *zebekiko* and *zorba,* then join them until sunrise. They are here to teach you! 800dr cover. Beer 700dr, cocktails 1500dr. Open daily 10pm-4am.

SIGHTS

The prime daytime activities on Mykonos are shopping and tanning. **Galatis,** left of Taxi Sq. (facing town), has lovely handwoven sweaters (from 10,000dr). Note the list of signatures of famous people, like Jackie O., who shopped here (tel. 22 255; open daily April-Oct. 9am-10pm). **O Liondis,** 55 Matogianni St., sells individually crafted leather sandals (from 2000dr; open daily 9am-midnight). Look for **Benetia** on the main shopping street in **Little Venice,** just down from **Paraportiani,** which sells beautiful, hand-embroidered white linen. These traditional embroideries and loomed fabrics imitate patterns from museums all over Greece (tel. 24 464; open daily 11:30am-3:30pm and 6:30pm-midnight).

Although cultural enrichment may not be a primary activity on Mykonos, several museums exist for those who are interested. The **Archaeological Museum** (tel. 22 325), on the paved road between the ferry dock and the center of town, has a 7th-century BC *pithos* (large terra cotta storage jar) with relief scenes from the Trojan War, and a bronze *kouros* (open Tues.-Sun. 8:30am-3pm; admission 500dr, students 300dr, European students free, seniors 300dr). The **Aegean Maritime Museum** (tel. 22 700), around the corner from the inland end of Matogiannis, contains ship models, rare ancient coins with nautical subjects, and navigational instruments (open daily April-Oct. 10:30am-1pm and 6:30-9pm; admission 200dr, students 100dr). The **Folklore Museum** (tel. 22 591) is in the 300-year-old house of a former sea captain, at the south edge of town, near the bus station, inland from the excursion boat docks. The lovely collection is open at convenient hours for beach-goers (open April-Oct. Mon.-Sat. 5:30-8:30pm, Sun. 6:30-8:30pm; free). **Lena's House** is a 300-year-old home with traditional 19th-century furniture. The home is part of the folklore museum and remains exactly as its owner left it (open Mon.-Sat. 6-9pm, Sun. 7-9pm; free). Next door is the **Paraportiani,** a cluster of white churches, probably the most famous of Mykonos's sights and on every other Greek postcard.

You will inevitably find yourself on the beach in Mykonos. Nearest to town after the unexceptional town beach is **Megali Ammos,** a 1-km walk past the windmills on the southwest corner of the harbor. **St. Stefanos Beach** is not spectacular, but very convenient (buses every 30min. from North Station 8:15am-2am, 10min., 210dr). Crowded **Psarou Beach** is a hop, skip, and jump from town (buses every 30min. from South Station 8:15am-2am, 15min., 210dr). Although all the beaches on Mykonos are nudist, the degree of nudity depends on where you go. The more daring beaches, **Plati Yialos, Paradise Beach,** and **Super Paradise Beach,** are reputedly the best. Reach the latter two by catching a bus from South Station to Plati Yialos (every 30min., 210dr), then take a *caïques* across the water. From Plati Yialos, *caïques* go to Paradise Beach (300dr), officially called Kalamopodi and packed with beach towels, and to Super Paradise Beach (380dr), the most popular gay beach on the island. Paradise can also be reached by the 7-km strip of road connecting it to town. For a more quiet sun-bathing experience choose **Kalafati, Panormos,** or **Elia beaches,** all of which are accessible by bus from North Station (290–320dr).

DELOS ΔΗΛΟΣ

The sacred heart of the Cyclades, Delos holds the famous **Temple of Apollo,** built to commemorate the birthplace of Apollo and his twin sister, Artemis. After Zeus impregnated Leto, he cast her out, fearing his wife Hera's wrath. Leto searched desperately for a place to give birth and at last came across this rocky island, bobbing in the sea. She declared that the child would stay forever at his birthplace, casting light upon the surrounding riches. At her word, the island stopped drifting, and Leto, reassured, decided to stay. Upon her son's birth, the island was bathed in radiance; its name, A-delos (meaning invisible) was changed to Delos because it could now be clearly seen. Immensely grateful, Leto promised to make the island the seat of Apollo's worship. The presence of the sanctuary made Delos a religious center.

The mortal history of the island has not been as charmed. Delos had long been a religious and commercial focus for the Cyclades when the Ionians dedicated it to the **cult of Leto** in the 10th century BC. By the 7th century BC, Delos had become the political and trade center of the Aegean League of Islands. Three centuries of struggle for power between the Delians and the Athenians ensued. During these years, the Athenians ordered at least two "purifications" of the island, the latter, in 426 BC, decreeing that no one should give birth or die on its sacred grounds. Delians who violated the edict were banished to nearby Rheneia. The Athenians later instituted the quadrennial **Delian Games,** which they always dominated.

After Sparta's defeat of Athens in the Peloponnesian War (403 BC), Delos enjoyed independence and wealth. Sweet prosperity soured, however, during the Roman occupation in the 2nd century BC. The island subsequently became the slave-trading center of Greece, where the transfer of as many as 10,000 slaves occurred daily. By the 2nd century AD, after successive sackings, the island was left virtually uninhabited apart from a few odd pirates. Today, its only residents are legions of leaping lizards and members of the French School of Archaeology.

The latter of the two have been excavating here since 1873. A map of the site is recommended, whether you choose to follow the tour detailed below, tag along with a guided tour, or improvise. For more information, a readable source is *Delos: Monuments and Museum,* by Photini Zaphiropoulou, which includes a map (1500dr, available at the entrance, at the museum, or at tourist shops in Mykonos).

Occupying almost an entire square mile of this very small island, the archaeological site is neatly sectioned off into the central part of the ancient city, including the Temple of Apollo and the Agora, and the outlying parts of the city, Mt. Kythnos, and the theater quarter. While it takes several days to explore the ruins completely, you can see the highlights in three hours or less. Most of your fellow ferry passengers will follow a similar route when they disembark; reverse the route if you want some privacy. Bring a water bottle; the cafeteria on site is expensive (soda, 600dr).

From the dock, head straight to the **Agora of the Competaliasts,** where Roman guilds built their shrines. Nearby are several parallel **stoas,** the most impressive of which were built by Philip of Macedon. This line of altars, pillars, and statue bases (you can still see the statues' prints) forms the western border of the **Sacred Way.** Follow this road to the **Temple of Apollo,** with its immense, partly hollow hexagonal pedestal that once sustained the weight of the 8m-tall marble statue of the god of light. The famous, **Delian Lions,** a gift from the people of Naxos to the holy island, lie 50m to the north. In the 7th century BC, nine marble lions were placed in a row on a terrace facing the sacred lake; only five remain here—a sixth, pirated by the Venetians, guards the entrance to the arsenal in Venice.

Proceed up the small crest left of the lions to the **House of the Hill.** Because the building was dug deep into the earth, this archetypal Roman house is still substantially intact. Downhill lies the **House of the Lake,** with a well preserved mosaic decorating its atrium and the desecrated **Sacred Lake.** A lone palm tree keeps watch over the surrounding shrubbery. Next to the cafeteria, the **museum** contains an assortment of archaeological finds from the island; unfortunately, the best sculpture from the site is in Athens (Delos museum open Tues.-Sun. 8:30am-3pm). From there, you can hike up the path on **Mt. Kythnos** (where Zeus watched the birth of Apollo). Along the way, you will pass several temples dedicated to the Egyptian gods. The elegant bust in the **Temple of Isis** depicts the sun, while the 120m hill affords a marvelous view of the ruins and islands. Although the climb is not especially difficult, wear comfortable yet sturdy shoes—some of the rocks that comprise the makeshift stairs dislodge easily. The **Grotto of Hercules** is on the way down. Its immense building blocks seem to date it to Mycenaean times, though some experts suggest it is a Hellenic imitation of Mycenaean architecture.

At the base of the hill, go towards the water to the **House of the Dolphins** and the **House of the Masks,** which contains the mosaic *Dionysus Riding a Panther.* Continue on to the **ancient theater,** which has a rather sophisticated cistern (as cisterns go), **Dexamene,** with nine arched compartments. Also try to explore the **House of the Trident,** graced by a mosaic of a dolphin twisted around a trident; the **House of Dionysus,** containing another mosaic of Dionysus and a panther; and the **House of Cleopatra.** The famous statue of Cleopatra and Dioscourides is sequestered in the museum; a plaster copy takes its place on the site (ruins open Tues.-Sun. 9am-2:30pm; 1200dr, students 600dr, European students free).

GETTING THERE

Delos is most accessible as a daytrip from Mykonos. **Boats** leave from the dock near town (not the dock for large ferries) Tuesday-Sunday every 30-45 minutes, 8:30am-11:30am, and return between 11am-3pm (25min., 1600dr round-trip). Most will let you explore the site for three hours. Guided tours, offered in several languages by each excursion boat company, are expensive (7500dr, including admission to the ruins). Take the free map that accompanies your admission ticket and eavesdrop on the groups at each site. Each boat line has several return trips in the afternoon, so you have some flexibility about how much time you spend exploring. Tickets can be bought at the dock. Other islands (especially Tinos, Naxos, and Paros) offer joint trips to Mykonos and Delos, but allow less time to explore the ruins.

IOS ΙΟΣ

If you're not drunk by the time you get here, you will be by the time you leave. On Ios, beers go down and clothes come off faster than you can say *"Opa!"* It has everything your mother warned you about—people swilling wine from the bottle at 3pm, wishing you slobbery "good evenings," drinking games all day along the beach, condoms scattered on dirt roads, men and women dancing naked in bars (of which Ios had 113 at last count), and oh so much more. Drinks here are cheap and plentiful; Ios imports one and a half mega-truckloads of beer a day—and exports the same number of empty bottles each morning. Though the island has settled down a bit in the past few years, it's still about ready to sink under the weight of well-built, suntanned 20-year-olds. There is little to do in Ios but sleep late, sunbathe in the afternoon, and join the drunken cavorting by night. Make the pilgrimage to this mecca of the young and the restless only if you're prepared for hangovers, the occasional groping hand, and the lustful stares of the inebriated.

The island quiets down in the off season. University students flee the scene, leaving locals behind to prepare for the next attack. September is an ideal time to visit Ios if you want to experience a beautiful yet slightly misbehaved Cycladic island.

ORIENTATION AND PRACTICAL INFORMATION

The good life centers around three locations, each 20 minutes apart along the island's paved road. The **port** (Yialos) is at one end of the road; the **village** (Chora), the focus of nocturnal activity, sits above it on a hill; and crowded **Mylopotas beach** rests over the hill on the other side of the village. Frequent buses shuttle from port to village to beach and back roughly every 10-20 minutes (8am-2am, 210dr).

Yialos

Ferries from Ios go to: Peiraias (4-5 per day, 7-8hr., 5160dr); Naxos (7-8 per day, 80min., 2295dr); Santorini (6 per day, 1¼hr., 1170dr); Paros (7-8 per day, 2½hr., 2605dr); Mykonos (2 per day, 4-5hr., 3190dr); Syros (2-3 per week, 5hr., 3635dr); Crete (3 per week, 5hr., 4015dr); Folegandros (3-4 per week, 1hr., 1750dr); Sikinos (3-4 per week, 30min., 1411dr); and less frequently to smaller Cycladic islands. **Flying Dolphins** serve: Rafina (daily, 4-5hr., 8160dr); Santorini (3 per day, 35min., 3225dr); Paros (3 per day, 1¼hr, 4895dr); Naxos (2 per day, 45min., 4270dr); Mykonos (2 per day, 2hr., 6380dr); Syros (1 per day, 2½hr., 7280dr); Andros (1 per day, 3½hr., 8640dr); Tinos (1 per day, 2½hr., 7050dr); and Amoros (1 every other day, 2hr., 4325dr). There are also four round-trip excursions per week to Sikinos (2000dr) and Folegandros (3000dr). The **port authority** (tel. 91 264; open 24hr.), is at the far end of the harbor next to Camping Ios.

Acteon Travel (tel. 91 343, -318, -002; fax 91 088) has offices all over the island, an English-speaking staff, free luggage storage, excursions around the island, stamps, maps, travel services, and a full-service **American Express** office. It is also the place to make or confirm airline reservations. The main office is by the bus stop in the port (open 8am-midnight). Staying in the port is a good idea if you want to avoid the late-night chaos of the village. On the waterfront, **Pension Irene** (tel./fax 91 023) offers clean, quiet rooms with bath and a view of the water (doubles 8000; triples 10,000). Head up the side street that faces you as you disembark from the ferry to find **Petros Place Hotel** (tel. 91 421). Complete with bath in every room, breakfast, an outdoor swimming pool, and poolside bar, Petros Place is ideal for those seeking a peaceful stay (doubles 10,000; triples 12,000). And you can always crash portside at the crowded **Camping Ios** (tel. 91 329; 1200dr per person, 1000dr per tent rental).

If the fast-food gyro joints don't tempt your appetite, choose **Enigma** (tel. 91 847; fax 91 407), on the waterfront. This is one of the few places in all of Greece that serves a dozen different baked potatoes (900-1000dr) and good onion rings (600dr). Gulp draft beer (600-700dr) while playing pool. To find serious drinking, climb the infamous "donkey steps" to the right of the paved road.

■ Ios Village

Miraculously, Ios Village has not become as trashed as its visitors. As you approach, the density of bars with storefront advertising gimmicks, the occasional dried side-walk vomit, and the odd comatose carouser will be enough assurance that you got off at the right port.

ORIENTATION AND PRACTICAL INFORMATION

You can do most of your "serious" business within five minutes, by foot, of the village bus stop on the paved road opposite the large, blue-domed church. The **Tourist Information Center** (tel. 91 135), immediately adjacent to the bus stop, is a private travel agency that sells ferry and hydrofoil tickets, provides currency exchange, helps with accommodations, and offers free luggage storage, maps, and safety deposit boxes (open daily 8am-midnight). The **OTE** (tel. 91 399) is a few minutes out of the village along a path starting from the main paved road after Sweet Irish Dream. Look for signs (open Mon.-Fri. 7:30am-3:10pm). Along the road heading to Kolitsani Beach, just past the OTE, you will find the English-speaking **police** (tel. 92 222, open 24hr.). Next to the main church, the **National Bank** (tel. 91 354) has an **ATM** and will handle all your MasterCard needs (open Mon.-Thurs. 8am-2pm, Fri. 8am-1:30pm). The village branch of **Acteon Travel** (tel. 91 004, -5) is just up the road from the bus stop. Cartoon maps and English information booklets are available free at most travel agencies in the village and port (open daily 8am-midnight). If you aspire to see more than the beach, you can rent a moped or a jeep at **Trohokinisi** (tel. 91 166), past the parking lot between the church and the main road (mopeds 3000-5000dr per day, cars 10,000-22,000dr per day). A license is absolutely necessary for both mopeds and automobiles. Two streets up in the densely packed village is the town square, where you can find **public toilets.** The **medical center** (tel. 91 227), full of travelers patching up wounds from drunken mishaps, is next to the bus stop at the back of the big yellow building (open daily 10am-1pm and 6-7pm). For **emergencies,** call 91 727, -827, (093) 400 423, or (093) 423 207 (open 24hr.). A **pharmacy** (tel. 91 562) is on the bar-infested street in the old village (open Mon.-Sat. 9am-2pm and 5-10pm). There is a **supermarket** in the complex on the main road. The **postal code** is 84001. The **telephone code** is 0286.

ACCOMMODATIONS

Ios is yet another case of hawks at the docks; make sure you are in a bargaining mood when you disembark. Depending on how the season is going, prices fluctuate between 2000-6000dr for singles, with bath 3000-7000dr; 2500-7000dr for doubles, with bath 3000-10,000dr; and 4500-9000 for triples, with bath 5000-12,000dr.

Francesco's (tel./fax 91 223). From the top of the "donkey steps," walk up the path to the square next to the church, take the uphill steps in the left corner of the square, then the first left. Rooms with a spectacular view of the harbor sit atop the hotel's terrace bar. Reservations encouraged. Doubles 5000dr, with bath 8000dr; triples 6000dr, with bath 9000dr.

Pension Markos (tel. 91 059; fax 91 060). From the bus stop, take the right (uphill) just before the supermarket. It's on another side street to the left, with a sign visible from the street. Friendly, clean, popular, with a happening pool. Bar serves breakfast all day (600dr). Reserve your room a few days in advance. All rooms with bath. Doubles 8000dr; triples 10,000dr.

Hotel Petradi (tel./fax 91 510), equidistant from the village and the beach on the main road. Every room has a balcony with a romantic ocean view. Large, pleasant patio. Quiet at night. Restaurant/bar downstairs. Doubles 8000dr; triples 9000dr.

Kolitsani View (tel. 91 061; fax 92 261). Follow the path past the OTE and look for the white archway. Approximately 10min. from the village action, it offers a quiet collection of spotless rooms with a family atmosphere. Expansive view of beaches and even Santorini. Free pick-up from the port. Doubles 7000dr, with bath 9000dr; triples 9000dr, with bath 13,000dr.

Pension Panorama (tel. 91 592, -186), a bit of an uphill hike on a path below the village, next door to Francesco's. The view makes up for the hike. Doubles 9000dr; triples 12,000dr. Continental breakfast 600dr.

Far Out Camping (tel. 92 301, -2; fax 92 303), at the far end of Mylopotas beach, is the hippest, most luxurious camping choice. Club Med at 1000dr per night, with a restaurant, bar, minimarket, basketball, volleyball, swimming pool, water slides, nightly movie, scuba diving (lessons open to public), showers, laundry, live music, and "happenings" with live bands and parties during summer. Open April-Sept. 1000dr per person; 400dr tent rental.

Camping Stars (tel./fax 91 612, -611), on Mylopotas beach. Quieter and less crowded than Far Out, with many of the same services, including a swimming pool. Open June-Sept. 1400dr per person; 500dr tent rental.

Camping Ios (tel. 91 329), at the port, is ideal for late-night arrivals. Open June-Sept. 1000dr per person.

FOOD

Interspersed among the omnipresent bars and discos in Ios village are several good, reasonably priced restaurants. You can't beat **Pithari,** near the National Bank, for Greek specialties. *Exohiko* (lamb wrapped in pastry) is 1800dr, chicken *methismeno* ("drunk chicken") 1200dr. For exquisite Greek cuisine and forgotten Greek recipes, look for **Lordos Byron** (tel. 92 125), uphill from the National Bank on the tiny street below the main drag. *Strapatsada* (special Greek omelette) is 1000dr, *fava* bean dip 900dr. Choose freely from the menu—everything is divine (open daily 7pm-midnight). There are also cheap, greasy gyro joints near the bars (350dr). Mylopotas Beach offers two quality international restaurants. **Harmony** (tel. 91 615), to the right at the bottom of the footpath leading to the beach from the village, offers good Mexican food (burritos 1600dr). Just down the slope is **Delfini,** with an enormous menu of Thai food (stir-fried vegetables with basil and garlic 1400dr). True gourmands make their way to **Polydoros** (tel. 91 132), 2km north of the port on Koubara Beach, for what's reputed to be the island's best food.

ENTERTAINMENT

Of Ios's alleged 113 bars, the majority are packed into the old village area. Some of the larger and louder hang-outs can be found along the main paved road. Smaller bars line the main pedestrian street in the village. Some bars offer happy hours early in the evening, but the real drinking doesn't begin until at least 11pm.

Sweet Irish Dream (tel. 91 141), a large building near the "donkey steps." Almost everyone ends up here, but most save it as the night's last stop. Come here after 2am to dance on tables. No cover before 2am. Beer 500-600dr; cocktails 700-800dr.

The Slammer Bar (tel. 92 119), just uphill from the main square in the Village. Serves specialty tequila slammers (shot glass filled with tequila, Tia Maria, and Sprite, slammed on the bar 600dr). Always packed.

Kalimera, lower down off the main strip. Perhaps the classiest bar, playing jazz and reggae. Beer 500-800dr; cocktails 1000-1200dr.

Dubliner (tel. 92 072), next to the bus stop. Proximity to Sweet Irish Dream makes it a great warm up—and the only place to enjoy Guinness on tap. The large outdoor terrace is the main attraction before midnight. Beer 500dr; cocktails 1000dr.

Scorpion Disco, on the perimeter of town, on the way to the beach. A dance emporium. Probably the craziest place on the island—not for the inexperienced or naive. 1000dr cover after 2am includes your first drink.

Blue Note, popular with Americans, Scandinavians, and those staying at Francesco's. Follow the main pedestrian path as it curves to the left. You will most likely have to ask for directions. Beer 500dr; cocktails 1000dr.

Anemos, a "block" from Blue Note, before the left-turning bend in the path. The only place to enjoy Greek music and dance *zebekika*. Very welcoming, but be prepared for a local crowd and vacationing Greeks. Cocktails 1000dr.

BEACHES

With the exceptions of a solitary monastery, some castle ruins, a modest pile of rubble at the north tip of the island reputed to be **Homer's tomb,** and the ancient town on the hill to the left of Ios town, the **beaches** are the place to be on Ios. Most head for **Mylopotas Beach** on foot (roughly 20min. downhill from Ios town) or by bus service from the port or village (daily 8am-1am, 210dr). The beach, like the town, has loudspeakers blasting everywhere. The outer reaches offer a modicum of privacy. The farther you go, the fewer clothes you will see (or wear). **Watersports** are available at the shack in the middle of the beach—look for the yellow *Body Glove* flags; windsurf (2000dr per hour), waterski (3000dr per hour), or snorkel (800dr per hour).

Of course, there are prettier and less crowded beaches on Ios. If you continue uphill from the OTE, look for the path that leads down to the secluded beach and crystal pool of water at the little **Kolitsani** bay (15-minute walk from Chora). Excursions leave daily for the nude beach at beautiful **Manganari Bay,** stopping—appropriately enough—at the monastery (11am, return 6pm; 2000dr). Nudist, secluded **Psathi** on the eastern coast is a 7km walk along donkey trails. An excursion goes to Psathi several times per week, stopping at the castle ruins (11am, return 6pm; 2000dr). Other nude beaches include **Koubara** (2km walk north from the port) and **Ag. Theodoti** near Psathi.

SANTORINI (THIRA) ΣΑΝΤΟΡΗΝΗ, ΘΗΡΑ

Plunging cliffs, burning black sand beaches, and deeply scarred hills make Santorini's landscape as dramatic as the cataclysm that created it. Even those with no interest in Santorini's intriguing past will find ample delights in its present—long stretches of beach, tiny cliffside towns, and spectacular landscapes forged by centuries of volcanic activity. Santorini's whitewashed homes are strewn against a cliffside, its ridges rising sharply out of the Aegean. The black beaches, stark against cobalt waters, and the searing-hot fields of pumice are unique in their beauty among the Greek islands. Blessed with fertile soil enriched with volcanic minerals, Santorini is the greenest of the otherwise barren Cyclades. Endless vineyards attest to the island's love of winemaking, a passion second only to the island's biggest industry—tourism.

From approximately 2000 BC to 1628 BC, one of the most advanced societies in ancient Greece flourished on the island, then called Thira. In 1628 BC, a massive volcanic eruption buried every sign of civilization beneath tons of lava and pumice. In the centuries since, fact and fiction have mingled, leading some to believe that Santorini is Plato's lost continent of Atlantis. More serious historical speculation has convinced many scholars that the eruption on Santorini triggered a tidal wave large enough to account for the destruction of several Minoan sites in Crete.

Modern Santorini is really only the eastern crescent of what was once a circular island, originally called "Strongili" (round). The explosion in 1628 BC left a crust of volcanic ash stretching over the hollow center of the island. When the crust caved in, water filled the resulting *caldera* (basin) that is now Santorini's harbor. The two islands to the west, **Thirasia** and **Aspronisi,** appear to be separate, but are in fact a continuation of the original island's rim.

ORIENTATION AND PRACTICAL INFORMATION

Santorini is easily accessible and incredibly crowded. Boats dock at one of three ports: Athinios, Thira, and Oia. **Athinios** is the most important and has frequent buses (at least 20 per day, 30min., 300dr) to Thira and Perissa Beach. Hostel-bound travelers can board the free shuttle bus to Thira Youth Hostel, Perissa Youth Hostel, or Youth Hostel Perissa-Anna. It is also possible to get free rides from the pension proprietors at the port. The port of **Thira** is a 587-step footpath below the town. The cable car departs every 20 minutes, 6:40am-midnight, and costs 700dr. You can also hire a mule for the same price.

Ferries depart for: Peirais (3-6 per day, 10hr., 5825dr); Ios (6-10 per day, 1½hr., 1775dr); Paros (8-10 per day, 5hr., 3100dr); Naxos (6-8 per day, 4hr., 2880dr); Mykonos (3-5 per day, 7hr., 3380dr); Iraklion (1-3 per day, 8hr., 3390dr); Syros (1-2 per day, 6hr., 4000dr); Rhodes (2 per week, 16hr., 6100dr); Sikinos (6 per week, 1925dr); Folegandros (5 per week, 1930dr); Anafi (3 per week, 1935dr); and Milos (3 per week, 3540dr). Three ferries per week go to: Sifnos (3058dr); Serifos (3335dr); and Kithos (2690dr). Two per week to: Kassos (3890dr); Karpathos (4565dr); and Thessaloniki (9300dr). One per week to Skiathos (7790dr). **Flying Dolphins** serve: Rafina (9403dr); Ios (3227dr); Paros (6210dr); Naxos (5765dr); Mykonos (6756dr); Syros (8017dr); Tinos (7852dr); and Amorgos (4493dr). **Olympic Airways** has daily **flights** to: Athens (21,300dr); Mykonos (15,100dr); Iraklion (14,700dr); Rhodes (21,900dr); and Thessaloniki (29,100dr).

Renting a moped may be the ideal way to travel around the island. During the summer, however, Santorini becomes densely crowded and moped dealers rent bikes to just about anyone. Inexperienced riders, poor bikes, and carefree drivers create a dangerous combination. If you choose to ride, make sure you are satisfied with the bike's quality, and be cautious. Travel by foot or bus (Santorini's service is excellent) may be a better option. The least painful choice is a half- (3000dr) or full-day (4500dr) bus tour. **Kamari Tours** (tel. 31 390, 31 455), with offices all over the island, is reputable. Other agencies may offer student discounts. There is a severe **water shortage** on Santorini; fresh water accounts for most of the price of rooms on the island.

Santorini (Thira)

■ Thira Town

The center of activity on the island is the capital city, **Thira,** which in Greek means "wild island." It is more commonly referred to as "Fee-rah" by Greek tourists and locals. Some say that the harbor below the town plunges into a bottomless abyss leading to the door between heaven and hell. Stepping off the bus from the port, you may conclude that hell is actually on this side of the door. First-time visitors have been known to wonder aloud if they have disembarked on the wrong island when confronted with the mess of glitzy shops, whizzing mopeds, and scads of tourists. Fortunately, the ugly roadside strip is only one aspect of this multi-faceted town. Thira is perched on a cliff and the short walk to the town's western edge, the *caldera,* reveals a stunning view of the harbor. Santorini's coastline, the neighboring islands, and its volcano make it a popular site for weddings and honeymoons. Although the town is overrun with tourists in summer, nothing can destroy the pleasure of wandering among the narrow cobbled streets, inspecting the craft shops, and arriving at the western edge of town in time to watch the sunset.

ORIENTATION AND PRACTICAL INFORMATION

Facing the street with the bus station behind you, a walk right and uphill will lead you to **Theotokopoulou Square,** full of travel agencies, banks, and restaurants. At the fork in the road, the street on the right is **25th Martiou Street,** the main paved road leading from the square north towards Oia. It is home to both of Thira's youth hostels, as well as other accommodations. If you head from the left branch north of the bus stop on to 25th Martiou and turn on to any westbound street, you'll find backstreets with many of the best bars and discos. Farther west is the *caldera*, where expensive restaurants and art galleries are overshadowed only by the spectacular view.

Tourist Police: (tel. 22 649) On the main road south of the bus depot. They share a building with the **police.** Open 24hr.

Port Police: (tel. 22 239) On the main road north of Theotokopoulou Sq.

Tourist Agencies: Dozens surround Theotokopoulou Sq. **Pelican Travel** (tel. 22 220, 23 667), on the northwestern corner of the square, has particularly efficient service. Ticketing done online. Currency exchange. Open daily 8am-11pm.

Banks: National Bank, on the avenue branching off from the main road south from the square. Offers currency exchange. Open Mon.-Thurs. 8am-2pm, Fri. 8am-1:30pm. The **Agricultural Bank** and **Commercial Bank** also exchange currency. Both open Mon.-Thurs. 8am-2pm, Fri. 8am-1:30pm.

American Express: (tel. 22 624) In the office of **X-Ray Kilo Travel and Shipping Agency** in the square. All AmEx services. Open daily 8am-11pm.

Flights: Olympic Airways (tel. 22 493). From the bus depot, go downhill on the main road, take the first left, then a right. Reserve 1-2 weeks in advance. Standby tickets possible (arrive 2hr. before take-off). Office open Mon.-Fri. 8:30am-4pm.

Buses: To: Perissa (25 per day, 30min., 370dr); Kamari (40 per day, 20min., 200dr); Akrotiri (15 per day, 30min., 360dr); Athinios (10 per day, 15min., 330dr); Oia (25 per day, 30min., 250dr); and the airport (12 per day, 30min., 230dr).

Taxis: tel. 22 555.

Moped and Car Rental: Try **Zeus Rent-A-Car** (tel. 24 013), next to Penguine laundry (12,000dr per day). For mopeds, try **Marcos Rental** (tel. 23 877), 50m north of the square. Free helmets included with every rental (3000-3500dr per day). Open daily 8:30pm-7pm.

International Bookstore: International Press (tel. 22 942), at the top of the plaza between Theotokopoulou Sq. and the cliff. Open daily 8:30am-midnight.

Laundromats: Penguine (tel. 22 168), north of the square on the left. For 5kg, wash 1050dr; dry 950dr; soap 200dr. Open daily 8:30am-9:30pm.

Public Toilets: 25th Martiou St., down and across the street from the bus depot.

Pharmacy: (tel. 23 444) 20m north of bus station. Open daily 8:30am-10:30pm.

Medical Center: (tel. 22 237) The first left off the main road down from the bus depot. Handles routine problems 9am-2pm; open for **emergencies** 24hr.

Post Office: (tel. 22 238; fax 22698). On 25th Martiou St. between the square and the bus stop. Open Mon.-Fri. 8am-2pm. **Postal Code:** 84700.

OTE: (tel. 22 399) 100m north of square on road to Oia. Open daily 7:30am-3:10pm. **Telephone Code:** 0286.

ACCOMMODATIONS

Santorini does not lack accommodations, but in summer the pensions and hotels are almost all booked by noon. The cheapest options, and the best bet if you arrive late, are the (non-HI) youth hostels in Thira, Perissa Beach or Oia; see **Southern Santorini** (p. 230) and **Northern Santorini** (p. 232). There are also good accommodations in private homes all over the island, so don't hesitate to branch out. The settlement of **Karterados,** 2km south of Thira, provides many options. Private doubles in outlying towns run as low as 2500dr. Head for **Karterados, Messaria, Pyrgos, Emborio,** or any of the small inland towns along the main bus routes. Some hawkers at the port misrepresent their rooms, so be clear about where you are going and what you are getting. In Thira, doubles run roughly 11,000-13,000dr in high season. Prices listed below are for peak season; rates decrease by as much as 50% in the off season.

Thira Youth Hostel (tel. 22 387), on the left roughly 300m north of the square, set back 25m from the road to Oia. Clean, quiet dorm rooms, a few even quieter "small dormitories," and pension-quality private rooms with baths. Hot showers 24hr., but bring your own toilet paper. Reception open 24hr. Owner enforces quiet after 11pm. No smoking in dorm rooms. Check-out noon. Open April-Oct. Dorm beds 1500dr; doubles 6000-8000dr. Sheets 200dr; pillowcase 100dr.

Kontohori Youth Hostel (tel. 22 722, -577), down a hill 400m north of the square. Look for a big yellow building next to the church at the base of the slope. 10% discount on stays longer than 5 days makes it popular among workers. Single-sex dorm beds. Reception open 24hr. Check-out noon. Hot showers 4-9pm only. Dorms 1200dr; doubles 7500dr.

Kamares Youth Hostel (tel. 24 472), north of the square with a turn-off before Kontohori hostel; just above Thira Hostel. Single-sex dorm rooms and beds available on the canopied roof. Reception open 8am-1pm and 5-9pm. Check-out noon. Hot showers 5-9pm only. Dorm beds 1000dr; roof 900dr.

Pension Petros (tel. 22 573; fax 22 615), one of a line of new, clean, and nearly identical pensions lining the road to Santorini Camping. Distinguishing feature is free transportation to and from the port. Family atmosphere—owners have five adorable daughters. All rooms with bath. Doubles 13,000dr; triples 16,000.

Villa Litsa (tel. 22 267), on 25th Martiou St. north of the square on a noisy street. Go up the green astroturf stairs. Large rooms with baths. Every 3 rooms share a kitchen. Open June-Sept. Doubles 10,000dr; triples 13,000dr.

Santorini Camping (tel. 22 944, 25 062; fax 25 065). Follow the blue signs leading east of the square. Lively atmosphere and shady campsites make this a great option for those who don't mind sleeping on the ground. Washing machine 1200dr (soap included). Swimming pool free for campers. Hot showers 5-9pm. Cafe, bar, and minimarket. Reception open 7am-midnight. Open April-Oct. 1300dr per person; 800dr per tent; 200dr per tent rental; 600dr per car; 400dr per motorbike.

FOOD

Nikolas Taverna (tel. 24 550), head uphill on the side street next to Pelican Travel, then take first right at the Hotel Tatakh. The *taverna* will be bustling with pleased diners on your right. Decipher the Greek-only menu, or choose blindly—you can't go wrong. Excellent beef stew with noodles (1500dr) and stuffed tomatoes (900dr). Celebrate the *taverna*'s 50th anniversary by showing your 1998 copy of *Let's Go* for a free glass of wine.

Restaurant Poseidon (tel. 25 480), down the stairs next to the taxi stand in the main square. Enormous portions of excellent Greek food; all entrees are served with 2 side dish helpings. Swordfish steak (1600dr), beef in tomato sauce (1400dr). Open daily 6am-2pm.

Restaurant Niki (NIKH), offers same view as other *caldera*-top restaurants without charging the same astronomical prices. Tuna *souvlaki* (1800dr), *kalamari* 1200dr. Open daily 11am-1am.

Taverna Simos (tel. 23 815), a 2min. walk uphill from the OTE. An overwhelmingly varied list of inexpensive appetizers may keep you from ordering a main course. Grilled red peppers (400dr), stuffed vine leaves (500dr), and the local speciality *fava* (500dr). Open daily noon-1am.

Alexandria's (tel. 22 510), at the far left of the *caldera* below Hotel Atlantis (meal-sized appetizers 2000dr). The cuisine is best described as Nouveau Greek—grandma's old recipes with creative new touches.

Mama's Breakfast Cafe (tel. 24 211), uphill from the main square, on the left side. Legitimately advertised as the best American breakfast, perhaps in all of Greece. Mama is a character, a one-in-a-million bundle of energy you must witness to believe. Perhaps it's her Maxwell House coffee, which she will undoubtedly tell you is "good to the last drop." Stuff yourself on Mama's special: 2 pancakes, 2 eggs, bacon, toast or coffee (1100dr, free coffee refills). Maple syrup smothers the stack.

To Limanakitou Vourvoulou, follow the signs to Vourvoulou Beach. A diamond in the rough—needs effort and an adventurous spirit to find, but worth the U-turns and dead-end streets. This fish *taverna* is authentic and inexpensive, an excellent combination of great food and warm hospitality. Not too many tourists make it out here—don't make the same mistake (open daily noon-midnight).

Popou (tel. 24 184), overlooking the *caldera* across the path from the Tropical Club. A seemingly out-of-place, dream-like candy store decorated with huge tubes of every kind of sugary concoction imaginable. Take a plastic bag and start scooping (350dr per 100g). 14 varieties of licorice. Open daily 9am-4pm.

ENTERTAINMENT

The bars are for early birds; after 2am, discos take over for some of the most intense, chic scenes in Greece.

Blue Note (tel. 24 211), across the street near the square. Draws a crowd to its free pool table. Empty bottles of Jack Daniels lining the counter top are evidence of owner's taste for whisky. Join him for a shot (800dr), a beer (500-800dr), or the bar's daily special cocktail (800dr). High up on the *caldera*, a native Californian mixes signature cocktails that are as tasty as they are creative (1500dr). "Sunset coffees" like the Bob Marley Frappe—dark rum, Kahlua, iced coffee, and cream—go well with the breathtaking sunset views over the *caldera*. Arrive by 8pm for prime seating on the balcony (open daily noon-4am).

Backpacker's Bar (tel. 22 853), where most budget travelers begin their evening. Cheap beer (500dr). Located near the youth hostels; not the place to meet locals.

Tithora Club (tel. 23 519), practically in the center of the main square, is the place for hard rock and headbanging beats. 1000dr cover includes your first drink (open daily 10pm-4am).

Trip into the Music (tel. 23 623), across from Nikolas Taverna on a side street parallel to the main road out of town. Plays a variety of tunes that keep its dance floor crowded. First beer included in 1000dr cover. Beers 700dr, cocktails 1500dr.

Kira Thira Jazz Club (tel. 22 770), next door to Trip. Offers a more mellow, relaxed scene. Sip beer (800dr) or sangria (1000dr) while enjoying the jazz music. Those with late-night stamina spend that energy dancing. Open daily 11pm-3am.

Koo Club (tel. 22025) and **Enigma** (tel. 22 466) both crank into the wee hours and charge high covers (1000-3000dr depending on the season), with drinks priced to match. Even so, the outdoor decks are cool places to watch the steam rise on the dance floors inside.

SIGHTS

Thira's **archaeological museum** (tel. 22 217), near the cable cars, holds an impressive collection of vases, mostly from the site of ancient Thira (open Tues.-Sun. 8am-3pm; 800dr, students 400dr). The private **Museum Megaro Gyzi** (tel. 23 077), housed in a restored Santorinian mansion near Kamares Hostel, has an engrossing collection of old maps, engravings, and Greek island photographs. The museum hosts several classical music concerts and temporary art exhibitions in July and August (open May-Oct. Mon.-Sat. 10:30am-1:30pm and 5-8pm, Sun. 10:30am-4:30pm; admission 400dr, students 200dr).

■ Southern Santorini

AKROTIRI

The archaeological site of **Akrotiri,** where extensive excavations are still underway, can prove bewildering. With the aid of a helpful guide book (1200dr), it is relatively easy to see everything on your own. Fifteen buses per day run here from Thira Town (350dr). The less adventuresome folks tag along with the guided tours. Bus tours (4000-4500dr through a travel agency) are coupled with a visit to **Profitias Ilias Monastery** in Pyrgos and a local wine-tasting. Professor Marinatos found the paved streets of Akrotiri in 1967, lined with houses connected by a sophisticated central drainage system. Each house had at least one room decorated with wall paintings, some of which are among the most magnificent in Greece. Since no valuables were found in the city, a common theory is that everyone escaped before the eruption (site open Tues.-Sun. 8:30am-3pm; admission 1200dr, students 600dr).

BEACHES

Santorini's two most frequented black sand beaches are **Perissa** and **Kamari** on the southeast coast. Perissa, the farther of the pair, is more popular with students and offers two youth hostels, camping, and a casual nightlife. The black sand sizzles in the sun—a straw mat and sandals are welcome accessories. Although referred to as a black sand beach, Kamari is actually covered in black pebbles, and the slippery sea-weed-covered rock bottom makes wading especially difficult. Both beaches are easily reached by bus. Harder to reach is **Red Beach,** named for the reddish rock formations you must climb over to get there.

Perissa

Youth Hostel Perissa-Anna (tel. 81 182), 500m along the road leading out of town, provides clean women's and mixed dorms, private rooms, cooking facilities, fresh spring water showers, the use of a nearby pool, and free safety deposit boxes. Reception is open 24 hours (beds 1500dr; rooms 2500dr per person; hot showers 9am-9pm; checkout 11:30am). Less than 100m away, the **Perissa Youth Hostel** (tel. 81 639; fax 82 668) offers dorm beds (1500dr), compartment beds (1700dr), room beds (2500dr), and private rooms (3500dr). The difference between them is the degree of privacy. Sheets, pillow and pillowcase (200dr). Guests use the kitchen facilities, 24-hour hot salt water showers, and a nearby pool. A continental breakfast is 500dr. 15% discount with an ISIC card. Enormous **Perissa Camping** (tel. 81 343) is adjacent to the beach and offers a beach bar, minimarket, kitchen facilities, and a restaurant serving traditional Cretan meals (snails 1400dr). The campgrounds are situated in one of the few tree-covered spots on the island. Check-out is at 1pm (1300dr per person; 800dr per tent). Rooms in private homes (you'll meet the proprietors at the dock) offer more privacy (doubles 6000-8000dr).

The delicious calzones, pizza, and pasta at **Bella Italiana** (tel. 82 671), near the end of the main road will make your taste buds hot for more. Over 10 varieties of each are prepared by an Italian chef who knows what he's doing. Try the house speciality pizza—the Bella Italiana—for ham, bacon, mushrooms, green peppers, and cheese piled on a thin crust (1650dr). Open daily 11am-1am. Across the street, the **Full Moon Bar** is the only spot on the island that serves Guinness on tap (1000dr). From 11am-4am, you can listen to the Stones and the Doors, watch MTV, Eurosport, or CNN, while sipping on 1500dr cocktails, 1000dr mixed drinks, or a 400dr Amstel. Half-price drinks during Happy Hour (9:30-11:30pm). Don't miss the special theme parties, including a full moon celebration starting at the bar then moving to the beach for a bonfire. Don't worry about the time—a bus leaves Perissa for Thira Town at 4am.

Kamari

Kamari Beach is closer to Thira and more popular with well-to-do tourists because of the upscale shops that line the waterfront. Forty buses per day travel from Thira (240dr), and a rocky **shuttle boat** scoots between Kamari and Perissa as well (every 30min., 9am-5pm, 800dr). The long beach is covered in umbrellas and lined with pricey hotels, cafes, and travel agencies. Doubles range from 8000-24,000dr. Contact **Kamari Tours** (tel. 31 390) or stop in the office on the waterfront if you have any questions or need assistance. The **Pension Golden Star** is on the road that goes inland from the beach at the Yellow Donkey Disco. It has clean double rooms with balconies (8000dr). Take the next side street inland to reach **Hotel Preka Maria** (tel. 31 266), where you can rent spotless doubles (10,000dr), triples (12,000dr), or furnished apartments (13,000dr). To pick up an inexpensive snack along the waterfront, head to **Ariston** (tel. 32 603). Betwixt the touristy restaurants and *souvlaki* shops, this bakery and small grocery sells fresh loaves of bread (50dr) and raisin bread twists (250dr; open daily 6:30am-11pm). The **Yellow Donkey Disco** (tel. 31 462) is one of the busier clubs along the waterfront of Kamari Beach. It's often crowded with people who come from all over the island to enjoy the 1000dr cocktails that come with a free shot (open daily 9pm-late). **Kamari Camping** (tel. 31 453), 1km inland along the main road out of town, is open June-September (1200dr per person; 1000dr per tent). The winery **Canava Roussos** (tel. 31 954, -278), 1km from the campsite, will both wine and dine you (200dr per glass; open daily 10am-8pm).

Monolithos

Those who prefer sandier beaches might want to check out **Monolithos Beach.** More popular with locals than with tourists, this small beach is easily accessible due to its proximity to the airport (15 buses per day, 230dr). If you want a bite to eat, the fish *taverna* **Skaramagas** (tel. 31 750) is the least expensive on the strip. Fresh seafood is caught by the family who owns the place; they keep what they need for the restaurant and sell the rest to other establishments. Many locals come here for lunch several times a week to enjoy the famed fish soup *kakavia* (1500dr), *kalamari* (1200dr), and great Greek salads (800dr; restaurant open daily May-Oct. 11am- midnight).

PYRGOS AND ANCIENT THIRA

Buses to Perissa stop in lofty **Pyrgos,** surrounded by medieval walls. Once a Venetian fortress, the town was conquered by the Ottomans, who remained here until 1828. The village's 25 blue- and green-domed churches dot the horizon. The **Profitis Ilias Monastery,** a 20-minute hike up the mountain from Pyrgos, graciously shares its site with a radar station. On July 20, the monastery hosts the **Festival of Profitis Ilias.** From Profitias Ilias, it is approximately a one-hour hike to the ruins of ancient **Thira.** The ancient theater, church, and forum of the island's old capital are still visible, though less spectacular than the Akrotiri excavations (open Tues.-Sun. 8am-3:30pm; free). Cheerful, whitewashed **Emborio,** some 3km inland from Perissa, has frequent bus connections to the beach and to Thira.

■ Northern Santorini: Oia OIA

Oia (pronounced EE-ah), is an intricate cliffside town on the northwestern tip of the island, famous for its dazzling sunsets and a fascinating mixture of devastation and renewal. The 1956 earthquake leveled this small town on the island's rocky north point. Its present 600 inhabitants have carved new dwellings into the cliffside among the shattered ruins of the old. Although the budget traveler will not thrive long in Oia, an afternoon visit affords enough time to wander the cobbled streets, window-shop at exquisite jewelry, craft, and embroidery shops, and glance at the menus of elegant restaurants before the riveting sunset. A 20-minute climb down 252 stone stairs at the end of the main road brings you to rocky **Ammoudi** beach, where a few boats are moored in a startlingly deep swimming lagoon. **Buses** run from Thira to Oia (25 per day, 20min., 250dr), and a few **ferries** dock at Oia before continuing to Thira or Athinios—check when you buy your ticket.

After a relaxing few hours spent lying on the rocks, and another few swimming in the beautiful blue water, climbing back up the cliff may seem like no small task. Re-energize before the climb with a meal of fresh fish at one of the three *tavernas* at the bottom of the stairs. Also make sure to buy a bottle of water before you begin your ascent. If the sun has left you feeling too lethargic, you can hire a **donkey** to carry you to the top (700dr per person).

In Oia, the Karvounis family can help meet all your tourist needs. **Karvounis Tours** (tel. 71 290, -291, -292; fax 71 291) answers questions on Oia and Santorini as a whole, in addition to selling both ferry and airline tickets. The family's **Youth Hotel Oia** (tel. 71 465; fax 71 291) is the classiest of Santorini's youth hostels. Painted bright white with bold blue trim, it boasts a superb view from its roof terrace and a bar open for both breakfast and evening drinks. Breakfast included (1500-3200dr per person; hot water 24hr.; wheelchair accessible). Its difficult to find short-term accommodations in Oia, as most proprietors expect a stay of at least five days.

Likewise, dining will cost you a bit more than in Thira, but some restaurants serve exceptional food. At the end of the main road in Oia, overlooking the *caldera,* is **Petros,** the oldest restaurant in Oia (tel. 71 263). Petros Jr. continues the family tradition of making homemade wines. His Santorinian tomato balls are especially delicious in June and July, when Santorini's fresh cherry tomatoes are available (900dr). Fresh, savory seafood is always grilled to perfection (*kalamari* 1200dr), while old Greek recipes provide a pleasant alternative to the common *moussaka.*

Melissa's Vegetarian and Piano Cafe (tel. 71 305) serves rather pricey, but meat-less lunches and dinners. After 7:30pm, enjoy the sound of live jazz piano music as you feast on *ratatouille* and basmati rice on the beautiful rooftop terrace (1900dr). Once you have eaten all your vegetables, splurge for one of the largest banana splits imaginable (more money, and calories, than your entire meal). Open daily 11:30am-3pm and 6pm-late. The Karvounis' **Neptune** (tel. 71 294), located in the main square near the church, serves traditional Greek specialities, including a lamb lemon special (1500dr) and a delicious *moussaka* (open daily 1-3pm and 6pm-12:30am). **Restaurant Lotza** (tel. 71 357) is ideal for lunch with a view, serving up curried chicken (1700dr), lasagna (1900dr), and yogurt with walnuts and fruit (1000dr; open daily 9am-midnight). **Cafe Greco** (tel. 71 014) has gyros in pita for 400dr (open daily 11am-1am). There is a small **grocery/bakery** (tel. 71 121) close to the square in which the buses stop. Follow the signs for the bakery for fresh loaves (150dr) and croissants and pies (170-350dr; open Mon.-Sat. 7am-9pm, Sun. 7am-2pm).

▓ Thirasia and Surrounding Islands

Santorini's unspoiled junior partner, Thirasia (pop. 300) is worthy of a detour. Built along the island's upper ridge, the villages of **Manolas** and **Potamos** have spine-tingling views of Santorini's western coast. Organized tour groups dock at one of two ports—Korfos or Reeva. From the former, the villages can only be reached by climbing a steep flight of 300 steps. The latter, however, provides a paved road leading up to both villages. Either way, you'll come across **Remetzo Taverna** (tel. 29 081) as you reach the top of the cliff; standard Greek fare for standard prices. There will also be a **minimarket** on your right. Manolas has only one hotel: **Cavomara** (tel. 24 523) offers a restaurant, pool, and doubles with bath for 10,000dr.

Excursions to Thirasia are often coupled with trips to the **volcanic crater** and **hot springs.** Tours can be booked at travel agencies on Santorini (1500-5000dr). Be warned that to get to the hot sulphur springs you'll have to swim through cold water first; to get to the volcano's crater you'll have to hike uphill for 30 minutes. **Theoskepasti agency,** in the main square in Thira, has daily trips to the volcano for 2000dr. As with most trips, reservations should be made a day in advance.

PAROS ΠΑΡΟΣ

The geographical center of the islands and third largest of the Cyclades, Paros seems to gracefully absorb the tourist masses that arrive each summer. Its historical claim to fame is its pure white marble, slabs of which have been sculpted into the renowned Venus de Milo and parts of Napoleon's mausoleum in Paris. Paros's golden beaches and tangled whitewashed villages make the island a favorite tourist destination. More importantly, Paros has the necessary means to accommodate tourists without fully relinquishing its idyllic Cycladic atmosphere; it has struck a careful balance between new world nightlife and old world serenity.

▓ Paroikia

Behind Paroikia's commercial facade, flower-filled streets wind beneath archways, past two-story whitewashed houses, a historic basilica, and windmills. Wander through the traditional *agora* (marketplace) to find trendy clothing, dazzling jewelry, local arts and crafts, and cozy coffee houses with outdoor terraces.

ORIENTATION AND PRACTICAL INFORMATION

From the ferry, most restaurants, hotels, and offices lie to the left (facing inland). Straight ahead, past the windmill and the tourist offices, is the main square, behind which a whitewashed labyrinth brims with shops and cafes. To the far right around the bend, a host of bars awaits—the island's party district.

Tourist Office: (tel. 24 528) To the right of the windmill, facing inland. **Currency exchange.** Information on buses, sights, and beaches, and free maps of the island. Open daily July-Aug. 8:30am-midnight.

Tourist Agency: The **General Travel Agency** (tel. 22 092; fax 21 983) is next door to the OTE. Has up-to-the-minute ferry, hydrofoil, and airplane schedules. Open daily 8am-1am.

Banks: National Bank (tel. 21 298), from the windmill, head inland to the main square and to the right—it's in the fortress-like building at the far corner, past the playground. **ATM** and **currency exchange** machine available 24hr. Bank open Mon.-Thurs. 8am-2pm, Fri. 8am-1:30pm.

Flights: Olympic Airways (tel. 21 900, 22 511; 91 257 at airport), in the main square. Open Mon.-Fri. 8am-3pm. 6 flights per day to Athens (14,500dr). Take a taxi to the airport (2000dr), or catch the bus to Aliki (280dr).

Buses: (tel. 21 395, -133). Complete schedule posted in the shack a few blocks to the left of the windmill (facing inland). Buses run to: Naoussa (20-30 per day, 15min., 230dr); Lefkes (8 per day, 25min., 250dr); Pounda (9 per day, 15min., 200dr); Aliki and the **airport** (10 per day, 30min., 280dr); Piso Livadi (8 per day, 40min., 380dr); Chrisi Akti (8 per day, 50min., 500dr); Drios (8 per day, 1hr., 500dr); Marpissa (8 per day, 35min., 400dr); Kamares (2 per day, 20min., 200dr); and the Valley of the Butterflies (8 per day, 10min., 200dr).

Ferries: Sail to: Peiraias (5-8 per day, 5-6hr., 4520dr); Naxos (6-10 per day, 1hr., 1470dr); Ios (4-9 per day, 2½hr., 2460dr); Santorini (6-9 per day, 3½hr., 2950dr); Mykonos (1-3 per day, 2hr., 1760dr); Syros (1-7 per day, 1½hr., 1620dr); Amorgos (6 per week, 3hr., 2710dr); Rhodes (6 per week, 16hr., 6520dr); Crete (8 per week, 8hr., 4660dr); Samos (6 per week, 6hr., 4050dr); Ikaria (6 per week, 4hr., 3050dr); Tinos (4 per week, 1800dr); Kos (4 per week, 4070dr); Sikinos (7 per week, 1840dr); Astypalea (3 per week, 4370dr); Koufonisi (3 per week, 2630dr); Folegandros (6 per week, 1920dr); and Rafina (1 per week, 3810dr).

Flying Dolphins: Catamarans and hydrofoils speed to: Santorini (2-3 per day, 6060dr); Mykonos (3-5 per day, 3350dr); Ios (2-3 per day, 4750dr); Naxos (2-3 per day, 2770dr); Syros (4 per week, 3070dr); Rafina (9 per week, 7870dr); Tinos (2-4 per day, 3350dr); Amorgos (1 per week, 5570dr); Koufonisi (2 per week, 5423dr); and Sifnos (variable, 2020dr).

Taxis: (tel. 21 500) Look inland and to the right of the windmill.

Luggage Storage: (tel. 23 582) Look for blue and yellow "Left Luggage" signs across from windmill in the first shop area (500dr per piece per day). Open 8am-1am.

Laundromat: For full- or self-service, go past bus station and look for **Top** (tel. 23 424), on right just after ancient ruins. Wash, dry, soap, and folding (optional) for 2000dr. Open daily 8:30am-11pm.

Public Toilets: Beside the small blue and white church to the left of the windmill.

International Bookstore: M.K. Bizas (**International Press;** tel. 21 247) is past National Bank; go straight and it's on your right. Large selection of English-language books (3000dr) and newspapers (380-400dr). Open daily 9am-2:30pm and 4-10pm.

Pharmacy: (tel. 22 223) Next to the self-service laundromat. Open daily 8:30am-1:30pm and 5:30-8:30pm. Others abound, particularly in the old town.

Medical Clinic: (tel. 22 500) Across the street from the toilets. Free physicals. Open Mon.- Fri. 7am-2:30pm. Open for emergencies 24hr.

Police: (tel. 23 333) are across the square behind the OTE, on the 2nd floor above the photo shops. Open 24hr. **Tourist police** (tel. 21 673), in the same building. Open 9am-3:30pm. **Port Police** (tel. 21 240), off the waterfront, past the bus station. Information about all sailings. Open 24hr.

Post Office: (tel. 21 236) On the left side of the waterfront, 2 blocks past the bus stop. Open Mon.-Fri. 7:30am-2pm. **Postal Code:** 84400.

OTE: (tel. 22 299) One block to the right of the windmill (its back borders the main square). Open Mon.-Fri. 7:30am-3pm. **Telephone Code:** 0284.

GREEK ISLANDS

Paros & Antiparos

Agios Pantes, **4**
Ancient quarries, **2**
Golden Beach, **7**
Mount Agioi Georgiou, **6**
Mount Agioi Theodoron, **5**
Mount Lagovardas, **1**
Mount Thapsanon, **3**

✈ Airport

Aegean Sea

Gaidouronissi · Vriokastro

Santa Maria
Lageri
Colybithres
Kamares
Kalami
Naoussa · Filisi
Ampelas
Marathi
⚓ Paros
Glyfades
Tsoukalia
Paros
Epano Fira
Kato Fira · Oros
Antiparos · Boutaria
Psichopiana
Prodromos
Marmara
Molos
Marpissa
Pounta
Logaras
Mesada
Vagia
Kamari
Voutakoy
Makronissi
Antiparos
Dryos
Dryonissi
Ageria
Alyki
Aspro Chorio
Agios Georgios
Glyfa
Trypiti

0 — 2 miles
0 — 2 kilometers

N

ACCOMMODATIONS

There are many hotels and rooms to let near the waterfront and in the old town, but a slew of new, inexpensive pensions have opened behind the town beach. Dock hawks often offer good deals and many represent better options in Naoussa, Piso Livadi, and Antiparos. Just make sure it's not too far from where you want to be. In the off season, rooms are 20-40% less than the prices listed.

> **Festos Pension** (tel. 21 635; fax 24 193) From the dock, walk left along the waterfront, toward the church. At the steps to the church, turn right, then left at the side street marked with an arrow and sign for "the Festos." 2500dr per person in the off season, increasing to 4500 per person in peak season. Friendly staff. Laundry 1000dr. Luggage storage 300dr. Check-out 10am. Reserve early.
>
> **Pelagos Studios** (tel. 22 725, -726; fax 22 708). Fully furnished, clean rooms with kitchen and private bath. Andreas and Vasili will send you off to your next destination with a barbecue feast—that is, if you ever decide to leave. Accommodations are peaceful, despite proximity to nightlife. Doubles: off season 550-7500dr; high season 16,000dr; triples: off season 9000dr; high season 16,000-20,000dr.
>
> **Parasporos Camping** (tel. 22 268, 21 100), 1500m south of the port with shuttle service. Showers, laundry, and kitchen. 1000dr per person; 500dr per tent.
>
> **Koula Camping** (tel. 22 081, -082), 400m north of town on the beach. Amenities include market, laundry, and kitchen. 1000dr per person; 500dr per tent.

FOOD

Plaza Pizzeria (tel.21 272), along the waterfront to the right of windmill. 30 pizzas to choose from, each baked in traditional wood oven. Open daily noon-2am.

Happy Green Cow (tel. 24 691), a block farther inland off the main square behind the National Bank. Delicious vegetarian food in a psychedelic setting. Stuffed potato rolls with cheese and walnuts are 2000dr. For a less expensive, yet mouthwatering meal, the *falafels* are a great choice for 1000dr. Open daily noon-1am.

To Tamarisko, near Mimikos Rooms—follow the signs. Lush flower garden, romantic setting. Traditional Greek cuisine—everything is homemade, including the menus! Excellent shrimp risotto with tomatoes and capers for 1450dr.

Levantes (tel. 23 613), near Hotel Dina on the "Market" street beyond the National Bank. Try roasted pepper rolls stuffed with feta, pine nuts, and capers (950 dr).

Nick's Hamburgers, next to Corfo Leon. Paros's first hamburger joint, established in 1977. 100% beef. Nikburger 430dr; Nikfeast (2 burgers, chips, and salad) 890dr. Only place to get fish and chips (950dr).

ENTERTAINMENT

Almost all of Paros's nightspots are along the waterfront, left of the windmill. On any given night, throngs of foreigners congregate on the strip, sit in circles around *ouzo* bottles, and sing songs. There are hangouts for English-speakers on the far end of the ferry dock, just before the small white bridge. **Saloon D'Or** and **Black Bart's Cafe Bar** are especially popular—the number of travelers in these bars gives them the aura of a foreign convention gone especially rowdy. **The Slammer Bar/7 Muses Disco,** specializes in tequila slammers for 500dr—there are posted instructions for the uninitiated. **The Paros Experience** consists of two mind-boggling party complexes which round out any night out on Paros. The larger of the two, at the far end of the strip of bars, contains under one roof **The Dubliner, Down Under, Cactus Shots Bar,** and the **Paros Rock Cafe.** Sit around or dance to any of the four tunes blaring simultaneously (beer 600-700dr, cocktails 1000dr). A little closer to town is the other boozing megaplex, containing **The Londoner, Tequila Bar,** and **Sodoma Dance Club** (beer 600-700dr, cocktails 1000dr).

SIGHTS

Anyone with a fondness for Byzantine architecture will be enraptured by the **Panagia Ekatontapiliani** (The Church of Our Lady of 100 Gates), an imposing 6th-century edifice that houses three separate churches, cloisters, and a large peaceful courtyard. Only 10 of the 100 doors are immediately obvious, so don't waste your time counting. The main structure is the mammoth **Church of the Assumption,** with three tremendous chandeliers. **Church of St. Nikolas** (the oldest of the three) flanks this central structure to the north, as does the **baptistry** (tel. 21 243), to the south. To reach the church, walk inland from the public garden. (Open daily 8am-9pm. Dress appropriately: no shorts.) There are two tiny museums in the courtyard, with the **Church Museum** on the right (open Mon., Wed., and Fri.-Sun. 9am-1pm and 5:30-9pm; admission 500dr) and the **Byzantine Museum** next to the entrance (open daily 9am-1pm and 5-9pm; admission 500dr). Behind the church next to the schoolyard, is the **Archaeological Museum** (tel. 21 231), which includes a 5th-century BC statue of wingless Nike and a piece of the Parian Chronicle (open Tues.-Sun. 8:30am-2:30pm; admission 500dr, students 300dr, Sun. free).

Just 10km south of town is the cool, spring-fed **Valley of the Butterflies** *(Petaloudes),* home to an enormous swarm of brown-and-white-striped butterflies. These amazing creatures cover the foliage, blending into their surroundings until they expose their bright red underwings in flight. In June, the butterflies converge on this lepidopterous metropolis to mate. You can visit by taking the bus from Paroikia that goes to Aliki (8 per day, 10min., 200dr). Ask to be let off at the *petaloudes* (butterflies). From there, follow the signs up the steep winding road 2km to the entrance. You can also take a tour from one of the various travel agents (2500dr), although it would be a shame to be whisked through here too quickly (open Mon.-Sat. 9am-8pm, Sun. 9am-1pm and 4-8pm; admission 230dr).

If you are wandering through Paroikia's old town, look for the **Frankish Castle,** whose walls were built with marble removed from the ancient **Temple of Athena.** You can actually spot the temple's columns in the Venetian structure. To get there, turn right after the bookstore and look for it near the top of the hill. At the top of the same hill is the charming, yet eerie, Byzantine **Church of Agios Konstantinos.**

■ Naoussa

Naoussa is a pleasant alternative to Paroikia. It is a natural harbor and a popular port, cradled on both sides by long, sandy arms in the shape of crab claws. Persians, Greeks, Romans, Venetians, Saracens, Ottomans, and Russians all anchored in the harbor. The tradition continues today as visitors from all over the world converge on Naoussa's magnificent beaches. Although much of the town has been usurped by this influx, a stroll along the harbor proves that beneath its tourist-friendly exterior, Naoussa remains a traditional Greek fishing village at heart.

ORIENTATION AND PRACTICAL INFORMATION

Naoussa's layout is not very complicated. From the bus stop facing the water, the road heading left past the little bridge leads to the beaches of **Kolimbithies** and **Monastiri.** Naoussa's commercial strip flanks the town on the right. If you walk along the waterfront, you will see how the harbor wraps around the town. To find the **police** (tel. 51 202, open 24hr.), walk over the bridge and along the ascending waterfront road. On your left, a flight of steep stairs ending at the Pension Hara also leads to the station. Turn right at the top. The police will be one block ahead on your right. The **medical center** (tel. 51 216; open Mon.-Fri. 9am-1:30pm) is on the commercial strip, directly across from the Zorbas restaurant. In an emergency, call the doctor at home (tel. 52 660). Farther down on the left is the **General Bookstore** (tel. 51 121), which sells English books. You will find the **post office** (tel. 21 236) 400m down the same road, just past the Santa Maria turn-off (open Mon.-Fri. 7:30am-2pm). The **pharmacy** (tel. 51 550; for emergencies 51 004) is on the waterfront, just to the right of the little bridge (open Mon.-Sat. 8:30am-2:30pm and 5:30-11pm, Sun. 10am-2:30pm and 5:30-11pm). The **National Bank** is along the marina (tel. 51 438; open Mon.-Fri. 8:30am-1:30pm). The **postal code** is 84401. The **telephone code** is 0284.

Buses run from Paroikia to Naoussa roughly every 30 minutes or every hour during *siesta* (30 per day, 15min., 230dr). There are also bus connections from Naoussa to: Santa Maria (2 per day); Ampelas (2 per day); Piso Livadi (7 per day); Drios (7 per day); and back to Paroikia (40 per day). Consult the detailed schedule at the bus stop booth. **Taxi boats** also leave Naoussa for nearby beaches. The little blue booth across from the first stretch of cafes on the waterfront sells round-trip tickets to: Kolimbithies (12min., 500dr); Monastiri (15min., 600dr); Laggeri (20min., 750dr); and Santa Maria (50min., 1500dr). If you are looking for the true Greek fishing experience, it will cost you 2500dr. A fishing boat takes curious tourists along to help drop the nets every Thursday morning at 7am and brings them back at 10am.

ACCOMMODATIONS

For a small town, Naoussa offers many hotels and rooms to let. Prices decrease by 20-40% in the off season. **Pension Hara** (tel. 51 011), at the top of the stairs heading to the police station, has clean rooms with balconies and refrigerators (doubles 11,500-15,000dr). **Hotel Aliprantis** (tel. 51 571, -648) is located right next to the bus stop. Directly below the hotel, a cafeteria and bakery owned by the same family will serve you breakfast (1000dr; doubles 8500-12,500dr). English-speaking Katerina at **Simitzi Tours** (tel. 51 113; fax 51 761), opposite the bus stop, rents studios with kitchens. (Open 8:30am-midnight in high season. Doubles 7000-11,000dr; quads 12,000-17,000dr. Rates depend on season.) Rooms to let cost roughly 5000-11,000dr for doubles and 6000-13,000dr for triples. There are two campsites near Naoussa. **Camping Naoussa** (tel. 51 595) awaits on the road to Kolimbithies (1300dr per person; 800dr per tent). **Camping Surfing Beach** (tel. 51 013, -491; fax 51 937), 4km toward Santa Maria, hosts waterskiing, windsurfing, and other summer fun stuff (1300dr per person; 800dr per tent).

FOOD AND ENTERTAINMENT

Naoussan kitchens are famed for cooking up superb seafood. If you follow the waterfront as it bends to the right, you will come to a crowded cluster of *tavernas*. **To Ouzeri ton Naftikon** is the embodiment of the traditional, unpretentious Greek *taverna* with excellent and cheap fresh fish (open daily 5pm-1am). **Diamantis** (tel. 52 129), behind the church, is an excellent choice for Greek fare (swordfish *souvlaki* 1300dr). For a divine eating experience, feast on the restaurant's specialty, lamb Diamantis, stuffed with feta cheese, tomatoes, peppers and onions, and grilled slowly (1650 dr). **Zorba's** (tel. 51 087), in the square in front of the church, offers a daily surprise on the menu (4-cheese tortellini 1400dr, *pastitsio* 950dr; open 24hr.; credit cards accepted). For dessert, **To Paradosiako** (tel. 52 240), is unbeatable for its *loucoumodes* (donut holes in syrup, 500dr) and traditional island sweets. From the commercial street, turn left at the Naoussa pastry shop and continue past the little white church. Look for a brown wooden sign and a pan of *loucoumodes* in the window (open daily 5:30pm-1am). There are quite a few low-key cafes and bars mixed in with the *tavernas*—look for dimmed lights and listen for groovy music. Late-night revelry occurs at **Varelathiko,** a huge wooden bar/disco with a beautiful outdoor deck. Reminiscent of an old-fashioned barn, the place is decorated with wine barrels and lanterns hanging from the ceiling. Head here for the latest in Greek music, a full bar, and all-night dancing (cocktails 1500 dr, cover 100dr). The main road through the square will take you to the front door, and so will the crowds going in the same direction. If you can't stay up that late, try your luck swatting mosquitoes at the **outdoor movie theater** next to Diamantis (shows nightly at 10pm). On the first Sunday in July, cruise around Naoussa's harbor and feast on free fish and wine as you watch traditional dancing at the **Wine and Fish Festival.** On August 23, festivities commemorate a naval victory over the Ottomans.

■ Around Paros Island

Cutting through the center of the island towards the east coast, you will reach **Marathi,** 5km from Paroikia. The marble quarries that made Paros famous in ancient times are nearby. Still considered to be among the finest in the world, Parian marble is translucent up to 3mm thick, one-third the opacity of most other marble. The quarries are now idle and difficult to find.

Lefkes, 5km from Marathi, was the largest village on the island in the 19th century when Parians moved inland to escape the swashbuckling pirates off the coast. Now it is a quiet village of 400 inhabitants with classic Cycladic architecture that makes it the prettiest town in Paros's interior.

Road meets sea at **Piso Livadi,** 11km from Lefkes. If you are not into Paroikia's nightlife, Piso Livadi can be a relaxing place to spend your hours on Paros. **Perantinos Travel & Tourism** (tel./fax 41 135), across from the bus stop, provides information on accommodations as well as an international phone (open daily 9am-10pm). Doubles range from 7000-9000dr, depending on the season and quality. Up the street from the bus stop toward Paroikia are two straightforward, clean hotels. **Hotel Piso Livadi** (tel. 41 309) offers doubles with bath for 10,000dr (triples with bath 12,500dr). The **Londos Hotel** (tel. 41 218) offers the same prices. Serene **Camping Captain Kafkis** (tel. 41 479) is roughly 1km back along the same road (900dr per person; 550dr per small tent; 700dr per large tent).

Buses run from Paroikia to **Pounda** (9 per day, 15min., 200dr) and **Aliki** (10 per day, 40min., 280dr), on Paros's west coast and home of pleasant, remote beaches. From Pounda, 30 boats per day cross to **Antiparos** (10min., 150dr). Boats also run from Paroikia's harbor to **Krios, Martselo,** and **Kaminia** beaches (every 15min. 9:30am-7pm, 15min., 340dr), all of which are relatively calm and secluded.

■ Antiparos

Antiparos is another quiet, easy going alternative. Those uninterested or unable to find rooms on Paros take refuge here. Literally "opposite Paros," Antiparos is so close to its neighbor that, according to local lore, travelers once signaled the ferryman on Paros by opening the door of a chapel on Antiparos. Its proximity to Paros and unique underground caves also make Antiparos a popular daytrip.

ORIENTATION AND PRACTICAL INFORMATION

Most of this small island is undeveloped—virtually all of its 700 inhabitants live in the town where the ferry docks, and there is no bus service (except to the stalactite caves). You will find a few waterfront restaurants and several hotels and pensions at the harbor. Tourist shops, *tavernas,* and bakeries line the street leading from the dock to the center of town, where a cluster of bars have opened. The center has a wide-open plaza with cafes under shady trees. Go through the stone archway to the right of the square to reach the **Castle of Antiparos,** a village built in the 1440s.

To get to Antiparos from Paros, take a direct boat from Paroikia (14 per day, 25min., 430dr one way), or one of the 25 daily buses to Pounda (15min., 200dr), followed by one of 30 daily boats to Antiparos (10min., 180dr one way). **Oliaros Tours** (tel. 61 231, in winter call 61 189; fax 61 496), on the waterfront next to the National Bank, assists with finding rooms (doubles with bath and refrigerator 4000-8000dr), and has boat and bus schedules. It also has an **international telephone** and **currency exchange.** The **National Bank** next door is open only in high season (Mon.-Fri. 9am-1pm). The **post office** is on the left side of the street leading from the waterfront to the square (open Mon.-Fri. 8am-1pm). The road bends left past the post office and passes the diminutive **OTE,** which is on the right just before the road opens into the main square (open Mon.-Fri. 8:30am-12:30pm and 5-10:30pm). The self-service **laundry** (wash, dry, and soap 2000dr; open daily 10am-2pm and 5-8pm) and **Arotho bookstore** (tel. 61 255) are closer to the water on the same street as the post office. Behind the unobtrusive wooden sign hides a stupendous collection of new and used books in many different languages. Ask to see the collection of Marvel, DC, and Image comics (500-1500dr; open 10am-4pm and 7pm-midnight). The number for the **police** is 61 202, for a **doctor** 61 219. **Postal Code:** 84007. **Telephone code:** 0284.

ACCOMMODATIONS

The **Mantalena Hotel** (tel. 61 206; fax 61 550), to the right of the dock (facing inland), has clean rooms with private baths (doubles 6000-12,000dr; triples 7000-14,000dr). A family-owned establishment for 37 years, the hotel welcomes guests with *kourabiethes,* an almond cookie. Conveniently located close to Sifneikos Beach, the **Antiparos Hotel** (tel. 61 358; fax 61 340) is an excellent choice. Similar in price to the Mantalena, it is also managed by a welcoming family. On the road to Camping Antiparos, the **Theologos Hotel** (tel. 61 244) offers sunny rooms with gleaming bathrooms (doubles 7000-10,000dr, depending on season). **Camping Antiparos** (tel. 61 221) is 800m northwest of town on Ag. Yiannis Theologos Beach (1000dr per person; 200dr per tent).

FOOD, ENTERTAINMENT, & SIGHTS

Some excellent restaurants include **Taverna Klimataria** (turn left down the alley next to the bookstore), under blazing pink azalea bushes (*kalamari* 1000dr; Greek salad 800dr), and **O Spyros** next to the National Bank on the waterfront (*kalamari* with pasta 1000dr, yummy *octopus stifatho* 1500dr). The latter has served authentic Greek cuisine for 30 years; its hard-kneaded phyllo dough—an ingredient that makes *spanakopites* (spinach pies) divine—is a family recipe passed down through the generations (tel. 61 323). At **Zorbas** (tel. 61 203), on the waterfront, *ouzo* and *gouna* (sundried fish) go hand-in-hand. For a meal, try the mussels and rice pilaf (1200dr) and taste the difference freshness makes (open daily 4pm-2am). Following the lead of neighboring islands, Antiparos's main inland square is packed with rock 'n roll bars and watering holes. Choose your favorite ambiance from among **Time Pub, Clown Pub, The Doors,** and many more (beers 400-700dr). Distinguished by an outdoor setting, **Cafe Yam** is a trendy spot to sip a cocktail. The whitewashed bar serves every drink imaginable from 10am-2am (beer 500-700dr, cocktails 1500dr).

Antiparos's main attraction is its cool, wet stalactite caves at the south end of the island. Names of the caves' famous visitors are written on the walls with their years of entry (alongside some of their less famous 20th-century counterparts who took it upon themselves to leave a mark). Some of the stalactites were broken off by Russian naval officers in the 18th century and "donated" to a St. Petersburg museum, while still more were destroyed by Italians during WWII. Despite the graffiti and history of theft, the caves, plunging 100m down into the earth, retain their beauty. Ask a ticket taker about the various stories associated with the caves—how Queen Amalia lost her earrings in 1840 or how a team of French archaeologists spent Christmas, 1673, inside. **Excursion buses** run from Antiparos's port every hour in the morning. (20min., round-trip 1200dr. Caves open 10:15am-4:45pm; admission 400dr.)

NAXOS ΝΑΞΟΣ

Alluring interior villages and tranquil beaches annually draw thousands to the Cyclades's largest and most fertile island. Naxos's rocky promontories, squat windmills, and demure villages tucked between rolling hills are all illuminated by an ancient constellation. After Ariadne, the daughter of King Minos of Crete, saved Theseus from her father's labyrinth, the young prince fled with her to Naxos. After they had spent the night there, Theseus, who said he was going to wash his hair, abandoned her. Ariadne wept at finding herself alone on the shore, but her despair was remedied when Dionysus, who had had quite an adventure himself, came along. Captured by pirates, he immobilized the ship's sails with spontaneously growing vines and turned the malevolent buccaneers into serpents and himself into a lion. He married Ariadne soon after arriving on Naxos. When she died, the gods put her bridal wreath among the stars where the Corona Borealis shines today.

Even without mythology, Naxos has one of the more colorful Cycladic histories. Parians, Cretans, Ionians, Athenians, Macedonians, Egyptians, Rhodians, Romans, Byzantines, Venetians, Ottomans, and Russians all ruled the island in succession. The island's agricultural industry, particularly its olive groves, affords it some freedom from a predominantly tourist economy. If you want to escape the armies of foreigners, you should head for the villages and avoid the waterfront.

■ Naxos Town

As you drift into the harbor, you can't help noticing **Portara,** the entrance to an unfinished temple. Naxos Town can be divided into two sections: the old, historic, mesmerizing half and the practical, less interesting newer half. The latter includes the buildings on the far side of town near Agios Georgios beach and the waterfront. Old Naxos lies behind waterfront shops, on the hill leading up to a Venetian castle. Ancient wooden porticoes and glimpses of the brilliant blue sea enhance the old-world charm. Low stone archways, flowers, and trellised plants engulf the homes that surround the castle, while nearby colorful markets bustle with activity.

ORIENTATION AND PRACTICAL INFORMATION

All ferries dock in Naxos Town. Maps can only get you so far; streets are poorly labeled and tend to be confusing. The dock is at the left end of town. Along the water-

Naxos

Agios Artemios, 1
Agios Mamas, 2
Agios Sozon, 3
Flerio, 4
Fotodoti, 5
Grotta, 6
Kalogiros, 7
Kastro Apalirou, 8
Moni Faneromenis, 9
Moni Hrissostomou, 10
Moni Ibsilis, 11
Moni Panagia, 12
Moni Pangias, 13
Panormos, 14
Pirgos Driovela, 15
Pirgos Himarrou, 16
Spilia Askiti, 17
Temple of Demeter, 18
Timios Stavros, 19
Za Spileo, 20

✈ Airport
⚓ Port

front, you will find stores and agencies that can meet all your needs, ranging from sunscreen to ferry tickets. At the right end of the waterfront is the main road out of town. Between this road and the shop-lined waterfront is the old town. The easiest entrance into this maze is behind the waterfront **Promponos** local goods shop. There is a sign at the rear of the square that reads "Welcome to the Old Market."

Tourist Office: (tel. 24 358 or 25 201; fax 25 200). A privately run tourist agency sits directly on the dock, but the *real* tourist office, farther along, has more of what you are looking for—advice on hotels and rooms to let; booking service for Naxos and all of Greece; bus, ferry, and hydrofoil schedules; **currency exchange;** international telephone; **luggage storage** (400dr); safety deposit boxes (400dr); and **laundry service** (2000dr). Sells guides on island walking tours (4000dr), lends *Let's Go* guides. English-speaking Despina is a miracle worker (for emergencies after hours, her home number is 24 525). Open 8am-midnight.

Tourist Agency: Zas Travel (tel. 23 330; fax 23 419), two offices along the waterfront and one in Agia Anna (tel. 24 027). Telephone, **currency exchange,** accommodations, **car rental,** and ferry/hydrofoil tickets. Open daily 8am-11pm.

Bank: The **National Bank** (tel. 23 053) offers **currency exchange.** Walk down the waterfront with the water on your right; bank is in the middle of the waterfront stretch in a yellow neoclassical building. A cash-spewing **ATM.** Open Mon.-Thurs. 8am-2pm, Fri. 8am-1:30pm. Several other banks line the waterfront.

Flights: An **Olympic Airways** desk is housed in **Naxos Tours** (tel. 22 095 or 24 000), at the right end of the waterfront. Two flights per day to Athens (18,000dr).

Buses: Depot directly in front of the ferry dock. Schedules at tourist office and the bus station across the street and to the left (facing inland). Arrive early; buses can be packed, especially to Filoti (7 per day, 340dr) and Apollonas (5 per day, 2hr., 1000dr). Also to: Agia Anna beach (every 30min., 15min., 280dr), via Agios Prokopios beach; Chalki (7 per day, 30min., 300dr); Apiranthos (6 per day, 1hr., 500dr); and Pyrgaki beach (4 per day, 1hr., 360dr).

Ferries: To: Peiraias (4-6 per day, 7hr., 4500dr); Paros (6-9 per day, 1hr., 1400dr); Ios (4-7 per day, 1½hr., 2100dr); Santorini (4-7 per day, 3hr., 2650dr); Mykonos (2-4 per day, 2hr., 1740dr); Syros (1-3 per day, 2½hr., 2050dr); Amorgos (1-3 per day, 3½hr., 2250dr); Crete (1 per week, 7hr., 4600dr); Iraklia, Schinoussa, Koufonisi, and Donoussa (1-2 per day, 1½hr., 1410dr); and Tinos (2-3 per day, 2½hr., 1900dr). Ferries occasionally sail to smaller Cycladic islands and the Dodecanese.

Flying Dolphins: To: Rafina (7285dr); Mykonos (3070dr); Ios (3740dr); Santorini (4795dr); Paros (2510dr); Andros (5435dr); and Amorgos (4445dr).

Taxis: (tel. 22 444) On the waterfront, next to the bus depot.

Motorbike Rental: Ciao (tel. 23 498), one block inland on the paved road to the right of the bus depot. Bikes start at 3000dr per day. Open daily 8am-midnight.

English Bookstore: Vrakas (tel. 23 039), behind a jewelry shop. Look for signs reading "gold-silver used books." Vrakas buys at half the original price, sells 200-1800dr. Open daily 9:30am-2pm and 6pm-midnight.

Public Toilets and Showers: Behind Toast Time on the street parallel to the waterfront. Turn left after Zas Travel and turn right. Toilets 100dr, showers 600dr (men and women separate). Open daily 8am-2pm and 5-11pm.

Pharmacies: (tel. 22 241) Next to the inland road, across from the bus depot and to the right along the waterfront. Open Mon.-Tues. and Thurs.-Fri. 8am-2pm and 6-9:30pm, Wed. and Sat. 8am-2pm. For after-hours emergencies inquire at the storefront window for phone number of stand-by pharmacy (*efimerevon*).

Health Center: (tel. 23 333, 22 661) Turn right past Hotel Hermes and continue along that road for about 500m; it is on your left. Has 14 doctors and can access a helicopter to Athens in emergencies. A taxi costs 700-1000dr. Open 9am-9pm.

Police: (tel. 23 100) On the main road heading toward Agios Georgios beach, 1km out of town. Open 24hr. **Port Police:** (tel. 22 300) Nikodemos St., near Porto Travel, directly above the town hall. Near bus depot on the waterfront. Open 24hr.

Post Office: Walk down the waterfront (water on your right), left after Hotel Hermes, and take your first right. Open Mon.-Fri. 7:30am-2pm. **Postal Code:** 84300.

OTE: Next to Hotel Hermes at the right end of the harbor. Open Mon.-Fri. 7:30am-3:10pm. **Telephone Code:** 0285.

ACCOMMODATIONS

Most hotels on Naxos fill to capacity in late July and August. Expect to pay 40-50% less during the rest of the year. Hotel representatives who meet the boat charge roughly 3000-4500dr for singles, 4000-8000dr for doubles, 7000-10,000dr for triples, and 5000-10,000dr for studios (doubles with kitchenette and bath). Put on your bargaining shoes and watch prices drop. Inexpensive rooms can be found by pursuing "Rooms to let" signs in Old Naxos Town.

Pantheon Hotel (tel. 24 335), head toward Hotel Chateau Zevgoli, then veer right past Koutaouki *taverna*, in heart of Old Naxos Town. 6 rooms in this tiny, family-run establishment. Expect to be well-taken care of. Kind owners (both retired teachers) welcome students. Doubles 4000-10,000dr.

Hotel Panorama (tel. 24 404), in Old Naxos near Hotel Dionysos (follow red-hand signs pointing the way). Clean and welcoming, especially suited for families. Very proud of the (you guessed it) panoramic view of the harbor and town. Singles 8000dr; doubles with bath 10,000dr; triples 11,000dr. Breakfast 800dr.

Hotel Anixis (tel. 22 112; fax 22 932), also near Hotel Dionysos. Sparkling rooms with bath. Glass-enclosed roof garden lets you enjoy breakfast while gazing at the Temple of Apollo. Doubles 10,000dr; triples 12,000dr. Breakfast 1500dr.

Hotel Chateau Zevgoli (tel. 22 993), follow the light blue signs in Old Naxos past Koutouki *taverna* toward the castle. Splurge for a night if you've been good so far. Indoor garden, bedside dried flowers. Doubles 15,000dr; triples 18,000dr.

Maragas Camping (tel. 24 552, 25 204; fax 24 552), farthest away but also the nicest and virtually on the beach. Shuttle bus service waits at the ferry docks, or take the frequent buses to Ag. Anna beach (every 30min, 280dr). 1000dr per person; doubles with bath 3000-6000; 300dr per tent.

Naxos Camping (tel. 23 500, -501), closest to town, 1500m along St. George's beach. Swimming pool. 1000dr per person; 300dr per tent. 10% discount for *Let's Go* readers.

FOOD

Galini (tel. 25 206), the best-kept secret in Naxos, 500m down the inland road past Hotel Hermes, and well worth the 10min. walk. It will be on your right just before the medical center. Recommending specific dishes is unnecessary—everything is cheap, fresh, and excellent. A very good idea to try it all. Open daily noon-2am.

Koutouki Taverna (tel. 23 389), in Old Naxos, go right if you enter the town at Promponas, then head uphill. Head here to fill a bottomless stomach. All portions are big, and entrees come with mixed vegetables, french fries, and rice (*souvlaki* 1300dr, stuffed peppers 1300dr). Open daily 6:30pm-1am.

Katerina's Restaurant Grill (tel. 23 733), on the corner of Papavasiliou and the post office side street. Greek cuisine with vegetarian options. Grilled eggplant 1200dr, stuffed tomatoes 1000dr. Breakfast menu. Open daily 7:30am-1am.

Kalee Karthia (tel. 22 537), on the waterfront. Authentic Greek grill clinging to traditions. Rabbit stew with onions 1200dr, *kokoretsi* (lamb viscera grilled on the spot) 1300dr. Vegetarians welcome. Open daily 7am-2am.

Giakoumis Taverna and Snack Bar Grill (tel. 24 561), one block behind the waterfront, across from port authority. Fast, inexpensive, good food, served to the sounds of traditional island music. *Souvlaki* pita/gyros 300dr, Greek salad 500dr. Owner makes his own wine. Open daily 8am-3am.

Cafe Picasso Mexican Bistro (tel. 25 408), in the post office square, heading toward St. George Beach. Some of the only real Mexican food you will find in Greece. Nachos 1500-1700dr, quesadillas 1200-1400dr. Ease the salsa with a glass of excellent sangria (500dr) or a frozen margarita (lime, 100dr). Open daily 7pm-2am.

Rendez-Vous: (tel. 23 858), you can't go wrong here with a pastry and prices are 20% lower if you take dessert to go. Especially delicious are the *loukoumades* (honey doughnuts, 650dr). Breakfast served. Open daily 6am-2am.

ENTERTAINMENT

Naxos's nightlife is not as frenetic as that of some of the other islands. Many people stroll the main promenade before heading to a bar, many of which offer happy hours in the earlier part of the evening (8-11pm) with drinks at half-price. For those who must dance, there are a few nearby discos as well (usually open at 11pm).

The Jam (tel. 24 306), behind OTE. Plays every style of rock plus a little reggae. Choose from 2002 different cocktails—the house specialty, the Naxos butterfly, is a good choice when all the options overwhelm. Open daily 7pm-3:30am.

The Rocks (tel 25 959), across the street. A similar atmosphere with a little more dancing incentive. Open daily 7pm-3am.

Musique Cafe, on the waterfront, offers a rotating special cocktail each night for 1000dr. Their DJ spins reggae, rock, and hip-hop. Open daily 7am-3am.

Empire Club (tel 25 167), on the water along the paved road next to the bus depot, where you head to bust some serious moves. Live disco/rock before midnight. 1500dr cover includes first drink. Open daily 10:30pm-3am.

Asteria Disco (tel. 22 173), five minutes from town on Ag. Georgios beach, plays the entire spectrum of dance music. Open daily 10:30pm-3am.

Cine Astra, on the road to Agia Anna just outside town. A more low-key adventure with 9 and 11pm films. About a 15min. walk. Tickets 1000dr.

SIGHTS

While in Naxos Town, walk around the old **Venetian Castle,** a series of mansions inhabited by the original Frankish and Venetian nobility. Uphill from the Hotel Pantheon, **The Castle** and **The Loom's** folk art merit a visit. The **Archaeological**

Museum is in a house where Nikos Kazantzakis, the author of *Last Temptation of Christ* and *Zorba the Greek,* studied. The museum contains vases, sculptures, jewels, and implements found in Mycenaean and Geometric chamber tombs (open Tues.-Sun. 8:30am-3pm; admission 500dr, students 300dr, free on Sun. and holidays).

From the waterfront, you can see the white chapel of **Myrditiotissa** floating in the harbor on a man-made islet. Nearby is the **Portara,** an intriguing marble archway on the hilltop near the port. According to myth, this is where Ariadne lost Theseus and found Dionysus; later, it was the site of Ariadne's palace. Excavation has debunked this romantic reasoning—in fact, the archway, along with the platform and some columns, is merely detritus from yet another temple to Apollo, this one unfinished. This is one of the few archaeological sites in Greece where you can actually climb all over the ruins. No admission, open 24 hours, no guards, and thus recommended for romantic sunsets or midnight star-watching.

■ Around Naxos Island

Mopeds can be ideal for reaching the popular beaches south of town and some nearby inland sights and villages. However, much of the island is mountainous and roads are often not in good condition; several people die each year on Naxos's more rocky, tortuous roads. Many travelers opt instead to take a morning bus to **Apollonas** (Apollon; 2hr., 1000dr), a small fishing village on the northern tip of the island. From Apollonas, you can slowly make your way back to Naxos alternating between bus and foot, stopping in towns like Korouida, Koronos, Apiranthos, Filoti, and Chalki. On the initial bus trip to Apollonas, examine the exhilarating scenery and note which areas you may want to investigate further on the way back.

The first hour of the ride from Naxos Town to Chalki takes you through cultivated mountainsides rich in olive trees, churches, and wildflowers that sprout each spring and summer. Before Chalki, there is a turn-off for **Ano Sangri,** an isolated town of winding flagstone streets 1km west of the road. You can get off the bus at the turn-off and walk the entire way from Naxos Town (roughly 1½hr.).

Chalki, a placid village surrounded by Venetian towers, marks the beginning of the magnificent **Tragea,** an enormous, peaceful Arcadian olive grove. Stop in at the **Panagia Protothonis,** the parish church of Chalki, right across from the bus stop. Restoration work there has uncovered wall paintings from the 11th through 13th centuries. The priest can let you in if the church is closed.

One of the more famous *kouroi* of Naxos lies a short walk from the harbor at **Apollonas.** At 10.5m long, this *kouros* is more massive, if less finely sculpted, than the one in Flerio, and is also incomplete. From the Apollonas bus stop, walk back along the main road uphill until you come to the fork in the road. Take a sharp right (onto the fork the bus did not take coming into town) and walk up until you see the stairs at the "προσ κουρο" ("Pros Kouro") sign. The walk takes about 20 minutes.

If you have a motorbike or car, an alternate route takes you from Naxos Town through Melanes to **Flerio,** where one of the magnificent **kouroi** of Naxos sleeps in a woman's garden. *Kouroi,* larger-than-life, Egyptian-influenced sculptures of male figures, were first made in Greece in the 7th century BC. This one was probably abandoned in its marble quarry because it broke before completion. Its owner runs a small *kafeneion* in the garden. From Flerio, backtrack and follow a road which passes through a trio of charming villages built in a river valley—**Kato Potamia, Mesi Potamia,** and **Ano Potamia**—before reaching Chalki. A map is essential.

Soon after leaving Chalki you will reach **Filoti,** a village where the Tragea ends and the road climbs the flanks of Mt. Zas. These slopes offer superb views extending all the way to Poros and the sea beyond. Serious hikers may want to check out the **Cave of Zeus,** most easily accessible from Filoti. Legend has it that this is the spot where the king of gods was raised by an eagle (from which he received the power of hurling thunderbolts). This 150m deep cave is a good 1½-hour trek uphill from Filoti. Determined mythologists, or those simply looking for a good hike with excellent views, should wear sturdy footwear, bring water and a flashlight, and should not come alone (two years ago it took a helicopter search crew a week to find a man who fell and injured himself here). If this excursion sounds appealing, head up the road to Apiranthos for 20-30 minutes until a dirt road branches off on the right. Follow this road to its end (passing through a gate on the way), just before a clearing with a drinkable **spring water fountain.** From there, keep going on, staying on the left (uphill) whenever possible. Look for red marks on stones, but do not expect any signs. Forty-five minutes more should bring you past some rather difficult terrain to a second potable fountain, just below the mouth of the cave. The grotto itself is large, cool, and rather slimy, but quite interesting to explore.

A 15-minute bus ride from Filoti brings you to the small town of **Apiranthos,** which houses the **Michael Bardani Museum** in a white building on the right side of the main street. The museum contains many remnants of Cycladic artifacts. Also in Apiranthos are a modest **folk art museum** and a **Geology Museum.** All three are "officially" open only early in the day (daily 8am-2pm). The museums lack posted hours, and the villagers will not necessarily open the doors for you. Many homes in Apiranthos are 300-400 years old, and lie in the shadows of the two castles that dominate the town. The mountain views from the edges of the town are stunning, and locals are cordial to the few tourists who come this way. From Apiranthos through **Koronos** and **Koronida,** a one-hour drive away, the road snakes through interior mountain ranges. The terraced landscape, laden with fruit and olive trees, plunges into the valleys below.

On your return trip from Apollonas to Chalki, you may want to get off the bus at Filoti (roughly 2km away) and walk through the **Tragea.** Footpaths off the main road will lead you into the dense grove. It is easy to get delightfully lost wandering among the scattered churches and tranquil scenery of the Tragea. Head west to return to the main road. A map is more than helpful here. Would-be hikers might pick up a copy of *Walking Tours on Naxos* by Christian Ucke, an exceedingly informative book available from the Tourist Office in both English and German (4000dr).

The most remote, uncrowded **beaches** and clearest waters are the farthest from town. Near town, the long sandy stretches of **Agios Georgios, Agios Prokopios, Agia Anna,** and **Plaka** border crystal blue water but may be crammed with sunbathers and unsightly modern buildings. All traces of authentic Greek culture are obliterated along these beaches, which are lined with hotels, rooms to let, bars, *tavernas,* discos, and *creperies.* Younger, more beautiful, and less clothed bathers begin to take over farther away from town. By Agia Anna, stunning nude sunbathers litter the shore. The beaches at **Mikri Vigla, Kastraki, Aliko,** and **Pyrgaki** are also accessible by bus from Naxos Town (4 buses per day, 360dr). Here desert meets sea; scrub pines, prickly pear, and century plants grow on the dunes behind you, shooing you towards the water. At Agios Georgios beach, **Flisvos Sportclub** offers windsurfing and cat-sailing rentals and lessons, and organizes weekly mountain bike excursions. The complex is complete with bar and restaurant (tel. 24 308; open daily 10am-6:30pm).

AMORGOS ΑΜΟΡΓΟΣ

In the case of Amorgos, Greek mythology has been supported by more recent archaeological discoveries. According to popular myth, King Minos of Crete, master of the infamous Minotaur, ruled a second kingdom on Amorgos. In 1985, the ancient Minoan civilization was discovered on the top of Mt. Moudoulia, affirming the legend. Today, Amorgos's stunning cliffside monastery, idyllic Chora, scattered churches, and assorted beaches offer a welcome respite from the throngs of tourists on other islands. Although the island's popularity has increased since the filming of *Le Grand Bleu* here in 1988, Amorgos is still the place to come for a few restful days. Ferry connections are relatively infrequent and generally stop at Amorgos' two ports in succession—**Aegiali** in the northeast and the larger **Katapola** in the southwest. Be sure to disembark at your desired port, because transportation between the two is sporadic.

■ Katapola

Katapola, the island's central port, is a welcoming village with windmills, white-washed houses, and narrow streets in the shadow of the remnants of a Venetian castle. It is small, quiet, and free of the bustle of many other Cycladic port towns.

ORIENTATION AND PRACTICAL INFORMATION

Across from the ferry dock is a **tourist agency** (tel. 71 201; fax 71 278). This is one of the few establishments on the island that accepts credit cards, and it offers helpful information, **currency exchange,** an international telephone, and ferry and hydrofoil tickets. If they do not sell the ticket you want, they will tell you where to buy it. Since there is no post office or OTE in Katapola, go there to take care of all that kind of business too. They sell stamps and phone cards, and handle registered mail. Open daily 8:30am-2pm and 5-11pm, longer in high season. The **port police** (tel. 71 259; open 24hr.) are on the right along the small street near the **pharmacy** (tel. 71 400; open Sun.-Fri. 9am-2pm and 6:30-9:30pm, Sat. 10:30am-1pm and 6:30-9pm); both are on a side street heading inland from the main square. The **medical center** (tel. 71 257) is along the waterfront as it bends around the harbor in the white building behind the two statues (next to the playground). For **medical emergencies** call 71 805.

Buses frequently connect the most desired destinations in Amorgos during summer. Buses run from Katapola to Chora about every hour 8am-midnight (10min., 220dr). Between 8am-7pm, the same bus continues on to Monastiri (from Kapapola 20min., 250dr; from Chora 10min., 220dr) and Agia Anna (from Katapola 25min., 250dr; from Chora 15min., 220dr). There is also a bus from Katapola to Aegiali roughly every two hours from 9:30am-10pm (45min., 450dr). From Amorgos (both ports), **ferries** sail to: Peiraias (4 per day, 8-13hr., 4685dr); Naxos (1-3 per day, 2½-4hr., 2280dr); Paros (2-3 per day, 2675dr); Mykonos (2 per week, 2945dr); Tinos (2 per week, 2965dr); Syros (5 per week, 3240dr); Andros (1 per week, 6hr., 3660dr); and Astypalea (2-3 per week, 3hr., 2909dr). Once a week, there is also a ferry to Kalymnos and Kos. **Hydrofoils** zoom to: Rafina (2 per week, 8975dr); Naxos (1 per day, 4420); Paros (1 per day, 5535dr); Santorini (1 per day, 4310dr); Ios (1 per day, 4140dr); Mykonos (1 per day, 6075dr); Tinos (1 per day, 6115dr); Syros (4 per week, 6665dr); and Andros (3 per week, 7505dr). **Public toilets** are at the beginning of the town beach across the street from **Motor Center Amorgos** (tel. 71 007, -777), where the helpful, English-speaking owner Thomas charges 2000-5000dr per day for a moped. Call a **taxi** at 71 255. The **postal code** is 84008. The **telephone code** is 0285.

ACCOMMODATIONS

It is probably wise to ignore the dock hawks and look for one of the amiable pensions or rooms to let. Prices are 20-40% lower in the off season.

Dimitri's Place (tel. 71 309), in a tiny olive grove. Walk along the harbor with the water on your left and take a right just before the small bridge. From there, look for the adorable "Dimitri's P(a)lace" sign. Dimitri welcomes you with a cup of Greek coffee and offers a range of rooms for a range of prices. Doubles with bath 6000dr.
Pension Anna (tel. 71 218; fax 71 084), also in a ravishing garden setting. Follow the signs on the inland road behind the small square with Pension Amorgos. It's a big white house with red shutters up behind the OTE. Doubles 3000-7000dr, with bath 4000-8500dr; triples 4000-8000dr, with bath 5000-9000dr. Studios with kitchen facilities: doubles 5000-10,000dr; triples 6000-14,000dr.
Pension Amorgos (tel. 71 013, -814), closer to the water. Has blue trimmed rooms and an open roof-top veranda with a view. Doubles and triples 4000-8000dr, with bath and kitchen 5000-9000dr.
Katapola Inn (tel. 71 007), on the waterfront, has simple but cheap rooms. Doubles and triples with bath 5000dr.
Community Campsite (tel. 71 802; winter 71 257) is a short walk from town. Cross the small bridge on the quay, and follow the signs. Peaceful and clean, the camp-

GREEK ISLANDS

site offers 24hr. hot water and meals for guests at a small cantina. 820dr-1000dr per person; 650dr-800dr per tent.

FOOD AND ENTERTAINMENT

Even though the waterfront is lined with *tavernas* and cafes, Katapola is not home to superb food. An exception is **Mourayio** (tel. 71 011), a fish *taverna* that serves traditional Greek cuisine as well as fresh seafood. You will find it smack in the middle of the waterfront as you disembark from the ferry. Local specialties included *patato* (meat and potatoes, 1400dr) and *fava* (bean paste, 800dr). Both are filling meals (open daily 10am-2am). **The Corner** (tel. 71 191), on the waterfront past most of the *tavernas,* has moderate prices for well-cooked food. *Pastitsio, moussaka, dolmades,* and *papoutsakia* are 1000-1100dr each (open daily noon-1am, live music 8pm-midnight). Two excellent options will satisfy your sweet tooth. The small and trendy creperie **To Kalderimi** (tel. 71 722) prepares delicious chocolate and banana crepes (1000dr) and meal-like cheese, ham, and tomato crepes (1100dr), to name a couple. Around the U-shaped waterfront, on the other end facing inland from the dock, **Thothoni** will overwhelm you with 36 flavors of ice cream, sherbet, and frozen yogurt. Not in the mood for ice cream? Order from the enticing cake-filled display case (ice cream 290-320dr per scoop; open April-Oct. daily 9am-2pm). Although nighttime entertainment is relatively subdued in Amorgos, there are a couple of good options to choose from. Near Thothoni, **Katerina's Moon Bar** serves excellent local liqueurs like *raki* (400dr), and delicious appetizers to the sounds of soothing music. Sample *dakos,* an island specialty—*paximathi* (dry bread) covered with tomato, onion, cheese and oregano (900dr). Although not on the menu, sea urchin is a salty accompaniment to your *ouzo* or beer. A block away, the waterfront bar **Le Grand Bleu** (tel 71 633), with a blue and white sign, capitalizes on the popularity of the movie from which it takes it name. Here, Cokes and beers cost 600dr but the showing of the movie *Le Grand Bleu* in English with Norwegian subtitles is free (open daily 8pm-3am). Across from the dock, **Erato Cafe Bar** faces you as you disembark. A good choice for excellent, authentic Italian pasta (*penne all'alrabita,* 1700dr) during the day, it transforms into a full bar at night. Don't worry, beer and cocktails (700-1400dr) are not limited to evening hours (open daily 2pm-3am).

For beaches, try **Plakes** and **Agios Panteleimonas,** a mere 10-minute walk from Katapola around the left end of the harbor and over the hill, and **Paradisia** in the south. A bus leaves Katapola for the latter at 10am daily and returns at 3pm (45min., 400dr). If you make it to this beautiful beach, ask the locals to direct you to the **Olympia shipwreck** *(navagio),* the remains of a boat that sank roughly 60 years ago.

■ Around Amorgos: Chora

Katapola literally means "below the town." In this case, the town above is Chora, also known as Amorgos, 6km from the harbor along the island's only significant paved road. Less convenient as a base for your stay, Chora is nonetheless a restful and ravishing option. Sights include a 14th-century Venetian fortress, a row of retired windmills perched precariously on the mountain ledge above town, 45 Byzantine churches, and the first high school in Greece, built in 1829 (on the left on way up to OTE).

Roughly 16 buses per day travel from Katapola to Chora (10min., 220dr), and 10 continue on to the monastery and Agia Anna (250dr). Chora is home to Amorgos's only **post office** (tel. 71 250), past the small square with the snack bar on the uphill end of town (open Mon.-Fri. 7:30am-2pm), and its main **OTE** (tel. 71 339), on the right at the very top of town (open Mon.-Fri. 7:30am-3pm). There is a **police station** (tel. 71 210) in the main square with the big church, next to Cafe Loza (open 24hr.; knock loudly after hours). The **medical center** (tel. 71 207), is on the main road into Chora from Katapola (open 24hr.). A branch of the **Agricultural Bank** operates in the small square with the snack bar (open Mon.-Thurs. 8am-2pm, Fri. 8am-1:30pm). If you decide to spend the night, look for "rooms to let" signs in town.

Pension Panorama is below the bus stop, and **Pension Ilias** (tel. 71 277), is on the road from Chora to Monastiri, toward the lower end of Chora. Both offer clean, stark rooms (doubles with bath 5000-9000dr). Several *tavernas* and cafes are tucked in the meandering streets. **Liotrivi** (tel.71 700), directly below the bus station, prepares delicious twists on traditional Greek dishes. Both *kalogiros* (eggplant with veal, cheese and tomato, 1500dr) and *exohiko* (lamb and vegetables in pastry shell, 1500dr) are house specialities. Adventurous gourmands should order the shark, prepared with garlic paste, mustard, and lemon sauce (1200dr; open daily noon-1am). Enhanced by an outdoor balcony and beautiful view, **The Sunset** is the only place for *soya moussaka* (100dr). Another worthwhile choice is the palatable grilled octopus and *patato* (1500dr). Head to **Vegana** (tel. 74 017) for an omelette (650-1100dr), every type of coffee imaginable, and sweet desserts. The atmosphere is relaxed—jazz, blues, 60s rock, and Greek folk music will eliminate the concerns of life (open 9am-3am).

In front of the main church in Katapola is a sign for the ancient town of **Minoa** (40-min. hike). This settlement was inhabited between the 10th and 4th centuries BC. Look for the base of the temple among the ruins with the bust of a statue still rising from within.

■ Around Amorgos : Chozoviotissa Monastery

A trip to Amorgos is incomplete without a visit to the **Chozoviotissa monastery** (tel. 71 274). From Katapola, you can catch a bus that goes through Chora. If you are in Chora, you may choose to go down the steps that begin at the top of Chora, past the OTE antenna. Both routes take you to the beginning of the 350-step staircase that climbs to the 11th-century whitewashed edifice. Wear comfortable shoes, a hat, and take plenty of water to tackle this hike. The monastery is built so flawlessly into the sheer face of a cliff that it appears to have grown there. Legend has it that attempts to build the monastery on the shore were twice thwarted by divine intervention before the workers discovered their bag of tools mysteriously hanging from the cliff, causing them to interpret the omen as advice on where to recommence construction. The monastery is undoubtedly one of the more exhilarating visual spectacles in all of Greece. If you complete the hike between 8am and 1pm (also 5-7pm in the summer), the monks may reward you with cold water, Greek liqueur, and *loukoumi* (Greek sweets). Before leaving, ask the monks to show you the downstairs exhibit, which includes writings, relics, and church items dating to the founding of the monastery. Wander through the chambers farther below to get a sense of the hamlet's serenity and solitude. Contrary to the sign posted at the base of the climb, spare clothing is available at the entrance, but it is more respectful for men to wear pants, and women dresses or long skirts; bare shoulders are not permissible.

The road from the turnoff for the monastery takes you to the lone and crystal waters of **Agia Anna;** two enchanting beaches await you. From the bus stop, one is at the end of the path through the clearing, the other at the bottom of the central steps.

TINOS ΤΗΝΟΣ

Tinos has been a place of religious significance for Greeks since the War of Independence, when a nun named Pelagia, guided by a vision, found a miracle-working icon of Christ and the Virgin buried in an underground church. The **Icon of the Annunciation,** also known as the *Megalochari* (Great Joy) or *Panagia Evangelistria*, is one of the most sacred relics of the Greek Orthodox Church. Each year on the Feasts of the Annunciation (March 25) and the Assumption (Aug. 15), thousands of pilgrims crowd the island and pray to the icon. Because of its strong ties to the Greek Orthodox Church, Tinos is often mistakenly overlooked by tourists seeking a more boisterous island experience. As a result, the breathtaking beauty, significant contributions of art history, and growing nightlife of Tinos have remained virtually undiscovered.

■ Tinos Town

Tinos Town garners special recognition for historical and religious reasons. The Panayia Evangelistria church and miraculous icon of the Virgin Mary make the town a spiritual center. On Aug. 15, 1940, the port rose to prominence when an Italian submarine torpedoed the Greek cruiser "Elli," which was docked in the harbor for the observance of a religious holiday. Mussolini declared war two months later.

Today, Tinos Town is the most visited part of the island. The plethora of souvenirs, hotels, restaurants and tourist-oriented services attracts domestic and international visitors, particularly during July and August. To avoid throngs of other backpackers and the island's famous windy conditions, visit in May or September.

ORIENTATION AND PRACTICAL INFORMATION

From the main dock next to the bus depot, walk left to the center of town to the sprawling **Leoforos Megalochares.** This wide avenue leads uphill to the Neoclassical facade of the **Panayia Evangelistria** church. Parallel to Leoforos Megalochares, **Evangelistrias Street** (nicknamed Bazaar St. by the locals) overflows with religious trinkets. The **police station** (tel. 22 100, -255), which also houses the **tourist police,** is located five minutes out of town on the road to Kionia. Facing inland, the **post office** is on the far right end of the waterfront, behind the small square (open Mon.-Fri. 7:30am-2pm). A few blocks up Leforos Megalochares on the right is the **OTE** (tel. 22 499; open Mon.-Fri. 7:30am-3:10pm). The **National Bank,** on the waterfront across from the bus depot, has an **ATM** (open Mon.-Thurs. 8am-2pm, Fri. 8am-1:30pm). For a **pharmacy** (tel. 22 272; fax 22 740), look for a green cross across the dock and to the left along the waterfront (open Mon.-Tues. and Thurs.-Fri. 8am-2pm and 6-9pm, Wed. and Sat. 8am-2pm). **Public toilets** are at the left end of the waterfront near Dolphin Sq., behind Hotel Lito.

Buses (tel. 22 440), leave from the station a few storefronts left of the National Bank. They depart two to seven times daily for: Pyrgos (700dr); Panormos (750dr); Kalloni (570dr); Steni (320dr); Skalados (400dr); Kionia (200dr); and Porto (200dr). A schedule is posted in the KTEL ticket agency across the depot. For a **taxi,** dial 22 470 or inquire at the blue booth to the right of the waterfront (available daily 6am-2am). Renting a **moped** is probably the best way to see Tinos, but take special care on the narrow gravel mountain roads. Try **Vidalis,** 16 Zanaki Alavanou St. (tel. 23 400), which is on the main road leading out of town off the right side of the waterfront.

The staff offers free information about the island (open daily 8am-10pm). Or try **Jason's** (tel. 22 583, 24 283), just before Alavanou St., on the waterfront (open daily 8am-10pm). Prices are 2500-3000dr per day for a moped and 6000-15,000dr per day for a car, depending on the model.

Tinos can be reached by frequent ferries and hydrofoils from Peiraias and Rafina near Athens, as well as Mykonos, Syros, and Andros. **Ferries** from Tinos travel to: Mykonos (4-5 per day, 30min., 1275dr); Andros (2-4 per day, 2hr., 1810dr); Syros (2 per day, 40min., 1195dr); Peiraias (2 per day, 5½hr., 4345dr); and Rafina (2-4 per day, 4hr., 3370dr). In high season, there is weekly service to Paros (1680dr) and Naxos (1890dr). A **catamaran** departs daily for: Mykonos (30min., 2410dr); Paros (1¼hr., 3385dr); Naxos (1¾hr., 3750dr); Rafina (3hr., 6925dr); and Amorgos (6¼hr., 6115dr). The agents at **K Sia Travel** (tel. 22 440) answer queries (open daily 7am-11pm). **Mariner** (tel. 23 193), next to the pharmacy, handles **flying dolphins,** which leave daily for: Mykonos (2410dr); Andros (3480dr); Rafina (7000dr); Paros (3385dr); Naxos (3750dr); Santorini (7665dr); and two times per week for Amorgos (6120dr). There is also an **excursion boat** to Mykonos and Delos (Tues.-Sun. depart 9am, return 6pm, 4000dr). The **postal code** is 84200. The **telephone code** is 0283.

ACCOMMODATIONS

Tinos has plenty of accommodations, except at festival time (Eastern Orthodox Easter week and occasionally on July and August weekends, when Athenians flock here). Most hotels are expensive, so try your bargaining skills with the crowd of smiling faces holding "Rooms to Let" signs when you disembark.

Loukas Apergis' Rooms (tel. 23 964, mobile phone 093 66 8888) are a good choice if the hustlers are too much. Take a left onto Zanaki Alavanou St. just before the post office, then the second left onto 25 Martiou at the second little park (the one with the little boy fountain) and look for signs on that street. Doubles 5000dr; triples 6000dr; both with bath. Ask about rooms in the countryside.

Mrs. Plyte (tel. 23 228) also has rooms in the same neighborhood with common baths and kitchens. Turn left at the first little park and at the top of the road look on your right for a white house with blue shutters above a woodshop. Inquire about rooms in the woodshop. Doubles 5000-7000dr; triples 7000-10,000dr.

Giannis (tel. 22 515) is for the hardy budget traveler. It is at the far right end of the waterfront. Simple but airy rooms in a traditional house with green shutters. Common baths, a kitchen, laundry facilities, and a lovely garden sitting area. Doubles 6000dr; triples with private bath and kitchen 12,000dr.

Tinos Camping (tel. 22 344, -548) is a clearly marked 10min. walk to the right-hand side of town. Well-kept, has kitchen and laundry facilities, showers, bungalows, and a bar/restaurant/cafe. 1000-1200dr per person; 700-800dr per tent.

FOOD AND ENTERTAINMENT

Pigada (tel. 24 240) is the first right off Evangelistrias St. and past a few other restaurants. Don't shy away from the exterior; the food is excellent. Try Greek *moussaka* (1200dr) or *dolmades* (1200dr).

Pallatha (tel. 83 516) is a fantastic find. Open year-round; serves authentic Greek cuisine and local specialities. Big portions, and the food is so good you will use the bread from next door to wipe your plate. Try fava beans and spinach (900dr), or local sausage and potatoes (1000dr). Open daily 11am-4pm, 6pm-1am.

Old-fashioned wood-burning bakery (tel. 24 317) is next door to Pallatha. Head to the new port, next to the only one on the island. Try amazing fresh bread (80-200dr). Open daily 7am-3pm and 5-11pm.

Peristeriones (tel. 23 425). Take the second left off Megalochores. Try the house specialty, vegetable fritters made with onion and dill (650dr). Open daily noon-3pm and 7:30-11:20pm.

Mesklies (tel. 22 151, -373) is the biggest and the best pastry shop in town. Two doors farther to the left, the same owner makes excellent pizza in a wood oven at his restaurant/pizzeria—also called Mesklies. After having pizza (1700-2500dr), spaghetti (1000-1700dr), or a calzone, top off your meal with the island's dessert specialty, *tyropitakia*. Unlike the more common cheese pie with the same name, *tyropitakia* of Tinos are made with sugar instead of salty feta cheese. The product is denser than cheese cake but just as good (open daily 7am-3am).

Most of the town's bars are on the water to the left of the harbor, behind Hotel Lito. **Metropolis Club** plays the latest Greek tunes for an often wall-to-wall crowd, while **Kaktos Club,** located inside a windmill behind the Panayia Evangelistria church, caters to American music lovers while providing them with an incredible hilltop view. Along the waterfront, **Fevgotas** has billiard tables and a TV tuned to MTV all night long. Prices at these nightspots are similar (beer 800-900dr, cocktails 1500dr).

SIGHTS

In 1822, Sister Pelagia, a Tiniote nun, had a vision in which the Virgin Mary instructed her to find an icon buried at the site of an ancient church, destroyed in the 10th century by pirates. A year later, the icon was housed, amid great rejoicing, in the **Panagia Evangelistria,** where it still resides. To the faithful, the find is evidence of the power and presence of the Holy Virgin. The relic reputedly has curing powers and is almost entirely covered with gold, diamonds, and jewels left at the church by people wishing to thank the Holy Mother for their good health. Countless *tamata*—beautifully crafted plaques praising the Virgin's healing powers—have won the Panayia the title "Lourdes of the Aegean." The most devout pilgrims make the journey up Leoforos Megalochares (the wide road rising from the sea to the church) on their knees to show their reverence. Others light offertory candles (100-1000dr donation depending on candle size). The **Well of Sanctification** flows below the marble entrance stairs in a chapel. It is a natural spring discovered during excavations, from which the faithful fill jugs for drinking or carrying as talismans. The spring is said to have been dry until the icon was unearthed; since then, it has flowed continuously. On March 25 and August 15, flocks of devout pilgrims arrive at the church. To the right of the well is the mausoleum of the Greek warship Elli, sunk by an Italian torpedo in 1940. To the left of the well, in an adjoining chamber, the spot where the icon was found is marked by a marble plaque and wooden icon.

There are lodgings and facilities in Tinos Town, but it so crowded on August 15 that the nearly 30,000 visitors sleep *everywhere*—along the dock, on the sidewalks, and even in the church itself. The next day, after making the 10km walk to the convent of Kechrovouni in a procession led by the icon, the masses depart on dozens of specially chartered ferries. No one will stop you here, but try to come modestly attired (long sleeves and pants or skirts, no bare shoulders) and be respectful of the Orthodox worshippers. Don't miss the oil painting of a weeping Mary Magdalene contemplating the crown of thorns in the gallery opposite the church entrance. A free English information booklet full of history, colorful reports of miracles, and explanations of holidays is available at the second floor to the right of the sanctum (tel. 22 256; open daily 7am-8pm; free). Tinos is also famed for its art, particularly its marble sculptures. After you visit the Panayia, drop by the church complex's art and archaeological museums, which features works by native Tiniotes (open 8:30am-3pm, hours variably extended in summer; free).

Tinos' **Archaeological Museum,** on Leoforos Megalochares across and uphill from the OTE, contains artifacts from Poseidon's sanctuary at Kionia, a first-century BC sundial, and a few vases from Xombourgo (open Tues.-Sun. 8:30am-3pm; admission 500dr, students 300dr). At **Kionia,** explore the ruins of the 4th-century BC temple of Poseidon and Amphitrite, then sit by the sea at the steadily touristed **Tinos** or **Stavros Beaches,** both near town. If you stay late at Stavros, enjoy the locally acclaimed **Chroma Bar/Homa Club.** A closer and equally crowded beach, **Agios Fokas,** is a short walk east (on the opposite side) of Tinos Town.

■ Around Tinos

Rustic Tinos will reward adventurers with secluded beaches and wonderful views of the verdant Tinos countryside. The best beaches on the island are outside of Tinos Town, a short bus ride away. **Agios Sostis, Porto, Panormos,** and **Kolimbithra** top the list. To get to spectacular **Kardianis** beach, take the Pyrgos bus to Kardiani and travel down the winding street from the main road. The 2000 **dovecotes** dotting the landscape have become the island's symbol. Built in medieval times, these small white buildings have intricate lattice-work, complete with nesting birds. No longer used to breed birds, abandoned *peristonies* are being transformed into striking summer homes. Stop by the picturesque town of **Pyrgos**, 33km northwest of Tinos Town (buses 3-5 times per day, 1hr., 700dr). With a marble quarry, Pyrgos has always been home to Tinos's artists and sculptors, including Giannouli Chalepas, whose *Sleeping Daughter* graces Athens's central graveyard. Today, it is also home to the only marble sculpting school in all of Greece. Two kilometers northeast of Pyrgos, Panormos Bay has a small beach and three *tavernas.* Be careful not to get stranded in the village—there are no night buses on Tinos and taxis are hard to find.

If you have wheels, investigate the delightful villages that encircle **Mt. Exobourgo,** 14km north of Tinos Town, and the precipitous site of the Venetian Fortress, **Xombourgo.** After withstanding 11 assaults, the 13th-century island capital fell to the Ottomans in 1715. It was the very last territorial gain of the Ottoman Empire. Climb the mountain from the east foothill (near the village of Xinara or Loutra), and indulge in the resplendent panorama.

SYROS ΣΥΡΟΣ

Syros's rise as a commercial power began with the Phoenicians who used the island as a sea port. Venetian control of the island, which began in the 13th century, solidified Syros's title as the trading capital of the Cyclades. The large Catholic population here is a vestige of this era. Many of the buildings in Hermoupolis date from this period, when rich merchants built mansions and erected monuments. But all good things must come to an end, and the advent of steam-powered ships coupled with the rise of Peiraias sent Syros into a nose dive. During the last 20 years Syros has managed to recover, due primarily to a shipbuilding industry which now keeps the island "afloat" year-round. This source of income has allowed the island not to concentrate on attracting large numbers of tourists. Particularly in Ano Syros, one of the two peaks on the island, diligent hikers can find relatively uncharted terrain.

■ Hermoupolis ΕΡΜΟΥΠΟΛΙΣ

With a Greek Orthodox church on one hill and a Catholic church on the other, Hermoupolis, the spiritual city of Hermes (god of commerce), rests serenely on its natural harbor. Despite its decline as a major port, the city remains the shipping center and capital of the Cyclades. Elegant Miaouli Sq. and the 19th-century mansions in Dellagrazia let us peek at Hermoupolis's opulent past and explain its former nicknames—the "Manchester of Greece" and "little Milan."

ORIENTATION AND PRACTICAL INFORMATION

The center of activity in Hermoupolis is **Miaouli Sq.,** two blocks up El. Venizelou St. from the winged statue at the center of the harbor. You can't miss the palatial town hall and large marble plaza. In Syros, **Gaviotis Tours** (tel. 86 606; fax 83 445), near the ferry dock and across from the bus depot, provides schedules and prices and sells tickets for ferries, hydrofoils, and flights (open 9am-10pm). The **National Bank** (tel. 82 451), on Kosti Kalomenopoulou St., in an elegant building at the end of the street the post office is on, offers **currency exchange** (open Mon.-Thurs. 8am-2pm, Fri.

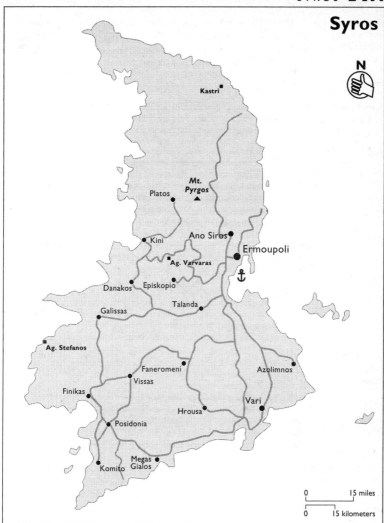

Syros

N

8am-1:30pm). For an **ATM,** try the **Credit Bank,** just off Venizelou St. near the post office. The **OTE** (tel. 82 799) is on the square (open daily 7am-11pm).

There are two-three daily **flights** to Athens (13,800dr). **Buses** (tel. 82 575) leave from the depot near the ferry dock and travel regularly to Galissas (18 per day) and nearby beaches Kini (6 per day) and Ano Syros (3 per day). Service is less frequent on Sunday, and a schedule is posted next to the buses. From Syros, ferries depart from the right of the harbor (facing the water) to: Peiraias (1-4 per day, 4½hr., 4100dr); Tinos (2-3 per day, 40min., 1240dr); Mykonos (2-3 per day, 1½hr., 1590dr); Andros (2 per week, 2100dr); Paros (1-2 per day, 1½hr., 1630dr); Naxos (1-2 per day, 2½hr., 2100dr); Ios (4 per week, 4hr., 3100dr); Santorini (1 per day, 5hr., 3850dr); Rhodes (2 per week, 5500dr); Kos (2 per week, 5250dr); and several of the smaller Cycladic islands. **Flying Dolphins,** departing from across the ferry docks (on the left, facing the water), speed daily to: Tinos (2300dr); Mykonos (3000dr); Paros (3080dr); Naxos (4020dr); Santorini (7880dr); and Ios (6660dr). **Sea Jets** run daily to: Rafina (1½hr., 6360dr); Tinos (15min., 2300dr); and Mykonos (35min., 3000dr). A high-speed catamaran carries cars and passengers daily to Peiraias (2hr., 8100dr).

Taxis (tel. 86 222) can be caught in front of the town hall. There is a **pharmacy** (tel. 82 248) on El. Venizelou St. (open Mon. and Wed. 8am-2:30pm, Tues. and Thurs.-Sat. 8am-1:30pm and 5:30-9pm; look for red cross). In case of emergency, the **hospital** (tel. 86 666) is at the left end of the waterfront (facing inland) at Platia Iroon (20min. walk from Miaculi St.). The **police** (tel. 82 620) are behind the theater off the upper right corner of Miaouli Sq. A **tourist police** officer is on duty in the mornings. The **post office** (tel. 82 596) is 40m down the second right off El. Venizelou (open Mon.-Fri. 7:30am-2pm). The **postal code** is 84100. The **telephone code** is 0281.

ACCOMMODATIONS

Hermoupolis has plenty of cheap rooms. Off-season prices are generally about 20-40% cheaper. There is a large map with names and phone numbers of hotels at the ferry dock. When staffed, the kiosk directly in front of you as you step off the ferry provides information on accommodations. Someone is likely to be there when boats arrive during the day in the summer. For clean rooms with high ceilings, try the tradi-tional house turned brand new **Villa Nefeli,** 21 Parou St. (tel. 87 076), along the waterfront and left on Hiou St., just before Venizelou. Parou is the first left off Hiou. Have a drink with the extra-friendly owner and his extra-passive dog on the roof gar-den bar, which has a full view of the harbor (doubles 6000-8000dr; triples 10,000-13,000dr). For a dose of luxury, head to **Ariadni Rooms to Let** (tel. 81 307, 80 245), on Nik. Fylini St. near the ferry dock (look for signs). Ariadni prides itself on a class "A" rating, and deservedly so—the rooms are spotless and radiant. (Show your *Let's Go* for a discount. Doubles 8000-13,000dr; triples 10,000-15,000dr depending on sea-son. Some rooms have a kitchen for the same price as the rooms without this perk, so call ahead if you plan on cooking.) For the full common bath experience, go to **Pen-sion Venetiko,** 2 Em. Roidi (tel. 81 686), two blocks from the lower right corner of the main square (facing inland). A sign welcomes all to a quiet bar in the pension's backyard (doubles 5000-7000dr).

FOOD, ENTERTAINMENT, AND SIGHTS

For excellent cuisine and friendly service, prepare for a climb and head to **Folia** (tel. 83 715), a *taverna* perched at the top of an endless flight of stairs. Head up the main road leading from the top right corner of the main square. Stay to the left of St. Nicho-las and keep going up, even after the road turns to stairs. Look for the sign on the left and turn onto Xenofontos street. After roughly 50m, take a right and head uphill to the restaurant. Three main dishes are particularly divine—the *kouneli stifado* (rabbit stew; 1250dr), the *arni rigonatto* (lamb cooked with oregano; 1300dr), and the only pigeon dish on the island (grilled and served with potatoes, 1100dr; open daily 5pm-1am). If your ferry arrives in Syros late at night and you're famished, try **Elysee** (tel. 81 741, 88 245), on the far right-hand edge of the harbor next to the port authority. Ely-see offers good pizza (1700-1900dr) and a hearty portion of spaghetti carbonara (1200dr), served until 4am. Show your *Let's Go* for a discount. In the square, next to the OTE, **"O Lucas"** serves good *moussaka* (1200dr) and *kanelonia* (crepe with chicken, 1200dr). Order a variety of small dishes and share with friends (tel. 80 677, open daily 9am-4pm and 7pm-1am). To satisfy that sugar craving, find **Kechayia** (tel. 88 076), on the waterfront corner of El. Venizelou. This amazing sweet shop prides itself on local specialties like delicious *loukoumi* (450dr for a big box) and *chalva-thopita* (a sweet concoction of almond paste mixed with nuts and chocolate, 350dr).

The waterfront and Miaouli Sq. buzz with activity at night. On the right-hand strip of the waterfront (facing inland), **Seasons** serves 35 varieties of beer and the neces-sary *mezethes* (finger food to whet your alcohol appetite). Don't bother asking what goes into the specialty cocktail *epoches;* it's a secret recipe (open 8am-3pm and 7pm-3am). The **Cotton Club,** a block farther left along the waterfront, offers similar drinks at similar prices. For the latest Greek music, stay along the waterfront at **Odyssea** or

Skiés. Both bars spin "top 40" Greek tunes and serve beer and cocktails until the early morning. **Kazino Eyéou** draws a crowd from all of the nearby Cycladic islands. The only casino on any of the surrounding islands, it mimics those in big gambling towns. Become a 24-hour member for 500dr and receive 300dr in chips as you enter the main door, across from the port (tel. 84 400; open 24hr).

Interesting sights and sounds abound at Syros's small **open market** between the lower left of Miaouli Sq. and the waterfront. Make the ascent to **Ano Syros,** a medieval Venetian settlement that is still home to Syros's Catholics. To get there, climb the steps behind Miaouli Sq. or take the bus from the waterfront. The **Archaeological Museum,** the entrance to which is at the upper left corner of the Town Hall, has a small collection of Cycladic Art (open Tues.-Sun. 8:30am-3pm; free). At the **Church of the Assumption** *(Kimisis Theotokou)* on St. Proiou St., view a painting created in 1562 at age 20 by **El Greco.** This painting's discovery on Syros helped confirm the painter's Greek origin.

■ Around Syros: Galissas

Galissas, a village to the west of Hermoupolis, has a busy beach. From Hermoupolis, 18 buses per day travel to Galissas, alternating between a direct 15-minute route and a 45-minute route that stops in other villages first (230dr). In Hermoupolis, buses leave from the depot near the ferry dock, where an up-to-date schedule is posted. Climb past the chapel of Agia Pakou on the left side (facing the water) to discover **Armeos Beach**—tiny, beautiful, and **nudist.** Clothing is definitely an option.

There is a dizzying collection of "Rooms to Let" signs at the bus stop. The rooms at **George's Restaurant** (tel. 42 066), up the main inland street from the bus stop, are decorated with hand-woven tapestries (doubles 6000-9000dr; triples 9000-12,000dr, depending on season.) **Angela's Rooms to Let** (tel. 42 855, -9), behind the mini-golf, has large, immaculate rooms surrounded by a spacious outdoor garden. A private bath and refrigerator are included (doubles 7000-10,000dr; triples 9000-13,000dr). Angela also has kitchen-equipped apartments suitable for up to four people (15,000-18,000dr). Also try **Tony's Rooms to Let** (tel. 42 482), at the end of the same street in the village (doubles 5000-8000dr; triples 6000-10,000dr). There are two **campgrounds** near Galissas beach, **Yianna** (tel. 42 418), and **Two Hearts** (tel. 42 052); representatives from each may greet you with shuttle buses at the dock. Yianna is more secluded and offers a *taverna,* minimarket, hot showers, kitchen, laundry, safe-deposit boxes, and a nightly disco (9pm-2am; cover including first drink 500dr). Camping is 1200dr per person, 350dr per small tent, and 600dr per large tent. Follow the signs from the bus stop. Two Hearts offers a restaurant and minimarket, but alas, no tunnel of love (1300dr per person; 650dr per tent; 5000dr per two-person cabin).

Galissas beach has most amenities: a *taverna* on the beach affiliated with the Dolphin Bay Hotel, a cheaper restaurant next door, mini-golf (next to Galissas Tours; open daily 7pm-1am), a few English language books at the Golden Corner, and video games in the cafe/bar next to Galissas Tours. Although Americans laugh at the name, the **Green Dollars Bar** contributes to the festivities with darts and a life-size chessboard in a courtyard (beer 400-500dr, cocktails 1000dr). If you exhaust the offerings at Galissas beach, **Galissas Tours** (tel. 42 801; fax 42 802), lets you make phone calls, change money, buy ferry tickets, rent mopeds (3000dr) or cars (9000-14,500dr), or take excursions around the island (mid-July to Aug., 2000dr to St. Stephanos Fisherman's Grotto; open Sept.-June 9:30am-2:30pm and 5-9pm; July-Aug. 9:30am-11pm).

Farther south along the coast are the beaches at **Poseidonia, Finikas, Angathopes,** and **Komito,** all connected by bus to Hermoupolis. The beach resort of **Vari** is most popular with families and package tour groups because of its shallow waters and relaxed atmosphere. North of Galissas is the tiny fishing village of **Kini.** If you happen to be in this picturesque hamlet on June 29th, the Church of St. Peter invites you and every other living thing within earshot to an all-night festival. The *kakavia* (fish soup) is plentiful and accompanied by the sounds of *baizoukia.*

ANDROS ΑΝΔΡΟΣ

Tiers of straw fields and stretches of green and purple growth are partitioned by a network of streams and stone walls, lying like a spider's web fallen on the face of Andros's hillside. Winding above splendid scattered beaches, the hour drive from the ferry landing at **Gavrio** to **Andros Town** is magnificent. The ruins sprinkled across the Andrian hills memorialize the island's checkered history of Ionian, Spartan, Venetian, and Turkish occupation. Despite this tumultuous past, Andros today is one of the most peaceful of the Cyclades. It is the perfect place for family holidays as well as an exciting outlet for singles seeking sun and fun. Islanders claim Andros has 300 beaches; come and find out for yourself.

■ Gavrio

Crowned by the three-domed Church of Saint Nikolas, the dusty port town of Gavrio has little else to offer tourists. Most visitors stay overnight to catch an early ferry, but you could also use Gavrio as a base to explore some of the best stretches of smooth sand between the port and the popular tourist beach town of Batsi.

Good **maps** are available at tourist shops (400dr). Facing inland, the **police** (tel. 71 220) are to the right on a road parallel to the waterfront, up the steps opposite the bus stop. The building is unmarked, so look for the Greek flag (open 24hr.). The **OTE** stands one block to the left of Hotel Galaxy, on a side street in a building with green shutters (open Mon.-Fri. 7:30am-3pm). The **post office** (tel. 71 254) is two blocks farther on the waterfront (open Mon.-Fri. 7:30am-2pm). The **Agricultural Bank** (tel. 71 478) is on the corner at the right-hand end of the waterfront facade (open for **currency exchange** Mon.-Thurs. 9am-2pm, Fri. 9am-1:30pm). A **pharmacy** is located in the left-center of the waterfront (tel. 71 329; open daily 9am-1:30pm and 6-10pm). For medical emergencies call the **hospital** at 22 222. The **postal code** is 84501. The **telephone code** is 0282.

To get to Andros Town, take one of the **buses** from the depot next to the ferry dock (5-7 per day, 1hr., 700dr). The same bus passes through Batsi (from Gavrio 15min., 250dr; from Andros Town 45min., 600dr). Check the schedules as early as possible. They tend to be erratic and structured around ferry arrivals and departures. From Andros, **ferries** sail to Athens's minor port, Rafina (2-5 per day, 2hr., 2330dr). They also head to Tinos (2-3 per day, 2hr., 1810dr); Mykonos (2-3 per day, 2½hr., 2575dr); Syros (2 per week, 2-3hr., 1815dr); Paros (1 per week, 2645dr); and Naxos (2 per week, 3½hr., 2870dr). There is daily **SeaJet** service to: Rafina (1hr., 4530dr); Tinos (50min., 3480dr); Syros (1½hr., 3595dr); Mykonos (15min., 5330dr); Naxos (2hr, 5930dr); and Paros (1¾hr, 5475dr). **Flying Dolphins** from Batsi zip to Tinos (1 per day, 3480dr); Mykonos (1 per day, 5335dr); Paros (4 per week, 5475dr); Naxos (4 per week, 5935dr); Ios (daily, 8455dr); and Santorini (daily, 9560dr). A **taxi** to Batsi costs 1200-1500dr and to Andros Town costs 3500-4000dr. You can rent a **moped** at **Andros Moto Rental** (tel. 71 605), behind the port authority (from 3500dr per day; open daily 8am-9pm).

Most accommodations are designed for longer visits and family groups, but simple rooming arrangements and camping are available. At the center of the waterfront, **Hotel Galaxias** (tel. 71 005, -228) has rather standard, simple, and beautiful rooms. (Singles 6000dr; doubles 7500dr; triples 9000dr. All with bath.) **Camping Andros** (tel. 71 444), has its own restaurant, minimarket, showers, and pool. There are signs to guide you from the OTE (1200dr per person, 800dr per tent).

Fix your own meals with goodies from the **Andrios Supermarket** (tel. 71 341), on the right end of the waterfront (open daily 6:30am-11pm). **Galaxias** (tel. 71 005), in the same building as the hotel, has traditional Greek dishes (stuffed tomatoes 900-1000dr, depending on local tomato prices). Get a pizza at **San Remo** (tel. 71 150), next to the post office (1400-1800dr). For breakfast, try the bakery **Gavrio**, next to the pharmacy (tel. 71 126; ham and cheese pita 350dr).

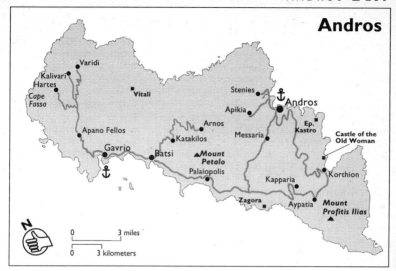

■ Batsi

Batsi, with its long stretch of golden sand and crystal-blue water, is the tourist capital of Andros. If you take a bus, sit on the right side to enjoy the scenery. Between Gavrio and Batsi, there are coves with pools, as well as beaches at **Agios Petros, Psili Ammos,** and **Kipri.**

ORIENTATION AND PRACTICAL INFORMATION

If you stay on the bus until Batsi, the main bus stop is at the end of the beach in a small square. The **taxi** stand is also there. There is a branch of the **National Bank** (tel. 41 400), to the right, continuing on the road to Andros Town (open Mon.-Fri. 8am-1:30pm). If you need an **ATM,** go to the **Ionian Bank** on the waterfront. The conveniently located **mobile post office** is down the road along the beach, inland from the Hotel Karanassos sign; the **post office** is across a dirt road from the hotel (open Mon.-Fri. 7:30am-2pm). On a street parallel to the main road, accessible from the stairs past the National Bank, is **Dolphin Hellas Travel** (tel. 41 185; fax 41 719) which offers **currency exchange,** information, and excursions. There are **taxi boats** that leave Batsi for other beaches on the island (up to 1200dr round-trip; open 9:30am-1:30pm and 6-9pm).

ACCOMMODATIONS

It is easier to find accommodations here than in either Gavrio or Andros Town, but they tend to be more expensive. Expect to pay 8000-10,000dr for a double at one of the beachfront hotels. Look for "Rooms to Let" signs or inquire at souvenir or tourist shops (6000-10,000dr). **Mrs. Tzoumoni** (tel. 41 211), has large, clean rooms with fully equipped kitchenettes. Her house is white with blue shutters, along the waterfront next to Supermarket Batis (doubles 6000-9000dr). **Hotel Karanassos** (tel. 41 480, -1), one block from the beachfront, is breezy and comfortable (doubles 6000-12,000dr; triples 8000-15,000dr; quads 10,000-17,000dr; breakfast 1000dr). Prices fluctuate with the season.

ENTERTAINMENT AND SIGHTS

To the left of the square, in a vine-covered setting along the waterfront, is the cafe/bar **Skala** (tel. 41 656). Listen to trendy music and choose from a vast variety of beers

(600-3000dr). If you want music with a faster beat, head to **Placebo** (tel. 71 800), half-way to Gavrio on the main road. The night club has a 1500dr cover including the first drink, but you can skip the cover and go into the bar (beer 800dr, cocktails 1200-1500dr). For daytime partying, take a taxi boat to the **Green Beach Club** (tel. 41 656), at the **Prasini Ammo beach,** where there is water polo, canoeing, windsurfing, and other beach fun around a bar (beer 500dr). Be sure to ask Argiris when he's planning his next beach party. On a quieter and more sophisticated note, check out the ruins of the ancient capital **Paleopolis** on the road to Andros Town, where remains of a the-ater and a stadium still stand. Roughly 2km southeast of Palaeokastro is the **Bay of Korthion,** with some of the finest swimming spots on Andros. The remnants of the **Castle of the Old Woman** are north of **Korthion.**

■ Andros Town (Chora ΧΩΡΑ)

A sophisticated village with striking neoclassical architecture, **Andros Town** is an intriguing destination. Built on a narrow peninsula, this town begins high above the water and slopes gently downhill to meet the sea. The wealthy Goulandris family has sponsored the construction of two amazing museums in town.

ORIENTATION AND PRACTICAL INFORMATION

The **post office** (tel. 22 260) where you can **exchange currency** (open Mon.-Fri. 7:30am-2pm) resides next to an open, airy square where **taxis** (tel. 22 171) queue. The **OTE** (tel. 22 099) is across from the central square on the left (open Mon.-Fri. 7:30am-3pm). The **National Bank** is on the left farther down, on the way to the water (open Mon.-Thurs. 8am-2pm, Fri. 8am-1:30pm), along with **pharmacies.** The **bus sta-tion** is coupled with a friendly restaurant, just to the right of the section of the town's main street which is closed to traffic. A full schedule is posted in the outdoor waiting area. Walk down the stairs next to the high blue domes of the church to find the town's center. The **police station** (tel. 22 300; open 24hr.) is at the far inland end of the main street. The **postal code** is 84500. The **telephone code** is 0282.

ACCOMMODATIONS

Rooms tend to be hard to find and expensive. **Hotel Egli** (tel. 22 303) fills up quickly; reservations are a good idea. (Singles 5000-8000dr; doubles 7000-10,000; triples 9000-12,000. Breakfast 1500-2000.) The expensive **Hotel Xenia** (tel. 22 270) lies down to the left (facing the water) from the main street, where the beach meets the upward slope. (Singles 6700-7700dr; doubles 9700-12,700dr; triples 12,500-15,500dr.) The numerous places on the beach get cheaper farther from the main strip. In high sea-son, doubles go for 5000-10,000dr.

SIGHTS

Following the main street downhill leads to a small square with outdoor cafes and a marble fountain. On the left is the **Archaeological Museum** (tel. 23 664), which has an excellent display on the Geometric village of Zagora and many later (through Byz-antine) marble relics, including a deservedly famous 2m-high statue of the messenger god Hermes (open Tues.-Sun. 8:30am-3pm; admission 500dr, students 250dr). Down the steps to the left of the square is the **Museum of Modern Art** (tel. 22 650), which prominently displays works by 20th-century Greek sculptor Michael Tombros. The weird noises from downstairs are not a mechanical failure but the clatter of the elec-tromagnetic "pieces" of the artist Takis. Don't miss the enormous temporary exhibi-tion space across the street a little farther downhill. Visiting exhibitions arrive every summer. One ticket is good for admission to both (open Mon and Thurs.-Sat. 10am-2pm and 6pm-8pm, Sun. 10am-2pm; admission 1000dr, students 500dr). Continuing straight through the square, through the white archway, you will find the free **Mari-time Museum of Andros** (open Mon. and Wed.-Sat. 10am-1pm and 6-8pm, Sun. 10am-1pm), which is somewhat of a letdown after the splendor of the first two museums. If it happens to be closed during open hours, the guard next door will give you a key. Proceed farther for a view of the walls of an off-island Venetian turret. After trekking around, head down the steps to the right of the square to a sandy beach.

MILOS ΜΗΛΟΣ

Much of Milos's claim to fame has been its association with celebrated artistic achievements—the Venus de Milo, Thucydides' Melin Dialogue, and the film *Bête Milo and Otis* are perhaps the most well-known. Today, Milos is recognized for the breathtaking beauty of its natural landscapes. Visitors must immerse themselves in the blue water of Paliochori, swim among the rock formations at Papatragas, wander the narrow alleys of Plaka, and embrace the warm hospitality of the Milians to fully appreciate the splendor of the Cycladic island.

▓ Adamas

This bustling port town is not the island's most attractive locale, but it can be a convenient base. Most of the island's nightlife and amenities are on Adamas's waterfront, and frequent buses can carry you to other parts of Milos.

ORIENTATION AND PRACTICAL INFORMATION

Across from the dock, a multilingual staff runs the **tourist information office** (tel. 22 445). Ask for brochures, maps, ferry and bus timetables, and a complete list of the island's rooms and hotels (open daily 10am-midnight). A helpful travel agency is **Milos Travel** (tel. 22 000, -200; fax 22 688), on the waterfront. The English-speaking staff sells most ferry tickets (open daily 9am-1:30am). The **National Bank** (tel. 22 077) is near the post office along the waterfront (open Mon.-Thurs. 8am-2pm, Fri. 8am-1:30pm). The **Olympic Airways** office, 25th Martiou St. (tel. 22 380; 22 381 at the airport), can also help with your travel needs (open Mon.-Fri. 8am-3pm). There are two to three daily Olympic Airways **flights** between Milos and Athens (12,700dr). The **bus stop** and **taxi stand** (tel. for both 22 219) are in a busy area on the waterfront. Taxis are available 24hr. A bus schedule (180dr) and a list of fixed taxi fares are posted.

From Milos, **ferries** follow a twisted and complex, yet well posted, schedule. The destinations are: Peiraias (2 per day, 8hr., 4600dr); Sifnos (2 per day, 1½hr., 1470dr); Serifos (2 per day, 3hr., 1575dr); Kithnos (1-3 per day, 2280dr); Kimolos (3 per week, 1290dr, and from Pollonia daily 700dr); Folegandros (3 per week, 1595dr); Sikinos (3 per week, 2530dr); Santorini (4 per week, 3100dr); Kassos (1 per week, 9hr., 4610dr); and Karpathos (10hr., 6140dr). Ferries also head to the Cretan ports of Agios Nikolaos (3 per week, 6hr., 4450dr) and Sitia (3 per week, 6½hr., 4670dr). You can rent a **moped** at **Speed** (tel. 23 254; 4000-7000dr per day), the shack next to the tourist office, or an automobile from the same spot (14,000-20,000dr per day with full insurance included (open daily 7:30am-10:30pm). The **pharmacy,** 25 Martiou St. (tel./fax 22 178, -011), is one block from the bus stop (open Mon.-Sat. 9am-2pm and 6-9:30pm). Along the waterfront you will find the **post office** (tel. 22 288; open Mon.-Fri. 7:30am-2pm), two doors down and on the second floor of the **port authority** (tel. 22 100; open 24hr.). The **postal code** is 84801 in Adamas, 84800 elsewhere on the island. The **telephone code** is 0287.

ACCOMMODATIONS

Although high-season prices may discourage the budget traveler, a little persistence in the side streets of Adamas will unearth more affordable private rooms. Few tourists look beyond the port for accommodations. To stay in Adamas, head along the main waterfront road and turn left after the supermarket on the left side of the fork in the road. Go straight to **Semirami's Hotel** (tel./fax 22 118, -117), where Petros and Nikos will welcome you to their comfortable establishment. Sit in the vine-covered garden and rest assured—you are in excellent hands. In August, reach up and help yourself to grapes (Sept.-June: doubles 6500dr; triples 7500dr; July-August: doubles 13,000dr; triples 15,000dr; breakfast 1000dr).

FOOD

While the two restaurants on the corner of the waterfront may not welcome English-speakers with open arms, the superb food makes up for it. Try the lamb cooked in lemon sauce (1350dr) or the broad beans (800dr) at **Kinigos** (tel. 22 349), around the first bend on the waterfront. **Floisvos** (tel. 22 275), before the bend in the waterfront, offers superb, cheap food (chicken and potatoes 1000dr). For an elegant dinner, ask for a table on the water at **Trapatseli's Restaurant,** a five-minute walk on the road to Achivadolimni Beach (yummy octopus in vinegar and olive oil 1250dr).

■ Around Milos

Six winding kilometers from Adamas, the town of **Plaka** rests upon the mountain tops. A **post office** (tel. 21 214) sits at the bus stop—follow the path leading left (open Mon-Fri. 7:30am-2pm). On the main road going through Plaka are an **OTE** (tel. 21 199; open 7:30am-3pm Mon.-Fri.), and farther down is the **medical center** (tel. 22 700, -01); ask the bus driver to let you off there. The Milos **police** (tel. 21 378) are in the square off the bus stop (open 24hr.). The terrace of the **Church of Panagia the Korfiatissa** leans into a view of verdant countryside and blue ocean only an arm's length away. Next door, the town's **Folk Museum** (tel. 21 292) has an eerie display of mannequins in household settings (open Tues.-Sat. 10am-2pm and 5-7pm, Sun. 10am-2pm; admission 400dr, students 200dr). Near the bus stop on the road to Tripiti, the **Archaeological Museum** (tel. 21 620) houses artifacts unearthed at Fylakopi, including the mesmerizing "Lady of Fylakopi" (open Tues.-Sun. 8:30am-3pm; admission 500dr, students 300dr, EU students free, seniors 300dr). For a truly spectacular view, head upward until you reach the **Panagia Thalassitra Monastery** at the top of the old castle. The 15-minute walk from the bus stop is more than worth it.

Accommodations in Plaka are predominantly rooms rented out by friendly families. One is of special note: Mr. and Mrs. Moraitis rent rooms in **Machi's House** (tel. 41 353), the hiding spot of the Venus de Milo after she was found in 1820 by farmer Theodnos Kentrotas. You can stay under the same roof for 8000-10,000dr.

Several *tavernas* line Plaka's main square near the police station. Walk away from this spot along the road to the catacombs and prepare instead to feast at the *taverna-ouzeri* **Plakiani Gonia** (tel. 21 024). The tomato balls are everything a vegetarian could desire (750dr). Add a serving of *pitarakia* (small cheese pies, 200dr) to complete an inexpensive meal.

South of Plaka, outside the small town of **Tripiti,** the **catacombs** (tel. 21 625), hewn into the cliff face, are the oldest site of Christian worship in Greece (open Mon.-Tues. and Thurs.-Sat. 8:45am-2pm; free). Archaeological finds in the ancient city on the hillside above the catacombs represent three periods of Greek history. You can still see part of the Dorian stone wall built between 1100 and 800 BC. A plaque marks the spot where the **Venus de Milo** was buried around 320 BC; she now resides in the Louvre. A well-preserved theater dating from the Roman occupation offers a riveting ocean view. A 20-minute walk downhill from Plaka on the road that goes through Tripiti will get you to the seaside village of **Klima.** This tiny fishing village, with its whitewashed houses looming over the waves, remains a beautiful representative of the Greek fishing community. **Pollonia** is a quiet fishing town with a pleasant beach. Boats run between Pollonia and the tiny island of **Kimolos** (2-3 per day). Kimolos Town and the port of Psathi are perfect places to unwind; few tourists venture there. Archaeology buffs will want to scramble among the ruins of **Filakopi,** 3km from Pollonia toward Adamas, where British excavations unearthed 3500-year-old frescoes (now displayed in the National Museum in Athens). There is a bus from Pollonia to **Papafragas** (every 45min., 15min., 220dr), where gangling rock formations surround a pool of clear blue water. Take the bus from Adamas and ask the driver to

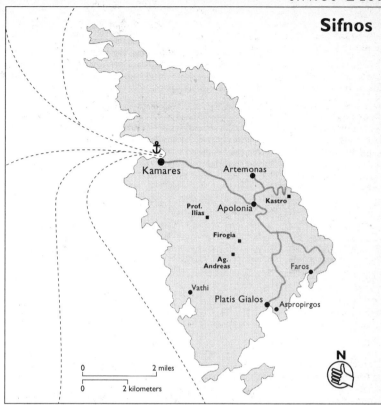

Sifnos

stop at Papafragas. Buses run frequently from Adamas to Plaka and Tripiti (every 30min., 15min., 230dr) and Pollonia (every 45min., 20min., 230dr).

There are several **beaches** with exceptional seascapes on Milos. Most are on the eastern half of the island, inaccessible by bus. Beaches of renown cling to the southeastern coast: **Paleochori** (6 buses per day, 25min., 350dr) and, northwest of Plaka, secluded **Plathiena.** Seven daily buses from Adamas journey to the more densely populated **Achivadolimni Beach** (15min., 350dr). On the southern coast, **Provatas** (8km from Adamas) is an ideal spot for a swim. Ask about the excursion boat at **Milos Travel.** This is an excellent way to see the beaches, fishing villages, lava formations of **Glaronissia,** and the enchanting blue waters of **Kleftiko** (tel. 22 000).

SIFNOS ΣΙΦΝΟΣ

In ancient times, Sifnos was renowned for the abundant gold, silver, and copper in its mines. Legend has it that each year the islanders, in order to placate Apollo, would send a solid-gold dancer to Delphi. One year, the locals decided to substitute a gold-plated egg. As a result of this insult, Apollo sank the Sifnian mines under the sea and cursed the land with infertility. Today, barrenness claims most of Sifnos's western half, where boats arrive. A short bus ride brings you to the whitewashed villages of Sifnos's eastern half. This side of Sifnos is affluent, with olive grove-gorged hillsides plunging down to rock caves and calm beaches. Tourism is more restrained than on most islands, and so accommodations are limited and simply not available in July and August. During high season your best bets are private rooms, camping, or reservations made several months in advance.

■ Kamares

Boats dock at Kamares, a magnificent harbor surrounded by formidable brown cliffs which stand in fierce contrast to the gentle emerald sea. Here you can secure a room, swim, dine, and meander into the shops featuring local ornate **pottery**; look for κεραμικο (ceramic) signs throughout the village.

ORIENTATION AND PRACTICAL INFORMATION

Just opposite the ferry dock, the **Community Information Office** (tel. 31 977) helps find rooms and decipher boat and bus schedules (hours depend on ferry schedule— someone will be here to greet you when you dock). The **port authority** (tel. 33 617) located next door has sea travel information (open 24 hr.). A visit to the **Aegean Thesaurus Travel Agency** (tel. 33 151, fax 32 190), located along the waterfront as you walk from the dock to town, almost always pays off. The friendly, English-speaking staff **exchanges currency,** finds accommodations, stores luggage (200dr, no time limit), organizes excursions around the island, and sells maps (250dr; open daily 9:30am-10pm, or until the last ferry arrives). From Sifnos, **ferries** head to: Peiraias (1-2 per day, 6hr., 4120dr); Milos (1-2 per day, 1½hr., 1600dr); Kimolos (1 per day except Sun., 1½hr., 1530dr); Serifos (1-2 per day except Fri., 1hr., 1500dr); Kithnos (1-2 per day except Fri., 2½hr., 2000dr); Folegandros (1-3 per week, 45min., 1620dr); Sikinos (1-3 per week, 2½hr., 1930dr); Santorini (1-3 per week, 4hr., 2920dr); Syros (2 per week, 4½hr., 2075dr); and Ios (1-3 per week, 3hr., 2610dr). There is weekly **hydrofoil** service to: Paros (1hr., 2030dr); Mykonos (1½hr., 6130dr); Tinos (2hr., 6245dr); and Rafina (6hr., 7350dr). Prices rise during high season. From Kamares, buses go to Apollonia at least every hour from 7:30am-10:30pm (190dr).

ACCOMMODATIONS

During high season, you are unlikely to find a budget hotel room; try private rooms, either by following "Room to Let" signs or by asking at one of the many waterfront *tavernas*. Off-season prices are roughly 1000-2000dr lower. (Doubles 6500-8500dr; triples 8000-11,000dr.) In Kamares, **Hotel Stavros** (tel. 32 383, 31 641; fax 31 709) has clean, pleasant rooms with baths, many with panoramic views of the harbor's beach. Stavros and his English wife also offer travel services and car rental. (Doubles 10,000dr; triples 12,000dr in high season.) For tighter budgets, there are also rear rooms with shared baths (3000dr). **Hotel Kiki** (tel. 32 329; fax 31 453) farther along the waterfront road toward Apollonia, offers spotless rooms, each with a bath, television, TV, and balcony overlooking the harbor. (Doubles 7500dr; triples 9000dr; prices roughly 40% higher in July and August. Breakfast 800dr.) Free-lance camping on Sifnos is illegal, but **Maki's Camping** (tel./fax 32 366) lies across the road from the beach in Kamares (open May-Oct.; 1000dr per person). Other campsites in more secluded parts of the island include calm, clean **Platis Yialos Camping** (tel. 31 786), amid trees and stone walls, a 10-minute walk inland from the Yialos Sq. bus stop (open July-mid-Sept.; 1000dr per person).

FOOD AND ENTERTAINMENT

Each *taverna* offers food of roughly the same quality and price, but many have seaside seating. For Greek food with a charming twist, try the waterfront **Kamares Ouzeri** (tel. 32 398). Among the specialties prepared by the English-speaking chef and staff are the stuffed chicken (1400dr), the shrimp *saganaki* (1700dr), and *tzatziki* (500dr). On the island of Sifnos, chick-peas are a local specialty found in a soup called *revithada* (700dr; served only on Sundays). It gets polished off early, so try it for lunch. There are also several **groceries** and **bakeries** that sell the local almond cookie delicacy, *amigdaloto*. The nightlife in Kamares is centered around two bars less than 100m apart. Closer to the dock, **Collage** (tel. 32 351) is on the second floor above a supermarket. Look for the sign hanging over an outdoor terrace. Enjoy freshly squeezed fruit juices (800dr), non-alcoholic cocktails (800-1000dr), and their alcoholic counterparts (1300-1500dr) while gazing over the water (open daily 11am-3am). Farther along the road, **Mobilize** (tel. 32 357) attracts a later crowd and keeps them dancing until sunrise. The DJ will accommodate requests while you enjoy the bar (open daily 10pm-6am).

■ Apollonia

Apollonia, the island's capital, serves as the island's central travel hub. Buses to **Kamares** (10min., 190dr) stop in the square in front of the post office, while those to villages and beaches like **Kastro** (190dr) and **Plati Yialos** (370dr) stop around the corner near the Hotel Anthousa. Buses run to all three at least once every hour.

Just about everything you need to conduct your important business stands in a row along the main square. **Aegean Thesaurus** (tel. 32 190, 31 145; open 9:30am-10pm), near the post office, is your source for **currency exchange, luggage storage** (200dr, no time limit), accommodation assistance, bus and ferry schedules, and island information packs (500dr). The neighboring **National Bank** (tel. 31 237) has an **ATM** (open Mon.-Thurs. 8am-2pm, Fri. 8am-1:30pm). There is an **OTE** (tel. 31 215, 33 399) a few doors down on the road back to Kamares (open 7:30am-3:10pm). From the other bus stop near Hotel Anthousa, head up the road to Artemonas to find the **medical center** (tel. 31 315) on your left and the **police station** (tel. 31 210) in a small white building on your right. The bus from Kamares drops you off at the main square; at the top is the **pharmacy** (tel. 31 833; open Mon.-Fri. 8:30am-1pm, 5:30-8pm; Sat. 10am-1pm). Next door is the **post office** (open Mon.-Fri. 7:30am-2pm). The **postal code** is 84003. The **telephone code** is 0284.

Summer vacancies are rare in Apollonia. Prices are generally lower in the off season. The **Hotel Sofia** (tel. 31 238) is just off the square; head up the wide paved road from the main square until you see it on your left above supermarket Sofia. Reservations should be made a month in advance (singles 6500dr; doubles 9000dr; triples 10,500dr; all rooms with private bath). **Hotel Anthoussa** (tel. 32 220), framed by trees and located above the pastry shop, has luxurious accommodations with daily cleaning service. Reservations are needed several months in advance (doubles 8000dr; triples 12,000dr; each 4000dr more in July and August).

Restaurants are excellent and not as expensive as their beautiful exteriors might suggest. The better *tavernas* are along the path across from the police. The restaurant at the **Sifnos Hotel** serves the island specialty—chick-peas served with olive oil and lemon, cooked all night in special ovens in another town. This delicacy is gone by dinner, so try it for Sunday's lunch. The fricasé is also a delicious choice—goat and rice covered with greens and baked in a ceramic pot (1800dr).

For Apollonia's nightlife, stroll along the street behind the museum. **Botzi** (tel. 32 358) a bar and coffee house, is likely to catch your eye or ear. Lit by candles that fill both levels and the outside terrace, this bar moves from folk music to jazz, then funk, as the night progresses. A beer will set you back 500dr when the place is relatively empty, and 1000dr when full. The cocktails are worth the extra 500dr, especially the carefully prepared and potent sangria. Drink slowly—the bar closes at 6am.

The **Museum of Popular Art** in the square features hand-woven laces, traditional dress, local pottery (still an important industry), and several unusual paintings. Telephone 31 341 to set up an appointment with the museum guide; otherwise, the museum has sporadic hours. Admission 200dr.

■ Around Sifnos

Travel in Sifnos is easy with the assistance of the map available at any kiosk (250dr). Pack some picnic treats to nibble as you go through Apollonia's adjacent hillside villages. The quiet but expansive village of **Artemonas,** a 10-minute walk from Apollonia, has a magnificent view and several fine mansions built by refugees from Alexandria. The enchanting village of **Kastro** is 3km east of Apollonia and can be reached by bus (15min., 190dr). This cluster of beautiful whitewashed houses and narrow streets rests on a mountain top overlooking the sea. You may find the tiny **archaeological museum** while walking through the former capital's streets (open

Tues.-Sun. 11am-2:30pm; free). There are no hotels, but ask around for rooms. Walk left at the base of the hill for the monastery of **Panagia Poulati.** The smooth alcove below reputedly offers the best swimming on the island.

To the south, **Faros** has several popular beaches. **Fasolou,** the island's only **nude beach,** is tucked away beneath promontories farther east. Continue west along the rocky hillside path past a dilapidated mine to reach a better beach at **Apokofto.** You can also reach Apokofto by getting off the bus to Platis Yialos at the Chrysopigi stop. At the far end of this bay, you will see the striking **Panagia Chrysopigi.** A bridge connects this 17th-century monastery's rocky islet to the mainland. The monastery (tel. 31 482) has rooms to let; make reservations about two months in advance (doubles 4000dr). Forty days after Easter, the two-day festival of Analipsos is celebrated at Chrysopigi. If the walk to Chrysopigi works up an appetite, the restaurant on the beach to the left of the monastery (tel. 71 295) serves authentic Sifnian cuisine. Mr. Lebesi prepares *mastelo* (lamb cooked in wine and spices, 1270dr) and *kaparosalata* (a salad of caper greens, 750dr; open daily noon-11pm). To go to Chrysopigi, take the bus to Platis Yialos and ask the driver to let you off at the monastery, then walk along the descending dirt path and cement stairs for 10 minutes. Allot twice as much time to get back to the main road.

SERIFOS ΣΕΡΙΦΟΣ

Serifos, acquiring its name from the ancient Greek word for "stony," owes its existence to the Gorgon Medusa. According to Greek mythology, Perseus, the son of Zeus and Danae, accomplished the impossible task assigned to him by King Polydictes, who sought to occupy Perseus while he occupied himself with Danae. Upon returning to Serifos and learning of the King's forceful advances, Perseus turned King Polydictes and his royal court into stone by showing them the severed head of Medusa—the very prize he had been sent to retrieve. Ravaged by a once thriving mining industry, the barren terrain contrasts sharply with the whitewashed houses of Chora that spill over the slopes of the island's highest mountain peak.

■ Livadi

All boats dock in Livadi. Don't let the single waterfront strip dismay you—you will find plenty to see, hear, taste, and smell on this concentrated main street.

ORIENTATION AND PRACTICAL INFORMATION

An island map which lists useful telephone numbers is available at kiosks (300dr). The **Milos Express Office** (tel. 52 135), located in the center of the waterfront strip next to a supermarket, offers hydrofoil and ferry tickets and schedules in English (open daily 9am-1pm and 7pm-midnight). The **police** (tel. 51 300) are up the narrow steps marked with a large Greek flag, less than 100m from the arrival dock. The **Ionian Bank,** equipped with an **ATM,** is hard to miss along the waterfront (open Mon.-Thurs. 8am-2pm, Fri. 8am-1:30pm). Serifos can be reached by regular **ferries** from Peiraias and other Western Cyclades, as well as occasional boats from Paros, Syros, Ios, and Santorini. From Serifos, ferries travel to: Peiraias (1-3 per day, 4½hr., 3620dr); Kithnos (4 per week, 1½hr., 1800dr); Sifnos (1-3 per day, 45min., 1480dr); Milos (1-3 per day, 2hr., 1665dr); Kimolos (3 per week, 2hr., 1740dr); Folegrandros (3 per week, 3hr., 1570dr); Sikinos (3 per week, 5hr., 2490dr); Ios (2 per week, 5½hr., 2800dr); and Santorini (1 per week, 6½hr., 2500dr). High-speed **flying dolphins** connect weekly to: Rafina (3½hr., 7380dr); Paros (1hr., 4000dr); and Mykonos (1½hr., 5800dr). For schedules and more information, contact **Krinas Travel** (tel. 51 488; fax 51 073). Farther along the waterfront, look for the green cross for the **pharmacy** (tel. 51 482, -205; open Mon.-Fri. 9:30am-2pm and 6-9:30pm; Sat. 10am-2pm). For **taxis,** call 51 245 or 51 435. The **telephone code** is 0281. The **postal code** is 84005.

ACCOMMODATIONS

Don't go to Serifos expecting people to aggressively offer rooms at the port. Instead, look for pensions on the waterfront, on the street parallel to the waterfront road, and on the road that bears left from the Milos Express office heading toward the campgrounds (doubles 5000-9000dr, depending on season and amenities). Arrive early or call the tourist police for information about reservations. Prices are 2000-4000dr less in winter. **Hotel Serifos Beach** (tel. 51 209, -468) is a block back from the beach, but easy to find by virtue of its large blue sign on the main waterfront road. Away from the main strip, rooms are comfortable and quiet (doubles 10,000-12,000dr; triples 12,000-14,400dr; breakfast 1000dr). **Hotel Areti** (tel. 51 479, -107; fax 51 547), on the first left as you step off the ferry, is a whitewashed building with blue shutters. With a backyard terrace and private balconies for each room, the hotel offers a beautiful view of the harbor. (Open April-Oct. Singles 6500-9500dr; doubles 8000-12,000dr; triples 9500-14,500dr. Prices vary seasonally.) **Coralli Camping** (tel. 51 500; fax 51 073), at the far end of the beach, is a 10-minute jaunt from the harbor. The campground has a bar, restaurant, and minimarket. (Doubles 12,000dr; triples with bath 14,000dr; quads 16,000dr. Breakfast 1000dr. Camping open May-Oct. 1300dr per person; 650dr per small tent; 1100dr per large tent.)

FOOD AND ENTERTAINMENT

One of the islanders' favorites for a delicious, well- prepared meal is **Mokkas** (tel. 51 242), one of the first *tavernas* along the waterfront. Come here for locally grown ingredients and deliciously prepared fresh seafood. Part owner Christina, herself a vegetarian, ensures that fellow herbivores have several enticing options to choose from. Try the stuffed tomatoes (800dr) or the *fasolakia* (green beans with tomato sauce and olive oil, 900dr). To find **Margarita's** (tel. 51 321), walk to the very end of the town beach (to the right facing inland) and over the little cement bridge. Do not despair if it looks like you are headed into uncharted territory—you're getting warmer. Look left for scattered tables, mismatched chairs, loose chickens, ducks, donkeys, sheep, inchworms, and other representatives of the animal kingdom. Preparations take time, but you will be rewarded with fresh vegetables and fish at incredibly low prices (eggplant 400dr, fish 800dr). For an inexpensive and filling meal, choose **Stamadis.** You can get fresh fruit at the **Marinos** market (tel. 51 279), on the waterfront past the main stretch of *tavernas* and shops (open daily 8am-2pm and 4:30pm-midnight). If you feel like unwinding after a hard day at the beach, the places to be are **Praxis,** in the middle of the waterfront, and **Metalio,** at the start of the road to Chora (beer 1000dr).

■ Around Serifos

Not surprisingly, the beaches here are a prime attraction. Closest to Livadi is the relatively crowded **Livadakia** beach (a 10-minute walk on the inland road to the right of the dock; there's a sign). A two-hour walk past Livadakia Beach leads to the adjoining sandy havens of **Koutalas, Ganema** and **Vaya Beach. Psili Ammos,** perhaps the island's best beach, is a 45-minute walk past Livadakia Beach in the other direction. **Karavi,** over the hill from Livadakia Beach, away from Livadi Harbor, is a popular **nude beach,** although many enjoy it clothed.

The northern part of the island offers small traditional villages, scattered churches, several monasteries, and traces of ruins. The rest of the island is fairly inaccessible without a car or moped, a map, and excellent driving skills. For **moped rental,** call **Blue Bird** (tel. 51 511; 3000dr per day). By car or moped, visit the **Monastery of the Taxiarchs,** 10km beyond Chora towards the village of Galini. Built in 1400 AD on a site where a Cypriot icon mysteriously appeared (and to which it returns whenever removed), the monastery houses an Egyptian lantern and several Russian relics, in addition to the enigmatic icon. Try to visit close to sunset in order to meet the lone monk, who has lived there for 20 years. Lucky visitors may be treated to coffee and cherries. Call 51 027 in the morning or afternoon to arrange a visit.

Dodecanese
ΔΩΔΕΚΑΝΗΣΑ

The Dodecanese are the best example of a cultural mosaic among the Greek islands. A succession of distinct ruling empires has left its mark on this region, and varying architecture keeps visitors guessing as to what they will stumble across around the corner.

After the Dorians settled here in ancient times, the region was captured in 1309 by the Knights of the Order of St. John, who remained until the Ottomans took control in 1512. Despite over three centuries of Ottoman influence, Greek culture and tradition persisted in the islands, due in part to the effects of underground schools organized precisely for this purpose. Despite their leadership role in motivating others to join in the 1821 Greek revolution, the Dodecanese did not immediately join the new Greek nation upon independence. The islands were then subject to a century of Italian control followed by German occupation in WWII.

Today, the layers of Dodecanese history are most clearly evident in the wide range of art and architecture that are characteristic of the islands. Attracted to this rare display of heterogeneity, tourists arrive daily by the hordes, despite the distance from mainland Greece. The islands' proximity to the Turkish coast also make them popular points of departure for visiting Turkey.

RHODES (RODOS) ΡΟΔΟΣ

Rhodes is the undisputed tourist capital of the Dodecanese. While the resort towns suffer from the maladies of commercialism, the sheer size of the island allows the interior regions, and many of the smaller coastal towns, to retain a sense of serenity. Sandy beaches stretch along the east coast, jagged cliffs skirt the west, and green mountains fill the interior where villagers continue their centuries-old traditions. Kamiros, Ialyssos, and Lindos show the clearest evidence of the island's classical past, while medieval fortresses slumber in Rhodes and Monolithos. Although modern hotels dominate city skylines and the major shopping streets and New Town beaches are crowded, soothing strolls are still possible in smaller villages and along the cobblestone streets of the Old Town.

■ City of Rhodes ΡΟΔΟΣ

Founded in 408 BC by the unification of three city-states, the city of Rhodes has served as the island's capital for over 20 centuries. In terms of regal majesty, the city knows no equal in all of Greece. The exceptional harbor, detailed architecture, and intricate layout, all designed by the architect Hippodamos, made Rhodes one of the ancient world's most beautiful cities.

The Knights of St. John left the most visible legacy on the city. The breathtaking palace and the grand fortress that surrounds the Old Town give the city a medieval flair. Lose yourself in the maze of narrow cobblestone paths that weave under ancient archways and delight in the prospect of discovering the city's hidden treasures.

ORIENTATION AND PRACTICAL INFORMATION

The city is divided into two districts: the **New Town,** stretching to the north and west, and the **Old Town,** below it, encapsulated within the medieval fortress walls. There are also three adjacent harbors. Most boat traffic uses the **Mandraki,** the New Town's waterfront. Private yachts, hydrofoils, and excursion boats dock here. Inter-

Rhodes

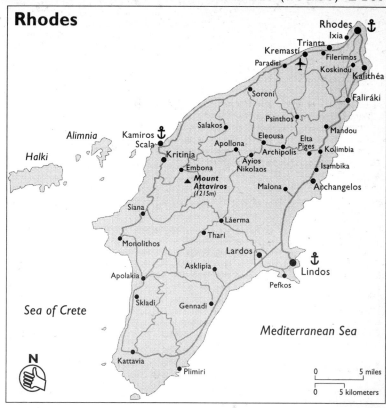

Rhodes ⚓
Ixia
Trianta
Kremastí
Paradísi
Filerimos
Koskinou
Kalithéa
Soroni
Faliráki
Psinthos
Salakos
Mandou
Alimnia
Kamiros ⚓
Scala
Eleousa
Elta
Piges
Apollona
Archipolis
Kolimbia
Halki
Kritinia
Ayios
Nikolaos
Embona
Isambika
▲ *Mount
Attaviros*
(1215m)
Malona
Archangelos
Siana
Láerma
Thari
Monolithos
Lardos
Asklipia
⚓
Apolakia
Lindos
Pefkos
Sea of Crete
Skladi
Gennadi
Mediterranean Sea
N
Kattavia
Plimiri
0   5 miles
0   5 kilometers

national and most domestic ferries use the **Commercial Harbor** outside the Old Town. **Acandia,** the harbor below it, provides a port for cargo ships. Beaches are located north beyond the Mandraki and along the city's west coast. **Rimini Square,** beneath the fortress' turrets at the junction between the Old and New Towns, has the city's tourist office, both bus stations, and a taxi stand. To get here from the Mandraki, walk to the base of the vase-shaped Mandraki and head one block inland along the park on the New Town side.

Tourist Office: (tel. 35 945) The tiny yellow building in Rimini Sq. Bus, boat, and excursion schedules, accommodations, and **currency exchange.** Open Mon.-Sat. 8am-9pm, Sun. 8am-3pm.

Greek National Tourist Office (EOT): (tel. 23 255, -655) At the corner of Makariou and Papagou St. in the New Town. Walk up Papagou several blocks from Rimini Sq. Extremely helpful resource for all travel needs. Open Mon.-Fri. 7:30am-3pm.

Budget Travel: Castellania Travel Service (tel. 75 860, -2; fax 75 861), in Hippocrates Sq. at the intersection of Sokratous and Aristotelous in the Old Town. Low prices on international travel, USIT ticketing, **ISIC** and **GO25 cards** issued (2600dr), international telephones, free **luggage storage,** the works. Open in summer daily 8:30am-11:30pm, in winter 8am-1pm and 4-8pm. **Triton Holidays,** 9 Plastira St. (tel. 21 690), in the New Town, is also well-regarded.

Consulates: The Voice of America (tel. 24 731), southeast of the city, just past Sigourou St. Handles consular matters, especially emergencies. Open Mon.-Fri. 8am-4:30pm. A **British** Vice-Consul is available Mon.-Sat. 8am-2pm through **Lloyd's Travel Bureau,** #23 25th Martiou St. (tel. 27 306, -247). **Turkish Consulate,** 10 Iroon Polytechniou St. (tel. 23 362, 24 603). Open Mon.-Fri. 8am-1pm.

Banks: Ionian Bank, 4 Symi Sq. (tel. 27 434), offers **currency exchange.** Open Mon.-Thurs. 8am-2pm, Fri. 8am-1:30pm, and Sat. 8:30am-1pm. The **National Bank** has an office in Museum Sq. with an **ATM** outside. Open Mon.-Thurs. 8am-2pm and Fri. 8am-1:30pm. In the New Town, the **National Bank** (tel. 27 031) in Kyprou Sq. also has **currency exchange** and an **ATM.** Open Mon.-Thurs. 8am-2pm, Fri. 8am-1:30pm, and Sat. 9am-1pm. Many other banks in New Town, but few in Old Town.

American Express: Rhodos Tours Ltd., 23 Ammohostou St., P.O. Box 252 (tel. 24 022). Open Mon.-Fri. 9am-1:30pm and 5-8:30pm, Sat. 7:30am-3pm.

Flights: Olympic Airways, 9 Ierou Lohou St. (tel. 24 571), near the central OTE. Open Mon.-Fri. 7:30am-9pm. Call 24 555 for reservations or 92 839 for the airport counter. The **airport** (tel. 91 771) is on the west coast, 17km from town, near Paradisi. Public buses run here 7am-midnight (1 per hr., 300dr). Arrive at least 1hr. before scheduled departure. **Domestic flights** to Rhodes are usually booked at least 2 weeks in advance. Flights to: Athens (5 per day, 24,600dr); Kos (3 per week, 11,000dr); Karpathos (4 per day, 12,500dr); Kassos (1 per day, 12,500dr); Kastellorizo (1 per day, 10,600dr); Thessaloniki (2 per week, 31,600dr); Crete (4 per week, 21,600dr); Santorini (4 per week, 22,600dr); and Mykonos (3 per week, 22,600dr). Off-season departures are less frequent and subject to change.

Ferries: Daily ferries to: Peiraias (2-3 per day, 14hr., 8305dr); Kos (2-3 per day, 3255dr); Kalymnos (1-2 per day, 4020dr); Leros (7 per week, 4375dr); Patmos (6 per week, 5210dr); Symi (4 per week, 1545dr); Tilos (4 per week, 2645dr); Nisyros (4 per week, 2685dr); Kastellorizo (3 per week, 3750dr); Thessaloniki (1 per week, 13,150dr); Chalkis (1 per week, 1945dr); Astypalea (2 per week, 4565dr); Samos (1 per week, 6110dr); Mitilini (1 per week, 7105dr); Alexandroupolis (1 per week, 10,665dr); and Limnos (1 per week, 8565dr). Two ferries per week sail to Peiraias via: Karpathos (4060dr); Kassos (4780dr); Crete (5970dr); Santorini (5910dr); Ios (5065dr); and Paros (5860dr). **Excursions** to Kos (10,000dr round-trip) and Symi (3000dr round-trip) stop at the monastery of Panormitis. **International ferries** head to: Limassol, Cyprus (2 per week, 17hr., 19,000dr in low season); Haifa, Israel (2 per week, 36hr., 31,500dr in low season); and Marmaris, Turkey (10,000dr).

Flying Dolphins: Hydrofoil service connects Rhodes with the northeast Aegean islands, Turkey, and the Dodecanese. To: Symi (2950dr); Tilos (5475dr); Nisyros (5555dr); Kos (6705dr); Kalymnos (8220dr); Astypalea (9315dr); Samos (12,035dr); Patmos (10,335dr); Leros (9075dr); Chalki (3685dr); Ikaria (11,845dr); and Fourni (11,845dr). Check travel agencies for current schedules.

Buses: Stations lie on opposite sides of Papagou St. at Rimini Sq. **East** served by KTEL. Schedules vary; call 27 706 or 24 268 for current details. To: Lindos (12 per day, 900dr); Faliraki (16 per day, 300dr); Archangelos (14 per day, 550dr); Kolimbia Beach (9 per day, 550dr); and Afandou (13 per day, 350dr). **West** served by RODA. For information, call 26 300. To: Paradissi Airport (24 per day, 300dr); Ancient Kamiros (2-3 per day, 870dr); Monolithos (1 per day, 1300dr); and Petaloudes (2 per day, 900dr).

Taxis: (tel. 27 666) In Rimini Sq. Radio taxis also available (tel. 64 712, -34, -56, -78, -90). Check the price list posted for destinations outside town. Open 24hr.

Road Emergencies: Dial 104.

Moped Rental: Mandar Moto, 2 Dimosthenous (tel. 34 576), in the Old Town. Take Sokratous to Hippocratous Sq. and continue on Aristotelous until Evraion Martiron Sq. Rentals 2500-4000dr per day. Open daily 8am-11pm.

Bike Rental: Mike's Motor Club, 23 I. Kazouli St. in the New Town (tel. 37 420). Mountain bikes 1500dr per day. Cobblestones in the Old Town and maniacal drivers in the New Town make roads here generally unsafe. Open daily 8am-8pm.

English Bookstore: Kostas Tomaras Bookstore, 5-7 Soph. Venizelou St. (tel. 32 055), in the New Town. Open Mon.-Fri. 8am-1pm and 5-9pm, Sat. 8am-2pm.

Libraries: Catholic Academy Library, 7 Dragoumi St. (tel. 20 254), off Diakou in the New Town. English books on the island's history and a few novels. Open Mon.-Tues. and Thurs.-Fri. 9am-2:30pm, Wed. 9am-2:30pm and 5:30-8pm. The library in the **Municipal Cultural Centre** (tel. 37 144), Rodiaki Epavli-King's Garden, has an English section. Open Mon.-Fri. 7:30am-2:30pm and 6-9pm, Sat. 8am-noon. The **Municipal Library,** 1 Aristotelous St. (tel. 24 448), in the Old Town. Open Mon.-Tues. and Thurs.-Fri. 9am-2pm, Wed. 9am-2pm and 5-7:30pm.

Laundromat: Lavromatik, #32 28th Octovriou St. (tel. 24 161), between Dragoumi and Fanouraki in the New Town. Self-service. Wash, dry, and soap 1800dr. Open Mon.-Fri. 9am-1:30pm and 4:30-8pm.

Public Toilets: Strategic locations in the New Town include Rimini Sq., next to the tourist office and the new market. In the Old Town, search out facilities at Orfeos and Sokratous St. Free, but B.Y.O.T.P. (Bring Your Own Toilet Paper).

Public Baths: Hamam (tel. 27 739), Arionos Sq. in the Old Town. Not your typical shower, but a good way to get clean. Single sex. 500dr. Open Tues. 1-7pm and Wed.-Sat. 11am-7pm.

Hospital: (tel. 22 222, 25 555) Erithrou Stavrou St. off El. Venizelou. Open for emergencies 24hr. **Visitor's clinic** open daily 5-9pm. Be prepared to wait for medical attention; patients line the corridors. **Medical Emergencies:** Dial 100.

Police: (tel. 23 294) Ethelondon Dodekanission St., 1 block behind the post office. Open 24hr. **Lost and found** open Mon.-Fri. 8am-2pm. The **tourist police** (tel. 27 423, 23 329), in the GNTO building, speak English. The **port authority** (tel. 22 220, 28 888), or Central Harbor Master, on Mandraki just left of the post office. Complete boat schedules. Open 24hr.

Post Office: Main branch (tel. 22 212, 34 873), on Mandraki St., along the waterfront and next to the Bank of Greece. Open Mon.-Fri. 7am-8pm, Sat. 7:30am-3pm, and Sun. 9am-2pm. **Parcel service** 7:30am-2pm. **Poste Restante** window takes a lunch hour. Also a **mobile branch** in the Old Town on Orfeos, near the Palace of the Grand Masters. From Museum Sq., head down Ipoton. Open Mon.-Fri. 7:30am-2pm. **Postal Code:** 85100.

OTE: 91 Amerikis St. (tel. 24 599), at the corner of 25th Martiou St. in New Town. Open 6am-11pm. **Telephone Code:** 0241 (for the northern half of the island), 0244 (below Kolymbia on the east), and 0246 (below Kalavarda on the west).

ACCOMMODATIONS

Old Town

Pensions are scattered about the narrow pebbled paths of the Old Town, the preferred resting place for most travelers. Low prices here inevitably mean low luxury, so prepare yourself. Winding streets are inconsistently named; bite the bullet and buy a map. Off-season prices run roughly 20-40% less than those in summer.

Hotel Andreas, 28 Omirou St. (tel. 34 156; fax 74 285). Rooms with bunk-beds are ideal for families. Roof terrace and bar hosts barbecue three times a month. Friendly, fun atmosphere. Doubles 6000dr, with bath 8000dr; triples with bath 10,000dr; quads with bath 12,000dr.

Pension Olympos, 56 Ag. Fanouriou St. (tel./fax 33 567). From Hippocrates Sq., go up Socratous St. and take a left on Ag. Fanouriou St. Look for the archway covered in pots and flowers. Spotless rooms with private baths and common kitchen facilities. Doubles 8000dr; triples 10,000dr.

Minos Pension, 5 Omirou St. (tel. 31 813). Immaculate rooms with clean common baths, but a little pricey for shared bathroom facilities. Doubles 8000dr; triples 10,000dr. Breakfast 900dr.

Rooms above Mango Bar, 3 Dorieos Sq. (tel. 24 877, 28 324). From Sokratous, take Ag. Fonouriou up to Dorleos Sq. to reach sparkling rooms above a bar with the cheapest draft beer in town (450dr per pint). All rooms with private bath. Singles 3000dr; doubles 5000dr; triples 7000dr. Breakfast 800dr.

Hotel Spot, 21 Perikleous St. (tel. 34 737). Newly renovated rooms with bathrooms that gleam like polished teeth. Doubles 8500dr.

Pension Sofia, 27 Aristofanous St. (tel. 36 181, 30 990), in Harritou Sq. From Sokratous St., turn onto Apellou St. south, pass the Sydney Hotel and Kavo D'Oro restaurant, then cross the parking lot to the right and look for the sign. Rooms have private baths. Doubles 6000dr; triples 7000dr.

Sydney Hotel, 41 Apellou St. (tel. 25 965), across from Kavo D'Oro. Wood-paneled rooms with bath. Doubles 9000dr; triples 11,000dr.

> **Hotel Stathis,** 60 Omirou St. (tel. 24 357). French and English spoken. Nightly folk music from nearby theater. Noon check-out. Laundry 950dr. Dorm beds 2500dr; singles 5000dr; doubles 7000dr. Breakfast 500dr.

New Town

The New Town is rather charmless, with its large apartment buildings and commercialized atmosphere; however, it is near the closest swimmable beach and has more than ample nightlife. Expensive hotels overshadow the coast, but affordable pensions can be found along the narrow streets of Rodiou, Dilberaki, Kathopouli, and Amarandou. Information about New Town pensions is available at the tourist office.

> **Hotel Capitol,** 65-67 Dilberaki St. (tel. 62 016, 74 154), has quiet, spacious rooms with private showers in a house once inhabited by Rhodes's mayor. Breakfast included. Singles 7000dr; doubles 8000dr; triples 12,000dr; quads 14,000dr.
>
> **Marieta Pension,** #52 28 October St. (tel. 36 396), is a charming, family-owned pension in a 60-year-old traditional villa. Rooms have ceilings and private baths. Doubles 8000dr; triples 12,000dr.
>
> **Marika's Rooms to Let** (tel. 21 910), on the corner of Diakou St. and Kodrigtonos. Clean doubles with private bath and shared kitchen facilities are 5000dr.

FOOD AND ENTERTAINMENT

Old Town

The Old Town's crowded thoroughfares are lined with *tavernas,* but the food tends to be mediocre, the waiters aggressive, and the prices high. Good food is hard to find; if you do, it will be on back streets.

A delicious exception is **Yiannis,** 41 Apellou St. (tel. 36 535), just off Sokratous. The food is prepared with care and the portions are huge (*stifado* 1400dr, *moussaka* 1000dr, and *Elliniko* plate with enough food for 3 people 1700dr). For excellent Italian food, go south on Pıthagora from Hippocrates Sq., turn right at Platonos, and left at a small square onto a larger one to find **Mediterraneo,** 29 Eschylou St. Tasty spaghetti smothered in tomato and basil is 1000dr, and vegetarian pizza is 1500dr.

The **Folk Dance Theater** (tel. 29 085), on Andronikou St. in the Old Town, stages hokey performances featuring dances and songs from all over Greece (shows May-Oct. Mon., Wed., and Fri. 9:10pm; admission 3000dr, students 1500dr). Evening **sound and light shows** (tel. 36 795) at the palace give an account of the Ottoman siege of the city during the Crusader occupation. It sounds enthralling, but don't expect much. The entrance is on Papagou St. in Rimini Sq. (English shows Mon.-Tues. 9:15pm; Wed. and Fri.-Sat. 10:15pm; Thurs. 11:15pm; admission 1000dr, students 600dr.) **St. Francis Church** (tel. 23 605), at the intersection of Dimokratias and Filellinon St., echoes with organ recitals Wednesday nights at 9pm. Check with the tourist office for performances in the **ancient theater** near Monte Smith. The **National Theatre** (tel. 29 678), off the Mandraki next to the town hall, stages occasional winter productions. **Rodon,** near the National Theatre, shows both new flicks and subtitled classics (daily shows at 8:30 and 10:30pm; admission 800dr).

Also in the Old Town, **Theater Bar** (tel. 27 887) has a mellow atmosphere where you can sip 1500dr cocktails to the sounds of acid jazz. Shake your booty at **Amazon,** a hoppin' disco with fountains, tropical waterfalls and a light show, or **Scorpio** (tel. 77 747), with a similar, more rock-oriented set up. **La Scala** is one of a cluster of discos near the beach outside of town (just after the intersection with Kennedy St.). At **Grand Master's Inn,** 64 Sokratous St. in the Old Town, two knights in armor greet guests from the balcony.

New Town

In the New Town, you will be overwhelmed by flashing fast food signs and Wendy's ~~rger billboards. Head to the New Market next to the bus station for fresh fruit. **Pan-**
~~**alth Foods,** 1 L. Fanouraki (tel. 35 877), has grains, pasta, vitamins, skin care
~~even Birkenstocks for the true yuppie traveler (open Mon.-Fri. 9am-2pm

and 5-9pm, Sat. 9am-2pm). For dessert, grab a crepe (600dr) at **La Case de la Crepe,** 6 Sokratous St. (tel. 21 698).

According to the effusive *Rodos News,* Rhodes has more discos per capita than London, Paris, New York, or Berlin. The piasters party in the New Town—most places start shaking around 11pm and don't fizzle out until 3am. Crowds flock to the clubs near the intersection of Diakou and Venizelou and along Orfanidou. Popular places have expensive drinks, while empty bars will cut deals. Orfanidou St. is referred to as **Bar Street.** The five-minute walk from end to end will give you a feel for each place's atmosphere, but be careful that the aggressive agents outside each bar don't pull you in.

Down Under Bar (tel. 32 982), **Cafe Charlie, Pete's Pub** (tel. 25 442), and **El Corazon Mexican Bar** (tel. 75 798) are all brimming with drunken revelers by midnight. **Bar Berlin** (tel. 32 250) on Orfanidou St., and **Valentino's** (tel. 34 070), off Apellou St. in the Old Town, are two gay bars. For true class, try Rhodes' tribute to Elvis, **Presley's** on Dragoumi St. in the New Town.

Outside the City

Excursion boats, tracing the beach-filled coast from Rhodes to Lindos, leave the city in the morning and return in the afternoon. They make several stops, including at Faliraki. Schedules and prices are posted at the dock along the lower end of the Mandraki (3500dr round-trip). **Waterhoppers** (tel. 38 146) offers **scuba diving** lessons and trips to Kalithea (lessons 12,000dr; non-diving passengers 6000dr; kids under 6 free; snorkeling free).

Rodini Park is a forested area outside the city with streams, trails, a restaurant, and some small, harmless animals left from the time when Rodini was a zoo. **Kalithea,** 10km south of Rhodes Town, features a deserted spa that once bathed rich Europeans. For food there is only the meager snack bar at the beach cove (not-so-fresh-looking cheese pie 350dr; soda 250dr). **Buses** run 15 times per day to Faliraki (300dr) and Lindos (900dr).

SIGHTS

Very few other islands can boast of being known for a sight that doesn't exist, and may never have existed. These bragging rights belong to the **Colossus of Rhodes,** a 35m bronze stature of Helios that may have stood astride the island's harbor. It was allegedly destroyed by an earthquake in 237 BC. Considered one of the **seven wonders of the ancient world,** the Colossus has been immortalized in tacky illustrations across the island. Two bronze deer now stand at the entrance to the port, each claiming a spot previously occupied by an enormous foot.

The Castello

There is nothing like redecorating to make a place feel more like home. The Knights of St. John knew this and thus gave the city of Rhodes an extensive face lift upon their conquest, replacing Hellenistic structures with medieval forts and castles. The result is unlike any other city in Greece.

The best place to begin exploring the Old Town is **Symi Square,** inside Eleftherias Gate at the base of the Mandraki. To the right, with your back to the arch, is the **Municipal Art Gallery,** with paintings by local artists (open Tues.-Sat. 8am-2pm; admission 500dr). Behind the 3rd-century BC **Temple of Aphrodite** in the middle of the square stands the 16th-century **Inn of Auvergne,** with an Aegean-style staircase on the facade.

Past Symi Sq. is **Argykastron Square,** with a relocated Byzantine fountain at its center. The 14th-century **Palace of Armeria,** now the **Archaeological Institute,** is on the right side of the square. It resembles a fortress with its small windows and lumbering Gothic architecture. Connected to the palace is the **Museum of Decorative Arts** with Dodecanese costumes, carved sea chests, and ceramic plates (open Tues.-Sun. 8:30am-3pm; admission 600dr, students 300dr). **Museum Square** is after the low archway; to its left is the **Church of St. Mary.** The Knights of St. John transformed this

11th-century Byzantine structure into a Gothic cathedral. Most of the rich interior frescoes were obliterated when the Ottomans remodeled the building into the Enderoum Mosque. The Italians then remade the mosque into a church once again, which has since retired to a quiet existence as an icon museum (open Tues.-Sun. 8:30am-3pm; admission 500dr, students 300dr).

Nearby, the **Inn of the Tongue of England** is a 1919 copy of it predecessor, built in 1493 but destroyed in one of the many battles fought to defend the city. Dominating the other side of the square, with its beautiful halls and courtyards, the former **Hospital of the Knights** is now the **Archaeological Museum** (tel. 27 674). Its treasures include the small but exquisite *Aphrodite Bathing* from the first century BC and the 4th-century *Apollo* (open Tues.-Fri. 8am-7pm and Sat.-Sun. 8:30am-3pm; admission 800dr, students 400dr, EU students free, seniors 400dr). The **Avenue of the Knights** (Ipoton St.), sloping uphill near the museum, was the main boulevard of the inner city 500 years ago. The Order of the Knights of St. John of Jerusalem consisted of seven different religious orders, called "tongues" since each spoke a different language. Their inns, now government offices that line both sides of Ipoton St., are not open to tourists. Because each tongue was responsible for guarding one segment of the city wall, parts of the wall are labeled "England" or "France" on the map.

At the top of the hill, a second archway leads to Kleovoulou Sq. To the right sits the pride of the city, the **Palace of the Knights of St. John,** with 300 rooms, moats, drawbridges, huge watch towers, and colossal battlements. The palace survived the long Ottoman siege of 1522 only to be devastated in 1856 by an explosion of 300-year-old ammunition left forgotten in a depot across the street. The Italians began rebuilding the castle at the beginning of this century. Determined to outdo even the industrious Knights, they restored the citadel and embellished many of its floors with mosaics taken from Kos (see p. 277). The interior decoration was completed only a few months before the start of WWII, so the Italians had little chance to savor the fruits of their megalomaniacal effort (open Tues.-Fri. 8am-7pm, Sat.-Sun. 8:30am-3pm; admission 1200dr, students 600dr). For an indescribable bird's eye view of the entire fortified city, wait patiently for a Tuesday or Saturday afternoon. Those with good balance and no fear of heights are permitted to walk along the city walls—an amazing, albeit brief, photo op (Tues. and Sat. 2:45-3pm; adults 1200dr, students 600dr).

Several blocks west of the south end of the Old Town off Diagoridon, a **stadium,** a small **theater,** and a **Temple of Apollo** have been partially reconstructed on the hill near Monte Smith. The stadium and theater are quite well preserved, but the temple lies in ruins. The few standing columns can be seen from the ferry; they're just before the last stretch of hotels (open 24hr.). The only other pre-Roman site is the ruined 3rd-century BC **Temple of Aphrodite.**

The Chora

To experience a different era of the city's history, turn right into Kleovoulou Sq. after the palace. After passing under several arches, turn left onto Orfeos St., better known as the **Plane Tree Walk.** The large **clock tower** on the left marked the edges of the wall that separated the knights' quarters from the rest of the city. The setup was identical during the Ottoman Era, but the boundaries changed; the Old Town housed the Muslims and Jews, while the Christians lived outside its walls. For 600dr, you can climb the tower and get a free drink for your trouble (open daily 9am-11pm). The **Mosque of Süleyman,** one block from the clock tower, dates from the early 19th-century with red-painted plaster walls, a garden, and a stone minaret. The original mosque on this site was built after Sultan Süleyman the Magnificent captured Rhodes in 1522. Its location makes it a good landmark in the Old Town (closed to the public).

The **Turkish library,** built in 1793 opposite the mosque, is full of 15th and 16th-century Persian and Arabic manuscripts (open daily 10am-1pm and 4-7pm; free, but the basket at the door implies a donation). The other Ottoman-era buildings and monuments in the Old Town are in various states of decay. One worth your time is the 250-year-old **hamam** (tel. 27 739) in Arionos Sq. Notice the dome with small carved stars that let the sunlight pour through (open Tues. 1-7pm, Wed.-Sat. 11am-7pm; admission 500dr).

Leading downhill from the Mosque of Süleyman is the main shopping strip, **Sokratous Street.** Continuing east along Aristotelous St. you'll reach **Martyron Evreon Square** (Square of the Jewish Martyrs) in the heart of the old Jewish Quarter. In 1943, 2000 Jews were taken from this square to Nazi concentration camps; only 50 survived. A little way down Dossiadou St. is the **synagogue,** restored by the survivors after the war. It is decorated by Oriental rugs covering the stone mosaic floor and hanging "eternal lamps." To see the synagogue's interior, ask Lucia, who lives above it, to contact the caretaker, Mr. Soviano, at 16 Polytechniou St. (tel. 27 344). Services are held Friday at 5pm; modest dress is required.

At Eleftherias Gate near Symi Sq. you'll find a small herd of **deer** in the moat. Eight hundred years ago, deer were imported to alleviate a serious snake problem. Apparently, the deer loved to impale the snakes with their hooves and antlers, and Rhodians have been grateful ever since.

The New Town and Mandraki

Look past the tasteless billboards and flashing advertisements; pearls of architectural ingenuity do exist in this initially repulsive display of modernity. Appreciate the fact that you are surrounded by trees; such lush plant life is rare in the Aegean Islands. Italian architecture dominates the modern business district. Mussolini-inspired stone buildings preside over wide Eleftherias St. The bank, the town hall, the post office, and the National Theater are the more imposing structures on the far side of the street. Directly opposite is the majestic **Governor's Palace** and a cathedral built by the Italians in 1925. The cathedral replicates St. John's Church, leveled in an 1856 explosion.

Named after Süleyman's admiral who died trying to capture Rhodes from the Knights of St. John in 1522, the **Mosque of Mourad Reis** is an important remnant of the Ottoman presence. The small, domed building inside is his mausoleum.

Three defunct **windmills** stand halfway along the harbor's pier. The **Fortress of St. Nicholas** at the end of the pier, built in 1464, guarded the harbor until the end of WWII (closed to the public). Greece's only **aquarium** (tel. 27 308, 78 320), also a marine research center in the Dodecanese, is at the northern tip of the island. Various creatures of the Aegean depths are exhibited (open April-Oct. daily 9am-9pm, Nov.-March daily 9am-4:30pm; admission 600dr, students 400dr).

▓ Faliraki

A smaller, yet more concentrated collection of the modern and tourist-oriented vices that plague the New Town, Faliraki should be sampled in small doses unless your taste is for the loud, the young, and the restless. The bars advertising wall-to-wall foam parties are named for alcohol-induced impotence (e.g. The Brewer's Droop). The raucous nightlife brings with it not only a shortage of peace and quiet but also a shortage of available accommodations—yet another reason to visit Faliraki as a daytrip.

ORIENTATION AND PRACTICAL INFORMATION

Located just 5km south of Kalithea and blessed with a sandy beach, Faliraki is considered a popular resort town. It consequently draws eager beach bunnies with their inflatable toys in hand. There are two main bus stops in Faliraki, one on the Rhodes-Lindos road and one on the waterfront. Directly opposite the waterfront bus stop, to the right of the main road connecting the beach with the Rhodes-Lindos highway (facing inland), is the **first aid station** (tel. 85 555). Dr. Zanettullis can be reached 24 hours at (094) 582 747 if he's not at the station (open daily 8am-6pm). The **pharmacy** (tel. 85 998) is on the main road up to the highway; look for the green cross (open daily 9am-10:30pm). There is a **taxi stand** next to the waterfront bus stop. **Buses** run between Rhodes City and Faliraki (15 per day, 300dr). The bus from Faliraki to Lindos leaves from the waterfront bus stop (10 per day, 700dr). Faliraki is also a base for boat trips to Lindos (4000dr), Kos (11,000dr), and Symi (3000dr). The **Travel Center** (tel. 85 520, 86 312), across from Ideal Hotel on the main road up to the highway, offers **currency exchange, telephones,** and safe-deposit boxes (open daily 9am-10:45pm).

ACCOMMODATIONS AND FOOD

There's a **campsite** (tel. 85 516, -358) off the main road 1500m before Faliraki; ask the bus driver to let you off. Facilities include TV, disco/bar, market, hot showers, and a pool (1200dr per person; 600dr per tent). Otherwise, lodgings in Faliraki are hard to find, especially in the high season, as most places rent their rooms to British package tour companies.

Dining in Faliraki means inhaling a burger, greasy fries and a soda at any of the endless stretch of fast-food stores. Your other option is to choose sugar instead of grease. The tiny sweet shop halfway between the main road and the beach, nestled in between a tourist shop and a side street, serves the gooey kind of *baklava* that leaves honey dripping down your face (300dr, and worth every penny).

ENTERTAINMENT

The beach teems with sunbathers during the day. As night falls, the volume rises at all bars on the main street, where uniformly priced beer (600-700dr) makes for a jubilant drinkfest. **Chaplin's** (tel. 85 662), on the beach at the base of the main road, is noisy with Friday afternoon karaoke competitions (shots 500dr). The self-titled "Factory of Cocktails" **Ziggy's and Charlie's** (tel. 85 324) is strategically located next to the bus stop on the beach. Choose one of two dozen specialty fishbowl cocktails (small 2600dr, large 4800d; open daily noon-3am). Up the main road, heading away from the beach, **Jimmy's Pub** (tel. 85 643), offers simultaneous CNN, ESPN, and MTV. Cheer on your team while chugging everything from delicious Guinness to less-delicious Bud (open noon-3am). The **Brewer's Droop,** a few doors down from Jimmy's Pub, shows a daily movie and is the place to go for frozen margaritas; choose from banana, pineapple, melon, or strawberry (1L jug serves 3-4 people, 2800dr; open daily noon-4am).

■ Between Faliraki and Lindos

Eleven kilometers farther south, just before Kolymbia, a road to the right leads to **Epta Piges.** The nature walks in this area are wonderful, but most people trek no farther than the inexpensive restaurant next to the main stream. It serves up mediocre food, but there's nothing else edible in sight (stuffed vegetables 800dr, *souvlaki* pita 300dr). The tunnel behind the restaurant leads to a beautiful hidden lake. There's no direct bus service, but you can ask any Lindos/Archangelos bus driver to let you off there. Continue inland past Epta Piges to visit the Byzantine **Church of Agios Nikolaos Fountoucli,** 3km past Eleousa, which has 13th and 15th-century frescoes. **Buses** stop at Eleousa (3 per day) on the way to Rhodes. Villagers in **Arthipoli,** 4km away, rent rooms.

A worthwhile stop if you have wheels is the **Tsambikas Monastery,** a Byzantine cloister atop Mt. Tsambikas. The asphalt ends at the Tsambikas Beach turn-off, but the road ahead takes you pretty far; you'll only have to walk the last kilometer. **Kolymbia** and **Tsambikas** beaches are sandy and peaceful. **Buses** run from Rhodes to Kolymbia (9 per day, 600dr). From Lindos to Kolymbia, two buses run daily and one returns the next morning (550dr). A bus leaves Rhodes for Tsambikas daily at 9am and returns at 4pm (550dr one way).

Roughly 10km farther down the road from Tsambikas (15km north of Lindos), take the turn-off to **Charaki,** where you can swim next to a hill topped by the crumbling **Castle of Feracios,** built by the Knights of St. John. Rooms and restaurants line the beach. **Buses** to Charaki leave from Rhodes (Rimini Sq.) three times per day (550dr).

■ Lindos

With whitewashed houses clustered beneath a soaring castle-capped acropolis, Lindos is perhaps the most picturesque town in Rhodes. Vines and flowers line narrow streets, and pebble mosaics carpet courtyards. Charm like this cannot stay a secret for long, and Lindos's hasn't. In summer, Lindos's packed streets make crowds in the City of Rhodes pale in comparison, and shop owners take advantage of the masses by charging astronomical prices for food and services. Lindos is also notoriously hot and short of rooms in the summer, making it a better place to visit outside of high season if possible. **Buses** run to Lindos from Rimini Sq. in Rhodes. Arrive early; they fill quickly. **Excursion boats** from Rhodes depart at 9am and return at 5pm, stopping elsewhere on the coast.

ORIENTATION AND PRACTICAL INFORMATION

Lindos is a pedestrian-only city. All traffic stops at **Eleftherias Square,** where the bus and taxi stations are. From there, **Acropolis Street** leads through the eastern part of town and up to the acropolis. **Apostolous Pavlou,** another main street, runs perpendicular to Acropolis St. just past the Church of the Assumption of Madonna, whose stone belfry rises above the middle of town. Houses are distinguished only by frequently changing numbers.

The rather unhelpful **tourist office** (tel./fax 31 288 or -900) in Eleftherias Sq. offers **currency exchange** and sells decent maps. The best is the watercolored "Lindos-Illustrated Map" (500dr; open daily 7:30am-10pm). **Pallas Travel** (tel. 31 494; fax 31 595) on Acropolis St. has an even better map of Lindos (free), offers currency exchange, and can plan various excursions (open Mon.-Sat. 8am-10pm, Sun. 9am-1pm and 4-109pm). Critical and not-so-critical services line the intersection of Apostolous Pavlou St. and Acropolis St. The **National Bank** is near this junction on Apostolous Pavlou (open Mon.-Thurs. 9am-2pm, Fri.-Sat. 9am-1pm), as is the **pharmacy** (tel. 31 294; open Mon.-Sat. 9am-10:30pm, Sun. 9am-3pm), just past Yianni's Bar. Sheila Markiou, an expatriate Bostonian, runs a superb **used bookstore** (tel. 31 443) with more than 7000 English, Italian, German, French, and Greek books. To get there, walk to Pallas Travel and bear right where the road forks; the library is up and to the left (open Mon.-Sat. 9am-8pm, Sun 9am-4pm). **Laundry** can be done at **Sheila's service** (1800dr wash, dry, and soap). The **medical clinic** (tel. 31 224) is to the left before the church (open Mon.-Sat. 9am-1:30pm and 6-8pm). There are **public toilets** across from the information office near the taxi/bus station (100dr). The **police** are at 521 Vas. Pavlou (tel. 31 223; open Mon.-Fri. 8am-3pm, 24hr. for emergencies). The **postal code** is 85107; **telephone code,** 0244.

ACCOMMODATIONS

Lindos is best seen as a daytrip; lodgings, even the tiniest spots, are hogged by European package tours. Arrive in the morning before the tour buses rumble in and ask the tour companies' offices if they have any empty rooms. The few free agents rent doubles for 5000-7000dr in high season; singles are difficult to find. For a good place to start looking, take the first left downhill after the donkey stand. This road leads down to the beach and is packed with pensions and private rooms. **Pension Electra** (tel. 31 266) offers a garden, terrace, and clean rooms. Look past the crumbling exteriors of neighboring buildings. Rooms include private bath, A/C, and fridge (doubles 12,000dr; triples 14,000dr). Less expensive rooms await in more remote corners. Inquire at Restaurant Stefany's on 230 Acropolis St. about rooms in **Pension Venus,** which has simple doubles (10,000dr).

FOOD AND ENTERTAINMENT

Eating on a budget in Lindos also poses a challenge. Restaurant prices range from expensive to exorbitant. The only cheap alternatives are *souvlaki-pita* bars, *creperies* (crepes start at 600dr), and grocery stores on the two main streets. "Snack bar" shops serve the healthiest option in Lindos (a bowl of yogurt with honey and fresh fruit 500-700dr). **Cyprus Taverna** (tel. 31 539) has rooftop tables below the acropolis where you can dine on Greek food with a Cypriot twist (*kleftiko* 1400dr, *hummus* 500dr). To prepare for the climb to the acropolis, or refuel upon your descent, stop off at the **Italian bakery** around the corner from the bookstore. Authentic *focaccia* (400dr) and *panzerotti* (700dr) draw constant crowds (open daily 8am-9pm). **Gelo Blu** (tel. 31 761) serves 18 flavors of delicious *gelato* made from natural ingredients (250dr per scoop). Strong espresso, cappuccino, and refreshing iced drinks accompany the chocolate fudge cake (open daily 9am-1am).

Lindos's nightlife is relatively tame (municipal law requires music to stop at midnight). If you are not ready to call it a day, head to **Amphitheatre** (tel. 288 549), an open-air nightclub not far out of town. Free cabs shuttle you from Lindos square to the dance floor, where you can rage with a view of both the acropolis and the sea (open daily midnight-4am; 1000dr includes first drink). Less energetic types might try **Jody's Flat,** on Apostolou Pavlou in the center of town. This beautiful bar, enhanced by a pebble mosaic floor and lush indoor garden, has board games, monthly foreign magazines, and daily papers (pint of beer 500dr; open 5pm-1am). The **Museum Bar** (tel. 31 446) is another more subdued option. Watch CNN, MTV, ESPN, or even the Discovery Channel on one of their three televisions. The sangria is fruity and refreshing (1000dr) and the coffee freshly brewed (400-600dr).

SIGHTS

Lindos's premier attraction, the ancient **acropolis,** stands amid scaffolding at the top of sheer cliffs 125m above town. The walls of a Crusader fortress further enclose the caged structure. Excavations by the Danish Archaeological School between 1902 and 1912 yielded everything from 5000-year-old neolithic tools to a plaque inscribed by a priest of Athena in 99 BC listing the dignitaries who visited Athena's Temple: Hercules, Helen of Troy, Menelaus, Alexander the Great, and the King of Persia. The winding path up to the acropolis is veiled in lace tablecloths sold by local women; the cobwebbed pall makes for a surreal ascent. Right before the final incline, don't miss the fabulous ancient Greek warship *(trireme)* carved into the cliffside as a symbol of Lindos' inextricable ties with the sea. The 13th-century **Crusader castle** looms over the entrance to the site. As you leave the castle, make a U-turn to your left to reach the imposing **Doric Stoa** (arcade), whose 13 restored columns dominate the entire level. The arcade, built around 200 BC at the height of Rhodes's glory, originally consisted of 42 columns laid out in the shape of the Greek letter "Π." The large stone blocks arranged against the back wall served as bases for bronze statues which have been long since melted down. The **Temple of the Lindian Athena** comes into view at the top of the steps. According to legend, a temple was built here as early as 1510 BC. All that remains today are parts of the temple built by the tyrant Cleoboulos in the 6th century BC. Once a tremendously important religious site, it's now one of the few ancient temples with inner walls still fairly intact; colonnades flank both sides. Donkey rides to the acropolis are a rip-off (1000dr one way), and the 10-minute walk is not too strenuous (acropolis open Mon. 12:30-6:45pm, Tues.-Fri. 8am-6:45pm, Sat.-Sun. 8:30am-2:45pm; admission 1200dr, students 600dr).

The graceful stone bell tower projecting from the middle of town belongs to the **Church of the Assumption of Madonna,** rebuilt by the Knights of St. John in 1489. Brightly colored 18th-century frescoes, retouched by the Italians in 1927, illuminate the interior (open daily 9am-1pm and 3-5pm; modest dress required). At the southwest foot of the acropolis are the remains of the **ancient theater.** The **Voukopion** is on the north side of the rock face, visible from the donkey path. This cave, which the Dorians transformed into a sanctuary for Athena, is believed to date from the 9th century BC and may have been used for special sacrifices that could be performed only outside the acropolis.

■ Western and Southern Rhodes

A string of high-rise hotels abuts the 8km stretch of sand west of Rhodes. The west end of this luxury hotel district is the town of modern **Ialyssos** (Trianda). The hotels were built in the late 60s and early 70s under Greece's military dictatorship. Along with Lindos and Kamiros, Ialyssos was once one of the three great cities on the island. The ruins are rather meager. Most impressive are the 4th-century BC **Doric fountain** ornamented with four lion heads, the adjacent monastery, and the **Church of Our Lady of Filerimos** (actually four conjoined chapels). The church and monastery occupy the site of a 3rd-century BC **temple to Athena and Zeus Polias.** On the stone floor just inside the doorway of the room to the left rests a remnant of the original Byzantine structure: a fish, the symbol of Christ, carved into one of the red stones. The path past the chapel leads to the ruins of a Byzantine castle (open Tues.-Fri. 8:30am-2pm, Sat.-Mon. 8:30am-3pm; admission 800dr, students 400dr).

Unfortunately, there is no easily negotiable road to Filerimos, but taxis from Rimini Sq. will make the trek for 3000dr round-trip. Aside from a moped, the only other alternative is the bus from Rhodes to modern Ialyssos (6 per day, 250dr), which stops 5km before the town. If you are blessed with a car, drive to Gennadi, less than 10 minutes outside of Lindos. Here, you can find fresh seafood that is both inexpensive and delicious. **Ta Mezedakia** (tel. 43 627) is a family-owned establishment serving up whatever the owner catches (open noon-1am).

Monolithos, on the island's southwest tip, is a tiny collection of scattered houses. The **Castle of Monolithos,** 2km west, is well worth the trip. In ruins, the fortress sits at the summit of a 160m-high rock pillar, and visitors can still walk inside. To get there, follow the only western road out of town. Despite its uninspired name, Monolithos's **Restaurant/Bar Greek Food** has decent entrees. Two buses leave Rhodes daily for Monolithos via Embona and Ag. Isidoros (2½hr., 1200dr).

In the south, the island assumes an entirely different character. Here in farm and goat-herding country, grassy yellow flatlands slope gradually into hills studded with low-lying shrubs. **Buses** run daily to Lardos (3 per day, 900dr) and Tuesday, Thursday, and Saturday to Asklipio (1000dr), Katavia (1300dr), and Messanagros (1200dr).

KOS ΚΩΣ

The booming nightclubs and packed bars of modern Kos do not pay adequate tribute to the impressive history of the island. In ancient times, Kos was a major trading power with a population of 160,000—eight times that of today. Having drawn attention to itself as an episcopal seat for the Byzantine Empire, the island became a target for predatory naval forces. The Knights of St. John prevailed in 1315, seizing control and turning Kos into one of their outposts. Since then, its history has mirrored that of the other Dodecanese in having Italian, German, and British governments.

The citizens of Kos are perhaps the island's biggest claim to fame. As the sacred land of Asclepius, god of healing, it seems appropriate that **Hippocrates,** the father of medicine, would also be from Kos. His 2400-year-old oath to healing is still taken by doctors. Not to be outdone by science, the island has also produced major contributors to literature. Both Theocutus and Philitus wrote their poetry here.

Today, Kos rivals Rhodes in the number of tourists that descend on the island each summer. Kos tends to draw more of the younger, louder, more intoxicated crowd. It also seems to be a favorite destination for package tours. Consequently, the raucous bars and mammoth hotels that line the otherwise beautiful beaches may dismay a casual traveler. Perseverance rewards those who take the time to look in the quiet nooks and glimpse traditional Greek hospitality.

GREEK ISLANDS

■ Kos Town

In Kos Town, minarets from Ottoman mosques stand beside grand Italian mansions and the massive walls of a Crusader fortress. The town is a repository of archaic, Classical, Hellenic, and Roman ruins. Unfortunately, it is also one of the more expensive places to visit in the Dodecanese. Package tour agents have made contracts with many of the pensions, leaving very few rooms for independent travelers. Despite this, the combination of ancient, medieval, and modern styles make Kos a pleasant city in which to wander, especially in the morning before the tours and the heat set in.

ORIENTATION AND PRACTICAL INFORMATION

As your ferry pulls into the harbor of Kos Town, you'll see only the colossal walls of the Castle of the Knights of St. John. If you walk left from the harbor (facing inland), the stately trees framing the **Avenue of Palms** (also called Finikon Street) make the island feel less imposing. Continuing along the waterfront past the Palms leads to **Vas. Georgios** and the rocky beach alongside it. Turn right onto the Palms and follow it to the next corner of the fortress and you will come upon **Akti Kountouriotou,** another waterfront street that wraps around the harbor. The city bus station, boats to Turkey, travel agencies, restaurants, and Kos's thriving nightlife can all be found here. Branching off Akti Koundouriotou inland are the town's main arteries. **Venizelou Street** leads through a row of travel agencies directly into the shopping district. **Megalou Alexandrou,** a few blocks down, heads to **Palaiologou Square,** the ruins of ancient Kos Town, and eventually to the inland villages. The town's other sandy beach originates near the end of Akti Koundauriotou.

Tourist Office: (tel. 28 724, 24 460) At the heart of Akri Miaouli, Hippokratous St., and Vas. Georgiou. Free maps (kiosks sell the same map for 250-300dr), information on excursions, events, lodgings, and ferry and hydrofoil schedules. Open Mon.-Fri. 7:30am-9pm, Sat. 7:30am-3pm.

Tourist Agencies: No single agency in Kos has comprehensive boat information. Two large ferry companies (DANE and GA) and two hydrofoil lines (Ilio and Dodecanese) serve Kos and its neighbors. **Pulia Tours,** 3 Vas Pavlou St. (tel. 26 388, 21 130; fax 26 388), near the waterfront end of this main road, sells DANE and hydrofoil tickets, organizes day excursions, offers **currency exchange** and helps you find a room (open daily 7am-11pm). **G.A. Office** (tel. 28 545; fax 24 864), on Vas Pavlou across from the National Bank, serves the other ferry and hydrofoil lines, and offers similar tourist services. Open daily 8:30am-10pm.

Banks: National Bank (tel. 28 517), in back of the Archaeological Museum, 1 block inland from the water on A.P. Ioannidi. 24hr. **ATM** accepts MasterCard and Cirrus. Open Mon.-Thurs. 8am-2pm, Fri. 8am-1:45pm. **Commercial Bank,** 7 Vas. Pavlou (tel. 28 825), inland from the City Bus station, advances money on Visa. Open Mon.-Thurs. 8am-2pm, Fri. 8am-1:30pm. After hours, **exchange currency** at the travel agencies along the waterfront.

American Express: (tel. 26 732) Follow Akti Koundouriotou to the dolphin fountain and look for it at the corner of Boubouliras St. Full AmEx services for cardholders. Open Mon.-Sat. 9am-2pm and 5-9pm.

Flights: Olympic Airways, 22 Vas. Pavlou St. (tel. 28 331, -2). To Athens (2-3 per day, 21,800dr) and Rhodes (2 per week, 9800dr). Open Mon.-Fri. 8am-3:30pm. On Sat.-Sun., call 51 567. Olympic runs a **bus** from Kos Town to the airport 2-4 times per day. Schedule posted in front window. Arrive 2hr. before departure (1000dr). Kardamena or Kefalos buses can let you off near the airport. Taxis from Kos Town to the airport cost 5000-5500dr.

Buses: (tel. 22 292) Leave from Kleopatras St. near inland end of Pavlou St. behind the Olympic Airways office. To: Tigaki (11 per day, 30min., 280dr); Marmari (10 per day, 35min., 280dr); Asfendiou-Zia (4 per day, 40min., 280dr); Pyli (5 per day, 30min., 280dr); Mastihari (4 per day, 45min., 450dr); Antimachia (6 per day, 40min., 350dr); Kardamena (6 per day, 45min., 450dr); and Kefalos (6 per day, 620dr). Full schedule posted by the stop.

Kos

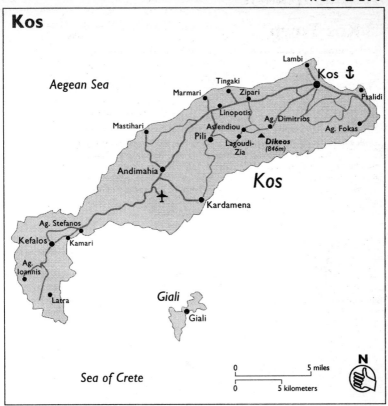

Aegean Sea

Lambi

Kos ⚓

Psalidi

Tingaki

Marmari

Zipari

Linopotis

Mastihari

Asfendiou

Ag. Dimitrios

Ag. Fokas

Pili

Lagoudi-
Zia

▲ *Dikeos*
(846m)

Andimahia

Kos

Kardamena

Ag. Stefanos

Kefalos

Kamari

Ag.
Ioannis

Giali

Giali

Latra

Sea of Crete

0   5 miles

0   5 kilometers

N

City Buses: 7 Akti Kountouriotou (tel. 26 276), on the water. Cheap tickets in front of the town hall. Fares 150-220dr, to: Agios Fokas (30 per day, 15min.); Nea Halicarnassus (34 per day); Marmaroto (8 per day); Therma (9 per day, 20min.); and Asclepion (16 per day, 15min.). Schedules at the station.

Ferries: Sail to: Peiraias (2 per day, 11-15hr., 7165dr); Rhodes (2 per day, 4hr., 3300dr); Kalymnos (2 per day except Sun., 1¼hr., 1500dr); Leros (1 per day, 2½hr., 2300dr); Patmos (1 per day, 4hr., 2700dr); and Astypalea (1 per week, 3300dr). Ferries travel weekly to: Thessaloniki (17hr., 11,000dr); Paros (5000dr); Naxos (5400dr); Syros (5500dr); and Samos (5500dr). Also, 1-2 boats per week set sail for: Nisyros (2400dr); Tilos (1800dr); Symi (2800dr); and Kastelorizo (3160dr). **Greek boats** to Bodrum, Turkey (near ancient Halicarnassus) every morning (12,000dr round-trip). **Turkish boats** leave in the afternoon and return the next morning (15,000dr round-trip). Since travel is international, it is not regulated by the Greek government—shop around and ask for student discounts.

Flying Dolphins: Two per day to: Kalymnos (2850dr); Leros (4000dr); Patmos (5500dr); and Samos (6200dr). Two per week to: Tilos (3500dr); Agathonisi (5500dr); and Astypalea (5850dr). Also to: Symi (1 per week, 4500dr); Lipsi (6 per week, 3360dr); Nisyros (3 per week, 3340dr); Fourni (3 per week, 7000dr); and Rhodes (2 per day, 6700dr).

Port Authority: (tel. 26 594) At the corner of Negalou Alexandrou and Akti Kountouriotou. Open 24hr.

Taxis: (tel. 22 777) Congregate near the inland end of the Avenue of Palms.

Moped/Bike rentals: Sernikos, 19 Herodotou St. (tel. 23 670). Take first right off Megalou Alexandrou—2 blocks down. Mopeds from 2500dr; bikes 500-1000dr. Moped license required for all rentals except mountain bikes. **Moto Holidays,** 21

Meg. Alexandrou (tel. 28 676). Mopeds from 3000dr; motorcycles from 5000dr; bicycles 300dr; mountain bikes 700dr.

Laundromat: 124 Alikarnassou St. Turn off Megalou Alexandrou on either Pindou or Kyprou St. and walk 2 blocks. Wash, dry, and soap 1500dr. Open Mon.-Fri. 8:30am-1:30pm and 5-9:30pm, Sat. 8:30am-4pm.

Pharmacies: 5 Va. Pavlou St. (tel. 22 346), next to the Commercial Bank. Open Mon.-Tues. and Thurs.-Fri. 8:30am-2pm and 5-9:30pm, Wed. and Sat. 8:30am-2pm. After hours, check the door for the number and address of the on-call pharmacy.

Hospital: (tel. 28 050) On Mitropoleas St., between El. Venizelou and Hippocrates (Ippokratous). **Emergency:** (tel. 22 300) Open 24hr. **Information:** (tel. 28 013).

Police: (tel. 22 222) On Akti Miaouli St. in the large yellow building next to the castle. Some English spoken. Open 24hr. **Tourist police** (tel. 25 462), in the same building. Open daily 7:30am-2pm.

Post Office: 14 Venizelou St. (tel. 22 250). Follow signs from Vas. Pavlou, which lead past Eleftherias Sq. and the fruit market and turn left onto Venizelou St. Open Mon.-Fri. 7:30am-2pm. **Postal Code:** 85300.

OTE: (tel. 22 499) Around the corner from post office, at the corner of L. Virona and Xanthou. Open Mon.-Sat. 7:30am-10pm, Sun. 8am-10pm. **Telephone Code:** 0242.

ACCOMMODATIONS

Hotel vacancies are rare during July and August, so start searching for rooms early. Most inexpensive places are on the right side of town (facing inland). It is best to seek out your own room (the dock hawks in Kos are notorious), but if your boat docks in the middle of the night, you may have no choice. Camping on the beach or in the park along the Avenue of Palms is illegal. Prices are generally 20-40% lower during the off season.

Pension Alexis, 9 Herodotou St. (tel. 28 798, 25 594), first right off Meg. Alexandrou, on the back left corner of the first intersection. Incomparable hospitality. If rooms are full, the proprietor will put you up with a mattress and sheets on the patio (1200dr) or cut you a deal at his elegant **Hotel Afendoulis** in the ritzier part of town. Balconies, common baths, and a guest book dating back to 1979. Prices flexible, especially if you are carrying *Let's Go*. Doubles 5500-6500dr; triples 7500dr. Breakfast 800dr.

Hotel Afendoulis, 1 Evrilpilou St. (tel./fax 25 321, 25 797). Evrilpilou is right down Vas. Georgiou. Well-kept rooms in a quiet part of town near the beach. All rooms with private bath. Doubles 7500-8500dr. Breakfast 800dr.

Rooms to Let Nitsa, 47 Averof St. (tel. 25 810), near the beach north of town. Super-clean rooms with baths and kitchenettes. Doubles 6500dr; triples 8000dr.

Hotel Hara (tel. 22 500, 23 198), corner of Chalkonos and Arseniou St., 1 block inland from the water. Private phones, baths, and towels provided. Singles 6600dr; doubles 8500dr; triples 9800dr. Flash your *Let's Go* for a discount.

FOOD

As a rule, try to avoid the waterfront cafes and restaurants—any hope of finding good, cheap food lies farther inland. The fruit and vegetable **market** in Eleftherias Sq. on Vas. Pavlou St. is inside a large yellow building with a picture of grapes over the doors. It caters to tourists and is therefore expensive. Cheaper fruit can be found in mini-markets (open Mon.-Fri. 7am-9pm, Sat. 7am-6pm, Sun. 10am-2pm).

Hellas (tel. 24 790) Take the first right off Meg. Alexandrou and look for it on your left after a few blocks. The best option in town. It serves immense portions of touristy, yet well-prepared Greek dishes. Lamb *kleftiko* 1500dr, *moussaka* 1200dr. Good vegetarian options available. Open noon-1am.

Ampavris (tel. 23 612), take the road to Ampavris past the Casa Romana; it's about 10min. from town. A true diamond in the rough and one of the few places on Kos to find authentic cuisine. Stuffed flower buds 900dr, Greek salad 700dr.

Taverna Theodoros, 22 Pindou St., the 4th right off Meg. Alexandrou, has delicious dishes. Stuffed tomatoes 900dr.

Far East (tel. 20 469), on Bouboulinas St., parallel to Meg. Alexandrou, is great for Chinese. Try the cashew chicken (1500dr) or sweet 'n' sour spare ribs (1500dr).

The Special (tel. 22 448), on Vas Pavlou St. across from the National Bank, will make you want to save room for dessert. An incredible sweet shop brimming with mouthwatering options. Divine baklava 350dr, and enormous croissants 350dr. Open until midnight.

ENTERTAINMENT

The nightlife in the pubs and bars all over Kos Town can be heard throughout the Dodecanese. Although tamer, Kos is considered the Ios of the Dodecanese. Prepare for crowds of people wearing skin-tight clothing and looking for a good time. Most bars are in two districts; the first includes the streets of **Exarhia** between Akti Koundouriotou and the Ancient Agora and around Vas. Pavlou. The **Cactus, Agora, Doors Music Bar,** and **Galatea** are practically indistinguishable. Beers will cost you 500-700dr at any of these places, while cocktails will set you back about 1200dr. Most places open at 9pm, fill by 11pm, and refuse to stop until about 4am. If you can squeeze in, **Saloon Tex** is the place to shake your thing on the dance floor, on the bar, on the tables. There is no cover, but drinks are 200-300dr more expensive than elsewhere.

The second bar district is **Porfiriou St.** in the north near the beach, where drinks are cheaper and the atmosphere more subdued. Beers at **Pub Cuckoo's Nest** and **Crazy Horse Saloon** are often accompanied by free shots (500dr). It is here that you will find the most popular discos on the island, two of which are **Kahlua** and **Heaven,** both located on the beach. Directly behind the dolphin statue at the base of Meg. Alexandrou, the **Fashion Club** completes the trio of these party complexes. Make sure you are well-dressed—people try to fit into a backdrop of carefully selected costumes. All discos charge a 2000dr cover, which includes your first drink. Dancing is best between midnight and 4am.

SIGHTS

The 15th-century **Castle of the Knights of St. John** was reinforced with elaborate double walls and inner moats in response to 16th-century Ottoman raids. As a result, it withstood innumerable attacks and is one of the best preserved examples of medieval architecture in all of Greece. Cross a bridge from the Plane Tree (see below) to enter the castle. The Order of St. John on Kos was originally dedicated to healing the sick, but you would never know it from the size of the fortifications (open Tues.-Sun. 8am-2:30pm; admission 800dr, students 400dr).

Before crossing the bridge, between the Palms and the ruins of the agora, you will see the gigantic **Plane Tree of Hippocrates,** allegedly planted by the great physician 2400 years ago. The tree, with a 12m diameter, is actually 500 years old; nonetheless, Hippocrates is said to have taught pupils and written books under its foliage. A spring next to the tree leads to an ancient sarcophagus that the Ottomans used as a cistern for the nearby **Hadji Hassan Mosque.** Behind the tree, the monumental former **Town Hall,** originally the Italian Governor's Palace, now houses police, justice, and governmental offices. The most impressive Ottoman structure is the **Defterdar Mosque** in Eleftherias Sq. Nearby, on Diakou St., is the abandoned **Synagogue of Kos,** in use until WWII. The city's Byzantine **Greek Orthodox Cathedral** is on the corner of Korai and Agios Nikolaou St.

The **archaeological museum** (tel. 28 326), is on the left in Eleftherias Sq., up Vas. Pavlou St. The museum features the celebrated statue of Hippocrates found at the Odeon of Kos. A 2nd-century AD Roman mosaic in the central courtyard depicts Hippocrates and a colleague entertaining the god Asclepios. (Open Tues.-Sun. 8am-2:30pm. Admission 800dr, students 400dr. No photographs permitted.)

The field of ruins bounded by Nafklirou St., Hippocrates St., and the waterfront is the **agora,** now dominated by a thriving cat population that sunbathes among the ruins. You will find a **temple of Aphrodite** and a more impressive 2nd-century AD **temple of Hercules** here (agora open 24hr.; free). Two short stairways off Grigoriou

St. (which runs along the southern edge of town) descend to the ruins. The main roads intersect Grigoriou St. 1km from the sea. The site itself is bordered by two Roman roads: the **Cardo** (axis), perpendicular to Grigoriou St., and the **Decumana** (broadest), parallel to Grigoriou and intersecting Cardo St. An ancient gymnasium, a swimming pool from the Roman era, and an early Christian basilica built over a Roman bath are all nearby. At the end of the Decumana, the 3rd-century AD **House of Europa**, protected under a modern wooden shelter, has a mosaic floor depicting Europa's abduction by a bullish Zeus (open 24hr.; free).

The **odeum,** a well-preserved ancient Roman theater, is across the street (open 24hr.; free). The 3rd-century AD **Casa Romana,** uncovered by an Italian archaeologist in 1933, is down Grigorious St. These ruins concealed the remnants of an even older (5th century BC) and more striking Hellenic mansion (open Tues.-Sun. 8:30am-3pm; admission 600dr, students 300dr, seniors 300dr). The meager ruins of a **Temple of Dionysus** are opposite the Casa Romana.

Much of the island's northern section is flat, and many roads have bike lanes which provide easy access to any number of beaches. If you take the main road east of town you will pedal past a sandy, crowded stretch on the way to the hot springs of **Thermae,** located near the road's end. **Lampi Beach** is at the northernmost tip of the island. Going west from there will take you all the way to the shady and busy **Tigaki** (10km west of Kos). The waterfront road is interrupted at **Aliki Lake,** so turn inland and cycle past fields with grazing livestock on the road parallel to the highway. **Marmari** and **Mastihari** are pleasant, longer rides. A hat and map are essential. If cycling does not interest you, buses run to Thermae (9 per day), Lampi (34 per day), Marmari (10 per day), and Mastinari (4 per day), but rides are often snug.

■ Asclepion

The Asclepion, an ancient sanctuary dedicated to the god of healing, lies 4km west of Kos Town. In the 5th century BC, Hippocrates opened the world's first medical school and encouraged the development of a precise science of medicine. Combining early priestly techniques with his own, Hippocrates made Kos the foremost medical center in ancient Greece. This past year, the Asclepion was named "peace capital of the world," and many new doctors still travel here to take their oaths.

Most of the ruins at the Asclepion actually date from the 3rd century BC. The complex was built into a hill on five terraces which overlook Kos Town and the Aegean. Remains of the ancient buildings are plentiful; it is easy to envision the structures as they once stood if you can ignore the swarms of tourists. A forest of cypress and pine trees, sacred in ancient times, adjoins the site, and 2nd-century AD Roman baths are inside. Explore the *natatio* (pool), the *tepidarium* (room of intermediate temperature), and the *caldarium* (sauna).

The most interesting remains at Asclepion are in the three stacked levels, called *andirons.* These contain the **School of Medicine,** statues of deities, and a figure of Pan, the mythical half-goat-half-human. Climb the 30 steps to the second *andiron* to see the best-preserved remains of the Asclepion, the elegant columns of the 2nd-century BC **Temple of Apollo,** and the 4th-century BC **Minor Temple of Asclepios.** The 60-step climb to the third *andiron* leads to the forested remains of the **Main Temple of Asclepios** and affords a view of the site, Kos Town, and the Turkish coast.

Buses motor to the Asclepion in summer (16 per day, 15min.), and the site is easily reached by bike or moped. (Follow the sign west off the main road and continue as straight as possible. Site open June-Sept. Tues.-Sun. 8:30am-7pm. Admission 800dr, students 400dr.) Taxis to the site should cost about 500dr.

■ Central Kos

The impact of package tours seeking "traditional Greek villages" is beginning to wear on the villages south of Kos Town. Where fertile fields once yielded tomatoes and olives, tourism is now the main crop. Nevertheless, the island's many paved roads make wonderful terrain for short trips by bike or moped. It is possible to go from Kos to Mastihari and then up to Pyli and Zia entirely on back roads. For those who prefer the bus, the main road leads first to the modern village of **Zipari,** which includes the ruins of the early **Christian Basilica of St. Paul,** 11km southwest of Kos Town. From there, a twisting road slowly winds through the green foothills of the Dikeos Mountains to **Asfendiou,** consisting of five small settlements, of which **Lagoudi** is the prettiest. It is easy to hike for hours and not encounter a soul. Buses from Kos go to Asfendiou-Zia (4 per day, 40min., 280dr). South of Lagoudi, the road narrows to a mule path and the hills become even less cultivated. A mere 8km farther (although a good portion of it is uphill), you will come to the compact ruins of old Pyli, which are 14th-century frescoes in a Byzantine church built within a castle. Buses go to Pyli from Kos (5 per day, 30min., 280dr). From Pyli, a twisting, potholed paved road climbs over the hills and descends into Kardamena.

The turn-off for the **Castle of Antimachia** is 1km before Antimachia on the main road to the left. Yet another legacy of the Knights of St. John, the fortress sits majestically on an isolated hilltop. For those who can't get enough of medieval architecture, the 20-minute hike up the hill will offer you another opportunity to marvel at medieval ruins. Otherwise, the castle in Kos Town is far more imposing. Antimachia is a relatively uninteresting town, but it does house the island's only operating **windmill,** which you can see to the left of the main road. Next to the windmill and across the street, visit the traditional house to watch the making of a wool carpet (open 9am-9pm; admission 100dr). The turn-off for Plaka is on the road to Kefalos, just 2500m out of Antimachia. This road provides access to a forested park inhabited by friendly peacocks. Pack a picnic and feed bread crust to these birds.

Mastihari and Kardamena are the two resorts of central Kos. Both offer beaches, streets with few cars, and several restaurants. **Mastihari,** north of Antimachia, is quiet, cozy, and popular among families. If you wish to make this more than a daytrip, try **Hotel Arant** (tel. 51 167; fax 51 168), equidistant from the bus stop and the beach (doubles with bath 8000dr). There are also many pensions and rooms available along the beach (doubles 8000dr). **For You Tourist Services** (tel. 51 149, -520), one block from the bus, helps find rooms (open 9am-9pm). **Boats** go to Kalymnos from Mastihari (3 per day, 810dr). Four **buses** per day leave Kos for Mastihari (45min., 410dr).

▓ Southern Kos

Southern Kos is covered by rolling hills, ravines, and occasional cow pastures. **Kefalos,** Kos's ancient capital and the only town of any real substance on the southern half of the island, is neither crowded nor terribly interesting. North of Kefalos is the picturesque little harbor of **Limionas.** Sit down for an excellent maritime meal at Limionas (tel. (0934) 22 002). The fish is cheap and freshly plucked from the store owner's fishing nets (*barbounia* 7500dr per kg, octopus 1200dr, Greek salad 700dr). The beach that stretches from Limionas to Mastihari is gorgeous and deserted.

Agios Theologos, just west of Kefalos, is one of the island's quietest and most beautiful beaches, a 4km hike from town. Because it is so hard to get to, you will probably have it all to yourself. At the Kefalos bus stop, take the dirt path that branches off to the right and begin your descent. It will take you about an hour, but the peace and quiet that awaits is worth the extra toil.

You will find the **best beaches** in all of Kos on the southeast shore of the island along the main road before Kefalos. Closer to Kefalos, where the road dips to sea level, **Ag. Stefanos** beach has been appropriated by Club Med. Private property signs and fenced-off areas make it clear that only paying guests are welcome in the resort. The beach, however, is open to the public and is a scenic place for a swim. The ruins of a Byzantine church meet the waves at the end of the dirt road that goes to the beach. The tiny island of **Kastri** is a short swim from the shore and tempts those who want to explore its rock formations—a perfect place to sunbathe. On the stretch up to Kardamene, **Camel** is a beautiful, mildly busy beach; **Paradise** has its own bus stop and is popular and more crowded; **Magic,** with a Hawaiian look to it, is farther north, empty, and temptingly blue. Ask the driver to let you out at any of the beaches.

KALYMNOS ΚΑΛΥΜΝΟΣ

Although the first inhabitants of Kalymnos have yet to be identified, archaeologists believe that the Phoenicians colonized the island around 2000 BC. The ruins at Embrio and Vathis suggest that this was a prosperous civilization. Doric and Persian tribes, Venetians, Genoese, the Knights of the Order of Saint John, Ottomans, and Italians all followed the Phoenicians.

But Kalymnos is not well-known for its ancient history. The island has always been famous for its sponge-diving industry. In years past, many men would depart for five or six months and dive for sponges in the Libyan Sea, south of Muammar Qadhafi's Line of Death. Today, the sponges lurk everywhere (warehouses, tourist kiosks, restaurant display-cases), harkening back to the island's glory days as the sponge capital of the world.

Unfortunately, the sponges are dying off, and Kalymnos's former staple industry is now in decline. The island's economy has been partially resuscitated by an influx of tourists on its western beaches. Most of the island's development clings to the coast, leaving the interior mysteriously barren. The rugged mountains, cascading into wide beaches and blue-green water, are unbelievably tempting to those willing to step off the beaten track.

■ Pothia ΠΟΘΙΑ

During the Italian occupation at the turn of the century, many locals painted their houses blue, Greece's national color, to antagonize the Italians. Pink and green buildings have since infiltrated Pothia's neighborhoods and, although slightly grayed, this relatively large town (population 10,000) remains more colorful than its white-washed Aegean counterparts. Pothia is not made to accommodate tourists; there are few rooms, few agencies, and few attractions. Before heading for the beach towns on the west coast, though, enjoy its rainbow architecture and the pride, authenticity, and genuine hospitality of the locals.

ORIENTATION AND PRACTICAL INFORMATION

Ferries arrive at the far left end of the port (facing inland). The road leading from the dock bends around the waterfront until it runs into the large, cream-colored municipal building, a church, and the town hall. A narrow shop-lined street, **Eleftherias** heads one-way inland at this point, leading to **Kyprou Square,** home to the **post office, OTE, police,** and **taxis.** The waterfront road continues past town hall, to a strip of delicious fish *tavernas* and one unparalleled sweet shop. The second most important avenue, **Venizelou** intersects Eleftherias at the end of the harbor near Agios Christos Church. Continue on this road to reach the western part of the island. Follow the harbor promenade past the police station to access the road to Vathis. Most streets in Pothia are unnamed, but following the landmarks is relatively easy.

Tourist Office: (tel. 28 583) Along the waterfront, in a small shack in the shadow of the Olympic Hotel. It's a little white house behind the kiosk and statue of Poseidon. English-speaking help with rooms, transportation, and sights. Bus schedules, photocopied maps of island and town. Open Mon.-Fri. 7am-2:30pm.

Port Authority: (tel. 24 444) In the yellow building across from the customs house, at the end of the dock. Updated ferry information. Open 24hr.

Tourist Agencies: There is no one agency to satisfy all your tourist needs—especially if you are looking at boat schedules. **Magos Travel** (tel. 28 777, -652), on the waterfront near the port police, sells hydrofoil tickets and G.A. ferry tickets. Open daily 8:30am-9pm. **DANE Sea Lines** (tel. 23 043, 24 083), next to the tourist office and clearly marked by a yellow flag, represents the other ferry line that serves Kalymnos. You will find any ferry information you could possibly need between the two offices. Open daily 8am-2pm and 5-10pm.

Bank: National Bank (tel. 29 794), on the waterfront, has an **ATM,** advances cash on MasterCard and Visa, and offers **currency exchange.** Open Mon.-Thurs. 8am-2pm, Fri. 8am-1:30pm.

Flights: Olympic Airways (tel. 29 265; fax 28 903), take the first left past the National Bank; it's 50m on the left, around bends. There is no airport, but the office is open for reservations. Open Mon.-Tues. and Thurs.-Fri. 8am-1:30pm and 5-8:30pm, Wed. and Sat. 8am-1:30pm.

Buses: Every hr. on the hr. 7am-10pm, buses leave for: Kastelli (50min.) via Chora (10min.); Panormos (15min.); Myrties (20min.); and Massouri (25min.). Fares 100-250dr. Six buses go to Vilhadia, 2 to Emborio, 4 to Vathis, 3 to Argos, and 3 to Plati Gialos. Buses to western towns leave from the town hall in harbor center. Buses to Vathis from the northeast corner of the waterfront. Purchase your tickets before boarding at Themis mini-market, next to the town hall, and insert them into the automated validating box on the bus, much like the system in Athens.

Ferries: Sail to: Peiraias (1-2 per day, 13hr., 6530dr); Leros (1-2 per day, 1hr., 1815dr); Patmos (1-2 per day, 3hr., 2350dr); Kos (1-2 per day, 1½hr., 1215dr); Rhodes (1-2 per day, 6hr., 4020dr); Astypalea (2 per week, 3hr., 2480dr); Lipsos (3 per week, 1885dr); Tilos (3 per week, 2445dr); Symi (3 per week, 3225dr); Nisyros (3 per week, 1745dr); and Thessaloniki (1 per week, 11,900dr). There is also service to Mastihari in Kos near the **airport** (3 per day, 1000dr). Kalymnos sends daily **excursions** to the small island of Pserimos between Kalymnos and Kos (1800dr round-trip), home to superior beaches and a few *tavernas.*

Flying Dolphins: Fast but more expensive and severely contingent on weather conditions. Daily to: Kos (3020dr); Leros (3560dr); Patmos (4680dr); Lipsos (4010dr); Ikaria (5975dr); Fourni (6515dr); Agathonisi (4815dr); Samos (5815dr); Tilos (3890dr); Nisyros (3015dr); Symi (6425dr); and Rhodes (8440dr).

Taxis: (tel. 24 222, 29 555) Congregate in Kyprou Sq. up Eleftherias St. 7am-9pm, taxis also operate as taxi buses; if there is a bunch of people going in one direction, the driver will take them all together.

Moped Rental: Costas Katrivesis (tel. 50 105), directly behind the port police at the end of the dock. Mopeds range from 2000-4000dr per day, with partial insurance. Open daily 8:30am-9pm.

Pharmacy: (tel. 29 338) Near the intersection of Eleftherias and Venizelou. Open Mon.-Tues. and Thurs.-Fri. 9am-1pm and 5:30-8:30pm, Wed. 9am-2pm.

Hospital: (tel. 28 851) On the main road to Chora, 1.5km from Pothia. Open 24hr.

Police: (tel. 22 100, 29 301) Go up Eleftherias St. and take the left inland road from the taxi square. In a blue and yellow neoclassical building on the right. Open 24hr.

Post Office: (tel. 28 340) On your right, just past the police station. Has **currency exchange.** Open Mon.-Fri. 7:30am-2pm. **Postal Code:** 85200.

OTE: (tel 29 599) From the taxi square up Eleftherias St., take the inland road on the right. Open Mon.-Fri. 7:30am-3:10pm. **Telephone Code:** 0243.

ACCOMMODATIONS

Securing a room in Pothia is hassle-free; pension owners await even late-night ferries and the tourist office shack is helpful when open. For true hospitality, head inland from the waterfront at the National Bank, take the first left, follow the bends, and look for signs to the Panorama Hotel. When the road splits at the embankment wall, go right: the first alley on the left leads to three flights of stairs. Haul yourself and your luggage to the top and meet **Katerina** (tel. 22 186), a replica of the stereotypical Greek grandmother—welcoming, compassionate, and concerned about your empty stomach. Family members can help you communicate about logistics, but food is a universal language. Katerina rents large, spotless rooms with tile floors, communal bath, and kitchen facilities (doubles 4000dr; triples 5000dr). The flower-covered home on the corner of the final alleyway near Katerina's is the hospitable **Pension Greek House** (tel. 29 559). Here you will find comfortable rooms with private bath and refrigerator (doubles 5000dr; triples 7000dr).

FOOD AND ENTERTAINMENT

The typical array of cafe/bars and modest *tavernas* is tightly clustered on Pothia's harbor. Most people enjoy a few drinks on the waterfront before heading to the clubs in Massouri.

Navtikos Omilos Restaurant (tel. 29 239), isolated at the end of the harbor, all the way on the left (facing inland). Depending on season, you will have front row seats facing either an amusement park (June-July) or the ocean. Very inexpensive, but prepare to dine with excursion groups from Kos, especially in afternoon. Spaghetti *neapolitana* 590dr, Greek salad 700dr. Open daily 8am-3pm and 6:30-11pm.

Xefteris (tel. 28 642), from the town hall, head up Eleftherias St., take the first right, then the first left directly into the *taverna*'s outdoor garden. A little more out of the way and less touristy. Oldest restaurant on the island. Traditional *taverna* serves authentic Greek cuisine, including island specialties like *dolmathes* (stuffed vine leaves, 1200dr) and stuffed zucchini (1200dr). Dessert is sinfully good. Do not pass up the opportunity to indulge yourself here. Open daily noon-1am.

Alachouzou (tel. 29 446), pass the church and continue along the waterfront. A Greek pastry lover's paradise. Sweet shop has been making only 5 types of desserts for over 35 years and has perfected all 5. *Galactobouri* (custard sandwiched between *phyllo* dough and drenched in sweet syrup, 350dr) is the house and island specialty; try it with homemade ice cream. Open daily 8am-1am.

MacDonuts (tel. 48 165), on right-hand side of Eleftherias St. in storefront with "1899" carved on the edifice. Best doughnuts in Aegean. Open 7:30am-midnight.

Yakinthos (tel. 24 016), serves beer (400-600dr), cocktails (800-900dr), and a variety of coffees and ice creams. Enjoy your choice as you people-watch. Open 9am-1am.

The Apocalypse, just past the town hall on the waterfront road. A little rowdier, noisier, and chic. Also a little more expensive, but has a packed dance floor. Open 10pm-3am.

Cine Oasis, at the end of a short alleyway plastered with movie posters. If bar-hopping is not pleasing, outdoor movie starts at 9:30pm, changes every night. Posters announce feature presentations. Adults 1400dr, children 1000dr.

SIGHTS

Learn first-hand about the island's historic **sponge industry.** The sponge shop of **Nikolas Gourlas** is on the waterfront near the port police. Mr. Gourlas speaks English and will be happy to show you around the factory where sponges are cleaned and chemically treated (sponge mementos from 500dr). Follow the blue signs from Venizelou St. to the **Archeological Museum of Kalymnos** (tel. 23 113), housed in the former mansion of Catherine and Nikolaos Vouvalis, turn-of-the-century sponge barons from Kalymnos (open Tues.-Sun. 10am-2pm; free). The **Marine and Folklore Museum** (tel. 24 862), a few doors down from the town hall, on the second floor, houses traditional island wares and clothing and explores the life and work of the island's sponge divers (open Tues.-Sun 10am-2pm; admission 500dr, students 250dr). The hilltop **Monastery of Agion Pantes and Agios Savvas** overlooks the town. Visitors can enter at the gate on the right side; the first chapel on your left contains the bones of canonized Saint Savvas in a sarcophagus. The nuns there may welcome you with water and an occasional sweet. The monastery is always open, but it is best not to disturb the nuns during their afternoon chores (free).

From the customs house, take the roads to the left to reach the beach at **Therma,** 2km away. Arthritic patients make pilgrimages to the sanitarium here to wade in its **sulphur mineral baths.** (Doctor's permission is required to bathe. Those without medical problems will not want to con a prescription; the baths have a strong phosphorous odor.) The main beach is crowded, but a short walk around the bend leads to a quiet swimming spot. The tranquil beach at **Vlichadia** (6km from Pothia), the island's only **scuba diving** site, is farther west from Therma (backtrack toward Pothia and then slightly north). Despite this attraction, an inconvenient bus schedule keeps Vlichadia Beach pleasantly peaceful. The rocky bottom makes it hard on feet.

■ Western Coast

Kalymnos sports two main roads: one runs northwest out of Pothia, the other northeast. A few kilometers along the northwest road, a side road to the left leads up to a fortress of the Knights of St. John, also called **Chrissocherias Castle.** A number of little chapels are hidden in its remains. Painted sections of wall indicate where privateers dug holes in search of treasure. The Byzantine **Pera Castle** looms north of Chrissocherias across the valley. The Knights enlarged and fortified this structure. Nine tiny white churches are scattered throughout the ruins and maintained by elderly Chorian women. Directly opposite lies the small village of **Argos**—once the ancient city of Argiens, now a suburb of Pothia. Pera Kastro and Argos overlook the town of **Chora,** once Kalymnos's capital but now little more than another one of Pothia's tentacles.

One kilometer or so beyond Chora, just after the road begins to descend into Panormos, a few white steps by the side of the road lead to the shell of the **Church of Christ of Jerusalem.** Byzantine Emperor Arcadius built this church to thank God for sparing him in a storm while at sea. The stone blocks with carved inscriptions are from a 4th-century BC temple to Apollo that stood on the same site. By incorporating and subordinating these architectural elements, the church came to be viewed as a symbolic victory over paganism (open 24hr.; free). The road branches at Panormos. One offshoot goes to **Kantouni,** a village with a less-than-spectacular beach. Staying at the hotel may be expensive, but the free outdoor swimming pool is open to the public. Also on the waterfront, the **Domus Bar/Restaurant** serves excellent food (Greek salad 800dr) and then clears the tables for a night of dancing. Try not to miss the rooftop sunset.

Another road from Panormos leads 2km to the sandy and less-crowded beach of **Plati Gialos.** You may consider staying at **Pension Plati Gialos** (tel. 22 014), perched on a cliff with a memorable view of the coastline (doubles 6000dr). Follow the paved road to the top of the hill, where you will find the pension's reception. Both the graysand beach at **Myrties,** 7km up the coast, and the pebbly one at **Massouri,** the next town, can be quite crowded. Massouri is well-known as the center of the island's nightlife. Establishments open late, and the clientele arrive even later. Since there is only one paved road running through Massouri, all the bars and clubs are within a five-minute walk of one another. The **Pink Elephant** boasts Guinness on tap (600dr), hard cider (600dr), and an assortment of cocktails (1000dr). The real hotspots are the dance clubs **Forum, Mike's,** and **Club Dorian Tropical.** Each charges a 2000dr cover that includes a free drink. The party starts after midnight.

Myrties's finest attraction, a short boat ride out of town (every 30min., 15min., 200dr), is the tiny, rocky islet of **Telendos,** severed from Kalymnos by an earthquake in 554 AD. A city occupied the fault line where the island cracked, and traces of it have been found on the ocean floor, but the rift is invisible from the surface. The Roman ruins on Telendos are modest at best, but a few small secluded beaches fringe the island. (Turn right from the ferry dock for the best beaches.) The **Byzantine Monastery of St. Constantine** is past the beaches to the right (open only for liturgy). Accommodations in Telendos are generally full only for a couple of weeks in August. Most pensions charge 3000-5000dr for a double. **Uncle George's Pension** (tel. 47 502), near the docks, has an excellent restaurant and clean rooms (doubles with bath 4000dr; studios with kitchenette and bath 5000dr). Inquire at the restaurant **Ailena** for similar rooms a little closer to the beaches (doubles 3500dr). **Galanomatis** (tel. 47 401) is farther along toward the beaches (doubles 4000dr). Before leaving Myrties, look back at Telendos. Many claim that a woman's profile is visible in the rock along the left side of the mountain (all right, stretch your imagination). According to residents, she is mourning her lost husband as she forlornly looks out to sea.

Back on Kalymnos, an empty beach stretches out at **Arginontas,** at the end of a long, narrow inlet. Both roads to the beach rise dramatically along cliffs that plunge into turquoise water. Though not the cleanest place on the island, **Vanzanelis'** (tel. 47 389), at Arginontas Beach, has a *taverna* and rooms with bath and refrigerator (doubles 7000dr; triples 8000dr.) Two buses from Pothia venture this far (250dr). The last village on the west side, **Emborio,** is unruffled and remote. **Harry's Restaurant** (tel. 47 434), 20m from the beach, provides good food and beds (doubles 8000dr; triples 9000dr; all with bath and kitchenette). The **Restaurant Themis** (tel. 47 277), the white building with blue trim facing the beach, has nice rooms, stately balconies and private baths (doubles 4000dr). A small boat makes an **excursion** from Myrties to Emborio daily at 10am (1800dr).

Although most of Kalymnos supports only grass and wildflowers, the valley at Vathis (6km northeast of Pothia) is a rich potpourri of mandarins, limes, and grapevines. The valley starts at the village of **Rina.** There is no beach here (swim off the pier), but the exquisite scenery and lack of tourists compensate for the lack of sand. On the north side of the inlet is **Daskaleios,** a stalagmite cave within swimming range. In Rina, the **Hotel Galini** (tel. 31 241) has decent rooms (doubles with bath and balcony 6500dr). The three *tavernas* on the tiny waterfront also rent rooms, but prices are similar to that of the hotel's and the rooms are not as well-maintained.

PATMOS ΠΑΤΜΟΣ

Declared the "Holy Island" by ministerial decree (signs at the port warn that nudity and other "indecent" behavior will not be tolerated), Patmos's historical and religious significance is evident. In ancient times, the people of Patmos worshipped Artemis, goddess of the hunt, who is said to have raised the island from the sea. Orestes built a grand temple to Artemis after seeking refuge on Patmos from the Furies, who were pursuing him for murdering his mother Clytemnestra.

While he was in exile from Ephesus, St. John established a Christian colony here and purportedly wrote *The Book of Revelations* in a grotto overlooking the main town. His words, "I…was on the isle that is called Patmos, for the word of God, and for the testimony of Jesus Christ…" could be considered the island's motto. In the 4th century AD, when the Christian faith spread with the Byzantine Empire, a basilica replaced the razed Temple of Artemis. In the 11th century, the fortified Monastery of St. John was built on a hill overlooking the entire island. Modern Patmos is lively and sophisticated, and thus far has managed to strike a delicate balance between its current popularity and solemn past. The common yellow flag with the black two-headed eagle is the age-old banner of the Byzantine Empire and Greek Orthodox Church.

Fashionable Religion

The latest accessory craze in Greece is a bracelet of black yarn tied in a series of knots. Although simple, these bracelets have taken the country by storm. Oddly enough, monks are some of the biggest suppliers of these trendy creations, which they make to raise money for their monasteries.

Each bracelet has 33 knots, symbolizing Christ's age at the time of his crucifixion. Each knot is tied so that three pieces of yarn cross uniformly, reminding the wearer of the Holy Trinity. The bracelets are often decorated with a single red bead, representing the blood of Christ. Monks wear these bracelets to encourage prayer. The monk recites one verse of prayer for each knot until he has gone around the entire loop. The current fashion craze has overlooked this decidedly religious symbolism in favor of accessorizing.

■ Skala ΣΚΑΛΑ

Built along a graceful arc of coastline, Skala is a neat and colorful port that gives only a hint of the island's diverse terrain. The town did not develop until the 19th century, when fear of pirates subsided and people began to live safely by the water. The main administrative buildings, which house the post office and customs house, were constructed during Italian occupation (1912-1943). Today, whitewashed churches are camouflaged among village buildings, but Skala also caters to the secular aspects of life: cafes, bars, *tavernas,* and shops are abundant. Skala is the most convenient place to stay on the island because inconvenient bus schedules make travel difficult.

ORIENTATION AND PRACTICAL INFORMATION

Skala's amenities are all within a block or two of the waterfront. Small ferries dock opposite the line of cafes and restaurants, while larger vessels park in front of the Italian building that houses the police and post office. The building borders the main square, where banks are located. Skala is on a narrow part of the island; if you walk away from the water you can reach the opposite coast in about 10 minutes.

Tourist Office: (tel. 31 666) In the big Italian building across the dock. Maps, brochures, bus schedules, information on all ferries, and help with accommodations. Ask for the free *Patmos Summertime* guide, which includes maps of Skala and the island. Open Mon.-Fri. 8:30am-10:30pm.

Port Authority: (tel. 31 231) To the left of the ferry dock (facing inland), next to the snack bar. Information on ferries. Open 24hr., but knock forcefully if it is late.

Tourist Agencies: All over the waterfront, but each offers information on only those ferry lines for which they sell tickets. Consult the tourist office or the port police for complete schedules and then ask where to buy your particular ticket. **Apollon Tourist and Shipping Agency** (tel. 31 356, -4; fax 31 819), is the not-so-helpful local agent for **Olympic Airways.** Open daily 8:30am-8:30pm.

Banks: National Bank (tel. 31 123, -774, -591), in the far end of the square. Cash advances on MasterCard and **currency exchange.** Open Mon.-Thurs. 8am-2pm, Fri. 8am-1:30pm. There is also an **ATM** next to the post office. Exchange at the post office and **Apollon Agency** as well.

Buses: Across the little park, left of the police station. 10 per day go to Chora (10min.), 7 of which continue to Grikou (10min.), and 4 to Kampos (15min.). All fares 190dr (children free). Schedule posted at bus stop or tourist office.

Ferries: Daily service to: Peiraias (10hr., 6430dr); Leros (1½hr., 1620dr); Kalymnos (2½hr., 2395dr); Kos (4hr., 2720dr); and Rhodes (10hr., 5300dr). Boats also run to Lipsi (4 per week, 1320dr) and Samos (6 per week, 2700dr). Ferries run once per week to: Lesvos (4525dr); Limnos (6780dr); Mykonos (3840dr); Syros (4135dr); Nisyros (2825dr); Tilos (3555dr); Naxos (3170dr); Paros (3620dr); Tinos (3875dr); and Symi (4650dr). Private **excursion boats** go to Lipsi (daily, 1500dr one way, 2500dr round-trip), and different beaches around the island (round-trip 1000dr). Check out the deals posted along the waterfront.

Flying Dolphins: Two per day to: Leros (30min., 3045dr); Kalymnos (1hr., 4570dr); and Kos (2hr., 5525dr). Two per week to Agathonisi (40min., 3665dr); and 4 per week to Lipsos (20min., 2465dr). Also to: Samos (2-3 per day, 1hr., 3490dr); Ikaria (1 per day, 50min., 3465dr); and Fourni (3 per week, 1hr., 3250dr).

Taxis: (tel. 31 225) Congregate in the main square 24hr. in summer, but difficult to catch in the *après*-disco flurry, and from 3-6:30am. Taxis to Chora 700-1000dr.

Car Rental: Patmos Rent-a-Car (tel. 32 203), turn left after the post office and look for it on your right (2nd floor). 9000dr and up. Open daily 8am-11pm.

Moped Rental: Express Moto (tel. 32 088), turn left after the tourist office and take the first right. New models 1500-5000dr per day. Open daily 8am-8pm.

Laundromat: Just Like Home, 5min. from the dock on the waterfront road toward Meloi and Kampos. 2500dr per 5kg load (wash, dry, and soap). Open Mon.-Fri. 9am-1pm and 5-8pm.

International Bookstore: International Press (tel. 31 427), behind the Pantelis Restaurant—look for the signs. Open daily 8am-9:30pm.

Pharmacy: (tel. 31 500) Behind Apollon Travel, on the first street parallel to the waterfront. Open Mon.-Tues. and Thurs.-Fri. 8:30am-1:30pm and 5:30-9pm, Wed. and Sat. 8:30am-1:30pm and 7-9pm, Sun. 11am-12:30pm and 6:30-9pm. Call 31 083 for after-hours emergencies.

Hospital: (tel. 31 211) On the main road to Chora, across from the monastery Apokalipsi (2km out of Skala). Open daily 8am-2pm. **Emergency:** Call the **police,** who know doctors' schedules and will contact them (tel. 31 087, -571).

Police: (tel. 31 303) Upstairs from the tourist office. Open 24hr. **Tourist Police** (tel. 31 303) also housed there.

Post Office: (tel. 31 316) On the main square, next to the police. Open Mon.-Fri. 7:30am-2pm. **Postal Code:** 85500.

OTE: Follow the signs in the main square. Open Mon.-Fri. 7:30am-3:10pm. The cafe-bar at the boat dock has an international telephone. **Telephone Code:** 0247.

ACCOMMODATIONS

Skala's hotels are often full in summer, but finding a room in a pension or private home is usually easy. Even boats arriving at 1am are greeted by a battalion of locals offering rooms. (Average prices: singles 4000dr; doubles 6000dr.) Off-season prices are generally lower by 20-40%. To find a room, walk left from the ferry dock and right onto Vas. Georgiou St. Roughly 50m on the left, after Pizza Zacharo, across from the basketball court, is a "rooms to let" sign. **Maria Paschalidis** (tel. 32 152, 31 347) runs a jubilant pension with spotless rooms, permeated by the fragrance of jasmine (doubles 6000dr, with bath 8000dr; triples 8000dr, with bath 10,000dr). Between Maria's rooms and Pizza Zacharo, above a Tae Kwon Do school, is **Pension Sofia** (tel. 31 501, -876). Knock on the second floor or ask next door on the right for the immaculate rooms. (Doubles with bath 7000dr; triples and quads with common bath 5000dr. Breakfast included.) Many rooms can be found on Vas. Georgiou St. and on the street that leads to the OTE. Two kilometers northeast of Skala, the excellent **Flower Camping at Meloi** (tel. 31 821), has a minimarket and cafe. It is a two-minute walk from Meloi Beach. Follow the waterfront road all the way to the right, facing inland; look for signs (1200dr per person; 750dr per tent; 750dr per tent rental).

FOOD

Several seafood restaurants featuring expensive fish entrees line the waterfront. There are several **grocery stores** clustered around the main square, as well as numerous **sweet shops.** Visit a sweet shop and try the Patmian dessert *pouggia,* a ball of honey and nuts (almonds, walnuts, or peanuts) covered in dough and sometimes smothered in powdered sugar (220-300dr), or Patmian cheese pie, a pastry shell filled with local cheese, eggs, milk, and cinnamon (380dr).

Grigoris (tel. 31 515), across from the bus stop at the corner of the road to Chora, has good and reasonably priced fare. Experience the swordfish *souvlaki* or grilled grouper (each 1400dr). Open daily noon-4pm and 6pm-1am.

The Old Harbor Restaurant (tel. 31 170), with its woodwork balcony on the waterfront road to Meloi, reputedly serves the island's best seafood. The best, however, does not come cheap. One medium-sized serving of *barbounia* will cost about 2500dr (800dr per kg). Open daily 6pm-midnight.

Pantelis (tel. 31 230), a cheaper but equally delicious option. Behind the central strip of cafes on the street parallel to the waterfront, this family restaurant will overwhelm you with its selection of Greek dishes. Over 50 choices each day, many are vegetarian. *Gigantes* 800dr, *kakavia* 1500dr. Open daily 11am-11pm.

Augerinos, on the road to the OTE, has excellent take-out *souvlaki-pita* (350dr).

ENTERTAINMENT

As befits such a sacred island, the nightlife here tends to be rather tame, more centered on promenading or casually sipping drinks than on rowdy carousing.

Arion (tel. 31 595), a cafe next to Apollon Travel. One of the more popular hangouts. Beers 500-850dr, cocktails 1200dr.

Adonis (tel. 32 040), just a couple storefronts down from Arion, serves similar drinks and excellent ice cream sundaes (1000dr). Open daily 7pm-3am.

Art Cafe (tel. 33 092) tends to draw an older crowd that comes to enjoy the jazz and blues that accommpany the terrace view. Open 9pm-3am.

Pépe Nero Bar (tel. 32 231), behind the tourist information office. The younger crowd heads here for Latin, funk, and soul music (i.e., everything you can dance to). Gets a little crowded, so be prepared to become closely acquainted with the person next to you. Open daily 1pm-3am.

Cine Meloi (tel. 31 579), start walking to Meloi and look for it on your left. A 15min. walk from the dock will get you to the 9 or 11pm showings of Hollywood hits under a starlit sky. A good alternative to the bar or cafe scene.

■ Chora ΧΩΡΑ

From almost any part of Patmos, you can see the white houses of Chora and the majestic, gray walls of the nearby Monastery of St. John the Theologian above. Roam Chora's labyrinthine streets, where gardens hide behind grand doors in the shelter of the monastery, and view the Patmos shoreline and the outlying archipelago.

ORIENTATION AND PRACTICAL INFORMATION

The town's convoluted layout makes it impossible to give precise directions. The map of Patmos available at kiosks and tourist shops comes with a questionable illustration of town. Take care of business before arriving; a few phonecard telephones and a mailbox at the bottom of the hill are the only links between Chora and the outside world. **Buses** travel to Chora from Skala (10 per day, 10min., 190dr). The bus stops at the top of the hill outside the town; this is also the point of departure for buses from Chora to Grikou. A taxi here from Skala costs 1000dr. If you decide to walk (4km and steep), the steps to Chora will be quicker and safer than the road.

FOOD AND ENTERTAINMENT

Vangelis (tel. 31 967), head toward the monastery and follow signs to the central square. Home to traditional Greek cuisine, is the talk of the town. Peek into the pots and pans; this is what good Greek food looks like. *Moussaka* 900dr. Grab a seat on roof garden an enjoy the view. Open daily noon-2pm and 6pm-midnight.

To Pantheon (tel. 31 226), near the bus stop, has less ambiance, but offers fried zucchini with garlic sauce (750dr) and wonderful octopus (1100dr). Open noon-1am.

Cafe Stoa (tel. 32 226), in the main square across from Vangelis, is your nighttime, alcohol-related entertainment. Enjoy a cheap cocktail (900dr). Be prepared to take a cab home if you are staying in Skala—the last bus from Chora leaves at 10:30pm, long before you will be ready to leave. Open daily 5pm-2am.

SIGHTS

The turreted walls and imposing gateway of the **Monastery of St. John the Theologian** (tel. 31 398) make it look more like a fortress than a place of worship. St. Christodoulos founded the monastery in 1088, nearly 1000 years after St. John's celebrated stay on the island. Pragmatic considerations proved more important than aesthetics, as the monastery was a constant target of pirate raids. The memorial to St. John was transformed into a citadel with battlements and watch towers. As you enter the courtyard, notice the 17th-century frescoes on the left that portray stories from *The Miracles and Travels of St. John the Evangelist,* written by John's disciple Prochoros. To the upper right, a fresco portrays St. John's duel with a local priest of Apollo named Kynops. When the Saint threw Kynops into the water at Skala, the heathen turned into stone. The rock is still in the harbor. Ask any local to point it out.

Continue to the **Chapel of the Virgin Mary,** covered with original 12th-century frescoes. In 1956, tremors revealed these frescoes buried beneath those that were on exhibit. The **treasury** guards icons, ornamented stoles (some of which were donated by Catherine the Great of Russia), a copy of St. Mark's Gospel, and an 8th-century Book of Job. Look for **Helkomenos,** an icon painted by El Greco near the end of the exhibit (admission 1000dr). The **Chapel of the Holy Christodoulos** holds the remains of the monastery's illustrious founder. Shortly after Christodoulos's death, many visitors attempted to appropriate his saintliness by carrying away his remains, so the monks built a marble sarcophagus and covered it with a silver reliquary.

Try not to visit the monastery at midday in summer because it becomes crammed with tourists. If you come in the off season, one of the monastery's 20 monks (there were once 1700) may volunteer to show you around. In summer, you will have to tag along with a guided group. (Monastery and treasure museum open Mon. 8am-1pm, Tues. 8am-1pm and 4-6pm, Wed. 8am-1:30pm, Thurs. 8am-1pm and 4-8pm, Fri.-Sat. 8am-1:30pm, Sun. 10am-noon and 4-6pm. Dress appropriately; no shorts or bare shoulders. If necessary, wrap a towel or shawl around legs or shoulders. Free.)

Halfway uphill on the winding road that connects Chora and Skala (2km from each) is a turn-off for another monastery, the **Apocalypsis,** a large, white complex of interconnected buildings. Most people come here to see the **Sacred Grotto of the Revelation** (tel. 31 234), adjacent to the Church of St. Anne. In this cave, St. John dictated the *Book of Revelation,* the last book of the New Testament, after hearing the voice of God proclaim "Now write what you see, what is to take place hereafter" (Rev. 1:19). Christians believe that when God spoke to St. John, he cleft the ceiling of the cave with a three-pronged crack representing the Holy Trinity. Silver plating marks the spot where St. John presumably slept. (Apocalypsis open same hours as Monastery of St. John. Dress appropriately. Free.)

▓ Around Patmos Island

The town of **Grikou,** only 5km southwest of Skala, is rapidly turning into a family beach resort. The beach itself is less than ideal, although there are watersport rentals available (paddleboats 1300dr per hour, waterskiing 5000dr per 10 minutes), and a rocky bottom makes wading uncomfortable. Rooms in the area are geared to families, offering kitchens and several bedrooms as a single unit. **O Flisvos** (tel. 31 380, -961) rents studios for up to three people above a shaded *taverna* overlooking the bay (with bath 12,000dr). Mopeds can continue 2km south to the secluded **Plaki Beach,** where the road degenerates. To reach the island's best beach, **Psili Ammos,** take the road to Grikov from Chora, then take the road that branches off to the right, headed for Thiakofti. At Thiakofti, park your moped and proceed down the dirt path, clearly marked with asbestos-painted rocks and handwritten signs. You will be sunbathing on a golden stretch of sandy paradise only 20 minutes later. Excursion boats leaving from Skala at 10am and returning at 4pm provide an easier route to Psili Ammos (1 per day, 1200dr). Although convenient, this option offers little flexibility. **Kambos** is another pleasant option for beachgoers. Perhaps not as beautiful as Psili Ammos, it has a sandy bottom and frequent bus service (4 buses per day, 15min., 190dr). In the north, **Lambi** is famed for its multicolored round pebbles. Arrange your own transportation, because buses do not go there.

ASTYPALEA ΑΣΤΥΠΑΛΑΙΑ

Few travelers venture to butterfly-shaped Astypalea, the westernmost of the Dodecanese islands. Jagged hills and secluded orange and lemon groves merit leisurely exploration. It is an excellent place to unwind and let off a little steam, but please do not repeat history. Astypalea's most infamous athlete, an Olympic boxer named Kleomedies, returned home after being disqualified from the ancient Games for fatally defeating his opponent. To vent his frustration, he destroyed the schoolhouse, killed all the children, and committed suicide. Amazing, considering the island's soothing atmosphere.

▓ Astypalea Town

Surrounded by tawny hills, Astypalea town is a hillside conglomerate of cubic dwellings. It is the only major city on the island, and most of the services and ammenities you'll need can be found here.

ORIENTATION AND PRACTICAL INFORMATION

Just before the town's small beach, the **police** (tel. 61 207) are in a small building (open 8am-7pm). The **OTE** (tel. 61 212, -5), is at the foot of the Paradissos Hotel (open Mon.-Fri. 7:30am-2pm). **M. Karakosta,** in the store under the Aegean hotel, is an agent of the **National Bank** (open Mon.-Thurs. 8am-2pm, Fri. 8am-1:30pm), while the small branch of the **Commercial Bank** on the waterfront has an **ATM** (open Mon.-Thurs. 8am-2pm, Fri. 8am-1:30pm). For transportation questions, try the **travel agency** just down the street from the bank (tel. 61 224; open Mon.-Fri. 9am-1pm). The **post office/currency exchange** (tel. 61 223; open Mon.-Fri. 7:30am-2pm) and several **supermarkets** (open 9am-1pm and 5-9pm) are all in this older section of town. In case of **medical emergency,** call the clinic at 61 222. **Ferries** arrive in Astypalea sporadically. Boats travel to: Peiraias (3 per week, 12-18hr., 5450dr); Kalymnos (3 per week, 3hr., 2420dr); Kos (1 per week, 3½hr., 4930dr); Rhodes (2 per week, 5hr., 4020dr); Paros (2 per week, 7hr., 3335dr); Naxos (2 per week, 5½hr., 3105dr); Santorini (1 per week, 4hr., 2850dr); and Amorgos (2 per week, 2-3hr., 2710dr). Ferries do not leave Astypalea every day, but excursion boats leave daily for the island's beaches. The **postal code** is 85900. The **telephone code** is 0243.

ACCOMMODATIONS

Rooms on the island fill up quickly in July and August, but those available are cheap (singles 5000dr; doubles 7000dr; triples 8000dr). Ask the **travel agency** for help. The **Hotel Aegean** (tel. 61 236), on the main road, has clean rooms with baths (singles 3500dr; doubles 4500dr; triples 5500dr). Your other two options are on the waterfront. **Paradissos** (tel. 61 224) and **Astynea** (tel. 61 209) offer similar, bare-minimum accommodations for similar prices (doubles 3500-5000dr; triples 5000-7000dr). **Camping Astypalea** (tel. 61 338) is 2½km east of town near Marmari; follow signs or take a bus toward Maltezana (1000dr per person; 750dr per tent).

SIGHTS

At the top of the hill, a striking row of windmills leads to the **castle,** a ramshackle Byzantine structure shedding segments of walls and windows. There is a clear view of the island and its flock of tributary islets from here. A 20-minute walk west (over the hill) from town will bring you to the sandy beach of **Livadia.** The beach is crammed with tents and children in July and August, but nude bathers can be found **Tzanaki Beach,** a 20-minute hike along the coast to the southwest. **Ag. Konstantinos** beach is accessible by a dirt road (1½hr. hike from Livadia).

In the other direction from Astypalea Town, the quiet fishing villages of **Maltezana** and **Analipsi** occupy the narrow isthmus. Home to some largely intact Roman mosaics, Maltezana is accessible by bus (2 per day, 150dr). The narrow natural harbor at **Vathi** is subdivided into **Exo** Vathi (outside) and **Esa** Vathi (inside). In winter, when the winds are too strong for boats to dock at Astypalea, the ferries go to the bay at **Ag. Andreas.** The lovely beach here is accessible by road. Another rocky road leads to the **Ag. Ioannis Monastery,** majestically balanced atop a hill.

KARPATHOS ΚΑΡΠΑΘΟΣ

Marking the midpoint between Rhodes and Crete, Karpathos is often seen only at a distance by those taking the overnight ferry. Karpathians embody Greece's famed hospitality, so those adventurous enough to disembark will enjoy a unique level of attention. In the mountains, residents preserve tradition almost religiously, but Karpathos Town straddles the line between quaint and cosmopolitan.

War and conquest mark Karpathos's history. Karpathians fought with Sparta in the Peloponnesian War in 431 BC and lost their independence to Rhodes in 400 BC. In 42 BC the island fell to Rome and in 395 AD was annexed by Byzantium. A few centuries later, Karpathos was ruled in turn by the Arabs, the Genovese pirate Moresco, the Venetians, and the Ottoman Empire. In 1848, the island became part of Greece, the country it is most closely related to in language and culture, but Ottoman rule ended only when the Italians conquered the island during WWI. Karpathos found itself ruled by the Germans for a couple years following the end of WWII.

■ Karpathos Town

Karpathos Town used to be referred to as Ta Pigadia, meaning "the wells." Before that, the town was called Possi, for "Poseidon Polis," but many objected to this name, which also meant "drinking about." Today, Karpathos Town is the island's administrative and transportation center.

ORIENTATION AND PRACTICAL INFORMATION

The best way to orient yourself in Karpathos Town is to bear in mind the Greek free spirit. The streets and square are not named, but do not fret. There are only two main roads. One, running along the water, is lined with *tavernas,* cafes, pharmacies, and the National Bank; the other, a block inland, runs parallel to the first and contains the post office, bakery, and signs for various guest houses. If you insist on buying a map, make sure it is up to date. The best places to purchase maps are **Karpathos** and **Possi Travel Agencies** (350dr). Maps of the area in tourist shops are often outdated.

Tourist Agencies: Karpathos Travel (tel. 22 148; fax 22 754), Dimokratia St., between the bus station and waterfront. Bus and boat schedules. Arranges accommodations, **rents cars** (43,400dr for 3 days), and **exchanges currency.** Sells tickets for excursions to Lefkos, Diafani, and Olympus. Open Mon.-Sat. 8:30am-1pm and 5:30-9pm, Sun. 9-11am and 6-8pm. Both Karpathos and **Possi Travel** (tel. 22 235; fax 22 252), around the corner on Apodimon Karpathion St., sell maps for 350dr. Open Mon.-Sat. 8:30am-1pm and 5:30-8:30pm, Sun. 9am-noon and 6pm-8pm.

Banks: National Bank (tel. 22 409, -518), opposite Possi Travel. **Currency exchange** and **ATM** that accepts Visa/MC. Open Mon.-Thurs. 8am-2pm, Fri. 8am-1:30pm.

Flights: Olympic Airways (tel. 22 150, -057), on the street parallel to the water. Flights to Athens (3 per week, 25,700dr) via Rhodes (4 per day, 25,700dr), and to Kassos (4 per week, 5800dr). Open Mon.-Fri. 8am-3:30pm.

Ferries: To: Peiraias (3 per week, 21hr., 7420dr); Iraklion (2 per week, 6hr., 3500dr); Kassos (3 per week, 1½hr., 1520dr); Paros (2 per week, 17hr., 4700dr); Rhodes (2 per week, 5hr., 4050dr); and Santorini (2 per week, 12hr., 4500dr).

Buses: 1 block up Dimokratia St. from town center. Serve most villages (300-1000dr); check the schedule at Karpathos Travel or call Manolis at 22 192.

Taxis: (tel. 22 705) Run 24hr. to all the villages (2000dr to nearby villages). Government regulated taxi prices are posted at the station on Dimokratia St.

Moped/Car Rental: Gatoulis Motorbikes (tel. 22 747), same street as the post office, but farther down the road leading out of town. 50cc bikes 3500dr per day. Cars 12,000dr per day plus tax. Open daily 8am-3pm and 5-8pm.

International Bookstore: John Pavlakos (tel. 22 389), next to Possi Travel, has writing supplies and guidebooks. Open Mon.-Sun. 9am-2pm and 5:30-11pm.

Pharmacies: Three near the water. All open Mon.-Fri. 8am-1pm and 5:30-8:30pm.

Medical Assistance: Contact the **Health Center** (tel. 22 228), a large white building 100m past Platia 5 October, on N.K. Matheou St. After 2pm, go directly to the center and ring the bell for emergency. No English spoken. Open 9am-2:30pm.

Police: (tel. 22 222) At the corner of Ethn. Anistassis St., next to the post office. They don't speak much English but try valiantly to help you. Open 24hr.

Post Office: (tel. 22 219) Take the uphill road right of the bus station. Open Mon.-Fri. 8am-1:30pm. **Postal Code: 85700.**

OTE: Past the post office, then left uphill. Open Mon.-Fri. 7:30am-3pm. **Telephone Code: 0245.**

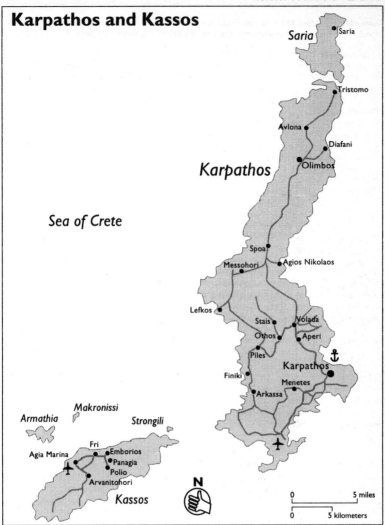

Karpathos and Kassos

Saria

Saria

Tristomo

Avlona

Diafani

Karpathos

Olimbos

Sea of Crete

Spoa

Agios Nikolaos

Messohori

Lefkos

Stais

Volada

Othos

Aperi

Piles

Karpathos

Finiki

Menetes

Arkassa

Makronissi

Armathia

Strongili

Fri

Emborios

Agia Marina

Panagia

Polio

Arvanitohori

Kassos

N

0   5 miles

0   5 kilometers

ACCOMMODATIONS

Illegal free-lance camping transpires mostly undisturbed on the town beach to the north. *Let's Go* does not recommend free-lance camping. Room prices are 1000-2000dr less in the off season.

Mertonas Studios (tel. 22 622, 23 079), 2 blocks left and uphill from the bus station, facing inland. Eva Angelos rents gorgeous, furnished studios with private baths and daily maid service that would make Mr. Clean weep with joy. Doubles with bath 5000-7000dr; winter double studios 50,000dr per month.

Harry's Rooms to Rent (tel. 22 188), just up the hill and to the left from the Avra Shopping Center at the center of town. The area is under construction—don't worry if it looks like there is little around. Modern, clean rooms with balcony and common bath. Singles 3200dr; doubles 4800dr; triples 5000dr.

Odyssey (tel. 23 240, -1, -2), next to Eva's, but farther down on the hill. Spotless studios and furnished apartments. Doubles 7000dr; quads 12,000 dr.

FOOD AND ENTERTAINMENT

Although waterfront taverns tend to be expensive and bland, better options lie away from the ferry dock, toward the beach along the paved waterfront road.

Sofia's Place (tel. 23 152), first on the road. Stop here if you crave grilled meat, although some salads and appetizers are vegetarian-friendly. The menu is complete with photos. Salty Karpathian sardines 750dr, lamb cutlets 1500dr.

Land and Sea (tel. 22 007), next door. Owner Yiannis serves large portions of excellent Greek cuisine. Choose his *stifatho* (beef in tomato sauce and onions, 1500dr) or *yiouvetsi* (lamb and *kritharaki* 1500dr). Open daily 11am-2am.

Kali Karthia (tel 22 256) has fresh and cheap fish since the owner's sons stock the restaurant daily. Grade A fish 7000dr per kg, kalamari cooked any way you crave it 1000dr. Open daily 7am-1am.

Kamarathos' Beehive, next to Karpathos Travel back along the waterfront. Has an endless variety of sweets. Open daily 7am-2am.

The Art Center, located in the center of the town near the mayor's office. For the artistically inclined. Minas Vlahos, the most acclaimed artist on Karpathos, captures the feeling of the island in work displayed in his tranquil studio. Hand-made cards 500dr. Open Mon.-Sat. 9am-1pm and 5-9pm.

The Rocks (tel. 85 700) mesmerizes with liquid lamps, and is one of three waterfront bars that are always crowded and serve beer (800dr) and cocktails (1200-1500dr). Open 8-9pm until late.

Symposium, on the waterfront, specializing in rock and rave, yet blessed with a quieter outdoor terrace. Open 8-9pm until late.

Eros (tel. 23 368), a dance bar that plays everything from Greek to hip-hop. Open 8-9pm until late.

To escape the waterfront and get down with the locals, prepare for an uphill climb or drive. Head straight out of town and follow the aimlessly scattered but carefully painted concrete blocks that mark the path to **Fillagri** (tel. 23 373), a unique bar and dance club. Overlook the island's largest olive grove as you party in an abandoned olive oil mill. With three indoor and one outdoor bar, the club handles over 800 thirsty customers each weekend night. For a smaller scene, head upstairs to **Gamma-3,** a bar that plays both Greek and foreign music (beer 700dr, mixed drinks 1000dr). Both places open before midnight, but only pick up around 1 or 2am.

▓ Southern Karpathos

The rest of southern Karpathos is known for its stone farmhouses, tiny isolated chapels, and cliff-top views of the sea. The towns of Menetes, Aperi, and Othos hold lively church festivals on August 6.

The hillside towns of **Menetes** and **Arkasa** are on a branch of the road south out of Karpathos Town. Menetes's huge church sprouts from the terraced houses below. Its marble pillars were salvaged from the ruins of an early Christian basilica. In the house in front of the church you will find Anna, the keeper of the keys. Ask at **Manolis Kafeneion** (tel. 81 356) for a key to the tiny **folk art museum** (free). In Arkasa, the remains of five parallel Cyclopean walls divide the peninsula southwest of town. **Buses** from Ta Pigadia leave for Arkasa (1-2 per day, 20min., 380dr); check the schedule for afternoon return times. **Taxis** from Ta Pigadia cost 2000dr.

The island's only other paved road leads north and then west out of Karpathos Town into lush hiking country. Freelance campers can be found on a small beach cove close to the sandy shore of Agios Nikolaos; follow the road from Arkasa to Agios Nikolaos, a five-minute walk from Anna's boarding house. **Aperi** became the island's capital in medieval times when Arab raids forced the Karpathians to abandon their coastal town. Today, it remains the island's spiritual capital. The church here holds the *Panagia* (Virgin Mary) icon revered throughout Karpathos. Legend has it that long ago a monk was chopping wood when blood suddenly spurted from one of the logs. The perplexed monk recognized the log as an icon of the Virgin Mary, and although the object disappeared several times, it always reappeared in an old church in Aperi. The monk understood that the *Panagia* wished to stay in that spot, and in 1886 a bishop's church was built (church open to visitors daily 8-11am, when overseer is present). Buses go to Aperi (3 per day, 300dr).

▓ Northern Karpathos

There are no good roads connecting the rural north and commercial south of Karpathos. A 1983 fire which devastated most of the Aleppo Pine Forests between Spoa and Olympus, eliminating any modernization that may have developed in this beautiful arid region. Daily **excursion boats** from Karpathos Town are the most reliable and scenic means of transport. Karpathos Travel offers combined boat and bus trips to Diafani (2hr. one way; 4500dr includes round-trip bus to Olympus). A boat journeys to the white beach of **Apela** and to the island of **Saria** north of Karpathos twice per week (from Diafani 1hr., round-trip 2500dr).

DIAFANI

Staying in languorous Diafani (Transparent) allows you to stick close to the beaches and the harbor of North Karpathos, but it has nothing more to offer than overpriced *tavernas* and a sleepy port. If exploring Olympus is your goal, however, take the first bus out of Diafani and absorb Olympus at your leisure (2 per day, 350dr). **Orphanos Travel and Shipping Agents** (tel. 51 410; fax 51 316), on the dock to the right of the *tavernas,* offers **exchange services,** room info, and ferry and excursion tickets. Ask about free boat trips to local beaches (open 8am-1pm and 2:30-10pm). There is no bank in Diafani. A telecard **phone** is in front of the travel agency. The **police** (tel. 51 213) are in the town center (open 24hr.). There is a **post box,** but the postman only rings three times per week. Rooms to let abound; expect to pay 3000-4500dr per single; 5000-7500dr per double. A **campsite** (tel. 51 288) offers pitches starting at 700dr per person, but it is rather disorganized and resembles free-lance camping.

OLYMPUS ΟΛΥΜΒΟΣ

Olympus is traditional, though no single word can convey the thoroughness of its isolation and insularity. Ethnologists and linguists have lauded the region's preservation of centuries-old customs. Several words in the local dialect date to 1000 BC. Eighty families seeking to escape attacking pirates founded the village, perched 1750m above sea level atop Mt. Profitis Ilias, in the 11th century. Each family built its own windmill, house, and church, which explains the innumerable chapels that dot the area today. The degree of isolation here makes the village and its inhabitants distinct from other areas and Karpathians. A history of migrant work that took Olympian men to Rhodes facilitated the matriarchal tradition that continues in the village today. Left behind to maintain the property and household while their husbands were away, women took control and responsibility over the family assets; houses are still inherited from mother to daughter. The radiant long-sleeved white shirts and flowered aprons worn by women, a striking contrast to their weathered skin, gives them an almost regal appearance. Plaster-sculpted nymphs, angels, eagles, and Venetian lions decorate the exteriors of traditional homes, while the interiors are filled with hand-embroidered linens and ceramic plates.

To travel between Olympus and Diafani, you can take a taxi or the small bus that leaves both Diafani (when the boat from Karpathos Town arrives) and Olympus daily. A dusty hike along the valley floor is another alternative if you have the time, energy, and drinking water.

Two **working windmills** overlook the cliffs on the west side of the village—here the women of Olympus grind flour for bread, which they bake in huge stone ovens smoldering under the hillside. Meanwhile, the men either idly play backgammon or musical instruments in the coffeehouses, or lead the overworked donkeys in the right direction. The **folk museum,** beneath one of the windmills (pick your way up the narrow village path), offers a glimpse of a 19th-century home, with tools and adornments. While you are there, check out the windmills. You can brave the tiny ladder inside and watch one whirl behind the scenes (open daily 10am-9pm).

Pension Olymbos (tel. 51 252), around to the left of the bus stop near the start of the village, rents old-style rooms with hand-carved beds (singles 2000dr; doubles 2500dr, with bath 5000dr). They also serve home-cooked food in the adjacent **taverna;** *pastitsio* and *moussaka* (each 1200dr), are worth every drachma.

Surprisingly, some of the best food in Olympus is served at the **Milos Tavern** (tel. 51 333), the restaurant that runs out of the windmill above the museum. Wait for the tour groups to leave, then enjoy the stuffed pitas baked in the wood-burning oven right before your eyes (350dr). For a heartier meal, choose the village's traditional meal, the pasta-like *makarounes,* served with cheese and sprinkled with onion (900dr). The *loukoumades* (honey-glazed doughnut holes) are great for dessert.

If you are willing to bound over stone walls, visit the oldest chapel on Karpathos, **Agia Triada,** one of two adjacent stone chapels easily visible from the town above (look down to the right of the bus stop for earthy red arched roofs). The frescoes inside are 13th- or 14th-century "aniconic" geometric paintings of birds and fish. The largest church in the village, **Kimisi tis Theotokov,** is arguably the most beautiful. Built of gold foil, the altar is absolutely priceless, and the handpainted scenes from the Bible that adorn the walls are breathtaking. If the priest is not there to let you in, ask at the folk museum for a key.

One of the few men you will see laboring in Olympus is the cobbler **Nichokis Kanakis,** who makes the leather boots that are standard footwear in the village. At 60,000dr per pair, these boots are not made for walking.

SYMI ΣΥΜΗ

The mountainous island of Symi is a small but prized showpiece of the Dodecanese. The famous **Panormitis Monastery** rests in a remote spot at the island's southern end, while the historic port of **Ghialos** adorns the northern tip. Monasteries were the only dwellings on these steep, barren shores until 19th-century commercial growth led to the construction of the port. During this period, shipbuilding, sponge-diving, fishing, and trade flourished, and Symi received concessions from the Sultans, eventually becoming the capital of the Dodecanese. Ships made in Symi still have a reputation for quickness and smooth handling. Ghialos is one of the lovelier ports in Greece. A string of islets leads boats into the harbor, where a rainbow of pastel houses welcomes visitors. To show its appreciation of this unique town, the Greek government declared the port of Symi a historic site in 1971. Many of the houses here date from the 19th century, but most were abandoned when the island's sponge-diving industry collapsed.

Symi remains poor while searching for an industry to replace sponge-diving. A growing emphasis on the cultivation of spices has given the island a glimmer of financial stability. In the meantime, locals depend heavily on tourism, anticipating the arrival of boats from Rhodes so customers can fill their stores. As a result, many locals seem overeager and aggressive. Since few tourists stay in Symi overnight, locals pull out all the stops. A growing population of foreign residents has given the island a slightly cosmopolitan flare to match the colorful mosaic of houses.

▨ Symi Town

Symi is the only significant town on the island, and is divided into two sections. Yialos, the port, has many of the island's visitor services.; the Chorio, perched 200 steps above the port, affords beautiful views of both the enchanting port and the fig orchard-covered mountains.

ORIENTATION AND PRACTICAL INFORMATION

Tourist Information: A touch-tone computerized screen is just to the left of where the ferries dock. Information on accommodations, transportation, and sights.

Travel Agency: Symi Tours (tel. 71 307), a block inland from the waterfront gold shop. Sells ferry, hydrofoil, and plane tickets, handles **currency exchange,** and helps find accommodations. Open daily 9am-2pm and 6-10pm.

Banks: National Bank (tel. 72 294), straight ahead from the dock and to the right after the footbridge where the harbor bends left. **ATM** services. **Ionian Bank** (tel. 71 122), on the waterfront, a couple of doors down, left of the ferry landing. **ATM.** Both banks open Mon.-Thurs. 8am-2pm, Fri. 8am-1:30pm.

Bus: A green van stops on the east waterfront past Ikonomou Square. On-the-hour transportation to Chorio (5min., 150dr) and Pethi (10min., 200dr).

Ferries: 2 per week to: Peiraias (7980dr); Kos (2460dr); Kalymnos (3225dr); Tilos (1835dr); and Nisyros (2410dr). Daily excursion boat from Rhodes can provide access to Rhodes's more comprehensive ferry service (2000dr one way to Rhodes).

Flying Dolphins: 4 per week to Rhodes (2500dr), 1 per week to: Kos (4785dr); Kalymnos (6640dr); and Astypalea (8155dr).

Taxis: (tel. 72 666) Most congregate near the bus stop on the east waterfront.

International Bookstore: (tel. 71 690; fax 71 773) On the waterfront near the pharmacy. Sells newspapers, magazines, and novels in several languages, including English. Fax services available. Open daily 8:30am-2pm and 5pm-midnight.

Public Toilets: Down an alley, left of Taverna Meraklis. Free.

Pharmacy: (tel. 71 888) On the waterfront, at the left side of the harbor, past Ikonomou Square. Open Mon.-Sat. 9am-2pm and 5-9pm, Sun. 9am-1pm.

Medical Center: (tel. 71 290) Next to the church, directly opposite Hotel Kokona. Open Mon.-Fri. 9am-1pm; after hours, call the police.

Police: (tel. 71 111) Next to the Ghialos clock tower, in a big white building on the waterfront. Open 24hr.

Post Office: (tel. 71 315), in the same building as the police, but up the flight of stairs on the left. Offers **currency exchange.** Open Mon.-Fri. 7:30am-2pm.

Postal Code: 85600.

OTE: Follow signs beginning at the Neraida restaurant. Inland along the left side of the park in the middle of the harbor. Open Mon.-Fri. 7:30am-3:10pm.

Telephone Code: 0241.

ACCOMMODATIONS

Most travelers do not spend the night, but the usual herd of dock hawks still awaits the arrival of ferries and hydrofoils. **Hotel Kokona** (tel. 72 620, 71 451), over the foot bridge and to the left of the old church tower, has pristine, welcoming rooms with baths and balconies that actually smell clean. (Doubles 8000-10,000dr; triples 10,000-12,000dr; quads 12,000-14,000dr. Breakfast 900dr.) **Helena Rooms to Let** (tel. 72 931), on the corner of Ikonomou Square, has comfortable rooms with private baths and A/C (doubles 7000dr).

FOOD

Taverna Meraklis (tel. 71 003), for piping-hot authentic food. Steer away from the waterfront, walk over the foot bridge, and go one block inland from Symi Tours. Overwhelming delicious Greek and island specialties. The *moussaka* and *pastitsio* (each 900dr) are truly fabulous. Open 10am-4pm and 6pm-1am.

Georgios' Restaurant (tel. 71 984), at the top of the 200 stairs to the Chorio. Authentic family-owned restaurant that serves more than the basic Greek menu, such as peppers florini (red peppers stuffed with feta, 1000dr), and lamb *exohiko* (lamb baked in aluminum foil with potatoes, cheese, and oregano, 1500dr). Enjoy the sounds of live folk music while you savor your meal. Open 7pm-2am.

Syllogos (tel. 72 148), continue up more steps. Named for and embodying the village meeting place. Service is superb, restaurant is spotless, and portions large. Come for several of Lemonia's specialties, like pork with leeks (1800dr) and fish with rosemary and lemon (both 1800dr). Terrace view. Open noon-3pm and 6pm-1am.

Igloo Ice Cream Shop, walk back down the stairs to the waterfront for dessert, and choose from the 40 flavors (1 scoop 300dr, 3 scoops 650dr).

Kantirmi Cafe (tel. 71 381), at the waterfront footbridge from which the cafe gets its name. Popular with foreign residents. Excellent daytime sandwiches (avocado and bacon 600dr) give way to beer (400-700dr), liqueurs (650dr), and cocktails (800dr). Conveniently located next to the ice cream stand, you can indulge in *galacto* paradise here as well. Open 9am-4pm and 6pm-2am.

ENTERTAINMENT

Jean and Tonic Pub (tel. 71 819), up the hill from George's. Cocktails (700dr) served 8-9pm and friendly conversation all night long. Jean, a British vacationer who loved Symi so much that she never went home, can help with accommodations.

Katoi Bar (tel. 71 752), over the bridge along the east waterfront. Popular among Greek residents. Greek music, good coffee, small tables for good conversation. Beer 600-800dr, long drinks 1000dr, cocktails 1000-1400dr, juice and coffee. Open daily 9am-noon and 7pm-2am.

Pat's Bar, near the Ionian Bank on the waterfront. English-speaking tourists come here for happy hour cocktails (700dr, 7:30-8:30pm).

Club, at the footbridge that seems to shake with the deafening bass beat. Everyone heads to this packed dance club once the music dies down at the bars (law requires this occur at midnight). Be prepared for a younger and more lustful crowd. 2000dr cover includes 1st drink.

SIGHTS

Panormitis Monastery, the grand Monastery of the Archangel Michael, friend of travelers, looms at the center of a remarkable horseshoe-shaped harbor in the southern part of the island and greets you with its chiming bells. The monastery was built in the 15th century at the spot where a local woman chanced upon an icon of Michael. Although it was brought to Ghialos, the icon kept returning to Panormitis. The palatial white buildings of the monastery, dominated by an elegant bell tower in the center, contains two small museums, one with ecclesiastical relics and worshippers' gifts and one with folkloric exhibits. (Both museums open daily 10am-12:30pm and when excursion boats visit. Admission 200dr for both.)

The small monastery church houses an exceptional wooden altar screen. The screen is famous throughout the Dodecanese for its wish-granting powers, and tokens in the museum represent supplicants' requests. Modest dress is required to enter the monastery. A gate attendant hands women wrap-around skirts to wear inside. No regular buses run to the monastery, but tour buses from Ghialos run four times per week (1hr.), and a boat from Ghialos heads here as well. All excursion boats from Rhodes stop here. There are free toilets to the left of the complex. If you get hungry, the bakery under the archway to the left has fresh goodies.

At Ghialos, the **Naval Museum** (tel. 72 363), housed in a yellow neoclassical building at the back of the main waterfront strip, recounts the history of sponge-diving on the island with equipment, photographs, and maps (open daily 10:30am-3pm; admission 300dr). A steep 20-30-minute hike ends at Chorio, the section of town fortified against pirate raids. Several sets of stairs lead up from the east side of the waterfront. The shadiest and most straightforward is the one farthest along the water, close to where the road heads uphill. Follow the road at the top of the stairs and you will see signs for the **archaeological museum** (tel. 71 114), housing classical and Byzantine pieces as well as island costumes and utensils. (Open Tues.-Sun. 10am-2pm. Admission 500dr, students 300dr, seniors 400dr, under 18 200dr.) Signs will lead you through a maze of streets to the ruins of the old **castle**.

Nos Beach, a 10-minute walk from Ghialos (head north along the waterfront, past the shipyard), is tiny but close to the port. The beach at **Nimborio,** 45 minutes on foot past Nos, is mediocre, but the views make the walk worthwhile. You can also take a taxi boat (800dr round-trip). **Pedi,** a short distance by bus, boasts radiant sands and refreshing water. Symi's tiny coves shelter a few excellent beaches at **Ag. Marina, Nanou,** and **Marathounda** on the east side of the island, which are accessible only by boat (daily, round-trip 1000dr). Boats also go to **Sesklia Island,** south of Symi (round-trip 3000dr). Excursion boats do not follow a set schedule. They all line up with destinations and prices posted in the morning.

NISYROS ΝΙΣΥΡΟΣ

Greece's *other* volcanic island, Nisyros is not quite as popular and dramatic as Santorini, but Nisyros has unspoiled island beauty, virgin landscape, and a community not yet infiltrated by the vices of tourism. With its volcano, clifftop monastery, and picturesque ghost town, Nisyros is a latent treasure of the Aegean. Small and unfrequented by travelers, rowdy backpackers come here to detox between parties in Kos and Rhodes.

■ Mandraki

Mandraki is Nisyros's tiny, whitewashed port town. While the area where the ferrys dock is quite dingy, the winding streets and gorgeous views of the sea make the city both pleasant and comfortable.

ORIENTATION AND PRACTICAL INFORMATION

The **port authority** (tel. 31 222; open 24hr.), the **police** (tel. 31 201; open 24hr.), and **post office** (tel. 31 249; open Mon.-Fri. 7:30am-2pm), which also offers **currency exchange,** are all housed in the white building on the dock with the Greek flag. The road continuing left around the bend (facing the water) leads into the town. **Enetikon Travel** (tel. 31 180; fax 31 168) is on that road on the right side in a tiny building on the rocks. A multilingual staff helps with boats, flying dolphins, accommodations, excursions, and faxes (open daily 9:30am-1:30pm and 6-9pm). Along the same road, parallel to the waterfront, you'll find **Alfa Rent** (tel. 31 438), in the first waterfront square, which has moped rentals (open daily 8:30am-9:30pm). Farther along the same path is the representative of the **National Bank** (tel. 31 459; open Mon.-Thurs. 8am-2pm, Fri. 8am-1:30pm) in **Diakomitalis Tours.** If you take the first left off the road from the dock into town, you'll reach the uptown square. The red cross on the left marks the **pharmacy,** which is usually open evenings. In a little office behind the town hall, Eleni Kendri sells tickets for ferries to the island and for **Olympic Airways** flights (tel. 31 230; open daily 7-9pm).

Two **ferries** per week serve Nisyros on their way to Rhodes (2200dr), Kalymnos (1300dr), Tilos (1200dr), Symi (2000dr), Kos (1300dr), and Peiraias (6057dr). **Flying dolphins** speed twice per week to Rhodes (5327dr), Tilos (2518dr), and Kos (2713dr). **Buses** on Nisyros run on their own time, but when they do turn on the engine, two per day head to Loutrs (5min.), Paloi (10min.), Emborio (20min.), and Nikeia (30min.). There are many private buses heading to the crater of the volcano, Stefanos. Ask around when you dock—most wait to meet incoming boats. There are two **taxis** on the island: **Babis'** (tel. 31 460) and **Irini's** (tel. 31 474). **Postal Code:** 85303. **Telephone Code:** 0242.

ACCOMMODATIONS

In high season, doubles range from 4000-7000dr; in off season rates may fall by up to 50%. Rooms are scarce but generally available except in mid-August, during the island's big festival for the Virgin Mary—prices shoot up with demand. On the road leading left from the dock (facing inland), **Hotel Romantzo** (tel. 31 340) has clean rooms with bath at negotiable prices. (Singles 3000dr. Doubles 4000dr. Triples 6000dr.) If you head to town, ask at **Taverna Nisyros** (tel. 31 460) for a double with bath and kitchenette. (Doubles 4000dr.)

FOOD

It is generally a good idea to wander away from the cafés and *tavernas* that attract most excursion visitors. A small sign points to **Fabrika** (tel. 31 552) on one of the little streets leading from the town hall square to the water. Go down the steps for books, music, and superb Greek *mezedes* at this cozy and friendly *ouzeri* (octopus 1000dr, *raki* 200dr, beer 400-500dr). Look a sign on the road parallel to the waterfront, pointing to **Tavernas Nisyros** (tel. 31 460), where Polyxeni cooks up a storm (Greek salad 450dr, *moussaka* 300dr, lamb chops 900dr). **Captain's** (tel. 31 225), at the water's edge, sells delicious *soumada* (almond juice), the island's specialty (1100dr per bottle), and cheap fish (swordfish filet 1500dr).

SIGHTS

As soon as you dock, it's obvious that the **volcano** is the island's main attraction. Tour guides and travel agents toting volcano signs crowd the dock—there's even a model of the island glorifying the volcano on the quay. Trips up to the **Stefanos crater** are often pre-booked, but you can join a group for 1000-1500dr. The bus ride is 20 minutes and you have 45 minutes to wander around in the crater. Another option is renting a moped, but drive carefully—the roads are narrow. There is no admission fee to the crater. The cafe on the site charges 350dr for a soda (open daily 8am-8pm). The toilet is behind the cafe. Inside the crater, you'll see piles of sulphur and jets of scalding steam against the island's gorgeous landscape. In some parts of the crater, you can hear the rumbling below. On the cliff at the end of the Mandraki is the **Panagia Spiliani Monastery**. The sacred icon of this monastery used to reside in a small cave just above Mandraki's port. It would mysteriously disappear from the sanctuary only to be found on the site of today's monastery. After several disappearing acts, the monks took it as a sign and built a new home for the icon, making a large replica of it in 1798 to display in the new church. The tender looks of Christ and the Virgin Mary have been known to grant relief from pain. The church also has relics of Agios Charlambos in its antechamber. Recently, on the rear face of the icon of the Virgin Mary, an altar boy discovered the iconographer's hidden portrait of Agios Nikolaos, which he had covered with an old cloth for over two centuries. Pictures of the back of this two-faced icon are displayed in the church as well. To get up to the monastery, climb the narrow uphill steps across from the church with the pink bell tower (monastery open daily 10am-3pm; free).

On those same steps up to the monastery is the tiny **Historical and Popular Museum** with folkloric exhibits on life on Nisyros (open Fri.-Wed. 10:30am-2:30pm and 6-8pm; free). The Cyclopean walls, built by the Venetians, are perched at the edge of Mandraki and extend to the monastery (open 24hr.; free).

On the road past the dock, a 10-minute walk from Mandraki, are the **thermal springs** of Loutra. Because of their therapeutic qualities, these springs are open only to visitors bearing a doctor's prescription. **Nisyros** also has few pleasant beaches, thanks to the steaming black volcanic rocks and sand, which torment the feet. Behind the monastery's cliff, along a waterfront path, is a small secluded beach (five-min. walk from Mandraki). On the road to Paloi is the island's best beach, **White Beach** (2km from Mandraki). Depending on demand, Enetikon Travel organizes trips to the nearby island of **Giali** for its better beaches (1900dr round-trip).

Saronic Gulf Islands

ΤΑ ΝΗΣΙΑ ΤΟΥ ΣΑΡΩΝΙΚΟΥ

Diverse, captivating landscapes and their proximity to Athens have made the Saronic Gulf Islands an enduringly popular destination. Narrow alleys and walkways barely separate houses that lead up to mountainous interiors dotted with ancient temples and tranquil monasteries. Many of the islands' beaches are pebbly, but the surrounding plush green hills make them some of Greece's most scenic swimming spots.

Despite geographic proximity, each island retains its own distinct character. Poros' magnificent lemon grove, Aegina's temple of Aphaia, Spetses' pine-filled forests and Hydra's fashionable waterfront attract countless Athenians seeking weekend getaways. The Saronic Gulf Islands' popularity also makes them among the most expensive in Greece, and free-lance camping is illegal.

AEGINA ΑΙΓΙΝΑ

Aegina's whitewashed buildings, narrow streets, horses decorated with brightly colored tassels, and aqua-hued water look as if they were produced in a Disney studio. Aegina is an easy daytrip for Athenians, so on summer weekends the island finds itself saddled with the bustle of Greece's capital. Nevertheless, the tourists who stay in **Aegina Town** are different from the typical scantily clad beach bums who frequent the other Saronic Gulf Islands, and behind the waterfront you will find a gritty little town that can be fun to explore. The beach crowd heads across the island to **Agia Marina** where sandy shores and strips of cafes and bars welcome all.

In ancient times, relations between Aegina and Athens were far less chummy. The little island made up for its size with spunk and initiative, consistently resisting Athenian political and military encroachment. The island produced the first Greek coins—the silver "tortoises" which gained great financial leverage throughout the Greek world—and Aegina's sprinters zoomed past the competition at the pan-Hellenic games. With the onset of the Persian War in 491 BC, the citizens of Aegina sided first with Xerxes' army, to the ire of the besieged Athenians. In 480 BC they returned to the Greek side and won the praise of the Delphic Oracle as the swiftest navy on the seas as a result of their performance at Salamis, the greatest of all Greek sea battles. Island life flourished and Aegina's inhabitants built the magnificent Temple of Aphaia during the next 30 years. But they eventually suffered the misfortunes of having taken the wrong side in the Athenian-Spartan clash and were thoroughly trounced by Athens in 459 BC. By 431, Athens had displaced Aegina's population with Athenian colonists. Sparta restored the native population to the island in 405.

To get to Aegina from Athens, take green bus #40 from almost anywhere in Athens and get off at the Public Theater *(Demotikon Theatron)* in Peiraias (30min., 75dr). From there, you can see the pier where ferries leave for Aegina. Alternatively, take the subway (75dr) to the stop at Peiraias and walk the few blocks to the ferry. From the Athens airport, take the bus #19 directly to Peiraias.

▓ Aegina Town

Ferries to the island dock in Aegina Town. The first thing you'll notice when you arrive is that you are in the "Pistachio Capital of the World." Kiosks with nuts by the kilo, pistachio preserves, candies, and free samples make this waterfront different from the rest in Greece. Even if you don't buy any, you're sure to try some before you leave; chef's sprinkle everything from pastries to entrees with the green flakes.

ORIENTATION AND PRACTICAL INFORMATION

The waterfront in front of and to the right (facing inland) of the quay is lined with overpriced cafes. To find more practical amenities, including cheap hotels, *tavernas*, and the bus station, turn left at the quay and follow the waterfront street.

Tourist Office: (tel. 25 588) In the town hall to the far right of the ferry quay. Offers general information and maps of Aegina. Open Mon.-Fri. 8am-2:30pm and 7-9pm, Sat.-Sun. 10am-1pm and 7-9pm.

Tourist Police: (tel. 27 777) 2 blocks up Leonardou Lada St., left of the quay. English spoken. Open daily 7:30am-10pm. **Port Police:** (tel. 22 328) On the pier. Provides updated ferry schedules. English spoken. Open daily 8am-2:30am.

Bank: National Bank (tel. 25 697), on the waterfront to the right of the quay past all the cafes. 24hr. **ATM.** Open Mon.-Thurs. 8am-2pm and Fri. 8am-1:30pm.

Buses: (tel. 22 787) To Agia Marina and Aphaia Temple (every 45min., 30min., 350dr) run 6:30am-7:45pm. If you are going to the temple, buy a round-trip ticket in Aegina Town. The bus station is in the park at the corner of the waterfront left of the ferry quay.

Ferries: To: Peiraias (1 per hour, 1½hr., 1350dr); Methana (3 per day, 1hr., 1000dr); Poros (3 per day, 2hr., 1100dr); Hydra (1 per day, 1500dr); and Spetses (1 per day, 2000dr). Ticket stands near the boat landing, but each stand represents only one company. Check with the port police for overall schedules.

Flying Dolphins: Ticket stand (tel. 27 462) next to the port police stand. Sells hydrofoil tickets to: Kythera, Nauplion, and Peiraias (16 per day, 35min., 1995dr); Poros (3 per day, 40min., 2230dr); Methana (1 per day, 25min., 1895dr); Hydra (2 per day, 1hr., 2840dr); Spetses (2 per day, 2hr., 4240dr); and Porto Heli (2 per day, 2hr., 4470dr).

English Bookstore: Giotis (tel 23 874), #25 along the waterfront, just right of the cafes. International books and magazines; small selection of used books in English. Open daily 7:30am-11pm.

Pharmacy: 19 Irioti St. (tel. 25 317), the second street inland parallel to the quay. Open Mon.-Sat. 7:30am-1:30pm, Tues.-Thurs. 7:30am-1:30pm and 4:30-8:30pm. There is always at least one pharmacy open Sun. 8am-11pm by rotation.

Medical Center: (tel. 52 222), 2km along the waterfront to the right of the ferry quay. If you have a problem call the tourist police and they will arrange transport.

Post Office: (tel. 22 398). To the left of the ferry landing on Kanari St. Cashes traveler's checks. Open Mon.-Fri. 7:30am-2pm. **Postal Code:** 18010.

OTE: (tel. 22 399) Up Aiakou St. to the right. Keep trudging up Aiakou when the street narrows into a walkway; the building has a monstrous rooftop satellite dish. Open Mon.-Fri. 7:30am-3:10pm. **Telephone Code:** 0297.

ACCOMMODATIONS

Rooms here are cheaper than on any of the other Saronic Gulf Islands. Even in the high season expect to find a double for around 4000dr. *Domatia* owners often meet the ferries, but as always bargain and discuss location before you follow them away.

Hotel Plaza (tel. 25 600), on the waterfront left of the ferries and around the bend. A little expensive, but the same owner has two other pensions, Christina and Ulrica, and he administers them from the desk of Hotel Plaza. All rooms have private bathrooms. Cheapest room in the high season 4000dr, in off season 3000dr.

Hotel Artemis (tel. 25 195), on Leonardou Lada St. up from the tourist police. Friendly management offers simple, spotless rooms decorated in pink and red. Singles 6000dr; doubles 8000dr; large triples or quads 12000dr. Breakfast 1200dr.

Hotel Xenon Pavlou (tel. 22 795), behind the church on the far right of the quay. Owned by the same kind-hearted man for 25 years. Offers comfortable rooms with balconies and psychedelic curtains. Singles 7000dr; doubles 8000dr.

Aegina

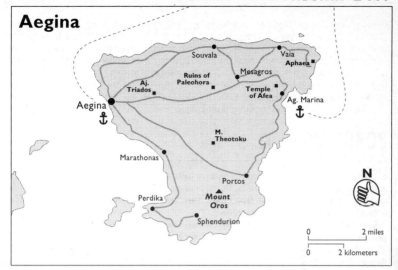

Souvala · Vaia · Aphaea

Ruins of Paleohora · Mesagros

Aj. Triados · Temple of Afea · Ag. Marina

Aegina ⚓

M. Theotoku

Marathonas

Portos

Perdika · Mount Oros

Sphendurion

N

0 — 2 miles
0 — 2 kilometers

FOOD, ENTERTAINMENT, AND SIGHTS

There are many no-frills *tavernas* along P. Irioti St., which runs parallel to the water-front one block inland along the right side of the harbor. **To Steki** (tel. 23 910) has a great atmosphere that includes an outdoor barbeque adorned with and a small TV tuned permanently to Greek music videos. To get here, turn up from the water after the movie advertisements and walk through the fish market (grilled octopus 1000dr, garlic-potato salad 400dr). **Bessis** (tel. 25 700), on the waterfront, offers a delightful array of sweets and pastries (*kataifi* 350dr), but don't be tempted by the sit-down ser-vice or 500dr will be tacked on to your bill.

Iris Club is one of Aegina's trendier nightspots. More sophisticated than your typi-cal beach bar, this roof-top club is the place to be between 9pm and 2am (drinks 1000dr, special 2-shot drinks 1300dr). **Anissis,** the outdoor **cinema** up Aiakou St., often shows American films (summers only; admission 1500dr). In the winter, you can see a film at **Titina.** Check the signs on the waterfront after the National Bank.

Aegina Town's archaeological fame rests tenuously on the last half-column of the **Temple of Apollo.** The 8m-tall Doric column dates to 460 BC and stands on Kolona hill, a short walk out of town to the north. A new archaeological museum has opened at the site (site and museum open Tues.-Sun. 8:30am-3pm; admission 500dr, students 300dr, EU students free, free on Sun.). The underground church of **Faneromeni,** a 15-minute walk inland just south of the town, houses a rare icon of the Virgin Mary. Locals say the night before construction was to begin on a site above Faneromeni, the architect had a vision in which he was instructed to dig instead. The man discovered the church and unearthed the icon (no regular hours, but if you want to visit, go to the tourist office where they will contact the church and arrange a time).

■ Around Aegina Island

On the road between Aegina and Agia Marina is the village of **Paleochora,** where the islanders once took refuge from invasions. Paleochora was once "the town of 300 churches." Only 15 remain, some with inspiring frescoes. Modest dress is required.

Two kilometers from Agia Marina rest the magnificent 5th-century BC remains of the **Temple of Aphaia.** Aphaia, daughter of Zeus, was a nymph-huntress worshipped solely on Aegina as a protector of women. Her temple, which is built on the founda-tion of an earlier 6th-century temple, boasts a rare and spectacular set of standing double-tiered columns. The Agia Marina bus from Aegina Temple stops right in front.

Determined and fit classicists can bicycle uphill to the temple from Aegina Town (11km, 14km via Souvala). The coastal route is much gentler and affords gorgeous views of rocky shores and other islands. To get to the temple from Agia Marina, walk to the end of town with the water on your right and then straight up Kolokotroni St. until it becomes a wooded trail. This is the footpath to the Temple of Aphaia. At night, peacocks roam the quiet hills by the temple (open Mon.-Fri. 8:15am-7pm and Sat.-Sun. 8:30am-3pm; admission 800dr, students 400dr). A small **museum** opens for 15 minutes every hour on the hour 9am-1pm.

POROS ΠΟΡΟΣ

Only a sliver of water separates the sinewy hills of the mainland from this tiny island. A mere three hours from Peiraias, Poros is actually two small, lush islands—Kalavria and Sphaeria—cut by a canal. Its name, meaning "passage," refers to the channel that forms its border with the Peloponnese.

The Kalavrian League, a seven-city council, met in Poros to ward off hostile naval powers and order the building of the Temple of Poseidon in the 6th century BC. Three hundred years later, the great orator Demosthenes, who improved his diction by speaking with marbles in his mouth, killed himself beside its columns. Poros was sparsely populated until Greeks arrived from Turkey in the 1920s.

■ Poros Town

Poros Town occupies most of tiny Sphaeria, while woods extend over rugged Kalavria. Less crowded than Aegina, Poros still overflows on the weekends. You can find serenity and spectacular views by climbing the narrow passageways that lead to the top of Poros Town and the hills beyond. The waterfront, especially near the ferry dock, seems consumed by tourism, but a walk left (facing inland) along the water takes you to a calmer area and establishments with slightly higher standards.

ORIENTATION AND PRACTICAL INFORMATION

Ferries (2hr., 1910dr) and **Flying Dolphins** (1hr., 3670dr) leave Peiraias for Poros several times per day. En route, the boats stop in **Methana**, a volcanic peninsula of the Peloponnese, known since antiquity for its therapeutic springs. In Poros Town, **hydrofoils** dock at the main landing in the center of town and car ferries tie up on the northwest side of town. The hydrofoil quay is the center of activity, with tourist agencies to the left, restaurants and souvenir shops in the center, and discos and bars to the right.

> **Tourist Police:** (tel. 22 256) On the waterfront, 500m to the right of the main ferry landing (open 9am-1pm). Same office and telephone number as the **regular police.** Helps find rooms. Open 24hr.
> **Bank:** The **National Bank** (tel. 22 236) is on waterfront, right of the ferry landing. Open Mon.-Thurs. 8am-2pm and Fri. 8am-1:30pm.
> **Tourist Agencies: Family Travel,** on the waterfront, opposite the ferry landing (tel. 23 473). English-speaking staff. Provides general info, sells ferry tickets, offers **currency exchange,** and finds rooms. Open Mon.-Fri. 9am-9pm. **Lela Tour** (tel. 24 439) offers showers for 500dr. Open daily 8am-10pm.
> **Ferries:** To Peiraias (5 per day, 2hr., 1910dr), stopping in Methana (½hr., 770dr) and Aegina (1hr., 1140dr). Ferries also run daily to Spetses (2hr., 1550dr) and twice a day to Hydra (45min., 9290dr). Small boat ferries to the far right of the quay go to Galatas on the mainland 24hr. (every 10min., 80dr).
> **Flying Dolphins:** (tel. 22 297) To: Peiraias (8 per day, 1hr., 3670dr); Aegina (7 per day, 40min., 2230dr); Hydra (8 per day, 30min., 1530dr); Spetses (6 per day, 1hr., 2450dr); and Monemvassia (daily, 3hr., 5455dr). Office open daily 6am-10pm.

Bike/Moped Rental: Kosta's (tel. 23 565) is on the waterfront to the left of main landing. Rents bikes (500dr) and mopeds (2000dr). Open daily 9am-10pm.

English Bookstore: (tel. 25 205) Up a flight of stairs on the waterfront near George's Cafe. Sells books and magazines in English and Spanish. Open daily 8am-midnight.

Laundromats: Suzi's Launderette Service, to right of the OTE (facing inland). Wash and dry 2000dr, drop-off only. 2hr. service. Open daily 9am-2pm.

Pharmacy: (tel. 24 793) In the open plaza on Iroon Square. 10m left of the post office. Open Mon.-Sat. 8am-2:30pm and 5-10pm.

Post Office: (tel. 22 275) Occupies the first square to the right along the water. Open Mon.-Fri. 7:30am-2pm. **Postal Code:** 18020.

OTE: (tel. 23 699) On waterfront to the left of the main landing. Open Mon.-Fri. 7:30am-3:10pm. **Telephone Code:** 0298.

ACCOMMODATIONS

During high season the cheapest double is listed at 7000dr, but try to bargain, especially on weekdays. Prices go way down in the off season.

KTM Pension (tel. 25 125). Their signs say "Best Price," and for once it is true. The pension has 10 neat rooms, all with private baths. To get there, turn left from the ferries and walk 500m, turning inland just before signs for the Agricultural Bank. Singles 4000dr; doubles 7000dr.

George Douros (tel. 24 780) has a block of rooms in the same area, all with private baths. If you want a kitchen, ask for a room downstairs. Doubles 8000dr; triples 10,000dr. Ask at **Lela Tours,** where George works, for more information.

Seven Brother Hotel (tel. 23 412), in the middle of the waterfront, 100m right of the ferry landing. Each large room comes with private bath and balcony. Singles 10,000dr; doubles 13,000dr. Prices negotiable. A/C 2000dr.

FOOD

Poros Town has many of the best restaurants in the Saronic Gulf. Restaurants line the harbor, and "charming" waiters try to convince tourists to sit down. Little distinguishes one from another, so you might choose between views or waiters. For a cheap make-your-own meal, stop in the **grocery stores** near the ferry landing.

Taverna Dendrakia stands out from the crowd. Set apart from the other restaurants, Dendrakia is about 1km left of the ferry landing. Their menu is very long and includes more than the standard *moussaka* fare. Choose between mussels or shrimp cooked in cream, garlic, or tomato sauce (1000dr). All meals come with free garlic bread and a serving of *ouzo*.

Lagoudera (tel. 22 389), on the wharf, right of the ferry landing. Offers mussels *saganaki* (1200dr) and stuffed tomatoes (1000dr). Open 10:30am-12:30am.

Seven Brothers (tel. 22 446), just back from the water in the center of the waterfront, has large portions of well-prepared food (from 900dr) and lively Greek dancing at 9pm on Monday nights. Try *orso* in a clay bowl or their lamb chops (1500dr).

Three Brothers (tel. 23 972) offers a boisterously Greek atmosphere. Entrees 900-2000dr. Open daily 7am-midnight.

George's Cafe (tel. 22 508), with its cute blue and white nautical decor, is located in the center of the quay. It offers a breakfast special of coffee, pastry, and orange juice (1150dr) along with an a la carte menu. Opens at 6:30am.

Vessala (tel. 25 890), a little farther away from town than Dendrakia, has home-made *kataifi* (250dr) to die for. Open daily 9am-10pm.

ENTERTAINMENT

Diana open-air cinema (tel. 25 204), to the left of Lela Tours, lets you experience a unique aspect of Greek movie culture. Sprawled out in a lawn chair on a roof and under the stars, cigarette and beverage in hand, you can view the American movies (subtitled in Greek) you missed six months ago (adults 1400dr, children 1000dr).

GREEK ISLANDS

Nightlife in Poros can be had at its bars and discos. The key difference between the two is that bars are required to shut off their music at 3am while discos keep up the beat into the wee hours. The majority of these establishments are located about 1km to the right of the ferry landing on the waterfront. Two of the most popular are **Korali** and **Sirocco.** Cover charges of 1000dr may pop up on weekends; expect drinks to cost 1000-1500dr. The **Posidonion** (tel. 22 435) is a hotel-resort-bar-disco located 2km above the other clubs. Hop in a taxi to get there.

■ Around Poros Island

In Poros Town itself, the **archaeological museum** (tel. 23 276) in the middle of the waterfront has some interesting inscriptions and photographs of the ruins at Troizen (open Mon.-Sat. 9am-1:30pm; free).

The island's main sight is the 18th-century **Monastery of Zoodochos Pigis** (Virgin of the Life-Giving Spring), nestled in an overgrown glade 6km from Poros Town. Since as early as 200 BC, monks have been quaffing the monastery's blessed, curative waters. Inside you'll find a spectacular gold-inlaid altarpiece depicting scenes from the lives of Jesus and the Apostles, as well as St. Barbara and St. Nikolas. Modest dress is required (open daily 8am-4pm). To get there, take the scenic bus ride from the stop next to the main port in town (every 20min. 7am-11pm, 20min., 150dr). Along the route to the monastery is the secluded beach of **Askeli.**

Unless you're a Greek history maven, the main incentive to visit the knee-deep rubble of the 6th-century BC **Temple of Poseidon** is the panoramic view of the gulf. The Athenian statesman Demosthenes took sanctuary from his Macedonian enemies here in 322 BC. Ignoring the temple's tradition of sanctuary, the Macedonians gave him only a few moments reprieve to write a farewell letter to his family. His captors mocked his cowardice as he sat chewing his pen, but the crafty orator died as they waited, having dipped the end of his quill in poison.

■ Near Poros Island

From Poros you can see **Galatas** just across a thin strait. The town on the Peloponnese mainland resembles Poros Town and is only the least bit less touristy. The farming land surrounding Galatas is beautiful, and the flat well-paved roads are perfect for bike riding. Boats run between Galatas and Poros every 10 minutes all day (5 min., 80dr). When you arrive, turn left (facing inland) to find the pleasant sand beaches of **Plaka** and **Aliki.** Plaka is just off the main road about 2km from Galatas, and Aliki is another kilometer down the main road (follow the signs). A gravel path 1km past the turn-off for Aliki is on the right of the road and leads up through the enormous lemon grove of Lemonodassos. If you are riding a bike, leave it here before going up the dirt road. It is a pleasant, but dusty 20-minute walk up to **Kardasi Taverna** (tel. 23 100), where you can find a cool glass of fresh lemonade (250dr), a view of windmills, and 30,000 lemon trees peering onto the sea.

HYDRA (IDRA) ΥΔΡΑ

At first blush, Hydra appears as only a snazzy version of the typical Greek port town: Neoclassical houses nestled quietly among steep limestone hills surrounding a bustling harbor. The uneasy knowledge that Hydra is unlike almost anywhere else you've been may come gradually, as the absence of rumbling cars, mopeds, or even bicycles sinks in. On the island you'll find donkeys, wild horses, boats bearing the sign "taxi," and steep roads and steps. The only automobiles are three garbage trucks. Once Hydra was a favorite of European artists and writers, but most foreigners today are well-heeled tourists looking for a beautiful spot not to create but to recreate. Nonetheless, the island still has an artsy feel with a relatively large expatriate artist community and a famous art school that sends young palette-laden students into the streets. Follow their lead to the peaceful back alleys where the only disturbance is the occasional bray of a donkey. Inexpensive boats traverse the waves from Hydra's port to far-off peaceful beaches.

ORIENTATION AND PRACTICAL INFORMATION

Most tourist agencies and accommodations on Hydra are centered around the pleasant but chic waterfront area accentuated by the clock tower. The crescent-shaped main street wraps around the harbor.

Tourist Police: (tel. 52 205) Along the main waterfront and left after the clock tower. Open 24hr. June-Aug.

Port Police: (tel. 52 279) Left from the dock and up a flight of stairs.

Tourist Agency: Saitis Tours (tel. 52 184), on the main waterfront. Very friendly staff offers information, **currency exchange,** and a free *Holidays in Hydra* guide. Open in summer daily 9am-9:30pm.

Bank: National Bank (tel. 53 233), on the waterfront. Open Mon.-Thurs. 8am-2pm and Fri. 8am-1:30pm.

Ferries: The **ticket office** is the first door on the left in the alley to the left of the National Bank. Ferries run once a day to Peiraias (2 per day, 3hr., 2150dr), stopping in: Poros (1hr., 950dr); Methana (1½hr., 1400dr); and Aegina (2hr., 1450dr). There's also a ferry to Spetses (1hr., 1100dr). From Spetses you can go to Portoneli.

Flying Dolphins: Ticket office (tel. 54 053) at the end of the alley on the left side of the main waterfront, next to Greco Gold. To: Poros (7 per day, 30min., 1530dr); Ermione (5 per day, 30min., 1700dr); Porto Heli (8 per day, 45min., 2335dr); Poros (7 per day, 30min., 1530dr); Spestes (7 per day, 30min., 2000dr); and Piraeus (13 per day, 1½hr., 4100dr). Open 6:15-7am, 8:30am-1:45pm, and 2:45-8pm.

Pharmacy: (tel. 52 059). Inland from tourist police and to the left. Open Mon.-Fri. 8:30am-1:30pm and 5-8:30pm, reduced hours on weekends.

Hospital: (tel. 53 150) A little inland and across the street from the OTE. Open 24hr. for emergency care.

Internet Access: HydraNet (tel. 54 150), left of pharmacy, then take first right. Call for hours. 500dr to send an email message.

Post Office: (tel. 52 262) In the alley to the left of the Bank of Greece. There are signs along the quay. Open Mon.-Fri. 7:30am-2pm. **Postal Code:** 18040.

OTE: (tel. 52 199) Located opposite the tourist police. Open Mon.-Fri. 7:30am-3:10pm. **Telephone Code:** 0298.

ACCOMMODATIONS

Hydra has the most expensive accommodations in the Saronic Gulf. Singles are practically nonexistent and doubles cost at least 7000dr. Finding a place without reservation on summer weekends can also be hard. **Sophia Hotel** (tel. 52 313), located smack in the center of the wharf for 62 years, is one of the cheaper places in town. Some rooms overlook the busy waterfront. The green iron-railed balconies will give the place away. Sophia has only six rooms, so reservations are recommended (open April-Oct; doubles 7700dr; triples 9900dr). **Rooms to Let Gloros** (tel. 53 679) are large and airy, each with private bath and balcony. It is in a back alley at the left corner of the waterfront, but get information by turning left when you get off the ferry and asking at Theano's Tourist Shop. **Pension Othon** (tel. 53 305) is up the same street as the Sophia. It features a beautiful view, newly painted rooms, and a shared bath with washing machine (singles 6000dr; doubles 8000dr; triples 10,000dr).

FOOD AND ENTERTAINMENT

You'll find the same types of restaurants on Hydra as elsewhere in Greece, but generally food is a little more expensive.

Christina's Taverna (tel. 53 615) has a menu that changes with the season, but they always serve vegetables (800dr) and a pork roll (1300dr), as well as both cheese and spinach pies (700dr). It's in a corner, 2 blocks from the water, displays no nameplate, and is hard to find. Your best bet is to ask directions, remembering that "Christina" is with a phlegmy "ch," not a "k" (open noon-3pm and 7pm-12:30am).

Restaurant Lulu (tel. 52 018), straight up from the dock on the same road as Sophia's Hotel, is a bargain. Food is served in small but tasty portions. Salads 500dr, *moussaka* 1000dr, veal dishes 1200dr.

The Garden (tel. 52 329) has a wide selection of reasonably priced food. Entrees 1000-2800dr. The quiet garden is pleasantly removed from the waterfront. To get there, follow the signs up the street from Saitis Travel (open 8pm-late).

Anemoni (tel. 53 136) is a dream for an after-dinner treat of Greek pastries (300-350dr), and portions are large. Or, try the fresh homemade ice cream (300dr). To find it, bear left up from the OTE. Open daily 7:30-12:30am.

Art Cafe (tel. 52 236), near the ferry landing, is relatively affordable. They offer ice cream (300dr), sandwiches (500dr), and *tyropita* (300dr). Open daily 7am-1am.

Hydra's clubs all have overpriced cocktails (1500dr), but die-hard dancers won't want to miss the scene. Most clubs are open nightly 8:30pm-6am, but don't bother showing up before 1am. Check out **Karos Music Club** (tel. 52 416) or **Disco Heaven** (up the whitewashed stairs) above the right end of the harbor for a more modern disco/dance club atmosphere. Quieter souls sit outside at the **Pirate Bar** (tel. 52 711) on the water and watch the world go by clad in sequined bra tops. Greek music fans head to **Saronicos** (tel. 52 389), underneath Disco Heaven. It stays open late into the night and boasts crazed Greek dancing on tables and the bar (open daily 9pm-6am).

SIGHTS

Despite its name, Hydra's land has always been too arid for lucrative agriculture. With few natural resources and refugee populations from the Peloponnese, Balkans, and Turkey, Hydra's inhabitants turned to managing the exports of others. Hydriots grew prosperous by dodging pirates and naval blockades during the late 18th and early 19th centuries and emerged in 1821 as financial and naval leaders in the revolt against the Ottomans. **Koundouriotis,** whose house is on a hill to the west of the harbor, was one of the many Hydriot leaders in the Greek War of Independence. To get to his house, walk up the narrow alley to the right of the Pirate Bar, which becomes Lignou St. Take the second alley on your right, turn right and go straight (and up) following the scenic path until you reach a small church in a shady pine grove. Koundouriotis's home is opposite the church. The view of the harbor is superb, but the house itself is usually locked. The houses of **Votsis** and **Economou,** two Hydriots who contributed to the island's naval fame, are closer to the crest of the hill, right on Voulgari St.

The **Orthodox Church,** built in 1806, bears the clock tower that dominates the wharf. Its peaceful courtyard seems completely removed from the bustling waterfront, and the beautiful icons make this chapel a calming stopping place (150dr donation requested, free postcard in return). Also interesting are the frescoes at the **Church of St. John** in the Platia Kamina (modest dress required at both churches). East of the harbor, set off by winding, anchor-flanked stairs, is the **Pilot School** of the Greek Merchant Marine, with paintings and models (open variably 8am-10pm; free).

The **Historical Archives Museum of Hydra** (tel. 52 355) is left of the ferry landing. This newly opened museum houses naval treasures such as tools, wood-carved ship decorations, and guns, as well as a large collection of water colors of Hydriot sailing ships. Don't miss the heart of Admiral Andreas Miaovlis, embalmed and preserved in a silver and gold urn (open daily 10am-noon; free).

An arduous (1½hr.) hike up A. Miaouli St. from the waterfront will take you to the **monastery** of Prophitis Ilias and, on a lower peak overlooking the harbor, the **convent** of Efpraxia. While the nuns at Efpraxia do beautiful embroidery work, Ilias is the prettier of the two and the monk may be willing to show you around. (Both open 9am-5pm. Modest dress required.) On the right of the harbor (facing inland) are three levels of flat rock perfect for sunbathing; leave your top at home to fit in with the other sunbathers. The beaches on Hydra are rocky ledges a short walk west from town. When the water is calm, small *caïques* run regularly to pretty **Palamida** and neighboring beaches on the west side. You should take food and drink with you; there's no place to buy it nearby. **Mandraki,** is easier to reach, either by a beautiful 30-minute walk along the water from the east end of town or by 15-minute boat ride (300dr). While convenient, Mandraki is less attractive and dirtier than others and is dominated by a new watersports center.

SPETSES ΣΠΕΤΣΕΣ

Ancient *Pitiusa*, or Pinetree Island, Spetses is a floating pine forest bordered by white and blue houses. With picturesque villages and rocky beaches, the island has become a playground for wealthy Greeks. A favorite among British tourists, Spetses offers a variety of moods. Its cafe, disco, and waterfront supply excitement, while its quieter interior provides the same serenity that prompted John Fowles to write *The Magus* here. Spetses was settled just in time to make a contribution to the Greek War of Independence in 1821. It was the first island to take part in the revolution, an event commemorated annually by ceremonies held near Agia Marina.

■ Spetses Town

The vast majority of Spetsiots live in Spetses Town, which is concentrated along the waterfront. Cafes and bars are strung along 4km of water, and little pebble beaches pop up about every 50m. All of this makes the town feel like a round-the-clock beach club. Jet-setters dock their yachts in Spetses's Old Harbor to the left (facing inland) of the ferry quay. One important detail—topless sunbathing is illegal on Spetses although this law is as well-heeded as the law requiring helmets on mopeds.

ORIENTATION AND PRACTICAL INFORMATION

Restaurants and shops form a 2km line on either side of the port. Facing inland, the old harbor is a 20-minute walk left of the boat landing.

Port Police: (tel. 72 245) On waterfront 50m left of ferry quay on 2nd floor. Posts ferry and hydrofoil schedules. Open 24hr.

Tourist Agencies: Several around the corner on the left side of the boat landing. **Meledon Tourist and Travel Agency** (tel. 74 497) is open in summer 9am-2pm and 4-9pm, in winter 10am-1pm. **Alasia Tours** (tel. 74 130) next door is open March-Oct. 8am-9pm. This is the only agency that sells ferry tickets.

Banks: National Bank (tel. 72 286), left of the OTE. Open Mon.-Thurs. 8am-2pm, Fri. 8am-1:30pm.

Ferries: Depart Spetses every afternoon for: Peiraias (4½hr., 2800dr); Poros (2hr., 1500dr); Methana (2¼hr., 1600dr); and Aegina (3hr., 2000dr). **Alasia Travel** sells tickets and posts the exact schedule. Small ferries leave for **Kosta** (4 per day, 15min., 300dr); look for signs on the dock.

Flying Dolphin: Ticket office (tel. 73 141), inland from the dock. **Hydrofoils** and **catamarans** to: Peiraias (in summer 5-7 per day, 2hr., 4830dr); Hydra (7 per day, 30min., 2020dr); Poros (5 per day, 1hr., 2450dr); Aegina (2 per day, 1½hr., 3700dr); Naupio (2 per day, 1hr., 2850dr); and Monemovassia (2 per day, 2½hr., 3775dr).

Bike Rental: Nameless shop (tel. 73 074), 50m to the right of the post office. Bikes 1500dr per day, motorbikes 3500dr per day. Open Easter-Nov. daily 9:30am-2pm and 4:30-6pm.

Pharmacy: Kapelaki (tel. 72 256) in the square at the end of the street parallel to the waterfront. Behind the port police. Open Mon.-Sat. 8:30am-1:30pm and 5:30-10pm, Sun. 10am-1:30pm and 5:30-9:30pm.

GREEK ISLANDS

First Aid Station: (tel. 72 472) Open Mon.-Fri. 8:30am-1:30pm; 24hr. emergency. Call police for doctor.

Police: (tel. 73 100) Follow signs to the Spetses Museum; 150m before museum. Also houses **tourist police** (73 744) in basement. Open mid-May to mid-Sept. 24hr.

Post Office: (tel. 72 228) Left of the ferry dock on the road parallel to waterfront behind Stelios Restaurant. Open Mon.-Fri. 7:30am-2pm. **Postal Code:** 18050.

OTE: (tel. 72 199) On the water to the right side of the Star Hotel. Open Mon.-Fri. 7:30am-10pm. **Telephone Code:** 0298.

ACCOMMODATIONS

Often crowded, Spetses is a relatively expensive island. Hotels are plentiful and very visible, but the larger ones overflow with tour groups. Look for something smaller, like the rooms offered by travel agencies in town. Both **Meldon Tours** and **Alasia Travel** have their own rooms starting at 6000dr for singles and 8000dr for doubles. They can also put you in contact with other *domatia*. Keep in mind that agencies take a percentage from *domatia* owners; you may do better bargaining at the ferry quay. Also consult the tourist police.

Hotel Dapia (tel. 72 295) offers airy rooms with private baths and fridges. Centrally located straight up from the quay. Singles 5000dr; doubles 8000dr.

Villa Christina (tel. 72 218) has comfortable rooms off a flower-filled courtyard. Follow the signs up from the street inland from the OTE, or the manager will pick you up from the ferry if you call ahead. All rooms have private bath shower. Open April-Oct. In August, call ahead. Singles 8000dr, 6000dr in low season; doubles 10000dr. Breakfast 10,00dr.

Villa Helena (tel. 73 194) is a 20min. walk to the old harbor. Turn inland at The Plaza, follow the mosaic path and climb the winding stairs. Look for a blue door. Has simple rooms with private bath. Doubles 7000dr.

FOOD AND ENTERTAINMENT

Restaurants, *tavernas,* and cafes abound in Spetses. Food tends to be more expensive than on the mainland, and only at certain places is it worth the price.

Patralis Tavern, a favorite restaurant among Athenian visitors to Spetses. To get to Patralis, turn right (facing inland) at the ferry quay and follow the sea for about 500m. Their original seafood recipes are scrumptious, the flavors unusually subtle. Be sure to try the grilled squid stuffed with seafood rice (2000dr), and the fresh tuna salad. Their home-made *retsina* is a must (400dr per mL). Catch it early in the season. Open Mon.-Fri. 10:30am-4pm and 6:30pm-1am.

Stelios (tel. 73 748), on the waterfront in the opposite direction, has traditional fare. Specialties include veal with pasta cooked in a ceramic pot (1600dr). The menu includes prix fixe options that include entrees and fruit desserts (2000dr). Open daily from noon until late, with a short break for siesta.

Politis (tel. 72 248), a coffee and pastry shop on the waterfront before the National Bank, serves full English breakfasts, which include coffee, fruit salad, eggs, bacon, toast, butter and jam (1300dr), outside by the water. Homemade pastries and biscuits baked by the same family for 36 years are a perfect mid-afternoon snack. Delicious *amigdaloto* (3400dr per kg; open daily 7am-midnight).

Spanos (tel. 22 516), on the walk toward Patralis, is a small bakery that sells fresh loaves (140dr) and crispies (like biscotti 750dr per kg) to locals. Come early—they sell out fast (open daily 6am-2pm).

Sports-watching Spetsiots gather for drinks at the **Socrates** bar (beers 500dr, drinks 1000dr). A younger crowd heads to **Mama's,** on the way to the Old Harbour, where drinks are more expensive, but way cooler. Trendy Athenians can be found in bars along the Old Harbor *(Palio Limani)*. Try **Mouraio, Bracera,** or **Naos.** Pulsating **Club Fever** (tel. 73 718), past the old Harbor, hosts popular all-you-can-drink orgies

(3000dr at the door) every Wednesday, Friday, and Sunday night beginning at 11pm—all the beer, wine, *ouzo,* and Metaxa you can drink.

For a mellow evening, try one of Spetses's two open-air cinemas. **Ciné Marina,** near the mansion of Laskarina Bouboulina, often shows English language films (1500dr), as does **Ciné Titania** (tel. 72 858). Marina is covered when it rains; Titania is always covered. Both have two showings nightly at 9 and 11pm.

SIGHTS

The **Anargyrios and Korgialenios College** (high school) is a 25-minute walk from town, to the right (facing inland), past the Poseidonian Hotel. John Fowles taught here and immortalized the institution and the island in his novel *The Magus.*

In the heart of the town is the **Spetses Museum** (tel. 72 994), housed in the crumbling, late-19th-century mansion of Hadjiyanni Mexi, Spetses' first governor. The imposing structure affords a great view of the island and houses coins, costumes, mastheads, folk art, religious artifacts, and a casket containing the remains of Bouboulina. The building itself is worth seeing, with an old island fireplace, stained glass windows, and carved wooden doors. Follow signs to get there (open Tues.-Sun. 8:30am-2:30pm; admission 500dr, students 300dr). The **House of Laskarina Bouboulina** (tel. 72416) is next to the park near the Dapia. Mme. Bouboulina was a ship's captain in the Greek War of Independence. Her heroic exploits are celebrated on Spetses with a mock naval battle in which a small boat is blown up the first Saturday after September 8th. (English tours every 30min. 10am-1pm and 5-7:30pm; admission 1000dr, children 300dr.) The **monastery of Agios Nikolas** stands opposite a square of traditional Spetsiot mosaics, just above the Old Harbor. Notice a memorial plaque commemorating Napoleon's nephew, who was pickled in a barrel of rum which was stored in a monastic cell at Agios Nikolas from 1827-32. The nuns give free samples of their homemade yogurt. Modest dress is required.

The water in Spetses is clean and clear, and all visitors seem to be ready to jump in at the drop of a hat despite pesky sea urchins. There are a couple of pleasant but crowded rocky beaches right in town and on the way to the Old Harbor. **Kaiki Beach,** a 1.5km walk to the right (facing inland) of the ferry quay, is just down from the Anargyrios and Korgialenios College. Long sandy beaches and lots of watersports make this a fun destination. Also close is **Paradise Beach,** past the Old Harbour. The island's prettiest beach, **Anagyri,** is a bus ride away. Catch the bus in front of Mama's Cafe (3 per day, 750dr round-trip). Ask at travel agencies for details about **Blueberry Hill Cove** and **Ligoneri.** The bus to these destinations leaves from in front of the Poseidonian Hotel (to the right of the quay). **Motorboats** leave the harbor for Anagyri as soon as they are full (10am-noon, returning from the beaches at about 4pm, 1500dr). **Sea taxis** cost a fortune and only help save money for groups of eight or more (7500dr for Anagyri). Since only registered cars are allowed on the island, land transportation is provided by horse-drawn carriages, which usually will not go past Kastelli Beach or Agia Marina.

Sporades ΣΠΟΡΑΔΕΣ

The jagged coasts and thickly forested interiors of the Sporades (Scattered Ones) were first colonized by Cretans who cultivated olives and grapes on the scattered islands until Athenians took over in the 5th century BC. The residue of ancient structures on these islands attests to the 2nd century BC Roman presence, the Venetians' 13th century rule, and Turkish rule until 1821 when the Sporades became Greek. Lush islands of fragrant pines, luxurious beaches, and abundant fruit orchards, the Sporades of today offer travelers (mostly Germans, Norwegians, and Brits), a smorgasbord of earthly delights. Although word has gotten out about the Sporades, and the islands' fledgling tourist facilities are quickly maturing, there are spots on this small archipelago that remain relatively quiet and inexpensive.

SKIATHOS ΣΚΙΑΘΟΣ

Falling short of the other Sporades in natural beauty, Skiathos compensates by playing host to a huge social scene. The incredible nightlife attracts more tourists each year. While the number of nightclubs increases, however, much of the older culture of the island is being lost. Your only recourse may be to read of the bygone era. Skiathos is one of the only places where you can find the writings of **Alexandros Papadiamantis** (1815-1911) in English translation. So either take a night away from the disco, or pack a book to the beach.

■ Skiathos Town

Skiathos Town has weathered the deluge of foreign tourists in much the same way as the coastline. The cobblestone streets of the commercial section are packed with loitering tourists and expensive stores. Residential neighborhoods with peaceful terraces and balconies, bursting with white gardenia blossoms and red geraniums, stand in contrast to the rows of *domatia* housing the tourists who flock to Skiathos Town to party. As *the* place to party in the Sporades, Skiathos Town never sleeps.

ORIENTATION AND PRACTICAL INFORMATION

The long waterfront, lined with travel agencies, *tavernas,* and various bike and car rental dealers, is intersected by **Papadiamantis Street,** where for each tourist agency there is also a jewelry store. Traveling inland, Papadiamantis is intersected by **Pandra Street** at the National Bank, and by **Evangelistra Street** at the post office. Parallel and to the left of Papadiamantis, beginning at Pandra, **Politechniou Street** houses a string of bars. On the far right of the waterfront, still facing inland, a road winds up to the airport and several beaches. On the far left, along a harbor perpendicular to the main waterfront, is a row of fishing boats that charter daily excursions. A mediocre map is available everywhere (500dr).

> **Tourist Police:** (tel. 23 172) On the right side of Papadiamantis St. in a small white building, inland past the OTE. Their *Summer in Skiathos* brochure has a map. Open daily 8am-9pm. The **police** (tel. 21 111), across the street and upstairs, are open 24hr. Although they speak very little English, they can help arrange *domatia* rooms.
>
> **Banks: National Bank,** midway up Papadiamantis St. on the left side, offers **currency exchange.** Open Mon. and Wed. 8am-2pm, Tues. and Thurs. 8am-2pm and 7-9pm, Fri. 8am-1:30pm, Sun. 9am-noon. Lines are long and slow July-Aug.
>
> **American Express:** 21 Papadiamantis St. (tel. 21 463, -4, fax 21 793), on the left before the post office, in the travel agency of Mare Nostrum Holidays. Provides all

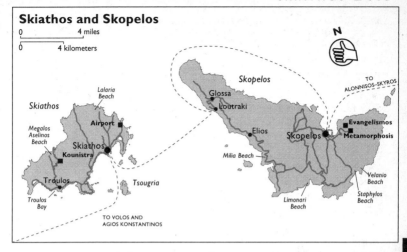

Skiathos and Skopelos

0 —————— 4 miles
0 —————— 4 kilometers

Skiathos

Lalaria Beach

Megalos Aselinos Beach

Airport

Skiathos
Kounistra

Troulos

Troulos Bay

Tsougria

TO VOLOS AND AGIOS KONSTANTINOS

Skopelos

Glossa
Loutraki

Elios

Skopelos
Metamorphosis

Evangelismos

Milia Beach

Velanio Beach

Limonari Beach

Staphylos Beach

TO ALONNISOS–SKYROS

N

tourist services, including **currency exchange**. Open Mon.-Sat. 8am-2pm and 5-10pm, Sun. 10:30am-1pm and 5-10:30pm.

OTE: (tel. 22 399) Right side of Papadiamantis St., 1 block inland from the post office. Open in summer Mon.-Fri. 7:30am-10pm; in winter Mon.-Fri. 7:30am-3pm.

Flights: Olympic Airways Office (tel. 22 200, -049), at the airport. Call 24hr. prior to take-off to confirm flight. Open Mon.-Fri. 8am-4pm. Taxis from the harbor to the airport cost about 1000dr. 2 flights per day to Athens (50min., 12,200dr).

Buses: Depart from the **bus stop** at the far right end of the wharf (facing inland), traveling along the main road and making 24 stops, ending at Koukounaries beach (every 15-30min., 7:15am-1am, 280dr). Schedule posted at bus stop on the wharf and at Koukounaries.

Ferries: Nomikos/Goutos Lines (tel. 22 209), located in the middle of the waterfront. Open daily 7am-10pm. Ferries travel to Skiathos most frequently from Agios Konstantinos, Volos, Skopelos, and Alonissos. From Athens, take the daily bus from the station at 260 Liossion St. (every hr., 6:15am-9:30pm, 2½hr., 2650dr) to Agios Konstantinos, and then the ferry (2-3 per day, 3½hr., 3500dr). From Volos, ferries run from Skiathos to Skopelos (3-4 per day, 1½hr., 1500dr) and Alonissos (3-4 per day, 2hr., 1800dr).

Flying Dolphins: (tel. 22 018) Look for the yellow signs at the center of the waterfront. Open daily 7:30am-9:30pm. Hydrofoils travel to Agios Konstantinos (3-4 per day, 1¼hr., 6600dr); Skopelos (9-11 per day, 35min., 2400dr); Volos (5-6 per day, 1¼hr., 5500dr); Alonissos (8-9 per day, 1hr., 3350dr); Platania (1-2 per day, 25min., 2650dr); and Thessaloniki (1 per day, 3¼hr., 9500dr).

Taxis: (tel. 21 460) Queue along the waterfront next to the "rooms to let" kiosk; prices are posted on the shack. Open 24hr.

Moped Rental: Numerous places along the waterfront, including **Avis** (tel. 21 458) and **Hertz** (tel. 22 430; fax 21 952). Both are open daily 8am-10pm. Mopeds begin around 300dr per day. Inquire about helmets and other tourist services.

English Bookstore: Skyline (tel. 23 647) on Evangelista St. Open daily 8:30am-midnight in summer 8:30am-2pm and 5-8pm in the winter. The best choices include translations of Papadiamantis' and Kazantzakis' books.

Laundromat: Snow White Self Service Laundry (tel. 24 256), behind the Credit Bank at the port. Wash 1800dr, soap 200dr, dry 500-1000dr, and iron 200dr each item, all while you visit with the English-speaking owner or sit at a nearby cafe. Open Mon.-Sat. 9am-10pm, Sun. 10am-10pm.

Pharmacy: (tel. 22 988) Look for the three green cross signs, first by the National Bank, second by the Post Office, and third past the school. All pharmacies open 8:30am-2pm and 6-10pm.

Medical Emergency and Hospital: (tel. 22 222) On the "Acropolis" hill behind Skiathos Town. Open 24hr., but emergencies only after 1pm.

Post Office: (tel. 22 011) At the intersection of Papadiamantis and Evangelistra St. Open Mon.-Fri. 7:30am-2pm. **Postal Code:** 37002.
Telephone Code: 0427.

ACCOMMODATIONS

Most tourists make reservations for July and August before they arrive, and tour groups often book most of the hotel rooms for summer almost a year in advance. Never fear, for although most hotel rooms and *domatia* are simply whitewashed doubles, usually something can be found if you are willing to pay the price. Be sure to bargain in the off season, especially if you are met with an offer at the port. Typical rooms run 6000-8000dr in winter, 8000-10,000dr in spring and fall, and 10,000-14,000dr in summer. Signs abound, particularly on Evangelistra and the streets parallel to it, but if you are stuck or tired of carrying your pack, pop over to the tourist police or the **Rooms to Let Office** (tel 22 990, -260; fax 23 852) in the wooden kiosk by the port (open daily 8:30am-midnight).

Pension Angela (tel. 22 962), to your left at the end of Papadiamantis St., offers typical, clean doubles with baths (6000-10,000dr depending on the season).
Australia Hotel (tel. 22 488), just left off Evangelistra, has no sweeping, panoramic views, but the simple doubles with baths are cheaper (5000-12,000dr).
Camping Koukounaries (tel. 49 250), lies on the bus route between stops 19 and 20. Has restaurant, minimarket, and campground 1km from the beach. A night runs 1500dr per person, 1000dr per tent, and extra for the usual amenities.

FOOD AND ENTERTAINMENT

The cheapest dining options in Skiathos are to hit the *gyro/souvlaki* (350dr) stands which line Papadiamantis and the waterfront or to forage in any of the numerous **supermarkets.** Any *taverna* away from Papadiamantis will cost you less than those which are right on the main drag. Walk down Politechniou toward the harbor, until it turns slightly to the right, and look for the blue sight for **Ellinikon Taverna,** featuring five or six different specialties each night for only 1000dr. While their vegetarian plate may be uninspiring, it nonetheless offers an alternative to the omni-present Greek salad. Continuing farther down Politechniou you will catch sight of **Taverna Stamatis and Angelos** and **Taverna To Steki,** which share a fluorescent-lit tent for outdoor dining. Both feature fresh seafood (entrees 1400-1800dr).

Although a quiet evening with a Papadiamantis translation in a waterfront cafe may strike your fancy, most visitors either dance the night away in one of the clubs lining the far right side of the coast, or drink at one of the innumerable bars and pubs on Politechniou St., Evangelistra St., or on Papadiamantis Sq. If you venture along the coast, choose whose blaring music you like best and shake your booty there with your 1500dr cocktail in hand. Most of these clubs close in the off season.

In town, decorated with a poster from *Casablanca,* **Kentavros** (tel 22 980) lies on Papadiamantis Sq. There, 700dr will buy you a beer and 1500dr a cocktail while everything from rock to jazz carries the night along in Skiathos's oldest bar. **Kalypso** (tel. 23 051), one of the classier places in town, is on the water above the restaurant of the same name; the door is on the street parallel to the waterfront road. The owner, who works at an Athens radio station, will guide you on a journey through classical, traditional, ethnic, and jazz music in the relaxed (and gay-friendly) atmosphere (beer 600dr, cocktails 1500dr).

For a much different adventure, grab a book off the shelf on your way into the **Admiral Benobow** (tel. 22 311), Politechniou's most eccentric pub. Better yet, chat with Brits Mick and Elaine who play oldies, rock, blues, and soul while serving imported beers for 500-700dr. Just down the street, see how the Greeks party at the pricey **Blue Chips Club** (beer 1000dr, cocktails 1500dr). If you're missing the classics of the 60s, 70s, and 80s, dance two floors down from Kentavros in the open-minded **Cafe Pixida.**

For more sedate entertainment, the open-air **Cinema Paradiso** (tel. 23 975) screens recent Hollywood hits in English with Greek subtitles (1500dr). Inquire at the American Express office for schedules as well as information regarding summer cultural and artistic events at the **Bourtzi,** on the far left of the harbor. Whatever you choose, remember that the night doesn't end until at least 4am. **Excursions** around the island and to neighboring islands can be arranged through any of the local travel agencies (3000-4500dr per person). As you walk inland, Papadiamantis Sq. lies to you right off of Papadiamantis St. Follow the signs to author Alexandros Papadiamantis' 140 year-old house, which now serves as the **Papadiamantis Museum,** housing his few possessions. The museum honors the 19th century realist who was one of Greece's most eminent prose writers. This is one of the few places where his short stories and novels are available in English. Information in the museum is also available in English (admission 250dr; open Tues.-Sun. 9:30am-1pm and 5-8pm)

■ Around Skiathos Island

The island's main paved road runs along the south coast from Skiathos Town to Koukounaries. Resort hotels dominate the beaches. A **bus** travels this route leaving the harbor in Skiathos Town (every 15-30min., 7:15am-1am, 280dr), with stops at many beaches, including **Megali Ammos, Nostos, Vromolimnos, Platanias,** and **Troulos.** The bus route and the road end at the pine grove beach of **Koukounaries,** where swaying branches shelter clear turquoise water and fine white sand. A short walk away is the curved yellow **Banana Beach,** slightly less populated than the others. From Koukounaries, take the paved road to the left of the bus stop, follow it to the bend, and make a right on the uphill dirt road. At the top, take the worn path through the gate on the left. The hike over the next hill leads to the **Little Banana Beach,** the island's nude beach which, popular with gay men, is the refreshing beach it claims to be if you are wanting (or willing) to bare all.

Just east of Troulos a road turns off for **Asselinos,** a beach on the north edge of Skiathos. For a calmer afternoon, take the high road which forks after 2km—the right branch leads uphill to **Panagia Kounistra,** a small monastery with a grape arbor and *averna* within its walls. West along the coast past **Lalaria Beach** are the ruins of the medieval walled **castle** (a 2hr. walk on a path from Skiathos Town). The Greeks built the castle during the 16th century to take refuge from marauding pirates. With independence in the 19th century, they abandoned this headland and began work on what has blossomed into present-day Skiathos Town. Two churches are all that remains of the ancient community, but the **Church of the Nativity** boasts fine icons and frescoes. For details on **boat excursions** around Skiathos and to neighboring islands, call the AmEx office or any other major tourist office along the waterfront, or ask at the "rooms to let" kiosk. Most trips cost 3000-4500dr per person.

SKOPELOS ΣΚΟΠΕΛΟΣ

Looming cliffs rising above the ocean gave this island the name, "Steep Rock From the Sea." Tempering the mountains' starkness, acres of pine, olive, and plum trees blanket the hills. Originally a Cretan colony ruled by King Staphylos, strategic Skopelos has been occupied by Persians, Spartans, Athenians, Romans, Franks, Venetians, and Ottomans. It was conquered in 1538 by the illustrious Ottoman admiral Khayr El-Din Barbarossa (Red Beard), who killed the entire population. Women practice traditional occupations of weaving and embroidery wearing the distinctive Skopelan *morko*—a silk shirt, short velvet jacket with flowing sleeves, and a kerchief.

■ Skopelos Town

Except for the front line of tourist offices and *tavernas* curving around the horseshoe waterfront, Skopelos Town is a delightful cobblestone maze stacked against the hillside. The tightly packed town is a jumble of Venetian, Byzantine, Macedonian, and Neoclassical architecture. Climb to the top of the castle walls on the left side of the harbor for a lovely view of the town.

ORIENTATION AND PRACTICAL INFORMATION

Boats dock at the concrete jetty on the left tip of the horseshoe as you look seaward. Behind you rises the old town. Tourist agencies, *tavernas,* and cafes line the waterfront. Behind the crowded eateries, one block past the Commercial Bank, **Galatsaniou Street,** a fashionable path rich with trinkets and goodies, darts upward. Buses and taxis depart from the right edge of town. Directly inland from the stop is a shady square (actually a triangle) affectionately known as **Platanos.**

Tourist Agencies: Most **exchange currency,** rent mopeds and cars, sell ferry and hydrofoil tickets, and arrange expensive excursions to neighboring islands. **Thalpos** (tel. 22 947, 23 466; fax 23 057), past the Commercial Bank, is on the 2nd floor. Open daily 9am-2pm and 6-8pm; extended hours in July and August.

Banks: National Bank (tel. 22 691), on the left side of the waterfront. Has 24hr. **currency changer.** The **Commercial Bank** (tel. 22 015) at the center of the waterfront has an **ATM.** Both banks open Mon.-Thurs. 8am-2pm and Fri. 8am-1:30pm, with additional hours in the summer.

Buses: Stop located on the right side of the waterfront as you face the sea. Bus service changes weekly. Buses serve: Panormos (30min., 340dr); Milia (35min., 460dr); Elios (45min., 460dr); Glossa (55min., 600dr); Stafilos (5min., 210dr); and Agnotas (15min., 210dr).

Ferries: Nomicos/Goutos Lines (tel. 22 363, 23 056, -5) run to: Ag. Konstantinos (2 per day, 4½hr., 3875dr); Volos (3-4 per day, 4½hr., 3225dr); Skiathos (4-5 per day, 1½hr., 1490dr); Alonissos (3 per day, 30min., 1240dr); Kimi (1 per week, 3hr., 4575dr); and Thessaloniki (3 per week, 6hr., 5050dr).

Flying Dolphins: Tickets sold by **Madro Travel** (tel. 22 145, -33; fax 22 941; open daily 6:30am-9:30pm). To: Ag. Konstantinos (3 per day, 2¼hr., 7925dr); Volos (5 per day, 2hr., 6610dr); Skiathos (7-11 per day, 45min., 2000dr); Alonissos (6 per day, 20min., 1850dr); Thessaloniki (1-2 per day, 4hr., 9500dr); and Kimi (2 per week via Skyros, 2½hr., 9500dr). You *must* arrive ½hr. before departure, as conditions often force the company to bus passengers to a sheltered port.

Taxis: (tel. 22 207, 23 100) Available at the waterfront, particularly near the bus stop, daily 7am-2am.

Moped and Car Rental: Shop around, as most travel agencies arrange rentals. Mopeds start at 2500dr per day, cars 10,000dr per day. Prices vary by season.

Laundromat: Several around town, including near Greca's Crêperie. Open Mon-Sat. 9am-1:30pm and 6-8:30pm. Wash 1800-2400dr; dry 1100dr, ironing available.

Pharmacy: (tel. 22 252) Across from OTE. Open Mon.-Fri. 9am-2pm, 5:30-11pm.

Medical Center: (tel. 22 222) Follow the left-hand road inland from Souvlaki Sq. until it dead-ends, then turn right and you'll see it shortly on the right. Open Mon.-Fri. 9am-2pm for free walk-ins; open 24hr. Mon.-Fri. for emergencies.

Police: (tel. 22 235) Behind the National Bank. Open 24hr.

Post Office: Follow the signs along the circuitous route to the office. Open Mon.-Fri. 7:30am-2pm. **Postal Code:** 37003.

OTE: (tel. 22 399) 100m uphill from the waterfront on Galatsaniou St. from the waterfront for 50m. Open in summer Mon.-Sat. 7:30am-10pm, Sun. 9am-2pm and 5-10pm; in winter Mon.-Fri. 7:30am-3:10pm. **Telephone Code:** 0424.

ACCOMMODATIONS, FOOD, & ENTERTAINMENT

If you don't get scooped up by hustlers, the cheapest accommodations can be found by wandering through the narrow labyrinthine streets behind the waterfront, looking for "rooms to let" signs and the EOT seal. The **Rooms and Apartments Association of Skopelos** (tel. 24 567) has an office in the small white building near the left edge of the waterfront (open daily 9:30am-1:30pm and 5:30-8:30pm). Singles and doubles average 5000-6000dr in June, 8000-10,000dr in July, and 10,000-12,000dr in August. If you want to make a reservation, try **Hotel Eleni** (tel. 22 393; fax 22 936) on the far right side of the waterfront, past the bus station (singles 6500-8500dr; doubles 8500-13,500dr). There are no campgrounds on Skopelos.

Platanos Sq. is home to many 350dr gyros. Nearby lies **Greca's Crêperie,** which earns local praise. A Parisienne artist, Greca came to Skopelos decades ago on a UNESCO project to help children. Ever since, she has run her crêperie for the love of it, offering delicious crepes (800-1200dr), her rare *joie de vivre,* and now internationally recognized prints (open daily 7pm-12:30am and for breakfast and lunch in summer). On the left side of the waterfront, **Molos** gains fame for its delicious vegetarian entrees (500-1000dr), Greek fare (starting at 1300dr), and friendly service. Good luck getting a seat to try the stuffed chicken (1200dr) at **Spyros Taverna,** on the waterfront near the Commercial Bank. Seafood, while available, is expensive.

Cafes lining the waterfront offer exotic ice cream sundaes in the afternoons and evenings. On the far left near the pier, the **Platanos Jazz Club** serves coffee and cocktails in the shade of a beautiful plane tree. Enjoy your drink (beer 600dr, cocktails 1500dr) or dessert to blues or new jazz music. More traditional jazz is served up in the **Blue Bar,** housed in a traditional Skopelan home. A wilder scene fills the streets behind Platanos Sq. all the way to the far right side of the harbor. **Anö Kato** and **Kounos,** on opposite sides of the street running away from the square, host the late night party-goers. Anö Kato plays only Greek music and is rumored to demonstrate the Greek festivities of table-dancing and glass-throwing; you'll need to stick around until at least 4am to find out. Kounos opens at 1am and shakes with everything from classic rock to rave (1000dr cover).

■ Around Skopelos Island

Mt. Palouki, facing the town across the harbor, conceals three **monasteries.** Two paved roads leave the town from the bus depot on the right end of the waterfront. To reach the monasteries, follow the left road, which circles the harbor, ascends the mountain, and becomes a dirt road 600m past the Hotel Aegean. At the next fork, 30 minutes by foot from town, two signs point the way to the monasteries. **Evangelismos** hails from the 18th century, but its enormous altar screen from Constantinople is 400 years older. Take the left-hand fork up the hot and winding mountain road for 45 minutes and start early in the morning before the heat and bugs intensify. If you are a dedicated monastophile or a masochistic hiker, descend back to the fork and climb an hour and a half to the **Monastery of Metamorphosis,** standing amid pines on a breezy knoll. The chapel, set in a flowery courtyard, dates from the 16th century. **Prodromou,** visible from Metamorphosis, sits on the next ridge. Once a monastery, this refuge is now a cloister dedicated to St. John the Baptist and inhabited by nuns. It's about a 2hr. walk from the original fork. A path described in *The Soto's Walking Guide* would shorten your trip (buy it at bookstores and shops; 2500dr).

Beaches line the coast south of Skopelos up to Loutraki. The first and busiest one, **Staphylos,** is long and sandy. Archaeologists discovered the tomb of the ancient Cretan general Staphylos on a nearby hillside, as well as a gold-plated sword dating from the 15th century BC, now displayed in the Volos museum. A large rock separates Staphylos from the quieter **Velanio.** Advertised as the only **nude beach** on Skopelos, it remains uncrowded. Past the sleepy fishing village of Agnostas, the bus stops at the beach of **Panormos.** From here a five-minute walk leads to the isolated **Adrina** beaches, named for the female pirate who once terrorized the islands. She leapt to her death from this cove when island residents cornered her.

At the end of the road, the hilltop town of **Glossa** overlooks Skopelos' second port. Glossa remains a quiet Greek town. For a superb hike from the village, walk the dirt track across the island to the **Monastery of Agios Ioannis,** which clings to a boulder above the ocean. Take the main road east from Glossa and turn left on the first dirt road to Steki Taverna, after which it's clear sailing. At the road's end a path drops to the sea, and stone steps, cut in the escarpment, lead up to the monastery. Allow at least four hours for a round-trip visit to Agios Ioannis, and bring at least a liter of water per person. Most of the road is navigable by motorbike.

ALONISSOS ΑΛΟΝΝΗΣΟΣ

On the quietest and least populated island of the Sporades, Alonissos' 2000 inhabitants enjoy magnificent beaches and pristine mountains. Archeological discoveries attest to Alonissos's ancient prosperity, but its story remains one of the more painful in Greece's tumultuous post-war history. In 1950, disease annihilated the once lucrative vineyards, and most men were forced into construction work in Athens. An earthquake in 1965 then destroyed the Old Town, and Patitiri developed as the island's new center as a result of government-directed housing projects.

Because of this devastation, Alonissos lacks polished beauty but remains one of the friendlier and less-touristed islands in Greece. The **National Marine Park** of Alonissos and the Northern Sporades protects the island's landscapes and helps to preserve the sedate, unruffled atmosphere. Come soon, though; architects and real estate agents are already setting up shop.

■ Patitiri

All boats dock at Patitiri which is, for all intents and purposes, the only town on the island. Above, the whitewashed Old Town clutches the slopes of the hill. As a city of concrete, Patitiri is neither the best nor the subtlest introduction to Alonissos, but it does provide an island hopping stopover and the gateway to the Marine Park.

ORIENTATION AND PRACTICAL INFORMATION

From the docks, two main parallel streets run inland, **Pelasgon** on the left and **Ikion Dolophon** on the right. In the center of the waterfront **Alonissos Travel** (tel. 65 188; fax 65 511) offers currency exchange, finds rooms, books excursions, and sells ferry tickets (open daily 9am-10pm). To the right, amiable, English-speaking Mr. and Mrs. Athanassiou at **Ikos Travel** (tel. 65 320, -648, -649; fax 65 321) provide similar services as well as excellent information about **ecological excursions** and handling **Flying Dolphin** ticketing. **Ferries** travel daily to: Agios Konstantinos (5½hr., 4100dr); Volos (2 per day, 5¼hr., 3550dr); Skiathos (3 per day, 2hr., 1800dr); and Skopelos (3 per day, 30min., 1200dr). Ferries run once a week to Kimi (2½hr., 4065dr) and Thessaloniki (6hr., 5630dr). **Flying Dolphins** leave for: Agios Konstantinos (3 per day, 2¾hr., 8500dr); Skiathos (10 per day, 1¼hr., 3000dr); Thessaloniki (1 per day, 4hr., 9500dr); and Volos (3-5 per day, 2½hr, 7300dr). Less frequently, they travel to Skyros and Kimi. **Taxis** (tel. 65 573) wait just to the right of the travel agencies, and although service stops at 2am, they can be called anytime. The red sign of the **laundromat,** farther inland on the left, shines daily 9:30am-2pm and 6-9:30pm.

Up Ikion Dolophon, the **National Bank** (tel. 65 777) lies on the left (open Mon.-Thurs. 8am-2pm, Fri. 8am-1:30pm). The **pharmacy** (tel. 65 540) is on the left (open 9am-1:30pm and 6-9pm except Sun. afternoons), but the pharmacist (tel. 65 165) can be reached 24hr. in an emergency. The **post office** (tel. 65 560) is farther inland on the right (open Mon.-Fri. 7:30am-2pm). Uphill, on the left, **Rent-A-Bike** (tel. 65 140) has rentals starting around 3000dr per day. You will need to purchase your own gas (about 500dr per tank), but the English-speaking owner can direct you to the gas station. The **police** station (tel. 65 205) and the **hospital** (tel. 65 208) sit at the top of the hill. **Postal code:** 37005. **Telephone code:** 0424.

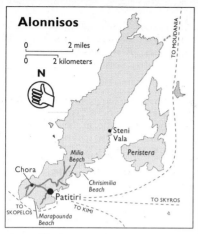

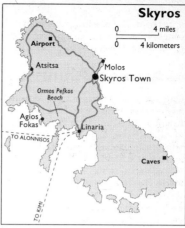

ACCOMMODATIONS

Domatia provide the best accommodations on Alonissos. You may be met with offers at the harbor, so remember to bargain. High season runs from late July through August, and reservations are recommended for this period. Although the **Rooms to Let Office** (tel./fax 65 577), next to Ikos Travel, offers its services daily 9:30am-3pm and 6-10pm, you may find a less expensive room by negotiating with locals and looking for signs with EOT seals on inland streets. Prices should range between 1000-6000dr per person. Inquire at **Boutique Mary,** on the right side of Pelasgon, for rooms with private baths at the **Dimakis Pension** (tel. 65 294; singles 5000-7000dr; doubles 8000-10,000dr). Off Pelasgon, follow signs uphill 1km to **Camping Rocks** (tel. 65 410), where 1000dr per person and 500dr per tent buys a spot next to their **disco,** which rocks *bouzouki* until 4am.

FOOD AND ENTERTAINMENT

On the left side of the waterfront, **Dolphin Restaurant** serves a 1100dr traditional Alonissos cheese pie. Locals hold the small *ouzerie* **To Kamaki** (tel. 65 245), on the left side of Ikion Dolophon, in especially high esteem. For a waterfront view, nothing can beat **Argo** (tel. 65 245), perched atop the cliff on the far right side of the harbor. Both specialize in local seafood and fish, but dinner will cost you at least 1400dr. Alternatively, follow the downward branch of the footpath to Argo, and with some bread and feta, the romance of moonlight, seascape, and Greek music will cost you far less.

After dinner, double back on the third branch of the footpath to reach the happening **Pub Nefli,** where locals and travelers dance and drink to the same commanding view of the sea. The barkeep will mix the club speciality, a *nefli*, on request. On the left end of the waterfront, Dennis and his sons entertain at the island's oldest bar, **Pub Dennis.** His exotic tropical cocktails cost at least 1500dr.

THE OLD TOWN (CHORA)

Set high on a hill to ward off pirate attacks, the Chora (Old Town) is now being rebuilt, mostly by Northern European vacationers. The town maintains its tradition through the **Christ Church.** Run by Papa Gregorias, village priest and local legend, the tiny chapel dates from the 12th century AD. The island's only **bus** runs between Chora and Patitiri hourly (9am-3pm and 7-11pm in the summer, 10min., 250dr). A schedule is posted at the stop across from Ikos Travel. **Taxis** are available (about 2000dr round-trip). A walk, however, affords as glorious a view as the town itself. Maps cost about 400dr, or you can start uphill on Pelasgon and just stay on the main uphill road. The parching walk from Patitiri takes about an hour and requires a liter of water per person. At the top, enjoy the **sunset** over the Aegean and **Kaphereas'** traditional almond sweets, which take a month to prepare and are not to be missed.

■ Around Alonissos

Only the south end of the island is inhabited, leaving the mountainous central and northern sections cloaked in pristine pine forests. A motorbike can traverse the length of the island, from Patitiri to Gerakas, at the northern tip, in about two hours. Many roads remain unpaved, so a map is useful. With little public transportation, your feet remain the best means of exploration of Alonissos. Ikos Travel provides information about ecological hiking trails on the island.

A 30-minute walk downhill leads to the beaches of **Vrissita, Megalo Mourtia,** and **Mikro Mourtia.** Steep, pine-clad slopes shelter these beaches on the southern tip of the island. Inquire at the port and in the travel agencies about boats traveling up the eastern coast to the sandy **Chrissi Milia,** where you can walk over 300m out into the clear water. Just north, at **Kokkinokastro,** swimmers occasionally find old coins. Here, the sea has inundated the ancient acropolis of Alonissos. Pot shards from Ikos, as it was then named, are among the significant archaeological discoveries. Farther north, the fishing villages of **Steni Vala** and **Kalamakia** remain only lightly touristed, although there are several *tavernas* and *domatia* available at Steni Vala. Perhaps the best, yet most expensive, way to see Alonissos and the **National Marine Park of the Northern Sporades** is by boat.

Either a 9500dr full-day tour or a 3000-4000dr charter boat will allow you to visit the various neighboring islands. A shipwreck off of Peristera significantly changed archaeologists' understanding of ancient shipping. **Cyclops Polyphemous** lived in the cave on Gioura until Odysseus and his crew came across him. Although many islands claim this distinction, Gioura's cavern and endangered brown goats with black crosses covering their spines and shoulderblades best fit the Homeric description. The park is designed to protect many such species once described by Homer, including the **Mediterranean Monk Seal.**

SKYROS ΣΚΥΡΟΣ

Rolling purple hills nibbled by goats, groves of fragrant pines, sandy beaches, and gnarled cliffs form the spectacular backdrop for daily life on Skyros. The island's idiosyncratic culture remains strong; throughout the entanglement of side streets, women embroider and weave rugs while men fashion sandals, ceramics, and intricately hand-carved wooden furniture. By far the quietest island of the Sporades, Skyros is also the largest and most isolated.

■ Skyros Town

Crowned by a Venetian castle, Skyros Town spills down from a rocky summit away from the sea. It was built on an inland cliffside as protection from pirate invasions. Today, its stark white cubist architecture remains unique among the Sporades. Its steep, narrow paths bear no resemblance to streets, so watch your step on the slick cobblestones and remember that what confounded pirates in the past will confuse you now. Your lost look and the simple question of "Brooke?" or "Kastro?" will receive a stream of Greek and a push in the right direction.

ORIENTATION AND PRACTICAL INFORMATION

Boats to Skyros dock at quiet **Linaria,** where they are met by a bus to Skyros Town (250dr). Still, ask drivers their destinations, as buses may be marked somewhat counterintuitively (e.g., "Topikon" for the town and "Skyros" for the beach). The bus stops right outside the maze of Skyros Town, but at least the main street, **Agoras,** runs straight uphill to the **central square** and taxi stand. From here it winds through *tavernas,* cafes, and tourist agencies before forking at Kalypso Bar and a kiosk. Turning left here and walking up what could never be a main street, you will arrive at another fork where a small sign points right to Brooke and museums. To find **Rupert Brooke Square,** continue "straight" on this cobbled path. The square, overlooking Molos and the sea, received its name from the famed English poet Rupert Brooke (1887-1915), who died here en route to Gallipoli during the disastrous Dardanelles campaign of WWI. He is depicted here in an uncharacteristically nude, bronze statue. The stairs to Brooke's left pass the archeological museum on their way to Molos. After a 15-minute walk downhill, the beach and many *domatia* will lie to the right.

Tourist Office: (tel./fax 92 789) Take the first right after the street with the post office. Information in English and help arranging accommodations. Open daily 7:30am-2:30pm, July-Aug. daily 9am-3pm and 6:30-11pm.

Travel Offices: Skyros Travel (tel. 91 123, -600), past the central square on Agoras St., is the agent for **Flying Dolphins** and **Olympic Airways.** Mr. Lefteris is a friendly agent who will know all the details of your travels before you leave the isolated island. Skyros organizes 1 boat trip per week to the south (6000dr), arranges bus trips (300dr per person), helps with accommodations, rents mopeds (3000dr per day) and sells island maps (500dr). Open daily 9:15am-2:15pm and 6:30-10:30pm. Their port office is open in accordance with the Dolphin schedule.

Banks: National Bank (tel. 91 802), up from the bus stop, on the left before the central square. Open Mon.-Thurs. 8am-2pm and Fri. 8am-1:30pm. 24hr. **ATM.**

Flights: (tel. 91 625) A military airport 20km from Skyros Town on the northern tip of the island can only be accessed by taxi (3500dr). 2-5 weekly flights to Athens (35min., 13,900dr).

Buses: From Skyros Town to Linaria (3-5 per day, 20min., 250dr), and Molos (3-4 per day, 10min., 200dr). Check Skyros Travel for posted schedule, which roughly corresponds to the ferry and dolphin schedule.

Ferries: Likomidis Lines (tel. 91 790), on the right past the bank, arranges ferry tickets. To Skyros, travel by bus from Athens to Kimi on Evia (2 per day, 3½hr., 2600dr). Ferries from Kimi's port area travel twice per day to Skyros (June-Sept., 2hr., 1959dr). There is no ferry service to the other Sporades.

Flying Dolphins: To: Alonissos (1-2 per day, 1¼hr., 6770dr); Skopelos (1 per day, 1¾hr., 7050dr); Skiathos (1 per day, 2¼hr., 8125dr); Volos (4 per week, 4½hr., 13,140dr); Kimi (1 per week, 45min., 4500dr); Marmaras (2 per week, 5½hr., 8310dr); and Thessaloniki (1 per week in high season, 6hr., 12,540dr).

Taxis: (tel. 91 666) Queue at central square, not to be confused with Rupert's square, which is at the far edge of town. Don't expect to call a cab late at night or during siesta hours.

Moped Rental: (tel. 91 223, -459) On your right as you walk out of town past the bus stop (3000-3500dr per day). There's another place (tel. 92 022) on your left before you reach the police station, and OTE offers motorbikes (2800-3500dr per day) and bikes (1500dr per day). Ask for a helmet. Open daily 9am-1pm, 6-9pm.

Medical Center: (tel. 92 222) Clinic with 2 doctors located at the edge of the village, 400m from the bus stop.

Pharmacy: On the right near the central square (tel. 91 617; open daily 8:30am-1pm and 6:30-11pm), and on the right past Skyros Travel (tel. 91 111; open 8:30am-2pm and 6pm-midnight).

Police: (tel. 91 274) Turn right just past Skyros Travel, and at the end of the road, take another right. It's the white building with light blue gates and trim.

Post Office: (tel. 91 208) The first right as you walk from the bus stop to the central square. **Exchanges currency** and cashes traveler's checks. Open Mon.-Fri. 7:30am-2pm. **Postal Code:** 34007.

OTE: (tel. 91 399; fax 91 599) Just across the street from the police, they are open Mon.-Fri. 7:30am-1pm and 1:30-2:30pm. **Telephone Code:** 0222.

ACCOMMODATIONS

Although there are rooms to let in tiny Linaria, to experience the Skyrian culture you should search the winding streets of Skyros Town. Wandering along the narrow stairs while carrying any sort of luggage will surely bring the simple question, *"Domatia?"* Even if you have a room, accept the offer just to see a Skyrian house. The Skyrians embellish their homes with family heirlooms of copperware, crockery, embroidery, icons, and hand-carved furniture. Initially, aristocratic families bought these prizes from pirates around the world. By the late 19th century, however, as the aristocracy moved to Athens, these possessions were being sold to the lower classes. The stark white architecture of the Skyrian home hides rooms cluttered by treasures, where even the bamboo ceilings are artwork. If you stay in a Skyrian house, remember to bargain for the price and look carefully for landmarks and house numbers, as the streets may be extremely confusing. You will probably miss the entire experience and pay much more if you are snatched up at the bus station or head to a travel agency.

For something simpler and closer to the bus stop, try the marble-floored rooms below the National Bank of Greece (tel. 91 459). A simple double runs 5000dr in low season and 7000dr in high season. Showers are shared, but there is no lack of water pressure. Next to the post office, **Hotel Elena** (tel. 91 738, -070) offers plain *domatia* with baths (singles 5000dr; doubles 8000dr; triples 9000dr).

If you want to soak up the sun, you can stay closer to the beach. At the end of the marble steps down from the naked poet statue awaits a house with blue railings and rooms decorated with the owner's carved-wood furniture (tel. 91 386; doubles with bath 8000dr). Next door a **campground** (tel. 92 458) offers the amenities of a restaurant and a mini-market, along with the opportunity to get back to nature with some horses in the same field (2500dr for two people with tent).

FOOD

As always, small, half-hidden *tavernas* offer deals and food superior to those of their better-situated counterparts. **Sisyfos** (tel. 91 505), 250m up from the bus stop past the National Bank on Agoras St., serves delectable vegetarian entrees (950dr) and a great variety of traditional Greek dishes (1100-1300dr). Choose your meal from the day's selection and ask the English-speaking owner about the myth of Sisyfos.

Tucked away in the maze of Skyros Town, **Kabanera** (tel. 91 240) features *rollo* (ground meat, cheese, and tomato wrapped in phyllo pastry, 1200dr). To find it, walk up Agoras to the first "fish taverna" sign and follow it and its successors. To grab a quick, cheap dinner, nothing beats the **souvlaki/pita/gyros stand** in the central square (250-300dr). Dessert comes from the unnamed **sweet shop** (tel. 91 005) along Agoras St. where the Skyrian specialty, *amigdolata* (sweet almond taffy covered in powdered sugar) costs about 300dr.

Of the collection of *tavernas* along the beach at Molos, **Milos** (tel. 91 378), the very last in the row, has the best lobster with pasta, a specialty of the island. In addition, Skyros, like the rest of the Sporades, produces much of the pine resin that flavors *retsina* in the country's larger distilleries. Its own brand of kegged *retsina* is among Greece's finest. Particularly good is *Kokkinelli* (rosé), from the barrel.

SIGHTS

Perched above Skyros Town, the thousand year-old **Monastery of St. George** and the **Castle of Licomidus** command magnificent, free views of Skyrian sunsets. (open daily Mar.-Aug. 7am-10pm, Sept.-Feb. 7:30am-6pm). Remember to dress modestly if you want to peek at the monastery's 11th-century fresco of St. George as you climb to the *Kastro*. Generally believed to be Venetian, the castle may be a stellar repair of an earlier Byzantine fortification. The reclining marble lion set in the stone above the gate dates from the 4th century BC, when Athenians taunted Skyrians with this symbol of Attic ascendancy. The steep hike uphill from anywhere on Agoras St. is much nicer in the evening and with water.

In July and August, house #995 is open as a **Traditional Skyrian House,** which you may be able to tour in the mornings or evenings for a few hundred drachmae. Farther downhill, to the naked Brooke's right, the **Faltaits Museum** (tel. 91 232) also boasts a model of a Skyrian home. The private collection of a Skyrian ethnologist, the museum displays embroidery, carved furniture, pottery, costumes, copperware, rare books, and relics from the island's annual carnival (open daily 10am-1pm and 5:30-8pm; free). Guided tours in English are provided, and you can inquire here or at the affiliated shop on Agoras Street about the **theater and music festival** in late July and August. To Brooke's left, the **Archaeological Museum** (tel. 91 327) holds significant artifacts found on the island. An English brochure describes its long history (open Tues.-Sun. 8:30am-3pm; admission 500dr, students 300dr).

Skyros remains a significant Greek island as a result of the unique revelry of the **Skyrian Carnival.** In February, forty days before Easter, an old man dressed in a goat mask and costume covered with clanging sheep bells, leads a young man dressed as a Skyrian bride, and a man mockingly dressed as a 17th-century European man, with one large bell hanging from his waist, on a wild, raucous dance through town to the monastery. The festival commemorates a legendary land dispute between shepherds and farmers, drawing upon many myths and religious customs. One hypothesis is that the transvestism refers to the warrior Achilles, who dodged the Trojan War draft on Skyros by dressing as a girl. When Achilles couldn't resist buying a sword from Odysseus, the well-worn traveler called his bluff. These days the only warriors you'll see are in the Greek military, as they sun themselves on their tanks .

The pleasant beach below the town stretches along the coast through the villages of Magazia and Molos, and continues around the point. Crowded and crawling with children in July and August, it's undeniably convenient. Ten minutes south of the town beach the local nude beach, ironically named *Tou papa to homa* (The Sands of the Priest), remains clean and uncrowded. In addition, the regular public bus, which runs from Linaria to Skyros Town, stops at the crowded **Ormos Mealos** beach.

■ Around Skyros Island

Thirty-five kilometers long and 5km wide at its narrowest point, most of Skyros is inaccessible. You can explore by car, motorbike, or one of the weekly bus or boat trips. Once home to nymphs, the natural spring at **Nifi Beach,** on the south side of Skyros, remains beautiful and deserted. Scenically barren beaches and **Rupert Brooke's grave** on the south portion of the island are accessible only by dirt paths and boat. Boats can also explore the sea caves at **Spilliés,** which once served as a pirate grotto, and **Sarakino Island,** once Despot's Island and one of the largest pirate centers in the Aegean. During Ottoman rule, merchant and war ships sought refuge in this natural harbor. As you travel, look for the endangered **Skyrian horses.**

Northeast Aegean Islands

ΒΟΡΕΙΟΑΝΑΤΟΛΙΚΑ ΝΗΣΙΑ ΤΟΥ ΑΙΓΑΙΟΥ

After centuries of resisting the Ottoman Empire, the northeast Aegean islands have learned how to stay closely guarded. Though pirates and Ottomans no longer pose a threat, many of the islands continue to isolate themselves from the influx of tourism in hopes of preserving their traditional atmosphere. Intricate, rocky coastlines enclose the thickly wooded mountains and bland port towns that give way to unspoiled villages and secluded beaches. A few miles off the Turkish coast, the islands have a sizable military presence; the large numbers of Greek soldiers may cause women traveling alone to feel uncomfortable. But travelers seeking undiluted Greek culture without the intrusion of foreign influence may well find it here.

CHIOS ΧΙΟΣ

When the mythical hunter Orion drove all the wild beasts from Chios, grand pine, cypress, and mastic trees sprouted on the vast mountainsides. Since antiquity, Chios has cultivated and exported *masticha,* a bitter-sweet, gummy resin used in varnishes, cosmetic creams, chewing gum, floor waxes, and color television sets. Long both a military base and a center of Greek shipping, Chios has only recently been opened to the tourist industry. As its striking volcanic beaches and medieval villages become more accessible, the island may become another hotspot for northern European package tours and for vacationers hopping between Greece and Turkey.

Sakız Adası, as Chios is known in Turkish, lies across a narrow strait from Çeşme, Turkey. Before Ottoman rule, this reputed birthplace of both Homer and Christopher Columbus hosted Venetians and Geonoese. The island gained modern fame in 1822, when a Greek nationalist rebellion failed and resulted in over 25,000 deaths.

■ Chios Town

Chios Town is home to many sailors (identifiable by their red license plates) and several wealthy ship owners (identifiable by their luxury cars). Ravaged by German troops during WWII, the unadorned waterfront, with its modern Athenian-style skyline, turns a rather indifferent face to the newcomer.

ORIENTATION AND PRACTICAL INFORMATION

Most services, buses, and taxis gather around **Vounakio Square,** the social center of town located two blocks inland from the right side of the waterfront (facing inland). Left from Vounakio lies the **market street,** pleasantly bustling and shaded in the morning. Most points of interest around the island are accessible only from Chios Town, the source from which all transit routes radiate. Every night the waterfront closes to traffic, cafes pack, and the Greek *volta* (promenade) begins, offering pleasant respite from the clamor that roars after the midday shutdown. This is the place to be between 9pm and 1am.

Tourist Office: 18 Kanari St. (tel. 44 389). Turn off the waterfront onto Kanari St., toward the square and look for the "i" sign. Open May-Sept. Mon.-Fri. 7am-2:30pm and 6:30-9:30pm, Sat.-Sun. 10am-1pm; Oct.-April Mon.-Fri. 7am-2:30pm. They provide lists of accommodations and reservation assistance.

Tourist Agencies: Hatzelenis (tel. 26 743; fax 26 531). As you face inland, walk to the white building on the right corner of the waterfront. They provide ferry info and ticketing for all lines except NEL, which has its own exclusive agency in the center of the waterfront. **Car rental** begins at 12,000dr in the high season, 6000dr

Chios (Hios)

PSARA

Agias Mata

Amani

Pellinaion

Kardamila

Marmaro

Inousses

INOUSSIS

PSARA

Volissos

Lagada

Sikiada

Aepos

Anavatos

Karies

Vrondados

MITILINI

Aegean Sea

Néa Moni

Chios

TSESME

Lithi

Ag. Georgios

Thimiana

Likouri

Kalimassia

Mesta

TURKEY

N

Nenita

Pirgi

0   5 miles

0   5 kilometers

Emporio

CHIO

SAMO

GREEK ISLANDS

per day in the off season, (unlimited mileage, full insurance, and all taxes included). Info about rooms, help finding accommodation, trips to Turkey, excursions, and **weekend currency exchange** are available Mon.-Sat. 7am-1:30pm and 6-9pm, Sun. 10am-1pm and 6-9pm, and often open when boats arrive late at night.

Banks: The **Ionian Bank,** 16 Kanari, is next to the tourist office and offers **currency exchange.** Open Mon.-Thurs. 8am-2pm, Fri. 8am-1:30pm, Sat. 9am-1pm. Also has a 24hr. **ATM.**

Flights: Olympic Airways (tel. 23 998), on the waterfront near the corner of Psychari St. Open Mon.-Fri. 8am-4pm. Flights to Athens and Thessaloniki.

Ferries: To: Samos (3 per week, 4½hr., 2800dr); Lesvos (daily, 3hr., 3200dr); Piraeus (daily, overnight, 5300dr); and Çeşme on the Turkish coast (2 per day, 45min., 8000-9000dr plus 5000dr port tax). A Greek and a Turkish line each serve this last route once per day. American and British citizens will have to purchase a visa if staying more than one day (by date) in Turkey. Ferries also sometimes travel to Alexandroupolis, Limnos, Lesvos, Samos, Patmos, Laros, Kos, Rhodes, and Crete.

Buses: (tel. 27 507) Leave from both sides of Vounakio Sq., right off the public gardens. Hatzelenis offers schedules and fare information. All one-way trips are less than 1000dr. **Blue buses** (tel. 22 079), on the right side of the square on Dimokratias St., are for travel within the immediate vicinity of Chios Town (9km), making 5-6 trips per day to Karfas, Vrondados, and Karies.

Taxis: (tel. 41 111) Cluster in the main square. Open 24hr.

Hospital: (tel. 44 303) 2km north of Chios. Open 24hr.

Pharmacies: Chios Town has more than 20. Notices on pharmacy doors indicate which are open on weekends.

Post Office: Follow Omirou St. 1 block inland after the Olympic Airways waterfront office. Open Mon.-Fri. 7:30am-2pm. **Postal Code:** 82100.

OTE: Across from the tourist office. Phones on waterfront. **Telephone Code:** 0271.

ACCOMMODATIONS, FOOD, AND ENTERTAINMENT

Most of Chios Town's accommodations are converted neoclassical mansions with creaky wooden staircases and high ceilings. In high season, when rooms become scarce, it's best to let a tourist agency call around for you. Ask at **Hatzelenis Tourist Agency** about the clean **Chios Rooms** on the opposite side of the waterfront (singles 3500dr; doubles 5000dr, with bath 6000dr). If they are full, Hatzelenis can help you find another inexpensive pension. Most of these cluster at the south end of the waterfront. You should be able to find single rooms to let for 4000dr and doubles for 5000dr. Prices remain relatively constant through both high and low seasons, with private bath an additional 1000dr. Tourist agencies also have info on **Chios Camping.**

A myriad of vendors hawk all kinds of food on the market street near Vounakio Square. Although locals praise the small *taverna* next door to Hatzelenis Tourist Agency (open for dinner), they warn that most waterfront *tavernas* cater to the undiscerning tastebuds of sunburnt tourists. Your best bet may be to lunch on the fresh *spanakopita* (spinach pie) or *tyropita* (cheese pie) available in **bakeries.** For full meals, ask the locals where they eat, and you're destined to find better fare.

Cafe-bars line the waterfront. Of these, locals flock particularly to **Remezzo** and **Metropolis.** A taxi ride (1300dr) will take you to a cluster of bars outside of town in **Karfos.** Of these, **Stasi** is the hottest and has the cheapest beer.

SIGHTS

Relics of the town's past encircle Vounakio Sq. The walls of the **Byzantine Kastro,** a castle reconstructed by the Genoese, enclose the narrow streets of the **old town.** The castle houses a tiny **Byzantine Exhibition** (open Tues.-Sun. 9am-3pm; 500dr). The **Turkish mosque** on Vournakio Sq. is actually a museum (open Tues.-Sat. 8am-1pm and Sun. 10am-3pm; free). The **Folklore Museum,** on the first floor of the **Korais Library,** is next to the **Mitropolis,** Chios Town's cathedral (open Mon.-Thurs. 8am-2pm, Fri. 8am-2pm and 5-7:30pm, Sat. 8am-12:30pm). Don't bother to follow the yellow signs leading to an archeological museum closed for renovation. Only 6km south of Chios Town lies the popular sandy beach Karfas, victim of Chios' latest burst of development. Nine kilometers north of town, beachgoers find the rocky shores of **Vrondados** and **Daskalopetra.** Blue buses from Vournakio Sq. travel to all three.

■ Around Chios

Pine-covered mountains 16km west of Chios Town cradle the impressive **Nea Moni** (New Monastery), built in the 11th century. An icon of the Virgin Mary miraculously appeared to three hermits who promptly founded the monastery with the aid of an exiled emperor. Over the centuries, the monastery complex has been rebuilt and enlarged, and today remains one of the world's most important Byzantine monuments. An earthquake in 1881 destroyed much of the complex itself, but most has been carefully restored. Don't miss the 11th-century mosaics in the inner narthex. Even their state of partial decrepitude can't hide the original artistry (open daily 9am-1pm and 4-8pm; free). **Anavatos,** 15km west of Nea Moni, is a staggeringly beautiful village with a tragic past. The women and children of the village threw themselves off the cliffs of this "Greek Masada" after their failed attempt to withstand an 1822 Ottoman invasion. Check with the bus station (Green bus) for excursions to both sites (2 per week). Taxi drivers may agree to drive you to the site, wait 30 minutes, and bring you back. From Chios, a **taxi-tour** of Nea Moni and Anavatos costs 8000dr (agree on a fare before leaving for the monastery). The road is hilly but well paved until Nea Moni, where it deteriorates into an uneven, rocky path, passable by car and motorcycle, but murderous on mopeds.

The villages in the southern half of the island, called *Mastichochoria,* are home to Chios's famous resin, produced by squat mastic or lentisk trees. **Pirgi** is called "mastic village" and is high in the hills 25km from Chios. The big attraction in Pirgi is not the mastic, but rather the unique black and white geometrical designs covering tradi-

> ### Craftsmen with a Fork and a Dream
>
> Although it is built in the twisting alleyways of a medieval castle, Pirgi is most recognizable for its *ksista*, the unique geometric patterns that coat walls of every house in the village. Instead of whitewashing homes as is common in the Cyclades, Pirgian craftsmen first coat each house with a paint made from the gray stone at Emborio. The houses are then whitewashed and, while the paint is still wet, the craftsmen form geometric patterns with a fork, creating the village's trademark design. After both coats have dried, artists add splendidly colorful designs to the otherwise black-and-white geometry.

tional buildings. Here you will find the **Women's Agricultural Tourist Collective** (tel. 0271 72 496), which arranges rooms in private farmhouses in Armolia, Pirgi, Olymbi, and Mesta. The female farmers, symbolized by the *melissa* (bee), will show you around their farms, but it's best to make reservations a few weeks in advance, especially in July and August. You can also make arrangements with village proprietors by asking at places with "rooms to let" signs.

Pirgi is also home to the 14th-century **Agioi Apostoloi** church, a replica of the Nea Moni. Sixteenth-century frescoes and paintings by a Cretan iconography school cover almost every inch of the interior. The caretaker must unlock the front gate for you; ask for Michalis Vassilis at 27 Mix. Kolika St., directly across from the OTE (open Mon.-Fri. 9am-3pm; 100dr donation is expected).

On the southern end of Chios lies the beach of **Emborio.** Its light brown volcanic cliffs contrast strikingly with the black stones and deep blue water below. The bus from Chios Town or Pirgi drops passengers off at the harbor. The first beach is up the only road to the right (facing the water). There's a smaller, less crowded shore up the stairs to your right. Good shoes are a must.

The poorer and less visited region, the north half of Chios is the silent partner of the *Mastichochoria*. Roughly 5km outside Chios Town, just past Vrondados, Homer held classes at the beach of **Daskalopetra.** After Daskalopetra, the main roads wind northwest along the coast past Marmaron to **Nagos** (30km away), which features a gray stone beach (perhaps a popular spot for cutting Homer's classes in antiquity). **Volissos** (40km west), Homer's legendary birthplace, is crowned by a Byzantine fort.

LESVOS (LESBOS) ΛΕΣΒΟΣ

Ironically, Lesvos's seemingly barren volcanic landscape has nurtured one of the richest cultural legacies in the Aegean. Once home to the musician Terpander, the poet Arion, the writer Aesop, and the 7th-century BC poet Sappho, Lesvos (often called Mitilini) now supports tourist haunts, indicating that its greatness remains in the fabled past. Yet even in this century, Lesvos has given rise to the Nobel Prize winning poet Odysseus Elytis, the neoprimitive artist Theophilos, art publisher Tériade, and the family of 1988 U.S. Presidential candidate Michael Dukakis.

According to legend, the population of Lesvos, Greece's third largest island, was once entirely female. The notion may owe its origin to the Athenian assembly's 428 BC decision to punish the recalcitrant residents of Mitilini by executing all adult males on the island. In reality, however, the assembly repealed the decision after some debate. Mitilini flourished as a cultural center for hundreds of years. Its inhabitants would be astonished to learn that the West has come to consider 5th-century Athens, not Mitilini, to be the zenith of Greek civilization. In particular, the Philosophical Academy, where Epicurus and Aristotle taught, brought Lesvos well-deserved fame.

Until recently, the island remained relatively remote and cultivated its own offbeat character—a blend of horse breeding, serious *ouzo* drinking, and leftist politics. Although Lesvos's major towns now host a growing number of foreign visitors, tourism has not reached Cycladean proportions. The island remains something of a mecca for (surprise!) lesbians and attracts long-term visitors taking weeks to explore the many historical sites and discovering the island's diverse landscape of tall pines, olive groves, corn fields, and barren hillsides.

■ Mitilini

This central port city and capital of Lesvos is picturesque... from a distance. Yachts and colorful fishing boats adorn the yawning harbor, while modern highrises and neoclassical mansions stand shoulder to shoulder on the ascent to the Amali mountains. Yet the decaying Gattelusi castle is only one indication that the city is crowded and crumbling. Her once grand mansions are in a state of decay—it is too expensive to restore them, yet illegal to tear them down.

ORIENTATION AND PRACTICAL INFORMATION

The city spreads chaotically along the waterfront road of **Pavlou Koudoutrioti,** with **Ermou Street** running parallel one block inland. In the most interesting quadrant of town, the **old market** advances inland from the waterfront, below the castle and to the right of the church. Get lost among the market's knotted streets and cobbled ways and shop in the aromatic fish market nearby.

Tourist Office: 6 James Aristarchou (tel. 42 511; fax 42 512), with your back to the tourist police, walk uphill one block; the office will be on your right. They offer information, free brochures, and maps. Open Mon.-Fri. 8:30am-3pm.

Tourist Police: (tel. 22 776), from the ferry, head left towards the interior harbor and main waterfront road. The official passport control building, at the corner of the pier, houses the tourist police. Open in summer 8am-9pm, in winter 8am-2pm.

Rooms to Let Office: One block inland from the center of the waterfront. Helps find accommodations. Open Mon.-Sat. 9am-1pm.

Bank: National Bank, in the center of the waterfront, has a 24hr. **ATM.** Open Mon.-Thurs. 8am-2pm, Fri. 8am-1:30pm.

Flights: Olympic Airways, 44 Kavetsou Ave. (tel. 28 659). Any ticketing agent can book flights to Athens (5 per day, 16,800dr) and Thessaloniki (1 per day, 20,600dr). Buy your ticket a week in advance. **Airport** (tel. 61 212).

Buses: Green buses leave from the intercity bus station (tel. 46 630) and service all destinations on the island. The station is behind Ag. Irinis Park, diagonally 1½ blocks from the south edge of the harbor. In summer, buses from Mitilini go to: Molyvos (4 per day, 1½hr., 1250dr); Sigri (2 per week, 2½hr., 1850dr); Skala Eressos (1 per day, 2½hr., 1850dr); Plomari (3 per day, 1¼hr., 800dr); and Petra (4 per day, 1¼hr., 1150dr). Fewer buses chug along on weekends. **Blue buses** (tel. 28 725), based on the waterfront, service local routes around Mitilini.

Ferries: Connect Lesvos to the northeast Aegean and beyond. **NEL Lines,** 67 Pavlou Koudoutrioti St. (tel. 22 220; fax 28 601), along the waterfront 3 blocks from the pier, is open 6am-9pm. In summer their ferries travel to: Peiraias (1 per day, 12hr., 6570dr); Limnos (4 per week, 5hr., 3950dr); Thessaloniki (2 per week, 12hr., 7800dr); Kavala (2 per week, 12hr., 6030dr); Chios (1 per week, 3hr., 3090dr); Syros (1 per week, 8hr., 5430dr); Andros (1 per week, 9hr., 5045dr); and Volos (1 per week, 12hr., 6000dr). Inquire about other lines which may connect to different islands. Ferries also run to Çesme, Turkey (at least 3 per week, 45min., 9000dr plus 5000dr Greek port tax and 3000dr Turkish port tax).

Hospital: (tel. 43 777) Southwest of the city on E. Vostani. Open 24hr. Dial 166 for an **ambulance.**

Post Office: (tel. 28 836), on Vourhazon St. near the intercity bus station. Signs pointing the way to the post office are behind the park (which has free **public toilets**), near the taxi stand. Open Mon.-Fri. 7:30am-3pm. **Postal Code:** 81100.

OTE: (tel. 28 299), 2 doors up from the post office. **Telephone Code:** 0251.

Lesvos

Andissa, 1
Argennon Akron, 2
Halinadou, 3
Klopedi, 4
Messon Temple of
Aphrodite, 5
Mithymna, 6
Ovriokastro, 7

Paliokastro, 8
Petrified Forest, 9
Sarakina, 10
Taxiarhes, 11

✈ Airport

⚓ Port

0   5 miles

0   5 kilometers

N

ACCOMMODATIONS AND FOOD

If you must stay in Mitilini, it is easiest to head to the Rooms to Let office, one block inland and well-marked by information signs. Singles should run you 4000-5000dr and doubles 7000dr.

Cafes and *tavernas* abound along the waterfront, and while locals dine in the north, tourists congregate in the south. In the cobbled streets, cheese pies, charmless croissants, and gyros abound. **Averof,** in the center of the waterfront, has traditional food and low prices. Remember that charm, too, has its price. For breakfast with the locals, saunter behind the local bus station onto Limnou St. and take the first right onto Thasou St. You will see them, they will see you. Expect a few stares, and real Greek coffee.

SIGHTS

The ubiquitous signs in Mitilini helpfully point tourists to the various sights. The **Archaeological Museum,** 7 Argiri Eftalioti St. (tel. 28 032), houses a collection of the island's artifacts. Accompanied by thorough descriptions of their role in Lesvian history, the artifacts include Mycenaean, Protogeometric, and Archaic pottery, Classical and Hellenistic vases and sculpture, and remnants from the Temple at Fressos. Don't miss the smaller building hiding behind the main museum quarters, which contains rare Aeolian tablets. Also, be sure to ask about the new museum expected to open in 1998. (Open Tues.-Sun. 8:30am-3pm. Admission 500dr, students and seniors 300dr, EU students free, Sunday free.)

GREEK ISLANDS

If you have a spare hour in Mitilini, visit the enormous late 19th-century **Church of St. Therapon,** on Ermou St., whose dome betrays Western influence. The church towers over the fish market's daily catch: sardines, octopi, and occasionally, small sharks (open daily 9am-7pm). Near the tall clock tower at the south end of the harbor is the impressive **Church of Agios Theodoros,** containing the bones and skull of its patron saint. From the ferry dock, all roads leading uphill will take you to the **Gattelusi Castle** (tel. 27 970). Surrounded by redolent pines above the town, the fortress protects its panoramic view over Mitilini and across to Turkey. Originally constructed by Emperor Justinian on the site of a Byzantine castle, it has since been repaired by the Genoese, Ottomans, and Greeks. The walls contain evidence from each epoch, capped by a telephone cable, the 20th century's contribution. The castle bears the name of Francesco Gattelusi, who received Lesvos as dowry in 1355 after he married the daughter of the Byzantine Emperor (open Tues.-Sun. 8:30am-3pm; admission 500dr, students 300dr). The highest point on the north side of Mitilini is the 3rd-century BC **ancient theater,** built during Hellenistic times. Here 15,000, spectators attended performances with near perfect acoustics. It was so impressive that it inspired Pompei to build Rome's first stone theater (open Tues.-Sun. 8:30am-3pm).

■ Near Mitilini

Only 4km south of Mitilini along El. Venizelou, the tiny, unassuming village of **Varia** surprises wayfarers with the **Theophilos Museum** (tel. 41 644), featuring the work of the famous neoprimitivist Greek painter Theophilos Hadzimichali (open Tues.-Sun. 9am-1pm and 4:30-8pm; admission 500dr). Next door, the **Musée Tériade** displays an excellent collection of Picasso, Miró, Leger, Chagall, and Matisse lithographs (open Tues.-Sun. 9am-2pm and 5-8pm; admission 250dr). Tériade, a native of Lesvos born Stratis Eleftheriadis, rose to fame as a leading publisher of graphic art in Paris during much of the 20th century. **Buses** to Varia depart from the Mitilini waterfront depot every 30 minutes. Or, head northwest 6km to a well-preserved Roman aquaduct at **Moria.** Buses to Moria also run about every 30 minutes from the waterfront.

▒ Northern Lesvos: Petra and Molyvos

With only 5km between them, the artists' colonies of Petra and Molyvos (Mithimna) lie at the northern tip of Lesvos. Both situated on long, lovely stretches of beach, the towns are Lesvos's most visited spots after Mitilini, yet prices remain quite reasonable. Molyvos conveys almost picture-perfect charm. Cobbled alleyways and stone houses topped with red tile roofs are all intricately stacked into a hill. Petra stretches along a sand beach and presses into the fertile plain behind it.

ORIENTATION AND PRACTICAL INFORMATION

Just up from the Molyvos **bus stop** (bear left at the fork), a small building on the left houses the **tourist office** (tel. 71 347), which provides maps, schedules, and help finding rooms (open 9am-3:30pm and 6:30-8:30pm). Next door, a **National Bank** has a 24hr **currency exchange** (open Mon.-Thurs. 8am-2pm, Fri. 8am-1:30pm). Nearby **Akti Rentals** (tel. 71 997), rents **mopeds** (3000dr per day), **cars** (10,000dr per day), and **jeeps** (18,000dr per day). They are open daily 8am-1:30pm and 5:30-10pm. Across the street, a stand sells **international newspapers.** Continuing uphill, a mobile **post office** on the main traffic route is open June-August, Monday-Friday 8am-2pm. Ascending the hill in a switchback, this steep, cobbled road winds through the town's center. Here you can find the local **laundry** (wash 1100dr, dry 600dr; open Mon.-Sat. 9:30am-2pm and 6-11pm) and **pharmacy** (tel. 71 427; open 9:30am-2pm and 6:30-11pm). On the next switchback, across from the main post office (open Mon.-Fri. 8am-2pm), a thickly shaded cafe serves as the local haunt for morning coffee. Signs direct you to the **police station** (tel. 71 222). The **postal code** is 81108; **telephone code,** 0253.

The bus stops in Petra at the central square opening onto the water. As you face inland, one street stretches in front of you. The **post office** is on this street, as is **OTE** (open Mon.-Sat. 7:30am-3:10pm). The **National Bank** lies on the street to the right (open Mon.-Thurs. 8am-2pm, Fri. 8am-1:30pm). The **Women's Cooperative of Petra** is on the same street as the National Bank. The balconies of their summer restaurant overlook the square, and they provide rooms to let throughout the community. Petra's **postal code** is 81009. The **telephone code** is 0253.

ACCOMMODATIONS AND FOOD

The best accommodations in both Molyvos and Petra are **rooms to let.** Your stay will be much simpler if you let the **tourist office** or **Women's Cooperative** help you with arrangements. If these offices are closed, or if you seek the adventure of finding your own rooms, take heart. Nearly every corner in both towns displays at least one room to let sign. Rooms with private bath start at 4000dr for singles, 6000dr for doubles, 7000dr for triples. Remember to bargain.

Beachfront **cafes** exist in both towns. On an inviting terrace shaded by large plane trees overlooking Molyvos and the Aegean, **Taverna Sansibala** serves traditional Greek entrees (1300-2000dr), as well as breakfast and lunch. In Petra, the **Women's Cooperative Restaurant** prepares delicious, home-cooked meals (1500dr).

SIGHTS

Although Molyvos has an **archaeological museum** and regular **exhibitions by local artists** in its town hall, and Petra boasts a **folk art museum,** the real attractions are the **beaches** around which these towns lie. If these beaches get too crowded, do not hesitate to take the rugged road north out of Molyvos toward **Eftalou.** This area is home to many secluded beaches beneath towering cliffs (5km northeast).

■ Southern Lesvos: Plomari

After arson destroyed the village of Megalochori in 1841, people resettled in the Turkish-inhabited region 12km south, now modern **Plomari.** From its earliest days, this southern coastal town has manifested a split personality—it is at once a no-holds-barred resort town (with discos, cheery *tavernas,* and all the other package tour trappings) as well as a fishing village, full of fishermen nailing octopi to telephone poles to dry in the sun. The overall effect, aided and abetted by Plomari's large *ouzo* industry, is cheerful and relaxing. The local product is far better than the bottled industrial variety. Try a sample at the **Barbayanni Ouzo Factory** (tel. 32 741), roughly 2km east towards Agios Isodoros on the way to Plomari (open Mon.-Fri. 8am-10pm and Sat. 8am-3pm). An annual week-long **Ouzo Festival** is held in late August and features song, dance, drunken tourists, and, of course, free *ouzo.* Large groups may receive a free tour. Throughout the summer, Plomari also hosts several religious celebrations and cultural events. The one-week **Festival of Benjamin** in late June commemorates the leader of the 1821 war with dancing and theatrical presentations in Greek.

ORIENTATION AND PRACTICAL INFORMATION

Manolis Stefanis at **Plomari Travel** (tel. 32 946) on Lesviou St. has information about everything in the area, from accommodations to excursions. To get to Plomari Travel from the **Commercial Bank** at the end of the square (open Mon.-Thurs. 8am-2pm and Fri. 8am-1:30pm), turn right into **B. Lesviou Square** and then take your first right up Lesviou St. The **OTE** (tel. 32 399) is in the main square (open Mon.-Fri. 7:30am-10pm) and the **post office** (tel. 32 241) is nearby (open Mon.-Fri. 8am-2pm). **Buses** go to Plomari (3-5 per day, 750dr) and Agiassos (5 per day, 460dr). The road hugs the **Bay of Geras,** and passes through the charming villages of **Paleokipos** and **Pappados.** The **postal code** here is 81200; **telephone code,** 0252.

SIGHTS

Beaches appear intermittently around Plomari. To reach rocky **Arnovdeli Beach,** turn onto Agios Nikolaou Rd. and follow the signs; it's a 15-minute walk south of town. If you continue straight on Agios Nikolaou you will come to **Agios Nikolaos,** a church sparkling with icons spanning 400 years. If you aren't into rocky coasts, the best beaches are at **Agios Isodoros,** 3km east of town along the main road.

Agiassos, a village 15km north of Plomari on the slopes of Lesvos's Mt. Olympus, remains a center for ceramic crafts. An **Orthodox church** here contains an icon of the Virgin Mary made by St. Lucas, originally destined for Constantinople in 330 AD. When the priest transporting it heard rumors of war, he feared for the icon's safety and deposited it in the church. On August 15 Agiassos hosts **Panagia,** a grand annual celebration in honor of the Virgin Mary. The village also boasts an **Ecclesiastical Museum** with Byzantine religious works (ask church officials and priests in town), a **Folk Museum** featuring traditional costumes, and a **library** with some English books.

■ Western Lesvos: Skala Eressos

Skala Eressos's seemingly endless beach stretches across the opposite end of Lesvos from Mitilini. Awarded the EU's Blue Banner award for cleanliness, its western half remains one of the few legal nude beaches on the island. Summer brings sunbathers—Lesvians and lesbians alike—to the birthplace of the poet Sappho.

ORIENTATION AND PRACTICAL INFORMATION

Between May and October, **Eressos Travel** (tel. 53 076; fax 53 576), one block inland from the waterfront, provides **currency exchange,** a kiosk for calls, excursion and accommodations information, and **car rentals** starting at 14,000dr per day (open Mon.-Sat. 8:30am-10pm, Sun. 8:30am-2pm). A stand sells **newspapers** across the street. A 24hr. **ATM** sits in the main square on the beachfront and, as you face the sea, signs point to the **post box** and card **phone** three blocks to the right. Further services, including the **police** (tel. 53 222), can be found in Eressos. The **postal code** is 81105. The **telephone code** is 0253.

ACCOMMODATIONS AND FOOD

Ask at **Eressos Travel** about the **Eressos House,** which has sparkling double rooms with private bathrooms and shared refrigerators (6000dr). Otherwise, they may be able to point you to other rooms to let. Of course, you can always count on the hotel hawkers at the bus station, or inquire at one of the many signs on Skala's wide streets.

Outdoor cafes and a serene view of the Aegean Sea surround the stone-layered **Square of Anthis and Evristhenous.** Restaurants with bamboo-covered wooden piers sit on the beach and serve up elegant sunset views of Sappho's Profile, along the ridge of the western mountains. At the end of the walkway is the **Bennetts' Restaurant** (tel. 53 624). Run by the Brits Max and Jackie Bennett, the restaurant has quite a few vegetarian options. Prices are reasonable, and you'll lick the platter clean (open mid-May to mid-Oct. daily 9:30am-3pm and 6-11pm).

SIGHTS

The early Christian basilica of **Agios Andreas,** three blocks north of the beach, once housed 5th-century mosaics, now located in Mitilini's Archaeological Museum. Behind the church, the **Skala Museum** displays 5th- and 6th-century vases, sculptured tombstones, Aeolian inscriptions, and an anchor from an Ottoman frigate used in the 1821 Greek War of Independence. In the museum yard rests the **tomb of St. Andrew.** Along the uphill road leading east lies the pilgrimage route for travelers visiting the remains of **Sappho's home** in Eressos. At dusk, the view from the hill is transcendent. The river, just west of Skala's center, serves as a habitat for many rare and exotic birds (peak **birdwatching** season runs between April and May). Farther inland at **Antissa** are the **petrified trees** of Lesvos, preserved by volcanic activity at least 700,000 years ago in one of only two such forests in the world (the other is on the Arizona-New Mexico border in the U.S.). Roughly 200 plant and animal fossils constitute the "forest," which requires a 90-minute walk to see properly. From Mitilini, take the bus to Sigri and walk or ride the 8km to the forest. From Skala, rent a moped or car, or check at Eressos Travel about tours.

SAMOS ΣΑΜΟΣ

With its sultry landscape and engrossing archeological remains, Samos is perhaps the most beautiful and certainly the most touristed island in the northeast Aegean. The island draws an older, more sedate crowd, and is quieter than many of the popular spots in the Cyclades and the Dodecanese. The wealthiest of the Aegean islands, Samos was home to many notable Greek architects, sculptors, poets, philosophers, and scientists. Among Samos's most famous residents were Epicurus, the moral philosopher, Aesop, the fable writer, and Aristarchus, the astronomer who argued that the sun was the center of the universe 1800 years before Copernicus. The island's most beloved native son is the philosopher Pythagoras, who is Samos's symbol.

Contemporary Samos enjoys a level of tourism somewhere between its less-frequented northern neighbors and the roaring popularity of the Cyclades to the west. Many people come to Samos simply to make the short hop to Kuşadası and ruins of Ephesus on the Turkish coast. The archaeological site is the most extensive and possibly the most evocative remnant of ancient Hellenic civilization. Founded around 1100 BC, Ephesus rapidly bloomed into the largest metropolis in Asia Minor (see **Ephesus,** p. 436). Alternately, those who are archaeologically impaired teeter to Samos to partake in the sumptuous local red wine *(kokkino krasi)* which oozes from village-made barrels and gives the island its 15 minutes of lush-ous fame.

■ Samos Town

With its wide white sidewalks, colorful fishing boats, and picturesque red-roofed houses nestled in the mountainside, Samos Town is among the northeast Aegean's more attractive ports. While the waterfront is a snarl of tourist shops and cafes, the residential lanes farther inland offer a collage of local lifestyles.

ORIENTATION AND PRACTICAL INFORMATION

Samos Town unfurls around a crescent-shaped waterfront. **Pythagoras Square,** easily identifiable by its four large palm trees, hosts banks, cafes, and taxis.

Tourist Office: (tel. 28 530, -582), on a side street one block before Pythagoras Sq.; follow signs from the waterfront. Open July-Aug. Mon.-Sat. 8:30am-2pm.

Tourist Agencies: Samos Tours (tel. 27 715), at the end of the ferry dock, provides info on everything from museum hours to accommodations. Free luggage storage. Open daily 6am-midnight and when boats arrive. **ITSA Travel** (tel. 23 605; fax 27 955), next door, offers similar services. Open daily 6am-2:30pm and 5pm-midnight.

Flights: Olympic Airways (tel. 27 237) has daily flights to Athens (4 per day, 1hr., 17,100dr). Open Mon.-Fri. 8am-4pm. Samos's **airport** (tel. 61 219) is 4km out of Pythagorion and can be reached only by taxi from Samos Town (2500dr).

Ferries: To: Peiraias via Ikaria (daily, 12hr., 6205dr); Naxos and Paros (5 per week, 6hr., 4020dr); Chios (4 per week, 5½hr., 2720dr); Fourni (4 per week, 2hr., 1800dr); Lesvos (1 per week, 8hr., 3700dr); and Patmos (3 per week, 2½hr., 4000dr). In summer, ferries also travel to the Cyclades, Syros (1 per week, 6hr., 3990dr) and Mykonos (1 per week, 6hr., 3925dr). Ferries to Kuşadası, Turkey, leave from Samos Town (daily at 8am and 5pm, 2hr.) Boats to Kuşadası cost 5000dr in addition to a 5000dr Greek port tax and a 3000dr Turkish port tax. Americans and Brits will also be charged a $20 fee for a

Turkish entrance visa; it is best to pay for it in U.S. dollars. If you stay overnight in Turkey and leave from Kuşadası, you will have to pay the tax again.

Flying Dolphins: Zip from Samos Town to Patmos in half the time and twice the *drachmae* as the ferries (1 per day, 1hr., 5500dr). Consult the waterfront agencies for the most recent schedule, including lines added in high season.

Police: (tel. 27 100) On the far right of the waterfront (facing inland); also doubles as the **tourist police.** Some English spoken.

Taxi Stand: (tel. 28 404) In Pythagoras Sq.

Motorbike Rental: Rent A Motor Bike Bicycle (tel. 23 756) is on the left side of the waterfront.

Laundromat: (tel. 28 833), near Georgiou's Taverna, 1 block to the left side of the waterfront. Wash 900dr; dry 700dr; soap 150dr. Open daily 8am-11pm.

Buses: To get to the **station,** follow the waterfront past Pythagoras Sq., turn left at Europe Rent A Car onto Lekati St., and continue 1 block. The bus schedule is posted here, but you can also pick up a copy at most tour offices.

Hospital: (tel. 27 426), to the left of the ferry dock (facing inland).

Post Office: (tel. 27 304) 1 block up from the waterfront behind the Hotel Xenia; turn at the immense palm tree and walk through the municipal gardens. Open Mon.-Fri. 7:30am-2pm. **Postal Code:** 83100.

OTE: Next to the post office. Open daily 7am-10pm. **Telephone Code:** 0273.

ACCOMMODATIONS

There aren't nearly enough rooms to go around on Samos, so finding one can be a chore. If the following are full, try the pensions around the Ionia.

Pension Ionia, 5 Manoli Kalomiri St. (tel. 28 782). Be skeptical of port-side room-hawkers who tell you it is full; they may be lying. To get there, turn right at the end of the ferry dock, left onto E. Stamatiadou St. before the Hotel Aiolis on the waterfront, and then take the second left onto Manoli Kalomiri St. The Ionia is 3 buildings of inexpensive, attractive rooms. Hot showers. Singles 2500dr; doubles 4000dr.

Hotel Artemis (tel. 27 792), in Pythagoras Sq. Offers clean rooms and suggests restaurants. Doubles 4000dr, with bath 5000dr.

Pension Trova, 26 Kalomiris St. (tel. 27 759), up the road just to the left of Pension Ionia. Singles 3000dr; doubles with bath 4500dr.

Pythagoras Hotel (tel. 28 601; fax 28 893), a 10-min. walk along the waterfront away from the town. Clean, well-maintained rooms and a restaurant downstairs. 24hr. hot water. Singles 3000dr; doubles with bath 4000dr.

FOOD, ENTERTAINMENT, AND SIGHTS

Christos (tel. 24 792), two blocks inland from the library, offers tasty Greek cuisine (each dish 1000dr). Another worthy local favorite is **Gregory's,** near the bus station at the right of the waterfront. **Chicken** (tel. 28 415) serves its namesake at low prices. Sweet, strong, and full of spirit, their local wine is everything it should be.

On the waterfront, the cafe/bar **Traffic** is popular with locals in the afternoon. They play recent American hits. The most popular bar at night is **Escape,** a five-minute walk on the way to the Pythagoras Hotel. A patio stretches out over the bay below, and the bar inside fills up as the drinks go down. By 3am, the party is underway at the discotheque **Totem,** a 250dr taxi ride from town.

Finds from local digs, including an impressive 4.75m-tall **Kouros** from 575 BC, have made their way to the recently-renovated **archaeological museum** (tel. 27 469), next to the post office (open Tues.-Sun. 8:30am-3pm; admission 800dr, students 400dr). Nearby, the Lilliputian but lovely **municipal gardens** contain caged birds, 200 varieties of flowers, and a little cafe (gardens free).

■ Pythagorion

Boats from Patmos and points south arrive in Pythagorion, the former capital of Samos. The town features numerous archaeological sites, quaint side streets, and proximity to some of the island's nicer beaches.

ORIENTATION AND PRACTICAL INFORMATION

Fourteen kilometers south of Samos Town, Pythagorion is served by convenient, hourly buses (20min., 280dr). The **bus stop** is on the main street running perpendicular to the waterfront. The **tourist office** (tel. 61 389) is in a pink building, halfway between the bus stop and the water (open daily April-Oct. 8am-10pm). On the same street is a **National Bank,** a 24hr. **ATM,** and a **post office.** The **tourist police** (tel. 61 100) are nearby, and the **OTE** is on the waterfront to the left of the intersection with the main street. The **port police** (tel. 61 225) are at the other end of the waterfront. **Taxis** can be called at 61 450. Most **pensions** surround the main street and are packed and pricey in summer (doubles 5000-7000dr). **Hotels** line both the waterfront and the main street.

SIGHTS

The ancient city of Pythagorion, once the island's capital, thrived during the second half of the 6th century BC under the reign of **Polykrates the Tyrant.** According to Herodotus, Polykrates undertook the three most daring engineering projects in the Hellenic world, all of them in and around Pythagorion. One of the more impressive is the **Tunnel of Eupalinos** (tel. 61 400), 1500m up the hill to the north of town, which diverted water from a natural spring to the city below. About 1.3km long, it is in remarkably good condition, although only about 200m are open to visitors (open Tues.-Sun. 9am-2pm; admission 500dr, students 300dr). Polykrates' second feat was the 40m deep **harbor mole** (rock pier), on which the modern pier now rests.

Polykrates' *magnum opus* stood 5km west of Pythagorion, toward Ireon. The goddess Hera had been worshipped on Samos for seven centuries when Polykrates decided to enlarge her temple. Supported by 134 columns, the 530 BC **Temple of Hera** (tel. 95 277) was 118m long, 58m wide, and one of the **seven wonders of the ancient world.** Damaged by fire in 525 BC, it was never completely reconstructed (open Tues.-Sun. 8:30am-3pm; admission 800dr, students 400dr).

While there are three buses per day from Samos and Pythagorion to the site, a walk along the beach will bring you to the temple at your leisure; there is a back gate leading directly onto the beach. If you can not enter through the gate, a path brings you inland to the main road and main entrance farther along the beach, past two houses. This inland path runs close to the route of the ancient **Iera Odos** (Sacred Way) from Pythagorion to the temple. You may want to wear a toga and bear libations in quirky jugs; it's a local custom (or at least it *was*).

On the south side of town rest the ruins of the **Castle of Lycurgus,** built during the beginning of the last century by (guess who) Lycurgus, a native of Samos and leader in the Greek War of Independence. The **Church of the Transfiguration,** built within the ruined walls, is a pale blue variation on classical Orthodox architecture and interior decoration (small donation is appreciated).

Blocks of columns, walls, and entablatures are strewn throughout Pythagorion like Lincoln Logs after a floorquake, and the presentation in the small **archaeological museum** is no different (tel. 61 400). In fact, only a little over half of the collection fits into the building; many of the ruins are haphazardly scattered on the sidewalk in front (open Tues.-Sun. 9am-2:30pm; free).

■ Northern and Western Samos

Built on a peninsula 10km west of Samos Town, the northern village of **Kokkari** deserves a spot on your Samos itinerary. White pebble beaches and clear waters encompass the village. The northern coast of Samos, particularly the stretch between Kokkari and Karlovassi, has a few deserted pebble beaches tucked away in little coves. Most of the coast is easily accessible from the road to Karlovassi.

Lemonakia Beach, 1km west of Kokkari next to Tsamadou, and the wide white beach just west of **Avlakia** are both alluring. You can trek into the mountains from the village of **Platanakia,** near **Agios Konstandinos,** in the "valley of the nightingales." The valley is famous for its lush greenery, tall trees, and the thousands of birds that wake up to sing in the mountain valley after midnight. They will lull you to sleep (or wake you up) at 3am. Hiking is best from May through June and especially during September, when the grapes from nearby vineyards are harvested and sweeten the air. The 16th-century monastery **Moni Vrontianis** rests near the village of **Vourliotes,** 5km south of Avlakia. **Karlovassi,** Samos's western port, is an unattractive city cluttered by empty modern buildings, but convenient for excursions to western Samos via bus or ferry. **Marathokampos,** 7km southwest of Platanos, is uncrowded and probably the easiest place on the island to find rooms. A couple of kilometers west of this peaceful coastal hamlet stretches the spacious beach at **Votsalakia;** another kilometer farther is an even better beach at **Psili Ammos.**

IKARIA ΙΚΑΡΙΑ

Ikaria is associated with one of the better-known Greek myths. Legend contends that Daedalus fashioned wings for his son Icarus to use in order to escape from Crete. Intoxicated with his newly acquired power, Icarus soared too close to the sun, melted his waxen wings, and plunged to his death near Ikaria's coast. Depite the island's mythological fame, Ikaria's has a very low-profile tourist industry. The notoriously idiosyncratic Ikarians have successfully resisted development; visitors (mostly Greek) come hoping to be healed by Ikaria's medicinal springs, renowned for their radioactivity and chemical composition. At one time, Ikaria was known for its thriving apricots, but locals got tired of "shaking the trees" to harvest the fruits. Now Turkey has the Ikarian apricot trees and Ikaria has only memories (sigh).

Split by a rocky mountain chain, the deceptively rugged landscape boasts up to 2500 species of plants, mostly herbs, that give subtle color and fragrance to the island. Large patches of Ikarian forest, devastated by a 1993 fire, are slowly returning. Most villages cling to the winding coastline. There is no bus service and many roads are in poor condition, so rent a manageable car or expect to walk. The two main port towns, the larger **Agios Kirikos** to the north and **Evdilos** to the south, are on opposite sides of the island. The mountains are separated by long, treacherous distances, and residents remain in relative isolation. Some villages' nocturnal habits, notably those of **Agios Christos,** have drawn heat from the Greek government, which wants to standardize business hours. Stores, including pharmacies, are open only in the mornings and evenings, often until 2am.

■ Agios Kirikos

Unassuming and congenial, Agios Kirikos is filled with whitewashed houses and the waterfront is lined with small cafes. As Ikaria's main port, Agios Kirikos is the most convenient place from which to coordinate travel on the island. The town's pier is marked by a large sculpture of Icarus plummeting to the ground, but getting here has become considerably easier and safer since Icarus's time. Coming off the ferry, walk up the pier onto the main waterfront road, then turn right to reach the town square.

ORIENTATION AND PRACTICAL INFORMATION

On the way to the town square from the ferry dock you will pass the **Sine Rex,** the town's former movie theater, and **Ikariada Travel** (tel. 23 322; fax 23 708), which offers friendly, English-speaking service and can arrange room or vehicle rental (open daily 8am-9:30pm). The **port police** (tel. 22 207) and **tourist police** (tel. 22 207) share a building; climb the steps to the left of Dolihi Tours and continue up the road (both open 8am-2pm). The island's only two **banks,** including the **National Bank** (tel. 22 553), are in Agios Kirikos, in the square near the ferry offices (open Mon.-Fri. 8am-2pm). After hours, tourist offices and big hotels offer **currency exchange.** Credit cards are not accepted on the island. About 100m up the street are the **post office** (tel. 22 222), to the right of the National Bank (open Mon.-Fri. 8am-2pm), and the **OTE** (tel. 22 399; open Mon.-Fri. 7:30am-3pm).

Ikaria's new **airport** offers service to Athens and is located on the northeastern tip of the island, near Fanari Beach. **Ferries** run to: Athens (1-2 per day, 10hr., 4200dr); Samos Town (2-3 per day, 3hr., 2000dr); Patmos (4 per day, 1½hr., 2800dr); Paros (3-4 per day, 4hr., 2600dr); and Mykonos (3 per week, 4hr., 3500dr). Boats alternate stops at Evdilos in the north and Agios Kirikos, where taxis await to shuttle passengers to the other port (2000-2500dr). Finding a hotel can be difficult on your first night, so make sure you know your port of arrival and call ahead for reservations. **Flying Dolphins** leaves for: Samos (4 per week, 1½hr., 4000dr); Patmos (4 per week, 1hr., 3800dr); and Fourni (4 per week, 30min., 2800dr). Three **caïques** leave for Fourni every week (1100dr). The **postal code** is 83300. The **telephone code** is 0275.

ACCOMMODATIONS, FOOD, & ENTERTAINMENT

Climb the stairs to the left of Dolihi and take your first left, just before the police station, to reach the new **Hotel Kastro** (tel. 23 480). Comfortable, modern rooms overlook the harbor (8000dr with bath and TV). To reach **Hotel Akti** (tel. 22 694), climb the same stairs to the left of Dolihi, but take your first right into a tiny, short, seemingly private alley and climb the steps; follow the new signs. Hotel Akti has a decidedly Greek appeal, enhanced by a plant-filled courtyard overlooking the Aegean Sea (singles 4500dr; doubles with bath 6500dr; triples 7500dr). On the way to Hotel Akti you'll pass the **Hotel O'Karras** (tel. 22 494), offering pink rooms and spacious baths (singles 2500dr, with bath 3500dr; doubles 4000dr, with bath 4500dr).

The **T'Adelfia Taverna,** the town's most established full-scale restaurant, offers summer "Greek nights," which include popular music (open daily 9am-2am; entrees from 700dr). At **Flik-Flak,** 1km out of town, get down to American favorites. Nearby **Aquarius** plays Greek music and hits from the age of *Hair*. There are some rocky **beaches** west of the ferry dock. To the east of town, you can clamber down to the sandy beaches and crystal blue water at the coves past the tourist police office.

▓ Northern Ikaria

EVDILOS

Heading north from Agios Kirikos, the tiny road to Evdilos offers breathtaking views of the coast as it snakes along sheer cliffs through florid hill country. From the island's eastern heights you can see Samos, Patmos, and the Fourni Archipelago. On the way to Evdilos, the road passes a few tiny villages and beaches, many of which offer services and accommodations. **Bus** service is unreliable and tourist routes operate only in July and August. The schedule reported by the tourist police is often inaccurate. **Taxis** may be your best bet; sharing a cab will cut costs. (Agios Kirikos to Evdilos 6000dr; Agios Kirikos to Armenistis 8000dr; Armenistis to Evdilos 2000dr.)

Evdilos, the island's minor port town, sports red-tiled roofs against a rural background. The **post office** sits at the top of a set of white stairs that lead to the right of the central square (facing inland). The **OTE** is past the post office, across from the church. There is a **health clinic** (tel. 31 228), numerous restaurants, and plenty of rooms to be let. The **beaches** near Kampos, 500m west of town, induce euphoria.

ARMENISTIS

Armenistis, 58km from Agios Kirikos, is sometimes called the "Greek Mexico" because of its relaxing environment. Although its population falls to 15 in the off season, it is the most touristed Ikarian haven. Life here, as elsewhere on Ikaria, sleeps the day away on sandy beaches and dances the night away. **Ikaros Rooms,** up the steps from the small beach, offers comfy rooms (singles 3000dr; doubles 4000dr). **Hotel Pashala** (tel. 71 302) is comfortable, with cheap, clean rooms and a pleasant restaurant (doubles 3500dr). **Livadi Camping** (tel. 41 349), on the beach roughly 300m before town, charges 500dr per person.

THASSOS ΘΑΣΟΣ

Thassos's imposing, dark green mountainsides differ strikingly from the chalky dry cliffs on many Greek islands. Villages, archaeological sites, and beaches are all engulfed in lush foliage, earning it the nickname "the Green Island." After recent fires, the forests are reviving. With still abundant vegetation, forested coastal drives, beekeeping, and jam-making, Thassos remains an island of natural riches.

In antiquity, the island thrived on the gifts from Hades, the god of wealth. Thassos escaped Athens's Delian League in 411 BC, only to be recaptured 22 years later. Nevertheless, the island maintained a veneer of wealth and independence. During Roman times, builders from all over the world sought Thassosian marble, and its gold mines made the island rich. Thassos was also the birthplace of Timoxenos, an athlete credited with some 1400 victories, and, for a few years, the home of Hippocrates. During medieval times, marauding pirates and Ottoman invaders drove the inhabitants to the interior of the island. It was conquered again by the Greeks in 1912.

▒ Limenas (Thassos Town)

Built atop the foundations of the ancient city, Limenas's streets wind around ruins. In this century, it has become the island's capital and tourist center. Accordingly, this lively if dusty port is more crowded and more expensive than the rest of the island.

ORIENTATION AND PRACTICAL INFORMATION

A central crossroad near the ferry landing connects the waterfront road and 18 Octovriou, the parallel street running one block inland. The central square lies about two blocks farther inland. A large blue sign at the dock lists the names and phone numbers of area hotels, pensions, and campgrounds.

Tourist Police: (tel. 23 111) On the waterfront. Open daily 8am-2pm and 6-10pm.
Tourist Agency: Thassos Tours (tel. 22 546, 23 225; fax 23 005). Continue left (facing inland) on the waterfront road from the port police toward the old port. Under the blue awning. They rent motorbikes (from 2000dr per day), suggest accommodations, and sell Dolphin and ferry tickets. Open daily 9am-11pm.
Bank: National Bank, at the main crossroad on the waterfront, has an automated 24hr. **currency exchange** and **ATM.** Open Mon.-Thurs. 8am-2pm, Fri. 8am-1:30pm.
Buses: The state (tel. 22 162) is across from the ferry landing, on the waterfront. Open 7:30am-8:15pm. Buses head west across the island to Limenaria, stopping at: Skala Prinos (11 per day, 30min., 330dr); Panayia (12 per day, 15min., 210dr); and Skala Potamia (12 per day, 30min., 290dr). Others trek to: Potos and Pefkari (10 per day, 1½hr., 850dr); Aliki Beach (5 per day, 1hr., 650dr); and Theologos (5 per day, 1½hr., 1050dr). Ask at the tourist police or the bus office for schedules.

Ferries: Run from Limenas to Keramoti (8-10 per day, 35min., 380dr), and from Prinos, another port on Thassos, to Kavala (8-10 per day, 2hr., 750dr). Be sure to note from which port, Limenas or Prinos, your boat leaves. If it leaves from **Prinos,** you can get there easily; bus schedules between Prinos and Leminas are synchronized with the ferries. To go to other islands, you must first return to Kavala for ferry connections. The gray port police building posts schedules.

Flying Dolphins: Hydrofoils zip between Thassos's main port of Limenas and nearby Kavala (7 per day, 45min., 1800dr) and Samothrace (3 per wk., 1½hr., 4340dr). Schedules are posted near the pier at the port police, and docked boats indicate upcoming departure times with signs on board. Tickets are bought on board or at Thassos Tours.

International Bookstore: Leather Plus (tel. 23 411), on the far right corner of the central square, has an eclectic selection of English, German, and Dutch novels available "for rent." Open more or less daily 9am-1:30pm and 5:30-11:30pm.

First Aid Hospital: In Prinos (tel. 71 100), open 24hr. Nearest hospital is in Kavala.

Police: (tel. 22 500) In the same building as the tourist police. **Port Police** (tel. 22 106), in a gray building at the waterfront's center. Open 24hr.

Post Office: Head inland from Thassos Tours and turn right at the fourth corner. Open Mon.-Fri. 7:30am-2pm. **Postal Code:** 64004.

OTE: Heading inland from Thassos Tours, turn right at the first corner, and it's on the left. Open Mon.-Sat. 7:30am-10pm. **Telephone Code:** 0593.

ACCOMMODATIONS

The sign in front of the bus stop includes some accommodation options but focuses on pricier hotels. Its worthwhile to hunt on inland streets for substantially cheaper pensions. Ask at Thassos Tours for suggestions.

Giorgos Raxos (tel. 22 778), on the right side of the waterfront (facing inland); look for the green-tiled house next to the barber shop. Rooms are spacious and clean. Doubles 6000dr; triples 7000dr.

Pension Philipus (tel. 23 076, -513). With the post office at your left, continue along the road, past the dry cleaners, and follow the bend. Philipus is on the left with a blue Philip sign. Doubles with bath and access to kitchen 6000dr.

Hotel Lena (tel. 22 933), next to the post office, offers clean doubles with private baths (6000dr).

Eleni Chrisatis-Mitroglou (tel. 22 032). On the street running at a 45-degree angle to the one with the post office; the doorway is surrounded with flowers. Clean doubles with bath cost 7000-8000dr.

Lean Dimon (tel. 22 080). Next door to the flowered doorway, the proprietor rents clean doubles with A/C, refrigerator, and private bath for 7000dr.

FOOD

Bougatsa and gyros abound just off the waterfront. Some 800m in from the port, past the overgrown "Sanctuary of Hercules," **Selinos Taverna** serves delicious grilled octopus appetizers (1200dr) and *kolikomezedhes* (zucchini burgers, 700dr) daily from 6pm to midnight. For a Greek meal, walk up toward Prinos and at the crossing look past the supermarket for **Toxotis,** a local favorite (open daily 1pm-1am).

SIGHTS

In addition to impressive remains of an **agora** and **acropolis** from the 6th and 5th centuries BC, the island flaunts a 4th-century BC Greek **theater.** The ruins are easy to find: turn right behind the old port and continue to a fork in the road, just beyond the ruins of the Temple of Dionysus. The middle path of the three leads to the theater. The archaeological sites are free and open during daylight hours, but the drama festival staged here has been suspended. Also under renovation, the **Thassos Museum** near the old port displays mosaic floors and sculptures found on the site, including a colossal 6th-century BC marble statue of Apollo with a ram draped around his shoulders. Currently under repair, the museum hopes to reopen in 1998.

The **Vagis Museum,** in the village of Potamia, displays sculptures of the famous Thessian artist, Polygnotos Vagis. After emigrating to America, Vagis (1894-1965) gained fame for his sculpture, which varies from classically influenced to abstract (open Tues.-Fri. 10am-noon and 6-7:30pm, Sat.-Sun. 10am-1pm; free).

Beachgoers may have difficulty choosing between Thassos' many beautiful sands. Between the ports of Panagia and Potamia, the popular golden beach of **Chrisi Ammoudia** stretches endlessly. On the southern edge of the island, the twin coves of **Aliki** hide more tranquil beaches. The northern one, surrounded by foliage, often remains isolated. The south beach cove, formed as sand shifted over a Roman marble quarry, shelters slabs of bleached white rock and crevices ideal for snorkeling.

SAMOTHRAKI (SAMOTHRACE) ΣΑΜΟΘΡΑΚΗ

Samothraki first welcomed Greek colonists in the 10th century BC. Soon after, the island achieved fame as a religious center, worshipping the *libiri,* twin fertility gods. Here at the **Sanctuary of the Megaloi Theoi,** Philip II of Macedon met his wife Olympia. After the requisite nine months, **Alexander** (the original "Great One") was born. Home to 999 churches but fewer than 3000 people, the starkly beautiful island rewards the occasional hardy adventurer. Fegari, the highest peak in the Aegean (1670m above sea level), rises from the stony, oblong isle. According to Homer, Poseidon rooted for the home team in the Trojan War from this summit.

■ Kamariotisa

Samothraki's port of Kamariotisa "welcomes" visitors with views of a barren peninsula and row of modern, minimalist windmills. Yet behind the trellises shading waterfront cafes, a small, but charmingly Greek village awaits. Although **Chora** is nominally the island's capital, Kamariotisa is where you go to do anything.

ORIENTATION AND PRACTICAL INFORMATION

Facing inland, on the left of the waterfront, a Greek flag marks the **port police** (tel. 41 305; open 24hr.). On the road running inland, next to the **National Bank** (open Mon.-Thurs. 8am-2pm and Fri. 8am-1:30pm), sits the **pharmacy** (tel. 41 581; open Mon.-Fri. 9am-2pm and 6-10pm, Sat. 9:30am-1:30pm and 7-9:30pm, Sun. 10:30am-12:30pm). Uphill on the left, a mini-market displays the **OTE** sign. The **post office** and another **OTE** are located in Chora.

Ferries connect Samothraki with: Alexandroupolis (3-5 per day, 2½hr., 2200dr); Limnos (1 per week, 3hr., 2330dr); and Kavala (5 per week, 4hr., 2730dr). **Flying Dolphins** travel to: Alexandropolis (1-3 per day, 1hr., 4300dr); Kavala (3 per week, 2hr., 5730dr); Thassos (3 per week, 1½hr., 4340dr); and Limnos (3 per week, 1½hr., 4530dr). For full schedule information inquire at the port police or at a travel agency. **Saos Tours** (tel. 41 505) is also the KTE. Scheduling information is available at the **bus station.** In summer, **buses** run 5-10 times per day around the island, leaving from the ferry dock to: Loutra; Profitos Ilias; Therma; Psira Potomos (390dr); Paleopolis, Alonia, and Chora (210dr); Lacoma and Kariotis (250dr); and the campsites (600dr). Check on which route your destination lies. **Taxis** wait on the waterfront between 8am and 1am. **Moped rentals** are available at the unnamed **garage** (tel. 41 511) opposite the ferry dock or at **Niki Rent Motor Bike's** colorful, flag-adorned lot across from the pharmacy (tel. 41 035). Rentals at both start at 4000dr per day. Niki also rents bikes (2000dr per day). Either way, don't forget a helmet. **Postal Code:** 68002. **Telephone Code:** 0551.

ACCOMMODATIONS

English-speaking **Saos** and **Niki Tours,** your all-purpose tourist agencies, can brief you on the current room situation in town and often help to find accommodations.

Doubles average 6000dr, with bath 8000dr, although in high season they can run much higher. Friendly, family-run **Vasiliki Karoyiannis** (tel. 41 165) has clean rooms with shared baths which start at 6000dr. Turn inland next to Niki Tours and the pension and *taverna* lie on your left. For slightly cheaper rooms with bath, continue uphill and turn right at the road's end. On your left next to the supermarket, a family (tel. 41 536) rents **rooms** with private bath starting at 5000dr. Do be certain that your room has windows, as some have only skylights, allowing no breeze as respite from the greenhouse effect. Inquire at any of the innumerable "rent rooms" or *"domatia"* signs, and remember to bargain.

FOOD, ENTERTAINMENT, AND SIGHTS

The restaurant beneath **Vasiliki Karoyiannis** (tel. 41 165) serves delicious Greek meals (Greek salad 800dr). To order, ask to see the kitchen and the daily creations which Mrs. Karoyiannis identifies for you in the international language of "Baa-aa" and "Moo" (1200dr). In the mornings try their delicious, fresh *lou kou mades* (Greek honey doughnuts, 500dr). You'll probably be able to get up early, for Samothrace earns no points for its nightlife. Waterfront cafe-bars are distinguished from *kafeneo* by their less rigid chairs and from *tavernas* by their lack of tablecloths. A few larger discos are located on the road outside of town, but not within walking distance.

Just 7km east of Kamariotisa lies **Paleopolis** and the **Sanctuary of the Great Gods.** This cult, culminating in rites at the Megaloi Theoi, originated with Thracian settlers and developed around 1000 BC. Samothrace thrived as a religious center, witnessing the rise of such dignitaries as Spartan King Lysander, Phillip II (father of Alexander the Great), and Herodotus, until paganism was outlawed in the 4th century AD.

Disclosure of initiation secrets was punishable by death, but as always, sources leaked information to the press. It appears that initiation into the cult consisted of two stages, the first of purification in the sanctuary and the second of rites in the Hieron, where five reconstructed columns now form the central visual attraction of the site. Ruins, including a theater and sacrificial altars, may be explored Tues.-Sun. 8:30am-8:30pm (admission 500dr, students 300dr, free on Sun.). The **Paleopolis Museum** (tel. 41 474), next to the ruins, houses artifacts including gargantuan entablatures from the Rotunda Arsinoe and the Hieron and a cast of the **Nike of Samothrace.** Also known as "Winged Victory," the statue was discovered and then looted in 1863 by a French consul. It now resides in the Louvre. Sign the book if you believe that it should be returned to Samothrace (open Tuesday-Sunday 8:30am-3pm; admission 500dr, students 300dr).

A short bus ride farther along the island brings you to the therapeutic waters of **Therma.** Although the plain, white building housing the baths can't compare with those of the Romans, it does provide facilities for both men and women. Private tubs cost 600dr, while common swimming pool-like baths are 400dr. All bathing must be done nude, and facilities for men and women are separate. Open daily 6-11am and 4-7pm. After your bath, sip coffee at the nearby shaded terrace cafe.

LIMNOS ΛΗΜΝΟΣ

It is said on Limnos that when one insensitive clod made a dirty joke about Aphrodite, the goddess put a curse on the island that caused the women to kill all the men. Only the king, helped by his daughter, escaped. The Argonauts, upon arrival, found only grieving widows on the island, but shortly thereafter, the repopulation of the island was underway. Limnos' scruffy hills, filled with bleating goats, shoulder vast expanses of golden wheat fields. Knuckled ridges of volcanic handiwork and fantastic rock formations fall away to long stretches of smooth beaches. Limnos is the northeast Aegean's best-kept secret.

GREEK ISLANDS

■ Myrina

The island's capital and primary port, Myrina is a charming, well-proportioned fishing village keenly aware of its beauty. The skyline, made strange by volcanic configurations, is dominated by an impressive Byzantine fortress, illuminated each night. Against the star-studded sky, its turreted tower achieves an almost ethereal silhouette.

ORIENTATION AND PRACTICAL INFORMATION

Myrina has two main **waterfronts** perpendicular to one another. **Romeikos,** the Greek coast, is the longer, prettier, and more popular waterfront, with cafe and *taverna* seating for spectacular sunsets behind Mt. Athos. **Turkikos,** the Turkish coast, is the active port, where ferries and hydrofoils dock. This harborfront fashions a plaza around which lie *tavernas,* ferry and tour agencies, and a few old hotels. **Kyda Street** leads inland past a variety of shops and into the town's **central square,** recognizable by its many **taxi stands** (tel. 23 820). The **OTE** (open Mon.-Sat. 7:30am-3:10pm) and the **National Bank** with a 24-hour **ATM** (open Mon.-Thurs. 8am-2pm, Fri. 8am-1:30pm) are both in the square. One block farther on Kyda St., Garofalidi St. runs to the right. Here you will find the **post office** (tel. 22 462; open Mon.-Fri. 7:30am-2pm) and a **laundry** (tel. 24 392; 1300dr per kg; open Mon.-Fri. 8:30am-2pm and 6-11:30pm, Sat. 8:30am-11:30pm, Sun. 11am-11:30pm). The **police** (tel. 22 201) are a few blocks past the post office. The **hospital** (tel. 22 222) is to the left of Garofalidi St., on the street farthest from the waterfront (open 24hr.). The **bus station** (tel. 22 464) is located in El Venizelou Sq., the second square along Kyda St. Although buses serve all the island's villages, you may get somewhere and find yourself unable to return; the soldiers who gather in El Venizelou to catch the night bus to the barracks get the best service. You may be better off seeing Limnos by renting a **bicycle** (1500dr), **moped** (3000dr), or **car** (10000dr). Inquire on the harborfront at one of the many agencies.

Ferries depart from the side of the port opposite the castle, a short hike from the port square. In high season, ferries run to: Kavala (4 per week, 6hr., 3510dr); Lesvos (5 per week, 6hr., 3890dr); Thessaloniki (2 per week, 8hr., 5100dr); Chios (3 per week, 10hr., 5090dr); Rafina (3 per week, 10hr., 5370dr); Peiraias (3 per week, 22hr., 6630dr); Alexandropolis (1 per week, 6hr., 3000dr); and Samothraki (1 per week, 4hr., 2500dr). Visit **Nicos Vayakos' Tourist and Travel Agency** (tel. 22 900; fax 23 560) in Mirina's port square for tickets and information on ferries (open 8:30am-2pm and 6:30-9pm). **Flying Dolphins** speed to Alexandropolis (3 per week, 3hr., 6200dr) and Samothraki (2 per week, 1½hr., 2500dr). In the middle of the main port square, a shop sells **international newspapers and books** daily from 7am-3pm and 5-11pm. **Postal code:** 84100. **Telephone Code:** 0254.

ACCOMMODATIONS, FOOD, AND ENTERTAINMENT

In high season, waterfront hotel rooms will cost at least 8000dr, so a better choice is to follow one of the many "Rooms to let" signs or ask at the tourist booth by the port. Just off the Romeikos waterfront, near Kosmos Pizzeria, look for the blue shutters on #8. **Katrina Bakaimi's** simple rooms (tel. 23 699) cost 5000dr for a single and 7000dr for a double. The clean, common bathroom is in the hall.

Typically, the waterfront *tavernas* are uniform in their prices and identical in their offerings. Try **Kosmos Pizzeria's** prime seating for the sunset behind Mt. Athos and delicious steamed mussels (1100dr). Later at night, stroll along the Romeikos among many cafe-bars, of which **Karagiozis Bar** is particularly popular, or right below the castle walls, where **Nefeli Cafe's** terrace perches.

SIGHTS

The **Kastro** which dominates the skyline and divides the waterfronts also houses several dozen deer. If you climb up and don't catch sight of them, you can at least enjoy the vista and ruins from the 7th-century BC fortress, reworked in the 13th century by the Venetians. **Romeikos Yialos** beach stretches across the opposite end of the waterfront. Directly across from the many sun worshippers, an **archaeological museum** displays artifacts from throughout Limnos (open Tues.-Sun. 9am-3pm).

The excavations at **Poliochni** are of particular importance, as the first of the seven levels is thought to date from almost 6000 years ago. It can be visited Tues.-Sun. 9am-3pm. On this half of the island, you can also see Aliki Lake, which dries in the summer to become a huge salt lick. Limnos holds an annual **festival** with concerts, traditional dancing, and exhibitions of local cheeses, honey, and wines, during the first ten days of August.

GREEK ISLANDS

Ionian Islands
ΝΗΣΙΑ ΤΟΥ ΙΟΝΙΟΥ

The Ionian islands have shared an historic fate distinct from mainland Greece. Situated on the country's western edge, the islands escaped Ottoman occupation, and were instead conquered at various times by Venetians, British, French, and Russians. Each of the Ionians' uninvited visitors left a lasting cultural, commercial, and architectural imprint. Despite its status as a British protectorate until 1864 and an Italian occupation during WWII, the islands are comparatively wealthy. Historical ties make the islands a favorite among Brits and Italians, as well as ferry-hopping backpackers who make the short trip from Italy.

CORFU (KERKYRA) ΚΕΡΚΥΡΑ

Odysseus praised Corfu's lush beauty when he washed onto its shores. Following this first visitor, the seas brought Franks, Venetians, and British, all leaving their undeniable marks on the architecture and culture of the island. Yet today, as international visitors ramble throughout the shuttered alleyways of a Neoclassical Venice, stroll along a Parisian esplanade, and sip tea while watching cricket on the grounds of a British imperial palace, they all seem to murmur "green, green, green." The verdant trees and brilliant flowers which tumble from hillsides down to fine sand beaches and sparkling blue waters attract most visitors. Even such a large island can only absorb so many tourists, however, and Corfu seems to have peaked in the late 80s and early 90s. In what is a blessing for budget travelers, tourists fled this resort destination and prices have correspondingly dropped.

■ Corfu Town

Corfu Town is the logical base for touring the island, as all ferries and most buses originate here. At the new port, a barrage of tourist agents proffering scooters, ferry tickets, and rooms greets every arrival. Apart from this melee, Corfu's two fortresses hulk over the waterfront, still guarding the old town. Quieter and more dignified, the narrow lanes near the Spianada (esplanade) and near Sanrocco Sq. present a mix of Byzantine, Venetian, and Greek architecture. The numerous souvenir shops and the preponderance of English-speakers have stolen the old town's traditional character, but not its charm of narrow streets, pastel and white neoclassical buildings, brilliant pink flowers, and stray cats.

ORIENTATION AND PRACTICAL INFORMATION

Familiarize yourself with the Theotokos family. Four of Corfu's main streets are named after members of this clan; you may pass from **N. Theotoki Street** to **M. Theotoki Street** to **G. Theotoki Street** to **I. Theotoki Street** without even realizing it. Use a map, and you'll be fine. Better yet, get lost in the **historic center** and bask in neoclassical splendor. On the north coast of town sit both the **new and old ports.** The new fortress, behind which sits Corfu's long-distance **bus station,** separates the two. The old town, at the center of historic Corfu, is a beautiful, befuddling maze of alleyways contained by the **Spianada,** an esplanade littered with chic cafes and the new fortress. To reach the Spianada from old port, simply follow the waterfront road (water on your left), walk through the arch of the British palace, and you will see the long set of cafes straight ahead and the park to the left. From there, any right will lead into the maze. From the new port, follow the same strategy, or turn inland onto

Corfu

Othoni
Othoni
Mathraki
Kato Mathraki
Ano Mathraki

Erikoussa
Erikoussa

Sidari
Peroulades
Avliotes
Karoussades
Agios Stefanos
Dafni
Agios Georgios
Makrades
Lakones
Paleokastritsa
Liapades
Gianades
Gouvia
Nimfes
Episkepsi
Loutses
Kassiopi
Pandokratoras
(906m)
Strinilas
Gimari
Ano Korakiana
Pirgi
Ipsos
Kato Korakiana
Dassia
Ptihia
Potamos
Kerkira
Pelekas
Perama
Gastouri
Agios Gordis
Benitses
Pendati
Ano Pavliana
Agios Mattheos
Gardiki
Moraitika
Messongi
Hlomos
Boukaris
Kouspades
Argirades
Lefkimi
Perivoli
Neochori
Paleochori
Spartera
Kavos

Ionian Sea

N

0   5 miles
0   5 kilometers

Napoleotos St., which becomes I. Theotoki. This leads you past **Sanrocco Square,** with the city bus terminal. Turn left along G. Theotoki, and head into old town. Any reasonably straight walk will bring you to the Spianada, the old fortress, and eventually the water.

National Tourist Office: (tel. 37 520) At Rizospaston Voulefton and Iak. Folila. The building is marked, and a sign directs you the first floor (by which they mean the second floor). Note that the information office has moved since the publication of even their own maps. Open May-Sept. Mon.-Fri. 8:30am-1:30pm and 5-8pm.

Tourist Police: (tel. 30 265) In the direction of Sanrocco Sq., with the old town at your back, walk along G. Theotaki. Turn right on I. Theotaki and take the first right. They're on the 4th floor. Open daily 7am-2:30pm.

British Consul: 1 Menekratous (tel. 30 055; fax 37 995), a few blocks down the street from the post office. Open Mon.-Fri. 8am-1pm. Call 39 211 in an emergency.

Banks: Corfu can't wait for you to spend your money. Banks with 24hr. **ATMs** line the larger streets, including **National Bank** on G. Theotoki St., near where it narrows and becomes Voulgareos. Banking hours generally Mon.-Thurs. 8am-2pm and Fri. 8am-1:30pm, although some have additional hours for **currency exchange** July-Aug. 4-6pm or 5:30-7:30pm, Sat. 8:30am-1pm. You can also try the currency exchange at the **airport** (open when planes arrive or depart).

American Express: Greek Skies Travel, 20A Kapodistriou St., P.O. Box 24 (tel. 30 883, 32 469), at the south end of the Spianada. Holds mail and cashes AmEx traveler's checks. Open Mon.-Fri. 8am-noon and 5:30-8:30pm, Sat. 8am-noon.

Room-Finding Services: Tourist agencies along Arseniou St. and Stratigou St., by the new port, find rooms in pensions. Many operate without commission and have information on cheap lodgings. Most open daily 8:30am-1:30pm and 5:30-9pm. Singles from 3000dr; doubles from 4000dr; triples from 5000dr; add 1000-1500dr for private bath. Prices negotiable for longer stays. Ask at the tourist police for rooms or call the **Association of Owners of Private Rooms and Apartments in Corfu** (tel. 26 133; fax 23 403) in the heart of the old town.

Flights: 20 Kapodistriou St. (tel. 39 910; airport 32 468), on the Spianada. A taxi ride takes only 5min. and is the only way to get to the airport unless your hotel or tour group has buses (before getting in, agree on a fare of roughly 1500dr). Planes go to Athens (3 per day, 50min., 19,200dr) and Thessaloniki (2 per week, 19,500dr). In summer, book 2-3 days ahead.

Buses: KTEL, behind the New Port on Avraniou St. (tel. 30 627 or 39 985). Pick up a handy timetable available at the station or from tourist agencies. Schedules for the main KTEL line are also posted on a billboard outside the new office behind Corfu Town's new fortress, from which the green KTEL buses leave. **Blue buses** leave from Sanrocco Sq., where schedules are printed on the signs. To: Paleokastritsa (7 per day, 400dr); Glyfada Beach (8 per day, 300dr); Kavos (10 per day, 500dr); Kassiopi (6 per day, 600dr); Sidari (11 per day, 550dr); Athens (2 per day, 7600dr); and Thessaloniki (1 per day, 7450dr). Buy tickets for Corfu destinations on the bus; all others in the bus office. Open daily 5:30am-8pm.

City Buses: #10 to Achilleon from Sanrocco Sq. (6 per day), #6 to Benitses (13 per day), #7 to Dassia (every 30min. 7am-10pm), #8 to Triklino (14 per day), #11 to Pelekas (7 per day). Fares for city buses average 130-190dr. Less frequent service on Sun. For information call 31 595 or ask at the booths in Sanrocco Sq. Schedules are seldom posted, so ask for a schedule.

Ferries: Book a day early in high season, especially to Italy—even deck-class sells out. Agents for the various shipping companies line Xen. Stratigou St., opposite the new port, so shop here for the lowest fares. Try **Fragline** and **Minoan** to Brindisi (daily 9am, 8hr., 4500-8000dr) and Patras (2 per day, 9hr., 5600dr). **Adriatica** and **Hellenic Mediterranean** recognize Eurail and Inter-rail passes. Ferries sail for: Ancona (2 per week, 23hr., 16,000dr); Bari (3 per week, 10hr., 10,000dr); and Venice (daily, 26hr., 18,000dr). Find out if the port tax is included in the price of your ticket when traveling to foreign ports. Ferry agencies, open all day in high season, follow regular store hours in the off season. **Corfu Mare** (tel. 32 467), at the new port beneath the Ionian Hotel, sells tickets. For updates on ferry schedules, contact the **port police** (tel. 38 425), in the customs house along the port, or the **port authority** (tel. 32 655 or 40 002).

Taxis: (33 811) At the old port, the Spianada, Sanrocco Square, and G. Theotoki St. Available by telephone 24hr.

Car Rental: A Fiat Panda should cost 10,000-12,000dr per day. Make sure quoted prices include the 20% tax. Third-party insurance is also usually included. You must have an international license to rent cars. Agencies along Xen. Stratigou all rent for roughly 10,000dr per day. **Hertz** and **Interrent/Europcar** tend to be more expensive. International car rental at **Greek Skies,** 20 Kapodistriou St. (tel. 33 410), has good prices, but requires you be 23 or older. Full payment in advance or major credit card required. Open Mon.-Fri. 8:30am-1:30pm and 5:30-8:30pm, Sat.-Sun. 8:30am-1:30pm.

Moped Rental: One of the most popular ways to see the island is by moped. Rental places abound, so don't pay more than 3000-4000dr per day. Make sure the brakes work and get a helmet. You're responsible for any damage to the vehicle, but the rental fee should include third-party liability and property damage insurance.

Luggage Storage: On Avrami St., directly across from the new port and above the bank on your right (400dr per day). Open 9am-10pm.

Laundromat: 42 I. Theotoki St. (tel. 35 304), just past Sanrocco Sq. Wash and dry 2500dr per basket. Open Mon.-Sat. 9am-2pm, and Tues., Thurs.-Fri. 5:30-8pm.

Public Toilets: On the Spianada near the pavilion and in Sanrocco Sq. Those on the Spianada are clean and wheelchair accessible.

Hospital: Corfu General Hospital (tel. 45 811, -2, -3; 24hr. emergency room 25 400). Walk down G. Theotoki, turn right at I. Theotoki and, as the road splits into 3 after one block, choose the middle course (Poluchroniou Koustanta St.). After 3 blocks this road forks. Bear right onto Iulias Andreadi St. and look right. For a list of

English-speaking doctors, call the Medical Association of Corfu (tel. 39 615) or the tourist office. For an **ambulance,** call 166.

Police: (tel. 39 509) In same building as tourist police.

Post Office: (tel. 25 544) On the corner of Alexandras St. and Rizospaston. Walk down G. Theotaki and turn left at Sanrocco Sq. The post office is in the yellow buildings, two blocks down on your right. Open Mon.-Fri. 8am-8pm for stamps and Poste Restante, Mon.-Fri. 7:30am-2:30pm for all else. **Postal Code:** 49100.

OTE: Main office at 9 Mantzarou St., off A. Theotoki St. Open daily 9am-midnight. Card phones on the Esplanade and in the white mobile buildings at both the old and new ports. **Telephone Code:** 0661 Corfu Town; 0662 south Corfu; 0663 north Corfu.

ACCOMMODATIONS

Hotels near the water fill up first, especially in high season, and the effectiveness of bargaining diminishes later in the day. Prices drop in the off season, and pension owners discount longer stays. Consider finding a room in a base town and taking advantage of Corfu's bus service for daytrips around the island. A good starting point is any one of the **room finding services** along the port. Although rooms to let will most likely provide the best accommodations at the best prices, it is easier to reserve a hotel room. Free-lance camping is practically impossible as well as illegal.

Hotel Hermes, 14 Rue G. Markora (tel. 39 268; fax 31 747), has clean, spacious rooms with bath by the daily market. Singles 6000dr; doubles 8000dr.

Hotel Ionian, 46 Xen. Sratigou (tel. 39 915), at the new port, offers inexpensive rooms with turf-carpet for mini-golf. Singles 5000dr; doubles 7000dr.

Hotel Astron, 15 Donzelot St. (tel. 39 505), on the waterfront to the left (facing inland) from the new port. Singles 7000dr; doubles 10,000dr.

Hotel Atlantis, 48 Xen. Stratigou (tel. 35 560), at the new port. Satellite TV, A/C, and private baths. Singles 8800dr; doubles 13,000dr.

FOOD

The premier restaurant areas are at the two ends of N. Theotoki St., near the Spianada and by the old port. Most places serve lunch outdoors until 3pm and dinner until 11pm. Tourist police strictly regulate all the restaurants in town, so the prices are fair and the cuisine monotonous. For a visual treat and fresh, inexpensive produce, head to the daily **open-air market** on Dessila St., near the base of the New Fortress (open 6am-2pm). Gyro stands abound (350dr), but as variety is the spice of life, try the delicious tomato and feta sandwiches (500dr) at the **Art Cafe,** in a garden behind the Palace of St. Michael and St. George. Below the palace on a small pier, a yellow building has been transformed into the **En Plo Cafe** and **Faliraki Restaurant,** where you can enjoy a cup of coffee or dinner right next to the sea. Although expensive and not very traditional, on a hot afternoon **Häagen-Dazs** sorbet can't be beat by any cafe frappe. They are in old town, one block off the Spianada.

Restaurant Bellissimo, 2 Kyriaki (tel. 41 112), off of N. Theotoki. Coming from the Spianada, look for their sign and turn right onto the narrow alleyway to Kyriaki. In a quiet square of its own. Nicely priced: stuffed vegetables 900dr, *sofrita* 1400dr.

Pizza Pete, 19 Arseniou St. (tel. 22 301), on the waterfront halfway between the Spianada and the old port, is very popular with both tourists and locals. Try the "Pete special" pizza (1700dr). Open April-Oct. daily 10am-3am.

Nautikon, 150 N. Theotoki (tel. 30 009), near the old port. A large place with appetizing food, some English-speaking staff, and 50 years of experience. Entrees 1300-1800dr. Open daily April-Oct. noon-midnight.

Faliraki Restaurant, on the corner of Kapodistriou and Arseniou St. Offers entrees (1700-1900dr) and beautiful views of the sunset over the Ionian Sea, while the waves virtually lap at your feet.

ENTERTAINMENT

In the evening, parade up and down the Spianada and its adjacent park; it stays alive until early morning. The demographics of a weekend evening lean heavily toward young girls and middle-aged tourists. Being seen has its price—cafes charge double what those in less popular locations do. Wander off the main catwalk into the streets of the old town for less touristy alternatives. Several **open-air cinemas** screen English language films (1500dr). If you can visit during Easter week, you'll be treated to the local tradition of smashing pottery to celebrate the Resurrection.

The east coast of Corfu is awash with **nightclubs** which cater mainly to British package tours. To the south, in Benitses and Kavos, the dancing can sometimes turn to fighting. There's less trouble in the resort towns of Gouvia, Dassia, and Ipsos north of Corfu Town, but you might find yourself forgetting you are in Greece. For bars and clubs that are both safe and authentically Greek, head north of Corfu Town past the old port along the port road. **Eidolo** plays only Greek music, while **Sax,** a favorite with the locals, is a classy, somewhat costly bar in a converted stable.

SIGHTS

Churches and Fortresses

Corfu's two most famous churches are the **Church of St. Jason and Sosipater** and the **Church of St. Spyridon.** The former, a 12th-century Byzantine stone structure located in a fishing neighborhood on the way to Mon Repos Beach, displays a dazzling array of silver and gold ornaments, medieval paintings, an impressive ceiling mural, and gorgeous Byzantine icons. The church was once covered entirely by murals of saints, but the islanders painted over them to prevent their destruction by the Ottomans. To get there, continue past the archaeological museum along the waterfront.

The Church of St. Spyridon, named for the island's patron saint, was built in 1590. Following plague outbreaks in the 17th century, residents of Corfu began parading the silver reliquary containing the remains of the saint around town every Palm Sunday and on the first Sunday of November. Each year he is given a new pair of slippers to replace the old pair he wears out wandering the island doing good deeds. In the right light, if you lift the gold cover, you can still see his oddly disconcerting grin beneath a black shroud behind the glass. St. Spyridon holds a **traditional festival,** with music and dancing on August 11. To find the church, take Ag. Spyridon off the Spianada; it's on your left. Both churches are open until 7pm.

Finished by the Venetians in the late 14th century, the **Palio Frourio,** just east of the Spianada, was thought to be impregnable. In 1864, however, the British blew it up before leaving Corfu to the Greeks. It was renovated for the European Socialist Party Leaders' Conference in 1993 and is now open to the public. On the grounds is the **Church of St. George,** now adapted to as a museum (site open Mon.-Fri. 8am-7pm and Sat.-Sun. 8:30am-3pm; admission 800dr, students 400dr).

The 375-year-old **New Fortress** (tel. 27 477), above the ferry ports, affords panoramic views of Corfu Town for sun-drenched picnics. The fort houses a small gallery of etchings, maps, and watercolors with nautical motifs, as well as an additional gallery with contemporary exhibits (open daily 9am-9pm; admission 400dr).

Museums and Archaeological Sites

At the north end of the Spianada stands the **Palace of St. Michael and St. George** (tel. 30 443). Unmistakably British, the palace was built as the residence of the Lord High Commissioner but now houses the **Municipal Gallery's collection** of Corfuit painting (open daily 9am-9pm; admission 300dr, students 100dr). The **Archaeological Museum,** 1 Vraila St., on the waterfront south of the Spianada, contains relics of the island's Mycenaean and classical past. A Gorgon pediment glowers over the collection, which includes many ancient coins from different regions (open Tues.-Sat.

8:30am-3pm and Sun. 9:30am-2:30pm; admission 800dr, seniors 600dr, students 400dr, children and EU students free).

Down N. Theotoki from the Spianada lies the Ionian Bank Building, which houses a **museum of paper currency** (tel. 41 552). Advertising itself as "one of the most interesting museums of its kind in the world," it is home to the first bank note printed in Greece and recommended by *Let's Go* for fanatical finance capitalists (open Mon.-Sat. 9am-1pm; free). Behind the old port lies the old **Jewish Quarter.** The **synagogue,** on Velissariou St., served the Jewish community from its construction in 1537 until 1940, when 5000 Jews were gathered on the Spianada to be sent to Auschwitz.

Corfu's most recently opened sight is the **Mon Repos Estate,** given by the British government to the Greek royal family in 1864. Since the royals' exile in 1967, the lovely neoclassical palace has fallen into disrepair, and large gardens filled with rare trees are overgrown. The grounds are now open to the public, largely because a **Temple to Artemis** rests in the garden. Just before the gated entrance to the estate is the entrance to the **monastery of St. Efthimeaus** (open daily 8am-1pm and 5-8pm). On the opposite side of the road is the **Archaeological Site of Paleopolis Roman Baths,** closed to the public but visible through the fence. Be careful crossing the street. The **Byzantine Museum,** which houses a vast collection of icons, is before Pizza Pete's, along the waterfront between the Spianada and the New Port. Look for the sign or the steps leading up to the building (open Tues.-Sun. 8:30am-3pm; admission 500dr, students and seniors 300dr, EU students free).

▓ Southern Corfu

Southern Corfu is home to the islet of Vlacherna. **Achillion Palace** stands nearby, 9km south of the port of Corfu in the village of **Gastouri.** Eccentric and ostentatious (but incredibly lovely), it was commissioned by Empress Elizabeth of Austria as a summer residence in honor of Achilles and Thetis. The Empress was obsessed with Achilles, probably due to the death of her favorite son, whom she felt resembled the god. Kaiser Wilhelm II of Germany spent his summers here until WWI diverted his attention. The gardens and view are especially cinematic; the 1981 James Bond flick *For Your Eyes Only* was filmed here (open 9am-4pm; admission 1000dr, students 500dr). Take bus #10 from Sanrocco Sq. (6 per day, 30min., 190dr).

Shallow but clear and pleasant, **Kavos Beach** lies at the island's southern tip, 47km from Corfu Town (buses every hr., 750dr). On the southwest coast stretches the gorgeous, sandy beach at **Agios Georgios** (2 buses per day, 550dr). The nearby, attractive **Vitalades Beach** remains one of Corfu's few deserted spots.

▓ Northern Corfu

Travel Advisory: Albania

On June 10, 1997, the U.S. State Department issued a **travel warning** advising against all unnecessary travel to Albania, and a **state of emergency** existed throughout that country at the time this book went to press. Armed gunmen still control much of the southern half of Albania, where several of the best archaeological sites arc located. While improved relations between Greece and Albania have made Albania's Ionian coast accessible to tourists in Greece, *Let's Go* strongly discourages people from traveling to Albania until the political situation improves.

The Kassiopi bus serves the northern coast. It leaves from the bus station and stops at every hamlet along the way (6 per day, 1¼hr., 600dr). Past Pirgi, the road begins to wind below steep cliffs. **Mt. Pantokrator,** on your left, towers 1000m above, while dramatic vistas of Albania come into view across the straits. After passing through Nissaki and Gimari you will reach **Kouloura,** 28km north of Corfu, with its Venetian manor-house, pebbled beach, marina, and matchless *taverna.* The right fork to **Kal-**

ami meanders down to a sandier beach where, in the 1930s, author Lawrence Durrell lived with his family, including his wacky brother Gerald. His small white house can still be seen (from the outside, at least). Buy the brothers' Corfu-inspired books (Lawrence's *Prospero's Cell* and Gerald's *My Family and Other Animals*) in **Lychoudis Bookstore.** Rooms are available for rent in both towns. The walk to Kalami or Kouloura from the main road takes 15 minutes.

On the northernmost coast of the island, the quieter beach resorts of **Roda Chanin** and **Sidari** provide excellent camping and beaches enveloped by cliffs. Sidari is particularly spectacular, especially the stretch of picture-perfect coves and sea caves along the shore toward Peroulades. A 5th-century BC temple has been found here.

Swimming on Corfu's west coast is like being trapped inside an all-blue kaleidoscope. The **Paleokastritsa beach** rests among some of the lovelier scenery in Greece, with six small coves and sea caves casting shadows over shades of blue. Renting a pedal boat is the best way to visit the caves where Odysseus supposedly washed ashore. The 13th-century fort of **Angelokastro** sits above the town, while a natural balcony, **Bella Vista,** rests halfway up. Jutting out over the sea is the bright white **Panagia Theotokos Monastery** with a collection of Byzantine icons, gorgeous views, and the skeleton of a sea monster. Come as early as possible, because it is a mess of tour buses by mid-morning. **Buses** run to Paleokastritsa from behind the new fortress (7 per day, 45min., 400dr).

Pelekas is ideal for watching sunsets over whitewashed villages in the hillsides. **Pelekas Beach,** a 30-minute downhill walk from town, attracts a large number of backpackers. Don't attempt to make the harrowing journey by moped. Bus #11 runs to Pelekas Town from Sanrocco Sq. (7 per day, 190dr). **Glyfada Beach,** 5km up the coast from Pelekas Town, is served directly by the Glyfada bus from behind the new fortress (8 per day, 300dr). It is far more touristed, but still picturesque. Both beaches, bracketed by scrubby cliffs, are remarkably shallow. Single women should watch out for smooth-talking Greek *kamakia* ("octopus spears," a.k.a. men) who cruise Glyfada. *Kamakia* make their living getting foreigners to pick them up and support them for a few days. They even have a union. Just ignore them.

A little north of Glyfada, accessible via dirt path off the main Pelekas road, lie the isolated beaches of **Moni Myrtidon** and **Myrtiotissa,** extolled by Lawrence Durrell as the most beautiful beaches in the world. A section of sand at Myrtiotissa is the island's unofficial nude beach. Everything here is very casual, although once in a while the local monks from the Monastery of Our Lady of the Myrtles complain to the police, who reluctantly bring offending nudists to court.

Agios Gordios, with its steep cliffs and impressive rock formations, is accessible by bus (7 per day, 45min., 260dr) and the setting for the **Pink Palace** (tel. (0661) 53 024, fax 53 025). An eternal pink *ouzo* circle for some, the "palace" is filled with the antics of frat parties and then some. Rooms vary significantly in quality (5000dr per person includes breakfast, dinner, and nightclub entrance).

ZAKINTHOS ΖΑΚΥΝΘΟΣ

A tour of Zakinthos's varied land and seascapes reveals an exceptional palette of colors—white cliffs rising from turquoise water, sun-bleached wheat waving in the shadows of evergreens, and magenta flowers framing the twisting streets. Unfortunately, if you stay in Zakinthos Town or on its neighboring beaches, all you'll see are the sweaty backs of other tourists. Zakinthos's best natural sights, including the famous blue caves, are in the north of the island. Anyone who ventures there will understand why the Venetians christened Zakinthos "Fior di Levante," the flower of the east.

■ Zakinthos Town

Tidy Zakinthos Town welcomes visitors to the east coast of the island with arcaded streets and whitewashed buildings. After an earthquake destroyed it in 1953, locals restored the city to its former state, making an effort to maintain the Venetian architecture in areas like the spacious Solomou Sq. to the right of the boat landing. It's a pretty town, but with all the other opportunities available, you may want to head for the more remote beaches.

ORIENTATION AND PRACTICAL INFORMATION

The waterfront runs between **Solomou Sq.** at the right end (facing inland) and St. Dionysus Church at the left end. Each end has a port where boats from the mainland dock. **Lombardou St.** runs along the water between the two ports and is lined with restaurants, gift shops, and ferry agencies. The first street parallel to Lombardou away from the water is **Filita Street,** home to the bus station. Behind it in order are **Foskolou, Alex. Roma** (the main shopping street), and **Tertseti.** Three blocks inland from stately Solomou Sq. is **Agiou Markou Sq.,** a gathering spot which houses outdoor restaurants and cafes.

Banks: National Bank (tel. 44 113), on Solomou Sq., has **currency exchange.** Open Mon.-Thurs. 8am-2pm, Fri. 8am-1:30pm, Sat.-Sun. 9am-1pm. The bank's **ATM** takes MasterCard and Cirrus. Other ATMs on Alex Roma and Lombardou.

Flights: The **airport** (tel. 28 322) is 6km south near Laganas. Flights to Athens (in summer 2 per day, off season 1 per day, 45min., 16,400dr, under 24 13,800dr). **Olympic Airways,** 16 Alex. Roma St. (tel. 28 611). Open Mon.-Fri. 8am-3:30pm.

Buses: 42 Filita St. (tel. 22 255), on the corner of Eleftheriou St., 6 blocks along the water from Solomou Sq., then 1 block inland. Long-distance buses piggyback on the ferry to Patras (4 per day, 3hr., 2800dr including ferry ticket) and then to Athens (4 per day, 6hr., 4500dr). Schedules for local service posted outside the bus station; complete list is available at the information window. Buses run to: Volimes (3 per day, 600dr); Vasiliko (Porto Roma); Geraka (2 per day, 30min., 260dr); Alykes (4 per day, 30min., 260dr); Argasi (5 per day, 210dr); Tsilivi (7 per day, 210dr); and Laganas (13 per day, 210dr). Buses run less frequently on weekends and the schedule changes often, so ask for the updated schedule at the desk.

Ferries: Arrive at Zakinthos Town port from Killini (4-6 per day, 1½hr., 1500dr) and also from Ag. Nikolaos to Pesado in Cephalonia (2 per day, 1½hr., 900dr). Tickets available at the **boat agencies** along the waterfront. For more information, call the **port police** (tel. 28 117).

Taxis: Line the side streets off the waterfront (tel. 48 400; 24hr.).

Car Rental: Hertz, 38 Lombardou St. (tel. 45 706). Cars from 15,000dr per day. Many moped places also rent cars. Must be over 21. Open daily 8am-2pm and 5:30-9:30pm.

Moped Rental: Your best bet is **EuroSky Rentals** (tel. 26 278), one block inland from the water on A. Makri. They are the cheapest (2000dr per day) and may not hassle you about not having a motorcycle license. Open daily 8am-10pm.

Hospital: (tel. 42 514, -515), above the city center. Walk down Lombardou St. until Ag. Eleftheriou. Follow this road inland until Kokkini St., where the road jogs right and becomes Ag. Spiridona. The hospital is at the end of this road (roughly 1km from the water). Open 24hr.

Police: (tel. 22 200), Lombardou and Fra. Tzoulati St., 5 blocks along the waterfront from Solomou Sq. Open 24hr. Laid-back **tourist police** (tel. 27 367) speak English, answer questions, and can help find rooms. Open daily 8am-10pm.

Post Office: (tel. 42 418), hard to find. On an unnamed side street between Alex. Roma and Tertseti near Damiri St. Offers **currency exchange.** Open Mon.-Fri. 7:30am-8pm. **Postal Code:** 29100.

OTE: 2 Dimokratias, between the 2 squares. Open daily 7am-2:30pm.

Telephone Code: 0695.

ACCOMMODATIONS

Rooms in Zakinthos Town tend to be expensive and scarce in July and August. Look for the signs that advertise *domatia*, and bargain in the off season. The **Ionion Hotel,** 18 Alex. Roma (tel. 42 511), offers rooms with big balconies and private baths (singles 4000d; doubles 6000dr). **Hotel Egli,** on Lombardou St., is two blocks from Solomou Sq. and has large, clean rooms (singles 5000dr; doubles 7000dr). **Rooms for Rent on St. Lucas Sq.** (tel 26 809) are on the waterfront, two blocks towards St. Dionysus from the tourist police. Rooms are large and clean with private baths. Prices are negotiable (singles 4000dr; doubles 6000dr).

FOOD

Finding food in Zakinthos is easy. Restaurants line the waterfront, Ag. Markou Sq., and every other establishment on Alex. Roma is a cafe or candy shop. Zakinthian specialities include *melissaki*, a nougat candy available at gift shops, and veal in tomato sauce. Fast food is ubiquitous, and a gyro will only cost you 350dr. **The Village Lion,** on the waterfront, is a little pricey, but has unbeatable indoor and garden seating (with live music). Most servings are big enough to share (mixed grill dishes 2000dr, salads 1400dr). **Molos Restaurant** (tel. 27 309) is another popular waterfront joint (*moussaka* 1250dr, stuffed tomatoes 1150dr). The **House of Latas** (tel. 41 585) is 2km above the city (follow the signs to Bohalis) near the Venetian castle. Spectacular views of Zakinthos and live local music are available every evening. Try the grilled swordfish (1800dr) and you won't be disappointed (open in summer 9am-midnight.) **Artos and Ugea Bakery** (tel. 23 134), on the corner of Alex. Roma and D. Stefaniou, is the perfect place to stock up for a picnic. They sell drinks, ice cream, and a delicious selection of cookies (1400dr per kg) and breads (200dr per loaf). **Coop Supermarket** (tel 22 262), on Lombardou near the police station, is a well stocked (open 8am-9pm). **San Marco,** which dominates Ag. Markous Sq., plays groovy English disco music for a diverse clientele (mixed drinks 800-1300dr).

SIGHTS

Zakinthos is famous for its **Church of Agios Dionysios,** named in honor of St. Denis, the island's patron saint. The church displays a silver chest which holds the saint's relics. The modest dress code is strictly enforced; a monk has long skirts to wrap around visitors clad in shorts. In Solomou Sq., the **Byzantine Museum** (tel. 42 714) houses icons from the "Ionian School," a distinctive local hybrid of Byzantine and Renaissance artistic styles (open Tues.-Sun. 8am-2:30pm; admission 800dr, students free). If you enjoy a good hike, climb 2km above town to the **Venetian Castle** where Solomos wrote the words to the Greek national anthem (open Tues.-Sun. 8am-2:30pm). To get there, follow Tertseti (later N. Koluva) to the edge of town and then the signs uphill to Bohalis, turn left after 1km, and follow the signs for the Kastro. The hike affords panoramic views of the island.

■ Around Zakinthos

The terrain and beaches on Zakinthos will easily lure you away from the pleasant port town. It's possible to see the entire island, including the otherwise inaccessible **western cliffs,** by boat. Shop around for a cruise on Lombardou St. Most tours leave in the morning, but require a reservation the night before (about 5000dr). KTEL also offers a **bus tour** of the island (every Sat. at 10:15am, 2500dr). **Boats** make excursions to the blue caves, turtle beach, and "Smuggler's Wreck." Inquire at the tourist police or agencies. To explore independently, tour the island by **moped** (there's at least one rental place at each beach) or by bus. Because the island is developing rapidly, many new roads won't appear on maps, so rely on a combination of road maps (400dr at gift shops) and asking directions.

The beaches at **Laganas,** 10km south, have been mangled by large hotels, souvenir stands, and tourists. If you must stay, try **Laganas Camping** (tel. 51 708), which has a pool (1500dr per person; 800dr per car; 800dr per small tent; 1000dr per large tent). Unscathed beaches carpet the peninsula extending out to the town of **Vasilikos,** 16km from Zakinthos Town, and are most plentiful near **Porto Roma.** Signs for rooms to let coat the road to Vasilikos, especially near **Agios Nikolaos Beach.** On the other side of Vasilikos, facing Laganas Bay, lies **Gerakas Beach.** Daily buses leave Zakinthos Town for Vasilikos (Mon.-Sat. 2 per day, 260dr).

From Zakithnos Town, walk to the beach along the asphalt road skirting the shore. **Planos,** just inland, has plenty of rooms. Buses run from Zakinthos Town to the beach (7 per day, 30min., 2000dr). **Zante Camping** (tel. 44 754) is Zakinthos' only campsite located on a beach. It has a cafeteria and minimarket (1300dr per person; 700dr per car; 950dr per small tent; 1100dr per large tent; 10% discount for *Let's Go* users). From Zakinthos Town, walk to the beach along the asphalt road parallel to the shore.

Alykes, 16km from Zakinthos Town, is more pleasant and less crowded than its counterparts in the south. Filled with romantic restaurants and fringed with soft, clean sand beaches, Alykes gets somewhat crowded, although less so than the other resort towns. **Montes** (tel. 83 101) is a vacation complex which lets large rooms with beautiful balconies and kitchens (5000-8000dr). Ask for an attic room. Downstairs there is a restaurant that serves excellent budget fare (*tzatziki* 400dr, *moussaka* 900dr, soup 300dr). Next door is a bakery and supermarket. Many other signs along the main drag advertise rooms to let. The **Apollo Restaurant,** on the edge of town, has fantastic chicken *souvlaki* (1100dr). Buses run to Alykis four times per day; the last bus returns at 7pm (260dr). Buses leave from Hotel Montreal at the far edge of town.

Buses from Zakinthos Town go to the sprawling old village of **Volimes** (3 per day, 600dr), where the residents specialize in needlepoint and crochet. Bring cash because this is the perfect opportunity to get a cheap, colorful rug, or other non-tacky present (no credit cards accepted). One kilometer east, up the hill in the upper part of the village (Ano Volimes), signs advertise rooms to let. Crumbling medieval bell towers and abandoned windmills dot the villages.

At the extreme northern tip of Zakinthos is the tiny village of **Korithi,** locally known as Agios Nikolaos, where the ferry to Cephalonia departs. Buses arrive only twice per week, so unless you have transportation, a taxi is probably the only way to get there. From the beach, you can hire a fishing boat to take you on a tour of the eerie **blue caves,** accessible only from the water. A one-hour excursion costs roughly 1500dr per person. You can also rent canoes and other small craft on the tiny beach. A drive between Korithi and Volimes through the northern farmlands of Zakinthos is breathtaking, and should not be missed by any visitor to the islands.

LEFKADA (LEFKAS) ΛΕΥΚΑΔΑ

Lefkada is distinguishable from its fellow southern Ionian Islands for many reasons. The Italians, not the British, are remembered as Lefkada's most influential colonists, the island is separated from mainland Greece by only a 50m canal, and the island was not devastated by the 1953 earthquake to the extent its neighbors were. In spots the island finds itself so swamped with tourists that the town's waterfront looks like one big souvenir stand. Those patches can be skirted, though, and it is possible to discover unspoiled beaches and explore fascinating towns on Lefkada.

According to Thucydides, Lefkada (Greek for white rock) was part of the mainland until 427 BC, when inhabitants dug a canal. The modern bridge which connects Lefkada to the mainland has only recently replaced the archaic chain-operated ferry built by Emperor Augustus.

■ Lefkada Town

Lefkada Town, directly across from mainland Greece, is a thinly touristed city next to a section of sea that looks like a vast swamp. It may be a poor copy of upscale Greek resort towns, but for that reason it offers a break from the commodities of heavy tourism—the gaudy signs, endless leather and jewelry stores, and fields of buses. Downtown consists of narrow pedestrian-only streets which feature an appealing, brightly painted architecture that's unique to the town.

ORIENTATION AND PRACTICAL INFORMATION

Lefkada was identified as Homer's Ithaka by the archaeologist William Dörpfeld. Today, Dörpfeld is the main street in Lefkada Town and runs right down the middle of the peninsula that comprises the city's downtown area. Dörpfeld and all the little winding streets that branch off it are for pedestrians and bikes only. Cars drive along the waterfront and inland of the peninsula. There is no tourist office, but the **tourist police** (tel. 26 450), 30 Iroon Politechniou, a few blocks to the right of Lefkada Town's bus station (facing the water), offer handy brochures and will help locate rooms (open daily 8am-10pm). In the same building is the **police station** (tel. 22 100; open 24hr.; English spoken).

For more detailed information about ferries, tours, or sights, try **Travel Mate** (tel. 23 581) at the tip of the peninsula. Look for the Eurocar signs (open 9am-2pm and 6-9pm). There is a **National Bank** along Dörpfield St. (open daily 8am-2pm, 24hr. **ATM**). Dörpfield also leads to the main square, filled with cafes and an occasional traveling music act.

From the bus station (tel. 22 364), on the waterfront with a gray and yellow striped awning, **buses** cross the canal to Athens (4 per day, 5½hr., 5700dr) and Aktion (4 per day, 340dr). The **local island buses** run to Nidri (13 per day, 30min., 280dr); Agios Nikitas (3 per day, 20min., 240dr); Poros (2 per day, 45min., 440dr); and Vasiliki (4 per day, 1hr., 650dr). Be sure to pick up a bus schedule at the station (or from tour offices) detailing additional transit routes and return times. **Ferries** link Lefkada with Ithaka and Cephalonia to the south. From Vasiliki in Lefkada, ferries make the run to Fiskardo on Cephalonia (3 per day, 1hr., 935dr), then to Ithaka (1¾hr., 935dr). From Nidri in Lefkada, ferries sail to Frikes on Ithaka (1 per day, 935dr). For Vasiliki ferry information, call 31 555; for Nidri 92 427. Travel offices have information and sell tickets. Lefkada may well be **excursion boat** paradise. Excursion boats run daily day-long cruises to Cephalonia, Ithaka, and Skorpios (every morning, roughly 3500dr). Boats also shuttle beach devotees to Lefkada's numerous cloistered beaches. Some also stop at the cave of **Papanikoli.** Inquire at waterfront kiosks, travel offices, or read the hard-to-miss signs aboard the little boats. The **post office** is on Dörfield (open Mon.-Fri. 7:30am-2pm). **Postal Code:** 31100. For the **OTE,** turn right off Stratigou Melas to Pataneromenis St., head back toward the waterfront, and look for the satellite tower (open daily 7am-10pm).**Telephone Code:** 0645.

ACCOMMODATIONS

Hotel Byzantion (tel. 22 629), at the waterfront end of Dörpfield, is more pleasant than other hotels in its price range. There are sinks in the rooms, bathrooms down the hall (singles 4000dr; doubles 8000dr.). Another budget option is to call the **Union of Pension Owners** (the tourist board can assist you) at 21 266. Expect private rooms to cost between 4000-8000dr depending on the season. **Santa Maura,** off Dörpfield about three blocks from the water, offers large bright rooms with sparkling private baths (singles 7000dr; doubles 10000dr.).

FOOD AND ENTERTAINMENT

Taverna Regentos, off the main square on Verrioti St. (turn right), has a delightful decor that matches the excellent quality of the traditional food (*moussaka* 800dr, grilled meats 1100dr; open 7:30pm-2am). **Taverna of the Nine Islands** is off Dörpfield St. before the square. Roses bloom over tables that line a charming narrow street (aubergines 900dr, salads 500dr). The restaurant begins serving dinner at 7pm.

The **folklore museum** is off the main square (turn right and follow the signs). The small museum offers a taste of old Lefkada and its Italian legacy (open Mon.-Fri. 10am-1pm and 7-10pm; 500dr). Make your way over to the bizarre **Phonograph Museum**, second left past the square; inquire at the meat market for access (open Mon.-Fri. 9am-1pm and 6-11pm). The **Archaeological Museum**, 1km down the road to Ag. Nikitas, is tiny and worthwhile for only the most dedicated, since the majority of Lefkada's treasures are in Athens or in Ioannina (open 9am-1:30pm; 500dr). Every year Lefkada hosts the famous **Folklore Festival,** now in its 34th year, in the second half of August.

■ Around Lefkada

While Lefkada Town has no sandy beaches, the northern half of the west coast offers miles of deserted white beached and clear water. Rent a moped (3000dr per day for *Let's Go* users at **Travel Mate/Eurocar** on the tip of the peninsula). The best stretch lies north of **Agios Nikitas.** The road there leads to the monastery **Moni Faneromenis** (tel. (0645) 22 275), with a sweeping view of the ocean and one resident monk (open daily 7am-10pm; free).

NIDRI

Nidri ensnares unwary travelers solely because it's the last stop of the otherwise delightful Frikes-Nidri ferry. The waterfront, crowded with pleasure boats, boasts a handsome view of the dappled coves of numerous small islands, but the town itself is little more than a strip of garish tourist shops and tacky cafes. The **post office** (open Mon.-Fri. 9am-1pm) and **OTE** (open Mon.-Fri. 9am-1pm and 5-10pm) are on the main street, parallel to and one block inland from the waterfront. **Buses** from Nidri go to Lefkada (17 per day, 30min., 260dr) and Vasiliki (8 per day, 300dr). "Rooms to let" signs are scattered along the main street. In July and August, when the island sags under the burgeoning weight of tourists, rooms are always full and prices are inevitably high (doubles from 10,000dr). In the off season expect a room for as low as 4000dr. eight kilometers north of Nidri, toward Lefkada, is **Camping Episkopos** (tel. (0645) 23 043; 1050dr per person; 800dr per small tent, 900dr per large tent, 500dr per car). **Thesimi Camping** is 5km south of Nidri (tel. (0645) 95 374; 1200dr per person, 900dr per small tent, 1000dr per large tent, 700dr per car). To escape the glitz but not the mosquitoes of Nidri, climb the 3km to **Neochori** at dusk. Three kilometers south is the tiny village of **Vliho,** accessible by bus from Lefkada (13 per day, 100dr), with a striking church in an idyllic setting of wildflowers and cypress trees.

VASILIKI

Vasiliki, at the south tip of Lefkada Island bears charms both tranquil and invigorating. Smaller and currently less touristed than Nidri, Vasiliki is becoming increasingly popular with the young international watersports crowd. Rated among the world's finest **windsurfing** resorts, Vasiliki is usually graced with consistent gentle winds in the morning, which rise to steady force-five gales in the afternoon. **Buses** run five times per day from Lefkada (550dr) and Nidri (300dr).

The main road running inland from the waterfront winds past the **post office** (open Mon.-Fri. 8am-2pm). The **postal code** is 31082. Just before the post office is **Samba Tours,** an all-purpose tour office willing to "help and advise by fax or phone" (tel. (0645) 31 520, -555; fax 31 522; open daily 8:30am-11pm). From Vasiliki, two **ferries** per day run to Fiskardo, Cephalonia (1hr., 1000dr), Ithaka (1¾hr., 1000dr), and Sami (2½hr., 1700dr). Inquire at the kiosk next to the pier. To contact the **health center,** call 31 065. The **police** (tel. (0645) 31 218; open 24hr.) are a short distance inland along the road; ask for directions.

Rooms are plentiful and signs easy to spot, particularly along the road leading uphill from the bus stop (on the waterfront and along the main post road). The popular **Vasiliki Beach Camping** boasts superlative amenities and rests a hop, skip, and a jump away from the beach. Head for the beach and make a right on the road running inland just before the Windsurfing Club (tel. (0645) 31 308, -457; fax 31 458; 1550dr per person, 1000dr per child, free for kids under 4; 1100dr per small tent, 1100dr per car). The **Galaxy Market** (tel. (0645) 31 221), around the corner at the back side of the ferry dock, lets tidy, simple rooms (singles 6000dr; doubles 7000dr).

Full meals can be inexpensive and well-prepared in Vasiliki, even in the waterfront cafes and eateries. Most have similar menus and prices, so choose your haunt according to what aspect of sun and sea seems most appealing. Give the **Alexander the Great Restaurant** a try; it is on the waterfront on the way to the beach (mixed salad with fresh parsley 500dr, fried *kalamari* with a touch of thyme 600dr). A haven for the high-spirited, **Zeus' Bar** serves up drinks to soothe the salt and sun weary. The orange juice and soda water (300dr) are particularly refreshing (open daily morning to late night. For a morning treat or for bus journey snack provisions, try the **bakery** above the bus stop. Scoop into their big barrels of tasty sweet rolls (molasses and a taste of caraway 50dr).

A **lighthouse** built on the site of the Temple of Lefkas Apollo sits at the southernmost tip of the island. Worshippers exorcised evil with an annual sacrifice here. The victim, usually a criminal or a mentally ill person thought to be possessed, was thrown into the sea from the cliffs. Live birds were tied to the victim's arms and legs for amusement as well as aerodynamic advantages. It was from these 70m cliffs that the ancient poet Sappho leapt to her death when Phaon rejected her. The cliff, called **Sappho's Leap,** is known in Lefkada as *Kavos tis Kiras* (Cape of the Lady).

ITHAKA (ITHAKI) ΙΘΑΚΗ

Like she did for Odysseus, Athena still bestows a blessing upon anybody lucky enough to wash up on one of the islets hidden along Ithaka's twisted coastline. When you first arrive at Vathi, the island's capital, your first sense of the island may be the overpowering impression that nothing is going on. If you are patient, however, the island will endear itself to you as it has to thousands who have come before.

According to legend, Ithaka is the island on which Penelope waited 20 years for Odysseus to return from the Trojan War. Olive trees sprout from its rocky mountain sides and pebbled coves dot its coast. These days Ithaka is visited by Scandinavian yachts and Italian vacationers, but many Anglophones blindly pass it by. The island, which only gears up for tourists between mid-July and mid-September, is coursed by walking trails and quiet roads.

■ Vathi

Ithaka's largest town wraps around its circular bay. In the evening, the dying sun deepens the tint of the pastel -colored houses and their red roofs, making Vathi one of the Ionian Islands' most beautiful towns. Since Vathi isn't over touristed, many of the locals are interested to meet travelers. This is especially true during the off season. Colorful fishing boats bob on the water, and the higher you climb, the more beautiful Vathi becomes.

ORIENTATION AND PRACTICAL INFORMATION

The ferry docks are to the right (facing inland) of the town square. Most points of interest are either on the waterfront or in the square. All directions—left and right— are given relative to someone facing inland. Most establishments have longer hours in the high season.

The web of **ferries** around the Ionian Islands enmesh Ithaka, but schedules vary drastically depending on the season. Check with helpful **Delas Tours,** located in the main square right off the water (tel. 32 104; fax 33 031; open daily 9am-11pm), but even they might only know the schedule for that month. In general, boats run between Frikes in the north on Ithaka to Nidri (2 per day, 2hr., 935dr). From Vathi, there are ferries to Sami on Cephalonia (1hr., 950dr). There are also boats from Piso Aetos to Sami (3 per day, 500dr) and to Astakos on the mainland (1 per day, 2½hr., 1850dr). Be sure to check boat schedules at your port of departure. For a **taxi,** call 33 030. Most **moped rental** places charge around 3000dr per day. Try your luck at **Rent-A-Bike** (tel. 33 243) behind the new cultural museum, as it may be the cheapest. The **hospital** can be reached at 32 222, or turn left and walk along the square until you see a sign reading "Hospital" (roughly 1km). Along the way, you will see the **police** station, where English is spoken (tel. 32 205; open 24hr.). The **port police** can be reached at 32 909. There is a **pharmacy** (tel. 32 251) left of the main square on the waterfront. The **post office** is in the main square (tel. 32 386; open Mon.-Fri. 7:30am-2pm). **Postal Code:** 28300. The **OTE** sits on the water left of the square (open Mon.-Fri. 7:30am-2:30pm). **Telephone Code:** 0674.

ACCOMMODATIONS

Your best bet is to find a private *domatia*. Sometimes proprietors will meet the ferry. It is possible to get a very good deal (3000-4000dr per night), but be sure to discuss price and distance before you follow them away from town. Prices spike in mid-July. If you need help finding a room call **Delas Tours** in the square or **Polyctor Tours** (tel. 28 300), open daily 7am-11pm in high season. The **Hotel Mentor** (tel. 32 433) lies on the water, left of the square and next to the OTE. This hotel's high prices may be flexible, but are, unfortunately, the lowest in town; in high season singles 10,800dr; doubles 14,500dr; breakfast included). **Camping** on the beach under the eucalyptus trees or any place else outside is generally tolerated, provided that campers clean up after themselves.

FOOD

The food is generally good in Ithaka, and prices are average for Greece. **Taverna To Trexantiri** (tel. 33 066) serves huge portions and is the hands-down favorite among locals (entrees average 1200dr, salads 500dr). **O Batis** (tel. 33 010), the last waterfront restaurant before the square, serves Greek favorites and good pasta (try the 4-cheese penne for 1100dr or the pizza for 1800dr). **Odysseus Restaurant** (tel. 32 381), 800m down the waterfront on the right (past the ferry landing), provides a beautiful view of night-lit Vathi (squid 1400dr, Greek salad 800dr, fried potatoes 400dr).

SIGHTS

The **Vathi Archaeological Museum** is small but free (open Mon.-Fri. 9am-3:30pm). Follow the signs from the water left of the town square. The brand new **Folklore and Cultural Museum** is a beautiful airy building that houses fully assembled bedrooms, kitchen, and sitting room from Ithaka's colonial period as well as photographs of the 1953 earthquake devastation. The Placards are soon to be translated into English (open daily 9:30am-2pm and 6-10pm; tel. 33 398; admission 250dr). Those with poetic imaginations may want to make the 45-minute, 4km climb up to the **Cave of the Nymphs,** where Odysseus hid the treasure which the Phoenicians bestowed upon him. To get here, walk around the harbor with the water on your right and follow the signs. The hike provides stunning views of Vathi. Bring a flashlight (admission 200dr). A two-hour hike southeast up a well-marked but rocky road leads to the Homeric **Arethousa Fountain,** along a steep mountain path through orchards. In summer, the fountain is dry. To find the path to the fountain, follow Evmeou St. up the hill until it turns to dirt and look for the signs. After a morning of hiking, spend an afternoon sifting through the multicolored stones of the beach at **Piso Aetos Bay,** 5.5km from town. There is a **Wine Festival** in Perahori on the last Sunday of July.

■ Around Ithaka

An excursion from Vathi will give you a chance to explore the scenic, remote villages scattered along Ithaka's rocky coast. The island's one **bus** runs north from Vathi, passing through the villages of Lefki, Stavros, Platrithiai, Frikes, and Kioni. The bus doubles as a school bus, and schedules are erratic. Check in town, but in the high-season, the bus usually runs three times per day (1hr., 350dr to Frikes). The bus route skirts both sides of the isthmus and offers superlative views of the strait of Ithaka and Cephalonia on the west and of the coastline on the east. Check the times of return buses before setting out; taxis from Kioni to Vathi cost roughly 4500dr.

Stavros, the highest point on the island might also merit a visit. The schoolmaster's wife has a key to a small museum at the alleged site of **Odysseus' Palace,** recommended for fanatical Homerists; a small tip is expected. Homer described this site as the place from which three different waters could be seen. Still visible from this point are the Bays of Frikes, Aphales, and Polis. Also worthy of a visit is the **monastery** at Kathara, on the highest mountain in Ithaka. To get there, take a taxi or moped to Anogi and follow the signs.

Ithaka's beaches are beautiful, if a trifle hard to reach. **Daxa** is the closest to Vathi. According to legend, this is where Odysseus landed when he returned to Ithaka. From Vathi, follow the main road out of town with the water on your right. On the other side of Vathi, **Filiatro** is also a gorgeous beach. **Gidaki**, the island's best beach, is only accessible by boat.

CEPHALONIA ΚΕΦΑΛΛΟΝΙΑ

Scientists and explorers have dubbed Cephalonia the "Island of Peculiarities." Surprisingly diverse environments—sandy beaches, subterranean caves, rugged mountains, and shady forests—can be found around the island and are the legacy of powerful earthquakes. Colonialism has also left its varied mark. Over the years, Cephalonia has been part of the Roman, Byzantine, Venetian, and British Empires. In this century, Cephalonia has endured a troubled history. When the Germans invaded in 1943, 9000 Italian soldiers occupying the island mutinied and resisted their Nazi "allies" for seven days. Only 33 Italians survived. Ten years later, a disastrous earthquake forced the island to rebuild. Because of this, only Fiskardo, which was relatively undamaged, retains the pastel Neoclassical look associated with the Ionian Islands. Cephalonia is ideal for a week-long vacation that allows time to explore all the island's beauty. An inconvenient bus network and multiple ports will frustrate the budget traveler or island-hopper.

■ Argostoli

The capital of Cephalonia, Argostoli is a busy, noisy town whose palm tree-lined streets are regularly jammed with traffic. Argostoli hosts an international **singing festival** in late August. The city boasts all the hassle of a large transportation hub without a hub's convenience. Check bus schedules carefully or you might find yourself here for days.

ORIENTATION AND PRACTICAL INFORMATION

Tourist Office: (tel. 22 248, -466) At the port. Provides free maps and candid advice on accommodations, restaurants, and beaches in the area. Also has a list of rooms to let. Open Mon.-Fri. 8am-10pm.

Tourist Police: Check inside the regular **police station** (tel. 22 815 or 22 200) on I. Metaxa across from the port authority. The tourist police is open, but has irregular hours.

Banks: National Bank of Greece on Drakopoulou, two blocks up from the water. Has an **ATM** (Cirrus, MasterCard, and Visa) and offers currency exchange. Open Mon.-Thurs. 8am-2pm, Fri. 8am-1:30pm.

Flights: The **Olympic Airways** office occupies 7 R. Vergoti St. (tel. 28 808, -81). Flights to Athens at least once per day (14,100dr). Office open Mon.-Fri. 8am-3:30pm. Their airport office (tel. 41 511) is open daily, but hours vary.

Buses: The bus station is on the south end of the waterfront (open 7am-8pm; tel. 22 281). Buses head to: Skala (2 per day, 550dr); Poros (3 per day, 750dr); Fiskardo (2 per day, 1½hr., 850dr); Sami (3 per day, 450dr); Ag. Gerasimos (3 per day, 300dr); and Kourkoumelata (3 per day, 250dr). There are also buses that piggyback on the ferry to Athens (7:45am and 1:30pm). Buses to Argostoli meet the ferry arriving in Sami (1 per day, 450dr). Service is reduced on Sat. No service on Sun.

Ferries: Unlike most islands, Cephalonia has several ports for different destinations. Buses connect Argostoli to other ports. From **Sami,** boats sail to: Ithaka (daily 3:30pm, 1hr., 1350dr), Patras (daily 8:30am, 3100dr), and Astakos (daily 8:45am, 1950dr). This is also the place to catch boats to Brindisi and Bori. From **Argostoli** boats go to Killini on the mainland (daily 2:30pm, 2725dr), and several boats shuttle to nearby Lixouri.

Car Rental: Myrtos Rent-a-Car (tel. 24 230 or 25 023), on the waterfront. Starts at 12,500dr per day. Open 9am-1:30pm and 6-9pm.

Moped Rental: Sunbird (tel. 23 723) near the port authority on the water, rents mopeds 2000dr per day and bicycles 1000dr per day. Open 8:30am-2:30pm and 5:30-9:30pm.

International Bookstore: Petratos Bookstore (tel. 22 546) one block up from the water on Ithakis. Foreign newspapers and magazines. Open daily 8am-8pm.

Post Office: (tel. 23 173), two blocks up from the water on Kerkyras. Open Mon.-Fri. 7:30am-2pm. **Postal Code:** 28100.

OTE: At the corner of Rokov Vergoti and Georgiou Vergoti. Open Mon.-Sat. 7:30am-3:10pm, Sun. 8:30am-1:30pm.

Telephone Code: 0671.

ACCOMMODATIONS

Hotel Allegro (tel. 28 684), up from the waterfront on Andrea Choïda, has double beds, private baths, and a cute little boy who speaks impeccable English (singles 4000dr; doubles 5500dr). **Hotel Tourist** (tel. 23 034) has sparkling rooms with balconies and TVs. Official prices may be discounted as much as 50% (singles 10,000dr; doubles 20,000dr; breakfast included).

FOOD

Restaurants that line the water are expensive and of mediocre quality. They serve fish (2000-6000dr) and *moussaka* (200dr) along with some Italian fare. **Igloo Cafe,** just off the waterfront on Andrea Choïda, serves economical sandwiches (500dr) and croissants (200dr). Another inexpensive option is to visit the exciting and well-organized farmers' market that takes over the waterfront near the bus station on Saturday mornings. Permanent fruit shops line the waterfront, 100m toward town from the bus station. **Mister Grillo** (tel. 23 702) is near the port authority. This restaurant offers plenty of vegetarian options including black beans in oil (600dr) and stuffed peppers (700dr).

SIGHTS

The town's main square is one block up from the water on Rokou Vergoti. The squat yellow building is Argostolis' **Archaeological Museum** (tel. 28 300; open Tues.-Fri. 8:30am-3pm, Sat.-Sun. 8:30am-1pm; admission 500dr). From Petratos Bookstore, go one block farther; you'll hit the square and the **Argostolian Archaeological Museum** (open Tues.-Sun. 8:30am-3:30pm; admission 400dr). From the museum, turn right onto R. Vergoti St. and continue two blocks to reach Corgialenios Library, which houses the **Historical and Folk Museum.** The museum is crammed with 19th-century household items. Argostoli's French coffee cups, English top hats, and antique dolls suggest a luxurious past. Best of all are the photographs of Argostoli during the last century, including shots of the damage from the devastating 1953 earthquake and ensuing reconstruction (tel. 28 835; open Mon.-Sat. 9am-2pm; admission 500dr).

■ Near Argostoli

The Venetian **Castle of St. George,** 9km southeast of Argostoli, rests on a hill over-looking the village of Travliata. Chug along the road to Skala and turn right when the road splits. **Buses** travel to the site (2 per day, 10min., 150dr). From the battlements, admire the panorama that once inspired Lord Byron (open Tues.-Sun. 8:30am-3pm; free). To swim at **Lassi,** one of the island's best sandy beaches, follow the road leading from the town to the airport. There are several options for exploring more of the island. Boats leave regularly for **Lixouri,** in the center of the west peninsula (every hr., 30min., 240dr). Once home to the satiric poet Lascaratos, Lixouri offers miles of practically tourist-free coastline. You can rent **mopeds** at several places in Lixouri; **buses** run to several smaller villages in the area.

A few beaches and interesting towns dot the island south of Argostoli. One of the best beaches is at **Ormos Lourda,** in the middle of the south coast; closer to Argostoli is **Platis Gialos** (7 buses per day, 30min., 150dr). Here visit one of Byron's adopted towns (though his house no longer exists) at **Metaxata,** or see **Kourkoumelata,** a village completely restored by a Greek tycoon after the 1953 earthquake. If you decide to stay, check out the comfortable **Hotel Kourkoumi** (tel. 41 645). Doubles with bath and breakfast are 6000dr. A multi-layered *tholos* tomb found in the village of **Dargoti** is thought to be Odysseus' grave, supporting the theory that Homer's Ithaka was really modern-day Cephalonia. **Poros,** on the southeast coast, is a modern coastal town with a beach; rooms to let are everywhere. Buses run from Argostoli (3 per day, 1½hr., 750dr).

On the night of August 15, the nearby village of **Omala** hosts a festival and a vigil in the saint's church. East of Argostoli is the monastery **Agios Gerasimos,** home of a monk's preserved corpse; the town goes wild on the saint's name days (Oct. 20 and Aug. 16). Contact the tourist office for more information. Omala also has an excellent **Archaeological Museum** (tel. 28 300; open daily 8:30am-3:30pm).

By far the best beach on the island is the pebble and sand beach at **Scala.** The town itself is prohibitively expensive (7000dr for plain singles), but the beach to the right of the rocks is heavenly. Three buses per day arrive from Argostoli; the latest returns at 5pm. If you must stay, ask at **Scalini Tours** for rooms, and catch a bite at the **Sun Rise Restaurant** (beef stew 850dr).

■ Sami

A small town on a harbor surrounded by lush green hills, Sami stays quiet during the day, offering a small ethereal pebble beach. By night the town waxes romantic to the glimmer of lighted ships in the harbor. The blue and white Hotel Kyma, two blocks from the ferry landing, points the way to Sami's main square, which you will hit if you follow the street from the hotel as it turns inland. There is no official tourist office, but the **police** (tel. (0674) 22 100; open 24hr.) may be able to answer your questions. **Sami Travel** (tel. (0674) 23 050) offers rooms, tickets to Italy, excursion tickets, and general information. It is located off Akti Posidonos St. (the one that runs along the port), at the end opposite the main square. The **Marketou Travel/Strintzis Line Office** (tel. (0674) 22 055 or 23 021), on the waterfront just to the left of the ferry landing in Sami, is also very helpful. You can exchange money at the **Commercial Bank of Greece** on Sami's waterfront (open Mon.-Thurs. 8am-2pm, Fri. 8am-1:30pm) or at most of the travel agencies. The **OTE** (open Mon.-Fri. 7:30am-3:10pm), is in the main square, as is the **post office (**open Mon.-Fri. 7:30am-2:30pm). **Postal code:** 28080.

Off-season lodgings in Sami cost 20-40% less. Try the **Hotel Kyma** in the town square. Many of the clean rooms offer spectacular views and cool breezes (tel. (0674) 22 064; singles 6000dr; doubles 10,000dr). The **Hotel Melissani,** several blocks back from the water on the left side of town as you face inland, offers lovely views of the harbor and surrounding hills (tel. (0674) 22 464; singles 15,000dr; breakfast included). **Hotel Ionian** in the main square across from the church offers rooms with a private bath (tel. 22 035; singles 5000dr; doubles 8000dr). The rooms above the **Riviera Restaurant** (tel. (0674) 22 777), on the waterfront, go quickly in the summer (doubles with bath 6000dr). **Karavomilos Beach Camping** (tel. (0674) 22 480) is set on top of the beach (look for a sign that says Hotel Kastro 250m), has a snack bar and small restaurant, and is clean and popular. The management also offers laundry services and a mini market (1450dr per person; 900dr per small tent; 1400dr per large tent; person with a sleeping bag 1500dr).

The underground caves of **Melissani** and **Drograti,** two sites near Sami, impress both troglodytes and surface-dwellers. Melissani, the more impressive of the two, can be reached by foot from Sami (30min.). Follow I. Metaxa and turn right at the sign for **Agia Efimia,** then follow the signs past the village of Karavomilos. At the lake, guides will show you around the two large caverns flooded with sparkling water, studded with stalactites, and squirming with eels. For best viewing, go when the sun is high (open 8am-8pm; admission 1100dr). To reach Drograti, 4km from Sami, head inland on the road to Argostoli and follow the signs (open until nightfall; admission 750dr). Just 10km north of Sami at the other end of the bay is the pretty harbor town of Ag. Efimia.

■ Around Cephalonia

Cliffs plunge into the sea along the coastal road north from Argostoli or Sami to Fiskardo. The pleasant beaches of **Agia Kyriaki** and **Myrtos** lie on this road. Signposts on the main road after the hamlet of Divarata advertise Myrtos, but swim cautiously there—the undertow can be powerful and sudden. Roughly 4km up the road are the fragrant gardens of **Assos,** joined by a narrow isthmus to an island with a Venetian **fortress.** A daily bus from Argostoli departs at 2pm, returning the next day at 6:45am (550dr). The 30-minute walk from the main road is challenging.

The road north ends at **Fiskardo,** the only town left undamaged by the 1953 earthquake and thus the only remaining example of 18th- and 19th-century Cephalonian architecture. Once called Panoramos, Fiskardo was magnanimously renamed after Robert Guiscard, a Norman, who died here in 1085 while attempting to conquer the town. A ruined church visible from the harbor is believed to predate Robert by some 800 years. Alongside the dilapidated old Venetian lighthouse, pine-sheltered campsites await. Rooms are expensive (doubles 7000-10,000dr), but the cheapest are on the road back to Argostoli. Here you may find singles as low as 4000dr. Try **Regina Rooms To Rent** near the bus stop. The **Panoramos** is Fiskardo's most accessible hotel (tel. 51 340; singles with bath 9000dr). Restaurants line the harbor and are fairly expensive. Fiskardo's beach is unbeatable, lying 500m out of town on the road back to Argostoli and offering flat rocks for sunbathing. In general Fiskardo is a bit intimidating for the budget traveler. One **bus** per day arrives from Sami (1hr., 650dr). Two buses arrive daily from Argostoli (1½hr., 850dr).

On August 15, an unusual and spooky festival in the village of **Markopoulo** in the southeast corner of the island celebrates the Assumption of the Blessed Virgin Mary. Celebrants hold an all-night church liturgy. According to local belief, during the service hundreds of small harmless snakes with black crosses on their heads appear and slither over the icons.

TURKEY TÜRKİYE

Cultural contradictions, as much as majestic landscapes and archaeological treasures, fascinate visitors to Turkey. This same land reared Homer, Midas, St. Paul, and Santa Claus. Today there are actually two Turkeys—one urban and cosmopolitan, the other rustic and parochial. It seems appropriate that Anatolia, the bridge between Europe and Asia, belongs to a secular state even though it contains the very first church in Christendom and hosts a largely Muslim population. The nude beaches, outrageous nightlife, and promiscuous natives and tourists alike baffle this conservative country's visitors. The country's heartland, however, remains virtually unaffected by tourism. All too many English-speaking residents shamelessly swindle tourists; the obliging folk in the country, on the other hand, rarely speak English but are nonetheless willing to help the occasional wayfarer. In the end, Turkey is among the world's ideal budget travel destinations.

Although the region of Eastern Turkey contains some of the most beautiful landscapes and sights in the country, single women and travelers who aren't fluent in Turkish may experience difficulties while traveling there. Moreover, the areas surrounding Diyarbakır and the border with Armenia are not safe for anyone to travel through. Sporadic fighting with Kurdish populations and strained relations with Armenia have resulted in pocketed war zones barring safe travel. Please keep these warnings in mind as you plan your trip through Turkey.

ESSENTIALS

■ Money

US$1 =165,370 Turkish Lira (TL)	100,000TL = US$0.60
CDN$1 = 118,672TL	100,000TL = CDN$0.84
UK£1 = 263,831TL	100,000TL = UK£0.38
IR£1 = 238,464TL	100,000TL = IR£0.42
AUS$1 = 122,903TL	100,000TL = AUS$0.81
NZ$1 = 105,903TL	100,000TL = NZ$0.94
SAR1 = 35,003TL	100,000TL = SAR2.86
1GRdr = 571TL	100,000TL = 175GRdr
C£1 = 303,371TL	100,000TL = C£0.33

All prices are quoted in U.S. dollars because inflation in Turkey tends to correspond roughly with the devaluation of the Turkish lira.

■ Once There

Government offices are open Monday-Friday 8:30am-12:30pm and 1:30-5:30pm and banks Monday-Friday 8:30am-noon and 1:30-5pm. **Food stores, bazaars,** and **pharmacies** have longer hours. During the summer, on the west and south coasts, government offices and other businesses close during the afternoons, but shops stay open until 10pm. **Museums** and **archaeological sites** in Turkey are open Tuesday-Sunday 9am-5pm. At all state-run museums, students with **ISIC** cards receive a 50% discount. Entrance to many museums is free with a **GO25** (FIYTO) youth card (see p. 9).

If you are in need of **medical care** in Turkey, an embassy or consulate can provide you with a list of English-speaking doctors, although they're common in most major hospitals. Istanbul has several foreign-run hospitals (see p. 392). Private hospitals generally provide a higher standard of care than public ones. Payment, with cash or a credit card, is expected at the time of treatment. For **emergency medical service** dial 112. For the **police,** dial 155. If your difficulties are not urgent, go to the nearest tourist office before trying the police; they can ease communication.

Be wary of English-speaking natives who approach you as friends. After befriending you, they'll offer to take you to a shop with "the best prices." Every time you spend a lira, your new best friend earns a commission (up to 50%). This scam is known as *hanut.* This also holds for people who approach you in bus stations offering accommodations. Have a hotel or *pansiyon* name in mind and tell the taxi driver that this is where you want to go. The taxi driver will more than likely be working on the same system and tell you that he knows of a better place. He may even say the place you want is full or has burned down. Stand firm.

Pensions that call themselves **aile** (family-style) try to maintain a wholesome atmosphere. Even if an establishment advertises 24-hour hot water, you may have to ask to have the hot water turned on in your room. Always carry toilet paper with you since many places don't have any; other **toiletries**—including condoms, sanitary pads, and usually tampons—are cheap and readily available, though less so in the eastern part of Turkey.

If you have Visa or MasterCard (Access or Eurocard), or even an internationally networked ATM card from your home bank, use **ATMs;** plentiful in Turkey, they will give you the best exchange rate. American Express cardholders can use Akbank ATMs; Pamukbank ATMs, among others, are connected to the Cirrus network. Remember to keep your currency exchange receipts, as some banks will not change lira back into dollars without a receipt.

■ Getting Around

Transport in Turkey can be both frustrating and time-consuming, but a little persistence will usually get you where you want to go. **Turkish Airlines** has direct flights once or twice weekly from Istanbul to Trabzon, Van, Diyarbakır, Erzurum, Izmir, and Ankara. Domestic flights average about US$80 one way, but passengers ages 12 to 24 may receive a discount. In some cities, an airport shuttle bus leaves from the downtown ticket office 30 to 90 minutes before flights (for an extra charge).

Frequent, modern, and cheap **buses** run between all sizeable cities. Many lines provide a 10% discount to ISIC-carrying students. You will need to go from booth to booth to piece together a complete schedule; one company may not divulge competitors' schedules. For long trips, try one of the more expensive bus lines. They usually offer larger seats, air-conditioning, a toilet, and tea for only about 50% more than ordinary companies. Reputable companies include Varan Tours, Ulusoy, Kamıl Koç, Pamukkale, and Çanakkale Seyahat. Try to buy a seat in advance, but keep in mind that changing your ticket can be difficult. In rural parts of Turkey, it is customary when catching buses simply to flag them down from the roadside without reserving a seat in advance. Try to spot the bus's destination sign in the front window. Drivers, who keep an eye out for passengers, stop only if they have an empty seat. A steward hops off to stow your baggage and then collects your fare.

Extensive **shared taxi (dolmuş)** service follows fixed routes between small towns or within large ones. These are usually vans or minibuses, though occasionally cars are in service as well (in Istanbul they are usually an expanded 1950 station wagon). They leave as soon as they fill up (*dolmuş* means stuffed), and are almost as cheap as municipal buses (which do not exist in some towns). Best of all, you can get on and off anywhere you like. Despite low fares, **trains** within Turkey are no bargain. They are slow and follow circuitous routes. First-class gets you a slightly more padded seat and more room, but most Turks travel second-class. Since couchettes are available, overnight train trips are preferable to overnight bus trips.

Turks drive on the right-hand side of the road. The speed limit is 50kph (31mph) in cities, 90kph (55mph) on the highways, and 130kph (80mph) on *oto yolu* (toll roads). Road signs in English make **driving** somewhat easier. Archaeological and historical sites are indicated by yellow signposts with black writing; village signs have

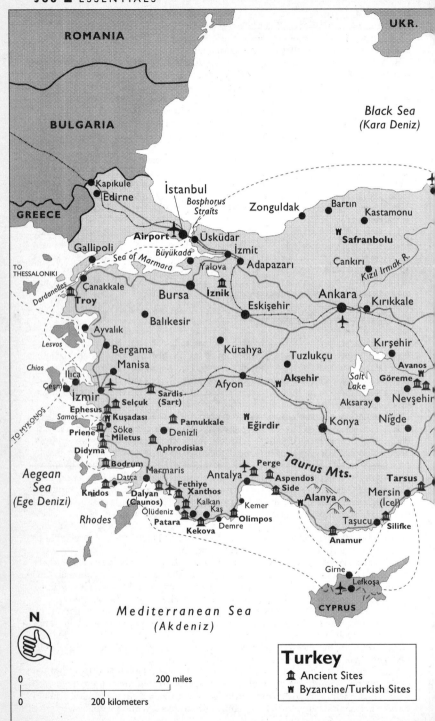

ROMANIA

UKR.

Black Sea
(Kara Deniz)

BULGARIA

GREECE

Kapıkule
Edirne

İstanbul
Bosphorus
Straits

Zonguldak

Bartın

Kastamonu

Airport

Üsküdar

Safranbolu

Gallipoli

Büyükada

İzmit

Çankırı

Kızıl Irmak R.

TO
THESSALONIKI

Sea of Marmara

Yalova

Adapazarı

Dardanelles

Çanakkale

Bursa

İznik

Eskişehir

Ankara

Kırıkkale

Troy

Balıkesir

Lesvos

Ayvalık

Kütahya

Tuzlukçu

Kırşehir

Bergama

Manisa

Afyon

Akşehir

Salt
Lake

Avanos

Göreme

Chios

Ilıca

Nevşehir

Çeşme

İzmir

Sardis
(Sart)

Aksaray

Niğde

Samos

TO MYKONOS

Ephesus

Selçuk

Pamukkale

Eğirdir

Konya

Kuşadası

Priene

Söke
Miletus

Denizli

Didyma

Aphrodisias

Aegean
Sea
(Ege Denizi)

Bodrum

Marmaris

Datça

Perge

Antalya

Taurus Mts.

Tarsus

Knidos

Dalyan
(Caunos)

Fethiye
Xanthos

Aspendos

Side

Mersin
(İcel)

Rhodes

Ölüdeniz

Patara

Kalkan
Kaş

Kemer

Alanya

Taşucu

Silifke

Kekova

Demre

Olimpos

Anamur

Mediterranean Sea
(Akdeniz)

Girne

Lefkoşa

CYPRUS

N

0   200 miles

0   200 kilometers

Turkey
🏛 Ancient Sites
♨ Byzantine/Turkish Sites

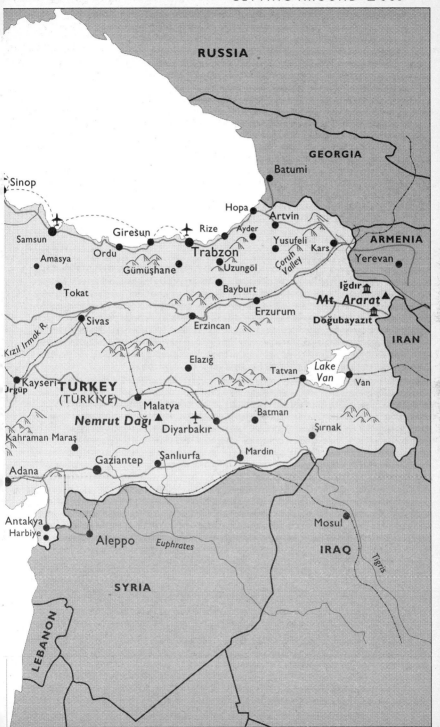

blue writing. Before taking your own car to Turkey, consider the likely effects poor roads will have on your vehicle. Official tourist literature warns against driving at night. If you get into an accident, you must file a report with the police. The **Turkish Touring and Automobile Association (TTOK)** can provide more information. Major offices include Maraşal Sevzi Çakmak Cad. 31/8 Beş Evler, Ankara (tel. (312) 222 8723); Antalya (tel. (242) 282 8140, -1, -2, or -3); and Istanbul (tel. (212) 231 4631).

As in Greece, in contests between pedestrians and motorists, Turkish drivers take the right of way. They rarely pause for pedestrians, so be alert when crossing the street. Those who decide to **hitchhike** in Turkey generally offer to pay half of what the trip would cost by bus. Hitchers in Turkey signal with a waving hand. *Let's Go* does not recommend hitchhiking as a means of transportation and urges readers to consider the risks inherent in hitching. Women should never hitch alone.

Ferries do not serve the west coast, but a **Turkish Maritime Lines (TML)** cruise ship sails between Istanbul and Izmir (1 per week, 21hr.). In summer, a weekly boat also connects Istanbul and Trabzon including intervening points on the Black Sea Coast. Istanbul has daily service to Bandırma. Larger ports have ship offices; otherwise, just get on the boat and find the purser.

TURKISH BUSES

Turkish drivers are notorious for recklessness. Anatolia's mountainous terrain and poorly maintained roads aggravate the problem. Even professional drivers for reputable bus lines are known for tearing over and around blind curves, dangerously risking passenger lives. Although road travel remains the most extensive, affordable, and modern way to get around Turkey, there are serious risks involved. You might consider safer options (such as by trains and ferries) despite the extra inconvenience. In Turkey, 22 people are killed in traffic accidents for every 100 million kilometers of vehicle travel; in the U.S., the comparable rate is 1.1 persons. (Source: *Association for Safe International Road Travel*)

For long trips there are always overnight buses; request a window seat in the middle of the bus, away from the driver's radio and behind the overhead window. Every so often a steward will come around spraying cologne; stretch out your palms to receive a squirt, then rub it over your face and neck. Every two to four hours or so, the bus will stop at a roadside rest complex where you can stretch your legs, use the toilets (10¢; paper extra), pray, and purchase overpriced cafeteria grub. The driver will announce the duration of the stop in Turkish before you get out, but it might vary by as much as 15 minutes either way, so keep an eye on your bus. Passengers who get left behind receive neither sympathy nor monetary compensation. If you get stranded, another bus going your way will probably visit the rest complex within a few hours; find the steward on board to buy a ticket for an empty seat. Nighttime travel is even more dangerous than daytime bus travel. Beware of tourist bureau advice to travel at night in order to maximize touring time.

STREET ADDRESSES

Since few Turkish cities follow a grid plan, maps can be difficult to use. To avoid confusion, a three-tiered addressing system is used. First comes the district, or *mahalle.* Then comes the nearest avenue *(cadde or bulvar).* Unless the address falls on this avenue, the side street off of it *(sokak, sokağı)* is specified next. Last comes the building's street number, prefixed by "No." A slash after the street number, or the word *kat,* introduces the number of the floor, if applicable. *Mahalle(si)* is abbreviated to **Mah.,** *Cadde(si)* to **Cad.,** *Bulvar(ı)* to **Blv.,** and *Sokak* (or *Sokağı)* to **Sok.** Thus, a complete street address in Turkey might look like *Çiğdem Mah. Atatürk Blv. Söğüt Sok. No. 6/2.* This book, which prints street numbers directly before the streets to which they refer, would list this address as *Çiğdem Mah. Atatürk Blv. 6/2 Söğüt Sok.* It means the second floor of 6 *Söğüt* St., off *Atatürk* Ave., in the *Çiğdem* District. Few addresses will contain all of these parts. In towns and rural areas, the street names—rarely used by residents—may not appear on maps. Here you will receive nonstandard addresses specifying the desired building's position relative to some visible nearby edifice (e.g., *Süleymaniye Camii Önü*, "in front of Süleyman's Mosque"). In these situations, the following prepositions will come in handy: **önü** (in front of), **arkası** (behind), **üstü** (on top of), **altı** (beneath), **yanı** (beside), and **karşı** (across from).

▦ **Keeping in Touch**

Mail to or from North America can take anywhere from one week to 17 days. Yellow signs make **post offices** (known as **PTT**) easily recognizable. PTT stands for Post Office, Telegraph, and Telephone. Large post offices in major urban areas are open Monday-Saturday 8am-midnight, Sunday 9am-7pm. Major PTTs in Istanbul are open 24 hours. Smaller post offices share the same hours as government offices (Mon.-Fri. 8:30am-12:30pm and 1:30-5:30pm). To send mail Poste Restante, write the person's name, *Postrestant,* and *Merkez Postanesi* (Main Post Office), followed by the town's name; use the postal code if you have it. Picking up letters sometimes costs a small fee. Check under both your first and last name, and have a form of identification handy. Specify *Uçak İle* (airmail) when requesting stamps, and write it on your mail (or ask for aerograms). Tell the vendor the mail's destination: *Avustralya, Kanada, Büyük Bretanya* (Great Britain), *İrlanda, Yeni Zelanda* (New Zealand), *Güney Afrika* (South Africa), or *Amerika*.

Turkey has a surprisingly good **phone** system. With few exceptions, even the smallest village is accessible by phone. The numbering system was revised in 1994, so beware of out-of-date listings. Local numbers now all have seven digits, and all area codes have three. (In small towns, all numbers will start with the same three digits, so you may occasionally be given a four-digit phone number.)

When making a **long-distance** call within Turkey, first dial 0, wait for the tone to change to a lower pitch, then dial the area code and the number. The number to dial for **information** is 118. To initiate an international call, first dial 0. When making a **direct international call,** dial 0, wait for the tone, then dial 0 again followed by the country code and the number, without pausing. There are four common phone tones: the dial tone, busy tone, and calling tone, as well as three short beeps followed by one repeated long beep, which means you need to dial again because your call is not going through properly. **Phone cards (telekart)** are very convenient and are available in denominations of 30, 60, or 100 units at PTTs. Some kiosks also sell them. Most phones take *telekart* while some take *jeton,* little coin-like tokens also available at PTTs. Regular coins are not accepted. *Telekart* are cheaper than *jeton* and easier to use, but villages often have a limited supply. Magnetic-card public phones are abundant in big cities and resort areas; they have on-screen instructions in English, French, and German. To make calling-card calls, dial the access number for your company (see **Calling There, Calling Home,** p. 45). Note that a card or *jeton* must be deposited, but the call is free. No credit will be deducted from your card, and your *jeton* will be returned to you. Calling card calls usually terminate after three minutes if you are calling from a public phone.

The cheapest way to make international **collect** (reverse-charge) calls is to contact an operator in the destination country. From *any* (working) payphone, dial: U.S. 0080012277, U.K. 00800441177, Canada 00800331177, Ireland 008003531177, or Australia 0800611177. Equally pleasant are *kontörlü telefon.* These are phones in the post office, and the officer tells you how much you owe at the end of your call. Note that there may be long lines for these phones, especially during the day. Try to use one late at night at one of the 24-hour PTTs. The same kind of phone is available at some hotels and restaurants, but it may cost you 20-500% more.

LIFE AND TIMES

■ History

ANCIENT TURKEY

Civilization has flourished in what is now Central Turkey since the 8th millennium BC, making it one of the world's oldest human-inhabited areas. This geographical region (known variously as "Anatolia" or "Asia Minor") has long mixed Asian and Western cultures. During the 3rd millennium BC (the Bronze Age), an early **Hittite** tribe settled in Central Anatolia. The Hittites developed techniques for forging iron weapons and spoke an Indo-European language considered by scholars to be closely related to modern European languages. Following the massive migration of Greek islanders at the end of the 2nd millennium BC, the Hittite empire collapsed. Cyrus extended the Persian empire along the coast of Asia Minor in the 6th century BC, using the region as a base for forays into Greece.

Two centuries later **Alexander the Great** invaded the region and routed the Persians. Great metropolises emerged after the 2nd century BC, when the coastline became the commercial and political core of the Roman province of Asia Minor. Following the creation of the Eastern Roman Empire in Byzantium (renamed Constantinople), Asia Minor prospered, becoming the center of Greek Orthodox culture, and overseeing a renewed empire stretching from the Balkans through Greece to the Levant and Egypt.

Turkic peoples began to migrate from Central Asia in the second half of the 8th century AD, moving west and establishing new states in eastern Iran, Afghanistan, and northern India. In the 11th century, **Seljuk Turks** from Inner Mongolia began the most significant Turkish migration, inhabiting the Muslim lands of Iran, Iraq, and Syria and the plains of central Anatolia. Although Seljuk power was momentarily eclipsed by Genghis Khan, the Seljuks were able to maintain their authority for a long period. The Byzantine ports along the coast began to wane in economic importance as land routes to Asia were monopolized by the various Seljuk fiefdoms in the interior. When Seljuk rule broke down in the 14th century, separate Turkish principalities picked up the pieces. A general named Osman claimed the northwest corner of Anatolia, and eventually united several fiefdoms to challenge and defeat the Greeks. From such origins grew one of the greatest empires in the history of civilization: the *Osmanlı,* or Ottoman Empire.

THE OTTOMAN EMPIRE

From the beginning of the 14th century to the middle of the 15th century, Ottoman rulers gradually gnawed away at the Byzantine Empire. In 1453, Constantinople fell to Mehmet the Conqueror. Renamed Istanbul, the city became the heart of a new and vigorous empire.

The Ottoman Empire incorporated Greece and Cyprus and penetrated into the Balkans as far as Belgrade. Under Selim I (1512-1520), Ottoman armies conquered Syria, Palestine, Egypt, and Arabia. In a feat of military and religious grandeur, the Ottoman sultan became guardian of the three holy places of Islam: Mecca, Medina, and Jerusalem. Under the sultans, governors (who were sometimes competing heirs to the sultanate) were sent to watch over the provinces. The sultans also granted **timars** (temporary, non-heritable land grants in return for military service) to maintain their power. In accordance with Islamic law, adherents to other monotheistic faiths paid the *cizye,* a special head tax, but were generally left to practice their faith as they wished. Greek Orthodox Christians, for example, fared far better under Muslim authority than they did under the crusading Franks. Many Jews, upon their expulsion from Spain in 1492, settled in parts of the empire and took up trade. Despite ruthless suppression of occasional rebellions, the early days of the Ottoman Empire brought relative peace and prosperity.

As Ottoman expansion slowed, the military tımar holders grew restless, missing the income they had gained from conquests. In order to reestablish military loyalty, Sultan Murad I created the first corps of **janissaries** (from *yeni çeri,* "new army") in the middle of the 14th century. Technically personal slaves of the Sultan, these (mostly Christian) sons of subjects were taken from the provinces and converted to Islam. Not all entered the military; some became *kulls,* the bureaucrats of the Ottoman state. Throughout much of the Empire's history, the Grand Vizier (Prime Minister) was a *kull,* as were many of the other high officers of the state, including the great architect Sinan.

Adherents to other monotheistic faiths paid a special head tax, but were generally left to practice their faith as they wished.

When **Süleyman** became Sultan (1520-66), the Ottoman Empire grew still further. He doubled the size of the empire, securing borders that stretched from the Balkans and Greece north to the Black Sea, west to Iraq, and south into Africa. Court administration was centralized, and literature, architecture, and decorative arts flourished. Süleyman's military conquests and garish lifestyle earned him the title of Magnificent among the Europeans. It was he who knocked at the gates of Vienna in 1529. He also earned the title of *Kanuni* (the Lawgiver) for combining the *şeriat* (Islamic jurisprudence) with the *ferman* (court decrees).

Süleyman's most influential wife, Roxelana, convinced the Sultan to name his less-than-magnificent son Selim as his successor. Selim turned virtually all matters of state over to the Grand Vizier. After his death (an intoxicated Selim had drowned in his tub in 1574), the palace was rife with infighting. Some scholars call this period the "rule of the women," as the wives of the potential sultans vied for power. Mothers ordered entire families strangled to ensure the throne for their own children. Kösem, a concubine of Sultan Murad (1603-17), scarcely survived banishment to Beyazıt upon the Sultan's untimely death, only to return triumphantly to the palace when her sons Murad IV and İbrahim became Sultans in rapid succession. Kösem even lived to see her grandson become Sultan, but in 1652 she was strangled to death by order of her own daughter-in-law.

Weakness at the top only encouraged abuses amongst the population. Religious and ethnic minorities, such as the Armenians, Kurds, Greeks, and Jews, faced increasing persecution. Following a period of devastating inflation caused by the Spanish discovery of American silver, the Ottoman administration weakened. After a series of disastrous military entanglements with Peter the Great and the Venetians, the Ottoman dynasty signed the Treaty of Karlowitz on January 26, 1699, consequently losing much of its Balkan territory.

END OF AN EMPIRE

Over the course of the next century, the Ottomans endured a series of setbacks at the hands of Europe and even its own provinces. In 1832, **Muhammad Ali,** nominally the Sultan's own governor of Egypt, invaded the Levant. He might have captured Istanbul itself had it not been for the intervention of the European powers. As the Ottoman government became increasingly weak militarily and more and more indebted to British and French bankers, the Empire became known as "the sick man of Europe." In the mid-19th century, after crushing conservative opposition, the Ottomans instituted a series of administrative reforms collectively known as the *tanzimat.* Besides providing *de jure* religious equality to all, the *tanzimat* attempted to regulate taxation and government conscription and to establish private ownership of land. Most peasants, however, believed that the government's reforms were merely covers for more tax-raising schemes. They therefore registered their land in the name of wealthy *shaykhs* and landowners instead of in their own names, thus allowing these elites to build up great estates.

Meanwhile, European powers concentrated on carving up and controlling Ottoman provinces. After assuming a "protectorate" over Cyprus in 1878, the British marched into the Nile to insure that bondholders who had invested in Egypt would be repaid. Meanwhile, as the self-proclaimed protectors of Greek Orthodox Christians everywhere, the Russians "liberated" Ottoman territory in the Crimea. Foreign missionary schools sprang up throughout the Ottoman Middle East. Arabs, ruled by Ottomans for more than five centuries, began to question Ottoman authority.

Although unrest in the early 1870s prompted the granting of an Ottoman constitution complete with elected parliament, Sultan Abdülhamid II (1876-1909) led a pan-Islamic counter-revolution and suspended all democratic reforms. The 1908 coup of the **"Young Turks,"** a secret Turkish nationalist organization which had burst from the officer corps, ended Abdülhamid's hold on power. Welcomed at first by most of the ethnic populations, the cadre of military officials who controlled the empire soon began to implement a strident plan of "Turkification." In accordance with Islamic law, the Ottomans had traditionally allowed minorities to open their own schools and keep their own languages and customs. But now the central government decreed that Turkish was to be the national language for non-Turkish-speaking Muslims and non-Muslims alike.

> On October 29, 1923, Mustafa Kemal, Atatürk, was elected the first president of the new Republic of Turkey.

The government of the empire sided with the Axis powers in WWI. As British officers led an Arab revolt against the Turks (a la Lawrence of Arabia), Turkish officials in the east began to "solve" their ethnic problems. A three-year period witnessed the death of more than 1½ million Armenian civilians after Armenian forces living in Turkey sided with the Russian army in an attempt to win their own independence. Officials in the German government expressed dismay with this development but did not interfere. The massacre of Armenians continues to be a cause of ethnic unrest in Turkey today.

THE TURKISH REPUBLIC

WWI proved to be the final demise of the Ottoman dynasty. Under the auspices of the League of Nations, Britain and France divided the Arab provinces after the Allied victory. Plans for the division of Anatolia were also drawn up, and Greece invaded in order to capture disputed territory. Such action was stifled, however, by the rise of **Mustafa Kemal,** an Ottoman general who was able to reorganize his army in time to defeat the Greeks. On October 29, 1923, Mustafa Kemal, dubbed **Atatürk** (Father of the Turks), was elected the first president of the new Republic of Turkey. Atatürk turned his back on Ottoman tradition. Equating modernization with rapid Westernization and secularization, Atatürk abolished the Caliphate, outlawed Muslim courts and the veiling of women, decreed that Turkish be written in Latin rather than Arabic script, and, for a time, ordered that the *adhan* (call to prayer) be recited in Turkish rather than classical Arabic. He also gave women the right to vote. These sweeping measures encountered strong resistance from the religious establishment.

After the rise of Mustafa Kemal, Turkey was determined to become a part of Europe. The **Republican People's Party** program of 1931 proclaimed the six principles of the modern Turkish state: republicanism, populism, nationalism, statism, secularism, and revolution. Changes were introduced to "re-educate" the public about Turkish achievements, and the government began a systematic campaign to purge foreign-derived words from the Turkish language. Eventually, Turkification triumphed over the competing ideals of Ottomanism and pan-Islamism.

Shortly before WWII, the increasingly autocratic Kemal died and was replaced by his associate İsmet İnönü. Though Nazi Germany's early successes resulted in a popular clamor to join the war on the side of Germany, the government remained neutral until the end of the war, when Turkey wisely joined the Allies. When the Soviets demanded that Turkey share control of the Bosphorus Straits and cede large pieces of eastern Anatolia to Soviet Georgia, the United States diverted military and economic aid to Turkey in the name of fighting communism. Today Turkey remains one of the largest recipients of U.S. aid.

WWII also led to the expansion of the Turkish military and its ability to play a role in Turkish politics. When a growing professional class demanded increased political participation, the **Democrat Party (DP)** broke off from the old **Kemalist Republican People's Party (RPP).** Throughout the 1950s, the government, dominated mostly by the DP, reduced censorship and expanded political rights. As the 1950s progressed, however, economic conditions deteriorated almost as fast as relations between the RPP and the DP. When the DP threatened to outlaw the RPP, unrest in the country peaked in student demonstrations and the army stepped in and took control.

After the eradication of the DP, the military's ruling National Unity Committee drafted a new constitution. Approved by voters in July 1961, the constitution established a bicameral parliament which jointly elects the president. Elections were held in October, and the army soon withdrew from politics. Many former DP members became influential in the new Justice Party (JP), which dominated elections after 1965. In 1970, after right-wing members of the JP split off and reconstituted the old Democratic Party, the army demanded the resignation of the government and again assumed *de facto* control.

RECENT YEARS

Following the coup in Cyprus which overthrew **President Makarios,** the Turkish army invaded Cyprus in July 1974, fearing that Cyprus would be annexed by Greece. Economic and arms embargoes soon followed and Turkey responded by closing foreign military installations. By the end of the 1970s, however, tensions decreased and most normal foreign relations resumed.

The military took power again in September 1980, when the government's control over the interior of the country declined precipitously. The military dissolved all opposition parties and tortured thousands of opposition leaders. By 1983, the military relinquished most of its hold on power and martial law ceased; elections that year brought the centrist **True Path Party** of **Turgut Özal** to power. Turkish assistance during the Gulf War against Iraq in 1991 proved economically debilitating and led to terrorist attacks against government installations and foreigners. But Özal's cooperation with the United States may well have led to a new international role for Turkey, which had lost its traditional strategic position at the end of the Cold War.

In May of 1993 the True Path Party voted **Tansu Çiller,** a woman, as its new leader. However progressive that victory may seem, the 1994 elections saw the emergence of Islamic fundamentalism as a political power at the state and local levels; fundamentalists captured the mayoral majorities of Ankara and Istanbul. In the wake of the Gulf War, **Kurdish separatists** stepped up their terrorist activity, prompting Çiller, in the spring of 1994, to turn the problem over to the military. Traditionally heavy-handed, the military began razing villages suspected of harboring rebels, and thousands of Kurdish villagers fled to the cities. In the spring of 1995, the Turkish military became determined to destroy the **Kurdistan Workers' Party (PKK),** a Kurdish party which they accused of financing terrorist activities through European drug trafficking. Thus, in an ironic turn of events, Turkey led a brief offensive into the power vacuum of northern Iraq, left by the departure of the U.S. forces after the Gulf War, in order to pursue Kurdish separatists. Strong threats of sanctions from the European Union (EU) may have contributed to this campaign's speedy conclusion.

As the European Community accelerated its drive toward unity, Turkey's role in the global economic arena stood undetermined. In 1987, Turkey applied for full membership, but was rejected in 1989 on the grounds that the completion of a previously defined European market was necessary before any expansion could be considered. Furthermore, the Commission of the European Communities noted Turkey's less than stellar human rights record, high rate of inflation, and control of Northern Cyprus as objections to granting Turkey membership. There is also a European fear that the number of Turks working in the rest of Europe will expand exponentially beyond the existing two million if visas are rendered unnecessary. In early 1995,

> **Turkey led a brief offensive into the power vacuum of northern Iraq to pursue Kurdish separatists.**

Turkey was finally accepted into the European Customs Union, on the condition that the Turkish parliament make hundreds of new laws and changes to the constitution by that October. Some of the changes have yet to be made. Meanwhile, Turkey has sought economic opportunity in the East, namely in the former Soviet Muslim republics of Kazakhstan, Tajikistan, and Uzbekistan.

In a surprising development in June 1996, Tansu Çiller formed a coalition government with **Necmettin Erbakan,** the fundamentalist Islam leader of the Welfare Party, some say in order to squelch an investigation of alleged corruption. Çiller had already formed a coalition government with **Mesut Yılmaz** (Motherland Party) after Erbakan won a majority of votes, but personality differences threatened the security of the nation, and both Çiller and Yılmaz resigned as Prime Minister. In the second election, after the collapse of the government, Erbakan won another majority of votes but was unable to take control without the support of another party. Meanwhile, Çiller became a target in a Welfare Party investigation into alleged corruption. After she formed her coalition with Erbakan, the investigation was dropped. It is unclear what the consequences of a fundamentalist Islamic leader will be in Turkey, but many nations, especially Israel (Turkey is Israel's only Middle Eastern ally), are worried. This recent shift of national politics is not so much a return to fundamental religious beliefs as it is a reaction to the growing disparity between the rich and poor populations of the country.

WHAT'S HAPPENING NOW

The military, which sees itself as the guardian of secularism, threatened to use force against any perceived religious threat. Under increasing pressure from Turkey's generals, Erbakan resigned as prime minister in June 1997 after just 11 months in power. By stepping down, Erbakan hoped to transfer all power to Çiller. But President Suleyman Demirel thwarted his plans by appointing Mesut Yılmaz as Çiller's partner in power. The new coalition of Yılmaz and Çiller brings together the political forces of Turkey's Left and Right, but still faces strong challenges as a minority coalition in parliament. At press time, the next elections were scheduled to be held in September or October 1997.

Erbakan's refusal to support the curtailment of religious education throughout Turkey initiated a feud with the military. Under Prime Minister Yılmaz, the Turkish parliament gave into the military's demands for less religious education. It passed a new law increasing compulsory secular education from five to eight years. Consequently, children cannot receive a religious education before the age of 14. In addition, the law phases out the junior high school sections of Islamic academies.

▒ Religion

About 95% of Turks are Muslim. Orthodox Christians of Greek, Armenian, and Syrian backgrounds, and Jews (mainly in Istanbul) compose the remaining population. Turkey does not have an official state religion, but every Turkish citizen's national identification card includes a space for it, filled out at birth by parents. While Atatürk set modern Turkey on a secular course, Islam continues to play a key role in the country's history and culture.

The Arabic word Islam means "submission." The most basic tenet of Islam is submission to God's will. Islam has its roots in revelations received from 610 to 622 AD by the prophet Muhammad, who was informed by the Angel Gabriel of his prophetic calling. These revelations are collected in the **Quran** and form the basis of Islamic belief. Muhammad is seen as the "seal of the prophets," the last of a chain of God's messengers which includes Jewish and Christian figures such as Abraham, Moses, and Jesus. The Quran incorporates many of the biblical traditions associated with all these prophets.

Staunchly monotheistic, Islam was met with ample opposition in 7th-century polytheist Arabia, leading to persecution in Muhammad's native city of Mecca. In 622, he

So You Want to Be a Dervish

Widely regarded as the "intellectuals" of mystical Islam, the whirling Dervishes wielded great political power from the Seljuk period until Atatürk dissolved the order in 1923. Their influence at court may partly have accounted for the Ottoman policy of religious toleration toward conquered peoples, especially in the Balkans and Eastern Europe. Atatürk reportedly found the Dervishes' monarchist and politically conservative beliefs to be inconsistent with the reforms he sought to implement. Not long after his death, the government ended the ban, and professional Dervishes are now free to whirl once a year during a week-long mid-December festival held in Konya (if that doesn't fit with your plans, you can also see genuine Dervish dances in Istanbul). The dances, in which the most adept Sufis (Islamic mystics) make as many as 60 revolutions per minute, are extraordinarily difficult to perform. Learning the dances involves gripping a partially buried spike with one's toes. One arm points down to Earth, the other upwards to Heaven, positioning the whirler as a symbolic channel unifying the energies from both.

and his followers fled to the nearby city of Medina, where he was welcomed as a mediator of a long-standing blood feud. This *Hijra* (emigration) marks the beginning of the Muslim community and of the Islamic (lunar) calendar. For the next eight years, Muhammad and his community defended themselves against raids and later battled the Meccans and neighboring nomadic tribes. In 630, Mecca surrendered to the Muslims, and numerous Meccans converted to the new faith. This established the pattern for *jihad* (struggle), referring first and foremost to the spiritual struggle against one's own desires, then to the struggle to make one's own Muslim community as righteous as possible, and lastly to the struggle against outsiders wishing to harm the Muslim community. Sadly, most Westerners have heard only of this last and least important aspect of *jihad.*

Islam continued to grow after the Prophet's death, as the four Rightly Guided Caliphs *(Rashidun)* who succeeded Muhammad led wars against apostate nomadic tribes. Faith in Islam was the strength of the Arab armies, which defeated the once mighty Persian empire by the year 640. The fourth Caliph, Muhammad's nephew and son-in-law Ali, was the catalyst for the major present-day split in the Muslim world. Ali slowly lost power and was murdered in 661. The *Shi'at Ali,* or Shi'ites, believe Ali to be the only legitimate successor to Muhammad, thus separating themselves from Sunni Muslims. Contrary to popular Western perception, Shi'ism is not a creed of fanaticism, but is Islam with a sharp focus on divinely chosen leaders (or *Imams*) who are blood descendants of the Prophet through Ali and his wife, the Prophet's daughter Fatima. Most Turkish Muslims today are Sunni.

Muslims do not believe that Muhammad was divine, but merely a human messenger of God's word. His actions, however, are sanctified because God chose him to be the recipient of revelation; several verses of the Quran demand obedience to the Prophet. The stories and traditions surrounding the Prophet's life have been passed on as *sunna,* and those who follow the *sunna* in addition to the teachings of the Quran are considered to be especially devout Muslims. The term Sunni is derived from *sunna.* The primary source for *sunna* is the *hadith,* a written collection of sayings attributed to Muhammad. A *hadith* must go through a rigorous verification process before it is accepted as legitimate; the tale must be verified by several sources, preferably those who saw the action with their own eyes.

Any place where Muslims pray is a mosque or *masjid,* best translated as "place of prostration." The *imam* (leader of prayer, not to be confused with the Shi'ite leaders) gives a sermon on Friday. In many areas of the Islamic world men and women still pray in different sections of the mosque. **Prayer is not a spectator sport,** and visitors should stay away during times of worship and always wear modest dress. Men in shorts may be particularly frowned upon. Shoes are usually removed before entering a mosque, and women should cover their heads as a courtesy even if it is not required (technically, men as well as women are supposed to cover their heads in the presence of God).

PILLARS OF ISLAM

> *Allahu akbar. Ash-hadu an la ilaha illa Allah. Ashadu anna Muhammadan rasul Allah. (God is great. I swear that there is no god but Allah. I swear that Muhammad is God's messenger.)*

These words compose the first lines of the Islamic call to prayer *(adhan)*, which emanates five times a day from live or recorded *muezzins* perched atop their minarets. The first line glorifies God *(Allah)*. The next two lines form the *shahadah* (the testimony of faith), which is the first of the five pillars of Islam. It reflects the unity of God *(tawhid)*, and the special place of Muhammad as God's final Messenger. Any person who wishes to convert to Islam may do so by repeating these lines three times, thereby completing the first pillar of Islam and becoming a Muslim.

The second pillar is prayer *(salat)*, performed five times per day, preferably following the call of the *muezzin*. However, if someone is unable to pray at that exact moment, the prayer may be performed whenever possible before the next call to prayer. Prayers, preceded by ablutions, begin with a declaration of intent and consist of a set cycle of prostrations. No group or leader is necessary for prayers; they constitute a personal communication with God. The person praying must face Mecca as he or she does so. The word for Friday in Arabic means "the day of gathering," the day on which communal prayer is particularly encouraged.

The third pillar is alms *(zakat)*. Every Muslim who can afford to is required to give one third of his or her income to the poor.

Muslims believe that Muhammad received the Quran during the month of **Ramadan.** Fasting during this holy month is the fourth pillar of Islam. Between dawn and sunset, Muslims are not permitted to smoke, have sexual intercourse, or let any food or water pass their lips; exceptions are made for women who are pregnant or menstruating, people who are sick, and people who are traveling—they must make up the fast at a later date. Fasting is meant to teach Muslims to resist temptation and thereby control all their unchaste urges. In addition, by experiencing hunger, they are meant to better understand the plight of the poor, and thereby be more thankful for the food which Allah has provided them. Ramadan also inspires a sense of community among Muslims. They break the fast every evening and begin a night of feasting, visits to friends and relatives, and revelry. In places like Cairo, the city stays up until just before dawn. During the month, offices and businesses not catering to tourists may be closed or keep shorter hours.

The last pillar, required only once in a lifetime, is pilgrimage *(hajj)*. Only Muslims who are financially and physically able to are required to fulfil this pillar by journeying to **Mecca** and **Medina** during the last month of the Muslim calendar. Those who make the trip talk about it for the rest of their lives. While *hajj* is essentially a re-creation of the path of the Prophet Muhammad, its effects are to unite Muslims and to stress the equal status of all people who submit to the will of *Allah*, regardless of gender, degree of wealth, race, or nationality. All pilgrims, from Gulf princes to Cairo street-sweepers, must wrap themselves in white cloth and perform the same rituals. If you are traveling during *hajj*, you may experience delays and general pandemonium in airports.

> **During Ramadan, between dawn and sunset, Muslims are not permitted to smoke or let any food or water pass their lips.**

As with any religion, degrees of interpretation and observance produce a wide range of practices. For more information, try *An Introduction to Islam* by Frederick Denny, *Islam: The Straight Path* by John Esposito, or *Ideals and Realities of Islam* by Seyyed H. Nasr. A sampling of Islamic texts can be found in Kenneth Cragg and Marston Speight's *Islam from Within*. If you feel inspired enough to study the Quran, read Muhammad Pickthall's translation, *The Meaning of the Glorious Koran*.

■ Architecture and Art

Turkey is an art and culture aficionado's dreamland. The waves of civilization that have swept across Anatolia have left a magnificent legacy of unique architecture, literature, and decorative arts.

ARCHITECTURE

Sultan Süleyman introduced unprecedented imperial patronage of the arts in Ottoman times. Under his rule alone (1520-1566), over 80 major mosques and hundreds of other buildings were constructed. Many of these mosques contain the remains of former sultans. **Divan Yolu,** Istanbul's processional avenue, boasts a spectacular collection of these structural wonders. The master **Sinan** served Suleyman and his sons as Chief Court Architect from 1538 to 1588, during which time he created a unified style for all of Istanbul and for much of the empire. Trained first as a carpenter and then as an elite soldier who marched the length of the Empire, Sinan forged an architecture influenced by early Islamic and Byzantine styles, but conforming to neither.

LITERATURE

To be Ottoman was, for many centuries, to be part of a palace culture that evolved separately from the cultures of the Sultans' subjects. Ottoman culture was designed to provide a common experience for a ruling class chosen from disparate ethnic, linguistic, and religious backgrounds. Perhaps the most obvious sign of this cultural heterogeneity was the use of the Ottoman Turkish language—an ornate combination of Persian, Turkish, and Arabic. Ottoman was the language of choice both for the administration and for literature. The creation of modern Turkish in the 1920s has resulted in the loss of the Ottoman administration's literary traditions to all but specialists. Modern Turkish literature looks back not to the early modern period, as is so often the case in Western traditions, but to earlier writings of Türkmen poets such as Celaleddin Rumi and Yunus Emre. Their verses survived the Ottoman centuries relatively unscathed and the Turkish used by these poets remains intelligible to a speaker of modern Turkish in a way that Ottoman is not. The *türkü* (modern Turkish folk song), for example, uses language and form that would be familiar to these late medieval poets.

The poems and songs of the frontier were often vivid portrayals of utopian societies. *The Book of Dede Korkut,* a collection of stories set in the age of the Oghuz Turks, represents this tradition, providing the English-reader with a good introduction to an important genre in Ottoman literature. Many of these works were rediscovered during the 19th century. The propagation of the tales of Nasreddin Hoca was part of this renewed interest in folk literature. Hoca was an amiable, anti-authoritarian, religious man whose exploits are known to every Turkish schoolchild.

Satire also has been an important element in Turkish literature. An early representative of modern Turkish writing, Namık Kemal is famous for his satire of the Ottoman Empire's shortcomings. Hikmet's critical poetry brought him both literary fame and exile, a common fate for writers who held political views unacceptable to the government. Aziz Nesin, a fervent republican and free speech advocate, is another writer who has expressed critical views. Some of his work is available in English. Perhaps the best known Turkish author is **Yaşar Kemal.** Nominated several times for the Noble Prize for Literature, his work has been consistently critical of Turkish society and government. As a result, the government recently charged Kemal with anti-Turkish activities. His most famous novel, *Memed, My Hawk,* is available in English. Orhan Pamuk is another talented and popular Turkish writer; his *White Castle* and *Black Book* are both easy to obtain and highly acclaimed.

DECORATIVE AND PERFORMANCE ARTS

Though the Quran discourages the artistic portrayal of living beings, nature motifs dominate Ottoman decorative arts. While standard arabesques inherited from earlier

Islamic art are common, court workshops developed distinctly Ottoman styles. The naturalistic styles include flowers and animals, while the *saz* (reed) style, thought to have been inspired by Chinese sketches on porcelain, features long, self-piercing leaves wound around abstract lotus blossoms. Similar but unrelated is the *rumi* style, which originated in Iran and features split leaves.

Music, dance, and theater have become more institutionalized in the past 150 years. Turkish music runs the gamut from *halk müziği* (folk music) to *özgün* (protest music) to *arabesk* and *taverna* (popular music). In 1971, concern over the integrity of Turkish culture prompted the government to establish the Ministry of Culture to ensure the propagation of "acceptable" Turkish art. The last decade has also seen the arrival of Turkish pop. Similar to the American music scene of the 1980s, new artists are popping up in every corner of Turkey. Today, several international arts and music festivals bring performers from all over the world to Ephesus, Istanbul, and other Turkish cities while the handicrafts of Turkish culture (carpets, meerschaum pipes, knit stockings, and elaborately inlaid wood) continue to be prized.

■ Language

Umm...

We've all heard the famous stories about foreign hosts who bungle their attempts to ingratiate themselves with English-speaking travelers abroad. Guests are cheerfully invited to take advantage of the washerwoman and cordially asked not to have children at the bar. An English-speaker who is a little shaky on her Turkish may experience the same kind of amusement when her hosts begin counting with *bir* (one), the very substance that may cause her to lose her *ability* to count later that evening. On the other hand, when it's her turn to speak, she may unfortunately miss the significance of the guffaws that her repeated *um*s elicit. On the lips of a Turk, this oft-repeated English stammer has a more *private* significance. The more fluent and modest speaker, knowing better, will only discuss her *am* with her gynecologist.

Once thought to be related to Finnish, Hungarian, and Mongolian, Turkish today is recognized as belonging to a distinct Turkic language group. This group includes languages spoken from Germany to China, including Azerbaijani, Kazakh, Khirgiz, Uyghur, and Uzbek. In his 1928 effort to forge a secular Turkish identity, Atatürk ordered the language written in the Roman alphabet rather than the Arabic script. Furthermore, Atatürk purged Turkish of many of its Arabic and Persian borrowings. While these words continue to be replaced by new Turkish ones, this linguistic cleansing is not absolute; Islamic terminology notwithstanding, common Arabic and Persian words such as *merhaba* (hello) remain.

Visitors with little or no experience with Turkish should not be intimidated. Pronunciation is entirely phonetic: each letter of the alphabet represents a single sound. There are only six new letters to learn: ş (sh), ç (ch), ğ (silent), ı, ö, and ü, two of which are already familiar to those who speak German. Moreover, grammatical gender does not exist, and Turkish case endings are so regular that one can count the exceptions on one's fingers (for pronunciations and a brief glossary, see p. 599).

English is widely spoken wherever tourism is big business—mainly in the major coastal resorts. In the rest of Anatolia, only university students tend to know English. It is a good idea to buy a phrasebook, such as the *Penguin Turkish Phrasebook* or *Harrap's Turkish Phrasebook*.

BODY VIBES

In Turkey, body language often matters as much as the spoken word. When a Turk raises his chin and clicks his tongue, he means *hayır* (no); sometimes a shutting or uplifting of the eyes accompanies this motion. Shaking your head sideways means *anlamadım* (I don't understand). More intuitively, *evet* (yes) may be abbreviated by a sharp downward nod. If a Turk waves a hand up and down at you, palm toward the ground, she is signaling you to come, not bidding you farewell. In Turkey the idle habit of snapping the fingers of one hand and then slapping the top of the other fist is considered obscene.

▓ Leisure

Many popular Turkish pastimes still take place in all-male enclaves. A favorite is visiting the local *kıraathane* (coffeehouse), where customers sip coffee or tea over games of *tavala* (backgammon). Another popular game is *OKEY,* which is basically the same as gin rummy played with tiles instead of cards. In Istanbul, you may still find men smoking *nargile* (hookahs). If you decide to purchase a *nargile* as a souvenir, take precautions to make sure customs officials do not mistake it for a bong. Traditional spectator sports include *yağh güres* (grease wrestling), *cirit oyunu* (tossing javelins at competitors on horseback), and *deve güresi* (camel wrestling). These are mainly regional and not as popular as the ubiquitous game of soccer. Virtually every man, woman, and child has a favorite *futbol* team, and games are notorious for getting out of control.

THE TURKISH BATH

It is worth your while to visit a *hamam* (Turkish bath) at least once while in Turkey. But just as a caution, some Turkish hamams are also gay pick-up joints, so you may want to be selective in the ones you choose to frequent. Also, many of the cheaper ones are breeding grounds for bacterial diseases. It is a good idea to check out the place before stripping down to your birthday suit. Because of the Islamic emphasis on cleanliness (pious Muslims perform ablutions before each of the day's five prayers), the baths have been a customary part of daily life since medieval times. Men and women use separate bath houses, or the same place on different days. Enter the bath house, deposit your clothes in a cubicle, don the provided *peştemal* (towel), and proceed to the sauna-like *göbek taşı* (large heated stone). Here, an attendant will give you a rub-down. Following the massage, you can bathe yourself or be bathed. Bring your own shampoo, soap, and towel, or pay to use theirs, and take care not to douse your neighbors since they might have just finished a ritual cleansing. The *kese* (abrasive mitt) will strip you of excess skin cells. Men should never drop their *peştemal;* cleaning one's lower half is therefore tricky, but not impossible.

▓ Food and Drink

It may come as a surprise that such popular Middle Eastern foods as hummus, falafel, and baba ghanoush are practically unknown in Turkey. Like other cuisine from the Balkans to the Persian Gulf, contemporary Turkish cuisine finds its roots in Ottoman cooking, which draws from the nomadic traditions of the Central Asian tribes and the many civilizations that swept through Asia Minor. An Assyrian cookbook found during recent excavations showed that similar dishes have been served for thousands of years. *Kebap* (kebab), the most famous of these dishes, exemplifies today's simple and hearty Turkish cuisine. Turkey still produces a food surplus and is one of the few places left in the Mediterranean where eating cheaply still entitles one to sample a great variety of dishes.

HOW IT'S DONE

In many *lokantalar* (restaurants), guests are shown into the back kitchen and encouraged to order by pointing. The kitchen probably will not display such staples as shepherd's salad, lentil soup, rice pilaf, or yogurt; their availability is understood. Prices, where listed, are by the *porsiyon* (portion), and an excellent way to increase variety while saving money is to order *yarım* (half) or *çeyrek* (quarter) portions for that fraction of the price. In this way, for example, one can cheaply and guiltlessly

---

But Aren't There Any Bagels?

Hotels often overcharge for traditional Turkish breakfasts, which are heavier than Continental breakfasts but lighter than American ones. They consist of tea or coffee, *ekmek* (bread from a fresh oval loaf), *peynir* (cheese), *tereyağ* (butter), and *reçel* (preserves) or *bal* (honey). Sometimes fresh *kavun* (melon) or a *yumurta* (hard-boiled egg) is included as well. Or you can purchase your breakfast *a la carte* from a pastry shop or open-air market. But Turks don't frequent pastry shops to feast on *baklava* or *kadayıf* for breakfast. *Börek,* a flaky layered pie filled with cheese or mincemeat, has the honor of satisfying Turks' early-morning hunger. Ubiquitous street vendors hawk *simit* (sesame-coated bread rings 10-25¢), which you may think of as the Turkish equivalent of a bagel.

---

sample the wide variety of *baklava* in a Turkish *pastane* (pastry shop). The same tip applies to street vendors of *döner kebap* (gyros) who tend to be stingy with the meat in thick pocket-bread sandwiches but give more than double the meat for double the price. Usually you can't bargain in restaurants, except when ordering fish, because prices are fixed by municipalities. Restaurant food is the notable exception to the rule that the tourist in Turkey should bargain for everything he buys.

When choosing an authentic, out-of-the-way *lokanta,* watch for eateries with cloudy water glasses on the tables. Successive local patrons of such establishments reuse these glasses without washing them; all they do is wipe off the rims with the colored sheets of paper provided. Although such places may serve safe and particularly cheap food, they probably will not have bottled spring water on hand. Moreover, restaurants that do serve bottled water tend to overprice it. Consequently, tourists who prefer water to soft drinks at meals should buy bottled spring water cheaply at a corner grocery store and bring it along into restaurants.

WHAT'S IN IT

An astonishing variety of simple meat dishes forms the heart of Turkish cuisine. Foremost among them, *kebap* means any food broiled or roasted in small pieces. Usually involving lamb or chicken, *kebap* cooking ranges from *şiş* (skewer) or *döner* (spit) broiling, to oven roasting. The result may be served on a plate or as a pocket-bread sandwich, and regional seasonings add personality. *Adana kebap* and *Urfa kebap* are spicy, the former as meatballs and the latter as stew. Originally from Bursa, the popular *İskender kebap* consists of *döner kebap* lamb strips on a mushy bed of yogurt-soaked bread pieces, topped with a tangy tomato sauce. *Kağıt* (paper) *kebap* describes a mixture of lamb and vegetables wrapped and cooked in paper, while *orman* (forest) *kebap* is a mutton and vegetable stew. Other variations on meat stew include *patlıcan kebap* (eggplant stew), *tas kebapı* (goulash), *güveç* (casserole), and *türlü* (generic, occasionally vegetarian stew). After *kebap,* the most pervasive meat form is the medallion-sized, grilled hamburger patty (*köfte*). Frequently mistranslated as "meatballs," these patties receive embellishments like embedded pine nuts (*içli köfte*). They are either skewered and roasted or served in a tomato broth with potatoes and vegetables. Rarer forms of meat include *bonfile* (sirloin steak), *pirzola* (lamb chop), and *pastırma* (pastrami-like smoked or sun-dried beef). For the brave there are even *kokoreç,* grilled intestines with spices. *Et* is the generic word for meat, while lamb is *kuzu,* beef *sığır eti,* and veal *dana eti.* Chicken, usually known as *tavuk,* becomes *piliç* when roasted.

Alcohol, though widely available, is frowned upon in the more conservative parts of the country. Restaurants that post *içkisiz* in their windows have none, while those with *içkili* are taking special pains to announce alcohol's availability. *Bira* (beer) is popular: *Efes Pilsen* and *Tüborg* are the leading brands. The best domestic white wines are *Çankaya, Villa Doluca,* and *Kavaklıdere.* The best red wines are *Yakut* and *Kavaklıdere.* Ice-cold *rakı,* an anise seed liquor with the taste of licorice, is Turkey's national drink. Customarily mixed in equal parts with water, which clouds it, *rakı* has acquired the name "lion's milk." It is similar to Greek *ouzo,* but even stronger. Istanbul's local specialty is *balyoz* (sledge hammer, wrecking ball). Demolition is the appropriate concept here: *balyoz* consists of *rakı,* whiskey, vodka, and gin mixed with orange juice.

There's an endless array of sweet things: *baklava,* a flaky pastry jammed with nuts and soaked in honey; *kadayıf,* a shredded-wheat dough filled with nuts and sugar; and *helva,* a crumbly sesame and honey loaf. There's also *lokum* (Turkish Delight), and *acıbadem kurabiyesi* or *badem ezmesi* (Turkish marzipan). Most restaurants serve some sort of fresh fruit or melon. *Tavuk göğsü* (chicken pudding), *sütlaç* (rice pudding), and *aşure* (fruit pudding) are all excellent. *Künefe* is a cheese dessert served hot.

Istanbul

Welcome to the only city in the world that stands on two continents: Istanbul, the home of some of the most splendid legacies of the Roman, Byzantine, and Ottoman Empires. Visitors to Istanbul will find a curious and irresistible harmony of architecture, art, culture, entertainment, and people. Opulent Ottoman architecture, built on an enormous scale, overlooks tiny, winding streets. Thousands of mosques sound the call to prayer five times daily (starting at 4:30am) as crowded, dusty markets filled with street merchants and peddlers sell gold, spices, aphrodisiacs, and more. Museums contain astonishing treasures: the hand of John the Baptist and the hair and mantle of the prophet Muhammad, as well as assorted treasures of art, jewelry, and gold.

■ History

The traces of the first known settlements in the Istanbul area date back to the paleolithic age. **Mycenaeans** settled the site of modern Istanbul around the 13th century BC. Two hundred years later, settlers had established various fishing villages here, one of which occupied the exact site of the **Topkapı Palace.** It was not until the **Megarian** colonists from Greece landed on the Asian shore of the Bosphorus around 700 BC, however, that the city's known history is recorded.

Later, the first stirrings of the **Byzantine Empire** emerged from the region. In the 7th century BC **Byzas** (Byzas... Byzantium... Are you beginning to see the connection?) consulted the "infallible" Oracle at Delphi, who told him his colonial excursion must settle "opposite the Land of the Blind." As Byzas sailed the Bosphorus, he spotted the Megarian settlement on the Asian shore at Chalcedon (now Kadıköy, one of the centers of Asian Istanbul). A quick turn to the left, though, and they knew where their new colony would lie. Overcome by the glory of the harbor of the Golden Horn on the European shore, they reasoned that the people at Chalcedon must have been blind to have ignored this site. Byzas and his crew settled here in 667 BC, and Byzas' sister Ramona gave the city its first name in his honor: **Byzantium.**

Infighting within the Roman Empire at the beginning of the 4th century AD determined the city's fate for the next millennium. The abdication of Diocletian in 305 caused a power struggle between **Constantine,** Emperor of the West, and his rival **Licinius** in the East. Constantine pursued his nemesis to the city (then called Augusta Antonina) and across the Bosphorus to Chrysopolis (Üsküdar), where he defeated Licinius in 324. Constantine, consolidating his power, declared Byzantium the "New Rome" and capital of his empire in 330. Following the emperor's inauguration, the city came to be known as **Constantinople.**

Constantine's rise to power spurred the spread of Christianity. His influence is evident in the edicts of the first and second Theodosiuses, who established Christianity as the state religion (in 380) and later forbade pagan practices throughout the Empire (435). During the 5th century, **Theodosius II** supervised the construction of several significant edifices including a new, fortified set of walls around the city, as well as **Aya Sophia** (St. Sofia, or the Church of the Holy Wisdom).

The region's pagan culture was dealt a crippling blow when in 529 when the emperor **Justinian** mandated the closing of all schools of pagan philosophy, including Platonic academies in Athens. A 532 insurrection (the **Nika Revolt**) nearly overthrew the government, but just as Justinian was on the verge of abdicating and fleeing, his wife convinced him that it was far nobler to stay and fight. Five days of bloodshed followed. Although victorious, Justinian faced a city in ruin. He eventually restored the city to twice its former majesty, but frequent warring, a horrible plague, and hefty taxes ultimately devastated the population. When **Heraclius** gained power, the entire empire was in shambles.

Heraclius set out to restore the city's splendor in 610. His success marked the coming of the **Byzantine** era. Under Heraclius' leadership the empire expanded into

Armenia, Syria, Egypt, Palestine, and Mesopotamia. **Basil II,** who reigned from 976 to 1025, presided over a renaissance for the empire and after years of Arab and Bulgar sieges. These victories earned Basil the moniker "Bulgaroctonus" (Bulgar-slayer). To celebrate his achievement, Basil blinded all but 10 of 10,000 survivors. The Bulgars never again saw the need to challenge Basil.

Following Basil's death in 1025 the city faced new challenges. The **Fourth Crusade** in 1204 resulted in yet another devastation of the city. The Crusaders, attacking from the sea walls in the Golden Horn, plundered the city and occupied it for 60 years. Venice was the lucky recipient of much of the pillaged art, and subsequently, the Latin West began to take a fresh interest in Greek civilization. Following Latin rule, the Empire was further debilitated by internal crises of leadership and skirmishes with the Ottoman Turks, who were steadily making territorial gains. Byzantine decline was paired with the rise of a new power, the **Ottoman Empire,** in western Asia Minor at the beginning of the 14th century.

By 1451, when **Mehmet II,** known as "Fatih," or "the Conqueror," came to lead the Ottomans, the Byzantine emperor controlled little besides the coveted capital city; Anatolia and most of the Balkans were already in Ottoman hands. Mehmet immediately began to orchestrate a siege of the city. Sparing no expense, his forces finished work on two fortresses on the Bosphorus in 1452 in anticipation of the conquest. Rumeli Hisarı and Anadolu Hisarı (the Castles of Europe and Asia) stood on opposite sides of the Bosphorus and enabled the Ottomans to control the strait. The Byzantine emperor tried to block the Golden Horn but could not foil Mehmet, who gathered all his boats at a cove and had them transported by slides to the other end of the Golden Horn at night. For his final bombardment of the Theodosian city walls, Mehmet insisted on purchasing the largest cannon yet invented.

The city fell to the Ottomans on May 29, 1453. Many believe that the prophet Muhammad foretold that a commander who bore his name would one day conquer the city, and Mehmet (Turkish for Muhammad) thus secured himself a place in heaven with his victory. The Sultan Mehmet then took to rebuilding and repopulating the city, transforming Istanbul into the exalted administrative, cultural, and commercial center of his empire. The Ottoman Empire witnessed the development of this city into an architectural treasury, best known for its collection of imperial mosques. With the expansion of the Ottoman Empire to Eastern Europe, the Middle East, and North Africa, the capital became one of the most cosmopolitan in the world. By the 19th century, however, the city's golden age had long passed. After WWI, Istanbul was occupied by Western powers.

Despite Istanbul's pivotal past, it was Ankara that served as the base for **Atatürk's** campaign for Turkish independence. Atatürk felt the former capital was linked to too many imperial memories and was too hard to defend from attack by gunboats. On October 29, 1923, Ankara was officially declared capital of the nascent Turkish Republic. Atatürk's modernization initiatives changed the color of the city, but Istanbul still exudes a confidence that is the product of 16 centuries of world prominence. In 1937, **Henri Prost** prepared a new city plan for Istanbul which has deeply influenced its recent development. Between 1960 and today Istanbul's population has increased fifteenfold—from 1.5 million to over 15 million inhabitants in 1997.

▓ Orientation

Waterways divide Istanbul into three sections. The **Bosphorus Strait** (Boğaziçi) separates Asia from Europe. The Turks call the western, European side of Istanbul **Aurupa** and the eastern, Asian side **Asya.** The area south of the **Golden Horn** is known as **Haliç.** Most directions in Istanbul are further specified by city precinct or district (i.e. Kadiköy, Taksım, or Fatıh).

The Asian side is mainly residential, while most of the historical sites, markets, mosques, and museums are situated on the south bank of the Golden Horn (Haliç), an estuary which splits the European half of the city. The modern north bank contains **İstiklâl Caddesi,** the main downtown shopping street, and **Cumhuriyet Caddesi,**

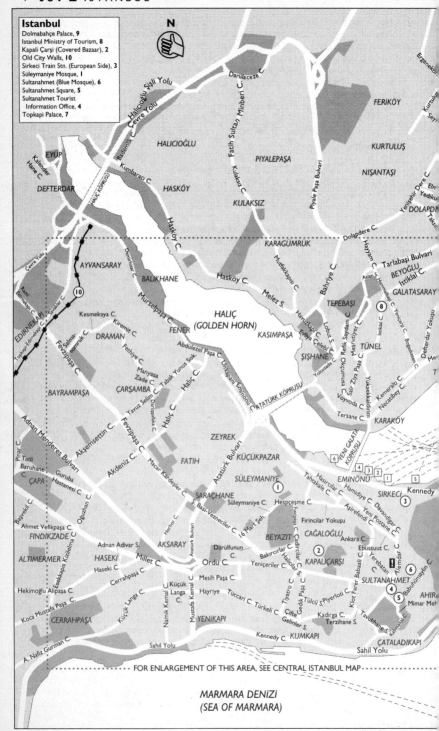

Istanbul

Dolmabahçe Palace, 9
Istanbul Ministry of Tourism, 8
Kapali Çarşi (Covered Bazaar), 2
Old City Walls, 10
Sirkeci Train Stn. (European Side), 3
Süleymaniye Mosque, 1
Sultanahmet (Blue Mosque), 6
Sultanahmet Square, 5
Sultanahmet Tourist
   Information Office, 4
Topkapi Palace, 7

N

FOR ENLARGEMENT OF THIS AREA, SEE CENTRAL ISTANBUL MAP

MARMARA DENIZI
(SEA OF MARMARA)

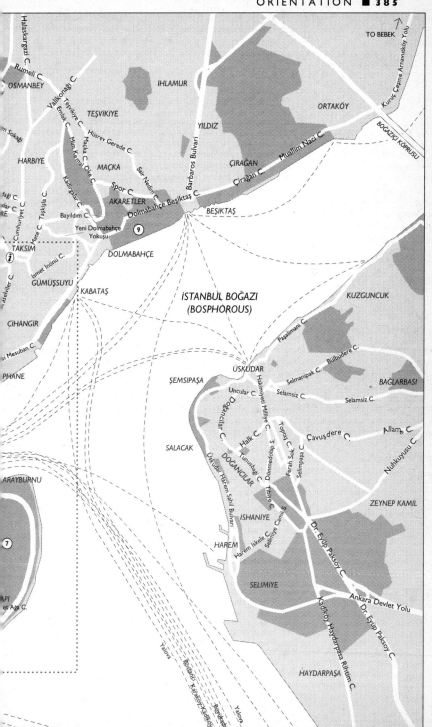

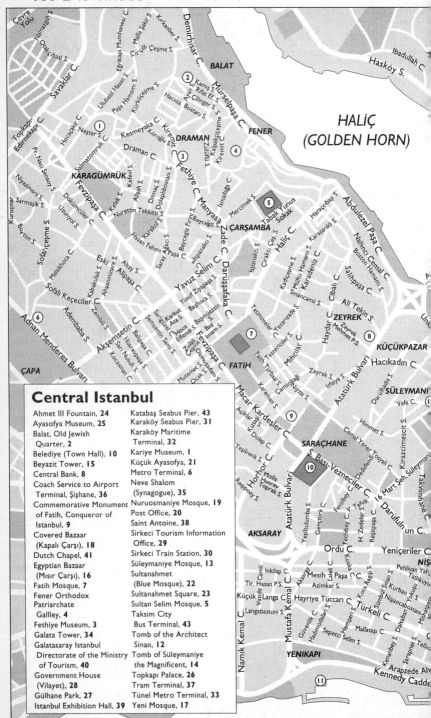

HALİÇ
(GOLDEN HORN)

Central Istanbul

Ahmet III Fountain, **24**
Ayasofya Museum, **25**
Balat, Old Jewish
  Quarter, **2**
Belediye (Town Hall), **10**
Beyazit Tower, **15**
Central Bank, **8**
Coach Service to Airport
  Terminal, Şişhane, **36**
Commemorative Monument
  of Fatih, Conqueror of
  Istanbul, **9**
Covered Bazaar
  (Kapalı Çarşı), **18**
Dutch Chapel, **41**
Egyptian Bazaar
  (Mısır Çarşı), **16**
Fatih Mosque, **7**
Fener Orthodox
  Patriarchate
  Gallley, **4**
Fethiye Museum, **3**
Galata Tower, **34**
Galatasaray Istanbul
  Directorate of the Ministry
  of Tourism, **40**
Government House
  (Vilayet), **28**
Gülhane Park, **27**
Istanbul Exhibition Hall, **39**

Katabaş Seabus Pier, **43**
Karaköy Seabus Pier, **31**
Karaköy Maritime
  Terminal, **32**
Kariye Museum, **1**
Küçük Ayasofya, **21**
Metro Terminal, **6**
Neve Shalom
  (Synagogue), **35**
Nuruosmaniye Mosque, **19**
Post Office, **20**
Saint Antoine, **38**
Sirkeci Tourism Information
  Office, **29**
Sirkeci Train Station, **30**
Süleymaniye Mosque, **13**
Sultanahmet
  (Blue Mosque), **22**
Sultanahmet Square, **23**
Sultan Selim Mosque, **5**
Taksim City
  Bus Terminal, **43**
Tomb of the Architect
  Sinan, **12**
Tomb of Süleymaniye
  the Magnificent, **14**
Topkapı Palace, **26**
Tram Terminal, **37**
Tünel Metro Terminal, **33**
Yeni Mosque, **17**

ISTANBUL
BOĞAZI
(BOSPHORUS)

MARMARA DENIZI
(SEA OF MARMARA)

N

lined with airline offices and hotels; both of these lead into **Taksim Square,** the center of the north bank. The **Sirkeci Train Station** lies just east of Eminönü, across from the tram station. Budget travelers converge in **Sultanahmet** and **Laleli** (also known as Aksaray), the area around the Aya Sophia mosque, south of and up the hill from Sirkeci. The main boulevard—leading west from Sultanahmet towards the university, the Grand Bazaar, and Aksaray—changes names from **Divan Yolu** to **Ordu Caddesi** as it nears Aksaray, right after the Çemberlitaş monument. Merchants crowd the district between the **Grand Bazaar,** east of the university, and the less touristy **Egyptian Bazaar,** just southeast of Eminönü. The **Kumkapı** district is south of the university and Yeniçeriler Caddesi. With help from a free map from the tourist office and a keen eye for the many landmarks, you can orient yourself through the maze of alleys that make up the city.

GETTING AROUND

If you come by plane, you'll arrive at either the international or the domestic terminal of **Atatürk Havaalanı** (Atatürk Airport); the two are connected by a free bus (theoretically every 20min., 6am-10pm). If arriving in the international terminal, take the "Havaş" bus to town (departs 10min. before the h.r, every hr., 5:50am-10:50pm; $2). This service goes through Aksaray and reaches the THY office in Taksim. Try to avoid the public bus system, especially if you are a unfamiliar with Turkish; you are likely to encounter a variety of problems. Other alternatives to the Havaş buses are taxis, but be wary, especially from the airport. If you do take an airport taxi, the fare should be $8-12 during the day, 50% more from midnight to 8am. Every taxi has a meter—make sure the driver uses it. If using a taxi, consider going to the nearby Yenibosna metro stop, from where you can go anywhere between Aksaray and Eminönü (30¢). If you are going to the Asian side, you can take a taxi to the Bakırköy seabus station from which you can reach Bostancı for a few dollars. Taxi service to either place should cost less than $5.

If you're like many budget travelers, you'll be heading for Sultanahmet. To get there from Aksaray, take the spiffy new tram five stops along Divan Yolu to the Aya Sophia mosque in Sultanahmet. You can buy a ticket at the little white booth across the road before boarding. Trams traveling in the direction "Sirkeci" go to Sultanahmet. If you want to reach some other destination, take the tram to either the Sirkeci stop or Eminönü— the last stop on the line. From Eminönü you can take ferries, seabuses, and public buses to most destinations in Istanbul. Sirkeci has the main train station on the European side and can connect you to some limited destinations in Europe. To get to Sultanahmet from the **Sirkeci Train Station,** take the tram two stops to Sultanahmet Station, where the tram diverges from the main road, then follow Babaîli Cad. uphill until it intersects Divan Yolu.

If you're coming from the Asian side by an intercity bus, get off at Harem to save yourself the journey to Esenler (about 2hr.), unless you want to travel over the Bosphorus bridges during a traffic jam. From Harem, you can take ferries to Sirkeci, near Eminönü, or *dolmuş* and public buses to Kadıköy, Üskidar, or other major destinations. If you are arriving in Istanbul by boat, you will get off at Sirkeci from where you can take ferries or trams to your final destination.

The new intercity **bus terminal** in Istanbul, the Esenler Otogar, is several miles from the city. The **metro** (every 5min. 6am-4pm, 35¢) links it and Aksaray station. *Otogar* is the name of the bus terminal's metro stop. From Aksaray metro station, cross the main road (Adnan Menderes Blv.), and walk down the nearest side street to its end; the Yusufpaşa train station will be in front of you. Catch the tram (direction *Sirkeci*) to Sultanahmet (6 stops, 35¢; buy ticket from the white booth before boarding). NOTE: *Topkapı bus station has recently closed, so beware of old maps.*

Buses in Istanbul are plentiful and cheap, though confusing for the newcomer. Tickets (35¢) are sold at booths at the larger bus terminals (such as Eminönü and Taksim) at kiosks marked *"Planktonluk."* At busy bus stops, they may be sold by street vendors for roughly 40¢. Stock up on tickets to avoid being stranded in the suburbs without a ticket seller for miles around. Short journeys require one ticket; longer trips

A Metro to Remember

Istanbul has one of the oldest functioning metros in the world. **Tünel** (The Tunnel), completed in 1873, is also the shortest metro ever built. It connects Karaköy to Beyoğlu, and the non-stop ride takes only a few minutes. The cable moving the single wagon up and down the steep path has snapped a few times in its history, but don't bother with the final letter home before trying the ride yourself: it's been a half century since its last mishap. The metro was built to transport rich foreigners from residential Beyoğlu to their banks, shops, and offices in Galata. Today you will find many passengers who are enjoying the trip, but during Ottoman times the metro was the focus of great controversies. Some Islamic clerics questioned whether it was Islamic "to put live men under the soil." A trip underground is worth your while just to get one of the tokens—they're collector's items in themselves. Take an extra home to prove you've traveled these well-worn tracks.

take two, especially those that cross a Europe-Asia bridge. Service begins at 6am and runs every five minutes or so on major routes. Buses are less frequent after dark and stop completely by midnight. Numbers and destinations are displayed at the front of the bus. For Sultanahmet, which has no bus station of its own, the nearest buses reach Beyazıt (to the north) and Eminönü (to the south and west). Bus #210 departs across from the back of the tourist office and runs up the European side of the Bosphorus to **Emirgan,** the home of superb teahouses (every hour Mon.-Fri. 7am-7pm, Sat.-Sun. 11am-6pm; schedule at the tourist office; 2bus tickets each way). Buses are inevitably slowed by Istanbul's considerable traffic. If you're not going far, walk.

A **dolmuş** (shared taxi), either a minibus or a vintage Chevrolet or Buick with fins and buffed chrome (lots from 1956), is faster than the bus and generally costs around 40¢. *Dolmuş* run on fixed routes, usually between the main bus stops in each quarter (if you ask they'll let you off *en route*). The assumption here is that a *dolmuş* only slows down for pick-ups and drop-offs, and it never actually comes to a full stop; know what you're doing beforehand. The most important thing to do prior to arriving in Istanbul is familiarize yourself with the city's layout and plan ahead of time. Try to use ferries, seabuses, metros, and trams as much as possible and avoid public buses, crowded *dolmuş,* and taxis.

SIDESTEPPING TOURIST PITFALLS

As in any heavily visited city, the touristy parts of Istanbul have fast talkers eager to unburden naive travelers of their money. Most of those who approach you in a friendly manner want to sell you something. Genuinely friendly Turks are generally less brash. Many Turks familiar with these same areas are eager to offer advice, give directions, or even invite you to tea, a forum in which they may try to satisfy their curiosity about a foreigner's culture while demonstrating their often minimal, but admirable, knowledge of MTV-imported English. Be wary of people who offer to "help" you buy a carpet. They are helping *themselves* to a commission that can easily be as large as 30-50% and will be tacked onto the price of your purchases. Also, exchanging money with people on the street isn't the greatest idea since fake bills are common. Please note that some discretion in displaying your travel guide in public (even, let's say, an innocuous *yellow* one) is usually warranted. A tourist peering into a guide is often a sign, saying either "I need help" or "I'm a sucker."

Most areas of Istanbul are relatively safe even at night, but some districts to avoid after sunset are the **Galata tower, Belgrade Forest, Beyazıt** (the neighborhood of Istanbul University), **Cihangir** (the area around the city walls), and the back streets of **Beyoğlu,** the area north of İstiklâl Cad., a fashionable shopping area by day, but a seething red-light district by night. While many regions of Turkey have been Westernized, the street culture is still undeniably different from one that you would find in, say, Milwaukee or even Kansas. Most catcalls are not threats even if they are annoying. In a situation in which you feel challenged or threatened, an alternative to ignoring the perpetrator is telling them in Turkish that you are uncomfortable. You might try *"Durun"* ("Stop"), *"Yeter"* ("Enough!"), or *"Beni rahat birakir misiniz"* ("Would you leave me alone?"). Find and memorize your own expressions to suit your needs and wants. But remember, these are hardly guaranteed-to-work formulas.

■ Practical Information

Tourist Office: In **Sultanahmet,** 3 Divan Yolu (tel./fax 518 1802; open daily 9am-5pm), north end of the Hippodrome, across from the Sultan Pub. In **Taksim,** in the Hilton Hotel Arcade (tel. 233 0592; open Mon.-Sat. 9am-5pm), and near the French Consulate (tel. 245 6876; open Mon.-Sat. 9am-5pm). Also offices in **Karaköy Maritime Station** (tel. 249 5776; open 8:30am-5pm), **Sirkeci Train Station** (tel. 511 5888; open daily 8:30am-5:30pm), and **Atatürk Airport** (tel. 663 0793; open 24hr.). Free country and city maps.

Tourist Police: In Sultanahmet, at the beginning of Yerebatan Cad., behind the obelisk in the park opposite the tourist office (24 hr. hotline tel. 527 4503, 528 5369; fax 512 7676). Open 24hr. In an **emergency,** call 155 from any phone.

Travel Offices: Gençtur, Prof. K. Ismail Gürkan Cad., Cağaloğlu Hamamı Sok., Kardeşler Iştlanı, 4th floor (tel. 520 5274, -5; fax 519 0864). Sells ISIC ($8), GO25 ($5), and provides a free Poste Restante service. Also organizes workcamps in villages. Open Mon.-Fri. 9:30am-noon and 1-5pm, Sat. 9:30am-1pm. **Seventur Travel Shop,** 2-C Alemdar Cad. (tel. 512 4183; fax 512 3641). Follow the Sirkeci tram tracks; a 1 min. walk past Aya Sophia, on the right. Sells ISIC and youth ID cards, provides free Poste Restante service, issues reliable plane and bus tickets (some agencies have been known to sell bogus tickets), and offers a shuttle to the airport (6am-midnight $4, midnight-6am $5). Check the schedule in the office. Open Mon.-Sat. 9am-1pm, Sun. 9am-6pm. **Indigo Tourism and Travel Agency,** 24 Akbıyık Cad. (tel. 517 7266; fax 518 5333), in the heart of the cluster of hotels in Sultanahmet. Open in summer daily 8:30am-7:30pm, in winter Mon.-Sat. 9:30am-6pm. Sells ISIC cards ($8) and GO25 ($5). Services include bus, plane, and ferry tickets, airport shuttle service, and Poste Restante.

Consulates: All are open Mon.-Fri. **Australia,** 58 Tepecik Yolu, Etiler (tel. 257 7050, -1); visas 10am-noon. **Canada,** 107/3 Büyükdere Cad., Gayrettepe (tel. 272 5174; fax 272 3427). **Greece,** 32 Turnacıbaşı Sok., Galatasaray (tel. 212 245 0596). **Ireland** (honorary), 26-a Cumhuriyet Cad., Mobil Altı, Elmadağ (tel. 246 6025); visas 9:30am-11:30am. **New Zealand** nationals should get in touch with the embassy in Ankara, 24/1 Kız Kulesi Sok. (tel. (312) 445 0556). **South Africa,** 106 Büyükdere Cad., Esentepe (tel. 275 4793; fax 288 2504); visas 9am-noon. **U.K.,** 34 Meşrutiyet Cad., Beyoğlu/Tepebaşı (tel. 293 7545); visas 8:30am-noon. **U.S.,** 104-108 Meşrutiyet Cad., Tepebaşı (tel. 251 3602); visas 8:30am-11am.

Banks: Currency exchange counters open Mon.-Fri. 8:30am-noon and 1:30-5pm. Most don't charge a commission. **ATMs** are scattered all over the city. Garanti Bankası branches are open on Sat. and during the noon breaks.

American Express: Türk Express, 91 Cumhuriyet Cad., 2nd floor (tel. 230 1515), up the hill from Taksim Sq. Handles lost checks and cards as well as other related business. Open Mon.-Fri. 9am-6pm. Their office in the **Hilton Hotel lobby,** Cumhuriyet Cad. (tel. 241 0248), deals with lost cards when Türk Express is closed. Open daily 8:30am-8pm. Neither gives cash advances or accepts wired money, as Turkish law requires it be done through a bank. AmEx's agent is **Koç Bank,** 233 Cumhuriyet Cad. (tel. 232 2600). Money is wired without fee if you accept Turkish *lira*; 1% fee for other currencies. To get a cash advance on your card, you must have a personal check or know the account number and address of your bank. Open Mon.-Fri. 8:45am-12:30pm and 1:30-4:30pm; cardholder services until 4pm. Cardholders can use Akbank ATMs all over Turkey for cash advances.

Flights: Atatürk Airport, 30km from the city. Has a terminal for domestic flights and one for international flights, 800m apart, connected by bus (every 20min. 6am-10pm). Take a *Havaş* bus from either terminal to the city (10min. before the hr. 5:50am-10:50pm, 30min., $2.50). The bus stops at Şişhane and Aksaray, where you can catch the tram to Sultanahmet.

Trains: Haydarpaşa Station, on the Asian side (tel. (216) 336 0475, -2063). Ticket office open 7:30am-11pm daily. Trains to Edirne (2 per day, $2.75). A convenient ferry connects the station to Karaköy pier 7, on the European side (every 20min. roughly 6am-midnight, 50¢). Pier is halfway between Galata Bridge and the Karaköy tourist office, where rail tickets for Anatolia can be purchased in advance at the **TCDD** (Turkish Republic State Railway) office upstairs. Office accepts couchette *(kuşet)* reservations for Ankara (2 days in advance, if possible). Tickets also available at Sirkeci station. Europe-bound trains leave from **Sirkeci Station** (tel. 527 0050, -1), in Eminönü (downhill toward the Golden Horn from Sultanahmet) to Sofia (2 per day, $31); Athens (1 per day, $62.50); and Munich (1 per day, $212). Call ahead to verify schedules and ask for student fares.

Buses: Intercity buses leave from the new **Esenler Otobüs Terminal** (tel. (212) 658 0036) in Esenler, several miles from downtown. To get there from Sultanahmet, take the tram 6 stops to **Yusufpaşa** (one stop beyond Aksaray), then walk (1min.) to the **Aksaray Metro station,** on the broad Adnan Menderes Blv. Take the metro to the *otogar* stop (15min., 35¢). Hundreds of buses leave here daily for virtually every point in Turkey and neighboring countries. **Varan Tours** (tel. 658 0277; fax 658 0280) is Turkey's most well-known company and is licensed to operate throughout Western Europe; **Ulusoy** (tel. 658 3000; fax 658 3010) serves Greece and domestic destinations; **Kamıl Koç** (tel. 658 2000; fax 658 2008); **Pamukkale** (tel./fax 658 2222). Most bus companies are authorized to go to Eastern Europe. *Unlicensed companies have been known to offer substantial discounts for Western European destinations and then abandon their passengers in Eastern Europe.* Frequent buses to Ankara (6hr., $12-15); Bursa (4hr., $8-10); Izmir (9hr., $14-17); Bodrum (13hr., $20-23); and Trabzon (14hr., $22-26). European service includes Athens (6 per week, 16hr., $24-27) and Vienna (1 per week, 36hr., $95). A station across the Bosphorus in **Harem** (tel. 333 3763)—accessible by ferry from Karaköy—serves Asia. Fares increase during summer and religious holidays. Reservations are recommended.

AKBİL: AKBİL, or the Akıllı Bilet, is new to the public transportation system. These electronic tickets can be used in metros, trams, seabuses, public buses, and double-deck buses. After depositing an initial $3.50, you can deposit credit to your AKBİL from any of the IETT public bus booths which has the sign "AKBİL satılır." AKBİL is convenient and ticket prices are usually 30-50% cheaper than cash fares.

Ferries (National and International): Turkish Maritime Lines has offices near pier 7 at Karaköy, just west of the **Haydarpaşa** ferry terminal. It is the building with the blue awning marked *Denizcilik İşletmeleri*. Ferries to Trabzon (and intervening points on the Black Sea coast) depart from Sarayburnu; after exiting the Sirkeci station, turn right, and walk for 5min. along the waterfront. These times, prices, and departure points change regularly; confirm at Turkish Maritime Lines. Although not from Istanbul, Turkish Maritime Lines (tel. 212 249 9222) also serves Venice and Northern Cyprus. Passenger boats leave for Bandırma, Auşa, Marmara Adası; whereas car ferries leave for Giresun (1 per week, 30hr.), Ordu (1 per week, 40hr.), Samsun (1 per week, 40hr.), Sinop (1 per week, 47hr.), Trabzon (1 per week, 50hr.) If you buy a combination ticket (boat-train) to Izmir ($10-25), you can sail to Bandırma and then take the train to Izmir (3 per week).

Ferries (Local): Ferries constitute a major part of Istanbul's public transport system. Some of the ferries to the north shore of the Golden Horn are commuter ferries. Since these leave in the morning and return in the evening, taking an evening ferry out could strand you. The following depart from the Sirkeci area; piers are clustered around Galata Bridge: Üsküdar (pier 1, every 20min. 6:30am-11pm); Kadıköy (pier 2, every 20min. 7:30am-9pm, 50¢); the Bosphorus (pier 3, $4 round-trip); Princess Islands (pier 3); Adalar (pier 5); Bağlat (pier 6, past the Galata Bridge); and Haydarpaşa railway station (pier 7, every 20min. 6am-midnight, 50¢). Timetables are posted at each terminal. Other ferries connect the various Istanbul suburbs. For details, buy the timetable *feribot tarifesi* (60¢) at any pier.

Seabuses: These fast and comfortable catamarans which carry up to 250 passengers each are one of the best ways to travel in Istanbul, but are also five times more expensive than ferries. You can recognize the piers and the booths by the painted

WESTERN TURKEY

blue dolphins. Timetables are distributed freely at the booths. You can get the latest updates from **Seabus Information** (tel. (216) 362 0444).

Taxis: Use of meters in taxis is imperative—make sure it's on and don't pay more than it says. One light on the meter indicates the day rate; two lights indicate the night rate (midnight-8am, fare 50% higher). Steer away from taxis whose drivers approach you in Sultanahmet and those waiting at the airport. Drivers seldom speak English; if you don't speak Turkish, write your destination down. If you have a problem, get the driver's licence number and the police will help.

International Bookstores: Aypa Bookstore, 19 Mimar Mehmet Ağa Cad., Sultanahmet (tel. 517 4492), behind the Blue Mosque. Foreign magazines and limited selection of newspapers. English and German spoken. Open daily 6:30am-8pm. **Robinson Crusoe 389,** 389 İstiklâl Cad. (tel. 293 6968, -77; fax 251 1735), is tasteful and upscale, selling books in English, French, German, and Russian. Full reference section, fantastic art books, *MAD* magazine, and computer database book searches. Open daily 9am-8pm. **International Press Büfe,** 91 İstiklâl Cad., offers numerous international magazines and newspapers at low prices, but no books.

Laundromats: Star Laundry, 18 Akbıyık Cad. (tel. 638 2302), below Star Pension. Wash and dry $1.25 per kg, minimum 2kg. English spoken. Open daily 8am-10pm. **Active Laundry,** at 14 Divan Yolu (tel. 513 7585), in the heart of Sultanahmet. Wash and dry $2 per kg; ironing 65¢. Open daily 8am-10pm. **Hobby Laundry,** 6/1 Caferiye Sok., in the Yücelt Hostel building. $2 per kg, minimum 2kg. Open daily 9am-6pm. **Vardar Laundry,** 15 Güzel Sanatlar Sok. (tel. 520 6658). $1.50 per kg, as well as washing and ironing of shirts ($1.50), jeans ($2), and skirts ($2.50). Open Mon.-Sat. 8am-8pm.

Hospitals: American Hospital, Admiral Bristol Hastanesi, 20 Güzelbahçe Sok., Nişantaşı (tel. 231 4050), is applauded by Istanbul natives and tourists and has many English-speaking doctors. The **German Hospital,** 119 Sıraselviler Cad., Taksim (tel. 293 2150), also hosts a multi-lingual staff and is more convenient to Sultanahmet. **International Hospital,** 82 Istanbul Cad., Yeşilköy (tel. 663 3000). Payment with cash or a credit card is expected at time of treatment at all of the above. The state-run **Taksim İlkyardım Hastanesi** (Taksim First Aid Hospital), 112 Sıraselviler Cad. (tel. 212 252 4300) offers cheaper services.

PTT: Istanbul has more than 100 post offices. The most convenient for those staying in Sultanahmet is the little booth opposite the entrance to Aya Sophia. **Main branch,** 25 Büyük Postane Sok. Stamp and currency exchange services open 8:30am-7pm. All PTTs accept packages; if a customs officer is not present, you will be directed to the **Kadıköy, Beyazıt,** or **Tophane** (on Rıhtım Cad.) offices. There is a **branch** off the west end of Taksim Sq. on Cumhuriyet Cad. convenient for mailing packages or making calls. Open Mon.-Fri. 8am-8pm, Sat. 8am-6pm. 24 hr. international telephone office in the building, but it does not arrange collect calls (see **Keeping in Touch,** p. 44). Card phones are the most convenient ones. You can get cards which have 30, 60, or 100 kontürs (credits). One credit lasts 2-10sec. during international calls.

Telephone Codes: 212 (European side) and 216 (Asian side); you have to dial the code when calling from one side to the other. **International calls** can be made from all pay phones, but often are cut off after 3min.

▓ Accommodations

Istanbul's budget accommodations are concentrated in the **Sultanahmet** district, just steps away from the city's most awe-inspiring sights. Budget prices start at about $4 for a cheap single or dorm bed. The side streets around **Sirkeci** railway station provide numerous singles and doubles in the $5-10 range, patronized mainly by working-class Turks. **Aksaray** offers dozens of hotels in every conceivable price range. Its streets are packed with Bulgarian and Romanian businesspeople, who often outnumber the Turks. Hotels in **Laleli** are the center of prostitution in Istanbul and should be avoided. The **Taksim** district is home to many of the city's five-star hotels and a smattering of budget lodgings. Rates rise by 20% in July and August.

SULTANAHMET

Yücelt Hostel (HI), 6/1 Caferiye Cad. (tel. 513 6150, -1; fax 512 7628; email ykeser@escortnet.com; http://www.travelturkey.com/yücelt.html), in the little alley to the left of Aya Sophia as you face the mosque's gate. To reach Aya Sophia from the Sultanahmet tram stop, follow the tracks downhill toward Sirkeci; Aya Sophia is the red-tinted mosque on your right. The hostel is a great place to meet travelers. Yücelt is one of only two Turkish hostels accredited by HI. Free luggage deposit. Laundry $1.25 per kg. Transport to airport. Showers included (7:30-10am and 7:30-10pm). Reserve rooms two weeks in advance in summer. 6-8 person dorm room $4-7; 3-4 person dorm room $6-9; doubles $8-11 per person; roof $2.50. Has non-smoking dorms. 10% discount for *Let's Go* readers. Free safe-deposit and bellydancing each week. V/MC/Eurocard. Cheap, decent meals available in the cafeteria, as are 85¢ beers during happy hour (10-11pm).

Orient Youth Hostel, 13 Akbıyık Cad. (tel. 517 9493; fax 518 3894), near Topkapı Palace. International mix of hip teens and experienced travelers alike eager to hang out in the breezy roof-terrace cafeteria (open for most meals). 24hr. hot water, A/C. Benefits include luggage room, safe, and a travel agency right by the reception-ist's desk. Has cable TV and video. Orient bar has free Friday belly dancing (beer $1, raki $2, no cover charge). Bring your own toilet paper and towel for communal bathroom use. Dorm beds $4.50; doubles $5.50 per person; quads $5; roof $3. Breakfast included.

Sultan Turist Otel, 3 Terbıyık Sok., Fez Travel Office at entrance (tel. 516 9260; fax 517 1626). Around the corner from the Orient Hostel. Turkish pensions don't get any better than the newly opened Sultan. Immaculate and highly professional. Great views of the Marmara from the roof restaurant/bar. Offers reasonably priced sandwiches and vegetarian sandwiches. Happy hour 5-8pm (beer 90¢). TV and VCR in common room. Safe-deposit and laundry services available. In-house travel office, and international phone services. Dorm beds $6.90; singles $16.50; doubles $20; triples $25. V/MC.

Hotel Anadolu, Yerebatan Cad. 3 Salkım Söğüt Sok. (tel. 512 1035; fax 527 7695). To get to Salkım Söğüt Sok. from the Sultanahmet tram, walk 50m down to Sirkeci along the tram tracks; take a left at the major intersection (Yerebatan Cad.); Salkım Söğüt Sok. will be the first right, roughly 20m up the street. Rudimentary, well kept rooms, a few with tiny balconies. Small terrace outside the front door. Hot and cold showers. English spoken. $12 per person. Roof beds $7 each.

Alp Guesthouse, Akbıyık Cad. 4 Adliye Sok. (tel. 517 9570 or 518 5728). Family-run guesthouse with spacious, spotless rooms, some with fine views, and Mediterra-nean-style ambience. Superb views from the terrace; barbecues held here, and drinks served until 11pm. Alp offers an airport transportation service, a safe, and a luggage room in the basement. All rooms with bath and shower. Singles $35; doubles $45 (large) and $50 (really large). Breakfast $5.

Bahaus Guesthouse, Akbıyık Cad. Bayram Fırını Sok. #11 (tel. 517 6697; fax 517 6697). A three-floor, comfortable hotel, with a terrace view of the Bosphorus. Free backgammon courses from the owner. 10% discount for *Let's Go* readers. Singles $15; doubles $25, with bath $30; triples $35, with bath $40; basement $5.

Hotel Pamphylia, Yerebatan Cad. 47 (tel. 526 8935 or 513 9548; fax 513 9549). Immaculate rooms, some with balconies and televisions. English and German spo-ken. Tiny terrace with a great view. Safe deposit. Singles $25; doubles $35; triples $50. Rates $5 less in winter. Breakfast included. V/MC accepted. Friendly staff, peaceful environment.

Hanedan Hotel, Akbıyık Cad., 3 Adliye Sok. (tel. 516 4869; fax 517 4524). Pleasant view from terrace. Beautiful cafeteria. Currency exchange. 24 hr. airport transport. 24 hr. hot water. Doubles $20, $26 with shower. Breakfast included.

Hotel Side Pension, 20 Utangaç Sok. (tel./fax 517 6590). Basic little pension. 3rd floor walls are lined with beautiful Ottoman-style tiles. Large, well kept rooms. Sin-gles $15, tiny singles $6; doubles $20, with bath $30. Breakfast included.

Hotel Park, Cankurtaran Mah. 26 Utangaç Sok. (tel. 517 6596; fax 518 9603; email hotelpark@ihlas.net.tr), in the heart of Sultanahmet. Friendly service, quiet envi-ronment, and terrace with colorful flowers. Rooms with bath have cable TV. Carpets sold in the foyer. Ask about a 10% discount for long stays (10+ days). Singles $25, with bath $35; doubles $35, with bath $45; triples $45, with bath $55; quads (with bath) $65. Breakfast included. Off-season prices lower. V/MC/AmEx.

Ottoman Guest House, Cankurtaran Mah. 6 Tevkifhane Sok. (tel. 518 0790; fax 518 0792). Take Tevkifhane Sok. across the little park between Aya Sophia and the Blue Mosque. Comfortable, with new furniture and a terrace. Luggage room, safe, travel agency contact, phone in rooms, and airport service ($3.50 per person). Doubles $28-30; triples $48-50. Bath and breakfast included. V/MC.

Poem Hotel, Akbıyık Cad. Terbıyık Sok. 12 (tel. 517 6836; fax 517 6836; http:// www.charminghotels.com.tr). Superb, luxurious rooms and baths. Nice view of the Bosphorus. 24 hr. hot water and service. Some rooms have a TV and A/C. Each room has a Turkish poem instead of a room number. Has a safe. Singles $50; double $70-75; triple $95. AmEx. Breakfast included.

Star Pansiyon, 18 Akbıyık Cad. (tel. 638 2302), opposite Orient Hostel. Spartan, but clean. 24hr. hot water. All rooms have bath with shower. The word on the street is that this is the place for toilet paper and towels. Doubles $20; triples $25.

Berk Guesthouse, 27 Kutlugün Sok. (tel. 517 6561; email evrensel@msn.com; http:/ /www.berkguesthouse.com). Family-run, clean, quiet, and comfortable. Classical music plays in the lobby. Has a safe. Discounts for stays over a week. Not open in the winter. Singles $40; doubles $50; extra bed $10. Breakfast included.

Alaaddin Guesthouse, 32 Akbıyık Cad (tel. 516 2330). Well furnished rooms. Buffet breakfast on terrace included. 24 hr. hot water and a safe. Singles $30; doubles $40; triples $55. Breakfast included. V.

Hotel Merih 2, 20 Alendar Cad. (tel. 526 9708). Small, simple rooms. 24 hr. hot water. Dorms $6 per person; doubles $16, with bath $22-26. Breakfast $2.

Londra Camping (tel. 560 4200), 1km from the airport, along the noisy and nerve-grating highway to Istanbul. No bus stop; take a taxi. Far from the center of town, but not its noise. Includes cafeteria, bar, and showers. $2.50 per person; $2 per tent; two-person bungalows $12.50.

TAKSIM

Hotel Santral, 26 Siraselviler Cad. Billurcu Sok. (tel. 251 8110), has rooms off Taksim Square. Breakfast included. Singles $50; doubles $75.

Vardar Palace Hotel, 54/56 Siraselviler Cad. Rooms feature satellite TV, phones, and fan. Although the prices are a little steep, they'll often discount up to 50%. Singles $70; doubles $90.

Hotel Plaza, 19-21 Siraselviler Cad. (tel. 245 3273). Many large rooms varying in price with the quality of the view. Doubles $45-50.

Otel Oriental, 60 Cihangir Cad. (tel. 252 6870). Clean rooms and new bathroom fixtures. Singles $50; doubles $70.

Hotel Nural, 12 Abdülhakhamit Cad. (tel. 235 1511). Rooms with A/C and TV. Singles $50; doubles $90. Offers discounts up to 30%.

▓ Food

Istanbul's budget dining options are superb. From the sandwich stands in the streets to the elegant seafood restaurants on the Bosphorus, you can expect high quality, kaleidoscopic variety, and reasonable prices. While Sultanahmet may be an optimal place to stay, it's not the premier eating locale—you'll fare much better in **Beyoğlu,** where a wide variety of eating establishments await you around İstiklâl Cad. The area around the busy pier of **Beşiktaş** is another place which has budget restaurants. **Kumkapı,** south of the Grand Bazaar, has numerous fish restaurants as well as entertainment. But prices here can be higher than average. **Çengelköy** is known for its simple fish restaurants, **Kanlıca** is reputed to have the most delicious yogurt in the city, and **Ortaköy** has great restaurants with views of the Bosphorus. Some of Istanbul's top restaurants are scattered along the Bosphorus straits, both on the European and Asian sides. Take any public bus going to Bebek or to Sarıyer to reach these more expensive places. For do-it-yourself meals, two **open-air markets** are centrally located—a general one next to Çiçek Pasajı in Beyoğlu, and a fruit market next to the

Egyptian Spice Bazaar *(Mısır Çarşısı),* the little thee-domed, three-arched structure beside the Yeni Mosque. It sells an astonishing and mouthwatering collection of sweets. For a quick stand-up lunch, the myriad of *kebapçı* and *köfteci* will easily fill you up for less than $3. Stop at a *büfe* (snack shop) for *tost* and a soft drink, both for less than $1. Even a meal at a cheaper *lokanta* shouldn't run you more than $3.50.

SULTANAHMET AREA

Many of the places here serve bland, international-style food or relatively tasteless Turkish fare in a cafeteria setting. There are a few exceptions.

Türkistan Aşevi, 36 Tavukhane Sok. (tel. 638 6525, -6; fax 518 1344). A veritable feast for the eyes and taste buds, this 3-part restaurant specializes in the cuisine of Turkistan. There are several variations of the 7-course lunch for $14 and the eight-course dinner for $17, all incredibly tasty. The meaty Harput marriage feast soup ($1.75), and the spicy *Saşlik* (Turkistani *şiş kebap,* $4) are great. Vegetarian *kebap* $3.15. V/MC/Eurocard. No alcohol served.

Dârüzziyâfe, 6 Şifahane Cad. (tel. 511 8414, -5; fax 526 1891), in the Süleymaniye Mosque. Main courses $4.50-6. Tour groups abound. Mellow atmosphere and attentive service. The specialty, *Sülemaniye Çorbası* is a must (meat and veggie soup, $1.75), as is the *çilek keşkül* (strawberry pudding, $1.50). Live Ottoman music on Sat. nights. No alcohol; it's part of a mosque. Open noon-11pm.

Pudding Shop, 6 Divan Yolu (tel. 522 2970; fax 512 4458), was a major pitstop on the Hippie Trail to the Far and Middle East in 1970s. Affectionately nicknamed the Pudding Shop by hippies, this family-owned establishment is now a lovely self-serve restaurant (meat dishes $2-2.50, veggie dishes $1.50) and super dessert stop. The creme caramel and *keşkül* (vanilla pudding) are sure to please, each for $1. The cappuccino rocks at only 65¢.

Cennet, 90 Divan Yolu (tel. 513 1416), on the right as you walk along Divan Yolu from Sultanahmet towards Aksaray, 3min. from the Sultanahmet tram. A full meal is $3-6. Specializes in Anatolian pancakes *(gözeme).* Open daily 10am-midnight.

Pandeli Restaurant, 1 Egyptian Spice Bazaar (tel./fax 522 5534). Main courses are $5-7, starters $4.75. Tasty *yaprak dolması* (stuffed vine leaves); and *hünkâr beğendi* (mashed eggplant with kebap, $5.75). Open Mon.-Sat. noon-3pm.

House of Medusa Restaurant, Yerebatan Cad. 19 Muhteremefendi Sok. (tel. 511 4116, 513 1428; fax 527 2822), on a cross street off Divan Yolu. This 4-floor, internationally renowned eatery is a must-see. Excellent Turkish cuisine in the 1st floor garden (open in summer), the 3rd floor divan area, and a fourth floor bar. Indeed, it's half restaurant, half museum. Delicious *piliç* (chicken stuffed with vegetables, $3.75), good vegetarian specialties ($2.75-4.25), and tasty pudding ($1.75) are best capped with their delicious Turkish coffee. Open daily 8am-midnight. Accepts major credit cards.

Backpacker's Underground Cafe, 14 Akbiyik Cad. Daily happy hour (5-8pm; large beer $1), and specialty sandwiches ($1.50-2.50). Conversation is good, interesting graffiti on the wall, and socially conscious music. Open 7:30am-11:30pm.

TAKSIM SQUARE

Taksim Square is a great place to go if you are missing the Golden Arches. In the heart of the square are a McDonald's, Pizza Hut, and other American fast food joints.

Patissiere Gezi, 5 İsmet İnönü Cad. A luxurious patissiere on Taksin Square. Great service compensates for higher prices. Try the delicious *rübli torte* (an almond carrot cake; $3).

Han Restaurant, on Cumhuriyet Cad. Has great deals on beer and fries ($1.50), beer and meatballs ($2), and other food.

KUMKAPı AREA

Kumkapı is a pleasant square with surrounding narrow cobblestone streets. Kumkapı is justifiably famous for its seafood. The district is lined with fish restaurants—there is

WESTERN TURKEY

nothing else here—making the area look like one giant restaurant. Prices are high by Istanbul standards (main courses $8-12), but it's worth coming here at least once. The trick in Kumkapı is to eat as many appetizers as possible since they are the most delicious and least expensive. Also, try to eat fixed menu options if possible. To get here from the Grand Bazaar, cross Divan Yolu and walk for roughly five minutes down the narrow Tiyatro Cad. to the square. Restaurant staff will beckon you into their establishments. This annoying habit doesn't reflect the quality of the food—even the best restaurants do it. There is a map showing the location of all restaurants just before you enter the square. One commendable choice is the **Yengeç Restaurant,** 6 Telli Odalar Sok. (tel. 516 3227). Open from noon to midnight, this establishment offers *bonfilet* ($7.50), catch-of-the-day ($9-15), attentive service, and nightly live "gypsy" music (8pm-midnight). One large fish is enough for two people.

İSTIKLÂL CADDESI

To get to İstiklâl Cad. from Sultanahmet, follow the tram lines to Sirkeci, take a left and follow the water, crossing the Galata Bridge and taking a left onto the first major thoroughfare; the Tünel station will be on your immediate right. The Tünel will take you to İstiklâl Cad. (every 5min. 8am-9pm, 20¢). İstiklâl Caddesi is a narrow, European-style boulevard combining Turkish and American fashion shops as well as more classic street vendors of *maraş* ice cream and *simit* (Turkish sesame pretzels). A 1915 San Francisco-esque tram runs down the middle (from the underground Tünel station to Taksim Sq., every 10min., 30¢). This district is a favorite for eating out, and at night it metamorphoses into Istanbul's main nightlife (and red light) district, but be careful. Between the Tünel and Taksim (on the left as you walk toward Taksim) is the famed **Çiçek Pasajı** (Flower Passage). It is here and in the many other side streets that one can find cheap but classy restaurants, bars, and cafes. The clientele is mostly Turkish—a good place to escape the tourist throng.

Şampiyon, Balık Pazarı. Famous all around Turkey; believed to prepare the best *kokoreç* in the country. Lamb innards are grilled, then cooked with spices and tomatoes. Try the *çeyrek ekmek kokoreç* which is the smallest portion ($1.50).

Cumhuriyet Meyhanesi (tel. 252 0886), at the far end of the fruit market. Turkey's top poets, artists, and journalists gather here in the evenings to discuss politics, culture, and other intellectual matters. Serves delectable items such as eggplant salad for $2.25. Open daily 10am-1am, possibly later.

Has Fırını, Kalyon Cukulluk Cad. #35. Melt-in-your-mouth fresh *kurabiye* for $2.50 per kg, or, for the health-conscious, *anasonlu galete* ($1.50 per kg), made with no fat or salt.

Cafe Gramafon, 3 Tünel Meydanı (tel. 293 0786), to your left as you come out of the Tünel station, offers an kitchen. The *Gramafon* filet and toast (sandwiches with veggies or meats, $4-8) are divine. Turkish coffee $1.75, cappuccino royal with amaretto, brandy, cacao, and espresso $3.75. Live jazz (Thurs.-Sat. after 10:30pm, $6.75 cover) attracts mixed crowds. Open daily 11am-2am.

Ağa Lokanta Restaurant, 7 Sakızağacı Cad., Beyoğlu (tel. (212) 249 3924). A traditional restaurant where the locals eat tasty Turkish food. Okra and spinach ($1.75), *sebze graten* ($2), *karışık komposto* dessert ($1). Great for vegetarians.

Tatlıses Lahmacun, 128 İstiklal Cad. Owned by Turkey's leading folk singer. Offers fast food *lahmacun* for 75¢ and *künefe* for $1. The 2-floor restaurant is ideal for meat lovers.

Duran Sandwich, 11 İstiklâl Cad. This sandwich shop offers more than 50 different sandwiches, from caviar to roast beef to edamer cheese. Prices range between 50¢ and $2.

Bursa Fast Food, 87 İstiklâl Cad. Three-story fast food restaurant serving traditional Turkish cuisine. Try the soup ($1), celery ($1.75), and artichokes ($2). Great vegetarian options. The third floor has beer. Clean, air-conditioned, and spacious.

Şimşek Karadeniz Pide Salonu, at the entrance of İstiklal Cad., in the alley to the right (tel. 249 4642). Offers great selection of pitas ($2.50-3.50).

Ali Muhiddin Hacı Bekir, 129 İstiklal Cad. This place has been around since 1777, and offers a great selection of sweets and Turkish delight. Try the *sakızlı lokum* ($5.75 per kg).

İnci Pastahanesi, İskitlâl Cad. 124-2 (tel. 243 2412, 244 9224). This shop has serviced the neighborhood for 52 years under the same owner. The shop's specialty is *profiterol,* a creme-filled cake smothered in chocolate sauce for a scandalously cheap $1.40 (open daily 7am-9pm).

■ Entertainment

NIGHTLIFE

Let's Go does not recommend club-hopping in a haphazard manner in Istanbul. Many clubs are reputable, but some are run by hustlers who have links with the nearby red light district. The hustlers will charge a lot—perhaps everything you've got—for a single drink. In one well-known scam, a couple of girls sit at your table and order drinks. You get hit for an exorbitant bill even if you haven't ordered anything. The demand for payment is likely to be backed up with an impressive and frightening display of muscle. If you don't have enough money with you, they may even take you back to your hotel and take it from your room. As always, exercise good judgment and try to stay with a group of friends.

A large part of the nightlife consists of excellent restaurants and coffeehouses. Western European-style nightlife—bars and nightclubs—is concentrated in the Taksim district, where the action starts at midnight and rages until dawn.

The nightclubs are located on İstiklâl Cad., Sıraselviler Cad. (the other main street which runs from Taksim Sq. to the Bosphorus), and in the little side streets which run off them. Be sure to try the local drink, *balyoz* ("sledge hammer" or "wrecking ball"). Demolition is the appropriate metaphor—*balyoz* consists of *rakı,* whiskey, vodka, and gin mixed with orange juice. **Kemancı** on Sıraselviler Cad., roughly a one-minute walk from Taksim, is a wild and loud rock bar that hosts live bands. Long hair and tattoos rule ($5 cover on weekends includes one drink, *rakı* and beer $2.50). **Bilsak,** Sıraselviler Cad., Soğancı Sok. No 7 (tel. 293 2774), is the place for a more mellow scene. The fifth floor hosts an intellectual, artsy crowd along with an incredible view of the Bosphorus. The best drink is "Aysel's in the Ditch"—a shot of tequila (shot glass and all) in a glass of beer ($5).

The **Carnival Pub,** in the fruit market beside the Çiçek Pasaji, is a loud and cavernous bar ($2 beers) where heavy metal and punk bands play. Live music every night—note the vintage Judas Priest paraphernalia. This may be the only place where you don't need to be dressed up to get in. You'll usually be the only tourist there, but people are friendly. **Leman Kültür,** on İmam Adman alley off İstiklâl Cad., is a spacious dimly lit bar with earth-tone decor and a funky spiral staircase. No live music, but billiard tables, good drinks, and a hip crowd listening to rock and jazz. It is owned by the

---

Carpet Buying in Turkey

Carpet and *kilim* buying in Turkey is a task for the expert bargainer. Merchandise is always overpriced, sometimes by as much as 50%, but the high quality can make it worth your while. "Shop around" is an understatement—you should seek out advice from several carpet/*kilim* vendors who speak English (as most do). The Grand Bazaar in Istanbul is the site of the most exorbitant prices, so beware. The name of the game is bargaining, so don't be afraid to stick by your bid if you know it's fair. Always get several independent opinions on the value of a carpet before you buy. Be sure to flip the carpet over to feel for knots (if you cannot feel any, it is probably machine made). Also, pull out a strand from the carpet and burn it; if it smells like wool, you know it is real. Be careful not to leave the store without a copy of insurance and shipping contracts, as well as a certificate of guarantee.

leading Turkish comic, Leman. Mellow your groove in the cozy alcove, **Asparagus Cafe and Bar,** on Büyükparmakkapı Sok., another alley off İstiklâl Cad., where the name of the game is relaxing to Anadolu Pop. Live music starts at 9:30pm. Right across the alley is **Hayal Kahvesi,** a popular haven for artists. Live music (rock/blues/ jazz) starts at 11pm. Keep an eye out for the awesome wooden menus and the sweet and satisfying house specialty, Hayal Cocktail ($4.25). **North Shield,** Çalıkuşu Sok. Levent is an authentic British pub and has an incredible variety of beers from around Europe. Lots of foreigners hang out here. The **Soldier Cafe and Bar,** 37 Ticarethane Sok, off Divan Yolu (tel. 511 3621), is filled with teens and twenty-somethings relax- ing during the day. Paintings of women in combat decorate the walls (open 11am- 4am). Young Turks also hang out in **Ortaköy** (ferry #22E, 22B, or 25 from Eminönü).

Around Sultanhamet, on İncili Çavuş Sok., try **Rumeli Cafe/Bar** which has open-air tables. A Bloody Mary is $4. **Adı the Bar,** 24 İncili Çavuş Sokak, is on the second floor. They don't let single males in. **2019,** Atatürk 100, Tıl Oto Sanayi Sitesi, has hard rock that nicely complements the car wreck decor. Gays, Istanbul's jet set, and assorted funky types frequent the bar. **VAT 69,** 7 İmam Adnan Sok., is open until early in the morning and is popular with gay men.

TURKISH BATHS

For a truly authentic **Turkish bath** *(hamam),* it's best to go to the nearby cities of Edirne and Bursa. Istanbul baths, however, can provide a reprieve for the down and dirty. The much-publicized **Cağaloğlu Hamamı** (tel. 522 2424), in Sultanahmet on Yerebatan Cad., is fancy, but avoid it if you are at all claustrophobic. It now charges between $10 and $20, depending on how much rubbing you want (open daily 8am- 10pm). Also try Istanbul's other famous *hamam,* the historical **Çemberlitaş Bath,** 8 Vezirhan Cad. (tel. 522 7974; fax 511 2535), 1584 product of master architect Mimar Sinan. With separate sections for men and women, it's one of the largest *hamam* in Istanbul and popular among Turks and tourists. A cathartic bath and massage costs $10; fresh orange juices $1. Before indulging in baths, female travelers should know that this Turkish tradition is male-oriented—most *hamams* have smaller facilities for women (open daily 6am-midnight). Keep in mind that Turkish massages are often severe by European and American standards.

■ Sights

Istanbul's incomparable array of world-famous churches, mosques, palaces, and museums can keep an ardent tourist busy for weeks, but five or six days of leg-work should be enough to acquaint you with the premier sights. A FIYTO card allows entry to most major museums for free; an ISIC card is usually good for half-price (see p. 9).

TOPKAPI PALACE

From the 15th to the 19th century, the **Topkapı Sarayı** (Topkapı Palace) was the nerve center of the Ottoman Empire. It faces Aya Sophia, with the Archaeological Museum situated between them. This magnificent maze of buildings and grounds, built by Mehmet II, was originally the site of the Ottoman government and the Empire's most exclusive schools. It was also the home of the Sultan and his sizeable entourage of wives, eunuchs, and servants. Don't be overwhelmed by the seemingly endless attractions—you can punctuate your tours inside the palace by sunning on the terraces or reposing in the rose gardens. Not to be missed are the **Second Court** and its huge East Asian porcelain collection, and the **Treasury,** which houses an ines- timable wealth of diamonds, emeralds, gold, and jade. Also not to be missed are the **Spoonmaker's Diamond** *(Kaşıkçı Elması),* the spectacular Topkapı Dagger, and some of St. John the Baptist's hand bones. Nearby, the **Pavilion of Holy Relics** con- tains remnants of the prophet Muhammad: his footprint, a lock of hair, a tooth, his original seal, and a letter written by his hand. The swords of four caliphs are on dis- play in an adjacent room. Be aware that this is a sacred place to Muslims.

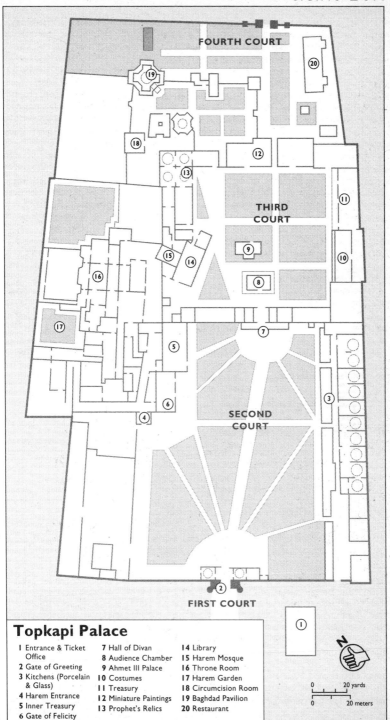

FOURTH COURT

THIRD COURT

SECOND COURT

FIRST COURT

Topkapi Palace

1 Entrance & Ticket Office
2 Gate of Greeting
3 Kitchens (Porcelain & Glass)
4 Harem Entrance
5 Inner Treasury
6 Gate of Felicity
7 Hall of Divan
8 Audience Chamber
9 Ahmet III Palace
10 Costumes
11 Treasury
12 Miniature Paintings
13 Prophet's Relics
14 Library
15 Harem Mosque
16 Throne Room
17 Harem Garden
18 Circumcision Room
19 Baghdad Pavilion
20 Restaurant

N

0   20 yards
0   20 meters

The **Harem** (the personal living quarters of the sultan and his wives), with its lush rooms and magnificent Iznik-tiled walls, is worth the additional admission fee (tours every 30min.; admission $2). It is not an original part of the palace as it was built during the reign of Süleyman the Magnificent. Prior to Süleyman, the palace was used only as an administrative center. To see it, take a tour. The **Circumcision Chamber,** near the patio throne overlooking the Bosphorus, is beautifully decorated with blue-green Iznik tiles. According to Turkish tradition, males were not circumcised at birth (as prescribed by Islam), but rather after they had come of age. Also on the palace grounds is the delicious **Konyalı Restaurant** which overlooks the Marmara Sea. Be warned that the great view comes at a not-so-great price. The palace grounds are open daily 9:30am-5pm. Admission is $3.30, students $1.30.

A museum complex lies through a gate marked "Archaeological Museum" downhill from the Topkapı Palace. The **Tiled Pavilion** (*Çinili Köşk*), once a petite pleasure retreat attached to Topkapı Palace, now houses the **Tile Museum.** Replete with yellows, blues, and greens, the building's own tiles constitute one of Turkey's best remaining examples of the Tabrizi Persian style, which the Ottomans increasingly avoided in favor of tiles with white backgrounds and naturalistic floral patterns (open May-Sept. Tues.-Thurs. and Sat.-Sun. 9am-4pm; admission $1.35). The **Museum of the Ancient Orient** has a buffet of Hittite, Babylonian, Sumerian, Assyrian, and Egyptian artifacts. Among them is a tablet on which part of the Hammurabi Code is inscribed, and another with a treaty between a Hittite ruler and the Egyptian Pharaoh Ramses II (open May-Sept. 9am-4pm; admission $1.35). The **Archaeological Museum** displays a prize-winning collection of early Greek, Hellenistic, and Roman marbles and bronzes, including a famous sarcophagus with carvings of Alexander the Great (open May-Sept. daily 9am-4pm; admission $1.35). The park on the **ramparts** of Topkapı Palace overlooks the Bosphorus and Golden Horn and offers a respite from Istanbul's sweltering streets.

The **Gülhane Park** outside the palace is popular among locals. There's frequently live Turkish music at night; the best artists draw large, loud, adoring crowds. Enter the park through the plastic booths (admission 50¢, students 35¢).

AYA SOPHIA

Aya Sophia (Haghia Sophia) was built by Emperor Justinian between 532 and 537 AD. After upstart plebeians destroyed a predecessor building during the Nika Revolt, Justinian built a new and improved church in an effort to cement imperial authority. Converted into a mosque after the Ottoman invasion in 1453, it was made a museum by Atatürk in 1935. Discussions have recently begun about whether to convert the building back into a mosque again or to keep it as a museum.

The church, 7570 square meters and 55.6m high, was the grandest building in the world when it was built. An elaborate marble square in the floor by the altar marks the spot where Byzantine emperors were once crowned. You can walk up the stone ramp on the left to the upstairs gallery to observe the remains of the famous wall mosaics of Christ and the Virgin Mary (museum open Tues.-Sun. 9:30am-4:30pm, gallery open Tues.-Sun. 9:30-11:30am and 1-4pm; admission $3.30, students $1.30).

BLUE MOSQUE

Sultan Ahmet I built the **Blue Mosque** (*Sultanahmet Camii*) opposite Aya Sophia in a brazen attempt to one-up Justinian. The mosque's formidable silhouette is unforgettable, and the interior of blue Iznik tiles is stunning. Sultan Ahmet was the sixth sultan after the Turkish conquest of Istanbul—hence, the six minarets. In its day, the mosque was most famous for the controversy over its minarets—religious leaders didn't want the sultan to match the number of minarets at Mecca. The ever-resourceful Ahmet averted the crisis by providing the money and workers necessary to build a seventh minaret at Mecca. The mosque has 16 balconies, symbolizing his role as the 16th sultan since the beginning of the Ottoman state. On the left side of the altar is the sultan's seal. Iron bars running across the domes indoors ensure that the whole

Kingdome Come

The Byzantine **Aya Sophia** offered inspiration to Sinan and the Ottoman archi-tects who preceded him. Built by the Emperor Justinian between 532 and 537 as the Church of the Holy Wisdom, it was distinguished by a large dome buttressed by two half-domes, and was for 900 years Constantinople's premier cathedral. Upon the Ottoman conquest in 1453, Mehmet the Conqueror converted the building into a mosque. So ponderous were the height and girth of Aya Sophia's central dome that, upon the cathedral's completion, Justinian supposedly pro-claimed, "O Solomon, I have surpassed thee!" Sultan Süleyman, whose name meant "Solomon," was well aware of his empire's classical heritage and consid-ered Justinian's gloating a personal challenge. Sinan made Süleyman's ambition a reality. It was Sinan who from 1568 to 1574 built the **Selimiye Mosque** in Edirne, which boasts a dome the size of Aya Sophia's, supported by eight columns, four axial half-domes, and a single half-dome in front. The size of Selimiye's central dome surpassed even that of Aya Sophia, and superior engineering ensured that it didn't collapse, as Aya Sophia's original dome did several times. Thus Sinan sur-passed Justinian, Süleyman surpassed Solomon, and Ottoman Classical architec-ture was born.

structure bends in earthquakes; it has withstood 20 so far. An underground pool also moderates the mosque's interior temperature, keeping it cool in the summer and warm in the winter. You may visit the mosque except during the five daily prayer times; modest dress is required.

Elsewhere in the Blue Mosque complex, visit the **tomb of Sultan Ahmet I,** which, like other imperial tomb *(türbe)*, houses the sarcophagi of the sultan and his immedi-ate family (open Wed.-Sun. 9am-4:30pm; 75¢ "donation").

To your right as you leave the Blue Mosque are the **Carpet and Kilim Museums,** with carpets and woven *kilim* from all over the Muslim world (open Tues.-Sun. 9am-4pm). It's worthy of a visit if you are interested in buying a carpet or *kilim* of your own, but keep in mind that the finer tapestries cost 50-100% more in Istanbul than in smaller towns.

SULTANAHMET

There are a few more sights back in the heart of Sultanahmet. The **Yerebatan Cistern** is a vast underground cavern where shallow water eerily reflects the 336 columns that support the structure. To get there, exit Aya Sophia's gate and cross the street to your right; it's the stone building on the left. Wooden walkways allow you to wander among the columns, while atmospheric lighting and classical music in the back-ground create an other-worldly effect. Underground waterways originally connected the cistern to the Topkapı Palace, but the passage was blocked to stop the traffic in stolen goods and abducted women (open daily 9am-5pm; admission $1.65).

The **Mosaic Museum** is in the gallery of shops below the mosque. It features mosa-ics dating from the 6th century, when the entire area was part of the Byzantine Impe-rial Palace. At press time, the collection was being renovated. It may not be open regularly during renovations (open Wed.-Mon. 8:30am-8pm; admission $1.25).

On the other side of the Blue Mosque is the ancient **Hippodrome,** a park where Byzantine emperors once presided over chariot races and circuses. The tranquility of the park today contrasts with its turbulent history. Long ago it was the site of violent uprisings and demonstrations. In 532, 30,000 people were massacred here as Justin-ian's troops put an end to the riots that had plagued Constantinople. In the Hippo-drome stands the granite **Egyptian Obelisk,** the upper part a 15th-century BC obelisk brought to Constantinople in 390 AD from Cairo. It was originally 25m high, but to move it had to be chopped it to 18.5m. The **Serpentine Column,** taken from the Temple of Apollo at Delphi, is a coarse column at the end of the Hippodrome. It was coated with bronze plates until members of the Fourth Crusade tore off the metal.

Across from the Hippodrome, next to Istanbul's legal administration buildings, stands the 16th-century **Ibrahim Paşa Palace.** This magnificent building houses a museum of Turkish and Islamic art featuring tiles, Qurans, and a fine carpet collection. The courtyard also houses a picturesque teahouse (open Tues.-Sun. 10am-5pm).

GRAND BAZAAR

The enormous **Grand Bazaar** *(Kapalı Çarşı)* is a vast, arched, colorful, chaotic marketplace which specializes in leather and carpets. You will get lost among the more than 4000 shops, but you'll probably enjoy it. The old part of the Bazaar is a jumble of shops selling hookah pipes, bright baubles, copper filigree shovels, Byzantine-style icons on red velvet, "ancient" Turkish daggers (made in Taiwan), silver flintlock guns with mother-of-pearl handles, chess sets, and hand puppets. Unfortunately, several warnings are in order. Hawkers prey on tourists. Fake and faulty merchandise is everywhere and the summer tourist invasion inflates prices by as much as 400%. Beware of bright, shiny *kayseri;* these shoddy imitations of Persian carpets are worthless, though people have been known to pay as much as $1000 for them. The gold is mostly 14-karat and is no more expensive elsewhere in Turkey. In short, it is better to look here than to buy. But if you know what you want, and know what price is reasonable, you may find a deal.

To reach the bazaar from Sultanahmet, follow the tram tracks toward Aksaray for five minutes until you see the large mosque on your right. Walk to the mosque, enter its side gate, and walk, with the park on your left, to the bazaar entrance (open Mon.-Sat. 9am-7pm).

At the opposite entrance of the bazaar is the **Sahaflar Çarşısı,** a used book market. A wide selection of books are sold here, along with Quranic inscriptions and university texts. The market opens onto a bustling square. Opposite stands the huge entrance gate of **Istanbul University,** which fronts a leafy, well-shaded campus that is a haven from the bustle of the city. Its tranquility is spoiled somewhat, however, by the constant presence of riot police resting languidly in the shade. You should avoid this area on Friday, especially after Friday prayers, as violent demonstrations sometimes pop up and are predictably squelched by the riot cops. The campus contains **Beyazıt Camii,** the oldest mosque in Istanbul.

SÜLEYMANIYE

The university walls to the left lead to the **Süleymaniye Camii** complex (completed in 1557), one of the three masterpieces of Sinan. Sinan served as Chief Court Architect under Ottoman Sultans Süleyman the Magnificent and his son, Selim. The name "Sinan" remains venerated in Turkey today, as he almost single-handedly codified Ottoman Classical architecture, a style so influential that generations of architects began imitating it shortly after the master's death. The huge Süleymaniye complex includes a mosque, seven *medreses* (religious schools), an *imaret* (charitable soup kitchen), and the *türbe* (tombs) of Süleyman and his wife Haseki Hürrem. It was intended as a center for Islamic higher education. Today it is said that there are buried treasures in the minarets. To the east of the mosque reposes a majestic courtyard; to the west a graveyard where Süleyman and Haseki Hürrem rest peacefully in opulent *türbe* drenched in Iznik tile (tombs open 9:30am-4:30pm; 75¢ "donation").

FATIH

A 20-minute walk northwest from the graveyard leads to the **Fatih Camii,** the imperial mosque complex of Sultan Mehmet II, notorious in European history books for seizing Constantinople in 1453, converting Aya Sophia into a mosque, and designing the Topkapı Palace. The Fatih Camii, nearly a century older than the Süleymaniye, remains impressive in its own right. The people of Fatih have a reputation for Islamic religiousity; you'll see many women covered from head to toe in *chador* and bearded men in Islamic dress here. The atmosphere differs markedly from the rest of Istanbul; some Turks liken it to Iran and call it *Küçük İran,* or "Little Iran." The mosque itself is usually crowded, and the rest of the complex serves as a meeting and recreation area for the community.

Somewhat northwest of Fatih is a mandatory stop for Byzantine art connoisseurs, the impeccably preserved **Kariye Camii.** It's a long way up Fevzipaşa Cad. near the Edirne Gate and is accessible by *dolmuş,* bus #58 from Eminönü, or any bus in the direction *Edirnekapı.* Having undergone the transition from Byzantine church to mosque, and mosque to museum, the building showcases superb 14th-century frescoes and mosaics. The realism and expressiveness of this strain of late Byzantine art influenced Giotto and other early Italian painters (open Wed.-Mon. 9:30am-4:30pm). From here you can also see the 7km of ruins that were once the **Theodosian Land Walls,** stretching from the Golden Horn to the Sea of Marmara. The only character to have ever crossed these looming, 5th-century ramparts was Mehmet the Conqueror.

EMİNÖNÜ

When you come within 200m of the Golden Horn you'll pass the **Rüstem Paşa Camii,** whose famous interior, almost entirely inlaid with Iznik tiles, compensates for a humble exterior. It was built in 1561 under Rüstem, a grand-vizier. The architect was the famed Sinan.

Soon after is the 17th-century **Yeni Camii,** whose steps afford a shaded resting place. It was built for Valide Sultan Safiye, mother of Mehmet II by a student of Sinan.

Beside Yeni Camii is the **Egyptian Spice Bazaar.** Egyptians once dominated the spice trade in Istanbul and this is where they held shop. This feast for the senses is much less touristy than the Grand Bazaar and does not sell leather or carpets. Instead, it is crammed with a mind-boggling array of sticky sweets, honeycomb cut straight from the hive, aphrodisiacs, spices, and gold.

Another Istanbul highlight are the **Bosphorus cruises.** Boats leave from Pier 3 beside the Galata Bridge in Eminönü ($3.35). When the ferry makes its final stop on the Asian side, have some fish *kebap,* mussels, or fried *kalamari* for $2-5 from the street vendors. Then walk up the hill for beautiful views of the Black Sea. Double-decker bus #210 also runs hourly from behind the tourist office to points along the European side of the Bosphorus and costs two bus tickets each way.

ACROSS THE GOLDEN HORN

Across the Galata Bridge is the 62m-high **Galata Tower,** built by the Emperor Justinian in 528. Genoese merchants rebuilt the tower in 1348 to spy on the old city. It still serves that purpose today, allowing for a spectacular view of the Golden Horn and the Bosphorus. The tower was also the take-off site for the first intercontinental flight, executed in a da Vinci-style hang glider. After hours, the tower degenerates into a pricey nightclub. From the Golden Horn, Galata Kulesi Sok. leads to the tower.

Along the Bosphorus sits **Dolmabahçe Palace,** the home of sultans from 1856 until the demise of the Ottoman Empire after WWI. The site of the palace was first used by Mehmet II as a royal pleasure garden shortly after the conquest of Istanbul. Soldiers guard the royal dock and the memory of Atatürk, who died in the palace on November 10, 1938, at 9:05am (all the clocks were stopped at that moment). Pseudo-French architecture reflects the sultan's pretensions of grandeur, even during the decline of the empire. Be sure to see the vast reception room, with 56 columns and a huge crystal chandelier weighing 4.5 tons. The palace's Bird Pavilion housed birds from all over the world (open Tues.-Sun. 9:30am-4pm; admission $5). From Eminönü, take the ferry to Beşiktaş (50¢) or bus #58. The number of daily visitors is limited, so go early.

Round out your tour with other sights scattered around the city, including **Askeri Müze,** the soldiers' museum in **Harbiye,** on the European side (tel. 140 6255). This is a 10-year-old's paradise—swords, armor, and other implements of war from the various cultures that have inhabited Asia Minor over the last few millennia garnish the walls. The Ottoman Military Band has live shows in the museum (open 9am-5pm).

Rumeli Hisarı (Thrace Castle), next to the second Bosphorus bridge on the European side, was an integral part of the Ottoman defense system. In wartime, a huge

WESTERN TURKEY

link chain was stretched from this fort to its mate **Anadolu Hisarı** (Anatolia Castle), across the Bosphorus on the Asian side. One link is on exhibit in the Askeri Müze. The fortress is composed of towers around a central courtyard. The view of the Bosphorus from atop the walls is spectacular.

Ortaköy is a liberal neighborhood favored by artists and young people; a church, synagogue, and mosque here are representative of the area's tolerance. It is a bit avant-garde and bohemian.

ASIAN ISTANBUL

The **TV tower** at Çamlıca Hill is Istanbul's highest point and offers views of the entire city and Bosphorus straits. There is a beautifully decorated Turkish cafe here, where classical Ottoman music plays and waiters wear traditional 19th-century costumes.

The best skyline views at sunset are to be had at **Salacak** in the city of Üsküdar, another home of excellent cafes and tea shops. Take the bus from Üsküdar, then the ferry to Çamlıca. The **Chamber of Florence Nightingale** in the Military Hospital in Haydarpaşa is open to the public. The **English Cemetery** in the Selimiye Barracks (one of the world's largest) is a beautifully maintained military cemetery for British soldiers who fell in the 1854 Crimean War against Russia.

Beylerbeyi Sarayı (tel. 321 9320) was the rococo-style summer palace of the Ottoman sultans. Built of white marble in the 19th century, it has a lovely garden teeming with magnolia trees (open daily 9am-4pm). Designed in the same style as Dolmabaçe Palace, it was used mainly to house visiting notables, diplomats, and politicians.

Some other areas of note: Bağdat Cad. in Kadıköy is the place for the Euro-chic (ferry from Piers 3 and 7, every 20min., 50¢). **Çengelköy** has excellent, cheap, and simple fish restaurants. **Anadoluhisarı** has small waterside restaurants and cafes. **Kanlica** is reputed to have the most delicious yogurt in all of Turkey. **Emirgan** is a peaceful village of old-style Turkish houses and excellent Turkish tea. An 1843 castle is nearby. Bus #210 heads to Kanlica, Emirgan, and Anadoluhisan. **İstiklâl Cad.**, the heart of modern Istanbul, is also worth a visit.

■ Near Istanbul: Eyüp

Eyüp, a popular Muslim pilgrimage site, houses the 15th-century tomb of Job, the companion of Muhammad who died during an Arab siege of the city in the 7th century. The Golden Horn ferries ride the waves to Eyüp twice hourly from pier 6 in Eminönü, above the Galata Bridge (35min., 45¢), or catch bus #55. You may see regally costumed young boys brought here by their families—the trip is customary for boys before circumcision. Once the refuge of the artists and the elite of the Ottoman Empire, today Eyüp is mostly a religious site, with Quran shops, the Eyüp Mosque, and lovely, spacious cemeteries. Since this is a quite conservative area, it is important to dress modestly. Avoid traveling in packs, making excessive hand gestures, and drinking alcohol in the open.

■ Near Istanbul: Büyükada

The fourth stop on the ferry ride to the Princess Islands, Büyükada is the largest and most enjoyable of the isles. When you get off the ferry, you'll find yourself in the heart of the commercial district. Fish restaurants border the shore; delicious *kebap* restaurants and *pastane* (pastry shops) line the streets in every direction. Primarily a popular summer retreat for natives of Istanbul, Büyükada offers lovely pinewood scenery, swimming, and peaceful walks farther behind the busy district. It's an excellent daytrip from Istanbul.

There are no cars or buses here. You'll survive—enjoy **walks** or a **horse-and-buggy** ride (starting from İsa Çelebi Sok.). Prices range from $2.50 for a short ride to $15 for an entire island tour (the tourists' favorite). You can also rent a bike for $2.50 per hour. **Ferries** depart from Eminönü or Kabataş on the north side; look for signs saying Sirkeci Adalar (from Eminönü, 6-7 per day, round-trip $2.50). A faster and slightly more expensive alternative is the **seabus** (operating from Bostancı and Kabataş in the summer). Many **pharmacies** are on Çınar Cad., to the right of the busy dock district. They alternate the hours they are open, as is standard Turkish policy, to make 24-hour service available. Check signs on the windows for details. In the **PTT,** 17 Balık Cad., is open in summer Mon.-Fri. 9am-9pm, Sat.-Sun. 9am-1pm; winter Mon.-Fri. 9am-6pm, Sat.-Sun. 9am-1pm. International phone service available. The **hospital** is Büyükada Hastanesi (tel. 382 6228), on 24 Lalehatun Cad. For **police,** go to 23 Nisan Cad. **Telephone Code:** 216.

Most of the hotels here are expensive and boast luxurious summer retreats with indoor everything (pool, disco, etc.). The **Ideal Aile Pansion,** 14 Kadıyoran Cad. (tel. 382 6857), is the exception. The pension is a haunted house-style masterpiece, with large rooms that are more like apartments than hotel rooms. Communal showers and bathrooms ($10 per person).

A horde of restaurants occupy the central commercial area by the dock. **Yeni Büfe** (tel. 382 6357; open daily 8am-11pm) has *lahmacun* (Turkish pizza on pita bread; 65¢), *döner* ($2.50), and *ayran* (50¢). A pastry shop recommended by islanders is **Dolci,** 23 Nisan Cad. (tel. 382 6349), which has outdoor seating, cheap lemonade, and *ayçöreği* for 35¢ (open daily 10am-1am).

Take a **horse and buggy ride** to Yörük Ali and Dil Uzantısı for a picnic or day at the beach. Another option is to take the buggy to **Luna Park** (ride should be no more than $7.50; 10-15min.) at the back of the island. **Donkey ride,** you plead? Rent one here ($10 for 30 min.). Ask the locals about the path to the stone-covered **beach** with perhaps the cleanliest swimming on the island. Clean is, however, a relative term. Pollution is a real problem around Istanbul, and the fact that locals can survive the microbes in the water does not mean that you can. **St. George's Monastery** is at the highest point on the island. Make sure to ask about the trails—hiking through the dense forest is forbidden in some places, and the guard in the watchtower overlooking the monastery may call the police.

Northwestern Turkey

◼ Edirne

Edirne is a quiet city located near the Greek and Bulgarian borders in Turkish Thrace. The city offers 5000 years of architectural history within a 1km radius. Its ancient name of Hadrianopolis derives from the Roman emperor Hadrian, who rebuilt the city in the 2nd century AD. The city was later incorporated in the Byzantine Empire. In 1363 Sultan Murat I conquered the area for the Ottoman Empire. Edirne then became the imperial capital and remained so for 91 years until Mehmet the Conqueror made Constantinople his new capital in 1453. Nonetheless, the city remained an important gateway between Europe and Anatolia; it was still the seventh largest city in Europe as late as the 19th century.

Today, the city no longer has a concentrated population area but is still a popular transit point for travelers en route to Istanbul and other eastern destinations. Edirne also plays host to the annual **Kirkpinar grease wrestling festival** held in the last week of June. The city's most important architectural structure is the Selimiye Camii, designed by the master architect Sinan. Its four minarets are the tallest in the Muslim world (230 feet). Other traces of Sinan's work can be seen in the various *hammam*s (baths) and bridges throughout the city.

ORIENTATION AND PRACTICAL INFORMATION

The triangle-shaped **Hürriyet Meydanı** is the center of Edirne, bounded by the **Eski Camii**, Kervansaray Hotel, and a row of shops. The Cafe Antik occupies most of the space inside the square itself. *Dolmuş* from the bus station drop you here. **Talat Paşa Cad.** is the city's main east-west thoroughfare, starting behind the Eski Camii and running through town to the Tunka River. If you walk on Talat Paşa Cad. away from Selimiye Camii, the first intersection will be **Saraçlar Cad.,** where the city's main shops are located. Continue down Talat Paşa Cad. to the tourist office at the next intersection. The street on your left is **Maarif Cad.,** where you'll find a variety of cheap accommodations. Returning to the square on Talat Paşa Cad., the magnificent Selimiye Camii will be in front of you, overlooking a park and tea gardens. If you walk to the left of the park on Selimiye Cad. you'll find the *dolmuş* terminal and further down the street the town's main shopping street. Keep going to the next intersection; the tourist office is on the corner. This street (on the left), Maarif Cad., is home to a good selection of inexpensive hotels. On your right is the beautiful **Selimiye Mosque** which overlooks a park. You can walk up the road to the left of the park and you will see on your left the main local bus and *dolmuş* terminal.

Tourist Office: 17 Talat Paşa Cad. (tel. 213 9208), 200m west of the Eski Camii, on your left after crossing Saraçlar Cad. Free maps. Open June-Aug. daily 9am-6pm, Sept.-May Mon.-Sat. 8:30am-5pm.

Bulgarian Consulate: 31 Talat Paşa Asfaldı (tel. 225 1069), 1km southeast of Eski Camii, on the road to Istanbul. Visas allow a 30-day stay. Foreigners should get express visas. Normally visas take a week to issue: tourist $31.50, transit $21, double transit $42. Express visas (issued the same day) are: tourist $46.50 and transit $31.50. Multiple entry: 3 months $42, 6 months $73.25, 1 year $105. Open Mon.-Fri. 9am-noon.

Trains: Two train stations serve Edirne, one on the road to **Istanbul** (tel. 225 1155 or 212 0914), and one in **Kapıkule** (tel. 238 2312), within walking distance of the Bulgarian border. To get to Kapıkule, take a *dolmuş* from in front of Rüstempaşa Kervansaray Otel (every 10min., $1), or a bus (every hr. until 6pm) from the local bus station. Kapıkule is the last stop. To: Istanbul (1 per day at 8am, 7hr., $2); Sofia (2 per day, 8hr., $19); Budapest; and 1 per day to points west in Europe (arrives from Munich early in the morning and leaves late at night).

Banks: Turkiye İş Bankasi on Saraçlar Cad. exchanges traveler's checks. There is also a **Baranti Bank** (open 9am-noon and 1-5pm).

Buses: Walk across the street from the *otogar* to take a *dolmuş* into Edirne. Buses to: Istanbul (every 30min., 3hr., $6); Keşan (5 per day, 1½hr., $4); Bursa (April-Dec. 2 per day, $9.50; Nov.-March 1 per night, $9.50); Ankara (2 per night, 10hr., $20); and Kapıkule (every 30min. until 9pm).

Hospital: Edirne Devlet Hastanesi (tel. (284) 225 4603). Public.

PTT: 17 Saraçlar Cad. **Telephones** and 24hr., although unreliable, **currency exchange.** They cash traveler's checks Mon.-Fri. 8:30am-5pm.

Telephone Code: 284.

ACCOMMODATIONS

Plenty of cheap options are scattered along Saraçlar Cad. and especially Maarif Cad., the first left after passing over Saraçlar Cad. on Talat Paşa Cad.

Hotel Kervansaray (tel. 225 2195; fax 225 0462), also known as Rüstempaşa, runs the length of Hürriyet Meydanı, Eski Camii Altı. It was built in the 1550s as an overnight resting place for camel caravans *en route* from Europe to the East. Recently renovated, its 100 rooms come with bath, toilet paper, TV, phone, and carpet, but still retain their quaint antique feel. The call to prayer resonates through the corridors and rooms at 4:30am. There's also a restaurant, parking, and an "American Bar" (whatever that means). Singles $18; doubles $32; triples $42. Breakfast included. V/MC.

Hotel Aksaray (tel. 225 3901), at the intersection of Maarif Cad. and Ali Paşa Ortakapi Cad., a couple of doors down from Efe Hotel. Cheaper and much more basic than its counterparts, it has small, plain rooms all with radio and telephone. Singles $5; doubles $8.75; triples $11.25. Rooms with bath cost considerably more.

Efe Hotel, 13 Maarif Cad. (tel. 213 6166, -466; fax 212 9446). Pleasant hotel with clean rooms including modern bathroom, telephone, and TV. Air-conditioned lobby and another "American Bar." Singles $27; doubles $38; triples $46; quads $63. Breakfast included. Discounts available for large groups.

Hotel Konak, 6 Maarif Cad. (tel. 225 1348 or 225 2148). Two words: no frills. Pleasant but a bit eerie, like it may have been used for an episode of *Scooby Doo.* Communal TV room. Singles $3.25; doubles $3.75; triples $4.25. $1 extra for room with bath.

Fifi Camping (tel. 235 7908), on the main Istanbul road, 8km from the center of town. Has its own restaurant, bar, and pool. Hotels in town are almost as cheap and more convenient. Camping $4 per person, tent rental $2, cars $2. V/MC.

FOOD AND ENTERTAINMENT

Edirne has three terrific tea gardens (*çay bahçesi*) with spectacular views of the city's main mosques. The **Sera** teahouse, in the park between the Selimiye Camii and Eski Camii, has a breathtaking view of the mosques. The atmosphere at the cafe is enhanced by a gentle fountain in the middle of the park. Tea (*çay*) is served either in a traditional small Turkish tea glass (20¢) or in a larger cup (35¢). *Aran* and *tost* both cost 35¢. Further down from the Selimye Camii, moving towards Üç Şerefli Camii is the recently opened **Tunca Cafe.** The cafe hopes to conjure visions of Barbados with its with fountains, small foot bridges and bamboo umbrellas, all in an area that was formerly a bus stop. You won't find sweets like baklava, but instead drinks (tea, coffee, and cappuccino), burgers, *tost,* and *dondurma.* A steady current of the nightlife streams past this tea garden. Further down from Selimye and covering most of the Hürriyet Meydani is the **Cafe Antik.** The cafe is bordered by the Eski Camii and Caravanserai on two of its sides. Its romantic atmosphere and table umbrellas give couples a sense of privacy. Selections are nearly identical to the other cafes, but with a greater variety of quick snacks (*karişik tost* 60¢, hamburger $1).

Edirne also has its share of cheap eats and sweet shops for those looking for a more substantial meal at a decent price. The **Çati Restaurant** (tel. 225 1307), located on Talat Paşa Cad. just a few doors down from the tourist office (away from the main mosques), has an excellent selection of food in a clean environment. Choose from a variety of cold *meze* for around $1, meat *köfte* (meatballs) for $2, and after-dinner sweets such as *kemalpaşa* for $1. Discounts available for large groups. Across from the Tunca Cafe, going towards the Municipal Building, is the **Beyti Kebap** (tel. 225 6624). This restaurant specializes in pitas and *Lahmacuns* at decent prices. Try their special *adana* plate for $3 or a double order of *shish kebap* (mixed dish) for $3.50, regular kebap dishes start at $1.75. A sweet view of Eski Camii from their outside seating enhances your meal. Another food option is the **Gaziantepo Kebap Salonu,** located on the same side of the street as the tourist office but before the Çati. Meals include *döner, adan kebap* and *şiş kebap* for $1.75. Salads run about 70¢. The place is small but has two levels; ask to see the "cow" on the second floor. Finally, closer to the Maarif Cad. strip of hotels, is the clean and delightful **Park Restaurant** (tel. 212 5041, 225 5657), which offers excellent food in a pleasant indoor setting. The manager speaks English and is happy to show you the specials of the day. *Adana, urfa* and *döner kebap* go for $1.75 while assorted *lahmacuns* are 50¢. The restaurant is down the street on 9 Maarif Cad.

For dessert, go to Saraçlar Cad. where several sweet shops *(pastanesi)* await your sweet tooth. **Cafe Muharipler** is located on the same side of the street as the PTT on the upper floor of the Vaklif İş Hani building. Tea (20¢), coffee (35¢), and colas (50¢) are offered along with a small selection of snacks (hamburger 70¢). Popular among the younger crowd in Edirne, it has a nice view of the city center. On the other side of the street is the three-story **Zoga Pastanesi,** a great place to start your day or get a quick sweet for the road. It is directly across from the PTT and is open 7am-11pm. Try their morning *Poğça* for less than 20¢. Just a bit further down the street, away from the central mosques, is the **Roma Pastanesi** (at #99). This sweet shop also boasts three floors and a *dondurma* machine at its entrance. It's the place to come for a delicious piece of cake ($3 per kg., open 7am-11pm).

SIGHTS

Edirne will enchant you with its Islamic medieval architecture, especially its mosques. The city's main sight is the **Selimiye Camii,** completed by the Ottoman architect Sinan. This work of genius, which includes 71m minarets, a 32m diameter dome and 999 windows, is the town symbol and can be seen towering above Edirne from several kilometers away. The exterior is impressive, but it's the interior that is unforgettable. It is vast and ornately decorated from dome to floor. The tiles inside the mosque are a brilliant red; indeed, their hue were long the envy of European ceramists. The mosque was completed between 1569 and 1575 at the behest of Sultan Selim II. Approach the mosque through an ancient shopping arcade, and then proceed up a small stone staircase (marked "Camii Giriş" and "Moschee Eingang") to the courtyard.

The nearby **Eski Camii,** completed in 1415, is quite distinct from the others architecturally: instead of one large dome, it has a series of small ones. Its interior is undergoing restoration, but part of it is still in use and can be visited. The final important mosque near the city center is the so-called **Üç Şerefli Camii.** The mosque was built between 1438 and 1447 on orders from Murat I. It is an important link in the evolution of Ottoman architecture with a dome 24m in diameter and a tall northwest minaret (overshadowed only by the Selimiye, built two centuries later). Notice the extensive floral motifs on the dome as well as the Quranic inscriptions in the same area. Some sections of the mosque are closed for renovation.

Edirne's other major sight is the **Beyazıt Complex,** a charitably endowed, spiritual and physical welfare facility a few kilometers from the center of town. To get there, walk along Talat Paşa Cad. until you reach the river, but don't cross the bridge; turn right and walk along the dirt path that runs parallel to the river. After a 10-minute walk you'll see a bridge on your left. Cross it, and walk four more minutes through pleasant countryside. The centerpiece of the complex is the **Beyazıt Camii,** a beautiful, single-domed mosque surrounded by multi-domed buildings which were designed to be schools, storehouses, and asylums. While these buildings are locked and no longer used, the mosque is usually open.

Be sure to visit the Beyazit Complex's **Museum of Health,** located to the right of the complex towards its entrance. The hospital was built during the 1480s and was one of the foremost centers of medicine in its time. The Ottomans used musicians here to help in the treatment of the sick (open 8:30am-5:30pm; admission 70¢).

Back in the center of town, there are several other sights worth a quick look. The **Bedesten,** on Hürriyet Meydanı, is a half-millennium-old covered market. Come here to buy leather goods, books, stationery, linens, and postcards. It is also a great place to escape from the sun. On the other side of Hürriyet Meydanı is the **Rüstem Paşa Kervansaray.** This multi-domed structure, designed in the style of the Eski Camii, was built as a resting place for medieval caravan trains. Much of it now serves as a university residence. The remainder is a hotel. Near the Selimiye Camii are two museums of minor interest. The **Ethnography Museum** exhibits clothing, carpets, and medieval armor (open Tues.-Sun. 10:30am-noon and 1-5pm; admission 60¢), and the **Turkish and Islamic Art Museum** contains examples of Ottoman architecture, Qurans, weapons, and glasswork (open Tues.-Sun. 8am-noon and 1:30-5:30pm, admission 70¢). The low prices and inspiring architecture may beckon you to sprawl out in reverie at one of Edirne's Turkish baths. Try Sinan's 16th-century **Sokollu Hamamı** (tel. 225 2193), beside the Üç Şerefeli Camii (open daily 8am-10pm for men, 10am-5pm for women; admission $2.25, with massage $5). Finally, Turkey's annual **grease wrestling** (*yağlı güreş*) tournament is held in Edirne in the last week of June. Travelers to Edirne during this time should call ahead, as the town is filled with spectators for the week-long festival.

▓ Çanakkale

As the coast's northernmost resort, Çanakkale faces the narrowest point of the Dardanelles, which in large part explains why the British chose to mount their WWI campaign here. Inexpensive accommodations and frequent bus connections to nearby sights and other cities make Çanakkale an easy base from which to explore Gallipoli and Troy. Because of its proximity to the site of the disastrous WWI battle, Çanakkale is particularly hospitable to New Zealanders and Australians, compatriots of the thousands who lost their lives at Gallipoli (Gelibolu). A handful of pubs cater to the Aussie and Kiwi traveler with friendly service and reasonable prices. But be warned if traveling in late April: April 25 is Anzac Day, commemorating the Allied invasion of the peninsula in 1915. Thousands of Australians and New Zealanders flock to the area around this time, which raises prices and makes budget accommodations scarce.

ORIENTATION AND PRACTICAL INFORMATION

Tourist Office: 67 İskele Meydanı (tel./fax 217 1187). From the bus station, take a left out the main doors, then take the next right onto Demircioğlu Cad. (following the "feribot" sign) and continue onto the docks. The office will be on your left just before the shore. If you arrive by ferry, the office is straight ahead to your right. Friendly English-speaking staff. Open 8:30am-7:30pm.

Tourist Agencies: Several agencies provide group tours of the Gallipoli Battle Sites and Troy. **Gallipoli tours** typically include transportation, breakfast or lunch, an English-speaking guide, and admission to the sites ($10). Tours of Troy are $7-8. **Down Under Travel Agency,** İsmetpaşa Mah., 14 Atatürk Cad. (tel. 814 2431), based on the European side of the Dardanelles at Eceabat, 7km from the Gallipoli battlegrounds; Çanakkale-based **Ana-Tur,** Cumhuriyet Meydani Özay İşhani Kat. 2, No.30 (tel. 271 5482 or 217 0771); and the 30-year-old **Troyanzac Travel Agency** (tel. 217 5847; fax 217 5849), to the right of the clock tower, offering car rental, private guides, hotel reservations, and general information in addition to summer Gallipoli tours leaving at 10am and 3pm, and tours of Troy leaving at 9am and 3pm. **R.S.L. House** (814 1065; fax 814 1900) offers the most relaxed tours of Gallipoli and arranges special boat tours of the Allied landing sites ($10).

Buses: Arrive every 1½hr. from Bursa (5½hr., $8.15); Edirne (stops at Eceabat for ferry to Çanakkale, 5hr., $8.75); Istanbul (5hr., $10.75); Pergamon (4hr., $8.15); Ayvalık (3½hr., $6.25); Ankara (12hr, $16.25); and Izmir (5hr., $8.75). Buses leave more often in the morning. *Dolmuş* ($1) run from Çanakkale (at the small bridge near the Sari Çay inlet) to Truva and Güzelyali (30min.).

Ferries: To Eceabat, 6am-midnight (every hr., in winter every 2hr., 50¢). In summer, ferries often leave early if they fill up. The smaller ferry to Kilitbahir is located to the right of the main docks (every 15min., 50¢). Travelers are free to pass between Greece and Turkey but exorbitant port taxes are imposed on international ferries.

Hospitals: Çanakkale Public Devlet Hospital (tel. 217 1098). **Özel Hastane Private Hospital** (tel. 217 7461), 1km from the tourist office, past the bridge with the *dolmuş* station.

Police Station: (tel. 217 1181) Off İnonu Cad., next to the post office.

Postal Code: 17100.

Telephone Code: 286.

ACCOMMODATIONS

Budget accommodations cluster around the clock tower, with many good restaurants and bars only a few steps away. It is best to check out a few places before settling on any one particular room.

Yellow Rose Pension, 5 Yeni Sok. (tel./fax 217 3343), around the corner about 50m from the clock tower. A popular backpacker hangout in Çanakkale, featuring a peaceful garden area, clean dorm rooms (single sex), screens on all windows (peace from the mosquitoes at last!), laundry facilities, and international phone and fax services. The film "Gallipoli," with Mel Gibson (hubba hubba), is shown every night for those who plan to tour the site. Singles $5; doubles $10; triples $15; roof $2.50. Breakfast $1.50.

Anac House, 61 Cumhuriyet Meydani (tel. 217 0156 or 217 1392; fax 217 2906), across from the taxi stand. Another popular meeting spot for Aussie and Kiwi backpackers. Laundry service and **internet access.** They can also arrange Gallipoli and Troy tours through Ana-Tur. Singles $6.50; doubles $11; triples $14; quads $17. Breakfast is $1.50 and they offer a $4 BBQ every evening from 6-7:30pm.

Hotel Efes, Saat Kulesi Meydani, 5 Fetvane Sok., one block from the clock tower behind the parking lot (tel. 217 3256). Simple, colorful, and airy rooms with negotiable prices surrounded by a rose-filled garden with a duck-filled fountain. Obscure location allows for noiseless sleep (except for the calls to prayer, and there's no escaping those). Singles $4.50; doubles $8.50; triples $10.50; quads $12.50. Rooms with bath are an extra $1.

Kervansaray Otel, 13 Fetvane Sok. (tel. 217 8192), across from Konak. A graceful time-worn structure with a fountain in the courtyard. Clean, sparse rooms with 4m-high ceilings. Hot water, kitchen, and laundry facilities. Singles $5.25; doubles $9.50; triples $14; quads $14.

Hotel Konak, 14 Fetvane Sok. (tel. 217 1150 or 217 1578), behind the clock tower to the left. Offers clean, spacious, but somewhat dark rooms. You can also use the TV in the large lounge area. Singles $5.25; doubles $9.50; triples $12.50; quads $14. Breakfast $1.25.

FOOD AND ENTERTAINMENT

Çanakkale has an array of restaurants serving meat and fish, as well as vegetarian meals. You can dine over the day's fresh catch in the harbor area and then wander inland a few streets for a nightcap. The city's ever-changing body of visitors also makes its bar scene a pleasant treat for those wishing to meet people from around the world—especially from Down Under.

The **Yeni Entellektüel** (217 5603), located on the harbor boardwalk toward the military museum, is a great place to start the evening. This hip little restaurant offers *soğuk meze* (cold appetizers) and grilled meat dishes as well as fish galore. Dine on octopus salad ($4.25), kalamari ($3.50), or fried mussels ($1.75). Cold dishes go for about $1. Open until 2am. Just up the block is the **Şehir Restaurant** (tel./fax 217 1070), with lots of seating both indoors and outside and great views of nearby Kilitbakir, where the Dardanelles come to their closest point. The restaurant specializes in fish, with mackerel as well as yummy octopus (both $2.75). The **Liman Yalova Restaurant,** 7 Gümrük Sokak, is located on the harbor just past Şehir (tel. 217 1045; fax 217 6360). While it looks quite expensive, the place is actually only a bit more than the other harbor restaurants. The sunset from their upper terrace is inspiring (open daily noon-12:30am). For food that is catered to the backpacker crowd, look for the **Aussi/Kiwi Restaurant,** 32 Yalı Cad. (tel. 212 1722). They have happy hours from 6-7pm and again from 10-11pm. The amiable owner Kemal offers hot and cold dishes, seafood, and genuine Kelloggs Corn Flakes. Prices are cheap and aimed especially toward travelers on a limited budget (free milk with every meal!).

For a taste of the nightlife, head over to the **Alesta,** 4 Yali Cad. (217 0839 or 212 8732). One of the funkiest places to be after sunset, this fashionably decorated club has an extensive and up-to-date CD selection, an English-speaking staff, and a happy hour every evening with *Marmaris* specials for 70¢ (open until 2am in the summer, midnight in winter). Located farther down toward the clock tower is the **TNT Bar** (217 0771). The live music here is great, and they've got two dance floors with plenty of room for partying. Play billiards for $2.75 per hour (open until 2am). Back up on 19 Fetvahane Sok. is the **Depo Disco Bar** (212 6813). The music is pumping and the drinks are cheap (beer for $1).

SIGHTS

The town has only a smattering of sights. The **archaeological museum** has artifacts from Troy, a fantastic statue of Hadrian, and busts of Augustus (open Tues.-Wed. and Fri.-Sun. 8:30am-5:30pm; admission $1, with ISIC 50¢). There's also a **fortress** with a vintage World War I cannon and warship to commemorate the Gallipoli battle. **Çimenlik Kalesi** (Grassy Castle), a castle-turned-naval museum, lies 200m past the clock tower (open Tues.-Wed. and Fri.-Sun. 9am-noon and 1:30-5pm; admission 40¢, students 15¢). About 55km southwest of Çanakkale lie the famed waters of the **Kestanbol thermal springs** (tel. 637 5223), reachable by *dolmuş* or taxi via Ezine (buses leave every 2-2½hr.). They boast of the minerals in the waters with special curative powers for people with skin, heart, and circulation problems (open daily 8am-midnight; men $3.75, women $2.50).

■ Near Çanakkale

GALLIPOLI (GELIBOLU)

Across the Dardanelles, on the European side, lies the battlefield of **Gallipoli,** known as Gelibolu in Turkish. In 1915-16, seeing an opportunity to secure the Balkan front, Winston Churchill proposed that Britain use its superior naval forces to launch an attack on the Dardanelles. The Allies would then conquer Constantinople, drive Turkey out of the war, and open communications with Russia. The British faced heavy bombardment at the narrowest part of the strait, so the British navy turned its forces to the peninsula. High Command sent wave after wave of Australian, New Zealander,

---

Piri Who?

Gallipoli is the birthplace of Piri Reis, a famous seaman and cartographer born in 1470. As an admiral in the Ottoman Navy, he scoured the bazaars in his many ports-of-call for new charts and maps. Using his extensive library of charts and diagrams, Reis drew a map of the world in 1513. In 1929, a group of historians, poking around in Topkapi Palace in Istanbul, found Piri Reis's map and were astonished to discover that the map showed the coastal outlines of South and North America. It also included precise data on Antarctica, supposedly not discovered until 1818! Further studies of Reis's map have concluded that his "original" charts may have been actually drawn from aerial pictures taken from high in the sky; the rivers, mountain ranges, islands, desserts, and plateaus are drawn with unusual accuracy. Reis is also well known for several other maps, including his so-called Kitapi Bahriye (Sail Map).

---

and British troops against the highly fortified Turkish positions here and suffered brutal losses. This battle launched its hero, **Atatürk,** on a rapid rise to his status as Turkey's founding father. Thousands of Australians and New Zealanders make pilgrimages to war cemeteries here, where over half a million men were killed, and 22,000 Allied dead lie buried. There is a dawn ceremony at the cove.

The battle sights and accompanying memorials are spread out, so your best bet is to see Gallipoli on an organized tour, most of which provide excellent English-speaking guides, transportation to each of the memorials, and breakfast or lunch (Çanakkale: **Tourist Agencies,** p.409). Also, be sure to bring along your swimsuit, since tours often make a short stop for a swim at **Brighton Beach** (the site the Allied forces originally intended as their landing area in 1915). For those wishing to visit the area on their own, take a *dolmuş* from Eceabat to the Kabatepe Museum (tel. 814 1297; open daily 8:30am-noon and 1-5:30pm; admission 75¢). From the museum, it is 4km to Anzac Cove, and 7km uphill to the Australian **Lone Pine Memorial.** From here, walk up toward the highest point on the peninsula to **Chunuk Baır**—the high ground taken by Turkish forces under Atatürk (then known as Kemal Paşa) to deny the Allies their goal of control over the Dardanelles. Today, the **New Zealand Memorial** shares space with a statue of Atatürk.

Tours don't always include the memorials at the southern tip of the peninsula (some 30km from Kilitbakik, the town directly across from Çanakkale at the Dardanelles' narrowest point), but can be easily seen on a separate trip. Take the smaller ferry from Çanakkale to Kilitbakik and then a minibus to the **Çanakkale Memorial** at **Melles Point,** the very tip of the peninsula. Be sure to check the minibus service before traveling to Kilitbakik.

TROY (TRUVA)

Troy lies 32km south of Çanakkale. The site was forgotten, until **Heinrich Schliemann,** a German-born American millionaire-turned-amateur archaeologist, decided to prove that the Homeric stories were not pure fiction. Staking out the most promising site along the coast, he hired local workers and began excavating. To the astonishment of fellow archaeologists, Schliemann uncovered the ancient city.

People raised on stories of the **Trojan War** should not expect imposing ruins; the city Homer wrote about came tumbling down 3000 years ago. But the remaining Bronze Age fortifications, given their age, are remarkably well preserved. The tacky wooden horse that assures you that you've reached Troy is a new addition. If you are familiar with the Homeric stories of Hector, Paris, and Helen, you will get the sensation that these immortalized characters played out the tragedy on this site. Nine distinct strata, each containing the remains of a city from a different period, have been identified and dubbed Troy I through Troy IX. An illustrated explanation of each stratum is available in the **Excavation House** (on your right after passing the horse; included in the admission ticket with same hours). Troy I dates from 3200 BC. The city of Homer's *Iliad* is now believed to be Troy VI, *not* Troy II, the city Schliemann excavated. Look out for house foundations, city walls, a temple, and a theater. Bring a bottle of water (unless you have a camel-like capacity for water retention) because you'll need it (open daily 8am-7:30pm; off season daily 8am-5pm; admission $1.50, students 75¢).

You can arrange a visit to Troy with a tour group or individually. The **Anzac House** (tel. 217 0156, -1392) arranges tours of the sight that leave at 9am ($8). The tour guide is Ali Efe from Ana-Tur (tel. 217 5482), a retired military officer with a good command of English and a pleasant personality. **Down Under Travel Agency** (tel. 814 2431, across the straits in Eceabat) also has an excellent tour ($7) conducted by İlhami ("T.J.") Gezici who speaks English well. **Troyanzac** (tel. 217 5849; located near the clock tower) also conducts summer tours of the fabled sight at 9am and 3pm (3hr., $8, conducted in English). If you are not inclined to take an organized tour, it is not difficult to arrange the trip yourself. Go to the *dolmuş* station at Çanakkale (straight down Demircioğlu Cad. and right onto Atatürk Cad. until just before the bridge; 10-15min.) and board one heading to Troy (every hr., 30 min., 95¢). The *dolmuş* will drop you off at the museum entrance, but it's still a 10-15 minute walk to the excavation area and wooden horse. You can try to arrange for the *dolmuş* to wait an hour or two, or you can catch another one later.

GALLIPOLI TOWN

Gallipoli is a city of mistaken identity. During WWI, Allied troops referred to the peninsula as Gallipoli since this was the nearest city on their maps. The Battle of Gallipoli, however, actually occurred many kilometers down the peninsula at Anzac Cove and Melles Point. Nonetheless, this seaside town makes a pleasant base for overnight trips to the sights found near Çanakkale. Its quiet atmosphere, fresh fish, and beach just 1.5km down the road make Gallipoli an ideal place to relax with friends before setting off for an emotional tour of the battlefields at Anzac Cove.

Gallipoli is easily accessible by bus from many points in Turkey. Çanakkale TRUVA (tel. (286) 566 1183, -2626) has buses from Istanbul (16 per day, $8.50), Izmir (9 per day, $9.25), and Ankara (several per day, $10.75). From Gallipoli, check out Radar Tur (tel. 566 6424) for non-stop bus services to Istanbul (8 per day, $7.25), Izmir (1 daily, $9), and Ankara (1 daily, $10.75). The Gallipoli bus station is in **Liman Meydani**, the square where most of the hotels, restaurants, and taxis are clustered. If you walk from the square across the bridge next to the old watch tower, you will come to the **Yilmaz Hotel,** whose English-speaking staff is the closest thing to a tourist office in the town. The street across from the hotel is **Atatürk Cad.** that leads up to several other hotels, the **PTT**, and several **pharmacies** and grocery stores. The **ferry** dock is on the waterfront and provides hourly service to Lapseki on the mainland (6am-1am, 50¢). There are plenty of **banks** scattered throughout town (on weekends, change money at the PTT). Near the harbor and to the right of the tower museum, Akbank (open 9am-12:30pm and 1:30-5pm) has an **ATM** that accepts Cirrus as well as V/MC. Other ATMs are located at Valuf Bank near the taxi stand and T.C. Ziraat Bankasi.

■ Bursa

Nestled in the shadow of the 2km-high slopes of Mt. Uludağ (literally "Great Mountain," or Mt. Olympus; see p. 417), Bursa is a city of fascinating contrasts. Along with Konya, Bursa is one of Turkey's two holy cities of pilgrimage. While many of the 14th-century mosques and tombs are still visited, Bursa has also become an industrial center with a wealthy resort area. The vast gardens, parks, and verdant plains at the center of a significant fruit production area contribute to the reputation of the city as "green." Green is also the symbolic color of Islam, making it doubly appropriate here. Mt. Uludağ, which gives the city its traditional moniker "Green Bursa," is home to Turkey's leading ski resort. As if this weren't enough, Bursa is famous for its silk trade, its local invention of İskender *kebap* (grilled meat in a dish of bread, tomato sauce, melted butter and yogurt), towel production, thermal springs, and sweet candied chestnuts, sold in nearly every pastry shop.

Osman, the founder of the Ottoman *(Osmanlı)* dynasty, besieged Bursa for nearly a decade; after his death in 1326, his son, Orhan Bey, made Bursa the capital of the blossoming empire until Edirne usurped the distinction 75 years later. Despite the ultimate demise of the Ottomans and the ascendancy of industry in Bursa, the well preserved monuments that are scattered throughout the city and the thermal baths in the **Çekirge** (Grasshopper) remain great attractions.

ORIENTATION AND PRACTICAL INFORMATION

To get to the center of town, take a bus marked "Heykel" from the new bus station (25¢) and get off at the first stop after the **Ulu Camii** (Great Mosque). Try to avoid taxis, since they cost about $10. Soon the city center will be connected to the new bus station by tram; until then, buses leave every 10-15 minutes.

Tourist Office: To get to the **main tourist office** (tel./fax 221 2359), go to the Ulu Camii side of Atatürk Caddesi, walk toward the statue of Atatürk, pass the fountain, and go down the stairs on your left. Helpful staff; worthless map. Open June-Sept. Mon.-Sat. 8:30am-noon and 1-5:30pm; Oct.-May Mon.-Fri. 8:30am-noon and 1-5pm. On weekends, use the office on Atatürk Cad. As you walk from the *heykel*, it lies about 100m before Ulu Camii. Open Sat.-Sun. 8am-5pm. Also, the **tourism information offices** in Eski Valilik Binais, Kat 1, Heykel (tel. 223 8308) and Orhangazi Parkı, Belediye Alt Geçit Garşısı (tel. 220 1848). Open Mon.-Fri. 9am-5pm.

Police: Call 155 or 271 1990 for emergencies.

Buses: Depart for Bursa from Istanbul's Esenler Bus Station (every 30min., 4 hr., $7). **Kamıl Koç,** İnönü Cad. Kamil Koç İş Merkezi #15, Kad 4 (tel. 223 7913, fax 223 7914), is generally safe and reliable. Routes connect Bursa to Ankara, Izmir, and other big cities (every 30min.). Bursa also has the most extensive **dolmuş** system in Turkey. Each car takes four passengers (40-60¢ per person). *Dolmuş* leave from Atatürk Cad., behind the *Adliye,* and the Atatürk statue in Heykel. A cable car (*teleferik,* tel. 327 7400) leaves for Uludağ daily and takes less than 20min.

Ferries: Ferries leave Istanbul and arrive in Yalova daily ($2.50), but are slow. There is also ferry service between Eskihisar and Topçular (every 20-30min.) on the way from Istanbul, and a daily ferry from Istanbul to Mudanya.

Seabuses: There are seabuses between Istanbul and Yalova, and Istanbul and Mudanya. Seabuses leave Istanbul from Kabataş, Kartal, Bostancı. The seabuses are speedy, comfortable, and safe, but are also pricey ($5) and are not in service during inclement weather.

Hospitals: Private **Vatan Hastanesi** (tel. 220 1040), on İnönü Cad. (left of clock tower). State **Devlet Hastanesi** (tel. 220 0020). Take a *dolmuş* from Atatürk Blv.

PTT: Across the street from Ulu Camii. Open daily 8am-9pm.

Currency exchange: There are numerous banks on Atatürk Cad. The exchange offices in Kapalı Çarşı (covered bazaar) are also available, but charger higher fees.

Postal Code: 16300.

Telephone Code: 224.

ACCOMMODATIONS

Özen Şükran Otel, 39 İnönü Cad. (tel. 221 5453). A small hotel with old furniture, and charming ambiance. Singles $8; doubles $12; triples $15. Bargain if you can.

Otel Deniz, 19 Tahtakale Cad. (tel. 222 9238). More expensive, but also more comfortable—small, quiet rooms around a pleasant courtyard. Hot showers on demand. Free do-it-yourself laundry. Singles $8; doubles $13.50.

Çeşmeli Otel (tel. 224 1511), on Gümüşçeken Cad., near the covered bazaar. There are fridges, TVs, and phones in some of the rooms. Female owners and friendly staff. Singles $12-15; doubles $20-24.

Saray Öteli, İnönü Cad. Matbaa Çık No. 1 (tel. 221 2820). Spacious, well-lit rooms. Communal bathrooms with sinks in every room. Safe and luggage room. Big rooms. Singles $6.

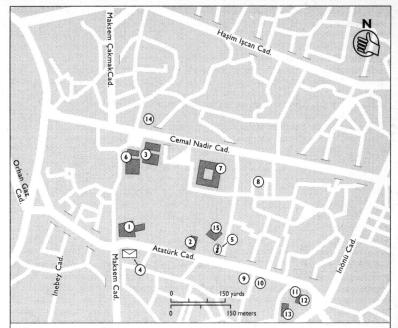

Bursa

Cable Car to Teleferik, 10	Dolmuş Stand, 11	Post Office, 4
Covered Market (Bedesten), 14	Flower Market, 8	Tourist Information, 5
Covered Market (Emir Han), 3	Heykel, 12	Turkish Bath, 6
Covered Market (Koza Han), 7	Koza Parkı, 2	Ulu Camii, 1
Dolmuş Stand, 9	Orphan Gazi Camii, 15	Government Building, 13

FOOD

Bursa is home to the tangy *İskender kebap*. Numerous restaurants creatively named "İskender kebap" specialize in the dish and are clustered in the area between the Atatürk statue and the Green Mosque. Bursa's **Kültür Parkı** district (take a *dolmuş* from Heykel, 30¢) has decent restaurants and cafes. Concerts, movies, or theater are also attractions. The **Arap Şükrü** district, near Altıparmak Cad., is next to the park and features fish restaurants, bars, and pubs. Picnickers can stock up in the **market** on Tahtakale near the budget hotels.

Kebapçı İskender (tel. 221 4615), 7 Ünlü Cad., at the corner of Atatürk Blv. and İnönü Cad., claims to have invented the *İskender kebap* (one portion $3.15). Order one and a half portions and a glass of grape juice (şira) like the locals do. Open daily 11am-10pm.

Gümüş Kebapçı (tel. 220 3401), on Gümüşçeken Cad., a block down from Atatürk Blv., is highly recommend by locals (kebap $3.50). Open 9am-9pm.

Lalezar, 14/c Ünlü Cad., farther up from Kebapçı İskender, is great for something different. Try the tasty vegetarian appetizers ($1.25) and great desserts, including *kadayıf* in milk and nuts (75¢).

Çiçek lagara (tel. 221 6526), near Ulu Camii, is one of Bursa's best meat restaurants. *Kaşarı köfte* (meatballs with cheese) cost $2.25 and *piyaz* (white bean salad) is 90¢. Do not leave this place before tasting their *sütlü kadayıf* (90¢).

Okyanus, near Heykel, has delicious pitas. Try pitas with cheese, meat, eggs, spinach, and *lahmacun*, all baked in a wood fire. A great meal is less than $3.

Gedelek Turşucusu, on İbrahimpaşa Cad, is another classic shop in Bursa. This place sells nothing but pickles and pickle juice; try a glass for 10¢. The juice is an adventure for a Western stomach!

Hanzade Bar/Restaurant (tel. 221 0052), Arap Şükrü Barlar Sok. No. 43, offers the catch of the day; prices range from $1.85-$10. Open daily noon-1am.

Berhar Süthanesi, near Bursa Erkek Lisesi behind the PTT, has great deserts and sweets. They have marvelous *keşkül* (pudding) for $1.

Kafkas (tel. 221 5549), 35 Atatürk Cad. is another good pastry shop. They offer delectable and reasonably priced chocolates, pastries, cakes, and, of course, candied chestnuts (*kestane şekeri*). They boast the best candied chestnuts in Bursa, but they are expensive. Open daily 7:30am-11:30pm.

SIGHTS

The city's layout perseveres from its days as the capital of the Ottoman Empire. Most of the mosques date back to the 14th and early 15th centuries. The famous **Yeşil Camii** (Green Mosque) and **Yeşil Türbe** (Green Mausoleum) are spangled inside and out in rich turquoise, cobalt, and occasional green Iznik tiles. Before the Ottoman capital moved to Edirne in 1402, the mosque served both religious and administrative functions for the Empire, as well as occasionally housing the sultan and his family (open in summer 8:30am-5:30pm; in winter 8am-5pm; mausoleum expects 25¢ donation). Across the way, finely carved wooden doors and small stained glass windows accentuate Yeşil Türbe's handsome turquoise interior. To get there, walk along Atatürk Cad. past the clock to Namazgah Cad., then turn left onto Yeşil Cad. after the small bridge. The **Turkish and Islamic Art Museum** (tel. 227 7679), including the **Ethnographic Museum,** is near the small bridge. It is located in the Green Medrese (Islamic school). The main *loggia,* or classroom, is now a display for traditional costumes. Many renowned scholars completed their education in this medrese, built by Hacı İvaz in 1424 (open 8:30am-12:30pm and 1:30-5pm; admission $1, students 50¢, free with ISIC).

The **Archaeological Museum** *(Arkeoloji Müzesi)* is in Kültür Park (tel. 220 2029). Don't miss the garden behind the museum which hosts an open-air exhibition of classical works (open Tues.-Sun. 8:30am-12:30pm and 1-5pm; admission 30¢). The **Ottoman House Museum** *(Osmanlı Evi Müzesi)* is in Muradiye Külliyesi (tel. 222 0868). See an old Ottoman home and learn a little social history (open 8:30am-12:30pm and 1-5pm).

The **Ulu Camii** (Great Mosque) is very different from the architectural style common in Istanbul. Rectangular layout and numerous supporting columns are characteristic of the style, and scholars believe that the nearby intricately carved wooden pulpit *(minbar)* represents an astrological chart. The mosque was built by Beyazıt to commemorate his victory in Nikopolis in 1396. It is said that Beyazıt vowed to build 20 mosques if he won the war; but once victorious, he built only the Ulu Camii with 20 domes, as if God would not notice. Walk west from Ulu Camii to the fortress *(hisar)* for a great view of the city. The park along Cumhuriyet Cad. are the **Mausoleums of Osman,** founder of the Ottoman Empire, and his son, Orhan. The **Emirsultan Mosque and Mausoleum** are near the Emirsultan cemetery. They were built by Sultan Bayezid's daughter Hundi Fatma Hatun. Today, locals take their sons here before their circumcisions.

In June and September, you can witness the silk production for which Bursa is rightly famous. The brilliantly dyed and patterned silk *(ipek)* can be purchased in the **Kapalı Çarşı (Bazaar)** or in **Koza Han,** by the tourist office, for $4-20 per square meter. You can also buy the silkworm cocoons themselves.

The **Eski Kaplıca bathing complex** (tel. 233 9300), Çekirge Meydanı, Kervansaray-Termal, was built by Justinian in the 6th century. Take the Çekirge *dolmuş* and get off at the luxurious Kervansaray Hotel. Eski Kaplıca will be on the right when you face the hotel (open daily 7:30am-11pm; entrance to baths $7.50, rubbing and massage $3 each). A short *dolmuş* ride just past the Kültürparkı and down the hill to the right will take you to **Yeni Kaplıca** (tel./fax 236 6968), 6 Yeni Kaplıca Cad., a bathing complex built for Süleyman the Magnificent in 1555. Three adjacent baths, fed by natural thermal springs, feature cavernous bathing pools (open daily 7am-11pm. Men $4.50 for first class bath, $3.25 for second class; women $2.25.). If you want a small and inexpensive *hamam* which still retains its local and authentic character, try **Mahkeme Hamamı** on İbrahimpaşa Cad. For around $2 you can have nice service in this historic bath.

■ Near Bursa: Mt. Uludağ

One of the many peaks in the ancient world once named Olympus, Uludağ looms over Bursa and is an excellent place for a morning hike, or a day away from the city.

To reach the **Uludağ cable car** station, take a *dolmuş* marked "Teleferik" (30¢) from behind Adliye and Heykel. The *dolmuş* leave from the underground stop for a ride that takes about five minutes. Get off at the last stop and you will see the Teleferik station (also called Teferrüç). The cable car leaves for Uludağ every 40 minutes between 8am-10pm (round-trip $5.75; no service during inclement weather). The first part of the ride takes eight minutes and takes you to Kadıyayla, which is 1231m high. There, you change to another cable car and travel for another eight minutes to Sarıalan. From there you can take a minibus to Uludağ Oteller Bölgesi, where all the resorts are. The ride takes 10 minutes and costs $1. If riding up a mountain on a single wire isn't your thing, you can get taxi or a *dolmuş* to Uludağ.

From Oteller Bölgesi, **hike** to the Kirazlıyayla Plateau, Sarıalan, or, if you're an experienced climber, the peak of Uludağ (2543m). Since all of Uludağ's hotels are expensive, the best thing is to imitate the locals who travel as early as possible to Uludağ after spending the night in Bursa. On the way to and from Uludağ, if you get hungry, try a bite at **Çam Et Mangal** (tel. 233 4694), 8km from Bursa, an open-air restaurant featuring a make-your-own barbecue.

■ Mudanya

Mudanya is the main port of Bursa. After its founding in the 7th century BC, it was ruled by Romans, Byzantines, and Crusaders. In 1321, the Ottoman Sultan Orhan conquered the town. It was around this time that the town's Latin name "Montania" changed to Mudanya. After WWI, the town was invaded by the British, then left to Greek control. The famous Mudanya Armistice, a turning point in Republican Turkey's War of Independence, was signed here. Today, Mudanya is Bursa's summer resort, and thus crowded with Turks in the high tourist season.

PRACTICAL INFORMATION AND ORIENTATION

The main entrance to the town is the Bursa Asfaltı, and the center of town is Cumhuriyet Meydanı. As you enter Mudanya, you can see the Atatürk statue to the left and the harbor to the right. The promenade along the beach is called İsmet İnönü Bulvari.

At the Cumhuriyet Meydanı, you can find the Kamil Koç offices with **buses** to major cities throughout Turkey. You can also take **minibuses** to Bursa Batı Garajı (Western Bus Station) for 55¢. The Istanbul Deniz Otobüsleri at the end of the same street offers **seabuses** to Istanbul at 7:30am (ex. Sun.). There are also seabuses going to Mudanya from Bostancı at 6pm and Yenikapı at 6:30pm, as well as a **ferry** from Istanbul daily at 9am. The **state hospital** is on Cumhuriyet Meydani (walk toward the coast), and a **private hospital,** Özel Mudanya Polikliniği (tel. 543 0020), is at the intersection of Mustafa Kemalpaşa Cad. and Mahkeme Sokağı, no. 9. The **PTT** is behind the Atatürk statue (open weekdays 9am-5pm). The **telephone code** is 244.

ACCOMMODATIONS AND FOOD

Mudanya is a great day trip from Bursa or even Istanbul, but unless you can afford to stay overnight at the **Montania Hotel,** do not stay overnight in Mudanya. The Montania is located in a renovated train station building. The station was built by the French in 1849 and today is equipped with 40 traditionally furnished rooms. All have color TV and minibar(tel. 544 6000, fax 544 6005; singles $60 negotiable; V/MC accepted).

Tarihi Yaşayanlar Börekçisi is a great pastry and pie shop serving *kol böreği* ($1), right next to the Cumhuriyet Meydani. You can also try the **Meria Cafe** for *çiğ börek* (40¢), cantık (40¢), and kiwi tea (25¢).

SIGHTS

Mudanya Mütareke Evi Müzesi (Armistice House Museum) is on 12 Eylül Cad., no. 8. (Sun.-Fri. 8am-noon and 1-5pm). The Mütareke Anıtı (the Armistice Monument) sits in front of the museum, sculpture of a bird with an olive branch in its beak. If you walk along the beach on 12 Eylül Cad., you can see the renovated and preserved houses of old Mudanya. Behind the Belediye there is the **Eski Camii** (old mosque) which dates from 1500. Be sure not to miss the **fountain** with Ottoman inscriptions in front of the mosque. Take a close look at the fountains which dot Mudanya's coast—the one in front of the mosque has beautiful Ottoman inscriptions—but resist the urge to quench your thirst here; the water is less than pure.

■ Yalova

Yalova has been a popular thermal resort—particularly for curing rheumatism—since the days of the Romans. A former Byzantine center and one of the more heterogenous cities in Turkey, both Greek and Armenian influences survive today. Later, Circassians from the Caucasus began to settle here in the 19th century, and the Arabic language signs scattered around the city testify to the huge influx of Arab tourists in the 1980s. When you land in this town on the southern shore of the Marmara Sea, you'll be in a busy commercial area, In the "town" of Yalova, visitors can find budget-priced hotels and restaurants. The main thermal center is in Termal and a beach is located at Çinarcik. Yalova is ideal for a daytrip from Istanbul or Bursa.

The most prominent reference point in Yalova is the stern-faced statue of Atatürk raising his right arm. The statue faces the water and is a convenient point of reference. Facing the statue, the **tourist office** (tel. (226) 814 2108; fax 812 3045; open summers daily 8am-noon and 1-5pm; in winter Mon.-Fri. 8am-noon and 1-5pm) is right behind you on İskele Meydani and offers free brochures. **Banks, pharmacies,** and **exchange offices** line Cumhuriyet Cad. which runs perpendicular to the back of the statue. From the statue, walk right 1½ blocks to find the *dolmuş* lot. To get to Termal, take a bone-rattling 20 minute ride in the yellow *dolmuş* marked "Termal" (35¢), or take the Çinarcik *dolmuş* (35¢) to visit the beaches and discos. You can pick up a Lüks Yalova Seyahat **bus** to Bursa for $2.10. **Seabuses** are available from the terminal in the harbor to Kartal, Kabataş, Sirkeci, and Kartal. The Adalar **ferry** is ideal for a trip to the islands around Istanbul. The **hospital,** Yalova Devlet Hastanesi (tel. (216) 814 1214), is at the intersection of Fatih Cad. and Koşu Yolu. Public. One block to the left (facing the statue), you'll find the **police station** (tel. (216) 813 0377), marked "Jandarma." The **PTT** is at 40 Gazipaşa Cad. (open daily 8:30am-12:30pm and 1:30-5pm; 7am-11pm for mail and faxes).

Yalova has an abundance of *kebap* restaurants and delicious pastry shops. Try **Şehir Lokantası** for a tasty bowl of soup (70¢) and kuzu tandır ($2.10). **Merkez 2,** near the *dolmuş* lot (tel. 814 3748), has clean, friendly service, and a comfortable atmosphere (İskender *kebap* $3.75, lamb tandur and cola $4.40; open in summer daily 8am-midnight; off-season 8:30am-9pm). **Husepoğlu,** on Gazipaşa Cad. no. 5 (tel. 812 4271) cooks all their dishes in a wood fire and only uses lamb. Try *acılı lahmacun* (65¢) and *ayran* (35¢). For delicious *saç kavurma* ($1.75) go to **Konyalı Lokantasi** (tel. 813 1346) to the left of the statue. **Yalova Pastanesi,** 4/1 Yali Cad. (tel. 814 1584; open daily 5:30am-1am), has finger-licking good tarts (chocolate cream with fruity top 70¢) and an excellent selection of cakes and chocolate.

TERMAL

The springs have a long history dating back to Greek times. The Roman Emperors Constantine and Justinian, the Ottoman Sultan Abdülhamid II, and the Turkish President Atatürk all used these springs. The surviving baths were built in the 16th century and renovated by Sultan Abdülhamid II in 1900. In 1929 Atatürk bought a farm in the area and Termal once again became a center of attention. We can't all be emperors, but we can all at least bathe where they did. Although the **Termal** (thermal) springs won't make you rich and powerful, they will give you a soothing and relaxing day.

To reach Termal from Yalova take a *dolmuş* to Termal (35¢). From the *dolmuş* stop, walk uphill (in the opposite direction of the Termal police station) on the right-hand side of the main road for five minutes. Climb the winding stairs on your right and hang another right at the top. Walk uphill for two minutes. The tourist village (*köy*) will be on your left.

Right at the entrance of Termal you can find a **police station.** The big maps by the minibus stop can help you orient yourself. The state-run **Turban Yalova Termal Hotels** (tel. 675 7400; fax 675 7413; singles start at $34, doubles at $49) is the main resort in Termal. Two hotels (Çamlık and Çınar) make up the resort. Despite being rather expensive by Turkish standards, these luxurious hotels are often crowded, and thus reservations are recommended. If the resort is too much of a budget-buster, either stay in Yalova or walk a few kilometers uphill from Termal and stop in Üvezpınar. You can find a cheap room there in one of the family-run pensions.

Termal is home to several baths. **Sultan Banyo** is the best, with private rooms, big bathtubs, and a nice atmosphere ($5.25 per hr., 2 people $8.40 per hr.; shampoo and soap 35¢, soda 70¢). **Valide Banyo** has separate sections for males and females (adults $1.75, children 70¢, boys under 3 bathe in the female section). There is also the **Kurşunlu** bath which has an open air pool, sauna, and bath (open 8:30am-10:30pm; pool $4.20, sauna $3.50 per 90 min.). If you want privacy and have done well in the stock market recently, ask for a private (but pricey) sauna ($46.40).

In addition to the thermal springs, Termal is blessed with yet another Atatürk museum, **Atatürk Köşkü** (open Tues.-Sun. 9am-noon, 1-5pm; admission 70¢). There are also some Byzantine ruins near the museum.

If you need a place to relax and have some fun, try **Methal Pub.** You can sip a $1.75 *cintonik* (gin and tonic) or devour *alabalık tava* ($2.80). The thermal spring area of Yalova offers a calming experience amid gardens, lush trees, and winding roads. The best promenade in Termal is the Aşıklar Yolu (the lovers' road), a remote and romantic path into the forest.

▨ Iznik

The history of Iznik, as the tourist office brochures aptly put it, "is very old." Iznik was first constructed in 316 BC by Antigonos, one of Alexander the Great's generals. In 310 BC, another general, Lysimachus, defeated Antigonos and renamed the city after his wife Nicaea. The Romans later invaded and built walls, theaters, and laid out the city's Hellenistic grid plan. Under the Byzantines, Nicaea hosted the First Ecumenical Council in 325 AD. Pressured by the Emperor Constantine, the assembly of bishops formulated and agreed upon the Nicene Creed, which states that God and Christ are one. Six more councils then convened to clear up other theological debates. The last council, called to resolve the issue of iconoclasm in 787, returned to Nicaea and met in the local Aya Sophia church. After a short period under the Crusaders and the Seljuks, Iznik fell to the Ottomans in 1331. A porcelain industry developed and thus began the production of the renowned blue Iznik tiles. Today, Iznik is a sleepy town except in the summer, when vacationers fill the few lakeside motels and tea gardens.

Iznik is calming, especially if you've been run down by the hustle and bustle of touristy Istanbul. To see an unforgettable indigo sunset, be sure and get a room with a terrace overlooking the serene Lake Iznik. Nightfall signals the hypnotic rhapsody of the nocturnal frogs. Sit on a bench along the lake and stare at the interminable sky of twinkling stars. The ruins here are in no way monumental, but the verdant hills and orchards and soothing waters of Lake Iznik may engage you for a day or two.

ORIENTATION AND PRACTICAL INFORMATION

Kılıçaslan Cad. and Atatürk Cad. separate Iznik into quarters and meet in the center at the Aya Sophia church. The lake is at the west end of town, and much of the city is enclosed by ancient walls.

Tourist Office: (tel. 757 1454; fax 757 1933). With your back to the bus station, walk 3 blocks to the right, turn left onto Kılıçaslan Cad., ascend the stairs, and follow the signs. Friendly staff speak broken English and offer free brochures. Open in summer daily 8:30am-noon and 1-5:30pm; off-season Mon.-Fri. 8:30am-noon and 1-5:30pm.

Buses: From Bursa (every 20 min., 6:30am-7:30pm; $1.45), with return trip every 30min., 8am-11pm. Atan Kardeşler buses are also available from Bursa ($1.75), offering warm cola and Turkish lemon cologne on the ride. Minibuses also go to Yenişehir, Osmaneli, and Gölcük. For schedules check the bulletin board in the bus station.

Ferries: Leave from nearby Yalova (58km) for Istanbul.

Police Station: 74 Kılıçaslan Cad., on the corner intersecting Atatürk Cad.

Hospital: Nearest hospital is in Yenişehir.

PTT: (tel. 757 1815), south of the tourist office on Kılıçaslan Cad. Offers **currency exchange** and cashes traveler's checks. Open daily 8:30am-12:30pm and 1:30-5:30pm.

Telephone Code: 224.

ACCOMMODATIONS

Burcum Motel, Kemalpaşa Mah., 20 Sahil Yolu (tel. 757 1011; fax 757 1202). A pleasant place to stay, with clean rooms and terraces facing the lake. All rooms have shower, toilet (even paper!), and telephones. 24hr. hot water when full, otherwise available 7:30pm-11am. Singles $10.70; doubles $17.85; triples $26.75. Breakfast included. Forego breakfast and pay less. V/MC accepted.

Cem Pansiyon, 24 Göl Kenarı, (tel. 757 1687), along the lakeside near Murat Pansion. Well kept rooms, some with terrace and superb views. Clean, huge communal bathroom and shower on every floor. Singles $7; doubles $14; triples $21. Breakfast included.

Hotel Babacan, Kılıçaslan Cad. 104 (tel. 757 1623), at the center of town. Modest hotel with communal bathroom. Singles $5.70; doubles $14.20.

FOOD AND ENTERTAINMENT

Restaurants by the lake offer inexpensive meals and breathtaking views. The **Kırık Çatal Restaurant,** next to the Burcum Motel, is a little more expensive, but the food is also a bit better. Languish on the shady patio as you gaze at the lake and enjoy the excellent service. **Çamlık Restaurant,** adjacent to Çamlık Motel, offers tasty appetizers for $1.25 including *tarator* (garlic yogurt with spices). Grilled Yayın balık (catfish), a regional specialty, is worth the $4 (open 7am-1am). In town, locals suggest **Karadeniz Pide Salonu,** 130 Kılıçaslan Cad. (tel. 757 0143), a small but cheap restaurant with good food (*lahmacun* 45¢, *Kıymalı Sandviç* in pita with veggies, $1.05). A popular pastry shop is the **Ceren Pastanesi,** on Kılıçaslan Cad. (tel. 757 1379). Ceren serves *poğaça* (pastry with cheese) and tea for less than 30¢ (open 5am-midnight).

SIGHTS

The **Aya Sophia Camii** (Saint Sophia or Church of the Holy Wisdom) at the town's central intersection was built as a church in the 4th century by the Byzantines. Osman, the founder of the Ottoman dynasty, converted the Aya Sophia into a mosque in 1331. The Chief Court *Mimar* (architect), Sinan, renovated the building during the reign of Süleyman the Magnificent (1520-1566). Today, it is decrepit and surprisingly small with a few pieces of religious art, including several fading frescoes (admission 70¢; open daily 9am-noon and 1-4:30pm). The aging **Murat Hamamı** (Turkish bath), just south of the Aya Sophia, still offers baths in the company of patrons who do not speak a word of English. (tel. 757 1011; open daily for men 6am-1pm and 6pm-midnight, for women 1-5pm only; bath 90¢, children 65¢; massage 90¢). The **Yeşil Camii** (Green Mosque), located near the tourist office in one of the quieter areas of town, was built by architect Hacı Musa in 1378. The shade and quiet here make the park a perfect place to have lunch and read in the afternoon sunlight (mosque open daily except during prayer times).

Murat I built the **Nilüfer Hatun İmareti** (charitable foundation) across the street from the mosque to honor his mother, the first Christian wife of an Ottoman sultan. The museum, established in 1960, displays many artifacts excavated in Iznik and briefly traces the history of Iznik tile-making. The exhibit includes coins and medals from the Seljuks, who conquered Iznik in 1078 (admission $1, students 50¢). In the winter, ask museum officials about keys to the following: the Aya Sophia; a 4th-century underground baptismal **spring;** and a **catacomb,** intricately decorated with Byzantine murals, 4km out of town (taxi to catacomb about $5, but be sure to bargain; $2 donation expected at the museum). The **roman theater,** the mosques around town, and the 16 **gates** of the city walls are also all worth a visit.

The **Huysuzlar (the Naughties) Tombs** are on Atatürk Cad. Because they don't face Mecca, the three graves are unlikely to be Muslim. Nonetheless, Muslim parents bring their naughty kids here hoping that the visit will calm them down.

Iznik's *faience* industry has not yet died. Shops along the main street sell earthenware tiles and plates decorated with opaque, colored glazes ($10 and up). Today's tilemakers occasionally let visitors watch the tilemaking process. Ask someone to show you the easy-to-find *fırın* (kiln), or follow the signs leading from the street that feeds into the bus station parking lot (no parking for tourists).

WESTERN TURKEY

Aegean Coast

Fabulous classical ruins and a sinuous coastline concealing sublime beaches have helped transform Turkey's once tranquil Aegean coast into an increasingly popular destination. Cradled by 5000-year-old mythology and history, the culture is intensely rich, offering an eye-full for photographer, archaeologist, nature-lover, and hedonistic nomad alike.

The coast's first foreign visitors were the ancient Greeks, who established several ports in the area. As Alexander the Great and subsequent Hellenic rulers pushed their Aegean empire eastward, the ports became the nerve centers of commerce along the major trade routes of the ancient world, growing even as Greek civilization declined. Today, Hellenistic ruins—especially extensive at Pergamon, Ephesus, Aphrodisias, and Heirapolis—stand as weathered testaments to the coast's heritage.

NORTHERN COAST

■ Ayvalık

Ayva means "quince" in Turkish, but this town is no haven for quince trees. Rather, Ayvalık's red rooftops and the turquoise waters of the Aegean form a pleasant juxtaposition that lends itself to the ineffable calm of the town. Known for its ornate Neoclassical buildings, Ayvalık was a wealthy Greek settlement until the 1923 population exchange. This small fishing village is reminiscent of a Greek town and it still makes its living from oil production. A mere 18km from the Greek island of Lesvos, Ayvalık features pleasant beaches and varied seafood. The town is situated in the Gulf of Edremit, and surrounded by 25 outlying islands, pine woods, and olive groves. The nearby sandy beaches at Sarımsaklı are clean, and have waters pleasant for swimming. Don't leave Ayvalık without exploring its less popular natural scenery on the small island of Cunda and the wild Badavut Beach just beyond touristy Sarımsaklı; you might discover more wildlife here than you previously thought. Ayvalık is a balanced mix of classic 19th-century architecture and genuine natural beauty.

ORIENTATION AND PRACTICAL INFORMATION

İnönü Cad., the main road, runs parallel to the coastline and turns into **Atatürk Cad.** after the bazaar area. The other main street is **Sefa Cad.,** which runs parallel to İnönü Cad. and Atatürk Cad. A bus from Çanakkale is $7.50; the ride takes 3½ hours. *Dolmuş* to the beaches can be found waiting on İnönü Cad., toward Çamlık on the left-hand side, a few streets after the Ayvalıl Tourism Society Booth (not to be confused with the government tourist office 1km south on İnönü Cad.). *Dolmuş* to Cunda (Alibey Adası) are found in the main square, where the **police station** is located toward the right-hand side facing the square.

> **Tourist Office:** (tel. 312 2753), in Cumhuriyet Meydanı (Republic Square) on the docks in the center of town. Open daily in summer 9am-1pm and 3-7:15pm.
> **Tours: Jade Tourism,** formerly Ayvalık tours (tel. 312 2740; fax 312 2470), on Gümrük Cad. 41-A, near Kıyı Motel, offers tours of Lesvos (1½hr., $65), Pergamon ($15), and nearby islands ($8). An agency of the same name is in Naci Bey Passage (along the seashore). Open in summer daily 8am-10pm; in winter daily 8am-6pm.
> **Currency Exchange: Günaydın Döviz** (tel. 312 1918), across from the Ekonomi Hotel, exchanges currency and cashes traveler's checks. Open daily 9am-6pm.
> **Buses:** *Dolmuş* bound for the bus terminal pass along the highway every 30min., on İnönü Cad. next to the Türkiye İş Bankası. Easy service to Çanakkale (roughly every hr., 3½hr., $5) and Izmir (roughly every hr., 1½hr., $3.25). Minibuses run to

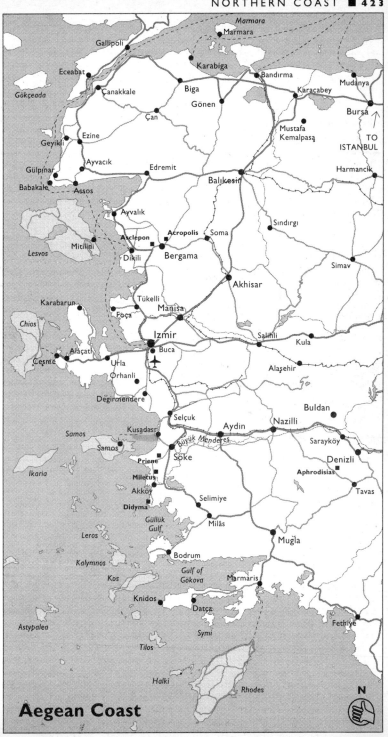

WESTERN TURKEY

Aegean Coast

Sarımsaklı beach and **Altınova beach** (every 15min.; 40¢), leaving from across the street from the tourist office.

Hospital: Ayvalık Devlet Hastanesi Public Hospital (tel. 312 1744). From the PTT, 300m along İnönü Cad, to the left (with your back to the sea).

Pharmacies: located in the main square and on İnönü Cad.

Police: İnönü Cad. (tel. 312 9500, -01).

PTT: İnönü Cad. (tel. 312 6041). Open 8:30am-11pm. **Traveler's checks** cashed 8:30am-5:30pm. **Postal Code:** 10400.

Telephone Code: 266.

ACCOMMODATIONS

The real essence of Ayvalık can be seen in its 19th and early 20th-century architecture. Influential Greek businessmen flocked to this city in the last decades before the population exchange. One should not miss the opportunity to stay in the city's historic houses. There are three pensions in particular that offer the traveler clean and historic accommodations. The prices are about as good as they come.

Taksiyarhis Pansiyon, İsmetpaşa Mah., 71 Maraşal Çakmak Cad. No. 71 (tel. 312 1494). Take the second street after the PTT and walk until you reach the church. This eclectic pension derives its name from a 9th-century Greek Orthodox Church located right across the street. The pension is removed from the busier town square and offers clean rooms, a book exchange, and sound advice. Ask about day-trips to Cunda Island, bike rentals ($5.40 per day), and laundry service ($5.40). Call in advance. Rooms are $5.40 per person. Breakfast $2.90.

Bonjour Pansion, Maraşal Çakmak Cad. Street 5, House 6 (tel. 312 8085). Walk about 200m from the Ayvalık Tourism Society Booth in the main square and take Maraşal Çakmak Cad. The pension is on the second street. This recently restored pension was the home of a French priest during the 1880s who acted as French ambassador to the Sublime Porte. All rooms have been restored to their former state. Doubles $17.15; triples $21.50. Breakfast $2.50.

Yah Pansion, PTT Arkası, No. 25 (tel. 312 2423, 312 3819). Located behind the PTT. In Turkish *yah* means "seaside residence" or "mansion," both applicable to this pension. The patron takes pride in the 106 year-old house. All rooms have views of the ocean, and some have balconies. $9 per person, breakfast included.

FOOD AND ENTERTAINMENT

Ayvalık still has a few restaurants which offer excellent food on uncrowded streets that have undergone little change since the 1920s. **Hüsnü'nün Yeri,** located on İnönü Cad., offers *meze* (appetizers) specialties. Vegetarian dishes are available. **Kardeşler Kebapçı** (tel. 312 1857), located just down the street from Hüsnü'nün Yeri, offers similar dishes with an emphasis on *kebap* ($2.15) and pitas (open daily 8am-2am). No matter where you dine in this area, the feeling of the old *meyhane* (bar, wine shop) is always present. For a more tourist-oriented spot, try the **Dayim Ocakbaşı,** across from the Ekonomi Hotel. For breakfast, pastries, or tea, try the popular **Odak Cafeteria** across the street from the Ayvaık Tourism Society Booth in the main square.

SIGHTS

Agios Yorgios (Çınarlı Camii) boasts beautiful Old and New Testament frescoes (open daily 9am-noon and 1-11pm). Several Byzantine churches that have since been converted into mosques house many of the city's treasures. The **Taksiyarhis Church** houses portraits painted on fish skins. Another church, on **Alibey Adası** (Sir Ali's Island, connected to Ayvalık via an artificial harbor), has remnants of frescoes on the walls. For a panoramic view of **Sarımsaklı** (one of Turkey's cleanliest natural beaches and where some of Turkey's finest artists have summer homes) and of Alibey, visit **Şeytan Sofrası,** "the Devil's Dinner Table." From far away, this large rock does look like a table. The story is that devils congregated here to dine. There is a monstrous footprint at the peak which is said to have been left by the hellraiser himself. Ordinarily, *dolmuş* (30¢) depart around sunset for the best viewing, wait 45 minutes, and then return. They do not, however, run if there are too few tourists. Sarımsaklı, 6km south of Ayvalık, is a growing, pricey resort town. Although hotels are expensive, the sandy beach is one of the finest in Turkey.

■ Around Ayvalık

Besides the major tourist sites of the beaches at Sarımsaklı and the town of Ayvalık itself, there is much to see in terms of sheer natural beauty in the surrounding islands, as each has its own sense of mystery and wonder. A bike tour of nearby **Cunda (Ali Bey) Island** is highly recommended as it gives the visitor to Ayvalık a grander perspective to the area than just the concrete jungle found at touristy Sarımsaklı. The tour of Cunda will bring the visitor to the deserted ruins of a Greek Orthodox church, beautiful and secluded swimming spots, and an ancient tower with an excellent view of the city. To rent a mountain bike, contact Herbert at the **Taksiyarhis Pansiyon** (tel. 312 1494). The pension has a limited number of bikes suitable for the trip which are rented out for $5.40 per day; locks and an air pump are provided. Bikes come with small storage cases suitable for water (bring plenty). There are some springs and wells along the way, but it is better to be safe than sorry; the duration is six to eight hours, depending on how long one allows for lunch and swimming. Bring bread and oranges which can be purchased at the town's bazaar area. Also, one should not stay out too late in the morning, as the middle of the day is extremely hot with little relief until late afternoon.

THE TOUR

Start heading north from Ayvalık's center, passing its *otogar* and bearing left after that point until you arrive at a short bridge to the first small island (**Lâle Adası**, or Tulip Island). Traveling from the town to this area should take no more than 30-45 minutes. There is a mediocre beach at the end of the bridge to the right. Follow the main road through this small island, passing over a second bridge that brings you to Cunda (Ali Bey) Island, and bear right when the road begins to diverge. The next major landmark is a windmill without any wings (all of this is on a map provided by Herbert, also found at the Ayvalıl Tourism Society). This is important in your trip since it's the start of dirt paths all the way up to the end of Cunda Island. Follow this path until you pass a natural mineral water fountain. If you need a rest or would like to take a swim, take a right to the small town located here and follow the paths to the beach area, where a small cafeteria and bar is located. This is the last such place for food or bottled water until the end of the trip. The trip to this area should be about 1-1½hrs. Continuing to the left of the water fountain (or returning from the town to the right), the dirt path will increase in intensity, taking you through fields of olive trees. After 30-40 minutes of riding through olive groves, you will see another secluded beach on the right. Note the small island in the bay with a deserted fortress called Güvercin Ada (Pigeon Island). Follow the beautiful beach to its very end (another 30min.) where you will arrive at a small farm area. To start the final trip to the monastery at the northeast corner of Cunda, you'll have to leave the bikes locked away at the farm (make sure they are put off to the side and away from the path travelled by some trucks). The path here is much too rough for bikes. You will now pass from one olive grove to the next until you arrive at a deserted village. Pass through the center of the village, and very soon you'll see red signs for the monastery. From there, it is a moderately steep climb, leveling off and then descending to the monastery. The monastery's central church *(katholikon)* is largely intact, but without any surviving frescoes inside. Other parts of the facility are not nearly as well-preserved and one should use caution when exploring.

▓ Pergamon (Bergama)

Pergamon (the ruins, as opposed to Bergama, the modern city) was once a dazzling center of cultural activity with one of the world's richest libraries; the ruins make it one of Turkey's finest archaeological sites. Bring your water bottle, slap on plenty of sun screen, and climb your way to the sights. Bergama's archaeological sights, towering 330m above the city, are extensive and impressive, but don't let them distract you from the 150-year-old Greek houses. And don't forget to visit the Kızıl Avlu (Red Basilica), which was one of the seven churches mentioned in the Book of Revelations (can you remember the other six churches?).

ORIENTATION AND PRACTICAL INFORMATION

The ruins of Pergamon are across the river from the modern city of **Bergama.** The city's main road winds its way to the ancient ruins. The road, from the new bus station in the direction of Izmir, is called **Izmir Cad.** From the PTT in the direction of İstiklal Meydanı, it is called **Uzun Çarşı Cad.,** but most people know that, by Izmir Cad., you mean the main road. Most of the pensions and local restaurants are in the direction of İstiklal Meydani, where taxis can be found for hire.

Tourist Office: (tel. 623 1862) From the new main bus station, go right onto the main road and walk 1km. It is on Cumhuriyet Meydanı, on the left coming from the bus station. If you reach the bust of Atatürk, you've passed it. Open April-Sept. daily 8:30am-7pm; Oct.-March Mon.-Sat. 8:30am-5:30pm.

Buses: Two terminals *(garaj)* serve Bergama. The old terminal (going toward the Kızıl Avlu), near the Basilica, runs buses to Izmir, Istanbul, Ankara, Bursa, and Soma. The new terminal (tel. 633 1545), across from Çamli Park on Izmir Cad., runs buses to the same major cities as well as minibuses to Ayvalık. Buses run to Bursa (3 per day, 5hr., $7), Izmir (every 30min. 6:30am-7:30pm, 1½hr., $2), Istanbul (2 per day, 9hr., $14). For information about the Bergama to Izmir route, call (tel. 632 3546) and for Bergama to Istanbul call (tel. 633 1545). All buses for both directions are run by Pamukkale Lines (tel. 31 1082 3546). When arriving, try to take a bus that trundles directly into Bergama; most buses from Izmir to Çanakkale drop you at the turn-off 7km away. Frequent *dolmuş* service to town is available (50¢). If you arrive at night, you may have to spend up to $6.25 on a taxi into town. The center of town is to the right as you exit the station.

Hospital: Bergama Devlet Hastanesı (tel. 633 2490, -1099). Walk from the bus station toward the PTT; where the park ends, walk uphill for 2min. and turn right.

Police: (tel. 632 7001), across and up the street from the PTT.

PTT: (tel. 632 3996) Izmir Cad. Some English spoken. Offers **currency exchange** (1% commission) after business hours. Open daily 8am-11pm.

Telephone Code: 232.

ACCOMMODATIONS

Pension Athena (tel. 633 3420), in a restored Ottoman house. Their motto, "Not the best, but we're trying to get there," is a charming reflection of the quality of both the rooms and the ambience. Hidden in the winding road beyond İstiklal Meydanı, it offers 24 hr. hot water, living room cable TV, and a tea garden. Rooms $5.25, with shower $7 (both are very clean). Kitchen available as well as laundry services $5. 10% discount for readers of *Let's Go* (just show them the book).

Pension Nike, Talatpaşa Mah. Tabak Köprü Çıkmazı, 2 (tel. 633 3901), after İstiklal Meydanı walk on the left road, go over a small bridge and enter the turquoise-blue stone house. Lush flower garden, and brightly colored, spacious rooms. Dinner menu available ($3-5). Kind owners offer self-made maps of archaeological sites. Singles $5; doubles $10. Breakfast $2.

Sayın Pension, Zafer Mah., 12 Izmir Cad. (tel. 633 2405), near the bus station outside of town. Turn left leaving the bus station; it's on the right. Functional rooms but little ambience. Most singles with shower $5.25. Breakfast $1.25. V/MC.

Acroteria, 11 Bankalar Cad. Eski Hamam Yani (tel. 633 1047; fax 633 1720). This pension is located on the right-hand side of the main road going toward İstiklal Meydani after the Çarşı Hamam. Rooms are clean with a shower and hot water. There is a restaurant, serving breakfast and dinner (with excellent view of the acropolis). Rooms are $8.60 per person with breakfast, $7 without.

FOOD AND ENTERTAINMENT

Bergama's intense heat during the daylight hours may discourage visitors from exploring the city's various restaurants and sweet shops. But at night, a gentle breeze cools the city, slowly revealing a decent selection of restaurants.

There are two Sağlam restaurants in Bergama managed by the sons of Yusuf Sağlam. The **Sağlam Restaurant,** 3 İstiklal Meydani (tel. 633 2046) at the central square is managed by İbrahim Sağlam and offers a family-style menu of various meat, fish and vegetarian plates. *Meze* go for $1 per plate, and mixed *shish-kebap* meals for $3.50 *(karışık izgara kebap)*. The other restaurant is the **Sağlam Restaurant** on 29 Hükümet Maydani (across from the municipal buildings, a few building down from the PTT going towards the new *otogar*). The food is southern Turkish cuisine with similar prices to its brother restaurant (*karışık izgara kebap* $3.50, pitas $1.40-1.75, *meze* $1.40). The real charm of this Sağlam Restaurant is its lovely garden-style seating and its two authentic Ottoman dining rooms (with seating for 25-30 people in each room). Both Sağlam restaurants are generally open from 8am-noon. Also in the central square area, across from the Sağlam Restaurant on İstakal Meydani is the **Maydan Restaurant,** 4 İstiklal Cad. (tel. 633 1793, 632 4522). This place offers excellent meals. Mixed *shish kebap* plates go for $3.50, with cold appetizers for a little over $1. All other meals are $1.75 (Open 7pm-2am).

For sweets or Turkish tea, there are two cafes: **Cafe Hülya** and **Cafe Manolya.** Cafe Hülya, 6 Belediye Hizmet Bınası (tel. 633 2183; fax 632 6245) is located past the PTT going toward the acropolis. It offers fresh sweets for $2.75 per kg.; baklava $3.10 per kg. (open 8am-1am). Cafe Manolya, 48 Hükümet Cad. (tel. 633 2583, 632 0549) is located a bit closer to the PTT (open 8am-12am).

SIGHTS

Pergamon's long history of fame began when Piletarus, a regional commander, seized the treasury he had been entrusted to keep and set himself up as king. Its ruins, over 30,000 acres, are located on two principal sites: the **acropolis,** which looms above the town (open daily June-Oct. 8:30am-7pm, Nov.-May 8:30am-5:30pm; admission $1.75, students 70¢, free with FIYTO), and the **Asclepion** (medical center) lying in the valley below (open daily June-Oct. 8:30am-7pm, Nov.-May 8:30am-5:30pm; admission $1.75, students 70¢, free with FIYTO). The theater, seating 3500 people, is also breathtaking. Under the direction of Galen, the most famous physician of the Roman Empire, Pergamon became the center of the cult of Asclepius, the Greek

Pergamon's Plethora of Problems

In ancient times, only the library in Alexandria surpassed Pergamon's, which contained more than 200,000 volumes. But Pergamon posed a real literary threat to the self-conscious Alexandrians. So Alexandria's denizens made what they thought was a brilliant strategic move: they limited the flow of Egyptian papyrus to Pergamon, thinking, hey, you can't write books without paper. But Pergamon's wily scientists were ready for this fiendish plot. To keep their library's stacks well-stocked, they invented a parchment made from goat hide. Soon, a mighty roar bellowed from jolly Pergamon as they foiled Alexandria's plot, but, alas, their joy was short-lived. When the Alexandrian library's fire suppression mechanism experienced a system-wide failure, Marc Antony plundered Pergamon's shelves and presented the pilfered publications to Cleopatra to replace the charred editions. Even if that were that the end of Pergamon's tales of woe, today's inhabitants would have just cause to view outsiders a bit suspiciously. Unfortunately, the story goes on from there. Pergamon used to be the home of one of the world's great artistic and cultural treasures, the Altar of Zeus. The Altar is the remains of a beautifully carved offering table. Today, Pergamonites can only see it if they travel to Berlin. Like Marc Antony, the Germans apparently think that Pergamon's treasures don't belong in Pergamon.

demi-god of healing and eponym of the Asclepion, which was both a temple and a place of healing. Supposedly, no patient left here unhealed. An impressive portion of the Asclepion remains include a marble colonnade, a theater, and healing rooms. The ruins of a huge gymnasium, a Roman circus, and the lavishly frescoed **House of Attalus** also lie scattered about. The most notable attraction is the mammoth **amphitheater,** capable of seating 10,000 spectators. On your way up to the **Royal Palaces,** write down a wish and tie it to a branch of the "wishing tree."

There are no buses to the ruins; walk, or, if too much smoking has debilitated your lungs, take a taxi (they run a meter; $5 to the top of the acropolis; $40 for transport to all sites, so share a cab). If you take a taxi it's best to be dropped off at the acropolis, and then to walk down through the rest of the ruins. To reach the acropolis, follow the main road past the **Kızıl Avlu,** or Red Basilica, which was originally built as a 2nd-century temple to the Egyptian god Serapis and converted into a basilica during the Byzantine Empire. This church has the distinction of being mentioned in the Book of Revelation as one of the Seven Churches of the Apocalypse (open 8:30am-7pm in summer, 8:30am-5:30pm in winter. Admission $1.40, students 70¢). The **Asclepion** is on the other side of town, 3km past the tourist office. (Do *not* take photos of the military base along the Asclepion; it is illegal, and armed soldiers take this law seriously.) The **Archaeological and Ethnographic Museum** displays artifacts such as earthenware statues (all arranged with full explanations) from Pergamon as well as a collection of traditional Turkish craft (open Tues.-Sun. 8:30am-7pm in summer, 8:30-5:30 in winter; admission $1.40, students 70¢).

Also don't forget to see some of Bergama's various earthen tombs used for ritual burial by the ancients. There are several large mounds of earth in the city, and one located past the *otogar* (heading toward the road to Izmir). Look for a sign pointing to the Asclepion (6km) and go down the street where a **Zafer Spor Derneği Lokalı** is located. You can't miss the mound (be sure to bring a flashlight). For a Turkish bath, there is the Çarsı Hamami (public bath) on Bankalar Cad. (near the Acroteria Pansion). The facilities are clean and a wash is $3.50, with a massage for an additional $3.50. (For men and women, open daily 7am-11:30pm.).

■ Izmir

Izmir (population 3 million), formerly ancient **Smyrna,** has risen from a tumultuous past to become Turkey's third largest city and second largest port. A western city with wide boulevards, plazas, and an arc-shaped waterfront, Izmir's industrialization has taken its toll. Izmir can be a fascinating destination, but in many places it's an industrial wasteland. Despite its seedier side, Izmir is known in Turkish as "Beautiful Izmir." While a stroll through the twisting alleyways in one of Izmir's residential districts may be enchanting, the exhaust fumes on the major boulevards will surely put to rest any thoughts of a Turkish wonderland.

Smyrna gained prominence in the 9th century BC and thrived before Lydians from Sardis destroyed the town in 600 BC. In 334 BC, Alexander the Great conquered Smyrna and refounded it atop Mt. Pagus, now called Kadifekale. During the Roman and Byzantine periods, the port of Smyrna again became prosperous and cosmopolitan. The diversion of the River Hermes protected Smyrna's harbor from silting, thereby rescuing it from the landlocked fate of its neighbors. In 1535, Suleyman the Magnificent brought trade to Smyrna by signing a treaty with France. The influx of Christian and Jewish merchants to Izmir gave prosperity to the city which, by the 19th century, had become a haven for migrants from mainland Greece. Following the Ottoman Empire's defeat in WWI, the Greek army occupied Izmir in hopes of uniting the area with mainland Greece. Turkish nationalist leader Mustafa Kemal (later Atatürk) defeated them when the Greeks overextended themselves in the Anatolian heartland. Greek forces left Smyrna on September 9, 1922, when the city's minority quarters went up in flames. The **Asia Minor Disaster,** as the events of 1922 came to be called, marked the end of Hellenic presence in Izmir.

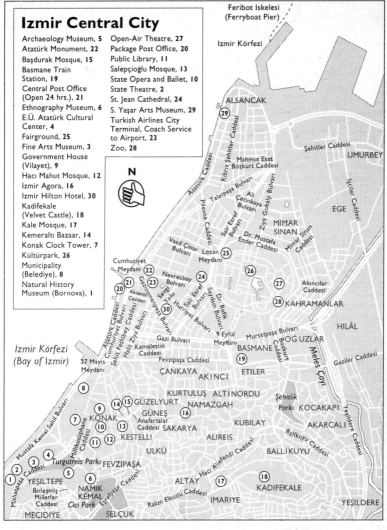

Izmir Central City

Archaeology Museum, 5
Atatürk Monument, 22
Başdurak Mosque, 15
Basmane Train Station, 19
Central Post Office (Open 24 hrs.), 21
Ethnography Museum, 6
E.Ü. Atatürk Cultural Center, 4
Fairground, 25
Fine Arts Museum, 3
Government House (Vilayet), 9
Hacı Mahut Mosque, 12
Izmir Agora, 16
Izmir Hilton Hotel, 30
Kadifekale (Velvet Castle), 18
Kale Mosque, 17
Kemeraltı Bazaar, 14
Konak Clock Tower, 7
Kültürpark, 26
Municipality (Belediye), 8
Natural History Museum (Bornova), 1

Open-Air Theatre, 27
Package Post Office, 20
Public Library, 11
Salepçioğlu Mosque, 13
State Opera and Ballet, 10
State Theatre, 2
St. Jean Cathedral, 24
S. Yaşar Arts Museum, 29
Turkish Airlines City Terminal, Coach Service to Airport, 23
Zoo, 28

Feribot İskelesi (Ferryboat Pier)

İzmir Körfezi

N

İzmir Körfezi (Bay of İzmir)

WESTERN TURKEY

ORIENTATION AND PRACTICAL INFORMATION

Izmir's principal boulevards radiate from rotaries, called *meydan*. **Cumhuriyet Meydanı**, on the waterfront, is the city's financial center and home to several travel agencies and consulates. Many budget hotels and inexpensive restaurants, along with several bus companies and the Aslancak **train station,** are located around **9 Eylül Meydanı,** the center of the Basmane district. From **Yeni Garaj** (the bus station), take municipal bus #50, 53, 56, 249, 250, or 260 to Basmane/Çankaya. Remember to buy your tickets (50¢) at the kiosk before you board. To get back to the bus station, take a bus from Basmane to **Konak Square** (Konak is the last of 3 stops), from which you can take bus #50, 56, or 60 to Yeni Garaj. **Konak,** 10 blocks south of Cumhuriyet Meydanı along the coastal **Atatürk Cad.,** is the center for metropolitan buses and *dolmuş.* Finding your way can be difficult, and street signs are hard to come by, so it is best to make the tourist office your first stop.

Tourist Office: The largest is the Central Office near the Hilton Hotel, 1/1D Gazi Osman Paşa Blv. (tel. 484 2148, 489 9278; fax. 489 9278). English spoken. Maps and other info. Open May-Oct. Mon.-Fri. 8:30am-7pm and Sat.-Sun. 8:30am-5:30pm, Nov.-Apr. Mon.-Sat. 8:30am-5:30pm. Also an office at the Yeni Garaj (486 2265; open daily 8am-11pm). Little English spoken.

Tourist Police: (tel. 489 0500, -6648).

Travel Agencies: There are 3 travel agencies on Gazi Osman Paşa Blv. recommended by both tourists and locals. **Ramtur,** 3/3 312 Gazi Osman Paşa Blv. Yeni Asır İşhani (tel. 425 2710, 483 3436; fax 483 3436; email orale@cakabey.ege.edu.tr). Don't be intimidated by the entrance; you can go right up to the 3rd floor. Arranges daily tours. **Opal Travel Agency,** 1 Gazi Osman Paşa Blvd. (tel. 445 6767; fax 489 8865). Reliable daily tours to Efes, Bergama, and Pamukkale. **Bintur Travel Agency,** 10/1 Gazi Osman Paşa Blv. (tel. 489 4100, 489 6564; fax 489 4228). Ticket sales and daily tours. All agencies open 9am-6pm.

Consulates: United Kingdom, Mahmut Esat Bozkurt Cad. 49 (tel. 463 5151; fax 421 2914), in Alsancak. **USA,** Amerikan Kültür Derneği, 2nd fl., Kazim Dirik Cad. (tel. 421 3643, -4).

American Express: (tel. 441 5843) Shares office space with **Koç Bank,** on Cumhuriyet Blv. (open Mon.-Fri. 9am-4:30pm).

Buses: For major intercity travel, go to the Yeni Garaj in Halkapinar (tel. 486 2265, -6; fax: 461 6652). Times and prices vary depending on the coach company. To: Istanbul (every 30min., 9hr., $22); Bursa (2 per day, 5hr., $7); Bodrum (ever hr. 7am-11pm, 4hr., $7); Kuşadası (every 30min., 2½hr., $7); Selçuk (get on the Bodrum bus and ask to be let off, 2hr., $3.50); and Ankara (8hr., $17). To go to the ancient city of Sardis, take the bus to Salihli and ask to be dropped off at the site (every 30min., 1½hr., $1.75).

Ferries: At the Yeni Liman 35220 Izmir (tel. 421 1484, -0094; fax 421 1481). 1 ferry per week goes to Istanbul (Sun., 19hr., from $15).

Hospitals: In Bornova, **Ege Üniversitesi Tip Fakültesi** (tel. 388 1920). **Alsancak Devlet Hastanesı** (tel. 463 6465), on Talatpaşa Blv., Alsancak. Also, **Yeşilyurt Devlet Hastanesı** (tel. 243 4343), Gazeteci Hasan Tahsin Cad., Yeşilyurt.

Medical Emergency: Call 112.

Police: (tel. 155; special "foreigners" department of the police tel. 482 2253, -1).

PTT: In Cumhuriyet Meydanı. 24hr. phone; cashes **traveler's checks** and offers **currency exchange** 8:30am-5:30pm. **Postal code:** 35.

Telephone Code: 232.

ACCOMMODATIONS

The small streets between Fevzipaşa Bulvarı and Gazi Bulvarı in the Basmane area are loaded with cheap hotels. Staying closer to the **9 Eylül Meydanı** will provide you with easy access to accommodations, taxis, and cheap eats. Beware of taxi drivers in Izmir: many work on commission and insist on driving you to hotels of *their* choice.

Bilen Palas Otel, 1369 Sok. No. 68 (tel. 483 9246). Located off 9 Eylül Meydanı opposite the Culture Park. Clean rooms have views of the 1369 Sok. below and may be noisy at night. Some rooms have a wash basin. Communal showers (always kept locked for safety), Turkish "pit" toilets, TV room on reception level. Singles $7; doubles $12.40; triples $17.25; quads $27.60.

Otel Divan, 1369 Sok. No. 61 (tel. 483 3675; fax 483 2243). Located a couple of doors down from Bilen on opposite side, it offers rooms with toilet, wash basin, shower, and TV. Makeshift garden for guests. Singles have access to a communal shower. Singles $7; doubles $12.40; triples $17.25; quads $27.60.

Güzel Izmir Hotel, 1368 Sok. No. 8 (tel. 483 5069). Just around the corner from the Bilen toward Fezi Paşa Bulvarı. Clean rooms at budget prices. Luggage storage, TV room, and public phone in the lobby. All rooms have showers. Singles $8.70; doubles $14.70; triples $22.

FOOD AND ENTERTAINMENT

Basmane Kebap Salonu, 157/A Fevzipaşa Blv. (tel. 425 5019), the dead-end street leading to the train station. A small, tidy place, the Salonu serves full meals ($5).

Ask for their specialty, *içli köfte* (meatballs with deep-fried batter, 50¢ each). Open daily 11am-midnight.

9 Eylül Merkez Lokantası, 9 Eylül Meydani No. 5/B (tel. 445 0531). A popular cheap eat with *köfte* ($1.66), *fasulya* ($1), and drinks ($1). Open 6am-11pm.

Kardelen Et Lokantası, 9 Eylül Meydani No. 3/A (tel. 441 4721). Another great Basmane cheap-eat with many vegetarian dishes. You can't miss their pink chairs out in front. Salads (86¢), *Lahmancun* (50¢), and kebaps ($1.40 to $2.75).

Club 33, 1469 Sok. No. 40, Alsancak (tel. 461 9782, 464 0470). Alsancak's hip-place to be in the "winter" months (Sept.-Jun.). Large dance floor on some nights holding up to 1000 people. Open 10:30pm-3am. Admission $7, which includes 2 drinks. Dress appropriately.

Au-Bar, 1471 Sok, No. 22 (tel. 464 3072, -3), in Aslancak. Winter club located next to the "33." Multilevel joint playing music well into early morning.

Sera Cafe, Atatürk Cad., No. 206/A, Alsancak (tel. 422 1939 or 422 4158). Fashionable cafe offers drinks, meals, appetizers, and live music. A bit pricier than the Basmane district, but the view of the harbor is inspiring at night. Serves breakfast ($2), and evening cocktails ($4.50). Also has a **La Sera** cafe-bar-restaurant on 190 Atatürk Cad. with similar offerings (tel. 464 2594, -5).

SIGHTS

Izmir's **agora** (marketplace) was built in the 4th century BC, destroyed by an earthquake in 178 AD, and subsequently rebuilt by Emperor Marcus Aurelius. The uninspiring remains are accessible from Anafartalar Cad. Walk south along 941 Sok. from the Otel Saray (open daily 8:30am-5:30pm; admission $1, students 50¢, free with FIYTO/ISIC). Above the city at Mt. Pagus is the most enduring of Alexander's legacies, the **Kadifekale,** originally built in the 4th century BC but frequently altered and restored by various conquerors (open 24hr.). The park within the walls of Kadifekale is at once unsavory and intriguing. The area may be unsafe after dark. Bus #33 from Konak ascends the mountain and offers a thrilling panorama of the bay. If you stroll along Anafartalar Cad. from its beginning at the Basmane station, you'll pass remnants of a less industrialized Turkey—*çay salonu* (teahouses), men smoking *nargile*, children and vendors filling the air with their cries, and colorful streets that eventually turn into Izmir's full-fledged **bazaar** (open Mon.-Sat. 8:30am-7pm). It is better to browse around at the bazaar during weekdays, because it is extremely crowded on Saturdays. Izmir's **archaeological museum,** near Konak Sq., displays statues of Poseidon and Demeter along with other antiquities (open Tues.-Sun. 8:30am-5:30pm; admission $2, students $1). There is an **Ethnographical Museum** next door which has folkloric items, including *kilims,* traditional costumes, and ancient weapons (open Tues.-Sun. 8:30am-5:30pm; admission $1, students 50¢, free with FIYTO/ISIC). Izmir's cosmopolitan character is most impressively revealed in its cultural events. The annual highlight, the **international festival** in late June and early July, brings classical and folk music concerts to Izmir, Çeşme, and Ephesus. For tickets and information, call the Izmir Hilton (tel. 441 6060; students $3.50-$10).

■ Near Izmir: Sardis (Sart)

Sardis was the capital of the Lydian Empire, which dominated Aegean Ionia from 680-547 BC. The Lydians embraced and embellished the existing Hellenic culture, providing the world with dice, balls, and coin minting.

Sardis boasts one of the seven churches mentioned in the Book of Revelation, which can easily be visited from Izmir or Kuşadası. Go to the Yeni Garaj and get on the bus to Salihli (every 30min., 1½hr., $1.75). Ask to be left off the highway in Sardis amid the scattered tea houses. The old city, including the gymnasium, baths, and synagogue, is located 100m up toward modern Sardis from the bus stop.

The entrance to the ruins leads to the **Marble Way,** lined by a row of **Byzantine shops.** At the end of the Marble Way, turn left to enter the **synagogue,** which has splendid 3rd-century mosaic floors. The imposing columns of the **gymnasium** shadow a **swimming pool,** affirming the historic grandeur of this ancient city. Go up the street that slips between two teahouses on the other side of the road and follow it 1km uphill to the **Temple of Artemis,** one of the largest in antiquity. Only a few columns remain, but their scrolled capitals are exquisite. Along the way to the temple you will pass an ancient Lydian gold refinery and a dome from a 12th-century Byzantine basilica, which was built atop a 5th-century church. The gymnasium complex and Temple of Artemis require separate admission fees (open in summer 8am-7:30pm, in winter 8am-5pm; 70¢, students 35¢). There is a **pyramid tomb** on the left side of the road leading to the Temple of Artemis. The path starts just before the lumber yard. The earliest of these tombs, located in the area northwest of the acropolis, date from the 6th century BC. Unfortunately, landslides have almost buried this once exceptional burial chamber. A **PTT** is located at the gymnasium entrance.

■ Çeşme

A breezy seaside village, Çeşme is built around a 14th-century Genoese fortress which was expanded and beautified by 16th-century Ottomans. Only one hour west of Izmir, Çeşme has deservedly gained popularity for its cool climate, peaceful beaches, crystal clear waters, friendly locals, and proximity to the Aegean and the Greek island of Chios. There is a festive nightlife in the discos, cafes, and bars along the marina. Nearby Ilıca is popular for its fancy thermal baths, yachting, and friendly (although ritzy) natives.

ORIENTATION AND PRACTICAL INFORMATION

If you are coming to Çeşme by bus, you will be dropped off a few hundred meters from the waterfront and the tourist information office. Along the way to the water is a shopping district with stores specializing in leather goods, jewelry and ceramics. Once you reach İskele Meydanı, head toward the ferries on the right for info.

Tourist Office: 8 İskele Meydanı (tel./fax 712 6653). From the bus stop, continue down the main road to the water, across from the castle and caravanserai. English, German, and French spoken. Maps, accommodation and price info available. Open daily in summer, Mon.-Fri. 8:30am-7pm and Sat.-Sun. 8:30am–5pm, in winter 8:30am-5:30pm. Closed weekends in the winter.

Travel Agencies: Hayne Tours, Izmir Cad. No. 154 (tel. 723 3346; fax 723 0068), located near Ilıca. Offers a variety of services, including car rental, tours, and plane, ferry, and bus ticket sales.

Ferries: Ertürk Tourism and Travel Agency, Beyazıt Cad. No. 7/8 (tel. 712 6768, 712 6876; fax 712 6223), located by the castle. Can arrange ferry travel between Çeşme and Chios (July-Sept. daily, May-June 3-5 per week, 1hr, $35 round-trip, not including steep port tax applicable to stays longer than 24hr.).

Bus Station: (tel. 716 8079) Walk 300m in the opposite direction from the tourist office toward the ferries, turning left before the small bridge and then walking straight to the station. Buses every 30min. from Üçkuyular in Izmir are very crowded on weekends. The last bus to Izmir from Çeşme during the summer is 9pm (1hr., $2). For info in Çeşme call 712 6499, in Izmir 259 3415.

Hospital: (tel. 712 0778).

Police: (tel. 712 6093), located in the back of the tourist office.

PTT: (tel. 712 6620, -348) On the waterfront in the opposite direction from the ferries, past a park with a statue of İsmer İnönü (open June-Sept. 8am-12am, Oct.-May 8am-8pm). **Postal Code:** 35930.

Telephone Code: 232.

ACCOMMODATIONS

Tarhan Pension, Musalla Mah., 9 Çarşı Sok. (tel. 712 6599), near the caravanserai (left after the "No Problem" cafe). Rooms are clean and cozy with a small table, chair, and showers with hot water. Owner speaks some English. Terrace and laundry service available. Singles $7; doubles $14; triples $24. Breakfast $1.75.

Tani Pension, Musalla Mah., 15 Çarşı Sok. (tel. 712 6238), next to the Tarhan Pension. Rooms in this comfortable family-style pension are clean and have marble floors. Terrace and laundry service, communal bathrooms with hot water, break-fast included. Singles $7; doubles $14; triples $21.

Yeni Kervan Pension, Musalla Mah. Kale Sokak (tel. 712 8496), turn right after the Tani Pension and walk 50m. All rooms have showers and balcony. TV lounge, pri-vate *bahçe.* Singles $10.50; doubles $17; triples $28; quads $34.50.

Alim Pension, Tarihi Türk Hamamı Yanı (tel. 712 7828; fax 712 8319), on the corner past the caravanserai and public bath house. Half the rooms have balconies over-looking a small orchard. Rooms are carpeted, have phones and showers. Singles $10; doubles $15; triples $24; quads $31. Breakfast $1.75.

Turiste Camping (tel. 722 1221; fax 722 1292), 8km from Çeşme near Altınkum Beach. Private beach. Water sports, restaurant, electricity and water. $5 per per-son; 2-person caravans $8.

Vekamp (tel. 717 2224), Ilıca Paşalimani, located near hot springs.

FOOD AND ENTERTAINMENT

Meals become more expensive farther down İskele Meydanı.

Flamingo Cafe and Restaurant, on the right before the street on the left near the Tarhan Pension. A no-frills place offering some of the least expensive food around. Spaghetti plates $2.40, mixed gill and rice $6, 10% discount for parties greater than 5.

Sahil Cafe and Restaurant, in the waterfront square. Has a pricier section by the waterfront and a fast food section toward the square. *Kebap,* salad and soda $5.

Körfez Restaurant, Bar and Disco, toward the PTT. Fast food and more expensive fare. During the day serves pizza, hot dogs and hamburgers. After 10pm a disco starts to groove in the adjacent room. Open until 4am in summer. Beer $2, soda $1.75, cocktails $5.

Lowry's Irish Pub, on the main shopping avenue. DJ spins tunes on small dance floor. Plenty of tables to enjoy a nice cold beer ($2; open until 4am).

Garden Pub, 16 İnlâlap Cad. (tel. 712 9215), a few doors up from Lowry's on the opposite side of the road. Open-air bar with a DJ and a Spanish-American motif. Open until 4am; drinks start at $2.

SIGHTS

The most impressive sight in Çeşme is the waterfront **castle** across from the tourist office. Historian Evliya Çelebi describes the castle, built in 1508 by Ottoman Sultan Beyazıt II to spy on Chios, as once having a staff of 185 people and 50 cannons. The castle was destroyed during 17th-century combat between the Ottoman Empire and Genoa. Rebuilt in the 18th century, the castle had lost its military function by the 19th century. The castle now houses an **Archaeological Museum** containing artifacts from the Çeşme area (open Tues.-Sun. 8:30am-noon and 1-5:30pm; 70¢).

Çeşme's other major attractions include its lovely **beaches,** easily accessible by the frequent *dolmus* service. There is a public beach only a short walk past the PTT, but the other major beaches are also worth visiting. Other beaches to explore are at Altınkum, Boyalık, Ildır and Erythrai. Boyalık is a 25-minute walk from Çeşme's town center. If you would like to test out Çeşme's **hot springs,** go to Ilıca, Şifne or Vecamp. In ancient times the springs were believed to cure the sick. *Dolmus* service around the peninsula runs until 11pm (sometimes midnight during peak season). Routes head east to Ilıca (6km, 50¢), and southwest to Altınkum (10km, 50¢, until 8pm).

For windsurfing enthusiasts, there is a school at Alaçatı (tel./fax 723 2896; local surf hotline tel. 716 9750). There are horse-riding facilites at Çanakbey Riding Center (tel. 712 9455 for reservations; stables tel. 712 9920). Finally, daily tours of Çeşme's **Don-key Island** (Eşek Adası) depart from the harbor near the PTT. Boats leave at 10:30am and return at 6pm ($14, lunch included).

EPHESUS AND ENVIRONS

■ Kuşadası

Kuşadası (the "Bird's Island") has something to offer almost any traveler. Located some 95km south of Izmir, Kuşadası is conveniently situated for daytrips to Ephesus, Selçuk, Priene, Miletus, and Didyma. Sandy beaches are a short distance away by *dolmuş*, as is a gorgeous National Park with lush, green forests and quiet mountain streams. By night, Kuşadası comes alive with cafes, bars, and dance clubs.

ORIENTATION AND PRACTICAL INFORMATION

Visitors arriving to Kuşadası by bus or ferry should brace themselves for the throngs of hustlers that will try to take you to their "bargain" accommodations. Hustlers work on commission and can be unrelenting. Try to have an idea where you want to go and don't be persuaded otherwise by the con men saying that the place is "closed" or "out of business." For a map, march straight to the **tourist information office** near the harbor before wandering into the city. Visitors disembarking from ferry-travel are advised to pay the port tax ($20) in U.S. dollars to avoid weak exchange rates.

The harbor master, the duty-free shop, the fish market, the passport police and the customs office are all in the port area. The bus station is about 2km east of the town center and frequent *dolmuş* connect it with Izmir (2hr.). *Dolmuş* also arrive from Selçuk and nearby smaller towns at a separate *dolmuş* stop about 1.5km from the **information office** in the port on İskele Meydanı. There's only one official office; other booths marked with an "i" for "information" are not official government offices and usually provide information about their own excursions. In the skyline, beyond the tourist office, are the turreted walls of an ancient Seljuk caravanserai (now a hotel), where itinerant merchants could once spend a night with their goods protected. The structure's turrets make a good reference point. Facing the caravanserai, **Kıbrıs Cad.** runs right and uphill, passing through a covered bazaar. Continue up the hill to **Aslanlar Cad.**, on which you'll find many cheap pensions. Left of the **Kervansaray Hotel** is the broad, pedestrian-only **Barbaros Hayrettin**. The **PTT, travel agencies,** and **banks** are also there. At the end of the street is a cubist medieval watchtower turned modern-day police station. Through the watchtower and along **Kahramanlar Cad.**, you'll reach the major artery out of town and, within a kilometer, the bus station.

Tourist Office: No. 13 Liman Cad., (tel. 614 1103; fax 614 6295), on İskele Meydanı in the port. Take a taxi from the bus station. Open daily in summer 8am-6pm; in winter 8am-noon.

Tourist Police: 2 Atatürk Blv. (tel. 614 1022), after the caravanserai.

Travel Agencies: Ekol Travel, with **WorldSpan,** Kıbrıs Cad., Buyral Sok 9/1 (tel. 614 9255, -5591; fax 614 2644). Cheap flights, ferry tickets, temporary baggage storage, room finding, message board, car rentals, and emergency help. English spoken. 15% discount on ferry tickets with *Let's Go*. English-speaking doctors. Open May-Nov. daily 8:30am-10pm; Dec.-April daily 8:30am-5:30pm.

Bank: Booths on the waterfront offer **currency exchange.** Open daily 8am-10pm. A **Koç Bank** is after the police station on Atatürk Blv. and has a 24hr. **ATM.**

Buses: Call ahead for tickets on the weekends. **Erbirlik** (tel. 614 9570) has service to Izmir (every 20min., 2hr., $2.70). **Pamukkale** (tel. 612 0928) has service to: Denizli (4 per day, 2½hr., $6.70); Istanbul (many per day, 11 hr., $18); Pamukkale (2 per day, 3hr., $8); and Bodrum (several daily, 2½hr., $46.70). **Kâmil Koç** leaves for Bodrum at 9:30am and returns at 6pm. Also has service to Ankara (10hr., $16.70).

Ferries: Ekol Travel undercuts the official rate. Flash *Let's Go* and ask for a 15% discount. Port taxes ($10) are included in the price of the ticket. Turkish boats leave daily in summer at 8:30am, returning at 5pm, only 2 per week in the off-season.

English Language Bookstore: Kuydaş Kitabevi, 8/B İnönü Blv. (tel. 612 8356; fax 614 9533), sells newspapers, magazines, guidebooks, and pulp novels. Open daily 7am-midnight. For cheaper stuff, try **Art Kitabevi,** 57 Sağlık Cad. (tel. 614 6454), near the PTT, which has an intriguing used book collection. Open until 12:30am.

Hospital: Kuşadası Devlet Hastanesı Public Hospital, Atatürk Blv. (tel. 614 1026, -1614; fax 612 2438), on the waterfront at the northern edge of town.

Police: (tel. 614 5350) On Hükümet Cad. Finds translators in emergencies.

PTT: (tel. 614 1212, -1034) Next to the caravanserai, halfway up Barbaros Hayrettin. Open daily 8:30am-7pm. **Telephones** available 24hr.

Postal Code: 09400. **Telephone Code:** 256.

ACCOMMODATIONS

Finding a pension in Kuşadası is rarely a problem, even for those traveling alone (unlike in Bodrum). Many are on Aslanlar Cad. and have high-season prices that can be haggled down. Don't be afraid of checking a few different places before settling on a room; good pension owners should not object.

Hotel Rose, 7 Aslanlar Cad. (tel. 612 2588; fax 614 1113; email sammy@superon-line.com). Run by the amiable Salman (a.k.a. Sammy) Kurt, who will do his best to make travelers comfortable. Comfortable rooms, bar and lounge, international phone, book exchange, and 24hr. hot water. Internet facilities available. Free luggage storage and transport to Ephesus. Half-price Turkish baths. Dorm beds $4; private rooms with shower $10; roof accommodations $2.50; breakfast $1.70; laundry $2 per kg; 10% student discount and 15% discount for *Let's Go*ers.

Park Pension, 17 Aslanlar Cad. (tel. 614 3917, 612 6912), down the street from Hotel Rose. In an old Greek home, it has colorful rooms, a garden, and restaurant. Breakfast included. Singles $6.70.

Hotel Sezgin, Kahramlar Cad. Zafer Sok. No. 15 (tel. 614 6489, -4225; fax 614 6489). Clean rooms and a comfortable atmosphere minutes away from the town center. Private baths, 24hr. hot water, laundry, and central heating. Lounge and bar area. Great fax. Singles $7; doubles $10; triples $15. Breakfast $2.50; BBQ dinner $4.

Önder (tel. 614 2413) and **Yat Camping** (tel. 614 1333), 2km north of town on Atatürk Blv. Take a Selçuk *dolmuş* or walk. Both have good facilities, including laundry ($2.50 per load) and swimming pools. Both campsites are $2.50 per person; tents $2; caravans $2.50; cars $1.25; electricity $1.25.

FOOD AND ENTERTAINMENT

There are many cheap restaurants on Kahramlar Cad. and its alley tributaries. Restaurants along the waterfront are expensive and crowded.

Sammy's Kebap House and Cafe, Hitit Sun Pasaji Kıbrıs Cad. Buyraı Sok. No. 1 (tel. 612 6042), down the street from the Hotel Rose near the waterfront. Choose from various *kebaps* ($1.50) and sandwiches.

Havana Restaurant, Grand Bazaar Buyraı Sok. No. 1 (tel. 612 7892), to the right coming down Kıbrıs Cad. to the harbor. No Cuban food, but you will feel relaxed in its bright environs. *Shish kebap,* fish, salad and wine ($5.25), beer (70¢).

Çınaraltı Restaurant (tel. 614 3332, -6281), in the Hotel Adakule Karşısı Kuştur Yolu; take the *dolmuş* heading to Selçuk and ask to be left off at Çınaraltı. Serves traditional Turkish meals. The specialty is *Çoban Kavurma* ($3).

Barlar Sok., parallel to Kahramanlar Cad., offers some great nightlife opportunities, including the clubs **Heaven, Green Bar** and **Step.** All offer live music and are open until 4am. **Ecstasy** is a groovin' disco with no cover during the week, $7 cover on weekends. Open until 4am. **The Temple** (tel. 612 5025), near the marina has a $10 cover during the week, $20 on weekends. Open until 4am. **Kaleiçi Hamamı,** 7 Eylül Sok. (tel. 614 1292), is near the PTT. Come prepared to open your body's pores. Bath and massage $20, $10 for guests of Hotel Rose.

WESTERN TURKEY

SIGHTS

Kuşadası's most important sights are its shopping areas and its several clean beaches. The **Grand Bazaar** and **Barbaros Mayrettin** are, contrary to what the shop owners will tell you, expensive places to shop. But it doesn't cost anything to browse (see **Carpet Buying in Turkey,** p. 397).

Kuşadası's beaches are clean but overcrowded. **Kadınlar Plajı** (Ladies Beach) is just 3km from the city and is easily accessible by *dolmuş* (35¢). There are **scuba** courses at the beach through the Balcı Pension (tel. 614 1410; fax 614 1730). For a longer coastline and fewer crowds, try the sandy **Karovaplajı** and **Yavansu Plajı.** Both can be reached by taking a *dolmuş* heading to Davutlan for 7km.

The best place for swimming, walking and picnicking is the **National Park** beyond Davutlan at Güzelçamlı (open 7am-7:30pm; 70¢ per person, $1 per motorcycle, $2.70 per car). The park's entrance is 30km from Kuşadası. There are four **beaches** in the park at various distances from the entrance (İçmeler, 1km; Aydınlık, 5km; Kavakı, 8km; and Karasu, 10km). There is also a canyon area 6km from the gate. Don't leave the park without seeing **Zeus Mağarası** (Zeus's Cave). It's full of water bubbling up from the ground, once rumored to have treasure hidden in its depths.

■ Ephesus (Efes)

Ephesus was one of the more important cities in the Roman Empire. Imagine being transported back two millennia: walking amidst its columned avenues, sitting in the city's theater, browsing through a scroll at the library. The city grew to be the second largest in the Empire and a gateway to the eastern world. Ephesus was also the city where the Virgin Mary and Apostle John spent some of their last days. The Ecumenical Council met here in 431 AD.

HISTORY

The origins of Ephesus are shrouded in legend. It was founded in a manner prescribed by the Delphic Oracle, which foretold that a fish and wild boar would point to the appropriate site. Its location has changed several times due to the continual recession of the harbor waters. Today, the ruins of the ancient port lie 10km inland from the coast.

Ephesians were reluctant to move, particularly because they sought to remain near the colossal city-protectress' shrine, the **Temple of Artemis.** The ancient traveler Pausanias deemed it the "most wondrous of the seven ancient wonders" and "the most beautiful work ever created by humankind." The first major structure built entirely of marble and the largest edifice in the ancient Greek world, the Temple of Artemis was four times as big as the Parthenon in Athens. Remarkably, this massive monument was actually built twice. The temple was set afire during the reign of Mad King Hesostratos in 356 BC, on the night of Alexander the Great's birth. According to legend, the pyro-king succeeded only because Artemis—watching over Alexander's birth at the time—was absent. Fittingly, Alexander himself restored the temple to its original dimensions and aura. Offerings by hundreds of thousands of pilgrims each year enabled the temple to grow so wealthy that it became the world's first bank. Today, little remains of the magnificent structure. Plundering Goths sacked the sanctuary in the 3rd century, followed by the Byzantines. You can see some of the original columns at the Aya Sophia in Istanbul.

Ephesus reached its zenith after 129 BC, when the Romans established the province of Asia with Ephesus as the capital. It was second only to Alexandria in population, with more than 250,000 inhabitants. The ruins today date primarily from this period. St. Paul, recognizing the significance of the metropolis, arrived in 50 AD and converted a small group of Ephesians to the new religion. Some perceived the development of Christianity as a threat to Cybele (mother goddess of Anatolia) and Artemis, and forced St. Paul and his followers to depart. Eventually, however, Ephesus became a center of Christianity in the Roman Empire.

Throughout its life, Ephesus waged a constant battle against silt from the neighboring Cayster River. It lost. Its harbor choked with silt, Ephesus transformed it into a marshy morass. By the 6th century AD, the recession of the sea had sealed the city's fate. The swamps became infested with malaria-carrying mosquitoes, which in turn triggered a tremendous epidemic that resulted in over 200,000 deaths.

ORIENTATION AND PRACTICAL INFORMATION

Disregard ominous signs at the travel agencies on Samos and in Kuşadası which insist that guided tours of Ephesus are "highly recommended." The tours are expensive (about $25 per day), and guides tend to rush you through the 2000-acre site (open daily 8am-6pm; admission to site $4.75, students with ISIC $2.40). The admission booth (tel. 892 6402) is helpful if you want to hire a guide beforehand. You can visit on your own with the aid of a good guidebook to Ephesus—about $5 in Kuşadası's souvenir shops or at the entrance to the site. Bring a water bottle; it gets toasty, and the refreshment stands at the site shamelessly overcharge.

To get to Ephesus from the Kuşadası bus station, take a *dolmuş* to Selçuk and tell the driver you want to get off at Ephesus. From the Selçuk train station, take any *dolmuş* toward Kuşadası. *Dolmuş* service is frequent in the summer ($1). It should drop you at the first Tusan Motel (there are two). Here, you will be met by taxi drivers offering to take you to the House of Mary ($16.70) or the top gate of the Ephesus site ($7). **Toilets** (15¢), a **post office** with orphaned guidebooks, and several expensive restaurants with chewy Turkish ice cream (if it's authentic, you can stretch it close to a yard) are located next to the Ephesus site entrance. If you want to stay near the site, the **Tusan Motel** (tel. 892 6060; fax 892 2665) is at the *dolmuş* stop on the road to Selçuk (singles $5). It has a pool and offers *kebap* dinners ($2.70).

The *dolmuş* that return to Kuşadası are sometimes full—you can go to Selçuk first if you want to be sure to get a seat. You should stop in Selçuk anyway to supplement your exploration of Ephesus with a visit to the impressive **Ephesus Museum** (see **Selçuk,** p.439). The **telephone code** is 232.

VISITING EPHESUS

If you don't take a guided tour, you'll probably approach the ruins from the road between Kuşadası and Selçuk, and your first glimpse of the site will be the outskirts of the ancient city.

Vedius Gymnasium

The most important of these remains is the **Vedius Gymnasium,** to the left as you proceed down the road to the main entrance. On the west end of the gymnasium courtyard (the main entrance is at the north end of the site) are **public toilets** and a source of potable but warm **water.** Farther down lie the contours of an enormous **stadium,** whose seats were removed to construct the Byzantine city walls. Just before the entrance stand the ruins of the **Double Church** where the Ecumenical Council met in 431 AD. The area can be reached via a dirt path to the right just after the gate.

Along the Arcadiane

Once you pass through the main entrance, you may not be able to resist heading straight to the center of the site and marveling at **Arcadian Street,** a magnificent, colonnaded marble avenue. Like the present-day tourist drag in Kuşadası, Arcadian St. was lined with shops and extended to the harbor, where visitors disembarked and trading ships docked with cargo from the Far East. The street liquefied into a small marsh, but many of the original columns have survived.

Once at the far end of the avenue, turn around for a dazzling view of the **Grand Theater.** With seating for 25,000 and remarkable acoustics, the amphitheater dominates the entire site, carved into the side of Mt. Pion. In ancient times the Ephesians celebrated the Festival of Artemis every April. Singing and dancing, the denizens marched 89 golden idols of the goddess to the Grand Theater. St. Paul also gave ser-

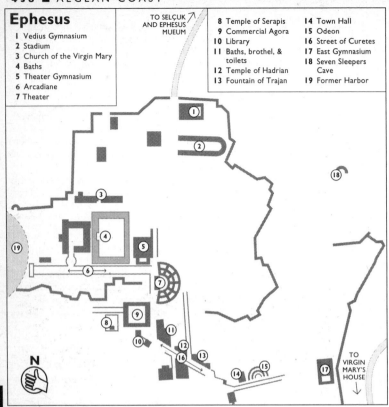

Ephesus

1 Vedius Gymnasium
2 Stadium
3 Church of the Virgin Mary
4 Baths
5 Theater Gymnasium
6 Arcadiane
7 Theater

TO SELÇUK
AND EPHESUS
MUEUM

8 Temple of Serapis
9 Commercial Agora
10 Library
11 Baths, brothel, & toilets
12 Temple of Hadrian
13 Fountain of Trajan

14 Town Hall
15 Odeon
16 Street of Curetes
17 East Gymnasium
18 Seven Sleepers Cave
19 Former Harbor

TO
VIRGIN
MARY'S
HOUSE
↓

mons here (open in summer daily 8:30am-6:30pm; in winter 8:30am-5:30pm; free).
Today, the theater hosts the **International Efes Festival,** held in late spring.

Along the Street of Curetes

In front of the theater is the slightly elevated **Marble Road (Street of Curetes),** built
by Nero, which once led all the way to the Temple of Artemis. Peek down one of the
small holes in the road for a glimpse of the sewage system. The **Commercial Agora,**
the main plaza of the city, is nearby. In the center of the colonnaded square stood a
huge **horologium,** a combination sundial and water clock. The Marble Rd. then leads
to the **Library of Celsus.** Almost entirely reconstructed by Viennese archaeologists,
its elaborately carved marble facade suggests the luxury of ancient Ephesus.

Across from the library at the corner of Marble Rd. and Curetes St. are the vestiges
of the **brothel** dedicated to the love-goddess Aphrodite. Romantic commerce took
place by candlelight in the small, windowless side rooms. A secret passage leads from
the library to the brothel. At the end of the brothel, farthest from the Grand Theater,
is a sacred pump whose water supposedly made barren women fertile. The statue of
Priapus, the god of fertility, was found here and is now displayed in the Ephesus
Museum in Selçuk. Between the brothel and the library is the **world's first known
advertisement**—a picture of a foot and a square containing an inscription. Supposedly, if cryptically, it was an ad for the brothel.

Uphill, the imposing ruins of the **Temple of Hadrian** dominate the left side of the
road. Renovation shows off the intricately carved facade. The marble archway contains friezes depicting the creation of the city of Ephesus, and a bust of the goddess
Cybele adorns the keystone. Beyond the temple and adjoining the rear of the brothel
are the **Baths of Scholastikia.**

Farther up the hill lie the ruins of the exquisite **Fountain of Trajan.** Various fragments found here have been piled to reconstruct the original structure. The statue of the Emperor Trajan that stood before the fountain has been destroyed—except for the base. The upper half of the site leads to the **Tomb of Memmius** on the left-hand corner. There is also a frieze of the goddess **Nike.**

Continuing up the path toward the top gate, you will pass the **odeon** (town hall) with the grand state **agora** on your right. The agora was the heart of political activity in the city from the 1st century BC until the city's final demise in the 5th century AD. On the left after the odeon lies the **House of Councils** and the upper **baths.** Be prepared to be harassed by hawkers after exiting the top gate.

Christian Sites

If you turn left after the hill of Trajan's fountain, you'll come to the **Grotto of the Seven Sleepers.** Many Christians believe that seven men fleeing persecution in the 3rd century hid in these caves. When they awoke, one of them went to buy bread and discovered that he and the group had been sleeping for 209 years. The story is more interesting than the site. Nearby is the **House of the Virgin Mary** (see p. 440).

■ Selçuk

The authentic "Turkishness" of Selçuk, for which the town has been deemed preferable to Kuşadası, has become aggressive and commodified. Although now inundated with carpet shops, souvenir dens, and lame *kebap* joints, flashes of the town's captivating history still glitter in places. Selçuk is smaller, less anonymous, and more beautiful than Kuşadası, and the archaeological sites outside of town offer respite from the commercial fervor. On Saturdays in summer, locals as well as tourists flock to the huge **Open Air Market,** featuring fresh fruit, cheeses, spices, and clothing. The Selçuk castle dominates the city's skyline for miles away. **Saint John's Basilica,** the wonderful **İsa Bay Camii** and the ruins of the **Temple of Artemis** lie below the castle. From Selçuk, the tranquil **House of the Virgin Mary** (Meryemana) can be reached by *dolmuş* or taxi (7km). Officially sanctified by the Vatican, this site on Bülbüdağı (Nightingale Mountain) is a often a stop on Christian holy treks.

ORIENTATION AND PRACTICAL INFORMATION

The main thoroughfares are the Izmir-Aydın road and the uniquely-named **Atatürk Cad.** The road from Kuşadası and Ephesus, **Sabahattındede Cad.,** intersects Atatürk Cad., forming the main crossroad of the town.

Tourist Office: Atatürk Mah. Agora Çarşısı 35-36 Ñirza Karşısı (tel. 892 6328, -6945), on the southwest corner of the intersection of Sabahattındede and Atatürk Cad. Their hand-drawn maps are a bit crude but adequate. Open in summer Mon.-Fri. 8am-7pm; in winter and weekends 9am-5pm.
Banks: There are several on Cengiz Cad.
Bus Station: At the intersection from which the Kuşadası *dolmuş* departs. Take a minibus to Izmir (every 30min., $1.50) at the bus station, or a larger bus on the street in front of the bus station. Stand on the opposite side and signal the driver (every 30min., 1½hr., $1.50).
Train Station: On Cengiz Cad.
Hospital: (tel. 892 7036) On the same corner as the tourist office.
Pharmacies: Scattered around the town center.
Police: (tel. 892 6016) Behind Cengiz Topel Cad., near the PTT.
PTT: 1006 Sok. No. 9 (tel. 892 6456), near a small square with a fountain facing the ruins on Cengiz Topel Cad. (open 8am-11pm, full services 8:30am-12:30pm and 1:30-5:30pm). **Postal Code:** 35920. **Telephone Code:** 232.

ACCOMMODATIONS

Pension hawkers on commission are increasingly common in Selçuk. Take advice only from the tourist office and other travelers.

Pansiyon Karahan, 9 I. Okul Sok. (tel. 892 2575), the 2nd right after the bus station heading north. Free service to Ephesus, beaches, and harbor. Clean, carpeted rooms, all with showers, balconies, secure locks, and comfortable beds. Management arranges boats to Samos (round-trip $35; 10% student discount). $6.70 per person, negotiable. Breakfast $2.50. Laundry $3.40. Make summer reservations 1 week in advance.

Barim Pansiyon I, Müze Arkası Sok. (tel. 892 6923), behind the museum off Turgutreis Cad. Carpeted and great decor—a bit like Tahiti, with grass mats on the floor and straw gazebos in the courtyard. Cool and quiet. 24hr. hot water; some rooms have bathrooms. Little English spoken. $6.70 per person. Breakfast $2.70.

Pansiyon Kirhan, Atatürk Mah. Turgutreis Sok. No. 24 (tel. 892 2257), behind the museum. An old Ottoman home with 4 comfortable, carpeted rooms to let. Garden, fireplaces, and 24hr. hot water. $5 per person. Breakfast $1.50.

Australian New Zealand Pension, 7 Prof. Miltner Sok. (tel. 892 6050), behind the museum (follow the signs). Spacious, lively garden. Free service to Ephesus and the beach. Trekking packages and tickets to Samos (same price as Karahan). Discounts (20%) for trekking groups larger than 7. $4 per dorm bed; private rooms $8, with shower $10. 15% discount for *Let's Go* readers. Laundry $4 per load.

Garden Camping, İsa Bey Mah. Kale Altı 4 (tel. 892 6165, -2489; fax 892 2997), behind the Selçuk Castle past the mosque. Peaceful location, electricity, swimming pool, laundry service, and clean bathrooms. $1.70 per person. Separate restaurant (tel. 892 2083) serves a full meal for $6.50.

FOOD AND ENTERTAINMENT

Restaurants here are less expensive than in Kuşadası. Most places speak some English as a result of a steady influx of tourists in the town. Don't expect to find a crazy nightlife in Selçuk but there are a couple of bars.

Özdamar Restaurant, Atatürk Mah. Cengiz Topel Cad. No. 65 (tel. 891 4097). Outdoor seating with excellent views of the Selçuk Castle. Choose from pizza, fish *kebaps, döner kebap* ($1.70-$2.40), cold dishes ($1), or mixed grill ($2.75).

Mine Restaurant, Atatürk Mah. Okul Sok. (tel. 545 3107), across from the Pansiyon Karahan. Similar selections to the Özdamar. *Tas kebap* (meat stew) $1.70; full breakfast $1.70; mixed grill $2.70.

Baget Sandwich Bar, Atatürk Mah. Koçak Sok. No. 5 (tel. 892 8050). The best place in town for pocket sandwiches ($1.70) and vegetarian options. Breakfast of tomato, eggs, honey, cucumber, cheese, tea and olives is $2. Open 7am-midnight.

Ekselans Cafe and Bar, Okul Sok. No. 18. Hip and environmentally conscious. There are 2 floors with picnic benches for seating. Backgammon boards available. Beer $1, cognac $1.50. Open 11am-midnight.

Pink Bistro Cafe-Bar, Atatürk Mah. Zaiyburg Cad. 24/A, close to the Ekselans. Large beer $1, cocktails $3.50-$4.

SIGHTS

Selçuk's archaeological sights have always been overshadowed by the towering majesty of its neighbor, Ephesus. The colossal and comparatively unadvertised **Basilica of Saint John** is a good place to escape the frenzied consumerism (that is, once you've slipped past the unctuous rug dealers and twinkling card stands near the basilica's entrance). The 6th-century church was constructed under the Byzantine emperor Justinian on the supposed site of St. John's grave (open daily 8am-6pm; $1.40, students 70¢). It was built on such an immense scale that, if reconstructed today, would be the seventh-largest cathedral in the world. Its stately, if somewhat sparse, remains are characterized by a strange combination of Roman imperial grandeur and early Christian grace. The cathedral's idiosyncratic character is made even stranger by an 8th-century wall built around it by invading Arabs, who used materials taken from the 1st-century gymnasium of Ephesus, a stadium where the Romans watched their infamous gladiatorial games.

The tranquil **House of the Virgin Mary** lies 100m off the road from Ephesus to Bülbüldağı (Nightingale Mountain). About five years after the death of Christ, St. John is said to have accompanied the Virgin Mary to Ephesus, where they lived in a small house on the slopes of Mt. Bülbül. The site lay forgotten for centuries until 1892, when an archaeologist discovered a 7th-century church that was built over the original site. It is a popular pilgrimage destination that both Christians and Muslims visit, leaving behind bits of tissue tied around branches of dwarf trees symbolizing wishes. You'll need to take a taxi to the mountain and have the driver wait ($16).

The stunning **İsa Bey mosque** lies at the foot of the hill on which the Basilica of St. John and the Ayasoluk castle stand. It was built in 1375 on the orders of Aydınoğlu İsa Bey and features columns taken from Ephesus, which the Ephesians in turn had pilfered from Aswan, Egypt. The mosque represents a transition between Selçuk and Ottoman styles. Restored in 1975, the mosque has regained much of the august simplicity that 600 years of wear and tear had eroded (open during prayer).

The **Temple of Artemis,** one of the **seven wonders of the ancient world,** used to be the largest temple on the planet. A lone reconstructed column now twists toward the heavens from a bog that roughly approximates the area of the temple's foundation (open 8:30am-5:30pm; free). Selçuk's **Ephesus Museum** (tel. 892 6010) is the home of most of the archaeological finds unearthed in the region since WWII. Those discovered earlier have been carted off to Vienna. The **statue of Priapus,** the randy little rascal that decorates postcards at nearly every stand in Turkey, is among the treasures you can still find here. The famous multi-breasted statue of Artemis, as well as exquisite busts of Eros, Athena, Socrates, the emperors Tiberius, Marcus Aurelius, and Hadrian, make this one of the more important collections of ancient art in the world (open daily 8:30am-6pm; $2, students $1).

Selçuk is also home to the famous **Camel Wrestling Festival,** held annually during the second week of January (contact tourist office for more information).

■ Near Seljuk

PRIENE (GÜLLÜBAHÇE)

Priene became prominent as a member of the Ionian Confederation of cities in the region of Smyrna (modern Izmir). The confederation controlled the Aegean coast after the decline of the Hittite empire, but Priene lingered in the shadow of its neighboring economic rival, Miletus. The city's population never exceeded 5000 and while its neighbors excelled in commerce, Priene devoted its resources to religion and sport. Now the city's ruins, on a plateau before the walls of Mt. Mycale, overlook the contortions of the River Meander.

Dolmuş stop by a cafe. To reach the site from there, follow the road that struggles up the slope and forks off to the right of the road to Miletus and Didyma. First you'll encounter the massive ancient walls that circumscribe the ruined metropolis constructed on the terraced slope of the mountain. From the main entrance, a path leads to what was once the main avenue of ancient Priene. The west side of the block (facing downhill) begins with the **Prytaneum,** the vaulted hearth of the city's sacred flame. Brought to Priene from Athens by the first settlers, the flame was extinguished only when the city was invaded and rekindled upon liberation. After the Prytaneum is the unmistakable **Bouleterion,** or Senate House, a well-preserved, elegant square auditorium. The interior chamber was equipped with a huge marble altar on which sacrifices were offered both at the opening and closing of senate sessions. Only the foundation of the altar remains.

Larger congregations convened just up the hill at the handsome **theater.** The front row retains five **thrones of honor** with dignified bases carved in the shape of lions' paws. Farther along the upper terrace, the **Temple of Athena** transports you back to the heyday of Hellenistic architecture. Alexander the Great financed the project, and Pytheos, the architect whose *chef d'œuvre* is the Mausoleum of Halicarnassus (one of the seven wonders of the ancient world), designed the structure. The temple retains largely intact front steps, interior floors, and five complete columns. Descend from the temple to visit the vast remains of the private houses of Priene, an unusual example of Ionian architecture.

Heading back toward the entrance of the site, you'll pass through the spacious **agora.** Women were allowed here only if accompanied by a man, either husband or slave. At the center, a public temple once hosted official ceremonies and sacrifices. Beyond the agora is the 3rd-century BC **Temple of Olympic Zeus.** Downhill, on the lip of the plateau, stand the **stadium** and **gymnasium,** with the names of many young athletes inscribed on their walls. On either side of the main hall were small rooms for bathing and exercise (open daily in summer 8am-6:30pm).

MİLETUS (MİLET)

Now surrounded by arid plains, Miletus once sat upon a thin strip of land surrounded by four separate harbors. Envied for its prosperity and its strategic coastal location, the city was destroyed and resettled several times. Eventually, it suffered the same fate as its Ionian confederates—the silting of its harbor and waters by neighboring rivers caused its decline. For centuries, Miletus was a hotbed of commercial and cultural development. In the 5th century BC, the Milesian alphabet was adopted as the standard Greek script. Miletus later became the headquarters of the Ionian school of philosophers, including Thales, Anaximander, and Anaximenes. The city's leadership, however, faltered in 499 BC, when Miletus headed an unsuccessful Ionian revolt against the Persian army. The Persians retaliated by wiping out the entire population of the city, massacring the men and selling the women and children into slavery.

The site's main attraction today is the **theater,** clearly visible from the Priene-Didyma highway. The strikingly well-preserved structure dates from Hellenistic times, though most of the visible portion was constructed by Romans. The theater could seat 15,000 and was originally positioned at the water's edge.

The remaining portions of Miletus are marshy in all but the summer months. To the right of the theater as you enter the site is a Selçuk **caravanserai** (perennially under restoration). Facing the theater, the footpath meandering to your right leads you to the **Faustina Baths** behind the theater, erected by the wife of the Roman Emperor Marcus Aurelius. To the left of the baths are the **North** and **South Agoras.** Next to the baths is the **Delphinium,** or sanctuary of Apollo Delphinus. The temple was first constructed to honor Apollo, who transformed himself into a dolphin and led the Cretans to Miletus. All of the temple's priests were sailors. If nothing else, visit the abandoned 15th-century **İlyas Bey Camii,** the peculiar dome-shaped structure just beyond the baths. The interior offers refuge from the heat as well as an exquisite *mihrab* (the ornate fixture pointing toward Mecca). There is a small **Archaeological Museum** about 500m before the main entrance. (Tel. (256) 875 5038, -5256. Site open in summer 8am-7pm; in winter 8am-5:30pm. Admission $1, students 40¢.)

DİDYMA (DİDİM)

Ancient Didyma was the site of a sacred sanctuary to Apollo and of an oracle that brought in most of the city's fame and wealth. The first Didyma oracles date from about 600 BC. The sanctuary was destroyed by the Persians 100 years later when they plundered Miletus. It lay deserted until Alexander the Great's arrival, which inspired the arid sacred spring to miraculously flow anew. The present sanctuary was begun during the 2nd and 1st centuries BC. Work continued until the 2nd century AD, but the original plans, like those for Alexander's empire, proved too ambitious and were never completed.

The **sanctuary** at Didyma ranked as the third-largest sacred structure in the ancient Hellenic world after its neighbors to the north, the Temple of Artemis at Ephesus and the Temple of Hera on Samos. Since virtually nothing remains of either of the latter two buildings, the sanctuary at Didyma stands alone as the best surviving example of such colossal temple architecture. It was built to last—many of its individual marble slabs weigh more than a ton. During the Roman period, the unfinished temple attracted pilgrims from all over ancient Greece. A church was constructed on the site in 385 AD after Emperor Theodosius I outlawed the solicitation of pagan oracles. The sanctuary was eventually incorporated into a church in the 5th century, but suffered extensive damage from an earthquake in 1500. The sacred road that ran from Miletus to Didyma ended at the temple gates. The statues that once lined the final stretch were plundered by the British in 1858 and have been replaced by souvenir shops.

Inside the main gate rests a bas-relief of a giant **Medusa head,** once part of an ornate frieze that girded the temple's exterior and now star of countless brochures. The building's full magnitude is apparent only when you climb up the stairway to the main facade. Still, you are seeing only a fraction of the original; all that remains of the more than 100 magnificent columns are the bases and lower sections. To transport such cumbersome chunks of marble, the Greeks constructed long shafts of stone leading to the temple site, lubricated them with soap, then slid the building materials over the slippery surface.

In front of the temple trickles the spring that the priestesses supposedly tapped when receiving prophecies from Apollo. Climb the steps to enter the forecourt. Through the **Hall of Twelve Columns** is the **Hall of Two Columns,** where visitors waited to hear the pronouncements. From here, 22 steps lead down to the **audition.**

In the southeast corner of the courtyard are traces of another **sacred fountain** as well as the foundations of a **naiskos,** a tiny temple that housed a venerated bronze statue of Apollo. The temple (tel. (256) 811 0035), which served as the site of the oracle, appears to have been erected in 300 BC, before the larger edifice was begun (open in summer 8am-7pm; in winter 8am-5:30pm; $1, students 40¢).

PAMUKKALE AND ENVIRONS

▓ Denizli

Denizli is only 22km from Pamukkale, where beautiful calcium formations have formed white terraces over the ages. It is also an hour's ride to the exciting archaeological site of Aphrodisias, thought to be potentially grander than Ephesus. More local sites include Laodicia, one of the seven churches mentioned in the Book of Revelations. After Izmir, Denizli is the fastest growing city in the Aegean Region. Two large statues of chickens, symbolizing Denizli's ties to the poultry industry, dominate major intersections.

ORIENTATION AND PRACTICAL INFORMATION

Visitors to Denizli will undoubtedly arrive at the hectic bus terminal *(otogar),* located at the intersection of **İstasyon Cad.** and **Cumhuriyet Cad.** The train station is located across the street on Izmir Blvd., where a small tourist office is also situated. Cheap pensions are behind the bus station on Doğan Cad. and Halk Cad.

> **Tourist Office:** (tel. 264 3971) In the train station. Comprehensive help, maps, general info, and English service. Open daily 8am-5:30pm.
> **Banks:** A large number of banks and **exchange offices** are located in Bayram Meydanı around the corner from the Ethnographic Museum.
> **Buses:** To: Izmir (8 per day, 4hr., $5.35); Pamukkale (every 30min., 30min., 40¢ by Belediye bus or *dolmuş*); Selçuk/Ephesus via Izmir (8 per day, 3hr., $4.70); Ankara (3 per day, 7hr., $10); Aphrodisias (9:30am, 1½hr., $6.70); Istanbul (2 per day, 10hr., $13.35); Kuşadası (1 per day, 3½hr., $5.35); Marmaris (2 per day, 4½hr., $5.35); Bodrum (4 per day, 4hr., $6); and Fethiye (9 per day, 4½hr., $5.35). There is a **luggage storage** *(emanetçi)* in the main bus garage, near the small PTT.
> **Trains:** Station is on Izmir Blvd, across from the bus station (tel. 268 2831). To: Izmir (4 per day, 6hr., $3.20); Afyon (6:40am, 6hr., $3.20); and Istanbul (5:25pm, 14hr., $7.33). 20% discount for students.
> **Pharmacies:** Most of the pharmacies are clustered on Hastane (or Doktorlar) Cad., near the hospitals, 1 street behind the Ethnographic Museum.

Hospitals: Denizli Devlet Hastanesi (tel. 265 3430, -1), directly ahead as you walk uphill on Hastane Cad. Public. **Özel Sağlık Hastanesi** (tel. 264 4311), located across from the Devlet Hospital. Private.

Police: (tel. 265 0034) Located at the intersection of İstiklal Cad. and İnönü Cad. Also a tiny police station next to the tourist office in the *otogar* (tel. 241 8920).

PTT: The main post office (tel. 263 5271) is located in the heart of the commercial district, where Mimar Sinan Cad. and Atatürk Cad. meet (across from the big park near the police station). Open 8am-noon and 1-5:30pm. There's a little PTT (tel. 261 1951) in the *otogar*. **Postal Code:** 20100.

Telephone Code: 258.

ACCOMMODATIONS

While rooms in Denizli may be cheaper than in Pamukkale, they are without many of the amenities as well. Alas, none of the pensions have pools.

Güntaş Pansiyon, 3/5 Halk Cad. Topraklık Mah. (tel. 263 3579), located on the street parallel to Izmir Yolu, 200m behind the *otogar*. Entrance is through the basement into a large eating room/TV salon with marble floors. Rooms have phone, bathroom/shower, balcony, and tiny closet space. Singles $5; doubles $10. Breakfast 70¢; dinner $1.

Ayyıldız Hotel-Pension, Doğan Cad. 615 Sok. No. 13 (tel. 261 8114), behind Halk Cad. near Izmir Blvd. Greets you with the feels and smells of home. Rooms are clean, and some have private bathrooms and showers. Singles $4.70; doubles $7.40; add $2 for private bathroom and shower.

Yıldız Pension, Halk Cad. 452 Sok. No 13 (tel 265 1266, 241 6013). Clean and close to the bus station. TV, bathroom, shower. 4 floors, with some balcony rooms. Singles $10; doubles $16.70.

Altın Pension, Topraklık Mak. 633 Sok. No. 4, just 20m from the back of the bus station. Basic rooms with showers and A/C. Breakfast included. Some rooms have balconies. Singles $10; doubles $13.40; triples $18; quads $24. Shower-free student rooms $3.40.

FOOD AND ENTERTAINMENT

Kervan Kebap Salon, Belediye Sarayı Alt. No. 10 (tel. 242 1144), near the Belediye Building, facing the Atatürk statue. Enjoy the excellent grilled cuisine while sitting on the patio. Or, take in the caravanserai motif inside. Salads $1, *lahmancun* 66¢, and döner kebap $1.70. Closes at 10:30pm.

Denizli Evi-Restaurant, İstiklal Cad. No 10 (tel. 263 1442), on the right hand side after passing the Yeni Ulu Çınar Camii from Atatürk Blvd. Excellent meals with superb service. Some balcony seating available. Cold dishes from $1.70, hot dishes from $1, lamb shish *kebups* $3.40. Closes at 11:30pm.

Istanbul Fast Foods, Çınar Mah. Atatürk Blvd. No. 106 (tel. 265 7446), near the police station. Name says it all. Inexpensive hot dogs and cheeseburgers are their specialties. Also consider pizza, spaghetti, and the mixed grill.

Madlen Pastanesi, D. Çınar Meydanı, İstiklal Cad. No 6/1 (tel. 264 3933), just a few doors down from the Denizli Evi. A large variety of sweets and pastries to satisfy your after-dinner sweet tooth. Baklava, *dondurma,* and other popular Turkish delights. Open 7am-1am.

SIGHTS

Denizli is not exactly brimming with touristic or historic sights, but the city is speckled with colorful mosques and lively markets. The **Atatürk Ethnographic Museum** (tel. 261 4029), located in the main city center *(merkez)* across from the Ulu Mosque on İstasyon Cad., has a small but impressive collection of folkloric clothing and traditional tools and *kilims* (open in summer Tues.-Sun. 9am-5pm, in winter Tues.-Fri. 9am-5pm; admission 35¢, students 15¢). Located 7km from Denizli is the **Akhan-Kervansaray,** the historic stopover site used by Seljuks and Ottomans on trade routes. The caravanserai gets its name (*Akhan,* meaning "white inn") from the white marble used in its outer walls. The 1100-square-meter complex was finished in 1252. You can get there by *dolmuş* or via the public buses that depart from the *otogar* (every 1-2hr., 25¢). Nearby is the **Myriokephalon,** a Roman settlement which is still under excavation. Located 8km from Denizli is **Laodicea,** one of the seven churches of St. Jean, mentioned in the Book of Revelations. To see Laodicea, ask the Pamukkale-bound *dolmuş* driver to drop you off. Bring plenty of water.

■ Pamukkale (Hierapolis)

Whether as Pamukkale (Cotton Castle) or ancient Hierapolis (Holy City), this village has been drawing the weary and the curious to its thermal springs for more than 23 centuries. The Turkish name refers to the extraordinary surface of the snow-white cliffs, shaped over millennia by the accumulation of calcium deposited by mineral springs. Legend has it that the formations are actually solidified cotton (the area's principal crop) that was left out to dry by giants. Dripping slowly down a vast mountainside, mineral-rich water foams and collects in bowls that terrace the decline, spilling over petrified cascades of stalactites into milky pools below. The museums accompanying the site are also impressive. Unfortunately the calcium terraces are now closed, having suffered for years at the feet of countless tourists' wading.

ORIENTATION AND PRACTICAL INFORMATION

As you stand in the central square with your back to the tourist map, the road to the tourist complex starts off straight ahead, then curves around to the left, past bus company offices and up the hill. The PTT is also up this hill. Technically, you've entered the site once you climb the hill, and you might be asked to pay the site fee just to get to the PTT. If you argue loudly in English, and ask to see an official sign stating the entrance fees, they'll probably let you in free.

The bus stops in Pamukkales Kölü, where hustlers working on commission will approach you to stay at "their" accommodations. To head to the Pamukkale site, walk toward the main road where you'll find a **tourist office** and the **police station** across the street from each other. Most direct **buses** that run to Pamukkale leave from Selçuk or Kuşadası (5-6 per day, 4½hr., $4.50). *Dolmuş* and minibuses to Pamukkale leave from the Denizli bus station, roughly 100m south of the train station. **Buses** run twice hourly between Izmir and Denizli via Selçuk. From Pamukkale, there are buses to: Bodrum (3 per day, 5hr., $6.25); Izmir (every hr., 4hr., $6.25); Selçuk and Kuşadası (2 per day, 4½hr., $7.50); Marmaris (5 per day, 4½hr., $7.50); Fethiye (6 per day, 5hr., $6.25); and Cappadocia (6hr.,$7.50). There are **pharmacies** in the village, across from the Mustafa Motel. **Net Bookstore** (tel. 272 2266), next to the Mustafa Motel, carries travel guides and pop novels (open in summer 8am-midnight). **Postal Code:** 20100. **Telephone Code:** 258.

ACCOMMODATIONS

Logistically, Pamukkale presents travelers with a dilemma. If it were closer to the coast, it would make a great daytrip from Kuşadası or Marmaris. Unfortunately, it takes a good four hours to get there by bus, so most daytrippers end up spending almost twice as long in transit as they do at the site. The best solution is to spend the night and see the few sights thoroughly, rather than rush the trip and return to the coast exhausted. If you stay, beware of bus station hustlers who have all kinds of stories to lure you to another joint. Ignore them and pick your own hotel.

Koray Hotel, (tel. 272 2300; fax 272 2095) in the middle of Pamukkale Village, toward the right of the bus stop. Rooms face inward to a beautiful garden area and a pool with thermal water from Pamukkale. TV salon, bar, and restaurant, as well as nightly belly dancing. All rooms with bathroom and shower. Single $7 in summer, $5.50 in winter. Breakfast $2.

Kervansaray Pension (tel. 272 2209; fax 272 2143) has clean rooms with excellent views. Showers and a small swimming pool. International phone. Breakfast included. Does *not* have hustlers at bus stations. Singles $10; doubles $13.40. 10% discount for *Let's Go* readers.

Öztürk Pension (tel. 272 2116, -2627) is a family-run pension with swimming pool and fish tank holding the evening's dinner special. Rooms with toilets, some with showers. Singles $6.70; doubles with showers $13.40; triples $16.70; quads $20. Dinners $2.70 (usually fish).

Coşkun Pension-Camping (tel. 272 2554), on the main road leading to Pamukkale, near the police and tourist offices. An ideal camping spot close to the site entrance. Evening meals served at restaurant. Communal showers for campers. Singles $2; caravan with electricity $6.70; breakfast $2.70. Staff speaks English.

FOOD AND ENTERTAINMENT

Most of the pensions in town serve lunch and dinner. Nonetheless, Pamukkale Village has a couple of restaurants to get you out of your room.

Han Restaurant (tel. 272 2792), in the town center. Specializes in *kebap* dishes. Try their house special *saç kebap* ($3.40), pitas ($2), or appetizers ($1.70).

Gürsoy Aile Restaurant (tel. 272 2267), close to the Han. Their house special is *Görsoy Börek* ($2.40). Also has a beautiful tea garden. Open 8:30am-1am.

Pamukkale Pizzeria and Restaurant (tel 268 8095), also in the town center. Relaxing restaurant offering a large variety of pizzas, desserts, cold dishes, and traditional Turkish plates. Terrace level has nice view. Pizza is $2-3, beer $1.

You won't mistake Pamukkale's nightlife for Times Square, but you can still get a quiet drink and listen to live music. Try the **Paşa Bar,** down the street from the Pamukkale Pizzeria, for traditional Turkish music. **Tiffany's,** next door to the Pizzeria, is a popular disco that spins American and Turkish tunes. **Eros,** next to Tiffany's, and the **Sevgi Bar** are also open late during the high season.

SIGHTS

The warm **baths** at Pamukkale bubble with oxygen. There are two series of terraces situated on either side of the main road down into the village. Elegant, shallow pools located in front of the Tusan Motel (near the highway) gradually become deeper as you go farther down the slope. The deepest, most intricately shaped, and most popular terraces are directly behind the nameless restaurant facing the main parking lot. The terraces are now closed to public bathing due to over use. There is an area near the Palmiye Hotel where small walkways still allow visitors to touch the top of the thermal waters. Unfortunately, bathing is forbidden here as well.

Between the motels soar the colossal vaulted archways of the **Hierapolis City Baths.** The visible portions of this first-century structure are all that remain of one of Asia Minor's greatest ancient tourist industries: hygiena. The springs of Hierapolis were particularly popular among vacationing Romans. After an earthquake leveled the spa in 17 AD, Hierapolis was promptly rebuilt, and it reached its heyday during the 2nd and 3rd centuries AD. The city bath's glossy marble interior has now been converted into a mediocre **Archaeological Museum** (tel. 272 2034; open Tues.-Sun. 9am-5pm; admission $1, students 35¢). Carved into the side of the mountain, the monstrous **Grand Theater** dominates the vista of Hierapolis. Almost all of the seating area for 25,000 is intact, and the various ornately sculpted decorative elements adorning the facade and stage area are well-preserved. In front of the theater are the remains of the 3rd-century **Temple of Apollo.** Behind the temple stands the **nymphaeum.** Nearby is the famous **Plutonium,** a pit that emits poisonous carbonic acid gas, a substance ancients believed could kill all living creatures except priests. The Turks call it Devil's Hole *(Cin Deliği).* Farther to the right lies a hot-water spring.

Down the road to Karahayıt are the north **city gate,** and the ruins of a 5th-century Christian basilica dedicated to St. Philip, martyred here in 80 AD. Outside the gate is the **necropolis,** holding some 1200 tombs and sarcophagi. People buried here believed that proximity to the hot springs and vapor-emitting cracks would ease their trip to the underworld.

You shouldn't leave Pamukkale without a savory dip in the **sacred fountain** at the Pamukkale Motel (75m past the archaeological museum). Warm, fizzy waters bubble at the spring's source, now blocked off to prevent divers from disappearing into its depths. On the pool's floor rest remains of Roman columns, toppled by the earthquake that opened the spring (open daily for pool use 8am-8pm; $3 per hour).

Admission to the Pamukkale site from either gate is $2.70, $1.40 for students (open daily 9am-5pm).

▒ Aphrodisias

In antiquity, Greeks made pilgrimages here to pay respects to the goddess of love, Aphrodite, and ask for her blessing. The village evolved into a metropolis, but only after King Attalos III bequeathed Pergamon to the Romans, spurring a massive exodus to this land of divine beauty and love. Aphrodisias was famed for its sculpture. Crafted from the white and bluish-gray marble of nearby quarries, the finer statues in the Roman Empire were often marked with an imprint from the Aphrodisian sculpting school. With the ascendancy of Christianity, temples were converted to churches, and the city's name became Stavropolis (City of the Cross).

ORIENTATION AND PRACTICAL INFORMATION

Getting to Aphrodisias is hard. The best way to see the ruins is to take a daytrip from Pamukkale. **Buses** leave daily at 10am and return at 5pm (2hr., round-trip $6.70). Some travelers take a bus or *dolmuş* from Denizli, Nazilli, or Kuşadası/Selçuk to the small town of Karacasu, and then hitch from there. Another option is to go to Aydın, accessible from Denizli, Selçuk, or Izmir by *dolmuş* or buses running at regular intervals. **Telephone Code:** 256. **Postal Code:** 09374 (Geyrr).

ACCOMMODATIONS AND FOOD

There are just two places to stay in Aphrodisias, both operated by the same guy (who speaks Turkish, French, and English). **Chez Mestan** is 400m down from the entrance to the site across from the stadium (tel. 448 8046, fax 448 8422). The pension, restaurant, and camping site offers elegant rooms, communal toilets, and 24-hour hot water. Doubles are $10, breakfast included. 20% discount for students. In the **restaurant,** choose from the pizza ($1.35), salads ($1), and fresh fish ($2.70). The **Aphrodisias Hotel-Restaurant** is 2km from the museum and 500m from the stadium (tel. 448 8132; fax 448 8422). This no-frills hotel offers clean rooms, central heating in the winter, rugs on the marble floors, toilets, and showers. Singles $13; doubles $20; triples $26. Ask for the 20% student discount. The rooftop **restaurant** has a traditional Turkish plate with salad, *meze,* grilled meats or fish, vegetables, and cheese ($5.40).

SIGHTS

While the stunning remnants of Aphrodisias have been scrutinized for decades, archaeologists believe that a great deal remains to be discovered. The ruins unearthed to date include a well-preserved Roman stadium and *odeon,* as well as a temple, an *agora,* a palace, and some thermal baths. Although getting to Aphrodisias is a hassle, the carefully preserved ruins make it worthwhile. Optimistic archaeologists believe Aphrodisias will outshine Ephesus in 50 years.

The highlight of a visit to Aphrodisias is the most well-preserved ancient **stadium** ever excavated. Even the marble blocks that once marked the starting line for foot races are still in the central arena, whose seating capacity was 30,000. Roman gladiators shed blood here in search of glory and prestige. The looming structure at the bottom of the hill is **Hadrian's Bath,** equipped with a sauna, frigidarium, and changing rooms. To the right is the **Temple of Aphrodite.** Although only a portion of its 40-column spiral-fluted Corinthian colonnade remains, the temple retains much of its former elegance. Dating from the first century AD, the shrine originally housed a famous statue of Aphrodite, similar in appearance to the many-breasted Artemis of Ephesus. So far, only copies of the original have been unearthed. Just to the south lies the **odeon,** or city council chamber, with its extraordinary blue marble stage. The nine columns nearby were resurrected as part of a building christened the **Bishop's Palace** by archaeologists, owing to the number of religious artifacts and statues unearthed on its premises. Some of the marble floors remain intact. Among the highlights of the site's must-see **museum** are megastatues of Aphrodite and a satyr carrying the child Dionysus. The site and museum are open daily in the summer from 8:30am-7pm, in winter 8:30am-5pm. Admission is $2 per site, students $1.

BODRUM PENINSULA

▓ Bodrum

Bodrum seems to be in a world of its own. Here travelers come to a focal point of divine beaches, forests, and quaint little islands known for their exquisite swimming coves. Then by night, the scenery shifts gears to the high-volume harborside of Bodrum where cafes, bars, and discos compete for the crowds. It is no surprise that Bodrum was a magnet for writers and intellectuals in the era before package-deal tourism. Bodrum was the site of the fabled remains of the **Mausoleum of Halicarnassus,** one of the **seven wonders of the ancient world.** Although the site no longer enjoys its former glory, some observers have thought that the nightclub Halikarnas is a wonder in its own right and among Europe's best open-air discos. No matter where you stay on the Bodrum peninsula, frequent *dolmuş* service (7am-midnight) connects to Bodrum for the best nightlife in Turkey.

HISTORY

Bodrum was built on the ancient city of Halicarnassus, a powerful port town and capital of ancient Caria (an Anatolian people who lived in the area around 1200 BC). Halicarnassus was known for its succession of **female rulers.** One ruler, Artemesia I, led a fleet against the Athenians in their war with Persia in 480 BC. Her story is related in the *Persian Wars* by Herodotus, another native of Halicarnassus. In 377 BC, Mausolus of Cairo came to power and made Halicarnassus his capital. Work on his tomb began during his reign and was completed under his wife's direction following his death in 353 BC. The tomb is the inspiration for the word "mausoleum." Roughly 25 years later, Alexander the Great razed the city.

Until 1925, Bodrum was a small fishing village of less than 2000 people. Then, the British-educated **Cevat Şakir Kabaağaç** settled here in political exile and began to write short stories about Bodrum and the surrounding area. A community of intellectuals flourished until tourists began to frequent Bodrum in the 1970s. A decade later, the town became one of the premier destinations for British and German package tours. Pensions and motels now cover the hillsides around the town. The Turkish intellectual and European package-tour communities lead separate lives in Bodrum, but the city has an atmosphere rare among resort towns, combining sophistication and a thrilling nightlife.

ORIENTATION AND PRACTICAL INFORMATION

Streets in Bodrum are poorly marked. The city's most prominent and easily recognizable landmark is the centrally located fortress *(kale),* from which several streets emanate. Cheap pensions lie along the bank to the right of the fort as you face inland. Breakwaters almost completely enclose the other port, which forms the more picturesque half of town. Ferries and yacht cruises depart from this harbor.

The main thoroughfare along the waterfront starts at the castle and runs along the enclosed left harbor—it begins as **Neyzen Tevfik Caddesi** along most of the harbor, and ends at the yacht harbor. Going right from the castle, the main commercial drag of **Cumhuriyet Caddesi** ends by the Halikarnas nightclub. Extending inland from the castle towards the bus station, **Kale Caddesi** is Bodrum's main shopping strip, lined with boat tour booths and sponge divers selling their precious finds. It eventually becomes **Cevat Şâkir Caddesi,** which runs past the PTT and the bus station, from which all inter-city buses, taxis, and *dolmuş* depart.

Tourist Office: 12 Eylül Meydanı (tel. 316 1091; fax 316 7694), at the foot of the castle. Room listings, bus info, and free brochures with maps. Helpful staff. Open April-Oct. daily 8:30am-7:30pm, Nov.-March Mon.-Fri. 8am-noon and 1-5pm.

Tourist Agencies: There are no shortages of agencies in Bodrum. **Karya Tours** (tel. 316 1914), at the ferryboat landing, organizes excursions all over Turkey. Ferry tickets to Kos and Datça, and daily excursion to Pirene, Miletus, and Didyma ($25; open 8am-9:30pm). **Apak Tours** (tel. 316 5244; fax 316 3998), on Cevat Şâkir Cad., down the road from the bus station, also offers boat excursions and daytrips. **Botour** (tel 316 8815; fax 316 8208), 24/A Cevat Şâkir Cad., on the right-hand side before arriving at the bus station. Similar services as the others plus **scooter rentals** ($20 per day; open 9am-10:30pm).

Currency Exchange: Available at the PTT 8am-midnight. There are also many exchange booths by the harbor on Kale Cad.; most do not charge commission.

Buses: Cevat Şâkir Cad. Popular destinations handled by **Pamukkale Coach Lines** (tel. 316 1369, -0650). To: Marmaris (8 per day, 3½hr., $4); Antalya (2 per day, 8½hr., $10); Izmir (every hour, 4hr., $6); Selçuk ($5); Fethiye (7 per day, 5hr., $6.70); Pamukkale (4 per day, 5hr., $6); Istanbul (4 per day, 14hr., $18.70); Kuşadası (3 per day, 2½hr., $5); Aydın (9:30am, 3½hr., $4). **Nevtur** has connections to Necşehir (Cappadocia) every day at 3pm ($16.70).

Ferries: Tickets sold through any travel agent. **Bodrum Ferryboat Association** (tel. 316 0882; fax 313 0205) has offices in the bus station and near the castle. Boats to Kos leave at 9am and return at 4:30pm (3-7 per week, 1hr., $13). Also a ferry to Datça Peninsula, 8km from Datça and 80km from Marmaris (9am and 5pm, 2hr., $6). Call in the off season.

Hydrofoils: Bodrum Express Lines, right after the Bodrum Ferryboat Assoc. (tel. 316 1087, -4067; fax 313 0077). Daily service to Kos (leaves Bodrum at 9am, returns at 4:30pm, 15min., $20 round-trip). Also "Kos-by-night" service available, as well as service to Rhodes, Marmaris, and Gallipoli.

International Bookstores: A 24hr. book fair with some English language books is located across from 06 Lokanta on Cumhuriyet Cad. Also, **Bodrum Kitabevi** (tel. 316 5948), off of Cumhuriyet Cad. after the Boschi appliance store. Offers English-language guide books, novels, and second-hand novels. Open 10am-1am.

Hospital: Bodrum Devlet Hastanesi (tel. 316 0880, -1, -2), Kıbrıs Şehitler Cad., uphill from the amphitheater. Public.

Police: 12 Eylül Meydanı (tel. 316 1218), next to tourist office at the foot of the castle. **Main branch** (tel. 316 1004), left on the main highway up Cevat Şâkir Cad.

PTT: (tel. 316 1212, -1560) On Cevat Şâkir Cad., 4 blocks from the bus station along the road to the harbor. Open in summer daily 8:30am-5:30pm, in winter Mon.-Fri. 8am-noon and 1-5pm. **Postal Code:** 48400.

Telephone Code: 252.

ACCOMMODATIONS

Pensions are plentiful in Bodrum, but require some advance planning and possibly sharing a room. When pension owners hear that you are a single person *(tek kişi)*, you will rarely have any luck in the high season. Calling ahead is a must in the summer, and be warned that you may end up near a bar blasting music until 4am.

Yenilmez Pansiyon (tel. 316 2520), along Neyzen Tevfik Cad., the road along the water to the right as you face the harbor. Turn right at the alley after Lowry's Irish Pub (but before Sini Restaurant), and walk 1min. up the winding path. Spotless rooms, bathrooms, and showers, 24hr. hot water, and great tea garden. Only a 10min. walk to the discos, but you're spared the noise. Doubles $20.

Polyanna Pension, No. 5 Ortanca Sok. (tel. 316 1528), a side street just before the Halicarnassis Disco end of Cumhuriyet Cad. If coming from the tourist office, turn left off Cumhuriyet Cad. at the White House Bar. Clean rooms with toilets and showers arrayed around a soaring atrium. Tables at ground level for backgammon. Terrace with view of the castle. Doubles with breakfast $16.70.

Uslu Pension, No. 35 Cumhuriyet Cad. (tel. 313 0665), across from the Korean restaurant. Communal bathrooms and clean rooms. Ask for a room in the back to minimize the noise from the main street. Doubles $13.40; triples $20.

Kocair Pension (tel. 316 8570), off Atatürk Cad. on 2426 Sok. No. 1 (leading to the 24hr. book fair). Simple furnishings with a garden area for reading. A 2min. walk to Cumhuriyet Cad. without all the noise. Doubles $24; triples $30.

Camping sites: Take a *dolmuş* to Gümbet.

FOOD

Bodrum is not a budget traveler's ideal destination for cheap eats. But the quality of octopus (mmmmmm, octopus) and squid is well-known in Turkey; it comes to the restaurants fresh every day. Nevertheless, there are a variety of restaurants, cafes, and bars which provide a decent meal without draining your wallet.

06 Lokanta, 156 Cumhuriyet Cad (tel. 316 8383), near the 24hr. book fair. A popular meeting spot located in the hub of the action on Cumhuriyet Cad. It has two levels with outdoor seating. A variety of hot dishes for $4-5. Open 24hr.

Cafe Mavsoleion, on the harborfront on Neyzen Tevfik Cad. Tepecik Camii Karşısı No. 120 (tel. 313 4555, -4636). Trendy restaurant offering a reasonable variety of dishes at reasonable prices. All grills come with chips and salad ($2.70-5.70).

Sultan's Beach House, Cumhuriyet Cad. No. 151 (tel. 316 0312, 313 3651), across from the public beach area. Comfortable indoor and outdoor seating with an animated staff. Pizzas from $3.40, spaghetti $4, beers $1. V/MC/AmEx accepted.

Sini Restaurant, Neyzen Tevfik Cad. No 90/A (tel. 316 3310), around the corner from the Yenilmez Pension. Seating under a vined-roof terrace with harbor views. Cold dishes are $1.40, main course grills $5.40-8.40. Closes at midnight.

ENTERTAINMENT

Nightlife rages all week long; just step out onto Cumhuriyet Cad. to see. Don't be fooled by the similarity between each club's bass woofer—each has its own unique feel. The following are just suggestions among many fun spots.

Halicarnassus Disco, Z. Müren Cad. at the end of Cumhuriyet Cad., 1500m from the center of town. There is no place in the world like this disco, but it has a hefty $14 cover. Different shows every night including live music and the obligatory laser show. Open until the early morning.

M&M Dancing, on Dr. Alim Bey Cad. 1025 Sok. No. 44 (tel 316 2725). This and Halicarnassus are the major open-air discos. No cover before 10pm, open at 6pm.

The Red Lion, on Cumhuriyet Cad., across from the public beach. One of the most popular tourist bars. Sports bar feel, with a small dance floor.

Mavi Bar, after the Red Lion and just before the ominous Halikarnas, this place is less noisy than others and has a top terrace with excellent views of the madness below. More of a Turkish hangout, but welcomes foreigners. Live music, comfortable couches. Not for intense dancing.

Melton Bar, back toward the Red Lion on Cumhuriyet Cad. A quaint bar with high stools and large open windows. Outdoor seating with English pop tunes.

Fora Disco and Bar, located farther back on Cumhuriyet Cad away from the Red Lion. A crowded place with a large dance floor. Make your way to the back of the bar where you'll find a deck on the harborside with a big screen TV.

SIGHTS

Greeting all visitors to Bodrum is the **fortress,** built by the knights of St. John during the 15th and 16th centuries. The castle was constructed over the ruins of an ancient acropolis and eventually used material from the nearby Mausoleum of Halicarnassus to reinforce the fortress in the years preceding the Turkish conquest of Bodrum in 1523. Over 249 coats-of-arms are found on the fortress's walls, belonging to former commanders. Despite its great size and durability, it surrendered to Süleyman's forces in 1523, not long after it was completed. The fortress's importance fell during Ottoman times and became a prison in 1895.

You'll be taken back to the Middle Ages in the **English Tower.** Hear violin music from the time and sample a glass of red or white wine (50¢ per glass). The English Tower is decorated with Turkish banners from through the ages as well as with English armor, weapons, swords, and decorative materials.

The **Gatineau Tower,** named after the 16th-century commander of the castle, houses a torture chamber. Twenty-three lonely stairs lead to a lower inner chamber, which bears the inscription *Inde Deus Abest* ("Where God Does Not Exist"). The **Snake Tower** hosts frequent art exhibitions. Also visit the **Glass Hall,** with the world's largest Islamic glass collection.

The castle also houses Bodrum's **Museum of Underwater Archaeology,** a bizarre assortment of shipwreck flotsam from sites along the surrounding Turkish coastline. A Byzantine courtyard in the central part of the castle houses the **Bronze Age Hall,** containing finds from a 1200 BC shipwreck. Huge jars found on board date from 1600 BC, and their artwork strongly suggests the existence of an ancient trade route between Crete and the Asia Minor coast. The museum also exhibits glassware *(cam)* recovered from a variety of ancient and medieval wrecks (castle open Tues.-Sun. 8:30am-5pm, museum open Tues.-Fri. 8:30am-5pm; admission to each $1.40, students 70¢).

The ruins of ancient **Halicarnassus** are Bodrum's better known, if less picturesque, attraction. Most of the remains were either destroyed or buried underneath the modern town of Bodrum. The city walls are visible at points, as are the meager remains of the **theater** on Kıbrıs Schitler Cad. The most famous of the ruins, the once wondrous **mausoleum,** consisted of a rectangular foundation and stone pedestal upon which the sepulchral chamber rested, supported by 36 Ionic columns. The 50m-high mausoleum, covered with a pyramidal roof, was crowned by a statue of Mausolus driving a chariot drawn by four horses and was one of the seven wonders of the ancient world. To get to the mausoleum's remains, turn onto Saray Sok. from Neyzen Tevfik Cad. It will be on your right at the end of the street (open Tues.-Sun. 8:30am–5:30pm; admission $1.40, students 70¢).

■ Near Bodrum

Bodrum's popularity among Turks stems largely from its location at the head of the enchanting **Bodrum Peninsula.** After a day of swimming and sunning, you can linger over dinner or partake in Bodrum's rousing nightlife. A few of the beaches on the south coast of the peninsula are accessible only by tour boats, which leave from the front of the castle (daily 9-11am, return 5-6pm). Known as *mavi yolculuk* (blue journeys), these tours are fine alternatives to all the archaic splendor of the ruins and the Teutonic masses plaguing the beaches around the city. Itineraries for the tours vary widely; check the tour schedule at the dock. Some popular destinations are **Kara Island,** the village of **Akyarlar,** and the beaches at **Baradakçı, Çapa Tatil, Yahşi, Kargı Bay, Bağla,** and **Karaincir.** Boat tours cost $12 per person for the day, $18 with lunch. In summer, boats leave daily from the castle and head to tranquil **Orak Island** (same prices), offering some of the better swimming spots on the peninsula—pristine and uncrowded. There are no cheap accommodations at any of these places, so daytrips are your best bet. Locals strongly advise against drinking the tap water, so stock up on Hayat, Pınar, and SultanSu.

WESTERN TURKEY

Less spoiled than the overpopulated south coast, the north end of the peninsula has rocky beaches and deep water. **Gölköy** and **Türkbükü,** once peaceful fishing villages, now host a large number of Turkish tourists and their yachts.

A 30-minute *dolmuş* ride from the *otogar* is the gorgeous sand paradise of **Yahşi,** the longest beach in Bodrum. Flanked by surfers, sunbathers, and pensions, the turquoise waters gleam, offering a more serene (if not less crowded) warmth than other beaches in the area. Yahşi is a popular refuge for Turkish families and tourists, so call in advance to ensure your spot under a striped umbrella.

Because the beach at **Bitez** is narrow, seaside bars have built pontooned docks over the water where you can order drinks while you sunbathe. The beach around the next large cove from Gümbet is peaceful but has no cheap accommodations. *Dolmuş* from the Bodrum bus station travel to both beaches. The most accessible point on the west coast of the peninsula, **Turgut Reis** is 18km from Bodrum. We've given you the scoop on the longest beach—here's the widest. It's a one-dimensional beach-eat-sleep tourist town, and the stretch of coast is usually crowded. There are a number of pensions in town, but they tend to fill up quickly in July and August. They line the street next to the beach to the right of the bus stop as you face the sea.

Words cannot do justice to the inspiring beauty of **Gümüşlük,** a tiny seaside paradise at the west tip of the Bodrum Peninsula. The Turkish name means "silvery," referring to ancient silver mines that were discovered in the area. Near the beach lie the ruins of ancient Mindos, a 4th-century BC port impregnable even to Alexander the Great. The site consists of the impressive city wall, 3m thick, and a Roman basilica. Gümüşlük's sparkling vistas, cool sea breezes, and relaxed atmosphere make it a great place to escape the frenetic hedonism of Bodrum.

■ Akyaka (Gökova)

Akyaka is a jewel of nature situated in the province of Muğla, at the head of the Gulf of Gökova. Fresh water from the mountains above continually cleanse its stunning beaches. Near the shore is a national park with camping. Special conservation land at the delta of the river teems with aquatic life, including fish, turtles, and ducks. Lovely riverside restaurants await farther up into the conservation area, where fish are caught only inches away from restaurant tables. On the other side of Gökova Bay, visitors can take a sail boat tour to the island of Cedia, whose unusually white sand is said to have been shipped from Egypt 2000 years ago for Cleopatra and Mark Antony's honeymoon.

ORIENTATION AND PRACTICAL INFORMATION

If you're arriving by boat, you'll have no problem acquainting yourself with the small town. Restaurants are on both sides of the pier. Coming by bus will leave you with two options. You can either take a direct minibus from Muğla (some 25min. away), or take any bus heading down to Marmaris and ask to be let off at Gökova. The 20-minute walk into town from here is pleasant and refreshing as the scent of pine trees surrounds you.

Travel Agency: To get to **Sunflowers Travel Agency** (tel./fax 243 5658), walk past the Belediye building almost to the sea, where you'll come to a square. Take a left where the "Why Not" bar is on Karanfıl Sok. Plans walking tours of the area and organizes tours of Dalyan. Open in summer 9am-11pm.

Jandarma: There are no police in this town as of yet, so contact the *jandarma* if you need help (tel. 243 5504 or dial 156).

Health Clinic: A small medical facility, **Saglik Ocagi,** is inside the Belediye building (tel. 243 5111).

Taxi: Akyaka Taxi (tel. 243 5194). 24hr. service.

Buses: There's 1 direct bus to Marmaris leaving at 10am and returning at 4pm (30min., $2.50). If you miss it, take a *dolmuş* heading toward Muğla and ask to be let off at the fork in the road (high above town). From here, flag down a bus heading to Marmaris. There is also a 6pm bus to Marmaris from Gökoava, but it needs at least 10 people to depart.

PTT: (tel. 243 5142) On the main road to Muğla, going toward Çinar Beach. Open daily 8am-5pm. **Postal Code:** 486050.

Telephone Code: 252.

ACCOMMODATIONS

There are several pensions in Akyaka, but call to be sure of getting a spot. Rooms are scarce in summer and singles are almost impossible to come by. Also, there is a designated camping site at the nearby national park with toilets, showers, small restaurants and public phones.

Murat Pension (tel. 243 5279), past Sunflowers Travel Agency on the end of Karanfil Sok. Clean rooms with wooden floors, communal toilets, showers, and 24hr. hot water. All rooms have mosquito-net windows, couches, and rugs. A 5min. walk to the beach. Only one single $10; doubles $14; triples $21.

Huzur Pension (tel. 243 5139, -5646), up the road to Muğla, across from the Belediye building. Showers, toilets, and 24hr. hot water. Kitchen in each facility. Quiet, shady tea garden extending into an olive grove. Doubles $14; triples $21.

Faith Apartments and Pension (tel. 243 5786), toward the Yücelan Hotel. Clean rooms with balcony, couch, kitchen, toilet, shower, and 24hr. hot water. View of the Gökova Gulf and pleasant night breeze. Doubles $14.

Camping: (tel. 243 5035) Available at the national park at the end of the beach. 50¢ entry to the park with free daytime use of the bungalows. Overnight camping farther up in the forest. Showers, toilets, and restaurants near site. $3.50 per person.

FOOD AND ENTERTAINMENT

Akyaka has a decent selection of restaurants in the village center and seaside. If you walk toward the Belediye and take a right before passing it, you'll see a road leading to a series of restaurants near a river. Prices are generally cheaper than in town.

Hali'nin Yeri (tel. 243 5173; fax 243 5373), the first restaurant you'll encounter by the river and conservation land. Selection of cold dishes, grilled meats, and fresh fish. Spectacular scenery. Access to harbor from their docks. Open until midnight.

Yosun Restaurant (243 5629), just past Hali'nin Yeri. Similar dishes. Has a small bridge leading to a terrace with seating on the river. Peaceful. Open until midnight.

Elalem Amca, on the same street as the Murat Pension. A bit pricier than the river restaurants, but the service and food are excellent. English-speaking staff. *Şiş kebap* $3, cold appetizers $1.50, ice-cream desserts $2. Open 10am-midnight.

"Why Not" Bar-Cafe, on the corner of Karanfil Sok. just past Elalem. Comfortable bamboo chairs and outdoor seating. A variety of brews. Large beer 80¢.

SIGHTS

The most obvious and delightful sight in Akyala is its **public beach.** The beach extends from the right of the pier to the entrance of the National Park. Palm trees on the beach combine with bamboo umbrellas to create a pleasant tropical feel. The beach has a sandbar extending nearly 100m into the gulf. Quaint, secluded swimming coves speckle the national park (admission 50¢).

Besides the fun of camping and walking in the park, there are also daily **boat trips** to the area's nearby islands, including **Cleopatra's Island.** Daily tours depart from the pier area (all include a lunch of fish, salad, fruit, and drink). On Monday, Wednesday, Friday, and Sunday, daily tours sail to Okluk Bay, Kargılı Bay, Karacaöğüt and İncekum beaches, Cleopatra's Island, and Dark Bay. Boats leave at 10am and return at 6pm. Inquire at the docks for more information ($6.75 per person).

■ Milas

Milas is a sleepy town about 30 minutes from the action in Bodrum. Come to Milas for a more traditional village atmosphere. There are no loud nightclubs here, just wonderful late 19th and 20th-century houses on cobblestone roads.

Milas is most renowned for its huge Tuesday **market,** where unbelievable deals can be found on almost anything. Look out for leather goods, carpets, crafts, and fine lacework. Just a bit outside the town center, on **Atatürk Boulevard** going toward the **Belediye** (city hall), is a small **archaeological museum** located next to a small park (tel. 512 3973; open daily 8:30am-5:30pm; admission 70¢, students 35¢).

Atatürk Blv. is especially beautiful at night when both of its ends are blocked off to allow for pedestrian traffic. Many cheap Turkish **restaurants** can be found here as well as beautiful **tea gardens** on your right side moving back to the museum. Strolling down the boulevard on the way to Bodrum you'll see a large statue of Atatürk on a horse with a modern amphitheater behind him.

If you must stay overnight in Milas, the **Park Hotel,** No. 51 Atatürk Blv. (tel. 512 8285) across from the large tea garden, provides small, viewless, adequate rooms. Communal toilets and showers (doubles $6.70).

Planes take off and land at the newly opened Milas Bodrum International Airport located on the outskirts of the town on the road to Bodrum (tel. 536 6569). Call **Turkish Airlines** for more info about flights, prices, and times (tel. 313 3172, 313 3173; fax 313 3174). To get to Milas from Bodrum, take a *dolmuş* marked "Milas" or with the company name "Milas Park." The last bus to Milas leaves at 7:30pm (30min., $1.35).

MARMARIS COAST

■ Marmaris

Marmaris is a major tourist center and a convenient base for travel to Rhodes via daily hydrofoil service in the summer. There's also lots of shopping in its labyrinth of shops or its covered bazaar. Although Marmaris has few sights (except a castle built by Süleyman the Magnificent in 1522 as a base against Crusaders), it is a refreshing break from the bustle of day-time Kuşadası or night-time Bodrum.

ORIENTATION AND PRACTICAL INFORMATION

You're never more than three blocks from the sea in Marmaris. **Kordon Caddesi,** which becomes **Atatürk Caddesi** at the statue, runs along the waterfront. The tourist office, castle, and marina are at the east end of the waterfront (to the left facing the water). From the bus station, cross the bridge over a channel of water and continue along the coast to reach the tourist office.

Tourist Office: 2 İskele Meydanı (tel. 412 1035), near the Roman statue on the harbor. Open in summer 8:30am-7:30pm; in winter Mon.-Fri. 8am-5pm.

Buses: To: Fethiye (every hr., 3hr., $5); Küyceğiz, Dalyan, Dalaman, and Gücek (every hr., $2.70); Muğla, Milas, and Bodrum (every 30min., 3hr., $5); Istanbul (7 per day, 13hr., $26); Ankara (3 per day, 10hr., $13.40); Izmir (every hr., 5hr., $8); Antalya (4 per day, 7hr., $10); and Datça (every hr., 1½hr., $3.40).

Hydrofoils: To Rhodes (9:30am and 4:30pm, 50min., $27.40 including $10 port tax). Give your passport to the travel agency the night before departure. There is no shortage of agencies that sell hydrofoil tickets on the harbor.

Ferries: To Rhodes (Fri. 9:15am, 1½hr., $14). Check in 45min. prior to departure. Call **Yeşil Marmaris** (tel. 412 1033, -2290; fax 412 0778) for more info. They are located around the corner from the tourist office going toward the new harbor. Small boats also travel to İçmeler (every 30min., 20min., $2.40).

Hospital: The public **Devlet Hastanesı,** Datça Yolu Üzeri (tel. 412 1029). From the tourist office, walk toward the Atatürk statue, then up toward the main road and take a right at the light. It's about 900m up the hill. Public.

Police: (tel. 412 1015) At the corner of Kordon and Fevzipaşa Cad., 3 blocks along the waterfront from the tourist office. Little English spoken. In **emergency,** call 155 or 156. The **passport police** (tel. 412 1696) are behind the new marina to the left of the tourist office as you face the water.

PTT: Fevzipaşa Cad. Three blocks along the waterfront toward the town center and 1 block inland from the tourist office. Open 8am-midnight. **Currency exchange** daily 8:30am-12:30pm and 1:30-4:30pm. **Postal Code:** 48700.

Telephone Code: 252.

ACCOMMODATIONS

Marmaris has quite a few reasonably priced pensions and hotels, most of which are booked in July and August. Arrive early in the day to secure a room.

Interyouth Hostel (HI), Tepe Mah. #45 42nd Sok. (tel. 412 3687; fax 412 7823), at the center of town. Watch out for the imposter Interyouth Hostel at Kemeraltı Mah. 14 İyilikataş Mevkii; it's actually the Aşem Motel. To get to the *real* hostel, go from the Atatürk statue and walk straight up Ulusal Egemenlik Blvd. MTV, book exchange, and boat excursions ($12 for hostel guests, $18 for others; lunch included). Breakfast in the terrace bar ($2.50), nightly spaghetti dinners (7:30pm, free for hostel guests). English spoken. Dorm beds $4.25; private rooms $6, 10% discount for ISIC, IYH, and GO25 holders. Laundry $5.

Maltepe Pansiyon (tel. 412 8456), facing the water. Walk away from the centrum to the right and turn right at the Disco and Cabaret. Follow this road and cross the footbridge. Clean, airy rooms, shady garden, friendly management, free laundry service (for small loads), and common kitchen. Singles $10; doubles $17; triples $23.50; quads $27; roof $5.

Hotel Lahti, Tepe Mah. 34 Sok. No. 11 (tel. 412 1958; fax 412 1804). Modern, clean, and cool. Singles $20; doubles $27; triples $33.

Bulut Apartments & Pension, PTT Çıkmazı Rıhtım Sok. No. 28 (tel. 412 5415), near Halil İbrahim Sofrası Restaurant. A clean and modern place with only double-bed rooms, all with toilet and shower. Some rooms have a refrigerator and small kitchen. No English spoken. Doubles $14.

FOOD AND ENTERTAINMENT

Marmaris has plenty of overcrowded, noisy, and expensive restaurants. For good, authentic, and cheap eats, look no farther than inside the bazaar where several restaurants are waiting to satisfy your appetite.

Özyiğut Restaurant, Tepe Mah. 53 Sok. Çarşı İçi No. 21 (tel. 412 3382), in the bazaar area. Come in, point to your food, and it's yours in seconds. Full meals $1-2. Don't be surprised if others sit next to you. Open 7:30am-midnight.

Halil İbrahim Sofrası, PTT Çıkmazı, No. 31. Cem Oteli Alti (tel. 413 1445). Located across from the PTT, near the Cem Hotel. This fast-paced Turkish restaurant serves great *döners* ($2.50). Open until midnight.

Grand Cafe Mozart, Org. Muğlalı Cad. No. 1-2-4 (tel. 413 8764), across from Tursem near the Maltepe Pension. A cafe, patisserie, and restaurant all in one. Authentic European meals (fish & chips wrapped in a newspaper, $5). Plays classical music hits and Viennese waltzes. Turkish breakfast $2.70; English breakfast $3; croissants $1. Open 7:30am-12:30am.

Greenhouse, Uzunyalı No. 80 (tel. 412 1861). One of several bars and cafes behind the tourist office on the street going toward the castle. The most popular bar in the area for locals and tourists alike.

SIGHTS

Marmaris itself has little to offer besides a large town beach and a **fortress,** built in 1522 by Süleyman as a military base for his successful campaign against the Crusaders (open Tues.-Sun. 8:30am-noon and 1-5:30pm; admission 70¢). Only 1500m away, **Günnücek National Park** features a small beach and picnic tables set against a forest fragrant with frankincense trees. To get there, follow the coastal road past the marina and across the wooden footbridge. Great views of the town and harbor.

While there is a **beach** in Marmaris proper, the better beaches and scenery in the area are accessible only by boat (an exception is the pretty **İçmeler beach,** reachable by *dolmuş*). Serving the bay, *dolmuş moto* (*dolmuş* boats) depart from the harbor along Kordon Cad. every morning for a variety of destinations. Full-day tours are $8.25 per person. Most boats make stops at **Paradise Island Beach** and then the **Akvaryum,** an aquarium. Tours also visit some phosphorous caves and the popular **Turunç Beach,** across the bay from Marmaris. Flanking Turunç to the north and south are the **Gölenye Springs,** whose waters reputedly cure intestinal ills, and the less crowded **Kumlu Buk Beach,** near the scanty remains of a fortress. Both are convenient by boat. Most of the mouth of the Bay of Marmaris is sealed off by the heavily wooded Nimara Peninsula. Along the far end of the peninsula are the fluorescent phosphorous caves near Alkoya Point, another stop for Marmaris's excursion boats.

Between the peninsula and the mainland is the tiny uninhabited village of **Keçi,** offering great views of the surrounding coastline. The fine sand beaches of **Kleopatra's Island** are a good daytrip. Also known as Sedir Adası, the island is laced with legend. Locals insist that Marc Antony imported the incredibly white sand from the Red Sea some 2100 years ago so his queen could enjoy afternoon rests. Others suspect that sand's purity is a function of its having mixed with fossilized plankton over the years. It is usually included in boat trips from Marmaris, but check at the dock.

■ Around the Coast: Datça Peninsula

The rugged, slim Datça Peninsula extends some 120km into the sea toward the Greek island of Symi. The ride to Datça may seem a bit terrifying at times, with sharp turns and sheer drops only inches away from the side of the road. Nonetheless, the bus ride will give you the opportunity to explore a less crowded and more beautiful seaside town. The harborside provides plenty of charter boats ready to take you to the ancient Dorian city of **Knidos.**

ORIENTATION AND PRACTICAL INFORMATION

The main road leading into Datça from Marmaris is known as **Atatürk Blv.** up until the Government Center *(Hükümet Konağı),* where it becomes **Yalı Cad.** The street then extends up toward the harborside and marina, where it is known as **Yat Limanı.** The Yat Limanı is closed to auto traffic from 6pm-8am in the summer to allow pedestrians to stroll.

The **tourist office, PTT,** and **police station** are all located within the same block at the Government Center near several **banks** that offer **currency exchange.** The **dolmuş** garage is directly across from the PTT. **Pir-Pak Laundry** (tel. (252) 712 2040) is at the end of Yalı Cad., past the taxi stand ($5 per load; open daily 8am-10pm). **Buses** travel to Marmaris every two hours or so (1½hr., $3.50). Call **Datça Koop** for reservations at 712 8292. The 6 and 8am buses go to Muğla as well. Visit **Pamukkale Turizm** (tel. 712 4149, -3101), near the Ziraat Bankası, for info on twice-daily service to Istanbul, Ankara, Antalya, and other cities. *Dolmuş* head to Mesudiye (swimming coves farther down the southern Datça coast) three times per day, and to Aktur every 30 minutes. In an **emergency** dial 156. The **telephone code** is 252 and the **postal code** is 48900.

ACCOMMODATIONS AND SIGHTS

There are mosquitoes aplenty in Datça, so stock up on repellent or tablets.

    Antalyalı Pension (tel. 712 3812) is centrally located and easy to find on Yalı Cad. From the bus station, pass the PTT and take the left fork; the pension is on the right. Rooms are large and guests have access to the kitchen on the terrace. Doubles $16.70; triples $20; quads $24.

Deniz Motel (tel. 712 3038) sits farther up the road. Take a left past the tourist office. All rooms have baths, balconies, and comfy beds. Breakfast included. Singles $10; doubles $18.40; triples $24.

Umut Pansiyon (tel. 712 3117), on the right side farther down the road. Great location, and 24hr. hot water. Singles $12; doubles $24; triples $36.

Huzur Pansiyon (tel. 712 3364; fax 712 3052), behind and above Umut. Balconies, sea views, and clean baths with toilet paper. Doubles $20; triples $30; quads $40.

Ilıca Camping (tel. 712 3400), on the beach beyond the harbor (turn right at the taxi station). A restaurant and two-person bungalows with private baths. Bungalows $6.70 per person; camping $3.40 per person; caravan with electricity $8.

People come to Datça for its two beaches. The beach across from the Government Center tends to be crowded, with tourists from all over staying at the vacation complexes nearby. The prettier and less frequented beach is to the right of Yalı Cad. and Yat Limanı. Check out the **fresh water spring** while you're there.

Datça's most significant historical site is the ancient city of **Knidos.** Built in honor of Apollo, Knidos was a wealthy port city and one of the original six cities of the Dorian League. A pair of **theaters** and **temples** dedicated to Dionysus and Demeter languish above the harbor. Outside this area are two medieval **fortresses** surrounded by an ancient necropolis. One of the artistic and intellectual centers of the ancient world, it was the home of Sostratos, designer of the Pharos lighthouse at Alexandria, and of the astronomer Eudoxos, who calculated the earth's circumference. The city was renowned in antiquity for its statue of Aphrodite.

Because Knidos is a government-regulated archaeological zone, pensions and restaurants are forbidden to operate. **Boat tours** leave for Knidos from Bodrum and Marmaris during the summer (ask at the tourist offices). From Datça, take one of the boat tours from the yacht harbor ($12.50 per person), or a taxi tour ($37.50-44 per car-load, negotiable).

▓ Dalyan and Caunos

The ancient city Caunos is on the river leading out of nearby Köycesiz. It was in this area that Caunos, son of Miletos, established a city dating from 3000 BC. Today the town of Dalyan is the starting point for tours of Caunos. From Dalyan, one can also see the rock tombs of the Lyceans, built into the faces of nearby cliffs. Dalyan's large number of pensions and cheap restaurants make it friendly to the wallet, but make sure your accommodations have mosquito-netted screens.

ORIENTATION AND PRACTICAL INFORMATION

Dalyan is a small town relatively new to the tourism. There are few street signs to help you find your way around except those of pensions seeking your business. The open area with a turtle statue, behind the PTT and mosque looking toward the river, is a good spot from which to get your bearings. Boats leaving for daily tours are on the river near this statue. Facing the river, go down the **Maraş Sokak** to your left, to find plenty of pensions, restaurants and a few bars.

For the **tourist office,** go to the open square with the turtle statue and enter the small passageway directly opposite the mosque (tel. 284 4235; open in summer 8:30am-noon and 1-6pm, in winter 8:30am-noon and 1-5:30pm). The **police** are near the tourist office (tel. 284 2031). A **health center** (*sağlık ocağı*) is on Maraş Sok. after the primary school (tel. 284 2033). Several pharmacies are also in the Maraş Sok. area. The **PTT** is in the square leading from the road to Ortaca and has **currency exchange** (open 8:30am-5:30pm). Several **banks** are on the road to Ortaca in the town center (open 8:30am-5:30pm). A **laundry** is on Maraş Sok. across from Dalyan Camping (tel. 284 4418; $4 per load; open 9am-midnight). **Buses** are available from Marmaris to Ortaca (every hr., 2hr., $2.70). There is no direct **dolmuş** service to Dalyan, so you must make a connection from Ortaca (every ½hr., 15min., 70¢); the station is behind the PTT. **Boat service** is available to many points in the vicinity, including tours to see the turtles and the hot springs. The **postal code** is 48840; **telephone code,** 252.

ACCOMMODATIONS

Pensions are abundant and inexpensive in Dalyan. Almost all pensions are relatively new and most have screened windows. Some have pools and views of the rock tombs. Try bargaining when possible.

Kristal Pension (tel. 284 2263, -3153), off Maraş Sok. A lovely pension with marble floors and tiles everywhere. Pool and a gorgeous terrace with a bar and ground level garden. Clean rooms with toilet, shower, and hot water. Screens. Breakfast included. Singles $10; doubles $17.

Albatross Pension (tel. 284 3287, -3288), on Maraş Sok. A lively place with a popular bar connected to the pension. Clean rooms with toilet, shower, and 24hr. hot water. Singles $7; doubles $10; triples $13.50.

Yunus Pension (tel. 284 2102; fax 284 3906), farther down Maraş Sok. away from the town center. Rooms with marble floors, toilets, showers. Some rooms with screens. Breakfast included. Singles $10; doubles $16.70.

Dalyan Camping (tel./fax 284 4157), past the Yunus on Maraş Sok. next to the river. A great campsite with views of both the rock tombs and the acropolis. New bathrooms and showers with hot water. Swimming possible. Breakfast and laundry available. Camping $4 per person; bungalows and caravans with electricity $10.

FOOD AND ENTERTAINMENT

Koşem Restaurant, on the riverside next to the Dalyan Co-op (tel. 284 2222). Excellent food and friendly service. Open-air seating or covered terrace. Clear views of the lit rock tombs at night. Try the *soğuk mezeler* ($1), grills ($2.70), and fish ($5).

Yöney Pastry and Bakery Shop (tel. 284 3072), right next to the PTT. Delicious selections of sweets and other Turkish delights. Comfortable indoor and outdoor seating. Open 7am-1am.

Crazy Bar on Maraş Sok., closer to the town center. The name sums up this lively Dalyan night spot. The interior design is made to look like a cave; farther back is a Pamukkale-like fountain. Beers $1.50, cocktails $5. Open until 4am.

Albatross Bar, on Maraş Sok. next to the Albatross Pension. Stools and tables right at the edge of the street. Good selection of music, and occasional live performances. Beer $1.50, whiskey $2.70, *rakı* $1.70. Open until 4am.

SIGHTS

Dalyam's most important site is the city of **Caunos.** As you proceed down the river by boat, the first sites you'll see are the ancient Lycian rock tombs that date from the 4th century BC. Continuing down the river, you'll encounter the **acropolis** with the ruins of the castle on top. You'll be let off at the base of the acropolis, where a small dirt path leads to the admission gate and site (tel. 284 3845; open in summer 8am-7pm, in winter 9am-5pm; admission $1.40, students 70¢). From the base of the acropolis, climb up to the **theater** for a panoramic view of the site and the beach in the distance. Facing the theater, the **basilica** is on your left. The ancient harbor of Caunos has several temple ruins in its vicinity, including a recently discovered fountain.

The last stop on daily boat tours from Dalyan is İztuzu Beach. The beach is heavily protected by environmentalist groups to preserve the natural habitat of the endangered **loggerhead turtle**. It is only open from 8am-8pm to allow these shy creatures to come out at night to lay their eggs. The beach is a 4.1km-long sandy strip of coastline. Bring water to the beach from Dalyan, if possible, as prices at the beachside concession stand are double those in town.

■ İçmeler

İçmeler is the next cove west of Marmaris, increasingly resembling its more famous neighbor. Named for the small village that is some 10km from Marmaris, İçmeler is now a full-blown concrete jungle down to the beach. Although luxury hotels and resorts have brought economic prosperity to this once sleepy village, it has also taken away the sense of peacefulness once associated with the cove. Nevertheless, its beach is slightly better than the one in Marmaris and does have some pleasant pensions with a "homey" feeling. The pensions are within walking distance of the beach while maintaining a pleasant distance from the crowded beachfront resorts. Frequent *dolmuş* service to Marmaris, only 10-15minutes away, make İçmeler a feasible alternative to lodging in Marmaris while staying in reach of its transportation system.

ORIENTATION AND PRACTICAL INFORMATION

There is **no tourist office** in İçmeler, but maps are available in the Marmaris office. **Dolmuş** run between İçmeler and Marmaris every 15 minutes from 7am-midnight (50¢). There's also **municipal bus service** to İçmeler; take the bus to its last stop. Dial 155 or 156 in case of **emergency.** See Marmaris for all other services (p. 454).

ACCOMMODATIONS

Stay away from places near the waterfront or botanical gardens area; they are expensive and overcrowded. Reasonably priced accommodations are right on the main road to Marmaris, just after entering the İçmeler area.

Palmiye Pension, Atatürk Cad. No. 3 (tel. 455 2085), is a family-run pension. Clean rooms, toilet, shower and 24hr. hot water. Shady garden area. Kitchen available to guests. English, German, and Greek-speaking staff. Doubles $20.

Podium Pension, Atatürk Cad. 156, Evler No.7 (tel. 455 3292, 455 2428), located a bit before the Palmiye with a rock garden, terrace, and tables for guests. Clean rooms with a communal bathroom. Doubles $14; triples $20.

Leydi Pension (tel. 455 2244). Go down Atatürk Cad. and take the first left after Palmiye. A quieter alternative to the Atatürk Cad. accommodations. Communal shower and toilets. Rugs on marble floors. Kitchen for guests' use. Two gardens. Rooms have couches for people with small children. Doubles $14; triples $20.

FOOD AND ENTERTAINMENT

Dining options are a bit more expensive than those found in the tourist areas in Marmaris. You may want to take the *dolmuş* to find cheap eats, but some places in İçmeler definitely deliver a hearty meal that's worth the extra cost. **Captain Bullshit's Place** is just this kind of place. Join Ali, Ibo, and Jimmy for an entertaining and tasty meal. They'll talk your head off, but they make excellent fish and chips ($6.75), chicken dinners ($5), and some Turkish plates. The bountiful servings and wide selection of music justify the high prices (open until midnight). To get there, take a left onto Kayabal Cad. going toward the old village.

İçmeler also has a happening nightlife on the beachfront. Live music thumps especially hard from the clubs on the left side of the beach (facing the water). **La Grotta** features live music nightly at 7pm, including the waltzes and Neopolitan musical style of the "Group un Sospiro." Later, the music becomes more progressive with "Aggressive" at 10pm. Enjoy comfortable couches and shady gardens in addition to the bar (wine $2.70, other drinks $4.70). The **South Beach Bar,** past La Grotta, bears graffiti claiming "Eric Clapton was here" (cola $1.75, beer $2). **Deniz Kapısı** (tel. 455 3017), on the opposite side of the beach, offers the lethal one-two punch of **Turkish folk dancing** and **karaoke** (cold appetizers $2, pizza $5.35, beer $1.75, gin $2).

SIGHTS

İçmeler's **beach** tends to be cleaner and slightly less crowded than Marmaris, and water sports are available in the area. **Parasailing** is a popular thrill but is a bit pricey ($24 per 10min.). For the same price, boat lovers can rent a high-powered **speed boat** for an hour and look cool frontin' on da beach. **Diving centers** also offer underwater recreation for all ages and skill levels. The **European Diving Centre** (tel. 455 4733; fax 455 4734), on the right side of the beach near the Gol-Mar Hotel, has excellent staff and equipment for beginners ($65 per day with equipment and pickup).

Black Sea Coast

The Black Sea Coast is bountiful and unspoiled, with a profoundly beautiful country-side. The region has long been overlooked by the majority of Turkey's tourists because of its short summer season. Cool breezes and heavy rainfall nourish the region's forests and thickly cultivated farmland that are more reminiscent of the northwest United States than a Middle Eastern country. Despite the isolation fostered by adjacent mountain ranges, trading posts like Sinop, Trabzon, and Amissos (now Samsun) have become commercial centers. They first exported local products and later profited from the silk route trade. The region still supports itself with exporting tea, cherries, and other crops, all of which have sustained the region for thousands of years. In recent years, commerce with Georgia and other former Soviet republics has brought added prosperity, but it has also led to a marked increase in prostitution. Religious fundamentalism in the region has also grown steadily in recent years. The Islamic Welfare Party won municipal elections in many towns, but the region still retains its liberal atmosphere. Just keep in mind that almost all of the men have their own pistol, and most know how to use it.

WEST TO TRABZON

Riding or driving along the Black Sea highway is one of the most beautiful drives in the world. There are several interesting cities to explore, outdoor octaves abound, and the natural scenery is spectacular. But **the ride is dangerous,** partly because of heavy traffic and partly because of the road conditions. Americans in particular, accustomed to a smooth ride on, say, the Indiana Toll Way (exit 77 for the home of the Fighting Irish), may also have a different idea of what a ride on highway should be like. *Let's Go* **strongly discourages hitchhiking** here and strongly suggests that **women not travel alone,** as in other parts of Turkey. Keep in mind as well that the region is rainy much of the year. Despite these drawbacks, a voyage along the scenic Black Sea highway between Istanbul and the Georgian border is nothing if not rewarding. You can easily rent a car or jeep (or even a mountain bike) in most cities.

■ Safranbolu

Safranbolu is a hidden jewel in the dusty lands of northwestern Turkey. An old Turkish town, it contains some of the best examples of early Ottoman architecture in Anatolia. Safranbolu was founded around 3000 BC. Since its beginnings as the Roman province of Paphlagonia, Safranbolu has come under Byzantine, Seljuk, and Ottoman rule. It was also an important location on the Silk Road. In part because of this rich historical past, Safranbolu now has hundreds of world-famous 18th- and 19th-century houses. The town was placed on the UNESCO World Cultural Heritage List in 1994 in recognition of the city's extensive efforts to preserve its cultural heritage. In addition to its famous homes, Safranbolu is also famous for its **Turkish delight** *(lokum)* and **saffron flower** *(safran).* Still relatively untouristed, Safranbolu, with its narrow streets and houses built of sun-dried brick, is arrestingly beautiful.

ORIENTATION AND PRACTICAL INFORMATION

Safranbolu has two distinct sections: the beautiful old town, and the dusty new one consisting of two long boulevards lined with five-story apartment buildings and of little interest. The heart of old Safranbolu and its center of transportation is the main square, **Mehmet Kurtulanı Meydanı.** Local and inter-city **buses, dolmuş,** and **taxis** leave from here. Standing in the square and looking toward the old baths, you will see four streets. On the extreme left, **Kastamonu Road** leads to Hıdırlık Tepesi, a hill

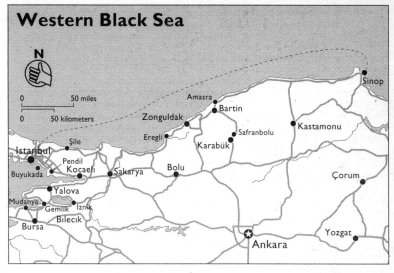

Western Black Sea

N

0   50 miles

0   50 kilometers

Sinop

Amasra
Bartin
Zonguldak
Eregli   Safranbolu   Kastamonu
Karabük

Istanbul
Şile
Pendil   Kocaeli   Sakarya   Bolu
Buyukada
Yalova   Çorum
Mudanya   Iznik
Gemlik   Bilecik
Bursa   Yozgat
★ Ankara

from which there is a superb view of the town. To the right of it is **Akın Sok.,** leading to the old *caravanserai,* is **Yukarı Çarşı Sok.,** which contains a tourist office and the Arasna Cafe-Bar Pansiyon. To the extreme right, **Hasan Dede Sok.** leads past the Tahsinbey Konağı and Paşa Konağı hotels to the old government house, now in ruins. Safranbolu is small, and most points of interest are within a five-minute walk. **Hilmi Bayramgil Sok.** runs to the new town.

There are two rival tourist offices in Safranbolu. On the main square, the office of the privately owned **Safranbolu Culture and Tourism Association** *(Kültür ve Turizm Vakfı),* Çeşme Mah., 1 Arasta Sok. (tel. 712 1047), supplies maps and information on sights and accommodations (open daily 8am-4pm, variably open until 9pm). More helpful is the government-run **Tourism Information Office** *(Turizm Danışma Müdürlüğü),* 7 Arasta Çarşısı (tel./fax 712 3863), which provides similar services (open daily 8:30am-5:30pm). Go down Yukarı Çarşı Sok., take the first left after the Aşiyan Otantik Cafe, then take an immediate right into the little shopping arcade. The Tourism Office's friendly staff will sell you an excellent map of the town for $1. You can reach the **police** by calling 712 1222.

There is a **telephone** in the main square of the old town, and another in the arcade opposite the tourist office. Both accept phone cards. In the new town, there are functional phones at the roundabout and on the main road. It is best not to use hotel reception phones, as they can be very expensive. Safranbolu is served by the Güven, Avrupa, and Ulusoy bus companies, which run to all major cities in Turkey. You can find buses to Istanbul and Ankara every hour. Ulusoy buses, which have a high-quality, safer service, can take you to Ankara for $3.50 or Istanbul for $9. Numerous other companies serve **Karabük,** a less-than-lovely steel manufacturing town 10km away, from which you can catch a frequent minibus to Safranbolu. **City buses** also make the journey every hour Monday through Saturday and every two hours on Sundays (25¢). A **taxi** from the bus station to old Safranbolu will cost $8-9; taxis are metered, and have the same rates as other Turkish cities. Most bus companies will take you to old Safranbolu for free. The **Ulusoy** office (tel. 725 4254, in Karabük 424 2111) is in the new town. Coming from the old town, turn right at the roundabout—it's roughly 15m down the street, on your right. The **Avrupa** office (tel. 712 4315) is 50m farther along, on your left. **Güven** (tel. 725 2145) is located on Sadri Artunç Cad. Bus employees seldom speak English; try to get tourist office personnel to make the call or to go to an office and buy a ticket.

The state **hospital** (tel. 712 1187) is in the new town, near Kaya Erdem Cad., behind the Kız Sağlık Meslek Lisesi. There are no **ATMs** in the old city; use the Yapi

Kredi Bankası or Ziraat Bankası machines in Kıranlar. Ziraat Banksı has an office in old Safranbolu on Çarşı Meydanı. The tiny **PTT** office is on Hamamönü Sok., next to the police station. If you need a bigger PTT, try the one in Bağlar, Sadri, Artunç Cad., which is open between 9am and 5pm. **Postal Code:** 78620. **Telephone Code:** 372.

ACCOMMODATIONS

Havuzlu Konak, 18 Beybağ Sok. (tel. 725 2883), is a luxurious, restored Ottoman villa. Rooms have delicate lace bedspreads, Ottoman couches, and brass tables. Bathrooms are larger than single rooms in most pensions. Reservations are recommended, and essential for Saturdays, when it fills with middle-class Turks on weekend trips. Stop in for a spot of *çay* even if you can't afford to stay—it's worth a look. The prices are high, especially in the summer (singles $25-40; doubles $45-65). Also sharing the upper price range are the **Paşa Konağı** and **Tahsin Bey Konağı**, 50 Hükümet Sok. (tel. 712 2014; fax 712 6062; email safranbolu@superonline.com.tr). Run by the same owner, the two villas will make a *paşa* out of you. Beautiful rooms with TVs and phones, oriental rugs, central heating, and a knockout view make them worth the extra *lira* (singles $30-37; doubles $42-58; triples $65; breakfast included). The **Arasna Cafe-Bar Pansiyon** (tel. 712 4170) has four rooms similar to the Konaks but without the views. Some are originals, some less authentic. Nevertheless, this place is classy, comfortable, and has a good bar ($12.50-15 per person, breakfast included). It's hard to miss the signs for the **Çarşı Pansiyon,** 1 Bozkurt Sok. (tel. 725 1079), where you can choose between standard pension rooms with shared bath and floor-tossed mattresses in rooms with private bath. This is the best budget option in town ($6.25 per person, breakfast included).

There are some pensions in the new town. You probably want to stay in these only if the ones in the old town are full. The **Konak Pansiyon,** 4 Kaya Erdem Cad., Sağlık Sok., 4 (tel. 725 2485), on the main road between the old and new towns, is comfortable (singles $11.75; doubles $18.75, all with shared bathrooms). The **Hotel Uz** (tel. 712 1086), just off the roundabout in the new town at the intersection of Baysal Sok. and Arap Hacı Sok., offers modern rooms (singles $23; doubles $30).

FOOD

For food, don't miss **Kadıoğlu Şehzade Sofrası,** Arasta Sok., #8, on the main square (tel. 712 5091). Their specialty is *kuzu kebap* (lamb baked in spices, $2). A three course meal will give you that six-months pregnant feeling for just over $4. The friendly owner may reward such an effort with a coffee on the house. The **Arasna Cafe/Bar** (tel. 712 4170) also features a full menu of similarly inexpensive Turkish cooking and live music after 9:30pm. The **Aşiyan Restaurant** (tel. 712 3412), opposite Arasna Cafe/Bar offers *yasım* (pasta, $2) in an old, historical house. The **Boncuk Cafe** in Yemeniciler Arastası (tel. 712 0067) is a nice place to stop and have *ispanaklı güzleme* (spinach pita, $1) and *Safranbolu gazozu* (a local soda, 30¢). For delicious baked goods, try **Tarihi Simit ve Çubuk Fırını** (tel. 712 1777) on Yukarı Çarşı Sok.

The local Turkish delight specialty is *fındıklı lokum,* a yellow delight with a hazelnut in the middle and covered with coconut dust. An excellent shop is **İmren,** 1 Arasna Çarşısı, in the little shopping arcade, several doors down from the government-run tourist office (open daily 8am-8pm). **Özkan Lokumlar,** on the street left of the tourist office, makes Turkish delight—stick your head into this ancient shop to see how it's made. You'll be stared at, but you may get a free sample. Also consider **Safran Pastanesi,** opposite Cinci Hanı, #13 (tel 725 2087). They have fresh baklava (60¢), homemade ice cream (75¢), and *su böreği* (cheese pie, 50¢) on Saturdays.

The **Beyaz Ev Pub** is behind Cinci Han facing Çarşi Meydani (tel. 725 2626). It offers live music after 9:30pm and inexpensive beer ($1) in a friendly environment. There are two discos next to White House; **Harabe Disco** and **Hangar Disco.** Although small-town Turkish discos won't conjure up visions of John Travolta, you can still pull out your best sequins and work on your moves.

SIGHTS

Any tour of Safranbolu should begin at **Yemeniciler Arastası,** the shopping arcade which houses the government Tourism Information Office (most shops open 9am-5pm). An oval-shaped complex, this was once home to Safranbolu's famous shoe industry. Now, candy stores and cafes, gift shops, and, yes, shoe stores crowd the intimate arcade. The Arasta gives one a unique glimpse into Turkey's past, albeit with more than a touch of touristy kitsch. The **Kaymakamlar Evi** (governor's residence) is the local museum. Enter through the courtyard, where the animals were originally kept. Various tools and utensils are on display here, including wooden cone *frustums.* These were filled with yogurt and water to make *ayran.* To get there from the market (at the back of the *caravanserai),* walk up the alley beside the T.C. Ziraat Bankası. The museum is the white building on the right (open Mon.-Fri. 8:30am-5:30pm; slipper charge 25¢). After wandering through the town's narrow streets, stroll up to **Hıdırlık Tepesi,** a lookout point at the town ramparts. Walk uphill along the snaking Kastamonu road for 10 minutes, then take the paved path on your right to the official-looking building with the Turkish flag. You can find a shop and **public bathrooms** here. After sipping tea for only 30¢, you won't mind paying the 10¢ to use the bathrooms.

In **Hıdırlık Tepesi,** you can see the grave of Candaroğly Hıdı Paşa, who conquered Safranbolu in 1358. Also visit the tomb of Hasan Paşa who was an important Ottoman notable exiled to Safranbolu in 1843. Mosque buffs will want to take a look at the **İzzet Paşa Camii** and **Köprülü Mehmet Paşa Camii.** After a long day in Safranbolu, nothing soothes weary bones like the baths at **Cinci Hamamı.** It has separate sections for men and women ($1.75).

▨ Amasra

Over 3000 years of trade and fishing have left Amasra the same quiet beach get away that Amastris, Alexander the Great's sister-in-law, was looking for. She founded the town on the site of Sesamos, an ancient Phoenician port. The midday sun sees young Turks and a handful of foreigners frolicking on the beach until an almost daily afternoon drizzle dampens the town's half-paved roads. A Byzantine Citadel and several Ottoman houses coexist with modern life; the fortress gates double as soccer goals.

ORIENTATION AND PRACTICAL INFORMATION

Amasra is accessible only by *dolmuş* from Bartin, about 15km to the south. Take a bus from Ankara, Istanbul (7½hr., $13), or Karabuk (2½hr., $3.25) to Bartin and then immediately hop on the *dolmuş* for Amasra (75¢). The road into town passes the little-used western beach, Küçük Plaj, and Sefa Park on the right, and then intersects Küçük Liman Cad. Küçük Liman Cad. winds left into the fortress, two blocks before the main beach, Büyük Plaj. The **PTT,** on the right opposite Küçük Liman Cad., has charge **phones** and card phones (open daily 8:30am-5:30pm). International operators are not always available from local phones, so come to town with cash and don't depend on a calling card. The government **tourist office,** one block east of the main square, offers little assistance beyond a pocket Turkish-English dictionary, so for information in English as well as **currency exchange** and **medical assistance,** visit the **pharmacy** (tel. 315 2323), next door to the PTT. Küçük Liman Cad. leads into the main square where *dolmuş* and **taxis** line up for the trip to Bartin. There is a **Türkiye Bankasi** here with an **ATM.** The town's only other ATM is at the **Ziraat Bankasi** on the beach road. The **postal code** is 74300. The **telephone code** is 378.

ACCOMMODATIONS

Otel Timur (tel. 315 2589, -90; fax 315 3290), and **Amasra Oteli** (tel. 315 1722; fax 315 3025), across from each other on Çekiciler Cad., one block back from the beach below the citadel, both offer clean rooms with private bathrooms and breakfast included ($10 per person). **Nur Turistik Pansiyon** (tel. 315 1015), offers clean rooms with views of the west harbor, common balconies, common bathrooms, and breakfast ($8 per person). At **Otel Belvu Palas** you will find beds on concrete floors and common bathrooms ($5 per person).

FOOD

The restaurants along Amasra's western harbor dish out the port's unsurprising specialty—fish. A full meal of salad, appetizers, fish, and drinks at **Canlibalik Restaurant,** 8 Küçük Liman Cad. (tel. 315 26 06) runs from $4-6. Cheaper options lie one block east of the main square at the **Sesamos Cafe,** where a burger and a drink cost $1 or at **Safak Restaurant,** which serves up *kebap* for $1.75 and pitas for $1. On Tuesday and Friday, a small **public market** offers local fruits, vegetables, and other goodies in the main square.

SIGHTS

Although the town was fortified as far back as the 3rd century BC, the **citadel** which stands today around a handful of modern residences dates from the 9th century, when Byzantines were fending off Russian raiders. It fell into the hands of Genoese merchants four centuries later and was surrendered without contest to the Ottomans in 1460. A 10-minute walk through the three tight gates and up around the walls should provide an ample fortress fix. Across the western harbor the **town museum** offers miscellaneous items, Hellenistic through Ottoman, including a collection of Ottoman pistols. Outside, moss-covered fragments of ancient columns and tablets with Hellenistic, Roman, early Christian, and Ottoman inscriptions languish through daily rains (open 8:30am-5:30pm, admission 75¢). A local **woodworking market** fills the narrow lane between Otel Timur and Küçük Liman Cad. with handmade cooking utensils and souvenir trinkets. There are a few **Ottoman houses** in town, but they are still occupied, so you will have to make friends to get a look.

■ Sinop

Sinop takes its name from a mythical nymph who spurned the advances of the thunderbolt-hurling god Zeus. Hoping to get her in his Olympian sack, he offered to grant her a single wish and she asked for eternal virginity. Bound to his promise, Zeus isolated her on the tiny mountain-enclosed peninsula, where modern Sinop now lingers, a town unspoiled by tourists. Uncrowded, but slightly littered, beaches and a wholesome nightlife provide escape from the urban grind and decadent "Natashas" (prostitutes from former Soviet republics) of Samsun and Trabzon. College students out of town for a beach holiday and old-timers nostalgic for their friends from the recently closed NATO base warmly welcome the few foreign travelers who straggle into town.

ORIENTATION AND PRACTICAL INFORMATION

The Sinop Peninsula juts north-eastward into the Black Sea. The town's main street, **Sakarya Cad.,** runs inland to the hills at the north end of the peninsula. The *otogar* is at the south end of town, enclosed by ancient fortifications and across the street from a prison. Several **buses** make connections to: Kastamonu ($7.50); Samsun ($5); Trabzon ($13); Karabük ($8); Ankara ($14.50); Istanbul ($19.50); and Izmir ($22). Atatürk Cad., the last right off the main road, leads down to the **PTT** (open 8am-11pm, full services 8:30am-5pm), which has 20 telephones. Across the square from the PTT on Kıbrıs Cad., the waterfront center of Sinop's nightlife, is the **tourist office** (tel. 261 7900) where little English is spoken (open 8am-6pm). The **TML ferry office** is to the south of the harbor (tel. 261 1424). The **hospital** (Atatürk Hastanesi) offers 24hr. service (tel. 261 4510). You can reach the police by dialing 155 or 261 1770. **Postal code:** 57000. **Telephone code:** 0368.

ACCOMMODATIONS

Formerly home to a significant U.S. Navy population, and now a popular vacation spot for young Turks, Sinop has plenty of reasonably priced rooms. Nestled between the *otogar,* the prison, and a mosque whose muezzin calls prayers with the most vibrato on the Black Sea Coast, **Gül Palas Otel** offers cheap dorm beds ($3.25) and a common bathroom. It is popular among the town's young tourists who bring their own toilet paper, bug spray, and ear plugs. On the quiet waterfront, southwest of the fortifications, **Yilmaz Aile Pension,** 11 Tersane Çarşisi (tel. 261 5752), offers clean rooms with common baths and waterfront views (singles $5; doubles $6.50; triples $9.75). Three doors down at **Uğur Hotel** (tel. 261 3742), there are rooms with common baths for solo travelers as well as larger rooms with private baths for families (singles $6.50; doubles $10.50; triples $19.50). English is spoken at the **restaurant** downstairs, which offers good fish and entertainment in the form of an energetic caged monkey named Çaplein ("playboy"). Campers can pitch their tents on the beach at **Gazi Piknik Ve Mesire Yeri** ($3.25 per tent). Coming into town, follow the sign to the campsite, right off the main road, 100m before the *otogar.*

FOOD AND ENTERTAINMENT

If, for some reason, the monkey at Uğur isn't in your plans, try **Saray** (tel. 261 1729) on the waterfront. You can select the fish there yourself in the kitchen. Most meals are $5-6 (open 8am-1am). For cheap *kebap* (60¢), roam the stands off Atatürk Cad. on the north side of the fortress, or head to the **Burg Cafe** on top of the Citadel's tower for a spectacular view and a meal ($1-2). If you must resort to American food, visit the **Cafe Gükkusage** on Kıbrıs Cad. A burger, fries, and cola are $1.50.

Akvaryum and **Karadeniz Lokantası** on Kurtuluş Cad. are two restaurants near the sea with reasonably priced seafood. **Yalı Kahvesi,** also by the seashore, is a nice place to enjoy your tea (35¢) as you chat with the locals. For those who miss good American food, **Barınak** is a must. Delicious food, excellent service, and a beautiful seaside location makes it a meeting place for foreigners (beer $1, chips $1.35). Near the intersection of Atatürk Cad. and Gazi Cad., **Hasıraltı Bar** is for those who would like to stay up late and throw back a few (beer $1).

Sunken Towns and Buried Ships

Over the millennia, coast lines bend, rivers shift meander, and hills rise, concealing the tangible remains of human history. Bustling with intercontinental trade for thousands of years, Anatolia's Black Sea coast is now a hot bed of archaeological research. A team of Turkish pre-historians, under the direction of Professor Önder Bilgi of the University of Istanbul, is unearthing a settlement outside the modern village of **İkizpepe.** Now a set of four land-locked mounds, 7km from the coast and 2km from the Kızlırmak River, İkizpepe was a riverside settlement (the Kızlırmak was then called Halyas) from the late Chalcolithic Period (3500 BC) to the middle Bronze Age (1750 BC). They have determined that of the two large mounds, one was a settlement while the other was a graveyard for the inhabitants of that settlement. Findings have revealed tree trunks as the principal architectural element, a highly developed metallurgy, and the use of monumental ovens. Surprisingly, skeletons found in the graveyard, many of which were colored red, have suggested a closer anthropological link to races on the coasts of Bulgaria, Romania, southern Russia, and the Caucuses than to the central Anatolian and pre-Mediterranean races. West along the coast in Sinop, an American team of archaeologists, led by Dr. Owen Doonan and Dr. Alex Gantos, are in the process of surveying coastal areas to determine where to search for ancient trade centers. The later stages of their project will bring them out to sea, where they hope to find both submerged land settlements and sunken pirate ships left intact. Since the Black Sea's low oxygen content is protective of sunken objects, they may find pirate ships complete with trunks of gold and pirates' bones.

ANATOLIA

Beach-goers have three options in Sinop: the littered but otherwise beautiful **Akliman Halk Plaji,** south of the *otogar* on the west coast; the **Bahçeler Halk Plaji** across the main road from the *otogar;* or the **Karakum Plaji,** a long walk or short *dolmuş* ride (30¢) down Kıbrıs Cad. northeast of town. After a day at the beach, Sinop vacationers, mostly Turkish college students, play backgammon and *erikriç* (a local strain of a game played with tiles) at the waterfront cafes on Kıbrıs Cad. After a few cups of tea and rolls of the dice, head north along the coast to **Telescope** and enjoy live bands (beer $1; cover $1.75; open 8pm-late). South through the fortress is **Diogenes Bar.** the official watering hole of the local American archaeological team (beer $1.25; open 8pm-late).

SIGHTS

Sinop's **fortifications** date from c. 770 BC when the port was settled by Miletian colonists. What stands today is a mish-mash of Pontic and Ottoman reinforcements. The **museum** at the end of the main road is most notable for a large Hellenistic sculpture of a deer appearing strangely unconcerned about being devoured by attacking lion. In the back of the museum lie the remains of the foundation of a **temple of Serapis.** A **photo exhibit** within the museum of Roman roads in Asia Minor reveals that it may have been easier to get around northern Anatolia 2000 years ago than it is now. (Open Tues.-Sun. 8am-5pm. Admission 60¢, students 30¢.) **Balatlar Kilisesi,** a 7th-century Byzantine church, is near the intersection of Radar Yolu and Kemalettin Sami Paşa Cad. The nearby prison once housed and inspired the famous leftist Turkish poet Sabahattin Ali. Two 13th-century Seljuk buildings, **Alaadin Camii** and the **Alaiye Medresesi,** are next to each other on the north side of Sakarya Cad.

■ Samsun

Its Hellenistic and Byzantine legacies burned away by a 15th-century fire, Samsun is a grimy, smelly industrial port which serves as a hub of transportation for the central Black Sea Coast. Those passing through are advised to hasten on their way out unless they possess an interest in industrial waste or the city's monument to Atatürk.

ORIENTATION AND PRACTICAL ORIENTATION

Samsun's *otogar* is 2km east of Cumhuriyet Meydani, the town's main square. The 20-minute walk to town, easier by **taxi** ($5) or **dolmuş** (30¢), reveals Samsun's filth. The **tourist office** (tel. 431 1228), where fluent English is spoken, is the most helpful office on the Black Sea Coast, ironically set in its least scenic town (open 8am-7pm). Two streets full of shops are a block or two south of the square. Gazi Cad. runs west and offers plenty of **banks** with **ATMs.** Istiklal Cad. runs east and has plenty of cheap eats as well as an **English bookstore,** Dünya Kitabevi (tel. 239 0849), with a few paperbacks and a selection of international newspapers and magazines. Kazimpaşa Cad. leads west of the main square to Gaziler Meydani, recognizable by its clock tower and home to the town's budget accommodations and restaurants. The **PTT,** open 8am-11pm, is on Kazimpaşa Cad., as is **Turk Telikom** with card **telephones.**

The **THY** office (tel. 431 3455), also on Kazımpaşa Cad., offers flights to Istanbul (1 per day, Mon.-Sat., 90min., $45, $30 students) and twice per week to Ankara (1hr., $35, $25 students). **Taxis** ($6.50) and **dolmuş** (30¢) can drop you at the airport from the square. A **ferry** running along the Black Sea Coast stops Tuesday evening in Samsun, goes east to Trabzon and Rize, and on Thursday morning heads back to Istanbul. Consult at the port (tel. 445 1605), 500m west of the main square, for specific times and prices. **Trains** run to Ankara daily (23hr., $8). If you are traveling by **bus** through Samsun and are determined to stop in town, ask to be dropped at Cumhuriyet Meydani where you can reserve a seat on a bus out of town with any of the bus companies, all of which have offices in the square. There are several daily connections to: Sinop (3hr., $3.25); Amasya (2hr., $3.25); Trabzon (6hr., $13); Ankara (8hr., $15); and Istanbul (12hr., $19.50). Prices are negotiable, so make the companies compete.

Less frequent connections include Izmir, Bursa, Rize, Hopa, Artvin, Tokat, Hatay, and others. The tourist office can help make reservations by phone. The **postal code** is 55000; the **telephone code** is 0362.

ACCOMMODATIONS AND FOOD

All of Samsun's cheap hotels crowd around Gaziler Meydani and little differentiates one from the next. **Divan Hotel,** 17-B Paşar Mah. Necipbey Sok. (tel. 431 3671), offers private rooms with clean, common baths ($6.50 per person). **Otel Deniz,** 42 Kale Mah. Bankalar Cad. (tel. 431 5878), is around the corner and similar facilities. **Otel Vidinli** (tel. 431 6050), in the main square offers more comfortable and expensive rooms with private baths (singles $35.50; doubles $50).

For a host of Turkish urban delicacies, as well as a fair dose of **Western fast food,** head to Gazi Cad. where **Krystal Restaurant** is most popular (meals $4-6; open daily 10am-midnight). **Huzur Tavuk Çuluk** (tel. 431 4965) serves tasty cheap *şiş kebap* or grilled chicken ($1.50). The staff speaks fluent French. Full tourist information on the Black Sea Coast offered to *ceux qui parlez français* (open 8:30am-10:30pm).

SIGHTS

Samsun's **archaeological museum**, across from the square, boasts a well-preserved, if not well-lit, Roman floor mosaic (open Tues.-Sat. 8:30am-5:30pm; admission 60¢, students 30¢). Otherwise the town holds little of interest to those without a deep interest in Atatürk. The park features an equestrian **statue of Atatürk**. On the west waterfront, there is a monument to the spot where **Atatürk** first stepped foot on Samsun's shore to begin the War of Independence. The **Atatürk museum,** also across from the square, has several photographs of the general and a number of his personal effects (open Tues.-Sun., 8:30am-5:30pm; admission 60¢, students 30¢).

■ Near Samsun: Tekkeköy Caves

Devoid of English speakers or serviceable restrooms, Tekkeköy is a grimy suburb 15km from grimy Samsun that recedes back into a river gorge with a surreal set of neolithic caves. Artfully carved, but small and quite scalable, the caves offer shade and calming drafts, as well as views of the river gorge and rolling hills to the south and Samsun's urban clutch on the Black Sea to the north. To get to Tekkeköy, hop on a *dolmuş* (40¢) from Samsun's main square and, after being dropped off in Tekkeköy, walk south and turn right before the bridge. Continue 1.5km on this dirt road until you reach the caves. Buses leave regularly back to Samsun (40¢) but restrict your visit to daylight hours. Have your passport handy as the local police, unused to tourists, may give you a momentary hassle on the streets.

■ Between Samsun and Ordu

If you are traveling between Samsun and Ordu, consider these places for a breather from the road or an over-night stay.

Yalçın Hotel (tel. (452) 423 1478) is 1.5km from **Fatsa** on the Kumru-Korgan highway, next to the OPET gas station. It is a surprisingly luxurious hotel, including a spacious lobby, restaurant, bar, sauna, disco, Turkish bath, pool, botanical garden, amphitheater, sports, and gym. Rooms have TVs, phone, and refrigerator. Singles $29; doubles $43; suite $50; extra beds $13. Visa accepted

Uzun Saçlının Yere is a famous tea house and cafe in **Medreseönü.** This is where many highway travelers stop and sip tea in crystal glasses (30¢). The owner, Uzun Saçlı, is the man with the longest hair in Turkey (95cm). Stop, enjoy your tea, and gaze over the Black Sea.

Vona Hotel (tel. (452) 517 1755; fax 517 1848) is in **Perşembe** on the Black Sea coast highway, 12km from Ordu. This seaside resort has a restaurant, bar, swimming pool, and soccer field, but, inexplicably, no baseball diamond. You can enjoy the sea either from the hotel's beach or your own balcony. Rooms have TVs, phone, bath, and 24hr. hot water. Breakfast included. Singles $20; doubles $33. Ask for student and group discounts.

Vonalı Celal Restaurant (tel (452) 587 2137) is 1km past the Çaka road tunnel in **Perşembe.** Truly a vegetarian's paradise, the restaurant has dozens of dishes cooked from dozens of plants collected all around the Black Sea. The menu has photos of the plants and the meals ($7-8). Be sure to try the pickles.

■ Amasya

Surrounded by steep cliffs into which the kings of Pontus carved their tombs in the 2nd and 3rd centuries BC and filled with medieval mosques and late Ottoman town houses (many of which offer accommodations, see below), Amasya is a quiet hill town within convenient reach of the Black Sea Coast. Although you may see few tourists in town, some locals take the opportunity to try to scam their relatively wealthier visitors. Industrious shoe-shine boys roam the streets with an English vocabulary that consists of "hello," "my name is," and "money." Wear sandals to avoid unwanted shoeshines.

ORIENTATION AND PRACTICAL INFORMATION

Amasya's main square is 1km southeast of the *otogar*. Most restaurants and services lie either on **Mehmet Paşa Cad.,** the road that runs along the southern bank of the Yeşiharmak "Green River," or on the main street of **Atatürk Cad.,** one block south of the river. The north bank is home to **old Ottoman houses** and the rising cliffs into which the tombs of the kings are carved. The **PTT** (open daily 8:30am-11pm) and **Turk Telikom,** with plenty of card **phones,** are on Mehmet Paşa Cad., 100m east of the main square. A helpful **tourist office** (tel. 218 7428) is located on the river, just west of the main square (open 10am-noon and 3-7pm). Slow, cheap **trains** run daily out of Amasya's rail station, 2km west of the main square to Samsun (60¢), Sivas ($1.20). **Buses** offer quicker, more comfortable service to: Samsun (2hr., $3.25); Trabzon (8hrs., $9.25); Konya (8hr., $9.25); Ankara (13hr., $10.50); and Istanbul (20hr., $18). The **postal code** is 05000, and the **telephone code** is 0358.

ACCOMMODATIONS

The full Amasya experience is incomplete without a night spent in one of the restored Ottoman houses along the river. More expensive than most lodgings in Turkey, their beautiful views and traditional decor make them worth the extra *lira*. Restored by its architect owner, **İlk Pension** (tel. 218 1689), 1 Hitit Sok., offers the most authentic rooms with clean, common baths (singles $22; doubles $29). On the north bank of the river, **Emin Efendi Pension** (tel. 212 1895), offers just as much Ottoman flavor in rooms overhanging the river (singles $17; doubles $25). East of Emin Efendi, **Zümrüt Pension** (tel. 216 2675) offers cheaper rooms with a more modern interior ($8 per person).

FOOD

Amasya's several **kebap** and **pita salons** are filled all day with locals escaping the sun, sipping tea, and taking in the familiar scenery. **Ocakbaşi Restaurant** (tel. 218 5692), on the west of the south bank, offers a full range of Turkish cuisine under shady trees (Meals $2-4). For a Cypriot twist on Turkish delicacies, head east on the south bank to **Kıbrıs Pide Ve Lahmacun Salonu** (tel. 212 2847). **Yela Pizza Lokantaşi** (tel. 218 6289), in the cobble stone streets east off the square, complements its Turkish offerings with Western standbys. Meals $3-6. Supposedly the best restaurant in town is in the **Öğretnen Evi** (teachers' hostel) on the northern bank of the river, across the bridge from the Atatürk statue. **Ali Kaya Restaurant,** near İlk Pension, is a safe haven for vegetarians running from ubiquitous *kebaps*.

SIGHTS

In the wake of Alexander the Great's roll through Anatolia, the hills of modern Amasya, formerly settled by Hittites, came under the jurisdiction of Greek-speaking Persians who called their kingdom Pontus. Their most famous leader, Mithradates II (281 BC), may be among those who were buried in the **tombs** carved out of the cliffs north of the city. From the square, head across the river and follow the yellow signs up the hill. The tombs, now covered with Turkish graffiti, are less impressive up close than they are from below. But the panoramic view of the valley and the city is beautiful (open 8:30am-6pm; admission 60¢, students 30¢).

A climb to the top of the cliff yields further views as well as a closer look at the **ancient fortress,** the oldest parts of which date back to the 3rd century BC, the newest the 1980s. The steep climb is commonly made up the northeast face. Follow yellow signs marked "Kale." Amasya has two museums: an **archaeological museum** in the main square with artifacts Hittite through Seljuk, and an **Ottoman house museum** on north side of the river with Turkish ethnographic museum and a gallery with several watercolor renderings of **Atatürk.**

Of the town's Seljuk and early Ottoman structures, the Seljuk **lunatic asylum,** the **Mustafabey Turkish bath,** and the **Mehmet Paşa mosque,** all east of the main square along the river's south bank, display a variety of styles employed from the early 13th century through the late 15th century. The lunatic asylum, whose recently restored interior columns betray a Hellenic influence on Seljuk architecture makes a nice stop for tea (30¢) after a hike to the citadel and tombs.

■ Ordu

Ordu is a hidden pearl on the coastline. A fire in 1883 robbed it of much of its ancient charm, leaving a thoroughly modern city in its place. When the Greeks and Armenians departed after the Turkish War of Independence, the town also lost part of its soul. Despite these misfortunes, Ordu is still a culturally rich city with a liberal atmosphere and friendly inhabitants.

ORIENTATION AND PRACTICAL INFORMATION

The **otogar** is on the eastern side of the city on the highway to Trabzon. The town is located on the shoreline. **Boztepe,** a 458m hill, is a great place for a panoramic view of the town as well as paragliding. **Kiraz Limanı** is a paradise 1km from the center of town where the green forest and blue sea meet.

The **tourist information office** (tel. 223 1606) is on 114 Atatürk Bul. (open Mon.-Fri. 9am-5pm). **Çotanak Tur Seyahat Acentası,** 112 Atatürk Cad. (tel 225 2054), is a travel office which sells Turkish Airlines tickets as well as other travel services. You can reach the **police** by calling either **155 in an emergency** or 223 1500. The state **hospital** is open 24hr. (tel. 224 4130). The **telephone code** is 452.

ACCOMMODATIONS AND FOOD

Turist Hotel (tel. 214 9115; fax 214 1950), on 134 Atatürk Bul. Central and inexpensive, but can be noisy at times. It has a restaurant and breakfast is included. Singles $13; doubles $23. 10% discount for groups.

Hotel Balıktaşı (tel. 223 0611; fax 223 0615) is on 13 Güzelyalı Mah. Sahil Cad., just outside of Ordu. By the sea, this hotel offers a bar, restaurant, conference room, sauna, fitness center, safe deposit, and pool. Rooms have TV, fridge, and bath. Breakfast included. Singles $40; doubles $60; triples $75. V/MC/EuroCard.

Belde Hotel (tel. 214 3987; fax 214 9398) is located in Kirazlimanı. It is a luxurious hotel with TV, fridge, phone, and bath in all rooms. Hotel goodies include: a restaurant, Turkish bath, fitness center, sauna, night club, beach, and pool. The hotel has an affiliated mountain house at the nearby **Çelikkıran Hill** (1600m) for you to enjoy the highland (paragliding, horse riding, and fishing). Singles $26; doubles $43; triples $56. V/MC/EuroCard.

The best place to try Ordu's fish is **Mıdı'nın Yeri,** on Kordon (Sahil Yolu Cad.). You can try *alablık* (trout) or *mezgit* with a salad starting at $7. **Ayışığı** is a wonderful place which combines the best **bar, cafe, movie theater, art gallery,** and **restaurant** in Ordu. This is where young people meet and enjoy themselves by the waves of the sea. **Turist Hotel's** restaurants also offers several dishes at reasonable prices ($4-5).

SIGHTS

The locals spend their evenings strolling the **Kordon** (shoreline). Street vendors sell boiled corn, sweets, and nuts to make the walk more pleasant. Ordu is world famous for its **hazelnuts** and **chocolates.** The **Safra factory** is in Ordu, supplying sweets to Turkey and the rest of Europe. Go visit **Safra shop** at Süleyman Felek Cad. and sample delicious sweets sold at ridiculously low prices. In July, Ordu hosts the **Golden Hazelnut Festival,** one of the liveliest festivals on the Black Sea coast. The most important event, however, is the **Volkswagen Beetle Festival** (VosVos Şenliği) in July. Hundreds of Beetles, what the Turks call "Turtles," come from all over Turkey to meet fellow VW lovers.

The **ethnography museum** is located in the Paşaoğlu Konağı (tel. 223 2596), Selimiye Mah. Taşocak Cad. This 19th-century Black Sea mansion has a traditionally decorated second floor worth seeing. Other historical sights include **Bolaman Konağı** (a mansion), **Yason Kilisesi** (a church), and **Eskipazar Camii** (a mosque). There are **rock tombs** in Büben Village and Dellikkaya, 10km from Ordu.

Çambaşı Yalası (highland, over 1850m, is a wonderful natural habitat where locals escape to enjoy the peace. Belde Hotel (tel. 214 3987), located in Kiraz Limanı, has a mountain villa and organizes trekking tours. If you have the energy and the will, climb the 3107m to see the crater lake **Karagöl.**

■ Trabzon

From its hilltop vantage point over the Black Sea, Trabzon has seen empires rise and fall, preserving a little of each in its architecture and life-style. Founded by the ancient Greeks as the port Trapezus, the city is best known as a trade center which attracted merchants from all over the world. Though important in the Greek and Roman periods, Trabzon reached its heyday after Alexius Comneni came to the city in 1204, fleeing Constantinople when the Crusaders sacked it. Comneni dubbed the city **Trebizond** and made it the capital of his empire. The dynasty he founded became the longest and one of the wealthiest in Greek history; its rulers lived off the profits of trade and nearby silver mines. The kingdom held out against the Ottomans until 1461 (even longer than Constantinople), postponing its demise by diplomatically marrying off its daughters, reputedly the most beautiful women in the world.

An industrial region of more than 1.4 million inhabitants, present day Trabzon has lost much of its romantic appeal as a stronghold of exotic princes. With the influx of impoverished immigrants from the Eastern Bloc came innumerable prostitutes; women traveling alone may be mistaken for prostitutes. A sultry atmosphere traps a noticeable stench in the city center. Rains wash it away from time to time, leaving the air crystal clear, for a day or so. Trabzon is greener than the cities on the Aegean and Mediterranean; its population is an ethnic bouillabaisse of Turks, Russians, Georgians, and assorted other ex-Soviets. Trabzon may either repulse or bewitch you with its fascinating history, industrial squalor, verdant beauty, and post-Cold War seediness.

ORIENTATION AND PRACTICAL INFORMATION

Tourist Office: (tel. 321 4659) In the southeast corner of the main square's park. Has maps and the dates of the huge highland festivals of late June and July. Open in summer Mon.-Sat. 9am-5:30pm, in winter Mon.-Fri. 9am-noon and 1-5pm.

Tourist Agencies: Afacan Tour, 40C İskele Cad. (tel. 321 5804, -6), 200m northeast of the main square. Can get visas for Georgia ($60 for 1 month, $110 for 3 months) and Azerbaijan ($40), as well as ship (7-15hr., $30-100) and flight schedules (every

ANATOLIA

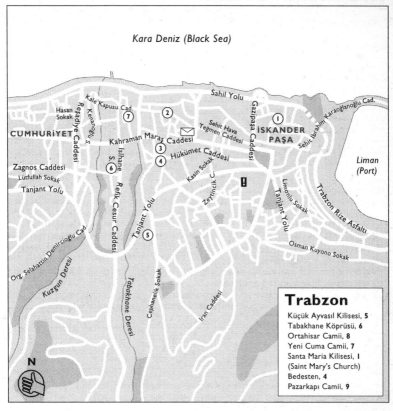

Kara Deniz (Black Sea)

Trabzon

Küçük Ayvasıl Kilisesi, 5
Tabakhane Köprüsü, 6
Ortahisar Camii, 8
Yeni Cuma Camii, 7
Santa Maria Kilisesi, I
(Saint Mary's Church)
Bedesten, 4
Pazarkapı Camii, 9

Mon., Wed., Fri., $100) to Sochi. They also operates daily tours of Trabzon and Sümela ($4); weekend tours of Uzungöl ($10) and Ayder ($10); and trekking expeditions in the Kaçkars and near Uzungöl.

Consulates: Those interested in traveling to Georgia, Russia, or Iran are probably best off working through a travel agency; applying directly to the consulate is a much cheaper, but less predictable method. **Georgian Consulate,** Gazipaşa Cad. 20 (tel. 326 2226). One-month visas $60; three-months $150; transit $30. Visa window open Mon.-Fri. 9am-1pm and 2-5pm. **Consulate of the Russian Federation** (tel. 326 2600), on Aranfil Cad. 200m southeast of the main square. Russian visa requests are even more complex; unless you have an invitation from a Russian, go to a travel agency. Open Tues. and Thurs. 9am-noon and 3-5pm. **Iranian Consulate** (tel. 322 4851), on Boztepe Cad., 1km southwest of the main square.

Flights: THY flies to: Ankara (2 per day, 1hr., $36, students $25); Izmir; and Istanbul (4 per day, 2hr., $47, students $35). Buses leave from the **THY office** (tel. 321 1680), at the southwest corner of the main square.

Buses: Run from the *otogar* 3km east of the main square. Two reliable bus companies are **Ulusoy** (tel. 325 2201) and **Metro** (tel. 325 7286). They have buses leaving for all major cities in Turkey. Check the schedule when you reserve your place a day in advance. Look for **Mahmutoğlu** for tickets to Georgia (Batum and Tblisi). The main square is reachable from via *dolmuş* marked *Otogar* or *Tıp Fak* (50¢).

Ferries: From June-Sept., **Turkish Maritime Lines** plies the waters of the Black Sea Coast from Istanbul to Trabzon. It leaves Istanbul Mon. at 2pm, stops at Sinop, Samsun, and Giresun, and arrives at Trabzon Wed. at 9:30am. The return voyage leaves Trabzon Wed. at 3pm and arrives in Istanbul Fri. at 1:30pm. Try to purchase tickets a week in advance at the **TML office** (tel. 321 7096), next to the tourist office ($16-35; 50% student discount). Open Mon.-Fri. 9am-noon and 1-5pm.

ANATOLIA

English Bookstore: Derya Kitap-Kırtasiye Pazarlama, 127 Uzun Sok. (tel. 321 1821), has a few English books.

Hospital: Nümune Hospital (tel. 223 4041) is west of downtown on Faik Dranaz Cad. off Kahramanmaraş Cad. Take a *dolmuş* marked "Hastane" or "Nümune" to the Nümune Hospital; get off at the Nümune Durağı.

PTT: Located halfway down Maraş Cad., the street directly west of the main square. Open 24hr. **Postal Code:** 61000. **Telephone Code:** 462.

ACCOMMODATIONS

It's difficult to find a decent, quiet hotel in Trabzon. Most of the cheaper hotels cluster around **İskele Cad.,** which runs northeast off the main square. They offer cheerless, basic rooms, and many have degenerated into borderline-brothels. Since the opening of the Georgian border up the coast, Trabzon has been swarming with Russian tourists and shoppers. They fill every hotel and are not shy about socializing well into the night. The secret to a restful stay is to seek out *aile oteli* (family hotels), places that stake their reputations on their healthy atmosphere for children. Couples, however, may be asked to present proof of marriage at such hotels.

Otel Anıl, 10 Güzelhisar Cad. (tel. 321 9566), is a real find. Spic-and-span, carpeted rooms with bath, TV, telephones, and Western toilets. Laundry service. Singles $12; doubles $18; triples $24. Breakfast $1.35.

Villa Pension (tel 321 7788), near Uzun Sok., is a clean and peaceful establishment with shared showers. $5 per person.

Erzurum Oteli, 15 Güzelhisar Cad. near İskele Cad. (tel. 322 5427), next to the Anıl, shares Anıl's views of the harbor. Clean doubles have private baths. $5 per person.

Gözde Aile Oteli, 7 Salih Yazıcı Sok. (tel. 321 9579), offers average rooms with showers. Families like it because it seems safe and reliable. Breakfast and meals available in nearby restaurant. Doubles $10; triples $15; quads $18.

Hotel Benli (tel. 321 1750), 100m east of the main square's south edge. Offers clean, cool, quiet, and odor-free rooms with telephones. Benli's has outworn the luxury status it enjoyed at its opening in 1958, but its price and charm make up for bathless rooms and basic toilets. Singles $6.65; doubles $10; triples $13.50.

FOOD AND ENTERTAINMENT

Trabzon's local cuisine is an exotic melange of fresh Black Sea fish, corn, potatoes, and peas from the fertile highlands south of the city. Vegetarians can feast on a boiled or barbecued corn on the cob, sold on many street corners for $1. A **fruit and vegetable market** lies 1.5km west of the square along Maraş Cad. (open daily 6:30am-9pm). Downhill west of the Luna Park on the shore, you'll find a **fish market** (open daily 7am-8pm).

Gelik Lokantası, 84 Uzun Sok. (tel. 326 2445), serves the range of dishes you expect from a *lokanta* in an exemplary state of cleanliness.

Uludağ Kebap Salonu, 43 Uzun Sok. (tel. 321 4120), dishes out *kebap* with gusto. Open daily 7am-10pm.

Kilim Mantı Salonu, 46 Uzun Sok, offers a treat nearly unknown to tourists called *mantı.* It is a delicious pasta dish like tortellini served in yogurt and seasoned with garlic, mint, hot pepper, and melted butter ($1.75). Open Mon.-Sat. 9am-9pm.

Özgür Restaurant (tel. 321 1319), next to the Özgür Otel on the south end of the central square. It specializes in comfort food like pizza ($2-3.35) and cheeseburgers ($1.35); a nice place to eat when you need a break from *kebap* and *ayran.*

Görele Pide Salonu (tel. 326 2278), has famous Görele pita. The best may be the cheese pita with egg ($3).

Tad Pizza and Burger, on the northeast corner of the main square (tel. 321 1238), boasts a $1 salad bar and serves a curiosity called *aşure,* a fruity pudding (70¢).

Beton Helva, 21 Uzun Sok. (tel. 321 2550), is great for dessert. Try the 50¢ blocks of *helva,* a sesame seed confection, and 50¢ glasses of clear grape cider.

Blue Sea Bar, Kemerkaya Mah. Mektep Sok. 51A Sahil Cad. (tel. 322 2733), across the highway from the shore. Name says it all. Beer $1.25. Open daily 11am-1am.

Kıbrıs Restaurant, just off the main square, is a pleasant terrace bar overlooking the east side of the square. Tables by the railing have front row seats for the occasional folk dance shows in the square. Beer $1.25.

Trabzon's long seaside terrace makes for a pleasant stroll; at the west end lies an **amusement park,** featuring rides and a video arcade (admission 15¢). Squeaky clean rejuvenation can be had for $3.35, including scrub and massage, at **Sekiz Direkli Hamam,** Pazarkapı Mah. (tel. 322 1012). Constructed by the Seljuks c. 1073 BC and used until 1916, it was renovated seven years ago with marble and wood paneling (open daily 6am-11pm, Thurs. 8am-5pm reserved for women only). The *hamam* is a mere 2km walk west following Maraş Cad. from the main square to where it turns downhill (follow the signs). A taxi costs $2-3 from the tourist office.

SIGHTS

The **Russian Bazaar** *(Rus Pazarı)* is the closed market area on Sahil Yolu. Entrance will set you back 15¢, but you can join in a market where thousands of people exchange goods from the ex-Soviet states. Don't forget to bargain.

The oldest Christian structure in Trabzon is the tiny 7th-century **St. Anne Church.** Head west from the square on Maraş Cad.; it's behind a cluster of newsstands and trees on your left, just before the mosque. At the top of the hill behind the town is **Atatürk Köşkü,** one of Atatürk's villas built at the turn of the century by a rich Greek. Though Atatürk stayed here only twice, the popular villa is now a museum fat with photographs and paintings of the "Father Turk." *Dolmuş* marked "Atatürk Köşkü" depart from the main square frequently. (Open in summer daily 8am-noon and 1:30-7pm; in winter 8am-noon and 1-5pm. Admission for Turks 35¢, students 15¢; 65¢ for all foreigners.)

Romantically set in a rose garden overlooking the Black Sea, the lovely 13th-century **Aya Sofya** church was once part of a monastery. Now a museum, it features fine frescoes and carvings. From the lower end of the square, take a *dolmuş* (35¢) marked "Aya Sofya" (open daily 8am-noon and 1:30-5:30pm; admission $1, students 65¢). Right next to the church is another museum—a traditional Black Sea house. In the garden, there is a traditional grain-silo and a cafe which serves beverages and snacks.

Within the walls of the old city is the **Ortahisar Camii,** formerly Panagia Chrisoke-falos Church, the main basilica of medieval Trebizond. Due north of Ortahisar Camii, on Amasya Sok., is the house where Süleyman the Magnificent was born. A statue of the turbaned sultan stands guard at the newly restored building. Behind the town rises the hill of **Boztepe.** Some 2.5km farther back into the hills is an Armenian monastery at **Kaymakli** with frescoes almost as impressive as those at Aya Sofya. *Dolmuş* to **Rize** for factory fresh tea, and **Akçaabat,** renowned for its *köfte,* leave frequently from the shore-hugging highway.

■ Near Trabzon: Sumela Monastery

No where else in northwestern Anatolia is the region's Byzantine legacy so breathtak-ingly combined with its thickly forested cloud-scraping hills than at Sumela Monas-tery, 40km southwest of Trabzon. Founded in the 4th century by Greek monks who, according to tradition, were visited by the Holy Virgin in a dream, Sumela's structures are built into a cliff side cave which provides natural protection from the elements. Many of the structures standing date from the 9th century. The monastery's "inner chapel" is a spectacular treat even for those who may think they've seen it all in Byz-antine monastic decoration. Frescoes cover not only the chapel's interior, but also the exterior shielded from harsh winds and rains by the overhanging caves. The fres-coes portray scenes from the Old and New Testaments, Genesis through Revelation, as well as enthroned Byzantine emperors. Don't expect to see any monks, however. Tolerated by the Ottomans, they were sent during to Greece during the population exchange. As a result, the monastery's frescoes have decayed and those at ground level have been tattooed with Turkish, Greek, and English graffiti. Even in this tat-tered condition, they remain unique and impressive.

The monastery's other structures, including the residences and kitchen of the monks, are currently in the midst of a long process of restoration by the Turkish government. The monastery and adjoining national park are accessible by car or by private tours from Ülüsoy or Afaçan Tours ($2.75). The ride to the park takes an hour and is followed by a 30 minute hike through the park (admission $1) to the monastery. A hike back down and a lunch of fish at the Sumela Restaurant on the way back to Trabzon follows. Be sure not to be rushed along on your tour. Pause while hiking to soak in the views of the monastery and cloud-drenched environs. Stick your head out of a monk's bedroom window to get a glimpse of a natural panorama, which can't be very different from what surrounded Sumela's devotees for centuries.

EAST OF TRABZON

The towns along this segment of the Black Sea coast are interesting more for their cultural makeup and serene damp atmosphere than for the few historical monuments they house. Most are small, quiet port and industrial towns. The primordial wildlands to the south are a sultry velvet of dense jungle and mist softening the jagged landscape. *Yayla,* or highland campgrounds, dapple the mountains, where natives of this region gather from as far away as Holland and Germany to relax and renew their cultural ties. Farther inland, people maintain autonomous, centuries-old traditions and styles of dress. The best places for campers to find an uncultivated spot are by the highway, on *yayla,* or along riverbanks. Locals are witty, welcoming, and hospitable; just respect their customs.

■ Uzungöl

Uzungöl, a pristine **trout-filled lake** hemmed in by steep fir-packed mountains, is 98km out of Trabzon via Çaykara. The slow and lumpy 20km ride from Çaykara follows a white water stream past hillsides of terraced hazelnut trees and corn. You'll see the lake as soon as the trademark twin yellow minarets poke into view. Continue 3km upstream by a small dam and out to a *yayla.* Between the lake and the dam, a handful of new hotel and restaurant complexes have sprung up to accommodate Turkish families, who come as much for the famous trout and rice pudding as for the scenery. Alcohol is not sold in Uzungöl. Campers either stake their tents for free upstream from the dam or at some of the hotels; indoor accommodations are on the expensive side.

ORIENTATION AND PRACTICAL INFORMATION

Reaching Uzungöl is a scenic adventure. From Trabzon, you can't reach Uzungöl directly unless you take a daytrip organized by a tourist agency. **Çaykara Tur** (tel. 322 5509) accepts phone reservations for its $12 tours. The tours leave Trabzon between 9 and 10am and return between 3 and 4pm. Otherwise, you can take a **dolmuş** marked "Çaykara" from the office of Çaykara Tur behind Trabzon's Russian bazaar *(Rus Pazari). Dolmuş* depart Çaykara every hour on the hour (7:30am-5:30pm, 1½hr., $1.35). From Çaykara, another *dolmuş* marked "Uzungöl" (every hr., 65¢) drops passengers off in front of the mosque with the twin minarets. We strongly recommend that you take a tour. Be aware that the journey is quite bumpy. Try to avoid weekends when the roads are extremely crowded.

ACCOMMODATIONS AND FOOD

Majestic cloud-ringed mountains, excellent fishing, and cool climate are reason enough for a visit. Uzungöl boasts neither ancient monuments nor interesting museums. Visitors come here to fish, swim, soak up the scenery, and relax. Some pleasant little pensions are scattered around the lake. Perhaps the best bargain is the **Uzungöl Pansiyon** (tel. (462) 656 6129), on the main road between the mosque and the lake. Free laundry ($3.75 per person, with bath; breakfast $1). The most famous and best

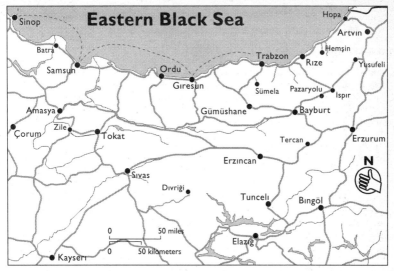

Eastern Black Sea

established resort is **İnan Kardeşler** (tel. (462) 656 6074) which boasts the area's **best restaurant.** Beautiful wooden two-person bungalows are $20 (breakfast included). Try to make reservations a week ahead. The cozy three-bedroom bungalows at **Orman Işletme Tesisleri** (tel. (462) 656 6010), across the lake, make superb bonding spots for up to eight people ($15 per bungalow). The brand-new **Önal Motel** offers great rooms with bathrooms and TVs for only $6.70 per person (breakfast included). It's right across from İnan Kardeşler. Ask for a second floor room.

For dinner, the restaurant at the **Sezgin Motel,** across the street from the motel, grills red-spotted trout from their farm ($3.50 per plate), which you can follow up with fresh rice pudding ($1). Near the PTT, **Gülalioğlu Restaurant** offers fresh fish and typical Turkish fare for low prices (full meal $3.15-4.50).

■ Rize

Rize is the tea capital of Turkey. Tourists are often directed to the hills south of town, where the Ministry of Agriculture conducts high level R&D in special tea labs, greenhouses, and gardens. If tea theory and research isn't your cup of tea, you may view Rize as merely a necessary overnight stop on the Black Sea highway.

ORIENTATION AND PRACTICAL INFORMATION

The main street in Rize is **Atatürk Cad.** Hotels and pensions line Atatürk Cad., Rize's main drag. Restaurants, shops, and teahouses line this and the parallel **Cumhuriyet Cad.** A large tea garden with a fountain is in the west part of town. In fact, all you'll probably see of Rize is packed into a kilometer of Atatürk Cad. West of the tea garden, by the mosque, is the **PTT** near the Atatürk statue (open daily 8:30am-5:30pm, mail service open 8:30am-12:30pm and 1:30-5:30pm). The **tourist office** (tel. 213 0408) is on the fourth floor of the Özel Idare Tessisleri, a building on the shore in the east part of town. They offer a brochure and general information, but their English skills may leave a little to be desired; you can probably get equally good advice from **travel agencies** (open Mon.-Fri. 8:30am-5:30pm). Try **Ritur** (tel. 217 8848; email i.h.yildiz@ihlas.net.tr). For **police** call either 213 0374 or, in an **emergency,** 155. The **state hospital** provides 24hr. service (tel. 213 0491). There is a **Turkish Airlines (THY)** office on Cumhuriyet Cad. (tel. 213 0591; open Mon.-Fri. 8:30am-5:30pm).

Dolmuş operate from the *otogar* to the town center. **Buses** head to all major Turkish cities at least once per day. Most destinations between Trabzon and Hopa are best left to highway *dolmuş* (under $3.50), but if you want to reach Trabzon in better time, with more space, and less cost, **Pamukkale Turizm** buses pass down the coastal highway (every 20min., $2.25). The **telephone code** is 464.

ACCOMMODATIONS AND FOOD

Budget rooms abound in Rize, but be prepared to be asked to produce proof of marriage if you are traveling as a couple. **Otel Efes** (tel. (464) 217 7555), two blocks up Atatürk Cad. across from Akbank, is sparkling clean. All rooms have bath and TV. (Singles $15; doubles $22.50; triples $30.) For a sea view, try **Otel Turist,** 26 Atatürk Cad. (tel. (464) 217 2009), east of the Otel Efes. Rooms are large, clean, and well furnished, most with bath, balcony, and TV. (Singles $15; doubles $25; triples $30. 20% student discount.) Another option is the **Keleş Hotel** (tel. 217 8641, fax 217 1895), near Cumhuriyet Cad. The rooms have TV, bath, and fridge ($13 per person). For an excellent cheap meal, try the **Bekiroğlu Restaurant,** 161 Cumhuriyet Cad. (tel. (464) 217 1380), near the Otel Efes (*kebap* $2.75). **Koğu** chain restaurants offer the best *kebap* ($3) in town as well as vegetarian options. The original is next to Otel Turist.

SIGHTS

To reach the **tea lab,** follow the road from the PTT by the central mosque about 800m to the hilltop (open daily 10am-5pm, sometimes later in the summer). Enjoy the Tea Research Institute's tea garden while sipping some of the best tea on the continent. **Atatürk's House and Ethnographic Museum** is on Müftü Mah, 2 Kirazlık Cad. (tel. 213 0425). This is the house where Atatürk stayed when he visited Rize in 1924 (open Tues.-Sun. 9am-noon and 1-5pm). The **Rize Kalesi** is a small stone fortress built on a 160m hill with a view of the town. Several other **highland** areas surround the region including Elevit with a waterfall, Palovit with a crater lake, Cimil with thermal baths, Anzer with its famous honey, and Kavrun with excellent camping and hiking.

■ Ayder

Forty kilometers east of Rize, in the Hemşin Valley of the Kaçkar range, is the mountain resort of Ayder (EYE-dare). The timber houses nestled in thick forests of this mist-shrouded village look as if they sprouted from the mountainside. On the forested far side of the valley, a slender brook cascades over crags fed by the melting snow at the mountain's peak, joining a roaring stream on the valley floor. The ebullience and colorful dress of the native Hemşin people are as good a reason to visit Ayder as the towering majesty of the site.

ORIENTATION AND PRACTICAL INFORMATION

If it weren't for the modern hot springs facility in the center, Ayder would look like an Alaskan gold-mining town. The one-street village houses a tiny **PTT** by the Ayder "Hilton" (open daily 8:30am-5:30pm). The booths of two rival **dolmuş** companies face each other across the main road. **Ulusoy** (tel. (462) 321 1281) buses leave Trabzon Ulusoy terminal at 8am ($3.35) and Rize at 9am ($2.35), returning at 5pm. There are also *dolmuş* to Çamlıhemşin (80¢) and to Pazar ($1.50). To go to Hopa, get the Pazar minibus and connect from there. Minibuses also run up to the *yayla* of Avusor (5km, $1.50), Lower Kavron (7km, $2.25), and Upper Kavron (12km, $2.25). Believe it or not, Ayder charges an **admission fee.** Your 50¢ will be collected upon entrance from an attendant in a booth 4km from the center of town. For **trekking information,** you should contact Kardelen Pansiyon or Pirikoğlu.

ACCOMMODATIONS AND FOOD

Because of the proximity of the springs, few hotels have any sort of shower. Most charge a standardized price of $5 per person. For rooms with bath, **Otel Ayder** (tel. (464) 657 2039, -40), the big, white, institutional building at the lower end of the main road, has six doubles. The rooms are clean to the point of sterility. (Open June-Sept. Singles $5; doubles with bath $13.) In the center of town is the inappropriately named **Ayder Hilton Hotel** (tel. (464) 657 2024; open March-Nov.). Rooms are

The Hemşin

Travelers in Ayder and the nearby valley may be astonished to discover the Hemşin, a merry, sometimes outrageous people that are distinctly different from the often solemn Central Anatolians. The Hemşin are said to have come from Georgia in recent times and to have lived isolated in the mountains until roughly 150 years ago. Intrepid and independent, they are known for their hospitality, revelry, and jovial drinking of *raki*. Although many Hemşin have moved to large cities and opened sweet shops for which they are famed, roughly 15,000 still live in the Hemşin Valley. Hemşin women wear brightly colored silk turbans imported from India, perhaps because the valley was once a stop on the silk road. To attempt to understand the Hemşin psychology, visit one of their *yayla* or summer villages. These tightly bunched shanty towns are inhabited during summer months by Hemşin who come from as far as Holland and Germany to get in touch with their homeland.

clean, but nothing more ($3.35-$4.65 per person; breakfast $1; lunch, dinner $3.35). Camping is free beyond the *yayla* and the cluster of buildings above it. That's also where you'll find the **Kardelen Pansion** (tel. (464) 657 2107), the secluded den of Muhammet Önçırak, mountain man and tour guide extraordinaire. Before ascending into the Kaçkars, you should consult the military issue map hanging on his wall (five drafty rooms available June-Aug.; $5 per person). Right near the PTT, **Hotel Saray** is a clean place to stay, but the rooms don't have a bath ($5 per person). Reservations a week ahead are advised.

Ayder is a good place to try *muhlama,* a melted mix of cheese, butter, and corn flour that looks like mashed potatoes and behaves like fondue. For a wholesome meal, try **Pirikoğlu Lokantası** (tel. (464) 657 2021). The owner, Adnan Pirikoğlu, is a good source of mountain information and will guide groups for about $50 per day. Try the local specialties *katneraç* (soup made of corn flour, milk, and butter, $1.35) and the desert (35¢). Full meals are $3.50 (open May-Oct. daily 6am-11pm). **Saray Et ve Balık Tesisler** (tel. (464) 657 2142) offers trout and grilled meat (full meal $5-6). If you are looking for a little something alcoholic, go to **Korkutlar Mini Market** (tel. (464) 657 2025). For **groceries** and local specialties like Ayder honey, tea, and "tea cologne," check out the really cheap **Kalkınma Kooperatifi Tanzim Satiş Reyonu.**

HOT SPRINGS

There are **hot springs** housed in a squat, steaming edifice completed only a few years ago. A dip in the marble bathing pools is an exhausting pleasure; as blood charges through every capillary in your body, you'll come to believe the legends about the curative effects of the water. (Open April-Oct. daily 7am-8pm. Regular bath $1.65, private bath $6.65.) The time limit for using the baths is one hour, but you won't want to stay in for more than five minutes.

■ Hopa

The Black Sea Highway continues along the coast from Ayder for roughly 60km, finally turning inland at Hopa. Like many of its fellow coastal cities, Hopa is void of tourist diversions, but is not an unpleasant place to spend a night if the need arises. Many stay in Hopa before visiting the Turkish border with Georgia in Sarp, just 30km away. Trade is lively in the dynamic border region, but the "highway" to Georgia is in terrible condition. The Kopmuş, Kemalpaşa, and Sarp **beaches** on the way to Sarp are theoretically used for swimming, but they aren't too clean. *Let's Go* does not recommend travel to Georgia due to a powerful extortionist mafia and periodic fighting.

ORIENTATION AND PRACTICAL INFORMATION

Most of Hopa lies on one of two streets. Several cafes and hotels are on **Cumhuriyet Cad.** and hotels, cafes, and other services are on the parallel **Orta Hopa Cad.,** behind

Cumhuriyet. Orta Hopa has Hopa's **PTT,** which provides the usual mail, telephone, and **currency exchange** services (open daily 8:30am-12:30pm and 1:30-5:30pm). Akbank and several others on the same street provide **ATMs** and currency exchange. Hopa's *dolmuş* and **bus stations** lie west of the bridge into town. *Dolmuş* and buses travel to all major cities once or twice per day. *Dolmuş* run every 20-30 minutes to nearby towns.

ACCOMMODATIONS AND FOOD

The best place to stay in Hopa is the **Hotel Papila** (tel. (466) 351 3641), located on the seashore on the eastern end of Hopa and has a nice view. It has a great view along with TV, bath, phone, 24hr. hot water, and a balcony with every room (singles $13; doubles $20; Visa accepted). Their restaurant also offers surprisingly delicious food. **Otel Huzur,** 25 Cumhuriyet Cad. (tel. (466) 351 4095), bills itself as "your home in Hopa," and indeed it could be. With clean, spacious rooms, A/C, showers, and bathrooms in each room, Huzur's prices are unbeatable (singles $3.35, $5 with bath; doubles $6.70, $10 with bath). **Otel Köşk,** 21 Orta Hopa Cad. (tel. (466) 351 3501), is meticulously clean and most rooms have bathrooms (singles $10; doubles $16.65; triples $23.25). Another clean and reliable hotel is **Hotel Ustabaş** (tel. (466) 351 5452), a luxurious resort with bath, phone, and a TV in each room. The staff is professional and friendly (singles $16.65; doubles $23.25; V/MC accepted). It also has a restaurant with live music.

Right at the entrance of the Hotel Ustabaş is the **Ustabaş Pide Kebap Restaurant,** where you can enjoy great pitas for $2-3. Just a few doors down from Otel Huzur, on the waterfront, **Beslen Lokantası** (tel. (466) 351 4957) offers an array of cheap, fresh, and finely prepared dishes (full meal $3.15-4.40).

■ Artvin

Chiseled into the mountain pass is the eerily tranquil town of Artvin, providing panoramic views of a largely deforested valley. The 15th-century citadel overlooking the highway, which both Georgians and the English sought to control within the last 100 years, receives few tourists today since Turkish soldiers still use it. Never mind, though—the nameless road that ribbons 5km up the mountainside to central Artvin puts the tower in its place; the view only gets better.

ORIENTATION AND PRACTICAL INFORMATION

Upon entering town, you may notice that lots of people carry guns. This should inspire a certain bit of caution during your visit to Artvin.

In vertical terms, the town occupies the space bounded by the **hospital** above and the **bus station** below, near the fortress by the river. Most bus companies have shuttle minibus services free of charge. You could also take a public bus (every 15-30min., 50¢). They all go to the center of town, the main street **İnönü Cad.,** home to hotels, restaurants, a *dolmuş* lot, a 24-hour **PTT** (İnönü Cad. 45), and a tea garden. This is really all you need in Artvin. There is a small **tourist office** (tel. (466) 212 3071) in Camii Meydanı, to the right of İnönü Cad. as you walk uphill. It has maps and brochures (open daily 8:30am-12:30pm and 1:30-5:30pm). Since Artvin's roads have the scariest turns and Turkey's most notorious drivers, stick to the town's main bus companies—Metro and Lüks Artvin Seychat. They service all the major cities in Turkey.

ACCOMMODATIONS AND FOOD

Many of Artvin's hotels feature low prices and good locations, but some are also frequented by prostitutes. A trio of clean, cordial, and untainted budget hotels hide down the stairs on the left side of İnönü Cad. as you walk uphill towards the *dolmuş* stop. The best hotel in Artvin is **Hotel Karahan** (tel. (466) 212 1800) on İnönü Cad. To reach the hotel, enter the building and take the elevator to the fourth floor. The rooms have TV, bath, phone, and a balconies with panoramic views. The hotel has a bar and restaurant, safe deposit, and an experienced, friendly staff (singles $30; doubles $50). It also boasts a travel agency which is open daily (8am-8pm) and has THY tickets and also helps with hunting tours. This travel agency is the best source of information and help in Artvin. The **Kaçkar Oteli** (tel. (466) 212 3397) has carpets, central heating, and shower. Some rooms have TV. They also offer free use of washing machine (singles $5; doubles $10; triples $16.65). **Otel Güven** (tel. (466) 212 1118), next door, offers large rooms, some with panoramic views. Hot water is unreliable and showers cost $1.25 each, but the manager speaks English ($3.75 per person). The state-run resort of **Köy Hizmetleri** has hot water and big rooms. It's clean and the service is great, but it tends to be full during festivals ($6.65 per person).

The watering hole for Artvin's elite, the **Hanedan Restaurant** (tel. (466) 212 7222) has a bar and porch with a view of the valley (*kebap* and beer $3; open daily 8am-11pm). Bar and view also come with the excellent food at **Nazar Restoranı** (tel. (466) 212 1709), at the lower end of İnönü Cad. It's decorated with bizarre posters and features delicious *meze* (open daily 10am-midnight). If you want to eat grilled meat and pickled plants from Artvin, try **Livane Restaurant.** In the evening, **Çağdaş Gazinosu** has live music after 8pm (open daily 9am-midnight).

For *rakı* and *meze*, **Ekfar Restaurant** at the intersection of İnönü Cad. and Ekfar Cad. offers the best view of the valley. The real bargain restaurant in town, **Saklıca Restaurant** ($2 per meal), is also the best hidden. To reach it, enter the narrow stairway opposite Karahan Hotel and turn left. Their menu includes several good vegetarian options.

SIGHTS AND ENTERTAINMENT

Artvin is close to many *yayla* that locals visit in summer. The plateau of **Kafkasör,** 11km from Artvin, hosts an annual **festival** on the third weekend of June. Kafkasör is technically a national park, and it is one of the most famous *yayla* of Turkey. Thousands of people gather here each year. The great view and the peaceful forest makes it a nice place to overnight.

Traditional dances and other performances are frequent, but the main events are **bullfights.** The bulls "wrestle" each other like the camels in Manisa, near Izmir. The winner's owner is honored; the bull gets squat. Kafkasör has the only bullfighting arena in Turkey. Artvin's Ottoman **hamam** (tel. 212 1158) is just down the street (open daily for both sexes 6am-10pm; bath $1.50, massage $1.50, scrub $1).

▓ Yusufeli

The small town of Yusufeli, stretching along the Barhal River, is fast becoming the **whitewater rafting** capital of Turkey. Too dangerous to raft before June, the famous Çoruh River, site of a 1993 rafting championship, passes only 6km away. Yusufeli's dry south side on the Kaçkar range also makes it an ideal trekking center.

ORIENTATION AND PRACTICAL INFORMATION

The tourist center of Yusufeli is the rectangular area remaining inside four streets named after Turkish politicians with military backgrounds: **Enver Paşa Cad., Fevsi Gakmak Cad., Mustafa Kemal Cad.,** and **İnönü Cad.** Most hotels occupy the upstream end of **İnönü Cad.** which passes the *otogar* lot, **pharmacies,** some decent alcohol-free restaurants, and eventually the **PTT** (open daily 7:30am-5pm) at the downstream end of town. The local **hospital** can be reached at (466) 811 2015. *Dolmuş* minibuses leave Yusufeli for Barhal, Uzundere, Hevek, and other nearby *yaylas* at least once a day in summer. Buses also run to most major Turkish cities.

ACCOMMODATIONS AND FOOD

Despite the increasing level of tourism here, the hotels are still not very developed or comfortable. Moreover, they are usually stuffed with trekkers and rafters. Always try to make reservations ahead of time.

The **Hotel Barhal** (tel. (466) 811 3151), on Asma Köprübaşı Cad., stands out for its private baths and river view and is probably the best place to stay ($3.35 per person). The owner rents six- and eight-person rafts and equipment at reasonable prices. And if there's no vacancy, you can ask the owner to arrange you a room in **Orman Tesisleri** (the Forest Ministry's resort). **Otel Keleş** (tel. (466) 811 2305), on the corner of İnönü Cad. and Halit Paşa Cad., features quality mattresses in modern, carpeted rooms with shared bath. Free laundry ($2.65 per person). The **Hotel Çiçek Palas,** 30 Halit Paşa Cad. (tel. (466) 811 2393), off İnönü Cad., offers clean, concrete-floored rooms, shared baths, and use of a stove ($3.35 per person).

One of the cleaner and more popular meeting places for tourists and nature lovers is **Çınar Lokantası** (tel. (466) 811 2365), overlooking the river beneath the Hotel Barhal. Its offerings include grilled meat, delicious trout, *rakı*, and vegetarian *meze* like *piyaz, pilaki,* and potato salad (open daily 9am-midnight; full meal $3.35). Blue inside and out, the **Mavi Köşk Restorant** (tel. (466) 811 2329), downhill from Hotel Barhal off İnönü Cad., is clean and has good food with a well-stocked bar (open daily 8am-1am; full meal $3.35). For tea and beverages, try **Pelanı Yeri** (tel. (466) 811 2008) opposite Hotel Barhal, which has tea for just 20¢. **Mahzen Restaurant,** next to Palanın Yeri, offers drinks next to Yusufeli's wooden suspension bridge (beer $1). **Yeni Sara Lokantası** (tel. (466) 811 3465) may not be a palace, but it does offer good vegetarian dishes ($1.50-2.35). For groceries the best alternative is **Tema Hipermarket,** on İnönü Cad., which has everything—even original German Haribo sweets. The air-conditioned store is open 9am-11pm and accepts Visa.

■ The Çoruh Valley

Yusufeli makes an excellent base for exploring the Çoruh Valley, home to half a dozen 10th-century **Georgian churches.** Begun in 730 AD and finished three centuries later, the **Işhan** church (35km from Yusufeli) was enhanced by a Byzantine dome in 1200 AD before its stewardship passed back into Georgian hands. The pilgrimage to Işhan is doubly worthwhile if only for the road's spectacular mountainscapes of tilted strata and ravine-wrinkled cliffs. The facade of the airy **Öşk Vank** church (50km from Yusufeli) has been preserved marvelously and features carvings of angels, patrons, and animals. If you are in the area, stop by; this is one of the most beautiful Georgian churches anywhere. Above the entrance you'll find a colorful band of frescoed faces next to the image of a church that may be Öşk Vank itself. From **Tekkale Village** (6km from Yusufeli), a rough, walkable road follows the stream for another 7km to a steep bank 50m below **Dörtkilise.** The ground outside makes good, free camping. Before ascending the Kaçkars, consider staying in Tekkale Village's little-known country pension **Dörtkilise Resting Camp** (tel. (466) 811 2908).

It's hard to get to the **Barhal church** (33km from Yusufeli), now a locked mosque whose main attractions are a few exterior carvings of small crosses, a lion, and a bird. The road to Barhal church passing through Sarıgöl by Barhal River has several fortresses nearby. Pay attention to the left bank of the river.

If you travel south toward Haho, you'll pass the pea-green **Tortum Lake,** supposedly formed 630 years ago when the peak of Mt. Hars collapsed into the Çoruh River valley. Locals claim there's a mosque on the lake floor and remnants of an inundated village. The Çoruh's real treat here, however, is **Tortum Falls,** a natural 50m cascade that the government turned into a hydroelectric plant in the 1950s. The **Şelale Tesisleri** restaurant owns a breathtaking view except mid-June through August, when the dam diverts the water. The falls are easily reached from the Erzurum highway which passes within 1km of them. You can tell the driver "Şelale" and sit back to enjoy the view—warped faces of mountain strata like one huge, prehistoric chunk of *baklava* ripped by time. A daily *dolmuş* departs from Yusufeli for each of the three nearby church villages in the afternoon, but doesn't return until morning. **Taxis** tour the area, but aren't cheap: İşhan $18; Öşk Vank $33; Dörtkilise $6; Barhal $45; and Haho $33. From the village of Uzundere, you can catch cheaper taxis to Öşk Vank and Haho.

Mediterranean Coast

During the second and first millennia BC, the area around Fethiye and Kaş formed the Kingdom of Lycia. The Lyceans, who reveled in fancy burial rites and monuments, are not remembered for much else. Rock tombs are carved into cliffs all along the coast, and Lycean sarcophagi litter the Lycean countryside and near-shore islands. The most significant of the Lycean cities remain in ruins at Xanthos and Patara.

Extending from the edges of Greece to the Syrian border, Turkey's Mediterranean coast is alternately chic, garish, and remote. Pine forests, hidden coves, and sandy beaches dot the stretch between Fethiye and Antalya. The swimming and sunbathing opportunities here are among the best in the world; thousands of visitors each year claim they've found "heaven on earth" in the Turkish coves and islands. Accommodations along the western segment of the Mediterranean coast are generally inexpensive. Farther east, broad ribbons of sand and concrete speckled with castles and ruins mark this stretch of shoreline, often called the "Turquoise Coast."

Distances on maps are deceiving: beyond Fethiye, the road winds through mountain terrain and becomes as slow as it is scenic. Boats run between northern Cyprus and the ports of Taşucu and Mersin; travel to southern Cyprus is impossible.

FETHIYE COAST

▓ Fethiye

The modern town of Fethiye is situated near the ruins of ancient Telmessos. Founded in the 4th century BC, this Lycean city was notorious for its astrologers, star gazers, palm readers, and oracles. The city fell under successive foreign regimes until the Knights of St. John or the Templar eventually built a fortress on top of the city's ruins. The Lycean Necropolis, which houses a tomb, survived a devastating 1958 earthquake that leveled everything else in Fethiye, although old-style architecture and winding, cobble-stone streets persist in the town to this day. With plenty of inexpensive pensions, Fethiye is a convenient base to explore the 12 islands of the Fethiye Gulf and is 15km from the famous Ölüdeniz, known for its spectacular sand beaches.

ORIENTATION AND PRACTICAL INFORMATION

Buses drop off at the bus station some 5km from the center of town, on the way to Ölüdeniz. If your bus company does not have coach service to the town center, simply leave the terminal and wait for a *dolmuş* heading to Fethiye. Hustlers working on commission may approach you to offer you a "good deal" for a room, and may even offer you a ride, but keep in mind that they usually charge more than the going rate. To find the **tourist office,** İskele Meydanı No. 1/A (tel. 612 1975), start walking down Atatürk Cad. after the last *dolmuş* stop, past the PTT, and down the road along the harborfront (where it becomes Fevzi Çakmak Sok.). It's on the waterfront across from the marina (open in summer 8:30am-7pm, in winter 8am-5pm). The **police** are next to the tourist office (tel. 614 1040; **emergency,** 155). Fetur, a **travel agency,** is next to the ancient theater on Fevzi Çakmak Sok. (tel. 614 2034, -2443). It has a full line of tourist services (open Mon.-Sat. 9am-7:30pm and Sun. 11am-7:45pm). You can **rent mopeds** at Abalı Rent, on the same street, starting at $20 per day (tel. 614 7979, -5412; open 8am-midnight). A **hospital** is on Atatürk Cad. near the final *dolmuş* stop (tel. 614 1499; for services 614 4017, -8). Several **pharmacies** are on Atatürk Cad, across from the PTT, as are several **banks** and **currency exchange offices.** Buses leave from the *otogar* on the road to the Ölüdeniz (tel. 614 3531) to: Antalya (12 per day, 4hr., $4.50); Marmaris (every hour, 3hr., $3.40); Bodrum (3 per day, 5hr., $6); Kuşadası via Selçuk (6½hr., $7.40); Izmir (11 per day, 7hr., $10); Istanbul (4 per day,

12hr., $20); Ankara (3 per day, 9hr., $13.40); and Bursa (2 per day, 12hr., $13.40). Frequent *dolmuş* service is available to Çalış Beach and Ölüdeniz from the *dolmuş* garage adjacent to the *otogar*. The **PTT**, on Atatürk Cad. near the Hamam Sok. area, is open 8am-midnight. The **postal code** is 48300; **telephone code,** 252.

ACCOMMODATIONS

Clean, inexpensive pensions can be found along **Sahil Yolu** (past the hospital on your left), as well as **Çarşı Cad.**

Pension Çetin, 100 Cad. Dolgu Sahası DSİ Yanı (tel. 614 6156; fax 614 7794), off Sahil Yolu near the Yakar. A clean pension with toilets, showers, and balconies in most rooms. Singles $6.70; doubles $13.40. Breakfast $1.50.

Yakar Motel, Sahil Yolu DSİ Yanı 14 (tel. 614 1557), along the harbor on the road to Çalış beach. Decent rooms with gorgeous views of the harbor. Has a shady, vine-covered terrace and lounge. Singles $6.70; doubles $13.40. Breakfast $1.50.

Ülgen Pension, Cumhuriyet Mah. Paspatur Mevkii Merdiven 3 (tel. 614 3491), high up in the Çarşı Cad. area. Clean enough rooms with gorgeous views of the town and rock tombs. Some rooms have private toilets and showers. Singles $5; doubles $10. Breakfast $1.50.

Özkan Pension (tel. 613 2020), at the very end of the boardwalk area at Çalış Beach (to your right, facing the water). Clean rooms with screens on all windows. Toilets, showers, and 24hr. hot water. Singles $6.70; doubles $13.40.

FOOD AND ENTERTAINMENT

Visitors to Fethiye can find several delicious eating spots near Çarşı Cad. area. Dining options near the harborside tend to be more pricey. On Çalış Beach across the harbor there's a boardwalk with restaurants, bars, and cafes, all with views of Fethiye.

Mağri Lokantası, Cumhuriyet Mah. Çarşı Cad. No 13/A (tel. 614 4074), a few doors down from the Pamukkale office. This is the less fancy of the two Mağri restaurants, but equally good in taste and atmosphere. Simple interior design with A/C. *Soğuk mezeler* $1.35, fish $6. Open until midnight.

Sedir Restaurant, Tütün Sok. No. 3 (tel. 614 1095), around the corner from the Mağri. Elegant outdoor seating. Serves pizza, including vegetarian varieties (ask for an "Americano"). Pizzas $2.50-4, grills $4. Open 9am-11pm.

Birlik Lokantası (tel. 612 2896), on Atatürk Cad., diagonal from the PTT. Come for complete traditional Turkish meals and ask to visit the kitchen to see what's fresh for the day. Rice $1, *soğuk mezeler* $1.70, grills $2.70. Open until midnight.

Rıhtım Pastanesi, Cumhuriyet Mah. Çarşı Cad. 13/3 (tel. 612 3831), on the same street as the Mağri and Pamukkale office. Don't worry about not having time for dessert; this *pastane* is open 24hr.

Disco Marina (tel. 614 9860), on Fevzi Çalmak Sok., past the tourist office moving away from town. You can't miss this club's signs posted everywhere. Open late.

The Music Factory (tel. 612 3778), on Hamam Sok., is a tourist favorite with outdoor seating. Open late.

SIGHTS

The road north into Fethiye ascends steep hillsides thick with pine trees and crickets. Isolated from the rest of Asia Minor, this region permitted the development of an insulated Lycean culture in ancient times. Believed to be the descendants of a pre-Hittite Anatolian people, the Lyceans remained independent until their quixotic stand against Cyrus' Persian armies in 545 BC. The city of tombs that remains, the **Necropolis of Telmessos,** is the most apparent remnant of Lycean culture (open 9am-6pm; admission $1). The facades of the cliff-hewn tombs replicate Greek temples down to the pediments, porticos, and cornices. The tombs themselves are thought to be facsimiles of Lycean homes. From the necropolis, the remains of the **Fethiye Tower** are visible. Connected to the road by several flights of steps just off Kaya Cad. (off Atatürk

Mediterranean Coast

SYRIA

Harbiye
Hatay (Antakya)
Adana
el (Mersin)
Silifke
Taşucu

Kuzey Kıbrıs
Cumhuriyeti
(Turkish Republic of
Northern Cyprus)

Gazimagusa

Karaman
Hotamış Lake
Konya
Anamur
Gazipaşa

Girne
Lefkoşa

G ney Kıbrıs Rum Y netimi
(Greek Cypriot Administration of Southern Cyprus)

G zelsu
Alanya

Beyşehir Lake
Aspendos
Perge
Side

Antalya Körfezi
(Antalya Gulf)

Eğirdir Lake
Isparta
Aksu
Antalya
Kemer
Olimpos

Acıgöl Lake
Burdur Lake

Kumluca
Finike
Demre
Kekova Ada

Akdeniz (Mediterranean Sea)

Denizli

Fethiye
Kalkan
Kaş

Meyisti
(Meis)

Leton
Patara
deniz

Dalyan
Dalaman

Muğla
Marmaris
Dat a

Rodos
(Rhodes)

Aydın
Knidos

Bodrum

Sel uk
Kuşadası
Sisam
(Sámos)
İstanköy (Kos)

İzmir
eşme

N

Ferry

80 miles

80 kilometers

ANATOLIA

Cad.) is the **Tomb of Amyntas,** identifiable by a 4th-century BC inscription on the left-hand column. Climb the 150 steps to the tomb to find a tiny chamber beyond the opening. Amyntas was thought to be a son of Hermapilas and a governor of Telmessos during the Hellenistic Period. You can enter the other tombs as well, though to reach them you must clamber around the rocks. The **Archaeological Museum,** one block down from the hospital towards the bus station, contains Lycean artifacts from neighboring digs (open in summer Tues.-Sun. 8am-7pm; in winter 8am-5pm; admission 70¢, students 35¢). There is a 400-year-old **Turkish bath** *(hamam)* located on Hamam Sok. No. 2, Paspatur Bazaar (tel. 614 9318). Full services include scrubdown, soap massage, and oil massage (open 7am-midnight; $10). Facilities for men and women.

Fethiye is also a perfect place to take a boat trip out to nearby islands. Operators typically offer a 12 island tour, or the Ölüdeniz and Butterfly Valley trip. Twelve island tours usually stop at Göcek Island for a quick swim, continue to the resort town Göcek, then on to Flat Island and finally to the Dock-Yard Island (where the ruins of an Ottoman dock-yard can be seen from the water). Other stops include **Cleopatra's Bath** (where bathing in the spring is said to make you look 10 years younger), the Step Cave, and tea at **Somanlık Bay.** Tours leave Fethiye at 10am and return to port at 6pm. They cost about $10, lunch and tea included.

The second kind of tour stops by the **Butterfly Valley** first, where church ruins are still visible. At **Ölüdeniz,** one can see the famous beach before going to the hot and cold thermal springs. The tour concludes with a stop at **St. Nicholas Island** and **Kueli Bay** for tea. Boats leave at 10am, returning at 6pm ($16.70, lunch and tea included).

■ Ölüdeniz

The highly romanticized Blue Lagoon is materialized in the serene, crystal clear lagoon of Ölüdeniz. While you have probably seen posters of this partially enclosed beach hanging on the walls of most Turkish hotels, no picture can convey the sheer beauty of this legendary site.

ORIENTATION AND PRACTICAL INFORMATION

Even from the east, visitors go to Ölüdeniz via Fethiye. During the summer, *dolmuş* depart the main minibus station every 10-15minute, 7:30am-11:30pm. The *dolmuş* to Ölüdeniz stop at a pebble beach; Ölüdeniz and most of its cheaper hotels are farther right, facing the water. To the left there is a string of bars, campgrounds, and restaurants. There is no tourist office, but the **Tourism Cooperative** (tel. 616 6950, -2), just up the Fethiye road from where it runs into the beach, helps with rooms and arranges boat trips and parasailing excursions (open 9am-midnight). The town has **grocery stores** and a **PTT** (open April-Oct. 9am-10pm) 50m to the right from the entrance to the lagoon. The **phones** in the PTT have been unreliable in the past; try the ones scattered around town. You can **exchange currency** at some of the larger campsites and at the grocery store to the right behind Derya Camping. **English-language newspapers** and magazines can be found at the newsstands along the beach. For **police,** call 616 6005. The **postal code** is 48300. The **telephone code** is 252.

ACCOMMODATIONS

Asmalı Camping (tel. 617 0137), located on the road past Tobiat Park's entrance just beyond Ölüdeniz Camping, is smaller than its neighbors, but it does offer extremely clean toilets and showers as well as a small **restaurant** near the road. Rented tents are new and clean (doubles $10). Bungalows are also clean and screened against mosquito assaults ($11.70). They also have regular **rooms** with baths ($20). **Ölüdeniz Camping** (tel. 617 0181) is roughly 300m north from the exit (to the right as you face the water), past the municipal beach, and not to be confused with Ölüdeniz Pension on the exit road. The site is a bit remote but is set at the edge of the lagoon and includes a small beach, market, and restaurant. They charge $1.65 per person, Tarzan-like tree house camping is $2 per person, $5 for 2-person caravans with electricity, and $8.75 per double bungalow. Breakfast is $1.65, and other meals are $3.75. **Deniz Camping** (tel. 616 6012; fax 616 6008) is to the left of the exit road facing the water. The ebullient Anthia Gurkan, an Englishwoman, is an experienced guide who can reserve plane and bus tickets as well as arrange trekking and paragliding adventures ($2 per person; $2 per tent; $4 per caravan; $4 per single bungalow; $8 per double bungalow).

The village of **Hisarönü** is another option, up the hill from the beach (5min. *dolmuş* ride, 35¢). It's growing in popularity because of its cheap pensions and hi-fi powered discos (your *dolmuş* might stop there on the way to Ölüdeniz). From the *dolmuş* stop, walk to the right (facing the water) 200m to the fork in the road. The national park is on your left, and on your right is the road to the campgrounds.

FOOD AND ENTERTAINMENT

Restaurants tend to be expensive along the boardwalk in Ölüdeniz, but the quality and service is usually good. There are also a few bars and discos for after-hours entertainment to celebrate your paragliding. Most campsites also offer evening meals.

Çetin Restaurant (tel. 616 6393), under the Çetin Motel, offers decently priced, delicious meals (chicken *ızgara* $5, casseroles $5; open daily 8am-11pm). **Dippy Dolly's Pancake House,** to the left from the exit road (as you face the water), serves gourmet confections (roughly $3.50). At night, revelers drink, mingle, and dance all night at any one of several discos. What do you do with a dingy basement and a stack of *Turkish Daily News* back issues? **Underground Disco** (tel. 616 7331) have made an air-conditioned booming disco where you can peruse old newspapers while you dance! A small dance pit adds to the intensity. It's in the Tokgöz Shopping Center up the road to Fethiye (beers $2; wine $2; cocktails $6.70).

SIGHTS

After seeing the Blue Lagoon of the Ölüdeniz from Tabiat Park, the next best thing is to see it from above by tandem paragliding. There are plenty of offices on the boardwalk that will show you their video and set you up. Passengers are driven to the top of Babadağ Mountain and given instructions on how to take off and land. Flight time varies with conditions. The whole thing takes about two hours and costs $115.

Some claim that the tranquil circle of the **Blue Lagoon,** at the tip of the beach, is where the movie of the same name was filmed. They are wrong, but this idyllic bit of land does fill with Speedo-clad beach creatures of another type from dawn to dusk. A quiet dip in these crystal waters, especially on weekday mornings and evenings when it is least crowded, is pure bliss. Enter the lagoon from Tabiat Park where potable water, bathrooms, and showers are all available. It's a 20-minute walk or 25¢ *dolmuş* ride from the exit road (admission 65¢, students 35¢, $2.50 per car).

Kaya and **Agia Nikola** islands were thriving Greek Christian communities until they were dispersed by invaders. Two popular excursions from Ölüdeniz visit the remains of these villages. Kaya is the larger of the pair, 10km away and accessible only by a dirt road. Tiny Agia Nikola Island is a more popular destination, with great swimming, a spine-tingling view of the coast, and the remains of a Byzantine basilica. **Explora Travel** (tel. 616 6316; fax 616 6274), on the main street next to Han Camping, books boat trips to Agia Nikola Island and **Butterfly Valley** for $19.40, including lunch. Visitors to the Butterfly Valley return reports of having found paradise on Earth. Boats leave from the main dock at about 10:30am and return at 6pm. Explora also offers comprehensive jeep safaris to **Saklıkent,** the ancient city of **Tlos, Patara Beach, Xanthos,** and trout farms for $27 per person including lunch (open April-Oct. daily 8:30am-midnight).

■ Patara

The old Lycean port city of Patara is 17km west of Kalkan. Choked with sand and brush, Patara's imposing ruins lie peacefully among a series of seaside hills. Until its harbor silted up, the city was the seat of the Roman governor of Lycia and the site of an oracle to Apollo. The **Mettius Modestus** arch, built in 100 AD, rests on the right of the road to the beach. A **necropolis** with numerous sarcophagi surrounds the gate. Along the path from the gateway to the sea lie the ruins of Roman baths, a Christian basilica, the **Baths of Vespasian,** and a theater.

ORIENTATION AND PRACTICAL INFORMATION

Getting to Patara is easy; take any bus between Fethiye and Kalkan and ask to be dropped off at Patara ($2). From there, you'll need to take a *dolmuş* running to the town center from the Antalya/Patara fork (2km, 70¢). To reach the site and the beach area, you'll need to catch yet another *dolmuş* from town (35¢). The ruins are near Patara's beach, making for an ideal post-sightseeing swim. The site is run by Antalya University and they charge a small fee to visit the site and beach area ($2, students $1). Frequent *dolmuş* to: Kalkan (½hr., $1.70); Kaş (1hr., $2.70); Kemer (4hr., $6.70); Olympos (3½hr., $6); Fethiye via Kınık (1¼hr., $3); and Antalya (5hr., $8). Call **Patara Taksi** for **taxis** (tel. 843 5050).

There is a **PTT** (tel. 843 5220) in the small town center up from the *dolmuş* station that **exchanges currency** (open in summer 8:30am-12am, in winter 8:30am-5:30pm). International **phones** are also available. The **postal code** is 07975. The **telephone code** is 242.

ACCOMMODATIONS, FOOD, & ENTERTAINMENT

A number of cheap pensions fill the small town center. Pension owners often organize rafting tours for guests as well. **St. Nikolas Pension** (tel. 843 5024, -5154), right before the fork leading to the beach or the town center, has clean rooms with toilet, shower, rugs, balconies, and screens on all windows (doubles $12; triples $15.50). **Flower Pension** (tel. 843 5164; fax 843 5034), on the main road to Fethiye past the St. Nikolas on the left, offers a garden, lounge area, screened windows, and balconies ($5 per person). **Rose Pension** (tel. 843 5165) is a family-run business with clean rooms, balconies, screened windows, and mosquito nets over the beds (singles $10). **Medusa Camping** (tel. 843 5193) is across from the *dolmuş* station. It is a spacious campground with lots of trees and shady spots. Deadheads will love the bar. It has some of the cleanest toilets and showers in Turkey ($2 per person; electricity $1).

Santa Claus Sure Was One Hip Cat

Next December 25th, when you're roasting chestnuts and frolicking 'neath the mistletoe, spare a moment of reflection for that good-natured Anatolian, the master of elves and toys, who travels around the world in one night to fill your stocking with goodies. On the day of his birth in Patara in 270 AD, St. Nicholas, or Claus as his close friends called him, is said to have stood up and folded his newborn hands in prayer. Claus's good deeds were many. In one of his journeys, he came across a landlord who had murdered three boys and pickled their bodies. A hopeless do-gooder, Saint Nick brought the boys back to life. The idea of Santa Claus as a bearer of gifts came into being when Nicholas, in another act of kindness, dropped a bag of gold into the window of a poor Anatolian family while they were sleeping. Despite these and other amazing deeds, his fame did not spread across Europe until the 13th-14th centuries, at which time the Dutch coined the term *Sinterklaas*. These days, jolly old Saint Nick's cheeks might not be quite so rosy since the Roman Catholic Church took away his sainthood in 1969 and excised his feast day from the church calendar, claiming that his miraculous works and acts of piety were nothing but old wives' tales.

There are plenty of restaurants and bars in Patara's town center. **Bistrot** (tel. 843 5108, -5231), on the road before the fork to the beach and Fethiye, is a cozy little eatery. Try their *içli köfte* special with large shepherd's salad and fruit for $8. Don't be bashful about asking for their special drink "The Bomb" (*boğma*) that will keep you going all night long (open until 3am).

Despite stories to the contrary, **Santa Claus** grew up in Patara, next to the sunny Mediterranean. St. Nicholas was famed for his annual gift-giving, and was martyred after becoming bishop of nearby Myra. You can visit his birthplace and then check out his church and grave near the village of Demre. The **Archaeological Museum** in Antalya houses some of his relics (see p.491).

KAŞ COAST

▓ Kalkan

Kalkan is the quintessential Turkish fishing village: a graceful breakwater encloses its harbor, as austere stone houses with wooden balconies huddle around the quay. Kalkan does not have much of a beach—just a bunch of rocks on the left of the harbor. More inviting sand, however, can be found nearby. Three kilometers along the road to Kaş, beneath a small metal bridge, lies the beach of **Kapıtaş,** where blue meets green, sun meets horizon, and Turkish guy in leopard-print Speedo meets blond gal from the Valley.

ORIENTATION AND PRACTICAL INFORMATION

Kalkan is on the main road between Fethiye and Kaş. Buses and *dolmuş* will drop you off on a hill with views of the town's shopping district and harbor. Proceed down the hill, where you'll pass the PTT and come to the shopping areas around which pensions are located.

The **tourist agency** Alinda/ABI, on Yalıboyu Mah. No. 18. (tel. 844 3108; fax 844 3101), is one of the first offices on your right when entering the main shopping district. An extremely friendly English-speaking staff can help you plan daytrips to the area's small islands and sites (open Apr.-Oct. 8:30am-11pm). They also **rent cars** ($45 per day). **Bus service** is available on Kâmil Koç (tel. 844 3111) to: Istanbul (7-8pm, 13hr., $21.40); Ankara (8:45pm, 10hr., $14.70); Selçuk (10:30am and 10:30pm, 8hr., $10); Izmir (10:30am and 10:30pm, 8hr., $11.40); Bursa (8:30pm, 10hr., $16.70); Dalaman (10:30am and 10:30pm, 3hr., $4); and Fethiye (several per day, 1½hr., $2). Frequent **dolmuş** service to Patara (½hr., $1.70) and Kaputaş (70¢). All departures are from *dolmuş* stop on the road up from the PTT. A 24hr. **hospital** (tel. 844 2244), the Tuana Medical Center, is up the road to the right before the *dolmuş* stop on Kalamar Cad. The **PTT** has **currency exchange** (open 8am-12am in summer; 8:30am-7pm in winter). The **postal code** is 07960; **telephone code,** 242.

ACCOMMODATIONS

Accommodations in Kalkan are reasonable, often offering pleasant views from their terraces. Most of the touristy part of the town is below the bus stop, past the PTT.

Çelik Pension, Yalıboyu Mah. No. 9 (tel. 844 2126). Offers very clean rooms, most with small balcony, toilets, and showers. 24hr. hot water. Reception is on roof-top terrace. Mosquito-netted windows. Breakfast included. Singles $10; doubles $15; triples $20, or ask for less expensive lower-level rooms (no balconies).

Kalamaki Pension (tel. 844 3312, -3649), farther down on Yalıboyu Mah. toward the lower left side of the main town. Beautiful, clean pension with a small atrium on the first two floors. Persian and Ottoman miniature paintings decorate the hallways. Lounge with book exchange. A terrace-level cafe offers excellent views of the harbor and town. Breakfast included. Singles $14; doubles $22.

Çetinkaya Pension (tel. 844 3307, -3096), Yalıboyu Mah., at the very bottom of the road toward the left side of town facing the water. Comfortable, clean rooms with toilet, showers, and netted windows. Breakfast included. Singles $17; doubles $20; triples $30.

Kervan Han Pension, Yalıboyu Mah. No. 49 (tel. 844 3684). From the center of the shops, go to your lower right facing the water. A family-run pension in the lower part of the shopping district. Comfortable, small rooms with harbor views, toilet, shower, and screens. Breakfast included, dinner $4. Singles $17; doubles $20.

FOOD

Kalkan is full of small, quaint restaurants ready to put a delicious meal in front of you. Most restaurants have views of the harbor to add to the romantic atmosphere.

Köşk Restaurant (tel. 844 3046), near the center of the shopping district. Delicious food and a pleasant view of the harbor. Try the grills ($2.60-5), vegetable dishes ($1.70), or spaghetti ($2.30-3). Open 9am-1am.

Belgin's Kitchen (tel. 844 3614, -3680), farther down the main shopping street, off to the right. Turkish food in a Turkish atmosphere. Dine on couches with rugs covering the floor. Nightly live music. Soup $1.50-2, stuffed grape leaves $2, Turkish ravioli (*mantı*) $3.40. Open until 11pm.

Jolly Roger (tel. 844 3284). Take a right coming down the hill from the *dolmuş* stop to get to this lively spot with plentiful vegetarian options. Unsurprisingly, it has a pirate motif inside. Tomato soup $2.35, vegetarian dish of the day $6, French toast and eggs $4. "Scottish" spoken. Open 8am-midnight.

Foto'nun Yeri (tel. 844 3464), across from the Jolly Roger. Watch your food cooked before your eyes. House specials are Turkish pancakes (*gözelme*) $1.70, and (Turkish ravioli (*mantı*) $3. Open 8:30am-midnight.

Merkez Cafe-Market (tel. 844 3054), in the center of the shopping district before the turn to Köşk. Selection of pastries and sweets. Garden under vine-terrace. Pudding $1, Turkish ice cream $1.35, baklava $1.35. Open 7am-midnight.

ENTERTAINMENT

Moonlight Bar (tel. 844 3043), down from the bus stop before the shopping district on the left, Yalıboyu Mahj. S. Yılmaz Cad. A popular nightspot with excellent musical selections. Softer rock in the earlier part of the evening, getting harder as the hour gets later. Beers $1.50, *rakı* $2, cocktails $6. Open noon-4am.

Elvis Bar (tel. 844 2387), off the town center toward on Hasan Altan Sok. Yes, even in Turkey. Terrace-level bar with small dance area. Happy hour 9pm-10:30pm. Beer $1, *rakı* $1.70, "Elvis" cocktails $4-6. Open 7pm-3am.

Yalı Cafe-Bar (tel. 844 3490), Yalıboyu Mah., near the small amphitheater. Another popular Kalkan nightspot with a decent-size interior bar and dance space as well as outside seating. Large selection of English pop tunes. Happy hour (buy 2, get 3) 6pm-10pm. Beer $1, *rakı* $1.70, cocktails $4. Open 1pm-3:30am.

■ Xanthos

Some 85km from Ölüdeniz and 22km from Kalkan rest the ruins of the ancient Lycean capital of Xanthos. **Lycean rock tombs** pepper the site, perched above the Eşen River. Unwilling to surrender during a revolt against the Persians, the Lyceans gathered everything they owned in Xanthos for a final stand. When all hope was lost, they set the city on fire and fought until their last soldier died. Years later, the Romans fortified Xanthos in return for its inhabitants' support during their invasion of Anatolia. Most of the ruins are from this period. Check out the **Roman city gate,** dedicated to Emperor Vespasian, and the **theater.** From the theater you can see the remains of the **acropolis** and a **Byzantine church.** Nearby are the **agora** and a **Byzantine basilica.** The **Xanthian Obelisk,** near the agora, bears an inscription which describes Lycean battles in the Peloponnesian Wars. At the end of the theater stands the 6th-century BC Lycean **Tomb of the Harpies,** decorated with a plaster cast of the mythological creatures being summoned to destroy invading armies. To get to Xanthos, take any *dolmuş* running between Fethiye and Kalkan or Kaş, get off at the village of Kınık, and follow the signs to the site (1½hr., $2).

The ancient ruins of **Letoon** are 10km southwest of Xanthos and date from the Roman and early Byzantine periods. Letoon, a Lycian religious sanctuary, was the place where the nymph Leto, mother of Zeus' children Artemis and Apollo, fled Hera's wrath. There are three temples at the site dedicated to Leto, Apollo, and Artemis. Scholars hope that an inscription found on the Leto Temple in Lycean, Greek, and Aramaic will prove as valuable in deciphering Lycean as the Rosetta Stone was in decoding hieroglyphics. There is no guard or information booth, and the area should not be visited after sunset.

■ Kaş

Kaş is a luscious little quark of civilization sandwiched between the sea and mountains. The serpentine road from Kalkan to Kaş passes glittering inlets dotted with pebbly beaches. The town is replete with inexpensive, hospitable places to stay, excellent restaurants, and enjoyable bars. A peninsula curves around from one side of the town's harbor, creating a calm, rock-lined lagoon ideal for swimming. Kaş is the place to explore the mountainous, ruin-strewn countryside, take a boat trip, dance to a hodge-podge of Turkish and American pop music in a bar, or wallow on the waterfront, cocktail in hand.

ORIENTATION AND PRACTICAL INFORMATION

Most of the town's activity centers around the small harbor along the main street, **Cumhuriyet Caddesi.** At its west end near the mosque, its name changes to **Hastane Caddesi.** Here it is intersected by **Elmalı Caddesi,** which heads uphill to the bus station. At its east end near the statue of Atatürk, Cumhuriyet is intersected by **Çukurbağlı Caddesi,** which leads to the PTT. From the Atatürk statue, Hükümet Cad. goes above the harbor to two beaches. The street going up the hill behind the tourist office—the one with most of the souvenir shops—is **Uzun Çarşı Caddesi.**

Tourist Office: 5 Cumhuriyet Meydanı (tel./fax 836 1238), to your left as you face the back of the Atatürk statue. English spoken. Area maps sold at bookstores. Open May-Sept. daily 8am-noon and 1-7pm; Oct.-April Mon.-Fri. 8am-5pm.

Tourist Agencies: Nearly all agencies offer tours to Kekova. Tour prices vary slightly, so shop around before purchasing a ticket. **Kahramanlar Tourism and Yachting** (tel. 836 1062; fax 836 2402), on Cumhuriyet beyond the mosque, offers numerous options. Buses and cruises and cars. **Simena Tours,** 1 Elmalı Cad. (tel. 836 1416), down the street from the *otogar,* books airline tickets in addition to the staple stock of tours to Kalkan, Demre, Patara, Xanthos, Saklıkent, Kekova, and Dalyan. Open daily 8am-8:30pm.

Buses: Station at end of Elmalı Cad., across from Petrol. **Pamukkale** office (tel. 836 1310). To: Antalya (every 30min., 4hr., $5.65); Fethiye (every hr., 2hr., $3.15); Marmaris (8:30, 10:30am, and 3:30pm, 5hr., $8.75); Bodrum (9am and 4:30pm, 7hr., $11.25); and Izmir (9:30am and 9:30pm, 9hr., $12.50).

International Bookstore: There is a small **used book emporium** a few meters up the hill from the Red Point Bar with an ambience and a bespectacled owner straight out of a Spielberg movie. **Smiley's Restaurant** has a surprisingly large book exchange, and the **Sarıcaoğlu Market** (with the Efes-Pilsen sign), between the Atatürk statue and the mosque, sells and trades books as well.

Laundromat: Habessos Laundry, 5 Uzun Çarşı Antik Sok. (tel. 836 1263), offers a friendly smile with a wash and dry for $6.25 per load. Open daily 8am-midnight.

Hospital: (tel. 836 1185) On Hastane Cad. From the tourist office, 500m past the mosque, before the campground. For **English-speaking health service,** call the town's polyclinic at 836 1014.

Police: (tel. 836 1024) 200m to the left of the tourist office, as you face the water.

PTT: (tel. 836 1430) On Çukurbağlı Cad. Walk down Elmalı Cad. from the bus station, then turn left before the Hacı Baba Restaurant. 200m through the parking lot

on the left. Open daily 8:30am-10:30pm. **Currency exchange** desk open 8:30am-5pm. **Postal Code:** 07580.
Telephone Code: 242.

ACCOMMODATIONS

The search for inexpensive accommodations in July and August will test your haggling and shopping skills. The pensions in Kaş are usually very clean and pleasant, but they tend to jack their prices up 20 to 40% in high season. **Smiley's Restaurant** offers free housing—you just have to dine there. More on this bargain-hunter's dream under **Food and Entertainment,** below.

Yalı Pension and Hotel, 50 Hastane Cad. (tel. 836 1870, -1132 for the pension), 1 block to the right of the mosque as you face the water. The hotel is on the right and the pension across the street. Both offer spacious rooms with carpets, couches, and balconies. The pension has slightly smaller rooms and a communal kitchen. Singles $8.75; doubles $13.75; triples $17.50. Breakfast $1.90.

Hotel Turquoise (tel. 836 1800), in the narrow street behind the statue (Askerlik Şubesi Yanı Sok.). Turquoise rooms with bathrooms. In-house Turkish textile boutique, and a terrace/bar with a sea view. Breakfast included. Singles $12; doubles $18; triples $24. Flash your *Let's Go* book and get a 10% discount.

Kısmet Pansiyon, 17 İlkokul Sok. (tel. 836 1879). From the bus station, follow the directions to the PTT onto Çukurbağlı Cad. Make a left 1 block after the Benetton store onto Postane Sok; Kısmet is at the top of the street. Bar and reception are on the roof. Roof patio with amazing view. Large, carpeted rooms. Laundry $3.15 per load. Breakfast included. Singles $6.75; doubles $11.25; triples $15.

Kaş Camping (tel. 836 1050, -2438), on Hastahane Cad., 100m past the amphitheater, or 500m past the mosque walking from behind the Atatürk statue. Sea view, hills, shade, and grass. Hot water is somewhat unreliable. $2.50 per person; $6.50 per double bungalow; $5.75 per caravan (electricity included). Breakfast $1.75.

FOOD AND ENTERTAINMENT

There's a fruit and vegetable **market** halfway between the bus station and the harbor, one block above the mosque on Elmalı Cad. Friday is market day.

Hacı Babi Pastanesi (tel. 836 2330), on Elmalı Cad., next to the vegetable market, is great for breakfast. Locals and tourists alike gather here to chat over plates of pastries and junk food. $4.50 will buy you enough sugar, sodium, and cholesterol to make your heart valves flutter with joy. Open daily 6:30am-1am.

Moonlight Bar, across from Kısmet Pension, offers a laid-back continental breakfast. Open daily 8am-1am.

Çınar Lokantası (tel. 836 2128), between the PTT and Otel Turquoise on Çukurbağlı Cad., offers pleasant atmosphere but is a tad crowded. *Kebap* $3. Open daily 8am-midnight.

Oba Restaurant (tel. 836 1687), on Çukurbağlı Cad., uphill past PTT on the vleft, serves up unbeatable Turkish-style home cooking. Cheap prices and good food.

Smiley's Restaurant (tel. 836 2812), behind the tourist office, is another good option. The energetic owner İsmail, a.k.a. Smiley, certainly lives up to his name. He started as a waiter and slowly worked his way up to become the manager of one of the most popular restaurants in town. Vegetarian specials $3.50-4.50. *Kebap* $3.50. *Let's Go* readers get 10% off. A new development: Smiley set up a charmingly traditional **hostel-esque thing** upstairs from the restaurant. You can stay in these rather comfy quarters for free on the condition that you eat your meals downstairs. Not bad, eh? And you still get the 10% *Let's Go* discount on your meals.

Eriş Restaurant, Cumhuriyet Meydanı 13 Ortança Sok. (tel. 836 1057), next door to Smiley's. Fancier and pricier than the restaurants along the harbor, but worth it. Full meal $5.50.

Chez Evy (tel. 836 1253). We know you're in Turkey and are desperately fusing with the local culture, but for a relaxing, romantic evening, Chez Evy is *the* place for a French restaurant decorated in laudably authentic Turkish decor. Up the street and around the corner from the Red Point Bar, Chez Evy is internationally renowned for its exquisite cuisine. Chicken $9.40, salad niçoise $3.75, crepes $1.90-3.75. If your *kebap* threshold has been saturated, walkez-vous to Chez Evy's.

Mavi Bar (tel. 836 1834), on the harbor by the tourist office, offers good music and dancing. Beer $1.25. Open daily 4pm-3:30am.

Red Point Bar (tel. 836 1605) is on the same street as the laundromats. You've probably seen a Red Point Bar in every tourist trap you've visited, but to experience the original, hit this perpetually jam-packed bar to make nicey-nicey with locals and tourists alike. Beer $1.25. Open daily 6pm-2:30am.

Elit Bar, from the start of the pier, take a right and pass between the teahouses on the shore. Romantics hit this bar, which has live music and a cozy atmosphere. Beer $1.50. Open daily 7pm-2:30am.

SIGHTS

The two beaches of Kaş lie in coves surrounded by rocky cliffs and covered with smooth stones. It takes considerable effort to scramble over the stones, but it's worth it. The entrance to **Küçük Çakil Plajı** (Little Pebble Beach) is at the top of the hill on Hükümet Cad., to your left as you face the harbor (200m left as you exit the tourist office). More determined sunbathers and swimmers frequent **Büyük Çakil Plajı** (Big Pebble Beach), 15 minutes down the road.

Kaş has several historic sights in or near the town. Most impressive is the **Hellenic Theater,** just past the hospital on Hastane Cad. as you leave town. The only intact ancient structure in Kaş, the theater rests on a solitary, elevated perch, overlooking the sea and the Greek island Kastelorizo. You can spend the night in the theater (bring a sleeping bag), but don't count on sleeping much: rowdy young people crowd in after the bars close at 3am and sing and play guitar for most of the night. Follow the footpath behind the theater roughly 50m to get to the 4th-century BC **necropolis.** Back in town, there's a free-standing **monumental tomb,** also from the 4th century BC (up Uzun Çarşı Cad. behind the tourist office). If you're lucky enough to be in Kaş on July 1, attend the **sea festival** on the harbor. Kaşians celebrate the bounty of the sea by picking up unsuspecting passersby and throwing them into the water, clothes and all. Swimming races are also held.

▨ Demre

Demre is a quiet agricultural town located down from the Beydağlari Mountains on the road which leads to Kaş. In ancient times, Demre was known as an important member of the Lycean League and sent three votes to the federal capital in Xanthas (the maximum number of votes was based on size and importance). St. Paul is said to have stopped in the city in 61 AD on his way to Rome. But for most, Demre is the diocese of St. Nicholas, better known to children all over the world as **Santa Claus.** The kind-hearted saint was actually born 60km west of Demre in Patara, but latter became Bishop of Myra in the early 4th century. St. Nicholas's reputation for helping the poor and needy, especially children, was well-known within his time and has since spread around the world. Today, a partially restored church stands at the spot where Father Christmas was buried on December 6, 343. An orthodox service is held on this day every year, honoring the Saint's contributions to humanitarian causes. Demre, also known as Kale (Castle), is an important center for greenhouses and ships its fruit and vegetables to all parts of Turkey.

ORIENTATION AND PRACTICAL INFORMATION

Demre is a remarkably uninspiring town with a simple layout. The **police station** is located near the **bus station.** Proceed to the main road where hotels and some pensions will be on the right or left side. Take a left and proceed to the next major intersection; take a right to find the **PTT** and a few budget hostels, or take a left to visit St. Nicholas Church (400m). Proceed up the main road (away from the bus station) to visit the Lycean city of Myra. A few pensions are also located down this way, going first past a series of greenhouses. **Myra Otogar Takşi** has taxis (tel. 871 4343; home: 871 5473). **Pharmacies** can be found on Ilkokul Cad. and Noel Baba Cad. (open 8:30am-6:30pm). There are **banks** and an **ATM** on Noel Baba Cad., next to **Türkiye İş Bankaşi** (on the way to St. Nicholas Church). The **telephone code** is 242.

ACCOMMODATIONS

There are a few pensions in the town which usually provide free service to the beaches and organize daily boat trips to **Kekova** ($11 per person). There are also relatively cheap hotels near the PTT, providing similar services for visitors.

Kent Pension (tel. 871 2042, -2721), located far up on the road to Myra. An extremely comfortable pension with enthusiastic, helpful management. Clean rooms with toilet, shower and 24hr. hot water. Garden-side accommodation also with toilet and shower. Shady lounge/bar area with a traditional "Turkish Corner." Breakfast included. All-you-can-eat dinner nightly $4 (if you don't like it, you don't pay). Motorbike rental $6.50 per day. Tours to Kekova by boat $11 per person, no lunch. Singles $13; doubles $16; triples $22.

Kekova Pension (tel. 871 2267). Take a right onto the main road after the bus stop; 100m down. Adequate accommodations with balconies in all rooms. Shower and 24hr. hot water. Breakfast included. Daily boat trips to Kekova also organized. Shady lounge area with tables and TV. Singles $10; doubles $13.33; triples $20.

Grand Hotel Kekova (tel. 871 4515, -16; fax 871 5366), across the street from PTT. Clean, fully-loaded rooms at a discount rate. English-speaking reception. Rooms have TV, phone (what a luxury), balcony toilet, shower, and 24hr. hot water. Free service to the beach. Breakfast included. $10 per person.

Camping (tel. 871 4019), across from the Myra site. Very clean toilets, showers, and solar-heated water. Located in a grove of lemon and orange trees. $7 per person (tent or caravan camping).

FOOD AND ENTERTAINMENT

Demre is unusually quiet and sparse in its dining options after the daily tour groups complete their rounds at Myra and St. Nicholas Church. Your best bet is to inquire about evening meals at your pension, which typically provide comfortable portions for all. Save the nightclubbing for Kaş, as there's nothing to speak of here.

Çinar Restaurant (tel. 871 3554), in the main intersection, diagonally across from the Belediye Cay Barçeşi. Homemade specialities like *döner kebaps* $3. Mixed grills $4-5. Variety of cold plates and vegetable plates $1-2. Open until 11pm.

Inci Pastanesi (tel. 871 5639), near St. Nicholas Church. A simply-decorated sweet shop with some indoor seating. Baklava $1 per portion. Open 8am-midnight.

SIGHTS

Myra

Demre's oldest site is the ancient city **Myra.** The city's name is derived from Lycean origins, meaning the "Most Brilliant." This is attested to by Myra's inclusion among the Federation of Lycia's six most important cities (along with the capital Xanthos, Patara, Olympos, Pinara, and Tlos), from among a total federation of 70 cities. The city's plan is divided into three areas: the "sea necropolis" on the southwest area of the site, the acropolis area and its surrounding walls, and the river necropolis. The rock tombs built in the sea and river necropolis are of particularly high quality. Some tombs are stylized to have the impression of wooden beams and even have slight traces of color. The river necropolis is less visited than the sea necropolis, but has a rock tomb which was painted on. To reach the river necropolis, follow a small path that runs parallel to the cliff area going east.

The site's other major attraction is a remarkably well-preserved **theater.** The complex has 35 consecutive rows of seats (6 rows above the *diazoma* and 29 below it).

The theater was destroyed by a devastating earthquake in 141 AD, but later rebuilt and modified to host gladiatorial games. Much of the stage area remains. (Open daily May-Oct. 7:30am-7pm, Nov.-April 8am-5:30pm. Admission $1, students 33¢. Restrooms to the right after the gate 33¢.)

Church of St. Nicholas

Demre's other major attraction is the Church of St. Nicholas. The church is thought to be built on the site of the famous saint's tomb (in the southern side of the complex). Though the church has its origins in the 4th century, the current structure dates from the 7th century. The architecture of the church represents a transitional period between early basilica types and later Greek orthodox designs of the middle Byzantine period. The church suffered damage as a result of the Arab invasion of the 11th century and was later restored. Frescoes remaining on the church's walls and domes date from this period. The final stage of the church's history up to recent modern times began in 1353, when Russian officials bought the church land in order to form a colony (later signed by both parties in Rhodes). The church again suffered from neglect until Czarina Anna Galicia ordered its repair in the mid-19th century. The church was later lost under debris and shifting sand from the Myras River, and not rediscovered until 1956. Excavations in 1989 have led to the discovery of many new rooms and findings. The original design of the church could have had a large dome over the central area of the church, whereas today it is a closed design from Russian restoration. (Open in summer daily 8am-7pm, in winter 8am-5pm. Admission $2, students $1. Toilets past the St. Nicholas statue 25¢.)

If you are looking for St. Nicholas's remains, go to the **Antalya Museum** (see p. 499). His original tomb was broken into in 1087, when Italian merchants hastily took his remains to Bari, Italy, leaving behind only those which appear in the Antalya museum. St. Nicholas's tomb is generally agreed upon by scientists and religious scholars to be located on the southern nave of the church. The Turkish government's efforts to bring the rest of St. Nicholas's remains to the church have fallen on the deaf ears of Vatican officials for the last 20 years.

Near Demre

The main attraction around Kaş is **Kekova,** a partially submerged Lycean city roughly two hours to the east. **Excursion boats** visit Byzantine ruins, Kekova, and two fishing villages that flaunt a cliff honeycombed with Lycean tombs and a hill crowned with a half-ruined castle. Both towns are surrounded by a dozen Lycean sarcophagi, some leaning on the village homes (tours $10). The **Blue Caves,** 15km from Kaş and home to the Mediterranean's only **seal colony,** are worth a visit. Try to swim in the mornings before the sea becomes rough. Nearby, 2km after Kalkan, is **Doves Cave,** which can be reached only by swimming. Opposite this grotto, the wide **Güvercinlik Cave** spouts a cold underwater stream. **Kemer** longs to achieve Spain's Costa del Sol's level of tourist saturation. While it fails to do so, Kemer does offer one of the few Mexican restaurants on the Turkish Mediterranean, and a multitude of overpriced, underoccupied hotels. Kemer does have nice beaches, however, and a pleasant pedestrian shopping area if you're out of leather jackets and Benetton accessories.

▓ Olympos

It is hard to say whether Indiana Jones or Han Solo would feel more at home in this remote outpost. Is it more challenging to live in a tree house, or to understand a society which, though equipped with washing machines and international phone lines, nonetheless lives (or at least puts up its guests) in tree houses? Of course, Olympos' earliest known fictional inhabitants were never played by Harrison Ford at all. The Greek gods called Olympos home thousands of years before today's thousands of backpack-toting tourists discovered the place.

Originally a powerful Lycean port city, Olympos was subsequently overwhelmed by Greek, Roman, and Byzantine invaders, each of whom left their mark on the

ANATOLIA

town's architecture. As late as the 12th century, Venetian and Genovese crusaders used the city as a resting point as they hacked their way to the holy land. In its heyday, the ancient city was home to more than 30,000 people.

ORIENTATION AND PRACTICAL INFORMATION

To get to Olympos from Antalya, take the Kaş bus and ask to be let off at Olympos (1½hr., $2). You'll be deposited at a rest station complex on the main road, with a restaurant, *gözleme* stand, and hotel. **Taxis** lie in wait here to whisk visitors off to Olympos proper, really no more than a road from the village of Çavuşköy to the ruins lined with pensions, restaurants, and campgrounds. There is no post office, PTT, pharmacy, bank, or police station. The friendly pension owners will accept U.S. dollars as well as *lira,* allow you to place international phone calls, and arrange any local sightseeing that might suit your fancy. Just remember to bring along any items necessary to maintain your personal hygiene standards. The $6.50 **taxi** fare can be worth it if you form groups, an easy feat in the summer when the Antalya-Kaş buses are full of Australian couples and extremely hip-looking German families heading for a holiday in the Olympos treetops. A still better bet is the frequent **dolmuş** service ($1.30), which will drop you off at the pension of your choice. Another *dolmuş* runs past all the pensions back to the main road every two hours. The **telephone code** is 242.

ACCOMMODATIONS

The Turkish government has classified Olympos as a *"sit,"* or archaeological site, the only apparent significance of which is a local ban on concrete. This means no asphalt roads (and thus no direct bus service) and no cement building foundations, a potential kiss of death to tourism. Resourceful Olympians have turned *sit* status to their advantage with the innovative treehouse pension, specimens of which line the dirt road to the beach and ruins. Unless noted, all prices include breakfast and dinner.

Kadir's Yörük Treehouses (tel. 892 1250), the first pension you will come to, is easily the most populous and Jedi-like of your lodging options. Prevailed over by the genial Kadir and his Australian helpmates, this mini-metropolis boasts a bar, restaurant (with vegetarian options), table tennis, volleyball, full-day treks to Chimaera, a general store, and a foam rubber bull donated by an "American film director." Accommodations range from tree houses ($6.50 per person) to cabins ($8 per person) to bungalows located in converted century-old grain huts ($10 per person). The treehouses range from 2-person boxes to 10-person beehive complexes.

Olympos Çamlık Pansiyon (tel. 892 1257), next up on the street, offers bungalows and motel-type rooms (alas, no treehouses) with shared bath for $6.50 per person.

Olympos Sheriff (tel. 892 1301) does treehouses for $5.50; 2-person room with private shower $16.15.

Türkmen Camping (tel. 892 1249) has the cheapest treehouses, with no decrease in quality, for $4.85.

Saban (tel. 892 1265), next door to Türkmen, offers treehouses planted in neat rows alongside orange trees, as well as particularly good dinners. $6.50 per person; $11.20 with private shower.

Orange Pansiyon (tel. 892 1243), next door to Bayram's, offers treehouses in orange orchards for $7. Styrofoam-insulated bungalows go for $9.

Gypsy Chimera Restaurant lets you camp out on its wide-pillowed divans for free. For $2.60, you can either use their blankets or set up a tent on the grounds.

Kadir's Pension (tel. 892 1110; fax 825 7209), closest to the sea, is run by Kadir of Kadir's Yörük who has, in this instance, restrained his ambition in order to yield a small, modest treehouse pension similar to its neighbors. $6.50 per person.

ENTERTAINMENT AND SIGHTS

Good food, convivial atmosphere, and a marvelous beach are really all the entertainment Olympos offers. The good news is that beer is alarmingly cheap; 70¢ for a pint of Efes. Past Kadir's Pension, a path choked with Amazonian vines and bits of ruined classical antiquity leads through a rocky gorge, crossing an icy freshwater stream to the sea. It's easy to get distracted on the pathways that veer off into the woods, thick with pine and fig trees, or to follow the stream along its course. The end of the trail, however, is no less bewitching. Clear azure waters lap against the pebbly, shaded shore, where the occasional wandering goat prompts goat jokes of varying levels of sophistication ("Look, here comes your girlfriend!").

The most cohesive collection of ruins looms over the water on a rocky, yet verdant cliff. To the left of the beach road over another creek, a pathway leads to an ancient **mausoleum** with two Greek-inscribed sarcophagi, suffering the wear of the centuries. Farther left on the path is the exquisite 5th-century **mosaic house,** whose floors were entirely covered with intricate tilework until an earthquake diverted the course of a stream and flooded the building with a meter of water. On the other side of the road across the stream, the decrepit **theater** and **medieval walls** have been damaged by the river and forest. The sea here tends to be very still, and you can swim out quite far without much effort, observing the partially excavated crumbling archways towering above, shrouded in vines, shrubs, and flowering bougainvilleas (admission to the ruins and beach $1.30, students 65¢).

Come to think of it, maybe it is *Star Trek*'s Mr. Spock, and not Han Solo, who would get the biggest kick out of Olympos. Second-century Olympians are known to have worshipped Vulcan (a.k.a. Hephaestos, god of fire and the forge), due to the city's proximity to **Chimaera,** the perpetual flame springing from the mountainside 7km away. They believed this flame to be the breath of the chimaera, a mythical beast that was part lion, part goat, and part serpent. Geologists have not yet produced a better explanation, but they suspect natural methane gas plays some role. In past centuries, the flame was even brighter than it is today; according to ancient reports, ships navigated by it. A Byzantine church now stands near the site. Tractor tours to Chimaera leave Olympos nightly at 9pm (2½hr., $2.50). Flag one down as it rumbles past your pension. Wear sturdy shoes and pants and bring a flashlight. More hi-tech and athletic daytime tours run about $6.50; many are organized by Kadir's Yörük.

ANTALYA GULF COAST

▓ Antalya

Forty years ago, Antalya was a provincial village known mostly for its large boys' boarding school. Today it is Turkey's premier tourist resort. Capital of the so-called Turquoise Riviera and served by tourist-laden airbuses from Munich, Moscow and Amsterdam, Antalya is a city of modern white buildings that has sprung fungus-like from the shoreline cliffs. Contemporary Antalya has encircled Kaleiçi (literally "inside the fortress") and the crescent-shaped old city, brimming with cobbled streets, Ottoman houses, pensions, restaurants, boutiques, and carpet dealers. Nested inside is the ancient and chic walled **yacht harbor** *(yat limanı)*, formerly a Roman marina, lined with pricey eateries and cutting-edge nightclubs.

The hulking Taurus Mountains tower over the bay's edge. Tourism has been good to Antalya. It has made the town wealthy, sophisticated and arrogant. It has an Internet Cafe. It has rich Russians (most leather store signs read "КОЖА", "DERİ," and "LEATHER," in that order). And once we told you it was "sophisticated," you knew it had to have a Benetton. The owner of Kaleiçi's English book store orders his stock in part from the Strand in New York and claims friendship with playwright John Guare *(Six Degrees of Separation)* and Stockard Channing (who starred in the movie). Antalya might overwhelm the casual visitor, but it is truly one of those places that live up to the cliche that there is something for everyone. Beaches, ruins, waterfalls, a first-rate museum, public transportation, lots of people, 5-star hotels and pensions, and restaurants serving the specialties of such diverse regions as İnegöl, Turkey (*inegöl köfte*) and Kentucky (Colonel Sanders's celebrated chicken of the 11 secret herbs and spices).

ORIENTATION AND PRACTICAL INFORMATION

1997 brought Antalya a new gargantuan shopping mall-like **otogar** replete with fountains, several **ATMs,** and sprawling mazelike bathrooms with Western toilets (rare in *otogars* and priced accordingly at 35¢ a shot—don't miss). Unfortunately, this wonderland is 4km out of town at the intersection of Namik Kemal and Dumlupınar Blv., known as the **Andolu Kavşağı.** For your purposes, this probably qualifies as the middle of nowhere. Frequent *dolmuş* (35¢) run to the city center. İşıklar is a convenient stop (look for the sign in the windshield), where Kazım Özalp Cad. intersects with Cumhuriyet Cad., marked by the brick-red fluted minaret and a stone clock tower.

Tourist Offices: The main office (tel. 241 1747) is in a restored mansion in the bowels of the old city, near the marina. Enter Kaleiçi beside the clock tower and walk under the "Welcome" arch. When the road ends after 800m, go left at the Türk Evi Otel. Eventually the road narrows and goes uphill. The tourist office is on your right, opposite the Aspen Hotel. English spoken. Open Mon.-Fri. 8:30am-5:30pm. The new city's tourist office (tel. 247 0541, -2) is on Cumhuriyet Cad. Open Mon.-Fri. 8am-7pm and Sat.-Sun. 9am-7pm. Both distribute free city maps.

Tourist Police: (tel. 243 1061, emergency 155; fax 345 4113) On a little street left of the Atatürk bust in the harbor.

Consulates: U.K., Dolaplıdere Cad. Pırıltı Sitesi, 1st fl. (tel. 247 7000; fax 243 1482). **The Turkish Republic of Northern Cyprus (TRNC),** Kışla Mah. 35th Sok. Dörteldemir Apt. 11 P.K. 633 (tel. 248 9847).

American Express: For cash transfers go to **Koç Bank,** on Atatürk Cad. opposite the Hadrian Gate, to the right with the gate to your back. Akbank's **ATM** for AmEx cards is on Kazım Özalp Cad. between the clock tower and bus station.

Flights: Antalya International Airport (tel. 243 4381, -2), on Cumhuriyet Cad. Offices in the same building as the smaller tourist office. Open Mon.-Fri. 8:30am-7pm and Sat.-Sun. 8:30am-5:30pm. Direct flights to: Istanbul ($65); Ankara ($55); Amman (2 per week); Lefkoşa; Tel Aviv; Vienna; and Zurich.

Trains: TCDD provides a bus service to Burdur (2hr.) which connects with its train to Istanbul.

Buses: Station at the Anadolu Kavşak 4km north of the city center, where Dumlupınar Blv. meets Namık Kemal Blv. (tel. 241 231). Buses to: Istanbul (10 per day, 15hr., $20); Ankara (12 per day, 12hr., $16); Izmir (5 per day, 12hr., $16); Rize (2 per day, 30hr., $27); Adana via Alanya (15 per day, 12hr., $16); Anamur (6hr.); Taşucu (8hr.); Mersin (10hr.); and Göreme/Ürgüp/Nevşehir (3 per day, 12hr., $16). The **inter-city bus terminal,** Doğu Garajı, is at the intersection of Aspendos Blv., Ali Getinkaya Cad., and İbni Sina Cad., 1.5km from city center on the airport road.

Dolmuş: *Dolmuş* (35¢) stop at blue signs marked "D" and run to Museum and Konyaaltı Beach (from Konyaaltı Blv. or İşıklar) and to Lale and Lara Beaches (from the *Doğu Garaj*). To get to Doğu Garaj from Atatürk Cad., take a right onto Ali Getinkaya Cad. Walk one block to the Start Hotel, then go right; you'll see *dolmuş* clustered on the street.

Ferries: Turkish Maritime Lines (tel. 241 1120) serves Venice May-Oct. Departs each Wed. and returns Sat. Prices range from $267-600.

Vehicle Rental: Available from many agents in Kaleiçi. They'll require a valid drivers license and a minimum age of 20. Daily fees start around $40 for a car, $30 for a motorcycle, $25 for a moped, and $12 for a bike.

English Bookstore: Owl Bookshop, Barbaros Mah. 21 Akarçeşme Sok. (tel. 243 5718). Off Hesapçı Sok., 500m into the old city on the left. The one-room Owl has: a kindly bearded proprietor, a black cat called Pythagoras, and an interestingly dated English-language selection: Ford Madox Ford, Mary McCarthy, F. Scott Fitzgerald, and Penguin classics about dialectical materialism. Back issues of *Harper's,* the *New Yorker,* and the unparalleled *Let's Go: Greece and Turkey* are also available. Open daily 10am-1pm and 3-7pm.

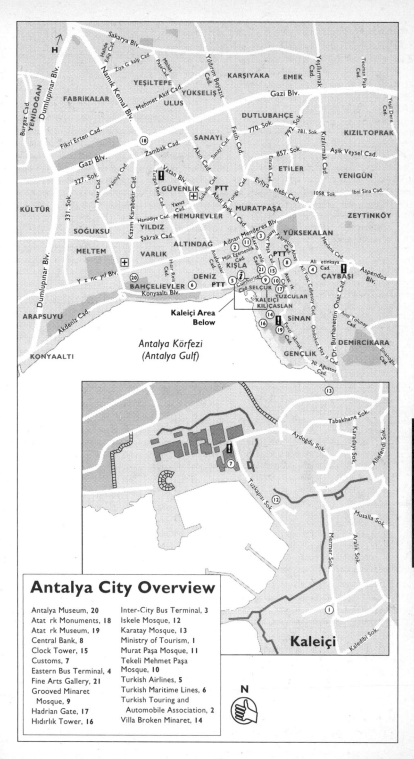

Antalya City Overview

Antalya Museum, 20
Atatürk Monuments, 18
Atatürk Museum, 19
Central Bank, 8
Clock Tower, 15
Customs, 7
Eastern Bus Terminal, 4
Fine Arts Gallery, 21
Grooved Minaret
  Mosque, 9
Hadrian Gate, 17
Hıdırlık Tower, 16

Inter-City Bus Terminal, 3
İskele Mosque, 12
Karatay Mosque, 13
Ministry of Tourism, 1
Murat Paşa Mosque, 11
Tekeli Mehmet Paşa
  Mosque, 10
Turkish Airlines, 5
Turkish Maritime Lines, 6
Turkish Touring and
  Automobile Association, 2
Villa Broken Minaret, 14

Laundromat: Yıkama Laundry, 28 Tabakhane Sok. (tel. 241 1174), beside the Anı Pansiyon. Wash'n'dry $5.50. Mysteriously enough, **Öz Ünaller Rent A Car,** 43 Hesapçi Sok. (tel. 248 9372; fax 248 4289), beside the Kesik Minaret, also has a laundry service. Drop a load off in the morning, and it comes back washed and dried around 7pm ($4.80, ironing 35¢ per piece). Both open daily 8am-10pm.

Hospital: Özel Antalya Kliniği, Işıklar Cad., Apt. No. 55/2 (tel. 243 6651; fax 243 3159). From Cumhuriyet Cad., walk down Atatürk Cad. to the park, bearing left to stay on the main road. The clinic is 1km down, on the left. 24hr. service includes ambulance and hotel visits. Doctors speak English, but receptionists do not.

PTT: To get to the **main branch,** head west on Cumhuriyet Cad. (with the sea to your left) and take the first major right onto Anafartalar Cad. Open daily 9am-5pm for stamps and currency exchange, 24hr. for phone calls. A **branch office** is on the harbor. Open daily 8am-6pm. There's another branch on İsmet Paşa Cad., the continuation of Atatürk Cad. north of Cumhuriyet Cad (open daily 9am-10pm). **Postal Code:** 07100.

Internet Access: Green Point Internet & Ice Cafe, 54A Cumhuriyet Cad. (tel. 248 5529; email greenpoint@aidata.com.tr). The refreshingly un-cyberhip decor seems to be modeled after the nearby McDonald's. Email/WWW access $2.60 per hr. Telnet available. Freshly squeezed orange juice $1.30. Open 9pm-12:30am.

Telephone Code: 242.

ACCOMMODATIONS

The best place to stay is within the ancient walls of **Kaleiçi;** the old city contains over 200 pensions and hotels. Unless otherwise stated, all include private shower and breakfast. Bargaining may help, especially for students.

Sabah Pansiyon, Kaleiçi Kılınçaslan Mah. 60 Hesapçi Sok. (tel. 247 5345, -6). A popular backpackers' hangout. Pleasant courtyard area. Singles $6.45; doubles $12-22 with breakfast; roof, couch, or floor $3; A/C $3; camping $2.50 per person.

Ninova Pension, Barbaros Mah. 9 Hamit Efendi Sok. (tel. 248 6114). A touch of luxury in a beautifully restored house. Wooden ceilings and floors in large rooms that are as clean as a whistle. Singles $16.15; doubles $26.

Anı Pansiyon, 26 Tabakhane Sok., Hesapçi Sok. (tel. 247 0056). This historic home, restored to a high degree of comfort, offers impeccable service. Rooms are smaller than at Ninova. Singles $16.15; doubles $26.

Hotel Villa Zürich, Kılınçaslan Mah. 18 Hidirlik Sok. (tel. 243 9349). Marble staircase. Rooms with A/C, phone, and often a sea view. Singles $16.15; doubles $26.

Mavi Pansiyon, Kılınçaslan Mah. 13 Tabakhane Geşidi, run by 3 brothers. Has almost entirely blue furniture and a pretty garden with fountain, TV, and guitar for guest use. Excellent meaty and vegetarian dinners; ask in the morning. Singles $6.45; doubles $11.45.

Bambus Motel Camping, 18 Lara Cad. (tel. 321 5263; fax 321 3550), on beautiful Lara Beach (accessible by *dolmuş* from Doğu Garajı). 24hr. hot water, electricity, and phones. Tents: 1-person $5.30; 2-person $7.45; 3-person $10.65. Caravans: 1-person $7.75; 2-person $9.70; 3-person $12.75.

FOOD

Even if you are not the tea and crumpets type, you might want to check out the **Tophane Çay Bahçesi** (Battlements Tea Garden), which stretches along the top of the rampart walls overlooking the harbor. It's easiest to enter from Atatürk Park on Cumhuriyet Cad. Around 4pm, half the city can be found here drinking Turkish tea (35¢) from narrow-waisted glasses (soft drinks 75¢, snacks 75¢-$1.25). For dinner, be careful you don't pay the "tourist price." As far as real food is concerned, Antalya is one of those places where the best and cheapest meals are to be had in holes in the wall—no atmosphere, baby.

Coming from the Old City, take a left off Cumhuriyet Cad. onto Kazim Özalp Cad. to get to the **Has Pide ve Kebap Salonu,** 30 Kazım Özalp Cad. (tel. 242 3709), for fresh pita and excellent, well-seasoned *Izgara* dishes (*şiş kebap,* pita, and a cold drink $2.90). Exit through the rear and you'll find yourself on a narrow back street behind the Hotel Maryot, where a small **Köfte ve Piyaz Salonu,** despite actually having sawdust on the floor, dishes up a delicious meal of *köfte* served with toast and fresh green peppers, salad, and a drink for under $2.60. On the inland side of Cumhuriyet Cad., heading towards the PTT, the **Bursa İnegöl Köftecisi** serves fantastic İnegöl *köfte* for $2.75. In Kaleiçi, **Eski Sebzeciler İçi Sokak,** a narrow covered alleyway lined with cheap outdoor *kebap* restaurants, is the place to try the local specialty, *tandır kebap,* mutton roasted in a clay pot. The touristy restaurants around the "Welcome to the Old City" arch tend to have good ambience, but overpriced, overrated food. Near the harbor, prices rise in direct proportion to the quality of the view and not the food. **Hisar Restaurant** (tel. 241 5281), uphill from the tourist office, has excellent fried calamari for $7.

ENTERTAINMENT

There is no shortage of nightlife in Antalya. **Club 29** in the harbor is the most happening scene, with a huge open-air dance floor jutting out over the sea. You enter at the top of a semicircular amphitheater-like area with bars and tables. As you descend the narrow stone steps to the water's edge, security guards inspect you with metal detectors and relieve you of $9 (first "drink" included). This place is the sound and light crew's fantasy, with megabass Euro, Turkish, and American pop blasted from all directions as the moon-and-starlight sky is augmented by underwater flood lamps illuminating the sea to its daylight turquoise. On weekends, mixed tourist and local crowds pack the floor until nearly daybreak. **Olympos,** in the 5-star Falez Hotel near Konyaaltı Beach, competes with a laser system, video bar, and occasional live music.

  Cinemas generally show English-language films with Turkish subtitles: **Oscar,** Zafer Sok. in the old city; **Ulusoy,** Kazım Özalp Cad.; and **Kültür,** Atatürk Cad., near the park are all quite cheap by Western standards ($2.60, students $2). The **Emperyal Casino** (tel. 249 3880) features unlimited food and drinks for a mere $6.75 initial purchase of chips. If you can assemble 15 people, the Ofo Hotel, which runs the casino, will pick you up at your hotel or pension and drive you home later. The flashy casino and low admission price ensure a mixed crowd.

ANTALYA MUSEUM

The Antalya Museum, 2 Konyaaltı Cad. (tel. 241 4528, -5386), winner of the 1988 European Museum of the Year Award, is among Turkey's most impressive museums, with 11 exhibition salons ranging from prehistoric times to the founding of the Turkish Republic (open in summer Tues.-Sun. 9am-6pm, in winter 1:30-5pm; admission $4, students $2). The museum is roughly 2½km from town along Cumhuriyet Blv., which changes name to Konyaaltı Blv. *Dolmuş* labeled "Konyaaltı/Liman" head left (with your back to the sea) along Cumhuriyet/Konyaaltı Blv., stopping at the large "D" signs. Ask to be let off when you see the yellow museum signs, before the *dolmuş* heads downhill to the beach.

Salon 1

Salon 1 is the **Children's Year Room,** established in 1985 and supposedly geared toward visiting children. Along with a 2nd-century multiplication table engraved on a stone tablet, the only other interesting thing in the room is the display of **children's banks,** from the plastic complimentary kind given to the children of İş Banka, Halk Bank, and Dışbank clients (these are shaped like footballs, soccer balls, and baseballs), to a bank of blue china marked FOR BABY, to a tin specimen decorated with a scene from The Lion King. The target audience appears to be either kids raised by wolves or rug-rats from another galaxy unfamiliar with 20th-century human civilization. A nearby plaque bears the somehow sinister message *"Hayat oyunla Başlar, oyunla biter"* (Life begins and ends with a game).

ANATOLIA

Salons 2 & 3

Meander on in to Salon 2, the **Hall of Natural History and Prehistory,** for an example of a **pithas burial,** a skeleton decomposing in a huge smashed urn. Salon 3, the **Hall of Rescue Excavations,** is a sort of *Rescue 911* of museum exhibits, containing, among other things, several gorgeous silver and ivory Phrygian statuettes daringly excavated from 8th-century tombs. A glass case nearby, lit by blue lights, is littered with "underwater findings" *(sualtı buluntular),* mainly barnacle-encrusted earthenware salvaged from 3rd-century shipwrecks. The gem of the collection is a magnificent illustrated Grecian urn, recovered in the face of untold adversity and mysteriously labelled "The Tibet Crater."

Salons 4-6

Salon 4, **The Salon of the Gods,** houses no less than three 2nd-century statues of Nemesis, along with her pals Zeus, Aphrodite, Tykhe, Athena, Artemis, Hygieia, Hermes, and Dionyseus, and their Egyptian sidekicks Serapis, Isis, and Harpokrates.

Salon 5, the **Salon of Small Works,** contains just that. Salon 6, the **Hall of Emperors,** is home to 2nd and 3rd-century marble busts of Roman rulers and aristocrats, among them Trajan, Hadrian, Spetimus Servus, Sabina, Faustina, Julia Domna, Julia Soemias, and Plankia Magna. All were excavated from Perge, and many are (sadly) headless.

Salons 7 & 8

Here in Salon 7, the **Hall of Tomb Culture,** lie seven beautiful sarcophagi. The one closest to the entrance once contained the remains of the Domitias Filiskas family. The hall also houses framed newspaper documentation of the smuggling of Turkish archaeological treasures to foreign lands. The 2nd-century Sarcophagus with Garlands, we learn, spent two illegal years in the **Brooklyn Museum** before being restored to the bosom of its native soil in 1994. The elaborate reliefs on the Heracles Sarcophagus have likewise been pillaged by unscrupulous foreign archaeologists.

Salon 8, the **Icon Hall,** is home to a small but interesting collection of Orthodox Christian icons. The 4th-century portrait of St. Nicholas accompanied by a few of his bones is particularly noteworthy.

Salons 9-11

Salon 9, the **Hall of Money and Jewelry,** contains a few of the **world's first coins,** minted between 640 and 630 BC by the Lydians. They were all forged from white gold or electrium (an alloy of gold and silver) until the reign of the last Lydian king, Croesius, the first to separate the two metals. Other displays include tiny Ottoman coins, early printed money, and an "Electrium Pin Head in Shape of a Duck."

Salon 10, the **Mosaic Salon,** contains an impressive floor mosaic from a Seleucid Agora, as well as some smaller 6th-century Byzantine works.

Salon 11, the **Ethnography Salon,** is replete with familiar Ethnography Museum artifacts: wooden spoons, musical instruments, enameled tiles, Ottoman costumes, oil lamps, a half-woven kilim on a wooden loom, and a model Bedouin tent occupied by two Bedouin mannequins cooking some kind of muttonous gruel over a hole in the ground. It also boasts four glass cases full of embroidered socks.

OTHER SIGHTS

Antalya's tiny **Fine Arts Gallery** (tel. 248 0008; fax 243 1089), a one-room affair at Kale Kapısı just above the "Welcome" arch, sponsors exhibits, lectures, poetry readings, and videos. Near the intersection of Cumhuriyet Cad. and the old city entrance, you'll see the red-tinted **Yivli Minare** (fluted minaret), dating from the 13th century. Down Atatürk Cad., on the right, stands **Hadrian's Gate,** built in 130 AD to commemorate the visit of the emperor Hadrian.

Through this gate to the old city, about halfway down Hesapçı Sok., is the **Kesik Minare** (Broken Minaret). The ruined mosque beside it was transformed from a Byzantine church by the Seljuks. The structure was actually built as a Roman temple before it was converted into a three-nave basilica in the 4th century. At the far end of Hesapçı Sok. is the **Hıdırlık Tower,** believed to have been built as a lighthouse in the 2nd century AD. Founded as Attaleia in the 2nd century BC by King Attalos II of Pergamon, Antalya's old city is still fortified by walls built by Greeks, Byzantines, and Seljuks. The Antalya Attın Portakal **Film Festival** held in the fall is a huge affair. Antalya is also known for its spectacular **waterfalls.** Upper and lower Düden Falls tumble from 40m and 20m respectively, and are accessible by *dolmuş* from **Pazar Pazarı** (in turn accessible from Doğu Garajı). Antalya's two main beaches are **Konyaaltı** and **Lara** (*dolmuş* service from Doğu Garajı).

■ Near Antalya: Perge

From the extensive remains of ancient Perge (16km from Antalya), it's easy to imagine what life must have been like in this prosperous town of over 100,000 inhabitants. The city was supposedly founded by Greek heroes after the Trojan War, but it did not earn its place in history until it sided with omnipotent boy wonder Alexander the Great. The **stadium,** which seated a crowd of 12,000, has a wall at the far end meant to protect spectators during the wild beast fights that took place here. Against the opposite hill, an impressive **theater** features finely rendered reliefs of Dionysus. Entering through the **Roman gate,** you'll see a large **agora** (market place) to your right, in which shops were arranged by trade and inspected by officials known as Agoranomas. Up ahead, two imposing **Hellenistic towers** mark the beginning of the long, colonnaded avenue leading to the **nymphaeum.** In ancient times, water flowed from here into a fountain that ran the length of the street. Don't miss the remains of the **public baths,** to your left (site open in summer daily 8:30am-6:30pm, in winter 8:30am-5:30pm; admission $2, students $1, parking 65¢). *Dolmuş* run from Doğu Garajı in Antalya to Aksu; Perge is a sweltering 2km walk from there.

■ Near Antalya: Aspendos

Arguably the most magnificent remaining Roman theater, **Aspendos** (tel. (242) 735 7038) lies 47km east of Antalya in the ancient land of Pampylia. It was built by the architect Zenon, son of Theodorus, under the reign of Marcus Aurelius (161-180 AD). Comprising five stage doors and 20 rows of seating with a capacity of 15,000, Aspendor was restored once by the Seljuks, who then used it as a caravanserai, and again by Atatürk, who declared it would be used once again as a theatre. The annual **Aspendos Opera and Ballet Festival** is still held here from June 7-24 (tel. (242) 243 6155, 248 0121), and artistic performances continue for most of the summer. A late July **Folk Festival** run by the Folkdance Music Youth Society, Istanbul Folklore (tel. (216) 410 2447, -2448), features an International Folk Dance Show with participating companies from Belgium, Finland, Moldavia, Latvia, Israel, Russia, Romania, Lithuania, Macedonia, Germany, Thailand, Holland, Kazakhstan, and Turkmenistan. Another highlight is the Mevlâna Sema Ritual, a Whirling Dervish exhibition, followed by Turkish folkdancing. Admission prices vary; shows begin at 9:30pm. The theater and attached museum (containing carved ivory masks and Roman theatre tickets) are open 8:30am-6:30pm. Admission is $2, students $1. To get there from Antalya, take the bus to Serik from Doğu Garajı; it's then a well-marked 4km to the site. You might be able to hitch a ride in summer; otherwise, walk or take a taxi (about $3.75).

▓ Side

Side (SEE-deh) contains all the ingredients necessary for a complete Mediterranean coast vacation: Hellenic ruins, parasailing, a fine museum, beautiful sandy beaches, and the self-proclaimed best disco in Europe. Shop for leather goods in the crowded pedestrian streets, study up on ancient history in the 7th-century Roman ruins, and tan under the sun. It's one-stop shopping—Mediterranean style.

ANATOLIA

ORIENTATION AND PRACTICAL INFORMATION

Side can be reached by direct buses from Antalya, but you will most likely be let off at the highway turn-off in Manavgat. From there, you can catch a *dolmuş* to Side or walk (3km). Walking has the advantage of taking you past the **tourist office** (tel. 753 1265). Your best bet is to ask to be let off the *dolmuş* when you see the office on your left. The tourist office is an inconvenience if you arrive at the *otogar,* but the staff is friendly and somewhat conversant in English (open in summer daily 8am-6pm, in winter Mon.-Fri. 8am-noon and 1:30-5:30pm). To get to the **PTT** (tel. 753 1796), exit the bus station to the left, turn left when you reach the main road, and go past the Luna Park amusement park. The hospital is just off the main street between Side and the highway, across from the tourist office. For a **medical emergency,** dial 753 1221. The **postal code** is 07330; **telephone code,** 242.

ACCOMMODATIONS

Many pensions line the main road as you walk through a series of gates and arches into town from Manavgat or the bus station. Follow the main drag past the ruins and into the pedestrian shopping street, taking a left at the Jungle Bar to get to **Pettino Pansiyon** (tel. 753 1272). One of the nicer places on the Mediterranean Coast, the pension has a beautiful courtyard area with bar and book exchange, vegemite, and excellent rooms with the standard pension amenities ($10 per person, breakfast included). The closest established camping area is the **Seving Pension** (tel. 753 1767), on the left from the center of town between the first and second gates, off a gravel road. Seving features a raised platform bar, perfect for watching the waves roll in ($4 per camping site for 1-3 people; $12 per 1-3 person bungalow room).

FOOD AND ENTERTAINMENT

No Mediterranean resort would be complete without seafood and a kickin' nightlife. Fine seafood can be had throughout the city. In most cases, the better the decor, the more expensive and less inspired the cuisine. Skip the Long John Silver routine and go where the locals go. If you do stay in the touristy part of town, **Pettino Restaurant** (tel. 753 1273), across from the Pettino Pansiyon, offers well-prepared Turkish favorites and seafood for not too many lira. You can also get a quick meal or an evening beer (or two or three) at the nearby **Blues Bar,** whose Welsh owner often sings and strums the guitar. The **Oxyd Disco,** touted by local pension owners as "the best in Europe," features laser shows, video screens, and screaming techno. The cover charge is $5, including your first beer. After that beers are $1.25 and drinks are more.

SIGHTS

You'll have no problem finding the ruins. When you enter Side, you'll see the **nymphaeum** memorial fountain which once had a marble facade depicting punishments administered to those who committed sexual sins or sins against the gods. Fortunately, Side today is as loose as it gets—get down, get dirty; chances are your neighbors are naughtier than you. While most ancient theaters were hewn into the hillsides, the 2nd-century AD **theater** of Side was built on level ground using arches. It's the largest in the area, seating 25,000 people (open daily 8:30am-5:30pm; admission $1, students 50¢). Other ruins include two **agoras.** The site is 1500m from the city and can be reached by following the beach to the west. The ancient **Roman baths** now house a great **archaeological museum** (open Tues.-Sun. 8am-noon and 1:30-7:30pm; admission $1.65, students 65¢). About 200m to the east stretches the best **beach** in Side, where some tourists unfurl sleeping bags on the sand or in one of the empty wooden shacks. To get there walk to the right directly out of the bus station about 2km (with the sea to your right) and turn onto the dirt road that leads to the water; the shacks will be off to the left.

EASTERN MEDITERRANEAN COAST

■ Anamur

Anamur, Turkey's southernmost point, is a city of many faces. The least attractive is the one facing the bus station, so don't be discouraged when you first arrive; this is the city center, heavy on dust and concrete. Most visitors stay in the prettier-faced harbor, with many pensions, a thriving nightlife, and free, uncrowded beaches with fine white sand and clear water. Anamur is also home to the magnificent ruined ancient city of Anemurium, perched 8.5km from town in the Cilician mountains and most renowned in international archeological circles for its 350-tomb necropolis.

ORIENTATION AND PRACTICAL INFORMATION

Buses drop off at the *otogar* (tel. 814 2019), where a small branch **tourist office** provides free maps and directions to the *dolmuş* stops (open Mon.-Fri. 8:30am-5:30pm). One *dolmuş* runs from the *otogar* to the right of the Atatürk statue in the main square, about 1km away. The *dolmuş* stop to İskele beach is to Atatürk's left. **Fergün Denizciler Şti. Ltd.** (tel. 814 4431), on İnönü Cad. in İskele, has recently begun **seabus** service to Girne in northern Cyprus, leaving İskele's harbor at 7pm on Friday and Sunday (2½hr., $14.35 round-trip). The main tourist office is just up the road from the bus station on Bulvar Cad. (Tel. 814 3529. Open in summer Mon.-Fri. 8am-noon and 1:30-5:30pm, Sat.-Sun. 9am-noon and 1:30-5:30pm, in winter Mon.-Fri. 8am-noon and 1:30-5:30pm.) **Buses** run to: Alanya (3hr., $5); Antalya (5hr., $6.25); Silifke (3hr., $5); and Mersin (5hr., $6.25). For a **medical emergency,** call the **hospital** (tel. 814 1086). There are several **ATMs** and **pharmacies** near the bus station. The **PTT** (tel. 814 1001) is in the bus station (open daily 8:30am-5:30pm, no exchange services Sat.-Sun.). The **telephone code** is 324.

ACCOMMODATIONS

Over a dozen pensions with similar facilities (private showers, balconies, breakfast) and prices (singles $8; doubles $12) pack the İskele area.

   Eser Pansiyon (tel. 814 2322) is the best place to stay. Run by two retired English-speaking schoolteachers and their dynamic son Tayfun, the rooms are charmingly idiosyncratic and the rooftop terrace is shaded by a grape arbor and distinguished by the fact that people actually use it. Great garden. $5 per person. Breakfast $1.70.
   Hotel Dolphine, 17 İnönü Cad. (tel. 814 34 35, -6; fax 814 1517), deserves recognition as the most affordable İskele hotel with A/C. Modern and otherwise unremarkable rooms also come with TV, shower, minibar, and phone. Breakfast included. Singles $11.70; doubles $20; triples $26.70.
   Yalı Mocamp (tel. 814 3474), on the main road around the army base, offers landscaped campsites, 3 wooden bungalows, and a bar on the beach. Camping $5 per person; $16-20 per bungalow.

FOOD AND ENTERTAINMENT

The İskele's main drag, İnönü Cad., bubbles over with fun restaurants and street food vendors. It's easy to find good *gözleme bazlama,* a large flat circle of dough spread with cheese (*peynir*), ground meat (*kıyma*), or potato mixture (*patates*), folded in half and fried in butter on a large black heated dome, usually by a woman sitting cross-legged on a platform three to four feet above street level (70¢). Anamur's classiest meal is to be had at the **Astor Restaurant** (tel. 816 5610), specializing in fish dishes (*şiş kebap* $6) and "Astor *köfte,*" a sort of croquette with potatoes and ground meat ($1.35). *Patlıcanlı şiş köfte,* meatballs with eggplant, is another good bet ($3.35). You can sit by the fountain and watch the owner's children torment the fish.

When the sun goes down, İnönü Cad. comes to life. The music is turned up, lanterns and strings of lights illuminate the streets to near-daylight brightness, traffic ceases, and the sidewalks overflow with food vendors, souvenir hawkers, and pedestrians looking to enjoy a cool evening. Many peaceful beachfront cafes and tea gardens are transformed into bopping joints with singing crowds dancing until dawn. The nightlife here is characterized by cheap Efes ($1.65 per pint) and a cheery atmosphere. You'll see nary a jaded socialite deadening the senses with vodka as you mingle with Anamur's friends and family in the various area bars and terraces. **Yakamaz Bar** features Western music, dancing, and a young crowd. Farther down the road, diners linger after dinner at the **Teras Bar and Restaurant,** where the music only *sounds* like a sing-along; all those voices actually belong to paid singers. Next to Astor, the mellower **Roza Bar** provides cool blue lighting and Turkish music. By the time you get there, you will have noticed that the top of the **Hermes Hotel** features a rooftop terrace bar where the music of choice is Van Halen and Quiet Riot.

SIGHTS

Anemurium

First established by the Phoenicians in the 4th century BC, the city of Anemurium fell to the Romans in the 3rd century AD, was Christianized in the 3rd and 4th centuries, reached its heyday in the 6th century, and was finally sacked by the Arabs in the 7th century. It hasn't been inhabited since. Today you can visit the Roman aqueducts, city walls, baths, Palaestra, gymnasium, odeon, amphitheater, Bouleuterion, and several churches, as well as a renowned **necropolis,** Asia Minor's most impressive city of the dead, boasting 350 tombs carved primarily out of single blocks of gray limestone. Most tombs hold a sarcophagus room as well as an antechamber serving as a chapel of the Heroes Cult, often decorated with fading frescoes. Some colored mosaics survive in the nearby **Necropolis Church.** Most of the houses where the living made their homes in Anemurium are still being excavated from under sand dunes. Also buried under a dune are the remains of a giant **oil lamp factory.** Some 700 terra-cotta oil lamps were unearthed all in one lot, indicating that they were about to be shipped elsewhere. This particular model of lamp is unique to the Anemurium. Wear pants and sturdy shoes to the site, as you will have to tangle with some bramble patches to explore thoroughly (open daily 7:30am-7:30pm; admission 70¢, students 35¢). Following the paved road uphill through the ruins, an absolutely gorgeous pebbled **beach** with bamboo umbrellas will appear on your left.

The lovely drive to Anemurium along the base of the Cilician Mountains passes many a hillside crammed with hundreds of glass greenhouses, home to Anamur's famous banana trees. *Dolmuş* will drop you off at the turn-off, from which point it's a 2km hike to the ruins. If you're staying at İskele, some hotels and pensions (Eser and Dolphine among them) occasionally organize fishing boat excursions to Anemurium. A taxi will also take you there, wait for you to look around/swim/have lunch, and take you back for an official $15 (but try bargaining).

Another alternative is to take a taxi directly to the ruins from the *otogar* ($3.65) and stay here instead, bypassing İskele altogether. Two tiny, idyllic family pensions await your disposal. **Anamuryum Ören Pansiyon** (tel. 835 1191) lets four cute and clean doubles with bucolic views ($6.75 per room). Guests can use the shared bathroom, kitchen, and washing machine for free. Next door, **Alper Pansiyon** (tel. 835 1113) offers clean, pretty rooms in a family home (complete with a Turkish translation of *Petit Larousse* on the bookshelves). Again, use of the tidy bathroom, kitchen, and terrace is free. Call ahead. One double and two quads go for $5 per person.

Mamure Kale

Dramatically jutting out into the sea, this *kale* is perhaps Anatolia's most impressive ancient castle. A 10m-wide moat encircles the structure and leads to the sea, which is fed by a nearby stream. After a history of conquest and possession by various parties, the castle reached its zenith under Sultan Mahmut Bey (1300-1305 AD), whose extensive renovations inspired the castle's present name. Today the remains are a veritable playground for all ages. A rewarding day can be spent navigating mazelike, wildflower-choked rooms, clambering up spiral staircases, and peering through slit-like windows at the sea. Come nightfall, Mamure's lights dazzle (open 8am-8pm; 75¢).

Dolmuş (30¢) run at least every half-hour from both the city center and the İskele area to **Pulla Camping** (tel. 827 1151), about 200m from Mamure. This sylvan and jolly camp ground sits atop a gorgeous sandy beach and boasts electricity, toilets, hot showers, picnic grounds, and a restaurant. In summer it is very popular with young adolescent Turkish youth. Another good lodging option is **Kale Pension and Restaurant** (tel. 827 1358), directly across from the castle, whose clean sunny rooms and private showers go for $6.75 per person, breakfast included.

Softa Kale

Though Mamure Kale is in better repair, Softa, built atop a craggy hill by crusade-era Armenian kings, offers even more breathtaking views. The rocky, cliff-lined shores give way at points to fine pale sand, and the Softa area is home to many a grape-arbored summer villa development. One of these is on the sprawling, Eden-esque grounds of two-star **Otel Alinko** (tel. 851 3998; fax 851 4696). All rooms have private baths (singles $13.35; doubles $20; triples $23.35). Guests have access to tennis courts, a teahouse and restaurant, and a fantastic **beach.**

Dolmuş continue 6.8km past Mamure/Bozdoğan to Softa/Bozyazi, but the actual castle isn't accessible by car. Wear pants and comfortable hiking shoes, as you'll have to climb the last bit on foot.

▨ Taşucu

While storming the Turkish Mediterranean, the tourists have overlooked Taşucu, mercifully leaving it free of Benettons, leather dealers, and resort hotels. What you will find is a small, friendly town with tiny pensions, free beaches, and tasteful amusement parks. While it is neither a cosmopolitan center nor the seat of glorious ancient civilizations, Taşucu is worth visiting in its own right if you don't mind fresh fish, great swimming, Ferris wheels, and a wholesome crowd that will remind you of bittersweet Sundays spent with your family at the shore. (Except that this is the Mediterranean and the beach is better.)

ORIENTATION AND PRACTICAL INFORMATION

The town's main square, where the bus or *dolmuş* will drop you off, looks out onto enticing blue water. The **PTT** (open daily 8am-7pm; no exchange services Sat.-Sun.) and several ferry boat offices sell tickets for the seabus and ferry to Girne (Kyrenia), and northern Cyprus. Unless you are into patronizing the underdog, stick with **Fergün Denizälik Şti. Ltd.** (tel. (324) 741 2323, -7311), the largest, richest, fastest, and most reliable of the passenger shipping companies. The **seabus** theoretically has daily departures at 11am, 1pm, and 3pm; arrive in the morning to make sure your chosen vessel will sail and then secure a ticket. (2½-5hr. depending on weather, one way $14.60, round-trip $26.75, 10% student discount.) The **ferry** operates on weekdays (overnight one way $10.70, round-trip $18.75, 10% student discount). Contact them to find out the ever-changing Taşucu port tax ($8.50 per entry or departure at press time). Schedules and taxes are likely to change. Intercity Antalya-Adana **buses** stop here, as well as buses to and from points east. For more extensive connections, *dolmuş* leave every half hour for **Silifke,** the region's transportation hub (and also home to an impressive **castle,** if you aren't sick of them yet).

ACCOMMODATIONS AND FOOD

The highway is only a two-minute walk from the sea. To the left, many pensions feature sunny rooms at similar prices. **Meltem Pansiyon,** 75 Sahil Cad. (tel. (324) 741 4391), all the way down to your left, is probably the nicest choice. All rooms have showers, kitchenettes, sea views, and balconies, and some have A/C that really works! (Singles $10, with A/C $13.30; doubles $13.30, with A/C $16.70.) Meltem tends to fill up fast so call ahead. Closer to the main square, all of the rooms in the **Tuğran Pansiyon,** 3 Sahil Cad. (tel./fax (324) 741 4493), have balconies and showers (singles $10; doubles $17). Two more excellent options are down the road. The **Barış Pansiyon** (tel. (324) 741 2838) offers all the amenities and ocean-front property (doubles $12.50). Down the street, you can't miss the blue and white compound of the **Taşucu Motel,** 8 Sahil Cad. (tel. (324) 741 4952, -2417; fax 741 2418), which has clean but worn rooms with showers, electric fans, and some sea and Ferris wheel views (singles $6.75; doubles $10).

Taşucu's seafood is both affordable and fresh. Do not miss the **Taşucu Balık Restaurant** on the main square. For around $8 you can have the catch of the day, an excellent eggplant appetizer, and a pint of Efes. Overlooking the harbor, **Denizkizi Restoran** serves good *izgara* ($2.75) and a large fish *şiş* ($6.20). At the **Gaziantep Pide Salon,** near the buses, delicious seasoned lamb chops with salad and fresh pitas cost just $1.85. Afterward, head up the beach to one of the many vendors offering ice cream so thick you will need a knife to cut it.

■ Adana

Adana, Turkey's fourth largest city, is appropriately named after Adanus, the god of weather. The average June-August temperature is 100°F with high humidity, and a persistent hot wind seems to issue from a giant invisible hairdryer. If you visit in summer the weather will probably occupy most of your waking thoughts.

Contemporary Adana is modern and has gotten rich from supplying cotton to the Turkish textile industry and *Adana kebap* (spicy minced lamb and herbs, flattened into strips and grilled) to Turkey's hungry mouths. The nearby U.S. military base at İncirlik provides a degree of Western influence. Adana has a giant *otogar* and many hotels, and its airport is a stopping point between North Cyprus, Antalya, and the Middle East. Transportation aside, there is little reason to come here. You can get *Adana kebap* virtually anywhere, and the cotton industry can survive without you.

ORIENTATION AND PRACTICAL INFORMATION

Adana is a large city with few street signs—not a good combination. The main street is the **E-5 highway,** which runs from the center of town past the bus station, and along the Mediterranean coast. In town, the landmarks on the E-5 are the big Akbank building, the overpass, and the minarets of the new Merkez Camii beside the river. With your back to the bus station, take a right at the Akbank onto Atatürk Cad. The **tourist office** (tel. 359 1994) is 10m ahead. The friendly staff speaks English and will supply you with maps (open Mon.-Fri. 8am-noon and 1-5pm). Continue along Atatürk Cad. and take the first right onto İnönü Cad. to reach several hotels. Past İnönü Cad., Atatürk Cad. changes its name to Saydam Cad. A 10-minute walk along here leads to the Atatürk statue. Beyond the Atatürk statue, down a side street to your left, is the main **PTT** (open 24hr.). You can turn left at the Akbank building onto Atatürk Cad. At the end, if you turn right, you will reach the **train station** (20min.). Opposite the station on İstasyon Cad. is a PTT (open 24hr., exchange services 8am-5pm). There is a small **PTT** on İnönü Cad (open 8am-5pm).

To get to the **THY Airlines** office, 1 Stadyum Cad. (tel. 454 1545), turn left out of the tourist office, walk straight, and go right after the second traffic circle (open Mon.-Fri. 8:30am-5:30pm, Sat. 8:30am-noon). Buses do not go to the airport, but *dolmuş* do. To get to the stop from the tourist office, turn right on İnönü Cad. and then left on Zia Paşa Cad. before the Öz Hotel. Past the museum and at the end of the block across from Hotel Kaza, board a *dolmuş* marked "Havaalanı" (airport).

To get to the center of town from the **Merkez Otogar** (bus station), located 5km away along the E-5, cross the road and take an E-5 *dolmuş*. Be sure to cross the road, because destination plates read *Barkal* in both directions (every 5min., 27¢). The *dolmuş* depart the E-5 about 1km before of the Akbank, one block short of the over-pass. Get off here and head for **Kurtulus Meydanı** (Rescue Square), across from İnönü Cad. **Taxis** are metered ($5-6). The larger **bus companies** offer free service to their central offices, clustered around the Akbank on the E-5. It is easiest to buy your ticket in advance from the offices on the E-5. Free service buses will then carry you to the station, 45 minutes to one hour before departure. There is a small **dolmuş station** on the E-5, by the river and opposite the Central Mosque, with services to local towns and villages. *Dolmuş* to Antakya also depart from here (every hr., 3½hr., $1.50), but run along the E-5 first—you can hail them at the Akbank building. *Dolmuş* to Mersin depart from the E-5, near the Akbank. Faster, more comfortable, and less frequent coach bus service to Mersin and Antakya is also available from the *otogar*.

Currency exchange bureaus *(Döviz)* cluster around Saydam Cad., the extension of Atatürk Cad., as you exit the tourist office to the right. **ATMs** are all over the place. To get to the **U.S. consulate** (tel. 453 9106), on the corner of the Atatürk Park, make a left out of the tourist office and pass through three traffic circles. **Foreign-language newspapers** are sold at **Yolgeçen Kitabevi** on Atatürk Blv. near the railway station, where you can pick up day-old copies of *USA Today* and the *International Herald Tribune.* The **postal code** is 01122. The **telephone code** is 322.

ACCOMMODATIONS

Unless you are broke, don't stay in the cheapest hotels—Adana's worst are pretty bad. An exception is the **Otel Mercan,** 5 Ocak Meydanı, Melekgirmez Çarşısı (tel. 351 2603), which is clean and quite plush for a hotel in its class. All rooms have private showers. Facing the Atatürk statue, look right—it is behind the construction site (singles $8; doubles $12). **Otel Duygu,** 14 İnönü Cad. (tel. 359 3916), is clean and comfortable with private showers and TV in each room. Some rooms have balconies. Posted prices are very high, but you can show your *Let's Go* guide for a discount (singles $21; doubles $36; breakfast $2). Across the street, the **İpek Palas,** 103 İnönü Cad. (tel. 351 8741), is similar, but cheaper (singles $19; doubles $30; breakfast $1.70).

FOOD, ENTERTAINMENT, AND SIGHTS

Adana's spicy namesake *(kebap)* will blow you away at **Yeni Onbaşlar,** on Atatürk Cad. opposite the tourist office (open daily 11am-10:30pm). It looks like it has not been renovated since the 50s (you might find this charming). **Limanı Lokantası,** in the arcade opposite the tourist office, serves standard *lokanta* fare (open 6am-9pm).

Walk along the E-5 toward the river to start your tour of the sights. You will pass the huge **Sabanci Merkez Camii** (Central Mosque), the "biggest mosque in the Middle East." Larger than the Taj Mahal, it was financed by the famous (in Turkey) multimillionaire Sakip Sabanci. It is still under construction—ask any local when it is likely to be finished, and he will shrug as only Mediterranean people can. Just before it, the **Archaeological Museum** displays Hittite sculptures, Roman jewelry, and bronze-age pottery (open Tues.-Sun. 8am-noon and 1:30-5pm; admission $1.35). Turn right and follow the river; you will soon pass a small **Atatürk Museum** (open Tues.-Sun. 8am-noon and 1:30-5pm; admission 70¢), and in five minutes you will be at the **Roman bridge,** built by the Roman architect Auxentus in the 4th century. Continue past it for five minutes and go right at the government building to reach the 19th-century **clock tower.** On the right before the clock tower is a park and just beyond it, the **Ulu Camii** (Great Mosque), built by Hailil Bey in 1507 and enlarged in 1541. (Halil is buried inside.) Past the clock tower is the **Bedesten,** a crumbling but bustling 16th-century market.

Continue on to reach **Yağ Camii** (Butter Mosque), an unusual structure that was converted from a church in 1501. The **Catholic church,** home to the city's small Christian community, is down the road to the right, 50m past the Atatürk statue and then down some narrow streets. Just off İnönü Cad. (follow the sign) is a small **Ethnographic Museum.** (Open Tues.-Sun. 8am-noon and 1:30-4pm. Admission $1.35.)

Outside of town is a none too beautiful dam and huge man-made **lake.** Pleasant tea gardens and restaurants are scattered along the shore. The municipality has erected sunscreens over the innumerable benches. A white *dolmuş* marked "Cemal Paşa" on top and "Göl" on the destination board, from opposite the tourist office, will take you all over Adana before stopping at the lake (every 10min., 27¢).

■ Near Adana: Tarsus

If fate ever forces you to spend two or three days in Adana, make the best of it and take a day trip to **Tarsus,** which is both the **birthplace of St. Paul** and the ancient capital of Roman Cilicia. Antony-Cleopatra groupies who have been retracing the couple's rendezvous points along the Eastern Mediterranean will also be interested to learn that the couple is said to have "met" here.

Mersin-bound *dolmuş* leave the stop outside the Merkez Camii every 15 minutes or so (5am-midnight, $1), stopping in Old Tarsus, where the main square commemorates St. Paul with **St. Paul's Well.** The nearby Roman arch is **Cleopatra's Gate.** It is unclear what connection St. Paul and Cleopatra actually have to these structures.

As a final stop, ask to be directed to Tarsus's **selâle,** or waterfall. You probably won't go into raptures over this waterfall, but several cool and pleasant cafes line the gorge. If you have a car you can take a pretty drive along the forest on the rim above. There is not much else in Tarsus, besides an American boys' boarding school. It's time to go back to Adana (sigh).

▓ Antakya (Hatay)

In Antakya, site of the ancient city of **Antioch,** the tourist levels and Mediterranean resort atmosphere subside considerably. You could probably turn the entire province of Hatay inside out without finding a single maraschino cherry, and don't expect your hotel to sponsor poolside aerobics or nightly lip sync contests. Come to Antakya not to pick up sexy foreign sports instructors on sparkling beaches, but to see the **Hatay Museum.** The museum is home to one of the world's best collections of **Roman mosaics,** assembled primarily by an archaeological team from Princeton University with the assistance of the British Museum and the Chicago Oriental Institute. Also, as you may or may not recall, it was in Antioch that "the disciples were called Christians for the first time." Visit **St. Peter's Grotto,** the church where Peter is said to have spoken the fatal words, half hidden in a cave on the southern side of Mt. Stauros. Furthermore, Antakya is a good place to bask in Syrian influence and **hummus,** largely unavailable in the rest of Turkey. The formidable Nur Mountains isolate this city from the rest of Turkey, and at the end of WWI, Hatay province became a part of France's Syrian protectorate. Aleppo (Haleb in Arabic) is a mere four-hour bus ride away (obtain your visa in advance in Ankara or Istanbul).

Kus I "the Satrap of Babil" Nicator, a general under Alexander the Great, founded Antioch in 300 BC and ruled over much of Asia from here. The population swelled to half a million, but growth was what you might call stormy and tumultuous. Internal strife, threats from the neighboring Persian and Roman Empires, 22 years of Egyptian invasions, and a catastrophic earthquake in 148 contributed to an atmosphere of panic and debauchery. In 64 BC the last Seleucid king, Antiochus XIII, gave up and ceded Antioch to the Romans.

By 42 BC, equipped with brand new city walls, an acropolis, amphitheater, courthouse, baths, and aqueducts, Antioch was the third largest city in the Roman Empire. But as they say, there is no rest for the wicked, and if 42 BC was the best of times, it was also the worst of times. Antioch simultaneously became known as a city of incredible wealth and incredible poverty as the Mediterranean's center of science, religious philosophy, commerce, and vice. There was a serious Parthian invasion in 40-39 BC. On the domestic front, religious, racial, and social differences sporadically erupted in violence and riots. Nature kicked in too, racking the city with countless earthquakes. One quake struck when the entire population was gathered in the Hippodrome, killing 250,000 of the city's 750,000 total inhabitants. Contemporary observers have made note of the eerie similarities between ancient Antioch and 20th-century Los Angeles. Oddly enough, it was during this time that the art of laying mosaics on floors—an activity requiring steady hands, steady floors, and, one would think, abundant peace and quiet, reached its peak as the greatest craftsmen of the world flocked to Antioch to create their masterpieces. Around 40 AD the Apostle Peter gathered the first Christian congregation here, intending to convince Antioch to curb its excesses.

After a series of brutal earthquakes, the desperate denizens even changed the city's name to Theopolis (City of God). More great earthquakes ensued, followed by a great fire. In 175-6 AD Marcus Aurelius cancelled the city's Olympic games in order to punish the citizens. In 540 AD the Persians invaded; in 542 a Great Plague wiped out the majority of the population. And in 573 the Persians burned the whole place down. By the time the Ottomans got hold of the city, Sassanians, Arabs, Byzantines, Crusaders, and Mamluks had all marauded through, and Antioch's former Californian splendor had been reduced to ruins, all of which bodes rather badly for Los Angeles. A glance at the city's crumbling walls along the surrounding mountain ridge will give you an idea of the city of yore's size, compared to the population of 150,000 here today.

ORIENTATION AND PRACTICAL INFORMATION

You will arrive at the **bus station,** 1km from the center. Nearly all **buses** pass through İskenderun (every 10min., 1hr., $1.15) and many through Gaziantep (every 30min., 3½hr., $3.70). They serve: Mersin (3 per day, 4hr., $4.25); Urfa (1 per day, 6hr., $10.25); Kayseri (2 per day, 8hr., $13.60); Ankara (10 per day, 11hr., $13.60); Antalya (2 per day, 11hr., $17); Izmir (3 per day, 16hr., $18); Samsun (2 per day, 16hr., $18); Istanbul (9 per day, 17hr., $18); Trabzon (2 per day, 22hr., $21.60); and Kars (1 per day, 22hr., $28). Mersin/Izmir coach buses stop in Adana (2hr., $3.45).

Buses to points east (Urfa, Diyarbakır, etc.) leave around 8pm and arrive in the early hours, around 3 or 4am. To avoid this, you can take one of the regular *dolmuş* from the bus station to **Gaziantep** (3hr., $3.50) and change there for connections. Buses head to: Aleppo (3 per day, $16) and Damascus, Syria (11am and noon, $23.50); Amman, Jordan (5 per week, $33); and daily to major cities in Saudi Arabia (Mecca, Riyadh, Medina, and Jeddah). Get your visas ahead of time in Istanbul or Ankara.

To reach the center of town, exit the bus station, turn left and left again onto İstiklâl Cad. Continue past the Türkiye İş Bankası to the river (700m). Cross the second bridge into the square with the Atatürk statue, without which we'd all be lost.

The **Archaeological Museum** and the **PTT** keep Atatürk company. The PTT is on the traffic circle, on Atatürk Cad. (open 24hr.). Walk 10 minutes down Atatürk Cad. (to the right of PTT) to reach the **tourist office** (tel. 216 0610), in the park opposite the circle. (Open Mon.-Fri. 8:30am-noon and 1:30-5:30pm. English, German, and French spoken.) Blue city **buses** leave from the center, in front of the Hotel Kent (every 20min. 6am-9pm, 15¢). **English-language books** can be found at **Ferah Koll. Şti.,** past Restaurant Nuri (open 7am-9pm). The **postal code** is 31050. The **telephone code** is 326.

ACCOMMODATIONS

Divan Hoteli, 62 İstiklâl Cad. (tel. 215 1518), offers clean 2-3 person rooms with balconies, private showers, and large windows (which make for good air circulation as there is no A/C). Free use of kitchen. $7 per person.

Hotel Saray, 3 Hürriyet Cad. (tel. 214 9001), just across the river from the square and offers new rooms with private bath. The minaret of the Ulu Camii will awaken you at prayer time. Breakfast included. Singles $9.30; doubles $13.80.

Jasmin Hotel, 14 İstiklâl Cad. (tel. 212 7171). Cheap, clean, waterless, and minimalist rooms. Rooftop terrace with TV. Singles $4.15; doubles $7; triples $8.30.

Hotel Orontes, 58 İstiklâl Cad. (tel. 214 5931, fax 214 5933). This two-star hotel offers rooms with A/C and TVs. Breakfast included. Singles $26.20; doubles $35.10.

ANATOLIA

FOOD AND ENTERTAINMENT

Among the specialties of the Hatay region are hummus, *İçli köfte,* often referred to here as *oruk,* a spicy *bulgur* wheat shell with red pepper stuffed with seasoned lamb and pine nuts. *Ekşi aşı* is a variation on *oruk,* covered in tomato sauce. *Kebap* is served with lemon and piles of fresh mint. For dessert, *künefe* (or *peynirli kadayıf*) is a *baklava*-style pastry stuffed with white cheese. These regional treats are not available in all of Antakya's eateries.

Restaurant Nuri, 9 Hürriyet Cad., has a cheap, authentic, delicious *lokanta.* Entrees about $2. Open daily 5pm-1:30am.

Saray Restaurant, under the hotel of the same name, is similar and almost as good.

Sultan Sofrası, 18 İstiklâl Cad., allows you to choose your food from the buffet in the glass case. Excellent *patlicanli kebap* (beef stew with eggplant, $2.15).

'46 Edem Dondurma (tel. 214 5336), has all your favorite fruit flavors, as well as three varieties of *dövme* ice cream: plain (*sade*), chocolate (*çikolata*), and the heavenly pistachio (*fistik*). *Dövme* (literally "beaten") is pounded, kneaded and stretched by machine to reach a thick gooey consistency.

SIGHTS

The mosaic collection in the **Hatay Museum** (a.k.a. the Archaeological Museum) has to be seen to be believed. Assembled over a millennium before color TV and the Pointillist School, thousands of tiny tiles create images of nearly photographic exactitude. For example, note the particularly charming wild pig in Salon I. She appears surrounded by the mythological figures Atalanta and Meleagar in "A Pig Hunt in Calydonia," the panel between "Spring" and "Summer" in *The Four Seasons* (2nd century AD; found in Harbiye). The most imposing mosaic in Salon IV (5th century AD; found in Yakto) is the giant hunting scene on the floor; climb the spiral staircase to the balcony for a complete view. The bust in the middle represents the spirit Megalopsychia. Directly across from the balcony you will notice a 2nd-century calendar mosaic depicting Oceanus, his wife Thetis, and a great many unrecognizable but incredibly vivid fish (several with more eyes than normal). Several panels illustrate Dionyseus in various stages of debauchery, including a 4th-century *Drunken Dionyseus* leaning on a satyr, and the 2nd-century *Mosaic of a Coma* in which Dionyseus, having passed out, is ministered to by the sleep god Hypnos. There is also a rather obscene 2nd-century *Happy Hunchback* mosaic for your viewing pleasure.

In the garden, glut your taste for symbolism with the illustration of Psyche about to waken the sleeping Eros. Also of interest is *The Evil Eye,* a scantily clad man running in horror from an enormous levitating eye radiating farming implements. (Open Tues.-Sun. 8:30am-noon and 1:30-5pm. Admission $2, students $1.05.)

To get to **Sen Piyer Kilisesi** (St. Peter's Church, a.k.a. St. Peter's Grotto) from the bus station, turn left and then take an immediate right onto İstiklâl Cad. Follow it one block to the twin gas stations and turn right, continuing 1.2km until you see a sign on the right. The church is 250m from the sign. The somewhat erratic city bus #6 will drop you off near the sign or you can take a taxi from town ($2.20). Founded by the Apostle Peter who preached here along with Paul and Barnabas, the original congregation coined the word "Christianity" to describe their new religion. Although the Christian community here is now tiny, it has never left Antakya. The church is built into a cave because the earliest services had to be conducted in secret. The subterranean spring dripping into a basin in the back is believed to have healing properties. A delegate of the French Commissary in Syria donated the nearby statuette of St. Peter. For more information on Christianity and Antakya call the **Antakya Catholic Church** at tel. 215 6703. Mass is held Sundays from 3-4:30pm.

The hillside near the church, riddled with the remains of caves, tunnels, and parts of Antioch's city walls, has been a holy spot since pagan times. A path zigzags 200m up to a high relief of Charonion (sometimes referred to as Haron or Charon), **Boatman of Hell.** A great plague reputedly struck the city of Antioch during the reign of Epiphanes, who was subsequently advised by an oracle to construct this likeness of

Charonion (the mythological gondolier who ferries souls to the underworld) high in the mountains. The huge woman's head beside the figure of the hellish boatman is believed to belong to the Syrian **Goddess of Hierapolis,** an underworld Mafiosa type whom the Byzantines frequently associated with Charonion (church open Tues.-Sun. 8am-noon and 1:30-5:30pm; free).

■ Harbiye

Originally named for Daphne the wood nymph, who was transformed into a laurel tree as protection from Apollo's amorous advances, the town of Harbiye and its attractive gorge has been a popular excursion spot since Roman times. Legend has it than Antony and Cleopatra were married here in another stop on their whirlwind Mediterranean love-in. A favorite tourist destination for years among Syrians and Iranians, Harbiye is beginning to win Western tourists as well with its fresh air, fantastic local food and breathtaking views. Nearly all of Harbiye's pensions are located on the gorge and have balconies.

ORIENTATION AND PRACTICAL INFORMATION

Dolmuş from Antakya's famed dual gas stations head for Harbiye every 10 minutes (8km away). To get to the stop from Antakya's *otogar,* turn left then right. Walk one block to the red and white gas station sign (another identical station is across the street). This is the *dolmuş* to Harbiye and Samandağ (both well-marked; 25¢). After 10 minutes, the Harbiye *dolmuş* passes under an arch marked "Harbiye Belediyesi" on the main thoroughfare (some call it Atatürk Cad., others Harbiye Cad.—in any case it's unmarked and residents don't seem to know or care what it's called). The **PTT** is on the right (open Mon.-Sat. 8:30am-12:30pm and 1:30-5:30pm), and the *dolmuş* veers right off the main road. Get off after the large pack of off-duty *dolmuş*. This is Harbiye's restaurant and pension street (Ürgen Cad. for the record, though you will not find a sign). It also contains the brand-new **Gözde Laundromat** (prices negotiable). The **postal code** is 31020. The **telephone code** is 326.

ACCOMMODATIONS

Numerous tiny family pensions dot the street with bright signs, usually in Turkish, English, and Arabic. These generally let 3-4 rooms, and the proprietors are very keen on renting you the whole place at once for a discounted price. The best all-around services, however, are offered by the larger **Turistik Hidro Oteli** and **Hotel Harbiye.** The newly-opened Hotel Harbiye (tel. 231 4212, -3060) offers shared kitchens on every floor and spacious, spotless rooms with private showers, TV, ceiling fans, excellent mattresses, and balconies overlooking the gorge ($10.35 per person; breakfast included). Rooms in **Hidro** (tel. 231 4006, -4657) feature private showers, starched white sheets, balconies with marvellous views, and remarkably high-quality free soap (singles $12; doubles $18; breakfast $3).

FOOD AND ENTERTAINMENT

Harbiye is deservedly renowned for its rendition of regional Hatay specialties like *ızgara* and *şiş tavuk* (chicken), *oruk* (spicy meatball in pastry), and *künefe* (baklava-style pastry with white cheese). Try them at the **Hidro Oteli** (see above) opposite the gorge at the *dolmuş* stop (*oruk* $2.50, *ızgara tavuk* $3.40, *künefe* or *peynirli kadayf* $1.50). Just up the road, the **Soner Restaurant** (tel. 231 2222) features similar prices and quality as well as a regular evening *chanteur.* Come early if you wish to avoid the Turkish nightclub scene. Try the ice cream at **Dedem Dondurma** on Atatürk Cad., opposite the Büyük Antakya Oteli. **Cafe Defne,** a beer garden under a grape arbor, overlooks the gorge (beer $1.70, entrees $2-4). Several tea gardens and cafes feature background Turkish music down in the cool, shady valley by the waterfall (*Harbiye Şelâlesi*).

Central Anatolia

The steppes, plateaus, and mountains of Central Anatolia form Turkey's agricultural hub, and contain some of the country's most authentic and hospitable villages. While the Aegean and Mediterranean Coasts (a.k.a. the "Turkish Riviera") have evolved into a crescent of tourist sites and Eurobeaches, and the Black Sea coast feels somehow like Eastern Europe, the essence of traditional Turkey is alive and well in the sparse but fertile mountains of Central Anatolia.

ANKARA AND ENVIRONS

■ Ankara

In many respects, Ankara plays Washington, D.C. to Istanbul's New York, Moscow to Istanbul's St. Petersburg. Though less charming and European than Istanbul, Ankara is also less pretentious and buzzes with a current of real life, urgency, and industry found nowhere else in Turkey. The fact that Ankara, like Moscow, has no river lends its semi-arid steppes and plains a central Asian atmosphere. Gazing at the billboards and terra cotta roofs on the hills along the highway from Esenboğa airport, visitors can easily imagine the days when merchants covered this distance by camel, carrying salt from central Anatolia's lakes. Indeed, travelers will feel oddly at home here in what was established over 3,200 years ago as an *en route* city, first named Ankuwash by the Hittites who founded it at the intersection of two Eurasian trade routes. Legend has it that Ankara was next ruled by the great Phrygian King Midas himself. Subsequently occupied by Lydians, Galatians, Augustan Romans, Byzantines, and Seljuks, Ankara was eventually appropriated by the Ottomans as the peaceful settlement of Angora, populated mainly by long-haired goats.

In 1923, after the Turkish War of Independence, **Atatürk** rebuilt the city more or less from scratch and more or less instantly. The Painting and Sculpture Museum, for example, was constructed, dedicated, and filled with contemporary Turkish art in just 18 months. Today, Ankara is an administrative metropolis of parks and tree-lined boulevards, pillared embassies, newspaper headquarters, and universities. And if its beautiful summer weather isn't enough to lure you, remember that Ankara is both the transportation hub of Turkey as well as a convenient base for securing visas for Eastern Europe, the Middle East, the former Soviet republics, and central Asia.

ORIENTATION AND PRACTICAL INFORMATION

The city's main street, **Atatürk Bulvarı,** runs north-south. At its north end, the **Ulus** and **Sihhiye** precincts offer dusty cement apartments, crowded markets, depressing lotto ticket vendors (often playing the harmonica), and monumental bronze statues of the likes of Atatürk and a giant Hittite reindeer. To the east of Ulus rises the **Citadel** (*Hisar*), a traditional Anatolian village scattered with upscale restaurants, and crowned by the 9th century **Ankara Fortress** (*Ankara Kale*). Ulus and the Citadel comprise the **Old City** (*Eskişehir*), where you'll find most of the sights and the cheapest hotels. A couple of kilometers south of Ulus is **Kızılay,** the center of the **New City** (Yenişehir), bustling with bookstores, bars, kebap houses, and students from the nearby Ankara, Başkent, Bilkent, Gazi, Hacettep, and Middle East Technical Universities. Two kilometers south of Kızılay lie **Kavaklıdere** and **Çankaya,** representing the most stately side of Ankara: lush residential areas of embassies, ministries, five-star hotels, and night clubs. Bus #391 runs the length of Atatürk Blv. from the main gate of the Citadel to the **Atatürk Tower.** In addition, a brand-spanking new subway system has its center in Kızılay. The bus terminal (**AŞTİ** on the signs, *otogar* to the

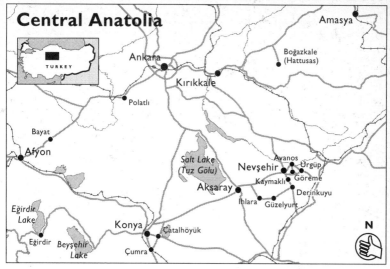

Central Anatolia

TURKEY

Amasya

Ankara

Boğazkale
(Hattusas)

Kırıkkale

Polatlı

Bayat

Afyon

Salt Lake
(Tuz Gölü)

Ayanos

Nevşehir

Ürgüp

Kaymaklı

Göreme

Akşaray

Derinkuyu

İhlara

Güzelyurt

Eğirdir
Lake

Konya

Çatalhöyük

N

Eğirdir

Beyşehir
Lake

Çumra

locals) in **Söğütözü** is 5km west of Kızılay, at the westernmost Ankaray subway stop; the railway station (*gar*) is 1.5km southwest of Ulus Sq. on **Cumhuriyet Blv.**

Tourist Offices: 121 Gazi Mustafa Kemal Blv. (tel. 488 7007, 231 5572; open Mon.-Fri. 8:30am-6:30pm, Sat.-Sun. 9am-5pm; reduced hours in the off season). Directly outside the Maltepe stop on Ankaray (from Kızılay, take the train headed toward AŞTİ). The staff speaks English and an assortment of other languages. Come here for free city and country maps, or to file a complaint with the **tourist police;** the tourist office will serve as your interpreter. The **airport tourist office** (tel. 398 0348, 398 0000, 398 1578) is open 24hr.

Embassies: Afghanistan, 88 Cinnah Cad., Çankaya (tel. 438 1121; fax 438 7745). **Albania,** 17 Ebüzziye Tevfik Sok., Çankaya (tel. 441 6103; fax 441 6104). **Australia,** 83 Nenehatun Cad., Gaziosmanpaşa (tel. 446 1180; fax 446 1188). **Azerbaijan,** 20 Cemal Nadir Sok., Çelikler Apt., Gankaya (tel. 441 2621; fax 446 2600). **Bosnia,** 98/ 8-9 Mahatma Gandhi Cad., Gaziosmanpaşa (tel. 446 4090; fax 446 6225). **Bulgaria,** 124 Atatürk Blv., Kavaklıdere (tel. 426 7455; fax 427 3178). **Canada,** 75 Nenehatun Cad. (tel. 436 1275, 427 3178; fax 446 2811). **Croatia,** 15/A Kelebek Sok., Gaziosmanpaşa (tel. 446 9460, 446 0831; fax 436 6212). **Czech Republic,** 100 Uğurnuncu Cad., Gaziosmanpaşa (tel. 446 1244; fax 446 1245). **Egypt,** 126 Atatürk Blv., Kavaklıdere (tel. 426 1026; fax 426 6478). **Germany,** 114 Atatürk Blv., Kavaklıdere (tel. 426 5465; for visas, 468 5906; fax 426 6959). **Great Britain,** 46A Şehit Ersan Cad., Çankaya (tel. 468 6230; fax 468 3214). **Greece,** 9-11 Zia Ül-Rahman Cad., Gaziosmanpaşa (tel. 436 8860; fax 446 3191). **Hungary,** 10 Gazi Mustafa Kemal Blv., Kızılay (tel. 418 6257; fax 418 8322). **Iraq,** 11 Turan Emeksiz Sok., Gaziosmanpaşa (tel. 468 7421; fax 468 4832). **Iran,** 10 Tahran Cad., Kavaklıdere (tel. 427 4320; fax 468 2823). **Israel,** 85 Mahatma Gandi Cad., Gaziosmanpaşa (tcl. 446 3605; fax 426 1533). **Jordan,** 18 Dede Korkut Sok., Aşagiayranci (tel. 440 2054; fax 440 4327). **Kyrgyzstan,** 11 Boyabat Sok., Eren Apt., Gaziosmanpaşa (tel. 446 8408; fax 446 8413). **Lebanon,** 44 Kızkulesi Sok. (tel. 446 7487; fax 446 1023). **Macedonia,** 30/2 Filistin Sok., Gaziosmanpaşa (tel. 446 9204; fax 446 9206). **Moldavia,** 49 Kaptanpaşa Sok., Gaziosmanpaşa (tel. 446 5627, 446 5527; fax 446 5816). **New Zealand,** 13/4 İran Cad., Kavaklıdere (tel. 467 9056; fax 467 9013). **Northern Cyprus,** 20 Rabat Sok., Gaziosmanpaşa (tel. 437 6031; fax 446 5238). **Oman,** 63 Mahatma Gandhi Cad. (tel. 447 0630; fax 447 0632). **Pakistan,** 37 Iran Cad., Gaziosmanpaşa (tel. 427 1410, -11; fax 467 1023). **Palestine,** 45 Filistin Sok. (tel. 436 0823; fax 437 7801). **Poland,** 241 Atatürk Blv., Kavaklıdere (tel. 426 1694; 427 3987). **Qatar,** 19 Karaca Sok., Gaziosmanpaşa (tel. 441 1364, -66; fax 441 1544). **Romania,** 4 Bükreş Sok., Çankaya (tel. 427 1241; fax 427 1530). **Russia,** 5

Karayağdız Sok., Çankaya (tel. 439 2122; fax 438 3952). **Saudi Arabia,** 6 Turan Emeksiz Sok., Gaziosmanpaşa (tel. 468 5540, -47; fax 427 4886). **Slovakia,** 245 Atatürk Blv., Kavaklıdere (tel. 426 5887, -97; fax 468 2689). **South Africa,** 27 Filistin Sok., Gaziosmanpaşa (tel. 446 4056; fax 446 6434). **Syria,** 40 Sedat Simavi Sok., Çankaya (tel. 440 9657; fax 438 5609). **Tunisia,** 42 Kuleli Sok., Gaziosmanpaşa (tel. 437 7812, 437 7720; fax 437 7100). **Ukraine,** 9 Cemal Nadir Sok., Çankaya (tel. 440 5289; fax 440 6815). **United Arab Emirates,** 10 Mahmud Yesari Sok., Çankaya (tel. 446 4090; fax 438 9854). **U.S.,** 110 Atatürk Blv., Kavaklıdere (tel. 468 6110; fax 467 0019). **Uzbekistan,** 14 Ahmet Rasim Sok., Çankaya (tel. 439 2740; fax 440 2740). **Yugoslavia,** 47 Paris Cad., Kavaklıdere (tel. 426 0354; fax 427 8345).

Banks: Bank lovers will delight in the profusion of banks all along Kavaklıdere, Kızılay, Maltepe, Ulus, and Sıhhiye—you literally cannot throw a stone without hitting a branch office. All large banks offer **currency exchange.** Slightly better rates are available at the change offices *(döviz)* along Atatürk Blv.

ATMs: 24hr. machines of varying reliability can be found on virtually every street corner. Akbank accepts MasterCard and Visa; Türkiye İş Bankası, Pamukbank, Vakıfbank, and Telebank Garanti Banka accept Cirrus, PLUS, Eurocard, MasterCard and Visa; Galkbank accepts Visa. Vakıfbank ATMs offer the most consistent Cirrus and PLUS service.

American Express: The main offices on Cinnah Cad. are now mere travel agencies. Akbank, Koçbank, or Türkiye İş Bankası will cash AmEx Traveler's Checks (and usually MasterCard Traveler's Checks as well). Don't forget to bring your passport. AmEx card-holders can send and receive moneygrams at the Koçbank in Ulus Sq.

Emergency Telephone Numbers: medical emergency, 112; police, 155 (regional police, 156); fire, 110; international operator, 115.

Flights: *Havaş* buses to **Esenboğa Airport** (tel. 398 0000) leave from Hipodrom Cad. (next to the train station), 1 per hr. ($5). Major carriers to and from Ankara include: Aeroflot, Air France, Alitalia, Austrian Airlines, British Airways, Iberia, J.A.L., K.L.M., Canadian Airlines, Lufthansa, Delta, and Swissair.**Turkish Airlines (THY),** 231 Atatürk Blv., Kavaklıdere (tel.: info, 419 2800, -25; sales, 468 7330), offers students (age 14-24) a 25% discount on direct flights to Istanbul (14 flights per day, 1hr., $60), Izmir (3 per day, 1¼hr., $50), Antalya (at least 1 per day, 1hr., $50), Adana (at least 1 per day, 1¼hr., $50), and Trabzon (2 per day, 1¼hr., $50). Try to buy tickets two days in advance, because the flights fill up. It is often easier to buy tickets from one of the private travel agencies visible between Kızılay and Kavaklıdere. Open Mon.-Sat. 8:30am-7:30pm, Sun. 8:30am-5:30pm.

Trains: Blue trains *(Mavi Tren)* serve Istanbul (1 per day, 1pm, 7hr., $8.50) and Izmir (1 per day, 9:15pm, 13hr., $8.50). Regular *(ekspres)* trains also serve Istanbul (5 per day, 8am-10:30pm; 7hr. during the day, 9½hr. overnight, $7), Izmir (1 per day, 15hr., $7.75), Adana (1 per day, 12hr., $7), Kayseri (1 per day, 7¼hr., $4.25), and Niğde (1 per day, 8:10pm, 8½hr., $5.50). Istanbul's train stations are Bostancı and Haydarpaşa; Izmir's is Basmane, where students get a 30% discount on all train tickets. Sometime this year, a commuter rail system (TCDD Banliyö) is expected to begin running between Sihhiye and Ankara's outlying suburbs.

Subway: Brand new trains on the east-west Ankaray line (stations marked by a white "A" on a green background) connect the bus station to Dikimevi, with stops in Tandoğan, Maltepe, Kızılay, and the Colleges (Kolej). 5-ride passes $1, 70¢ for students. Runs 6:15am-midnight. Service on the north-south Metro line (white "A" on red background), also passing through Kızılay, has not started yet, but may by the time you arrive.

Buses: The **terminal** (a.k.a. *AŞTI* or *Otogar*), 5km west of Kızılay in Söğütözü, is connected to all points in the city by local buses, *dolmuş,* and taxis. It is also the westernmost stop on the Ankaray line. *Dolmuş* (60¢) run when full to Ulus. Their dropoff point is Hisarpark Cad., in the middle of the cheap hotel area. A taxi for the same trip should cost about $5.50. City buses (30¢) also make the trip. As with Istanbul, scores of companies connect Ankara with nearly every point in Turkey, and buses depart around the clock. To: Istanbul (34 per day, 7½hr., $10.50); Izmir (about 20 per day, 8½hr., $12.25); Antalya (11hr., $10.50); Konya (3½hr., $5.60); Trabzon (12hr., $14); Sungurlu (to Boğazkale) (3hr., $5.25). Student discounts sometimes available upon request. Schedules and prices change. Private bus companies such as **Varan** (34/1 Izmir Cad., Kızılay, tel. 418 2706, 224 0043) and **Ulusoy**

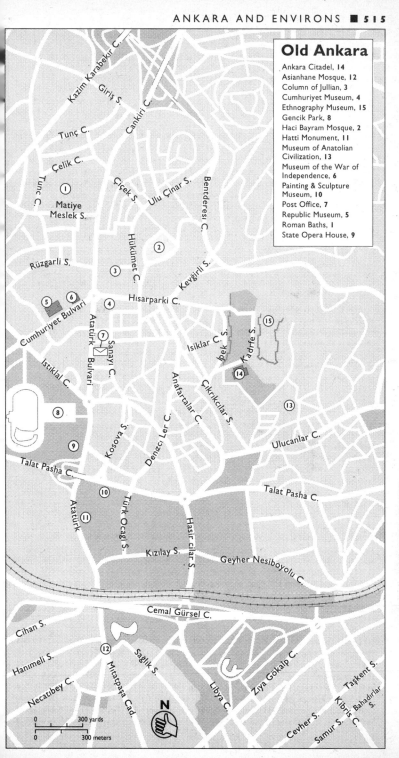

Old Ankara

Ankara Citadel, 14
Asianhane Mosque, 12
Column of Jullian, 3
Cumhuriyet Museum, 4
Ethnography Museum, 15
Gencik Park, 8
Haci Bayram Mosque, 2
Hatti Monument, 11
Museum of Anatolian
Civilization, 13
Museum of the War of
Independence, 6
Painting & Sculpture
Museum, 10
Post Office, 7
Republic Museum, 5
Roman Baths, 1
State Opera House, 9

ANATOLIA

(18/A İnkılap Sok., Kızılay, tel. 418 5212, 224 0172) offer faster, more expensive and posh (coach buses, complimentary tea and coffee) service to major destinations (Varan's service to Istanbul is 6hr., $19, students $17).

Car Rental: Depar Rent A Car (17/A Büyükelci Sok., Kavaklıdere, tel. 426 9354, 426 9355, open daily 8am-8pm) and **Alara Rent A Car** (1/A Güniz Sok., Kavaklıdere, tel. 426 5475; fax 426 5263) rent Şaphins (a make of Fiat), $35 per day, $195/week, $800/month, and air-conditioned Toyotas for $84 per day, $525 per week, $1,021 per month.

Lost and Found: *Kayıp Eşya* in Esenboğa (tel. 398 1517, 398 0550) and the bus terminal (tel. 224 1000), as well as the Head Security Office (*Emniyet Müdürlük*), İskitler Cad. (tel. 384 0606, 384 6445).

City Buses: Ankara has a furiously busy, beehive-like bus system. Buses come in three flavors: red, green, and blue. Red and green buses are government-run, blue are private. Buy tickets for red and green buses (30¢) from booths near major bus stops or street vendors. On the blue buses, pay conductors once on board (30¢). Conductor sits at desks halfway down the buses. *Dolmuş* within the city cost 35-60¢, depending on distance.

Library: National Library (*Millî Kütüphane*), Bahçelievler (tel. (4) 212 6200; fax 223 0451). Free entry with photo ID (a guard at the front door will hold your card until you leave the library), this multi-level, rose marble CD-ROM equipped library can be reached via *dolmuş* (30¢) from Kızılay's **Güvenpark.** Study salons open Mon.-Fri. 9am-9pm, Sat.-Sun. 9:30am-6:30pm; stacks open Mon.-Fri. 9am-noon, 1:30-4:30pm.

English Bookstores: ABC Bookshop, 1 Selanik Cad., Kızılay (tel. 434 3842), 2 blocks north and ½ block east of the main square. Good selection of English books. While Ankara has no English bookstores per se, most bookstores in Kızılay offer a fair range of (in order of abundance) Wordsworth Classics (a cheerless line with emphasis on Eliot, Austen, and Hardy), Steven King's œuvres, and nonfiction (*Fisk's Introduction to Linguistics, Michael Jackson: The Real Truth*). Open daily 9am-7pm. An especially good selection can be found at **Tahran Kitabevi** (19A Selanik Cad., tel. 417 2550, open daily 9am-12:30pm, 2-7pm) and **Dost Kitabevi** (4 Konur Sok., tel. 418 8327, open Mon.-Sat. 9am-7:30pm, Sun. noon-6pm). From spring to fall the **open-air book market** on Karanfil Sok. is the place to go for cheap back issues of U.S. magazines (*Newsweek,* 4¢, *Cosmopolitan,* 3 for 70¢, full-year color J.C. Penny catalog $1.75).

Turkish-American Cultural Association: 20 Cinnah Cad., Kavaklıdere (tel. 426 2644, fax 468 2538, email ak01-k@servis2.net.tr, http://www.ekosis.com.tr/taa). Cinnah Cad. branches off from Atatürk Blv. south of Bakanlıklar. Take any bus marked "Kavaklıdere" from the stop across from the Ulus PTT. There is less reason to come here now that the American Association Library has been permanently closed, but if you're in the area, stop by to catch up on your MTV, shown on the 70s-decorated, glass-enclosed front lobby. Small selections of U.S. magazines (also free coupons for the Kavaklıdere Kentucky Fried Chicken) in the Graphica Cafe (coffee and mediocre pastry, $1, open Mon.-Fri. 9am-9:30pm, Sat.-Sun. 9am-4pm). Frequent photography, painting, and craft exhibits. Occasional nostalgia nights, ballroom dances, happy hours, and concerts. They also offer monthly "workshops" (e.g. Bank Strategy and Performance, Patchwork Quiltmaking).

Laundromat: Self-service launderette (*Ekspres Çamaşir*) in the Beğendik shopping mall under the Kocatepe mosque in Kızılay. Go up the motorized ramps to the luggage department, and take a right; exit at the end of the corridor; turn left. Open daily 9:30am-9pm, wash and dry $2.75. Free locker storage. Ironing about 50¢ per article.

24-Hour Pharmacy: Ankara's pharmacies (*eczane*) take turns being open 24hr. For listings of on-duty (*nöbetci*) pharmacies, consult the *Hürriyet* daily newspaper (same page as movie listings). On-duty establishments should also have a sign in the front window.

Hospital: Bayındır Tıp Merkezi, Kızılırmak Mah. #3-3A 28th Sok. (tel. 287 9000), and **Sevgi Hastaesi,** 28 Tunus Cad., Kavaklıdere (tel. 419 4444, -60) are among Ankara's best private hospitals. **Hacettepe Üniverite Tıp Fakultes Hastanesi,** Hazırcılar Cad., Samonpazarı (tel. 310 3545), and **Ankara Üniversitesi Tıp Fakült-**

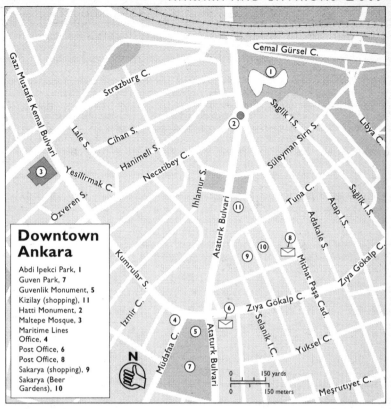

Downtown Ankara

Abdi Ipekci Park, 1
Guven Park, 7
Guvenlik Monument, 5
Kizilay (shopping), 11
Hatti Monument, 2
Maltepe Mosque, 3
Maritime Lines Office, 4
Post Office, 6
Post Office, 8
Sakarya (shopping), 9
Sakarya (Beer Gardens), 10

esi Hastanesi, Tıp Fakültesi Cad., Dikimevi (tel. 319 2160), are the largest university hospitals.

Internet Access: InterplaNET Club, 47/1 Karanfil Sok., Kızılay. Computer use $3 per hr. at one of the 5 Pentium workstations (Windows 95, Netscape, Telnet, word processing, and Sound Blaster). Black-and-white and color printing available, tea served upon request. Soundtrack ranging from Metallica to Madonna and wallpaper printed with tiny surfers sets a hyper-global atmosphere. Open daily 9am-9pm.

PTT: On Atatürk Bulvarı in Kızılay and in Ulus. Both open 24hr. In the train station, open daily 7am-11pm. Poste Restante open Mon.-Sat. 8:30am-5:30pm. **Telephones** at every PTT as well as at the bus and train stations. **Postal Code:** 06443. **Telephone Code:** 312.

ACCOMMODATIONS

If Kavaklıdere's and Gankaya's five-star hotels are not up your alley, Kızılay and Ulus will be your two main accommodation centers. If you can afford the slightly higher rates, the lively student-oriented, largely traffic-free Kızılay is a more pleasant prospect then the dustier, noisier Ulus, though Ulus is nearer to most of the sites. Women traveling alone should know that the there is about a 70-30 male-female ration of pedestrians in the evenings.

Kızılay

Otel Ertan, 70 Selanik Cad. (tel. 418 4084, 425 1506). Going south along Atatürk Blv., take the fourth left after McDonald's onto Meşrutiyet Cad., then the third right onto Selanik Cad. Decent rooms with showers and a garden in front. Peaceful, yet close to the Kızılay nightlife. Singles $12.30; doubles $17.60.

ANATOLIA

M.E.B. Özel Ülkü Kız Öğrenci Yurt, 61 Karanfil Sok. (tel. 419 3715, -3067), between Akay Cad. and Meşrutiyet Cad. off of Atatürk Blvd. This girls' dormitory is open to women travelers from July-Sept., providing clean, relatively safe lodgings with shared bathrooms/showers and a cafeteria. 24hr. hot water. Singles $7; doubles $14; triples $16.

M.E.B. Özel Çağdaş Erkek Öğrenci Yurt, 15 Neyzen Tevfik Sok., Maltepe (tel. 232 2954, -5). Coming out of the Maltepe Ankaray stop onto G.M.K. Blv., make a right (away from the tourist office) uphill onto Neyzen Tevfik Sok. These dormitories located between G.M.K. Blv. and Gençlik Cad. serve as a coed hostel from June 1-Sept. 1. Singles, doubles, triples, and quads $12 per person.

Hotel Ergen, 48 Karanfil Sok. (tel. 417 5906). Recommended by the tourist office, Ergen offers clean rooms equipped with televisions and private showers. Breakfast $2; no hot water 2-8pm. Singles $25; doubles $45.

Ulus

Ulus is packed with extremely cheap hotels, some more Dostoevskian than others. To find them from the train station, take Cumhuriyet Blv. straight to the equestrian statue in Ulus Sq., which marks the center of town. On your left will be a sports club complete with parachute tower; Gençlik Park will be on your right. (This is roughly a 20min. walk, so take a taxi if you are burdened with baggage.) From the bus station, take Ankaray to Kızılay and head north on Atatürk Blvd.

Hotel Taç, 35 Çankın Cad., (tel. 324 3195, -6). North of the statue, Atatürk Blv. becomes Çankın Cad.; this is a busy, well-lit street which makes lodging here safer, noisier, more convenient to the Roman ruins, and slightly more expensive than elsewhere in Ulus. Charming elevator and clean, attractive, strangely-shaped rooms with private showers: singles $10.50, $7 without shower, breakfast $1.75.

Hotel Kale, Anafartalar Cad. 13 Alataş Sok. (tel. 311 3393, 310 3521). From the statue follow Hisarpark Cad. toward the Citadel and turn right on Anafartalar Cad. A brand-new, clean, and pleasant hotel. All rooms have private showers, televisions, and sofas. Singles $10; doubles $18. Breakfast $2.

Marmara Otel, 17 Demizciler Cad. (tel. 324 2740). From the statue take Anafartalar Cad. and bear right onto Demizciler Cad. Clean but spartan singles, $3.50; doubles $7; triples $10. All toilets are "à la turka"—a hole in the ground with footprints on either side (awkward for women wearing shorts or pants). No showers; the Turkish bath next door, **Marmara Hamami,** costs $3.50.

Otel Şan, 8/C Şan Sok. (tel. 311 0943, -9998). Heading away from the statue on Anafartalar Cad., Şan Sok. is the 4th street on the left. An old-fashioned hotel with a 1920s feel. Closets have locks. Singles (without shower) $5.30; doubles $9.15 ($12.70 with shower); triples $17.60.

Bulduk Otel, 26 Sanayı Cad. (tel. 310 4915, -16, -17), parallel to Atatürk Blv. just south of, yes, the statue. Offers televisions in each room—eureka! Singles (with bathtub) $14; doubles (with half-size tub) $21.25; triples (with shower) $26.40.

Efes Hotel, 12 Demizciler Cad. (tel. 324 3211, -12; fax 311 5137). For just $12 (single), $19.50 (double), or $24.75 (triple) you can stay in the hotel with the same name as Turkey's favorite beer. It even has an elevator! Private showers in all rooms. Breakfast $1.75.

Otel Oba, 9 Posta Cad. (tel. 312 4128, -29). Clean. Elevator. Singles $7 ($8.50 with shower); doubles $11.25 ($15.50 with shower); Roger, Oba and out.

Otel Yavuz, Anafartalar Cad., 6 Konya Sok. Clean. Elevator. Singles $6; doubles $11.25 ($15.50 with shower).

Camping

D.S.i Kampi, Bayindir Barajı, tel. 372 2731. By car, take the road to Samsun, past Kayaş; the campground will be on your right. *Dolmuş* service runs from Demizciler Cad., Ulus (30¢). There is a gas station and cafe nearby. State-operated; open May 1 until it gets too cold; camping $1.00 per day; free use of toilets, showers, and laundry; 24hr. hot water.

FOOD

The main culinary neighborhoods are Kızılay (mid-range), Gençlik Park (cheap), the Citadel (upscale, touristy), and Kavaklıdere (upscale, trendy). In addition, just southeast of the Atatürk Tower, **Hoşdere Caddesi** lays claim to many good restaurants, as does Ahmet Mitat Sok., the side street one block south of it. If restaurant life does not suit your wallet, you'll be placated at the many supermarkets. **Gıma,** with branches on Atatürk Blv. in Kızılay and on Anafartalar Cad. in Ulus, and **Beğendik,** under the Kocatepe mosque in Kızılay (at the south end of Mithat Paşa Cad.), are comprehensive mercantile vortices. At these stores, you can stock up on rugs, furniture, electronics, watches, shoes, linens, toys, cosmetics, life insurance, and, by the way, food. The **Migros** chain (look for the *MMM* symbol) restricts itself to supermarket wares and has branches on Celalbayar Blv. in Maltepe and on Uğur Mumcu Cad. in Çankaya.

If you number among those who travel to escape mass consumerism, refuge awaits you at the small, hyper-specialized food stores lining the streets of Kavaklıdere, Kızılay, and Ulus. **Bread** baked daily at bread *(ekmek)* stores is about 14¢ a loaf. The grocery stands overflow nearly year-round with exotic fruits. In the spring, try the orange-yellow Malatyan plums *(malatya erik)* that are tart and tangy but totally unrelated to standard plums. The glamorous name alone is worth the $3.50 per kg. In late summer peaches *(şeftali)* and figs *(incir)* are a must. For snacks try Ankara's *simit*, something between a pretzel and a sesame bagel (10¢). Corn-on-the-cob *(mısır)* is 20¢, and *helva* (multi-colored dish-sized wafers) are 35¢.

Helva is also sold at cake shops *(pastane)*, but the best deal by far at these shops is the ice cream *(dondurma)*. Turkish ice cream is not very creamy and comes primarily in fruit flavors (18¢ per scoop). Other specialty stores of interest are *kuruyemiş* shops which sell coffee beans and nuts.

The Citadel

To get to the restaurants, do not enter the Citadel via the steps at Hisarpark Cad.—the Citadel is a confusing labyrinth. Instead, enter via the gate uphill from the Museum of Anatolian Civilizations. Several traditional Turkish restaurants are clustered around the main square inside the gate. All of them are high-class (not *kebap* joints) but reasonably priced. **Kale Washington,** on the square just to your left, offers tasty fare on an open-air, canopied terrace (*imambayıldı* (stuffed eggplant) $2.50, main courses roughly $5.25).

Kavaklıdere / Gaziosmanpaşa

Several upscale restaurants, favored by the employees of the nearby embassies, line Noktalı Sok., the road leading uphill on the right of the Sheraton Hotel (main courses $5-7) in this area. At **Paul Boulangerie,** you can look at exposed bricks while dining on crepes ($2.10) or panini sandwiches ($3), while the **Daily News Cafe,** decorated entirely with newspapers, will transport you to a pseudo-Greenwich Village as you enjoy standard pub food with a Turkish twist. Arjantin Cad. will feel like another planet as you float from **Beethoven Restaurant, Cafe, and Bar** (canned techno by day, live Turkish/American guitar music by night; omelettes $1.75) to the art nouveau **Cafe Kahve** ("buffalo burger" $3.85, chocolate soufflé $3). Just around the corner, **Buzilika Restaraunt, Cafe & Bar** (66 Nenehatun Cad., tel. 436 57 54, -3460, -3354; fax 436 22 49) tempts jaded palates with a menu rich in delicacies (artichoke hearts with tuna salad $4.25, calamari $3.85, *Dom Perignon* $140). **Cafemiz,** decorated with Toulouse-Lautrec murals, dishes up a delicious *kestane kup* (chestnut puree, vanilla ice cream and raspberry sauce, $2), as well as entrees running the gamut from the indecipherable French (puff pastry with mushrooms, $2.45) to the California/ Thai (Bangkok curry chicken salad, $2.80). For less expensive, *kebap*-type dining, look for Hoşdere Cad., south and to the right of the Atatürk Tower. Take the first left off Noktalı Sok. after the Sheraton. The stand-up **Dürümland,** 9/B Filistin Sok., 20m down the street to your left, serves some of the best *döner kebap* you'll taste anywhere, wrapped *dürüm* style in pita ($1.75). If you prefer to meet your *kebap* sitting down, head back to the taxi stand; below the Chinese take-away is the **Ayfa Cafe.** A good-sized "pizza" (pita with lamb, onions and tomato) and *çoban salatası* (toma-toes, onion, cucumber, pepper, parsley, lemon, and olive oil) runs about $4. While you're here, why not make Chinese fast food more than just a cartographical aid to your Ankara sojourns? Yuming Bozkus, a Taiwanese-born musician with a doctorate in piano performance from the University of Michigan runs the sparkling, formica-tiled **Yuming'in Cin Mutfaği** (tel. 446 6864, -65), on the corner of Mahatma Gandhi Cad. and Kahraman Kadin Sok. in GOP, around the corner from the Migros supermar-ket branch. Tasty egg rolls wrapped in Turkish *yufka* (crisp, paper-thin dough similar to Greek) are two for $1.30. *Specialité de la maison* is Yuming's special chicken ($2.45). Free delivery. The nearby branch of **Divan Pastane** (Turkey's finest) sells delicious caramel *(karamelize)* and apricot *(kaysi)* ice creams (20¢ per scoop), Turkish delight *(lokum)*, and candied chestnuts *(kestane şejerkerlemesi,* ($7/lb).

Kızılay

Some of Kızılay's streets have been turned into pedestrian zones bustling with restau-rants, bars, and cafes. It's hard to go wrong here; just follow the crowds and avoid "fast-food" joints. Prices are pretty uniform ($3.75 for salad, entree, and a drink). Kızılay's cheapest possible meal is probably the 85¢ *döner* at **Döner Cafe** on Olgunar Cad. **Düveroğlu,** 18 Selanik Cad., serves delicious *şiş kebap* for $2.80 (open daily 10am-1am). The **ABC Cafe,** 1 Selanik Cad., in the basement of the ABC Bookshop, plays classical and jazz music while Ankara students sip the excellent house coffee and look intellectual (open until 7pm). The chic but uncomfortable black metal fold-ing chairs at **Cafe M,** 40 Selanik Cad., are generally already taken by collegiate hip-sters (*muzlu süt* 85¢, *tiramisu* $1; open until 10:30pm). While the yuppie cafes of Kavaklidere and GOP stay open until the wee hours doing a lively business in alco-holic beverages and Euro-something pastries, the more academic and hardcore Kızılay has a separate bar scene which begins after the coffeeshops close. Manic dancers should be warned, however, that Kızılay's nightlife is of the chat-over-a-beer/listen-to-live-music variety. If what you really want is to tear up the floor with your mad moves, head instead to the nightclubs and discos scattered around Kavaklidere, GOP, and oddly enough, **Gankaya**—-the district containing the Presidential Mansion and most of Ankara's ambassadorial residences—that happens to be home to **No Name Club** (16/2 Gevre Sok.), **Paradise Disco** (34 Farabi Sok.), and **Disco Neron** (6 Dosteli Sok.).

Ulus

For slightly more upscale dining, hop uptown to the **Çiçek Lokantası,** 12 Çankırı Cad. Established in 1932, this classy establishment boasts an indoor fountain, white tablecloths, and traditional Turkish cooking. You will be taken to the kitchen and shown their selection of soups, cold appetizers ($2.10), and hot dishes ($4.25). You can also order just about any *izgara* you can think of (open daily 7am-10pm). The **Yavaz Lokantası,** 15 Konya Sok. (tel. 311 8508), is another of Ulus' nicer offerings, with a quiet "family room" *(aile salonu)* in addition to its main dining area. (In this set-up, although you're free to sit wherever you choose, Turkish women and couples will *always* sit in the *aile* room, which tends to be furnished better than the men-only "main" room. Single women who do not sit in the *aile salon* will probably be stared at by the clientele and politely questioned by the staff.) Entrees here run from $2.70-$4. **Kale Pilsen/Kale Hamburger** (tel. 311 1125), a few doors down from Yavaz offers standard Turkish cafe fare at standard Turkish cafe prices (entrees $1.75-2.50) in a pleasant marble dining area.

ENTERTAINMENT

Metropol Sanat Merkezi movie house in Kızılay 76 Selanik Cad. (tel. 425 7478) offers 6 screens of artsy, mostly American and French selections (tickets $2.80, stu-dents $2.10). You can also catch up on American first-run flicks at the **open-air cin-ema** on the roof of the Kavaklıdere Sheraton (tel. 468 5454), with nightly 9:30pm screenings for $5.30. There's no popcorn, but there is a **bar** (first drink on the house, additional cocktails about $2.75). Unfortunately, national cinematography is represented in Ankara almost exclusively by Turkish soft-core pornography. Take the Ankaray to access Maltepe's many such theaters. Chances are there won't be subtitles, but you can probably figure out the plot using context clues. Back in Kızılay, the **Ankara French Cultural Center** (Ankara Fransiz Kültür Merkezi/Institut d'Etudes Françaises), 15 Ziya Gökalp Cad. (tel. 431 1458; fax 433 0500), boasts frequent jazz, baroque, classical guitar, and troubadour-type concerts (about $1.50), art exhibits, and French movie screenings (English or Turkish subtitles; $1.25), as well as a library with substantial CD-ROM facilities and several French daily newspapers and fashion magazines.

From Nov. 1-June 15, the terra cotta, pillared **State Opera and Ballet House** (Devlet Opera ve Balesi), Atatürk Blv. Opera Meydani, Ulus (tel. 221 0248), and the nearby **Presidential Symphony Orchestra Hall** (Cumhurbaşkanliği Senfoni Orkestrasi Konser Salonu) 38 Talatpaşa Blv., Ulus (tel. 310 7290), offer daily performances (tickets $2.45, $2.10, and $1.75; 50% student discount).

Kızılay

Pub life is centered on **İnkilâp Sok.** and the even livelier **Bayındır Sok.,** two and three blocks to the left of Kızılay Sq. as you look south. Roam the traffic-free streets and pick the crowd you want to hang with. On the second floor of a corner building at Bayındır and Sakarya Cad., the tiny but happening **Blues Bar** blasts Euro pop—you'll hear it before you see it. Also, don't miss **Forza Cafe and Bar,** across the street from **Büyük Ekspress** on Bayindir Cad., where Turkish folk singers earn laughter and applause from the local crowd. Take a left on this street (Sakarya Cad.) away from Atatürk Blv. for one block to reach the **Z-Pub,** another crowded hotspot where Turkish music is the rage. At the far end of Selanik Cad., just past the Ertan Hotel, **Brothers Bar** entertains a large college crowd with hip Turkish tunes. Near Sihhiye, on Mithat Paşa Blv., the **S.S.K. Işhane** (Life Insurance Office Building) throbs with the kick-bass of about a dozen small live music bars. The youngest and coolest crowd seems to be packed into the cubicle-like **Gölge Bar,** grooving to live grunge. **Ada Bar** favors heavily-synthesized male-female slow rock duets (*a la* "Somewhere Out There," only in Turkish). A few couples can usually be found swaying in each other's arms on the tiny dance floor while, at the surrounding tables, distressed-looking twenty-somethings smoke cigarettes and gaze at a giant reproduction of Klimt's *The Kiss.* **Mavi Bar** has frequent (live) unplugged sets, and the third-floor **Kalem Bar** features traditional Turkish *saz* (like a banjo) and *davul* (a kind of drum) tunes. Framed photos of Louis Armstrong and Duke Ellington set an atmosphere of generic classiness. Kızılay's bar prices are fairly uniform: a pint of Efes, the local favorite, goes for $1.05-$1.40; mixed drinks, cognacs, etc. from $2.80-3.50.

Kavaklıdere

Kavaklıdere offers much more upscale, less crowded entertainment than Kızılay—bars are spread throughout this residential area and can sometimes be hard to find. **Jazz** bars on Billur Sok., just uphill from the McDonald's on Tunali Hilmi Cad., have live Turkish music most nights. On Paris Cad. in Giziosmanpaşo, **Disco 777,** a cavernous cement disco the size of an airport parking garage, rocks nightly from 9pm-4am nightly (cover $5.30; students $2.10; first drink free). The **Kuğlu Park Cafe and Restaurant** in Kavaklıdere's Kuğlu (Swan) Park is a nice place for lunch overlooking a pond with its many ducks and somewhat less plentiful swans (*tavukizgara*, $3.15; *Goban salata*, $1.05; open 9:30am-12:30am).

Ulus

Gençlik Park is crammed with cheap restaurants, and also contains a garish yet dingy amusement park and an artificial lake with rental pleasure boats. This can be a rather depressing place, reminiscent of the pleasure park where Pinocchio was corrupted. It's at its best in the early evening, when the lights first come on. Ulus also contains most of the city's **baths** (a bath and massage usually runs to $3).

ANATOLIA

SIGHTS

Anıt Kabir (Atatürk's Mausoleum)

Upon Atatürk's death, Turkey held an international contest to select a plan for his **mausoleum**. The winner, Emin Onat's simple, monumental, Hittite-influenced **Anıt Kabir,** took nine years to complete and now covers 750,000 sq. meters near Tandoğan Sq. To get there, take Ankaray to Tandoğan and follow the Anıt Kabir signs. You'll pass the **TMT Cleaning Equipment** store (tel. 215 3152; vacuum cleaners $210 and up), a residential area, then an unmarked entrance guarded by two soldiers.

It's a 10-minute uphill walk from the gate to the mausoleum entrance where six unhappy statues of men and women represent the grief of the Turkish nation upon its father's death. **Lion's Way,** the broad stone promenade leading to the mausoleum with **Atatürk's sarcophagus,** is lined with 24 lions, symbolizing power. They are arranged in pairs, Hittite style. The mausoleum complex claims no less than nine towers as well as two giant victory reliefs, a museum, and a hall of honors. Objects on display include Atatürk's '36 Lincoln sedan, tie clips, and an excellent series of photographs commemorating Atatürk's career and social life: visiting an elementary school teachers' conference, Atatürk at a masquerade ball (dressed as himself), Atatürk sitting in on a convention of female factory workers, etc. Other photographs show cloud formations shaped like Atatürk's profile taken after his death, suggesting that even the sky mourns his loss. In the Reform Tower is the **Cinevision salon,** which shows non-stop period documentaries, including some very moving posthumous propaganda films with Chopin soundtracks. "Tell us heavens, tell us flag, clouds, birds, mountains—where is Atatürk now?" Wrap up your tour with a stop at the gift shop for your favorite Atatürk paraphenalia: Atatürk post cards, plaques, clocks, and photos (museum open Nov.-Feb. 9am-noon and 1:30-4pm, Feb.-Oct. 9am-noon and 1:30-5pm, closed Mondays; admission free).

Museum of Anatolian Civilizations

At the feet of the Citadel, the **Museum of Anatolian Civilizations** rightly numbers among Turkey's most famous museums. Walk to the top of Hisarpark Cad., turn right at the Citadel steps (without ascending them), and follow the Citadel boundaries to the entrance. This restored 15th-century Ottoman building houses a collection of astoundingly old artifacts tracing the history of Anatolia, from a 6th millennium BC bone and obsidian razor to Bronze Age golden ear plugs. Equally impressive is the room of 3,300 year-old hieroglyphic tablets. English labelling is not as extensive or coherent as it could be, but the catalogue ($7) explains all. Private guides lurk on the benches outside the main doors and can be hired for a one-hour tour for about $15 (museum open Tues.-Sun. 8:30am-5:15pm; admission $2.10, students, $1.05).

Other Museums

The **Ethnographic Museum,** 1km south of Ulus off Atatürk Blv., displays clothing, calligraphy, woodwork, a model room from a dervish lodge, and a golden *tuğbu* tree with its roots in heaven and its branches reaching down to earth, rendered by Sultan Mahmud II's daughter, Adile (open Tues.-Sun. 8:30am-12:30pm and 1:30-5:30pm; admission $2.80). Next door the **Painting and Statue Museum** (*Resim ve Heykel Müzesi*), commissioned by Atatürk, documents the development of modern Ottoman and Turkish painting, from its birth over 160 years ago through its Cubist and Naive periods to the present day. Over the stairs in the front hallway, two giant oil paintings depict a wolf leading the first Turkic peoples to Anatolia from Central Asia, and Atatürk leading the nation upwards from the ashes of the Ottoman Empire.

Mosques

The pure white **Kocatepe Mosque,** completed in 1987, shines as one of the world's largest and most beautiful mosques. Billed as a 16th-century mosque utilizing 20th-century technology, it continues the architectural dialogue between the buildings of Sinan, the famous Ottoman architect, and the central dome and half-domes recalling the Blue Mosque, built by Sinan's successor in Istanbul. Don't miss the stunning stained glass and tiled interior containing a model of the mosque at Medina—a present from King Fahd of Saudi Arabia to the people of Turkey in 1993. Kocatepe is particularly striking at night, when moths sleep on the white flagstones overlooking the illuminated city and the enormous round crystal chandeliers inside are lit up. After your visit, you can do a little shopping at the Beğendik supermarket and mall, ultra-modern, and air-conditioned, directly underneath the mosque.

The small 13th-century **Aslanhane Mosque** (Ahi Şerafettin) in the Citadel is also worth a visit, with its beautiful old carpets, Corinthian pillars, and a tiled alcove. Roman ruins in Ankara are poorly preserved and aren't worth a lot of your time if you're going to visit the Aegean or Mediterranean coasts where the old baths, aqueducts and theaters are more impressive.

Roman Ruins

If this is your last and only opportunity to see a piece of Rome, however, you may want to check out the **Roman Baths,** a five-minute walk up Çankırı Cad. from the equestrian statue (open Tues.-Sun. 8:30am-noon and 1:30-5:30pm; admission 70¢), and the **Column of Julian.** The nearby **Temple of Augustus,** built in 25 BC over the site of earlier temples to Cybele (an Anatolian fertility goddess) and the Phrygian moon god, was later converted to a Byzantine church.

Other Sights

In the same general area are the 15th-century **Hacı Bayram Mosque,** the old **Parliament** (where Turkey was proclaimed an independent republic), and the **zoo** (Atatürk Orman Çiftliği) in an expansive, tree-filled park. A few kilometers south soars the **Ataküle Observation Tower.** Bus #391 runs from the Citadel and Ulus to the tower via Kızılay and Kavaklıdere; bus #613 from Ulus only. You can literally see all of Ankara from its observation deck (admission 50¢).

■ Boğazkale

Put your Greeks and Romans back on the shelf—welcome to Hittite Country. Nowhere in the world is the former glory of this 4000-year-old Indo-European civilization more evident than in their ruined capital, **Hattuşaş.** The ancient city is on the outskirts of present-day Boğazkale, just over 200km east of Ankara and 30km off the Samsun highway (see p. 466). The great Hittite kings occupied Hattuşaş for four centuries beginning in 1600 BC, during which time their armies vied with the Egyptians for control of the fertile lands and trade routes of Mesopotamia. The saga featured such episodes as the conquest of Syria (14th century BC) and a showdown with the mighty pharaoh Ramses II (1298 BC). Historians remain unsure where to place responsibility for the the razing of Hattuşaş. It may have been the hostile Kashka of the Black Sea region, embittered vassals of the Empire, or perhaps the "Sea People," invaders from Greek islands and city-states, including the Trojans. In any case, archaeologists from the German Oriental Society and the German Archaeological Institute have unearthed enough of the ruins to reveal the city's vanished splendor.

Two kilometers northeast of the site, **Yazılıkaya,** an open air temple with 100 of the 1000 or so gods of the Hittite pantheon represented in bas-relief, merits a visit, as does Boğazkoy's small **museum.** It takes about 3½ hours to get from Ankara to Boğazkale by public transport, whereupon the loop passing through the site makes an 8km walk. The hike is painless and beautiful, passing through a wild landscape of cliffs and valleys set against misty blue mountains. If you are in a hurry, you can take a taxi or try to hitch a ride from site personnel, who seem to do a lot of gratuitous driving around.

ORIENTATION AND PRACTICAL INFORMATION

If you don't have a car, the easiest way to get to Boğazkale is through **Sungurlu,** 30km west. The **Sungurlu Seyahat** bus company (tel. (312) 224 0129, -0159) runs daily buses from Ankara (every hr., 3hr., $4.75). Buses head back hourly from the Sungurlu Seyahat office next to the park, and it's easy to catch onward connections to Ankara and Istanbul. The bus will drop you off either on the main highway or in a parking area next to a huge park and tea garden in the center of town. Taxi drivers lurking on the highway have been known to tell tourists that there is no *dolmuş* service to Boğazkale. This is a lie. *Dolmuş* (30min., 65¢) leave every 30 minutes outside a grocery store in town on Lise Cad., 100m from the other side of the parking lot/tea garden. A private taxi is $10 for a one-way trip to Boğazkale, $15-20 for a full tour of the ruins. Once you get there, **Osman Soyal,** the village carpet dealer (tel. 452 2821) gives guided car tours of Hattuşaş and Yazılıkaya for $6 per person.

Boğazkale only has one street to speak of. A good place to disembark from the *dolmuş* is at the well-marked museum on the town's fringe. Farther in, you'll hit **Aşıkoğly Motel and Restaurant** and **Hattuşaş Pension.** Next to Aşıkoğlu, the Boğazkale İlce Sağlık Ocağı (tel. 452 2007) is a 24-hour **clinic** with ambulance service. Pass the carpet store and a small grocery to reach a **pharmacy** and **bakery** *(fırın)* at the end of the street. Next door, the **PTT** is open 8:30am-noon and 1-5:30pm. There are currently **no ATMs** here, but there are several in Sungurlu. The **postal code** 19310, while the **telephone code** is a scintillating 364.

ACCOMMODATIONS AND FOOD

The area's only restaurants are in the pensions. Outside of that, you must rely on the bakery and grocery store for sustenance.

Kale Motel and Restaurant (tel. 452 2189; fax 452 2189) is on the road to Yazılıkaya. Coming out of the museum, turn right, and take another right at the Petrol Ofisi gas station. The motel will be on your left. Gorgeous hilltop views make Kale an unbeatable preview to a hike. All rooms have balconies or terraces and access to showers. Restaurant serves excellent semolina bread with its meals (a good *saç tava* is $2.60). Breakfast included. Singles $6.45; doubles $13; triples $16.15; camping $2.60 per tent. Show your copy of *Let's Go* for a 25% discount.

Başkent Pansiyon (tel. 452 2567; fax 452 2037), on the same road as Kale closer to the museum, features neat and clean rooms with carpeting, private shower, and "slide projection services." $8.50 per person, including breakfast.

Hattuşaş Pension and Restaurant (tel. 452 2013; fax 452 2957), right up the hill from the museum, boasts private showers and lovely views of the countryside from the back room. The rooms currently do not have private toilets, but they should be added by autumn 1997. $6.45 per person. Breakfast $1.30. Children under 12 get a 70% discount. Major credit cards accepted.

Aşıkoğlu Motel and Restaurant (tel. 452 2004; fax 452 2171) has welcomed guests for over 35 years. Across from the museum, Aşıkoğlu offers a fine Turkish restaurant and clean rooms with toilets and showers. Breakfast included. $6.45 per person. Open dinner buffet $5.

Atila Camping (tel. 452 2101) has a swimming pool amid its camping space. Clean showers and bathrooms make "roughing it" not so rough. Take a right out of the museum and keep going past the gas station. $3.75 per person.

SIGHTS

Dolmuş from Sungurlu pass right by the modest **Boğazkale Museum** (tel. 452 2006), where an excellent selection of Hittite bureaucratic red tape, a collection of paraphernalia spanning stone stamps and deeds inscribed on stone tablets in cuneiform, is labelled in Turkish and German. Another case contains crosses and other findings from a Byzantine church of post-Hittite Hattuşaş. The museum curator "loves university students" and will go out of his way to help them plan a hike of the sites (open daily 8am-5:30pm).

Yazılıkaya

The temple of Yazılıkaya is best visited between 11am-1pm, when the sun is directly overhead; shade from the towering grotto easily obscures the bas-relief deities. To get there, head right out of the museum and make your first right at the Petrol Ofisi gas station; the site is another 2km or so down the road.

Yazılıkaya comprises two chambers and a roofless sanctuary containing reliefs of gods and goddesses on parade. Goddesses appear in profile, wearing long, trailing robes; gods, most wearing kilts, face forward, and their rank can be inferred by the number of horns on their hats. The deities' names are often inscribed over their heads, preceded by an oval ("god" in hieroglyphics).

To the left, **Chamber A** contains the famous 2.6m-high Great King relief representing King Tudhaliya IV (c. 1250-1220 BC) standing on two mountains under a winged sun disk. The bouquet-like object in his right hand is actually his name in hieroglyphics. Back and to the right, **Chamber B** contains a relief of 12 gods, representing the 12 months of the year (open daily 8am-6pm). See Kurt Bittel's *Guide to Boğazkale,* available for $4.80 in Turkish, English, and German from the museum shop, for a more detailed introduction and description to the site.

Hattuşaş

Coming out of Yazılıkaya, head left and then follow the yellow "Hattusha" (the city's Hittite name) signs to get back to Hattuşaş. The road following the 6km wall that encircles the ruins first passes by **Büyük Mabed,** a temple of the weather god of Hatti and the sun goddess of Arinna. A drawbridge over two pools of water granted the only entrance to the original temple. The big green rock inside was a wedding gift from the King of Egypt to his son-in-law, the King of the Hittites. Today, visitors enter the temple through the *propylon,* or processional entrance. Farther in are the temple's warehouses, where thousands of cuneiform tablets documenting goods sold and received were found in 1907.

Continuing up the hill and to the right, the road passes the Hittite kings' ruined summer castle and then the **Aslanlıkapı,** a gate consisting of two crumbling doorways framed by lion statues (one headless, the other missing only its canines). Note the grooves about 6m above the ground for the hubs of entering chariot wheels. A photographic computer simulation posted nearby shows what the gate might have looked like in its 13th-century BC heyday. Farther uphill, the Yerkapı Ground Gate leads to a 71m long tunnel. On the other side, steps lead up to the **Sfenksil Kapısı,** a gate whose four original sphinxes have, over the past 33 centuries, been reduced to one. Looking down, you can observe several razed temples *(mabbet)* and a Byzantine church, now little more than giant blueprints marked out by limestone blocks. The plum tree to your left as you pass through Sfenksil Kapısı marks the point where the cuneiform and hieroglyphic Boğazkale tablets in the Museum of Anatolian Civilization (see p. 522) were excavated. Also in the museum is the larger-than-life figure carved in relief found at the **Kralkapı** (King's Gate), just down the hill. Originally believed to be the gate's namesake king, this fellow is actually a war god, and now stands in plaster reproduction *in situ.*

Farther along you will come across hieroglyphic **Chamber 1** and the more interesting **Chamber 2.** Commissioned by King Shupilulima II around 1200 BC, the chamber was originally located in the castle **Güney Kale** in the valley below, having been moved to its current location (for whatever reason) by German archaeologists. The enclosed cult chamber contains a relief of the king holding a symbol with an inscription mentioning a "divine earth road," suggesting that this was the cult's symbolic entrance to the underworld. The **Büyük Kale,** a ruined complex of archives, offices, and royal apartments linked by courtyards, rounds out the tour (open 8am-5:30pm; admission $1.40, students 70¢).

ANATOLIA

KONYA AND ENVIRONS

▓ Konya

In Roman times, St. Paul favored Konya (then called Iconium) with a visit and sparked the city's transformation into a significant Christian center. The Seljuks swept through Asia Minor in the 11th century, making Konya their capital. They replaced its churches with the greatest mosques of the era. In 1228, the Afghani Islamic philosopher Celâleddin Rumi, known to his followers as Mevlâna (our master), settled in Konya. After his death, his disciples founded a Sufi order which later became known for its "Whirling Dervishes," who sought to achieve ecstasy and unity with God through controlled trance-like spinning. Today, Muslims often stop in Konya to visit Mevlâna's tomb before embarking on the pilgrimage to Mecca.

Konya numbers among Turkey's conservative Islamic cities. If you are respectful of its religious traditions, you'll find the residents amiable and welcoming. Women should avoid sleeveless shirts, and be aware that it is impolite for either sex to wear shorts. Whatever your clothes, you're certain to experience a different type of "hospitality" from Konya's numerous street carpet hustlers, who will try to lure you to their shops. These middlemen get a 30% commission that is inevitably added to your price; if you want to buy a carpet, go alone (see **Carpet Buying in Turkey,** p. 397).

ORIENTATION AND PRACTICAL INFORMATION

Konya's main street runs between the turquoise **Mevlâna tomb** and the circular **Alâaddin Bulvarı,** which embraces **Alâaddin Tepsi** (Alâaddin Hill), actually a prehistoric burial mound from which neolithic tombs, artifacts, and human skeletons have been excavated. The 500m closest to the Mevlâna tomb is called **Mevlâna Caddesi,** the other half **Alâaddin Caddesi.** Konya's sights, hotels, and restaurants are all clustered within this small area. Frequent **trains** run between Alâaddin Blv. and the **bus station** *(otogar),* 3km from town. The **railway station** is 2km from the town center. When you exit, you'll see the road to town marked by a roundabout to your right. Walk along this street to get to town, passing Atatürk Stadium and the Atatürk statue. Take the second left onto Atatürk Blv. after the statue, and then bear right on Alâaddin Blv. after 500m. Any *dolmuş* marked "Istasyon" or "Gar" will take you back to the train station; *dolmuş* marked *"otogar"* run, uncannily, to the bus station.

The **tourist office,** 21 Mevlâna Cad. (tel. 351 1074; fax 350 6461), is across the street from the Mevlâna Müze. The staff speaks English and French. They provide free city and regional maps, but take their accommodation and carpet shop advice with a grain of salt (open Mon.-Fri. 8am-noon and 1:30-5:30pm). Buses leave the *otogar* 3km out of town on A. Hilmi Nalcacl Cad. (tel. 235 4649, -4647), headed for: Silifke (7 per day, 3hr., $7); Ankara (15 per day, 3hr., $7); Izmir (10 per day, 8hr., $10.50); Eğirdir (5 per day, 3½hr., $6.45); and Aksaray (11 per day, ½hr., $4). Nighttime buses run to Istanbul ($11) and Nevşehir/Göreme (3 per day, 4hr., $7.75).

Pharmacies are scattered all over town, especially on the streets of Alâaddin and Melvâna Cad. The pharmacy on night duty *(nöbetçi)* is posted in all pharmacy windows and at the hospitals. **Sağlik Hastanesu** is the hospital on Hastene Cad., Iktap Sok. (tel. 233 8204, 235 6795). The receptionists don't speak English, but most doctors do. For **medical emergencies,** dial 112. Your **PTT** needs will be met on Alâaddin Cad., to your left as you face Alâaddin Tepsi. The office is open for your pleasure 24 rockin' hours per day. There is also a smaller branch at the bus station (open daily 7am-11pm). The **postal code** is 42000, while the intriguing **telephone code** is 332.

ACCOMMODATIONS

Many hotels and pensions are clustered in small alleys along Konya's main drag. Rooms are considerably more expensive than in other cities, and bargains are hard to find, as the pension owners here seem to actually obey their cooperative agreement. Prices range from $12 to $15 per person. Be aware too that male-female duos will have trouble finding a room together without either the same last name or a bona fide marriage certificate.

Otel Çeşme, Istanbul Cad. 35 Akifaşa Sok. (tel. 351 2426), offers tidy rooms with bath, fake bricks, TV, and stained glass. Breakfast included. Singles $13; doubles $17; triples $23.25.

Yeni Köşk, Yeni Aziziye Cad. 28 Kadılar Sok. (tel. 352 0671, 350 1329; fax 352 0901), is conveniently and peacefully located a couple of blocks off Mevlâna Cad. It features well-scrubbed rooms with showers and TVs. Singles $15.50; doubles $19.35; triples $24.50. Breakfast $2.25.

Hotel Dergâh, 19 Mevlâna Cad. (tel. 351 1197, -7661, -1774; fax 351 0116). Conveniently located next door to the tourist office, idiosyncratic 3-star Dergâh features rooms with nice decor ($26 per person) and rooms with not-so-nice decor ($16 person). Both categories of rooms feature a private shower. Some of the cheaper rooms also seem to belong to Dergâh's custodial staff, who can occasionally be seen sitting on the floor, drinking tea. Breakfast included.

Hotel Sema, 15 Mevlâna Cad. (tel. 350 4623; fax 351 0116), has 3 stars, a fish tank in the lobby, and clean but unspectacular rooms. Singles $14.50. Breakfast $2.50.

FOOD AND ENTERTAINMENT

The local speciality is *fırın kebap,* a chunk of oven-roasted mutton served unceremoniously on a pita, sometimes under the alias *tandır kebap.* Konya is also renowned for its Turkish pizza, here called *etliekmek.* With the tourist office on your left and the Mevlâna in front of you, go right roughly 100m, passing by the left-hand side of the Balıkçı Otel, then turn right again just before the third roundabout to find a bare brick wall and plastic Pepsi sign which conceal a 150-year-old Konya house serving some of the **best food** you'll have in Turkey. Specialities are *gebzeli çöp kebap* (*kebap* with eggplant, $2), *çöp şiş,* and *etli yaprak sarması* (meat-stuffed grape leaves with yogurt, $1.50).

For your coffee needs, **Ankara Pastanesi,** on Alâaddin Cad., serves a delicious, frothy Nescafé. Coming from the Mevlâna, it's past the post office on your left. Near the Mevlâna Museum at 3 and 30 Mevlâna Cad., **Deva Restaurant** and **Şifa Lokantasi** serve typically hearty *fırın kebap* for about $3. A single portion will render you fuller then you previously imagined possible. If a day of Konya appreciation has left your back tense and knotty, head to the **Şems Mah. Hamam,** 7 Serfettin Cad. (tel. 353 0093), in a restored Seljuk building beside the Selimiye Mosque (entry $2.75, complete bath and massage $6.50, tip $2-4 depending on service). Most of Konya's restaurants are nonalcoholic, and **nightlife** is restricted to bars in the larger hotels.

SIGHTS

Mevlâna Tekke

The interior of the **Mevlâna Tekke** is among Turkey's more spectacular sights. Inside the mausoleum, originally part of a Whirling Dervish lodge, are the turbaned tombs of the philosopher Mevlâna, his sons, and several other Dervishes. The mausoleum also houses several Maneluke crystal chandeliers and the **Nisan Tas,** a bronze cauldron in which Dervishes used to collect April rainwater believed to have medicinal properties. It is now a sort of shrine; if you wear shorts, the museum staff will loan you a sarong to wrap around your legs as you enter, and you must remove your shoes and carry them with you in a plastic bag (also provided at the door). Women might want to lower their heads. In a back room, several hand-written Qurans are on display, including one that fits into a tiny silver pillbox. Around the courtyard, a few rooms once used as Dervish dormitories and offices now contain Dervish mannequins in full costume, posed in natural habitats (open Mon. 10am-6pm and Tues.-Sun. 9am-6pm; admission 65¢, students 35¢).

Around Alâaddin Tepesi

Konya's other major attractions are tame by comparison. Most are situated on or around **Alâaddin Tepesi,** built on what some say are countless layers of yet-unexcavated layers of civilizations stretching back to the Bronze Age. Closer to the surface are a park and some pleasant tea gardens, crowned by the hilltop **Alâaddin Camii,** an early 13th-century mosque in the Syrian Seljuk style. The mosque reopened in the summer of 1995 after 11 years of restoration, and now sports a more modern decor. The imposing bicycle helmet-like edifice you'll notice on the other side of the hill is a **Seljuk Palace** built during the reign of Sultan Kılıç Arslan II (1156-1192 AD).

Nearby, on Alâaddin Blv., is the **Karatay Medrese,** built under Sultan İzettin Keykavus II by Emir Celâleddin Karatay. The Quran and Islamic Law were taught to young Seljuks here in the 13th century. Today, it is a **Tile Museum** (tel. 351 1914). The interior itself is a marvellous example of Seljuk tilework, with a magnificent turquoise, blue, and white-tiled dome over a square central pool. Displays include tiles from Kubadâbâd Palace, near Beyşehir Lake, as well as ceramic plates and lamps from Konya. Most of the tile decorations are geometric designs, but you can also catch occasional birds, fish, and almond-eyed people in elaborate hats (open Tues.-Sun. 9am-noon and 1:30-5:30pm; admission 65¢, students 35¢).

Also on Alâaddin Blv., next to McDonald's, is the **İnce Minare Medrese,** which serves as Konya's **Stone and Woodwork Museum** (tel. 351 3204). Probably the best part of the museum is the massive stone portal, whose arch is engraved with Arabic script and **bas-relief artichokes.** The slender minaret which was, in Turkish, the school's namesake was struck by lightning in 1901, but it's been rebuilt. Inside are Seljuuk and Ottoman stone carvings, many of which have spent centuries outside in God's great open spaces and are somewhat blurrier for the wear. A woodwork exhibit includes carved doors and window shutters, *yazma* stamps, and a wooden ceiling (open Tues.-Sun. 8am-noon and 1:30-5:30pm; admission 65¢, students 35¢).

Konya's **Archaeological Museum** includes a nice courtyard with rose bushes, stone lions, a fountain, a peacock mosaic, and a large room containing several interesting 3rd-century Roman sarcophagi, including one illustrating the labors of Hercules. Other items on display include tiny Roman ivory collapsing combs and toothpicks, and numerous 9000-year-old stone blobs, some sharper than others, labelled as neolithic spoons, axes, mortars, needles, and even a figurine (open Tues.-Sun. 9am-noon and 1:30-5:30pm; admission 65¢, students 35¢).

Take a left out of the Archaeological Museum gates to get to the **Ethnographic Museum** (tel. 351 8958), which has the same hours and prices as its neighbor, but was closed for renovations at the time of the writing of this book. It's expected to re-open in 1998 and the collection is one of Turkey's most highly acclaimed.

On Atatürk Blv., just off Alâaddin Blv., you'll find **Atatürk's house** (tel. 351 3206), a small museum of the great man's personal effects. Displays include Atatürk's overcoat, complete with its "Harrod's Ltd. London" label, and memorabilia celebratingKonya's role in the Turkish independence struggle (open Tues.-Sun. 9am-4pm; admission 65¢, students 35¢).

A Dizzying Poet

Celaleddin Mevlâna Rumi, founder of the order the Dervishes and perhaps the greatest of all the Persian mystic poets, made his home in 13th-century Konya after leaving his native Balkh (now part of Afghanistan) upon the Mongol invasion in 1222 AD. Revered both as a poet and a prophet, Rumi is said to have used his spiritual powers to repel the invasion of Hulegu Khan's Mongol hordes in 1256. For 700 years, the passionate elegance of his verses has inspired readers from Istanbul to Samarkand, Muslim India, Arabia, and Africa. He is not widely known in the West, but English literature has felt his impact through translations made by early 19th-century Orientalists. For English-speaking readers, *I Am Wind, You Are Fire* by Anne-Marie Schimmel is an excellent introduction to the life and teachings of Rumi, while Coleman Barks is renowned for English translations of his poetry.

Other Sights

Back in the Mevlâna area, on the other side of the huge Üçler Cemetery from the Mevlâna Museum, is the **Koyunoglu Museum and Library,** 25 Kerimded Çeşme (tel./fax 351 1857). This museum houses the private collection and archives of A.R. İzzet Koyunoğlu (1900-1974), a private collector who spent virtually his entire life accumulating this vast agglomeration of stuff. Thanks to his generosity, you can wander through the two floors taking in such artifacts as paleolithic arrowheads, stuffed birds, first-century glass vases, agate geodes, fossilized moose antlers, mammoth legbones, marbled paper, and tea sets (open Tues.-Sun. 8am-noon and 1:30-5pm; admission $1.30, students 35¢).

Next door, the **Koyunoglu Konya House** is a restored 19th-century Ottoman house decorated in period style (open Tues.-Sun. 8am-noon and 1:30-5pm; admission $1.30, students 35¢).

The **Aziziye Mosque,** a five-minute walk from the Mevlâna, off Mevlâna Cad. to the left, is built in 18th-century Baroque style, unusual for Turkey. The windows are larger than the door for extra light, and the dome is self-supporting.

Konya's bazaar lies between the Aziziye Mosque and the PTT. About halfway along Mevlâna Cad., steps covered by glass panels lead down to the **underground gold bazaar** *(yeraltâ altın pazarı).*

■ Near Konya

A brief trip to **Sille,** 8km away, makes an excellent morning excursion. Sille-bound bus #64 leaves the municipal bus stop (on Lâaddin Cad., across from the PTT) every 30 minutes, letting you off in the middle of Sille's main street, distinguished by the existence of stores and, of course, a bust of Atatürk. The PTT is ahead and around the corner (open daily 8:30am-5:30pm). Despite the lack of a tourist office, you should have no trouble finding your way around.

Most visitors come to Sille to visit the **Aya Elena Kilisesi,** a 4th-century Christian church decorated by more recent frescoes (open Tues.-Sun. 9am-4pm; admission 65¢). The two caves to the left of the church were once used as human dwellings. To get there, ask the driver to let you off at the Aya Elena Kilisesi sign. There are two. If you find yourself let off near a manure farm, walk up the road until you see the second one, near a row of garages. The church is now partially concealed by a house.

Near the town of **Çumra,** 50km south of Konya, the advanced neolithic community of **Çatahöyük,** dating back to the 8th millennium BC, vies with Jericho for the coveted title of "World's First City." Çatahöyük is most famous for its Cult of the Mother Goddess findings. The Mother Goddess, a large woman with wide hips symbolizing abundance, is usually represented by small statuettes. Sometimes she is shown giving birth, other times accompanied by a bull and a wildcat. A goddess of many names, she was known as Hepat to the Hittites, Cybele to the Phyrgians, and Artemis to the Greeks.

Most of Çatahöyük's drawings and artifacts were either plundered by the Dutch or moved to Ankara's Museum of Anatolian Civilizations. Little remains on-site but a few crumbling walls. If you would like to see them, *dolmuş* head six to seven times daily from Konya's *otogar* to Çümra (45min., 65¢), then find a taxi to take you the remaining distance ($20 round-trip).

▒ Eğirdir

Eğirdir's recently released tourist brochure is a triumph of Romantic stream-of-consciousness lyricism: "We are waiting You to Eğirdir. Sun is hot, refreshing wind, transparent lake, best combination of blue and green amusing, colorful companion...." Eğirdir puts a refreshing twist on the standard Turkish beach holiday. This small ex-fishing town, discovered during the tourism boom in the 1980s, is surrounded on three sides by Turkey's largest lake, Lake Eğirdir (540 sq. km). Situated 916m above sea level in the Central Taurus mountains, summer temperatures here are 5° to 10°F

ANATOLIA

cooler than on the Mediterranean and Aegean Coasts. The lake yields unparalleled carp and bass, and in the fall, orchards fill with Starking and Golden Delicious apples. Eğirdir contains 27 pensions and makes a convenient stop-over either between the Antalya area and Konya/Cappadocia or the Aegean coast. The town is also notable for its 1000-bed **Bone Hospital** (Kemik Hastanesi), the biggest in the Middle East, as well as for a giant Turkish **commando base** perched on a hill by Isparta Road.

ORIENTATION AND PRACTICAL INFORMATION

Here in Eğirdir, the Seljuks built the world's only walk-through minaret, which is poised atop an archway in the town center. The archway leads east past municipal headquarters (Belediye) to the Lydian King Croesus's crumbling 5th-century fortress, now crowned by a blue and white EĞIRDIR sign. The **bus station** sits directly between the arched minaret (part of the **Hizirbey Mosque,** built in the 13th century) and the lake shore. It may help to envision Eğirdir as a giant Pinocchio-like nose in profile, facing east, with two growths on the tip. The growths are actually two small islands, linked to the fortress road by bridges. The closer one, little more than a float-ing tea garden, is called **Canada** (JAHN-ah-dah), which means "soul island" or "life island." Half of the town's pensions are located on the more bulbous **Yeşilada** (Green Island).

While these hip, picturesque budget lodgings are the most popular with backpack-ers and are almost all on the lake front, there are no real beaches on Yeşilada (though you can clamber down the rocky shore and swim wherever you like for free). For sand and beachside cafes, head west and then north on **2nd Sahil Yolu,** which leads along the upper surface of the nose up toward the eyebrows, eventually leading to the usually idle train station, and then on to Isparta. You will pass a few **banks,** the **PTT,** and the **tourist office** before following the road right past a small beach, **Yazla Plaj.** Originally intended as a retreat for secondary school teachers, it is now open to pedants and public alike. A **soldiers' casino** *(askeri gazinosu)* and several pensions are nearby. Past the Köşk Pension at the top of the hill, signs point to **Altinkum Plaj** (Golden Sand Beach), considered by most residents to be Eğirdir's finest. Some 11m further is the less crowded **Bedre Plaj.** Returning to the underside of the Nose, **Yen-mahalle** (New Neighborhood) Road begins beside the bus station, 100m south of the archway, and continues past the modern hospital on to Konya. In the center of the town, around the arched minaret, stands several restaurants, pensions, and small hotels, as well as an outdoor marketplace. You can shop for sundresses, economy-sized jugs of vegetable oil, and large scythes here.

Tourist Office: #13 2nd Sahil Yolu (tel. 311 4388; fax 312 2098). From the bus sta-tion gate (a map stands outside), walk straight and follow the road as it curves to the left and up. English, French, and German spoken by staff seldom on duty simul-taneously. Open Mon.-Fri. 8:30am-5pm; sometimes open on weekends.

Trains: (tel. 311 4694) 2km west of town center, off 2nd Sahil Yolu. 1 train per day to Istanbul (5:10pm, 12hr.). For Ankara, change in Eskişehir. 1 train per day to Izmir (10:50pm, 10hr.); change in Isparta. Open daily 6am-noon and 5-7pm.

Buses: (tel. 311 4036) Just south of town center. Buses leave daily for: Afyron (5 per day, 3hr., $6.50); Antalya (7 per day, 3hr., $6.50); Konya (8 per day, 3½hr., $6.50); Nevşehir (4 per day, 6hr., $14); Izmir (6 per day, 7hr., $13); Ankara (4 per day, 7hr., $11.70); and Istanbul (1 per day, 10hr., $17). Frequent **local buses** and *dolmuş* leave 7am-10pm from behind the mosque, across the street from the bus station (25¢), running from Yeşilada to town (1.5km) and from town to Altinkum Beach (3km).

Luggage Storage: Open roughly 6am-8pm at the bus station (75¢).

Hospital: Sağlik Ocaği, Güney Sahil Yolu (tel. 311 4855, -6490).

PTT: 2nd Sahil Yolu (tel. 311 4591), on the way to the tourist office. Information and Poste Restante open 24hr.; other services at your disposal Mon.-Fri. 8:30am-noon and 1:30-5:30pm. **Postal Code:** 32500.

Telephone Code: 246.

ACCOMMODATIONS AND CAMPING

While the town center contains a few modern, depressing hotels, Eğirdir's best lodging offering is the **Classy but Affordable Pension-Restaurant,** which awaits both on Yeşilada and on the continuation of 2nd Sahil Yolu toward the train station. Upon arrival at the *otogar,* you may be besieged by pension staff intent on leading you to their establishments. You can save $2 or 3 a night if you let them bid on you with their rivals. The pensions themselves are similar, though Yeşilada currently seems to be a more trendy area. 2nd Sahil Yolu, though not lacking an international backpacking clientele, is slightly less touristy. Most Yeşilada pensions do not have single rooms and will make you pay for double occupancy during high season (June-Sept.).

Köşk Pension-Restaurant, 37 Yazla Mah. (tel. 311 4382, -6350), at the top of 2nd Sahil Yolu, 800m from town. Most rooms with private shower and water views. Rooftop terrace boasts breathtaking vista of lake and surrounding mountains. Fresh fish caught daily. English spoken. Boat tours available. Free car service to and from town and the beaches—a driver is usually waiting at the Tuborg/Pepsi sign across from the *otogar,* or you can call for pick-up. Köşk, owned by the Egirdir area's Pepsi distributors, features a free "Pepsi Tur" every Sun., shuttling guests in a Pepsi truck some 25km south to the scenic Čandir Canyons, for two *"otentic"* (authentic) rooms, featuring log-panelled and wicker basket-weave-covered walls, tree stump bedside tables, wine bottles, padlocks, and a lot of calico. Singles $7; doubles $11.

Halley's Pansiyon, Yeşilada Mah., No. 6 (tel. 312 3625). Keep right as you enter the island. Second oldest pension in town, it is alive with backpackers. The hallway to the reception passes through a lush and verdant greenhouse. Come in Sept. to sample the grapes. Free rowboat for guest use. English spoken. All rooms with private shower. Singles $8; doubles $14; triples $20. Breakfast $1.65, dinner $5.

Sahil Pansiyon Restaurant, Yeşilada Mah., No. 21 (tel. 312 2167). Super-bright, simple, clean rooms with big windows, private showers, and lower-than-norm prices. Free *otogar* pick-up. Singles $4.80; doubles $9.70. Breakfast $1.30.

Sefa Sega Pansiyon, Yeşilada Mah., No. 5 (tel. 311 4877). Nestled 100m from the shore in a tiny cherry orchard among grape arbors and rose bushes, rustic Sefa Sega is the prime place in Eğirdir to escape any nagging bourgeois roots. Lock yourself in a room in this old tile-roofed village house (with or without private shower), compose 12-tone operatic songs, and think antisocial thoughts, emerging only for a home-cooked supper. Doubles $13; triples $19.35. Bargain if you are alone.

Altinkum Plaj Camping, Altinkum Plaj (tel. 311 4857), roughly 2km past the tourist office; bear right at "major junction" sign after Köşk Pension. *Plaj*-bound *dolmuş* leave from across the bus station approx. every 15min. Camp on Eğirdir's best-loved beach and enjoy access to electricity, hot showers, and telephone ($1.30 per small tent, $3.20 per large tent). Rent a small (double occupancy) concrete hut for either $6.45 (with private shower and toilet) or $3.20 (a mere cement shell).

FOOD, ENTERTAINMENT, AND SIGHTS

The people of Eğirdir cook a mean fish. The local specialities are carp (*sazan,* usually served whole), bass (*levrek,* generally filleted and fried in a light tomato flavored batter), and crayfish *(kerevides),* all prepared with varying degrees of skill by the pension-restaurants of Yeşilada. Many of these offer tables very close to the lake's edge. A more luxurious meal can be had at the **Kervansaray Restaurant** (tel. 311 6340; fax 311 6390), boasting a fine wine list, extensive menu (comprising a nice *meze* selection and *Izgara çeşitler* as well as fish), and lakefront terrace. *Levrek* here comes in a light, crisp tomato batter that must be tasted to be believed ($2.60). **Kemer Lokantası,** by the bazaar on 2nd Sahil Yolu, features a variety of excellent traditional stew-like dishes for low prices (entrees $2-4).

After hours, the **Disco Bar** next door is the town's *bamam,* near the bazaar. This place features a music hall, dancing area, and full bar with tables on an outdoor terrace overlooking the city.

ANATOLIA

Eğirdir's free beach is **Yazla Plaj,** on 2nd Sahil Yolu. **Antinkum Plaj,** some 1.5km farther and served by *dolmuş* from the town center, is more impressive (entrance 35¢; parking 60¢). Eğirdir will not disappoint nature lovers, adventurers, or cave enthusiasts. Twenty-seven kilometers to the east lies the 1.5km-long **Zindan Cave,** which served the Romans as a temple dedicated to Eurymedon. Bring a flashlight.

Forty kilometers southeast of Eğirdir near the village Sağrak stands the ruined Pisidian city of **Adada,** now consisting of an ancient temple's fallen columns, sarcophagi, and an amphitheater. Coins have been found here dating to the first century BC. Only 25km south of town, **Lake Kovada National Park** teems with wildlife, drawing butterfly collectors in the spring. Avid walkers can follow a popular stretch of the **King's Road,** by which Lydian rulers once traveled from Ephesus to Babylon. The trail passes through the Çandir Canyons near Lake Kovada. Many pensions can be coerced into running excursions to these sights, especially if you can get a group together.

CAPPADOCIA

The Biblical land of Tabal, later named Katpatukya under the Persian Empire (585-332 BC), is known today as Cappadocia. The region lies within the Nevşehir-Niğde-Kayseri triangle, bordered by four extinct volcanoes. Ten million years ago, the volcanoes spewed 100-150m of lava and ash on the enclosed Lyconian marsh. These deposits subsequently hardened into a layer of soft rock called *tufa.* A variety of natural disasters, flooding from the Kızılırmak River, rain, and wind shaped the *tufa* into a striking landscape of cone-shaped monoliths called *peribaca* ("fairy chimneys" in Turkish) grouped in cave-riddled valleys and along ridges. Chunks of hard basalt trapped on the surface of the prehistoric sludge often protected the *tufa* underneath from wind erosion, thus forming particularly weird-looking fairy chimneys consisting of a giant basalt boulder capping a *tufa* tower.

Homo sapiens have been onto Cappadocia's charms since about 3000 BC and it has hosted Assyrian, Hittite, Cimmerian, Medean, Persian, Macedonian, Roman, Byzantine, Seljuk, and Ottoman civilizations. Cappadocia has also been a cradle of religion. The **Mother Goddess** cult was born here during the Chalcolithic Age. Starting from about 525 BC, the fire-worshipping Zoroastrian Persians revered Erciyes and Hasan as holy mountains. In the second half of the first century AD, Christianity was imported by several traveling apostles (among them St. Paul, who was born in Tarsus). In hiding from the Romans, these early Christians dug homes and churches, many of them decorated with exquisite frescoes, into the *tufa.* Part of Cappodocia's unearthliness comes from the appearance of the so-called "moonscapes:" stairs, windows, and sentry holes have been carved into the already eerily-eroded rock. Many of these "troglodyte dwellings" are still used as houses, storage rooms, or stables, while others have been converted to hotels or remain empty. Later, the Byzantines developed earlier subterranean storage rooms into vast underground cities.

The many-headed Cappodocian tourism industry focuses on Ürgüp and Göreme, which means that you probably will too, for convenience's sake. If you can only spare a day or two, it is probably easiest to stay in Göreme, see the spectacular **Open Air Museum,** and then take a day trip to the **underground cities** of Derinkuyu and Kaymaklı (many local companies run a ½-day tour to the Ihlara Valley; $15).

GETTING AROUND

Transportation in the region includes minibuses, guided tours, bikes, mopeds, and car rentals from any of the numerous agencies in Ürgüp and Göreme. **Car rentals** starts at about $38 per day. Prices skyrocket for automatic transmission: **Europcar** (tel. 341 3488, -4315) in Ürgüp rents automatics with A/C for $88 per day. **Bicycles** go for $1.40 per hour or $10.60 per day; **mopeds** $5.20 per hour or $17.60 per day; and **motorcycles** $45.75 per day. Some agencies offer **horse rental.** A **minibus** runs (50¢) from the Ürgüp *otogar* to Göreme (Open-Air Museum), Çavuşin, Zelve, and

Avanos weekdays June-September. One bus leaves Ürgüp every two hours (8am-6pm); another leaves Avanos at 9, 10am, 1, 3, 5, and 7pm. This means that a bus arrives at each town every hour. The rest of the year, you have to backtrack to Nevşehir from Göreme (30¢) or Ürgüp (50¢), or by the Avanos-Nevşehir bus (catch at the Göreme PTT, Mon.-Fri. 7am-6pm, Sat. 7am-5pm; 25¢). You can get off at Nevşehir's tourist office or bus station, and catch your next bus from the same place.

Guided tours of Cappadocia's major sites are available from agencies in Göreme Ürgüp. You might find Göreme a little less intimidating—shady things seem to be afoot in Ürgüp's tourism industry, probably because there are nearly as many different agencies as there are tourists. Tours are $20-35—a good deal if you want to see as much as you can as quickly as possible. The agencies occasionally permit haggling, and all give 20% student discounts. The most expensive tours are not necessarily the best. Package tours are convenient for visiting **Soğanlı** and the **Sultan Marsh's Bird Heaven** (Sultansatlığı Kuş Cenneti), a bird-watching marsh complete with ornithological museum. Some tours also go off the main road between Derinkuyu and Ihlara to take in **Güzelyurt** and the **Crater Lake**—a volcanic crater filled with water. If you want to hike through Ihlara Valley, you can spend the night in Ihlara, hike the valley, and return independently the next day. Güzelyurt is less than 10km away and most pensions will drive you for free or a small charge.

■ Göreme

Göreme abounds with fairy chimneys and cave-houses, easily making it Cappodocia's most visited town. More than sixty pensions have sprung up in the last few years, and the main square is full of restaurants, carpet dealers, bike rentals and tour agencies. Göreme is not as cute as Ürgüp, the other main tourist center, and places a slightly heavier emphasis on doing things in caves; most bars and discos are in caves. Many restaurants and virtually all pensions offer one or more "cave rooms." Göreme's main attraction is the **Open Air Museum,** and it also makes a good base for exploring the **Rose Valley** and the **Pigeon Valley.**

ORIENTATION AND PRACTICAL INFORMATION

Göreme's **bus station** in the main square contains the private, hotel-run **tourist office** (tel. 271 2316, -7; fax 271 2569; http://www.wec-net.com.tr/belediye/goreme), which gives information only on lodgings. Standing with the bus terminal lengthways behind you, the main road to a mosque runs on your right. To get to the Open Air Museum, walk 100m and take a right at the first major intersection. The **PTT** (open daily 8:30am-12:30pm and 1:30pm-5:30pm) is on the main road at this junction, to your left. There is another office (open daily 9am-5pm) in the Dösim handicrafts building by the entrance to the Open Air Museum, 1km away from Göreme proper. You'll also find two **banks** here (open daily 8:30am-5pm or later, April-Nov. only). The Göreme Sağlik Ocağı **hospital** (tel. 271 2126), located near the PTT, is indicated by signs with a white "H" on a blue background. Behind the *otogar,* across from the Göreme Belediye Handicrafts Market, uphill next to Yama Tours, is a laundromat (tel. 271 2179; $3.50 per load wash; $1.75 dry or iron; open daily 8:30am-8pm). **Postal Code:** 50180. **Telephone Code:** 384.

ACCOMMODATIONS

Göreme's pension owners have settled on a common price scale: dorm beds $4, private rooms $7 per person, $9 with shower. The bus *otogar*'s tourist office is full of posters for the dozens of pensions, and most will pick you up if you call them from the terminal.

Paradise Pansiyon (tel./fax 271 2248), on the road to the Open Air Museum, has two fairy chimney rooms, 5 beds each, with shared bathrooms. Also has 9 other 2, 3, and 4-person rooms. Turkish breakfast is $1.40. If you ask in the morning, they'll fix you an *ızgara* dinner with salad, *pilar,* and watermelon ($3.50). For $2.10 they will wash a load of your laundry (or use the machine for free).

Ufuk Motel and Pension, next door to Paradise, offers 4 of the valley's rare cave rooms with private showers, as well as 11 clean regular rooms (with and without private showers). Dinner—soup, salad, *pilar, ızgara,* and dessert—costs $5.30.

Peri Pansiyon (tel. 271 2136; fax 271 2589), the next pension on the street, has 9 rooms in fairy chimneys and 6 regular rooms; all but 4 have private showers. Breakfast ($1.75) and five-course dinners ($4.60) are served in a pretty courtyard.

Ottoman House (tel. 271 2616; fax 271 2351; email indigo@wec-net.com.tr; http://www.wec-net.com.tr/indigo) is on Orta Mahalle. The Australian-Turkish run inn offers slightly posher lodgings for a slightly higher price. Marble floors, rooftop terrace, restaurant, bar, and nice furniture (singles and doubles $10 per person).

Köse Pansiyon is in the glad just past the PTT. Everything from the handwritten business cards, to the makeshift Ottoman divans, to the daily vegetarian dinner menus ($3.50) contribute to a communal mellow, all-natural atmosphere suggestive of small liberal arts colleges in Vermont. Beside a dorm room, Köse offers 4 triples with shared bathrooms and 5 doubles with private showers.

Panoramic Terrace Pension (tel./fax 271 2040), far to the left of the main street from the *otogar,* boasts **10 cave rooms with private showers,** 3 regular rooms, 1 fairy chimney room, and a panoramic terrace, all with views. If you give them a ring, somebody will pick you up from the bus station in the family car. They also offer breakfast ($1.40), dinner ($3.50), and laundry ($5.60 per kilo).

There is no shortage of camping options in Göreme, most of them on the road to the Open-Air Museum. At **Göreme Dilek Camping** (tel. 271 2396), across from Peri Pansiyon, campsite and pool are nestled among phallic rock structures ($4.50 per site; $8 tent rental; $10 per caravan). **Kaya Camping,** a 5-10 minute walk uphill from the museum, has a superb vista of the valley opposite.

FOOD AND ENTERTAINMENT

Mehmet Paşa Bar and Restaurant, one of Göreme's most elegant eateries, is located in a restored 1826 Ottoman mansion. Choose your meal from the glass counter at the top of the stairs. The excellent *meze* selection ($1.40) includes *patlıcan kızartma* (fried eggplant) and *sarma* (stuffed grape leaves). To get here, take the first right on the road to the mosque (coming from the bus station), then head left and up a steep hill. Open 8:30-12:30am.

Orient (tel. 271 1346), opposite the Yüksel Motel, will entertain your appetite for $2.50-$6 per entree, including vegetarian dishes and a decent *saç tava* ($3).

Asena Family Cafe and Tea Garden (tel. 271 2582), across from Belediye's Handicrafts Market, serves delicious *ızgara* platters with olives and cucumbers ($2).

Flintstones Bar, next to Peri Pansiyon, is run by the dashing and English-speaking Mustafa, and features an 8-10pm happy hour (Efes by the ½L only 70¢).

Escape Bar, located in a converted donkey barn below the giant fairy chimney with the Turkish flag. Bellydancing is featured at 11pm two or three nights a week.

SIGHTS

The **Rose Valley,** between Göreme and Çavuşin, makes a wonderful hike through eerie landscapes of fairy chimneys and bizarre multi-colored rock formations. Tour groups don't come here, so you'll have the place all to yourself. From Göreme, take the first left on the road to the Open Air Museum. Walk for five minutes, then go right; you'll be rewarded with views of a magnificent vista. Descend into the valley from here. You'll probably wander off the several paths and get lost from time to time, but eventually you'll end up in **Çavuşin.** The Avanos-Nevşehir bus and the Avanos-Zelve-Göreme-Ürgüp minibus back to Göreme are available until 6pm. After that, a taxi from Çavuşin costs roughly $4.

In town, the castle-sized fairy chimney with the Turkish flag on top, between the bus station and the carpet emporium, is believed to have been used as a **Roman burial ground.** The most impressive concentration of sights in the region is at the

Open-Air Museum, 1km out of Göreme on the Ürgüp road, containing six Byzantine churches, a convent, and a kitchen/refectory. In the 4th century, St. Basil founded one of the first Christian monasteries here, setting down religious tenets that influenced the teachings of St. Benedict and subsequently the entire Western monastic movement. The church in the hill before the main entrance to the museum is called **Tokalı Kilise,** comprising three smaller churches and a chapel. Three other churches near but not actually inside the museum are **Aynalı,** across from Kaya Camping 600m uphill from the museum entrance; **Saklı,** only discovered in 1957; and **El Nazar,** which you will pass on the right on your way from town to the museum (currently closed for repairs). Behind the Tokalı Church about 250m from the entrance are the **Church of Mother Mary** and the 10th-century **Church of St. Eustathios.** Inside the museum **Elmalı Kilise** is currently closed, but you can visit the **Çarıklı** and **Yılanlı** churches as well as the **Chapels of St. Barbara and St. Basil.** Yılanlı Kilise is also known as St. Onuphrius Church. Conflicting stories circulate regarding St. Onuphrius, the hermaphroditic-looking individual you will notice on your right as you enter. According to one legend, there was once an Egyptian girl called Onophirios who was so beautiful that she could not drive away all the men who wanted to ravish her. She prayed for assistance and was granted a long white beard and mustache, which solved all her problems. Other sources have it that St. Onuphrius belonged to a 4th-century commune of Egyptian "hermits" (forget the fact that these "hermits" all lived together). When St. Paphnutius visited them, he was impressed by the moral fervor and self-control of Onuphrius, who is therefore depicted with a long beard to represent wisdom and full breasts to represent...some kind of big-heartedness? Onophirios/Onuphrius, whoever he/she really was, stands today behind a young palm tree whose position prevents any conclusive answer.

By far the most spectacular frescoes in the museum are those of **Karanlık Kilise** (Dark Church), thus named because light enters through only one very small window in the narthex. It opened in 1997 after 12 years of renovation. The entrance fee is an annoying $7, but it is well worth it to see the 12th-century frescoes preserved in the natural gloom (ticket sales April-Oct. 8am-5:30pm, 8am-4:30pm in winter).

■ Near Göreme

UÇHISAR

To get to Uçhisar from Göreme, take the half-hourly bus to Nevşehir (30¢) and get off at the road junction. It is less than 1km to Uçhisar's Kale, a magnificent rock-carved **fortress** (open 8am-sunset; 70¢). Downstairs is a small grocery store and a photography exhibit by İrtan Ölmez, the fellow responsible for the greater part of Cappadocia's brochure and postcard photographs. The **Kale Cafe** just outside has fabulous views, acceptable *şiş kebap* ($2.40), and the good-natured staff offers to stay open as long as you keep ordering food and drinks.

On the way to Çavuşin-Zelve from the Göreme Open Air Museum you will pass the old village of Uçhisar, with a six-story fairy chimney you can climb, several souvenir stands, and a few decked-out camels (rides $1-$5). Uçhisar is full of lovely, quiet spots to stay should you decide to prolong your visit to Cappadocia, with many especially pleasant, Francophone pensions on the road just below the fortress. Among these numbers the **Uçhisar Pension** (tel. 219 2662), boasting a beautiful view and an open buffet breakfast served on a rooftop terrace (singles $10.40; doubles $17.30, with shower). There is also **Le Jardin des 1001 Nuits** (tel. 219 2293), a sort of nine-room apartment complex of fairy chimneys.

The walk to Göreme will be much easier if you manage to find the **underground tunnel** (unlit—bring a flashlight) on the valley floor. Otherwise it is a moderately difficult hike. Wear hiking boots and be prepared to get a little lost. A good place to descend is from the dirt road a sharp right just past the onyx factory, toward the mosque. A distant terra cotta building with a Turkish flag will appear to the left across the valley. This is your target—the road to Göreme passes right next to it.

ÇAVUŞIN-ZELVE

Both the Ürgüp-Avanos minibus and the Göreme-Avanos bus pass through Çavuşin (2km from Göreme), known for the ancient 5th-century hilltop **Church of St. John the Baptist,** the oldest church in the region and a former pilgrimage site. To reach the church, walk into town past the main square and take the left fork. Go left and uphill after the Walnut Cafe, keeping left at the forks. The church is at the end of the path. This part of Çavuşin is a bit eerie. Lots of empty, brown Greek mansions, abandoned because of the danger of falling rocks earlier this century, create a post-nuclear ghost town effect. The 10th-century **Çavuşin Church**, on the main road beside the turn-off to the village (look for the steps leading up to the rock face), has some well-preserved frescoes (open daily 8am-7pm; admission $1.40).

Like Avanos, Uçhisar, and Mustafapaşa, Çavuşin makes both a good daytrip from Göreme or Ürgup and a nice place to stay for a few days. The **Green Motel** (tel. (384) 532 7050; fax 532 7032), up the main road just past the town square, provides rooms, camping grounds, and good, affordable Turkish food. The German and English-speaking innkeeper will also arrange **horseback riding** ($5.30 per hour. Singles $12; doubles $21.10; triples $26.40; camping $3.50 per tent; tent rental $5.30). Çavuşin is also woodsier than most of Cappadocia, making for shady picnic spots.

Nearby, both **Panorama Pansiyon** (tel. 532 7002) and **Turbel Pansiyon** offer secluded and comfortable rooms with good views for $7 per person, breakfast included. It has solar power only, so when it reaches its maximum 18-person occupancy, late risers might have to take cold showers. Though a little out of the way and lacking private showers, these pensions feel less gimmicky than the ruined-Greek-mansion scene in Ürgüp or the cave scene in Göreme. Traditional Turkish fixed menu dinners are about $5.

Five kilometers uphill from Çavuşin (and one stop away on the Ürgüp-Avanos minibus) lies the village of **Zelve,** which houses the **Zelve Open Air Museum** (the last stop on the minibus route). It is virtually as stunning as Göreme's but much less visited, since most people have already been to Göreme by the time they get to Zelve, (and there are only so many rock-carved 9th-13th-century churches a person can stomach). The **Direkli Kilise** has many highly detailed reliefs from the iconoclastic period (during which representational art was forbidden). Also of note are **Balıkı Kilise, Üzümlü Kilise,** and **Geyikli Kilise.**

AVANOS

The banks of the nearby wine-colored Kızılırmak, Turkey's longest river, have been providing the potters of Avanos with red, iron-rich clay since history began. Roughly a hundred workshops crowd the area, especially the cobbled Old Town, most of them called "Chez (Somebody)" for the benefit of the town's many French visitors. **Chez İsmail, Chez Barış, Chez Galıp,** and, alarmingly enough, **Chez Rambo** are among the many studio/shops located primarily in caves or old whitewashed Greek buildings. Watch the potters at work or try your own hand at the giant foot-powered wheels. For whatever reason, Avanos seems to be Cappadocia's most **internet-savvy** town, and even the smallest and most unlikely looking pensions and ceramics stores are likely to have web sites and email addresses.

Unless you are eager to delve deeply into Avanos's considerable art and pottery scene, Avanos is best visited as a day trip from Göreme or Ürgüp. Belediye **buses** head to Avanos from the Göreme *otogar* every half hour 8am-7pm. Göreme Belediye buses (30¢) also run to Nevşehir every half hour, 7am-6pm. Either of these will drop you at Avanos's *otogar*. The **tourist office** (tel. (384) 511 4360), located in the *otogar,* gives out free town maps, regional brochures, and directions to Avanos's widely-scattered pensions (open daily 8:30am-5pm, sometimes later in peak season). To get to the center of town, walk along the bus route and turn right across the bridge onto Atatürk Cad. The main square, marked by several terra cotta statues (remarkably all depicting artisans—there is no Atatürk), is 250m farther. To your left, an uphill stone path leads to the well-marked Old Town, where most of the ceramics studios as well as a few

> ## "I never take hair by force."
>
> When checking out the Old Town pottery scene, stop by *chez* **Chez Galip** (tel. 511 4240, 4577; fax 511 4543; http://business.wec-net.com.tr/galip; http://www.wec-net.com.tr/Avanos/galip), home to what owner Galip Körükçü claims is the **world's first hair museum**. The walls and ceiling of the museum are covered by 10,000 snippets of hair, thoughtfully labelled with the donors name, address, and telephone number. Here is the actual text from Monsieur Galip's interview with *Let's Go*:
>
> MG: Have you seen how pots are made?
> LG: Yes, thanks. Actually, I'm very interested in the Hair Museum, I saw the signs outside. Is it in this building?
> MG: Will you have some tea?
> LG: No thanks. Could you possibly tell me a little about the Hair Museum?
> MG: Of course, follow me. This is the world's first hair collection. I opened it in '79. I only take hair from ladies.
> LG: Why do you only collect ladies' hair?
> MG: Why not?
> LG: Fair enough.
> MG: I'll give you a brochure. Look here, every page has color photos. The tourism office tries, but they can't manage a brochure this good. Did you go to the tourism office yet?
> LG: Yes, you're right, their brochure didn't have color photos.
> MK: Why don't I cut a little of your hair?
> LG: Oh, no, that's okay.
> MK: Why not?
> LG: Thank you, but I'd just as soon you didn't.
> MK: It's up to you. I never take hair by force. You can write that down.

pensions and cafes can be found. **ATMs** are numerous at the many branch banks here. **Kirkit Voyages**, around the corner from the Kirkit pension, also arranges guided horse tours (2hr.; $7; ½ day $12.70; full day $21.15) and rents French mountain bikes ($14 per day). Just past the square are the **PTT** (open daily 7am-11pm) and the striking **Büyük Avanos Mosque.**

If you do decide to prolong your stay in Avanos, a fine selection of pensions and affordable hotels lies at your disposal. The **Sofa Hotel** (tel. (384) 511 4489, -78; fax 511 4489; http://www.hotels.wec-net.com.tr/data/sofa), just across the bridge into town up the first hill on the left, offers beautiful rooms decorated in the traditional Turkish style and a small tea garden (singles $20; doubles $20). **İlhan's Guesthouse,** 1 Zafer Sok. (tel. 511 4828), right next door with some river views, is another good pension ($7 per person, all rooms with private bath; 15% discount for *Let's Go* users). The **Kirkit Pension** (tel. 511 3259; fax 511 2135; email kirkitşwec-net.com.tr; http://www.hotels.WeC-NeT.com.tr/data/kirkit), on the way to the *otogar*, offers lodgings in a restored Ottoman stone house ($7 per person, $8.80 with private bath). Behind the Ziraat Banka and next to the mosque, on the bank of the Kızılırmak, **Mesut Camping and Restaurant** (tel. 511 3545) charges $4.20 per tent.

Atatürk Cad. is full of fine restaurants between old and new town. The **Sarıkaya** dining experience is much like eating in one of those Japanese steak houses where meals are prepared on a hibachi grill at your table—pricey, a little embarrassing, not particularly authentic, but entertaining nonetheless.

Carved (unsurprisingly enough) into a hillside, Sarıkaya offers "Turkish banquets" with folklore, music, and dancing for about $15 per person. The **İlter Mantı Evi** specializes in *mantı* (tiny boiled meat-filled dumplings served with yogurt, $1.75). **Tafana** serves *ızgara* and *tandır* dishes with excellent fresh pita and pinto beans ($1.75). Many small, pretty *kafeleriya*-type joints line the river. **Beyaz Saray Kafeteriya** serves pita or *ızgara* dishes with salad ($1.40).

ANATOLIA

■ Ürgüp

Ürgüp is more compact and less geologically oriented than Göreme, with few cave hotels and no rock-carved churches. The bizarre rock formations and early Christian dwellings are interspersed with vineyards and old Greek mansions recalling sunny Mediterranean milieux. Göreme is an easy 10-minute *dolmuş* ride away, and Ürgüp's *otogar* and rental agencies offer access to most Cappadocian points of interest.

A word of warning: some of Ürgüp's **tourist agencies** are pushier and more irritating than their counterparts in Göreme. The folks at **Erko Tours,** however, located in the *otogar*, are reliable and will not jump down your throat trying to sell you a carpet. Speaking of carpets, think twice before buying one in Cappadocia. Carpet stores abound here, not because it is Turkey's carpet-making hub, but because of the influx of tourist dollars. Scams, especially "artificial aging," are not unusual.

ORIENTATION AND PRACTICAL INFORMATION

The extremely helpful Ürgüp **tourist office** (tel. 341 4059), inside the garden on Kayseri Cad., provides maps, bus schedules, and helps arrange tours (open April-Oct. daily 8:30am-7:30pm or later; Nov.-March Mon.-Fri. 8am-5:30 and Sat.-Sun. 9am-5pm). You may direct any bus schedule-related questions to the helpful and English-speaking Aydın Altan at **Nevtur** (tel. 341 4302, -3330) in the *otogar*. Coming out of the tourist office, head right and take your first right uphill to get to the **PTT** (open daily 8:30am-5:30pm; **currency exchange** closed noon-1:30pm). Instead of going up the hill, just head right out of the garden for 80m or so to the **bus station.** You'll also see several **ATMs** and **rental agencies.** The main square is 20m ahead, marked by the Sofa Restaurant, a bath house, and an Atatürk statue. The road forks uphill into two smaller roads, both full of pensions and hotels. Call the **hospital** (tel. 341 4031) or the **Cappadocia Health Center,** 28 Dumlupınar Cad. (tel. 341 5427, -28; fax 341 3492), in an emergency. **Postal Code:** 50400. **Telephone Code:** 384.

ACCOMMODATIONS

Hotel Asia Minor (tel. 341 4645), behind the Atatürk statue, is a beautiful 150 year-old Greek mansion with reproductions of rock-church frescoes on the lobby walls and a lovely garden. Singles with bath $8.80-$14. Breakfast included.

Hotel Akuzun (tel. 341 3869, -66), across the street, has friendly service and clean, modern facilities. Drinks are served on a rooftop terrace and breakfast outside in a rose garden. Some rooms have balconies and bathtubs, and all have private showers. Singles $15; doubles $25; triples $38.

Hotel Elvan, İstiklal Cad., II Barbaros Hayrettin Sok. (tel. 341 4191, -3455), is a little farther downhill and to the left. Its family-run atmosphere offers comparable quality. Breakfast is served in an carpeted lounge, and rooms have arched ceilings and stone walls. Cleanliness borders on obsessive; the toilet bowls sparkle.

Hotel Surban (tel. 341 4761, -03; fax 341 3223). If instead of a right you take a left uphill behind the Atatürk statue, fortune will again shower you with many accommodation options, among them this large, modern locale. Laundry $1.40 per piece. Singles $14; doubles $21; triples $28. Breakfast included.

FOOD AND ENTERTAINMENT

The three major tourist-oriented eateries are: **Sofa Restaurant,** stuffed in the courtyard of an antique inn between the bus terminal and the Atatürk statue, **Şömine Cafe and Restaurant** across the street next to the taxi stand, and the newly-opened **Kervan Restaurant** to the right of Şömine (as you approach from the tourist office). All offer extensive menus of Turkish and Western dishes as well as some local specialties. The big thing here is food cooked in a *tandir*—an underground clay charcoal oven similar to the Indian tandoori. *Tandir* specialties include *güveç* (eggplant and other vegetables), *kiremit kebap* (lamb or chicken cooked with onion, tomato, mushroom and cheese), and *kuru fasulye* (pinto beans, tomato, and onion).

While Sofa, Şömine, and Kervan offer decent food and ambiance, the best food in town tends to turn up in some of the smaller restaurants. **Kardeş ler 2 Pizza,** 5 Suat Hayri Cad. (tel. 341 2376), has truly first-rate pita and *ızgara* as well as *tandır* dishes ($2.50-$3). The *piliç* joints on İstiklal Cad. serve rice and a loaf of bread for $3.50. Inside the *otogar*, the **Ocakbaşı Restaurant** (tel. 341 3277) serves surprisingly tasty *ızgara* ($3) and cold *meze* dishes ($1.40), with an emphasis on southern specialties. One of the best of Ürgüp's restaurants is the family-run **Han Çirağan** (tel. 341 4169; fax 341 4181), between the bath house and the Harem Disco. The place is no slacker ambiance-wise; the building is a 200-300 year-old caravanserai and some rooms are still used by merchants in horse-drawn carriages. They serve excellent *melemen* ($2.45), *güvec* ($2.80), and mixed grill ($4.25).

If you find yourself still energized after a day of trooping through Ürgüp's narrow cobblestone streets, the **Harem Disco** (at the foot of the road to Hotel Surban) blasts Turkish and European techno daily until 4:30am in a cave lit by candles, a fireplace, and blue lights reflecting off a disco ball (no cover). A nightly half-Turkish, half-tourist crowd heads to the **Armağan Disco,** across the street from the Kapadokya Market (under the "Born To Be Free" neon sign), where disco tunes and Turkish pop precede an occasional belly dance act. They also have several (relatively) quiet stone-cut rooms with divans and carpets, making Armağan the most conducive of Ürgüp's establishments to privacy and coherent conversation.

The connoisseur may be aware that Cappadocia is one of Turkey's major viticultural regions, with its center in Ürgüp. Just uphill from Hotel Surban, the renowned **Turasan Winery,** supplier of 98% of Cappadocia's wines (2.5 million liters per year, plus exports) offers free tours and tastings in its rock-carved wine cellar. You can also buy cheap wine here—the 1995 vintage is $2 (the more robust '89 $5.25). Several wine shops around the main square also offer free tastings.

While you are at the tourist office, you might as well step next door to check out Ürgüp's **museum** (open daily April-Oct. 8am-5pm; 70¢, students 35¢). You may also want to drop in at the (coed!) **Tarihi Şehir Hamamı** in the main square. A complete bath with massage/scrub and sauna is $5.30 per person (open daily 8am-11pm).

■ Near Ügüp: Mustafapaşa

The fascinating moonscape valleys and rock-cut Greek orthodox churches of Mustafapaşa seem to be unknown to the entire world except for the Mustafapaşans themselves and several French walking-tour groups. Although a few new and still-dormant hotel-like edifices sprawling along side roads suggest that tourism is on its way in, for now at least this is Cappadocia's proverbial undiscovered gem. It absolutely merits a day-trip from Ürgüp—or even, should you really dig subterranean churches or French hikers, a few days' stay.

Dolmuş make the 5km run from Ürgüp's *otogar* to Mustafapaşa throughout the day (20¢ each way). The *dolmuş* deposit you in Mustafapaşa's square, containing a now-defunct fountain and enclosed by a few restaurants, shops, hotels, and an old caravanserai, now used as a carpet bazaar. The shop labeled "Information" doubles as the **tourism office** (open daily June-Aug. 8:30am-7:30pm). On the wall to the left of the door, an imaginatively-scaled diagram (200m in some places appears as long as 10km in others—be sure to read the labeled distances) indicates the location of the closest sites. The churches are mostly kept locked, but for 70¢ (students 35¢) the information folk will lend you the keys.

To the northwest of the old fountain, a gravel road leads downhill 1km past the Paça Restaurant to the 7th-century Byzantine **Aios Vasilyos Church.** The visible portion of Aios Vasilyos is an uninspiring stone cubicle the size of a port-a-john, but two flights of stone stairs lead down to a magnificent subterranean church. Because it's carved into the side of the valley, occasional windows let in enough daylight for you to admire the many frescoes. One window served as a sentry post: when the sentry noticed undesirables approaching, he could roll an enormous boulder in front of the only window accessible from ground level, thus sealing the place off.

Right next door to Aios Vasilyos, **Paşa Kamping** (tel. 353 5018), patronized mostly by French backpackers, allows you to set up camp overlooking the valley and use the swimming pool, bathroom and showers (24hr. hot water) for $3 per person. If you like, they will fix you a traditional Turkish dinner for $4 extra. The **Şarap Farbrikası** winery, in a cave 200m to the east of the old fountain in the square, offers free tours and tasting, as well as the opportunity to enjoy a picnic lunch with a bottle of the famous local $2 wine. Follow the road leading southwest of the fountain for a hilly 2km to reach **Gömede Valley,** Mustafapaşa's most striking site. On your way you will pass the **Hotel Pascha** (tel. 353 5004), a restored Greek mansion, where 12 well-restored singles, doubles, and triples with lovely views and private showers go for $7 per person (breakfast $1.75).

Because few pains have been taken to make Gömede Valley more accessible to visitors, some athleticism is required to get around. Hiking boots and a flashlight will make this a more pleasant experience. Once your soul and day pack have been adequately prepared, you will find that Gömede's pluses far outweigh its minuses. The valley has no admission fee and it's off the packaged tour circuit, so you can spend half a day here roaming through the cave dwellings, cave-churches, cave-wine cellars, cave-jails, cave-cemeteries, and other caves, without seeing a single other living soul except the occasional French *à pied* excursion. Keep a check on your exploratory instincts. Many caves and tunnels are not fully explored, and there is a rumor of an undiscovered 5km tunnel linking the various citadels and villages of Cappadocia. It might be unpleasant to stumble into it by accident.

Entering the valley, you will notice an **information office** to your left. Like many of Cappadocia's finest institutions, this office is located in a cave. The valley's "keeper" actually lives here. The bad news is, as you might find when you arrive, he's often gone out for some firewood or something and has locked the place up. The good news is that he'll probably return soon and can point the way to **Tavşanlı Kilise,** the 1100-year-old **Kimistavros Church,** and the 1200-year-old **Karakilise.**

■ Nevşehir

Although Nevşehir is not especially interesting, it is the region's transportation hub. Even if you buy what looks like a direct bus ticket from Göreme or Ürgüp, what you are really getting is probably a *servis* shuttle to Nevşehir and then a regular bus onward from there. Also, the only public transportation available to Aksaray, Penh-kuyu, and Kaymakılı from Ürgüp and Göreme is through Nevşehir. Don't stay here if you have time to take a *servis* bus to Göreme or Ürgüp, which are more charming.

ORIENTATION AND PRACTICAL INFORMATION

The two main streets in Nevşehir are the north-south **Atatürk Bulvarı,** and the perpendicular **Lale Cad.** While standing in the main bus/car park with the terminal at your back, you'll see **Lale Cad.** running uphill on your right. Atatürk Blv. is a 10-minute walk up Lale Cad. If you take the Nevşehir Belediye bus from Ürgüp or Göreme, one of the stops before the main terminal is on Lale Cad. outside the Göreme and Nevşehir ticket agencies. If you turn left at the intersection, you'll see the **tourist office** (tel. (384) 213 3659), offering free maps and brochures. English and German is spoken (open Mon.-Fri. 8am-5:30pm, Sat.-Sun. 9:30am-5:30pm). **Dolmuş** leave from outside the tourist office for most parts of Cappadocia and also stop at the main bus station (every 30min. 7am-7pm, off season 7am-5pm). Next door, the **hospital** can be reached at (384) 213 1200. Atatürk Blv. has everything—restaurants, pharmacies, shops, a Cappadocian tea garden, several **ATMs,** and a 24-hour **PTT.** If you're particularly interested in **mosque-bath-medressa complexes,** there is an 18th-century one commissioned by Damat İbrahim Paşa at the western end of Lale Cad.

ACCOMMODATIONS AND FOOD

Nevşehir might not put you up in a cave or restored Ottoman house, but all the following are clean and pleasant alternatives. The **Şems Otel** (tel. 213 3597; fax 213

0834), on Atatürk Blv., has well-furnished rooms with private showers for $8.80 per person (breakfast $1.75). Down the street, the two-star **Epok Otel,** 39 Atatürk Blv. (tel. 213 1168, 213 1487; fax 213 1642) offers similar rooms but with an in-house restaurant and lounge (singles $17.60; doubles $24.65; breakfast $1.40; dinner $5.30). **Hotel Seven Brothers,** Kayseri Cad. 23 Tusan Sok. (tel. 213 4979, -8178; fax 213 0454), just off Atatürk Blv. to the south of the tourist office, has TVs in every room and a motorized shoe shine machine in the lobby ($10.60 per person). Nearby, **Otel Nisa,** 35 Yeni Kayseri Cad. (tel. 213 5843, 212 6168; fax 213 5843), has TVs and private showers in its rooms, some with balconies (singles $10; doubles $15). The **Açlan Gaziantep Kebap Salon,** 8 Tartaroğlu Sok. (tel. 212 0990 or 212 2525), serves delicious *kebap* with fresh pita for about $2.50 (the specialty is *Adana kebap*).

■ Kaymakli and Derinkuyu

In 1962 a farmer in the village of Derinkuyu lost a chicken. After looking around the farm all afternoon, he found the truant foul in a small cave and stumbled upon the famous underground city of Derinkuyu. Cappadocia contains almost 200 such underground cities, all carved from *tufa*. Kaymaklı and Derinkuyu are the two largest, 20km and 29km south of Nevşehir on the Niğde road respectively. *Dolmuş* run to Nevşehir every 30 minutes, 6:30am-7pm (70¢).

Earliest written mention of Hellenic communities in Derinkuyu and Kaymaklı appears in Xenophon's *Anabasis,* dating them to at least the 4th century BC. The first levels of these cities are actually believed to have been built by the Hittites around 2000 BC, either for storage or to escape attack from enemies. Most of them, however, were constructed by Christians between 1300 and 1800 years ago to avoid Sassanid raids. Thousands of people lived in Derinkuyu and Kaymaklı for months at a time. Strict discipline was enforced, and some pillars have holes drilled for chaining and torturing transgressors. It was forbidden for anyone to leave while the cities were occupied, lest their departure give away the hideouts. Strangely enough, **no toilets** have been conclusively found in either Derinkuyu or Kaymaklı.

Derinkuyu, 85m deep with a 120m well and eight levels open to the public, is slightly more impressive and offers sizable rooms and halls, good lighting, and relatively easy access. In both cities, the tunnels were built low and tortuous to hamper the progress of invaders. They are also dank and chilly; bring a sweater. Derinkuyu houses an entire missionary school, formerly known as Melagobia, as well as the standard grape-treading areas, storage cellars, churches, refectories, living quarters, and stables. Kaymaklı, smaller than Derinkuyu at 35m, boasts a more complex structure. The village has been built around the underground city, so residents can enter storage areas through tunnels in their courtyards. One of Cappadocia's famous "blocked" tunnels is rumored to span 9km from Kaymaklı back to Derinkuyu.

In both cities, red arrows lead down, blue arrows up. Both cities also have uncharted tunnels, so be careful. Remember, these cities were designed to foil potential trespassers by tricking them into falling to their deaths with sudden drops hidden behind corners. (Both sites open daily 8:30am-7pm, off season 8:30am-5pm. Admission $1.50, students 75¢.)

▓ Ihlara

For centuries thousands of Greek Christians found the Ihlara valley a refuge for sedentary life while their nomadic Turkish neighbors grazed their flocks over the grassy plains above. Although the valley is still somewhat off the beaten track, it is becoming more mainstream every year. A dozen years ago there were no pensions and no public transport. Now there is a daily *dolmuş*, a number of pensions, and two restaurants.

GETTING THERE

Getting to Ihlara is relatively painless. Many Göreme tour agencies run a half-day tour covering the valley's major churches, as well as the underground cities of Derinkuyi and Kaymaklı. If you want to do a thorough hike, you'll have to either arrange a one-way excursion and get dropped off in Ihlara at the end of the day ($25 per person for two people; discounts available for groups over 5) or throw yourself at the mercy of Ihlara Belediye's public transportation. **Dolmuş** depart Monday-Saturday from Aksaray's bus station at 11am, 3, and 6:30pm, arriving at the main square of Ihlara village one hour later. The other buses depart Ihlara at 7, 7:30am, and 1pm (70¢ each way). From Ürgüp to Göreme, take the half-hourly bus to Nevşehir and one of the seven daily buses onto Aksaray (8:45am-6pm, 1¼hr., $1.75). Because of the eccentric bus schedule, you probably can't hike the valley in a daytrip, or even with a single overnight in Ihlara. One option is to take the 3pm or 5:30pm bus from Aksaray, settle into your pension and have a meal, do the hike the next day, and leave the following morning. About 10km south from the last turn-off to Ihlara, the bus from Aksaray will pass the town of **Selime,** pockmarked with the windows and doors of former troglodyte habitations. Hikers usually enter here, or at the village of **Yaprakhisar,** just around the bend. Ten minutes later, the bus will stop to let passengers off at Ihlara's handful of pensions, then continue 1km downhill to the main square. Except for the excellent restaurant (lunch $3.50) at the official entrance to the gorge, little food is served outside the pensions. **Hospital** (tel. 453 7006). **Police** (tel. 451 2008). **Postal Code:** 68570. **Telephone Code:** 382.

ACCOMMODATIONS

Accommodations in Ihlara charge per person, not per room. The Famille and Akar pensions offer private *dolmuş* service from Aksaray and will run you to the valley entrance or to Selime for free in the morning. You can hike through the valley back to Ihlara village. Ihlara Pansiyon offers free car or tractor excursions to Hasandağ, complete with a *saç tava* picnic and Turkish music.

Bişkinler Ihlara Pansiyon (tel. 453 7077) has basic rooms, all with balconies, hot water, shower, and toilet. Recently has come under new and dynamic management. Quite a bargain, both in the restaurant, bar, and pension. Breakfast included. $7 per person. Camping $3.50 per tent; $7 per caravan.

Pansiyon Anatolia (tel. 453 7440, -7182; fax 453 7439) is comfortable and clean, with some private showers and balconies. Breakfast included. $7 per person; camping $1.75 per tent; tent rental $4.25.

Pension Famille (tel. 453 7098), where French is the language of choice, offers comfortable rooms in a family home. Breakfast included. $7 per person; dinner, including home-made yogurt, $4.90.

Pansiyon Akar (tel. 453 7018) has clean, comfortable rooms with balconies and private baths. Those at the back have views of Mt. Hasan. $10 per person; fixed menu dinner $5. Breakfast included. The **grocery store** below sells picnic supplies and some personal hygiene items.

HIKING THE VALLEY

The Ihlara Valley consists of 14km of the north-south Melendiz River, from Selime to Ihlara village. Most people visit the valley on guided tours from Göreme or Ürgüp; these take tourists on a walk from its **official entrance,** 2km from Ihlara's pension cluster, to **Belisırma,** 3km north, where there's a restaurant and a campsite. To reach the entrance from Ihlara's main square, go uphill towards Aksaray 1km and take the first main intersection to your right (it's signposted "Ihlara Valley 2km"). The official valley entrance (unmarked from below) allows you to see the highlights without a hike: hundreds of concrete steps lead directly to the rich, frescoed-rock churches (entrance open 8am-7pm; admission $1.75, students 75¢).

But don't feel trapped in by the officialism—in reality, you have lots of flexibility in visiting the valley. To hike the 10km south from **Selime** back to Ihlara, take the 7 or 7:30am Aksaray bus and get off at Selime. Ask the locals to point you to the valley entrance *(vadi girişi).* The views are best in the downstream direction. In the other direction, time your arrival in Selime to catch the 5:30pm Aksaray-Ihlara bus. A 7km hike starts in **Yaprakhisar** (the Aksaray bus passes through there as well). The flat and well-worn path does involve a few scrambles among the boulders north of Belisırma.

The popular **Sümbüllü** and **Ağaçaltı** churches flank the official entrance stairs at the valley floor. The Sümbüllü is noteworthy for its rock facade and five deep, arched bays separated by pillars. Spectacular blue and white angels ring the Christ figure on the well-preserved dome of the Ağaçaltı. Another 30m south past the Ağaçaltı (to the right after descending the entrance stairs, away from Belisırma) lies the **Pürenliseki Church,** whose faded walls enclose the many martyrs of Sivas. The **Kokar Church,** 70m farther along, celebrates biblical stories with colorful frescoes and ornate geometrical ceiling crosses. Also worth seeing is the **Yılanlı Church**, which gets its name from a display of Satan's serpents (Yılanlı means snake). To reach it, backtrack from the Kokar to the steps at the official valley entrance and cross the wooden bridge. The church lies 100m to your left, up the concrete steps.

AKSARAY

The main reason to visit Aksaray is to catch public transport on to Ihlara. Fortune smileth upon those who arrive in Aksaray via the Nevşehir Belediye bus (7 per day 8:45am-6pm, $1.70), for they shall be dropped at the **bus station** in town. Intercity Nevşehir-Konya buses deposit you instead at a Mobil station on the ring road, 2.5km from the center. Taxis ($1.50) are hassle-free, or ask someone to point the way to the *şehir merkez* (town center). After 500m, you will pass soccer fields on your left. The **police** can be reached at 212 6650 or 212 1185. Aksaray is home to a very large, quite modern **hospital** (tel. 212 9100, 213 1043, -5207), located at the entrance to town. The **PTT** is just off the public garden one block past the main square on the same road as the bus station. Turn right at the garden (open daily 8:30am-5:30pm). **Postal Code:** 68100. **Telephone Code:** 382.

If you need to stay in Aksaray, exit the bus station by the Pension Çakmak, cross the street, and continue down the opposite road. Eventually you'll come across **Aksaray Pansiyon** (tel. 212 4133), offering large, clean rooms, a wicker-roofed terrace, sunny TV salon, and a free kitchen (singles $5.25; doubles $10; triples $12.75). Back near the bus station, the **Ihlara Pansiyon** (tel. 213 6083), on Eski Sanayı Cad., has pleasant, well-lit rooms (singles $5.25; doubles $10; triples $12.75; breakfast $1). If you get hungry, check out **Kent Lokanta** near the Otel Yuvam. They offer tasty and cheap rotisserie chicken ($1.50). **Sultan Lahmacun** (1 Kalealtı Cad.; tel. 212 4220) serves only three dishes: *lahmacun* (50¢), rice pudding (*sütlaç*, 55¢), and lentil soup (70¢).

▓ Tokat

It was 47 BC and King Pharnake II was not a stupid man. He knew that the problems lurking beneath the surface of the Pontic Kingdom would have to be reckoned with. There was only one possible course of action: attacking the Roman provinces of Armenia, Cappadocia, and Galatia. Later, somewhere near Alexandria, a young soldier rushed into Julius Caesar's tent. "Caesar!" the messenger cried, "the Pontic armies are planning a siege on Anatolia!" The emperor raised his majestic head and turned with blazing eyes to the messenger. "Very well," he said, "to Anatolia at once!" The road to Amasya shimmered in the central Anatolian sun as Caesar and his men encountered Pharnake's troops between Tokat and Zile. The Pontic soldiers were at the same time a terrible and wonderful sight, as they urged their foaming horses and their murderous scythe-wheeled chariots forward. Nonetheless, it took Caesar only five hours to defeat the Pontic army. Surveying the carnage with a slight smile, the emperor allowed himself a moment of exhilaration. Victory was sweet, coming so shortly after his return from Egypt. "A message to Rome," he cried, "Veni! Vidi! Vici!" providing the Tokat's Tourism Directorate 2000 years later with possibly the lamest slogan in Asia Minor: "I came, I saw, I fell in love!"

Conquering? Falling in love? Ugh, how recherché! Not to mention messy, complicated, and expensive. Instead, try a visit to Tokat. The unique blend of Black Sea and

Central Anatolian ambiance, the first-rate museums in the Gök Medresi and the Latifoğlu Mansion, the crafts workshops in Taş Han, and the Ballica Cave all make Tokat a worthwhile stop, especially on the way to the Black Sea coast from Cappadocia.

ORIENTATION AND PRACTICAL INFORMATION

Mountains and jagged promontories surround the town on three sides, crowned at one point by a **kale** (stone fortress). The main street, Gazi Osman Paşa Bulvari (GOP Blv.), runs north-south, with the heart of the town (Cumhuriyet Alanı) located about 2km from the *otogar*. If your bus arrives late at night, you might want to take a taxi into town (about $3).

Banks: The handful of banks on GOP Blv. offer identical ATM services as their Ankara counterparts (see **Ankara—Practical Information,** p.512).

Buses: Tokat Seyahat provides the most comfortable and reliable service. Offices both at the *otogar* and across the street from the PTT (near the Turistik Otel) in Cumhuriyet Alanı. Buses go to Ankara (7 per day, 6hr., $11); Istanbul (4 per day, 11hr., $13.40); Sivas and Amasya (1 per day, 2hr., $3.15); and Kayseri (2 per day, 4½hr., $6.35). 10% student discount.

Local Transportation: You can probably walk everywhere you want to go in town, but *dolmuş* (20¢) and local buses (30¢) run the length of GOP Blv.

Hospital: Devlet Hastanesi, Ardola Sok. (tel. 214 5400), south of the main square on the road to Sivas.

Emergency Telephone Numbers: Medical emergency, 112; police, 155 (regional police, 156); fire, 110; international operator, 115.

PTT: In Cumhuriyet Alanı. Poste Restante, telex card, and other services 8:30am-6pm; telephones available 24hr. Postal code is 60000.

Telephone Code: 356.

ACCOMMODATIONS

Temar Turistik Hotel, 10 Cumhuriyet Cad. (tel. 212 7755), just off GOP Blv., directly across from the PTT. Airy, clean rooms all have private showers, some with nice views of the Ali Paşa Mosque. Singles $7; doubles $9 ($10.50 with TV); triples $14. Laundry facilities in basement. Breakfast ($1.75) is in the roomy 2nd floor lobby.

Hotel Çağri, GOP Blv., tel. 212 1028. Winding staircases, dark hallways, and faux mahogany furniture characterize this pleasant and cheap establishment. Singles $6, with bath $8; doubles $12; triples $14, with bath $18.

Hotel Çamlica, 86 GOP Blv. (tel. 214 1269). Relatively clean, with large windows and pleasant atmosphere. Singles $8.50 ($10.50 with bath); doubles $14, with bath $18; triples $18, with bath $21; quads $21, with bath $28. Discounts on stays longer than 2 days, but the shared showers are $1.50. TVs are available for an extra charge. Breakfast $1.50. Laundry facilities are free for guests.

Plevne Otel, 83 GOP Blv. (tel. 214 2207). Comparable in quality to Çamlica. Singles $8, with bath $10; doubles $15, with bath $20. Breakfast $2. Laundry available.

Büyük Tokat Oteli, Demirköprü Mevkii (tel. 228 1661, fax 228 1660), 3km from Cumhuriyet Alanı. From the PTT, head north on GOP Blv. and make a left on the Demirköprü Mevkii, following the signs to the hotel. If you always wanted to stay in a 4-star hotel, this might be your big chance. Singles $22.50; doubles $34, breakfast included. All rooms have A/C and private bathtubs. Otherwise, they aren't much better than their cheaper counterparts in town. The main perks are the swimming pool, *pastane*, wine shop, barber shop, and restaurant.

Camping: Permitted in Gümenek (9km away) and on the shores of the lake behind the dam (35km away).

FOOD

Although famous for its wines, Tokat is no culinary capital. The two local specialties are *Tokat kebap* (skewered lamb, potatoes, and eggplant, $3.50), and *çokelekli* (pita bread filled with crumbled cheese and lamb or potatoes, 40¢). *İskender* (lamb cut from a *döner* kebap and served slathered in yogurt), tomato garlic sauce, and melted butter, can be good but is particularly nasty when ill-prepared. If you are at all picky about your food, it is better to stick to the simplest possible fare.

Inexpensive restaurants line GOP Blv. and its neighboring streets. The smaller and less extravagant the building, the cheaper the food. **Sofra Restaurant** on GOP Blv. serves fine *Tokat kebap,* as does **Cim Cim** across the street. Sofra has pleasant second-floor seating with nice views of the town. Cim Cim is a little gloomier and sepulchral, but, unlike Sofra, serves beer. Vegetarians tired of *çokelek* can try *nohut* (stewed chickpeas) at many of the restaurants, but beware that uninvited chunks of lamb sometimes turn up in such dishes. And, while tofu hasn't made it to Turkey yet, those wishing simply to avoid the red meat scene may do so at the **Burai Restaurant,** which serves half rotisserie-baked chickens ($1.75) and a unique chicken *döner* ($1.50). It is open 8am-11pm and is located north of the PTT.

SIGHTS

The most widely visited sight in Tokat is the **Blue Seminary** *(Gök Medrese),* located across from the fortress on GOP Blv. (admission 70¢, 35¢ for students; open 8:30am-12:30pm and 1:30-5pm). The seminary dates back to 1277 and was used as a hospital until 1811. The focus is on artifacts unearthed at the Hanözü, Sebastopolis, and Maşat Höyük archaeological digs between Tokat and Zile from 1975 to 1984. Glut yourself on fragmented Hittite vases, Bronze Age objects, Ottoman executioners' swords, and more. In the calligraphy gallery, note the 7½-meter long Ottoman diploma required of all tradesmen, listing the owner's every credential from family background to school performance to completed pieces. Other especially intriguing items on display include early Ottoman cocaine receptacles, a wooden *kilim* loom, and a wax model of the Diocletian-era martyr Christinae entombed in a labelled glass coffin (whose resemblance to Snow White stops with the faithfully reproduced bloody gash across her throat). Legend has it that she was killed by her Christian family for eloping with a Muslim. For better or for worse, another attraction of Tokat's museum is the **40 Girls' Mausoleum** *(Kirkkizlar Turbesi),* containing 20 coffins painted the color of cotton candy. Museum staff claim that the interred bodies are the seminary's architect and his 19 closest relatives. An alternative legend is that 40 young female nurses who were poisoned during the seminary's hospital days lie here, stacked two per pale pink coffin. The seminary owes its name to the brilliant turquoise tiles decorating the central courtyard *(gök medrese* means "sky seminary"). The enamel on these tiles uses a formula which modern-day enamel technology has never been able to reproduce.

Next door to the *Gök Medrese* is the **Taş Han** inn/caravan *serai.* Once a major stop on the Ottoman silk route, the small store and workshops here now specialize in selling tourist merchandise, including *yazmalar,* Tokat's famous gauze scarves printed with wood-block floral designs. The smithery shop in No. 32 overflows with fascinating Ottoman tidbits, much of it quite valuable, from giant mortar and pestles to spiked chain whips. Perhaps the *han's* most interesting shop is operated by a bee enthusiast, who stocks Tokat with bee-keeping costumes, masks, honey-harvesting equipment, bee hormones, powdered pollen, vitamins for bees suffering from malnutrition, and more. A jar of honey *(bal)* is $3.50; honeycomb $5.

You also can't help but see the 425-year-old **Tarihi Ali Paşa Hamam** in Cumhuriyet Alani. Intentionally or not, its roof sings—nay, shouts—a glorious architectural ode to the human breast. The roof is comprised of two giant side-by-side domes over the women's section, while the several smaller domes over the men's section are studded with nippled glass bulbs. A complete bath costs $2 (open 9am-5pm). On the same side of the street, several blocks south of the baths, is the splendid **Latifoğlu Konaği,** a richly decorated 19th-century Ottoman family mansion. The sign is easier to see coming north from the clock tower. Enter through the garden; if the door is locked, knock; admission 70¢, students 35¢; open Tues.-Sun. 9am-12:30pm and 1:30-5pm). The hilly, stone-paved **Sulu Sokak** to the west of the clock tower brims with equally nice, though less well-maintained, Ottoman homes.

At the summit of Sulu Sok., in his home at 26 Ayvaş Paşa Mahallesi, Duran Atilgan (tel. 212 0437) operates a **zurna** shop. Incredibly loud, these oboe-like woodwind instruments are used in Turkish folk music. Altigan, a self-taught virtuoso, performs on request. If you can't find the house, ask passers-by for "Duran Amja". He'll even sell you a zurna (starting at $10).

■ Near Tokat: Ballica, Pazar, and Kat

A new paved road 25km from Tokat winds up White Mountain (*Akdağ*) 1916m to the entrance of the **Ballica Mağaralar.** Stalactites and stalagmites of awe-inspiring size have been forming on the Permo trias marble and limestone walls of these caves since the Pleistocene Era at a rate of 1cm every 400 years. Evidence suggests that some of the caves had human inhabitants in the Hittite period. Unseasonably cool in the summer and warm in the winter, Ballica is made up of eight irregular chambers. Climbing hundreds of stone-hewn stairs into a horizonless landscape of both jagged and bulbous green rock, punctuated only by the dripping of water and the chattering of bats, visitors have ample opportunity to indulge in catacomb fantasies. The caves are a popular stop for elderly asthmatics who believe the air of the caves will help their breathing (admission $1.75; open 9am-6pm). There is also a cafe just outside the entrance. *Servis* buses leave Tokat's Cumhuriyet Alanı for Ballica weekdays at 11am and weekends at 9am and 1pm (4hr., $1.50). For a group of more than two people, it might be worth the $28 to hire a taxi to Ballica and back. On the way, you can stop in the village of **Pazar,** which boasts the interesting ruins of an old caravan *serai* and the **Belediye İşhani Sosyal Dayanişma Vakfı** (a blanket and *kilim* school). It's in the back of the building across from the Helediye Hotel on Pazar's main road; turn toward the PTT and the entrance will be to your left. The school's students and faculty don't speak a word of English, but will cheerfully display their wares, serve you free tea, and let you try your hand at *kilim* weaving.

Budget travelers with ailments of the body, heart, or mind might want to check out the **healing spring** in Kat. Take the Kat Kasabasi bus from Cumhuriyet Alanı in Tokat. The local tradition is to make a wish in the glade beside the spring and then tie a handkerchief to a branch and drink the spring's water.

EASTERN ANATOLIA

■ Kayseri

Once the capital of Cappadocia (and still its largest metropolis, with a population of 425,000), Kayseri is the present-day capital of **Turkish cold cuts.** This is the place to go for *pastırma* (spicy, well-salted, sun-dried beef or veal with aged garlic, pepper, and parsley), *sucuk* (extremely spicy, well-salted beef sausage resembling a long, thin salami), and *salam* (well-salted Turkish salami, similar to *sucuk* but less spicy). Other conspicuous attractions are Kayseri's **airport** (the closest to Göreme and Ügüp) and **Erciyes Dağı** (Mt. Aergius), a hulking extinct volcano 25km south of the city which in the winter becomes one of Turkey's few **ski resorts.**

Originally named Caesaria under the reign of Roman emperor Tiberius (14-37 AD), contemporary Kayseri boasts several points of historical interest, including a Medical Museum housed in the world's first medical university (Gevher Neribe tip Fakultesi). Vacationing ghouls will appreciate Kayseri's wealth of preserved tombs (14 or 6, depending who you ask). Perhaps the most distinctive relic of ancient times is the 6th-century fortress, or citadel (*kale* or *hisar*), remarkable for its size, excellent condition, ominous appearance (it is built entirely from volcanic rock), and urban integration—while most citadels look down on the city from an inconvenient height, Kayseri's is downtown. There is no Hittite theme park in the fortress yet, but the interior has been converted into a shopping mall-esque bazaar, replete with countless gold jewelers and two *kebap* houses. At night, the buttresses are lit with strings of white Christmas tree lights for a gingerbread effect. All things considered, Kayseri merits a one- to two-day stopover en route to Cappadocia proper.

ORIENTATION AND PRACTICAL INFORMATION

The **otogar** is on Osman Kavuncu Cad., which meets Park Cad. and Hastane Cad. at **Düvenönü Meydani** (square), where the Beğendik supermarket and the Hotel Almer are located. Walking away from Düvenönü Meydani on Park Cad., you will arrive at the fortress. To your right, Nazmi Toker Cad., a.k.a. **Bankalar Cad.** distinguishes itself with its vast number of **banks.** Many inexpensive restaurants can be found on the back streets parallel to Bankalar Cad. Kayseri's second main square, marked by the PTT and the clock tower, is **Cumhuriyet Meydani,** at the corner of the fortress where Park Cad. meets Sivas Cad. and Talas Cad. Following Talas Cad. away from the fortress, you will pass the Hunat Mosque Complex and the Tourist Office, eventually ending up at the Döner Kümbesi (Revolving Tomb) near the Archeological Museum and the Seyyid Burhaneddin Türbesi (tomb).

Tourist Office: 61 Kagan, Pazari (tel. 222 3903, 231 9295; fax 222 0879), next door to the Hunat Mosque Complex. English, French and German spoken. Open 8am-5pm (daily in summer, weekdays only in winter).

Airport: Kayseri's **Erkilet Airport** (tel. 338 3353) offers 2 flights daily to Istanbul (1¼hr., $60) and some flights to Germany and France. Purchase tickets from the THY office on 1 Yildırım Cad., (tel. 222 3858; fax 222 4748). Buses from Erkilet to Cumhuriyet Meydan $1.40.

Trains: Kayseri's **gar** at the end of Hastane Cad. (tel. 231 1313) provides daily trains to Ankara ($4.25) and Istanbul ($7), among others, and 3 trains per week to Tatvan (17hr., $14). Buses are faster and more reliable.

Buses: Buses from the *otogar* on Osman Kavuncu Cad. (tel. 336 4373) run to most major destinations, including Istanbul, Izmir, Antalya (12hr., $18.50), and Ankara (5hr., $6). Minibuses to Ürgüp leave from a stop on Osman Kavuncu, a little closer to Düvenönü Meydani, every 2hr. from 8am-6pm (1½hr., $2).

Hospitals: The **Ericyes Tip Fakultesi Hastanesi** (tel. 437 4901, -2, -3, -5) and the **Özel Gülhane Sağlik Merkezi,** 24 Kiçikapu Cad. (tel. 222 4854, -35, 222 0450). Both have ambulance service and English-speaking doctors.

PTT: On Sivas. Cad. in Cumhuriyet Meydani. Lobby and telephones open 24hr. Poste Restante and currency exchange 8am-5pm. **Postal Code:** 38000
Telephone Code: 352.

ACCOMMODATIONS

Hotel Çamlıca, Bankalar Cad., 14 Gürcü Sok. (tel. 231 4344, 232 3493, 232 2354, 222 4368). Despite the warehouse-like stair landings, the clean and pleasant rooms are reasonably priced. Singles $7, with shower $10.50; doubles $17.50, $21. Breakfast included and served in a suburban living room-type lobby complete with sofa, fish tank, giant bookshelves, and Atatürk portrait.

Hotel Yat, 14 Talas Cad. (tel. 232 7378, 232 3595). Definitely the most postmodern joint in town. Even the name is a pun: *yat* means both "go to bed" and "yacht" (hence the hotel's nautical decor). Upon entrance the weary traveler is confounded by an illusory maze made by 4 perpendicular floor-length mirrors kaleidoscoping an admirable collection of paint-by-number seascapes. A winding staircase leads to the appropriately rickety, turquoise-lacquered reception desk. The rooms are very colorful, with bright orange telephones complementing the glossy blue and green walls. The 8 rooms have balconies. Singles $7.75, with shower $8.75; doubles $12.25, $14. Breakfast $1.50.

Hotel Meydan, 12 Osman Kavunucu Cad. (tel. 336 5135), down the street from the *otogar.* Clean but stark rooms. Floor bathrooms have only *a la turka* toilets. Front rooms are noisier, but have balconies. Singles $5.50; doubles $10; triples $10.50; quads $14. Free laundry service and use of kitchen.

Hotel Hisar, 24 Osman Kavunucu Cad. (tel. 336 6644). Down the street from and comparable to Hotel Meydan, Hisar's prices go up 25% in the winter. In summer singles $6.50; doubles $11.25; triples $16; quads $21. Free laundry facilities.

ANATOLIA

Hotel Çapari, 12 Donanma Cad. (tel. 222 5278; fax 222 5282). Donanma Cad. runs parallel to Park Cad., 1 block north. This mid-range, 2–star hotel boasts a restaurant, elevator, and rooftop sauna, as well as very clean, comfortable, well-furnished rooms. Hotels of this quality and price range are fairly plentiful in Düvenönu Meydani. Singles $23; doubles $30; triples $46. Breakfast included.

FOOD

Inexpensive picnic fare is easy to find. Kayseri's many bread shops sell loaves of fresh bread for about 12¢. *Pastırma* goes for about $3.60 per kg, *sucuk* about $2.90 per kg. Vegetarians might consider Kayseri's specialty cheese, *tulum peyniri*, or *bal* (honey, $2.50-$3.25 per jar), both sold at most of the multitude of dried meat stored with *pastırma* hanging in the windows.

As far as restaurants go, locals overwhelmingly recommend the **İskender Kebap Salonu,** a three-story affair on Millet Cad. behind the fortress. A traditional meal of *iskender kebap* and *ayran* (a drink made with yogurt and buttermilk) is just $3.25. Around the corner, the **Dinçerler Et Lokantası** serves excellent *tavuk çöpşiş* (cubes of chicken grilled with tomatoes on wooden skewers), *piliç*, *köfte*, or *ızgara köfte*. Stop at the nearby branch of the famous **Divan Pastane** for some *fıstıklı baklava* (4 pieces for $1) or ice cream (7¢ per scoop).

At 10A Park Cad., between Duvenönü and Cumhuriyet Meydani, **Avcılar İskender** (tel. 222 7045) serves first-rate *köfte* and *piliç şiş* ($2), accompanied by delicious fresh *pide tost* (grilled cheese, $1) and *kuru fasulye* (pinto beans, $1). The second-floor dining room has some nice views of the street and several fish tanks inhabited by large, bug-eyed, flat-faced bass—always good for a laugh. On Osman Kavuncu Cad., **Ocakbaş** also has good *kebap* and *ızgara* dishes with first-rate pita for similar prices. A note on nightlife (of lack thereof): Kayseri is *not* a city that parties until dawn. Even the restaurants shut down by 10 or 11pm.

SIGHTS

Early in the 13th century, Alâdin Keykubad, Sultan of the Anatolian Seljuks (1219-1237), captured the Alanya fortress from its Persian ruler, Kir Vart. One of the conditions of Vart's surrender was that his daughter Hunat (meaning "lady" in Persian) Mahperi Hatun would become the sultan's wife. After her marriage, Lady Hunat, as she is redundantly referred to in English brochures, converted to Islam and commissioned the **Hunat Hatun Complex (Külliyesi),** made up of the **Hunat Hatun Cami** (mosque), **Türbe** (tomb), **Medrese** (school), and **Hamam** (bath) located across from the fortress near Cumhunyet Meydani.

The Hunat Hatun Medrese now serves as Kayseri's **Ethnographic Museum** (admission 70¢, students 35¢; open 8:30am-12:30pm and 1:30-5pm), with an assortment of coins, guns, costumes, household objects, etc. Of particular interest are a bunch of creepy-looking Roman door-knockers shaped like clenched fists, several attractive Armenian icons, and a replica Turkmen nomad's tent. In the summertime you can see the real thing along the roads up to Mt. Erciyes. Turkmen set up camp on the mountains to raise sheep and harvest wool. When the weather gets cold, they sell the sheep in the city and either move on or return to their home villages.

Student travelers especially should note that, like Tokat's "Sky Seminary," the "Lady Hatun Seminary" also houses a tomb. Remove your shoes before climbing the stair to the domed stone chamber containing the three coffins. The one with hieroglyphics belongs to Lady Hunat herself; beside her rests her grandson, Seljuk Hatun. The occupant of the coffin closest to the entrance has not been identified.

South of the Kale, just off Talas Cad., check out the **Gürgüpoğlu Konağı,** a beautifully restored 18th-century stone mansion. Nearby on Tenmuri Cad. stands the **Atatürk Konağı,** the 19th-century stone-cut house where Atatürk stayed in 1919 when he came to Kayseri as the leader of the Assembly of Representatives. Documents and photographs commemorating this visit are on display upstairs. As with most Atatürk-related sites, admission is free.

On a traffic island further down Talas Cad. you will find the 13th-century **Döner Türbesi.** No, this is not where the Seljuks buried their uneaten *döner kebap*—in Turkish *döner* means "revolving" or "rotating" (you will have noticed that *döner* cooks on a rotating spit). That said, the 12-sided, cone-roofed tomb does not revolve, either. Nor are visitors allowed inside, although you can peer through a metal grate in the wall at a blue plastic watering can that somebody has left on the floor. Brochures claim that the tomb "belongs to Sultan Shah Cinan." If this means that he is interred here, his remains are nowhere in evidence (unless they have been placed in the watering can sometime after the 13th century). The exterior of the tower is decorated with interesting bas-relief, representing among other things, two-headed eagles, lions and the "tree of life."

To the naked eye, the nearby **Sıçalı Kümbet** (Glass Tomb) suggests glass even less than the Revolving Tomb suggests revolving; however, this cylindrical, domed building was once covered with glazed tiles. Taking a left at the Döner Türbesi, you will come to the **Seyyid Burhaneddin Türbesi,** an inarguably five-star tomb nestled in a little park. Built in the early 13th century for Burhaneddin Tirmizi, the first *mevlâna* teacher at Hunat Hatun Medrese, the tomb is a more sacred place than a typical tourist attraction. It includes two separate and heavily-frequented prayer rooms for men and women. If you decide to go inside to admire the crystal chandeliers and tiled ceiling, remember to either leave your shoes outside or carry them with you in a bag. Women might want to wear a head scarf.

Across from the Seyyid Burhaneddin Türbesi on Kişla Cad., the **Archaeological Museum** (admission 70¢, children 35¢) displays artifacts such as pottery and metalwork from the Assyrian trading colonies (1850-1720 BC) unearthed in Kültepe, an excavation site 20km northeast of Kayseri believed to have been first settled some 6000 years ago.

In May 1993, NASA named a newly discovered mountain on Venus after the Seljuk princess Gevher Nesibe Sultan in recognition of her contribution to modern science. When Gevher Nesibe Sultan died of tuberculosis in 1204, her elder brother, Giyasettin Keyhüsrev Sultan, commissioned a medical center to be built in her name according to her wishes. The hospital was to treat everyone for free, and patients, doctors, and medical students were to be admitted regardless of religion. The **Gevher Nesibe Tibbiyesi** opened in 1206 to become the world's first medical school, as well as its most technologically advanced hospital. Today its two seminaries, Giyase ve Şi faiye Medreseler, house the **Ericyes University Medical Museum,** where you can take a tour of a 13th-century operating room, mental ward, clinic, and hospital (admission $1.40, students 70¢).

Considering the many difficulties of running a large-scale electricity-free hospital, it's hard to decide whether to be glad or sorry you weren't a citizen of 13th-century Kayseri. The skylight in the operating room *(ameliyat hane)* concentrates maximum sunlight on the operating table. Pharmacists used a darkroom to mix the same sorts of medicines we buy today in brown light-resistant bottles. The equally well-planned *hamam* managed to heat both halves of the building during Kayseri's snowy winters. Perhaps most remarkably, the mental hospital *(Akil Hastanesi)* is equipped with one the earliest known P.A. systems: sound vents in the upper corners of the stone cells enabled a single person upstairs to address all the patients at once. In case you were wondering, the semicircular charts on the walls match the first initials of all hospital employees with personal information.

Of course this seminary is not without a tomb of its own—look out for the low-flying sparrows when descending the stairs to the **Gevher Nesibe Sultan Mescidi ve Sandukası** (little mosque), where the princess is interred.

Other alcoves are dedicated to relevant quotes from the Quran ("Whoever saves one life has in a way resurrected us all"); hospitals founded by Turkish women (from Gevher Nesibe to Valide Sultan in 1845); and Atatürk's brushes with the medical world, including a photograph of a syringe, labeled (in Turkish) "THE LAST INJECTION OF *EXTRAIT HEPATIQUE* ADMINISTERED TO ATATÜRK BEFORE HIS DEATH BY DR. M.K. BERK. GIFT OF DR. M.K. BERK".

■ Near Kayseri: Erciyes Dağ (Mt. Erciyes)

Switzerland meets steppe on Mt. Erciyes—at 3916m, the tallest mountain in Central Anatolia. From certain angles Erciyes looks quite the unwelcoming, treeless extinct volcano—parts are snow-covered year round. On its northern face, however, fruit orchards and vineyards thrive from 1100 to 1600m, while the upper peaks are covered with typical Alpine vegetation—yes, that means *eidelweiss*.Demographically as well as visually, Erciyes offers an eclectic mix. From late October to March skiers flock to the 2215m-high Tekir Yaylası (ski track) which is equipped with a chair lift, two teleskis and three beginner's lifts. The only tourist hotel on the mountain is the nearby **Kayak Evi** (tel. 342 2051). Vesin, the hotel's Turkish and German-speaking ski instructor, will guide hikers as well from June to September. IN the summer, Erciyes is popular with Kayserians escaping the city's heat for some fresh mountain air a *mangal* (barbeque), as well as with gypsy camps and Turkmen nomad sheep farmers who settle there for months at a time.

CYPRUS ΚΥΠΡΟΣ

The history of the island of Cyprus is preserved in the tangible remains of its complex past. Ancient temples, Roman mosaics, remote monasteries, castles, mosques, and the Green Line are monuments to the island's eternal role as both peaceful meeting place and bloody background for East and West. The land abounds in natural beauty from the sandy beaches of Agia Napa to the Troodos range, to the cool mountain air of Platres. The island caters to diverse travelers and remains generally clean, pleasant, and grime-free, even in its most industrial cities. This environment attracts tourists from all over the world. The people of Cyprus are friendly and hospitable, adding to the ever-increasing popularity of the island as a tourist destination, especially among Brits and Arabs. Most residents speak English. Traveling in Cyprus is generally more expensive than in Greece, but Cyprus has some budget options.

Note: Because of the large number of streets named "Leoforos Archbishop Makarios III" in Cyprus, we (like the Cypriots) have abbreviated it to "Makarios Ave."

ESSENTIALS

▓ Money

US$1 = C£0.54 (Cypriot Pounds)	C£1 = US$1.83
CDN$1 = C£0.39	C£1 = CDN$2.56
UK£1 = C£0.87	C£1 = UK£1.15
IR£1 = C£0.79	C£1 = IR£0.90
AUS$1 = C£0.41	C£1 = AUS$1.94
NZ$1 = C£0.35	C£1 = NZ$2.25
SAR1 = C£0.11	C£1 = SAR6.81
100GRdr = C£0.19	C£1 = 418GRdr
TL10,000 = C£0.03	C£1 = TL303,371

> Note: throughout this section, Cyprus pounds will be indicated by £.

▓ Getting There

The third largest island in the Mediterranean after Sicily and Sardinia, Cyprus lies 64km from Turkey, 160km from Israel and Lebanon, and 480km from the nearest Greek island. The Republic of Cyprus is accessible from Greece and other European and Middle Eastern countries by airplane or boat. Limassol can be reached by sea from a seemingly unlimited number of points, and finding a boat agency to facilitate your trip should not be difficult. By plane, Cyprus is accessible on **Olympic Airlines** (U.S. tel. (800) 223-1226), **Egypt Air** (U.S. tel. (800) 334-6787), **Cyprus Airways** (U.S. tel. (212) 714-2310), and other airlines. Student fare on Olympic (age 12-28) or Cyprus Airways (age 12-24) is US$190 round-trip from Athens to Larnaka; you'll need to show a letter from your university or an ISIC.

▓ Once There

TOURIST ORGANIZATIONS

Tourist offices in Cyprus are extremely helpful and efficient. There are offices in Limassol, Nicosia, Larnaka, Paphos, Agia Napa, and Platres. The main office is the

Cyprus Tourism Organization, P.O. Box 4535, 19 Limassol Ave., Nicosia CY 1390 (tel. (2) 337 715); in the **U.S.,** 13 E. 40th St., New York, NY 10016 (tel. (212) 683-5280). The CTO offices provide excellent free maps and information on buses, museums, events, and other points of interest. A particularly helpful publication available at tourist offices is *The Cyprus Traveler's Handbook* (free). Officials generally speak English, Greek, German, and French. In the north, there are tourist offices in Famagusta and Girne.

TRANSPORTATION

A reliable highway system serves much of Cyprus, but caution is required on the winding mountain roads. Cars drive on the left side of the road in the south and on the right in the north. Rented cars may not cross the Green Line. The south also has several British rotaries, some of which can be particularly intimidating for American drivers. Transportation is almost nonexistent after 7pm. Shared **taxis** run regularly Monday through Friday between Limassol, Paphos, Larnaka, and Nicosia (£2-3.50). Hitchhiking is uncommon, and neither locals nor tourists are likely to offer rides.

Buses to the **Troodos Mountains** depart once daily from both Nicosia and Limassol. Renting wheels is the best option for mountain excursions. There is no direct bus connection from Paphos to Nicosia or Larnaka; you must pass through Limassol. Bus service throughout Cyprus is less frequent in the winter. There is one island-wide **bus schedule** which is available at tourist offices. This schedule provides all necessary information, including prices for buses and private taxi service. All Cypriot rental cars have manual transmission and standardized rental rates. The cheapest compact cars should cost no more than £17 per day, small motorbikes £5, and larger motorcycles £7-8 (most dealers rent two-seat motor bikes, but operating with two riders may result in a fine). Cypriot law requires that seatbelts be worn in front seats, and an international driver's license or a national driver's license from your home country is required. A temporary Cypriot driver's license, good for six months, can be obtained from district police stations with a photo ID and £1.

CROSSING THE GREEN LINE

Crossing the infamous Green Line **from the south** is relatively easy, if you follow the strict regulations. Don't even try to get information on northern Nicosia on the Greek-Cypriot side. Greek-Cypriots have not crossed the line for over 20 years. You will not be permitted to cross if you are a Greek citizen or if you are of Greek descent.

Head for the **Ledra Palace Checkpoint** between the Greek-Cypriot and Turkish walls. This former hotel, its interior gutted and its exterior marred by bullet holes, stands on neutral territory and houses UN troops.

You will show your passport on the Greek-Cypriot side and again on the Turkish side, where you'll also fill out a general information form in order to receive a special visitor's visa (£1). They will not stamp your passport. *Do not let them stamp your passport.* If they stamp your passport, you will not be readmitted to Greek Cyprus. They will, however, give you a form to be stamped by someone at another window. Hold on to this form—you will need it to cross back after your visit.

If your travels originate from the north, and you have a Turkish stamp in your passport, you can never enter the south. Northern authorities may stamp a separate piece of paper if you ask. The quickest way to get to South Nicosia, therefore, is to first fly to London, and then to the south. This trick will only work if you don't have a Northern Cyprus stamp on your passport. A cheaper, but much slower, way is to go by seabus (or ferry) to Taşucu in Turkey, take a bus from there to Marmaris, from there a ferry to Rhodes, and finally a ferry to Southern Cyprus. Travel time: about two days. To be safe, ask the Turkish authorities not to stamp your passport, as a Taşucu stamp gives away that you've been to Northern Cyprus (though this isn't always a problem).

Some reminders: (1) You may enter Northern Cyprus between 8am and 1pm, but must return by 5pm. No exceptions. (2) Cars are not allowed—you must cross by foot. (3) As in other areas of Nicosia and Cyprus, do *not* take pictures of anything that

Cyprus

N

20 miles

20 kilometers

TO MERSİN

TO LEBANON

TO TAŞUCU

TO ALANYA

Mediterranean Sea

Apostolos Andreas Monastery

Dipkarpaz

Cape Elaia

Famagusta Bay

Cape Greco

Salamis

Gazimagusa (Famagusta)

Agia Napa

Karpaz

Larnaka

Green Line

KIBRIS
(Turkish Republic Of Northern Cyprus)

Bellapais Abbey

Girne

Lampousa

Kition

Zygi

Airport

Nicosia

Dhal

Chapelle Royale

Stavrovouni Monastery

Akrotiri Bay

Karavostasi

Lefke

Kakopetria

Republic of Cyprus

Kourion

Limassol

G zelyurt

Vouni

Troodhitissa Monastery

Platres

Troodos Mtns.

Sanctuary of Apollon Ylatis

Episkopi

Cape Kormakiti

Morphou Bay

Episkopi Bay

Kokkina

Stavros Psokas

Kykko Monastery

Panagaia Chryssorogiatissa Monastery

Petra tou Romiou

Chrysochou Bay

Polis

Agios Georgios

Paphos

CYPRUS

has to do with the military or police. (4) As you will be forewarned on the Greek side, you are not allowed to buy anything on the Turkish side. If you wish to buy food, you must exchange your Cypriot pounds for Turkish lira. Also, you cannot bring items from the south to the north—they will be confiscated. (5) Finally, if you have a problem, ask the UN soldiers with the blue berets for assistance.

PRACTICAL INFORMATION

Post offices are open Monday through Friday from 7:30am-1:30pm (1pm in the summer). Some have afternoon hours from 3:30-5:30pm (summer 4-6pm). *Poste Restante* (see **Keeping in Touch,** p.44) is available only in Nicosia, Larnaka, Paphos, and Limassol (10¢ per piece). Letters from the south must have a 1¢ refugee stamp.

Southern Cyprus has fairly reliable **telephone service** (administered by **CYTA**). Direct overseas calls can be made from nearly all public phones. **Telecards,** which are sold at banks and kiosks, make international calls more convenient. They can be used only in special phones and are available in denominations of £3, 5, and 10. Private phones in hotels may carry a 10% surcharge. For **ambulance, fire,** or **police** in the South, dial 199.

In general, off-season prices (Oct.-May) are about 20% less than the rates quoted in this book. Nicosia, Troodos, Paphos, and Larnaka all have **HI youth hostels.** Although Cyprus has few formal campgrounds, you may sleep on beaches and in forests. Choose your site discreetly and leave it as clean as you found it. Be careful if you camp unofficially; women should be especially wary and never camp alone.

LIFE AND TIMES

■ Government

The government of the **Republic of Cyprus** (the southern part of the island) is based on a 1960 constitution that was devised by governments in London, Athens, and Ankara. Never intended to be a permanent document, it was meant as a compromise among the British, Greek, and Turkish governments over control of the island. The constitution created a government that remains deeply divided along Greek and Turkish lines. The republic's President must be a Greek-Cypriot while the Vice-President must be a Turkish-Cypriot. These officials are elected in separate elections, and both retain the right to veto legislation. All government positions and agencies are divided along a controversial 70% Greek 30% Turkish split, which is meant to reflect the nation's population. Before a bill can pass in the 100-member parliament (which meets in Geneva), it requires both an overall majority and a majority within each of the Greek and Turkish coalitions. Originally intended as a compromise, this provision has been the cause of frequent deadlock.

On the other side of the Green Line lies the **Turkish Republic of Northern Cyprus (TRNC).** Founded on November 15, 1983, the government is led by President Rauf Denktaş. Northern Cyprus is a parliamentary democracy similar to the British system. The official language is Turkish and the official currency is the Turkish lira. Most of the 150,000 Northern Cyprus residents are Turkish-Cypriot. About 40,000 of these are Turks who emigrated from mainland Turkey. Roughly half the population speaks English, and many older residents are fluent in Greek.

■ History

ANCIENT CYPRUS

The remains of round stone dwellings indicate settlement on Cyprus as early as neolithic times, dating back to roughly 7000 BC. Cyprus first achieved local importance in the **Bronze Age** due to its wealth of copper ore. Linguists are unsure whether *Kypros,* from which the word "copper" is derived, first referred to the island or the metal itself. The Bronze Age witnessed an increase in Cyprus' trade and cultural exchange with neighboring countries.

The most dramatic change in island culture was fostered by the arrival of the **Mycenaeans** from the Peloponnese in the **Middle Bronze Age,** initiating a Hellenic tradition that has carried over to the present. From 1400 to the mid-12th century BC, Mycenaean traders visited the island regularly, spreading the use of the Greek language and introducing written notation for commerce. The arrival of **Phoenician** traders and colonists in the first millennium BC introduced yet another fresh cultural impulse to the island. The Phoenicians shared political control with the Greeks until the arrival of the **Assyrians** in the 7th century BC, who dominated the island for 100 years. After the waning of Assyrian power, the Egyptians briefly took hold of the island, but were soon overthrown by the Persian king. There was significant resistance to Persian rule by Cypriots, notably in the efforts of pro-Hellenic Evagoras I, who forced Persians out of Salamis and spread Greek throughout his kingdom.

> With the conversion of the Roman governor, Cyprus became the first country in the world to be ruled by a Christian.

As Persian expansion stagnated, **Alexander the Great** absorbed Cyprus into his growing empire. In 295 BC, following Alexander's death, Ptolemy claimed Cyprus for Egypt. Cyprus prospered under the succession of Ptolemics. While cultural and religious institutions remained unchanged, the Greek alphabet came to replace the local syllabic script. Two centuries later, in 58 BC, Rome took advantage of Ptolemy's declining fortunes by annexing Cyprus. Christianity was introduced to the island in 45 AD by the apostle Paul and the Cypriot apostle Barnabas. The spread of Christianity continued for the next three centuries, and, with the conversion of the Roman governor in 46 AD, Cyprus became the first country in the world to be ruled by a Christian.

BYZANTINE RULE TO THE OTTOMAN EMPIRE

When Constantinople was proclaimed the capital of the eastern half of the divided Roman empire, the stage was set for the synthesis of Roman civic thought, Greek philosophy, and the Greek Orthodox tradition in Cyprus. During these centuries, the island endured several disasters—two devastating earthquakes in 332 and 342, a 40-year drought that severely scarred the island, and fierce Arab raids in the 7th century that once again proved the island's vulnerability to foreign attack. At the same time, however, many new towns were founded, and established towns expanded significantly. In 1191, **Richard the Lionheart,** en route to the Crusades in Jerusalem, quickly overran the island, which proved indispensable in provisioning the Christian armies. After robbing the island of its treasures, King Richard sold Cyprus to the **Knights Templar,** who in turn passed responsibility on to Guy de Lusignan, a minor French noble who had been involved in the Crusades.

The **Lusignan Dynasty** (1192-1489) ruled through a feudalistic system of class privileges and hierarchy that oppressed the lower classes and suppressed Cypriot culture and religion. Despite French subjugation of the locals, the Lusignan era left a legacy of impressive Gothic architecture in the form of churches, cathedrals, and castles. As setbacks in Palestine forced the Crusaders into full retreat, the Lusignans invited Crusader families to set up camp on the island. By the late 13th century, Cyprus had become the wealthiest island in the eastern Mediterranean. Yet in 1489 the **Venetians,** profiting from the Lusignans' dynastic intrigues, annexed the island. They remodeled and strengthened Cypriot military defenses, but were still no match for the Ottoman Empire. In 1570, following a two-month siege, Nicosia surrendered to the Ottomans. The fall of Famagusta one year later marked the beginning of the **Ottoman period** in Cyprus.

Cypriots welcomed the Ottoman abolition of feudalism, and the peasants acquired land under the new system. The Orthodox Church also flourished in this period, serving as a powerful administrative machine for the sultan. As the Empire weakened in the 19th century, Britain found itself defending Ottoman territories in the face of Russian expansionism. In July of 1878, British forces landed peacefully at Larnaka and assumed control of Cyprus as a second military base. **Britain** entered into an arrangement with Turkey in which the island's excess revenue was used to pay off Ottoman war loans. Although Cypriots did not enjoy political self-determination under the British, they benefited from the construction of many public works—roads, bridges, drinking and irrigation water supplies, a railway line, schools, and hospitals.

CYPRUS IN THE 20TH CENTURY

In 1954, **General George Grivas,** in conjunction with **Archbishop Makarios,** founded the EOKA (National Organization of Cypriot Fighters), an underground *enosist* movement. When the United Nations vetoed the Greek request to grant Cyprus self-government in 1955, General Grivas and the EOKA initiated a round of riots and guerilla warfare aimed at the British government. In response to increased EOKA activity, the underground Volkan (Volcano), under the leadership of **Rauf Denktaş,** founded the TMT (Turkish Resistance Organization). TMT was a paramilitary organization designed to fight the *enosists* and to push for **taksim,** or partition of the island between Greece and Turkey. Weary of the perpetual violence but unconvinced that either *enosis* or *taksim* was viable, Britain, along with the foreign ministers of Greece and Turkey, agreed in 1959 to establish an independent Cypriot republic. On August 16, 1960, Cyprus was granted independence and became a member of the U.N. and the British Commonwealth.

The new **constitution** stipulated that a Greek Cypriot president and a Turkish Cypriot vice-president were to be appointed through popular election and that the Greek to Turkish ratio in the House of Representatives would be 70:30. In 1959, Archbishop Makarios became the republic's first president, and Fazıl Küçük, leader of the Turkish Cypriot community, was elected to the vice presidency without opposition. In 1963, Makarios proposed 13 amendments to the constitution, intended to facilitate bicommunal life, which included the abolition of the president's and vice-president's veto power and the introduction of majority rule. When the Turkish government threatened to use military force if these amendments were implemented, renewed violence broke out between the EOKA and TMT, resulting in the division of Nicosia along the Green Line. In February 1964, the U.N. dispatched a "temporary" peace-keeping force that has been renewed indefinitely.

> The U.N. reduced their peacekeeping mission, leaving Cyprus to resolve their situation without much international intervention.

In 1968, Makarios and Küçük were both re-elected by an overwhelming majority, although in the years following they were subject to several coup plots, notably one by former ally General Grivas who returned to Cyprus in 1971 to found the militant EOKA-B and to revitalize the call for *enosis.* Intermittent violence exploded into an international affair in 1974 when the Greek Cypriot National Guard, assisted by the military **junta** in Greece, overthrew Archbishop Makarios and replaced him with **Nikos Sampson,** a notorious EOKA gunman who favored immediate *enosis.* Five days later the Turkish army invaded Cyprus from the north in order to protect Turkish Cypriots from the National Guard. Early in 1975, the North declared itself the Turkish Federated State of Cyprus (TFSC), officially partitioning the island.

In November 1983, Turkish-occupied Cyprus proclaimed itself independent as the Turkish Republic of Northern Cyprus (TRNC). Though only Turkey has recognized the new state, the TRNC has established trade relations in Europe and with several Arab states. Led by Rauf Denktaş, the TRNC lags far behind the Republic of Cyprus economically but is generally supported by Turkish-Cypriots who, in recent years, have been joined by thousands of settlers from mainland Turkey. In 1992, the U.N. reduced their peacekeeping mission significantly, leaving Cypriots to resolve their situation without much international intervention.

Glafkos Clerides, former head of the conservative Democratic Rally (DISY), became head of the Republic of Cyprus in 1993. The re-election of Denktaş in the

North has helped the negotiation process, and, in conjunction with U.S. involvement, resolution seems possible in the near future. Both Turkey and Greece are eager to win the favor of the U.S. and the E.U. Greek officials are hopeful for the Republic of Cyprus's acceptance into the European Union, with talks on the matter beginning in 1998

Turkey, however, objects to the proposal, warning that it would seek unification with Northern Cyprus if the Republic of Cyprus joins the European Union. In early August 1997, Turkey and Northern Cyprus had already agreed to work toward partial defense and economic integration. The agreement, which incensed the Greek government, came just five days before UN-sponsored talks between the two sides were supposed to yield greater cooperation.

■ Nicosia (Lefkosia) ΛΕΥΚΩΣΙΑ

Landlocked Nicosia, the capital of the Republic of Cyprus, is a city of walls. The ramparts and barbed wire of the Green Line separate the city from the Turkish side of the city, and the enormous **Venetian walls** separate the new city from the old. Today, Nicosia is a sprawling metropolis with an expanding suburbia. Greek Cypriots call their city Lefkosia, but the use of Nicosia is common and inoffensive.

Built on the ancient Roman town of Ledra, Nicosia first prospered under the Lusignan dynasty. When Lusignan power waned, Venetians arrived in 1489. In 1567, they built huge walls to ward off Ottoman cannons. The walls didn't work; three years later the Ottomans conquered Nicosia in seven weeks, and ruled the city for several hundred years. The Ottoman era closed when the British arrived in 1878. When Cyprus won independence in 1960, Nicosia became its capital.

The city has taken measures to restore the old **Laiki Yitonia,** the pedestrian shopping district, where the cobblestone streets are crammed with shops and restaurants. The recent proliferation of museums and monuments reflects the town's eagerness to maintain its spirit and cultural heritage. Unfortunately, the only major attraction in the city is the Green Line, and in general Nicosia seems geared more towards bureaucrats than backpackers and is best seen as a day trip. Larnaka is a better base from which to explore the east coast. For the true Cyprophile Nicosia offers a chance to interact with the local population on its own terms, without the frills of tourism.

ORIENTATION AND PRACTICAL INFORMATION

The easiest way to orient yourself in Nicosia is to refer to the ominous Green Line, which runs east-west at the north end of the city. The line splits the **Old City** within its circular Venetian walls. When you walk down the streets divided by the border, you are confronted by sheet metal barriers or white and blue dividers. Do *not* ignore the signs forbidding photography that are scattered throughout the area. The southern part of Nicosia within the walls contains most budget lodgings, museums, and sights. From **Eleftherias Square,** Evagoras St. heads southwest into the **New City.** Intersecting Evagoras are Makarios Ave., Diagoras St., and Th. Dervis St., which leads away from the city to the youth hostel. The New City is much busier than the old and is the center of Nicosia's nightlife. Be sure to get the free **map** from the tourist office.

Tourist Office: (tel. 444 264) 35 Aristokypros St., in the Laiki Yitonia. Entering Eleftherias Sq., turn right and follow signs from the post office. Route maps, a complete list of village buses, and free copies of *Nicosia: This Month.* A 2 hr. walking tour of Nicosia (Mon.-Tues., and Thurs. 10am) and a tour through the old suburb of Kaimakli leave from here (Mon. 10am). Tours are free and conducted in English. Open Mon.-Fri. 8:30am-4pm, Sat. 8:30am-2pm.

Embassies: Australian High Commission, 4 Annis Comninis St. (tel. 473 001; fax 366 486), 500m east of Eleftherias Sq. off Stassinou Ave. Open in summer Mon.-Fri. 7:30am-3:20pm. **Egypt,** 3 Egypt Ave. (tel. 465144; fax 462 287), open Mon.-Fri. 8am-2pm. **Greece,** 8 Lordou Vyronos (tel. 441 880; fax 473 990), open Mon.-Fri. 9am-noon. **Israel,** 4 I. Grypari St. (tel. 445 195), open Mon.-Fri. 9am-noon. **Leba-**

non, 1 Vas. Olgas (tel. 442 216; fax 467 662), open Mon.-Fri. 9am-noon. **Syria,** 1 Androkleous St. (tel. 474 481; fax 446 963), open Mon.-Fri. 8am-2:30pm. **U.K. High Commission,** Alexanderou Pauli St. (tel. 473 131; fax 367 198), west of the old city. Open Mon.-Fri. 8-11:30am. **U.S.,** Metochiou and Ploutarchou (tel. 476 100; fax 465 944). Open in summer Mon.-Fri. 8am-4pm; in winter 8am-5pm.

Banks: Bank of Cyprus, 86-88-90 Phaneromeni St. (tel. 477 774), offers **currency exchange.** Open Mon.-Fri. 8:15am-12:30pm. Convenient branch in Laiki Yitonia on Drakos St. (tel. 365 959). Open Mon.-Sat. 8:30am-noon and also Mon. 3:15-4:45pm.

American Express: A.L. Mantovani and Sons, 2D Agapinoras St. (tel. 443 777), 1km south of Solomos Sq. down Makarios Ave. Open Mon.-Fri. 8am-12:45pm and 3:30-6:30pm.

Buses: Kemek, 34 Leonides St., south of Solonos Sq. (tel. 463 989), and **Kolo Kassi** (tel. 347 774), on Salaminos St. by the entrance to the Old City. Buses to: Limassol (3-4 per day, £1.50); Larnaka (4-7 per day, £1.50); and Platres (5 per week, £2). **EMAN** bus stop, down a flight of steps 50m east of the post office, runs similar routes. **City buses** (tel. 473 414) run from Solonos Sq. daily 5:30am-7pm. A bus to Agia Napa runs on Sundays at 9am and returns at 5pm (£2).

Taxis: To Limassol (£2), Paphos (additional £2.50). Taxis to Larnaka (£2.30) run every 30min. 6am-7pm.

International Bookstores: Philippides & Son, 10 Paleologos Ave. (tel. 462 984), opposite the post office. Well-stocked, slightly pricey resource for travel guides, fiction, and Greek literature in translation. **The American Center,** 33B Homer Ave. (tel. 473 45), around the corner from the museum, is a fully automated information center, complete with the latest in CD-ROM technology. Open Sept.-July Mon.-Fri. 10am-12:30pm and 2-4pm.

Library: British Council, 3 Museum Ave. (tel. 442 258; fax 477 257), two doors down from the museum. Books, videos, and tapes. Open Sept.-June Mon. and Thurs.-Fri. 9am-1pm, Tues.-Wed. 9am-1pm and 3-6pm.

Hospital: (tel. 451 111) At the intersection of Omirou and Nechrou. Open 24hr.

Police: (tel. 303 090). 150m east of Paphos Gate on Rigenis St., inside the wall. Open 24hr. **Emergencies:** Dial 199.

Post Office: Main Office (tel. 303 231) on Constantinos Paleologos Ave., east of Elefthenias Sq. within the walls. Open in summer Mon.-Tues. and Thurs.-Fri. 7:30am-1pm and 4-7pm, Wed. 7:30am-1pm; in winter Mon.-Tues. and Thurs.-Fri. 7:30am-1pm and 3-6pm, Wed. 7:30am-1pm. Branch offices on Dhigenis St., Palace St., and Loukis Akitas Ave. (tel. 302 531). **Postal Code:** 1903.

CYTA: 14 Egypt Ave. (tel. 470 200). Sells £3 telecards, good for about 30min. of local phone time. Telecards work in pay phones anywhere on the island. Open Mon.-Fri. 7am-7pm. **Telephone Code:** 02.

ACCOMMODATIONS

Most of Nicosia's budget accommodations are within the city walls and are tolerably clean. If you don't like the room you're shown, ask to see another—the degree of cleanliness and comfort tends to vary widely.

Youth Hostel (HI), I Hadjidaki St. (tel. 444 808), 1km into the New City. Popular with young people from around the globe. Kitchen and yard provide meeting spots for travelers. Bring bug repellant. Showers included. £4 per person. Sheets £1.

Royal Hotel, 17 Euripides St. (tel. 463 245), on a side street off Ledra, at the corner of Euripides and Aeschylus, in the old town. Clean rooms with fans, and most with shower. TV Lounge. Breakfast included. Singles £8.25; doubles £13.50. A/C £2.15.

Tony's Bed and Breakfast, 13 Solon St. (tel. 466 752), in the Laiki Yitonia. Rooms range widely in size, but all have TV, radio, phone, and fridge. A/C units, operated by special coin (£1 for 7hr). Full English breakfast included. Singles £11-15; doubles £18-22; triples £27; quads £32.

Rimi Hotel, 5 Solon St. (tel 463 153). Recently renovated flats, all with private bath. Singles £23; doubles £28; triples £36; breakfast at downstairs restaurant included.

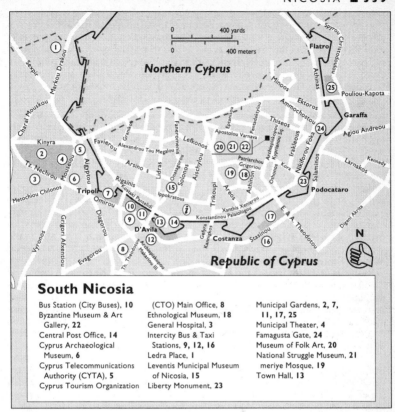

South Nicosia

Bus Station (City Buses), **10**
Byzantine Museum & Art
  Gallery, **22**
Central Post Office, **14**
Cyprus Archaeological
  Museum, **6**
Cyprus Telecommunications
  Authority (CYTA), **5**
Cyprus Tourism Organization

(CTO) Main Office, **8**
Ethnological Museum, **18**
General Hospital, **3**
Intercity Bus & Taxi
  Stations, **9, 12, 16**
Ledra Place, **1**
Leventis Municipal Museum
  of Nicosia, **15**
Liberty Monument, **23**

Municipal Gardens, **2, 7,
  11, 17, 25**
Municipal Theater, **4**
Famagusta Gate, **24**
Museum of Folk Art, **20**
National Struggle Museum, **21**
  meriye Mosque, **19**
Town Hall, **13**

FOOD AND ENTERTAINMENT

Dining choices in Nicosia range from *tavernas* with live music, to pubs, pizzerias, and full restaurants. The touristy joints around Laiki Yitonia serve Cypriot cuisine in cool surroundings. The smaller restaurants in the Old Town cater more to locals.

Mattheos (tel. 475 846), behind the Phaneromeni Church (near a small mosque). Good food for low prices. Shaded tables outside. *Koupepia* (stuffed grape leaves) and *moussaka* £2.75 each. Open daily 5am-7pm.

Faros Barbeque Boss, 6 Tillirias St. (tel. 463 326). Take away joint offering any kind of *kebab* you desire complete with pita, fried potatoes, rice, and salad (£1.25-3.20). Open daily noon-3pm and 7-10pm.

Berlin #2 Cafe (tel. 474 935), corner of Lefkon St. Savor your *kebab,* salad, and pita (£2.50) in the shade of the Green Line. A real U.N. guard is in the background. Open Mon.-Tues. and Thurs.-Fri. 7:30am-6:30pm; closes early on Wed. and Sat.

Byzantine (tel. 477 085), 1 block from the tourist office, is a wooden-beamed restaurant with a shady courtyard. Offers *meze* (£5), *moussaka* (£3.50), and salad (£2.25). Open Mon.-Sat. 8am-5pm.

Natural Choice, 11 Chytron St. in the new city (tel. 362 674), convenient to the youth hostel. All food is homemade at this fresh foods eatery. Outdoor seating under huge umbrellas; bright airy interior. Wash down your seasonal stuffed veggies or chicken curry (£2.50) with a huge slab of sugar-free apple pie (75¢).

Odyssea Pub, Eleftherias Square (tel. 451 174). Unselfconsciously local, popular watering hole frequented by twenty-something Cypriots. Open daily 8am-4pm.

For the most inexpensive eating in Nicosia, head to the **municipal market** on the corner of Digenis Akritas and Kallipolis Ave., a huge warehouse filled with a variety of food stands. You can buy fresh feta in blocks and make your own salad, while hanging pigs will make you either ravenous or vegetarian (open daily 6am-1pm and 4-6pm). A colorful streetside **produce market** opens on Wednesdays near Eleftherias Sq. along Constantinos Paleologos Ave. (open Wed. 9am-1pm and 4-6pm).

SIGHTS

The **Makarios Cultural Center** (tel. 430 008) occupies the Old City buildings of Archbishopric Kyprianos Sq., a former 15th-century Gothic monastery. Several interesting museums are clustered here. The **Byzantine Art Gallery** hosts the island's largest collection of icons (open Mon.-Fri. 9am-4:30pm; admission £1). The **Folk Art Museum** (tel. 463 205) presents Cypriot masterpieces of woodcarving, embroidery, pottery, basketry, and metalwork from the 18th to 20th centuries (open Mon.-Fri. 9am-5pm and Sat. 10am-1pm; admission £1). A guide to the collection costs 50¢. The neighboring **Greek Independence War Gallery** (tel. 302 465), founded in 1961, contains photographs and other items from the struggle for *enosis,* the union of Cyprus with Greece (open Mon.-Fri. 9am-4:30pm and Sat. 9am-1pm; admission 50¢). Also in the area is the **St. John Cathedral Church,** built in 1662 by Archbishop Nikiforos (open Mon.-Fri. 8am-noon and 2-4pm, Sat. 9am-noon).

Near the Archbishopric is the **House of Hadjigeorgiakis Kornesios,** known as **Konak Mansion,** at 18 Patriarch Gregory St. (tel. 302 447). A famous dragoman (Ottoman interpreter) lived in this luxurious, 18th-century structure (open Mon.-Fri. 8am-2pm, Sat. 9am-1pm; admission 75¢). Nearby is the **Ömeriye Mosque,** easily recognizable by its huge minaret. The **Turkish Baths,** on 8 Tillirias St. (tel. 477 588), are across from the mosque. (Open for women Wed. and Fri. 8am-3pm; for men Wed. and Fri. 3-7pm, Tues., Thurs., and Sat.-Sun. 8am-7pm. Admission £4.)

A marble monument depicting 14 Cypriots, each representing a period of the island's history, is down Korais St. from the Archbishopric. Nearby, along the Venetian Walls at the end of Theseus St., is the recently restored **Famagusta Gate,** which served as the main entrance to the medieval city. Built in 1567, it now hosts plays, concerts, and lectures (open Mon.-Fri. 10am-1pm and 4-7pm; free).

In the Laiki Yitonia, the **Leventis Municipal Museum** on Hippocratis St. (tel. 451 475), won the European Museum of the Year award in 1991. The exhibit chronicles the history of Nicosia, beginning with the modern city, back to 3000 BC (open Tues.-Sun. 10am-4:30pm; free). The **Cyprus Jewelers Museum,** 7-9 Odos Praxipou, is opposite the tourist office. Though small, it is worth visiting. The 18th- to 20th-century collection includes gold and silver plates, spoons, and jewelry hand crafted in the *filigree* and *skaleta* techniques (open Mon.-Fri. 10am-4:30pm; free).

The **Cyprus Museum** (tel. 302 189) has the most extensive collection of ancient art and artifacts on the island, from the pre-Hellenic periods through the Byzantine era. Lovers of archaeology may find hours of fun comparing local jewelry from many periods of civilization, while everyone will feel dwarfed by the larger-than-life terra cotta figures of ancient Cypriots (open Mon.-Sat. 9am-5pm, Sun. 10am-1pm; admission £1.50). The colorful **botanical gardens,** whose aviaries showcase most of the island's indigenous species, are next to the archaeological museum and behind the Garden cafe (open daily 8am-10pm; free). The **Green Line** is Nicosia's main attraction. The only spot on the border where photography is permitted is on Ledra St., where the military has erected a makeshift shrine to the north.

■ Larnaka ΛΑΡΝΑΚΑ

The remains of **St. Lazarus** lie in the city's central church and give the island its name from the ancient Greek word for coffin: *larnax.* According to tradition, Lazarus came to **Kition** (upon whose ancient ruins Larnaka was built) as the island's first bishop after being resurrected by Christ. Larnaka, one of the oldest continually inhabited cit-

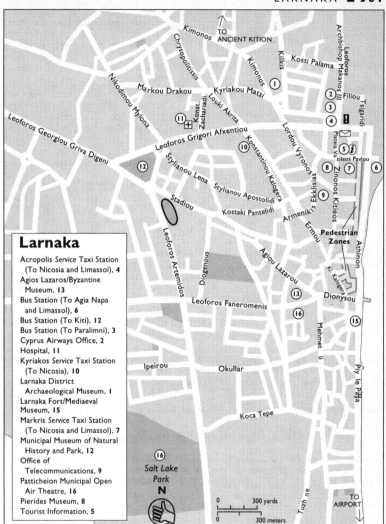

Larnaka

Acropolis Service Taxi Station
  (To Nicosia and Limassol), 4
Agios Lazaros/Byzantine
  Museum, 13
Bus Station (To Agia Napa
  and Limassol), 6
Bus Station (To Kiti), 12
Bus Station (To Paralimni), 3
Cyprus Airways Office, 2
Hospital, 11
Kyriakos Service Taxi Station
  (To Nicosia), 10
Larnaka District
  Archaeological Museum, 1
Larnaka Fort/Mediaeval
  Museum, 15
Markris Service Taxi Station
  (To Nicosia and Limassol), 7
Municipal Museum of Natural
  History and Park, 12
Office of
  Telecommunications, 9
Patticheion Municipal Open
  Air Theatre, 16
Pierides Museum, 8
Tourist Information, 5

ies in the world, retains monuments from each major phase of its long history. A segment of the ancient city walls and some Bronze Age temples can be found in the north of town. Elsewhere in the city, the Hala Sultan Tekke Mosque dates back to the first Arab invasion of Cyprus (647 AD), while the graffiti reading *"Hellas, Enosis, EOKA"* elicits memories of the violent movement for union with Greece just a few decades ago. Larnaka, however, is curiously indifferent to its long history and has become a modern tourist center offering visitors a long beach bordered by numerous cafes and restaurants. Quieter and cleaner than Limassol, sunny Larnaka (pop. 65,000) charms visitors, and while it is a bit less expensive than neighboring Agia Napa, rooms are just as scarce in summer.

ORIENTATION AND PRACTICAL INFORMATION

Athinon Avenue, also known as the "Palm Tree Promenade," runs along the waterfront and is Larnaka's most popular attraction. In summer, masses of barefoot young

Cypriots and sandal-clad foreigners fill its cafes, restaurants, pubs, and beaches. Quaint French-style lamp posts illuminate the strip every evening as mobile vendors and amusement rides create a carnival atmosphere. **Vasileos Pavlou Square,** where most practical facilities are located, is a block west of the north end of Athinon Ave.

Cyprus Tourism Organization Office: Vasileos Pavlou Sq. (tel. 654 322). Hours vary widely depending on the season, but it is generally open Mon.-Tues. and Thurs.-Fri. 8:15am-2:15pm and 3-5:45pm, Wed. 8:15-2:15pm, Sat. 8:15am-1:15pm. There is also an **airport branch** (tel. 643 000; open 24hr.).

American Express: Stassinou St. (tel. 652 024), in the office of **A.L. Mantovani and Sons,** across from the C.T.O. No traveler's checks or currency exchange. Provides money check forms for those drawing funds from AmEx cards. Guarantees personal checks for acceptance at local banks. Open Mon.-Fri. 8am-1pm and 3:30-7pm, Sat. 9am-noon; reduced hours in winter.

Bank: 24hr. ATM, traveler's checks and currency exchange at the **Bank of Cyprus,** next to AmEx office. Open Mon.-Fri. 8:30am-12:30pm and also Mon. 3:15-4:45 pm.

Airport: (tel. 692 700) Most flights into Cyprus land at the Larnaka airport. Bus #19 runs to town. (14 per day in summer, 6:20am-7pm; in winter 6:20am-5:45pm, reduced service Sat. pm and no service Sun. 50¢.) Taxis cost £3 to get to St. Lazarus Sq. in the center of town.

Buses: Leave from Athinon Ave. by the marina on the seafront. Look for a sandwich board on the sidewalk with the schedule. **Kallenos Buses** (tel. 654 890, -50) go to Nicosia (7 per day, Mon.-Fri. 6:30am-4pm; 4 per day Sat. until 1pm; £1.30) and Limassol (4 per day, Mon.-Fri. until 4pm; 3 per day Sat. until 1pm; £1.50). **EMAN** (tel. 721 336) buses to Agia Napa leave from the same spot (Mon.-Sat. 8:30am-5:30pm; 4 per day Sun. 8:30am-4:30pm; £1.30). **P.E.A.L.** (tel. 650 477; fax 654 977) buses leave from St. Lazarus Sq. and stop at St. Helenis, Artemidos Ave., Meneou, Kiti, and Tersefanou (13-14 per day, 6:20am-5:45pm and 7pm, no 7pm bus in winter; 60¢).

Service Taxis: Makris (tel. 652 929, 655 333), Vasileos Pavlou Sq., opposite the Sun Hall Hotel. **Akropolis** (tel. 655 555), at the corner of Markarios Ave., opposite the police station, and **Kyriakos,** 2C Hermes (Ermou) St. (tel. 655 100). All run to Limassol (every 30min., Mon.-Fri. 6am-6pm, £2.60) and to Nicosia (£2.10). *Service* taxis also run from Nicosia to Limassol (£3) and from Limassol to Paphos (£2.30). *Service* taxis will pick up and drop off anywhere in the city. Call ahead. On Sun., the companies alternate, running until early afternoon. Prices may be higher (by roughly 50¢). **Private taxis** are shamelessly expensive but offer 24hr. service. Contact Makris for a private taxi.

Car Rental: Phoenix Rent-A-Car, 65 Makarios Ave. (tel. 623 407, 622 314; fax 650 460). Prices from £15 per day. Unlimited mileage. Minimum age 25.

English Language Bookstore: Academic and General Bookstore, 41 Ermou St. (tel. 628 401). A comprehensive offering of new and used books as well as current magazines in English. Selection includes British and American fiction, Cypriana, classics, English and Greek (in translation) poetry and a full complement of *Let's Go* books. Offers student discounts.

Hospital: (tel. 630 300) Off Grigori Afxentiou Ave., at the intersection of Agias Elenis and Konst. Zachariada St.

Police: (tel. 630 200), on Makarios Ave., one block north of the tourist office. English spoken. Open 24hr. **Fire:** tel. 199.

Internet Access: Web Internet Cafe, 54 Lordou Vyronou St. (tel. 654 954; email webcafe@webcafe.com.cy; http://www.webcafe.com.cy). Offers the most (perhaps only) accessible internet connection in town. Browsing, cruising, email, games £2 per hour. Printing 20¢ per page. Email may be sent and received through the cafe's address.

Post Office: Main branch (tel. 630 18, -178), Pl. Vasileos Pavlou. Open Sept.-June Mon.-Tues., and Thurs.-Fri. 7:30am-1:30pm and 3-6pm, Sat. 9-11am, July-Aug. Mon.-Fri. 7:30am-1:30pm and 4-7pm, Sat. 9-11am. **Postal code:** 6900. There is a branch in **St. Lazarus Sq.** (tel. 630 182). Open Sept.-June Mon.-Fri. 8am-1:30pm, and Thurs. 8am-1:30pm and 3-6pm; July-Aug. Mon. and Fri. 7:30am-1:30pm. **Postal code:** 6902. Note that each post office has a separate postal code.

CYTA: 7-9 Z Pierides (tel. 132 or 640 257), follow Lordou Vyronos toward the seafront. Office is on the right, before Zinonos Kitieos. **Phone cards** in £3, 5, or 10 amounts (open June-Aug. Mon.-Fri 7:30am-7pm, Sat. 7:30am-1pm; Sept.-May Mon.-Fri. 7:30am-6pm, Sat. 7:30am-noon). **Telecard phones** throughout the city. **Telephone Code:** 04.

ACCOMMODATIONS

The town's hotels and pensions tend to fall into three distinct categories—luxury hotels, flats, and dives. Cleaner and cooler than the dives, flats are hip alternatives to regular hotels in Larnaka. Prices tend to be £5-7 less in winter.

Youth Hostel (HI), Nikolaou Rossou St. in St. Lazarus Sq. (tel. 621 188). Has 3 large rooms (all male, all female, and co-ed) with 10 beds each and 1 room for a family. Open 24hr., but front desk is not manned 24hr. Guests can sign in anytime. Ideal for the weathered traveler in need of cheap lodgings and the company of other wanderers. Bring sheets (or rent them for £1) and bug repellant. £3.50 per person.

Petrou Bros. Holiday Apartments, 1 Armenikis Ekklisias St. (tel 650 600, -1; fax 655 122). Centrally located two blocks from the seafront. Offers immaculate and spacious modern flats with bathrooms, showers, telephones, kitchens, A/C, balcony, 24hr. reception, and sun roof. Laundry and travel services, parking, breakfast, and access to a pool are also available (£1-2 each). Doubles £18; quads £28; 6 person £35. 30% off-season discount.

Harry's Hotel, 2 Thermopylon St. (tel. 654 453), near Marina Pier, the second left inland from the tourist office. Common room downstairs with rag-tag couches, TV, fridge, and common bath/shower. Bar and modest garden patio. Midnight curfew. Singles £8; doubles £13. Breakfast £1.

Pavion Hotel, 11 Faneromeni St., St. Lazarus Sq. (tel. 656 688), offers clean rooms, most with balconies overlooking St. Lazarus Church. Singles £13; doubles £18; quads £30. Breakfast of toast and coffee included.

Petalmo Hotel Apts., 50 Lordou Vyronou St. (tel. 658 600, -1; fax 658 602). Family-run furnished flats. Double studios £16; double suites £19; quads £26.

FOOD AND ENTERTAINMENT

Most of Larnaka's restaurants and bars are on the waterfront which bustles night and day with amusements for tourists and kids alike. Larnaka also offers an array of international cuisines. Chinese, Armenian, Lebanese, Italian, French, and Indian food all is available. Prices include 10% service charge and 8% V.A.T.

1900 Art Cafe, 6 Stasinou St. (tel. 653 027). Run by a painter and journalist, the cafe fosters the exchange of intellectual and artistic ideas over carafes of local wine (£2.50), tea (90¢), or coffee (50¢-£1). The *milopita*, or apple pie, is their specialty (£1.10). Vegetarian dishes also available. A tasteful and obscure selection of Greek folk music lends sonic ambiance. Friday nights offer performances by Cypriot and Greek folk musicians. Bookshop, bar, fireplace, and display of local artists' works upstairs. Cafe open Mon.-Sat. 8:30am-2:30pm and 6pm-1am, Sun. 6pm-1am.

Nitro Cafe (tel. 664 909), on the corner of Leoforos Grigori Afxentiou and Lordou Vyronos, specializes in coffee (£1) and desserts (£1.25-1.75). Sandwiches are £1.20. Open daily 10am-6am, so their patrons will never lack a hip place to chat. D.J. spins a soulful mix of House, American R&B, and Greek pop.

Mauri Helona (tel. 650 661), at the beginning of Mehmet Ali St., at St. Lazarus Sq. Offers *mezedes* (£5-6) and a cute logo—an alcoholic turtle. The entrance is filled with skeletal marine remains and toy turtles. A group of singers and musicians gathers until midnight on Wed., Fri., and Sat. nights. Fish £3.75-4.75, chicken £2.75, rabbit £4, pork £2.75. House wines £3-4, beer £1.25. Opens for dinner at 6pm.

Elitor: The Patisserie, 35 Gr. Afxentiou Ave. (tel. 656 929, 657 097). Delectable *baklava*, pastries, and *kouriabiedes* (powdery almond cookies) for 4¢ each or £3.50 per kilo. Ice cream cakes £3-4. Open 7:30am-9pm.

Megalos Pefkos (tel. 628 566), at the southern end of the harbor by the fortress, has relatively inexpensive fish. Swordfish and *meze* on menu.

The Hobo Pub and Restaurant (tel. 624 993), near the north end of Leoforos Athinon. Pleasant rooftop restaurant and good chicken *kebab* (£3). Breakfast £1.30-2, pizza £2-3.50, pasta £2-2.50.

The Tuck Inn, open 24hr. and located in the middle of Athinon Ave. This fast food joint and kiosk offers the cheapest meal in town. Eat in or take out.

SIGHTS

The ancient city of **Kition** is the oldest spot in Larnaka, although most of it is now underground. Settled in the early 13th century BC and abandoned soon after, Kition was rebuilt in 1200 BC by refugees from the Peloponnese. The city was damaged in wars with the Phoenicians and Egyptians (4th century BC) and leveled by earthquake and fire in 280 BC. Ruins reveal part of an ancient Cyclopean wall, the large **Temple of Astarte** (the Phoenician goddess of fertility), and four small temples. (Open Sept.-June Mon.-Fri. 7:30am-2:30pm, Thurs. 7:30am-2:30pm and 3-6pm; July-Aug. Mon.-Fri. 7:30am-2:30pm. Admission 75¢).

The **Larnaka District Archaeological Museum** (tel. 630 169) boasts neolithic finds from the Larnaka District. The **Kition Archaeological Site** lies 500m northeast of the museum and has a small collection with objects from neolithic to Roman times. (Museum and site both open Sept.-June Mon.-Fri. 7:30am-2:30pm, Thurs. 7:30am-2:30pm and 3-6pm; July-Aug. Mon.-Fri. 7:30am-2:30pm. Admission 75¢.)

The private **Pierides Foundation Museum** (tel. 651 345, 652 495) on Zinonos St. is the former home of Demetrios Pierides (1811-1895), a cultured man and collector of Cypriot artifacts. His descendants have continued this tradition and still occupy the top floor of the house. Prehistoric Cypriot idols are displayed in china chests. Pots take the place of end tables, and antique maps of Cyprus hang in lieu of wallpaper. Artifacts abound from 3000 years of Cypriot history, including Byzantine and traditional art. In the adjacent yard, classical and modern sculptures stand side by side. (Open Mon.-Fri. 9am-1pm and 3-6pm, Sat. 9am-1pm, Sun. 10am-1pm; reduced hours in winter. Admission £1.) The **Municipal Museum of Natural History** on Stadiou St. (across from the stadium) houses 5000 Cypriot insects which are individually labeled. It attracts those with an open mind. Three kinds of extinct snakes have been stuffed, and other preserved local animal species are arranged in panoramic displays. Outside there are live versions (so the kids don't have nightmares for the rest of their lives) of turkeys, buzzards, hamsters, canaries, sea gulls, a flamingo, and a peacock. A park for all ages and a playground for children under 10 surrounds the museum. (Open Mon.-Fri. 10am-2pm, 4-6pm, Sat 10am-1pm. Admission £1.)

Housed in the old customs warehouse at the end of Athinon Ave., the new **Tornaritis-Pierides Museum of Paleontology** (tel 658 848) boasts fossils from Cyprus and around the Mediterranean. Pieces in the collection date back 500 million years and include the now-extinct pygmy elephant whose migration to Cyprus is not yet fully understood. Call in advance to arrange a tour from the curator. (Open Tues.-Fri. 10am-1pm and 5-8pm, Sat. 10am-1pm, Sun. 7-10pm; admission £1, children 50¢.)

At the south end of the port, a small **medieval fortress** peers over the water's edge. Built by Venetians in the 15th century and rebuilt by Ottomans in 1625, the fort contains artifacts and photographs from Kition and other local excavations, as well as early Byzantine artifacts and a medieval armory (open Mon.-Fri. 7:30am-7:30pm, reduced hours in the off season; admission 75¢).

The first left north of the fortress leads to the **Church of St. Lazarus,** which is built over the saint's tomb. In the Gospel story, Christ resurrected Lazarus after the latter had been dead for four days. The revived Lazarus journeyed to Cyprus, became the island's first bishop, and lived in Kition another 30 years before dying again. The church was built in the 9th century and has been burnt and rebuilt several times since then. You can visit St. Lazarus's tomb by descending steps near the iconostasis. The church's belfry was added in 1857. In the courtyard there is a small museum (tel. 652 498) with ecclesiastical art. Modest dress is required. (Open Mon.-Tues., and Thurs.-Fri. 8:30am-1pm and 4-6:30pm, Wed. and Sat. 8:30am-1pm. Admission 50¢. Greek Orthodox services Sun. 6-9:30am.)

At the north end of Athenon Ave. is **Larnaka's Marina,** upon which couples and families warm up for their *voltas* (nightly strolls) among the palm trees. The **town beach** (a dismal mixture of packed dirt and cigarette butts) manages to satisfy the vacationers who bake there. The bustling beach also offers **water sports:** canoes (£3.50 per hr.), pedalboats (£5.50 per hr.), sail boards (£4.50 per hr.), water-skis (£5.50 per ride; £6 per lesson), jet skis (£10 per 15min.), mini-boats (£7 per 15min., £12 per 30min.), or banana boats (£3.50 per person). Beautiful, less crowded beaches are farther northeast on the way to Agia Napa.

■ Near Larnaka

The **Hala Sultan Tekke Mosque** is located at the edge of a salt lake and surrounded by palm trees. Also called the Tekke of Umm Haram, the mosque was constructed during the Arab invasion of Cyprus (647 AD) and rebuilt in 1816 over the site where Umm Haram (Mohammed's maternal aunt) fell off a mule and broke her neck. Three gargantuan stones—reputed to have been quarried in Mecca—surround her grave in back of the mosque. The mosque also houses the tomb of the great-great grand-mother of Jordan's King Hussein. She died in exile in Cyprus in 1929. Bus #6, bound for Kiti, leaves St. Lazarus Sq. (in summer 12 per day, 8am-7pm, in winter last bus at 5:45pm, 15 min., 50¢), and travels west to the Hala Sultan Tekke Mosque. Ask the driver to stop at the mosque, or you'll end up in Kiti. To be dropped at the turnoff, tell the bus driver you're going to "Tekke." From there, walk along the paved road for 1km. The mosque (open in summer daily 7:30am-7:30pm; free) is next to the **Larnaka Salt Lake.** In winter, the lake is covered with pink flamingos, but in summer it dries up, and the flamingos hop away. Legend has it that St. Lazarus created the lake from an old woman's vineyard as punishment for her lack of hospitality.

You can also take bus #6 all the way to the village of **Kiti** (25min. from Larnaka), which boasts the church of **Panayia Angeloktisti** (literally, "Built by the Angels"). Again, ask the driver to stop there. This church was built in the 11th century, but it retains a section built several hundred years earlier. The mosaic in the central apse, representing the Virgin Mary with Christ surrounded by the Archangels Michael and Gabriel, is one of the more important works of art on the island. The narthex of the church was built in the 14th century by the Gibelet family, one of the most promi-nent Latin noble families of medieval Cyprus (open Mon.-Fri. 8am-4pm, Sat. 10am-4pm, Sun. 9am-noon and 2-4pm).

Forty kilometers from Larnaka and 9km off the main Nicosia-Limassol road is **Stavrovouni Monastery** (Mountain of the Cross). According to tradition, the monas-tery was constructed by order of St. Eleni in 327 BC on a site called Olympus, where a pagan temple had stood. At the time, Eleni, mother of the Roman Emperor Constan-tine, was returning from Palestine where she had found the Holy Cross. She pre-sented a fragment to the monastery, where it is kept in the church's iconostasis. Although their founder was female, the monks do not allow women into the monas-tery. There are no buses to Stavrovouni, but you can go to Kornos and walk up to the peak. A taxi costs roughly £25 (open daily sunrise-noon and 3pm-sunset, closed for Green Monday Feb. 26 -27). The neolithic settlement of **Choirokoitia** is 32km from Larnaka (open Mon.-Fri. 7:30am-5pm, Sat.-Sun. 9am-5pm; admission 75¢). The **Tradi-tional Museum of Embroidery and Silversmithing** is in Lefkara, 40km from Larnaka (open Mon.-Sat. 10am-4pm; admission 75¢).

▓ Agia Napa ΑΓΙΑ ΝΑΠΑ

Twenty years ago, Agia Napa was a quiet farming and fishing village. Most tourists went to Famagusta, 16km to the north, allowing Agia Napa's ruined monastery and white sandy beaches to lie peacefully vacant. But when Turkey occupied Famagusta in 1974, Agia Napa was transformed almost overnight into a tourist center replete with marble and brass glitz, all the while absorbing a large refugee community from

Northern Cyprus. Over the years, Agia Napa has developed a raucous nightlife popular among foreigners.

ORIENTATION AND PRACTICAL INFORMATION

Agia Napa's center is home to banks, restaurants, and shops. The **Hellenic Bank** is on Markarios Ave. (Tel. 721 488; fax 722 636. Open Mon.-Fri. 8:30am-12:30pm and Mon.-Tues., Thurs.-Fri., 3:30-6:30pm. Fewer hrs. in winter. 24hr. ATM.) The **bus station** is next to the bank. A Cyprus Air representative, **AirTour-Cyprus**, 28 Makarios Ave., is near (Tel. 721 265, fax 721 776. Open in summer Mon.-Tues., Thurs.-Sat. 8am-1pm and 4-6:30pm, Wed. and Sat. 8am-1pm. Reduced hrs. in winter.) There are many places to rent bikes, including **Angelos Motosport,** 15 Al Nissi Ave. (tel. 721 695). Walk down Makarios Ave. toward the beach and take the only right back toward Larnaka (open 8:30am-6:30pm; motorcycles, mopeds, and bikes £2-7.20 per day).

Buses make the 41km trip from Athens Ave. in Larnaka to the **EMAN station,** opposite the Leros Hotel in Agia Napa. (9 per day Mon.-Sat. 8:30am-5:30pm; 4 per day Sun. 8:30am-4:30pm. Returning to Larnaka 10 per day Mon.-Sat. 6:30am-5pm; 4 per day Sun. 9am-4pm; £1 one way). The **post office** is on D. Liperti St. (open Mon.-Fri. 7:30am-1:30pm, Sat. 9-11am). **Postal Code:** 5330. The **C.T.O.** (tel. 721 796) is on Kyrou Nerou. (Open Mon.-Fri. 8:30am-2:30pm, and also Mon. and Thurs. 3-6pm. Reduced hours in winter.) **Telephone Code:** 03.

ACCOMMODATIONS

Half of the buildings in town are luxury hotels full of Europeans on box-lunch tours. Inexpensive rooms are elusive and, in August, nearly nonexistent. To get to **Xenis Rooms** (tel. 721 086), go up the road to Paralimni until you have to turn. A left and then a right at Mary's Supermarket will take you there—it's at the top of the hill. Rooms have baths and kitchens (doubles £10; two-night min. stay). Just before Xenis Rooms, across from Mary's Supermarket is **Paul Marie Hotel Apts.** (tel. 721 067), which boasts currency exchange, its own pool table, bar, and rooftop pool (doubles £20; quads £30). On Makarios Ave., flats are available above the **Cinderella Leather Shop** (tel. 722 148; singles £13; doubles £15). The **campground** is 3km from town (tel. 721 946; £1.25 per person, £1.50 per tent) and near crowded **Nissi Beach.**

FOOD AND ENTERTAINMENT

Raven's Rook (tel. 722 427), above the Hellenic Bank and near the tourist office, serves meals in a pleasant rooftop garden (tuna salad £2.60, *kebab* £2.95). **The Square Pub & Cafe,** in the central square, has inexpensive food and outdoor seating with a nice view of the square and monastery (Greek salad £1.60, *moussaka* with salad £2.40). **Jasmin Kebab House** (tel. 721 436) on D. Solomou St. offers the cheapest takeout in town, complete with a Cypriot flair (chicken *kebab* £1.30). Its 11am-5am daily hours conform to the town's wild tourist population. The **Hard Rock Cafe** (tel. 722 649), opposite the monastery, holds a dubious claim to membership in the American chain, but the burgers (£1), merchandise (£7 t-shirts), and modest collection of memorabilia attain the desired effect (open Mon.-Sat. 11am-2am, Sun. 5pm-2am). A **fruit market,** on Pappoulis St. near Cross Road, sells fruits and vegetables as well as fresh breads, olives, pastries, and drinks (tel. 723 372; open in summer Mon.-Sat. 7am-8pm, Sun. 8am-1pm; in winter Mon.-Tues., Thurs.-Fri. 7am-8pm, Wed. and Sat. 7am-1pm, Sun. 8am-1pm).

Agia Napa boasts the most intense nightlife in Cyprus. **String Fellows,** 9 Nissi Ave. (tel. 723 566), a 60s, 70s, and 80s dance club, and the **Kool Club,** 3 Makarios Ave., up from the monastery square on the right, are huge places on the downswing which rarely fill but are still fairly popular. The really happening places to be from 1-5am are **Pizazz** off Makarios Ave. and **VIP's** on Makarios Ave. Agia Napa also has a thriving pub scene. **Minos Pub,** up from the monastery square, has a jukebox and music every night, but more important to its patrons are the draft beers (£1-1.60 per pint) and strong drinks (£1.50). The **Makedonas,** within a minute's stumbling distance of Minos, has drinks for just £1 all night.

SIGHTS

Deserted beaches lie between Larnaka and Agia Napa, past the army base. Closer to Agia Napa, the better beaches are north and south of **Protaras** (10km from Agia Napa). Opposite the tourist office is the 16th-century Venetian **Monastery of Agia Napa.** Within its walls you'll find a beautiful courtyard with flowers, plants, trees, and an octagonal, dome-covered, marble fountain. The huge sycamore outside the west entrance is famous in Cyprus. Every summer Sunday at 8pm, locals perform Cypriot **folk dances** in the square near the monastery. The monastery's small chapel is off the main courtyard (open daily 6:30am-8pm). While inside, you might hear the well which still supplies water to the chapel's cave. The well's appearance is connected to the Miracle of Panagiya. During pirate attacks, Christians would seek refuge in the chapel's cave. Once, the pirates occupied the town for several days. The people in the cave were on the brink of dehydration. When, according to local Christian belief, the Virgin appeared to the people, she pointed to the fresh water coming from the corner of the cave. Since then, the water has never run dry. Services are held every Saturday at 6pm.

Close to Agia Anargyri and 8km east of Agia Napa is **Cape Greco.** You'll find no tourists here, no half built concrete hotels, no *tavernas,* and no sand—just rocky coves cascading into the magnificent blue sea. The cape has remained undeveloped because of a military radar installation, giving James Bond aspirants the chance to swim off the rocks beneath two space-age radar dishes. Two kilometers north of Paralimni, a stone's throw from the green line, is the small village of **Dherinia.** Several tourist lookouts nearby provide views of the "ghost" of occupied **Famagusta;** construction cranes stand exactly as they did a quarter of a century ago.

■ Limassol (Lemesos) ΛΕΜΕΣΟΣ

The island's second largest city and port of entry for most passenger ferries, Limassol is a cordial introduction to a striking island. Accordingly, there is a constant barrage of cultural festivities to entertain foreigners and natives alike. Rapid growth and a lack of urban planning have nurtured an endless row of hotels stretching east along the coast. The region's jewels, a gorgeous beach and the extensive Roman and Hellenic ruins of Kourion, lie 10km to the west on the Akiotisi Peninsula.

ORIENTATION AND PRACTICAL INFORMATION

Centrally situated in Cyprus's south coast and 50-70km from other major cities in southern Cyprus, Limassol is the transportation hub of the island. Passenger boats arrive at the **new port,** 5km southwest of the town center. As you enter the arrivals terminal, a **tourist desk** to your right has excellent free maps. Bus #1 runs to the port from the station near the Anexartisias St. market and bus #30 runs from the port to downtown Limassol (every 30min., Sat. every hr., 35¢). After ships arrive, buses wait near the customs building; otherwise, the stop is outside the port gates. A taxi to town costs £2.50. If you're headed for another major town, call the appropriate *service* taxi, and you'll be picked up at the port at no extra charge. In town, most shops, services, and sights can be found within a few blocks of the waterfront, especially along **Saint Andrew Street.**

Cyprus Tourism Organization: 15 Spiro Araouzos St. (tel. 362 756), on the waterfront 1 block east of the castle. Open July-Aug. Mon. and Thurs. 8:15am-2:15pm and 4-6:30pm, Tues.-Wed. and Fri. 8:15am-2:15pm, Sat. 8:15am-1:15pm; Sept.-June Mon. and Thurs. 8:15am-2:30pm and 3-6:30pm, Tues.-Wed. and Fri. 8:15am-2:30pm, Sat. 8:15am-1:15pm. An office at the **port** (tel. 343868) is open immediately following arrivals. Another office is in **Dassoudi Beach,** 35 George I Potamos

Yermassoyias (tel. 323211), opposite the Park Beach Hotel, open as the Limassol office.

Tourist Agencies: Salamis, 28 Octovrion St. (tel 355 555), offers package tours and cruises. **American Express,** 1 Archiepiskopou Kyprianou St. (tel. 362 045), in the offices of **A. L. Mantovani and Sons.** Open for AmEx transactions Mon.-Tues. and Thurs.-Fri. 9am-noon and 3:30-6:30pm.

Buses: KEMEK terminal, corner of Irenis and Enosis St. To: Nicosia (Mon.-Fri., 4 per day, Sat., 3 per day, £1.50), Paphos (1 per day, £1.50); and Larnaka (leaves from old port; 4 per day, £1.70).

Taxis: To: Nicosia (£3); Larnaka (£2.60); and Paphos (£2.50). Less frequent service Sept.-May. Taxis run 6am-5:30pm. No shared taxis on holidays.

Bike and Moped Rentals: Agencies cluster on the shore road, near the luxury hotels. Motorbikes £6.50 per day. For longer rentals, you'll find lower rates in Polis.

English Bookstores: Teveza's Book Swap Shop, 51 Kitoukyrianou. Open Mon.-Sat. 9am-1pm.

Laundromat: (tel. 368 293) Kaningos St. off Markarios Ave., near the Archaeological Museum. Same-day service or do-it-yourself. Wash £2, dry £1. Open Mon.-Tues. and Thurs.-Fri. 7:30am-1pm and 2-5pm.

Pharmacy: There are pharmacies all over town. Call 1402 for 24hr location.

Hospital: Government General Hospital, outside Limassol near the village Polemidia; take the #15 bus. There are many private doctors and clinics.

Police: (tel. 330 411) On Gladstone and Leondios St. next to the hospital.

Post Office: Main office (tel. 330 190), Gladstone St., next to the central police station. Open May-Sept. Mon.-Tues. and Thurs.-Fri. 7:30am-1:30pm and 4-6pm, Wed. 7:30am-1:30pm, Sat. 9-11am. **Postal Code:** 3900.

CYTA: On the corner of Markos Botsaris and Athinon St. All phones in Limassol use telecards except a few in the port. **Telephone Code:** 05.

ACCOMMODATIONS

Without many flats or a youth hostel, Limassol offers its best budget accommodations in the form of quirky guest houses a few blocks inland. Solo travelers, especially women, may prefer the more upscale hotels on the waterfront.

Guest House Ikaros, 61 Eleftherias St. (tel. 354 348). *Twin Peaks* comes to Limassol. Tapestries, fish tanks, animal skins, and chandeliers. Rooms are large and clean. Shared bath is off a lovely garden; sinks are on the open-air patio. Each day, first shower free, second is 50¢. Call to reserve in high season. Singles £5; doubles £10.

Continental Hotel, 137 Spiro Araouzos St. (tel. 362 530). 2-star hotel on the waterfront. Some rooms have balconies with sea views. All rooms with bath, shower, and radio. Breakfast included. Singles £15; doubles £25; triples £35. A/C £2.

Stalis Guest House, 59 Eleftharias St. (tel. 368 197), next to the Ikaros. Rooms are clean enough with a bed, chair, and dresser. Toilet and shower off an outdoor veranda with hanging laundry. Most bring their own towels, but they have some if you need one. Singles £3; doubles £5.80.

Hotel Metropole, 6 Iphigenias St. (tel. 362 686), off Saint Andrews St. Centrally located clean rooms, most of which have their own bath. Singles £6; doubles £9.

FOOD AND ENTERTAINMENT

There are a plethora of Cypriot *tavernas,* small *kebab* houses, and cafes lining the streets of Limassol. The best option for the health- and wealth-conscious traveler may be the **Central Market.** This huge warehouse spills onto the sidewalk and is filled with fresh produce, meat, seafood, and bread vendors (open Mon.-Tues. and Thurs.-Fri. 6am-1pm and 4-6pm, Wed. 6am-1pm). You can put together a cheap, delicious lunch of grapes, a loaf of fresh bread, and local *halloumi* cheese for less than £1.

Mikri Maria, 3 Ankara St. (tel. 357 676). The owner of this endearingly unpretentious restaurant serves delicious Cypriot food cooked over hot coals. The grilled *lountza* and *halloumi* is delicious, as is the refreshing *tzantziki.* Diners enjoy the

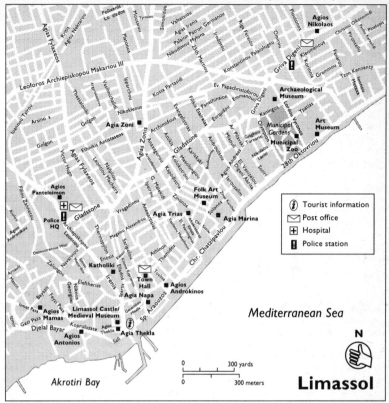

Limassol

streetside tables in summer and guitar playing inside in winter. Open Mon.-Sat. 7pm-10:30 or 11pm.

CyberNet Cafe, (tel. 745 093; email cafeinf@zenon.logos.cy.net; http://www.geoci-ties.com/Athens/5106) is popular among youth who come to drink, smoke, play games, and chat. It represents the highest evolution of the video arcade, and has the most accessible **Internet** capabilities in town, including Netscape and telnet access (£2.50 for the first hour, £1 per hour thereafter). Open daily noon-2am.

Richard and Berengaria, 23 Irinis St. (tel. 363 863), opposite the castle. This tiny *kebab* serves inexpensive local specialties like *shettalia* (£1) and *halloumi* sand-wiches (75¢). Cypriot brandy sour (65¢).

Edo Lemosos, 111 Irinis St. (tel. 353 378). Traditional Greek guitar music late into the evening; summer outdoor seating in a large tree-covered, candle-lit courtyard. *Meze* £7.75. ½ bottle of local brandies £3.75. Musicians indoors in winter. Open daily 9:30pm-12:30am.

Skoozi!, 292 Saint Andrew St. (tel. 642 549), 1 block from the Guest House Luxor. Soups, salads, sandwiches, and pasta for a hip, local clientele. Young Cypriots enjoy jazz, trance, and opera music wafting over the stone floors and Byzantine arches. Delicious crepes (banana with *ganache* £2.60). Many kinds of coffee (65¢).

In addition to the *tavernas,* there are many bars and nightclubs. Those along the coast near Dassoudi Beach are overrun by 16-year-old tourists who help create the wild pickup scene; **Whisper's, Temptations,** and **Basement Disco** can be fun if that's what you're in the mood for. According to locals, the hotter clubs are **La Bubu** and **Opu Opu** near Elias beach and Hawaii Beach. Close to Dassoudi Beach is **Sismos** (Earthquake), which is quite popular with local twenty- to thirty-somethings.

CYPR

SIGHTS

The **Limassol Castle** is the only building of historical significance in the city, where Richard married Queen Berengaria in 1191. It was then destroyed by earthquakes and Genoese assaults, and the only traces of the old Byzantine fort are in the western wall of the building. In the early 14th century, the Knights Templar fortified the castle's walls and covered the Gothic windows. Later, the Knights of St. John converted the great Western Hall into a Gothic church and the chapel into a series of prison cells. The Ottomans claimed the castle in 1570, and the capacious West Hall was used as a prison under the British regime until 1940.

The **Cyprus Medieval Museum** (tel. 330 419) is the final incarnation of the castle. (Open Mon.-Fri. 7:30am-5pm, Sat. 9am-5pm, Sun. 10am-1pm; off season Mon.-Sat. 7:30am-5pm. Admission £1.) The **Archaeological Museum** (tel. 330 132), on the corner of Kaningos and Vyronos, contains an assortment of funerary *stelae,* jewelry, statues, and terra cotta figurines (open Mon.-Fri. 7:30am-5pm, Sat. 9am-5pm, Sun. 10am-1pm; admission 75¢). On Byron St., closer to the sea, are the **public gardens** and town **zoo,** the largest in Cyprus (both open daily 9am-noon and 3-6pm; reduced hours in the off season; admission 50¢). The **folk art museum,** 253 Agios Andreas St. (tel. 362 303), one block east of the intersection of Zenon and Agios Andreas, houses 19th- and 20th-century embroidery and costumes. (Open Mon.-Wed., Fri. 8:30am-1:30pm and 3-5:30pm, Thurs. 8:30am-1:30pm; reduced hours in the off season. Admission 30¢.)

Limassol's **Reptile House** (tel. 372 770), at the Old Port near Limassol Castle, showcases poisonous scaly critters from around the world (open daily 9am-5pm; admission £1, children 50¢). The city's long stone beach might be a little too rocky and too near the busy port for the discerning beachgoer, but a new breakwater has made the area more pleasant for swimming. **Dassoudi Beach,** 3km east of town, is far better; take bus #6 from the market on Kanaris St. (every 15min., 40¢). The ebullient **Ladies Mile Beach** at the new port is also popular (take bus #1).

Limassol is host to a wide array of special events throughout the year. At summer's end, Limassol's gardens are transformed into a modern-day tribute to the ancient wine god, Dionysus. In the Limassol **wine festival,** participants are given a bottle to fill with as much of the local wine as they can handle. Between trips to the casks, digestion is aided by music, dance, and theater performances. A bottle of your favorite vintage makes a great souvenir at the evening's close (open late Aug. to early Sept. 6-11pm, admission £1.50). At the end of June, actors from around the world trek to Limassol to take part in **Shakespeare Nights** (tel. 363 015). **Carnival,** 50 days before Orthodox Easter (usually in Feb.), is celebrated more intensely in Limassol than anywhere else in Cyprus. Details are available at the tourist office and in *This Month's Principal Events.*

■ Near Limassol: Akrotiri Peninsula

The **Kolossi Castle** 9km west of Limassol played a crucial role during the Crusades. Both the Knights Templar and the Knights of the Order of St. John briefly made the castle their headquarters. When the latter knights moved to Rhodes in 1310, Kolossi, with its wealth of vineyards, remained their richest overseas possession (open June-Sept. daily 7:30am-7:30pm, Oct.-May 7:30am-5pm; admission 75¢). To reach Kolossi, take bus #16 from the bus station in Limassol (every 20min., 40¢).

Outside the British base of Akrotiri, the small resort town of **Pissouri** frolics year-round with Her Majesty's soldiers. Built on a cliff of enticing views, Pissouri has several bars and *tavernas.* The **Bunch of Grapes Inn** has both a restaurant and rooms (doubles £25; breakfast included).

The remarkably well-preserved ruins of **Kourion,** are 12km west of Limassol. First settled during the neolithic period, Achaïans from Argos colonized Kourion during the 14th and 13th centuries BC. It became famous for its **sanctuary to Apollo** (8th century BC) and its **stadium** (2nd century AD), both west of the main settlement. In the 4th century AD, the same earthquake that destroyed several other Cypriot coastal cities leveled Kourion. The city was rebuilt in the 5th century only to be burned in the 7th century during an Arab raid.

The impressive **amphitheater** is used for **Shakespeare Nights** in June, occasional summer concerts and theatrical productions, and weekend theater in September. The earliest structure on the site was a small theater built in the 2nd century BC. During Greek and Roman times, the theater was used for dramas, but by the 3rd century AD, civilization had progressed to animal fights and professional wrestling.

Across the road from the basilica lie a group of ruins under excavation. In the northwest corner are the remains of the **House of Gladiators** and its mosaic gladiator pinups. Try to avoid plummeting into the nearby cisterns. The **House of Achilles,** facing the highway at the end of the excavation site, is fenced off, but you can get the key at the ticket office or climb in through the narrow path following the fence along the road. (Open June-Sept. daily 7:30am-7:30pm, Oct.-May daily 7:30am-5pm. Admission £1.) The nearby **Museum of Kourion** in Episkopi village provides clear explanations of the artifacts. (Open Mon., Wed., Fri. 7:30am-2:30pm, Thurs. 7:30am-2:30pm and 3-6pm. Admission £1.)

Buses leave Limassol Castle bound for ancient Kourion and Kourion Castle. (Every hr. on the hr., 9am-2pm, return from ancient Kourion 11:50am, 2:50, and 4:50pm. 60¢.) Mopeders to Kourion usually go via Episkopi village. There are no signs for Kourion until you're within about 2km of the site, so a good map is essential.

■ Troodos Mountains ΤΡΟΟΔΟΣ

In this serene mountain range, isolated villages nestled amid cool, pine-covered hills provide refuge from the sun-baked coastal cities. Tiny hamlets and Byzantine churches dot the countryside while remote monasteries and pine forests ward off the summer heat. Hikers and campers in particular will find a small paradise here. What is usually a peaceful and rejuvenating natural experience in June and early July, however, can turn frustrating and costly in August when the urban crowds descend on the area, especially on weekends. From January to March, **Mt. Olympus**, the highest point in Cyprus (1951m), is host to hundreds of skiers.

Public transportation to the area and between the villages runs infrequently, and even scheduled stops can be unreliable. The best way to get around is to rent some wheels or make a friend with a car. Some hitch, but *Let's Go* does not recommend it. It's difficult to maintain a rigid schedule here. In the mountains, no town has motorbike rentals, but you can easily rent mopeds or cars in Limassol, Paphos, Polis, or Nicosia if you are over 25. Mountain roads, however, are tortuous, winding, bumpy, and always steep.

PLATRES

The most accessible city in the Troodos by public transportation, **Platres** will most likely be your first stop in the region. **Zingas Bus** (tel. (02) 463 154) in Nicosia runs to Platres at 12:15pm, returning at 6am (Mon.-Fri., £1.50). From Limassol, **Kyriakos** (tel. 364 114), a *service* taxi, leaves at 11:30am, returning at 7am (Mon.-Fri., £2.50). A private **taxi** from either city costs £15-20. You can rent **Mountain bikes** from **Top Hill Souvenirs** (tel. 421 729) on the main street, down the hill from the post office. There are some great bike routes in the Troodos, and the staff is happy to help you find them (4-gear bikes run £4 per day; open daily 10am-6pm).

Platres is divided into the **pano** (upper) and **kato** (lower) sections. The tourist facilities are in Pano Platres. The **tourist office** (tel. 421 316) is left of the parking lot in the main square (open Mon.-Fri. 9am-3pm, Sat. 9am-2pm). The **post office** sits to the left of the tourist office. (Open in summer Mon.-Fri. 7am-noon and 3-5pm, in winter Mon.-Fri. 8-10am and 3-5pm.) The **Bank of Cyprus** is opposite the tourist office (open Mon.-Fri. 8:15am-12:30pm and 3-5:30pm). The **hospital** (tel. 421 324) is below Pano Platres (open 24hr.). The nearest **pharmacy** (tel. 922 020) is in Kakopetria (open Mon.-Fri. 8am-2pm, Sat. 8am-1:30pm). The **police** (tel. 421 351) are opposite the tourist office in a converted military chapel. **Postal code:** 4815 in Kato and 4820 in Pano Platres. The **telephone office,** next to the post office, sells phone cards (open Mon.-Fri. 7:30am-1:30pm). **Telephone Code:** 05.

The **Village Restaurant** (tel. 421 741) offers some local flavor on a terrace with gorgeous views of the southern coast. Clean, modern rooms are available above the restaurant (£5 per person). Two large **grocery stores** are across the street from the restaurant. **Soforla Supermarket** (tel. 421 666) and **Cherryland** (tel. 421 414) stock standard supplies and a huge selection of ice cream bars (Soforla open daily 7:30am-9pm; Cherryland open daily 7am-10pm). North of Platres on the road to Troodos, **Psilo Dentro** (tel. 422 050) serves sumptuous trout from its fish farm under a beautiful canopy of tall trees (whole trout £4.20; open daily 8am-5pm).

Near Platres is the cordial lace and wine village of **Omodos,** next to the famous **Monastery of the Holy Cross.** After a tour of the **folk museum** in the monastery, visit the restored **wine press** (*linos*). You can buy a bottle of local, dry wine (£2) or the fiery *tsipoura,* a Cypriot whiskey. As you return to Kato Platres, signposts lead to the red-tiled village of **Phini.** The **Pilavakion Museum** (tel. 421 508) focuses on *pitharia* (large, red ceramic jars), wine-making equipment, and the "Pithari Sauna" used in traditional Cypriot obstetrics to avoid post-pregnancy stretch marks (if you call ahead, they'll open for you; admission £1). The family-run **Neraida Restaurant** (tel. 421 680) serves fresh trout (£4.50), *meze* (£5), and *kleftiko* (£4). The restaurant boasts chairs of a unique, but now virtually extinct, village design (open Feb.-Nov. daily 8am-11pm).

TROODOS

Though just 10km north of Platres, **Troodos** is accessible only by **bus** from **Clarios Bus Co.** (tel. 453 234) in Nicosia (Mon.-Fri. 11:30am, returns 6:30am; £1.10). A private **taxi** from Nicosia costs £17. You can either hike (at least 2hr.) or take a taxi (£5) from Platres. The **police** (tel. 421 623), just outside of town, offer **CYTA** info, but keep unreliable hours. For more reliable services, head to Platres or Limassol.

The **Troodos campground** (tel. 422 249), 2km north of the main square in a pine forest (£1 per person), provides laundry facilities, a minimarket, a bar/restaurant, and a first aid station. The **Jubilee Hotel Bar** (tel. 421 647), just outside of town, is a favorite of British expats. The **Troodos Youth Hostel** is the roomiest, cleanest, and most relaxing of the island's hostels (£4 per person, £1 for sheets). The caretaker sometimes offers camel rides.

Three self-guided **nature trails** originate in the Troodos area. The first is 8.5km long and goes from the Troodos post office to Chromion, passing various villages. A 3km trail leaves from the coffee shop in Troodos Sq. and finishes at a divine lookout point. Shorter but even more captivating is the 2km path following a stream from the presidential palace in Troodos, built by, among others, the famous French poet Arthur Rimbaud, and finishing at beautiful **Kaledonia Falls** near Platres (45min.). The tourist office has a pamphlet outlining the trails, and it's helpful to get a guidebook and map for starting points.

Eight monks and a myriad of animals make their home in the modern **Troodhitissa Monastery,** 5km from Platres on the Prodromos-Platres road. Dedicated to the Virgin Mary, the original monastery was built in 1250 to house one of her miracle-working icons. During the chaos of the iconoclastic movement during the 8th century, a monk hid an icon of the Virgin Mary in Troodos, where a miraculous pillar of fire protected it. More than a century later, a sign revealed the site of the monastery, which still stands today (open daily 6am-noon and 2-8pm).

KAKOPETRIA AND ENVIRONS

Picturesque **Kakopetria,** literally "bad rock," is the most popular town in the northern part of the mountains. According to local legend, the large rock perched on the hillside was supposed to bring good luck to newlyweds. That is, until one day when the rock rolled over and crushed a couple.

The town has several hotels, including the **Rialto** (tel. 922 438) and the **Hellas** (tel. 922 450). Rates vary widely according to tourist traffic (doubles £10-45). The **Bank of Cyprus** is in the main square (open Mon.-Fri. 8:15am-12:30pm), near the **post office** (open Mon.-Wed. and Fri. 7:30am-1:30pm, Thurs. 7:30am-1:30pm and 3-6pm). The **police station** (tel. 922 420, -255) is up the street from the bank. A **pharmacy** is below the Rialto Hotel (open 9:30am-9pm), and a doctor (tel. 3077) is a few doors down. **Telephone code:** 02.

Kakopetria and its smaller neighbor **Galata** have five Byzantine churches between them; the most beautiful is **Agios Nikolaos tis Stegis,** on a dirt road 4km southwest of Kakopetria. The interior of this 14th-century church is painted with strikingly unique frescoes. While more common in Roman Catholic settings, such icons are very rare for Greek Orthodox Churches (open Tues.-Sat. 9am-4pm and Sun. 11am-4pm). **Buses** to Kakopetria travel from Nicosia (12-14 per day Mon.-Sat. in summer, £1.10). A delicious dinner with a view of the Old Village can be had at **Maryland at the Mill** (tel. 922 536). The church of **Panagiatou Arakou,** 16km southeast of Kakopetria, is another repository of elaborate 12th-century frescoes, including Christ Pantokrator (on the inside of the dome). South of the church is the comely vineyard village of **Agros,** with the only rooms in the vicinity.

PRODROMOS

About three buildings comprise Prodromos which is more a tribute to asceticism than to tourism. Prodromos, 10km northwest of the town of Troodos, is the second-highest hill resort in the area, after Troodos. Relax at the nearby **Stephos Cafe** before heading to **Pedoulas,** a small village to the north of Prodromos, featuring the **Church of Archangel Michael** which has mural paintings dating from 1474. Up the street from the church is the **CYTA** and the **police** who answer most tourist questions. Across the street is the mini **post office. Postal Code:** 4840. **Telephone Code:** 02.

Kykko Monastery, in the northwest part of the mountains, 14km from Pedoulas and 33km from Troodos, enjoys more wealth and prestige than any other monastery on the island. The monastery was founded in the early 12th century when a hermit, after curing the Byzantine Emperor's daughter, was given the Apostle Luke's own Icon of the Virgin Mary. The monastery has burned down numerous times, but the celebrated icon has survived intact. As the icon is thought too holy to be viewed directly, it is completely ensconced in mother of pearl and silver casing. After entering the monastery's palatial courtyard, you may think you've wandered into a large luxury hotel with 400 beds for visitors, the circa-1800 buildings seem more suitable for hosting revelry than religion. A supermarket, a tourist pavilion with prices only an extortionist could love, and several sweet shops are close to the monastery.

Kykko gained new fame this century as a communication and supply center during the Cypriot struggle and as the monastic home of Archbishop Makarios III. Only 1.5km away were the secret headquarters of the first military leader of the struggle, "Dighenis" (General George Grivas). **Makarios's tomb** is just 2km farther in the high hills west of the monastery. The site, guarded at all times by two Greek Cypriot soldiers, is partially open to the east. Makarios requested the opening so on the day of Cypriot reunification, sunlight would enter his tomb and he could celebrate with his people. Just above the tomb is a path leading up to an icon of the Virgin, called the *throni* (small throne). The bushes alongside the path are laden with scraps of clothing placed there by sick children hoping to be cured.

■ Paphos ΠΑΦΟΣ

When the Egyptian Ptolemies conquered Cyprus, they made Paphos their capital. The city grew fabulously wealthy and developed into a cosmopolitan commercial center. Paphos maintained this exalted position under the Roman conquerors, but a 4th-century earthquake ended its supremacy. The Cypriot capital, and the accompanying political and social prestige, moved to Salamis (near modern Famagusta).

CYPRUS

Paphos shrunk to a small village until recently, as it has risen again as the tourist capital of the Republic of Cyprus. Sights of historical interest—classical, Byzantine, medieval, and modern—surround the city to a far greater extent than in Agia Napa, its resort rival on the southeastern coast. Paphos also boasts far more scenic beaches than the equally historic Larnaka or Limassol. Paphos has been a place of honor for Aphrodite, goddess of beauty, and its rolling hillsides and finely curved coastline evince her continued blessings since the 12th century BC.

ORIENTATION AND PRACTICAL INFORMATION

The city of Paphos is divided into two sections. The upper **Ktima Paphos** (referred to simply as "Paphos") is centered around Kennedy Sq., where most of the city's shops, budget hotels, and services are located. The lower **Kato Paphos** lies roughly 1km to the south, and hosts luxury hotels, holiday villas, and most of Paphos's nightlife. Everything listed below is in Ktima Paphos, unless otherwise noted.

Cyprus Tourist Organization, 3 Gladstone St. (tel. 232 841), across from Iris Travel. Hours vary. The **airport C.T.O.** (tel. 422 833) is open when flights arrive.

Budget Travel: Iris Travel, 10A Gladstone St. (tel. 237 585), opposite the C.T.O. Ferry tickets to Rhodes, Crete, and Israel (student discounts up to 20%). Airline tickets to London and Greece (student discounts up to 40% if age 24-28, depending on airline). Rents cars (£13-22 per day, unlimited mileage; must be over 25) and apartments (from £5 per person). Open in summer Mon.-Fri. 8am-1pm and 4-7pm, Sat. 8am-1pm; in winter Mon.-Fri. 2:30-5:30pm.

Banks: Many concentrated around Kennedy Sq. **Bank of Cyprus,** Evagorou St., with **ATM.** Open Mon.-Fri. 8:30am-12:30pm.

CYTA: Grivas Digenes Ave. (tel. 230 228). Open daily 7:30am-7:30pm.

Airport: C.T.O. (tel. 422 641). Contrary to popular belief, there is a second international airport in Cyprus. Although most flights arrive in Larnaka, Paphos International Airport receives various European airlines and many chartered flights. Opens when flights arrive. Offers **currency exchange** and a C.T.O. branch. Private taxis from city center £5, from Kato Paphos £5. No bus service.

Buses: Nea Amoroza Co., 79 Pallikaridi St. (tel. 236 822), across from the ESSO station. Minibuses run to Polis (10 per day, Mon.-Fri. 6:30am-7pm, £1). Some go to Pomes (£1.15 from Paphos). **KEMEK** (tel. 234 255) goes to Limassol from the Mitropolis Bldg., off Thermopylon St. (2 per day, £1.25). Change buses in Limassol for Nicosia or Larnaka. **Excursion buses** make the run to Palaepaphos Museum and Aphrodite's birthplace (3 per day, £1.15). Bus #30 makes stops at larger hotels.

City Buses: Municipal buses run hourly between Ktima Paphos and Kato Paphos (30¢). Catch one in Ktima Paphos, just up the road from the post office, in Kato Paphos at any of the yellow benches on the road to town. Buses also go to Coral Bay (20 per day, 40¢). Schedules in the tourist office.

Taxis: Go to Limassol (every hr. 6am-6pm, £2.30).

Moped Rental: There are several shops in Kato and Ktima Paphos. Prices range £2.50-6.50.

International Bookstore: Axel Bookshop, 62-64 Makarios Ave. (tel. 232 404). Books about Cyprus and novels in English. Open Mon.-Sat. 8am-1pm and 4-7pm.

Pharmacies: Can be found on just about every corner in Paphos.

Hospital: Paphos General, Neophytos Nicolaides St. (tel. 240 111). Free first aid. English spoken. A long walk, so take a taxi. **St. George's Private Hospital,** 29 Eeleftherios Venizelos Ave. (tel. 247 000, fax 241 886), on the way to the youth hostel. Casualty and ambulance services. English spoken. Open 24hr.

Police: Grivas Digenes Ave. (tel. 240 140) in Kennedy Sq., opposite the Coop Bank. English spoken. Open 24hr. For **emergencies,** dial 199.

Post Office: Main branch on Leoforos Eleftheriou Venizelou. Open Mon.-Tues., and Thurs.-Fri. 7:30am-1:30pm and 3:30-5:30pm (afternoon hours for stamp purchase only), Wed. 7:30am-1:30pm, Sat. 9-11am. There is a smaller office (tel. 240 223) on Nikodhimou Mylona St. Open Mon.-Fri. 7:30am-1:30pm, Sat. 9-11am. The post office in **Kato Paphos** is on Ag. Antoniou St. (tel. 240 226).

Postal Code: 8900 (in Ktima Paphos); 8903 (in Kato Paphos).

Telephone Code: 06.

ACCOMMODATIONS

Finding inexpensive accommodations in Paphos is a chore. Solo travelers should stick to the youth hostel or, if finances permit, one of the nicer hotels; groups might try renting an apartment. The following are in Ktima (upper) Paphos, unless otherwise noted. Prices are higher in Kato Paphos, but the nightlife is better.

Youth Hostel (HI), 37 Eleftheriou Venizelou Ave. (tel. 232 588), on a residential street northeast of the town center. From the square, follow Pallikaridi to Venizelou, and turn right—a 10min. walk from town. £4 per night. Sheets £1.

Park Mansion Hotel, off of Pavlou Ave. behind the park just outside of Kennedy Sq. (tel. 245 646). Elegant but affordable rooms vary in size, but all offer a bathroom and A/C. Pool downstairs. Breakfast included. £13 per person.

Kiniras Hotel, 91 Makarios Ave. (tel. 241 604). Costly, but classy and clean. All rooms with private bath and phone. Has restaurant and lovely patio. A/C available at £2 per day. Breakfast included. Singles £20; doubles £30.

Hotel Trianon, 99 Makarios Ave. (tel. 232 193). Toned-down exterior in keeping with the older interior. Rooms are reasonably clean, but common bathrooms leave much to be desired. You may feel more comfortable here if you are traveling in a group. Singles £5; doubles £8-12.

Zenon Gardens Geroskipou Camping (tel. 242 277), east of the tourist beach on the sea, 3km from Paphos Harbor. Minimarket, restaurant, and kitchen. Open March-Oct. £2 per site; £2 per 3 people; £1 per small tent.

FOOD AND ENTERTAINMENT

While most restaurants in Kato Paphos are geared to pound-laden foreigners, there are some cheap options. **Peggy's Miranda Cafe** in Kennedy Sq. serves continental breakfast (£2) and hosts a book swap. Run by and for British expatriates, it offers a cultivated local flavor (open Mon.-Tues. and Thurs.-Fri. 7am-6:30pm). One of the newer restaurants in the area, **Surfcafe,** 1 Gladstone St. (tel. 253 125), across from the police, is classy and reasonably priced (sandwiches £1-1.50, beer 80¢). The cafe also boasts internet on two computers (£1 per hr.). Soft music and traditional meals grace the peaceful garden of the **Kiniras Hotel,** where you can also find Zodiac cocktails (meals and drinks from £4). Sugar-starved travelers will enjoy the sweet shop **Athens,** 47 Evagora Pallekaride (tel. 232 613). In Kato Paphos, **Hondros,** 96 Pavlou St. (tel. 234 256), is one of the older restaurants in the area, founded long before the town's tourist boom. Sit under the bamboo-covered terrace beneath the grapevines and eat lamb *kleftiko* off the spit (£3.75; open daily 11am-4pm and 7pm-midnight).

The two most popular **beaches** stretch along **Geroskipou** and **Coral Bay.** Geroskipou is well touristed with snack bars, while Coral Bay is sandier, less crowded, and frequented by locals. Bus #11 from Ktima Paphos goes to Yeroskipou (every 20-25min., 40¢), and #15 goes to Coral Bay from Yeroskipou (every 20min., 40¢).

SIGHTS

Kato Paphos

Apostolou Pavlou Ave., which connects Kato and Ktima Paphos, must have seen just as much traffic centuries ago, as it is clustered with monuments to the Roman, early Christian, Byzantine, and medieval periods of Cypriot history.

The mosaic floors of the **House of Dionysus,** the **House of Theseus,** and the **House of Aion** (tel. 240 217; admission to all three £1) are the city's more dazzling ancient spots. Discovered accidentally by a farmer plowing his fields in 1962 and excavated by a Polish expedition, the largely intact mosaics covered 14 rooms of the expansive Roman House of Dionysus. The floors depict scenes from mythology and daily life with vibrance and a subtle use of the stones' natural hues. Farther towards the water rests the **House of Theseus** complex, dating from the 2nd to the 6th centuries AD. The ruins reveal a luxurious building with marble statues and columns and mosaic floors. The two mosaics of Theseus and Achilles are accessible by walkways.

CYPRUS

To the north of the mosaics, you'll find the remnants of an *agora* beside the limestone Roman **odeon**—a small, roofed semi-circular theater. Built in the 2nd century AD, the odeon accommodates 3000 and is still used for performances. (Open in summer daily 7:30am-7pm, in winter 7:30am-5pm. Admission £1.) Built in the late 7th century on a hill overlooking the harbor, the **Byzantine Castle** *(Saranda Kolones)* was intended to protect inhabitants from Arab pirates. To get there, take Sophia Vembo St. off A. Pavlou Ave. When an earthquake destroyed the castle in 1222, the Lusignans built the **Paphos Fort** at the end of the pier, which was later rebuilt by Venetians and the Ottomans (open Mon.-Fri. 7:30am-2:30pm, Thurs. 3-6pm, Sat.-Sun. 9am-5pm; admission 75¢).

The musty **Catacombs of Agia Solomoni,** along the road between Ktima and Kato Paphos (opposite the Apollo Hotel), include a chapel with deteriorating Byzantine frescoes. Dedicated to St. Solomoni (Hannah), the chapel sits on the site of the old synagogue. Part of the deepest chamber is filled with lucent water, which you may not notice until you're drenched in it. A tree with handkerchiefs draped from its branches marks the entrance to the catacombs on A. Pavlos Ave. The tree is said to cure the illnesses of those who tie a cloth to it. St. Paul was allegedly whipped for preaching Christianity at **St. Paul's Pillar** (both free and open 24hr).

Ktima Paphos

The **Archaeological Museum** on Grivas Digenes Ave (tel. 240 215); 1km from Kennedy Sq., houses an array of Bronze Age pottery, tools, sculpture, statues, and artifacts from the House of Dionysus and the House of Theseus (open Mon.-Fri. 7:30am-2:30pm and 3-5pm, Thurs. 7:30am-2:30pm and 3-6pm, Sat.-Sun. 10am-1pm; admission £1). Don't miss the **Ethnographic Museum,** 1 Exo Vrysi St. (tel. 232 010), just outside of Kennedy Sq. The garden sports a 3rd-century BC Hellenistic tomb, Christian catacombs, and *kleftiko* ovens. (Open Mon.-Sat. 9am-5:30pm, Sun. 10am-1pm. Admission £1. Guidebooks in English £3.) The **Byzantine Museum,** 26 25th Martiou St. across from the Ethnographic Museum (tel. 232 092), has icons and religious relics from local monasteries and churches. (Open Mon.-Fri. 9am-12:30pm and 4-7pm, Sat. 9am-12:30pm, reduced hours in winter. Admission 75¢.)

West of Ktima Paphos, a signposted road runs 1km to Paleokastra's **Tombs of the Kings** (tel. 240 295)—a misnomer, since those interred in these stone tombs were merely local aristocracy. The larger tombs consist of an open court encircled by burial chambers, with Doric columns carved out of the underground rock and stairways leading down to the interiors. The tombs, from the Hellenic and Roman periods, were also used as hideouts by early Christians fleeing persecution. To the north of the tombs lies **Paleoeklisia** (literally "old church") with fragments of Byzantine frescoes. (Both open June-Sept. Mon.-Fri. 7:30am-5pm, Sat.-Sun. 9am-5pm; Oct.-May 7:30am-sunset. Admission 75¢.)

■ Near Paphos

The area around Paphos contains some of Cyprus's greater treasures. Adjacent to the modern village of **Kouklia** lie the ruins of the great **Temple of Aphrodite** (tel. 432 180) and **Paleopaphos** (Old Paphos), once the capital of a kingdom encompassing nearly half of Cyprus. The sites are most easily seen from the excursion buses. Renting a moped is not advisable—the road is very dangerous. The temple itself was the religious center of the island and a destination for pilgrims from every corner of the Roman world. Built in the 12th century BC, it thrived until the 4th century AD, when the edicts of Emperor Theodosius and a series of earthquakes reduced it to rubble. The scant remains—merely piles of rocks—make little sense without a guide. *A Brief History and Description of Old Paphos,* published by the Department of Antiquities, is available in the adjoining **Paleopaphos Museum.** (Museum and temple open Mon.-Fri. 7:30am-5pm, Sat.-Sun. 9am-4pm. Admission to ruins, city, and museum 75¢.)

The **Monastery of Agios Neophytos,** with icons, Byzantine frescoes, and painted caves and buildings, lies 9km north of Paphos, near Coral Bay Beach. Roughly 100m from the monastery complex are three rock caves carved out by Neophytos and covered with beautiful 12th-century frescoes. You can get here by taking the bus to Tala (6 per day Mon.-Fri., 4 per day Sat.-Sun.) and then walking to the monastery. Bring a flashlight (open daily 7:30am-noon and 3pm-dusk; admission 50¢).

■ Polis ΠΟΛΙΣ

Aphrodite, who came to Polis to bathe, was one of this coastal resort's first visitors. The goddess of beauty no longer bathes alone. Tourism has gained a foothold in Polis, which is smaller, cheaper, and more relaxed than Paphos, 37km to the south. Accessible by minibus and taxi, Polis is a popular Cypriot base for budget travel.

ORIENTATION AND PRACTICAL INFORMATION

Polis boasts some stellar examples of traditional Cypriot architecture—large rounded wooden doors and stone masonry. At the end of the winding main street is the *platia* (open 8am-1pm), home to several locally flavored cafes and all of the town's tourist services. The **CTO** office (tel. 322 468), the island's newest, offers enthusiastic and helpful advice for daytrips and accommodations (open Mon.-Sat. 9am-1pm and 2:30-5:45pm). The **police** (tel. 321 451; open 24hr) roost one block from the square in the direction of the beach and speak some English. Around the *platia* you'll find three **banks** (all open Mon.-Fri. 8:30am-noon; reduced hours in the off season). The **Popular Bank** and the **Bank of Cyprus** offer afternoon currency exchange (Mon. 3:15-4:45pm). The **post office** (tel. 321 539; open Mon.-Fri. 7:30am-noon and 1-2pm) and **Spirides Taxi Service** (tel. 516 161) are also on the *platia*. The **Lemon Garden** (tel. 321 330) rents and sells **sports equipment** such as diving equipment, jet skis, and mountain bikes (£1.50-4 per day). **Pegasus** (tel. 321 374, 322 156) in the *platia* rents cars, mopeds (£4 per day, 4 day minimum), mountain bikes (£3 per day, 3 day minimum), and apartments. Two **pharmacies** (tel. 321 253 and tel. 321 167) are down the street from the post office. The **hospital** (tel. 321 431) is on the way to the campsite, about a 6-min. walk from the *platia*. **Postal Code: 8905. Telephone Code: 06.**

ACCOMMODATIONS

Several restaurants along the road east to the Baths of Aphrodite provide free or almost-free camping and the use of facilities. **Campground** (tel. 321 521), 1km from the town center in a fragrant, seaside eucalyptus grove, is open from March to October (£1 per person; £1.50 per tent). The **Akamas Hotel** (tel. 321 330), at the beginning of the main street, has clean, tiny rooms with shared baths and a quiet courtyard (singles £5; doubles £10). The **Lemon Garden** (tel. 321 443) is definitely worthwhile for its unique combination of quality rooms, food, and atmosphere. All rooms come with kitchenette, private bath, A/C, and view (doubles £14-16; larger rooms £16-20). Also, look for inexpensive rooms in private households down the hill from the Bank of Cyprus, along the road to the beach, or inquire at a cafe. Rooms go for about £5-6 per person. Next to the church before Vomos Taverna, **Mrs. Charita Antoniou** (tel. 321 989) rents spacious rooms with access to a common bath and kitchen. The three front rooms open onto a porch (£5 per bed).

FOOD AND ENTERTAINMENT

Vomos Taverna (tel. 321 143) serves drinks and snacks by the beach. In town, **Arsinoe** (tel. 321 590), across from the church, is run by a fisherman's family and serves their daily catch (swordfish £3.50, fish *meze* £4.50; open daily 8am-1pm and 7pm-1am). Nearby, the **Kebab House** sells scrumptious *souvlaki* for £1.50. There's a beachside disco, but a more appealing option is to wander over to **Brunnen,** located down some steps, just before the Akamas Hotel. Marios has turned this dilapidated Turkish house into a sprawling **garden bar** (large beer £1; breakfast served; open daily 9:30am-2pm and 5pm-2am).

SIGHTS

The **Baths of Aphrodite,** a shady pool carved out of limestone by natural springs, are 10km west of Polis. It is reportedly where Aphrodite married Akamas, the son of Theseus. Aphrodite came here to cleanse herself after her nocturnal exploits, and according to legend whoever bathes in the pool stays forever young. The pool of **Fontana Amorosa,** 8km away, can be reached by foot via a narrow trail overlooking the sea. Buses run from Polis to the Baths (Mon.-Fri. 9:30, 10:30am, and 2:30pm; 50¢). The church of **Agios Andronikos** in Polis was built in the 15th century, but was converted to a mosque during the latter half of the 16th century by invading Ottomans who plastered over its frescoes. Now the plaster is being removed and the church restored. Ask for a key from the CTO to see the church yourself.

AROUND POLIS REGION

Pristine **beaches** and a small selection of inexpensive lodgings characterize the road from Polis to the baths of Aphrodite. The port town of **Lachi,** 2km west of Polis, offers some hotels and a pleasant stretch of coastline (tel. 32 11 14 or 23 67 40 for more information; bus from Polis 40¢). A long sand beach stretches below the **Baths of Aphrodite tourist pavilion,** 1km west of Lachi. Beyond the baths is **Ttakkas Bay,** a cove many consider the best beach on this part of the coast. **Ttakkas Bay Restaurant,** above the beach, serves fresh fish and has a terrace with a nice view (fish *meze* £4; open daily 9am-midnight).

The coastline and **beaches** east of Polis are just as lovely as those to the west. Between Polis and Kato Pirgos, roughly 65km to the east, there are no rooms to let, no seaside *tavernas,* and no free-lance camping—only placid farming villages and deserted stretches of sand. The village of Kokkina is currently occupied by the Turkish military, which necessitates a 45-minute detour through the mountains.

It is difficult to tour the area without wheels. **Minibuses** (tel. 23 67 40, 23 68 22) pass through Polis from Paphos (10 per day Mon.-Fri. 6:30am-7pm, 5 per day Sat. 9am-4pm; £1). Some minibuses from Paphos continue on to Pomos (£1.15). Two **buses** from Kato Pirgos also stop here. Passing cars are rare, but those that come by will usually stop. This is not, however, recommended; *Let's Go* would never, ever, recommend hitchhiking. The second half of the journey is treacherous for mopeds—you may want to rent a car.

NORTHERN CYPRUS
Kuzey Kıbrıs Türk Cümhuriyeti

It's hard to tell the guests from the hosts in the real life social studies textbook that is northern Cyprus. It is a collage of ancient Egyptian statuaries, Roman ruins, Byzantine frescoes, Ottoman minarets, French abbeys, and proto-urban concrete. On top of all this, it is suffocatingly gorgeous. Northern Cyprus offers some of the loveliest, quietest beaches and historical sights in all of the Mediterranean.

ESSENTIALS

▨ Money

US$1 =165,370 Turkish Lira (TL)	100,000TL = US$0.60
CDN$1 = 118,672TL	100,000TL = CDN$0.84
UK£1 = 263,831TL	100,000TL = UK£0.38
IR£1 = 238,464TL	100,000TL = IR£0.42
AUS$1 = 122,903TL	100,000TL = AUS$0.81
NZ$1 = 105,903TL	100,000TL = NZ$0.94
SAR1 = 35,003TL	100,000TL = SAR2.86
1GRdr = 571TL	100,000TL = 175GRdr
C£1 = 303,371TL	100,000TL = C£0.33

> All prices are quoted in U.S. dollars because inflation in northern Cyprus tends to correspond roughly with the devaluation of the Turkish lira.

▨ Getting There

The international boundary that divides Cyprus remains nearly impossible to cross. One-day passes are available on the southern side of the Green Line, but only with stringent restrictions (see **Crossing the Green Line,** p. 552). By far the easiest way to enter is via Turkey. Ferries and sea-buses depart more or less daily from Mersin (İçel), Alanya, Anamur, and Taşucu to Girne. Less frequent ferries also run from Mersin to Mağusa. Turkish airlines are the only companies that fly into northern Cyprus; flights come and go from Lefkoşa to most major airports in Turkey.

▨ Once There

> Exercise extreme caution when driving in northern Cyprus. Tortuous roads, tortured drivers, and scores of tourists unfamiliar with driving on the left-hand side of the road provide less than optimal road conditions.

Ah, the buses of northern Cyprus. Ephemeral, fleeting creatures, you will rarely see one when you need one. Reliable *dolmuş* run between the larger cities, but service to local points of interest range from the arthritic to the nonexistent. To do any real sight seeing, you have to rent a car; guided tours do only a cursory job and the Turkish Republic of Northern Cyprus's (TRNC) taxis charge standardized, exorbitant rates for excursions into the countryside. You need to have either an international driver's permit or a national driver's license from your home country to rent a car here. In theory, though seldom in practice, you must also be 25 or older. If you don't take out the maximum possible collision insurance, many agencies require a hefty cash deposit.

Tourist offices can be found in Mağusa, Girne, and Lefkoşa. Emergency medical treatment at hospitals is free for foreigners.

For an **emergency ambulance** dial 112; **police** 155; **fire** 199.

■ Keeping in Touch

To send letters to northern Cyprus, use the postal code 'Mersin 10, Turkey'. A sample address is: Amy Alberts, Dome Hotel, Girne, Northern Cyprus, Mersin 10, Turkey. The TRNC has its own internationally accepted stamps.

To call from abroad, dial 90 (Turkey) as the country code, followed by 392, the **area code** for northern Cyprus. At press time, neither public phonecards from mainland Turkey nor American calling cards (e.g., AT&T, MCI) worked in northern Cyprus. Most post offices sell special TRNC phonecards that work in all pay phones.

■ People, History, and Government

Turkey is the only country that recognizes the northern 37% of the island as the TRNC, and Atatürk's picture graces the walls of offices, lobbies, and waiting rooms everywhere. Although Turkish is the official language, more than half the population speaks English, and many older residents speak Greek. Of the 150,000-odd residents of northern Cyprus, more than half are either Turks who came to do their military service in the mid-70s and never went back, and Cypriots from the south who relocated when Cyprus split in 1983. A few hundred Brits and Germans also live here, with a good number of bonus Brits dropping in on their holiday homes in the summer.

Being an out-of-the-way spot, Cyprus has been a popular banishment site for years. Emperor Constantine V gave icon-worshipping nuns and monks the choice of either marrying and leaving the church, or being blinded and sent to Cyprus. After the Ottoman conquest of the island in 1571, sultans typically banished officials who had incurred their disfavor to the walled port city of Mağusa (Famagusta).

The TRNC came into existence on Nov. 15, 1983. President Rauf Denktas is also an amateur photographer; you can pick up a copy of his handsomely bound book *Fotoğraflari ve Rauf Denktaş* at most local bookstores. The TRNC is a parliamentary democracy based on the British system. The official currency is the Turkish lira. Please see p. 556 for more on the Cypriot situation.

■ Lefkoşa (North Nicosia)

The sounds of growth, construction, and urban traffic outside the Old City cannot redress the silence one finds near the **Green Line**—the series of oil-drum, barbed-wire, and steel barricades separating the capital city of North Nicosia from the South. The violence of the conflict is not audible; it registers only the stale silence of intermittent peace. Lefkoşa teems with green-clad troops who pack together at street corners or around ATMs. They are youths instructed to be kind to tourists and who occasionally snap photos of each other in the desiccated grassy knolls that inlay the city's main square. While the **Girne Cad.** has been modernized and even glitzed up a bit for tourists, much of the Old City, especially in the east and along the Green Line, is a ghost town of crumbling walls and stray barbed wire.

Budget travelers may not feel very welcome in Lefkoşa. The few hotels with Western amenities (fresh towels, air-conditioning) ask US$20-40 per person and lack charm. The many pensions generally cater to locals who can't afford apartments and live here instead. Inexpensive restaurants crowd the area near the Girne Gate; *döner kebap* and *Öz Amasyali* are popular lunch options. Nightlife is a contradiction in terms; the streets are dead at 10pm. All in all, it is probably best to see Northern Nicosia in a daytrip (buses from Girne are about US$1).

**Lefkoşa
(Northern Nicosia)**

Büyük Hamam (Great Bath), 4
Clinic (Poliklinik), 14
Covered Bazaar, 2
Cyprus Turkish Airlines Terminal, 18
The Green Line, 13
K. Kaymaklı Martyr's Memorial
  (Şehitler Anıtı), 16
Kyrenia Gate Tourism Information
  (Girne Kapısı), 11

Lapideri Museum, 5
Main Post Office, 6
Museum, 20
Old City Walls, 1
Parcel Post Office, 16
Police Headquarters, 8
Sultan Mahmut Library, 3
Telecommunications Office, 15
Tourism Information, 19

T.R.T. Cyprus Office (Kıbrıs
  Bürosu), 9
Turkish Embassy, 12
The Turkish Museum
  (Türk Müzesi), 10
The Venetian Column, 7

ORIENTATION AND PRACTICAL INFORMATION

Arriving by bus from other parts of Northern Cyprus, you'll be dropped at the **bus station** *(otogar)*, 1km from the old city. Take the street perpendicular to the Girne Rd., which runs beside the bus station, to get to town. The **Girne Gate** and the old city walls lie 1km farther. The tourist office is at the entrance to the gatehouse. From here, **Girne Caddesi,** the main street, runs to the main square, **Atatürk Meydanı,** and continues to the Green Line.

If you arrive from the south at the **Ledra Palace** crossing, a roundabout (with a Turkish victory monolith in the middle) is 500m up the street. Follow the city walls to the Girne Gate. To reach the bus terminal, continue up this street (bearing left at the fork); it is a 15-minute walk.

Embassies: Only **Turkey** has a full embassy in Northern Cyprus, at Bedrettin Demirel Cad. (tel. 227 2313). The following countries have "representative offices," which offer some consular services: **Australia** (tel. 227 1115), in the Saray Hotel, open Tues. and Thurs. 9am-noon; **Germany,** #15 28 Kasım Sok. (tel. 227 5161); **U.K.,** 23 Mehmet Akif Cad. (tel. 227 1938, open Mon., Wed., and Fri. 7:30am-1:30pm, Tues. and Thurs. 7:30am-1:30pm and 4:30-5pm); **U.S.,** 20 Güner Türkmen Sok. (tel. 227 2443, open Mon.-Fri. 8am-3:30pm).
Currency Exchange: Several offices along Girne Cad. Open Mon.-Fri. 8am-1pm and 2-4pm. **Banks** close at noon. **ATMs** near Atatürk Meydanı.
Telephones: Pembe Telefon, 30m to the right of the post office, has metered booths and sells phonecards. Open Mon.-Fri. 7:30am-2pm and 3:30-5:30pm. The

Government Telecommunications Dept. is on Arif Salim Cad., one third of the way between Girne Gate and the bus station.

Flights: The airport is 17km from town, but it is serviced only by Turkish Airlines. Taxis from the airport $15-20; be sure to fix the fare in advance. **Cyprus Turkish Airlines** (owned by Turkish Airlines) has an office on Atatürk Meydanı (open Mon.-Sat. 7:30am-2pm and 3:30-6pm). Flights to Istanbul, Izmir, Ankara ($60 one way, $100 round-trip) and London (1 per day, $225 one way, $400 round-trip).

Buses: Buses leave from city station. With Girne Gate at your back, go right, bearing left at the fork. Hourly buses to: Mağusa ($1.25); Güzelyurt ($1.50); and Lefke ($2.25). Buses also run to numerous small villages, 1 per day in each direction, arriving in Lefkoşa by 7am and leaving in the mid-afternoon.

Dolmuş: Several departures from the bus station per hour to Girne ($1). You may also catch a slightly cheaper *dolmuş* off the main street leading away from the Girne Gate. Services run from 7am-5pm.

International Language Bookshop: Rüstem Kitabevi, 26 Girne Cad. Generally a lousy selection, but they do have English-language fiction and books on Cyprus. Hours vary.

Hospital: (tel. 228 5441) On the road to Girne, roughly 700m from the Victory Monument. Look for the Hastane sign.

Police: (tel. 228 3311) Girne Cad., close to Atatürk Meydanı.

Post Office: (tel. 228 5982) Sarayönü Sok. From the Girne gate, take a right off Atatürk Meydanı. Open Mon. 7:30am-2pm and 3:30-6pm, Tues.-Fri. 7:30am-2pm and 4-6pm, Sat. 8:30am-12:30pm.

Telephone Code: 22.

SIGHTS

The Green Line is tangible evidence of the tensions on the island. The sensitivity of the politics surrounding it is matched only by the coarseness of its construction. In places, the "line" is a barbed- or chicken-wire fence, sometimes screened with oil drums. Other places, it's a steel barrier or a wall blocking a road. Take a right off Atatürk Meydanı and walk alongside the old British courthouse for five minutes; any street to your left will drop you off at the Green Line. In certain sections of the line—especially near the Bedesten—the morning light seems to penetrate the stone and wood remains of the buildings that once linked the northern and southern halves of the city. *Photography is prohibited.*

The **Selimiye Mosque/St. Sophia Cathedral** is a bizarre sight; a seemingly ancient (1326 AD) cathedral looms in the shadow of its more recent additions—two soaring Islamic minarets. Despite the prayer rugs *(seccade)* and Islamic calligraphy, it still feels like a church. From Atatürk Meydanı, with Girne Gate at your back, continue down Girne Cad., looking left for its twin minarets. Beside it is the **Bedesten,** the Orthodox cathedral of St. Nicholas which dates from the 14th century. Ottomans converted it into a covered market and later a barn. The **city walls** date from 1570.

Face the Green Line and follow it to your right to reach the **Derviş Paşa Museum.** The former mansion of a notable 20th-century Cypriot newspaper owner, it has been converted into a small museum housing a collection of clothing and household goods (open daily 9am-7pm, but often closes around lunchtime; admission $2, with ISIC 50¢). The **Mevlevi Tekke,** near the tourist office, was once an Islamic monastery and is now a small museum housing life-size models of whirling dervishes and a collection of Islamic artifacts. (Open Mon. 9am-2pm and 3:30-7pm, Tues.-Fri. 7:30am-2pm. Admission $2, with ISIC 50¢.)

■ Near Lefkoşa

LEFKE

On the road stretching from Güzelyurt to Gemikonaği, on the far western rim of northern Cyprus, lies a patch of Mediterranean coastline given short shrift by most tourists. A few gritty travelers find their way here (elderly British ones, for the most part). The area around Lefke doesn't have the beaches or facilities of Girne, nor the mutable history of Lefkoşa, but it does have one precious characteristic: distance. Distance from other tourists, distance from the low-rise, whitewashed cityscapes of most North Cypriot civilization, and distance from some of the last stubborn remainders of "modernity." Shepherds brandish genuine crooked staffs, and locals are prone to wave to you more often than one might expect.

Two local objects draw the gaze of most tourists to this region. The first, and most worthy of your 95¢, is the **Soli Ruins.** The residue of 2000 years of practice at building cities (proving that city planning may, in fact, be the world's oldest profession), the Soli site first attracted Assyrians around 700 BC. Later populated by Greeks, it derives its name from Solon, the Athenian philosopher. The city changed hands, was razed, and rebuilt as often as would any city planner. Today, it boasts a gorgeous, semi-circular Roman amphitheater (currently being renovated), a few city ruins, and a basilica floor inlaid with mosaics (admission 95¢, with ISIC 50¢). Simply follow the road from Güzelyurt; it is the main road from Lefkoşa heading west. Without turning off toward Lefke, continue straight and follow the signs that clearly mark the ruins. If traveling by bus, buy a ticket to Lefke and let the driver drop you off at the turn; from there, the hike is roughly 2-3km. Otherwise, take the bus into Lefke and find a taxi. Drivers will wait for you to examine the Soli site, but it will cost you more. Renting a car or jeep is the preferred option, though much more expensive ($30 per day, $5 for insurance, and $10-15 for gas). Car rental outfits abound in Girne while Lefkoşa hosts two or three that rent for $10 less.

The second most popular destination near Lefke lies 10km west along the same road that leads to the Soli Ruins. The educational value of the **Vouni Palace** ruins, however, is eclipsed by the relief you feel having survived the drive up the road that brought you there. The road to Vouni is a treacherous one with endless blind curves and thousand-foot drops. Even if you don't think you're scared of heights, you very well may be here. Delicate-stomached travelers should take a taxi and close their eyes. The Vouni site itself is not so impressive, but the view of the Mediterranean and Güzelyurt Bay is stunning.

Lefke is starved for accommodations, but if you choose to spend an evening near Lefke, you may want to try the **Soli Inn.** Just past Lefke and along the same road which extends to the Soli and Vouni ruins, the Soli Inn stands as visitors' sole hope in an infrequently touristed area. Students from nearby **Lefke University** make up its main traffic. Composed of thirteen bungalow-style rooms (all capable of housing 4-5 guests), the Soli Inn charges a modest $20-25 per person, including breakfast.

Finally, the **Liman Restaurant & CMC Bar** provides the most compelling reason to visit Lefke. Look for its sign on the main road eastbound; it appears just after you have gone straight past the turnoff for Lefke proper. Located across from the monstrous copper slag-heaps and mining equipment left over from the Cyprus Mining Corporation (hence, CMC), the *liman* (port) reveals a small part of the island's history. The mine started up in 1917, after an American (dare we say "capitalist"?) geologist came to Cyprus on hearing it was an "island of copper." The entire operation was once run by steam and by Cypriots, though it shut down upon the Turkish invasion in 1974. Along the walls of the CMC Bar, masks, mining helmets, and WWII-era *curioso* fill, but do not clutter, the space. The Liman Restaurant serves a friendly plate of fish and chips for $5 from noon to 10pm. The CMC Bar opens at 8am and closes at 1am. Along with a drink at the bar (roughly $1-2), view ancient Roman driftwood. Just ask the proprietor. Incidentally, the land on which the Liman Restaurant and CMC Bar stands is American soil, along with a third of the town of Lefke (greedy imperialists).

GÜZELYURT

Güzelyurt is a large and none-too-interesting market town. Visit it to see **Agios Mamas,** a beautiful, perfectly preserved icon-filled Greek Orthodox church. Check out the **Tomb of Mamas,** an Orthodox saint, inside. It is believed that the moisture which occasionally oozes from the tomb is a cure-all for disease and a pacifier of storms. To visit the church you must first pay to enter the **Museum of Archaeology**

and Natural History next door; the curator will admit you to the church. The museum contains a collection of stuffed animals and birds downstairs and ancient pottery upstairs; look for the two-headed lamb and the lamb with eight legs. Upstairs is the famed black-faced, multi-breasted statue of **Ephesian Artemis** from Salamis, which was recovered from the sea in the 1980s. This image appears on numerous postcards and books around northern Cyprus.

■ Girne (Kyrenia)

The Mediterranean seems to sit affectionately beside the city of Girne, separated from it by thick wall 500m long. The semi-circular harbor created by the wall is rimmed by fish restaurants, bars, and open-air cafes. Lazy, luxuriant Girne oozes Britishness. If that's what you're after, you can bet on horse and dog races broadcast live from the U.K. at the Dome Hotel Casino; stay in the Lord Kitchner room at the aptly named Nostalgia Hotel; shop for Earl Gray tea at any of the local grocery stores; and get your fried liver-and-onions fix and pay for it in sterling instead of lira at the city's plentiful British pubs. Upscale watch and sunglasses shops line the side streets, and imported liquors fill the shelves of the local markets. Despite the ritzy image, however, budget travelers can survive and prosper here.

ORIENTATION AND PRACTICAL INFORMATION

A wide, grassy mall fills the coast from the harbor to the **Dome Hotel,** a rambling white plaster colonial institution that marks Girne's center of gravity. At the other end of the wall rises the massive **Kyrenia Castle,** in which Queen Carlotta, the last true monarch of the Lusignan dynasty, resisted the 15th-century siege led by her illegitimate half-brother, the future James II.

Ferries from Turkey arrive at the **new harbor,** 2km from town. *Dolmuş,* when available (usually in the afternoons), run to the **main square** for 75¢; a taxi to the old harbor (where most of the hotels and upscale restaurants are located) costs $3.50. To make this journey by foot, exit the port gates on your right and continue 500m down the road. Take a right at the main intersection onto **Cumhuriyet Cad.** Just 1.5km past the post office is the roundabout in the main square. Beyond the roundabout stands a dry modern-art-type fountain; behind it, to the left, runs **Hürriyet Cad.,** the main street in town, lined with shops and a few hotels. The streets to the right lead to the seafront; the nearest ones, to the old harbor. Arriving overland, you'll be dropped at the **bus station.** Exiting, turn right and walk to the International American University (700m). Go left at this intersection—the main square is 800m down the road.

Tourist Office: Walking out of Girne along Hürriyet Cad., the office will appear on your left, 500m past the Dorana Hotel. Open Mon. 7:30am-1:30pm and 3:30-6pm, Tues.-Fri. 7am-1:30pm. Free city maps of Girne, Lefkoşa, and Mağusa.

Banks: Banking hours are Mon.-Fri. 8am-noon, with some variation. **ATMs** on Hürriyet Cad. near the castle, provide V/MC/Eurocard/Cirrus/Plus services. **Vakıfbank,** in the main square, cashes traveler's checks. Bring your passport.

Exchange offices: Many are scattered along the street leading from the Atatürk statue left and up to Hürriyet Cad. Cash only, open Mon.-Sat. approx. 9am-8pm.

Expatriates' Notice Board: In front of the post office. Provides information on local events, apartment rentals, etc.

Buses: Run hourly to Mağusa, Güzelyurt, and Lefkoşa from the bus station. From the main square, walk up Lefkoşa Rd. (beside Vakıfbank) for 800m—you should pass Shell and Esso stations on the way. Hourly *dolmuş* run to Lapta.

Ferries: Tickets can be purchased from **Fergün Ferries** on the main square. Daily **seabuses** to Taşucu (Turkey) are fast and cushy. Slower ferries also run to Taşucu.

Taxis: Countless underpatronized Mercedes-Benz taxis lurk at stands on every street corner. None of them have meters, relying instead on a standardized printed list of fares. Trips within town, including the new port, officially cost $3.50, $6 for 3-8km outside of the city, $8.25 for 8-11km, and $10.50 for 11-16km. Try bargaining.

Car Rental: Atlantic (tel. 815 3053), in the Dome Hotel, offers Renaults for $20 per day and Jeeps for $27 per day (insurance $8). Free pick-up from all points in northern Cyprus, including the port and airport. **Sun** (tel. 815 2302), across the street, offers similar deals and also rents automatic Nissans with A/C for $33 per day.

International Bookstore: The British owned **Green Jacket Bookshop,** 20 Temmuz Cad. (tel./fax 815 7130), roughly 1.5km from town, offers a random selection of English-language novels, nonfiction, and history/guidebooks on Cyprus. The management also serves, of all things, baked potatoes. To get here from the main square, walk to the end of Hürriyet Cad. and keep going along the coastal road for 700m—it's on the left across from the petrol station. Open Mon.-Fri. 9am-1pm and 4-7pm, Sat. 9am-noon. **BBD** news agents on Hürriyet Cad. near the square have a small selection of British and German newspapers.

Hospital: Alcıcek Hospital (tel. 815 2266, -2254), Cumhuriyet Cad., roughly 100m past the post office. There is a **doctor** (tel. 815 3528) at Hüseyin Cenkler.

Police: (tel. 815 2014, -2125) Just off the harbor behind the **Harbor Club,** on the road immediately beside the castle.

Post Office: Cumhuriyet Cad., off the main square. Open Mon.-Fri. 7:30am-2pm and 4-6pm, Sat. 8:30am-12:30pm. Parcel office open Mon., Wed., and Fri. 9:30am-12:30pm. **Postal Code:** 9900, "Mersin 10, Turkey" from abroad.

Telephones: In the main square, beside Cumhuriyet Cad. They accept only TRNC phonecards. The **Telekomunikasyon Dairesi** opposite the post office sells them. Open until 2pm. They come in 30, 60, and 100-unit cards costing 95¢, $1.90, or $2.80, respectively. **Telephone Information:** tel. 192. **Telephone Code:** 392.

ACCOMMODATIONS

Harbor-front hotels here are the most expensive, but the most comfortable. If you're going to be splurging on lodgings at all in the course of your Cypriot travels, this is the place. Although some of the pensions in town are dingy and patronized by employees of Girne's shipping industry, decent lodgings are easy to find, especially if you make your reservations in advance; motels and pensions fill up faster than the hotels.

Motel Elizel, 3 Bafra Sok (tel. 815 4774). From Girne's main road heading towards the Dome Hotel, 1 block from the square, take a right (at the taxi stand) and follow the road until you see the sign. Spacious, clean rooms, some with balconies. Breakfast and private shower included. Singles $10; doubles $16.75; triples $23.50.

Castle Motel, 1 Bafra Sok. (tel. 815 3942), across the street from Elizel. Offers clean rooms dwarfed by gigantic beds and equipped with private showers and high-tech hot and cold-blowing electric fans. Breakfast included. $8.30 per person.

Bingöl Motel (tel. 815 2749), Hürriyet Cad., on the main square. Rooms are basic but comfortable. Breakfast and private showers included. Singles $11.75; doubles $23.25. The jovial proprietor Loka offers a 10% discount to *Let's Go* bearers.

Kanguru Pansiyon, 25 Canpolat Sok. (tel. 815 4587), between the harbor and Hürriyet Cad. You can't miss the kangaroo sign. Clean, hostel-like rooms with fans, balconies, showers, and lawn-furniture tables and chairs. Singles $6.75; doubles $10.

New Bristol Hotel (tel. 815 2321), Hürriyet Cad. Offers spacious, comfortable rooms with A/C. Breakfast and private shower included. Singles $15; doubles $22.

Nostalgia Hotel (tel. 815 3079), just behind the harbor near the Icon Museum, offers great wooden headboards and tables, A/C, TV, and baths, in rooms named for Cypriot personalities like Lala Mustafa Paşa and Cleopatra. The Sultan Selim II room boasts a canopy bed 3.5m high. Breakfast included. $20.25 per person.

FOOD

The harbor, lined with tiny and adorable seafood restaurants, is the most obvious place to dine. The standard $7.50 fish and chips combo, if neither wildly delicious nor an outstanding bargain, makes a pleasant enough dinner when accompanied by the ravishing twilight harborside views. In the angular, white-walled streets uphill from the harbor, several cafes and small restaurants supply more bodacious, bargain food to the more bodacious, bargain-seeking traveler. It's best to avoid the fish here;

stick to your mainland *döner* and *ızgara* favorites. Girne is also a city of many **super-markets,** a good source of cheap fresh bread and olives for picnics, as well as such British delicacies like potted meats and digestive biscuits.

Dünya, 15 Karaoğlanoğlu Cad. (tel. 822 2392), about 4.5km outside of Girne on the road through Karaoğlanoğlu. Located in the backyard of an old summer home, it serves complete, $8.30 fixed-menu dinners only—a stupefying selection of cold *meze*, hot *meze*, fresh fruit, and all the alcohol you can drink. Thanks to its alcohol policy, Dünya attracts a particularly jovial crowd. Open 7pm-midnight.

Yama (tel. 822 2888), next door to Güler's Fish, serves fantastic *meze* (95% vegetarian) and a unique *mantı* stuffed with cheese or chicken instead of ground lamb.

Niazis (tel. 815 2160; fax 815 5665), on Kordon Boyu Cad., opposite the Dome Hotel. Established in Limassol in 1949, this Cyprus institution moved to Girne in 1974, along with many of Limassol's Turks. For 46 years its specialty has been full *kebap*, a mixed *ızgara* grill served with *meze* ($7).

Piccolino Ristorante Italiano (tel. 815 8266), uphill and behind the harbor. Run by a British mother-daughter team, this tiny place serves first-rate pasta and fish in large portions, accompanied by fresh garlic bread. Dine on spaghetti bolognese ($6.75) or fresh tuna ($7) under the stars in their whitewashed courtyard.

Dedem, located in the main square, serves a couple of stew-type specials as well as good *döner kebap* ($3.50). Open from lunchtime until about 6:30pm.

Planter's Bar & Bistro, 159 Karaoğlanoğlu Cad. (tel. 822 2219), between Dünya and Yama. Well worth the trek for the colonial atmosphere. 99% British crowd sips Bloody Marys and whiskey and soda. Dig into your steak and kidney pie ($9.50) in an outdoor dining room with palm trees, candles, jazz, and English-speaking waiters. Prices on the English-only menu are listed in pounds sterling only. While the food is good, portions can be minuscule—six shrimp wrapped in bacon with salad will set you back $12.

Güler's Fish, off to the right of Karaoğlanoğlu Cad. about 100m past Dünya, has views of the sea and serves four fresh fish, fried whole, with chips for $7; $10.30 with *meze*, salad, and fruit.

ENTERTAINMENT

Beach-going, street-walking, stuff-buying, sun-avoiding, and nap-taking are Girne's most popular entertainment activities, though more active leisure can be found as well. Several local bars host large and young weekend crowds. **Cafe 34,** on the harbor, earns the highest marks for its tasteful indoor and terraced outdoor drinking areas which become jammed on Friday and Saturday nights in high season. Just off the harbor, behind the taxi stand and next to Hotel British, **Cafe Esquire** hosts a smaller, virtually all-male crowd who come for the blaring American music, pool tables, and video games that actually talk to you in Japanese. **Sunset Beach** comes equipped with an **outdoor disco** (tel. 821 8330) teeming with local youth on summer weekends. Five to six hundred natives swallow up the 15-20 tourists who make a Friday or Saturday night there. The club is open Monday through Saturday 11pm-3:30am, or perhaps until the last dance-dazed teenage disco queen staggers out into the night. Look under the listing for Sunset Beach for directions (p. 587).

SIGHTS

The preeminent sight in Girne is the huge medieval **castle** at the harbor's mouth. Built by the Byzantines with material plundered from the ruins of a now nonexistent Roman city, it was fortified by the Lusignans and refortified by the Venetians.

Upon entering through the first tunnel of Girne castle, you'll be greeted by strains of Palestrina choral music, which drift with varying audibility through the inner maze of rooms, hallways, and courtyards. Turn left through the next tunnel to reach the only remaining structure from the Byzantine period, a small chapel.

In the courtyard, ghostly fragments of the past waft through the **dungeon** where King James's wife threw his mistress Lady Jeanne after she gave birth to the king's son. This is now a sort of **torture museum;** peer two stories down through a raised grating at a languishing, scantily-clad plaster mannequin representing the unlucky Lady Jeanne along with various grisly scenes involving other bloodied mannequins.

From the courtyard, notice the row of brown, locked doors on the upper level; these prison cells were last used by the British in the 1950s to house EOKA terrorists (see **Cyprus in the 20th Century**, p. 556). Also in the courtyard, the **Shipwreck Museum** contains the remains of the world's oldest known trading ship, dating from the time of Alexander the Great (300 BC). Some of the cargo, including **9000 blackened almonds** (the crew's main staple), is on display in the museum as well (castle and museums open daily 8am-7pm; admission $1.40, students 15¢).

Behind the Hotel British, **Archangelos Church** contains an interesting **Icon Museum** (tel. 815 5313) where 18th and 19th-century icons fill the ground floor and three-tiered balcony. From the fourth-floor balcony you can look across at the magnificent altarpiece depicting Christ sitting in a large golden chalice, surrounded by levitating winged-angel heads, many of whom bear an eerie resemblance to **Doris Day** (open 9am-1pm and 3-7pm; admission $1.40, students 15¢). Girne's **Fine Arts Museum,** an enchanting seaside stone cottage which once belonged to an English governor, lies 1km down the street from the Dome Hotel. Because of the intervening militarized zone, you have to take a circuitous route to get there: walk along Hürriyet Cad. until you reach Kocatepe Sok., take a right, passing the military hospital; the well-marked museum is on your left. Two salons of Euro-paintings (including the requisite oils of windmills and nursing mothers) give way to several adorable gabled rooms of yellow porcelain Chinese horses, red and gold dragons, and Mt. Fuji fire screens (open Mon.-Fri. 8am-7pm and Sat. 8am-3pm; admission $1.40, students 15¢)

The north coast beaches are some of the finest in Cyprus. A few are free, but most are not, and sit below monolithic, multi-storied resorts or "bungalow-style" condo developments. For a small fee (usually around $3), you can storm these beaches. **Kervon Saray,** the best of the area's free beaches, lies near the village of Karaoğlanoğlu, several kilometers west of Girne. To get there, either take the Girne-Lapta *dolmuş* (35¢) from the stop by the roundabout and get off when you see the "Güler's Fish" sign on your right, or take a taxi (about $3). To reach **Acapulco Beach,** perhaps the loveliest of the pay beaches, head down the coastal road eastbound on the Bellapais side of Girne. The beach is well-marked, and about 4km from the center of town. It

---

Those Loony Lusignans

In terms of historical narrative, Girne's castle stands as a giant monument to the dysfunctionality of the Lusignan family, a notoriously zany bunch. In the Middle Ages, Raymond de Lusignan's wife, the lovely Countess Melusine, was said to morph into a serpent from the waist down every Saturday before eventually turning into a dragon which even now haunts her castle in Poitou.

John II ruled Cyprus from 1432-1458 under the dominating influence of his unscrupulous and ambitious second wife, Helena Palaeologa. The couple had only one child (Carlotta), but John's mistress, Marietta of Patras, bore him a son some years later, later to become King James II. In a move that foreshadowed Mike Tyson's boxing career, Helena bit off Marietta's nose in a fit of jealousy.

Carlotta fared much worse. Widowed, then orphaned, then remarried to the insipid nonentity Louis of Savoy, she managed in her loneliness to grow quite close to her half-brother James. The Lusignan High Court, sensing James was a threat to the purity of their line, poisoned the friendship and drove James to Cairo where his dynamic ways won the support of the Mamluk Sultan, who loaned him a fleet with which to claim the Cypriot crown from his half-sister. In 1460, James took the entire island except for the castle of Girne, in which Carlotta withstood his attacks for 4 years with only the sickly Louis for moral support.

Peter I, arguably the greatest of the Lusignan kings, was similarly lacking in family values. Having gotten his favorite mistress, Lady Jeanne d'Aleman, with child, he went off to Egypt to recruit soldiers and funding for the Crusades. Peter was later ambushed, assassinated, and dismembered by mutinous barons while in bed with his other favorite mistress, Lady Echive de Scandelion.

CYPRUS

rests in front of a yawning resort called, not surprisingly, Acapulco Resort. The beach costs $3 per day, and you can also rent windsurfing equipment (about $5) or a bicycle (about $3) here. If you decide to wrinkle under the sun for an afternoon, be warned: on a good weekend the beach gets a thousand other people intent on sharing your rays. **Sunset Beach** is in the opposite direction from Acapulco, along the same road, 1km past the turn-off for Kervon Saray. A little cheaper than the Acapulco ($2), it also lacks both the equipment and glaring popularity.

■ East of Girne

BEYLERBEYI (BELLAPAIS)

This tranquil hillside village 6km from Girne contains one of northern Cyprus's most notable sites, the stunning Gothic **Bellapais Abbey.** Founded by French monks fleeing the Arab sacking of the city in the 13th century, 30m-high cypress trees now tower above the delicately arched cloisters and silvery olive groves descending to the sea. And the abbey grounds come with music! An all-Mozart soundtrack is piped in nonstop through various hidden speakers. The **Kybele Restaurant** inside the gorgeous courtyard overlooking the sea, serves good if slightly pricey food (fish *şiş kebap* $6.40). It also features a wine house (restaurant open 11am-11pm, abbey open daily 9am-5pm; admission $1.40, students 15¢). **Erol's Restaurant** (tel. 815 3657), 1km from Bellapais on the main road to Girne in Ozanköy village, serves stellar Cypriot cuisine well worth a stop on the way back from the abbey. Two dozen types of *meze!* Make reservations in advance.

ST. HILARION CASTLE

Ten kilometers from Girne, off the Lefkoşa road, towers **St. Hilarion Castle.** Together with the **Bufavento** and **Kautava** castles, St. Hilarion formed part of the Byzantine's early warning system in the Five Finger Mountain area. The three Lusignan castles are so fairy tale-perfect that Walt Disney reportedly used them as architectural models when animating *Snow White and the Seven Dwarfs* and *Sleeping Beauty.* Of the three, St. Hilarion is the best-preserved, most accessible, and in some ways the most fun since it alone was used as a vacation home by the Lusignan royalty (and not just an emergency military fallout shelter by the British). St. Hilarion was built in the 10th century and renovated by the Lusignans in the 12th-13th centuries. The Venetians, who didn't need castles, roughed the place up a bit 200 years later. Though further damaged by a fire in 1995, St. Hilarion has reopened and is looking remarkably fit for its years (open daylight hours; admission $1.40, students 15¢). Walking to the castle is prohibited; there's a military base on the way up. You'll have to rent a car or take a taxi ($16 for a trip to both Hilarion and Bellapais). On Mondays and Fridays, **Apple Tour** (tel. 815 5499; fax 815 1894), on Ecevit Cad. in Girne, offers half-day tours of the castle and abbey for $20, including admission fees.

■ West of Girne: Karaman (Karmi)

A small hill village, Karaman lies 10km southwest of Girne. Known as Karmi before 1974, it was abandoned by the Greeks during the war. Literally propped on the side of a mountain, the village offers views of Girne, good hiking, a European atmosphere, and many walking trails. No bus will take you here, but Karaman is popular among tourists, and rental cars fill the parking lot of the old **Orthodox Church.** Walking to Karaman is possible, if tiring; the road leading up to the village is contorted and steep. Head west along the coast road to Karaoğlanoğlu and take a left at the sign. Once nameless, its streets have recently been given lush names such as Geranium Way, Plum Road, and Azalea Alley. These "streets" may look like private steps. They are not, and in the summer months they are well-planted and heavily fragrant.

Numerous walking trails lead away from the village; **free maps** of the trails are available at Crow's Nest Pub. Diehard hikers may want to walk along the **Forestry Mountain Road.** It is 40 beautiful kilometers from St. Hilarion to the Lapta area, but not all hikes are so long. The **Karaman Steps** provide a panoramic stop, although getting there requires good hiking shoes and pants, since they often seem less like steps and more like bramble-covered, minced rock. Follow the main village road past Karaman; when the road forks, go right up the steep hill.

A number of excellent restaurants are located in the Karaman area. The **Crow's Nest Pub,** located behind the old Orthodox Church, serves good English pub food, lots of snacks, and a make-your-own dinner (choose the meat, sauce, chips or rice, and salad). An amiable bar, its proprietor is also a mine of information (open Mon.-Sat. noon-3pm and 7pm-midnight, Sun. noon-3pm). The **Karaman Shop** in front of the Crow's Nest is the only grocery in the village (open early-12:30pm and 6:30-8:30pm). The **Levant Restaurant** (tel. 822 2594), along the main village road, offers Cypriot and Eastern Mediterranean fare (open Tues.-Sun., bar opens at 6pm, dinner service at 7pm—they have their priorities straight). The **Treasure** (tel. 822 2400), located farther along the village road toward Girne, offers English and Cypriot meals. The fish casserole ($8) and the *muluhiya*—a vegetable dish cooked with lamb, tomatoes, onions, and lemons—are both good bets. The Treasure's balcony rests over the precipice leading to Girne. Reservations are a good idea (opens Thurs.-Tues. at 7pm).

■ Mağusa (Famagusta)

An obese port sequesters the sea around Mağusa—a port you may have met already as the anonymous "seaport in Cyprus" where Shakespeare set his great tragedy *Othello.* In Shakespeare's time Mağusa was still the world's richest, wildest, most cosmopolitan and glamorous city, *the* trading post between Christian West and Muslim East—a sort of agglomeration of modern-day New York, Paris, and pre-Chinese Hong Kong. In short, a city absolutely screaming to be the setting of an iambic murder-suicide melodrama about a jealous Moor. Every language could be heard in the streets, from Greek to French, Norse to Persian, Georgian to Amharic. The harbor throbbed with ships hailing from every great port from Venice to Tripoli to Alexandria. Mağusa itself was, in addition to a point of transit, a supplier of countless luxury exports: cloth woven with threads of gold, lace of Levarka, Commanderia wine (whose vinegar preserved exotic pickles), topaz crystals (marketed as "Paphos diamonds"), madder root, indigo, saffron, and gum mastic (collected from the beards of goats) were all hot commodities shipped west. Cypriot beeswax from Mağosa was even shipped to the silver mines of Bolivia in the remote peaks of the Andes.

Stories are told of the two Netsorian Lachas brothers, the city's wealthiest merchant-princes, at whose banquets the tables were piled with precious stones intended as party favors. Both the hearth and the kitchen stoves were fuelled with great fragrant sandalwood logs in order to perfume guests and meal alike. According to a visiting Westphalian priest, another merchant gave his daughter, upon her marriage, "jewels more precious than all the ornaments of the Queen of France." The incredible riches poured into hunting, jousting, and the procuring of women gradually earned Mağusa, even by the 14th century's none-too-rigorous standards, a reputation of depravity. St. Bridget of Sweden was especially gloomy in her indictment of "the new Gomorrah." Presumably unnerved, the citizens of Mağusa commenced church-building with their typical zeal so that at one point 365 churches stood within the fortified walls; one for every day of the year (today 17 remain).

ORIENTATION AND PRACTICAL INFORMATION

Buses stop on the Lefkoşa road. Disembark and turn right. After 250m you'll see the impressive **Victory Monument** in the center of a roundabout. Behind it are the old city walls. Follow the road outside the walls and after 500m you'll pass the tourist office; 400m farther and you'll be at the sea. On the left is the **Canbulat Bastion** and past it, the port where **ferries** from Turkey arrive. The vacated **Maraş,** now a military zone, lies to the right. The museums, old churches, and the Othello Tower are all within the old city, as is the *otopark* where you can catch the Salamis Bay Hotel bus to Salamis.

Tourist Office: Fevzi Çakmak Blv., opposite the city wall. Free city maps. Open in summer Mon.-Fri. 7:30am-2pm, in winter Mon.-Fri. 8am-1pm and 2-5pm.

Banks: Akbank on Liman Yolu, running between Lala Mustafa Paşa mosque and the Namik Kemal Museum, has one of the city's few **ATMs,** with V/MC/Electron/Cirrus/Plus services.

Buses: To Lefkoşa (every hr., 1hr., 7:30am-5pm, $1.25). Rare village buses head to random points in the region, including Karpaz Peninsula. Buses arrive in Mağusa Mon.-Fri. by 7am, in time for the typical 7:30am start to the working day, returning to the villages from the station between 2 and 5pm.

Dolmuş: S. Göçmen Nakliyat Şti. Ltd. (tel. 366 6347, -5456) runs half-hourly service to Lefkoşa ($1.05), leaving from Ayhan Niyazi Yolu, past the roundabout on your left. 25m farther, **Virgo Trans** (tel. 366 4313, -6347), owned by the same people, has hourly air-conditioned vans to Girne ($1.40).

Ferries: Although faster, cheaper, more comfortable sea-buses to Taşucu are available from Girne, **Turkish Maritime Lines** (tel. 366 5786) does operate ferries to Mersin every Tues., Thurs., and Fri. at 1pm (8hr., $39 round-trip, students $17). Tickets must be bought in advance from their office, 25m down the right fork from the roundabout.

Hospital: Polat Paşa Blv. (tel. 366 5328).

Police: İlker Karter Cad. (tel. 366 5310, -21).

Post Office: On İlker Karter Cad., the street to the left of the tourist office as you face it; the post office is 300m along, on the left. Open 7:30am-12:30pm. The smaller branch office next to the ramp near Land's Gate in the bastion has more convenient hours, but no public phones. Open 8am-2pm and 3-6pm.

Telephones: 60 Polat Paşa Blv., the street to the right of the tourist office as you face it. They sell phonecards and have two cardphones in the lobby. Open 7:30am-8pm. **Telephone Code:** 36.

ACCOMMODATIONS

You're not exactly spoiled for choice of accommodations in this town because most people visit Mağusa on daytrips from Girne or from Salamis's four-star hotels. Nonetheless, a couple of excellent and inexpensive hotels do await you.

Otel Portofino, 9 Fevzi Çakmak Blv. (tel. 366 4392, -93; fax 366 2949), just down the street from the tourist office, offers enormous, clean rooms with balconies and private showers. Front rooms overlook the harbor; triples and quad rooms all have sofas and refrigerator. Breakfast included. Singles $12.15; doubles $19; triples $26.50; quads $32.

Altun Tabya Otel, 7 Kizilkule Yolu (tel. 366 5363, -3404), just to your right as you enter the old city, offers smaller rooms with ceiling fans, balconies, and private showers. Breakfast included. Singles $20.70; doubles $27.60; triples $34.50.

FOOD

The old city is peppered with cafes with varying degrees of charm and consumerist philosophy. Leading between the Namik Kemal Museum and Lala Mustafa Paşa mosque all the way to the wall by the port, Liman Yolu is home to a number of pleasant restaurants.

Ağagez Börek & Simit Fırıni (tel. 366 3061), on İlker Karter Cad. Hüsseyin Ağagez and his three daughters serve up delicious *sertme börek,* giant pastries filled with ground lamb, cheese, or potatoes ($1.05).

Desdemona Kebap & Meze Sarayı, a newly opened place on the road between Othello Tower and the Canbulat Museum, serves *meze* meals—20 different hot and cold appetizers in lieu of a main course. A full *meze,* enough for two people, is $8.60, coffee included. Tack on salad, bottled water, and fresh fruit for $15.20.

Viyana Kebap House, 19 Liman Yolu (tel. 366 6037), has decent *kebaps* served in a gorgeous grape bower surrounding a fountain. Adana *kebap* $1.75.

Petek Pastane, facing the city walls at the end of Liman Yolu, supplies Mağusa with every kind of Turkish sweet and pastry imaginable. Take-out or stuff your face in a roomy faux-Parisian salon with indoor fountain. Delicious gooey *döume* ice-cream with chopped pistachios is $1 per bowl. 20% discount for students.

SIGHTS

The **city walls** and surrounding **moat,** the result of 20 years' labor by the Venetians in the 16th century, are a sight to behold. Nonetheless, they failed in their task: after a vicious year-long siege, the city fell to the Ottomans in 1571. Climb up the two ramps to the **Rivettina Bastion** to get an idea of the thickness of the walls. The other bastion, the one with the lighthouse near the museum, is **Canbulat Bastion.** From the top of Rivettina you'll notice what looks like a large French Gothic cathedral with a minaret. It is in fact a large French Gothic cathedral with a minaret! Having taken **St. Nicholas Cathedral** from the Venetians, the Ottomans removed all of the statuary and stained glass representations of the human form (prohibited in Islam), slapped down some carpets, erected the minaret, and *voila!* the **Lala Mustafa Paşa Mosque.** At one point, the cathedral contained a sarcophagus unearthed by the Venetians in Paphos and believed to be the authentic "Tomb of Venus." After taking the island the British moved the tomb to a cemetery in Maras and buried a (dead) bureaucrat in it.

Facing the mosque's entrance, go right for a few blocks to reach the **Church of St. George of the Greeks.** Built in the 15th century, it combines both Gothic and Byzantine styles. Its original domed roof was destroyed in the Ottoman invasion; cannonball marks can still be seen on some walls, especially those facing Canbulat Bastion. Back on the other side of Lala Mustafa Paşa, the **Church of St. Peter and St. Paul,** converted to the **Sinan Paşa Mosque,** is a Latin stone church complete with flying buttresses built by a 14th-century merchant from the profits of a single business transaction. Across the road, a car park infringes on the site of the **Venetian Governor's Palace,** but enough walls and ruined staircases still stand to clamber around in.

Next to Sinan Paşa is the **Namik Kemal Museum** in a building where Namik Kemal (1840-1888), the Ottoman poet, was exiled from 1873-1875 for criticizing the sultan. The upper story contains some first editions, photographs, correspondence, and amusing Namik Kemal anecdotes. In a small room downstairs, a gray-faced mannequin of the great writer sits slumped at a writing desk with a blue Faber pencil lying limply between two fingers. Outside is the **Zindan Dungeon,** where visitors can peer through one of two metal grilles into a vaulted stone cell (museum open 9am-noon and 2–4:30pm; admission $1.40, students 15¢).

Follow Liman Yolu between the museum and Lala Mustafa Paşa until you get to the city wall, then take a left onto Cambulat Yolu to get to the 13th-century **Othello's Tower,** the city's oldest building. At ground level, notice the old medieval hall and the dark passages and shafts. Peter Scaliger, the last of the Veronese ruling family, was imprisoned in one of these for 11 years by the Venetians (open approximately 8am-5pm daily; admission $1.50, students 15¢). Opposite Othello's Tower, the **Church of St. George of the Latins** is merely an attractive shell. Then again, so are all the actors on Baywatch, and that's the world's highest-rated TV show.

Continue away from Othello's Tower and the sea to pass, on your left, the twin chapels of the **Knights Templar** and the **Knights of St. John of Jerusalem,** usually kept locked. Next, go straight to reach the **Nestorian Church,** or **Church of St. George the Exiler,** dating from the 14th century. There are a few more old churches near the city wall to your left as you face the sea, but this is now a military zone. If you take a right instead of a left at Petek Pastane, you'll wind up at **Canbulat Museum,** in the bastion. Displays include the tomb of the Ottoman commander and a 16th-century hand-printed Quran. (Open Mon. 7:30am-2pm and 3:30-6pm, Tues.-Fri. 7:30am-2pm. Admission $1.40, students 15¢.)

The beaches around Mağusa are among the largest and most beautiful on the island. **Palm Beach,** located beneath a large hotel from which the beach takes its name, is the closest. From Canbulat Bastion, follow the sea 1km. **Glapsides Beach,** located 14km north of Mağusa, is a broad and wide strip of sand popular with the city residents and university students. Other, quieter beaches can be found up the coast toward the Karpaz Peninsula.

CYPRUS

■ Near Mağusa: Salamis

Legend has it that Salamis, one of the nine ancient cities of Cyprus, was founded in the 11th century BC by **Teucer,** a hero in the *Iliad;* Salamis may have been Homer's birthplace. It was at one time the capital and richest city on the island. The oldest anecdote about Salamis appears in the fifth book of Herodotus, who writes that during the Ionian Revolt of 502 BC, the Persian of Amathus decapitated Onesilos of Salamis and hung his head over the city's gates. When the head became hollow, a swarm of bees moved in and filled it with honeycomb. Interpreting this as a pro-Onesilos gesture on the part of the gods, the Amathusians made yearly sacrifices to their former Salamisian enemy.

In 392 AD, the Emperor Constantius exempted Salamis from taxes in recognition of the damage done to it by the great earthquakes of 332 and 342. In gratitude, the citizens changed Salamis's name to **Constantia,** which stuck through the end of the Byzantine period (1192). It was destroyed by Arab invaders in the 7th century, after which its inhabitants fled to Mağusa. Geologists believe that a severe climate change must have caused the entire city to be covered in sand until its excavation 1000 years later. Salamis was thus spared the looting of the rowdy Middle Ages.

Salamis is 18km from Mağusa. If you haven't already broken down and rented a car, · infrequent, unpredictable buses will drop you at the signposted turn-off. Another choice is the Salamis Bay Hotel Bus, which departs from the 4-star hotel and can drop you off at the turn-off about 80m from the entrance to the site (2.5km from the ruins). It leaves at 10am and 1pm and returns from the *otopark* on Cafer Paşa Sok. in Mağusa (70¢). The bus is intended primarily for hotel guests, but unless you land an atypically rule-loving driver, you won't get kicked off. If you dislike the free-loading stigma, consider staying a night at the **Salamis Bay Hotel** (tel. 387 8201, -6; fax 378 8209, -8337), where the price is quite reasonable for what you get. Large well-furnished rooms have air-conditioning, private bath, TV, minibar, direct-dial phone, free breakfast, free use of the sauna, pool, and tennis courts, and a beach (singles $26; doubles $33).

Roman Salamis

Immediately to the right of the entrance stands Salamis's best preserved building, the **Palaestra,** or gymnasium, built by the Emperors Trajan and Hadrian after an earthquake destroyed the city in 76 AD. Unfortunately, virtually none of the ruins are labeled, and there is no brochure or map, so you'll have to do a little guesswork. The Palaestra was for the use of patrician Roman citizens only; the much more plentiful slaves were responsible for transporting the 50-ton stone columns to Salamis in small wooden boats from Turkey, Greece, and Italy. The Palaestra's swimming pool is surrounded by beautiful marble headless statutes. The heads were pilfered for use as garden ornaments in the 16th and 17th centuries when such things were fashionable.

Beside the Palaestra lie the elaborate baths, comprising the **sudatorium** with baths kept between 86-95°F, the **caldarium** (steam baths, about 77°F), and the **frigidarium** (64-68°F). Also keep an eye out for the occasional mosaic.

To the left, you can lose yourself in the labyrinth of corridors and ruined walls that were once part of residences and public buildings. You also have another opportunity here to marvel at the Romans' endearing and technically sophisticated concern with temperature control. Under many floors, air vaults supported by 2m pillars of terra cotta tile have been exposed. These were **hypocausts,** connected by air ducts to outer furnaces kept stoked day and night by slaves. Nearby is the theater, built around 200 AD under the reign of Augustus. The lower seats are original; those higher up are a 1960s reconstruction. The original seating capacity was 15,000, and the theater was used for gladiator shows and bawdy plays. Other than the old city walls, the only other recognizable relic is the **agora** at the end of a 48km stone aqueduct, surrounded by a by a wrecked colonnade. The city also contains a **Temple of Zeus,** with a podium from which to view the agora, and three basilicas: **St. Epiphanos, Kanpanopetras,** with some interesting mosaics and views, and a third with baptismal basins but no name (site open daily during daylight hours; admission $1.40, students 15¢).

Coming out of the theater, follow the paved road, bearing right at forks, until you get to the main road; cross the street and follow the sign to the St. Barnabas Museum. On the way, you'll pass the interesting **Royal Tombs Museum.** Over 150 of the underground tombs of the kings of Salamis have been excavated and numbered so far. The kings have long ago disintegrated and their grave treasures scattered between other, distant museums, but you can peer through the plate windows at several royal horse skeletons unearthed near the surface of the tombs. From this yard you can also access the stone mausoleum called, for reasons unclear, **St. Katherine's Prison,** dating back to 700 BC. It has yielded countless archaeological curiosities, including an ivory-panelled throne and a bronze cauldron decorated with griffins, now in a southern Cyprus museum (open 8am-sunset; admission $1.40, students 15¢). A couple of hundred meters down is the St. Barnabas Monastery, officially the **St. Barnabas Icon and Archaeological Museum.** According to some, St. Barnabas was a Cypriot Jew from Salamis who was educated in Jerusalem and returned to Cyprus with St. Paul in 45 AD to spread Christianity.

Christian Salamis

The two saints were initially ill-received in Paphos, where Paul was bound to a pillar and beaten, but he then converted the Proconsul to Christianity and Cyprus became the first nation in the world with a Christian ruler. Barnabus, besides helping Paul for several years, was also a scribe, and used to carry a copy of the Gospel of Matthew. He was eventually stoned to death as a traitor by Jews. Some 430 years later, St. Barnabas appeared in a dream to Archbishop Anthemios of Salamis, revealing the location of his grave and the existence of the Gospel. The Archbishop ordered the opening of the grave and found the body identifiable by the hand-written Bible. The Archbishop took the martyr's remains to Emperor Zeno is Istanbul, who declared the autonomy of the Church of Cyprus (previously granted by the Council of Ephesus but challenged by the Patriarchs of Antioch) and commissioned the Monastery of St. Barnabus to be built at the burial site.

The church, which owes its Greek Orthodox appearance to the renovations of Archbishop Philotheas in 1756, houses a fabulous collection of 19th and 20th-century icons. Now an archaeological museum, the monastery contains a very nicely-arranged and labelled range of artifacts, from 9000-year-old rocks to Byzantine **sgraffito** ware scribbled with Picasso-like portraits to possibly the only 2600-year-old toys you will ever see—tiny horse-drawn chariots with real turning wheels. Finally, 150m from the monastery is the **chapel tomb of St. Barnabas.** It is usually unlocked, but if not, get the key from the custodian. The actual body has since been moved to Jerusalem (open daily 8am-6pm; admission $1.40, students 15¢).

▓ Karpaz Peninsula

The Karpaz is northern Cyprus's most remote and inaccessible region. The Karpaz Peninsula extends for roughly 65km into the Gulf of İskenderun and at points is as wide as 20km. The topography resembles a cross between Israel and Los Angeles, with arid, gently sloping hills covered with scrub and wildflowers. Along its main road—the paved road—fields and occasional olive and mulberry groves descend to the sea, although the formerly rich juniper forests have been largely depleted by fires. Sociologically, the peninsula presents the last study of cohabiting Greek and Turkish Cypriots. In **Dipkarpaz,** the largest village in the peninsula, 400 of the 3000 inhabitants are Greek. The two cafes in the village are ethnically distinct; the one with the signs in English is for Greeks. The community exists peacefully if not entirely harmoniously. In 1991, the marriage of a Greek and Turk inspired angry demonstrations.

Accommodations, among other things, are rather scarce on the Karpaz. A few kilometers past **Yenierenköy,** the Karpaz's second largest village, site of the last petrol station, and easternmost point on the peninsula accessible by bus, the small but attractive **Hotel Theresa** (tel. 374 4267, or after 5pm tel. 374 4368) sits next to the 16th-century Therisos Church. It boasts electricity, private showers, a telephone, hot water, and a good restaurant (vegetarian dinner $4.75). Breakfast included (singles $16; doubles $25). In April, Theresa tends to fill up with foreign botanical groups who come to investigate the area's unique vegetation. A nearby island is also known for its bird-watching opportunities. The English-speaking proprietor rents out fishing boats and can direct you to various hiking trails leading to some **Egyptian statues,** an ancient city wall, and gate, and a nameless church with a baobab tree growing out of the floor. His wife, a **medical doctor,** is available for emergency treatment.

The road through Yenierenköy (and past Hotel Theresa) will take you straight to Dipkarpaz. To reach the end of the peninsula, Zafer Burnu (literally "Victory Nose" and somewhat less literally, "Cape Victory"), turn right after Dipkarpaz's Atatürk statue, and rattle down to the sea. The narrow road winds through hills populated almost exclusively by sheep and the occasional shepherd; along the inside seam of the peninsula, vast expanses of sandy beach stand unoccupied. The 37km drive to the Cape spans a landscape equally conducive to the deepest meditation and to the deepest psychosis. Help stave off the violent madness by making sure you have enough gas before you leave—there are no petrol stations after Yenierenköy. Between 2-3km from Zafer Burnu, you'll see signs to Turtle Beach (also called "Big Sands Beach" as well), where **Sea Turtle Restaurant and Camping** (tel. 372 2199) let small wooden, two-person bungalows ($10; breakfast included), if you eat at the restaurant, you can also camp there for free (and use the showers, bathrooms, and phone).

The massive beach with its fine white sand is among the last in the Mediterranean used by the endangered Caretta-Caretta and **Green Turtles** for egg-laying. During July and August, you can observe the turtles frantically paddling sand to dig holes as deep as 1m in which to lay their eggs.

As far as Karpaz's sights are concerned, your first stop should be **Kantara Castle** at the base of the peninsula, perched 724m above sea level in the Five Fingers. The view alone justifies the trip. On a clear day you can see Turkey's Taurus Mountains. Built by Richard the Lionhearted in the 12th century, Kantara was used by the Lusignans and Venetians, then abandoned in the 16th century. To get there from Mağusa, turn off at Boğaz and follow the signs. Three kilometers from the Hotel Theresa, in the village of **Sipahi** (on your right as you follow the village road) lies a ruined 6th century Byzantine basilica with some preserved mosaics. Entrance is free.

The peninsula's real claim to fame is the Greek Orthodox **Apostolos Andreas Monastery,** set in a vast, empty square, at the tip of Zafer Buran, approximately 25 poorly paved kilometers from Dipkarpaz. Some Christians believe that St. Andreas traveled to Palestine on a ship navigated by a half-blind captain. St. Andreas struck a rock where the monastery now stands, bashing open a magical spring which restored the captain's sight. Although St. Andreas was always an important figure locally, a 1912 "miracle" landed Apostolos Andreas on the international pilgrimage circuit. A Greek mother was reunited with her son who had been kidnapped 17 years earlier after St. Andreas appeared to her in a dream and told her to make a pilgrimage to Apotolos Andreas. Karpaz was then visited by thousands en route to Jerusalem, although its only pilgrims today are Greeks from Dipkarpaz who file down to the icon-filled chapel in a progression of rattle-trap 1950s-era buses. The monastery is open daylight hours and is free.

Transportation to the Karpaz is difficult if you don't have a car. There are village **buses** from Lefkoşa (11am) and Mağusa (noon), but only as far as Yenierenköy, leaving you to negotiate another 60km, not to mention a ride back. The quoted cab fare to Dipkarpaz and back is a depressing $135. You can bargain a bored taxi driver down to about $50 for the whole enterprise, including a stop at the monastery, but most companies won't go any lower. If you can't rent a car, your best bets is a guided tour. Apple Tours (see **Bellapais,** p. 588) offers a $40 day full-day tour every Monday and Wednesday, visiting Kantara, some churches, a beach, and Apostolos Andreas.

APPENDIX

HOLIDAYS AND FESTIVALS

■ Greece

Jan. 1: Feast of St. Basil. Carrying on a Byzantine tradition, Greeks cut a New Year's sweet bread called *Vassilopita*, baked with a coin inside. The person who gets the slice with the coin is that year's lucky person.

Jan. 6: Epiphany. Celebrated in the West as the day the Magi appeared in Bethlehem to greet the baby Jesus; in the Eastern church Epiphany is recognized as the day Jesus was baptized by St. John. In Greece, *kallikantzaroi* (goblins) appear between Christmas and Epiphany. Village bonfires scare them away. At Epiphany, waters are blessed and evil spirits leave the earth. Crosses are thrown into harbors all around Greece and the young men who fetch them are considered blessed.

Feb. 8-March 2: Carnival. Three weeks of feasting and dancing before the Lenten fast begins on March 2. Notable celebrations occur in Patras and Cephalonia.

March 25: Greek Independence Day. Commemorates the 1821 struggle against the Turkish Ottoman Empire. Also a religious holiday, the Feast of the Annunciation, when the angel Gabriel told Mary of the Incarnation.

April 17: Good Friday. People carry candles in a procession through town or around the church in one of the Greek church's most moving liturgies.

April 19: Easter. The most holy day in the Greek calendar. After a midnight mass that is followed by a meal, celebrations on Easter Sunday typically include feasting on spit-roasted lamb and red-dyed hard-boiled eggs, followed by dancing.

April 23: St. George's Day. Celebration in honor of the dragon-slaying knight. Festivities at Limnos, Chania include horse races, wrestling matches, and dances.

May 1: Labor Day. Also Feast of the Flowers. Wreaths of flowers hung outside people's doors. The odd Communist demonstration.

June 8: The Day of the Holy Spirit. This national religious holiday takes place 40-50 days after Easter and is celebrated differently in each region.

June 7: Pentecost. Celebrated 50 days after Easter.

Aug. 15: Feast of the Assumption of the Virgin Mary. Celebration throughout Greece, particularly on Tinos, in honor of Mary's ascent to Heaven.

Sept. 8: The Virgin's Birthday. In some villages an auction is held to determine who will carry the Virgin's icon. The money is used to provide a village feast.

Oct. 26: Feast of St. Demetrius. Celebrated with particular enthusiasm in Thessaloniki. The feast coincides with the opening of new wine.

Oct. 28: National Anniversary of Greek Independence. Called "*Ohi* Day" in honor of Metaxas's famous "*Ohi*" (No) to Mussolini.

Nov. 17: Commemoration of the rise of the Greek university students against the junta of 1974. Speeches are presented at the University of Athens.

Dec. 24-25: Christmas. As part of the festivities, children traditionally make the rounds singing *kalanda* (Christmas carols).

■ Turkey

Dec. 30, 1997-Jan. 28, 1998: Ramadan (Ramazan). A month-long Islamic holiday during which Muslims abstain from eating, drinking, smoking, and sex between dawn and sunset. Each day's fast is broken with a feast. Only one or two restaurants may be open during the day in the smaller towns and inland, and in such areas it is inappropriate to eat or drink openly during the daytime. The dates for Ramazan change with the lunar calendar, so these dates are only accurate for 1997.

Jan. 1: New Year's Day.

Jan. 29: Sugar Holiday (Şeker Bayramı). A three-day holiday celebrating the end of Ramazan, an occasion for gift-giving and sweets for children. Eating and drinking in public is encouraged. Banks and holidays close all three days.

April 23: National Sovereignty and Children's Day (Ulusal Egemenlik ve Çocuk Bayramı). Commemorates the first meeting of the Grand National Assembly in Ankara in 1920. An international children's festival is held in Ankara.

May 1: May Day. May 1 is Turkey's labor day; labor protests abound.

April 7-April 10: Festival of Sacrifice (Kurban Bayramı). The most important holiday of the year, this festival recalls Abraham's sacrificial offering of Ismael to God on Mt. Moriah. 2½ million sheep are slaughtered each year in Turkey to honor the faith and piety of Abraham. Offices close for up to a week. The dates for Kurban Bayramı change with the lunar calendar, so these dates only apply for 1997.

May 19: Youth and Sports Day. Mustafa Kemal Atatürk decided to commemorate Turkey's youth and tomorrow's future on this day.

Aug. 30: Victory Day. Anniversary of the final rout of Western invaders, 1922.

Oct. 29: Republic Day (Cumhuriyet Bayramı). Largest civil holiday commemorates Atatürk's proclamation of the Turkish Republic in 1923. Ubiquitous parades.

Nov. 10: Marks the anniversary of Atatürk's death in 1938. At 9:05am (the time of death), all of Turkey stops for a moment of national mourning; horns are blown.

Dec. 19, 1998-Jan. 17, 1999: Ramadan.

▧ Cyprus

Both southern and northern Cyprus observe not only Greece and Turkey's holidays, respectively, but also hold their own regional and local festivities. Consult the C.T.O. or the T.C.I.O. for more information.

CLIMATE

Temp in °C Rain in mm	January Temp	Rain	April Temp	Rain	July Temp	Rain	October Temp	Rain
Athens	12.0	62.0	19	23.0	33.0	6.0	23.0	51.0
Salonika	5.5	44.0	15	41.0	26.5	22.0	17.5	57.0
Ankara	0.0	40.5	11	40.3	23.0	13.5	13.0	24.4
Antalya	10.0	247.5	16	43.3	28.0	2.4	20.0	62.6
Istanbul	5.0	109.0	12	46.0	23.0	34.0	16.0	81.0
Trabzon	6.0	85.2	11	58.4	22.0	37.0	15.0	113.2
Nicosia	10.0	76.0	18	18.0	29.0	1.0	21.0	25.0

TELEPHONE

▧ City Codes

Greece 30

Aegina	0297	Kalamata	0721	Paleochora	0823
Agia Galini	0832	Kalambaka	0432	Parga	0684
Agios Nikolaos	0841	Kalavrita	0692	Paros	0284
Agria	0423	Kalymnos	0243	Patmos	0247
Alexandropoulis	0551	Kardamili	0721	Patras	061
Amorgos	0285	Karpathos	0245	Petalidio	0722
Andritsena	0626	Karpenisi	0237	Piraeus	01
Andros	0282	Karystos	0224	Poros	0298
Arachova	0267	Kastoria	0467	Pouri	0422

Astypalea	0243	Kavala	051	Pylos	0723
Athens	01	Kea	0288	Rafina	0294
Cape Sounion	0292	Kellini	0623	Rethymnon	0831
Cephalonia	0671	Kimi	0222	Rhodes	0241
Chalkida	0221	Kithnos	0281	Samos	0273
Chania	0821	Kos	0242	Samothraki	0551
Chios	0271	Kyparissia	0761	Serifos	0281
Chora Sfakion	0825	Kythera	0735	Sifnos	0284
Corfu	0661-3	Lefkada	0645	Sithonia	0375
Corinth	0741	Lesvos	0251	Sitia	0843
Delphi	0265	Lia	0664	Skiathos	0427
Dimitsana	0795	Limni	0227	Skopelos	0424
Edessa	0381	Limnos	0254	Skyros	0222
Epidavros	0753	Litohoro	0352	Sparta	0731
Eritrea	0221	Matala	0892	Symi	0241
Galaxidi	0265	Methoni	0723	Syros	0281
Gythion	0733	Metsovo	0656	Thassos	0593
Hersonissos	0897	Milos	0287	Thebes	0262
Ierapetra	0842	Monemvassia	0732	Thessaloniki	031
Igoumenitsa	0665	Mt. Athos	0377	Tinos	0283
Ikaria	0275	Mycenae	0751	Tripoli	071
Ioannina	0651	Mykonos	0289	Volos	0421
Ios Village	0286	Nauplion	0752	Xilokastro	0743
Iraklion	081	Naxos	0285	Zagora	0426
Isthmia	0746	Neapolis	0734	Zakinthos	0695
Ithaka	0674	Olympia	0624		
Itilo	0733	Osios Loukas	0267		

Turkey 90

Adana	322	Fethiye	252	Marmaris	252
Ankara	312	Göreme	384	Olimpos	242
Antakya	326	Hopa	466	Ölüdeniz	252
Antalya	242	Ihlara	382	Pamukkale	258
Aphrodisias	256	Istanbul (Euro)	212	Patara	242
Artvin	466	Istanbul (Asia)	216	Pergamon	232
Ayvalık	266	Izmir	232	Rize	464
Bodrum	252	Iznik	224	Safranbolu	372
Bursa	224	Kâhta	416	Selçuk	232
Çanakkale	286	Kalkan	242	Taşucu	324
Çeşme	232	Kars	474	Trabzon	462
Datça	252	Kaş	242	Urfa	414
Edirne	284	Konya	332	Ürgüp	384
Eğirdir	246	Kuşadası	256	Yusufeli	466

Cyprus 357

Agia Napa	03	Nicosia	02	Podromos	0295
Larnaka	04	Pano Platres	05	Polis	06
Limassol	05	Paphos	06		

■ Country Codes

Country	Access Number
Australia	61
Canada	1
Cyprus	357
Greece	30
Ireland	353
New Zealand	64
Northern Cyprus	90 392
South Africa	27
Turkey	90
U.K.	44
U.S.A.	1

■ Calling Home

Company / Country	Access Number
AT&T	
Greece	00 800 1311
Turkey & Northern Cyprus	00 800 12277
Cyprus	080 90010
MCI	
Greece	00 800 1211
Turkey & Northern Cyprus	00 800 11177
Cyprus	080 90000
Sprint	
Greece	00 800 1411
Turkey & Northern Cyprus	00 800 14477
Cyprus	080 90001

TIME ZONES

Greece, Turkey, and Cyprus are all two hours ahead of GMT, seven hours ahead of EST, and ten hours ahead of PST.

Daylight savings time (spring ahead, fall back…) is: between the last Sunday of March and last Sunday in September in Greece and southern Cyprus; and between the first weekend of April and last weekend in September in Turkey and northern Cyprus.

WEIGHTS AND MEASURES

■ Conversion Chart

1 centimeter (cm) = 0.39 inches	1 inch = 2.54cm
1 meter (m) = 3.28 feet	1 foot = 0.31m
1 kilometer (km) = 0.62 miles	1 mile = 1.61km
1 gram (g) = 0.04 ounces	1 ounce = 28g
1 kilogram (kg) = 2.2 pounds	1 pound = 0.45kg
1 liter (l) = 0.26 gallons	1 gallon = 3.76l
1 Imperial Gallon (U.K.) = 1.2 gallons	1 gallon = .83 Imperial Gallons
°F = (°C x 1.8) + 32	°C = (°F - 32) x .56

■ Temperature Conversions

To convert from Fahrenheit degrees into Celsius, subtract 32 and multiply by 5/9.
To from Celsius to Fahrenheit, multiply by 9/5 and add 32.

°C	-5	0	5	10	15	20	25	30	35	40
°F	23	32	41	50	59	68	77	86	95	104

GLOSSARY

■ Greek

The table of the Greek alphabet (only 24 letters) below will help you decipher signs.
The left column gives you the names of the letters in Greek, the middle column
shows the printed lower case and capital letters, and the right column provides the
approximate pronunciations of the letters.

alpha	α A	*a* as in father
beta	β B	*v* as in velvet
gamma	γ Γ	before vowels, *y* as in ya-hoo; otherwise a hard *g* as in guest pronounced in the back of the throat
delta	δ Δ	*th* as in there
epsilon	ε E	*e* as in jet
zeta	ζ Z	*z* as in zebra
eta	η H	*ee* as in queen
theta	θ Θ	*th* as in health
iota	ι I	*ee* as in tree
kappa	κ K	*k* as in cat
lambda	λ Λ	*l* as in land
mu	μ M	*m* as in moose
nu	ν N	*n* as in net
ksi	ξ Ξ	*x* as in mix
omicron	o O	*o* as in row
pi	π Π	*p* as in peace
rho	ρ P	*r* as in roll
sigma	σ (ς), Σ	*s* as in sense
tau	τ T	*t* as in tent
upsilon	υ Y	*ee* as in green
phi	φ Φ	*f* as in fog
xi	χ X	*ch* (*h*) as in horse
psi	ψ Ψ	*ps* as in oops
omega	ω Ω	*o* as in glow

Greetings and Courtesies

Good morning	ΚΑΛΗΜΕΡΑ	kah-lee-ME-rah
Good evening	ΚΑΛΗΣΠΕΡΑ	kah-lee-SPE-rah
Good night	ΚΑΛΗΝΥΧΤΑ	kah-lee-NEE-khtah
yes	ΝΑΙ	NEH
no	ΟΧΙ	OH-hee
please/you're welcome	ΠΑΡΑΚΑΛΩ	pah-rah-kah-LO
thank you (very much)	ΕΥΧΑΡΙΣΤΩ	ef-hah-ree-STO (po-LEE)
excuse me	ΣΥΓΓΝΩΜΗ	seeg-NO-mee
hello (polite, plural)	ΓΕΙΑ ΣΑΣ	YAH-sas

hello (familiar)	ΓΕΙΑ ΣΟΥ	YAH-soo
OK	ΕΝΤΑΞΕΙ	en-DAHK-see
What is your name?	ΠΩΣ ΣΕ ΛΕΝΕ	pos-se-LEH-neh
My name is ...	ΜΕ ΛΕΝΕ	me-LEH-neh ...
Would you like some red wine?	ΜΗΠΟΣ ΘΕΛΕΙΣ ΛΙΓΟ ΚΟΚΚΙΝΟ ΚΡΑΣΙ;	ME-pos THEL-ees LE-go KO-kee-no kra-SEE?
Mr./Sir	ΚΥΡΙΟΣ	kee-REE-os
Ms./Madam	ΚΥΡΙΑ	kee-REE-ah

Directions

Where is ... ?	ΠΟΥ ΕΙΝΑΙ	pou-EE-neh ... ?
I'm going to ...	ΠΗΓΑΙΝΩ ΓΙΑ	pee-YEH-no yah ...
When do we leave?	ΤΙ ΩΡΑ ΦΕΥΓΟΥΜΕ	tee O-rah FEV-goo-meh?
restaurant	ΕΣΤΙΑΤΟΡΙΟ	es-tee-ah-TO-ree-o
post office	ΤΑΧΥΔΡΟΜΕΙΟ	ta-khee-dhro-MEE-o
market	ΑΓΟΡΑ	ah-go-RAH
museum	ΜΟΥΣΕΙΟ	mou-SEE-o
pharmacy	ΦΑΡΜΑΚΕΙΟ	fahr-mah-KEE-o
bank	ΤΡΑΠΕΖΑ	TRAH-peh-zah
church	ΕΚΚΛΗΣΙΑ	eh-klee-SEE-ah
hotel	ΞΕΝΟΔΟΧΕΙΟ	kse-no-dho-HEE-o
room	ΔΩΜΑΤΙΟ	dho-MAH-teeo
suitcase	ΒΑΛΙΤΣΑ	vah-LEE-tsah
airport	ΑΕΡΟΔΡΟΜΙΟ	ah-e-ro-DHRO-mee-o
airplane	ΑΕΡΟΠΛΑΝΟ	ah-e-ro-PLAH-no
train	ΤΡΑΙΝΟ	TREH-no
bus	ΛΕΩΦΟΡΕΙΟ	leh-o-fo-REE-o
ferry	ΠΛΟΙΟ	PLEE-o
ticket	ΕΙΣΙΤΗΡΙΟ	ee-see-TEE-ree-o
hospital	ΝΟΣΟΚΟΜΕΙΟ	no-so-ko-ME-o
port	ΛΙΜΑΝΙ	lee-MA-nee
toilet	ΤΟΥΑΛΕΤΑ	twa-LE–ta
police	ΑΣΤΥΝΟΜΙΑ	as-tee-no-ME-a
archaeology	ΑΡΧΑΙΟΛΟΓΙΑ	ark-ha-o-lo-GEE-a
bar	ΜΠΑΡ	BAR
doctor	ΓΙΑΤΡΟΣ	yah-TROS
right	ΔΕΞΙΑ	dhek-see-AH
left	ΑΡΙΣΤΕΡΑ	ah-rees-teh-RAH
here, there	ΕΔΩ, ΕΚΕΙ	eh-DHO, eh-KEE
open, closed	ΑΝΟΙΧΤΟ, ΚΛΕΙΣΤΩ	ah-nee-KTO, klee-STO

Prices

How much?	ΠΟΣΟ ΚΑΝΕΙ	PO-so KAH-nee
I need	ΧΡΕΙΑΖΟΜΑΙ	khree-AH-zo-meh
I want	ΘΕΛΩ	THEH-lo
I would like ...	ΘΑ ΗΘΕΛΑ	thah EE-the-lah ...
I will buy this one	ΘΑ ΑΓΟΡΑΣΩ ΑΥΤΟ	thah ah-go-RAH-so ahf-TO
Do you have?	ΕΧΕΤΕ	Eh-khe-teh
Can I see a room?	ΜΠΟΡΩ ΝΑ ΔΩ ΕΝΑ ΔΩΜΑΤΙΟ	bo-RO nah-DHO E-nah dho-MAH-tee-o
bill	ΛΟΓΑΡΙΑΣΜΟ	lo-gahr-yah-SMO
newspaper	ΕΦΗΜΕΡΙΔΑ	eh-fee-meh-REE-dha
water	ΝΕΡΟ	ne-RO
good	ΚΑΛΟ	kah-LO

| cheap | ΦΤΗΝΟ | ftee-NO |
| expensive | ΑΚΡΙΒΟ | ah-kree-VO |

Time

What time is it?	ΤΙ ΩΡΑ ΕΙΝΑΙ	tee-O-rah EE-neh?
yesterday	ΧΘΕΣ	k-THES
today	ΣΗΜΕΡΑ	SEE-mer-a
tomorrow	ΑΥΡΙΟ	AV-ree-o
first	ΠΡΩΤΟ	PRO-to
morning	ΠΡΩΙ	pro-EE
evening	ΒΡΑΔΥ	VRAH-dhee
later tonight	ΑΠΟΨΕ	ah-PO-pseh
last	ΤΕΛΕΥΤΑΙΟ	teh-lef-TEH-o

Numbers

zero	ΜΗΔΕΝ	mee-DHEN
one	ΕΝΑ	Eh-nah
two	ΔΥΟ	DHEE-o
three	ΤΡΙΑ	TREE-ah
four	ΤΕΣΣΕΡΑ	TES-ser-ah
five	ΠΕΝΤΕ	PEN-dheh
six	ΕΞΙ	E-ksee
seven	ΕΠΤΑ	ep-TAH
eight	ΟΚΤΩ	okh-TO
nine	ΕΝΝΙΑ	en-YAH
ten	ΔΕΚΑ	DHEH-kah
eleven	ΕΝΔΕΚΑ	EN-dheh-kah
twelve	ΔΩΔΕΚΑ	DHO-dheh-kah
thirteen	ΔΕΚΑΤΡΙΑ	DHEH-kah TREE-ah
fourteen	ΔΕΚΑΤΕΣΣΕΡΑ	DHEH-kah TES-ser-ah
fifteen	ΔΕΚΑΠΕΝΤΕ	DHEH-kah PEN-dheh
sixteen	ΔΕΚΑΕΞΙ	DHEH-kah E-ksee
seventeen	ΔΕΚΑΕΠΤΑ	DHEH-kah ep-TAH
eighteen	ΔΕΚΑΟΚΤΩ	DHEH-kah okh-TO
nineteen	ΔΕΚΑΕΝΝΙΑ	DHEH-kah en-YAH
twenty	ΕΙΚΟΣΙ	EE-ko-see
thirty	ΤΡΙΑΝΤΑ	tree-AN-dah
forty	ΣΑΡΑΝΤΑ	sa-RAN-dah
fifty	ΠΕΝΗΝΤΑ	pen-EEN-dah
sixty	ΕΞΗΝΤΑ	ex-EEN-dah
seventy	ΕΒΔΟΜΗΝΤΑ	ev-dho-MEEN-dah
eighty	ΟΓΔΟΝΤΑ	og-DHON-dah
ninety	ΕΝΕΝΗΝΤΑ	en-EEN-dah
hundred	ΕΚΑΤΟ	ek-ah-TO
thousand	ΧΙΛΙΑ(ΔΕΣ)	hil-ee-AH(dhes)
million	ΕΚΑΤΟΜΜΥΡΙΟ	eka-to-MEE-rio

Problems

Do you speak English?	ΜΙΛΑΣ ΑΓΓΛΙΚΑ	mee-LAHS ahn-glee-KAH?
I don't speak Greek	ΔΕΝ ΜΙΛΑΩ ΕΛΛΗΝΙΚΑ	dhen mee-LAHO el-leen-ee-KAH
I don't understand	ΔΕΝ ΚΑΤΑΛΑΒΑΙΝΩ	dhen kah-tah-lah-VEH-no
I am lost	ΧΑΘΗΚΑ	HA-thee-ka
I am ill	ΕΙΜΑΙ ΑΡΡΩΣΤΟΣ	EE-meh AH-ross-toss

| Where is my toothbrush? | ΠΟΥ ΕΙΝΑΙ ΤΗΝ ΟΔΟ–ΝΤΟΒΟΥΡΤΣΑ ΜΟΥ | pou EE-nay teen o-DHON-dho-voo-tsa mou? |
| Help! | ΒΟΗΘΕΙΑ | vo-EE-thee-ah |

■ Turkish

Be aware that certain letters and combinations of letters in Turkish are pronounced differently than the English. Turkish is a phonetic language: each letter has only one sound, and this is always pronounced distinctly. Words are usually lightly accented on the last syllable; special vowels, consonants, and combinations include:

Turkish	English
c	*j* as in jacket
ç	*ch* as in check
ğ	lengthens adjacent vowels
ı	(no dot on the "i") *i* as in hit
i	*ee* as in peace
j	*zh* as in pleasure, or *j* as in French *jadis*
ö	*ö* as in German *könig*, or *eu* as in French *deux*
ş	*sh* as in short
u	*oo* as in boot
â	dipthong of *ea*, or faint *ya*
ü	*ew* as in cue
ay	*eye* as in pie
ey	*ay* as in play
oy	*oy* as in toy
uy	*oo-ee* as in phooey

Greetings and Courtesies

good morning	*günaydın*	gewn eye-DUHN
good evening	*iyi akşamlar*	ee-YEE ahk-sham-LAR
good night	*iyi geceler*	ee-YEE geh-jeh-LEHR
yes, no	*evet, hayır*	EH-vet, HIGH-yuhr
please	*lütfen*	LEWT-fen
thank you (formal)	*teşekkürler*	tay-shayk-kewr-LEHR
thank you (informal)	*sağol*	SAA-ohl
you're welcome	*bir şey değil*	beer shay DEE-yeel
pardon me	*affedersiniz*	ahf-feh-DEHR-see-neez
hello	*merhaba*	MEHR-hah-bah
good bye (said by a guest)	*allaha ısmarladık*	aw-LAH-huss-small-duck
good bye (said by a host)	*güle güle*	gcw-LAY-gew-lay
beautiful, good	*güzel*	gew-ZEHL
okay	*pekiyi*	PEHK-ee-yee
What is your name?	*İsminiz ne?*	ees-meen-eez NEH
Would you like some white wine?	*Biraz beyaz şarap itermisin?*	beer-az bay-az sharap ist-aer-me-sin?
My name is ...	*İsmim ...*	ees-MEEM
Mr./Sir	*Bay*	Bye
Ms./Madam	*Bayan*	Bye-AHN

Directions

Where is... ?	*...nerede?*	...NEHR-eh-deh
I'm traveling to...	*...ya seyahat ediyorum*	...ya say-yah-HAHT eh-dee-OHR-room
How near is it?	*Ne kadar yakın?*	NEH-kah-dahr yah-KUN

post office	*postane*	post-aaaah-NEH
museum	*müze*	mew-ZEH
hotel	*otel*	oh-TEL
room	*yer, oda*	OH-da
toilet	*tuvalet*	too-vah-LET
airport	*hava alanı*	hah-VAH-ah-lahn-uh
bus	*otobüs*	oh-toh-BOOS
doctor	*doktor*	dohk-TOHR
grocery	*bakkal*	bahk-KAHL
pharmacy	*eczane*	ej-zaaaah-NEH
bank	*banka*	BAHN-kah
police	*polis*	poh-LEES
left, right	*sol, sağ*	sohl, saah
passport	*pasaport*	pahs-ah-PORT
train	*tren*	trehn
ticket	*bilet*	bee-LET
here, there	*burada, orada*	BOOR-ah-dah, OHR-ah-dah
open, closed	*açık, kapalı*	ah-CHUHK, kah-pah-LUH

Prices

How much is it?	*Kaç para?* or *Ne kadar?*	KACH-pah-rah NEH-kah-dar
I want ...	*Óistiyorum*	ees-tee-YOH-room...
a double room	*iki kişilik oda*	ee-KEE kee-shee-leek OH-dah
a twin-bedded room	*çift yataklı oda*	CHEEFT yah-tahk-LUH OH-dah
I do not want any.	*Yok.*	YOHK
cheap, expensive	*ucuz, pahalı*	oo-JOOZ, pah-hah-LUH
bill (as in check)	*hesap*	hessahp
water	*su*	soo

Time

What time is it?	*Saat kaç?*	SAH-aht kahch
yesterday	*dün*	dewn
today	*bugün*	boo-GEWN
tomorrow	*yarın*	YAHR-uhn

Numbers

zero	*sıfır*	SUF-fuhr
quarter	*çeyrek*	chay-REK
half a...	*yarım*	yahr-UHM
one	*bir*	beer
...and a half	*Óbuçuk*	boo-CHOOK
two	*iki*	ee-KEE
three	*üç*	ewch
four	*dört*	duhrt
five	*beş*	besh
six	*altı*	ahl-TUH
seven	*yedi*	yeh-DEE
eight	*sekiz*	seh-KEEZ
nine	*dokuz*	DOH-kooz
ten	*on*	ohn
eleven	*on bir*	OHN-bir
twelve	*on iki*	OHN-ee-kee

thirteen	on üç	OHN-ewch
twenty	yirmi	yeer-MEE
thirty	otuz	OH-tooz
forty	kırk	kirk
fifty	elli	ehl-LEE
sixty	altmış	ahlt-MUSH
seventy	yetmiş	yet-MEESH
eighty	seksen	sehk-SEN
ninety	doksan	dohk-SAHN
hundred	yüz	yewz
thousand	bin	been
million	milyon	meel-YOHN

Problems

I don't understand.	Anlamadım.	ahn-LAH-mah-duhm
Do you speak English?	İngilizçe biliyor musunuz?	EEN-ghee-leez-jeh bee-lee-YOHR-moo-soo-nooz
I don't speak Turkish.	Türkçe bilmiyorum.	TEWRK-cheh BEEHL-mee-yohr-oom
I'm lost!	Yolumu kaybettim!	YOHL-loo-moo KIGH-bet-tim
I am ill.	Hastayım.	hahs-TAH-yuhm
Where's my toothbrush?	Diş fırçam nerede?	deesh fir-cham naer-eh-de?
Help!	İmdat!	im-DAHT

Greek Language Index

Greek Name	English Name	Page
ΑΓΙΑ ΓΑΛΗΝΗ	Agia Galini	192
ΑΓΙΑ ΝΑΠΑ	Agia Napa	565
ΑΓΙΟΣ ΝΙΚΟΛΑΟΣ	Agios Nikolaos	206
ΑΓΟΡΑ	Agora	83
ΑΘΗΝΑ	Athens	66
ΑΘΩΣ–ΑΓΙΟΝ ΟΡΟΣ	Mount Athos	132
ΑΙΓΙΝΑ	Aegina	303
ΑΛΕΞΑΝΔΡΟΥΠΟΛΗ	Alexandroupolis	134
ΑΛΟΝΝΗΣΟΣ	Alonissos	320
ΑΜΟΡΓΟΣ	Amorgos	245
ΑΝΔΡΟΣ	Andros	255
ΑΡΕΟΠΟΛΗ	Areopolis	177
ΑΡΓΟΛΙΔΑ	Argolis	138
ΑΡΓΟΣ	Argos	147
ΑΡΚΑΔΙΑ	Arcadia	163
ΑΣΤΥΠΑΛΑΙΑ	Astypalea	292
ΑΧΑΙΑ	Achaïa	153
ΒΕΡΓΙΝΑ	Vergina	125
ΒΙΚΟΣ	Vikos Gorge	117
ΒΟΛΟΣ	Volos	104
ΓΑΛΑΞΙΔΙ	Galaxidi	97
ΓΥΘΕΙΟ	Gythion	175
ΔΑΦΝΗ	Daphni	86
ΔΕΛΘΟΙ	Delphi	91
ΔΗΛΟΣ	Delos	221
ΔΗΜΗΤΣΑΝΑ	Dimitsana	165
ΔΙΑΚΟΦΤΟ	Diakofto	158
ΔΩΔΕΚΑΝΗΣΑ	Dodecanese	266
ΔΩΔΩΝΗ	Dodoni	117
ΕΔΕΣΣΑ	Edessa	125
ΕΛΛΑΔΑΑ	Greece	47
ΕΠΙΔΑΥΡΟΕ	Epidavros	152
ΕΡΜΟΥΠΟΛΙΣ	Hermoupolis	252
ΕΥΒΟΙΑ	Evia	98
ΕΥΡΥΤΑΝΙΑ	Evritania	111
ΗΓΟΥΜΕΝΙΤΣΑ	Igoumenitsa	112

Greek Name	English Name	Page
ΗΗΡΑΚΛΙΟΝ	Iraklion (Heraklion)	184
ΗΠΕΙΡΟΣ	Epirus	112
ΘΑΣΟΣ	Thassos	340
ΘΕΣΣΑΛΙΑ	Thessaly	104
ΘΕΣΣΑΛΟΝΙΚΗ	Thessaloniki	118
ΘΗΒΑ	Thebes	97
ΘΗΡΑ	Thira (see Santorini)	226
ΘΡΑΚΗ	Thrace	133
ΙΕΡΑΠΕΤΡΑ	Ierapetra	209
ΙΘΑΚΗ	Ithaka	358
ΙΚΑΡΙΑ	Ikaria	338
ΙΟΣ	Ios	222
ΙΤΕΑ	Itea	96
ΙΩΑΝΝΙΝΑ	Ioannina	115
ΚΑΒΑΛΑ	Kavala	135
ΚΑΛΑΜΑΤΑ	Kalamata	166
ΚΑΛΑΜΠΑΚΑ	Kalambaka	108
ΚΑΛΑΒΡΥΤΑ	Kalavrita	159
ΚΑΛΥΜΝΟΣ	Kalymnos	284
ΚΑΜΑΡΕΣ	Kamares	261
ΚΑΡΠΑΘΟΣ	Karpathos	293
ΚΑΡΠΕΝΗΣΙ	Karpenisi	111
ΚΑΡΥΣΤΟΖ	Karystos	101
ΚΑΣΤΟΠΙΑ	Kastoria	127
ΚΕΡΚΥΡΑ	Corfu	346
ΚΕΦΑΛΛΟΝΙΑ	Cephalonia	360
ΚΟΠΙΝΘΙΑ	Corinthia	138
ΚΟΡΙΝΘΟΣ	Corinth	138
ΚΠΗΤΗ	Crete	182
ΚΥΘΗΡΑ	Kythera	179
ΚΥΚΛΑΔΕΣ	Cyclades	216
ΚΥΛΛΗΝΗ	Killini	159
ΚΩΣ	Kos	277
ΛΑΚΩΝΙΑ	Laconia	171
ΛΑΡΝΑΚΑ	Larnaka	560
ΛΕΜΕΣΟΣ	Limassol (Lemesos)	567
ΛΕΣΒΟΣ	Lesvos	329

Greek Name	English Name	Page
ΛΕΥΚΑΔΑ	Lefkada	355
ΛΕΥΚΩΣΙΑ	Nicosia (Lefkosia)	557
ΛΗΜΝΟΣ	Limnos	343
ΛΙΝΔΟΣ	Lindos	275
ΛΟΥΤΡΑΚΙ	Loutraki	143
ΜΑΚΕΔΟΝΙΑ	Macedonia	118
ΜΑΚΡΥΝΙΤΣΑ	Makrinitsa	106
ΜΑΛΙΑ	Malia	205
ΜΑΝΗ	Mani	175
ΜΑΤΑΛΑ	Matala	190
ΜΕΘΩΝΗ	Methoni	170
ΜΕΣΣΗΝΙΑ	Messenia	166
ΜΕΤΕΩΡΑ	Meteora	107
ΜΕΤΣΟΒΟ	Metsovo	109
ΜΙΚΟΝΟΣ	Mykonos	216
ΜΗΛΟΣ	Milos	258
ΜΟΝΕΜΒΑΣΙΑ	Monemvassia	178
ΜΥΚΗΝΑΙ	Mycenae	145
ΜΥΚΟΝΟΣ	Mykonos	216
ΜΥΣΤΡΑΣ	Mystra	174
ΝΑΞΟΣ	Naxos	240
ΝΑΥΠΛΙΟ	Nauplion	149
ΝΗΣΙΑ ΤΟΥ ΑΙΓΑΙΟΥ	Aegean Islands	326
ΝΗΣΙΑ ΤΟΥ ΙΟΝΙΟΥ	Ionian Islands	346
ΝΙΣΥΡΟΣ	Nisyros	300
ΟΛΥΜΠΙΑ	Olympia	160
ΟΛΥΜΠΟΣ	Mount Olympus	128
ΟΛΥΜΒΟΖ	Olymbos	297
ΟΡΟΣ ΠΗΛΙΟ	Mount Pelion Peninsula	106
ΠΑΛΕΟΧΟΡΑ	Paleochora	200
ΠΑΡΓΑ	Parga	114
ΠΑΡΟΣ	Paros	233
ΠΑΤΜΟΣ	Patmos	288
ΠΑΤΡΑΣ	Patras	154
ΠΑΦΟΣ	Paphos	573
ΠΕΙΡΑΙΑΣ	Peiraias	87
ΠΕΛΟΠΟΝΗΣΟΣ	Peloponnese	138
ΠΛΑΚΙΑΣ	Plakias	196

Greek Name	English Name	Page
ΠΟΘΙΑ	Pothia	284
ΠΟΛΙΣ	Polis	577
ΠΟΡΟΣ	Poros	306
ΠΥΛΟΣ	Pylos	169
ΠΥΡΓΟΣ ΔΙΡΟΥ	Pirgos Dirou	178
ΡΕΘΥΜΝΟ	Rethymnon	193
ΡΟΔΟΣ	Rhodes	266
ΣΑΜΟΘΡΑΚΗ	Samothraki	342
ΣΑΜΟΣ	Samos	335
ΣΑΝΤΟΡΙΝΗ	Santorini	226
ΣΕΡΙΦΟΣ	Serifos	264
ΣΗΤΕΙΑ	Sitia	210
ΣΙΘΩΝΙΑ	Sithonia	131
ΣΙΦΝΟΣ	Sifnos	261
ΣΚΑΛΑ	Skala	130, 288
ΣΚΙΑΘΟΣ	Skiathos	314
ΣΚΟΠΕΛΟΣ	Skopelos	317
ΣΚΥΡΟΣ	Skyros	322
ΣΠΑΡΤΗ	Sparta	172
ΣΠΕΤΣΕΣ	Spetses	311
ΣΠΟΡΑΔΕΣ	Sporades	314
ΣΤΕΜΝΙΤΣΑ	Stemnitsa	165
ΣΥΜΗ	Symi	298
ΣΥΡΟΣ	Syros	252
ΤΑ ΝΗΣΙΑ ΤΟΥ ΣΑΡΩΝΙΚΟΥ	Saronic Gluf Islands	303
ΤΗΝΟΣ	Tinos	248
ΤΡΙΠΟΛΙΗ	Tripoli	163
ΤΡΟΟΔΟΣ	Troodos Mountains	571
ΦΟΙΝΙΚΟΥΝΤΑΣ	Finikountas	171
ΧΑΛΚΙΔΙΚΗ	Halkidiki	131
ΧΑΝΙΑ	Chania	197
ΧΕΡΣΟΝΗΣΟΣ	Hersonissos	203
ΧΙΟΣ	Chios	326
ΧΩΡΑ ΣΦΑΚΙΩΝ	Chora Sfakion	202
ΥΔΡΑ	Hydra	309
ΖΑΓΟΡΙΑ	Zagoria	117
ΖΑΚΥΝΘΟΣ	Zakinthos	352

Index

A

Acandia 267
Accommodations in
  Greece 52
Achaïa 153
Achaïa Clauss winery 157
Acrocorinth 142
Acropolis 80
Acropolis Museum 83
Adamas 259
Adana 505
address abbreviations 368
adhan 376
Aedipsos 102
Aegean Turkey 422
Aegina 303
Aegina Town 303
Agamemnon 145
Agia Anna 248
Agia Barbara 108
Agia Galini 192
Agia Kiriaki 132
Agia Kyriaki 363
Agia Napa 565
Agia Nikola 485
Agia Pelagia 180
Agia Roumeli 200
Agia Triada 102, 108
Agios Andreas 157
Agios Christos 338
Agios Dionysios, Church
  of 354
Agios Fokas 251
Agios Georgios 351
Agios Kirikos 338
Agios Mamas 583
Agios Nikitas 357
Agios Nikolaos 108, 206, 355
Agios Nikolaos tis Stegis 573
Agios Theologos 283
Agrafiotis River 112
Aigai, ancient 126
Aile 365
airlines 30
Akçaabat 473
Akrotiri 230
Akrotiri Peninsula 570
Aksaray 543
Akyaka 452
Akyarlar 451
Alâaddin Tepesi 528
Albania 351
Alberts, Amy 580
Aleppo 507
Alexander the Great 56, 370
Alexandroupolis 134
Ali 375
Aliki 308, 342
Aliki Lake 282

Almiros 208
Alonissos 320
alternatives to tourism 21
Alykes 355
Amasra 463
Amasya 468
Ammoudi 232
Amorgos 245
Amorgus 245
Anıt Kabir 522
Anadolu Hisarı 404
Analipsi 293
Anamur 502
Anavatos 328
Andros 255
Andros Town 257
Anemurium 503
Ankara 512
Ano Potamia 244
Ano Sangri 244
Antakya xiii, 507
Antalya 495
Antalya Gulf Coast 495
Antalya Museum 493, 498
Antioch 507
Antiparos 239
Antonius 130
Aoos River 117
Apela 296
Aperi 296
Aphrodisias 443, 447
Apiranthos 245
Apokofto 264
Apollonas 244
Apollonia 263
Apostolos Andreas
  Monastery 594
Arachova 95
Arcadia 163
Areopolis 177
Arginontas 287
Argolis 138
Argos 147, 287
Argostoli 360
Arkasa 296
Armenia 364
Armenistis 340
Armistice House
  Museum 418
Art in Greece 60
Art in Turkey 377
Artemis, Temple of 436, 441
Artemonas 263
Arthipoli 274
artichokes, bas-relief of 528
Artvin 478
Asclepion 282
Asian Istanbul 404
Askeli 308

Aslan Aga Mosque 116
Aspendos 500
Assos 363
Astraka 117
Astypalea 292
Asya 383
AT&T 45, 598
Atatürk 372, 383, 398, 400,
  412, 414, 415, 416, 419,
  422, 435, 439, 440, 444,
  450, 454, 455, 456, 459,
  464, 465, 467, 468, 469,
  475, 481, 482, 497, 498,
  500, 505, 510, 512, 522,
  536, 538, 540, 548, 549,
  582
Atatürk Havaalanı
  (Airport) 388
Atatürk Museum 419, 467
Atatürk Park 498
Atatürk Stadium 526
Atatürk statue 418
Atatürk, Aspendos and 500
Atatürk, bust of 496
Atatürk, cloud
  representations of 522
Atatürk, Cyprus and 580
Atatürk, death of 403
Atatürk, Harrod's and 528
Atatürk, house of 528
Atatürk, museum of 467, 507
Atatürk, personal effects
  of 467, 528
Atatürk, portrait of 547
Atatürk, real name of 372
Atatürk, sarcophagus of 522
Atatürk, statue of 417, 454,
  502, 506, 584
Atatürk, villa of 473
Athenian Agora 83
Athens 66
Athens Festival 79
Athens Flea Market 80
Athens, history of 66
Atlantis 89
ATMs 13, 365
Atreus 145
Aurupa 383
Avanos 536
Avlakia 338
Aya Sophia 400, 401
Aya Sophia (Iznik) 421
Ayder 476
Azogizes 201

B

Bagla 451
Balkan Wars 57
Ballica 546

Banana Beach 317
Baradakçı 451
Barba 130
Baseball xii
Batsi 256
Baywatch 591
Bellapais 588
Bellapais Abbey 588
Bergama 425
Beulé Gate 82
Beydağlari Mountains 491
Beylerbeyi 588
Beyoğlu 389
bisexual, gay, and lesbian
  travelers 25
Bitez 452
Black Sea Coast 460
Black Sea Highway 460, 474
Blue Caves 493
Blue Lagoon 485
Blue Mosque 400
Bodrum Peninsula 448, 451
Bogazkale 523
Bosphorus 383
Bosphorus cruises 403
Boston Red Sox xii
Boztepe 473
Brewers, Milwaukee xi
Büben Villiage 470
budget travel agencies 29
Bursa 413
Buses in Greece 50
Buses in Turkey 365, 368
Butterfly Valley 485
Büyük Çakil Plajı 491
Büyükada 404
Byzantine Empire 56
Byzantine Museum 85

C

Caesar, Julius 543
camping and the
  outdoors 41
Camping in Greece 54
Çanakkale 409
Canbulat Museum 591
Çapa Tatil 451
Cape Greco 567
Cape Sounion 89
Cappadocia 532
car insurance 10, 51
Caretta-Caretta turtles 594
cash cards 13
Castelian Spring 93
Castello 271
Catacombs of Agia
  Solomoni 576
Çatahöyük 529
Cave of Perama 117
ÇavuŞin 536
Central Anatolia 512
Central Crete 184
Central Kos 282
Cephalonia 360

Çesme 432
Chalki 244
Chalkida 98
Chalkis 98
Chania 197
Charaki 274
charter flights 35
children, traveling with 27
Children's Museum 85
Chimaera 495
Chiona Beach 212
Chios 326
Choirokoitia 565
Chora 180, 287, 291
Chora (Amorgos) 247
Chora (Andros) 257
Chora Sfakion 202
Chozoviotissa 248
Chrisi 209
Chrisi Ammoudia 342
Cilician Mountains 503
Çiller, Tansu 373
Cirrus 13
city codes 596
Clerides, Glafkos 556
Climate 596
clothing and footwear 28
collect calls in Greece 55
collect calls in Turkey 369
Colossus of Rhodes 271
Constantia 592
Constantine 56
Constantinople 382
consulates and embassies 3
Corfu 346
Corinth Canal 138
Corinth, ancient 141
Corinthia 138
Çoruh Valley 480
Cotton Castle 445
country codes 45, 598
credit cards 12
Crete 182
Crusades 383
Çümra 529
Cunda (Ali Bey) Island 425
currency 10
customs 7, 8
Cyclades 216
Cyprus 551
Cyprus Tourism
  Organization (CTO) 552
Cyprus, Northern 579

D

Daphni 86
Daphni, Monastery of 87
Dargoti 362
Daskalopetra 329
Daxa 360
Day, Doris 587
daylight savings time 598
Death, Line of 284
Dellikkaya 470

Delos 221
Delphi 91
Delphi, Oracle of 92
Demre 491
Dendra 149
Denizli 443
Denktaş, Rauf 556
Derinkuyu 541
Dervishes 375, 528
Dherinia 567
Diafani 297
Diakofti 180
Diakofto 158
Diastavrosi 130
Didim 442
Didyma 442
dietary concerns 26
Dipkarpaz 593
disabled travelers 25
Dodecanese 266
Dodoni 117
Dolmabahçe Palace 403
dolmuş 365
döner 380
Dragon Lake 117
driving in Greece 51
driving in Turkey 365
driving permits 10, 51
Düden Falls 500
Dukakis, Michael 329
Duluth 119

E

Eastern Anatolia 546
Eastern Crete 202
Ecclesiastic Art
  Museum 135
Edessa 125
Edirne 406
Efes 436
Egirdir 529
Egyptian Spice Bazaar 403
El Greco 187, 190
Elafonissi 202
Elias 153
embassies and consulates 3
Emborio 288, 329
Emergencies in Greece 50
Emergencies in Turkey 365
Eminönü 403
Enipeas River 130
enosis 556, 560
Ephesus 434, 436, 437
Epidavros 152
Epirus 112
Epta Piges 274
Erbakan, Necmettin 374
Eretria 99
Essentials 1
Euboea 98
Eurail 51
Evdilos 338, 339
Evia 98
Evritania 111

Evros River 133
express mail 44
Eyüp 404

F

Faliraki 273, 274
Famagusta 589
Faros 264
Fatih 402
Fatsa 467
Ferries in Greece 52
Ferries in Turkey 368
Fethiye 481
Fighting Irish 460
Filiatro 360
Filoti 244
Fiskardo 363
Flerio 244
Florina 117, 128
Fodele 190
Folklore Festival 357
Food in Greece 64
Food in Turkey 379
footwear 28

G

Galata (Cyprus) 573
Galata Tower 403
Galatas 308
Galaxidi 97
Galissas 254
Gallipoli 411
Gallipoli Town 413
Gamila 117
Gandhi, Jennifer 44, 54
Gastouri 351
Gavdos 201
Gavrio 255
gay travelers 25
Gaziosmanpaşa 519
Gelibolu 411
Gerakas 355
Giali 302
Gidaki 360
Girne 584
Glossa 319
glossary 599
Glossary, Greek 599
Glossary, Turkish 602
Glyfada 352
Glyfatha Lake Cave 178
Gökova 452
Golden Horn 383
Golfo 114
Gölköy 452
Göreme 533
Gortinia 190
Goulandris Museum of
  Cycladic and Ancient
  Greek Art 84
Gournia 209
government information
  offices 1
Grand Bazaar 402

Grand Meteoron 107
Greek Folk Art Museum 85
Greek glossary 599
Greek Holidays and
  Festivals 595
Greek Independence War
  Gallery 560
Greek Popular Musical
  Instruments Museum 85
Greek Telephone
  Organization 54
Green Line 552
Green Mosque 416, 421
Grikou 292
Grivas, General George 556
Gulf of Corinth 138
Güllübahçe 441
Gümüşlük 452
Güzelyurt 583
Gythion 175

H

Hadrian's Arch 84
Haghia Sophia 400
Hair Museum 537
hajj 376
Hala Sultan Tekke
  Mosque 565
Halkidiki 131
Halyas River 465
hamams 379
Harania 208
Harbiye 403, 510
Hard Rock Cafe 204
Harem 400
Hatay 507
Hatay Museum 507
Hattuşaş 523, 525
Hellenic Center of Mountain
  Sports 96
Hellenic Chamber of
  Hotels 53
Hellenic Railways
  Organization 51
Hellenic Theater 491
Hemşin 477
Hera, Temple of 337
Heraklion 184
Hercules 152
Hermoupolis 252
Hersonissos 203
Hidirlik Tepesi 463
Hierapolis 445
Hijra 375
History of Greece 55
History of Turkey 370
hitchhiking 38
Hitchhiking in Greece 52
Hitchhiking in Turkey 368
Hittites 370
holidays and festivals 595
holidays and festivals in
  Greece 595
holidays and festivals in

Turkey 595
Homer 55, 329
Hopa 477
hostels 39, 52
Hotels 53
House of Aion 575
House of Dionysus 575
House of Theseus 575
Hydra 309
Hydrofoils in Greece 52

I

Ialyssos 277
İçmeler 458
identification cards for
  youth, students, and
  teachers 9
Idra 309
Ierapetra 209
Igoumenitsa 112
Ihlara 541
Ikaria 338
Ikizpepe 465
Ilias Lalounis Jewelry
  Museum 85
Indiana Toll Way 460
insurance 20
insurance, car 10, 51
Internet resources 2
Ioannina 115
Ionian Islands 346
Ios 222
Ios Village 223
Iraklion 184
Islam 374
Istanbul 382
Istanbul, history of 382
Isthmia 144
Istiklâl Cad. 396
Itea 96
Ithaka 358
Ithaki 358
Itilo 169
Izmir 428
Iznik 419

J

Jewish Museum 85
jihad 375
Justinian 382, 419

K

Kadmos, House of 98
Kakopetria 572
Kalamata 166
Kalambaka 108
Kalami 141, 351
Kalamitsa 137
Kalavrita 159
Kaledonia Falls 572
Kalo Chorio 208
Kalogeros 130
Kalymnos 284
Kamares 261
Kamari 231

Kamariotisa 342
Kambos 292
Kampos 339
Kantara Castle 594
Kapitaş 487
Kapsali 180, 181
Kara Island 451
Karaincir 451
Karaköy 389
Karaman 588
Karathona 152
Kardianis 252
Kargi Bay 451
Karitena 160
Karlovassi 338
Karmi 588
Karpathos 293
Karpaz Peninsula 593
Karpenisi 111
Karystos 101
Kas 489
Kassandra 131
Kastoria 117, 127
Kastro 263
Kat 546
Katapola 246
Katarrakton Waterfall 126
Kato Paphos 575
Kato Pirgos 578
Kato Potamia 244
Kavaklidere 519, 521
Kavala 135
Kavos 351
Kaya 485
Kaymaklı 473
Kaymakli 541
Kayseri 546
Kazantzakis 188
kebap 380
keeping in touch 44
Kefalos 283
Kekova 493
Kerkyra 346
Kesariani 86
Kibris 579
Killini 159
Kimolos 260
Kionia 251
Kiti 565
Kition 560, 564
Kizilay 517, 520, 521
Kizlirmak River 465
Klafsion 112
Klima 260
Knidos 456, 457
Knossos 188
Kokkari 337
Kokkino Kastro 102
Kolymbia 274
Konak Mansion 560
kontörlü telefon 369
Konya 526
Konyaalti 500
Korithi 355

Kos Town 278
kosher concerns 26
Kouklia 576
Koukounaries 317
Kouloura 351
Koundouriotis 310
Kourion 570
Kourkoumelata 362
Krendi 112
Ktima Paphos 576
Küçük Çakil Plajı 491
Küçük, Fazıl 556
Kueli Bay 484
Kumkapı 395
Kusadasi 434
Kuzey Kibris Türk
  Cümhuriyeti 579
Kykko Monastery 573
Kyrenia 584
Kyrenia Castle 584, 586
Kythera 179, 180

L

Lachi 578
Laconia 171
Laganas 354
Lake District 128
Lake Kovada National
  Park 532
Lake Marathon 90
Lâle Adası 425
Lambi 292
Lampi 282
Language in Greece 59
Language in Turkey 378
Lara 500
Larnaka 560
Larnaka Salt Lake 565
Lassi 362
Ledra Palace
  Checkpoint 552
Lefka Ori 199
Lefkada 355
Lefkas 355
Lefke 582
Lefkoşa 580
Lefkosia 557
Lemonakia 338
lesbian travelers 25
Lesbos 329
Lesvos 329
Let's Go Picks xiii
Letoon, ancient 489
Levadia 94
Leventis Municipal
  Museum 560
Limenas 340
Limni 102
Limnos 343
Lindos 274, 275
Literature in Greece 61
Literature in Turkey 377
Litohoro 128, 130
Livadi 180, 264

Lixouri 362
LKIDIKH 131
Loutraki 143
luggage 28
Lusignans 587
Lycabettos Theater 79

M

Macedonia 118
Macedonian Museum of
  Contemporary Art 124
Magusa 589
mail 44
Mail in Turkey 369
Makarios 373, 556
Makarios, tomb of 573
Makrinitsa 106
Malia 204
Maltezana 293
Mamure Kale 504
Mandraki 266, 273, 311
Mani 175
Manolas 233
Marathokampos 338
Marathon 90
Marathonisi 175
Markopoulo 363
Marmari 282
Marmaris 454
Marmaris Coast 454
Marshall Plan 57
Masada, Greek 328
masjid 375
Mastihari 282
Matala 190
Mavromati 168
Mavrovouni 176
McDonald's 72, 395, 497,
  521, 528
MCI 45, 598
Mecca 374
Mediterranean Turkey 481
Medreseönü 467
Mega Spilaeou 158
Megali Idhea 57
Mehmet II 383
Menetes 296
Mesi Potamia 244
Messene, Ancient 168
Messenia 166
Metaxata 362
Meteora 107
Methoni 171
metric conversions 598
Metro (Istanbul) 389
Metsovo 109
Mevlâna Tekke 527
Milas 454
Milet 442
Miletus 442
Mili 102
Milos 258
Milwaukee 389
Milwaukee Brewers xii

Minoa 248
Minoan Palace 206
Mithimna 332
Mitilini 330
Molyvos 332
Monastery of Agia Napa 567
Monastiraki 75
Monemvassia 178
money matters 10
Moni Chrisoskalitissis 201
Moni Faneromenis 357
Moni Myrtidon 352
Monolithos 232, 277
Montes 355
Mopeds in Greece 51
mosque 375
Mt. Athos 131, 132
Mt. Exobourgo 252
Mt. Hymettus 86
Mt. Ochi 102
Mt. Olympus 128
Mt. Palouki 319
Mt. Pantokrator 351
Mt. Parnassos 96
Mt. Psalida 128
Mt. Simvolo 135
Mt. Stauros 507
Mt. Uludağ 413
Mt. Velouchi 111
Mt. Verna 128
Mudanya 417
muezzin 376
Muhammad 374
Muhammad Ali 371
Museum of Anatolian
  Civilizations 522
Museum of Modern Greek
  Art 110
Music in Greece 63
Mustafa Kemal (see also
  Atatürk) 372
Mustafapaşa 539
Mycenae 145
Mykonos 216
Mykonos Town 216
Myra 492
Myrina 344
Myrtiotissa 352
Myrtos 363
Mythology 62
Mytikas 130, 131

N

Nagos 329
Naoussa 237
NASA 549
National Archaeological
  Museum (Athens) 84
National Gallery
  (Athens) 85
National Marine Park of the
  Northern Sporades 322
Naughties Tombs 421
Nauplion 149

Navarino, Battle of 57
Naxos 240
Naxos Town 240
Necropolis Church (in
  Anemurium) 503
Necropolis of
  Telmessos 482
Nemea 144, 145
Neo Itilo 169
Neochori 357
Nevşehir 540
New Corinth 138
Nicaea (Iznik) 419
Nicosia 580
Nicosia, northern 580
Nidri 357
Nisyros 300
Northeast Aegean
  Islands 326
Northern Cyprus 579
Northern Karpathos 296
Northern Nicosia 580
Nos 300
Notre Dame, University
  of 460
nude beaches 219, 225,
  245, 264, 265, 352
Nur Mountains 507
Nymphs, Cave of the 359

O

Odeum, Ancient
  (Patras) 157
Oia 232
older travelers 25
Ölüdeniz 484
Olympia 160
Olympia, Ancient 162
Olympic Airways 50
Olympos 493
Olympus 297
Omala 362
Omalos 199
Oracle at Delphi 92
Orak Island 451
Ordu 467, 469
Ormos Lourda 362
Ormos Mealos 325
Ortaköy 404
Orthodox Church 59
Osios Loukas 94
OTE 54
Othello's Tower 591
Ottoman Empire 370
ouzo, festival of 333
Özal, Turgut 373

P

packing 27
Palace of the Knights of St.
  John 272
Palaikastro 212
Palamida 311
Paleochora 200, 306

Paleokastritsa 352
Paleopaphos 576
Paleopolis 343
Palio Chora 102
Pamukkale 443, 445
Pamvotis, Lake 115
Panayia Angeloktisti
  Church 565
Papandreou, Andreas 58
Parga 114
Parliament, Athens 86
Paroikia 233
Paroli 174
Paros 233
Parthenon 80, 82
passports 4
Patara 485, 486
Patitiri 320
Patras 154
Patras Festival 157
Pazar 546
Pedi 300
Peiraias 87
Pelekas 352
Pella 124
Peloponnese 138
Peloponnesian Wars 56
Pensions 365
Pergamon 425
Perissa 231
Persembe 467
Petalion Gulf Coast 89
Petra 332
Phaistos 190
Philippi 137
phone codes 596
Pillars of Islam 376
Pindos Mountains 108
Pirgi 328, 329
Pirgos Dirou 178
Pistachio Capital of the
  World 303
Plaka 75, 77, 260, 308
Plaki 292
Plakias 196
Plane Tree of
  Hippocrates 281
planning your trip 1
Platanakia 338
Plateau of the Muses 131
Platis Gialos 362
Plato 56
Platres 571
Plomari 333
PLUS 13
Poliochni 345
Pollonia 260
Poros 306, 362
Poros Town 306
Poseidon's Foot 178
Post Offices in Greece 54
Post Offices in Turkey 369
Poste Restante 54
Potamos 180, 233

Pothia 284
Potomas 180
Priene 441
Prionia 130
Profitis Ilias 130
Prosimni 149
Protaras 567
Prousos, Monastery of 112
Psili Ammos 292, 338
Pylos 169
Pyrgos 232, 252
Pythagrion 337

Q

Quran 374

R

rack-railway 158
Rafina 89
Ramadan 376
Ramnous 90
Rashidun 375
Reis, Piri 412
Religion 374
Religion in Greece 58
Religion in Turkey 374
Republic of Cyprus 551
Rethymnon 193
Rhodes 266
Rina 288
Rio 157
Rize 475
Roda Chanin 352
Rodos (Rhodes) 266
Romeikos 344
Rooms to Let 53
Rose Valley 534
Roussolakos 212
Royal Tombs Museum 593
Rumeli Hisarı 403

S

Sabanci Merkez Camii 506
safety and security 14
saffron flower 460
Safranbolu 460
Sakız Adas (Chios) 326
Saklıkent 485
Salamis 592
salat 376
Samaria Gorge 199
Sami 362
Samos 335
Samothrace 342
Samothraki 342
Sampson, Nikos 556
Samsun 466
Santorini 226
Sarakino Island 325
Sardis 431
Saria 296
Saronic Gulf Islands 303
Sart 431
Scala 362
Schinias 90

Schliemann, Heinrich 146, 412
security 14
Selimiye Camii 408
Selinitsa 176
Seljuks 370
Sen Piyer Kilisesi 509
Serifos 264
seven wonders of the world 162, 271, 436, 448
shahadah 376
Shi'ism 375
shopper 30
Sidari 352
Side 501
Sifnos 261
Sille 529
Simitis, Constantinos 58
Sinan 408
Sinop 464
Sipahi 594
sis 380
Sithonia 131
Sitia 210
Skala 130, 288
Skala Eressos 334
Skiathos 314
Skolio 130
Skopelos 317
Skyros 322
Skyros Town 322
Socrates 56
Softa Kale 504
Soli 583
Southern Karpathos 296
Southern Kos 283
Southern Rhodes 277
Southwestern Crete 202
Sparta 172
Spetses 311
Sphaeria 306
Spilia 130
Spilliés 325
sponges 286
Sporades 314
Sprint 45, 598
St. Hilarion Castle 588
St. Lazarus 560
St. Lazarus, Church of 564
St. Nicholas Island 484
St. Nicholas, Church of 493
St. Paul 576
St. Paul, cell of 137
St. Paul's Well 507
St. Peter's Grotto 507
Star Trek xi
Stavros 360
Stavrovouni Monastery 565
Stefani 130
Street Addresses in Turkey 368
student identification 9
study abroad 21
Styx River 115

Suleyman 371
Süleymaniye 402
Süleymaniye Mosque 402
Sultanahmet 393, 395, 401
Sultanahmet Camii 400
Sumela Monastery 473
Sunnism 375
Syntagma 75, 77
Syros 252

T

Taksim 394, 395
Tarsus 507
Tasucu 504
Taurus Mountains 495
Taygetus Mountains 169
teacher identification 9
Tekkeköy Caves 467
Telephone Codes 596
telephones 45
Telmessos, ancient 481
Temple of Aphrodite 576
Temple of Astarte 564
Temple of Athena Nike 82
Temple of Olympian Zeus 84
Temple of Pronaia Athena 93
Termal 419
Teucer 592
Thassos 340
Therma 286, 339, 343
Thermae 282
Thessaloniki 118
Thessaly 104
Thira 226
Thira Town 227
Thira, Ancient 232
Thirasia 233
Thission 75
Throne of Zeus 130
ticket consolidators 33
Tigaki 282
Time Zones 598
Timfristos Mountains 111
Timvos Marathonas 90
Tinos 248
Tirintha 152
Tiryns 152
Tlos 485
toilets 53
Tokat 543
Tolo 152
Tomb of the Unknown Warrior 86
Topkapı Palace 398
Tornaritis-Pierides Museum of Paleontology 564
Toumba 130
Trabzon 470
Trains in Greece 51
Trains in Turkey 51, 365
transliteration 59
travel agencies 29

traveler's checks 11
traveling with children 27
Treasury of Marseilles 93
Trianda 277
Tripi 174
Tripiti 260
Tripoli 163
Troodhitissa Monastery 572
Troodos 572
Troy 412
Truva 412
Tsamadou 338
Tsambikas Monastery 274
Ttakkas Bay 578
Tulip Island 425
Tünel 389
Turgut Reis 452
Türkbükü 452
Turkikos 344
Turkish Airlines 365
Turkish Baths 379, 398
Turkish Cyprus 579
Turkish delight 460
Turkish glossary 602
Turkish Holidays and
  Festivals 595
Turkish Touring and
  Automobile
  Association 368
Turkish-American Cultural
  Association 516
Turquoise Coast 481
Turquoise Riviera 495
turtles, Caretta-Caretta 594

Tylissos 190

U

Uçhisar 535
Ulu Camii (Great
  Mosque) 416
Uludağ 417
Ulus 518, 520, 521
Ürgüp 538
Uzungöl 474

V

Vai 213
Valtos 114
Varia 332
Varlaam Monastery 108
Vasiliki 357
Vasilikos 355
Vathi 293, 358
vegetarian concerns 26
Venus de Milo 258, 260
Vergina 125
Vikos Gorge 117
Virgin Mary, house of 440
visas 7
Vitalades 351
Vlichadia 286
Vliho 357
Volimes 355
Volissos 329
Votsalakia 338
Vouni 583

W

weights and measures 598

Western Crete 193
Western Kalymnos 287
Western Rhodes 277
when to go 1
women travelers 24
women's health 19
work abroad 23
World's First City 529

X

Xanthian Obelisk 488
Xanthos 485
Xepatomeni 208
Xombourgo 252
Xyloskalo 199

Y

Yahşi 451, 452
Yalova 418
Yazılıkaya 524
Yenierenköy 593
Yesil Camii 416
Yialos 223
Yilmaz, Mesut 374
Young Turks 372
youth identification 9
Yusufeli 479

Z

Zagoria 117
zakat 376
Zakinthos 352
Zakros Gorge 212
Zelve 536

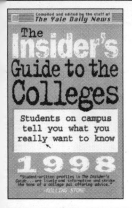

★Let's Go 1998 Reader Questionnaire★

Please fill this out and return it to **Let's Go, St. Martin's Press,** 175 Fifth Ave., New York, NY 10010-7848. All respondents will receive a free subscription to *The Yellowjacket,* the Let's Go Newsletter.

Name: _____

Address: _____

City: _____ **State:** _____ **Zip/Postal Code:** _____

Email: _____ **Which book(s) did you use?** _____

How old are you? under 19   19-24   25-34   35-44   45-54   55 or over

Are you (circle one)   in high school   in college   in graduate school   employed   retired   between jobs

Have you used Let's Go before? yes no **Would you use it again?** yes no

How did you first hear about Let's Go? friend   store clerk   television   bookstore display   advertisement/promotion   review   other

Why did you choose Let's Go (circle up to two)? reputation budget focus   price   writing style   annual updating   other: _____

Which other guides have you used, if any? Frommer's $-a-day   Fodor's   Rough Guides   Lonely Planet   Berkeley   Rick Steves   other: _____

Is Let's Go the best guidebook? yes no

If not, which do you prefer? _____

Please rank each of the following parts of Let's Go 1 to 5 (1=needs improvement, 5=perfect). packaging/cover   practical information   accommodations   food   cultural introduction   sights   practical introduction ("Essentials")   directions   entertainment   gay/lesbian information   maps   other: _____

How would you like to see the books improved? (continue on separate page, if necessary) _____
_____

How long was your trip?   one week   two weeks   three weeks   one month   two months or more

Which countries did you visit? _____

What was your average daily budget, not including flights? _____

Have you traveled extensively before? yes no

Do you buy a separate map when you visit a foreign city? yes no

Have you seen the Let's Go Map Guides? yes no

Have you used a Let's Go Map Guide? yes no

If you have, would you recommend them to others? yes no

Did you use the Internet to plan your trip? yes no

Would you use a Let's Go: recreational (e.g. skiing) guide   gay/lesbian guide   adventure/trekking guide   phrasebook   general travel information guide

Which of the following destinations do you hope to visit in the next three to five years (circle one)? South Africa   China   South America   Russia   Caribbean   Scandinavia   other: _____

Where did you buy your guidebook?   Internet   chain bookstore   independent bookstore   college bookstore   travel store   other: _____